HANDBOOK OF

Psychological Assessment, Case Conceptualization, and Treatment

Michel Hersen, Editor-in-Chief

HANDBOOK OF
Psychological Assessment, Case Conceptualization, and Treatment

Volume 2 **Children and Adolescents**

Volume Editor
David Reitman

BICENTENNIAL
1807
WILEY
2007
BICENTENNIAL

John Wiley & Sons, Inc.

Library of Congress Cataloging-in-Publication Data:

Handbook of psychological assessment, case conceptualization, and
    treatment / editor-in-chief, Michel Hersen.
        p. ; cm.
    Includes bibliographical references and index.
    ISBN-13: 978-0-471-77999-5 (cloth) Volume 1: Adults
    ISBN-13: 978-0-471-78000-7 (cloth) Volume 2: Children and Adolescents
    ISBN-13: 978-0-471-77998-8 (cloth) Set 1. Psychology,
Pathological—Handbooks, manuals, etc.   I. Hersen, Michel.   II. Rosqvist, Johan.
    III. Reitman, David
    [DNLM: 1. Mental Disorders—diagnosis.   2. Mental Disorders—therapy.
    WM 141 H2374 2008]
    RC454.H352 2008
    616.89—dc22   2007026314

Printed in the United States of America.

10 9 8 7 6 5 4 3 2 1

Contents

Preface to Volume 2

Many books have been written on assessment, conceptualization, and treatment separately, yet there is no resource that links all three critical issues in systematic fashion. Given the recent surge in interest in the relation between assessment and intervention, and the crucial role that conceptualization plays in linking these activities, we believe that this work will fill a very significant gap in the literature. We hope that this volume of the *Handbook of Psychological Assessment, Case Conceptualization, and Treatment* will be well received by students and practitioners alike and that it contributes to your understanding of the complex issues involved in the provision of psychological care to children and adolescents.

In this volume on *Children and Adolescents*, the chapters are divided into three parts. Part I (General Issues) has 8 chapters that deal with an overview of behavioral assessment with children and adolescents, diagnostic issues, behavioral conceptualization, developmental issues, an overview of behavioral treatment with children and adolescents, the role of the family in treatment, medical and pharmacological issues, and ethical issues.

The bulk of this volume is presented in the 16 chapters comprising Parts II and III, where the authors detail assessment, conceptualization, and treatment issues relevant to specific disorders appearing on Axis I or Axis II of the *Diagnostic and Statistical Manual of Mental Disorders (DSM)*. Part III features problems that are less prominently featured in the *DSM* but are nevertheless commonly encountered in clinical practice with children and adolescents (e.g., firesetting, neuropsychological disorders, substance abuse).

To ensure cross-chapter consistency in our coverage of the disorders (or clinical problems), the chapters appearing in Parts II and III begin with a general description, followed by information about diagnosis and assessment. Conceptualization is highlighted in all chapters, and the authors were encouraged to consider developmental issues, parenting, life events and genetics, peer socialization factors, physical and drug influences, and cultural diversity. The conceptualization is followed by a review of empirically supported treatments (including medical and pharmacological interventions) relevant to the clinical problem.

We believe that the way this volume is structured should enhance its value as a teaching tool so that students will have a more holistic view of psychopathology, its etiology, and its ultimate remediation. The case descriptions were included to help our experts communicate to students about the subtle but important interplay among assessment, conceptualization, and treatment.

Works of this scope are a team effort, and all of the contributors should be thanked for the long hours of sweat equity invested in this volume. Thanks are also due to Dr. Michel Hersen (series editor) and his longtime editorial assistant, Carole Londeree, who keeps everything running so smoothly. We thank Cynthia Polance and Christopher Brown for their work on the indexes. And finally, but hardly least of all, we thank our editorial friends at John Wiley, who understood the importance of this project and who helped us keep on track to completion.

My personal gratitude extends to my friends and family, especially my wife, Ann, and our dearly departed feline companion, Hadley (aka "the Foozebeast").

DAVID REITMAN

Fort Lauderdale, Florida

Contributors

R. Matt Alderson, MS
Department of Psychology
University of Central Florida
Orlando, Florida

Ashley Austin, PhD
Community-Based Intervention
    Research Group
Florida International University
Miami, Florida

Jennifer S. Baldwin, PhD
School of Psychology
University of New South Wales
Sydney, Australia

Christopher T. Barry, PhD
Department of Psychology
University of Southern Mississippi
Hattiesburg, Mississippi

Sara Chapman, BS
Center for Psychological Studies
Nova Southeastern University
Fort Lauderdale, Florida

Catherine Cheely, BA
Department of Psychology
University of South Carolina,
    Barnwell College
Columbia, South Carolina

Heather Christiansen, MS
Center for Psychological Studies
Nova Southeastern University
Fort Lauderdale, Florida

Christine A. Conelea, BA
Department of Psychology
University of Wisconsin–Milwaukee
Milwaukee, Wisconsin

Krystal T. Cook, BA
Departments of Educational Psychology
    and Psychology
Texas A&M University
College Station, Texas

Lisa W. Coyne, PhD
Department of Psychology
Suffolk University
Boston, Massachusetts

Mark R. Dadds, PhD
School of Psychology
University of New South Wales
Sydney, Australia

Amanda Jensen Doss, PhD
Departments of Educational Psychology
    and Psychology
Texas A&M University
College Station, Texas

T. David Elkin, PhD
Department of Psychiatry & Human
    Behavior
University of Mississippi Medical Center
Jackson, Mississippi

Ian M. Evans, PhD
School of Psychology
Massey University
Palmerston North, New Zealand

Farahnaz K. Farahmand, BA
Psychology Department
DePaul University
Chicago, Illinois

Jan Faust, PhD
Center for Psychological Studies
Nova Southeastern University
Fort Lauderdale, Florida

Christopher A. Flessner, MS
Department of Psychology
University of Wisconsin–Milwaukee
Milwaukee, Wisconsin

Abby H. Friedman, MS
Department of Psychology
West Virginia University
Morgantown, West Virginia

Patrick C. Friman, PhD
Clinical Services and Research
13603 Flanagan Blvd.
Boys Town, Nebraska

Charles J. Golden, PhD
Center for Psychological Studies
Nova Southeastern University
Fort Lauderdale, Florida

Kathryn E. Grant, PhD
Psychology Department
DePaul University
Chicago, Illinois

Alan M. Gross, PhD
Department of Psychology
University of Mississippi
University, Mississippi

Benjamin L. Hankin, PhD
Department of Psychology
University of South Carolina,
    Barnwell College
Columbia, South Carolina

Laurie B. Kaufman, BA
Department of Psychology
University of Vermont
Burlington, Vermont

Lee Kern, PhD
College of Education
Lehigh University
Bethlehem, Pennsylvania

Elizabeth Brestan Knight, PhD
Department of Psychology
Auburn University
Auburn, Alabama

Ian Kodish, MD, PhD
Psychiatry Residency Training Program
University of Washington Medical Center
Seattle, Washington

Michael J. Kofler, MS
Department of Psychology
University of Central Florida
Orlando, Florida

Elizabeth Kolivas, BA
Department of Psychology
University of Mississippi
University, Mississippi

Scott H. Kollins, PhD
Department of Psychiatry
Duke University Medical Center
Durham, North Carolina

Joshua M. Langberg, PhD
Cincinnati Children's Hospital
    Medical Center
Cincinnati, Ohio

Jon McClellan, MD
Psychiatry Residency Training Program
University of Washington Medical Center
Seattle, Washington

Bryce D. McLeod, PhD
Department of Psychology
Virginia Commonwealth University
Richmond, Virginia

Tracy L. Morris, PhD
Department of Psychology
West Virginia University
Morgantown, West Virginia

Jessica D. Pickard, BA
Department of Psychology
University of Southern Mississippi
Hattiesburg, Mississippi

Joseph S. Raiker, BS
Department of Psychology
University of Central Florida
Orlando, Florida

Mark D. Rapport, PhD
Department of Psychology
University of Central Florida
Orlando, Florida

David Reitman, PhD
Center for Psychological Studies
Nova Southeastern University
Fort Lauderdale, Florida

Jennifer Ret, MS
Department of Educational Psychology
Miami University
Oxford, Ohio

Lorraine E. Ridgeway, MS
Department of Psychology
Auburn University
Auburn, Alabama

Patrick Riordan, BA
Department of Psychology
University of Mississippi
University, Mississippi

Malcolm M.S. Roland, MD
Sleep Disorders Center
University of Mississippi Medical Center
Jackson, Mississippi

Julie A. Schumacher, PhD
Department of Psychiatry & Human
    Behavior
University of Mississippi Medical Center
Jackson, Mississippi

Kerry Silvia, MA
Department of Psychology
Suffolk University
Boston, Massachusetts

Julie Snyder, MS
Center for Psychological Studies
Nova Southeastern University
Fort Lauderdale, Florida

Talida State, MA
College of Education
Lehigh University
Bethlehem, Pennsylvania

Timothy R. Stickle, PhD
Department of Psychology
University of Vermont
Burlington, Vermont

Paul S. Strand, PhD
Department of Psychology
Washington State University Tri-Cities
Richland, Washington

Sarah B. Stevens, MS
Department of Psychology
West Virginia University
Morgantown, West Virginia

Lindsay M. Stewart, MA
Center for Psychological Studies
Nova Southeastern University
Fort Lauderdale, Florida

Eric F. Wagner, PhD
Community-Based Intervention Research
    Group
Florida International University
Miami, Florida

T. Steuart Watson, PhD
Department of Educational Psychology
Miami University
Oxford, Ohio

Tonya S. Watson, PhD
Department of Educational Psychology
Miami University
Oxford, Ohio

Robert Westerholm, MA
Psychology Department
DePaul University
Chicago, Illinois

Emily Wetter, BA
Department of Psychology
University of South Carolina,
  Barnwell College
Columbia, South Carolina

Emerson M. Wickwire Jr., MS/MA
Department of Psychiatry & Human
  Behavior
University of Mississippi Medical Center
Jackson, Mississippi

Douglas W. Woods, PhD
Department of Psychology
University of Wisconsin–Milwaukee
Milwaukee, Wisconsin

PART I

GENERAL ISSUES

CHAPTER 1

Overview of Behavioral Assessment with Children and Adolescents

DAVID REITMAN, HEATHER CHRISTIANSEN, AND JULIE SNYDER

Behavioral assessment has evolved rapidly since Hersen and Bellack (1976) first surveyed the field over 30 years ago. Child behavioral assessment (CBA), in particular, has grown increasingly complex. Whereas the earliest treatments of behavioral assessment focused on broad areas of concern such as "behavioral excesses" and "behavioral deficits," contemporary efforts "suggest a field that is becoming more inclusive, and at the same time more highly specialized" (Reitman, 2006, p.3). Much of the growing specialization in behavioral assessment has been fueled by the *Diagnostic and Statistical Manual of Mental Disorders* (*DSM;* American Psychiatric Association, 2000). Indeed, *Child Behavioral Assessment* (Ollendick & Hersen, 1984) devoted only a single chapter to diagnostic issues. By contrast, a recent special section of the *Journal of Clinical Child and Adolescent Psychology* (see Mash & Hunsley, 2005) emphasizes the *DSM* taxonomy yet reveals limitations in *DSM*-focused assessment that has broad implications for CBA (see Kazdin, 2005; Pelham, Fabiano, & Massetti, 2005). In this overview, we discuss CBA past and present and offer some perspectives on the future of research and practice in this ever-developing field.

DEFINING CHILD BEHAVIORAL ASSESSMENT

Over the past 25 years, efforts to define behavioral assessment and evaluate its adequacy have been numerous (Haynes, 1998; R. O. Nelson, 1983; Reitman, 2006). In one of the earliest attempts to define the field, Ollendick and Hersen (1984, p. 6) defined CBA as "an exploratory hypothesis testing process in which a range of specific procedures is used in order to understand a given child, group or social ecology and to formulate and evaluate specific intervention strategies." Through the 1980s, CBA continued to be defined in relation to traditional, psychodynamically informed

Table 1.1
Purposes of Evidence-Based Assessment

Purpose	Definition and Example
Diagnosis and case formulation	Determining the nature or causes of the presenting problems (formally or informally)
Screening	Identifying children who have or are at risk for a particular problem and who might be helped by further tests or treatment
Prognosis	Generating predictions about the course of the problems if left untreated; recommendations for possible courses of action to be considered and their likely impact on the course of the problems
Treatment design and planning	Selecting or developing and implementing interventions designed to address children's problems by focusing on elements identified in a diagnostic evaluation
Treatment monitoring	Tracking changes in symptoms, functioning, psychological characteristics, intermediate treatment goals, and variables determined to cause or maintain problems
Treatment evaluation	Determining the effectiveness, social validity, consumer satisfaction, and cost-effectiveness of intervention

Source: "Evidence-Based Assessment of Child and Adolescent Disorders: Issues and Challenges," by E. J. Mash and J. Hunsley, *Journal of Clinical Child and Adolescent Psychology, 34,* 2005, p. 366. Reprinted with permission.

assessment. Thus, for example, behavioral assessment was described as emphasizing cross-situational variability, whereas traditional assessment assumed stable personality traits (see Mash & Terdal, 1988). Although older definitions of CBA are helpful in contrasting traditional assessment and early CBA, these definitions seem less capable of revealing the subtle but important differences in assessment practices that have emerged in contemporary CBA. Many authors have taken note of the plethora of behavioral assessment methods and their diverse functions (see Elliott & Piersel, 1982; Hawkins, 1979; Kelley, 2003), and recent interest in evidence-based assessment has highlighted this diversity. Most recently, Mash and Hunsley (2005) have argued that contemporary CBA is comprised of a complex array of assessment operations, including (a) diagnosis and case conceptualization, (b) early identification (screening), (c) prognosis, (d) treatment design and planning, (e) treatment monitoring, and (f) treatment evaluation (see Table 1.1 for details). Reitman (2006) reviewed previous definitions of CBA (including Hersen & Ollendick's) and suggested that recent developments in behavioral theory could signal an opportunity to refine our understanding of behavioral assessment. To this end, we briefly explore the relationship of conceptualization and assessment before presenting a revised definition of child behavioral assessment.

CASE CONCEPTUALIZATION AND ASSESSMENT

Case conceptualization is the process of developing hypotheses about client difficulties, including historical events, antecedent events, and other factors contributing to the maintenance of presenting problems (Freeman & Miller, 2002). According to Eells (1997), conceptualization has four basic purposes. First, conceptualization is a tool for organizing complicated and contradictory information. This process of collecting, organizing, and integrating clinical information is especially important for students and beginning therapists. Second, case conceptualization can serve as a blueprint for treatment planning. Third, the process of identifying important clinical issues can foster the development of a working alliance between therapist and client. Fourth, the development of a good working alliance may neutralize obstacles to treatment and client resistance, thus enhancing treatment outcome. It is most notable that in Eell's description of case conceptualization, the line between assessment and treatment is inexact, and the processes seem more complementary than one might surmise based on the rather independent development of assessment and treatment literatures in contemporary clinical child psychology.

Conceptualization efforts can be traced to the diagnostic approach used in Hippocratic and Galenic medicine (Eells, 1997). Hippocratic physicians integrated the information obtained from a comprehensive examination and observation of all five senses to clarify the underlying cause of the presenting symptoms. A Greek physician, Galen of Pergamum, was the first to emphasize the importance of understanding the anatomic structures and function as the foundation of disease. Galen used experimentation to understand anatomy, and the notion of testing formulations remains an important part of some forms of behavioral case conceptualization. For example, some behavioral clinicians use functional analysis to identify possible cause-and-effect relations between environmental events and maladaptive behavior (Freeman & Miller, 2002). An additional aspect of case formulation that was adopted from medicine is the practice of obtaining posttreatment information to confirm the conceptualization (i.e., diagnosis).

Many clinical scientists regard the case conceptualization as a working hypothesis that may include a variety of factors, such as information about early childhood trauma, developmental history, biological influences, maladaptive schemas, or reinforcers (Eells, 1997). Because conceptualization itself is generic, the specific hypotheses that arise from this process are themselves a function of the theory of psychotherapy and psychopathology adopted by the clinician (Orvaschel, Faust, & Hersen, 2001). Thus, good case conceptualization is regarded as rooted in an identified theory. Theoretical assumptions about the relevance of certain kinds of information vary from theory to theory, alter the clinician's perception of abnormal behavior, and, most important from an assessment perspective, influence the selection of behaviors that need to be assessed (and, presumably, changed; Eells, 1997).

Taking a slightly different view, Meier (1999) characterizes case conceptualization as a two-level process. Level 1 consists of descriptive information that informs the process of hypothesis development, and level 2 consists of the prescriptive recommendations generated from the hypothesis. The descriptive level includes the history of the presenting problem; previous psychological problems; developmental, social, and medical history; stressors; and mental status examination results. The similarity of level 1, the descriptive level, to contemporary *DSM*-focused assessment is readily apparent. The prescriptive level emerges from the hypotheses about the function of the target behavior and offers a treatment plan (Eells, 1997). Prescriptive-level case conceptualizations include the type of therapy, frequency and duration, therapy goals, obstacles that may interfere with treatment, prognosis, and referrals for adjunctive interventions. As will be shown later in the chapter, many, but not all, CBAs use functional assessment to generate definitions of target behavior problems, document important antecedent and consequent events, and gain a better understanding of the functions of problem behavior (Freeman & Miller, 2002). A key question explored in this chapter is the weighting of these assessment practices (i.e., descriptive or prescriptive) in contemporary and future CBA.

BEHAVIORAL CONCEPTUALIZATION AND CHILD BEHAVIORAL ASSESSMENT

In a conceptual analysis and historical overview of behavior therapy, Hayes, Follette, and Follette (1995) suggest that behaviorism has passed through four stages: an initial stage in which Watson's (1914/1967) methodological behaviorism distinguished itself, a second stage in which behavioral researchers in the operant tradition (e.g., Azrin, Baer, Risley) explored applied problems, a third stage characterized by the ascendance of cognitive theory, and a fourth stage in which the methodological and cognitive streams blended to form contemporary, mainstream behavior therapy (i.e., empirical-clinical psychology). Although the methodological and cognitive streams merged, the operant tradition continued to evolve. Extending Hayes et al.'s argument, we suggest that behavioral assessment has evolved along lines comparable to behavior therapy. We argue here that the distinction drawn between the methodological-cognitive and contextual-operant traditions in *behavior therapy* can be readily extended to *behavioral assessment*.

Since at least the early 1980s, two rather distinct streams or traditions in contemporary applied behavioral work are apparent: the empirical-clinical and the contextual (operant). Drawing on experiences in the operant laboratory, so-called radical behaviorists came to value data derived from repeated observations and direct manipulation of consequences (contingencies). Championed by B. F. Skinner, the operant tradition enjoyed widespread acceptance throughout the post–World-War II period and through the 1960s and early 1970s. Also described as contextualism (see Hayes et al., 1995), the operant tradition became known as applied behavior analysis, with many successful applications in child populations and adult (institutional) settings. By contrast, the mechanistic/structural or neobehavioral view pioneered by Watson, Wolpe, and Beck matured in the context of adult outpatient practice and is today closely identified with cognitive and cognitive-behavioral therapies. With respect to assessment practices, the demands of working with adults and children with internalizing problems such as anxiety and depression led methodological behaviorists to relax emphasis on direct observation and promoted a greater reliance on self-reports and behavioral rating scales. Because contingency control and access to clients and their cognitions may be limited, methodological behaviorists are also more tolerant of inference and, perhaps, more sensitive to the challenges associated with gathering data from outpatients. For their part, contextual behaviorists went on to refine methods for developing contingency (functional) analysis (e.g., Iwata, Dorsey, Slifer, Bauman, & Richman, 1982/1994).

By 1990, the discrepancies between the two traditions had become sufficiently large that Gross was compelled to comment on "drift" from early definitions of behavioral research and practice appearing in *Behavior Therapy*. Specifically, he pointed out that earlier research and practice in behavioral assessment emphasized individualized, direct assessment of behavior and minimized inference. Other key features of behavioral assessment were the development of functional hypothesis and repeated, ongoing assessment to ensure that incorrect analyses would be modified to achieve treatment goals (for details, see Table 1.1; Mash & Terdal, 1988; Silva, 1993). With hindsight, it can now be said that the drift noted by Gross and decried by others (Krasner, 1992) pointed to the continued evolution and divergence of the two streams of behavior therapy. Interestingly, in recent years, rating scales have emerged as the most commonly used form of behavioral assessment (Cashel, 2002; Reitman, 2006), at least in the methodological tradition. Further, cognitively oriented child clinical work, while emphasizing the rigorous empirical, data-based, and objective aspects of laboratory research, placed greater emphasis on topographical-structural descriptions of child behavior problems and relatively less emphasis on contingency analysis and context than was characteristic of earlier approaches to behavioral assessment (see Mash & Terdal, 1988).

At the time Ollendick and Hersen (1984) crafted their oft-cited definition of behavioral assessment, the *DSM* had scarcely begun to include information relevant to behavioral work with children. However, given the diverse purposes associated with behavioral assessment today, it seems unlikely that any one definition can meaningfully capture the complex functions of CBA. Returning to Mash and Hunsley's (2005) discussion, the past 20 years of CBA have emphasized the diagnostic, epidemiological, and prognostic functions of behavioral assessment, while less attention has been paid (until recently) to its other purposes, specifically, informing treatment design and promoting efficient treatment monitoring and evaluation (see Kazdin, 2005; Mash & Hunsley, 2005). Put in Ollendick and Hersen's terms, contemporary CBA can be thought of as involving two distinct but potentially complementary approaches to hypothesis testing. One approach involves assigning individuals to categories (i.e., establishing differential diagnosis and/or comorbidity). Some authors have identified this approach as "taxonomic diagnosis" (Mash & Wolfe, 2005). We here suggest that the term *diagnostic assessment* be applied when CBAs seek information intended to inform diagnosis. Further, when the nature of the hypothesis testing concerns not which diagnosis is most appropriate, but the purpose, cause, or function of behavior, this activity may be called *functional assessment.* This form of behavioral assessment can also be understood as "problem-solving analysis" (Mash & Wolfe, 2005). Functional assessment is distinguished from *functional analysis* because no attempt is made to manipulate sources of control in the former case (Alberto & Troutman, 2003). Both diagnostic and functional assessment can thus be included under the larger domain of "behavioral assessment."

For the purposes of this chapter, examples of diagnostic assessment include such activities as conducting interviews with the express purpose of isolating symptoms of *DSM* disorders and establishing their onset or prevalence as well as level of functional impairment (needed to establish diagnosis). Additionally, use of parent, teacher, or child self-ratings to determine the presence or absence of symptoms needed to meet the threshold for establishing deviance from a normative sample would also be considered diagnostic assessment. By contrast, use of interviews (whoever the respondent) to elicit information about the circumstances that give rise to problem behavior as well as the factors that seem to influence the frequency of the problem would be considered functional assessment. In addition, behavioral observations conducted to test hypotheses about function (e.g., whether oppositional behavior was related to escape- or attention-based reinforcement, or both) would be consistent with functional assessment. Simply counting behavioral problems or symptoms, regardless of how well the target behavior is defined, is not functional assessment—unless there is an effort to gather information about setting events, antecedents, and consequences. (See Table 1.2 for additional facets of diagnostic and functional assessment.)

Table 1.2
Behavioral Assessment: Diagnostic and Functional Approaches

Type of Behavioral Assessment	Diagnostic	Functional
Purpose	Identify diagnostic category that best fits symptom presentation.	Identify environmental influences (broadly construed) on behavior in context.
Commonly used methods	Use diagnostic interview, Likert-type rating scales (age- and/or gender-normed), observations/self-monitoring (presence/absence).	Use functional-diagnostic interview (identify setting events, antecedents, behavior, and consequences; ABCs), observations/self-monitoring (emphasizes identifying manipulable ABCs and setting events). Rating scales used less frequently.
Outcomes	Pre- and (sometimes) posttreatment assessment.	Outcome data used to evaluate effectiveness and guide clinical decision making on a session-by-session basis.
Treatment logic	Diagnosis dictates treatment. Diagnostically focused treatment manuals with empirical support.	Interventions designed to meet functional needs, teach and shape skills that permit acquisition of reinforcement in a socially acceptable manner. Treatment selection based on manipulating factors that influence setting events, discriminative stimuli, or motivational operations.

From "Overview of Child Behavioral Assessment" (pp. 4–24), by D. Reitman, in *Clinician's Handbook of Child Behavioral Assessment*, M. Hersen (Ed.), 2006, New York: Elsevier. Adapted with permission.

Based on the conceptual analysis offered here, we argue that CBA should be redefined as a multidimensional approach to data collection and analysis in which a range of procedures is used to facilitate clinical decision making for children or groups of children. It has been suggested that diagnostic and functional assessment constitute two different but potentially complementary approaches to clinical decision making. After 20 years of being estranged, it appears that greater balance between diagnosis-driven and functional assessment is on the horizon (see Kazdin, 2005; Mash & Hunsley, 2005; McMahon & Frick, 2005; Pelham et al., 2005; Reitman & Hupp, 2003). Finally, as discussed at the close of this chapter, it is possible, and perhaps even profitable, to engage in both types of assessment activity. However, to appreciate the merits of these approaches, one must be able to distinguish between them (Cone, 1998; Haynes, 1998).

CONTEMPORARY TRENDS IN CHILD BEHAVIORAL ASSESSMENT

There have been numerous efforts to classify the various forms of behavioral assessment. Among the most notable efforts to accomplish this task was Cone's (1978) behavioral assessment grid or BAG, which offered a taxonomy of assessment tools based on the kinds of information obtained (i.e., contents: cognitive, motor, etc.), methods used to obtain the information (e.g., interview, self-report. ratings), and universes of generalizability (e.g., time, setting). Most forms of behavioral assessment have previously been reviewed, including general reviews (see Reitman, Hummel, Franz, & Gross, 1998) and reviews that focus on one or more of the grid elements in the BAG (e.g., direct observation: Roberts, 2001; interviews: Orvaschel, 2006; lab-based or computerized assessment and activity assessment: Rapport, Kofler, & Himmerich, 2006). Readers interested in detailed accounts of the various forms of behavioral assessment are referred to those sources. A more compelling question for the purposes of this overview concerns the detection of time-related trends in CBA.

To examine trends in behavioral assessment over the past 40 years, Reitman (2006) conducted an informal electronic database search (i.e., PsychInfo) of dissertations, books and book chapters, and journals. These sources were examined for the terms "behavioral assessment," "direct observation," "functional assessment or functional analysis," "parent report or parent rating,"* "teacher report or teacher rating,"* and child-related synonyms (e.g., child, children, adolescent*). The results suggested remarkable growth in CBA research overall. In addition, although growth in entries including the term "direct observation" (a frequently identified core element of behavioral assessment) have not kept pace with "behavioral assessment," there has been substantial growth in publications involving parent and teacher ratings and functional assessment. Overall, since 1960, publications in child behavioral assessment appear to have outpaced general child assessment by roughly 5 to 1. During that same period, growth in projective assessment has been flat. Notably, in the 10-year span from 1990 to 2000, research featuring parent and teacher ratings appeared roughly 800 times (each) compared to 200 publications featuring functional assessment (see Figure 1.1).

TRENDS IN ASSESSMENT RESEARCH: DIVERGENCE OF THE STREAMS

The methodological-cognitive and contextual traditions in behavioral assessment have been evolving more or less independently for the better part of the past 25 years. Next we highlight the major events contributing to development of each behavioral

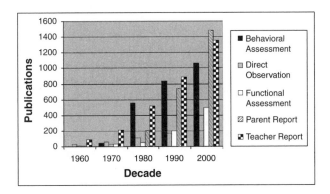

Figure 1.1 Publications trends in child behavioral assessment by decade. *Note*: Publication data from 2000 to 2004 were doubled to estimate the most recent decade. From "Overview of Child Behavioral Assessment" (pp. 4–24), by D. Reitman, in *Clinician's Handbook of Child Behavioral Assessment*, M. Hersen (Ed.), 2006, New York: Elsevier. Adapted with permission.

assessment tradition. The methodological-cognitive stream has influenced and been influenced by the *DSM,* whereas assessment activity in the contextual stream has been organized around the functional assessment construct.

THE RISE OF DIAGNOSTIC ASSESSMENT

Since the introduction of *DSM-III* (American Psychiatric Association, 1980), the *DSM* has enjoyed greater acceptance with each revision. A landmark in this evolution concerns the addition of a separate section in the *DSM-III* focusing on "disorders usually first diagnosed in infancy, childhood, or adolescence" and acknowledgment in *DSM-III* and the research literature that adult forms of psychopathology such as depression and anxiety might also be observed in children. Concern among behavioral practitioners about the implications of widespread acceptance of *DSM* and the medical model has certainly waned since the inception of behavior therapy (Follette & Hayes, 1992). Indeed, one consequence of the increased acceptance of the *DSM* nosology has been to blur the distinction between traditional assessment and behavioral assessment (see Table 1.2). In addition to economic pressures to adopt the system, several factors have contributed to the *DSM*'s greater acceptance among CBAs, including the *DSM*'s atheoretical approach (but see Krasner, 1992, for another view), improvements in interrater reliability, greater attention to developmental factors, and reductions in the level of inference required to identify symptoms (Mash & Wolfe, 2005).

Greater specialization appears to be another trend in contemporary CBA, no doubt related to greater acceptance of the *DSM* nosology. Today's clinical child researchers and practitioners readily acknowledge distinctions between internalizing and externalizing problems, and many describe their expertise in such terms (e.g., child-externalizing). Subspecialization in assessment practices is also beginning to emerge, and this development may fuel further subspecialization among child practitioners. For example, in the externalizing domain, interviews and rating scales tend to dominate lists of assessment practices for the disruptive behavior disorders (e.g., Attention-Deficit/Hyperactivity Disorder [ADHD], Oppositional Defiant Disorder, and Conduct Disorder), but state-of-the-art ADHD assessment is likely also to include direct observation (either analogue or naturalistic), supplemented by laboratory tests and self-report data (Gordon, 1997; Reitman & Hupp, 2003). By contrast, because of concerns about parents' ability to provide useful information and adolescents' willingness to supply it, file reviews and permanent product records (e.g., disciplinary records, classroom attendance logs; Frick, 1998; Patterson, Reid, & Dishion, 1992) have become staples in the diagnostic assessment of Conduct Disorder.

Choice of assessment targets and measurement strategies may also be influenced by research. For example, developmental psychopathologists have found that aggressive behavior may be expressed differently by boys and girls and that outcomes associated with conduct problems may be related to time of onset (Robins & Rutter, 1990). Similarly, McMahon and Frick (2005) note that important developmental considerations may even dictate assessment of social and community-based risk factors that diverge significantly from assessment procedures in general outpatient clinics (e.g., assessment of callous-unemotional traits, use of analogue assessment procedures). Many of the changes in the forthcoming *DSM-V* will attempt to redress shortcomings in the *DSM*'s treatment of developmental issues (Pine et al., 2002).

Finally, greater specialization is also apparent in research involving internalizing disorders such as anxiety disorders. Specifically, parents may be limited in their ability to provide diagnostic information and children may be reluctant or unable to talk about their fears. Behavioral avoidance tests (BATs) have been utilized to provide clearer evidence of impaired functioning than can typically be acquired via pencil-and-paper assessments. In some cases, BATs go beyond diagnostic considerations and are used to obtain functional assessment data in a manner comparable to the use of functional analysis in applied behavioral assessment (Silverman & Kurtines, 1996). Because mood and anxiety disorders among adults have largely been diagnosed with self-reports (e.g., Beck Depression Inventory, State-Trait Anxiety Inventory), measures of cognition and affect have been readily assimilated into assessment practices with children and adolescents (see Reynolds, 1994; Velting, Setzer, & Albano, 2004). In contrast to research and clinical work with children and adolescents diagnosed with internalizing problems, consideration of cognitive and affective variables has been less frequently observed in research involving externalizing children (see Pelham, Wheeler, & Chronis, 1998).

REBIRTH OF FUNCTIONAL ASSESSMENT

At one time, contingency analysis (also known as A-B-C [antecedent-behavior-consequence] analysis) was such a fundamental part of behavioral assessment that it scarcely warranted mention. Early CBA efforts routinely began with careful spec-ification of target behaviors, setting events, antecedents, and consequent conditions (see Hawkins, 1986). As behavioral assessment matured, the assessment of context began to incorporate systemic factors and macrosocial factors such as the school en-vironment. Although formal assessment of family factors was not common (e.g., the use of paper-and-pencil measures of family functioning), the development of parent-directed interventions (Patterson, 1965) and clinical work with children in institutions such as schools and hospitals has long demanded a high level of concern about the social environment (e.g., Van Houten et al., 1988). In contrast to the view that be-havioral analyses must be simplistic or linear, Patterson and Reid's (1970) case study of a highly noncompliant and antisocial boy hypothesized numerous contextual fac-tors (e.g., family stress, poverty) that might have contributed to maintenance and generalization failures. Goldiamond's (1984) nonlinear analyses of parenting are also symbolic of the more complex forms of functional assessment that have failed to re-ceive sufficient attention in past reviews of behavioral assessment. Through the 1980s, Forehand and colleagues (e.g., Forehand & McCombs, 1988) conducted pioneering research on the relation of maternal depression and marital function to treatment outcome, thus setting the stage for assessment of a much broader range of child-, parent-, and family-level variables (Chronis, Chako, Fabiano, Wymbs, & Pelham, 2004). Nevertheless, by the early 1990s, functional assessment seemed to play a much less important role in mainstream child research in externalizing and internalizing populations, where evidenced-based treatments have tended to emphasize manual-ized interventions based on *DSM* taxa (see Reitman, 2006, for an extended discussion).

Although functional assessment appeared to wane in mainstream behavior therapy with children, it remained a cornerstone of ideographic treatments conceived in the applied behavior analytic tradition. Indeed, following refinements of well-described procedures for conducting functional analyses (see Iwata et al., 1982/1994), there has been an explosion of research in select populations of children and adolescents that are well-suited to experimental analyses. Specifically, functional analyses of problem behavior for children with developmental disabilities have become routine in this population. Since the mid-1990s, functional analyses have been used almost to the exclusion of other methods, although rating scales and interviews are sometimes utilized (see O'Neill et al., 1997). Functional analyses involve direct manipulation of setting events, antecedents, or consequences (in analogue or in vivo situations) to test hypothesized relations between these manipulations and behavior change. Although brief, modified versions of functional analysis are now being adapted to suit the demands of children with typically developing functional capacity and a wider range of behavioral challenges (e.g., Northup & Gulley, 2001), they are not yet in widespread use. Functional assessments that do not involve direct manipulation of the child's environment have been increasingly utilized with higher functioning children, particularly as part of functional behavioral assessments mandated under the Individuals with Disabilities Education Act (1997; Alberto & Troutman, 2003; Noell, 2003). Growth in functional assessment in some school systems has been so rapid that experts have suggested that the rate of growth is too fast to ensure the development of high-quality, effective behavior support plans (see Sasso, Conroy, Peck-Stichter, & Fox, 2001). Finally, there has been increasing attention to functional assessment in the area of school refusal behavior. One study demonstrated that prescriptive treatments based on the function of school refusal appeared more effective than nonprescriptive treatments in which a standard treatment was applied without matching treatment to function (Kearney & Silverman, 1999).

Trends in Training and Practice

If assessment practices are to change, changes are likely to begin with graduate training. Twenty years ago, Elbert and Holden (1987) reported that child clinical interns were far more likely to utilize projective tests (75% to 88%) than either behavioral interviews (44% to 58%) or behavioral checklists (11% to 33%). A more recent survey indicated that training directors perceived training in cognitive-behavioral therapy as valuable, but the benefits associated with training in behavioral assessment were not evaluated (Stedman, Hatch, & Shoenfeld, 2001). By contrast, Elliot, Miltenberger, Kaster-Bundgaard, and Lumley (1996) found that the top five assessment practices among practicing behavior therapists were (defined as the percentage of clients that received it) interviews (94%), direct observation (52%), rating scales (49%), self-monitoring (44%), and interview with significant others (42%). Although results were not stratified by population (i.e., child versus adult), it is striking that academics were more likely than practitioners to report that clients completed standardized rating scales (67% versus 48%). Unfortunately, although both practitioners and academics reported use of direct observation with over 50% of their clients, details about the nature of the observations were not provided.

In the school system, utilization of functional assessment has been boosted by legislation that requires meeting due process requirements associated with changes in a child's educational placement (Noell, 2003). Nevertheless, while an increasingly strong database supports the efficacy of functional assessment when used with persons with developmental disabilities, limited data support the clinical utility of functional assessment with higher functioning children in school settings (Gresham, 2004; Nelson-Gray, 2003; Noell, 2003). Leaders in school-based assessment have voiced concern about widespread dissemination of functional assessment practices in advance of solid empirical data and have called for more research (see Gresham, 2004; Sasso et al., 2001). Toward that end, a recently published study attempted to adapt functional assessment procedures to the school setting by developing function-based interviews and rating scales for teachers. Data from this preliminary study revealed that interrater agreement on a rank order of behavioral function was low (Kwak, Ervin, Anderson, & Austin, 2004). By contrast, another study suggested that agreement across measurement methods (e.g., interview and ratings) was acceptable and that treatment response was enhanced when informed by functional assessment (Newcomer & Lewis, 2004).

Despite some of the promising developments in CBA in recent years, there are significant economic challenges to overcome before empirically sound assessment can be more widely practiced. For example, anecdotal reports from CBAs suggest that reimbursement for traditional clinic-based testing has been limited in recent years (Kelley, 2003). McGlough and Clarkin (2004) note that many third-party payers distinguish between *evaluation* or *assessment* (sometimes called an intake or biopsychosocial interview) and *testing* (defined as norm-based, standardized evaluation intended to inform treatment planning or clarify complex diagnostic questions), with significant limitations being placed on the latter, more time- and resource-intensive efforts. So far, at least two studies suggest that practitioners working with children and adolescents feel that their ability to practice has been negatively affected by managed care (Cashel, 2002; Piotrowski, Belter, & Keller, 1998).

Although not limited to assessment, one implication of testing constraints imposed by managed care is a reduction in utilization of tests with limited or suspect psychometric qualities. Thus, though still popular, the use of projective tests, especially the Rorschach, appears to be declining. Notably, significant reductions in the administration of IQ and achievement tests are also evident (Cashel, 2002). This may reflect reductions in unnecessary or superfluous psychoeducational testing (e.g., as part of a battery of tests given without regard to presenting problems), but these reimbursement policies may also inhibit the administration of measures that contribute to treatment outcome or treatment monitoring. Given that well over half the children diagnosed with common externalizing problems like ADHD may have academic problems or learning disabilities (Lyon, Fletcher, & Barnes, 2003), reductions in psychoeducational assessment may constitute a legitimate threat to the hypothesis-testing approach endorsed by Ollendick and Hersen (1993). Without some form of psychoeducational assessment, the ability of the clinician to rule out the contribution of academic difficulties (e.g., poor tool skills) to behavioral problems may be hampered as well (see Allyon & Roberts, 1974; Witt & Beck, 2000).

Outside of managed care, behavioral assessment in the schools is likely to continue as dictated by federal law and local implementation policies. One factor that seems likely to impact the course of behavioral assessment concerns the emergence of RTI, or the response to intervention movement (Willis & Dumont, 2006). Advocates of RTI have argued strongly against perpetuation of the status quo in psychoeducational assessment and placement. Interestingly, assessment practices designed to inform treatment decisions are integral to attempts to reform intervention in the classroom, a theme that is also echoed in recent efforts to promote empirically based assessment in clinical practice settings. Interestingly, restrictions or limitations placed on psychoeducational testing by HMOs in the public sector and potentially by RTI advocates inside of schools could represent an opportunity for curriculum-based measurement, a system of assessment and intervention that is clearly based on a behavioral approach to instruction (see Shinn, 1989). Some curriculum-based techniques are similar to procedures employed in functional analysis in that they manipulate academic performance parameters (e.g., task difficulty) to clarify the function of behavioral problems in the classroom (O'Neill et al., 1997). Many curriculum-based approaches also offer significant time savings relative to traditional psychoeducational testing (Witt & Beck, 2000). However, unless the utility of these procedures can be clearly established, it seems improbable that third-party payers will authorize payment for these services. For CBAs to take advantage of new technologies, efforts must be directed to educating both consumers and third-party payers about the empirically supported benefits of diagnostic *and* functional assessment.

In contrast to traditional assessment measures, sharp increases have been noted in the use of behavioral rating scales (e.g., Child Behavior Checklist or Conners' Rating Scales) by a theoretically diverse group of American Psychiatric Association-member clinicians working with children and adolescents (Cashel, 2002). Inquiring about HMO-related changes and their likely impact on their assessment practices, only rating scales (e.g., Behavior Assessment System for Children, Child Behavior Checklist, Conners' Parent Rating Scale, and Teacher Report Form) were expected to be utilized more frequently in future assessments. Cashel ultimately concluded that ease of use and interpretation may explain *both* the rising interest in behavioral rating scales and the continuing popularity of some forms of projective testing (e.g., Draw-A-Person, Sentence Completion, Bender-Gestalt). Users of behavioral assessment methods such as rating scales noted benefits in tracking client progress and modifying treatment focus and a desire to adhere to ethical guidelines concerning assessment and treatment (see Hatfield & Ogles, 2004; Lambert & Hawkins, 2004).

Taken together, existing studies of clinical practice suggest that widely available, well-normed, easily administered, and resource-efficient measurement tools would be welcomed by both third-party payers and clinicians. Diagnostic assessments utilizing efficient measures stand to gain, whereas traditional testing and more labor- and cost-intensive approaches may be in jeopardy. In school settings, the use of functional behavioral assessment has not always enjoyed widespread acceptance, but it appears to be on the rise, following legislation mandating its use.

THE FUTURE OF BEHAVIORAL ASSESSMENT: EVIDENCE-BASED ASSESSMENT

These are exciting times for CBA enthusiasts. Surveying the landscape of assessment in clinical practice, behavioral assessment has become commonplace, even among eclectic and nonbehavioral practitioners. A recent study suggested that interest in outcome assessment among behavioral and cognitive-behavior therapists working with children may well be higher than among other clinicians. Hatfield and Ogles (2004) reported that among a heterogeneous sample of 874 American Psychiatric Association-member child clinicians, only 37% reported routinely utilizing some form of measurement to track outcomes. However, that number rose to 50% among cognitive-behavioral therapists, and 54% among child clinicians in general (it was likely even higher among child clinicians with a cognitive-behavioral orientation, but these data were not reported).

In CBA research, there has been rapid growth in the number and variety of assessment tools and an explosion of studies examining their reliability and validity. However, despite the advances noted earlier, at least two major issues are likely to preoccupy behavioral scientists for the next decade and beyond. The first issue concerns the validity and utility of existing assessment practices, a problem noted by Nelson and her colleagues nearly 20 years ago (Hayes, Nelson, & Jarrett, 1987). A second and related issue was raised by Kazdin (2005) and parallels the distinction between efficacy and effectiveness noted by Weisz and Weiss (1993). If empirically based assessment methods developed in research settings are seldom used in clinical practice, there is ultimately little need for such research. We close the chapter with a discussion of earlier attempts to improve the validity of assessment practices and possible solutions to problems presently confronting CBAs.

EVIDENCE-BASED ASSESSMENT

Ollendick and Hersen (1984, p. 4) argued that behavioral assessment has historically "been directed toward a description of current behavior and a specification of organismic and environmental conditions that occasion and maintain it." An important question addressed in this overview concerns how well that description applies to CBA as it is practiced today. As we have shown, rather than attending to factors that occasion problem behavior (in an ideographic sense), most research in CBA has largely focused on diagnostic assessment. Consequently, less attention has been devoted to the kinds of research activities needed to establish the reliability and validity of methods to evaluate treatment response. Further, only a limited amount of research that has occurred since the mid-1980s has concerned itself with the kind of assessment practices described by Ollendick and Hersen, and most of that work can be found in a small number of journals that emphasize the treatment of persons with developmental disabilities. Interestingly, the tenuous connection between *DSM* diagnosis and treatment success (see Pelham et al., 2005) has led clinical researchers to reexamine the relationship between assessment practices, treatment planning, and treatment outcome. Inasmuch as behavioral assessment was once defined by a strong link between assessment and treatment (see Gross, 1990; Hawkins & Mathews, 1999; Hayes, Nelson, & Jarrett, 1986), such questioning may well set the stage for a significant reprioritization of assessment practices, at least in university and research-based settings.

Given that diagnostically focused assessment has become the dominant assessment model employed by contemporary CBAs, it is somewhat surprising that so little work has been done to establish what Nelson-Gray (2003) calls "the treatment utility of assessment" for diagnostic assessment (Pelham et al., 2005). Defined as "the degree to which assessment is shown to contribute to beneficial treatment outcome"(Nelson-Gray, 2003, p. 521), the treatment utility of assessment derives from the concept of incremental validity (see Hayes et al., 1986, 1987). That is, to justify any evaluation practice, assessment methods and procedures must result in greater or more rapid treatment success than either no assessment or an established assessment practice. Alternatively, a given assessment approach might foster results comparable to an established procedure, but do so with fewer resources. A key aspect of determining the treatment utility of an assessment procedure is *experimental manipulation* (for details, see Hayes et al., 1986; Nelson-Gray, 2003) of some aspect of the assessment process (e.g., who has access to functional assessment data). Only when experimental manipulation occurs can the incremental validity of a given behavioral assessment practice be known (Johnston & Murray, 2003).

Recent interest in incremental validity gave rise to an important special section of the *Journal of Clinical Child and Adolescent Psychology* (Mash & Hunsley, 2005).

For example, in a review of common procedures employed in the assessment of ADHD, Pelham et al. (2005) argue that the use of lengthy structured interviews is of questionable utility for diagnosing the disorder. Instead, they suggest that brief measures completed by both parents and teachers, and brief observations and records containing information about a child's seatwork performance, are likely to be better indicators of an ADHD diagnosis. However, the determination of a measure's contribution as an aid to diagnostic efficiency or accuracy is not synonymous with treatment utility. Indeed, if diagnosis itself lacks treatment utility, then all assessment efforts directed toward diagnosis suffer.

Because of questions concerning the incremental validity of existing assessment practices for ADHD, Pelham et al. (2005) suggest that clinicians de-emphasize ADHD diagnosis and allocate more time to the functional assessment of problem behaviors associated with the diagnosis (i.e., outcomes; see Table 1.1). Functional behavioral assessments (FBAs) require that therapists identify the antecedents and consequences of problem behavior and systematically evaluate a number of competing hypotheses about the factors maintaining the behavior (e.g., Is the child's arguing a function of parent or sibling attention, escape from demands, or attempts to coercively obtain tangibles?). Although research has yet to demonstrate that the treatment utility of FBA is greater than the treatment utility of *DSM-IV* diagnostic criteria for ADHD, Nelson-Gray (2003) identified a number of experimental studies providing evidence to support the treatment utility of FBA for problem behaviors such as self-injury.

With respect to diagnostic assessment in CBA, Acierno, Hersen, and Van Hasselt (1998) argue that refinements in *DSM* taxonomies might produce more homogeneous groupings that could improve outcomes for structured, manualized, diagnosis-driven treatment approaches. Improved outcomes would provide indirect evidence of treatment utility. Cone (1998, p. 41) notes that such topographical behavioral assessments (what is here called diagnostic assessment) "could be subjected to functional evaluation. If assessment produced data describing topography that was then used successfully for some purpose, the assessment would be seen as functionally useful," even if it was not derived from a functional assessment. Similarly, Nelson-Gray (2003) suggested that even personality assessment (e.g., conscientiousness) could have treatment utility if, for example, a parent's "low conscientiousness" score predicted dropout or poor compliance with homework assignments. If "low scorers" could be distinguished, given a modified form of treatment based on their conscientiousness score, and demonstrated improved treatment outcome, the assessment data would have established treatment utility (Nelson-Gray, 2003, p. 522, terms this "the methodology of obtained differences"). Nelson-Gray also suggests that when diagnostic groupings are more heterogeneous, there may be a greater need for functional assessment methodologies.

Because many manualized treatments are based on a diagnosis-to-treatment model, the treatment utility of diagnostic assessment could be evaluated in that context (Acierno et al., 1998). For example, major empirically supported parent training models are relatively silent on the topic of functional behavioral assessment and appear to take a "structural" approach to treating externalizing problems (e.g., Hembree-Kigin & McNeil, 1995). Put another way, many manualized empirically supported parent-training programs neither explicitly teach functional assessment principles nor advise altering one's treatment approach based on the function of the behavioral problems displayed by the child. This is not an indictment of parent training approaches per se, but it raises questions about the merits of diagnostic and functional assessment in contemporary behavioral practice with families. Mischel (1979, as cited in Ollendick & Hersen, 1984, p. 740) once raised concerns about personality assessment that still have salience in the present context:

> My intentions . . . were not to undo personality but to defend individuality and the uniqueness of each person against what I saw as the then prevalent form of clinical hostility: the tendency to use a few behavioral signs to categorize people enduringly into fixed slots on the assessor's favorite nomothetic trait dimensions and to assume that these slot positions were sufficiently informative to predict specific behavior and to make extensive decisions about a person's whole life.

With diagnostic assessment substituted for personality, ought we not question whether diagnostic assessment produces data that inform "extensive decisions" such as developing treatment plans and making placement recommendations that may strongly affect a young person and his or her family? If diagnostic assessment and the treatment-from-diagnosis logic underlying many manualized treatments are insufficient to produce positive outcomes, can functional assessment be offered as a viable alternative or supplemental approach? If so, it must be acknowledged that the treatment utility of functional assessment for persons not diagnosed with developmental disabilities has yet to be established (Nelson-Gray, 2003).

In addition to the many issues raised previously, questions about incremental validity can also be extended to multimodal assessment. Consensus regarding the need for multimodal assessments has become so uniform that the absence of data needed to inform clinical decision making or resolve inconsistencies across raters (e.g., parents, teachers, and self-report) might be surprising. In fact, concerns about combining information exist in both functional and diagnostic assessment traditions (Miltenberger, 2000; Youngstrom, Loeber, & Stouthamer-Loeber, 2000). Beyond questions of disagreement, critical questions also remain about the incremental validity of specific behavioral assessment practices utilized with children, including the computerized assessment of attention (Reitman et al., 1998), direct observation (Tryon, 1998), and teacher ratings (Handwerk, Larzerlere, Soper, & Friman, 1999; J. R. Nelson, Benner, Reid, Epstein, & Currin, 2002).

APPLIED ASSESSMENT

Whatever is claimed about the importance of incremental validity and empirically based assessment, it matters little if these bold initiatives do not translate into changes in clinical assessment practices. For many years, practitioners complained that the treatment research literature did not inform clinical practice (Barlow, 1981). Only recently have concerted efforts to address some of these concerns come to fruition (see Chorpita, 2007). Incidentally, modular treatments may increase the importance of assessment, as these kinds of interventions appear to require more specific information about functional impairments and response to treatment (see Chorpita, 2007).

Unfortunately, practitioners seeking to document and evaluate their effectiveness in outpatient settings have rarely been offered much that would be of use in clinical practice. One legitimate effort to assist practitioners was undertaken by Hawkins and colleagues (see Hawkins & Mathews, 1999; Hawkins, Mathews, & Hamdan, 1999), who advocated that clinicians adopt a level one research model that emphasized a labor-nonintensive, free-wheeling kind of accountability that should improve one's effectiveness as a clinician. The level one approach dictates that clinicians system-atically monitor clinical outcomes—without any need to scientifically prove what is causing those effects. A similar approach has recently been advocated by Lambert and his colleagues (Harmon, Hawkins, Lambert, Slade, & Whipple, 2005), with prelimi-nary data showing that simple feedback to therapists based on systematic monitoring of clinical outcomes is very beneficial to client progress.

While determining treatment outcomes is the main focus of studies that might evaluate the utility of assessment, Hodges (2004) provides additional insight into the ways that assessment could be integrated into all stages of therapy. For example, when conducted during intake sessions, assessment can enhance therapist and parent agree-ment concerning the selection of intervention targets. Following this discussion, the therapist may utilize assessment information to develop a treatment plan that directly addresses the needs of the child, as well as the identified strengths and weaknesses of the family. Even when presenting problems are carefully identified, treatment selec-tion may still be challenging. For example, Hodges points out that a comorbid diag-nosis makes it difficult for the clinician to select an empirically supported treatment that will address both disorders. Likewise, Nelson-Gray (2003) explains that some disorders have more than one empirically validated treatment; however, no specific decision-making criteria currently exist to aid clinicians in selecting one treatment over another.

Although the development of empirically sound, user-friendly tools for managing and evaluating individual response to treatment have lagged behind the progress in *DSM*-based diagnostic practices, help may be on the way. To address many of the issues raised earlier, Kazdin (2005) has recommended adopting the following principles concerning the revision of existing behavioral assessment measures and the development of new measures and methods. Specifically, he recommended that more research be devoted to measures that:

- Are acceptable to clients and therapists (seen as reasonable, relevant, and worth-while)
- Are feasible to administer (brief, user-friendly)
- Are easily adapted to track individualized patient concerns (e.g., goals)
- Can be used repeatedly and retain validity and be bidirectional (e.g., permit assessment of "getting worse" and "getting better")
- Can be applied across, or are relevant to, different treatments
- Lend themselves to assessment of change in meaningful units (e.g., have real-life referents)

At this point, it is unclear how Kazdin's (2005) recommendations will be received; however, it should be noted that much of what Kazdin suggests fits well within the behavior analytic (contextual) paradigm, which has long emphasized the importance of tracking socially meaningful behaviors, systematically, over time (see Hawkins & Mathews, 1999).

RAPPROCHEMENT: BLENDING DIAGNOSTIC AND FUNCTIONAL ASSESSMENT

Although the functional and diagnostic approaches can be distinguished, there have been efforts to combine these approaches, often with the implicit though untested assumption that such efforts would enhance treatment outcome. One approach to blending diagnostic and functional approaches was introduced by Hawkins (1979), who argued that child assessment should be conceptualized as a "funnel." At the wide end of the funnel, child functioning is evaluated broadly, followed by a progressively more targeted behavioral assessment. Scotti, Morris, McNeil, and Hawkins (1996) elaborated on this model and suggested that functional assessment could be integrated with diagnostic assessment. Scotti et al. (1996) noted that functional assessment was not served well by the *DSM*'s existing axial format, but they did not recommend abandoning it. Instead, they argued that Axes I and II could be retained unchanged, with Axes III and IV adapted and refined to facilitate a more detailed (functional) account of setting events, antecedents, and consequences. Axis V would make better use of empirically supported measures to track outcomes.

It is presently unclear whether this blend of diagnostic and functional assessment is common practice among CBAs, but such a combination could ultimately prove to have strong incremental validity. In the absence of clear empirical data to guide clinical decision making, the consensus approach among CBAs seems to begin with treatment based on a largely diagnostic approach (i.e., treatment from diagnosis). If treatment results are unsatisfactory, functional assessment may then be utilized to enhance standard care (see Reitman & Hupp, 2003).

SUMMARY

Behavior therapy has undergone many changes since its inception in the 1950s. During its formative years, behavior therapy focused heavily on the development of more effective treatments, but the importance of behavioral assessment practices was relatively unappreciated until the late 1970s and early 1980s. Since the early 1980s, trends in therapy have continued to drive changes in assessment practices. Most recently, concerns have arisen over the merits of some forms of behavioral assessment. Specifically, questions have arisen about diagnostic assessment, especially in the realm of treatment monitoring and outcome evaluation. As a result, the next decade may well feature more research evaluating the utility of functional behavioral assessment and greater appreciation for the diverse functions of behavioral assessment in child behavior therapy. Finally, as with the evidence-based treatment movement, there appears to be a large gap between the assessment practices utilized by university and grant-funded researchers and assessment activities in clinical practice settings. The greater empirical scrutiny that is being brought to bear on assessment in clinical practice appears consistent with societal trends emphasizing demands for accountability outside of and within the mental health system (Lambert & Hawkins, 2004). Although preliminary data suggest the need for changes in assessment practices to accommodate the realities of clinical practice, there are only limited data concerning guidance on empirically based assessment as it should be practiced in the field.

REFERENCES

Acierno, R., Hersen, M., & Van Hasselt, V. B. (1998). Prescriptive assessment and treatment. In A. S. Bellack & M. Hersen (Eds.), *Behavioral assessment: A practical handbook* (4th ed., pp. 47–62). Boston: Allyn & Bacon.

Alberto, P., & Troutman, A. (2003). *Applied behavior analysis for teachers* (6th ed.). New York Prentice-Hall.

Allyon, T., & Roberts, M. D. (1974). Eliminating discipline problems by strengthening academic performance. *Journal of Applied Behavior Analysis, 7,* 71–76.

American Psychiatric Association. (1980). *Diagnostic and statistical manual of mental disorders* (3rd ed.). Washington, DC: Author.

American Psychiatric Association. (2000). *Diagnostic and statistical manual of mental disorders* (4th ed., text rev.). Washington, DC: Author.

Barlow, D. H. (1981). On the relation of clinical research to clinical practice: Current issues, new directions. *Journal of Consulting and Clinical Psychology, 49,* 147–155.

Cashel, M. L. (2002). Child and adolescent psychological assessment: Current clinical practices and the impact of managed care. *Professional Psychology: Research and Practice, 33,* 446–453.

Chorpita, B. F. (2007). *Modular cognitive-behavioral therapy for childhood anxiety disorders.* New York: Guilford Press.

Chronis, A. M., Chako, A., Fabiano, G. A., Wymbs, B. T., & Pelham, W. E. (2004). Enhancements to the behavioral parent training paradigm for families of children with ADHD: Review and future directions. *Journal of Child and Family Psychology Review, 7,* 1–27.

Cone, J. D. (1978). The behavioral assessment grid (BAG): A conceptual framework and a taxonomy. *Behavior Therapy, 9,* 882–888.

Cone, J. D. (1998). Psychometric considerations: Concepts, contents, and methods. In A. S. Bellack & M. Hersen (Eds.), *Behavioral assessment: A practical handbook* (4th ed., pp. 22–46). Boston: Allyn & Bacon.

Eells, T. D. (1997). Psychotherapy case formulation: History and current status. In T. Eells (Ed.), *Handbook of psychotherapy case formulation* (pp. 1–25). New York: Guilford Press.

Elbert, J. C., & Holden, E. W. (1987). Child diagnostic assessment: Current training practices in clinical psychology internships. *Professional Psychology: Research and Practice, 18,* 587–596.

Elliot, A. J., Miltenberger, R. G., Kaster-Bundgaard, J., & Lumley, V. (1996). A national survey of assessment and therapy techniques used by behavior therapists. *Cognitive and Behavioral Practice, 3,* 107–125.

Elliott, S. N., & Piersel, W. C. (1982). Direct assessment of reading skills: An approach which links assessment to intervention. *School Psychology Review, 11,* 257–280.

Follette, W. C., & Hayes, S. C. (1992). Behavioral assessment in the DSM era. *Behavioral Assessment, 14,* 293–295.

Forehand, R. L., & McCombs, A. (1988). Unraveling antecedent-consequence conditions in maternal depression and adolescent functioning. *Behavioral Research and Therapy, 26,* 399–405.

Freeman, K. A., & Miller, C. A. (2002). Behavioral case conceptualization for children and adolescents. In M. Hersen (Ed.), *Clinical behavior therapy: Adults and children* (pp. 239–255). Hoboken, NJ: Wiley.

Frick, P. J. (1998). *Conduct disorders and severe antisocial behavior.* New York: Plenum Press.

Goldiamond, I. (1984). Training parent trainers and ethicists in nonlinear analysis of behavior. In R. F. Dangle & R. A. Polster (Eds.), *Parent training* (pp. 504–546). New York: Guilford Press.

Gordon, M. (1997). *How to operate an ADHD clinic or subspecialty practice* (1st ed., rev.). DeWitt, NY: GSI Publications.

Gresham, F. M. (2004). Current status and future directions of school-based behavioral interventions. *School Psychology Review, 33,* 326–343.

Gross, A. M. (1990). An analysis of measures and design strategies in research in Behavior Therapy: Is it still behavioral? *Behavior Therapy, 13,* 203–209.

Handwerk, M. J., Larzerlere, R. E., Soper, S. H., & Friman, P. C. (1999). Parent and child discrepancies in reporting severity of problem behaviors in three out-of-home settings. *Psychological Assessment, 11,* 14–23.

Harmon, C., Hawkins, E. J., Lambert, M. J., Slade, K., & Whipple, J. L. (2005). Improving outcomes for poorly responding clients: The use of clinical support tools and feedback to clients. *Journal of Clinical Psychology, 61*, 175–185.

Hatfield, D. R., & Ogles, B. M. (2004). The use of outcome measures by psychologists in clinical practice. *Professional Psychology: Research and Practice, 35*, 485–491.

Hawkins, R. P. (1979). The functions of assessment: Implications for selection and development of devices for assessing repertoires in clinical, educational, and other settings. *Journal of Applied Behavior Analysis, 12*, 501–516.

Hawkins, R. P. (1986). Selection of target behaviors. In R. O. Nelson & S. C. Hayes (Eds.), *Conceptual foundations of behavioral assessment* (pp. 331–385). New York: Guilford Press.

Hawkins, R. P., & Mathews, J. R. (1999). Frequent monitoring of clinical outcomes: Research and accountability for clinical practice. *Education and Treatment of Children 22*, 117–135.

Hawkins, R. P., Mathews, J. R., & Hamdan, L. (1999). *Measuring behavioral health outcomes: A practical guide.* New York: Plenum Press.

Hayes, S. C., Follette, W. C., & Follette, V. M. (1995). Behavior therapy: A contextual approach. In A. S. Gurman & S. B. Messer (Eds.), *Essential psychotherapies: Theory and practice* (pp. 128–181). New York: Guilford Press.

Hayes, S. C., Nelson, R. O., & Jarrett, R. B. (1986). Evaluating the quality of behavioral assessment. In R. O. Nelson & S. C. Hayes (Eds.), *Conceptual foundations of behavioral assessment* (pp. 463–503). New York: Guilford Press.

Hayes, S. C., Nelson, R. O., & Jarrett, R. B. (1987). The treatment utility of assessment: A functional approach to evaluating assessment quality. *American Psychologist, 42*, 963–974.

Haynes, S. N. (1998). The changing nature of behavioral assessment. In A. S. Bellack & M. Hersen (Eds.), *Behavioral assessment: A practical handbook* (4th ed., pp. 001–21). Boston: Allyn & Bacon.

Hembree-Kigin, T. L., & McNeil, C. B. (1995). *Parent-child interaction therapy.* New York: Plenum Press.

Hersen, M., & Bellack, A. S. (1976). Preface. In M. Hersen & A. S. Bellack (Eds.), *Behavioral assessment: A practical handbook* (pp. ix–x). New York: Pergamon Press.

Hodges, K. (2004). Using assessment in everyday practice for the benefit of families and practitioners. *Professional Psychology: Research and Practice, 35*, 449–456.

Individuals with Disabilities Education Act Amendments of 1997, Pub. L. No. 105-17, 20 U.S.C. §1400 *et seq.*

Iwata, B. A., Dorsey, M. F., Slifer, K. J., Bauman, K. E., & Richman, G. S. (1994). Toward a functional analysis of self-injury. *Journal of Applied Behavior Analysis, 27*, 197–209. (Reprinted from *Analysis and Intervention in Developmental Disabilities, 2*, 3–20, 1982)

Johnston, C., & Murray, C. (2003). Incremental validity in the psychological assessment of children and adolescents. *Psychological Assessment, 15*, 496–507.

Kazdin, A. E. (2005). Evidence-based assessment for children and adolescents: Issues in measurement development and clinical application. *Journal of Clinical Child and Adolescent Psychology, 34*, 548–558.

Kearney, C. A., & Silverman, W. K. (1999). Functionally-based prescriptive and nonprescriptive treatment for children and adolescents with school refusal behavior. *Behavior Therapy, 30*, 673–695.

Kelley, M. L. (2003). Assessment of children's behavior in the school setting: An overview. In M. L. Kelley, D. Reitman, & G. H. Noell (Eds.), *Practitioner's guide to empirically based measures of school behavior* (AABT Clinical Assessment Series, pp. 7–22). New York: Kluwer Academic/Plenum Press.

Krasner, L. (1992). The concepts of syndrome and functional analysis: Compatible or incompatible? *Behavioral Assessment, 14,* 307–321.

Kwak, M. M., Ervin, R. A., Anderson, M. Z., & Austin, J. (2004). Agreement of function across methods used in school-based functional assessment with preadolescent and adolescent students. *Behavior Modification, 28,* 375–401.

Lambert, M. J., & Hawkins, E. J. (2004). Measuring outcome in professional practice: Considerations in selecting and using brief outcome instruments. *Professional Psychology: Research and Practice, 35,* 492–499.

Lyon, G. R., Fletcher, J. M., & Barnes, M. C. (2003). Learning disabilities. In E. J. Mash & R. A. Barkley (Eds.), *Child psychopathology* (2nd ed., pp. 520–586). New York: Guilford Press.

Mash, E. J., & Hunsley, J. (2005). Evidence-based assessment of child and adolescent disorders: Issues and challenges. *Journal of Clinical Child and Adolescent Psychology, 34,* 362–379.

Mash, E. J., & Terdal, L. G. (1988). Behavioral assessment of child and family disturbance. In E. J. Mash & L. G. Terdal (Eds.), *Behavioral assessment of childhood disorders: Selected core problems* (2nd ed., pp. 3–65). New York: Guilford Press.

Mash, E. J., & Wolfe, D. A. (2005). *Abnormal child psychology* (3rd ed.). Belmont, CA: Thompson Wadsworth.

McGlough, J. F., & Clarkin, J. F. (2004). Personality disorders. In M. Hersen (Ed.), *Psychological assessment in clinical practice: A pragmatic guide* (pp. 117–145). New York: Brunner-Routledge.

McMahon, R. J., & Frick, P. J. (2005). Evidence-based assessment of conduct problems in children and adolescents. *Journal of Clinical Child and Adolescent Psychology, 34,* 477–505.

Meier, S. T. (1999). Training the practitioner-scientist: Bridging case conceptualization, assessment, and intervention. *Counseling Psychologist, 27,* 846–869.

Miltenberger, R. G. (2000). Strategies for clarifying ambiguous functional analysis outcomes: Comments on Kennedy. *Journal of Positive Behavioral Interventions, 2,* 202–204.

Mischel, W. (1979). On the interface of cognition and personality: Beyond the person situation debate. *American Psychologist, 34,* 740–754.

Nelson, J. R., Benner, G. J., Reid, R. C., Epstein, M. H., & Currin, D. (2002). The convergent validity of office discipline referrals with the CBCL-TRF. *Journal of Emotional and Behavioral Disorders, 10,* 181–188.

Nelson, R. O. (1983). Behavioral assessment: Past, present, and future. *Behavioral Assessment, 5,* 195–206.

Nelson-Gray, R. O. (2003). Treatment utility of psychological assessment. *Psychological Assessment, 15,* 521–531.

Newcomer, L. L., & Lewis, T. J. (2004). Functional behavioral assessment: An investigation of reliability and effectiveness of function-based interventions. *Journal of Emotional and Behavioral Disorders, 12,* 168–181.

Noell, G. H. (2003). Functional assessment of school-based concerns. In M. L. Kelley, D. Reitman, & G. H. Noell (Eds.), *Practitioner's guide to empirically based measures of school behavior* (AABT Clinical Assessment Series, pp. 37–61). New York: Kluwer Academic/Plenum Press.

Northup, J., & Gulley, V. (2001). Some contributions of functional analysis to the assessment of behaviors associated with attention deficit hyperactivity disorder and the effects of stimulant medication. *School Psychology Review, 30,* 227–238.

Ollendick, T. H., & Hersen, M. (1984). An overview of child behavioral assessment. In T. H. Ollendick & M. Hersen (Eds.), *Child behavioral assessment: Principles and procedures* (pp. 3–19). New York: Pergamon Press.

Ollendick, T. H., & Hersen, M. (1993). Child and adolescent behavioral assessment. In T. H. Ollendick & M. Hersen (Eds.), *Handbook of child and adolescent assessment* (pp. 3–14). Needham Heights, MA: Allyn & Bacon.

O'Neill, R. E., Horner, R. H., Albin, R. W., Sprague, J. R., Storey, K., & Newton, J. S. (1997). *Functional assessment and program development for problem behavior: A practical handbook* (2nd ed.). Pacific Grove, CA: Brooks/Cole.

Orvaschel, H. (2006). Structured and semi-structured interviews. In M. Hersen (Ed.), *Clinician's handbook of child behavioral assessment* (pp. 159–179). New York: Elsevier.

Orvaschel, H., Faust, J., & Hersen, M. (2001). General issues in conceptualization and treatment. In H. Orvaschel, J. Faust, & M. Hersen (Eds.), *Handbook of conceptualization and treatment of child psychopathology* (pp. 3–7). Oxford: Elsevier.

Patterson, G. R. (1965). Responsiveness to social stimuli. In L. Krasner & L. Ullman (Eds.), *Research in behavior modification* (pp. 157–178). New York: Holt, Rinehart and Winston.

Patterson, G. R., & Reid, J. B. (1970). Reciprocity and coercion: Two facets of social systems. In C. Neuringer & J. L. Michael (Eds.), *Behavior modification in clinical psychology* (pp. 133–177). New York: Appleton Century Crofts.

Patterson, G. R., Reid, J. B., & Dishion, T. R. (1992). *Antisocial boys*. Eugene, OR: Castalia.

Pelham, W. E., Fabiano, G. A., & Massetti, G. M. (2005). Evidence-based assessment of attention deficit hyperactivity disorder in children and adolescents. *Journal of Clinical Child and Adolescent Psychology, 34,* 449–476.

Pelham, W. E., Wheeler, T., & Chronis, A. (1998). Empirically-supported psychosocial treatments for attention deficit hyperactivity disorder. *Journal of Clinical Child Psychology, 27,* 190–205.

Pine, D. S., Alegria, M., Cook, E. H., Costello, E. J., Dahl, R. E., Koretz, D., et al. (2002). Advances in developmental sciences and DSM-V. In D. J. Kupfer (Ed.), *A research agenda for DSM-IV* (pp. 85–122). Washington, DC: American Psychiatric Association.

Piotrowski, C., Belter, R. W., & Keller, J. W. (1998). The impact of managed care on the practice of psychological testing: Preliminary findings. *Journal of Personality Assessment, 70,* 441–447.

Rapport, M. D., Kofler, M. J., & Himmerich, C. (2006). Activity measurement. In M. Hersen (Ed.), *Clinician's handbook of child behavioral assessment* (pp. 125–157). New York: Elsevier.

Reitman, D. (2006). Overview of child behavioral assessment. In M. Hersen (Ed.), *Clinician's handbook of child behavioral assessment* (pp. 4–24). New York: Elsevier.

Reitman, D., Hummel, R., Franz, D. Z., & Gross, A. M. (1998). A review of methods and instruments for assessing externalizing disorders: Theoretical and practical considerations in rendering a diagnosis. *Clinical Psychology Review, 18,* 555–584.

Reitman, D., & Hupp, S. D. A. (2003). Behavior problems in the school setting: Synthesizing structural and functional assessment. In M. L. Kelley, D. Reitman, & G. H. Noell (Eds.), *Practitioner's guide to empirically based measures of school behavior* (AABT Clinical Assessment Series, pp. 23–36). New York: Kluwer Academic/Plenum Press.

Reynolds, W. M. (1994). Assessment of depression in children and adolescents by self-report. In W. M. Johnston & H. F. Johnston (Eds.), *Handbook of depression in children and adolescents* (pp. 209–234). New York: Plenum Press.

Robins, L. N., & Rutter, M. (1990). *Straight and devious pathways from childhood to adulthood*. New York: Cambridge University Press.

Roberts, M. W. (2001). Clinic observations of structured parent-child interaction designed to evaluate externalizing disorders. *Psychological Assessment, 13,* 46–58.

Sasso, G. M., Conroy, M. A., Peck-Stichter, J., & Fox, J. J. (2001). Slowing down the bandwagon: The misapplication of functional assessment for students with emotional or behavioral disorders. *Behavioral Disorders, 26,* 282–296.

Scotti, J. R., Morris, T. L., McNeil, C. B., & Hawkins, R. P. (1996). DSM-IV and disorders of childhood and adolescence: Can structural criteria be functional? *Journal of Consulting and Clinical Psychology, 64,* 1177–1191.

Shinn, M. (1989). *Curriculum-based measurement: Assessing special children.* New York: Guilford Press.

Silva, F. (1993). *Foundations of behavioral assessment.* New York: Sage.

Silverman, W. K., & Kurtines, W. M. (1996). *Anxiety and phobic disorders: A pragmatic approach.* New York: Plenum Press.

Stedman, J. M., Hatch, J. P., & Shoenfeld, L. S. (2001). Internship directors' valuation of preinternship preparation in test-based assessment and psychotherapy. *Professional Psychology: Research and Practice, 32,* 421–424.

Tryon, W. W. (1998). Behavioral observation. In A. S. Bellack & M. Hersen (Eds.), *Behavioral assessment: A practical handbook* (4th ed., pp. 79–103). Boston: Allyn & Bacon.

Van Houten, R., Axelrod, S., Bailey, J. S., Favell, J. E., Foxx, R. M., Iwata, B. A., et al. (1988). The right to effective behavioral treatment. *Behavior Analyst, 11,* 111–114.

Velting, O. N., Setzer, N. J., & Albano, A. M. (2004). Update on advances in assessment and cognitive-behavioral treatment of anxiety disorders in children and adolescents. *Professional Psychology: Research and Practice, 35,* 42–54.

Watson, J. B. (1967). *Behavior: An introduction to comparative psychology.* New York: Holt, Rinehart, and Winston. (Original work published 1914)

Weisz, J. R., & Weiss, B. (1993). *Effects of psychotherapy with children and adolescents.* Newbury Park, CA: Sage.

Willis, J. O., & Dumont, R. (2006). And never the twain shall meet: Can response to intervention and cognitive assessment be reconciled? *Psychology in the Schools, 43,* 901–908.

Witt, J. C., & Beck, R. (2000). *One-minute academic functional assessment and interventions: "Can't" do it . . . or "won't" do it?* Longmont, CO: Sopris West.

Youngstrom, E., Loeber, R., & Stouthamer-Loeber, M. (2000). Patterns and correlates of agreement between parent, teacher, and male adolescent ratings of externalizing and internalizing problems. *Journal of Consulting and Clinical Psychology, 68,* 1038–1050.

CHAPTER 2

Diagnostic Issues

AMANDA JENSEN DOSS, KRYSTAL T. COOK, AND BRYCE D. MCLEOD

The *Oxford English Dictionary* defines "diagnosis" as "identification of a disease by careful investigation of its symptoms and history; also, the opinion (formally stated) resulting from such an investigation" ("Diagnosis," 1989). Mental disorders were first documented in Egypt around 3000 BC, and the first system for identifying psychiatric diagnoses was developed in India in 1400 BC (Mack, Forman, Brown, & Frances, 1994). Nevertheless, childhood* psychopathology was largely neglected as an area of study prior to the twentieth century (Rubinstein, 1948), and the first version of the prevailing diagnostic system in the United States, the *Diagnostic and Statistical Manual of Mental Disorders* (*DSM*; American Psychiatric Association, 1952), contained only two categories of childhood disorders. Over the past 50 years, significant advances have been made in our understanding of childhood psychopathology and in methods of assessing the mental health needs of children. The purpose of this chapter is to review contemporary perspectives on the purpose of diagnosis, predominant classification systems, and diagnostic methods. We close the chapter with a discussion of the many factors (e.g., developmental and cultural considerations) that complicate diagnosis in clinical practice.

WHY DO WE DIAGNOSE?

Diagnosis serves several important purposes. Diagnoses facilitate communication among professionals about clinical practice and research settings. Diagnoses allow clinicians to summarize their clients' problems when communicating with other professionals. Diagnoses also permit integration of research findings across studies and allow clinicians to access the research findings most relevant to their clients. Indeed, matching treatments to diagnoses has gained increased attention in the past decade. The empirically supported treatments (EST) movement spearheaded by the American Psychological Association's Division 12 has attempted to increase

---

*Throughout the chapter, we use the terms "child" and "children" to refer to both children and adolescents, unless otherwise indicated. We use the term "client" to refer to the child being diagnosed.

clinicians' awareness and use of efficacious treatment approaches (Chambless & Ollendick, 2001). To accomplish these objectives, the American Psychological Association (Chambless et al., 1996, 1998) and others (e.g., Lonigan, Elbert, & Johnson, 1998) have generated lists of therapies that have passed some threshold of research support for the treatment of particular disorders (e.g., treatments for depression, Attention-Deficit/Hyperactivity Disorder [ADHD]). Because the lists are organized by *DSM* categories, the treating clinician must assign a diagnosis. Though the EST movement is based on the assumption that treatment should be matched to diagnosis, this assumption is largely untested (Nelson-Gray, 2003). Research is needed to establish the treatment utility of using diagnoses to determine treatment choice (Nelson-Gray, 2003).

Diagnoses are also the primary basis of third-party service authorization. Many clinics and insurance providers require clients to meet criteria for a diagnosis to qualify for services in publicly funded community-based service settings. Diagnosis also plays a role in qualifying children for some types of special education services under the Individuals with Disabilities Education Improvement Act of 2004 (IDEIA). Requiring diagnoses for service authorization raises a number of issues that are discussed later in the chapter.

Finally, diagnoses can be used to monitor treatment outcomes. Optimally, children who meet criteria for a disorder at treatment onset will no longer meet criteria at the end of treatment. Surprisingly, psychotherapy research has primarily focused on symptom improvement during therapy, with less emphasis on whether a client is "cured." Increasingly, the field is placing greater emphasis on whether treatments produce "clinically significant" change or represent a return to, or significant progress toward, "normal" functioning (Jacobson & Truax, 1991). Indeed, determining whether someone continues to meet criteria for a diagnosis at the end of treatment is one important indicator of clinically significant change.

CATEGORICAL AND DIMENSIONAL SYSTEMS OF CLASSIFICATION

Since Hippocrates developed his dimensional model of psychopathology based on the balance of humors within the body and Plato countered it with a categorical model of "divine madness," one of the fundamental debates about psychological disorders has been the issue of dimensional versus categorical classification (Mack et al., 1994). Though the pendulum of prevailing opinion has swung back and forth between the two sides of the issue, today the prevailing model is the categorical approach, most noticeably applied in the *DSM-IV-TR* (American Psychiatric Association, 2000) and the *International Classification of Diseases* (ICD-10; World Health Organization, 1993). Here, we briefly define the main characteristics of categorical and dimensional classification approaches and outline their respective strengths and limitations.

CATEGORICAL CLASSIFICATION

The categorical model of classification is based on the idea that mental health difficulties are best conceptualized as distinct disorders. Based on the medical model —that psychiatric diagnoses are disease entities similar to medical diseases—categorical approaches assume that individuals either do or do not have a particular diagnosis. To determine whether someone meets criteria for a diagnosis, clinicians assess for the presence or absence of the specific symptoms comprising the diagnosis, including their duration and associated impairment.

Originally developed in 1952 by the American Psychiatric Association to facilitate communication among professionals, the *DSM* has undergone five revisions. In the *DSM-I* and *DSM-II* diagnoses were largely defined according to a specific theory of psychopathology (i.e., psychoanalytic theory). Though the *DSM-I* and *DSM-II* represented a notable advance, generating diagnoses in terms of a single theory of psychopathology limited acceptance of the system (Follette & Houts, 1996). To gain wider appeal, diagnoses in the *DSM-III* (American Psychiatric Association, 1980) were rendered atheoretical; explicit references to particular theories were avoided. Subsequent versions of the *DSM* have employed work groups comprising researchers and clinicians to refine existing or propose new diagnostic categories based on research rather than theory.

The most recent version of the *DSM* is the fourth edition, text revision (American Psychiatric Association, 2000). The *DSM-IV-TR* uses a multiaxial system. The first axis includes Clinical Disorders and Other Conditions That May Be a Focus of Clinical Attention (e.g., anxiety, depression). Personality disorders and Mental Retardation are listed on Axis II. Axis III is used to report general medical conditions associated with mental disorders. Psychosocial and environmental problems that may contribute to the diagnosis and treatment of a mental disorder are reported on Axis IV. Finally, Axis V contains the Global Assessment of Functioning Scale, where clinicians rate an individual's overall functioning on a 0 to 100 scale. The manual contains descriptions of each disorder, including explanations of associated features, culture-, age-, and gender-specific features, as well as information on the course and prevalence of the disorder. Diagnoses are assigned following a polythetic format, in which only a subset of a larger set of symptoms is required to meet criteria for a given disorder. For example, a diagnosis of Major Depressive Disorder (MDD) requires the presence of 5 of 9 symptoms, one of which must be depressed mood (or, for children, irritability) or loss of pleasure in activities (American Psychiatric Association, 2000). Though this structure was designed to account for variation in symptom presentation across individuals, some have suggested that within-diagnosis heterogeneity promotes diagnostic confusion (Clark, Watson, & Reynolds, 1995).

DIMENSIONAL CLASSIFICATION

Dimensional systems conceptualize psychopathology as existing along a diagnostic continuum. Rather than considering psychopathology to be either present or absent, the dimensional model posits that symptoms vary naturally across the population, with low levels of symptoms being associated with lower impairment and higher levels of symptoms warranting clinical attention. This model of psychopathology has been advocated among researchers of adult psychopathology, particularly for the personality disorders (e.g., Widiger & Samuel, 2005). Thomas Achenbach and his colleagues have spearheaded the movement to develop a dimensional assessment system for childhood psychopathology, employing what they termed the "empirical approach" to the classification of psychopathology (Achenbach & Edelbrock, 1978). This work has resulted in the Achenbach System Empirically Based Assessment (ASEBA; Achenbach & Rescorla, 2001). Though other dimensional systems have been developed (see Rating Scales later in the chapter), we briefly describe the development of the ASEBA system to illustrate a typical dimensional approach to classification.

The ASEBA was developed to assess behavior, competencies, and personality (Achenbach & Rescorla, 2001). The system was empirically developed by administering a scale consisting of common childhood symptoms to large groups of children and then applying factor analysis to detect common factors of psychopathology (Achenbach, 1966, 1978; Achenbach & Edelbrock, 1979). These studies found that childhood psychopathology seemed to be organized into two "broadbands" of behavior: internalizing (i.e., symptoms directed inward, such as depression and anxiety) and externalizing (i.e., symptoms directed outward, such as aggression or delinquency) problems. Falling within these broadbands were "narrowband" syndromes, consisting of more fine-grained groupings of symptoms. The ASEBA has been revised over time, and the current version has a factor structure consisting of the internalizing and externalizing broadbands and eight narrowbands: Aggressive Behavior, Anxious/Depressed, Attention Problems, Rule-Breaking Behavior, Social Problems, Somatic Complaints, Thought Problems, and Withdrawn/Depressed (Achenbach & Rescorla, 2001).

Dimensional measures such as the ASEBA assume that symptoms are distributed continuously across the population. Normative samples are used to study the occurrence of symptoms within the population to determine whether a given symptom profile falls outside of what would be considered "normal" childhood behavior. For example, the current version of the ASEBA was administered to approximately 2,300 children from the 48 contiguous states, using a strategy to ensure that the ethnicity, region, and socioeconomic status of the sample were representative of the U.S. population (Achenbach & Rescorla, 2001). From this sample, age and gender subgroups were created, and the means and standard deviations of these subgroups were used to create norms. Norms are important because they allow comparison of a given child's score to scores of other children of the same age and sex. Most often, T scores are created to locate the individual within the normative sample. T scores have a mean of 50 and a standard deviation of 10, and T scores of 70 or greater (i.e., 2 standard deviations above the mean) are usually considered to be in the clinical range.

Relative Merits of Categorical and Dimensional Approaches

The debate between categorical and dimensional approaches to classification has been contentious. Next, we briefly summarize key issues in this debate, highlighting the strengths and limitations of each approach.

The Structure of Psychopathology   The central difference between categorical and dimensional approaches to classification is their conceptualization of the structure of psychopathology. Categorical approaches are based on the notion that symptoms are either present or absent, whereas the dimensional approaches argue for a continuous distribution of symptoms. Studies in both the child and adult literature suggest that many *DSM* diagnoses may be better represented by dimensional models than by dichotomous groupings (e.g., Hankin, Fraley, Lahey, & Waldman, 2005; Kendler et al., 1996).

A related issue raised by some critics is that categorical models imply that clients who do not meet criteria for a diagnosis are not impaired. Evidence suggests that clients do not have to meet formal criteria for a diagnosis to experience functional impairment (e.g., Angold, Costello, Farmer, Burns, & Erkanli, 1999), and the presence of symptoms is a risk factor for developing more severe psychopathology (Costello, Angold, & Keeler, 1999). Dimensional approaches have the advantage of representing the full range of impairment for an individual.

Comorbidity   Another common concern about categorical systems are high rates of comorbidity. Comorbidity refers to the co-occurrence of two or more disorders in the same client, either concurrently or over the life span. Research has found that psychological disorders co-occur at a rate higher than would be expected by chance (Angold, Costello, & Erkanli, 1999) and that comorbidity may be the rule rather than the exception among children with psychopathology, especially in clinical settings (e.g., Jensen & Weisz, 2002). High rates of comorbidity have led some to suggest that, rather than representing distinct disease entities, many "disorders" are instead markers of broader, underlying dimensions of psychopathology. Indeed, as mentioned earlier, support for underlying internalizing and externalizing factors of psychopathology have been found in child (e.g., Achenbach & Edelbrock, 1978) and adult (e.g., Krueger, Caspi, Moffitt, & Silva, 1998) samples, although studies have also supported finer-grained distinctions between syndromes (e.g., Achenbach & Edelbrock, 1978; Burns, Boe, Walsh, Sommers-Flanagan, & Teegarden, 2001).

Clarity of Communication   The main advantage of categorical approaches may be their clinical utility (First, 2005). Many decisions based on diagnostic information are categorical in nature, including whether someone qualifies for services and whether someone would benefit from a given treatment, decisions most easily made based on categorical information (i.e., Does this person have a diagnosis?). Even the authors of dimensional measures of psychopathology have acknowledged this need by creating clinical cutoff scores, which essentially allow clinicians to generate categorical information from dimensional measures. However, as discussed by Widiger and Samuel (2005), even when applied this way, dimensional measures have the advantage of being able to use different cutoffs for different purposes (e.g., one cutoff to qualify for outpatient treatment and another for hospitalization).

DIAGNOSTIC TOOLS AND METHODS

Practitioners use myriad tools and methods to generate diagnoses. To frame our discussion of these methods, we first describe factors that one should consider when choosing a diagnostic method. We then reference these factors as we discuss specific methods.

STANDARDS FOR EVALUATING THE QUALITY OF DIAGNOSTIC METHODS

Until recently, setting standards for evaluating the quality of diagnostic methods has received little attention. In their introduction to a 2005 special section of the *Journal of Clinical Child and Adolescent Psychology* on evidence-based assessment (Mash & Hunsley, 2005a), Mash and Hunsley (2005b) discuss the lack of clear guidelines for determining whether assessment measures are evidence-based (i.e., have sufficient research support to recommend their use). They suggest that the field generate guidelines for evidence-based assessment similar to those used to identify ESTs (see Chambless & Ollendick, 2001) and propose factors that might be included in the guidelines. Though Mash and Hunsley discuss guidelines designed for assessment tools intended for a variety of purposes, many of their suggestions also apply to diagnostic tools.

One important aspect to consider when evaluating the quality of a diagnostic method is the psychometric quality of the measure (Mash & Hunsley, 2005). Psychometric properties include reliability, validity, and measurement utility and are important because they speak to a measure's ability to provide accurate information. *Reliability* is the consistency of a person's score on a measure (Anastasi, 1988). For example, a thermometer is considered reliable if it provides the same temperature over repeated assessments. Three types of reliability are important to consider when evaluating the quality of a measure: internal consistency, interrater reliability, and retest reliability. *Internal consistency* assesses whether all questions in a measure contribute consistently to the overall measure score. Low internal consistency indicates that the questions might not all assess the same construct (e.g., depression). *Interrater reliability* assesses whether the same results would be obtained if a different clinician administered or scored the measure. *Retest reliability* assesses whether the same score would be obtained if the person completed the measure a second time.

A second category of psychometric quality is *validity*, or how well a measure assesses what it is supposed to assess (Anastasi, 1988). For example, a thermometer is considered valid if it indicates the correct temperature. Discussions of validity have traditionally referred to specific types of validity (e.g., construct validity, concurrent validity). However, the 1999 *Standards for Educational and Psychological Testing* guidelines generated by the American Educational Research Association, the American Psychological Association, and the National Council on Measurement in Education, recommend conceptualizing validity in terms of the type of evidence in support of a measure's validity. Here, we briefly describe the *Standards* definitions of "evidence based on relations to other variables" (p. 13). Interested readers are referred to the *Standards* for a more thorough discussion.

One important category is *convergent and discriminant evidence* (related to the traditional concepts of convergent, convergent-discriminant, and discriminant validity). This evidence is concerned with whether a measure converges with measures of similar constructs and diverges from measures of different constructs. A second category is *test-criterion relationships* (related to the traditional concepts of concurrent and predictive validity). This evidence indicates whether a measure is related to some present or future outcome that is thought to be theoretically related to the construct the measure is supposed to be assessing. In the case of a diagnostic instrument, an important test-criterion relationship might be whether people who are assigned diagnoses by the instrument also show high levels of functional impairment that would be anticipated to result from the disorder. Finally, the *Standards* discuss *validity generalization,* which refers to the extent to which a measure's test-criterion relationships would be expected to generalize to a different setting from the one in which the measure was originally validated. In sum, validity is extremely important because it indicates whether a measure is indeed measuring what the clinician expects it to.

A final category of psychometric quality is what we refer to here as *measurement utility* (to distinguish it from treatment utility), or a measure's ability to classify individuals correctly into groups. There are four types of measurement utility, which are

Gold Standard Diagnosis

Measure Results	Diagnosis Present	Diagnosis Absent
Diagnosis Present	True positives (a)	False positives (b)
Diagnosis Absent	False negatives (c)	True negatives (d)

$a/(a + b)$ = Positive predictive power
$d/(c + d)$ = Negative predictive power
$a/(a + c)$ = Sensitivity
$d/(d + b)$ = Specificity

Figure 2.1 Four Types of Measurement Utility

illustrated in Figure 2.1. In this figure, the results of a measure are compared to those of a gold standard of diagnosis (i.e., a measure that is thought to generate the correct diagnosis). Measurement utility is determined by the measure's ability to correctly identify people who do or do not meet diagnostic criteria, and is evaluated along four criteria. *Sensitivity* refers to the likelihood that persons with a disorder will be classified by the measure as having the disorder. *Specificity* refers to the likelihood that persons without the disorder will be classified as not having the disorder. It is important to consider these indicators together when assessing a measure. Take, for example, a test that indicates that 100% of the population has a given diagnosis. This measure would have perfect sensitivity, as all people with the diagnosis would be classified as having it, but the test would not be useful because its specificity would be 0!

In recent years *positive predictive power* (PPP) and *negative predictive power* (NPP) have also been used to generate estimates of diagnostic validity. Although more difficult to understand, PPP and NPP are regarded as superior by some authors (e.g., Widiger, Hurt, Frances, Clarkin, & Gilmore, 1984) because they incorporate information about base rates into the estimate of test accuracy. Thus, PPP is the proportion of persons that test positive for the disorder that actually have the disorder. Likewise, NPP indicates the proportion of persons that test negative for the disorder that actually do not have the disorder. In conditional probability terms, the relation is stated as the likelihood of having or not having the disorder (diagnosis) given a positive or negative test result. Widiger et al. argue that NPP and PPP are superior to sensitivity and specificity:

> Although the sensitivity and specificity rates remain useful, the single most informative statistic does appear to be the PPP of a symptom, because it presents, in a single value, the conditional probability of a disorder given the symptom, the central question faced by the diagnostician. (pp. 1006–1007)

In addition to these psychometric concerns, the practicality of a measure should be considered when one is choosing a diagnostic tool. Clinicians often must consider the cost of administering a measure. Factors that contribute to cost include the amount of time required to administer or complete the measure, the financial cost of administering the measure, time spent scoring and interpreting the measure, equipment required (e.g., computers to score the measure), and training time (Jensen Doss, 2005; Yates & Taub, 2003). The level of training required to administer the measure (e.g., whether a trained clinician must administer the measure) also contributes to costs (Jensen Doss, 2005). Another practical consideration, largely neglected in the assessment literature, is the acceptability of measures to clients and whether an assessment measure might negatively impact the client-clinician relationship (Mash & Hunsley, 2005). Finally, when working with diverse populations clinicians must also take into consideration whether an instrument is available in the client's native language.

Balancing these practical considerations with psychometric quality can be challenging. Several authors (e.g., Hunsley, 2003; Johnston & Murray, 2003) have raised the importance of considering the *incremental validity* of a measure when trying to make such decisions. Incremental validity addresses the question "Does the procedure or method *add* to the assessment process in a way that improves the outcome?" (Johnston & Murray, 2003, p. 496). In the context of diagnosis, incremental validity speaks to whether a given measure improves one's ability to assign a correct diagnosis above and beyond other methods available to a clinician. Information regarding the incremental validity of an instrument can be helpful as providers consider other practical issues related to diagnosis, such as the cost of an instrument. For example, as Johnston and Murray discuss, a lengthy, expensive diagnostic battery would not be justified *if* the same results could be obtained through less costly methods. Given the limited research available on the incremental validity of measures for children, additional clinically relevant research in this area is needed to aid clinicians trying to choose assessment tools to use in real-world clinical settings (Johnston & Murray, 2003).

Types of Diagnostic Methods

As the previous section illustrates, there are several factors to consider when choosing a diagnostic approach. These factors must be weighed against one another, taking into account the specific context in which a diagnosis is to be generated and utilized. Fortunately, a wide range of diagnostic tools and approaches exist. Next, we discuss categories of commonly used diagnostic methods. Though these approaches are useful in gathering the information needed to assign a diagnosis, use of a single approach is unlikely to produce the most accurate diagnosis. To form a complete diagnostic picture, several authors have advocated using a combination of instruments with strong psychometric properties and (a) clinical interviews to gather family history; (b) discussions with collateral reporters, such as teachers; (c) medical record reviews; and (d) mental status examinations (Basco et al., 2000; Leckman, Sholomskas, Thompson, Berlinger, & Weissman, 1982; McClellan & Werry, 2000a).

Unstructured Interviews   The traditional method of diagnosis is the unstructured interview, in which a clinician interviews a child and/or parent, guided by his or her clinical expertise, to gather the information needed to determine a diagnosis. Surveys indicate that the unstructured clinical interview is the assessment method used most often by clinicians (e.g., Cashel, 2002), and many clinicians employ this as their only method of diagnosis (Anderson & Paulosky, 2004). Unstructured interviews typically take 1 to 2 hours, during which the clinician asks about the presence, frequency, and duration of symptoms and factors that might be contributing to the symptoms, such as the child's home situation, developmental history, academic performance, and family history of psychopathology.

Unstructured interviews have several advantages over other diagnostic tools. Unlike the standardized interviews and rating scales, unstructured interviews allow clinicians to tailor questioning to the client and apply clinical expertise to probe for additional information. Moreover, few standardized instruments include thorough assessment of contextual factors that may be contributing to a child's symptoms, such as individual and family history (although see Table 2.1 for exceptions).

Unstructured interviews also have several disadvantages. Because the clinician does not follow a predetermined set of questions, unstructured interviews are more susceptible to clinician bias than structured methods. Research has shown that clinical decision making is subject to several information-gathering biases that may influence diagnostic outcomes (Angold & Fisher, 1999; Garb, 1998, 2005). First, clinicians often decide on a diagnosis before collecting all relevant data and then seek information to confirm that diagnosis while ignoring information that is inconsistent with the diagnosis. Second, clinicians combine information in ways that do not conform to *DSM* criteria, perhaps because they base decisions on whether their client conforms to a predetermined cognitive schema regarding the prototypical client with the diagnosis (Garb, 2005). Third, clinicians might base diagnostic judgments on the most readily available cognitive pattern (Angold & Fisher, 1999; Garb, 1998); thus, clinicians may be less likely to assign low base rate disorders even when diagnostic signs are present. Additional biases thought to impact clinician data gathering and decision making include a bias to perceive psychopathology over normative behavior and biases based on stereotypes about gender, ethnicity, and/or age (Garb, 1998).

Researchers have questioned the reliability and validity of interviews based solely on clinical judgment because unstructured interviews are susceptible to these biases. The seminal work in this area was Meehl's (1954) book *Clinical versus Statistical Prediction: A Theoretical Analysis and Review of the Evidence,* which suggested that statistically based models for making decisions, such as mathematical algorithms, are at least as accurate, if not more so, at making clinical decisions as clinicians. This position has been supported by numerous studies, including a recent meta-analysis finding a small but significant advantage of statistical methods over clinical methods when the two were used to make a decision based on the same set of information, although the two appeared to be equally effective for assigning diagnoses (Aegisdottir et al., 2006). These findings suggest that, in terms of assigning a final diagnosis, mathematical methods may be more efficient, although perhaps not more accurate, than a clinician. However, as this meta-analysis included only studies in which the two forms of decision making were based on the same information, it did not take into account threats to reliability and/or validity that might result from biases during the information-gathering stage of diagnosis.

To address this issue, many researchers have compared diagnoses assigned by clinicians to those generated through use of research diagnostic interviews consisting of standard rules for information gathering (see Standardized Interviews section). These studies were combined in a recent meta-analysis (Rettew, Doyle, Achenbach, Dumenci, & Ivanova, 2006) indicating that the overall agreement between clinician- and researcher-generated diagnoses for children is *kappa* = .15, which is considered poor agreement (Landis & Koch, 1977). This lack of agreement does not necessarily mean that the research instruments are correct and the clinicians are incorrect, but when compared to gold standard diagnoses generated by experts, research interviews

Table 2.1

Standardized Diagnostic Interviews for Children

Interview Name	Type	Ages	Reference	Content	Format(s)	Administration Time
National Institute of Mental Health Diagnostic Interview Schedule for Children (NIMH DISC)	RBI	6–17 (child version 9–17)	(Shaffer, Fisher, Lucas, Dulcan, & Schwab-Stone, 2000)	>30 *DSM-IV* diagnoses	Clinician administered computerized interview; self-administered computerized voice version available for child report	90–120 min. per informant
Children's Interview for Psychiatric Syndromes (ChIPS)	RBI	6–18	(Weller, Weller, Fristad, Rooney, & Schecter, 2000)	20 *DSM-IV* diagnoses; psychosocial stressors; child abuse/neglect	Clinician administered paper-and-pencil interview	21–49 min. per informant
Schedule for Affective Disorders and Schizophrenia for School-Age Children (K-SADS)	IBI	6–18	(Ambrosini, 2000; Kaufman et al., 1997)	>30 *DSM-IV* diagnoses; psychosocial and health history	Clinician-administered paper-and-pencil interview	90 min. per informant; additional time required to score

have been found to be more accurate (Basco et al., 2000). Taken together, these studies do not support the psychometric quality of unstructured interviews alone as a method of diagnosis.

In terms of practical considerations, unstructured interviews are likely to be more acceptable to clients than more structured methods, as they can be tailored to individual clients and allow clients to influence the course of the interview. As mentioned, unstructured interviews may be the best way to gather information not covered by standardized interviews; however, given the biases noted, clinicians may want to consider generating a list of questions they want to cover in these areas to guide the interview.

Standardized Interviews   In an effort to address the low reliability of unstructured interviews, researchers have developed standardized interviews. These interviews have traditionally been placed in two categories based on their level of structure: structured and semi-structured. In structured interviews, the interviewer administers a standard set of questions guided by strict rules for their administration. In contrast, semi-structured interviews allow interviewers to use clinical judgment to modify the interview by asking additional questions or clarifying the wording of interview questions. Angold and Fisher (1999) objected to this terminology, arguing that the essential difference between these two classes of interviews is not the structure of the interviews, but rather the role of clinical judgment. They proposed the term "respondent-based interview (RBI)" for interviews that follow a set script without the interviewer interpreting the respondent's answers and "interviewer-based interview (IBI)" for those with a standard set of questions, but in which the interviewer makes the final interpretation as to whether a symptom or diagnosis is present.

Both interview formats have several characteristics in common. Both typically consist of diagnostic modules designed to gather information following *DSM* criteria for specific diagnoses. For example, these interviews will typically contain a depression module, consisting of questions to assess the absence or presence of every *DSM* symptom of Major Depressive Disorder, the frequency and duration of each symptom, and the associated impairment, information required to assign a *DSM* diagnosis of MDD. Within each module, both RBIs and IBIs consist of contingency rules to guide the questioning. For example, if a parent answers yes to the question "Has your child felt depressed in the past year?," the interviewer would then ask about the frequency, duration, and impairment associated with the symptom of depression. If the parent answered no to this question, then the interviewer would ask about a different symptom. Because of these contingency rules, both RBIs and IBIs require a trained interviewer or, in the case or RBIs, a computer to guide the interview.

The essential difference between RBIs and IBIs, as mentioned, is the role of the interviewer. Respondent-based interviews were developed for use in large epidemiological studies. Given that these studies typically consist of thousands of diagnostic interviews, it was advantageous to develop an interview that could be administered by someone without clinical training. To achieve reliability across lay interviewers, RBIs consist of yes/no questions administered in a standard format. Typically, interviewers are not permitted to change the wording of questions, nor are they allowed to probe for more information from the interviewee. In addition to being less costly to administer, RBIs are highly standardized and reliable and lend themselves to computerization, further cutting down on staffing costs (Shaffer, Fisher, & Lucas, 1999). However, RBIs also have several limitations, including an inability to address invalid responses, difficulty characterizing atypical symptom presentations, and perhaps lower acceptability to interviewees relative to IBIs, as the interviewer has less control over the pace of the interview (Shaffer et al., 1999).

Interviewer-based interviews, on the other hand, were developed for administration by trained clinicians. As such, IBIs consist of a structured set of questions but typically allow the interviewer to use clinical judgment to tailor the interview. For example, an interviewer may clarify the meaning of a question, repeat or restate a question, or probe an answer with additional questions. The use of clinical judgment also allows IBIs to incorporate open-ended questions. Compared to RBIs, IBIs have several advantages, including (a) increased understanding of the interview results, (b) the ability to cross-check information, (c) the use of efficient open-ended questions, and (d) the ability to repeat questions to increase the quality of responses (Angold & Fisher, 1999). However, IBIs also have several disadvantages, including (a) the need for intensive training, (b) the need for a higher level of quality control, and (c) difficulty comparing the meaning of symptoms across IBIs due to differences in coding rules across interviews (Angold & Fisher, 1999).

Numerous RBIs and IBIs have been developed for use with children and their parents. In 2000, McClellan and Werry edited a special section of the *Journal of the American Academy of Child and Adolescent Psychiatry* dedicated to these interviews (McClellan & Werry, 2000b).The authors presented reliability and validity data for several standardized interviews, three of which are summarized in Table 2.1. In general, the psychometric quality of these instruments is high, although some authors have raised the possibility that these interviews, especially RBIs, may generate false positives, perhaps due to interviewers not being able to clarify questions for confused respondents (e.g., Breslau, 1987; Jensen & Weisz, 2002).

When examining practical considerations, these interviews can be costly to administer. As seen in Table 2.1, these interviews are lengthy (the ChIPS is a notable exception; Weller et al., 2000). Most clinicians obtain diagnostic information from children and parents, so the total time needed to generate a diagnosis can be extensive. In some settings, however, use of RBIs can save clinician time by gathering diagnostic information through a computerized or layperson interview prior to the intake with the clinician. Recently, the DISC developers have constructed a measure called the DISC Predictive Scales (DPS) to screen for diagnoses warranting further assessment (Lucas et al., 2001). The DPS significantly decreases the amount of time associated with a DISC administration. In addition to costs associated with interview and staff time, the financial costs of these interviews varies widely, ranging from interviews that are free to administer (e.g., K-SADS; Kaufman et al., 1997) to interviews that require use of copyrighted score sheets for every administration (e.g., ChIPS; Weller et al., 2000).

Despite significant attention to psychometric factors in the development of clinical interviews, few authors have assessed the acceptability of these interviews to children and parents. One exception is the DISC, where developers found that approximately half of interviewees reported that the interview was too long, but the majority still indicated they would "tell a friend to participate" (Shaffer et al., 2000). Finally, several of these interviews (e.g., DISC, ChIPS) are available in Spanish.

Rating Scales   A rating scale is a "measure that provides relatively rapid assessment of a specific construct with an easily derived numerical score, which is readily interpreted, whether completed by the youth or someone else, regardless of the response format and irrespective of application" (Myers & Winters, 2002, p. 115). Numerous rating scales exist, including questionnaires and checklists designed to assess one specific problem domain and multidimensional scales that cover a wide range of problem areas. Problem-specific rating scales are most useful when confirming or ruling out a diagnosis and are discussed in other chapters in this volume that focus on specific problem areas. In contrast, multidimensional scales are most useful for assessing a broad range of psychopathology and are the focus of this discussion. See Table 2.2 for commonly used multidimensional scales for children.

Most multidimensional rating scales ask parents, youths, or teachers to rate a list of symptoms as present or absent, or on a Likert scale for severity of the symptom (e.g., the ASEBA system employs a scale of 0 = Not true, 1 = Somewhat or sometimes true, and 2 = Very true or often true; Achenbach & Rescorla, 2001). Often, these scales consist of parallel child-, parent-, and teacher-report versions, allowing for standardized assessment from multiple perspectives and facilitating comparison across reporters. Most multidimensional rating scales measure child problems in domains similar to those contained in the *DSM* (e.g., depression, anxiety) but do not directly assess whether a child meets criteria for a *DSM* diagnosis. Ideally, these rating scales have norms available to facilitate comparison of one's client to other, similar children. All of the scales in Table 2.2 have norms available based on age and sex.

Compared to other methods of diagnosis, rating scales have several advantages. First, relative to unstructured interviews, rating scales facilitate a more consistent and systematic approach to clinical assessment (E. L. Hart & Lahey, 1999). Second, the availability of norms provides a concrete assessment of a child's level of symptoms relative to other, similar children. Third, rating scales are more time-efficient than interview methods; the time to administer these measures ranges from 5 to 20 minutes. Finally, these measures do not require extensive training, although training is needed to interpret results. Rating scales also have disadvantages. Unlike IBIs, rating scales do not have procedures in place to probe for additional information about a symptom (E. L. Hart & Lahey, 1999). In addition, in settings requiring the assignment of a *DSM* diagnosis, rating scales have to be augmented with further assessment to determine whether a client actually meets *DSM* criteria (Jensen Doss, 2005).

The psychometric quality of rating scales in Table 2.2 is quite high. Most rating scales completed by parents and teachers have high internal consistency and test-retest reliability; child-report scales have somewhat lower but adequate reliability (E. L. Hart & Lahey, 1999). When choosing a rating scale, measures with clearly defined anchor points and more than two raters tend to have higher reliability and/or validity, especially when completed by someone who knows the child well (Nunnally & Bernstein, 1994; O'Leary & Johnson, 1979). The quality of the measure's norms is also important to consider. Ideally, the normative sample is large enough to provide stable estimates of the population mean and standard deviation and is representative of the population under consideration (Anastasi, 1988). To evaluate the norms it is vital to consider client characteristics; if a client is very different from a scale's normative sample on characteristics that might impact the meaning of his or her scale score (e.g., cultural factors, see later discussion), it is better to find a measure with more appropriate norms.

As noted, rating scales have the advantage of requiring little staff time, other than the time required to score and interpret the measure, although additional assessment is required for assignment of a *DSM* diagnosis. Most measures are copyrighted and cost $1 to $2 per administration, although the SDQ is available for free on the Internet (Youth in Mind, 2006b). Similar to diagnostic interviews, few authors have assessed

Table 2.2
Multidimensional Rating Scales for Children

Interview Name	Reference	Content	Reporters (Child ages)	Completion Time
Achenbach System of Empirically Based Assessment (ASEBA)	(Achenbach & Rescorla, 2001)	8 syndromes; Internalizing and Externalizing scales; Total Problem scale; 6 DSM-oriented scales	Child (11–17); parent & teacher (preschool: 1.5–5, school-age: 6–18)	15–20 min. per informant
Behavior Assessment System for Children (BASC-2)	(Reynolds & Kamphaus, 2004)	Varies by reporter. Total of 18 Clinical scales, 10 Adaptive scales, and 10 optional Content scales	Child (child: 8–11, adolescent: 12–21); parent & teacher (preschool: 2–5, child: 6–11, adolescent: 12–21)	10–30 min. per informant
Conners' Rating Scales—Long Versions	(Conners, 1997)	Varies by reporter. Total of 12 subscales, 3 global indices, and 3 ADHD DSM-IV scales	Adolescent (12–17); parent & teacher (3–17)	15–20 min. per informant
Strengths and Difficulties Questionnaire (SDQ)	(Bourdon, Goodman, Rae, Simpson, & Koretz, 2005; Goodman, 1997)	5 subscales; Total difficulties score	Adolescent (11–16); parent & teacher (preschool: 3–4, school-age: 4–16)	4–5 min. per informant

the acceptability of rating scales to children, parents, or teachers, although Goodman and Scott (1999) found that mothers were twice as likely to prefer the SDQ to the parent-report ASEBA form. Finally, all scales in Table 2.2 are available in Spanish and the Conners' scales are available in French. The SDQ is available in 60 languages, although normative data are available only from Britain, Finland, Germany, Sweden, and the United States (Youth in Mind, 2006a).

DIAGNOSTIC CONSIDERATIONS

Though there are relatively clear criteria for assigning diagnoses and many user-friendly methods available to do so, rendering diagnoses for children is actually a very complex process. In the following sections, we discuss several factors that contribute to this complexity.

DEVELOPMENTAL CONSIDERATIONS

In arriving at a diagnosis for children it is important to consider their level of cognitive and linguistic development (Sattler, 2001). Social, cognitive, and biological factors can each influence the expression and experience of symptoms and syndromes (Cicchetti & Toth, 1998). It is therefore important for clinicians to understand how cognitive and linguistic factors impact the expression of child psychopathology and incorporate this knowledge into their diagnostic procedures (Schniering, Hudson, & Rapee, 2000). In the following section, examples of how developmental factors influence childhood psychopathology are provided as well as suggestions on how to ensure that diagnostic procedures are developmentally sensitive.

Development and the Expression of Symptoms Developmental factors can influence how a specific symptom is expressed in children, adolescents, and adults (Weiss & Garber, 2003). Consider, for example, how dysphoric mood, a core symptom of MDD, varies with development. Weiss and Garber note that children may express dysphoric mood by appearing sad and crying, but may be unable to report on their affective state due to limited cognitive and linguistic development (Poznanski, Cook, Carroll, & Corzo, 1983). In contrast, dysphoric mood in adolescents may be expressed as increased irritability, whereas adults are more likely to talk and reflect about feeling sad (Weiss & Garber, 2003). As this example illustrates, to generate a correct diagnosis clinicians and researchers must be aware of how symptoms manifest across developmental stages. Unfortunately, this can be challenging, as the *DSM* does not consistently describe developmental variations in symptom presentation.

Development and the Experience of Syndromes Developmental factors can also determine whether youngsters can experience specific symptoms (Schniering et al., 2000; Weiss & Garber, 2003). Cognitive and linguistic limitations may preclude young children from experiencing symptoms such as worry, hopelessness, guilt, and low self-esteem. This is because some symptoms require children to develop insight, an understanding of emotion, or a sense of self (Dadds, James, Barrett, & Verhulst, 2004; Fiske & Taylor, 1991; Flavell, 1985; Harris, 1989; D. Hart & Damon, 1986; Harter, 1999; Schwartz & Trabasso, 1985; Vasey, 1993), which may not develop until late childhood or adolescence. It is therefore essential that clinicians take into account how developmental factors can influence the expression of symptoms and syndromes and focus on those symptoms appropriate for a youngster's developmental level (Klein, Dougherty, & Olino, 2005; Weiss & Garber, 2003).

Developmentally Sensitive Diagnostic Procedures   To ensure that diagnostic assessment procedures are developmentally sensitive, clinicians must be aware of the interplay between developmental level and the expression and experience of symptoms. This requires that clinicians apply a *normative developmental approach,* which involves applying knowledge of basic developmental processes to view psychopathology against a backdrop of normal child development (Dadds et al., 2004; Silverman & Ollendick, 2005; Warren & Sroufe, 2004). The progression of fears across childhood into adolescence provides an example of how a normative developmental approach can inform the diagnostic process. Gullone (1996) noted that fears begin in infancy with a fear of separation from caregivers, progress to a fear of social situations in childhood, and then in adolescence become more generalized. Thus, when considering a diagnosis of Specific Phobia, a clinician must assess whether a fear is appropriate given the child's developmental level; for example, an intense fear of the dark in adolescence is not in line with normal development. Adopting a normative developmental approach can therefore help clinicians decide whether a given behavior is congruent with a child's developmental level, which can help inform the diagnostic process.

Ensuring that diagnostic procedures are developmentally sensitive also necessitates that clinicians understand how developmental factors can influence children's abilities to report on their own symptoms. Developmental factors, such as language development and comprehension, determine a child's ability to interpret and understand symptoms and constructs embedded within a clinical interview or self-report measure (Schniering et al., 2000). For example, children and adolescents have been found to interpret instructions on a self-report measure of worry in different ways, indicating that each group had a different understanding of worry (cf. Dadds et al., 2004). Children and adolescents may therefore have a different understanding of symptoms, which can result in miscommunication and inaccurate diagnoses. The greatest potential for reporting to vary with development is when self-report measures used with children are downward modifications of adult measures (Schniering et al., 2000; Silverman & Ollendick, 2005), as adults may have an understanding of the constructs different from that of children and adolescents.

Diagnostic procedures must also take into account how developmental factors influence a youngster's ability to understand and express emotion. For example, young children may show behavioral signs of emotional distress but find it difficult to describe their affective state. At other times, they may express affective distress in terms of somatic complaints (Sattler, 2001). Clinicians must therefore take into account how development level may influence a youngster's ability to describe subjective experiences when deciding how to collect information to inform a diagnosis (e.g., behavioral observation, parent interview). Moreover, due to the potential for miscommunication, it is important that clinicians clearly define the meaning of symptoms when assessing children and encourage them to speak up if they do not understand a concept or question (Sattler).

CROSS-INFORMANT CONSIDERATIONS

Using multiple informants in the diagnostic process can help supplement information provided by children, as parents and teachers may have information that can corroborate or clarify aspects of the child report. Young children do not appear to be reliable sources of diagnostic information (Johnston & Murray, 2003), so multiple reporters are necessary for an accurate diagnosis. Older youths are better able to reflect upon their internal state and covert behaviors; thus, for internalizing and antisocial symptoms, adolescent report adds incrementally to teacher and adult report (e.g., Cantwell, Lewinsohn, Rohde, & Seeley, 1997; Johnston & Murray, 2003). Using teachers as informants can supplement information provided by parents. Teachers have access to information concerning classroom behavior or social behavior that parents do not and thus may provide new information that allows for more accurate assessment of externalizing behaviors occurring outside of the home environment.

Although there is great utility in gathering information from several sources, incorporating this information into a single diagnostic decision is challenging. Low agreement among informants is a persistent problem. Achenbach, McConaughy, and Howell (1987) published a seminal meta-analysis of 119 studies on cross-informant agreement about child emotional and behavioral problems. They found that agreement between informants was generally modest, with higher agreement between informants with similar roles (e.g., mothers and fathers; mean $r = .60$) than informants with dissimilar roles (e.g., teachers and parents; mean $r = 28$). They also found low agreement between children's self-ratings and those of other raters (mean $r = 22$). These low levels of agreement have been called "one of the most robust findings in child clinical psychology" (De Los Reyes & Kazdin, 2005, p. 483).

Many child factors can impact agreement, including age, sex, ethnicity, and social desirability (i.e., the child's wish to cast himself or herself in the best light possible; De Los Reyes & Kazdin, 2005). Though Achenbach and colleagues (1987) originally found that agreement was higher for younger children, others have found higher agreement for older children (e.g., Grills & Ollendick, 2002) or have found no relationship between age and agreement (e.g., Choudhury, Pimentel, & Kendall, 2003). Findings have also been mixed regarding the impact of sex, ethnicity, and social desirability on agreement. The child factor found to most consistently impact agreement is problem type, with agreement typically higher for externalizing than internalizing symptoms (Achenbach et al., 1987; Duhig, Renk, Epstein, & Phares, 2000).

Parent and family characteristics have also been found to negatively impact agreement, including family distress (e.g., marital distress and child externalizing problems; Christensen, Margolin, & Sullaway, 1992) and maternal psychopathology. Mothers who have a history of mental health problems, such as depression, are more likely to overrate and overgeneralize their child's symptoms compared to mothers who lack a psychiatric history (e.g., Boyle & Pickles, 1997; Chilcoat & Breslau, 1997; Conrad & Hammen, 1989).

At present, there is no standard algorithm for combining the information from multiple informants, although several methods have been suggested (Renk, 2005). As noted, developmental factors influence which informants provide reliable information on particular disorders (Bird, Gould, & Staghezza, 1992). As such, one possible approach is to combine information based on which reporter is a more accurate reporter of the symptoms in question. Other methods that have been suggested include relying on a single reporter or assigning diagnoses based on consensus between different informants (Verhulst & Koot, 1992).

CULTURAL CONSIDERATIONS

Culture is defined as "an integrated pattern of human behavior that includes thought, language, action, and artifacts and depends on man's capacity for learning and transmitting knowledge to succeeding generations" (Frisby & Reynolds, 2005, p. 5). Variables such as nationality, ethnicity, and acculturation level are commonly studied in research on culture and diagnosis. Here, we briefly review three ways in which culture may influence the diagnostic process: (1) the expression of psychopathology; (2) child, parent, and teacher reports about psychopathology; and (3) obtaining information about and interpreting symptomatic behavior. Given the complexity of this topic, interested readers are referred to other comprehensive reviews for a more thorough discussion of diagnosis and culture (e.g., Cohen & Kasen, 1999; Tsai, Butcher, Munoz, & Vitousek, 2001).

Culture and the Expression of Psychopathology   There is some evidence that the expression of psychological distress may vary across cultures. For example, several authors have found higher rates of anxiety among African American children than among European American children (Hembree, 1988; Reynolds, Plake, & Harding, 1983). The *DSM-IV* acknowledged cultural variability in symptoms by including a section of "culture-bound syndromes," or syndromes that are thought to occur only within certain cultures (American Psychiatric Association, 2000). These syndromes are primarily seen in adults, although one of them, *mal de ojo* (fitful sleep, crying without cause, diarrhea, vomiting, and fever), is found in children in Mediterranean cultures (American Psychiatric Association, 2000).

Cultural variation in the expression of symptoms could be due to value differences. For example, one culture might place a higher value on child compliance than another, perhaps leading to lower rates of child externalizing disorders in that culture. Cross-cultural differences in symptom expressions could also be due to differences in the acceptability of psychological symptoms. For example, some authors have found that Latino children have higher rates of somatic symptoms than Caucasian children (e.g., Pina & Silverman, 2004), perhaps suggesting a greater acceptability of expressing medical than psychological symptoms among Latinos. Complicating our understanding of cultural variation in symptoms is the fact that it is unclear whether many observed cultural differences in symptoms are true differences or are due to cultural differences in response patterns or culturally biased assessment (Brewis & Pineda, 2001; Cohen & Kasen, 1999).

Cultural Influences on Reports of Psychopathology   To identify a diagnosis and receive treatment for mental health problems, individuals need to report their symptoms to a clinician. There are cultural differences in behaviors people consider problematic. For example, in violent communities, aggression is often a means of survival and is the modeled form of resolving conflicts (Atkins, McKay, Talbott, & Arvanitis, 1996). Therefore, some parents may not report aggressive behaviors to a clinician or see these behaviors as problematic, even if those behaviors are associated with child impairment in other settings, such as school. If the person being interviewed is not concerned about a particular symptom, he or she is unlikely to tell a professional about it unless specifically asked; therefore, cultural differences in concern about particular behaviors can lead to differences in the information obtained during an interview. This is particularly likely to happen when a clinician relies on unstructured interviews that do not systematically assess a broad range of symptoms.

Culture can further impact reports of psychopathology due to differences in beliefs about the appropriateness of telling someone about a child's symptoms. For example, some authors have suggested that Asian American parents may be less likely to report externalizing behaviors because of the possible cultural stigma and negative perceptions attributed to these types of behaviors (Nguyen et al., 2004). To minimize the impact of reporter variability on the diagnostic process, it is recommended that clinicians use multimethod, standardized procedures to ensure coverage of symptoms that the parent, child, or teacher might not discuss unless specifically asked.

Cultural Influences on the Assessment of Psychopathology Though structured methods might help alleviate some of the impact of reporter variability, they are not without their own problems. Often, the measures used in the diagnostic process were developed with Caucasian participants and may or may not apply cross-culturally. Many interviews and checklists have separate norms by age and sex, but most do not have separate norms by ethnicity. As mentioned, the ASEBA is one of the most widely used dimensional systems for assessing children's problem behaviors; however, there is limited research on the impact of race and ethnicity on ASEBA scores (Nguyen et al., 2004), and some research suggests there may be a need for separate norms or additional items for that system to apply to different ethnic groups. For example, Lambert, Rowan, Lyubansky, and Russ (2002) found that treatment-seeking African American parents reported child behavior problems that did not match items on the ASEBA. In general, cultural bias in measures of childhood psychopathology is understudied, and there is a need for additional research in this area (Cohen & Kasen, 1999).

Because of cultural biases in reports of psychopathology, measures that lack cultural sensitivity, and likely biases in the way clinicians interpret the information gathered in the diagnostic process, the final diagnoses assigned have the potential to be culturally biased. Mak and Rosenblatt (2002) studied this phenomenon using the diagnoses assigned in a large public mental health system. They found that African Americans were overrepresented and Asian Americans were underrepresented among children diagnosed with severe emotional disturbances relative to their representation in the population. Furthermore, there appear to be disparities in qualification for special education. African Americans and Native Americans tend to be overrepresented in special education, and Latinos and Asian Americans are generally underrepresented compared to Caucasians in most states (Losen & Orfield, 2002).

Culturally Competent Assessment To avoid potential biases in the diagnosis of children, it is important for clinicians to be aware of the role of culture in the diagnostic process. Although the field lacks clear, systematic suggestions for culturally sensitive practice (Bernal & Saez-Santiago, 2006), it has been suggested that culturally sensitive practice includes (a) awareness of culture; (b) knowledge of aspects of culture (e.g., norms, values, customs); and (c) the ability to distinguish between culture and psychopathology (Zayas, Torres, Malcolm, & DesRosiers, 1996). The American Psychological Association (2003; American Psychological Association, Office of Ethnic Minority Affairs, 1990) has published guidelines for multicultural practice, research, and education to assist providers in becoming culturally competent.

SETTING CONSIDERATIONS

Diagnoses are used in a variety of settings, including clinical, educational, pediatric, and juvenile justice settings. The purposes and processes of diagnosis vary across these settings. Here, we briefly review the unique diagnostic considerations within each.

Diagnosis in Clinical Settings   In clinical settings (i.e., outpatient, day treatment, residential, and inpatient mental health settings), diagnosis is often the first priority when a new client begins treatment, as typically clients must meet criteria for a *DSM* diagnosis in order to be treated. Diagnoses are required for treatment reimbursement by most insurance providers, so clinicians must assign a diagnosis prior to initiating services. Clinicians often practice in institutional settings (e.g., community mental health centers) where long waiting lists are commonplace. Such systems typically only admit or treat clients with the highest need and use diagnosis and functional level to set admission criteria.

These requirements present challenges to clinicians. Services cannot typically begin until a diagnosis is generated; however, clinicians have limited time to devote to the diagnostic process. Insurance providers may authorize only a 60-minute intake assessment, which limits the time clinicians can dedicate to the diagnostic process. Given the productivity requirements under which many clinicians work, there are few incentives, and likely disincentives, to utilize assessment procedures that take more than the time allotted by the insurance provider. Thus, clinicians must generate a diagnosis to justify services, but their compensation does not depend on the accuracy of the diagnosis. Indeed, as many as 25% of children receiving diagnoses from clinicians do not meet criteria for any diagnoses, according to research interviews (Jensen & Weisz, 2002; Lewczyk, Garland, Hurlburt, Gearity, & Hough, 2003).

Neither are there incentives to update diagnosis during treatment. Though the assignment of at least one diagnosis is often required for services to begin, there may be little incentive to assess for the presence of additional diagnoses (i.e., comorbidity) once this requirement has been satisfied. Studies on the agreement between clinician-generated diagnoses and standardized interviews suggest that this is likely the case. Clinicians are significantly less likely than research interviewers to assign more than one diagnosis (Jensen & Weisz, 2002).

Diagnosis in School Settings   Diagnosis in school settings presents unique challenges compared to other settings. In these settings, *DSM* diagnosis plays an important but not decisive role in determining eligibility for special education services and the design of school-based intervention plans. In the United States, the 2004 IDEIA mandates that if a child has a disability hindering his or her education in the regular classroom, the child must receive special school services.

Because IDEIA requires that a disorder must impact a child's educational performance in order to qualify the child for services, a diagnosis alone does not automatically satisfy eligibility requirements. Typically, schools will require additional determination of a link between symptoms and academic performance. Unlike other settings that rely on the *DSM* to define functional impairment, IDEIA specifies 13 eligibility categories, the precise definitions of which differ across states. In addition, IDEIA requires that a functional behavior assessment be used to confirm functional impairment and develop intervention plans. Because of these federal guidelines, clinicians completing psychoeducational assessments for use by schools must be educated in IDEIA, as the results of assessments not conforming to these guidelines will be of little value to parents hoping to qualify a child for educational or behavioral supports under federal law.

Diagnosis in Juvenile Justice Settings   Research on rates of mental illness in juvenile justice settings indicates that more than half of incarcerated youths have a diagnosable mental disorder (e.g., Teplin, Abram, McClelland, Dulcan, & Mericle, 2002; Wasserman, McReynolds, Lucas, Fisher, & Santos, 2002). Therefore, mental health professionals employed in juvenile justice settings are increasingly involved in the screening, diagnosis, and treatment of incarcerated youths. However, as with the educational system, diagnosis in juvenile justice settings presents unique challenges.

First, unlike youths in other settings, incarcerated youths are separated from their caregivers, schools, and peers. Consequently, incarceration may preclude or inhibit access to collateral reports of child symptoms. Second, the high-stress environment in which these youths find themselves could influence their reports, perhaps leading to higher symptom reports than would be obtained in a less stressful environment. Third, their reports might also be negatively impacted by a fear of disclosing information that could be used against them in court (Bailey, Doreleijers, & Tarbuck, 2006). Such fears may not be completely unwarranted, as some assessments (e.g., competency to stand trial) are not covered by client-provider confidentiality (Zerby & Thomas, 2006).

Diagnosis in Pediatric Settings   Pediatric settings are a common point of contact for mental health services (Ziv, Boulet, & Slap, 1999) and have the potential to be an important access point to mental health services for children and their families. However, the available evidence suggests that detection rates are low in pediatric settings and that diagnostic procedures do not conform to existing guidelines or use standardized measures (Gardner, Kelleher, Pajer, & Campo, 2004; Hoagwood, Kelleher, Feil, & Comer, 2000). Because primary care clinicians are responsible for a significant proportion of the prescriptions for psychotropic medication written for children, the need for accurate diagnostic procedures in this setting is especially notable (Gardner et al., 2004; Hoagwood et al., 2004). Staff and clinician time is limited in pediatric settings, so assessment procedures used in these settings must be easy to administer and score (Gardner et al., 2004). Computerized assessments, such as the DISC or CBCL, could reduce clinician time associated with administering and scoring measures and produce reports easily accessed by clinicians. The use of brief, standardized measures could potentially improve diagnostic practices among primary care clinicians. However, as noted previously, there remains a need for more research on how changes in diagnostic practices influence treatment outcomes in community-based settings.

ETHICAL CONSIDERATIONS

It has been argued that the most important ethical obligation a clinician engaged in the diagnostic process has is to assign an accurate diagnosis (Reich, 1999). Diagnoses can have a significant impact on the lives of children, including determining whether they receive treatment and potentially impacting how society views them (Corrigan & Kleinlein, 2005). Due to the role diagnoses play in determining service eligibility, clinicians may feel pressure to assign a diagnosis even when one is not present because not assigning a diagnosis would prevent a child from receiving services (Jensen & Weisz, 2002). It is also important to remember that psychopathology, or abnormal behavior, is defined in part by our social norms and that assigning a diagnosis can lead to stigma, that is, fear of being labeled mentally ill, or the harm the label might bring (e.g., Corrigan & Kleinlein, 2005). Stigma has been related to poor therapy engagement (Corrigan & Kleinlein, 2005), so clinicians must carefully weigh the impact the assigned diagnosis can have on the child.

SUMMARY

The classification of childhood psychopathology is an important and complex process. A wide range of measures have been developed to assist clinicians, although future research is clearly needed on issues such as the incremental validity of these instruments, their cultural and developmental sensitivity, and their acceptability to clients and other informants. As the debate between dimensional and categorical models of psychopathology continues and advanced statistical methods are increasingly used to test these models (e.g., taxometric methods; Meehl, 1995), it is likely that our systems for classifying psychopathology will change. Consequently, contemporary child and adolescent practitioners will need to carefully monitor the literature to maximize their ability to accurately diagnose and treat the children and families in their care.

REFERENCES

Achenbach, T. M. (1966). The classification of children's psychiatric symptoms: A factor-analytic study. *Psychological Monographs: General and Applied, 80*(7), 37.

Achenbach, T. M. (1978). The child behavior profile: Pt. I. Boys aged 6–11. *Journal of Consulting and Clinical Psychology, 46*(3), 478–488.

Achenbach, T. M., & Edelbrock, C. S. (1978). The classification of child psychopathology: A review and analysis of empirical efforts. *Psychological Bulletin, 85*(6), 1275–1301.

Achenbach, T. M., & Edelbrock, C. S. (1979). The child behavior profile: Pt. II. Boys aged 12–16 and girls aged 6–11 and 12–16. *Journal of Consulting and Clinical Psychology, 47*(2), 223–233.

Achenbach, T. M., McConaughy, S. H., & Howell, C. T. (1987). Child/adolescent behavioral and emotional problems: Implications of cross-informant correlations for situational specificity. *Psychological Bulletin, 101*(2), 213–232.

Achenbach, T. M., & Rescorla, L. A. (2001). *Manual for the ASEBA school-age forms and profiles.* Burlington: University of Vermont, Research Center for Children, Youth, and Families.

Aegisdottir, S., White, M. J., Spengler, P. M., Maugherman, A. S., Anderson, L. A., Cook, R. S., et al. (2006). The meta-analysis of clinical judgment project: Fifty-six years of accumulated research on clinical versus statistical prediction. *Counseling Psychologist, 34*(3), 341–382.

Ambrosini, P. J. (2000). Historical development and present status of the Schedule for Affective Disorders and Schizophrenia for School-Age Children (K-SADS). *Journal of the American Academy of Child and Adolescent Psychiatry, 39*(1), 49–58.

American Educational Research Association, American Psychological Association, & National Council on Measurement in Education. (1999). *Standards for educational and psychological testing.* Washington, DC: American Educational Research Association.

American Psychiatric Association. (1952). *Diagnostic and statistical manual of mental disorders.* Washington, DC: Author.

American Psychiatric Association. (1980). *Diagnostic and statistical manual of mental disorders* (3rd ed.). Washington, DC: Author.

American Psychiatric Association. (2000). *Diagnostic and statistical manual of mental disorders* (4th ed., text rev.). Washington, DC: Author.

American Psychological Association. (2003). Guidelines on multicultural education, training, research, practice, and organizational change for psychologists. *American Psychologist, 58*(5), 377–402.

American Psychological Association, Office of Ethnic Minority Affairs. (1990). *Guidelines for providers of psychological service to ethnic, linguistic, and culturally diverse populations.* Retrieved August 3, 2006, from http://www.apa.org/pi/oema/guide.html.

Anastasi, A. (1988). *Psychological testing* (6th ed.). New York: Macmillan.

Anderson, D. A., & Paulosky, C. A. (2004). A survey of the use of assessment instruments by eating disorder professionals in clinical practice. *Eating and Weight Disorders, 9*(3), 238–241.

Angold, A., Costello, E. J., & Erkanli, A. (1999). Comorbidity. *Journal of Child Psychology and Psychiatry, 40*(1), 57–87.

Angold, A., Costello, E. J., Farmer, E. M. Z., Burns, B. J., & Erkanli, A. (1999). Impaired but undiagnosed. *Journal of the American Academy of Child and Adolescent Psychiatry, 38*(2), 129–137.

Angold, A., & Fisher, P. W. (1999). Interviewer-based interviews. In D. Shaffer, C. P. Lucas, & J. E. Richters (Eds.), *Diagnostic assessment in child and adolescent psychopathology* (pp. 34–64). New York: Guilford Press.

Angold, A., Prendergast, M., Cox, A., Harrington, R., Simonoff, E., & Rutter, M. (1995). The Child and Adolescent Psychiatric Assessment (CAPA). *Psychological Medicine, 25*(4), 739–753.

Atkins, M. S., McKay, M. M., Talbott, E., & Arvanitis, P. (1996). DSM-IV diagnosis of conduct disorder and oppositional defiant disorder: Implications and guidelines for school mental health teams. *School Psychology Review, 25*(3), 274–283.

Bailey, S., Doreleijers, T., & Tarbuck, P. (2006). Recent developments in mental health screening and assessment in juvenile justice systems. *Child and Adolescent Psychiatric Clinics of North America, 15*(2), 391–406.

Basco, M. R., Bostic, J. Q., Davies, D., Rush, A. J., Witte, B., Hendrickse, W., et al. (2000). Methods to improve diagnostic accuracy in a community mental health setting. *American Journal of Psychiatry, 157*(10), 1599–1605.

Bernal, G., & Saez-Santiago, E. (2006). Culturally centered psychosocial interventions [Special issue]. *Journal of Community Psychology: Addressing Mental Health Disparities through Culturally Competent Research and Community-Based Practice, 34*(2), 121–132.

Bird, H. R., Gould, M. S., & Staghezza, B. (1992). Aggregating data from multiple informants in child psychiatry epidemiological research. *Journal of the American Academy of Child and Adolescent Psychiatry, 31*(1), 78–85.

Bourdon, K. H. M. A., Goodman, R. P. D., Rae, D. S. M. S., Simpson, G. M. S., & Koretz, D. S. P. D. (2005). The Strengths and Difficulties Questionnaire: U.S. normative data and psychometric properties. *Journal of the American Academy of Child and Adolescent Psychiatry, 44*, 557–564.

Boyle, M. H., & Pickles, A. R. (1997). Influence of maternal depressive symptoms on ratings of childhood behavior. *Journal of Abnormal Child Psychology, 25*(5), 399–412.

Breslau, N. (1987). Inquiring about the bizarre: False positives in Diagnostic Interview Schedule for Children (DISC) ascertainment of obsessions, compulsions, and psychotic symptoms. *Journal of the American Academy of Child and Adolescent Psychiatry, 26*(5), 639–644.

Brewis, A. A., & Pineda, D. (2001). Population variation in children's behavioral symptomatology. *American Journal of Physical Anthropology, 114*, 54–60.

Burns, G. L., Boe, B., Walsh, J. A., Sommers-Flanagan, R., & Teegarden, L. A. (2001). A confirmatory factor analysis on the DSM-IV ADHD and ODD symptoms: What is the best model for the organization of these symptoms? *Journal of Abnormal Child Psychology, 29*(4), 339–349.

Cantwell, D. P., Lewinsohn, P. M., Rohde, P., & Seeley, J. R. (1997). Correspondence between adolescent report and parent report of psychiatric diagnostic data. *Journal of the American Academy of Child and Adolescent Psychiatry, 36*(5), 610–619.

Cashel, M. L. (2002). Child and adolescent psychological assessment: Current clinical practices and the impact of managed care. *Professional Psychology: Research and Practice, 33*(5), 446–453.

Chambless, D. L., Baker, M. J., Baucom, D. H., Buetler, L., Calhoun, K. S., Crits-Christoph, P., et al. (1998). Update on empirically validated therapies, II. *Clinical Psychologist, 51*(1), 3–16.

Chambless, D. L., & Ollendick, T. H. (2001). Empirically supported psychological interventions: Controversies and evidence. *Annual Review of Psychology, 52*, 685–716.

Chambless, D. L., Sanderson, W. C., Shoham, V., Bennett Johnson, S., Pope, K. S., Crits-Christoph, P., et al. (1996). An update on empirically validated therapies. *Clinical Psychologist, 49,* 5–18.

Chilcoat, H. D., & Breslau, N. (1997). Does psychiatric history bias mothers' reports? An application of a new analytic approach. *Journal of the American Academy of Child and Adolescent Psychiatry, 36*(7), 971–979.

Choudhury, M. S., Pimentel, S. S., & Kendall, P. C. (2003). Childhood anxiety disorders: Parent-child (dis)agreement using a structured interview for the DSM-IV. *Journal of the American Academy of Child and Adolescent Psychiatry, 42*(8), 957–964.

Christensen, A., Margolin, G., & Sullaway, M. (1992). Interparental agreement on child behavior problems. *Psychological Assessment, 4*(4), 419–425.

Cicchetti, D. V., & Toth, S. L. (1998). The development of depression in children and adolescents. *American Psychologist, 53*(2), 221–241.

Clark, L. A., Watson, D., & Reynolds, S. (1995). Diagnosis and classification of psychopathology: Challenges to the current system and future directions. *Annual Review of Psychology, 46,* 121–153.

Cohen, P., & Kasen, S. (1999). The context of assessment: Culture, race, and socioeconomic status as influences on the assessment of children. In D. Shaffer, C. P. Lucas, & J. E. Richters (Eds.), *Diagnostic assessment in child and adolescent psychopathology* (pp. 299–318). New York: Guilford Press.

Conners, G. K. (1997). *Conner's rating scales—revised: Technical manual.* New York: Multi-Health Systems.

Conrad, M., & Hammen, C. (1989). Role of maternal depression in perceptions of child maladjustment. *Journal of Consulting and Clinical Psychology, 57*(5), 663–667.

Corrigan, P. W., & Kleinlein, P. (2005). The impact of mental illness stigma. In P. W. Corrigan (Ed.), *On the stigma of mental illness: Practical strategies for research and social change* (pp. 11–44). Washington, DC: American Psychological Association.

Costello, E. J., Angold, A., & Keeler, G. P. (1999). Adolescent outcomes of childhood disorders: The consequences of severity and impairment. *Journal of the American Academy of Child and Adolescent Psychiatry, 38*(2), 121–128.

Dadds, M. R., James, R. C., Barrett, P. M., & Verhulst, F. C. (2004). Diagnostic issues. In T. H. Ollendick & J. S. March (Eds.), *Phobic and anxiety disorders in children and adolescents* (pp. 3–33). New York: Oxford University Press.

De Los Reyes, A., & Kazdin, A. E. (2005). Informant discrepancies in the assessment of childhood psychopathology: A critical review, theoretical framework, and recommendations for further study. *Psychological Bulletin, 131*(4), 483–509.

Diagnosis. (1989). *The Oxford English Dictionary* (2nd ed., OED Online). Retrieved July 11, 2006, from http://dictionary.oed.com/cgi/entry/50063060.

Duhig, A. M., Renk, K., Epstein, M. K., & Phares, V. (2000). Interparental agreement on internalizing, externalizing, and total behavior problems: A meta-analysis. *Clinical Psychology: Science and Practice, 7*(4), 435–453.

First, M. B. (2005). Clinical utility: A prerequisite for the adoption of a dimensional approach in DSM [Special issue]. *Journal of Abnormal Psychology: Toward a Dimensionally Based Taxonomy of Psychopathology, 114*(4), 560–564.

Fiske, S., & Taylor, S. (1991). *Social cognition.* Reading, MA: Addison-Wesley.

Flavell, J. H. (1985). *Cognitive development.* Englewood Cliffs, NJ: Prentice-Hall.

Follette, W. C., & Houts, A. C. (1996). Models of scientific progress and the role of theory in taxonomy development: A case study of the DSM. *Journal of Consulting and Clinical Psychology, 64*(6), 1120–1132.

Frisby, C. L., & Reynolds, C. R. (2005). *Comprehensive handbook of multicultural school psychology.* Hoboken, NJ: Wiley.

Garb, H. N. (1998). *Studying the clinician: Judgment research and psychological assessment.* Washington, DC: American Psychological Association.

Garb, H. N. (2005). Clinical judgment and decision making. *Annual Review of Clinical Psychology, 1*(1), 67–89.

Gardner, W., Kelleher, K. J., Pajer, K. A., & Campo, J. V. (2004). Primary care clinicians' use of standardized psychiatric diagnoses. *Child: Care, Health, and Development, 30*(5), 401–412.

Goodman, R. (1997). The Strengths and Difficulties Questionnaire: A research note. *Journal of Child Psychology and Psychiatry, 38*(5), 581–586.

Goodman, R., & Scott, S. (1999). Comparing the Strengths and Difficulties Questionnaire and the Child Behavior Checklist: Is small beautiful? *Journal of Abnormal Child Psychology, 27*(1), 17–24.

Grills, A. E., & Ollendick, T. H. (2002). Issues in parent-child agreement: The case of structured diagnostic interviews. *Clinical Child and Family Psychology Review, 5*(1), 57–83.

Gullone, E. (1996). Normal fear in people with a physical or intellectual disability. *Clinical Psychology Review, 16*(8), 689–706.

Hankin, B. L., Fraley, R. C., Lahey, B. B., & Waldman, I. D. (2005). Is depression best viewed as a continuum or discrete category? A taxometric analysis of childhood and adolescent depression in a population-based sample. *Journal of Abnormal Psychology, 114*(1), 96–110.

Harris, P. L. (1989). *Children and emotion: The development of psychological understanding.* Oxford: Blackwell.

Hart, D., & Damon, W. (1986). Developmental trends in self-understanding. *Social Cognition, 4*(4), 388–407.

Hart, E. L., & Lahey, B. B. (1999). General child behavior rating scales. In D. Shaffer (Ed.), *Diagnostic assessment in child and adolescent psychopathology* (pp. 65–87). New York: Guilford Press.

Harter, S. (1999). *The construction of the self: A developmental perspective.* New York: Guilford Press.

Hembree, R. (1988). Correlates, causes, effects, and treatment of test anxiety. *Review of Educational Research, 58*(1), 47–77.

Hoagwood, K., Kelleher, K. J., Feil, M., & Comer, D. M. (2000). Treatment services for children with ADHD: A national perspective. *Journal of the American Academy of Child and Adolescent Psychiatry, 39*(2), 198–206.

Hunsley, J. (2003). Introduction to the special section on incremental validity and utility in clinical assessment. *Psychological Assessment, 15*(4), 443–445.

Individuals with Disabilities Education Improvement Act of 2004. Public Law 108–446. (2004).

Jacobson, N. S., & Truax, P. (1991). Clinical significance: A statistical approach to defining meaningful change in psychotherapy research. *Journal of Consulting and Clinical Psychology, 59*(1), 12–19.

Jensen, A. L., & Weisz, J. R. (2002). Assessing match and mismatch between practitioner-generated and standardized interview-generated diagnoses for clinic-referred children and adolescents. *Journal of Consulting and Clinical Psychology, 70*(1), 158–168.

Jensen Doss, A. (2005). Evidence-based diagnosis: Incorporating diagnostic instruments into clinical practice. *Journal of the American Academy of Child and Adolescent Psychiatry, 44*(9), 947–952.

Johnston, C., & Murray, C. (2003). Incremental validity in the psychological assessment of children and adolescents. *Psychological Assessment, 15*(4), 496–507.

Kaufman, J., Birmaher, B., Brent, D., Rao, U., Flynn, C., Moreci, P., et al. (1997). Schedule for Affective Disorders and Schizophrenia for School-Age Children—Present and Lifetime version (K-SADS-PL): Initial reliability and validity data. *Journal of the American Academy of Child and Adolescent Psychiatry, 36*(7), 980–988.

Kendler, K. S., Eaves, L. J., Walters, E. E., Neale, M. C., Heath, A. C., & Kessler, R. C. (1996). The identification and validation of distinct depressive syndromes in a population-based sample of female twins. *Archives of General Psychiatry, 53*(5), 391–399.

Klein, D. N., Dougherty, L. R., & Olino, T. M. (2005). Toward guidelines for evidence-based assessment of depression in children and adolescents. *Journal of Clinical Child and Adolescent Psychology, 34*(3), 412–432.

Krueger, R. F., Caspi, A., Moffitt, T. E., & Silva, P. A. (1998). The structure and stability of common mental disorders (DSM-III-R): A longitudinal-epidemiological study. *Journal of Abnormal Psychology, 107*(2), 216–227.

Lambert, M. C., Rowan, G. T., Lyubansky, M., & Russ, C. M. (2002). Do problems of clinic-referred African-American children overlap with the Child Behavior Checklist? *Journal of Child and Family Studies, 11*(3), 271–285.

Landis, J. R., & Koch, G. G. (1977). The measurement of observer agreement for categorical data. *Biometrics, 33*, 159–174.

Leckman, J. F., Sholomskas, D., Thompson, D., Berlinger, A., & Weissman, M. (1982). Best estimate of lifetime psychiatric diagnosis: A methodological study. *Archives of General Psychiatry, 39*(8), 879–883.

Lewczyk, C. M., Garland, A. F., Hurlburt, M. S., Gearity, J., & Hough, R. L. (2003). Comparing DISC-IV and clinician diagnoses among youths receiving public mental health services. *Journal of the American Academy of Child and Adolescent Psychiatry, 42*(3), 349–356.

Lonigan, C. J., Elbert, J. C., & Johnson, S. B. (1998). Empirically supported psychosocial interventions for children: An overview. *Journal of Clinical Child Psychology, 27*(2), 138–145.

Losen, D., & Orfield, G. (2002). *Racial inequity in special education: Executive summary for federal policy makers.* Cambridge, MA: Harvard University, The Civil Rights Project. Retrieved July 24, 2006, from www.thecivilrightsproject.harvard.edu/research/specialed/IDEA_paper02.php.

Lucas, C. P., Zhang, H., Fisher, P. W., Shaffer, D., Regier, D. A., Narrow, W. E., et al. (2001). The DISC Predictive Scales (DPS): Efficiently screening for diagnoses. *Journal of the American Academy of Child and Adolescent Psychiatry, 40*(4), 443–449.

Mack, A. H., Forman, L., Brown, R., & Frances, A. (1994). A brief history of psychiatric classification: From the ancients to DSM-IV. *Psychiatric Clinics of North America, 17*(3), 515–523.

Mak, W., & Rosenblatt, A. (2002). Demographic influences on psychiatric diagnoses among youth served in California systems of care. *Journal of Child and Family Studies, 11*(2), 165–178.

Mash, E. J., & Hunsley, J. (2005a). Developing guidelines for the evidence-based assessment of child and adolescent disorders [Special issue]. *Journal of Clinical Child and Adolescent Psychology, 34*(3).

Mash, E. J., & Hunsley, J. (2005b). Evidence-based assessment of child and adolescent disorders: Issues and challenges. *Journal of Clinical Child and Adolescent Psychology, 34*, 362–379.

McClellan, J., & Werry, J. S. (2000a). Introduction- Research psychiatric diagnostic interviews for children and adolescents. *Journal of the American Academy of Child and Adolescent Psychiatry, 39*, 19–27.

McClellan, J., & Werry, J. S. (2000b). Research psychiatric diagnostic interviews for children and adolescents. [Special issue] *Journal of the American Academy of Child and Adolescent Psychiatry, 39*(1).

Meehl, P. E. (1954). *Clinical versus statistical prediction: A theoretical analysis and a review of the evidence.* Lanham, MD: Aronson.

Meehl, P. E. (1995). Bootstraps taxometrics: Solving the classification problem in psychopathology. *American Psychologist, 50*(4), 266–275.

Myers, K., & Winters, N. C. (2002). Ten-year review of rating scales: Pt. I. Overview of scale functioning, psychometric properties, and selection. *Journal of the American Academy of Child and Adolescent Psychiatry, 41*(2), 114–122.

Nelson-Gray, R. O. (2003). Treatment utility of psychological assessment. *Psychological Assessment, 15*(4), 521–531.

Nguyen, L., Arganza, G. F., Huang, L. N., Liao, Q., Nguyen, H. T., & Santiago, R. (2004). Psychiatric diagnoses and clinical characteristics of Asian American youth in children's services. *Journal of Child and Family Studies, 13*(4), 483–495.

Nunnally, J. C., & Bernstein, I. H. (1994). *Psychometric theory* (3rd ed.). New York: McGraw-Hill.

O'Leary, K. D., & Johnson, S. B. (1979). Psychological assessment. In H. C. Quay & J. S. Werry (Eds.), *Psychopathological disorders of childhood* (Vol. 2, pp. 210–247). New York: Wiley.

Pina, A. A., & Silverman, W. K. (2004). Clinical phenomenology, somatic symptoms, and distress in Hispanic/Latino and European American youths with anxiety disorders. *Journal of Clinical Child and Adolescent Psychology, 33*(2), 227–236.

Poznanski, E. O., Cook, S. C., Carroll, B. J., & Corzo, H. (1983). Use of the Children's Depression Rating Scale in an inpatient psychiatric population. *Journal of Clinical Psychiatry, 44*(6), 200–203.

Reich, W. (1999). Psychiatric diagnosis as an ethical problem. In S. Bloch, P. Chodoff, & S. A. Green (Eds.), *Psychiatric ethics* (3rd ed., pp. 193–224). New York: Oxford University Press.

Renk, K. (2005). Cross-informant ratings of the behavior of children and adolescents: The "gold standard." *Journal of Child and Family Studies, 14*(4), 457–468.

Rettew, D. C., Doyle, A., Achenbach, T. M., Dumenci, L., & Ivanova, M. (2006). *Meta-analyses of diagnostic agreement between clinical evaluations and standardized interviews.* Manuscript under review.

Reynolds, C. R., & Kamphaus, R. W. (2004). *The Behavior Assessment System for Children manual* (2nd ed.). Circle Pines, MN: AGS Publishing.

Reynolds, C. R., Plake, B. S., & Harding, R. E. (1983). Item bias in the assessment of children's anxiety: Race and sex interaction on items of the Revised Children's Manifest Anxiety Scale. *Journal of Psychoeducational Assessment, 1*(1), 17–24.

Rubinstein, E. A. (1948). Childhood mental disease in America: A review of the literature before 1900. *American Journal of Orthopsychiatry, 18*, 314–321.

Sattler, J. (2001). *Assessment of children: Cognitive applications.* La Mesa, CA: Author.

Schniering, C. A., Hudson, J. L., & Rapee, R. M. (2000). Issues in the diagnosis and assessment of anxiety disorders in children and adolescents. *Clinical Psychology Review, 20*(4), 453–478.

Schwartz, R. M., & Trabasso, T. (1985). Children's understanding of emotions. In C. E. Izard, J. Kagan, & R. B. Zajonc (Eds.), *Emotions, cognition, and behavior* (pp. 409–437). New York: Cambridge University Press.

Shaffer, D., Fisher, P. W., & Lucas, C. P. (1999). Respondent-based interviews. In D. Shaffer, C. P. Lucas, & J. E. Richters (Eds.), *Diagnostic assessment in child and adolescent psychopathology* (pp. 3–33). New York: Guilford Press.

Shaffer, D., Fisher, P., Lucas, C. P., Dulcan, M. K., & Schwab-Stone, M. E. (2000). NIMH Diagnostic Interview Schedule for Children Version IV (NIMH DISC-IV): Description, differences from previous versions, and reliability of some common diagnoses. *Journal of the American Academy of Child and Adolescent Psychiatry, 39*(1), 28–38.

Silverman, W. K., & Ollendick, T. H. (2005). Evidence-based assessment of anxiety and its disorders in children and adolescents. *Journal of Clinical Child and Adolescent Psychology, 34*(3), 380–411.

Teplin, L. A., Abram, K. M., McClelland, G. M., Dulcan, M. K., & Mericle, A. A. (2002). Psychiatric disorders in youth in juvenile detention. *Archives of General Psychiatry, 59*(12), 1133–1143.

Tsai, J. L., Butcher, J. N., Munoz, R. F., & Vitousek, K. (2001). Culture, ethnicity, and psychopathology. In P. B. Sutker & H. E. Adams (Eds.), *Comprehensive handbook of psychopathology* (3rd ed., pp. 105–127). New York: Kluwer Academic/Plenum Press.

Vasey, M. W. (1993). Development and cognition in childhood anxiety: The example of worry. In T. H. Ollendick & R. J. Prinz (Eds.), *Advances in clinical child psychology* (Vol. 15, pp. 1–39). New York: Plenum Press.

Verhulst, F. C., & Koot, H. M. (1992). *Child psychiatric epidemiology: Concepts, methods, and findings.* Thousand Oaks, CA: Sage.

Warren, S. L., & Sroufe, A. (2004). Developmental issues. In T. H. Ollendick & J. S. March (Eds.), *Phobic and anxiety disorders in children and adolescents* (pp. 92–115). New York: Oxford University Press.

Wasserman, G. A., McReynolds, L. S., Lucas, C. P., Fisher, P., & Santos, L. (2002). The voice DISC-IV with incarcerated male youths: Prevalence of disorder. *Journal of the American Academy of Child and Adolescent Psychiatry, 41*(3), 314–321.

Weiss, B., & Garber, J. (2003). Developmental differences in the phenomenology of depression. *Development and Psychopathology, 15*(2), 403–430.

Weller, E. B., Weller, R. A., Fristad, M. A., Rooney, M. T., & Schecter, J. (2000). Children's Interview for Psychiatric Syndromes (ChIPS). *Journal of the American Academy of Child and Adolescent Psychiatry, 39*(1), 76–84.

Widiger, T. A., Hurt, S. W., Frances, A., Clarkin, J. F., & Gilmore, M. (1984). Diagnostic efficiency and DSM-III. *Archives of General Psychiatry, 41,* 1005–1012.

Widiger, T. A., & Samuel, D. B. (2005). Diagnostic categories or dimensions? A question for the Diagnostic and Statistical Manual of Mental Disorders (5th ed.) [Special issue]. *Journal of Abnormal Psychology: Toward a Dimensionally Based Taxonomy of Psychopathology, 114*(4), 494–504.

World Health Organization. (1993). *The ICD-10 classification of mental and behavioral disorders: Diagnostic criteria for research.* Geneva, Switzerland: Author.

Yates, B. T., & Taub, J. (2003). Assessing the costs, benefits, cost-effectiveness, and cost-benefit of psychological assessment: We should, we can, and here's how. *Psychological Assessment, 15*(4), 478–495.

Youth in Mind. (2006a). *Normative data.* Retrieved July 6, 2006, from http://www.sdqinfo.com/b8.html.

Youth in Mind. (2006b). *Questionnaires and related items in English and translation.* Retrieved July 6, 2006, from http://www.sdqinfo.com/b3.html.

Zayas, L. H., Torres, L. R., Malcolm, J., & DesRosiers, F. S. (1996). Clinicians' definitions of ethnically sensitive therapy. *Professional Psychology: Research and Practice, 27*(1), 78–82.

Zerby, S. A., & Thomas, C. R. (2006). Legal issues, rights, and ethics for mental health in juvenile justice. *Child and Adolescent Psychiatric Clinics of North America, 15*(2), 373–390.

Ziv, A., Boulet, J. R., & Slap, G. B. (1999). Utilization of physician offices by adolescents in the United States. *Pediatrics, 104,* 35–42.

CHAPTER 3

Behavioral Conceptualization

PAUL S. STRAND, LISA W. COYNE, AND KERRY SILVIA

Behaviorism has traditionally been identified with learning theory (Kanfer & Phillips, 1970). Despite the strong historical connection between the two, it would be a mistake to equate them. Behaviorism and behavioral interventions are defined by something larger than any set of learning principles, no matter how basic or far-reaching. Behaviorism is an *epistemological commitment* to a functional understanding of behavior. As such, behaviorism is defined by a set of rules for exploring and explaining complex behavior. Those rules require that explorations target organism-environment interactions and that explanations be made in terms of experimentally defined, observable behavioral processes (Donahoe & Palmer, 1994). It is the goal of this chapter to describe this commitment and to discuss the clinical conceptualizations and interventions that arise from it.

From its inception, behaviorism has been concerned with the improvement of individual well-being. This is not surprising considering the circumstances of its genesis. Behaviorism arose as a reaction to then dominant currents in American and European psychology—namely, introspectionism and psychoanalysis. As such, it was incumbent upon early behaviorists to quickly and decisively illustrate the usefulness of the new approach (Rilling, 2000). Elements within the nascent movement demanded rapid progress as well. As the dominant philosophical influence on behaviorism, pragmatism emphasized "effective action." In philosophical terms, both pragmatism and behaviorism share a commitment to *successful working* (Hayes, Hayes, & Reese, 1988; Morris, 1988). Indeed, hardly a decade passed from the birth of behaviorism in 1913 to its first clinical application (Jones & Watson, 1924).

CONDITIONING CONCEPTUALIZATIONS

CLASSICAL CONDITIONING

The earliest behavioral conceptualizations of psychological and emotional disorders were derived from experimental studies of classical conditioning. Also referred to as Pavlovian or respondent conditioning, classical conditioning describes a phenomenon in which behavior originally elicited by a stimulus or stimulus class comes to also be elicited by some other stimulus or stimulus class. For example, to the extent that a neutral stimulus such as a tone signals the presentation of food, the tone may elicit behavioral reactions that are nearly identical to those elicited by the presentation of food. This *transfer of function* that defines classical conditioning arises out of a history in which the tone (conditioned stimulus) repeatedly occurs in close temporal proximity to the presentation of the food (unconditioned stimulus).

It was Pavlov's enduring contribution to psychology to document this process, which very quickly was recognized as a possible explanation for human emotional responses and emotional disorders (Pavlov, 1960). Importantly, however, explaining human emotional processes in terms of behavioral processes observed in animals constitutes a behavioral *interpretation*. Although interpretation is a legitimate scientific activity, the ultimate goal of science is to subject phenomena to an *experimental analysis*. An experimental analysis constitutes an empirical demonstration of causal relationships between two or more variables.

The first experimental demonstration of classical conditioning in the context of human emotional functioning involved the conditioning of a fear response in a 4-year-old boy, subsequently known as "Little Albert" (Watson & Rayner, 1920). In a controlled laboratory environment, Little Albert was repeatedly presented with a live rat and then exposed to a loud and aversive noise. Importantly, prior to being paired with the aversive noise, Little Albert's emotional response to the animal's presence was characterized by curiosity and delight. However, as a result of the repeated pairing of the aversive noise (unconditioned stimulus) and the rat (neutral stimulus), the boy's response to the rat changed from "delight" to "fright." This new emotional reaction arose as a result of the repeated pairing of the unconditioned stimulus (aversive noise) with the neutral stimulus (rat), thus rendering the rat a conditioned stimulus and the "new" response to the rat (in absence of the loud noise) a conditioned emotional response.

Weeks after training, fear continued to be elicited by the presentation of the rat. Moreover, stimuli resembling the rat, including a rabbit and a fur coat, also elicited the conditioned response. Therefore, the conditioned response *generalized* across similar stimuli and time and appeared extreme and irrational to anyone unfamiliar with the training experienced by the boy.

The experiment with Little Albert suggested that classical conditioning could offer an account of the development of emotional reactions such as fear and avoidance. Only a few years later, Watson attempted to extend the classical conditioning model, moving from an explanation of fear conditioning to the use of the technology to "cure" or modify it. The process, known as *counterconditioning*, was illustrated with another young boy, Peter, who displayed a fear of rabbits (Jones & Watson, 1924). To reduce this fear, a rabbit was presented to Peter shortly after he was given candy to eat. The pairing of the candy and the rabbit led to the rapid elimination of Peter's fearful response. Jones and Watson attributed the new emotional response (the absence of fear and avoidance) to the repeated pairing of the feared object with a competing emotional response (eating).

It is of historical interest that Watson did not describe the initial response as having been eliminated or extinguished, as did subsequent models of conditioning (e.g., Rescorla & Wagner, 1972). Rather, consistent with current thinking and experimental data (Bouton, 2000; Rescorla, 1996), Watson argued that the original response survives but is interfered with or "masked" by more recently acquired conditioned responses.

Therefore, it would not have been surprising to Watson and colleagues that the "spontaneous" reemergence of prior responses—particularly in novel settings and as a function of time-since-training—constitutes a major limitation of the effectiveness of counterconditioning as a clinical intervention (Bouton, 2000).

Classical Conditioning and Clinical Interventions The clinical applicability of counterconditioning to anxiety disorders was enhanced by the pioneering work of Joseph Wolpe (1958). Prior to his work, counterconditioning consisted primarily of exposing an individual to a feared or avoided stimulus, and perhaps encouraging activities or behaviors inconsistent with avoidance. Wolpe devised a clinical approach that involved not only exposure but also a second activity, systematic relaxation training. Termed *systematic desensitization*, clients or patients are trained in relaxation techniques that involve deep breathing and increased awareness of physiological signs of stress, such as muscle tension and changes in heart rate. Only after some level of mastery of such techniques would Wolpe expose subjects to feared objects or situations.

In addition, Wolpe (1958) advocated graduated or systematic exposure according to the discomfort elicited by the stimuli. So, rather than exposing spider-phobic persons to spiders, he might initially expose them to pictures of spiders or even simply invite them to think about spiders. Then, in the presence of such stimuli, clients were encouraged to reduce their own anxiety through the use of the previously learned relaxation techniques. Only after indicating reasonable comfort with a less anxiety-provoking stimulus would the client be introduced to the most feared object or situation. Through this graduated process, phobic individuals obtained mastery over their avoidance behaviors and feelings of anxiety.

Criticisms of Classical Conditioning Interventions Respondent conditioning can be thought of as a process by which reflexive behaviors come under stimulus control. Avoidance behaviors, such as those characteristic of anxiety disorders in children, are thought to have developed at least in part due to actual experiences (i.e., children with a simple phobia of animals may have been frightened or hurt by an animal in the past). However, individuals with phobias often report no prior frightening or life-threatening experiences with the feared object or situation. Therefore, although respondent conditioning makes for a sensible explanation of phobic avoidance, traditional accounts cannot fully encompass the breadth of phobic presentations, nor can they fully account for how phobic behavior develops (Mineka & Zinbarg, 2006). This constitutes a primary criticism of classical conditioning as a model for the development of phobias and other avoidance-based psychological disorders. Conceptual and experimental advances on this basic paradigm that have attempted to overcome this important shortcoming are discussed later. Specifically, evolutionarily based "preparedness" and language processes specific to humans are discussed as factors explaining the emergence of fearful reactions to novel stimuli.

OPERANT CONDITIONING

A second empirical pillar of behavioral interventions is operant conditioning. Like classical conditioning, the operant conditioning model emerged out of laboratory work with nonhumans. Closely associated with the work of B. F. Skinner, it was not long before laboratory work was extended to developing new treatment methods for adults and children.

Operant conditioning is concerned with the effect of prior consequences on future behavior. For example, how does the future likelihood and rate of a child's tantruming behavior relate to how a parent responds to such behavior in the present? Several decades of experimental and applied research have shown that behaviors such as tantruming and arguing are strongly influenced by their consequences (Patterson, 1982). Operant conditioning, sometimes referred to as Skinnerian or instrumental conditioning, is concerned with the way behavior functions as an "instrument" for producing outcomes and the extent to which the rate and likelihood of behavior is sensitive to such consequences. To the extent that future behavior can be predicted, influenced, or controlled by its consequences, it qualifies as *operant behavior* (Catania, 2000).

Operant behavior is defined with respect to what is called the *three-term contingency*. The *behavior* of the organism and its *consequences* constitute two of the three terms. The other term, the *antecedent*, refers to the context in which the functional relationship occurs. If a consequence is more likely in the presence of some stimulus, that stimulus signals the likely instrumentality of future behavior. For example, an "Open" sign in a doorway signals the likelihood of gaining entry by turning the doorknob or pushing it open. Antecedent stimuli that serve such a signaling function are termed *discriminative stimuli.*

The antecedent, the behavior, and the consequence constitute the ABCs of the operant account of behavior. In addition to these three terms, organismic and contextual variables—such as physiology and learning history—are sometimes referred to as constituting additional terms (Michael, 1982; Sidman, 1986). This is in recognition of the fact that such variables may affect the degree to which a behavior is, at that moment, sensitive to its consequences. The three-term contingency is the cornerstone of an operant view, in part because it highlights variables that can be manipulated. For example, consider a child thought to have a difficult temperament (an organismic variable), as operationalized by sharper or faster peaks in physiological responding and shorter latency to crying or loudly vocalizing when novel stimuli are introduced. Independent of presumptions about the child's level of biological vulnerability, behavioral interventions still involve a careful analysis and modification of the environmental events thought to influence problem behavior (either antecedents or consequences, or both). The primary reason that behaviorists emphasize environmental rather than organismic factors concerns the readiness with which antecedents and consequences can be manipulated to produce changes in behavior. Moreover, it is a primary position of behaviorism that many behaviors that on casual inspection appear to be involuntary or unchangeable are in fact responsive to environmental contingencies (Ader, 1997; Ainslie, 2001).

Operant Conditioning and Clinical Interventions   Many behavioral treatments for children, adolescents, and their families are founded on principles of operant conditioning. These include behavior change techniques that rely on contingency management. Some of the most frequently utilized interventions involve differential attention, planned ignoring, and time-out from positive reinforcement (see Miltenberger, 2001).

The treatment logic underlying the use of differential attention techniques derives from the observation that for many individuals, social attention is reinforcing. Early applied behaviorists working with families attempted to help parents use contingent social attention to improve child behavior. Specifically, parents were taught to provide a great deal of attention and affection to children following desired behaviors and to withhold attention and affection following less desirable behaviors. Withholding attention is sometimes referred to as planned ignoring.

Differential attention and planned ignoring represent contingency management of *primary reinforcers.* Primary reinforcers are those that individuals seek naturally, or without training. In addition to attention, primary reinforcers include food, sex, a comfortable and stimulating environment, and sleep. Of course, even primary reinforcers are not reinforcing in all circumstances for all people. Food does not serve as a positive reinforcer for most people after a large meal, and does so rarely, if ever, for adolescents or young adults diagnosed with Anorexia Nervosa.

In addition to differential attention and planned ignoring, time-out from positive reinforcement, usually called *time-out,* was developed as a contingency management technique (Wolf, Risley, & Mees, 1964). Like planned ignoring, time-out involves attempting to reduce some undesirable behavior by having it result in reduced contact with reinforcing objects and situations. Time-out involves limiting a child to an unstimulating place (i.e., a chair facing the corner or a room with no toys) for some specified time period (Roberts & Powers, 1990). Time-out constitutes a key intervention strategy for managing oppositional child behavior (McMahon & Forehand, 2003).

Weaknesses of time-out as a clinical approach include the fact that some children escape from or refuse to remain in the time-out area. One response has been to provide an aversive contingency for such behavior, such as spanking. This is an ironic response, however, given that time-out is touted as an alternative to spanking. Another possible response is to physically restrain the child in the time-out area. This solution may be problematic if escape behavior is in the service of generating parental attention. This might explain why physical restraint is less effective than spanking as a means of responding to children who escape from time-out (Roberts & Powers, 1990).

These techniques—differential attention, planned ignoring, and time-out—constitute just a few examples of efforts to manage behavior by controlling primary reinforcers. Another widely used contingency management approach, the *token economy,* represents an attempt to affect behavior through the use of secondary reinforcers (Swiezy, Matson, & Box, 1992). That is, a token economy shapes behavior through the contingent presentation of secondary reinforcers (money, poker chips) that may be exchanged for more primary reinforcers (e.g., play time, toys, food, field trips). Modern applications of the token economy date to the 1950s and 1960s, but early precursors or approximations date at least to the 1850s (Rodriguez, Montesinos, & Preciado, 2005). The token economy represents a clear example of direct contingency management with a focus on affecting behavior by controlling its consequences and have been successfully implemented in numerous settings, including hospitals, work environments, homes, and schools (Miltenberger, 2001).

Functional Assessment   A defining element of contingency management approaches is the need to identify the nature of the contingencies that control behavior. Systematic attempts to identify controlling contingencies are frequently termed *functional analyses* or *functional assessment* (Shriver, Anderson, & Proctor, 2001). A functional analysis involves manipulating the environment to identify the contingencies that affect behavior. For example, numerous studies have identified at least two functions of aggressive behavior: One involves escape or avoidance, and the other involves attention seeking (see Shriver et al., 2001). The probability and rate of aggressive behavior can vary as a function of the withdrawal of certain types of social demands, such as instructions issued by caretakers, hereafter termed an "escape function" for aggression. Alternatively, for other children, or, for the same child in different circumstances, aggressive behavior may "produce" or be "functionally related" to social attention from caretakers.

In addition, certain forms of aggression, such as self-injurious behavior, have been shown to serve a communicative function (Carr, 1977; Iwata, Dorsey, Slifer, Bauman, & Richman, 1982). That is, the self-injurious behavior of some individuals terminates in response to predictable actions on the part of caregivers, including help with difficult tasks or the presentation of food or enjoyable objects. Based on these findings, Carr and Durand (1985) proposed a treatment called *functional communication training*, in which individuals are taught to signal caretakers using nonaggressive behaviors. Simultaneously, caretakers are trained to respond to nonaggressive child behavior, ignoring aggression.

Another function of both aggressive and self-injurious behavior on the part of children and adults may be *control* (Schramm, 2006; Wahler & Dumas, 1986). Schramm describes the *control child* as one whose oppositional or uncooperative behavior is not ultimately directed at attention or escape. Rather, "escape or attention behavior occurs purely as a means to an end—that end being the goal of maintaining or controlling a position in the interaction or relationship" (p. 89). The functional nature of the behaviors exhibited by control children is most fittingly described under the rubric Oppositional Defiant Disorder (American Psychiatric Association, 2000). However, the severity of the problems that arise from control behavior may occasion more severe diagnostic labels. For example, a child might meet the criteria for an Autism Spectrum Disorder if his or her efforts at control during early childhood severely delay his or her acquisition of behavior, social, and general learning skills. Importantly, controlling behavior may not be the cause of autism, but it may impair the emergence of behavioral, social, and learning skills that free a child from the debilitating symptoms that define the disorder.

Schramm (2006) notes that the idea of control as a primary function of behavior is rejected by many behavior analysts because it may distract from identifying simpler functions of behavior. Nevertheless, the construct is appealing to the extent that contingency management plans targeting attention or escape are ineffective. Importantly, the same basic behavioral framework employed to change behavior motivated by escape and attention seeking is utilized for behavior motivated by control, although with some modifications reflecting the unique effects of control-seeking behavior on the mood and behavior of caretakers (Schramm, 2006).

The primary goal of functional assessment is to determine the purpose or function of behavior. By identifying that function, it becomes possible to affect the behavior via contingency management or through training alternative behaviors. Most individualized programs derived from a functional analysis utilize both contingency management and skills training in an attempt to generate alternatives to aggressive, dangerous, and unwanted behavior. In addition to being implemented at the level of individuals, programs that utilize some combination of contingency management and skills training have also been developed and successfully implemented at the level of classrooms (van Lier, Muthen, van der Sar, & Crijnen, 2004) and schools (Anderson & Kincaid, 2005).

Criticisms of Operant Conditioning Interventions   Criticisms of contingency management strategies abound, ranging from claims that they are ineffective to claims that they are iatrogenic and immoral (Kohn, 1993). Science may be ill-suited to answer questions of morality (but see Plaud & Vogeltantz, 1992, for an alternative view), but it can be most appropriately applied to questions of treatment efficacy. Encouragingly, decades of research show that contingency management is frequently an effective tool for reducing maladaptive behavior and increasing adaptive behavior (Pelham, Wheeler, & Chronis, 1998). Nevertheless, the positive impact of contingency management may not be realized in new settings or when it becomes clear that previously established contingencies are no longer operative. Therefore, an area for future research in contingency management concerns the development of procedures that maximize generalization and maintenance effects (O'Callaghan, Reitman, Northup, Hupp, & Murphy, 2003).

MODERN CONCEPTUALIZATIONS

Classical and operant conditioning are the two pillars on which behaviorism rose, and many behavioral conceptualizations still rely heavily on these conditioning paradigms. Classical conditioning involves learning about relations between signals and significant events, and operant conditioning involves learning about relations between one's own behavior and those significant events. Despite these differences, and contrary to earlier views, a consensus is emerging that operant and classical conditioning are part and parcel of a single, universal learning principle (Donahoe, Burgos, & Palmer, 1993; see also Ader, 1997; Ainslie, 2001). That is, the apparent distinction reflects different experimental preparations and environmental circumstances, not fundamentally different forms of learning. Nevertheless, the distinction between classical and operant conditioning is useful for identifying the conditions giving rise to learned responses and is, therefore, maintained in the experimental and applied literatures.

Behavior Therapy and Cognitive-Behavioral Therapy

Despite assertions that all behavior can be understood in terms of basic conditioning processes (Skinner, 1957), most practitioners have viewed conditioning as inadequate with respect to explaining complex human behavior (Bandura, 1977; Beck, Rush, Shaw, & Emery, 1979). What is missing, according to critics, is an account of the influence of internal states and experiences on behavior. To remedy the alleged problem, conceptualizations based on conditioning models were augmented with explanatory constructs from cognitive psychology. The result is a hybrid of behavioral and cognitive concepts and interventions that is known as cognitive-behavior therapy (CBT).

The emergence of CBT reflects the growing dominance of interpretations of behavior that emphasize covert internal experiences. Psychopathology, for example, was (and is) cast in terms of overt behavioral outcomes, as well as cognitive or information-processing deficits. Targets of treatment include content-based shifts in individuals' faulty thoughts, beliefs, attributions, and schemas. For example, negative automatic thoughts and depressive rumination are thought to lead directly to the development of episodes of depression. Similarly, mothers' negatively biased appraisals of their toddler's behavior predict overreactive discipline (Lorber, O'Leary, & Kendziora, 2003). According to the cognitive perspective, positive change at the level of overt behavior will be most efficient to the extent one can alter faulty or maladaptive cognitive content.

Some behaviorists see negative implications of cognitive theorizing. The complaint is that hypothetical constructs—like those previously posited by psychoanalysts and introspectionists—are merely "labels posing as explanations." Like previous concerns about the scientific standing of psychoanalysis, there are doubts that cognitive explanations will yield to falsification or promote functional accounts of behavioral processes. Worse, cognitive accounts could divert behavioral scientists from the development of methodologies that are better suited to facilitating behavior change (Hayes, 2004; Jacobson & Gortner, 2000; Strand, Cerna, & Skucy, 2007; Wolpe & Rachman, 1960).

Describing cognitive theories of language, Palmer (1998, p. 4) notes, "A common tactic is to infer a neural mechanism with just those properties necessary to explain the behavior under study and then to assert that this mechanism is innate." It is a primary epistemological commitment of behaviorism to avoid this reification error. That is, most behaviorists reject explanatory hypothetical constructs that have not been subjected to experimental analysis.

Reification errors may be less likely to occur in cognitive models of psychopathology than in cognitive models of language. That is because, as an applied discipline, clinical psychology is committed not to explaining behavior, but to changing behavior. In this way, the epistemological commitments of behaviorism and clinical psychology overlap (Hayes & Berens, 2004). Many cognitive-behavioral clinicians insist that cognitive variables are manipulable, which serves as the justification for such therapeutic techniques as cognitive restructuring (Beck et al., 1979). To the extent that cognitions are subject to manipulation, the fundamental disagreement about cognitive constructs becomes less a matter of philosophical legitimacy and more a matter of practical utility. The question becomes, Does manipulating cognitive variables add to the clinical utility of behavioral interventions?

We are aware of two domains of empirical evidence relevant to this debate. Most famously, it exists with respect to the treatment of adult depression. The results of a decade of investigations exploring the multiple components of cognitive-behavioral therapy for depression have called into question the value of cognitive components (Dimidjian et al., 2006; Gortner, Gollan, Dobson, & Jacobson, 1998; Jacobson et al., 1996). That is, despite their intuitive and theoretical appeal, cognitive components add nothing to, or even reduce, the effectiveness of interventions for depressed adults that employ behavioral components. Those behavioral components, termed *behavioral activation*, include techniques to help depressed individuals make contact with reinforcers via increasing their overall activity level and reducing social avoidance (Ferster, 1973; Kanter, Baruch, & Gaynor, 2006; Kanter, Cautilli, Busch, & Baruch, 2005).

The second source of data bearing on this question involves the role of social cognitions and emotion regulation in the treatment of child Conduct Disorder. According to Dodge (Crick & Dodge, 1994), a primary difference between aggressive and nonaggressive children involves how they experience, perceive, interpret, and react to social information. For example, a common empirical finding is that aggressive children are more likely to attribute hostile intent to peers in ambiguous social situations (e.g., De Castro, Slot, Bosch, Koops, & Veerman, 2003; Dodge & Somberg, 1987). Moreover, they have also been found to generate fewer and more aggressive solutions to hypothetical difficult social interactions than do nonaggressive children. These social information-processing deficits have been conceptualized as the basis for higher rates of aggressive behavior (Dodge, 1991; Crick & Dodge, 1994). Accordingly, interventions have been developed for aggression that target faulty or maladaptive cognitions (Conduct Problems Prevention Research Group, 1999a, 1999b; Lochman & Lenhart, 1993).

Similarly, a growing body of research illustrates that parental attributions regarding child behavior predict overreactive parenting (Lorber et al., 2003; Miller & Prinz,

2003). It follows, then, that efforts to alter parent attributions might affect parent behavior toward the child and, in turn, affect child behavior and development. Indeed, several studies exploring this and other mediational and moderator hypotheses lend support to the contribution of social cognition for understanding childhood aggression (Nix et al., 1999). Cognitive interventions may have utility in reducing overt aggressive behavior by altering the behavior of parents and how children respond to environmental triggers for aggressive behavior.

RELATIVITY OF REINFORCEMENT

In addition to fostering research into cognitive mechanisms, challenges posed by cognitive models of child psychopathology have inspired increasingly sophisticated behavioral models. For instance, because of research illustrating that conduct problem children could not be distinguished from control children in terms of differential reinforcement for their coercive and aggressive behavior, Maccoby (1992) argued against reinforcement theory as an explanation for childhood aggression.

Partly in response to this criticism, Snyder and Patterson (1995) tested a *matching law* formulation of aggression in families. According to the matching law, behavior is not a function of the absolute amount of reinforcement available for a given behavior; rather, it is a function of its reinforcers *relative to* reinforcers that accrue to behavioral alternatives (a ratio; Herrnstein, 1970; McDowell, 1982; Snyder et al., 2004; Strand, 2000a). Therefore, the rate of aggressive behavior may be drastically different across two children despite identical consequences for aggressive behavior. Such outcomes are possible given different consequences for *nonaggressive* behavior for each child.

Consistent with this logic, Snyder and Patterson (1995) found no differences in the absolute rate of reinforcement for aggressive behavior for a sample of conduct problem and control children. However, there were significant differences in terms of the *relative* effectiveness of such behavior. That is, for aggressive children, noncoercive behavior was ineffective at terminating conflict bouts with parents, whereas coercive means were effective. For control children, noncoercive behavior was more effective than coercive behavior at terminating conflict bouts. The relative payoff for child coercion in home settings predicted child coercion in the home setting several weeks later and child arrests over the subsequent 2 years (Schrepferman & Snyder, 2002).

These data suggest that conduct problems may arise as a result of parents doing a poor job of disciplining their children, but they do not rule out the possibility that aggressive children are simply more adept at coercive social tactics than nonaggressive children. Nevertheless, the importance of the Snyder and Patterson (1995) study and follow-up studies (Lucyshyn et al., 2004; Schrepferman & Snyder, 2002) lies in the fact that they show the power of the *relative* principle of reinforcement to predict behavior. They suggest efforts to reduce unwanted behaviors by increasing positive reinforcement for alternative behaviors (McDowell, 1982; Strand, 2000a).

The conceptualization that gave rise to the matching analysis just described is called *coercion theory* (Patterson, 1982). It assumes that coercive interactions within families begin with parent commands or instructions. Antisocial children typically respond to parent commands with coercion or aggressive acts that facilitate escape or termination of the command. To the extent that parents give in (i.e., terminate their command) without obtaining child compliance, the child's coercive behavior was successful (i.e., reinforced) and will be more likely to occur in the future.

Interestingly, Dumas and Wahler (1985; Wahler & Dumas, 1986) found that only 10% of coercive exchanges between conduct problem children and their parents began with a parental command. Instead, most coercive sequences appeared to arise out of the blue, with no predictable antecedent to child aggression. Wahler and Dumas reasoned, therefore, that mechanisms other than those posited by coercion theory may be at work. Perhaps child-initiated aggression was not always a bid to escape from a command, but rather a bid to escape from an unpredictable family environment. That is, the function of at least some child coercive episodes is to generate predictability (see also Schramm, 2006).

Consistent with the hypothesis, research shows that humans and nonhumans prefer predictable over unpredictable environments and will behave so as to increase predictability (Wahler & Dumas, 1989). Moreover, Wahler and Dumas (1986) found that mothers of conduct problem children behaved in a more predictable fashion when their children were coercive compared to when they were not. Wahler (1994, 1997) elaborated on the basic theme of the predictability hypothesis, arguing that conduct problems arise from the absence of continuity and predictability in the lives of conduct disordered youth.

Coercion theory and the predictability hypothesis are not mutually exclusive (Strand, 2000b). Each details a functional account of coercive child behavior. They are in agreement that children actively participate in shaping their environments. They are also in agreement that coercive behaviors learned at home generalize to out-of-home environments, and that if coercive tactics or efforts to control an unpredictable situation come to dominate a child's behavioral repertoire, that child will be less proficient at behaving in ways necessary for sustained and satisfying relationships.

TWO-FACTOR LEARNING THEORY

In addition to conceptualizations inspired by operant conditioning, conceptualizations of child Conduct Disorder may also be described by principles of respondent conditioning. For example, the two-factor theory of anxiety posits that escape from classically conditioned aversive stimuli is maintained via operant reinforcement. To the extent that parents give in or respond harshly to child coercion because of the emotional flooding that such behavior elicits, the two-factor theory provides an explanation for those maladaptive parenting behaviors. That is, one aspect of poor parenting is a conditioned emotional response. Thus, it stands to reason that treatment should perhaps address parents' capacity to tolerate negative arousal elicited by aversive child behaviors, in addition to targeting operant parent behaviors (Vasta, 1982).

This classical conditioning formulation suggests a different intervention strategy than the operant conditioning model. For instance, replacing efforts to train parents to better manage child behavior, intervention might involve systematic desensitization. That is, parents might be taught relaxation training and new methods for interacting with their children, while being exposed to aversive child behavior. The goal is to reduce maladaptive conditioned emotional responses on the part of parents, as these inhibit and interfere with the learning of more adaptive responses (Cavell, 2000; Cavell & Strand, 2002).

Also consistent with the principles of respondent conditioning is a structured intervention for compliance-problem children proposed by Ducharme (1996; Ducharme, Atkinson, & Poulton, 2000). Errorless compliance training conceptualizes noncompliance as a conditioned emotional response arising from frequent failures. It relies on the empirically supported idea that high-frequency behaviors have a momentum or persistence that is independent of immediate contingencies (Strand, 2000a). In errorless compliance training, parents are taught to make requests of their children that have a high likelihood of occurrence. So, for example, a parent might ask for frequent "high fives." At each successive phase of training, parents request increasingly difficult behaviors. Prior to moving to the next level, however, practice, praise, and encouragement are provided until compliance is at or near 100%. Rates of child compliance have been shown to improve dramatically as a result of this treatment, suggesting that the momentum generated for high-likelihood requests generalizes to low-likelihood requests. Errorless compliance training has been utilized effectively across a variety of diagnostic categories and in home, school, and inpatient settings (Ducharme & DiAdamo, 2005).

Many operant-based strategies for managing noncompliance and problem behavior focus on suppression of problem responses through reductive consequences. Errorless compliance training and other interventions stemming from classical conditioning provide nonaversive alternatives for reducing aversive child behavior. The relativity of reinforcement and behavioral momentum are modern developments in behaviorism, in the sense that they focus on how a change to one behavior affects other behaviors (Strand, 2000a, 2002).

RELATIONAL CONCEPTUALIZATIONS

Relational frame theory (RFT) is another lens through which externalizing disorders and family management issues may be conceptualized. The theory provides a functional account of human language and cognition that derives from advances in the experimental analysis of verbal behavior (Hayes, Barnes-Holmes, & Roche, 2001). These advances have led to a reconceptualization of psychopathology that focuses on the ways verbal rules and derived relational responding may affect behavior. Recent attempts have been made to apply an RFT conceptualization to behavioral parent training programs (Coyne & Wilson, 2004). Specifically, parents may respond to children's aggressive behavior in narrow, inflexible ways, such as escalating punitive responses or acquiescing to children's demands for the purpose of terminating, avoiding, or escaping aversive interactions. The avoidance functions of maladaptive parenting behaviors predominate and are difficult to change in behavioral parent training treatments. It is often hard to convince parents to try alternative behaviors, even though those to which they cling do not bring about desired outcomes.

Behavioral treatments arising from research on derived relational responding seek to go beyond traditional respondent or operant approaches addressing directly conditioned emotional responses to child misbehaviors. The principles of RFT suggest a model of failed parent-child interactions based on indirectly conditioned processes, which may be useful in addressing issues of treatment motivation and engagement that may foster the development of more varied, flexible behavioral management strategies.

To appreciate the potential contribution of derived relational responding to traditional conditioning processes, it is essential to consider how stimulus events acquire their behavior regulatory functions. Responses to stimuli may be *directly* (as in the case of classical or operant conditioning) or *indirectly* acquired. Indirectly acquired functions are mediated by language. Stimulus functions acquired in this way are termed *derived.* The psychological functions of particular stimuli cannot be fully captured without appreciation of their surrounding network of verbal relations.

There are two important ideas inherent in derived relational responding that extend classical conditioning models. First, the psychological properties of events could be much broader and more complex than those attained by simple classical conditioning. Second, humans respond to indirectly acquired stimulus events as if they are *actual* or *real.* For example, if a parent has the thought "I am a failure," he or she may respond to this thought as real or *true,* despite the fact that he or she may never have experienced someone evaluating him or her in this way. Moreover, due to the pervasiveness of human language processes, the thought "I am a failure" may belong to an extensive functional class of stimuli. This class may perhaps include parenting behaviors, thoughts about their own children, and comparisons of their own child to others. Contact with any member of this functional class (e.g., perceptions of one's child, the child's misbehavior, the child's negative or contextually inappropriate affect) may elicit the psychological properties of the thought "I am a failure." Importantly, avoidance responses acquired in the presence of some members of the class may transfer to other members of the class. Parents may attempt to avoid contact with any or all members of this functional class in an effort to terminate the unpleasant stimuli. Given how quickly functional classes form and how broadly they are distributed, behavioral attempts at avoidance predominate, thus leaving only a narrow and inflexible band of responses at parents' disposal. This broad avoidance constitutes what has been called *experiential avoidance,* or attempts to control, suppress, or alter unwanted private events. Engagement in experiential avoidance is thought to contribute to enhancing the behavior regulatory functions of unwanted private events, as well as increase their frequency and intensity. Moreover, it also may foster insensitivity to actual environmental contingencies, as is the case in rule-governed behavior (Hayes, 1989).

Conceptualized in this way, principles of derived relational responding could have important implications for treatment. In classical conditioning models, individuals participate in exposure-based treatment so that they may habituate to feared stimuli and extinguish avoidant repertoires with respect to those stimuli. Treatment based on RFT may be considered a special class of exposure, which utilizes a collection of therapeutic techniques called *defusion* strategies. The goal of defusion techniques is not habituation to feared stimuli, but to help individuals to experience thoughts about or evaluations of given stimuli as merely thoughts and evaluations, rather than actual or real events necessitating avoidance responses. In so doing, defusion assists individuals in developing a broader, more flexible repertoire of behavioral responses to the stimulus in question.

In the case of our "failed" parent, a therapist would walk that individual through a set of exercises in which he or she would be encouraged to experience the thought "I am a failure" as simply a thought rather than an aversive event that may be perceived as truth. Thoughts perceived as what they are (simple, psychological events) rather than literal truths are less likely to elicit avoidance, or more specifically, attempts to modulate or minimize internal experience. Instead of avoidance, the parent would be encouraged to simply note the thought, laugh about the thought, or say the thought aloud, and to engage in whatever parenting behaviors may be appropriate. Because the parent's attention is no longer focused solely on his or her own internal experience, the parent might become more aware of and responsive to a broader range of environmental contingencies. Consequently, defusion strategies do not attempt to change the content of thoughts; rather, they seek to alter the regulatory behavior or *psychological functions* of those thoughts for individuals. Through multiple exemplar training, avoidance behaviors should be reduced, and the client expected to begin engaging in more flexible, adaptive, approach-oriented strategies.

Experimental studies of RFT have found that cognition alters the impact of other behavioral processes (Hayes, Luoma, Bond, Masuda, & Lillis, 2006). Specifically, individuals who have been taught that stimulus A is larger than stimulus B, and who have been shocked in the presence of stimulus A, show a greater emotional response to stimulus B, even though the shock has never been directly paired with stimulus B (Dymond & Barnes, 1995). To review a simplified illustration, see Figure 3.1. Solid arrows denote direct conditioning processes, and dashed lines denote indirect conditioning processes. In Step 1, participants are directly trained that A is larger than B, and they derive that B is *smaller than* A indirectly. Likewise, in Step 2, participants are directly trained that when A is presented, they will experience a shock. They derive, again indirectly, that when shock occurs, it will be in the presence of stimulus A. Step 3 denotes the derived relation between stimulus B and shock, even though this relationship has never been directly trained. Thus, B elicits a greater emotional response

Step 1. Direct conditioning: A is larger than B.

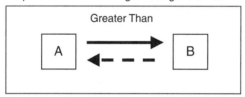

Step 2. Direct conditioning: A paired with shock.

Step 3. Indirect conditioning: Participant derives relationship between B and shock, even though never directly paired.

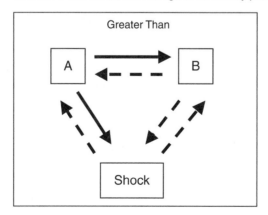

Figure 3.1 Illustration of transfer of functions through derived relations.

than stimulus A simply by virtue of its membership in this relational frame. In addition, a number of experimental studies have demonstrated that contextual features of a given situation regulate the relations made among stimuli and the intensity of their psychological functions (e.g., Wulfert & Hayes, 1988).

In acceptance and commitment therapy (ACT), a behavioral treatment derived directly from principles of RFT, individuals are introduced to the concept of "valuing" (Hayes, Strosahl, & Wilson, 1999). Valuing is perhaps best described as working toward meaningful pursuits, for instance, "being a loving parent" or "having a good relationship with one's children." Values are not goals, in the sense that they are not end points, but rather are verbal constructions that allow individuals to continue working in a particular direction (Wilson & Murrell, 2004). The difference between a goal and a value is the difference between "going to California" and "going West." The former is an end point that can be directly experienced; the latter organizes a continuous stream of behaviors. In this kind of clinical experience, parents may work toward learning to perform a well-defined set of behavior management strategies, but also toward more meaningful or valued ideas that may reinforce the pursuit of skill development. Thus, if parents are required to practice new skills that have as their immediate consequences discomfort, they may be more likely to persist. Consider the example of planned ignoring. Parents who remain focused on the valued pursuit of, say, "helping my child become a good citizen" may be more likely to persist in utilizing techniques that are focused on the immediate short-term goal of reducing tantrums. Allowing parents to work for verbally constructed rewards is another way in which derived relational responding extends traditional respondent and operant conceptualizations of behavior change.

Derived relational responding principles would suggest that we cannot fully describe parenting behavior without ascertaining the functional properties of parents' experienced events during their interactions with their children. Nor can we expect to predict behavior without elucidating the ways that those psychological functions are acquired through both direct and verbal learning processes. Addressing these issues may be central to initiating and maintaining treatment participation. Additionally, there may be great potential for using applied principles of derived relational responding to enhance and extend positive outcomes of parent training programs targeting conduct problems.

The same verbal processes that negatively affect parent-child relationships are implicated in both adult and childhood anxiety disorders. Specifically, children or adults who experience anxiety symptoms may frequently engage in experiential avoidance. A hallmark of internalizing disorders is difficulty tolerating one's own anxiety and physiological responses to it, which serve as antecedents to behavioral avoidance. Motivational factors involving children undergoing exposure-based treatment may also be dealt with using defusion strategies and valuing. Techniques such as these have been used with some success in a variety of anxiety and mood issues with adults, and a number of efforts are under way to adapt them to childhood disorders (Coyne & Wilson, 2000; Greco, Heffner, & Poe, 2005; Murrell, Coyne, & Wilson, 2005; Wicksell, Dahl, Magnusson, & Olsson, 2005).

BIOBEHAVIORISM AND BEHAVIORAL NEUROSCIENCE

Although behaviorists rely heavily on reinforcement history as an explanation for both normal and abnormal functioning, they do not eschew the contributions of biological structure and functioning. Psychological disorders are conceptualized as relatively stable patterns of action that arise out of an organism's history of interacting within an environment. Nevertheless, behavior is not determined solely by contingencies. Rather, the structure and functioning of the nervous system constrains or mediates behavioral outcomes. For example, computer simulations of neural networks illustrate that stable response patterns emerge as a result of exposure to certain reinforcement contingencies; however, the exact nature of those patterns differs depending on the complexity of the neural network (Burgos & Donahoe, 2000; Donahoe, Burgos, & Palmer, 1993). Therefore, one cannot characterize behavior simply in terms of reinforcement contingencies; one must also know something about the structure of the behaving system that is interacting with the environment (Dickins et al., 2001; Timberlake, Schaal, & Steinmetz, 2005). Importantly, because neither the structure of the organism nor the environment is static, as time unfolds distinctions between structure and function become blurred.

BIOBEHAVIORAL AND NEUROCOGNITIVE CONCEPTUALIZATIONS OF PSYCHOPATHOLOGY: THE CASE OF ATTENTION-DEFICIT/HYPERACTIVITY DISORDER

Scientists who emphasize cognitive constructs in their conceptualizations of child psychopathology refer to their efforts as *cognitive neuroscience* or *cognitive neuropsychology;* scientists who rely on behavioral constructs refer to their efforts as *behavioral neuroscience* or *biobehaviorism.* The differences between these approaches can be elucidated by exploring recent conceptualizations of Attention-Deficit/Hyperactivity Disorder (ADHD).

Attention-Deficit/Hyperactivity Disorder is characterized by inattentiveness, overactivity, and impulsiveness. The etiology of the disorder is almost universally recognized to involve maladaptive brain processes to varying degrees. However, which processes are maladaptive, and how they give rise to ADHD, is open to debate. Cognitive neuropsychological models emphasize a disordered frontal cortex—hypothesized to give rise to deficiencies in executive functioning—as the basis for the disorder (Barkley, 1997). Executive functions refer to complex behaviors associated with frontal lobe functioning that include planning, problem solving, delay of gratification, and inhibiting prepotent responses (Hayes, Gifford, & Ruckstuhl, 1996). According to the theory, the deficits that define ADHD are a relatively direct manifestation of faulty brain processes. That is, the link between brain functioning and the defining symptoms of ADHD is not mediated by reinforcement. The theory is cognitive to the extent that it does not limit explanations to constructs that are based on a direct experimental manipulation.

An alternative conceptualization is the dynamic developmental theory (DDT) proposed by Sagvolden and colleagues (Johansen, Aase, Meyer, & Sagvolden, 2002; Sagvolden, Johansen, Aase, & Russell, 2005). It is in agreement with cognitive neuropsychology models that ADHD reflects maladaptive neurological processes. Specifically, Sagvolden and colleagues argue that the disorder reflects hypofunctioning dopamine activity within mesolimbic areas of the brain, which gives rise to widespread faulty neurotransmitter activity. This neurological process affects learning. Specifically, it reduces the likelihood that the behaviors of ADHD individuals will come under the control of all but the most immediate reinforcers—resulting in inattentiveness and impulsiveness. Additionally, the altered brain functioning adversely affects extinction processes such that ineffectual behaviors are not efficiently pruned from the repertoires of ADHD individuals—resulting in overactivity.

According to its authors, the DDT provides a more parsimonious and more complete explanation for the symptomatology and developmental course of ADHD than do competing theories. It differs from neurocognitive theories in that it is consistent with the epistemological commitments of behaviorism; explanatory constructs derive from the experimental analysis of neural and behavioral events only. As such, the DDT accepts behavioral mediators, such as reinforcement gradients and extinction, while rejecting cognitive mediators, such as executive functioning. Moreover, the model maintains that symptomatology arises over the course of some developmental time frame. It is the *developmental process* of learning that is affected by altered brain functioning and that gives rise, over time, to the defining symptoms of ADHD. Cognitive conceptions, on the other hand, do not specify a developmental or time-dependent process for the emergence of the complex behaviors that define ADHD.

Sagvolden and colleagues (2005, p. 415) focus on the role of the three-term contingency as the basic force dictating the bidirectional interaction between brain and behavior: "The vulnerability consists, in particular, of inefficient reinforcement and extinction processes." Nevertheless, DDT differs from traditional behavioral models of psychopathology in that it postulates reinforcement history not only as an *independent variable* affecting behavior, but also as a *dependent variable* affected by brain structure and function. As such, ontogenic reinforcement history is not the primary factor distinguishing ADHD and non-ADHD individuals; the primary difference between them concerns not *what* they have learned, but *how* they learn.

That ADHD might result from differential sensitivity to reinforcement rather than differences in environmental experiences, across individuals, could pose a challenge to traditional behavioral conceptualizations. Specifically, Sagvolden and colleagues (2005) are skeptical about the efficacy of contingency management in the treatment of ADHD. They argue that both current and future functioning of individuals with ADHD is most likely to be normalized via psychostimulant medication, not through contingency management. Nevertheless, it remains the case that the DDT identifies outcomes for individuals with ADHD as being determined not by faulty brain processes, but by the behavioral repertoires that arise (or fail to arise) over the course of development. Because these repertoires are operants, they are at least theoretically subject to change through contingency management. As such, Catania (2005) expresses greater optimism than Sagvolden about the potential effectiveness of next-generation contingency management approaches to treating ADHD. In particular, Catania conceives of computer-based training aimed at helping children develop the capacity to respond to delayed rather than immediate outcomes as a potentially effective nonpharmacological intervention.

CONCEPTUAL ERAS

Behavioral conceptualizations of psychopathology have increased in number over the years. Table 3.1 organizes these conceptualizations into three distinct eras. The table is presented as a heuristic for viewing the progressive nature of behavioral psychology and as a point of reference for generating competing (and complementary) behavioral conceptualizations of clinical disorders. Each era is defined in terms of a set of concepts and methods that have given rise to distinct formulations for understanding and impacting psychopathology. The dates refer, approximately, to when

Table 3.1
Historical Eras of Behavioral Conceptualization

Conceptualization	Concepts/Methods	Applications
Absolute reinforcement (1920–present) [Mechanistic]	Law of effect Cumulative record Response rate Conditioned avoidance	Direct contingency management (i.e., Token economy)
Relative reinforcement (1980–present) [Relativistic]	Matching law Concurrent schedules Molar behaviorism	Management of reinforcement Response rate contingencies for behavioral alternatives
Relational learning (1990–present) [Relational, Functional-contextual]	Derived stimulus relations Matching-to-sample Generalized operants Higher order operants Stimulus classes Bidirectional relations Experiential avoidance	Interoceptive exposure Reinforced variability Cognitive defusion Multiple exemplar training Valuing Acceptance

the concepts and methods began to influence clinical conceptualizations. The eras are open-ended with respect to time because each allows for a valid conceptualization of psychopathology; later ones do not negate earlier ones. Nevertheless, later conceptualizations have sometimes resulted in advances in our ability to predict and influence behavior (McDowell, 1982; Patterson, 2005) and in an expanded subject matter for behavioral investigations (Hayes et al., 2001) and interventions (Coyne & Wilson, 2004; Schramm, 2006).

The *absolute reinforcement* conceptualization highlights the study of environmental effects on behavior without reference to other behaviors. The emphasis is on cumulative changes in the frequency and duration of a behavior; interventions involve managing the consequences of behavior. *Relativistic reinforcement* conceptualizations challenge the notion that behavior is solely a function of its consequences. They contend that behavior is a function of its consequences *relative to* the consequences that accrue to other forms of behavior. From this perspective, behavior cannot be understood in terms of a cumulative record, but must be studied with respect to its relative strength or relative probability (i.e., response ratio). Interventions involve management of a wider network of reinforcement contingencies and an emphasis on response-response relationships. Although the clinical applications of this conceptualization were discussed in the early 1980s, its most transformative effects were not realized with respect to children until the mid-1990s, when the principle of relative reinforcement was shown to account for differences in aggression across clinical and nonclinical samples (Snyder & Patterson, 1995).

The conceptual ramifications of *relational learning* have not yet been fully realized in behaviorism (Hayes & Berens, 2004). The approach denotes advances in behavioral conceptualizations of verbal behavior that began in the mid-1980s (Hayes, 1984), whose clinical significance became clearer in the 1990s (Dougher, 2000; Hayes et al., 1999; Kohlenberg & Tsai, 1990). Also termed post-Skinnerian, the conceptualization highlights the ability of humans to apply lessons across a variety of contexts.

According to relational conceptualizations, what makes verbal humans unique is their capacity to learn and to arbitrarily apply a relational repertoire to a wide range of situations (Strand, Barnes-Holmes, & Barnes-Holmes, 2003). Unfortunately, the sophisticated verbal capacities are a double-edged sword with respect to happiness and well-being. In particular, the propensity to avoid (or at least try to avoid) certain kinds of experiential states is considered a primary source of human suffering (Hayes & Gifford, 1997). Relational learning could lead to a revised basic research agenda for behaviorism and to clinical interventions that bear little resemblance to traditionally behavioral interventions (Hayes & Berens, 2004). Nevertheless, this conceptualization is behavioral to the extent that it is consistent with the epistemological commitments of behaviorism. Indeed, by pushing the boundaries of behavioral investigations, recent conceptualizations may clarify the essence of behaviorism (Donahoe & Palmer, 1989; Hayes, 1986).

SUMMARY

Behaviorism remains, at its core, a commitment to a set of rules for explaining complex behavior. The constraints are those of natural science and involve rejecting explanations that invoke constructs that have not been the subject of experimental investigation. Some have argued that the price of these self-imposed constraints is too high; it prohibits the study of what is most interesting and most important about people. Nonetheless, behaviorism has generated a surprisingly rich assortment of clinical conceptualizations and interventions and vibrant research and theory about the nature of language and cognition. It has also contributed to parsimonious conceptualizations of the interaction between neural organization and behavioral organization and how that interaction may give rise to complex disorders such as ADHD. We suggest that the richness and variety of behavioral conceptualizations has arisen not despite behaviorism's self-imposed constraints, but because of them.

REFERENCES

Ader, R. (1997). The role of conditioning in pharmacotherapy. In A. Harrington (Ed.), *The placebo effect: An interdisciplinary exploration* (pp. 138–165). Cambridge, MA: Harvard University Press.

Ainslie, G. (2001). *Breakdown of will.* Cambridge, MA: Harvard University Press.

American Psychiatric Association. (2000). *Diagnostic and statistical manual of mental disorders* (4th ed., text rev.). Washington, DC: Author.

Anderson, C. M., & Kincaid, D. (2005). Applying behavior analysis to school violence and discipline problems: Schoolwide positive behavior support. *Behavior Analyst, 28,* 49–63.

Bandura, A. (1977). *Social learning theory.* Englewood Cliffs, NJ: Prentice-Hall.

Barkley, R. A. (1997). Behavioral inhibition, sustained attention, and executive functions: Constructing a unifying theory of ADHD. *Clinical Psychology Review, 21,* 971–978.

Beck, A. T., Rush, A. J., Shaw, B. F., & Emery, G. (1979). *Cognitive therapy of depression.* New York: Guilford Press.

Bouton, M. E. (2000). A learning theory perspective on lapse, relapse, and the maintenance of behavior change. *Health Psychology, 19,* 57–63.

Burgos, J. E., & Donahoe, J. W. (2000). Structure and function in selectionism: Implications for complex behavior. In J. C. Leslie & D. Blackman (Eds.), *Experimental and applied analysis of human behavior* (pp. 39–58). Reno, NV: Context Press.

Carr, E. G. (1977). The motivation of self-injurious behavior: A review of some hypotheses. *Psychological Bulletin, 84,* 800–816.

Carr, E. G., & Durand, V. M. (1985). Reducing behavior problems through functional communication training. *Journal of Applied Behavior Analysis, 18,* 111–126.

Catania, A. C. (2000). Ten points every behavior analyst needs to remember about reinforcement. In J. C. Leslie & D. Blackman (Eds.), *Experimental and applied analysis of human behavior* (pp. 23–37). Reno, NV: Context Press.

Catania, A. C. (2005). Attention-deficit/hyperactivity disorder (ADHD): Delay-of-reinforcement gradients and other behavioral mechanisms. *Behavioral and Brain Sciences, 28,* 419–424.

Cavell, T. A. (2000). *Working with parents of aggressive children: A practitioner's guide.* Washington, DC: American Psychological Association.

Cavell, T. A., & Strand, P. S. (2002). Parent-based interventions for aggressive, antisocial children: Adapting to a bilateral lens. In L. Kuczynski (Ed.), *Handbook of dynamics in parent-child relations* (pp. 395–419). Thousand Oaks, CA: Sage.

Conduct Problems Prevention Research Group. (1999a). Initial impact of the Fast Track Prevention Trial for conduct problems: Pt. I. The high risk sample. *Journal of Consulting and Clinical Psychology, 67,* 631–647.

Conduct Problems Prevention Research Group. (1999b). Initial impact of the Fast Track Prevention Trial for conduct problems: Pt. II. Classroom effects. *Journal of Consulting and Clinical Psychology, 67,* 648–657.

Coyne, L. W., & Wilson, K. G. (2004). Cognitive fusion in impaired parenting: An RFT analysis. *International Journal of Psychology and Psychological Therapy, 4,* 469–486.

Crick, N.R., & Dodge, K.A. (1994). A review and reformulation of social information-processing mechanisms in children's social adjustment. *Psychological Bulletin, 115,* 74–101.

Crick, N. R., & Dodge, K. A. (1996). Social-information processing mechanisms in reactive and proactive aggression. *Child Development, 67,* 993–1002.

De Castro, B. O., Slot, N. W., Bosch, J. D., Koops, W., & Veerman, J. W. (2003). Negative feelings exacerbate hostile attributions of intent in highly aggressive boys. *Journal of Clinical Child and Adolescent Psychology, 32,* 56–65.

Dickins, D. W., Singh, K. D., Roberts, N., Burns, P., Downes, J. J., Jimmieson, P., et al. (2001). An fMRI study of stimulus equivalence. *NeuroReport, 12,* 405–411.

Dimidjian, S., Hollon, S. D., Dobson, K. S., Schmaling, K. B., Kohlenberg, R. J., Addis, M. E., et al. (2006). Randomized trial of behavioral activation, cognitive therapy, and antidepressant medication in the acute treatment of adults with major depression. *Journal of Consulting and Clinical Psychology, 74,* 658–670.

Dodge, K. A. (1991). Emotion and social information processing. In J. Garber & K. A. Dodge (Eds.), *The development of emotion regulation and dysregulation: Cambridge studies in social and emotional development* (pp. 159–181). New York: Cambridge University Press.

Dodge, K. A., & Somberg, D. R. (1987). Hostile attributional biases among aggressive boys are exacerbated under conditions of threat to the self. *Child Development, 58,* 213–224.

Donahoe, J. W., Burgos, J. E., & Palmer, D. C. (1993). A selectionist approach to reinforcement. *Journal of the Experimental Analysis of Behavior, 60,* 17–40.

Donahoe, J. W., & Palmer, D. C. (1989). The interpretation of complex human behavior: Some reactions to parallel distributed processing in J. L. McClelland, D. E. Rumelhart, & the PDP Research Group (Eds.). *Journal of the Experimental Analysis of Behavior, 51,* 399–416.

Donahoe, J. W., & Palmer, D. E. (1994). *Learning and complex behavior.* Needham Heights, MA: Allyn & Bacon.

Dougher, M. J. (Ed.). (2000). *Clinical behavior analysis.* Reno, NV: Context Press.

Ducharme, J. M. (1996). Errorless compliance training: Optimizing clinical effectiveness. *Behavior Modification, 20,* 259–280.

Ducharme, J. M., Atkinson, L., & Poulton, L. (2000). Success-based, noncoercive treatment of oppositional behavior in children from violent homes. *Journal of the American Academy of Child and Adolescent Psychiatry, 39,* 995–1004.

Ducharme, J. M., & DiAdamo, C. (2005). An errorless approach to classroom management of child noncompliance in a special education setting. *School Psychology Review, 34,* 107–115.

Dumas, J. E., & Wahler, R. G. (1985). Indiscriminate mothering as a contextual factor in aggressive-oppositional child behavior: "Damned if you do and damned if you don't." *Journal of Abnormal Child Psychology, 13,* 1–17.

Dymond, S. & Barnes, D. (1995). A transformation of self-discrimination response functions in accordance with arbitrarily applicable relations of sameness, more than, and less than. *Journal of the Experimental Analysis of Behavior, 64,* 163–184.

Ferster, C. B. (1973). A functional analysis of depression. *American Psychologist, 28,* 857–870.

Gortner, E. T., Gollan, J. K., Dobson, K. S., & Jacobson, N. S. (1998). Cognitive-behavioral treatment of depression: Relapse prevention. *Journal of Consulting and Clinical Psychology, 66,* 377–384.

Greco, L. A., Heffner, M., & Poe, S. (2005). Maternal adjustment following preterm birth: Contributions of experiential avoidance. *Behavior Therapy, 36,* 177–184.

Hayes, S. C. (1984). Making sense of spirituality. *Behaviorism, 12,* 99–110.

Hayes, S. C. (1986). The case of the silent dog: Verbal reports and the analysis of rules—A review of Ericsson and Simon's protocol analysis: Verbal reports as data. *Journal of the Experimental Analysis of Behavior, 45,* 351–363.

Hayes, S. C. (Ed.). (1989). *Rule-governed behavior: Cognition, contingencies, and instructional control.* New York: Plenum Press.

Hayes, S. C. (2004). Acceptance and commitment therapy, relational frame theory, and the third wave of behavioral and cognitive therapies. *Behavior Therapy, 35,* 639–665.

Hayes, S. C., Barnes-Holmes, D., & Roche, B. (Eds.). (2001). *Relational frame theory: A post-Skinnerian account of human language and cognition.* New York: Kluwer Academic/Plenum Press.

Hayes, S. C., & Berens, N. M. (2004). Why relational frame theory alters the relationship between basic and applied behavioral psychology. *International Journal of Psychology and Psychological Therapy, 4,* 341–353.

Hayes, S. C., & Gifford, E. V. (1997). The trouble with language: Experiential avoidance, rules, and the nature of verbal events. *Psychological Science, 8,* 170–173.

Hayes, S. C., Gifford, E. V., & Ruckstuhl, L. E. (1996). Relational frame theory and executive function: A behavioral approach. In G. R. Lyon & N. A. Krasnegor (Eds.), *Attention, memory, and executive function* (pp. 279–305). Baltimore: Paul H. Brookes.

Hayes, S. C., Hayes, L. J., & Reese, H. W. (1988). Finding the philosophical core: A review of Stephen C. Pepper's "World hypotheses: A study in evidence." *Journal of the Experimental Analysis of Behavior, 50,* 97–111.

Hayes, S. C., Luoma, J. B., Bond, F., Masuda, A., Lillis, J. (2006). Acceptance and commitment therapy: Model, processes, outcomes. *Behaviour Therapy, 44,* 1–25.

Hayes, S. C., Strosahl, K. D., & Wilson, K. G. (1999). *Acceptance and commitment therapy: An experiential approach to behavior change.* New York: Guilford Press.

Herrnstein, R. J. (1970). On the law of effect. *Journal of the Experimental Analysis of Behavior, 13,* 243–266.

Iwata, B. A., Dorsey, M. F., Slifer, K. J., Bauman, K. E., & Richman, G. S. (1982). Toward a functional analysis of self-injury. *Analysis and Intervention in Developmental Disabilities, 2,* 3–20.

Jacobson, N. S., Dobson, K. S., Truax, P. A., Addis, M. E., Koerner, K., Gollan, J. K., et al. (1996). A component analysis of cognitive-behavioral treatment for depression. *Journal of Consulting and Clinical Psychology, 64,* 295–304.

Jacobson, N. S., & Gortner, E. (2000). Can depression be de-medicalized in the 21st century? Scientific revolutions, counter revolutions, and magnetic field of normal sciences. *Behaviour Research and Therapy, 38,* 103–117.

Johansen, E. B., Aase, H., Meyer, A., & Sagvolden, T. (2002). Attention-deficit/hyperactivity disorder (ADHD) behavior explained by dysfunctioning reinforcement and extinction processes. *Behavioral Brain Research, 130,* 37–45.

Jones, M. C., & Watson, J. B. (1924). A laboratory study of fear: The case of Peter. *Pedagogical Seminary, 31,* 308–315.

Kanfer, F. H., & Phillips, J. S. (1970). *Learning foundations of behavior therapy.* New York: Wiley.

Kanter, J. W., Baruch, D. E., & Gaynor, S. T. (2006). Acceptance and commitment therapy and behavioral activation for the treatment of depression: Description and comparison. *Behavior Analyst, 29,* 161–185.

Kanter, J. W., Cautilli, J. D., Busch, A. M., & Baruch, D. E. (2005). Toward a comprehensive functional analysis of depressive behavior: Five environmental factors and a possible sixth and seventh. *Behavior Analyst Today, 6,* 65–81.

Kohlenberg, R. J., & Tsai, M. (1990). *Functional analytic psychotherapy: Creating intense and curative therapeutic relationships.* New York: Plenum Press.

Kohn, A. (1993). *Punished by rewards.* Boston: Houghton Mifflin.

Lochman, J. E., & Lenhart, L. A. (1993). Anger coping intervention for aggressive children: Conceptual models and outcome effects. *Clinical Psychology Review, 13,* 785–805.

Lorber, M. F., O'Leary, S. G., & Kendziora, K. T. (2003). Mothers' overreactive discipline and their encoding and appraisals of toddler behavior. *Journal of Abnormal Child Psychology, 31,* 485–494.

Lucyshyn, J. M., Irvin, L. K., Blumberg, E. R., Laverty, R., Horner, R. H., & Sprague, J. R. (2004). Validating the construct of coercion in family routines: Expanding the unit of analysis in families of children with developmental disabilities. *Research and Practice for Persons with Severe Developmental Disabilities, 29,* 104–121.

Maccoby, E. E. (1992). The role of parents in the socialization of children: An historical overview. *Developmental Psychology, 28,* 1006–1017.

McDowell, J. J. (1982). The importance of Herrnstein's mathematical statement of the law of effect for behavior therapy. *American Psychologist, 37,* 771–779.

McMahon, R. J., & Forehand, R. L. (2003). *Helping the non-compliant child: Family-based treatment for oppositional disorders* (2nd ed.). New York: Guilford Press.

Michael, J. (1982). Distinguishing between discriminative and motivational functions of stimuli. *Journal of the Experimental Analysis of Behavior, 37,* 149–155.

Miller, G. E., & Prinz, R. J. (2003). Engagement of families in treatment for childhood conduct problems. *Behavior Therapy, 34,* 517–534.

Miltenberger, R. G. (2001). *Behavior modification: Principles and procedures.* Belmont, CA: Wadsworth/Thomson.

Mineka, S., & Zinbarg, R. (2006). A contemporary learning theory perspective on the etiology of anxiety disorders: It's not what you thought it was. *American Psychologist, 61,* 10–26.

Morris, E. K. (1988). Contextualism: The world view of behavior analysis. *Journal of Experimental Child Psychology, 46,* 289–323.

Murrell, A. R., Coyne, L. W., & Wilson, K. G. (2005). ACT with children, adolescents, and their parents. In S. C. Hayes & K. D. Strosahl (Eds.), *A practical guide to acceptance and commitment therapy* (pp. 249–273). New York: Springer.

Nix, R. L., Pinderhughes, E. E., Dodge, K. A., Bates, J. E., Pettit, G. S., & McFadyen-Ketchum, S. A. (1999). The relation between mothers' hostile attribution tendencies and children's externalizing behavior problems: The mediating role of mothers' harsh discipline practices. *Child Development, 70,* 896–909.

O'Callaghan, P. M., Reitman, D., Northup, J., Hupp, S. D. A., & Murphy, M. A. (2003). Promoting social skills generalization with ADHD-diagnosed children in a sports setting. *Behavior Therapy, 34,* 313–330.

Palmer, D. C. (1998). The speaker as listener: The interpretation of structural regularities in verbal behavior. *Analysis of Verbal Behavior, 15,* 3–16.

Patterson, G. R. (1982). *Coercive family process.* Eugene, OR: Castalia Press.

Patterson, G. R. (2005). The next generation of PMTO models. *Behavior Therapist, 28,* 27–33.

Pavlov, I. P. (1960). *Conditioned reflexes* (G. V. Anrep, Trans.). New York: Dover. (Original work published 1927)

Pelham, W. E., Wheeler, T., & Chronis, A. (1998). Empirically-supported psychosocial treatments for attention deficit hyperactivity disorder. *Journal of Clinical Child Psychology, 27,* 190–205.

Plaud, J. J., & Vogeltantz, N. D. (1992). On the goodness of Skinner's system of naturalistic ethics in solving basic value conflicts. *Psychological Record, 42,* 457–468.

Rescorla, R. A. (1996). Preservation of Pavlovian associations through extinction. *Quarterly Journal of Experimental Psychology: Comparative and Physiological Psychology, 49*(B), 245–258.

Rescorla, R. A., & Wagner, A. R. (1972). A theory of Pavlovian conditioning: Variations in the effectiveness of reinforcement and nonreinforcement. In A. H. Black & W. K. Prokasy (Eds.), *Classical conditioning: Pt. II. Current research and theory* (pp. 64–99). New York: Appleton-Century-Crofts.

Rilling, M. (2000). John Watson's paradoxical struggle to explain Freud. *American Psychologist, 55,* 301–312.

Roberts, M. W., & Powers, S. W. (1990). Adjusting chair timeout enforcement procedures for oppositional children. *Behavior Therapy, 21,* 257–271.

Rodriguez, J. O., Montesinos, L., & Preciado, J. (2005). A 19th century predecessor of the token economy. *Journal of Applied Behavior Analysis, 38,* 427.

Sagvolden, T., Johansen, E. B., Aase, H., & Russell, V. A. (2005). A dynamic developmental theory of attention-deficit/hyperactivity disorder (ADHD) predominantly hyperactive/impulsive and combined subtypes [Including commentaries]. *Behavioral and Brain Sciences, 28,* 397–468.

Schramm, R. (2006). *Educate toward recovery: Turning the tables on autism.* Available from www.knospe-aba.de.

Schrepferman, L. M., & Snyder, J. (2002). Reinforcement mechanisms in behavior parent training associated with the long term alteration of child antisocial behavior. *Behavior Therapy, 33,* 339–359.

Shriver, M. D., Anderson, C. M., & Proctor, B. (2001). Evaluating the validity of functional behavior assessment. *School Psychology Review, 30,* 180–192.

Sidman, M. (1986). Functional analysis of emergent verbal classes. In T. Thompson & M. D. Zeiler (Eds.), *Analysis and integration of behavioral units* (pp. 213–245). Hillsdale, NJ: Erlbaum.

Skinner, B. F. (1957). *Verbal behavior.* New York: Appleton-Century-Crofts.

Snyder, J., & Patterson, G. R. (1995). Individual differences in social aggression: A test of a reinforcement model of socialization in the natural environment. *Behavior Therapy, 26,* 371–391.

Snyder, J., Stoolmiller, M., Patterson, G. R., Schrepferman, L., Oeser, J., Johnson, K., et al. (2004). The application of response allocation matching to understanding risk mechanisms in development. *Behavior Analyst Today, 4,* 335–345. Retrieved June 6, 2006, from http://behavior-analyst-today.com/vol-4/BAT-4-4.pdf.

Strand, P. S. (2000a). A modern behavioral perspective on child conduct disorder: Integrating behavioral momentum and matching theory. *Clinical Psychology Review, 20,* 593–615.

Strand, P. S. (2000b). Responsive parenting and child socialization: Integrating two contexts of family life. *Journal of Child and Family Studies, 9,* 269–281.

Strand, P. S. (2002). Treating antisocial behavior: A context for substance abuse prevention. *Clinical Psychology Review, 22,* 707–728.

Strand, P. S., Barnes-Holmes, Y., & Barnes-Holmes, D. (2003). Educating the whole child: Implications of behaviorism as a science of meaning. *Journal of Behavioral Education, 12,* 105–117.

Strand, P. S., Cerna, S., & Skucy, J. (2007). Assessment and decision-making in early childhood education and intervention. *Journal of Child and Family Studies, 16,* 209–218.

Swiezy, N. B., Matson, J. L., & Box, P. (1992). The good behavior game: A token reinforcement system for preschoolers. *Child and Family Behavior Therapy, 14,* 21–32.

Timberlake, W., Schaal, D. W., & Steinmetz, J. E. (Eds.). (2005). Special issue on the relation of behavior and neuroscience. *Journal of the Experimental Analysis of Behavior, 84,* 305–692.

van Lier, P. A. C., Muthen, B. O., van der Sar, R. M., & Crijnen, A. A. M. (2004). Preventing disruptive behavior in elementary schoolchildren: Impact of a universal classroom-based intervention. *Journal of Consulting and Clinical Psychology, 72,* 467–478.

Vasta, R. (1982). Physical child abuse: A dual-component analysis. *Developmental Review, 2,* 125–149.

Wahler, R. G. (1994). Child conduct problems: Disorders in conduct or social continuity? *Journal of Child and Family Studies, 3,* 143–156.

Wahler, R. G. (1997). On the origins of children's compliance and opposition: Family context, reinforcement, and rules. *Journal of Child and Family Studies, 6,* 191–208.

Wahler, R. G., & Dumas, J. E. (1986). Maintenance factors in coercive mother-child interactions: The compliance and predictability hypotheses. *Journal of Applied Behavior Analysis, 19,* 13–22.

Wahler, R. G., & Dumas, J. E. (1989). Attentional problems in dysfunctional mother-child interactions: An interbehavioral model. *Psychological Bulletin, 105,* 116–130.

Watson, J. B., & Rayner, R. (1920). Conditioned emotional reactions. *Journal of Experimental Psychology, 3,* 1–14.

Wicksell, R. K., Dahl, J., Magnusson, B. & Olsson, G. L. (2005). Using Acceptance and Commitment Therapy in the rehabilitation of an adolescent female with chronic pain: A case example. *Cognitive and Behavioral Practice, 12,* 415–423.

Wilson, K. G., & Murrell, A. R. (2004). Values work in acceptance and commitment therapy: setting a course for behavioral treatment. In S. C. Hayes, V. M. Follette & M. M. Linehan (Eds.) *Mindfulness and acceptance: Expanding the cognitive-behavioral tradition* (pp. 120–151). New York: Guilford Press.

Wolf, M. M., Risley, T. R., & Mees, H. (1964). Application of operant conditioning procedures to the behavior problems of an autistic child. *Behavior Research and Therapy, 1,* 306–312.

Wolpe, J. (1958). *Psychotherapy by reciprocal inhibition.* Stanford, CA: Stanford University Press.

Wolpe, J., & Rachman, S. (1960). Psychoanalytic "evidence": A critique based on Freud's case of Little Hans. *Journal of Nervous and Mental Diseases, 131,* 135–148.

Wulfert, E., Hayes, S. C. (1988). Transfer of a conditional ordering response through conditional equivalence classes. *Journal of the Experimental Analysis of Behavior, 50,* 125–144.

CHAPTER 4

Developmental Issues

CHRISTOPHER T. BARRY AND JESSICA D. PICKARD

Ayoung person presents for psychological services. Among other emotional and behavioral concerns, the parents are most worried because the child regularly drinks alcohol. Suppose that the child is 16 years of age. Suppose instead that the child is 9 years old. In this instance, professionals and laypersons alike can clearly understand the different implications of the same behavioral symptom based on developmental level (here, indicated by age).

The importance of developmental issues in measuring and assessing, understanding, conceptualizing, preventing, and treating psychological phenomena pervades all clinical activities with youth and their families. However, the previous example notwithstanding, it may also be the case that such considerations are not fully appreciated. Indeed, current diagnostic nomenclature does not include different symptom sets or criteria based on development. The closest that the *Diagnostic and Statistical Manual of Mental Disorders* (*DSM-IV-TR*) comes to such a consideration is the requirement of a certain age of onset of symptoms for some disorders (e.g., prior to age 7 for Attention-Deficit/Hyperactivity Disorder, prior to age 18 for Mental Retardation, and Conduct Disorder by age 15; American Psychiatric Association, 2000). Such age-of-onset requirements attempt to take into account apparent qualitative differences in syndromes emerging before and after these age cutoffs. This approach still falls far short of encompassing many clinically relevant findings from recent clinical, experimental, and developmental research. The purpose of this chapter is to provide examples of such findings, as well as to guide assessment, conceptualization, and treatment of child and adolescent difficulties in a manner that takes into account the importance of developmental processes.

Because of significant individual variability in the timing of developmental processes, in genetics, and in environmental factors, we cannot rely on a person's age alone to determine his or her developmental level or to understand a given child's psychosocial history or developmental course. Although it is important to be knowledgeable about typical age-related developmental processes and milestones, chronological age itself does not yield a definitive understanding. Aside from typical developmental progressions and changes, it has been suggested that we also consider the individual's response to transitions as an important indicator in psychology and related fields (O'Connor & Rutter, 1996). Epidemiological research can then further guide our understanding by delineating what responses to transitions are normative or nonnormative, as well as what transitions themselves are normative or nonnormative (e.g., children experiencing parental divorce is becoming more normative). In addition to the question of developmental normality, we should seek continued knowledge of the current and future functioning associated with various developmental trajectories.

Findings in the emerging field of developmental psychopathology underscore the vital need to understand the *course* and *trajectory* of common child and adolescent difficulties, particularly for case conceptualization and treatment, as well as mediator and moderator variables in the development of such difficulties (Cicchetti & Cohen, 1995). This field merges the disciplines of child development and child psychopathology (Kamphaus & Frick, 2005) and, in short, emphasizes the role of empirical evidence from these disciplines in informing the assessment, conceptualization, and treatment of youth. Data from developmental psychopathology may be particularly valuable in the context of child and adolescent assessment, yet clinical application has lagged (Mash & Hunsley, 2005). It is hoped that continued discussion and investigation of developmental issues will beget increased consideration of development in the provision of psychological services to children.

This emphasis on understanding development for work with youth does not negate the rapidly advancing knowledge of the impact of development throughout the life span and, consequently, the importance of development in the assessment, conceptualization, and treatment of adults. Rather, highlighting the role of development for youth speaks to the rapid rate of change during this period of life, as well as the importance for caretakers to understand developmental challenges of youth, given the relatively limited autonomy of children and adolescents (Schroeder & Gordon, 2002).

With up to 20% of children estimated to have diagnosable psychopathology, between 5% and 9% estimated to have severe functional impairments (Costello et al., 1996, as cited by Tolan & Dodge, 2005; Schroeder & Gordon, 2002), and high rates of change during childhood and adolescence, it is incumbent upon adults in a caretaking role (e.g., parents, teachers, clinicians, physicians) to have knowledge of both normal and abnormal development. Aside from the many clinical and subclinical issues that might warrant attention from mental health professionals, an understanding of development is also critical for understanding the antecedents and manifestations of youth psychological difficulties (Steinberg, 2002). Furthermore, this understanding should inform decisions as to who needs intervention, who should be involved in intervention, and the targets of intervention.

The information that follows is an attempt to synthesize the rapidly emerging findings from the area of developmental psychopathology, particularly as they will shape evidence-based clinical practice. For roughly the past 2 decades, much has been written about the benefits of infusing principles of and findings from developmental psychology into clinical work (e.g., Cicchetti, 1993; Kamphaus & Frick, 2005; Rutter & Garmezy, 1983), not the least of which is that these principles and findings can (and must, in our view) inform interventions for children and adolescents (Weisz, 1997). A relatively more formal integration of developmental science and clinical science, although relatively recent, currently shapes the manner in which services are delivered from the initial assessment until services are discontinued.

ASSESSMENT

Much of the current focus on developmental norms as an assessment standard can be traced to the work of G. Stanley Hall in the early twentieth century (Boyd & Bee, 2006). Therefore, the idea of understanding an individual in the context of what is normal or typical for someone in his or her population—defined by gender, culture, developmental level, and so on—is not a new one. Normative comparisons allow a clinician to determine if a child's behavioral or emotional presentation is abnormal relative to others with similar developmental and historical backgrounds. However, it is also incumbent upon professionals to consider the relations among different facets of development to determine if that presentation is clearly deviant or simply an exaggeration of a normal developmental process (Kamphaus & Frick, 2005). For example, symptoms of separation of anxiety are fairly common among preschool-age children (see Masi, Mucci, & Millipiedi, 2001; Silverman & Ollendick, 2005). Significant separation anxiety during this time might have different implications for assessment and treatment than symptoms of separation anxiety for a 10-year-old child, for whom the presence of such symptoms would be nonnormative.

Thomas and colleagues (Thomas, Chess, & Birch, 1968) similarly laid a foundation for the approaches to assessment that are widely advocated today. Specifically, Thomas et al. argued that some characteristics may both represent symptoms of a current problem and predict the development of later, and potentially more severe problems. The varied developmental course of numerous individual difference variables suggests a need to implement assessment strategies that sample multiple domains. The work of Jerome Kagan and colleagues (e.g., Kagan, Snidman, & Arcus, 1993) illustrates the relative stability of general dimensions of child temperament (i.e., inhibited versus uninhibited). Although such general tendencies may remain stable throughout development, other intrapersonal characteristics (e.g., specific anxiety symptoms) seem to exhibit less stability, and specific personality characteristics become more easily identifiable throughout development (Shiner, 1998).

Comprehensive assessments of cognitive, social, emotional, behavioral, and contextual variables for young children may have prevention and intervention benefits. For example, a child at risk for later and/or heightened conduct problems can be identified early, and this early identification facilitates the likelihood of successful intervention (Lochman & Conduct Problems Prevention Research Group, 1995). However, the identification of specific risk factors for individuals deemed at risk is not sufficient. That is, assessment, as noted by Achenbach (2005, p. 541), should entail "initial broad-spectrum assessment, to identify strengths and problems, narrower spectrum assessment of targets for intervention, ongoing assessment during the course of interventions, and outcome assessment." Professionals working with children and adolescents must be mindful of the ongoing nature of assessment and case conceptualization, as well as considerations involving the methods, informants, and domains that constitute an assessment.

METHODS

To determine whether a given presenting problem is cause for concern, we first consider developmental norms (Schroeder & Gordon, 2002). Decades of research yielding representative developmental norms have revealed that a given behavior may be normal at certain developmental periods and abnormal at others. In the context of assessment, it becomes clear that the employment of some norm-referenced strategy is necessary for adequate case conceptualization and subsequent treatment. Presently, rating scales or standardized tests are used routinely to address this need.

Furthermore, there is little dispute that child and adolescent assessment is truly comprehensive only when it encompasses evaluation of multiple domains, in multiple settings, by multiple informants. Nevertheless, satisfying these criteria alone does not ensure that one has adequately considered all relevant developmental factors. We emphasize the point made previously that age alone cannot be considered an adequate reflection of the child's developmental level or the sole indicator of the degree to which his or her behavior is abnormal or impaired. For example, Steinberg (2002) notes that a broad range of developmental variables should be assessed in evaluating an adolescent's developmental status (e.g., physical maturation, school transitions, abstract reasoning abilities, sexual activity, relationships with parents and peers) and, further, that these factors are far more relevant indicators than age alone.

Wright, Zakriski, and Drinkwater (1999) note that many commonly used tools that have a normative basis do not address *situational variability or fluctuations in behavior* that are often present for youth. Wright and colleagues note that rating scales typically include a list of items (e.g., "Hits others") designed to assess the target child's general propensity toward certain behaviors or characteristics. Situational variability, they conclude, is addressed simply through aggregating data from informants across different settings. The approach to aggregation can and perhaps should change with development (see later discussion; Kamphaus & Frick, 2005). Seeking information about specific contextual antecedents to a child's behaviors would seem to result in assessments that more accurately describe a child's typical presentation.

Gathering information about contextual variability can be best accomplished by direct observation of the child in his or her important contexts and/or by designing items that address variability in the important day-to-day situations faced by a young person. Examples of the latter approach include such measures as the Home Situations Questionnaire and the School Situations Questionnaire developed by Barkley (1997). These scales require a parent or teacher informant to indicate whether compliance is a problem in a given situation and then rate the severity of the problem in each endorsed situation. Altering the situations (e.g., "while playing with other children") assessed in such a measure for various age groups and applying this technique to more varied problems would likely be a useful strategy for recognizing the important contexts in which young people function and how those contexts change with development. Nevertheless, as they currently exist, ratings of behavior—even if the intent is to rate behaviors in context—are limited by the item content and scope of the particular measure selected.

Behavioral observations are also considered an important tool for highlighting contextual factors in child and adolescent assessment, with developmental level playing an important role in the selection of the context for observation (e.g., parent-child for younger children; peers for adolescents). Observations may focus on solitary play, play interactions with caretakers, and play with same-age peers for younger children, and behavior in both structured (e.g., classroom) and unstructured (e.g., interactions with others) settings. A limitation of behavioral observations is the difficulty associated with defining and observing instances of behavior, especially covert behaviors and multifaceted behavioral constructs that are considered developmentally significant (e.g., emotions, motivation, cognition). Observational methods offer the assessor considerable flexibility and allow the user to tailor to the assessment and focus on the contextual variables that are most likely to influence the occurrence of the behaviors. In addition, a focus on direct observation of behavior is often indicated for many young clients based on the types of child referrals often made for psychological services (Kamphaus & Frick, 2005) and the difficulties associated with asking children about their internal states.

Although most rating scales fail to produce much information about contextual factors, their convenience and relatively large and inclusive standardization samples make them a cost-effective addition to assessment batteries. Widely used omnibus rating scales for children such as the Achenbach system (Achenbach & Rescorla, 2001) and the Behavioral Assessment System for Children, second edition (Reynolds & Kamphaus, 2005) demonstrate sound reliability and validity as well as item content geared toward the experiences of children and adolescents. An additional benefit of rating scales or structured interviews or tests is their amenability to research. The extensive research on such assessment tools has enabled clinicians to be better informed consumers. For example, research has discovered several response tendencies or biases that are characteristic of structured interviews and rating scales. The order of item presentation (e.g., with items presented earlier being more likely to be endorsed on structured interviews; P. S. Jensen, Watanabe, & Richters, 1999) and the emotional functioning of the person completing a rating scale (e.g., parents under stress may overreport the child's symptoms; see Kamphaus & Frick, 2005) may be important biasing factors. These findings underscore the importance of considering not only the context of the child's behavior, but also the context in which well-accepted assessment strategies are implemented.

Rating scales that are broad in scope have the advantage of allowing the clinician to determine the relative significance of different types of problems exhibited by the client. That is, in addition to determining if the presenting complaints are developmentally normal or abnormal, these tools can help distinguish between types of psychopathology and level of impairment and ultimately aid case conceptualization and treatment recommendations.

PROCESS AND OUTCOME IN DEVELOPMENTAL PSYCHOPATHOLOGY

As Kamphaus and Frick (2005) illustrate, the concepts of equifinality, in which the same developmental outcome (e.g., delinquency) can be the result of different developmental processes (e.g., poor parental monitoring, impulsivity, negative peer affiliations), and multifinality, in which the same developmental process (e.g., parental divorce) can lead to a variety of outcomes (e.g., lower school achievement, increased internalizing symptoms, no significant problems) are vital to a contemporary understanding of developmental psychopathology. Research in the areas of child assessment and treatment has addressed the concepts of equifinality and multifinality through research on intervening variables (e.g., mediators and moderators) and through studies of the relations between risk and protective factors and outcomes.

Although being located at a particular developmental stage or level increases the probability of some behavioral issues (e.g., substance use during adolescence), knowledge of symptoms and developmental stage alone are unlikely to predict outcomes for a particular individual (Kamphaus & Frick, 2005). Assessment methods should therefore focus on the individual, as others at the same developmental level with the same problem may well have experienced different precipitants to the problem.

Risk factors may also operate differently for individuals proceeding along a generally normal developmental path than for those who are at the extremes—particularly negative extremes—of development (O'Connor & Rutter, 1996). For example, individual or environmental risk factors are thought to have a compounding effect, such that the addition of more risk factors significantly increases the likelihood of maladjustment (e.g., Forehand, Biggar, & Kotchick, 1998). It is also important to view risk and protective factors not as stable, static entities but to consider their developmental precursors or driving forces (O'Connor & Rutter, 1996), necessitating a focus on present *and* past functioning.

Clinical interviews, particularly unstructured interviews, permit flexible questioning and allow the respondent to provide detailed information about presenting problems (Schroeder & Gordon, 2002). Unfortunately, because of their susceptibility to clinician bias, unstructured clinical interviews lack a strong evidence base (Mash & Hunsley, 2005). Structured interviews help negate this issue but suffer from practical shortcomings, such as their rigidity and length (i.e., Kamphaus & Frick, 2005). Nevertheless, because of limited evidence of the differential utility of any particular assessment method and the advantages of the clinical interview noted previously, it remains the most widely used assessment method (Mash & Hunsley, 2005; Peterson, 2004).

Quite obviously, the content and pacing of interviews conducted directly with children or adolescents vary as a function of their developmental level. In general, child informants in interview formats are considered unreliable until the child attains approximately 8 or 9 years of age (Kamphaus & Frick, 2005). However, Schroeder and Gordon (2002) have suggested that younger child interviewees may provide some useful information about their environment, perceptions of others, and rudimentary coping strategies. Along with concerns about the reliability and validity of adult versus child informants, research has also noted potential differential utility of informants across different developmental levels.

INFORMANTS

The first informant in many psychological assessments is the referral source. Therefore, understanding the presenting issues and referral question from the perspective of the referral source is an important initial task. Schroeder and Gordon (2002) have noted that gaining a sense of what led to the referral at a given time is essential. Whether the answer is a maladaptive response to a specific precipitating event, persistent problems that are seemingly resistant to current intervention strategies, or the exacerbation of a more chronic problem, the clinician tries to understand the developmental course of the problem by reconstructing the sequence of events that led to the client's being in his or her care.

As with all individuals, children shape, and are shaped by, their environment, making some degree of situational variability in functioning expected. Consequently, assessment information should be collected from multiple informants for children and adolescents. Data obtained from informants who see the child in the same setting will presumably (but not always!) yield similar information about the child's behavior. The inclusion of data from different informants across settings lends itself to the assessment of the child across contexts, but it is confounded to some degree by variability associated with the respondent, which is to be expected (Kamphaus & Frick, 2005; Schroeder & Gordon, 2002; Youngstrom, Loeber, & Stouthamer-Loeber, 2000).

Variability across contexts and persons may be particularly useful for diagnosis and treatment planning (Ferdinand, van der Ende, & Verhulst, 2004).

Developmental status plays a central role in the selection of informants. As noted previously, it is generally recognized that child self-report on rating scales and in structured interviews is unreliable prior to age 9 (for reviews, see Kamphaus & Frick, 2005; Schroeder & Gordon, 2002). Unstructured interviews may also be of limited utility. As child self-report becomes more reliable and potentially useful into adolescence, the validity and utility of parent, but especially teacher, report becomes more uncertain. Importantly, it is not the *reliability* of adult informants that would be in question. A parent or teacher might be capable of providing reliable information about an adolescent but would likely lack sufficient opportunity to provide a clear, detailed picture of his or her functioning (Edelbrock, Costello, Dulcan, Kalas, & Conover, 1985). In addition, although parents may well have many opportunities to observe their adolescent, the adolescent may engage in some relevant behaviors (e.g., covert delinquent activity) outside of the home environment or in private.

As suggested, research has indicated that parents often are unaware of their child's internalizing symptoms (Kolko & Kazdin, 1993; Sourander, Helstelae, & Helenius, 1999). With development, a young person is thought to be capable of providing not only increasingly reliable and valid information but also unique and useful information about his or her behavioral and emotional functioning. This advantage of self-informants does not necessarily hold across domains; evidence suggests that parents are more accurate informants of hyperactivity than are children (Loeber, Green, Lahey, & Stouthamer Loeber, 1989, 1991). Youth and their parents may also disagree on the severity of symptoms (Yeh & Weisz, 2001), which does not render one informant's report more valid per se (Ferdinand et al., 2004) but may have important implications for treatment planning.

Disagreements among informants may be indicators of important variables in case conceptualization and eventual treatment outcome. Ferdinand and colleagues (2004) found that parent-child discrepancies in externalizing and internalizing symptoms were risk factors for later psychopathology and problem behaviors. Longitudinal evidence has also suggested that child-parent disagreement on anxiety symptoms is predictive of slower treatment progress (Kendall, Panichelli-Mindel, Sugarman, & Callahan, 1997). Discrepancies between parent and teacher reports of externalizing symptoms—particularly with teachers reporting more problems—may be related to current or past difficulties in the parent-child relationship, such as parental neglect or poor parental control (Ferdinand et al., 2004). Therefore, research on informants of child and adolescent psychopathology underscores the need to obtain information from multiple informants across settings. Different informants may provide important and unique information across different areas of youth functioning that has implications for subsequent treatment.

Domains

It has been well documented that in youth clinical populations, "comorbidity is the rule, rather than the exception" (Mash & Hunsley, 2005, p. 367). Specifically, children who have problems in one area of functioning tend to have problems in other areas. Gaining information about the domains of relative strength or difficulty for a client or patient has definite treatment implications, as the combination of difficulties could be predictive of response to different forms of intervention (Kamphaus & Frick, 2005;

Kazdin & Weisz, 2003). More likely, co-occurrence of problems may influence the specific design or targets of intervention. For example, although some evidence suggests that a comorbid diagnosis of Attention-Deficit/Hyperactivity Disorder (ADHD) and Conduct Disorder does not predict a child's responsiveness to stimulant medication (Pliszka, 1989), the presence of both conduct problems (e.g., temper tantrums, aggressiveness) and the distractibility and impulsivity associated with ADHD should influence the targets of behavioral interventions for children and adolescents comorbid for these problems.

The need to assess a comprehensive set of domains (e.g., physical health, emotional, behavioral, social) and to not confine the assessment to a particular stated problem area is clear. However, the potential significance of particular domains often vary according to development. Common practice among child clinicians is to assess the child's prenatal history (e.g., complications, health of mother, exposure to drugs or alcohol) and the child's developmental history, particularly in reaching important developmental milestones (e.g., walking, language, toileting). Assessment of such early developmental history is important for conceptualization of a number of developmental concerns, including mental retardation and learning disabilities (Kamphaus & Frick, 2005; Schroeder & Gordon, 2002). Furthermore, it is important to gain some sense of the child's current developmental level in a variety of domains (e.g., physical, cognitive, language, social, temperament and personality) and to compare this present functioning to others in the same environment or at the same expected developmental level (Schroeder & Gordon, 2002). Areas of functioning such as sleep, appetite, and developmentally appropriate self-care also are often relevant concerns throughout the life span.

Assessments of current child functioning should also vary in their relative emphasis on different domains. For example, with very young children, motor and language development will be crucial targets of assessment, as functioning in both of these domains is an important indicator of the child's cognitive development. Measures geared toward infants and toddlers (e.g., Bayley, 2005; Wechsler, 2002) place a heavy emphasis on the assessment of motor functioning and receptive and expressive language. The focus of a mental health professional's assessment of older children might cover social functioning, academic functioning and achievement, and mood and stress. Into adolescence, greater emphasis may be placed on the evaluation of risk-taking behavior (broadly defined) that would not have been a typical concern for younger clients (e.g., substance use and abuse, sexual promiscuity, dangerous driving habits). Although assessment of each of these domains reflects its importance in the context of the existing developmental demands on the child or adolescent, they are also relevant to long-term development. For example, although some level of adolescent risk-taking behavior is considered developmentally appropriate (Zuckerman, Eysenck, & Eysenck, 1978), the long-term consequences of such behavior must also be considered (Resnick et al., 1997). To engage in developmentally meaningful case formulation and treatment, one must first have engaged (and continue to engage) in developmentally meaningful assessment.

CONCEPTUALIZATION

The importance of development in the conceptualization of child and adolescent psychopathology includes onset, course, culture and context, concurrence with stressful life events, comorbidity, and goodness of fit with the environment. Falvey (2001) cautioned against the use of cognitive heuristics in case conceptualization and treatment planning. We echo this concern, noting that arriving at a case conceptualization with certainty after only a cursory assessment of any one of the variables previously mentioned may be as likely to do harm as to be helpful. Nevertheless, we also hope to communicate how the consideration of variables such as those described in this section can actually result in more comprehensive and thoughtful case conceptualization and treatment tailored to a youth's healthy developmental needs. Although general statements certainly can be made—even cross-culturally—about the developmental demands and features of various phases of childhood, it is important to note that an individual's mastery of developmental tasks is, in part, a function of his or her genetics, multiple contexts, and interactions with others (Schroeder & Gordon, 2002). It is also worth noting, and perhaps is self-evident, that the assessment process previously discussed should be conceived of as an ongoing, self-correcting process that begins with the first client contact and continues through assessment and treatment to the termination of care. Thus, many of the issues noted in the Assessment and Treatment sections apply equally to the case conceptualization taking place during those clinical activities.

Case conceptualization is a difficult, yet critical, clinical activity, as it requires the integration of large amounts of information, including relevant research findings and pertinent idiosyncratic client factors. The ability to perform this integration is perhaps most difficult for child and adolescent cases, as the information will likely include multiple informants from multiple settings and variables such as the client's current developmental level and previous developmental course. It is important for a clinician in deriving a case conceptualization to consider concurrently how he or she will convey this information to persons involved in the case, including, in most instances, the child. We also feel that parent perception of the "causes" of a child's difficulties may aid in case conceptualization and in how the conclusions to be presented by the clinician will be received. To be comprehensive and useful, a consideration of the child's and family's strengths and weaknesses should be conveyed, an opportunity for questions to be asked about the results and recommendations should be provided, and inclusion of important figures in the client's subsequent care (e.g., child, parent, teachers, physicians) should be standard practice (see Schroeder & Gordon, 2002).

DEVELOPMENTAL ONSET

Age of onset (or developmental onset) is a key moderating variable in the presentation of different emotional and behavioral symptoms and may predict differences in etiology, course, or outcome (O'Connor & Rutter, 1996). One of the best examples of the use of developmental onset in the conceptualization of child and adolescent psychopathology is Moffitt's (1993) description of childhood-onset and adolescence-limited conduct problems. Moffitt comprehensively reviewed the Conduct Disorder literature noting that (a) conduct problems or antisocial behavior is relatively persistent across the life span for individuals who have a childhood (i.e., preadolescent) onset of such behaviors (e.g., Moffitt, 1991); (b) there is a peak of the number of individuals involved in some delinquent or antisocial activity during adolescence (Farrington, 1983); and (c) for the majority of individuals who initiate antisocial behavior during adolescence, the course of this behavior is very time-limited (Blumstein & Cohen, 1987; Farrington, Ohlin, & Wilson, 1986). That is, the age of onset of conduct problems appears to be indicative of whether the behavioral pattern represents an atypical developmental process that may predict persistent and perhaps severe conduct problems (i.e., childhood onset) or whether the behavioral pattern is an exaggeration of a normal developmental process that will desist with further development (i.e., adolescence-limited; Moffitt, 1993).

Adolescence in and of itself is a time associated with an increase in externalizing, internalizing, and addictive problems (Steinberg, 2002). Recent efforts have been made to consider these issues "in the context of adolescence as a developmental period" (p. 124) rather than focusing on the particular emotional and behavioral features associated with specific age groups. Rather than age per se, developmental events may be strong precipitants for the onset of a particular problem or clinical disorder. For example, it is quite rare for eating disorders such as anorexia and bulimia to exist prior to puberty; however, there is striking evidence of a change in body image beliefs and satisfaction around the time of puberty for females. The results published by Field and colleagues (1999) in their cross-sectional study of body image perceptions are striking in this regard. Specifically, for 9- and 10-year-olds, the proportion of females who thought themselves overweight was lower than the proportion who actually were. However, for the 11-year-olds, the converse was true, with a slightly larger percentage thinking they were overweight than actually were. This disparity was progressively larger for the 12-, 13-, and 14-year-olds. For 14-year-olds, 33% of the girls thought themselves overweight, though only 15% actually were. Therefore, the pattern of body image concerns—and presumably, potential eating disorders—suggests a rather sharp increase in the risk for such problems around the time of puberty rather than a linear and gradual increase in prevalence throughout the life span.

Precursors of problems in childhood may also differ from the precursors of adolescent problems (see Holmbeck & Kendall, 2002). Again, in the area of conduct problems, Moffitt (1993) asserted that there may be at least subtle biological differences between youth who exhibit conduct problems prior to adolescence and their same-age peers. Moreover, comorbid ADHD and learning disabilities are more often associated with early than later onset of these problems. Taken together, biological factors and early onset may explain the relative stability and consistency of these problems throughout childhood. Conversely, according to this conceptualization (Moffitt, 1993), adolescent-onset conduct problems, by virtue of their instability and inconsistency, appear to be more sensitive to environmental influence (e.g., adolescent peers encouraging or discouraging delinquent activity).

Based on such considerations, the use of empirically based subtypes for conduct problems has been advocated. Empirically based subtypes of conduct problems reflect the influence of onset, context, and similar variables described previously (Dodge & Pettit, 2003). For example, a professional might design a treatment approach much differently for clients with an early versus a later onset of conduct problems. Another example of a potentially important designation is to consider if aggressive behaviors by a client are primarily reactive, proactive, or both (Dodge & Pettit, 2003). Such a practice would more closely incorporate well-established developmental considerations into child and adolescent case conceptualization and subsequent intervention.

COURSE

Of utmost importance in the discussion of developmental course is determining what developmental pathways place a young person at risk for developing severe or varied problems and what pathways might prevent problems or their exacerbation. Included in these pathways are multiple variables and processes that influence the outcome, making the consideration of developmental course more complex and more closely tied to the individual (see Cicchetti & Toth, 1997).

Patterns regarding the typical developmental course of psychological phenomena have also been well-researched. However, Cicchetti and Toth (1997, p. 318) have noted that it is important to "understand the diversity in process and outcome" pertaining to risk factors and disorders. In a broad sense, it is important to consider potential shifts that might alter the developmental course at different developmental stages relative to normative developmental processes. Such shifts may be particularly pronounced during adolescence, given the multiple changes and transitions occurring (Cicchetti & Rogosh, 2002). For example, although cross-sectional research has shown increases in self-esteem throughout childhood (e.g., McCarthy & Hoge, 1982), longitudinal research has shown a decline in global self-esteem in early adolescence (e.g., Robins, Trzesniewski, Tracy, Gosling, , & Potter, 2002) followed by an increase in self-esteem as one enters late adolescence and throughout adulthood (e.g., Greene & Way, 2005; Robins & Trzesniewski, 2005; Wigfield, Eccles, MacIver, Reuman, & Midgley, 1991).

Adults who are in a mentoring or caretaking role would be well advised to be aware of such developmental patterns so as to be more likely to respond reasonably. This response should include consideration of the developmental history (e.g., prior self-esteem or mood) of that individual. That is, in determining whether a self-esteem issue should be regarded as a departure from normality, one must consider both the individual's prior history as well as the typical developmental course for similar individuals within that developmental period. Part of this consideration is the recognition of not only the substantial heterogeneity within a cohort of children or adolescents but also the heterogeneity of presentation for a psychological construct or diagnostic category.

Cicchetti and Toth (1998) offer an informative discussion of the role of developmental course and heterogeneity in their presentation of youth depression. They note that a more sophisticated understanding of the varied developmental presentations of depression could improve the identification of many cases of child and adolescent depression that presently go untreated. First, youth may manifest symptoms of depression differently (see Christ, 1990). Additionally, not only is depression in children and adolescents often comorbid with other problems (e.g., anxiety), but these problems may predate depression for many youth, which has important treatment implications (Kovacs, 1996). Importantly, it has also been suggested that the similarity in lifetime prevalence rates of depression between adolescents and adults suggests that, for many adults, the origin of depression may be during adolescence (Cicchetti & Toth, 1998). Cicchetti and Toth also cite evidence that the gender ratio of adolescent depression approximates the gender ratio of adult depression (Lewinsohn, Clarke, Seeley, & Rohde, 1994). The essential message as it pertains to youth depression is that considering developmental course, as well as the various ways in which depression may manifest in this population, could improve the likelihood of identifying children in need of services and better target prevention efforts (Cicchetti & Toth, 1998).

Concomitant with considering the course and presentation of a problem is considering the child's present age and developmental level. The degree to which a symptom or set of symptoms is a problem depends, in large part, on whether it is deviant from a typical developmental course. Therefore, case conceptualizations must include developmental interpretations (Kamphaus & Frick, 2005). For instance, the meaning behind bed-wetting for a child younger than 5 would be conveyed much differently than that for an 8-year-old. Likewise, many childhood fears are transient and not necessarily predictive of enduring or future anxiety problems. The child's level of anxiety and its persistence over time signal the potential need for clinical attention (Silverman & Ollendick, 2005). With examples pertaining to virtually any domain of psychological functioning, the ethical problems inherent in providing blanket explanations or inter-pretations of a child's symptom(s) to parents without considering development are self-evident.

The stability of youth personality—and even the appropriateness of applying the term "personality" to youth—is a point of contention. It stands to reason that be-cause so many changes are occurring during childhood and adolescence relative to adulthood, many youth emotional, behavioral, and social characteristics would be less stable than in adulthood. Indeed, as noted by Shiner (1998), although much re-search has been devoted to temperament in early childhood and to personality in later adolescence, little attention has been devoted to potentially stable individual differ-ences from middle childhood to early adolescence. Perhaps this relative lack of focus is a function of the multiple transitions occurring during that developmental period. Thus, identification of stable personality characteristics may be more difficult and less useful for such an age group. On the other hand, a growing body of literature (e.g., Branje, van Lieshout, & van Aken, 2004; Frick & Dantagnan, 2005) has identified some clinically meaningful personality characteristics or styles among older children and younger adolescents. For example, in applying the concept of psychopathy-linked personality features, often dubbed callous-unemotional traits (e.g., Frick, O'Brien, Wootton, & McBurnett, 1994), to youth, it has been found that characteristics such as lack of empathy, lack of guilt, and shallow affect are predictive of relatively stable and severe problem behaviors (Frick & Dantagnan, 2005). Other research reveals some areas of functioning to be more stable in youth (e.g., intellectual functioning; A. R. Jensen, 1980) than others (e.g., mood during adolescence; Dumenci & Windle, 1996). In summary, the clinician's challenge is to conceptualize a child's strengths and diffi-culties in the context of meaningful, identifiable attributes, while also recognizing the transient nature of many observed and potentially measurable characteristics.

CULTURE AND CONTEXT

Although psychological constructs and levels of functioning may demonstrate vari-able courses across and within individuals, a young person's context may place him or her at lesser or greater risk for more varied problems over time. The influences involving the individual and his or her contexts are reciprocal (Hartup, 1979). For example, a young person in a hostile family environment may experience episodes of internalizing symptoms, including depression, but the young person might also demonstrate a propensity toward behavioral problems that could be a factor in creat-ing a hostile family environment in the first place. To further underscore the role of the individual in how, or the degree to which, the environment plays a risk or protective role, O'Connor and Rutter (1996) noted that individuals may differ genetically in the degree to which they are sensitive to the environment. Similarly, individual difference variables may predict adaptability in the face of change in the environment. Indeed, some research suggests that gender is one such important intrapersonal variable, as boys and girls differ in their level of risk in response to environmental factors such as poverty (Elder, 1979) and parental divorce (Needle, Su, & Doherty, 1990).

Nevertheless, there is little question as to the influence of a variety of contextual variables on youth development. Such variables include, but are not necessarily limited to, prenatal and perinatal factors, family, school, media, cultural values, neighborhood environment, socioeconomic status, ethnicity, age of parents, and specific incidents such as divorce, moves, and traumatic events (Dodge & Pettit, 2003). Although both individual temperamental and contextual factors will themselves change over time, the fact that their relation is mutually influential will not (Dodge & Pettit, 2003). From a developmental standpoint, a contextual factor may exert an influence on the individual's later response to other contextual factors. For example, attachment theorists dating to Bowlby (1969) have suggested that early bonds with caretakers lead the child to form an internal working model that is used in relating to others later in life (e.g., peers, romantic partners). In addition, a given contextual variable such as family environment may still be differentially associated with different indicators of functioning. B. Henry, Caspi, Moffitt, and Silva (1996), for example, found that a positive family environment was related to a reduction in risk for violent behaviors among adolescents but was not as strong a protective factor against nonviolent offenses. Therefore, we must understand the developmental outcomes associated with early and/or ongoing exposure to contextual risk or protective factors—an understanding that includes careful consideration of potential moderating conditions.

To add further complexity to the case conceptualization process, it is necessary not only to consider issues such as potential precipitating factors in the child's environment and, as discussed earlier, the child's functioning relative to developmental norms, but also to understand differences in risk-outcome relations and prevailing ideas of developmental normality within the child's cultural context. Regarding attachment, for example, it has been suggested that specific types of early attachment experiences may not lead to similar outcomes across cultures (Lopez, Melendez, & Rice, 2000). It has been noted that insecure-avoidant attachment styles among German infants may be more normative and reflective of an emphasis on infants attaining greater independence from an early age in that culture (Grossmann, Grossmann, Spangler, Suess, & Unzner, 1985). For assessment purposes, there may also be cultural differences in the normality of scale elevations on a particular domain. For example, a given score may appear to be an elevation in relation to the general normative sample, but the child may be functioning well within the normative range when compared to individuals of the same cultural background. This notion is consistent with Weisz's (1989) idea of an adult distress threshold model, which could be used to predict at what point adults in a culture would seek help for their child's behavioral or emotional symptoms. Moreover, the *perception* of others in that context regarding severity, normality or abnormality, and need for intervention of the problem has important implications for the child's adjustment. Suvannathat (1979) noted that parents in Thailand tended to accept a wide range of child behavioral presentations that may shape, and be shaped by, their ideas of how to address child behaviors (see Weisz, McCarty, Eastman, Chaiyasit, & Suwanlert, 1997). It is necessary, then, to conceptualize a client's presentation within his or her cultural context, which includes reconciling how characteristics may be considered psychopathological in some, but not all, cultures.

The typical developmental course of constructs associated with emotional, behavioral, and social functioning may also vary as a function of culture. It was noted earlier that a decline in self-esteem often occurs upon the transition to adolescence, with subsequent increases in self-esteem (e.g., Wigfield et al., 1991). However, research on adolescent group differences has found higher self-esteem among African Americans compared to European Americans (Twenge & Crocker, 2002), with the early adolescent decline in self-esteem being most pronounced among Asian Americans. Nevertheless, on the whole, the self-esteem of adolescents across different ethnic groups tends to increase with age, with African American and Latino Americans having the highest self-esteem levels in late adolescence compared to European Americans (see Greene & Way, 2005). It has been hypothesized that a so-called African American self-esteem advantage may result from the social support provided by family, peers, and/or community members (Chapman & Mullis, 2000; McCreary, Slavin, & Berry, 1996), which encourages autonomy in African American adolescents—a period when demonstrating increased autonomy is a normal developmental process—and acts as a buffer against social stigma (Chapman & Mullis, 2000).

Even parenting practices like the use of corporal punishment must be considered in the context of development and culture. Research has shown that parental monitoring and supervision are particularly important dimensions of parenting for adolescents (see Dodge & Pettit, 2003), whereas use of corporal punishment tends to diminish significantly from childhood to adolescence (Frick, Christian, & Wootton, 1999). Deater-Deckard, Dodge, Bates, and Pettit (1996) provide an example of the latter, suggesting that low-income African American parents viewed the use of corporal punishment less negatively, which in turn influenced the extent to which such practices predicted risk (see Gershoff, 2002).

Context clearly plays a role in the individual's functioning, but research has indicated that childhood and adolescence present their own unique *developmental* contexts as well (Kamphaus & Frick, 2005; Steinberg, 2002). That is, young persons' strengths and weaknesses need also be considered in light of their stage of development. For example, an adolescent may present differently behaviorally, emotionally, and socially not necessarily as a function of environmental changes such as a move, parental divorce, or new school, but as a function of factors associated with a given stage of development (e.g., more time with peers, school structure allowing for increased autonomy, greater responsibility, more privileges). A common thread in all sections of this chapter is that development itself is an important contextual factor that influences the presentation and perception of child psychological functioning.

COMORBIDITY

As noted, comorbidity is a critical aspect of child and adolescent assessment and, consequently, of case conceptualization. Comorbidity deserves attention in this section as well because a case conceptualization cannot be accurate or, more important, useful for designing and planning intervention unless it clearly includes a consideration of strengths and weaknesses in a number of domains. For example, the presence of sexual acting-out behavior may take on very different meanings depending on developmental level (e.g., a 7-year-old versus a 16-year-old), the severity of the behavior (e.g., verbal remarks versus sexual assault), and the youth's functioning in other areas (e.g., no significant problems versus changes in mood and daily functioning, increased defiance). Taking the presenting complaint at face value without consideration of comorbidity or other developmental factors prevents the acquisition of information critical to the design of potential interventions.

Another issue to address regarding comorbidity is that empirically based treatments for youth (e.g., Barkley, 1997; Kendall, 2000; McMahon & Forehand, 2003) tend to be designed for a particular set of issues, usually organized around a *DSM-IV* syndrome. The role of multiple presenting complaints in predicting outcomes associated with these interventions has not been well studied. Thus, comorbidity represents a challenge and an opportunity to refine and develop interventions that should be better suited to cases seen in clinical practice. In addition, although the early onset of problems in mood and behavior is suggestive of significant and enduring problems (e.g., Moffitt, 1993), attempting to address areas of concern earlier, even if complex and multifaceted, should bode well for prognosis. Recognition, particularly early recognition, of comorbidity in the assessment, conceptualization, and treatment of youth should enhance the services provided to youth and their families.

GOODNESS OF FIT

Conceptualizing a problem faced by a child or adolescent (or even an adult) as a static issue best captured by a categorical label ignores the reciprocal influences on the individual and his or her environment. Attention to reciprocity would seem especially important for young people for whom both aspects of this reciprocal relation are frequently changing. The work of Thomas and Chess (1984) is quite influential in this regard. Thomas and Chess proposed that individual-environment interactions are transactional; for example, a child and parent constantly influence each other through their responses to each other. The likelihood of a particular outcome, then, is a function of the continuous transactions between the individual and his or her environment. Similar to Bronfenbrenner's (1979) ecological theory of development, we would predict that the more proximal the environmental factor (e.g., parents), the more influence that factor would have on the individual's subsequent responses. Likewise, relatively proximal protective factors can buffer against problematic transactions that result from some risk factors (Cicchetti & Toth, 1998). Such models have been advocated in the conceptualization of youth depression (e.g., Cicchetti & Toth, 1998) and delinquency (e.g., Stouthamer Loeber, Loeber, & Farrington, 1993). These models emphasize that relations between nature and nurture as they affect child development should be considered evolving rather than static.

A good match between a person and his or her context would likely increase the chances of transactions leading to continually positive outcomes. One variable that should shape such a match is the child's developmental level. For example, it would be expected that, by and large, as a child progresses through adolescence, the parent(s) would respond by encouraging more independence and responsibility and providing less assistance with self-care. According to this view, responding to changes in the adolescent's development either "too early" or "too late" could give rise to increased parent-child conflict and/or making the adolescent more vulnerable to risk factors. Conceptualizing this fit should be a natural extension of the assessment process and would most certainly have implications for treatment recommendations.

Aside from the adjustments necessary to cope with the typical developmental changes and transitions, children and their primary caretakers often must adjust to acute and/or chronic life stressors. Such factors can be within the child's immediate context (e.g., divorce, loss of job) or in the larger social context (e.g., poverty; Schroeder & Gordon, 2002). In addition to assessing what stressors are present and the timing of those stressors vis-à-vis the child's development and presenting problems, it is critical to conceptualize a child's or family's strengths and difficulties in terms of how they have adjusted to acute incidents and how they continue to cope with more chronic ones. Doing so will prevent clinicians from taking themselves as well as their clients down a treatment road that will surely lead to an impasse. To borrow from Maslow (1971), it may be short-sighted to require a family to allocate significant resources (in time and, perhaps, materially) needed to implement a complex token economy and behavior management plan when a family lacks basic emotional and material resources needed to provide adequate food, safety, and shelter. Although such a behavioral strategy may well be an effective means to increase desired behaviors, the more salient need for that family is to take care of basic needs. Thus, our treatment plans must be sensitive to the more general needs of the family and their present social ecology.

TREATMENT

Although adequately addressing developmental issues in child and adolescent assessment and case conceptualization involves knowledge of developmental norms, familiarity with relevant research, and clinical skill in applying this wealth of information to the individual client, the challenge of considering developmental issues is as evident, if not more so, in devising a treatment plan for the client. Developmental level plays an integral role in the structure of the intervention, the involvement of parents and school officials, targets of treatment, and the contexts in which treatment is applied. As might be gleaned from the issues discussed earlier, treatments should increase in effectiveness relative to the extent to which they are geared toward the unique issues faced by the child, consider multiple facets of the child's developmental history, and adhere to the relevant empirical literature in developmental psychopathology. Early intervention is considered most effective, but prevention or intervention programs designed in ways that allow application of at least some aspects of the program across stages of youth development and cultures have also been advocated (Dodge & Pettit, 2003). Such programs, particularly those with supporting empirical evidence, are extremely rare, perhaps because of the physical, cognitive, and social distinctions between children and adolescents.

It has been argued that because treatments are often very similar for children, adolescents, and adults, relatively little attention has been devoted to examining the effectiveness of interventions as a function of development (Weisz & Hawley, 2002, as cited by Steinberg, 2002). Indeed, some evidence suggests that therapies for depression developed with adult populations can be effective with youth (Kovacs & Bastiaens, 1995). Some child and adolescent intervention programs have also successfully treated such problems as anxiety (e.g., Kendall, 2000), even though the criteria used to define such problems are virtually the same as those used for adults. Nevertheless, it stands to reason that the optimal interventions for children and adolescents will be geared toward the unique developmental features of youth emotional and behavioral functioning.

Across intervention strategies, but depending on the setting and the developmental level of the child or adolescent, it is typically the case that the clinician will speak to a parent, guardian, or caretaker first to gain a sense of the presenting problems and history. However, if treatment is anticipated, then other issues aside from the important factors discussed earlier must also be addressed during the assessment process. For example, with a younger child for whom parent management training seems indicated, it is important for the clinician to gauge the parents' expectations for therapy, to assess the parents' motivation and current emotional functioning, and to establish a positive therapeutic relationship (Schroeder & Gordon, 2002). For an adolescent with whom an emphasis on individual work is planned, these initial activities with the parents still typically have some importance, but they are likely not as crucial to treatment success. Instead, greater emphasis will be placed on the ability of the clinician to engage the adolescent in the therapy work. Unfortunately, as noted previously by Weisz (1997), little research has been conducted to ascertain the child's or adolescent's cognitive understanding of the therapeutic process.

The advantages and disadvantages of the child's presence during the parent interview have been discussed elsewhere (Schroeder & Gordon, 2002). Still, most clinicians seek the opportunity—regardless of the youth's age—to speak with the parents or guardians privately about their concerns at the outset of treatment because they are more likely than the child to have initiated the referral. Similar considerations arise concerning whether the parents are present in the initial child interview and therapy session. As has been discussed by others (e.g., Kamphaus & Frick, 2005), the benefits of having the parents present at the very beginning of contact with the child—whether oriented toward assessment or intervention—typically outweigh the disadvantages in terms of increasing the child's comfort level, allowing the parents to assist in the explanation of what visits with the clinician will involve, and establishing rapport. Of course, the parents' role in each of the aspects of the beginning of clinical work would presumably be diminished for older children and adolescents. A discussion of additional developmental considerations in various aspects of child and adolescent intervention follows.

STRUCTURE OF SESSIONS AND INVOLVEMENT OF PARENTS AND SCHOOL OFFICIALS

An obvious variable in the conduct of treatment that has developmental implications is the actual structure of sessions (i.e., how therapy is conducted). Weisz (1997) noted that although children should be able with time to increasingly integrate therapeutic concepts into their everyday lives, it is likely the case that such developmental advances happen over a longer period of time than most therapeutic contacts. Therefore, it is unlikely that development per se has a noticeable influence on therapeutic gains beyond what may be attributable to the therapist-client relationship, the repetition and practice of coping skills, and support and skills offered to parents. To try to capitalize on developmental progressions in cognition and self-awareness as the primary mechanism of change for any client is probably misplaced by virtue of the slow nature of such changes.

With this point in mind, it still is necessary to consider developmental issues associated with how therapy sessions are conducted. These issues are more logistical than factors such as the tone of therapy sessions or the role of the therapist, issues that will largely be based on developmental considerations and theoretical orientation. Instead, we refer to considerations such as with whom the therapist meets, in what order, and for how long. On the one hand, it may make sense to meet with the child or adolescent for a longer period of time and/or first during the session so that the young person remains at the forefront of the sessions. On the other hand, it may be necessary to consult with parents at the outset to get a clear picture of the young person's functioning since the previous session. That is, the parents may have a number of issues to be addressed in session about which a child or adolescent might be less than forthcoming. Other than the likely higher emphasis on parenting practices with very young clients as opposed to adolescents, we suspect that this issue essentially comes down to the individual client as well as the therapist's style and preference.

Although parenting or family-based interventions exist for adolescent clients (e.g., Barkley, Edwards, & Robin, 1999; Kumpfer & Alvarado, 2003) and may well be indicated in many cases, much of the focus on parenting interventions has been on the preschool and early school-age years (e.g., Barkley, 1997; McMahon & Forehand, 2003). The relative de-emphasis of family involvement in treatment reflects natural developmental changes. This statement should not be taken to mean that family members or other adults play no role in the development of adolescents or young adults. Instead, Schroeder and Gordon (2002) note that parents are charged with helping children cope with normal developmental changes and tasks throughout their lives. This assistance ranges from being responsible for all self-care in infancy to providing support on educational, occupational, and financial decisions in adulthood. The level of effort, monitoring, and time required of parents in the early years dictates that parents will be centrally involved in interventions geared toward helping children meet their developmental demands in the behavioral, emotional, and social arenas.

In short, a central developmental task for parents is to adapt their practices to the changing developmental needs of the child, and our approaches to intervention often follow suit. The number and significance of early parent-child interaction variables that can be predictive of behavioral functioning are vast (e.g., punishment strategies, consistency of discipline, empathic responding to child's needs; Dodge & Pettit, 2003). Moreover, interactions between parents and children differ substantially across development, ranging from basic instruction in social behavior (e.g., teaching right from wrong) in early childhood to complex discussions of relationships, sexuality, and behavioral choices in adolescence. As the child matures, parents typically encourage and allow more independence and individual responsibility. Similarly, with psychological treatment, youths often assume more responsibility for their improvement, and the sophistication of in-session treatment comes to more closely resemble adult psychotherapy.

Adolescents present unique challenges in this regard. They are old enough to request treatment but are still, particularly early in adolescence, dependent on parents for making arrangements for such services, including transportation and payment (Steinberg, 2002). Because it is atypical for adolescents to actively solicit psychological services, significant tension may arise between adult caretakers requesting services and adolescents who object to the very services being offered.

As described in the Assessment section, the role of school officials in therapy also changes throughout a young person's development. Elementary school teachers, for instance, may be quite involved in developing treatment plans for younger clients, particularly if the referral issue is related to school functioning. However, because high school teachers tend to have less contact with any given student, they and other school officials may be less integral to ongoing treatment. We are not suggesting that school officials are not important influences in the lives of adolescents, as they may in fact have central roles. Rather, the referral issues associated with adolescent clients may or may not be closely tied to school-related concerns and must be evaluated on an individual basis.

TARGETS

Identifying the appropriate targets of treatment should be relatively straightforward once a professional has completed assessment and case conceptualization, particularly concerning the relative primacy of various presenting issues. We therefore will not reiterate previous points in this and prior sections. Instead, we here summarize briefly some examples of typical targets of treatment at different developmental stages.

Children's developmental level has an important influence on the selection of intervention targets. For example, sensory stimulation is an important consideration in the sensory, cognitive, and language development of an infant or toddler, but is not commonly a primary target in adolescent interventions. Additionally, improvements in parenting skills (e.g., use of praise, consistency of expectations, clarity of commands, punishment for misbehavior) are a key component of psychosocial interventions for toddlers and school-age children, but not all parenting skills have equal importance across the developmental spectrum. For example, time-out is far less likely to be recommended for older adolescents; instead, family-based interventions are more likely to focus on the encouragement of parental monitoring and perhaps alterations of the emotional environment in the home (see Patterson, 2005). Individual therapy with the adolescent is also more likely to be recommended.

As alluded to earlier, internalizing problems, such as depression, involve a different approach to intervention based on developmental differences in symptom presentation. For very young children, intervention may involve psychoeducation with parents, as well as work with the parents and the child concerning somatic complaints that may be manifestations of stress or depression (Carlson & Kashani, 1988). In recent years, a variety of interventions for older children and adolescents have emerged for both anxiety and depression. Importantly, the authors have begun to more actively incorporate developmental considerations in the design and implementation of these empirically based interventions (see Kazdin & Weisz, 2003; Kendall, 2000).

Peer Context

We address peer context in this section as assessment approaches do not commonly include detailed consideration of peer issues, such as social status and group entry skills, beyond the reports of typical informants (i.e., parents, teachers, child). However, as noted, peers represent a potentially influential developmental context for a young person, and peer-related risk and protective factors are often a focus of treatment. The sheer amount of time that an adolescent spends with his or her peers (up to twice as much as with parents; Steinberg, 2005) highlights the importance of considering peer relationships and what protective and risk factors are part of those relationships in assessment and treatment planning. Prior to adolescence, it is likely the behaviors demonstrated by the client toward peers (e.g., aggression) or the lack of age-appropriate peer contacts would be targets of treatment. However, during adolescence, intervention may be focused on these issues, but may also include myriad other issues (e.g., peer pressure, peer deviance, parent-child conflict over peer issues, coping with peer rejection).

Peer context is a particularly salient variable for assessment, conceptualization, and treatment for youth, given the patterns of behavioral and emotional functioning associated with peer factors. For example, evidence has supported the notion that affiliation with deviant peers is related to the likelihood of a young person's having conduct problems (e.g., D. B. Henry, Tolan, & Gorman-Smith, 2001; Viatro, Tremblay, & Bukowski, 2001). It is also the case that very early play behavior, particularly the manner in which a preschool-age child enters a play situation with a peer or group of peers, is predictive of social acceptance by peers (Fantuzzo, Coolahan, & Mendez, 1998). Parent-child disagreements over time spent with peers or the particular peers with whom the youth associates may also need to be addressed in therapy. Therefore, in some form or fashion, peer and social functioning will be an integral part of much clinical work involving youth of all ages (e.g., Prinstein, Borelli, Cheah, Simon, & Aikins, 2005).

FUTURE DIRECTIONS

The issues discussed in this chapter have been presented in the context of mental health service provision to children, adolescents, and their families. However, it is often the case that children with whom we work are referred by professionals in other disciplines (e.g., pediatricians, medical specialists, school officials), or that we make referrals to such professionals. Therefore, the ability to communicate about the importance of development in the assessment, conceptualization, and treatment of children to allied professionals is crucial. Likewise, it is important to have knowledge of developmental manifestations of the problems encountered by other professionals in their work (e.g., milestones in acquiring various academic skills). Undoubtedly, it is asking a lot for child mental health professionals to be well-versed in both the emerging findings in developmental psychopathology and in their application to education and the health professions more generally.

In addition, the advancement of knowledge regarding the different clinical presentations of a problem (e.g., conduct problem behaviors) in childhood, adolescence, and adulthood is necessary. Incorporation of developmental considerations into existing classification systems would likely improve case conceptualization, communication, and treatment, as classification systems are often the basis for decisions about treatment options, including setting, modality, availability of reimbursement, and the inclusion of professionals from different disciplines. Moreover, developmentally sound classification systems can further inform future research, which in turn could improve clinical practice in child and adolescent mental health.

Making these advancements is only half of the battle. More attention should be paid to developmental protective factors and to defining the strengths of youths. As noted, it is understood that risk factors may have a compounding or additive effect (e.g., Dodge & Pettit, 2003; O'Connor & Rutter, 1996), yet a single protective factor (e.g., parental monitoring) could neutralize multiple risk factors (e.g., poverty; Buckner, Mezzacappa, & Beardslee, 2003). It stands to reason that additive effects may also be noted for protective factors—a relatively easy phenomenon to demonstrate in parent-child transactional models—although current evidence for such an effect is limited.

Finally, as our field moves toward further development and refinement of evidence-based treatments and embarks upon the more recently described mission of developing evidence-based assessments (see Mash & Hunsley, 2005), we must consider how we might use information that is derived from these assessments. Understanding child and adolescent strengths and weaknesses within a developmental context is a necessary function of any work with youth, but there are risks associated with this activity. Given the numerous *changes* experienced by children and adolescents, designating or labeling a child as having early-onset conduct problems (i.e., being at risk) could itself carry risks. For example, early identification could help identify important risk factors or treatment targets, but may also alter environmental risk factors (e.g., educational outcomes) that could result in a negatively self-fulfilling prophecy. On the other hand, knowledge of developmental norms should not lead parents or mental health professionals to dismiss the aberrant behavior of a teenager when intervention might prevent more enduring or severe patterns of delinquency. With all of the emerging findings in developmental psychopathology, it is still necessary to consider the relations among the many variables affecting youth functioning as probability-based rather than absolute.

SUMMARY

In this chapter, we provided an overview of the research and theory that concludes something very intuitive: that developmental changes influence the manifestation of psychological constructs. Further, given the sheer number and rate of such changes during childhood and adolescence, a necessary conclusion is that professionals working with children and adolescents in any capacity must concern themselves with the developmental context in which a young person is functioning. We have devoted attention to important developmental considerations in clinical child assessment (e.g., methods, informants, domains, comorbidity) and how these considerations, along with specific developmental issues (e.g., course, onset, context and culture, environmental goodness of fit), aid in case conceptualization and subsequent treatment planning. Moreover, intervention activities with child and adolescent populations are affected by the manner in which the assessment is conducted and the case is conceptualized and the selection of treatment targets. None of these clinical activities can happen in a developmental vacuum.

We are encouraged by the sound empirical attention that has been devoted to these issues and the convergence of evidence on some issues pertaining to both developmental and clinical psychology (e.g., multifinality and equifinality). Professional experience backed by attention to growing empirical evidence should enhance our appreciation of the complex developmental influences that inform our understanding of youths' strengths and weaknesses. After all, it is likely a multitude of developmental factors that render the topographically similar behaviors of a 9-year-old and a 16-year-old (discussed at the outset of this chapter) very different indeed.

REFERENCES

Achenbach, T. M. (2005). Advancing assessment of children and adolescents: Commentary on evidence based assessment of child and adolescent disorders. *Journal of Clinical Child and Adolescent Psychology, 34,* 541–547.

Achenbach, T. M., & Rescorla, L. A. (2001). *Manual for the ASEBA preschool forms and profiles.* Burlington: University of Vermont, Department of Psychiatry.

American Psychiatric Association. (2000). *Diagnostic and statistical manual of mental disorders* (4th ed., text rev.). Washington, DC: Author.

Barkley, R. A. (1997). *Defiant children: A clinician's manual for assessment and parent training* (2nd ed.). New York: Guilford Press.

Barkley, R. A., Edwards, G. H., & Robin, A. L. (1999). *Defiant teens: A clinician's manual for assessment and family intervention.* New York: Guilford Press.

Bayley, N. (2005). *Bayley Scales of Infant Development* (3rd ed.) San Antonio, TX: Psychological Corporation.

Blumstein, A., & Cohen, J. (1987). Characterizing criminal careers. *Science, 237,* 985–991.

Bowlby, J. (1969). *Attachment and loss: I. Attachment.* New York: Basic Books.

Boyd, D., & Bee, H. (2006). *Lifespan development* (4th ed.). Boston: Allyn & Bacon.

Branje, S. J. T., van Lieshout, C. F. M., & van Aken, M. A. G. (2004). Relations between Big Five personality characteristics and perceived support in adolescents' families. *Journal of Personality and Social Psychology, 86,* 615–628.

Bronfenbrenner, U. (1979). Contexts of child rearing: Problems and prospects. *American Psychologist, 34,* 844–850.

Buckner, J. C., Mezzacappa, E., & Beardslee, W. R. (2003). Characteristics of resilient youths living in poverty: The role of self-regulatory processes. *Development and Psychopathology, 15,* 139–152.

Carlson, G. A., & Kashani, J. H. (1988). Phenomenology of major depression from childhood through adulthood: Analysis of three studies. *American Journal of Psychiatry, 145,* 1222–1225.

Chapman, P. L., & Mullis, R. L. (2000). Racial differences in adolescent coping and self-esteem. *Journal of Genetic Psychology, 161,* 152–160.

Christ, M. G. (1990). *A four-year longitudinal study in boys: Phenomenology and comorbidity of conduct disorder.* Unpublished doctoral dissertation, University of Georgia, Athens.

Cicchetti, D. (1993). Developmental psychopathology: Reactions, reflections, projections. *Developmental Review, 13,* 471–502.

Cicchetti, D., & Cohen, D. J. (1995). Perspectives on developmental psychopathology. In D. Cicchetti & D. Cohen (Eds.), *Developmental psychopathology:* Vol. 1.*Theory and methods* (pp. 3–22). New York: Wiley.

Cicchetti, D., & Rogosh, F. (2002). A developmental psychopathology perspective on adolescence. *Journal of Consulting and Clinical Psychology, 70,* 6–20.

Cicchetti, D., & Toth, S. L. (1997). Transactional ecological systems in developmental psychopathology. In S. S. Luthar, J. A. Burack, D. Cicchetti, & J. R. Weisz (Eds.), *Developmental psychopathology: Perspectives on adjustment, risk, and disorder.* New York: Cambridge University Press.

Cicchetti, D., & Toth, S. L. (1998). The development of depression in children and adolescents. *American Psychologist, 53,* 221–241.Deater-Deckard, K., Dodge, K. A., Bates, J. E., & Pettit, G. S. (1996). Physical discipline among African American and European American mothers: Links to children's externalizing behaviors. *Developmental Psychology, 32,* 1065–1072.

Dodge, K. A., & Pettit, G. S. (2003). A biopsychosocial model of the development of chronic conduct problems in adolescence. *Developmental Psychology, 39,* 349–371.

Dumenci, L., & Windle, M. (1996). A latent trait-state model of adolescent depression using the Center for Epidemiologic Studies—Depression Scale. *Multivariate Behavioral Research, 31,* 313–330.

Edelbrock, C., Costello, A. J., Dulcan, M. K., Kalas, R., & Conover, N. C. (1985). Age differences in the reliability of the psychiatric interview of the child. *Child Development, 56,* 265–275.

Elder, G. H. (1979). Historical change in life patterns and personality. In P. B. Baltes & O. G. Brim (Eds.), *Lifespan development and behavior* (Vol. 2, pp. 117–159). New York: Academic Press.

Falvey, J. E. (2001). Clinical judgment in case conceptualization and treatment planning across mental health disciplines. *Journal of Counseling and Development, 79,* 292–303.

Fantuzzo, J., Coolahan, K., & Mendez, J. (1998). Contextually relevant validation of peer play constructs with African-American Head Start children: Penn Interactive Peer Play Scale. *Early Childhood Research Quarterly, 13,* 411–431.

Farrington, D. P. (1983). Offending from 10 to 25 years of age. In K. Van Dusen & S. A. Mednick (Eds.), *Prospective studies of crime and delinquency* (pp. 17–38). Boston: Kluwer-Nijhoff.

Farrington, D., Ohlin, L., & Wilson, J. Q. (1986). *Understanding and controlling crime.* New York: Springer-Verlag.

Ferdinand, R. F., van der Ende, J., & Verhulst, F. C. (2004). Parent-adolescent disagreement regarding psychopathology in adolescents from the general population as a risk factor for adverse outcome. *Journal of Abnormal Psychology, 113*, 198–206.

Field, A. E., Camargo, C. A., Taylor, C. B., Berkey, C. S., Frazier, L., Gillman, M. W., et al. (1999). Overweight, weight concerns, and bulimic behaviors among girls and boys. *Journal of the American Academy of Child and Adolescent Psychiatry, 38*, 754–760.

Forehand, R., Biggar, H., & Kotchick, A. B. (1998). Cumulative risk across family stressors: Short- and long-term effects for adolescents. *Journal of Abnormal Child Psychology, 26*, 119–128.

Frick, P. J., Christian, R. C., & Wootton, J. M. (1999). Age trends in the association between parenting practices and conduct problems. *Behavior Modification, 23*, 106–128.

Frick, P. J., & Dantagnan, A. L. (2005). Predicting the stability of conduct problems in children with and without callous-unemotional traits. *Journal of Child and Family Studies, 14*, 469–485.

Frick, P. J., O'Brien, B. S., Wootton, J. M., & McBurnett, K. (1994). Psychopathy and conduct problems in children. *Journal of Abnormal Psychology, 103*, 700–707.

Gershoff, E. T. (2002). Corporal punishment by parents and associated child behaviors and experiences: A meta-analytic and theoretical review. *Psychological Bulletin, 128*, 539–579.

Greene, M. L., & Way, N. (2005). Self-esteem trajectories among ethnic minority adolescents: A growth curve analysis of the patterns and predictors of change. *Journal of Research on Adolescence, 15*, 151–178.

Grossmann, K., Grossmann, K. E., Spangler, G., Suess, G., & Unzner, L. (1985). Maternal sensitivity and newborns' orientation responses as related to quality of attachment in northern Germany. *Monographs of the Society of Research in Child Development, 50*(1–2, Serial No. 209), 233–256.

Hartup, W. W. (1979). The social worlds of childhood. *American Psychologist, 34*, 944–950.

Henry, B., Caspi, A., Moffitt, T. E., & Silva, P. A. (1996). Temperamental and familial predictors of violent and nonviolent criminal convictions: Age three to eighteen. *Developmental Psychology, 32*, 614–623.

Henry, D. B., Tolan, P. H., & Gorman-Smith, D. (2001). Longitudinal family and peer group effects on violence and nonviolent delinquency. *Journal of Clinical Child Psychology, 30*, 172–186.

Holmbeck, G. N., & Kendall, P. C. (2002). Introduction to the special section on clinical adolescent psychology: Developmental psychopathology and treatment. *Journal of Consulting and Clinical Psychology, 70*, 3–5.

Jensen, A. R. (1980). *Bias in mental testing.* San Francisco: Freeman.

Jensen, P. S., Watanabe, H. E., & Richters, J. E. (1999). Who's up first? Testing for order effects in structured interviews using a counterbalanced experimental design. *Journal of Abnormal Child Psychology, 27*, 439–446.

Kagan, J., Snidman, N., & Arcus, D. (1993). On the temperamental categories of inhibited and uninhibited children. In K. H. Rubin & J. B. Asendorpf (Eds.), *Social withdrawal, inhibition, and shyness in childhood* (pp. 19–28). Hillsdale, NJ: Erlbaum.

Kamphaus, R. W., & Frick, P. J. (2005). *Clinical assessment of child and adolescent personality and behavior* (2nd ed.). New York: Springer.

Kazdin, A. E., & Weisz, J. R. (2003). *Evidence-based psychotherapies for children and adolescents.* New York: Guilford Press.

Kendall, P. C. (2000). *Cognitive-behavioral therapy for anxious children: Therapist manual* (2nd ed.). Ardmore, PA: Workbook Publishing.

Kendall, P. C., Panichelli Mindel, S. M., Sugarman, A., & Callahan, S. A. (1997). Exposure to child anxiety: Theory, research, and practice. *Clinical Psychology: Science and Practice, 4*, 29–39.

Kolko, D. J., & Kazdin, A. E. (1993). Emotional/behavioral problems in clinic and nonclinic children: Correspondence among child, parent and teacher reports. *Journal of Child Psychology and Psychiatry and Allied Disciplines, 19,* 75–95.

Kovacs, M. (1996). Presentation and course of major depressive disorder during childhood and later years of the lifespan. *Journal of the American Academy of Child and Adolescent Psychiatry, 35,* 705–715.

Kovacs, M., & Bastiaens, L. J. (1995). The psychotherapeutic management of major depressive and dysthymic disorders in childhood and adolescence: Issues and prospects. In I. M. Goodyer (Ed.), *The depressed child and adolescent: Developmental and clinical perspectives* (pp. 281–310). New York: Cambridge University Press.

Kumpfer, K. L., & Alvarado, R. (2003). Family-strengthening approaches for the prevention of youth problem behaviors. *American Psychologist, 58,* 457–465.

Lewinsohn, P., Clarke, G., Seeley, J., & Rohde, P. (1994). Major depression in community adolescents: Age of onset, episode duration, and time to recurrence. *Journal of the American Academy of Child and Adolescent Psychiatry, 33,* 809–818.

Lochman, J. E., & Conduct Problems Prevention Research Group. (1995). Screening of child behavior problems for prevention programs at school entry. *Journal of Consulting and Clinical Psychology, 63,* 549–559.

Loeber, R., Green, S. M., Lahey, B. B., & Stouthamer Loeber, M. (1989). Optimal informants on childhood disruptive behaviors. *Development and Psychopathology, 1,* 317–337.

Loeber, R., Green, S. M., Lahey, B. B., & Stouthamer Loeber, M. (1991). Differences and similarities between children, mothers, and teachers as informants on disruptive child behavior. *Journal of Abnormal Child Psychology, 19,* 75–95.

Lopez, F. G., Melendez, M. C., & Rice, K. G. (2000). Parental divorce, parent-child bonds, and adult attachment orientations among college students: A comparison of three racial/ethnic groups. *Journal of Counseling Psychology, 47,* 177–186.

Mash, E. J., & Hunsley, J. (2005). Evidence based assessment of child and adolescent disorders: Issues and challenges. *Journal of Clinical Child and Adolescent Psychology, 34,* 362–379.

Masi, G., Mucci, M., & Millipiedi, S. (2001). Separation anxiety disorder in children and adolescents: Epidemiology, diagnosis, and management. *CNS Drugs, 15,* 93–104.

Maslow, A. H. (1971). *The farther reaches of human nature.* Oxford, England: Viking.

McCarthy, J. D., & Hoge, D. R. (1982). Analysis of age effects in longitudinal studies of adolescent self-esteem. *Developmental Psychology, 18,* 372–379.

McCreary, M. L., Slavin, L. A., & Berry, E. J. (1996). Predicting problem behavior and self-esteem among African American adolescents. *Journal of Adolescent Research, 11,* 216–234.

McMahon, R. J., & Forehand, R. L. (2003). *Helping the noncompliant child* (2nd ed.). New York: Guilford Press.

Moffitt, T. E. (1991, September). *Juvenile delinquency: Seed of a career in violent crime, just sowing wild oats—or both?* Paper presented at the Science and Public Policy Seminars of the Federation of Behavioral, Psychological, and Cognitive Sciences, Washington, DC.

Moffitt, T. E. (1993). Adolescence-limited and life-course persistent anti-social behavior: A developmental taxonomy. *Psychological Reports, 100,* 674–701.

Needle, R. H., Su, S. S., & Doherty, W. J. (1990). Divorce, remarriage, and adolescent substance abuse: A perspective longitudinal study. *Journal of Marriage and the Family, 52,* 157–169.

O'Connor, T. G., & Rutter, M. (1996). Risk mechanisms in development: Some conceptual and methodological considerations. *Developmental Psychology, 32,* 787–795.

Patterson, G. R. (2005). The next generation of PMTO models. *Behavior Therapist, 28,* 27–33.

Peterson, R. L. (2004). Evaluation and the cultures of professional psychology education programs. *Research and Practice, 35,* 420–426.

Pliszka, S. R. (1989). Effect of anxiety on cognition, behavior, and stimulant response in ADHD. *Journal of the American Academy of Child and Adolescent Psychiatry, 28*, 882–887.

Prinstein, M. J., Borelli, J. L., Cheah, C. S. L., Simon, V. A., & Aikins, J. W. (2005). Adolescent girls' interpersonal vulnerability to depressive symptoms: A longitudinal examination of reassurance-seeking and peer relationships. *Journal of Abnormal Psychology, 114*, 676–688.

Resnick, M., Bearman, P., Blum, R., Bauman, K., Harris, K., Jones, J., et al. (1997). Protecting adolescents from harm: Findings from the National Longitudinal Study of Adolescent Health. *Journal of the American Medical Association, 278*, 823–832.

Reynolds, C. R., & Kamphaus, R. W. (2005). *A clinician's guide to the Behavioral Assessment System for Children (BASC)*. New York: Guilford Publications.

Robins, R., & Trzesniewski, K. (2005). Self-esteem development across the lifespan. *Current Directions in Psychological Science, 14*, 158–162.

Robins, R. W., Trzesniewski, K. H., Tracy, J. L., Gosling, S. D., & Potter, J. (2002). Global self-esteem across the lifespan. *Psychology and Aging, 17*, 423–434.

Rutter, M., & Garmezy, N. (1983). Developmental psychopathology. In E. M. Hetherington (Ed.), *Manual of child psychology: Vol. IV. Social and personality development* (pp. 775–912). New York: Wiley.

Schroeder, C. S., & Gordon, B. N. (2002). *Assessment and treatment of childhood problems* (2nd ed.). New York: Guilford Press.

Shiner, R. (1998). How shall we speak of children's personalities in middle childhood? A preliminary taxonomy. *Psychological Bulletin, 124*, 308–332.

Silverman, W. K., & Ollendick, T. H. (2005). Evidence based assessment of anxiety and its disorders in children and adolescents. *Journal of Clinical Child and Adolescent Psychology, 34*, 380–411.

Sourander, A., Helstelae, L., & Helenius, H. (1999). Parent-adolescent agreement on emotional and behavioral problems. *Social Psychiatry and Psychiatric Epidemiology, 34*, 657–663.

Steinberg, L. (2002). Clinical adolescent psychology: What it is, and what it needs to be. *Journal of Consulting and Clinical Psychology, 70*, 124–128.

Steinberg, L. (2005). *Adolescence* (7th ed.). New York: McGraw-Hill.

Stouthamer Loeber, M., Loeber, R., & Farrington, D. P. (1993). The double edge of protective and risk factors for delinquency: Interrelations and developmental patterns. *Development and Psychopathology, 5*, 683–701.

Suvannathat, G. (1979). The inculcation of values in Thai children. *International Social Science Journal, 31*, 477–485.

Thomas, A., & Chess, S. (1984). Genesis and evolution of behavioral disorders: From infancy to early adult life. *American Journal of Psychiatry, 141*, 1–9.

Thomas, A., Chess, S., & Birch, H. B. (1968). *Temperament and behavior disorders in children*. New York: New York University Press.

Tolan, P. H., & Dodge, K. A. (2005). Children's mental health as a primary care concern: A system for comprehensive support and service. *American Psychologist, 60*, 601–614.

Twenge, J. M., & Crocker, J. (2002). Race and self-esteem: Meta-analyses comparing Whites, Blacks, Hispanics, Asians, and American Indians and comment on Gray-Little & Hafdahl (2000). *Psychological Bulletin, 128*, 371–408.

Viatro, F., Tremblay, R. E., & Bukowski, W. M. (2001). Friends, friendships, and conduct disorders. In J. Hill & B. Maughan (Eds.), *Conduct disorders in childhood and adolescence* (pp. 346–378). New York: Cambridge University Press.

Wechsler, D. (2002). *WPPSI-III administration and scoring manual*. San Antonio, TX: Psychological Corporation.

Weisz, J. R. (1989). Culture and the development of child psychopathology: Lessons from Thailand. *Rochester Symposium on Developmental Psychopathology:* Vol. 1. *The emergence of a discipline* (pp. 89–117). Hillsdale, NJ: Erlbaum.

Weisz, J. R. (1997). Effects of interventions for child and adolescent psychological dysfunction: Relevance of context, developmental factors, individual differences. In S. S. Luthar, J. A. Burack, D. Cicchetti, & J. R. Weisz (Eds.), *Developmental psychopathology: Perspectives on adjustment, risk, and disorder.* New York: Cambridge University Press.

Weisz, J., & Hawley, K. (2002). Developmental factors in the treatment on adolescents. *Journal of Consulting and Clinical Psychology*, 70, 21–43.

Weisz, J. R., McCarty, C. A., Eastman, K. L., Chaiyasit, W., & Suwanlert, S. (1997). Developmental psychopathology and culture: Ten lessons from Thailand. In S. S. Luthar, J. A. Burack, D. Cicchetti, & J. R. Weisz (Eds.), *Developmental psychopathology: Perspectives on adjustment, risk, and disorder.* New York: Cambridge University Press.

Wigfield, A., Eccles, J. S., MacIver, D., Reuman, D. A., & Midgley, C. (1991). Transitions during early adolescence: Changes in children's domain-specific self-perceptions and general self-esteem across the transition to junior high school. *Developmental Psychology*, 27, 552–565.

Wright, J. C., Zakriski, A. L., & Drinkwater, M. (1999). Developmental psychopathology and the reciprocal patterning of behavior and environment: Distinctive situational and behavioral signatures of internalizing, externalizing, and mixed-syndrome children. *Journal of Consulting and Clinical Psychology*, 67, 95–107.

Yeh, M., & Weisz, J. R. (2001). Why are we here at the clinic? Parent-child (dis)agreement on referral problems at outpatient treatment entry. *Journal of Consulting and Clinical Psychology*, 69, 1018–1025.

Youngstrom, E., Loeber, R., & Stouthamer Loeber, M. (2000). Patterns and correlates of agreement between parent, teacher, and male adolescent ratings of externalizing and internalizing problems. *Journal of Consulting and Clinical Psychology*, 68, 1038–1050.

Zuckerman, M., Eysenck, S. B., & Eysenck, H. J. (1978). Sensation seeking in England and America: Cross-cultural, age, and sex comparisons. *Journal of Consulting and Clinical Psychology*, 46, 139–149.

CHAPTER 5

Overview of Behavioral Treatment with Children and Adolescents

ELIZABETH KOLIVAS, PATRICK RIORDAN, AND ALAN M. GROSS

Ever since Rosenzweig (1936) used a line spoken by the Dodo bird in *Alice's Adventures in Wonderland* (Carroll, 1865/1988: "Everyone has won, and all must have prizes") as an analogy for the idea that all forms of psychotherapy are equally effective, the dodo hypothesis has persisted in psychology and psychotherapy research. While the argument that most forms of psychotherapy do not significantly differ in terms of efficacy appears to have merit (e.g., Luborsky, Singer, & Luborsky, 1975; Smith, Glass, & Miller, 1980), at least one notable and consistent exception to this proposed equivalence has been demonstrated. In the realm of child and adolescent psychotherapy, meta-analytic research continues to demonstrate the superior efficacy of behavioral interventions over nonbehavioral interventions (Casey & Berman, 1985; Esser, 2005; Weisz, Weiss, Alicke, & Klotz, 1987).[1]

Behavior therapy is a form of treatment based on learning theory that has proven effective in addressing a wide range of problems that may arise in childhood or adolescence.[2] Its central goals are to reduce or remove patterns of maladaptive functioning, be they cognitive, behavioral, or physiological, and to enhance or produce adaptive behaviors. From a behavioral perspective, maladaptive functioning is conceptualized as a product of learning; therefore, behavior therapy begins with a functional analysis of the environmental contingencies believed to shape and maintain maladaptive behaviors. With this information, the behavior therapist attempts to intervene by manipulating or creating environmental contingencies that will foster adaptive behaviors and/or extinguish maladaptive ones. In contrast to some other forms of therapy, it is the rule rather than the exception that behavioral therapies will involve not only the child, but also his or her parent(s), guardian(s), and/or teachers. Behavioral

---

[1]This conclusion has been criticized (e.g., Shirk & Russell, 1992), but the preponderance of the evidence appears to support the overall superiority of behavioral therapies for children (e.g., Weiss & Weisz, 1995).
[2]Hereafter, unless specifically stated otherwise, the words "children," "childhood," and their variations are intended to encompass the terms children and adolescents, childhood and adolescence, and so on.

interventions are characterized by continuous evaluation of observable behavior and modification of the intervention approach until the desired ends are obtained.

Since the inception of behavior therapy, its proponents have placed a strong emphasis on empirical demonstrations of treatment effectiveness. Through its focus on observable behaviors, behavior therapy directly applies the scientific method to treatment evaluation. Each intervention is therefore conceived as a testable hypothesis. Many forms of behavioral intervention are based on well-researched and established principles of learning and have themselves faced the rigors of empirical testing. From the early twentieth century until today, these methods have generated a remarkable number of efficacious behavioral treatments.

Despite a limited number of assumptions, behavioral techniques have addressed a wide range of childhood and adolescent concerns, ranging from primarily physical problems such as enuresis and hyperactivity to traditional mental problems such as anxiety and phobias. In addition to the treatment of psychopathology, behavior therapy has also proven useful in improving behavioral health (S. J. Allen & Kramer, 1990) and promoting the use of effective child rearing (Bourke & Nielson, 1995) and classroom management practices (L. J. Allen, Howard, Sweeney, & McLaughlin, 1993).

Recent research on the prevalence of emotional and behavioral problems among children and adolescents in the United States and abroad underscores the importance of developing empirically validated treatments for these populations. Approximately 46% of all U.S. residents will meet the criteria for a *Diagnostic and Statistical Manual of Mental Disorders* (*DSM-IV*) disorder in their lifetime, with 50% of these individuals experiencing onset before the age of 14 (Kessler, Berglund, Demler, Jin, & Walters, 2005). In line with these data, the U.S. Department of Health and Human Services (1999) reports that approximately 20% of U.S. children and adolescents experience diagnosable behavioral, emotional, or developmental problems. It appears that similar rates can be observed across cultures: The World Health Organization (2001) estimated that 10% to 20% of children and adolescents worldwide experience some form of psychopathology.

This chapter reviews common behavior therapies in use with children and those responsible for their welfare. Some issues relevant to behavior therapy with children are detailed, followed by a review of general principles of behavior therapy that inform specific therapeutic techniques. Finally, the various classes of behavioral treatments for children and some of the ethical issues surrounding the use of behavioral treatments with children are also addressed.

ISSUES IN BEHAVIOR THERAPY WITH CHILDREN

Countless studies have demonstrated the efficacy of behavioral therapeutic techniques for children, yet the implementation of these treatments is not without challenges. The unique characteristics of the child and adolescent population creates a number of potential pitfalls for the behavior therapist in terms of assessment, diagnosis, treatment selection, and implementation. Much of this difficulty is due to the rapid developmental change throughout childhood, as well as the fact that the rate and trajectory of this change is idiosyncratic across children. Consequently, it is difficult to identify the appearance of a particular behavior or failure to achieve a particular developmental milestone as problematic based on overall developmental level. Nevertheless, consideration of a child's developmental level is important in treatment selection and interpretation, as a developmentally delayed child may lack the skills to comprehend or benefit from a particular treatment, or, conversely, a more sophisticated child may view particular components of a treatment as condescending.

Several clinical and developmental issues complicate the assessment and treatment of child and adolescent psychopathology. For example, interrater reliability is especially problematic with this population, as self-, parent, and teacher ratings of a given child's psychopathology can be wildly discrepant (De Los Reyes & Kazdin, 2005). Additionally, in a phenomenon known as heterotypic continuity, the same child may display the same underlying pathology in different ways at different ages (Cicchetti & Rogosch, 2002). Furthermore, as represented in the concepts of multifinality and equifinality, respectively, children initially sharing the same pathology or environmental challenges may experience different developmental outcomes, and children may develop the same form of pathology along very different routes (Cicchetti & Rogosch, 2002).

In considering these phenomena, one can generate a number of recommendations for the practice of behavior therapy with children. For one, they clearly highlight the need for careful analysis and consideration of child problems, as well as potential treatments for them, in the context of their overall pattern of social, emotional, cognitive, and physical development. Thus, the effective behavior therapist should have a working knowledge of developmental norms, as empirical data on normative developmental processes and milestones can be extremely valuable. With this information, the behavior therapist is in a better position to develop accurate case conceptualizations, evaluate the viability of various treatment options, and implement treatments with a greater awareness of potential pitfalls and opportunities based on the child's developmental levels.

Principles of Behavior Therapy

The vast majority of therapeutic techniques that fall under the heading "behavior therapy" are based on principles of learning theory developed through the seminal work of two researchers who remain the figureheads of behavioral psychology. Ivan Pavlov's (1927) work on associative responding served as the basis for what became known as classical or respondent conditioning. B. F. Skinner (1953) demonstrated the importance of contingencies in shaping and maintaining behavior, a phenomenon known as operant conditioning. Although other theories and principles have influenced some forms of behavior therapy, most of the best known and most efficacious behavioral techniques for children are directly extrapolated from classical and operant conditioning principles.

Pavlov's landmark findings, incidentally uncovered during physiological research on dogs, demonstrated an unusual phenomenon that has been applied with great success in a number of behavior therapy techniques. His work on classical conditioning showed how the temporal pairing of a neutral stimulus with a stimulus that reliably produces a reaction in an organism will eventually result in the neutral stimulus producing the same reaction. Formally stated, a neutral stimulus (i.e., one that produces no response) becomes associated with an unconditioned stimulus, or one that reliably produces an unconditioned response. Through repetitive pairings where the neutral stimulus precedes the unconditioned stimulus, the neutral stimulus comes to generate the same response even in the absence of the unconditioned stimulus. At this point, the previously neutral stimulus becomes known as a conditioned stimulus, and the response it generates is dubbed a conditioned response. Although Pavlov's work focused on physiological reactions in dogs, behavior therapists have exploited the fact that this same phenomenon can account for certain types of both physiological and emotional responding in humans.

Perhaps more influential in the practice of behavior therapy, if less original in its origins (e.g., Thorndike, 1898), was B. F. Skinner's work on operant, or instrumental, conditioning. Building on Thorndike's law of effect, which revealed that animals could learn to associate the performance of certain behaviors with particular consequences, Skinner showed how the consequences of a behavior come to affect the probability of the performance of that behavior in certain circumstances. When environmental stimuli signal the presence of reinforcers or punishers in the environment, this will increase or decrease, respectively, the probability of the occurrence of behavior that the organism has come to associate with these particular outcomes. Behavior therapists have successfully applied the principles of operant conditioning to their clinical work to develop various methods to increase or decrease the recurrence of target behaviors in children.

BEHAVIORAL TREATMENTS

Reinforcement Techniques   Positive reinforcement is a fundamental behavior therapy technique that is a direct application of Skinnerian operant conditioning. In contrast to other forms of operant control designed to remove problem behaviors (e.g., extinction and punishment), positive reinforcement is meant to address problems that have been conceptualized as behavioral deficits. Simply put, positive reinforcement consists of introducing a reinforcer, or reinforcing stimulus, after the child performs a desired behavior in order to increase the probability of future performance of that behavior. Consequently, a reinforcer is defined as any stimulus introduced after the performance of a behavior that increases the probability of the reoccurrence of the behavior it follows. That this definition is unstable and somewhat circular is both essential and unfortunate, the former because these characteristics reflect the inevitable idiosyncrasy in what constitutes a reinforcer, and to what degree it acts as one, both among and within children (e.g., the reinforcing properties of candy vary substantially among different children based on age, personal taste, etc., but also vary within a particular child based on contextual factors like food deprivation or satiation); the latter because it precludes the possibility of a definitive, empirically established index of the reinforcing properties of various stimuli. These factors often necessitate that clinicians, parents, teachers, and children themselves collaborate to identify effective and appropriate reinforcers on a case-by-case basis.

While the obvious and basic premise behind positive reinforcement can reasonably be supposed to predate recorded human history, behavioral science has elevated our understanding of contingency management from the dubious realm of common sense to empirical knowledge. Along the way, a variety of factors have been demonstrated to influence the effectiveness of reinforcers and inform the practice of behavior therapy with children. For one, despite the aforementioned variability of effectiveness in and among potentially reinforcing stimuli, some attempts have been made to rank the reinforcing properties of various stimuli (e.g., Witryol & Fischer, 1960). Although this line of research failed to identify strict hierarchies of reinforcing properties of various stimuli, contemporary research has demonstrated the efficacy of various methods for selection of reinforcers (e.g., single-stimulus presentation method: Pace, Ivancic, Edwards, Iwata, & Page, 1985; paired-stimulus presentation method: Fisher et al., 1992; multiple-stimulus method: DeLeon & Iwata, 1996; free-operant assessment methods: Roane, Vollmer, Ringdahl, & Marcus, 1998). Excepting the relatively weak single-stimulus method, these methods appear to be roughly equivalent, while possessing unique benefits and drawbacks.

Other research on applied reinforcement has examined the general properties and relative effectiveness of different types of reinforcers. Five main classes of reinforcers have been described in the literature: material, social, activity, covert, and token. Material reinforcers, such as candy, money, and toys, are generally most effective with young children (e.g., Terrell & Kennedy, 1957).[3] However, due to the arbitrary nature of material reinforcement for specific behaviors and the pervasiveness of social reinforcers (e.g., praise, smiles, attention) in the environment, some authors (e.g., Rimm & Masters, 1979) suggest that material reinforcers should be used sparingly and in the context of reinforcement programs that emphasize social reinforcers.

Other classes of reinforcers may also be of use to the clinician looking to implement positive reinforcement programs with children. Contingent positive self-evaluations, or covert reinforcement, may be challenging for the behavior therapist to implement, but research has shown the important role it can play in reinforcing child behavior (e.g., Masters & Santrock, 1976). Covert reinforcement may also be efficacious in the treatment of anxiety problems in children (Cautela, 1993). Another type of reinforcer, access to preferred activities, involves making performance of a desired behavior contingent upon performance of the target behavior, a practice based on the experimental work of Premack (1965).

Finally, token reinforcers have received a great deal of empirical attention and have proven successful with children in a variety of contexts (see Kazdin, 1982). Token reinforcers are typically worthless items (e.g., stickers, points) that are delivered contingent on performance of target behavior and that can eventually be exchanged for backup reinforcers (e.g., material reinforcers, preferred activities). Token reinforcers are often favored because they can be delivered flexibly, giving the behavior therapist, parent, or teacher the option of frequent and immediate delivery of relatively less valuable tokens or infrequent delivery of more valuable tokens, as the situation warrants. Token reinforcers are typically utilized in the context of a formal token economy system, which may involve individual (McGoey & DuPaul, 2000) or group (e.g., classroom, household) contingencies or both (Anhalt, McNeil, & Bahl, 1998). Many token systems also combine reinforcement-based token systems with punishment contingencies (i.e., response cost), discussed later in this chapter.

Other empirical work has informed clinical recommendations for the implementation of positive reinforcement techniques with children. For example, after selecting and verifying the effectiveness of a particular reinforcer, the reinforcer should be made strictly contingent on performance of the target behavior, as noncontingent reinforcement has been shown to severely undermine target performance (e.g., Lattal, 1974). Also, the reinforcing properties of a stimulus are generally maximized by immediate delivery of the reinforcer after performance of the behavior (e.g., Dews, 1960; Terrell & Ware, 1961).

Other research has delineated the nature of the relationship between quantity of reinforcement and its effectiveness. For example, the quantity of reinforcement

---

[3]Interestingly, in another study that underscores the importance of case-by-case evaluation of reinforcers, Terrell and colleagues (Terrell, Durkin, & Wiesley, 1959) found that the reinforcing properties of material versus nonmaterial incentives differ significantly between children of different socioeconomic backgrounds.

positively correlates with the probability and rate of performance of the target behavior, suggesting that a larger delivery of a particular reinforcer will produce a greater likelihood and rate of target performance. However, this relationship carries an important caveat, as it breaks down at the point of satiation, where the reinforcing stimulus loses, at least temporarily, its reinforcing properties (Skinner, 1953). This suggests two implications for the clinician. The first is to have reasonable expectations about where the point of satiation for a particular reinforcer may lie and to try to stop short of it. Second, it is advisable that the clinician have a "reinforcement menu" (Homme, 1971) prepared in case satiation is reached prematurely.

Another important consideration in the use of positive reinforcement techniques is the scheduling of reinforcement delivery. In general, the most effective approach is to begin with a continuous schedule, where the performance of the target behavior is immediately and consistently followed by reinforcement. However, once the response is established, the introduction of an intermittent schedule of reinforcement maximizes target response maintenance and improves resistance to extinction (Skinner, 1953).

The discussion to this point has presupposed that the target response is already part of the child's behavioral repertoire. However, this is often not the case. When a child needs to learn a new behavior, shaping procedures can be used. Shaping consists of reinforcing successive approximations of the target behavior until the desired response is achieved. To begin this process the behavior therapist must identify a response already in the child's repertoire that is somewhat similar to the target behavior. Reinforcement for that response is then delivered continuously but is gradually made contingent upon performance of "successively closer approximations" of the target behavior.

PUNISHMENT TECHNIQUES

Punishment techniques are commonly used in behavior therapy with children. Like positive reinforcement, punishment techniques aim to modify the probability of behavior by applying operant principles; however, punishment procedures attempt to eliminate maladaptive responses as opposed to engendering preferred ones. Unlike positive reinforcement, punishment procedures are generally believed to carry a greater risk of side effects, and the potential benefits and drawbacks need to be carefully considered before they are employed with children.

The chief concern regarding the use of punishment with children is that it may be counterproductive to the aims of behavior therapy. For one, the use of punishment may entrench the very behaviors targeted for removal (Kazdin, 1989). Furthermore, the use of punishment, particularly physical discipline, carries a distinct possibility of creating other undesirable responses, such as aggression or avoidance. Nonetheless, the risk of side effects varies considerably among punishment techniques, and in certain situations (e.g., dangerously self-injurious behavior, failure of less restrictive treatment options) the use of punishment may be indicated.

Although a variety of specific punishment procedures exist, in its simplest form punishment involves the introduction of aversive stimuli (positive punishment) or the removal of reinforcing stimuli (negative punishment) upon the performance of the target maladaptive behavior. Positive punishment (e.g., mild electric shock, spanking) is generally regarded as having the most potential for harm to the child, and consequently is usually reserved for situations where the behavior poses an immediate threat to the child or someone else. As in positive reinforcement, the effect of the stimulus on behavior determines its utility as a punisher.

Because of the heightened risks and ethical considerations surrounding physical punishment, the most widely used forms of punishment eschew the application of aversive physical stimuli. One example of such a punishment procedure is overcorrection. Overcorrection is a form of positive punishment in which the child is induced to perform an exaggerated corrective response after performance of an undesirable behavior. Originally developed by Foxx and Azrin (1972, 1973) to eliminate behavioral problems in institutional settings, overcorrection has proven useful with a wide range of child behaviors, including toilet training, thumb sucking, and disruptive classroom behaviors (see Axelrod, Brantner, & Meddock, 1978, for a review).

Foxx and Azrin (1973) originally described two separate forms of overcorrection, which are often combined, in phases, to maximize their impact. The restitution phase consists of making amends for performance of the undesired behavior and correcting or improving the situation (Axelrod et al., 1978). Examples of restitution include cleaning up a broken item as well as the rest of the room where the behavior occurred, or apologizing for calling someone a name and for previous instances of name-calling. The second phase, positive practice, consists of practicing incompatible, correct behaviors in the target situation (Axelrod et al., 1978). Examples of positive practice include practicing journaling as a more appropriate way of expressing anger or practicing socially appropriate ways of expressing disagreement with peers.

Whereas overcorrection represents a form of positive punishment, several other common aversive techniques rely on the principle of negative punishment. The first of these, time-out, involves removing or separating the child from all sources of reinforcement for a specified period of time. For example, upon performance of the target behavior, the child might be removed from an environment with access to toys and peers and placed in isolation for several minutes. This practice has been shown to be effective for numerous behavior problems, including oppositional behavior (Roberts & Powers, 1990), Conduct Disorder (McGuffin, 1991), and sibling aggression (Jones, Sloane, & Roberts, 1992).

Several considerations are relevant to the use of time-out procedures. First, although time-out can be successfully employed with older children and adolescents (e.g., Kendall, Nay, & Jeffers, 1975), its employment is easiest with younger children, who can most easily be removed from their environment. Second, research findings on time-out length have important implications for implementation. The general guideline is that time-out length in minutes should be equivalent to the child's age in years. However, additional time may need to be added for noncompliance with time-out rules. To impose additional time without providing reinforcing attention, the parent, teacher, or clinician is advised to count out additional minutes on his or her hand (Reitman & Drabman, 1996). Despite the general guidelines concerning time-out duration, there remains considerable ambiguity concerning how to maximize effectiveness. Some research suggests that longer time-outs are more effective (e.g., Burchard & Barrera, 1972). However, Kendall, et al. suggest that the effectiveness of time-out length may be relative to previously experienced time-outs, with the use of longer time-outs undermining the effectiveness of previously successful shorter ones.

Response cost is another therapeutic technique that relies on negative punishment. The technique involves the removal of a positive reinforcer upon performance of an undesirable behavior. However, response cost techniques are generally embedded within larger behavioral interventions such as a token economy or contingency management procedures (to be covered later in the chapter). An example of a response cost procedure is a system whereby a child loses part of his or her allowance every time a given undesirable behavior (e.g., swearing, yelling, hitting) is performed. This procedure has been shown effective for a variety of behavior problems, including excessive crying (Reisinger, 1972), various behaviors related to Attention-Deficit/Hyperactivity Disorder (ADHD; Luman, Oosterlaan, & Sergeant, 2005), disruptive behavior among preschoolers (Conyers et al., 2004), noncompliance (Little & Kelly, 1989), and sleep problems (Piazza & Fisher, 1991).

Although techniques such as response cost, overcorrection, time-out, and sometimes even physical punishment have their place in child behavior therapy, aversive techniques should not be used without an adjunct reinforcement plan. Without reinforcement for alternative behaviors, there can be little expectation of long-term behavior modification through the use of punishment. In some cases, there will be clear opportunities for positive reinforcement of specific adaptive behaviors or behaviors incompatible with the target maladaptive behavior. In other cases, alternative adaptive behaviors may need to be reinforced to compete with the undesirable behavior.

Behavior therapists have developed several types of differential reinforcement schedules that can be used with punishment programs. These schedules aim to increase the frequency of acceptable behaviors through reinforcement, while reducing the occurrence of the targeted maladaptive behavior through punishment. In extreme cases the therapist may want to begin with a differential reinforcement of low rate responding schedule. In this approach, reinforcement is delivered for the target behavior occurring at some specified frequency below its baseline rate of occurrence (e.g., M. H. Epstein, Repp, & Cullinan, 1978). Another approach is the differential reinforcement of other behavior schedule, which consists of reinforcement delivery when the target behavior has not been performed for a predetermined amount of time (e.g., Conyers, Miltenberger, Romaniuk, Kopp, & Himle, 2003). When feasible, the differential reinforcement of incompatible responding schedule may be the most desirable. This schedule is designed to reinforce behaviors that are topographically incompatible with the behavior targeted for reduction (e.g., Friman, Barnard, Altman, & Wolf, 1986). Last, the differential reinforcement of alternative behavior schedule is defined as reinforcement of other adaptive behaviors that are not necessarily incompatible with the target behavior (e.g., Marcus & Vollmer, 1996).

EXTINCTION

Extinction is another operant technique aimed at reducing the occurrence of undesirable behavior. Unlike the previously considered techniques, however, it cannot be properly labeled a reinforcement or punishment procedure. This is due to the fact that extinction does not involve the introduction or removal of any particular stimulus, but rather the withholding of previously experienced positive reinforcement. By identifying and removing the reinforcing stimuli that maintain the target behavior, it is assumed that the behavior will eventually cease. Indeed, there is much empirical support for the effectiveness of this procedure. However, successful implementation of an extinction procedure requires a great deal of diligence, and numerous challenges and problems can arise.

Extinction procedures begin with the identification of the stimulus or stimuli reinforcing the problem behavior. Due to the complexity of organic reinforcement systems in the child's environment, this can be a difficult task. Nonetheless, correct identification of behavioral reinforcers is essential to the extinction procedure. Awareness of several factors can aid in this process. First, reinforcers for a target behavior may appear consistently or intermittently, and different reinforcers may serve to maintain the same behavior across settings. Additionally, maintaining reinforcers can take different forms. For example, they can be social reinforcers such as peer or adult attention (e.g., talking out in class for attention), negative reinforcers such as escape (e.g., throwing tantrum to avoid a chore), or material reinforcers such as money or candy (e.g., aggressive behavior toward peers to extort money). Through observation of the child in the natural environment, the clinician should make hypotheses regarding the reinforcers maintaining the behavior. To ensure that the maintaining reinforcers have been correctly identified before beginning the extinction procedure, the hypothesized reinforcers should be systematically manipulated to observe the effect they have on the child's responding (Coyne & Gross, 2001).

Once the reinforcers maintaining the target behavior are identified, they must be systematically withheld for extinction to occur. It is imperative that reinforcement for the target behavior is consistently withheld, as intermittent reinforcement of the behavior will make it more resistant to extinction and lengthen the process. Along the same lines, time to extinction will be a function of the preexisting, natural reinforcement schedule for the behavior; consistently reinforced behaviors can be expected to decrease and extinguish more quickly than intermittently reinforced behaviors.

Extinction procedures can produce several undesirable side effects that the clinician should be prepared to address. During the extinction process, the occurrence of a phenomenon known as an "extinction burst" is likely. Extinction bursts represent brief but potentially significant increases in the severity and/or occurrence of the behavior during the extinction process. Adherence to the extinction procedure will eliminate these, but these bursts can be highly disruptive and troubling. Accordingly, they may increase the likelihood of reinforcing responding by teachers and caregivers. Such responding can severely undermine the procedure and increase resistance to extinction. Furthermore, extinction procedures may produce other undesirable behaviors such as crying or aggression. In both cases, it is suggested that the clinician use positive reinforcement for appropriate behaviors to minimize the occurrence and impact of extinction bursts and peripheral undesirable behaviors (Handen, 1998; Kazdin, 1989). Last, a phenomenon known as "spontaneous recovery" is common to the use of extinction procedures. Here, a behavior eliminated by extinction suddenly reoccurs. If no reinforcement is provided, the behavior will quickly disappear again.

Given the potential side effects, extinction procedures are not appropriate for all behavior problems. When the reinforcers maintaining the target behavior cannot be clearly identified, extinction is contraindicated. Also, extinction procedures should not be used when reinforcing contingencies cannot reliably be controlled and withheld, as intermittent reinforcement is highly undesirable. Inadvertent intermittent reinforcement may be likely when there are numerous caretakers, some of whom do not understand or are unwilling to implement the procedure, or when social reinforcers such as peer attention are extremely difficult to control. The risk of extinction bursts may be intolerable in certain circumstances, such as classroom settings, where they may lead to disruption of the entire class.

Nonetheless, extinction procedures have been used effectively to treat a number of problem behaviors in childhood and can be a powerful therapeutic tool given the right circumstances. Numerous studies have shown the efficacy of extinction programs in reducing the severity and frequency of temper tantrums in young children (McCurdy,

Kunz, & Sheridan, 2006). Extinction is also considered a well-established treatment for childhood sleep problems such as bedtime refusal and night wakings (Mindell, 1999). Furthermore, there is a great deal of empirical support for the efficacy of extinction procedures in treating food refusal among children (McCartney, Anderson, & English, 2005). Numerous other types of childhood behavior problems have been successfully treated with extinction procedures, including ADHD-related behaviors (Douglas & Parry, 1994), self-injurious behaviors (Pace, Iwata, Cowdery, & Andree, 1993), and aggressive behaviors (Egan, Zlomke, & Bush, 1993).

CONTINGENCY MANAGEMENT

In clinical applications with children, operant procedures are generally employed in the context of a contingency management package. Rather than being used alone, reinforcement, punishment, and extinction techniques are combined to achieve a variety of behavioral goals. Contingency management packages provide the benefit of undermining maladaptive target behaviors while simultaneously reinforcing adaptive responses. These packages tend to be devised by a therapist in conjunction with the child's caregivers and teachers, who are generally responsible for implementation of the programs. In many instances, especially with older children and adolescents, the child will also be involved in program construction. Although contingency management programs can take a variety of forms, most of these programs can be described as contingency contracting or token economy programs.

Contingency contracting and token economy programs show a great deal of overlap, and the terms are often used loosely in different contexts, but there are some general distinctions between them. First, contingency contracting procedures generally involve shared decision making and even negotiation with the child regarding terms of the contract details (e.g., Kelley & Stokes, 1984), whereas token economy programs tend to be devised and implemented solely by therapists, parents, and/or teachers (e.g., Anhalt et al., 1998). Second, strictly defined, token economies use inherently worthless items as immediate reinforcers that can be accumulated and traded for larger material reinforcers. In contingency contracting, a wide variety of different reinforcers and/or punishments can be included in the terms of the contract. Despite these differences, both systems employ operant techniques such as positive reinforcement and response cost to modify behavior. However, contingency contracting often includes a wider array of operant techniques, including extinction, time-out, and overcorrection.

Based on contingency contracting research, Williams and Gross (1994) provide five criteria for developing an effective contingency contract for a child. First, the contract should delineate all reinforcers the child can potentially earn. Second, the contract must specify the behaviors that delivery of these reinforcers will be made contingent upon. The relationship between specific behaviors and specific reinforcers needs to be described accurately and thoroughly to avoid disagreement. Third, punishment clauses in the contract must also be clearly specified. Fourth, bonus clauses should be included to reward long-term improvements in specific behavioral areas. Fifth, the contract should include a section describing under what terms and conditions the contract can be terminated or renegotiated.

Contingency contracts have been successfully employed for a number of childhood behavior problems. Case study evidence has shown support for using contingency contracting to increase on-task behaviors in both ADHD-diagnosed students

(Flood & Wilder, 2002; Pelham, Wheeler, & Chronis, 1998) and general student populations (L. J. Allen et al., 1993). Other studies have shown that contingency contracting can be successfully employed to treat school refusal (Kearney & Tillotson, 1998) and to increase academic productivity in disadvantaged youth populations (Kelley & Stokes, 1982, 1984). Other studies point to its effectiveness for treating anxiety, fears, and phobias (Babbitt & Parrish, 1991; Barrios & O'Dell, 1989). Contingency contracting has also been successfully employed in weight reduction programs (L. H. Epstein, McKenzie, Valoski, & Klein, 1994), treatment of nocturnal enuresis (Luciano, Molina, Gómez, & Herruzo, 1993), and a program to improve personal grooming (S. J. Allen & Kramer, 1990).

CLASSICAL OR RESPONDENT CONDITIONING TECHNIQUES

Respondent conditioning has long been considered a central and necessary component of evidence-based behavioral treatments for children. Techniques based on the principle of respondent conditioning have proven especially useful for the treatment of anxiety-related disorders (Albano, Causey, & Carter, 2001), which represent one of the most prevalent forms of psychopathology experienced by children and adolescents (Costello & Angold, 1995). More specifically, exposure-based therapies are considered core elements of effective treatments for childhood Obsessive-Compulsive Disorder (OCD; Abramowitz, Whiteside, & Deacon, 2005), Separation Anxiety Disorder, Social Phobia, Generalized Anxiety Disorder (GAD; Velting, Setzer, & Albano, 2004), and specific phobias and childhood fears (King, Muris, & Ollendick, 2005). Preliminary evidence also supports the use of exposure to treat children with Posttraumatic Stress Disorder (PTSD; for a review, see Feeny, Foa, & Treadwell, & March, 2004).

The two most common behavioral interventions developed directly from basic respondent or classical conditioning principles include brief or graduated exposure therapy, also referred to as systematic desensitization, and prolonged or intense exposure therapy, referred to as flooding. Both categories of exposure can be used alone or in combination with other treatment strategies for children and adolescents. Exposure involves repeatedly introducing a feared stimulus to the child in a controlled, therapeutic environment until the stimulus no longer produces a fear response. Thus, the child learns that the feared negative consequences do not actually occur. Fear-producing stimuli or situations can be introduced directly into the child's environment (i.e., in vivo exposure), symbolically (e.g., presenting photos or videos of feared stimuli), vicariously (e.g., watching a model), or, more recently, virtually (e.g., using computer simulation; Rothbaum, Hodges, Smith, Lee, & Price, 2000). In vivo exposure is generally preferred over other modes of delivery, as it tends to produce the greatest and most rapid reductions in fear.

Systematic Desensitization   Using respondent conditioning principles, Wolpe (1958) devised a graduated exposure-based treatment known as systematic desensitization to inhibit maladaptive emotional and behavioral responses to anxiety-provoking stimuli. According to Wolpe (1969, p. 15), "If a response inhibitory of anxiety can be made to occur in the presence of anxiety-provoking stimuli it will weaken the bond between these two stimuli." Wolpe (1969) originally outlined three sets of operations employed in systematic desensitization with clients: (1) training in progressive relaxation, (2) development of anxiety-producing stimulus hierarchy, and (3) pairing deep relaxation with graduated exposure to anxiety-producing stimuli on the hierarchy. In his chapter on systematic desensitization with adults with phobias, Wolpe (1969, pp. 91–149) provides detailed instructions for employing progressive relaxation techniques, constructing anxiety hierarchies, including several examples, and implementing the desensitizing procedure.

Before exposure can be introduced to therapy, a child must learn progressive relaxation techniques or other competing/anxiety-inhibiting responses. Relaxation training refers to techniques used to teach clients to purposely tighten and then relax the muscles of the body. Clinicians slowly guide children through the process of tightening and releasing the major muscle groups of the body, usually several times during a session over several sessions. The number of sessions necessary to teach relaxation, as with exposure, varies considerably depending on the severity of the presenting problem and cognitive, developmental, and cultural factors. The ultimate goal is for the child to be able to successfully relax major muscles on demand; thus initial therapist-guided relaxation exercises are audiotaped for use in homework assignments between sessions.

Although researchers have cautioned against using progressive relaxation with children under the age of 9 (Kratochwill & Morris, 1991), suggestions and examples of ways to adapt progressive relaxation strategies for young children and children with cognitive disabilities have been presented in the literature (Harvey, 1979; Walker, 1979). However, adolescents with phobic disorders appear to learn and benefit from the progressive relaxation suggested by Wolpe (1969; King et al., 2005).

Using previously published progressive relaxation exercises (e.g., Lazarus, 1971), Koeppen (1974) developed a relaxation exercise script for grade school children. Recognizing the difficulty young children may have learning the various major muscle groups, he encouraged the use of fantasy and metaphors (e.g., replacing feelings of butterflies in the stomach with images of a lazy cat) in relaxation exercises with children (Koeppen, 1974). Heffner, Greco, and Eifert (2003) examined 33 nonclinical preschool children's compliance and preference of metaphorical versus literal instructions after a progressive relaxation exercise. Children were equally compliant regardless of instructions used; however, children rated the metaphorical instructions more positively than the literal instructions.

Emotive imagery is a variant of systematic desensitization originally introduced by Lazarus and Abramovitz (1962). In this technique, positive images or other fantasies, such as a child's favorite superhero, are incorporated into imaginal exposure sessions to induce feelings of mastery, competence, and positive emotions for the purpose of counteracting an anxiety-related response. The use of emotive imagery may be helpful with younger children or those who have difficulty learning or engaging in traditional relaxation exercises. Relaxation exercises and emotive imagery attempt to evoke positive feelings that are incompatible with an anxiety response elicited by feared stimuli. King, Heyne, Gullone, and Molloy (2001) recently provided case examples and outlined a list of guidelines for using emotive therapy with children.

Once proficient in progressive relaxation techniques or emotive imagery procedures, the child is asked to generate a list of anxiety-provoking cues, thoughts, situations, and other stimuli usually falling under a specific feared and avoided category (e.g., snakes, flying, contamination, trauma-related event). Feared cues and stimuli surrounding these categories are listed hierarchically from least to most anxiety provoking. Clients are instructed to include many benign, low- and medium-range anxiety-producing events so exposure can progress in a systematic, graduated fashion. The use of self-monitoring techniques has been advocated in the literature to assist children in identifying anxiety-provoking cues, situations, and stimuli. For example, children and adolescents can use daily diaries to record anxiety-provoking events, their antecedents and consequences, subsequent physiological responses, intensity of anxiety experienced, and behaviors used to cope with stressors (e.g., avoidance and escape responses; Beidel, Neal, & Lederer, 1991). Diary entries can be used to select items for the fear hierarchy.

Next, exposure sessions begin with relaxation exercises until a deep state of relaxation is induced. Exposure begins with items at the lowest end of the fear hierarchy. Progression to higher items on the fear hierarchy occurs gradually, at a pace dependent on the child's level of distress. During exposure to fearful stimuli, clients are asked to simultaneously or alternately engage in behaviors that compete with anxiety. These later exposure sessions are also audio-recorded for use in homework assignments. Treatment is continued until extinction takes place and the child's anxiety reactions are eliminated.

Flooding   Flooding refers to a prolonged, intense exposure procedure. In contrast to the brief and gradual presentation of low to more intensely anxiety-provoking stimuli used in systematic desensitization, flooding exposure begins with the introduction of stimuli listed much higher on the fear hierarchy. Thus, these stimuli elicit the most anxiety in clients. During flooding, exposure to the highly aversive stimulus or situation can last for an extended period of time, depending on how long it takes the child's anxiety to reach a peak, then begin to subside. Just as with gradual exposure, several modes of stimulus presentation, such as in vivo and imaginal, are available. Again, in vivo flooding (i.e., exposure to actual anxiety-provoking stimuli) is the preferred method.

Like systematic desensitization, flooding procedures are primarily used to treat anxiety-related disorders such as phobias, OCD, and PTSD. In contrast to the adult literature, Saigh, Yule, and Indamar (1996) noted that few empirical investigations have been carried out demonstrating the effectiveness of flooding procedures with children. However, they reviewed a number of experimental flooding studies, mostly single case trials that provide support for the use of this technique to treat children with PTSD. It was pointed out that some children may have difficulty imagining traumatizing events and tolerating extended exposure sessions. In these cases, incorporating additional techniques such as asking children to draw pictures associated with the traumatic event and then having them provide verbal descriptions of their drawings was recommended. In addition, they warn that flooding procedures may be contraindicated in some cases, such as those involving comorbidity, Conduct Disorder, or decreased mental capacity.

Bouchard, Mendlowitz, Coles, and Franklin (2004) outlined a number of guiding principles in conducting exposure with children and adolescents. For example, they stressed the importance of including a strong educational component and rationale for treatment, eliminating any distracters from the therapeutic environment, incorporating emotive therapy techniques such as superhero characters into the scripts of imaginal exposure and relaxation exercises, providing multiple replications of relaxation training and exposure sessions, establishing a strong therapeutic alliance, and ensuring high levels of parental involvement. Additionally, as treatments for child anxiety disorders typically incorporate cognitive components, the authors point out that younger children may need a stronger behavioral component, reserving complicated cognitive tasks typically included in cognitive-behavioral treatment packages for use with adolescents.

BEHAVIORAL PARENT TRAINING

Parent training programs are one way of implementing behavior modification systems for children. Although they can take a variety of specific forms, these programs aim to educate parents in contingency management so they can effect behavioral change in their children. Given the relatively limited amount of contact between therapist and child in traditional clinical settings and the extensive interaction between the child and his or her parents in everyday life, parent training is an attractive approach for modifying children's behavior. Furthermore, there is considerable and legitimate doubt regarding the generalizability of behavioral interventions limited to clinical and/or classroom settings (e.g., DuPaul & Eckert, 1997; Stokes & Baer, 1977). Parent training programs rest on the premise that training parents in behavioral techniques and principles can produce long-term behavioral change in children efficiently and effectively. Indeed, there is a large body of empirical support for these claims.

Behavioral parent training programs can take a variety of forms but tend to share general features. In general, behavioral parent training programs involve clinicians teaching parents how to properly identify behavior problems, assess their intensity and context, and develop and implement plans to modify the child's behavior (Breismeister & Schaefer, 1998). However, some programs aim to provide parents with a broad understanding of behavioral principles and techniques to maximize adaptability (e.g., Patterson & Gullion, 1968), whereas others focus on addressing specific behavioral problems or disorders (e.g., Barkley, 1987). Despite the various programs and presenting problems, parents are taught that consistency and immediacy are critical to any contingency management procedure.

A substantial and growing research base supports the use of behavioral parent training for a variety of childhood behavior problems. Behavioral parent training programs, particularly those based on systems developed by Patterson and Gullion (1968) and Webster-Stratton (1984), have been deemed empirically supported treatments for ADHD (Pelham et al., 1998) and OCD and Conduct Disorder (Brestan & Eyberg, 1998). More recent meta-analytic research (Maughan, Christiansen, Jenson, Olympia, & Clark, 2005) has shown parent training programs to be effective for treating externalizing and disruptive behaviors in general. Other studies and reviews have concluded that behavioral parent training programs are effective for treating antisocial behavior (Serketich & Dumas, 1996) and various specific, overt behaviors such as enuresis, crying, stuttering, and phobias (Graziano & Diament, 1992).

Behavioral parent training programs are not only efficacious, but they also appear efficient and applicable in a variety of settings. For example, Bourke and Nielson (1995) estimated that by training 10 parents who have an average of three children and spend 3 to 4 hours with them each day, these children would experience a cumulative total of 700 hours of behavior modification per week. Furthermore, recent research has examined the implementation of parent training programs with resistant and difficult parents (Smagner & Sullivan, 2005), a single parent (Briggs, Leary, Briggs, Cox, & Shibano, 2005), and fathers (Tiano & McNeil, 2005). Some contemporary research has also begun to examine how specific child traits like temperament (Hawes & Dadds, 2005), sex, and socioeconomic status (Kim, Arnold, Fisher, & Zeljo, 2005) influence outcomes in behavioral parent training programs.

Modeling

Modeling procedures represent an extension of traditional behavioral principles based on the influential work of Albert Bandura. Bandura (e.g., Bandura, 1962; Bandura, Ross, & Ross, 1961) showed how learning could occur without direct participation by the subject, but instead by observation of a model. This line of research demonstrated that learning processes similar to classical (Bandura, Grusec, & Menlove, 1967) and operant (Bandura, 1965) conditioning could take place by proxy, opening up the door for a new but not entirely unfamiliar class of behavioral treatments. Since then, a wide variety of successful behavioral treatments for children have been developed on the basis of modeling principles.

Modeling procedures employ individuals who perform a target behavior to help the child learn it. These techniques generally fall into one of three broad classes. In simple modeling (Vasta & Novak, 1975), the child is merely exposed to performance of the behavior. In participant modeling (Newman & Tuckman, 1997), children are encouraged to perform the behavior after it is modeled for them. Covert modeling (Krop & Burgess, 1993) is an imaginal procedure where the child is encouraged to vividly imagine a model or himself or herself performing the target behavior.

A number of common variations characterize different modeling techniques that can be used with children. For example, in graduated modeling procedures (Bandura et al., 1967), the child is presented with graduated exposure to increasingly difficult behaviors. Modeling with reinforcement (Kazdin, 1974) techniques have the child observe the model being rewarded after performing the target behavior, and guided modeling procedures have the therapist or model giving the child feedback while practicing the modeled behaviors. Symbolic modeling procedures (Wurtele, Marrs, & Miller-Perrin, 1987) involve watching models perform the target responses on film. In addition to these features, modeling procedures can be implemented as either coping or mastery procedures. In the former, the child observes a model struggling with the target situation and trying a number of behaviors before finding a successful one. In the latter, the model immediately demonstrates a successful behavior. Research suggests that coping models are generally more effective than mastery modeling procedures (Cunningham, Davis, Bremner, Dunn, & Rzasa, 1993; Meichenbaum, 1972).

Despite the numerous variations that exist today, Bandura (1969, 1977) identified four essential components of successful modeling procedures. First, they require that the child pay attention to the modeled behavior and the situation in which it occurs. Second, the child must retain this information. Third, they require that the child reproduce the target behavior. Fourth, the child must be motivated to reproduce the target behavior. Other research indicates that the effectiveness of modeling procedures is also contingent on variables such as how well the children recognize the consequences in the modeling situation and in their own practice of the behavior, the amount of time the child spends practicing the behavior, and the extent of verbal coding of the modeled response (Thorpe & Olson, 1997).

Modeling procedures have garnered a great deal of empirical support for treatment of childhood behavior problems. These procedures have been especially successful in the treatment of fears and phobias (e.g., Glasscock & McClean, 1990; King & Ollendick, 1997; Mendez & Garcia, 1996). They have also been successfully used for training social skills (Carlyon, 1997; Matson, Foe, Coe, & Smith, 1991) and have shown promise in the treatment of various other childhood behavior difficulties, such as learning problems (Lonnecker, Brady, & McPherson, 1994), anger management (Marion, 1994), aggression (Vidyasagar & Michra, 1993), and elective mutism (Holmbeck & Lavigne, 1992).

ETHICAL CONSIDERATIONS

A number of ethical considerations are relevant to the use of behavior therapy with children. Foremost among them are issues of treatment selection and confidentiality. Some of these concerns will be familiar to any therapist who works with children, but unique features of behavior therapy can create situations that warrant attention before implementing a behavioral intervention with a child. As with other aspects of treatment with children, the child's or adolescent's age will play a major role in determining the relevance of these concerns, as well as possible options for addressing them.

One of the main ethical concerns surrounding behavior therapy with children is the issue of treatment selection and direction. As opposed to psychotherapy with adults, which is by and large self-initiated, behavior therapy with children usually begins with a parent or teacher referring the child for treatment. Additionally, in many cases, the child has little or no say in what treatment will be used and how it will be implemented. Often this can result in confusion or resentment. In some cases (e.g., severe self- or other-injurious behavior, limited cognitive capacity), this is unavoidable. However, studies have shown that adolescents tend to sufficiently comprehend treatment issues and their own rights in treatment programs (Belter & Grisso, 1984; Kaser-Boyd, Adelman, & Taylor, 1985), suggesting that they should play an active role in treatment decisions. Even with younger children it is advisable to attempt to discuss treatment issues and decisions, as is often done in behavior contracting programs. Thus, it is important that therapists take the time to articulate the procedures and rationale for treatment to child clients and their parents.

Another major ethical issue in child behavior therapy is confidentiality. Because both the child and the parents (and, in some cases, teachers) are closely involved in treatment, it is difficult to maintain confidentiality with the child. Additionally, most states allow parents access to the child's mental health records. For these reasons it is important that all involved parties negotiate confidentiality issues before treatment begins. It is essential that the therapist clearly convey what level of confidentiality the child or adolescent can expect during treatment, as well as what level of disclosure the parent can expect. Although this issue tends to be more salient with older children and adolescents, any effective therapeutic relationship requires trust on the part of the child.

SUMMARY

We have reviewed the major behavior therapy techniques and procedures used for the treatment of child and adolescent disorders. Child behavior therapists rely on operant conditioning techniques, such as positive reinforcement, punishment, and extinction, and therapies derived from classical conditioning principles, such as systematic desensitization and flooding. The broad range of intervention strategies has produced treatments for a wide range of childhood problems. For example, some anxiety disorders and elimination disorders such as nocturnal enuresis have been successfully treated exclusively with respondent conditioning techniques (Mellon & McGrath, 2000; Mowrer & Mowrer, 1938). However, the complexities of common childhood disorders such as Conduct Disorder, ADHD, OCD, and Social Anxiety Disorder, which frequently present comorbidly (Angold, Costello, & Erkanli, 1999), often require treatments that include a combination of operant and respondent conditioning techniques.

Research suggests that treatment packages combining behavioral techniques with psychopharmacological medications (Pelham & Gnagy, 1999), observational learning techniques, and cognitive components (e.g., cognitive restructuring, thought stopping, and self-talk) may increase long-term treatment effectiveness and reduce relapse rates for certain childhood disorders (Velting et al., 2004). While comprehensive treatment packages derived from a variety of theoretical models are sometimes necessary, reinforcing practices and strong parental involvement remain central to any child treatment program.

Behavior therapy's grounding in empirical methods has allowed it to enjoy prominence in the movement toward evidence-based practice. The recent focus on brief, empirically supported treatments has prompted the manualization of a number of treatment programs with strong behavioral components, such as parent-child interaction therapy (for a review, see Herschell, Calzada, Eyberg, & McNeil, 2002) and cognitive-behavioral therapies for child anxiety disorders (Kendall, 2000). In the realm of anxiety disorders, ongoing longitudinal studies support long-term maintenance of treatment outcomes (Kendall, Safford, Flannery-Schroeder, & Webb, 2004). However, the extraordinary cost of implementing comprehensive treatment protocols that combine behavioral, cognitive-behavioral, and pharmacological components, particularly in terms of the demands placed on those involved in treatment (i.e., therapists, caregivers, teachers, and children), warrants additional consideration of the most effective and efficient treatment components. Additional research is necessary to determine which treatment modalities are most effective and efficient for specific disorders and to identify variables that might impact treatment success or failure, such as childhood (e.g., diagnostic comorbidity, ethnicity, age) and parental (parental psychopathology) factors.

REFERENCES

Abramowitz, J. S., Whiteside, S. P., & Deacon, B. J. (2005). The effectiveness of treatment for pediatric obsessive-compulsive disorder: A meta-analysis. *Behavior Therapy, 36*(1), 55–63.

Albano, A. M., Causey, D., & Carter, B. (2001). Fear and anxiety in children. In C. E. Walker & M. C. Roberts (Eds.), *Handbook of clinical child psychology* (3rd ed., pp. 291–316). New York: Wiley.

Allen, L. J., Howard, V. F., Sweeney, W. J., & McLaughlin, T. F. (1993). Use of contingency contracting to increase on-task behavior with primary students. *Psychological Reports, 72,* 905–906.

Allen, S. J., & Kramer, J. J. (1990). Modification of personal hygiene and grooming behaviors with contingency contracting: A brief review and case study. *Psychology in the Schools, 27*(3), 244–251.

Angold, A., Costello, E. J., & Erkanli, A. (1999). Comorbidity. *Journal of Child Psychology and Psychiatry and Allied Disciplines, 40,* 55–87.

Anhalt, K., McNeil, C. B., & Bahl, A. B. (1998). The ADHD classroom kit: A whole classroom approach for managing disruptive behavior. *Psychology in the Schools, 35,* 67–79.

Axelrod, S., Brantner, J. P., & Meddock, T. D. (1978). Overcorrection: A review and critical analysis. *Journal of Special Education, 12*(4), 367–392.

Babbitt, R. L., & Parrish, J. M. (1991). Phone phobia, phact or phantasy? An operant approach to a child's disruptive behavior induced by telephone usage. *Journal of Behavior Therapy and Experimental Psychiatry, 22*(2), 123–129.

Bandura, A. (1962). Social learning through imitation. In M. R. Jones (Ed.), *Nebraska Symposium on Motivation* (pp. 211–274). Lincoln: University of Nebraska Press.

Bandura, A. (1965). Influence of models' reinforcement contingencies on the acquisition of imitative responses. *Journal of Personality and Social Psychology, 1*(6), 589–595.

Bandura, A. (1969). *Principles of behavior modification.* New York: Holt, Rinehart, & Winston.

Bandura, A. (1977). *Social learning theory.* Englewood Cliffs, NJ: Prentice-Hall.

Bandura, A., Grusec, J. E., & Menlove, F. L. (1967). Vicarious extinction of avoidance behavior. *Journal of Personality and Social Psychology, 5*(1), 16–23.

Bandura, A., Ross, D., & Ross, S. A. (1961). Transmission of aggression through imitation of aggressive models. *Journal of Abnormal and Social Psychology, 63*(3), 575–582.

Barkley, R. B. (1987). *Defiant children: A clinician's manual for parent training.* New York: Guilford Press.

Barrios, B. A., & O'Dell, S. L. (1989). Fears and anxieties. In E. J. Mash & R. A. Barkley (Eds.), *Treatment of childhood disorders* (pp. 167–221). New York: Guilford Press.

Beidel, D., Neal, A. M., & Lederer, A. S. (1991). The feasibility and validity of a daily diary for the assessment of anxiety in children. *Behavior Therapy, 23,* 505–517.

Belter, R. W., & Grisso, T. (1984). Children's recognition of rights violation in counseling. *Professional Psychology: Research and Practice, 15,* 899–910.

Bouchard, J. D., Mendlowitz, S. L., Coles, M. E., & Franklin, M. (2004). Considerations in the use of exposure with children. *Cognitive and Behavioral Practice, 11,* 56–65.

Bourke, M. L., & Nielson, B. A. (1995). Parent training: Getting the most effective help for the most children. *Journal of Psychological Practice, 1,* 142–152.

Breismeister, G. H., & Schaefer, C. E. (1998). *Handbook of parent training.* New York: Wiley.

Brestan, E. V., & Eyberg, S. M. (1998). Effective psychosocial treatment of conduct disordered children and adolescents: 29 years, 82 studies, and 5,725 kids. *Journal of Clinical Child Psychology, 27,* 180–189.

Briggs, H. E., Leary, J. D., Briggs, A. C., Cox, W. H., & Shibano, M. (2005). Group treatment of separated parent and child interaction. *Research on Social Work Practice, 15*(6), 452–461.

Burchard, J. D., & Barrera, F. (1972). An analysis of timeout and response cost in a programmed environment. *Journal of Applied Behavior Analysis, 5*(3), 271–282.

Carlyon, W. D. (1997). Attribution retraining: Implications for its integration into prescriptive social skills training. *School Psychology Review, 26*(1), 61–73.

Carroll, L. (1988). *Alice's adventures in wonderland.* New York: H. N. Abrams. (Original work published 1865).

Casey, R. J., & Berman, J. S. (1985). The outcome of psychotherapy with children. *Psychological Bulletin, 98,* 388–400.

Cautela, J. R. (1993). The use of covert conditioning in the treatment of a severe childhood phobia. In J. R. Cautela & A. J. Kearney (Eds.), *Covert conditioning casebook* (pp. 126–134). Pacific Grove, CA: Brooks/Cole.

Cicchetti, D., & Rogosch, F. A. (2002). A developmental perspective on adolescence. *Journal of Consulting and Clinical Psychology, 70*(1), 6–20.

Conyers, C., Miltenberger, R. G., Maki, A., Barenz, R., Jurgens, M., Sailer, A., et al. (2004). A comparison of response cost and differential reinforcement of other behavior to reduce disruptive behavior in a preschool classroom. *Journal of Applied Behavior Analysis, 37*(3), 411–415.

Conyers, C., Miltenberger, R. G., Romaniuk, C., Kopp, B., & Himle, M. (2003). Evaluation of DRO schedules to reduce disruptive behavior in a preschool classroom. *Child and Family Behavior Therapy, 25*(3), 1–6.

Costello, E. J., & Angold, A. (1995). Epidemiology in anxiety disorders in children and adolescents. In J. S. March (Ed.), *Anxiety disorders in children and adolescents* (pp. 109–124). New York: Guilford Press.

Coyne, L. W., & Gross, A. M. (2001). Behavior therapy. In M. Hersen & V. B. Van Hasselt (Eds.), *Advanced abnormal psychology* (2nd ed., pp. 481–505). Dordrecht, The Netherlands: Kluwer Academic.

Cunningham, C. E., Davis, J. R., Bremner, R., Dunn, K. W., & Rzasa, T. (1993). Coping modeling problem solving versus mastery modeling: Effects on adherence, in-session process, and skill acquisition in a residential parent-training program. *Journal of Consulting and Clinical Psychology, 61,* 871–877.

DeLeon, I. G., & Iwata, B. A. (1996). Evaluation of a multiple-stimulus presentation format for assessing reinforcer preferences. *Journal of Applied Behavior Analysis, 29,* 519–532.

De Los Reyes, A., & Kazdin, A. E. (2005). Informant discrepancies in the assessment of childhood psychopathology: A critical review, theoretical framework, and recommendations for further study. *Psychological Bulletin, 131*(4), 483–509.

Dews, P. B. (1960). Free-operant behavior under conditions of delayed reinforcement: Pt. 1. CRF-type schedules. *Journal of the Experimental Analysis of Behavior, 3,* 221–234.

Douglas, V. I. & Parry, P. A. (1994). Effects of reward or nonreward on frustration and attention in attention deficit disorder. *Journal of Abnormal Child Psychology, 22*(3), 281–302.

DuPaul, G. J., & Eckert, T. L. (1997). The effects of school-based interventions for attention deficit hyperactivity disorder: A meta-analyses. *School Psychology Review, 26*(1), 5–27.

Egan, P. J., Zlomke, L. C., & Bush, B. (1993). Utilizing functional assessment, behavioral consultation and videotape review of treatment to reduce aggression: A case study. *Special Services in the Schools, 7*(1), 27–37.

Epstein, L. H., McKenzie, S. J., Valoski, A., & Klein, K. R. (1994). Effects of mastery criteria and contingent reinforcement for family-based weight control. *Addictive Behaviors, 19*(2), 135–145.

Epstein, M. H., Repp, A. C., & Cullinan, D. (1978). Decreasing obscene language of behaviorally disordered children through the use of a DRL schedule. *Psychology in the Schools, 15*(3), 419–423.

Esser, G. (2005). Verhaltenstherapie mit kindern und jugenlichen: Forschungsstand und perspektiven [Behavioral therapy with children and adolescents: Status of research and outlook]. *Verhaltenstherapie and Verhaltensmedizin, 26*(1), 19–39.

Feeny, N. C., Foa, E. B., Treadwell, K. R. H., & March, J. (2004). Posttraumatic stress disorder in youth: A critical review of the cognitive and behavioral treatment outcome literature. *Professional Psychology: Research and Practice, 35*(5), 466–467.

Fisher, W., Piazza, C. C., Bowman, L. G., Hagopian, L. P., Owens, J. C., & Slevin, I. (1992). A comparison of two approaches for identifying reinforcers for persons with severe and profound disabilities. *Journal of Applied Behavior Analysis, 25,* 491–498.

Flood, W. A., & Wilder, D. A. (2002). Antecedent assessment and assessment-based treatment of off-task behavior in a child diagnosed with attention deficit-hyperactivity disorder (ADHD). *Education and Treatment of Children, 25*(3), 331–338.

Foxx, R. M., & Azrin, N. H. (1972). Restitution: A method of eliminating aggressive-disruptive behaviors of retarded and brain-damaged patients. *Behavior Research and Therapy, 10,* 15–27.

Foxx, R. M., & Azrin, N. H. (1973). The elimination of autistic self-stimulatory behavior by overcorrection. *Journal of Applied Behavior Analysis, 6,* 1–14.

Friman, P. C., Barnard, J. D., Altman, K., & Wolf, M. M. (1986). Parent and teacher use of DRO and DRI to reduce aggressive behavior. *Analysis and Intervention in Developmental Disabilities, 6*(4), 319–330.

Glasscock, S. E., & McClean, W. E. (1990). Use of contact desensitization and shaping in the treatment of dog phobias and generalized fear of the outdoors. *Journal of Clinical Child Psychology, 19,* 169–172.

Graziano, A. M., & Diament, D. M. (1992). Parent behavioral training: An examination of the paradigm. *Behavior Modification, 16*(1), 3–38.

Handen, B. L. (1998). Mental retardation. In E. J. Mash & R. A. Barkley (Eds.), *Treatment of childhood disorders* (2nd ed., pp. 369–415). New York: Guilford Press.

Harvey, J. R. (1979). The potential of relaxation training for the mentally retarded. *Mental Retardation, 17,* 71–76.

Hawes, D. J. & Dadds, M. R. (2005). The treatment of conduct problems in children with callous-unemotional traits. *Journal of Consulting and Clinical Psychology, 73*(4), 737–741.

Heffner, M., Greco, L. A., & Eifert, G. H. (2003). Pretend you are a turtle: Children's responses to metaphorical versus literal relaxation instructions. *Child and Behavior Therapy, 25*(1), 19–33.

Herschell, A., Calzada, E., Eyberg, S. M., & McNeil, C. B. (2002). Parent-child interaction therapy: New directions in research. *Cognitive and Behavioral Practice, 9,* 9–16.

Holmbeck, G. N., & Lavigne, J. V. (1992). Combining self-modeling and stimulus fading in the treatment of an electively mute child. *Psychotherapy, 29,* 661–667.

Homme, L. E. (1971). *How to use contingency contracting in the classroom.* Champaign, IL: Research Press.

Jones, R. N., Sloane, H. N., & Roberts, M. W. (1992). Limitations of "don't" instructional control. *Behavior Therapy, 23*(1), 131–140.

Kaser-Boyd, N., Adelman, H., & Taylor, L. (1985). Minors' ability to identify risks and benefits of therapy. *Professional Psychology: Research and Practice, 16,* 411–417.

Kazdin, A. E. (1974). Effects of covert modeling and model reinforcement on assertive behavior. *Journal of Abnormal Psychology, 83*(3), 240–252.

Kazdin, A. E. (1982). The token economy: A decade later. *Journal of Applied Behavior Analysis, 15*(3), 431–445.

Kazdin, A. E. (1989). *Behavior modification in applied settings* (4th ed.). Pacific Grove, CA: Brooks/Cole.

Kearney, C. A., & Tillotson, C. A. (1998). School attendance. In T. S. Watson & F. M. Gresham (Eds.), *Handbook of child behavior therapy* (pp. 143–162). New York: Plenum Press.

Kelley, M. L., & Stokes, T. F. (1982). Contingency contracting with disadvantaged youths: Improving classroom performance. *Journal of Applied Behavior Analysis, 15*(3), 447–454.

Kelley, M. L., & Stokes, T. F. (1984). Student-teacher contracting with goal setting for maintenance. *Behavior Modification, 8*(2), 223–244.

Kendall, P. C. (2000). *Cognitive-behavioral therapy for anxious children: Therapist manual* (2nd ed.). Ardmore, PA: Workbook Publishing.

Kendall, P. C., Nay, W. R., & Jeffers, J. (1975). Timeout duration and contrast effects: A systematic evaluation of a successive treatment design. *Behavior Therapy, 6*(5), 609–615.

Kendall, P. C., Safford, S., Flannery-Schroeder, E., & Webb, A. (2004). Child anxiety treatment: Outcomes in adolescence and impact on substance use and depression at 7.4-year follow-up. *Journal of Consulting and Clinical Psychology, 72*(2), 276–287.

Kessler, R. C., Berglund, P., Demler, O., Jin, R., & Walters, E. E. (2005). Lifetime prevalence and age-of-onset distributions of DSM-IV disorders in the National Comorbidity Survey replication. *Archives of General Psychiatry, 62*(6), 593–602.

Kim, H., Arnold, D. H., Fisher, P. H., & Zeljo, A. (2005). Parenting and preschoolers' symptoms as a function of child gender and SES. *Child and Family Behavior Therapy, 27*(2), 23–41.

King, N. J., Heyne, D., Gullone, E., & Molloy, G. N. (2001). Usefulness of emotive imagery in the treatment of childhood phobias: Clinical guidelines, case examples, and issues. *Counseling Psychology Quarterly, 14*(2), 95–101.

King, N. J., Muris, P., & Ollendick, T. H. (2005). Childhood fears and phobias: Assessment and treatment. *Child and Adolescent Mental Health, 10*(2), 50–56.

King, N. J., & Ollendick, T. H. (1997). Treatment of childhood phobias. *Journal of Child Psychology and Psychiatry, 38*(4), 389–400.

Koeppen, A. S. (1974). Relaxation training for children. *Elementary School Guidance and Counseling, 9*(1), 14–21.

Kratochwill, T. R., & Morris, R. J. (1991). *The practice of child therapy* (2nd ed.). New York: Pergamon Press.

Krop, H., & Burgess, D. (1993). The use of covert modeling in the treatment of a sexual abuse victim. In J. R. Cautela & A. J. Kearney (Eds.), *Covert conditioning casebook* (pp. 153–158). Belmont, CA: Brooks/Cole.

Lattal, K. A. (1974). Combinations of response-reinforcer dependence and independence. *Journal of the Experimental Analysis of Behavior, 22*(2), 357–362.

Lazarus, A. A. (1971). *Behavior therapy and beyond.* New York: McGraw-Hill.

Lazarus, A. A., & Abramovitz, A. (1962). The use of emotive imagery in the treatment of children's fears. *Journal of Mental Science, 108,* 191–195.

Little, L. M., & Kelly, M. L. (1989). The efficacy of response cost procedures for reducing children's noncompliance to parental instructions. *Behavior Therapy, 20,* 525–534.

Lonnecker, C., Brady, M. P., & McPherson, R. (1994). Video self-modeling and cooperative classroom behavior in children with learning and behavior problems: Training and generalization effects. *Behavioral Disorders, 20,* 24–34.

Luborsky, L., Singer, B., & Luborsky, L. (1975). Comparative studies of psychotherapies: Is it true that "everyone has won and all must have prizes"? *Archives of General Psychiatry, 32,* 995–1008.

Luciano, M. C., Molina, F. J., Gómez, I., & Herruzo, J. (1993). Response prevention and contingency management in the treatment of nocturnal enuresis: A report of two cases. *Child and Family Behavior Therapy, 15*(1), 37–51.

Luman, M., Oosterlaan, J., & Sergeant, J. A. (2005). The impact of reinforcement contingencies on AD/HD: A review and theoretical appraisal. *Clinical Psychology Review, 25*(2), 183–213.

Marcus, B. A., & Vollmer, T. R. (1996). Combining noncontingent reinforcement and differential reinforcement schedules as treatment for aberrant behavior. *Journal of Applied Behavior Analysis, 29*(1), 43–51.

Marion, M. (1994). Encouraging the development of responsible anger management in young children. *Early Child Development and Care, 97,* 155–163.

Masters, J. C., & Santrock, J. (1976). Studies in the self-regulation of behavior: Effects of contingent cognitive and affective events. *Developmental Psychology, 12,* 334–348.

Matson, J. L., Foe, V. E., Coe, D. A., & Smith, D. (1991). A social skills program for developmentally delayed preschoolers. *Journal of Clinical Child Psychology, 20,* 420–433.

Maughan, D. R., Christiansen, E., Jenson, W. R., Olympia, D., & Clark, E. (2005). Behavioral parent training as a treatment for externalizing behaviors and disruptive behavior disorders: A meta-analysis. *School Psychology Review, 34*(3), 267–286.

McCartney, E. J., Anderson, C. M., & English, C. L. (2005). Effect of brief clinic-based training on the ability of caregivers to implement escape extinction. *Journal of Positive Behavior Interventions, 7*(1), 18–32.

McCurdy, M., Kunz, G. M., & Sheridan, S. S. (2006). Temper tantrums. In G. G. Bear & K. M. Minke (Eds.), *Children's needs III: Development, prevention, and intervention* (pp. 149–157). Washington, DC: National Association of School Psychologists.

McGoey, K. E., & DuPaul, G. J. (2000). Token reinforcement and response cost procedures: Reducing the disruptive behavior of preschool children with attention-deficit/hyperactivity disorder. *School Psychology Quarterly, 15,* 330–343.

McGuffin, P. W. (1991). The effect of timeout duration on frequency of aggression in hospitalized children with aggressive disorders. *Behavioral Residential Treatment, 6,* 279–288.

Meichenbaum, D. H. (1972). Examination of model characteristics in reducing avoidance behavior. *Journal of Behavior Therapy and Experimental Psychiatry, 3,* 225–227.

Mellon, M. W., & McGrath, M. L. (2000). Empirically supported treatments in pediatric psychology: Nocturnal enuresis. *Journal of Pediatric Psychology, 25,* 193–214.

Mendez, F. J., & Garcia, M. J. (1996). Emotive performances: A treatment package for children's phobias. *Child and Family Behavior Therapy, 18*(3), 19–34.

Mindell, J. A. (1999). Empirically supported treatments in pediatric psychology: Bedtime refusal and night wakings in young children. *Journal of Pediatric Psychology, 24*(6), 465–481.

Mowrer, O. H., & Mowrer, W. M. (1938). Enuresis: A method for its study and treatment. *American Journal of Orthopsychiatry, 8,* 436–459.

Newman, E. J., & Tuckman, B. W. (1997). The effects of participant modeling on self-efficacy, incentive, productivity, and performance. *Journal of Research and Development in Education, 31*(1), 38–45.

Pace, G. M., Ivancic, M. T., Edwards, G. L., Iwata, B. A., & Page, T. J. (1985). Assessment of stimulus preference and reinforcer value with profoundly retarded individuals. *Journal of Applied Behavior Analysis, 18,* 249–255.

Pace, G. M., Iwata, B. A., Cowdery, G. E., & Andree, P. J. (1993). Stimulus (instructional) fading during extinction of self-injurious escape behavior. *Journal of Applied Behavior Analysis, 26* (2), 205–212.

Patterson, G. R., & Gullion, M. E. (1968). *Living with children: New methods for parents and teachers.* Champaign, IL: Research Press.

Pavlov, I. P. (1927). *Conditioned reflexes.* New York: Oxford University Press.

Pelham, W. E., & Gnagy, E. M. (1999). Psychosocial and combined treatments for ADHD. *Mental Retardation and Developmental Disabilities, 5,* 225–236.

Pelham, W. E., Jr., Wheeler, T., & Chronis, A. (1998). Empirically supported psychosocial treatments for attention deficit hyperactivity disorder. *Journal of Clinical Child Psychology, 27,* 190–205.

Piazza, C. C., & Fisher, W. (1991). A faded bedtime with response cost protocol for treatment of multiple sleep problems in children. *Journal of Applied Behavior Analysis, 24,* 129–140.

Premack, D. C. (1965). Reinforcement theory. In D. Levine (Ed.), *Nebraska Symposium on Motivation* (pp. 123–180). Lincoln: University of Nebraska Press.

Reisinger, J. J. (1972). The treatment of "anxiety-depression" via positive reinforcement and response cost. *Journal of Applied Behavior Analysis, 5,* 125–130.

Reitman, D., & Drabman, R. S. (1996). Read my fingertips: A procedure for enhancing the effectiveness of time-out with argumentative children. *Child and Family Behavior Therapy, 18*(2), 35–40.

Rimm, D. C., & Masters, J. C. (1979). *Behavior therapy: Techniques and empirical findings* (2nd ed.). New York: Academic Press.

Roane, H. S., Vollmer, T. R., Ringdahl, J. E., & Marcus, B. A. (1998). Evaluation of a brief stimulus preference assessment. *Journal of Applied Behavior Analysis, 31,* 605–620.

Roberts, M. W., & Powers, S. W. (1990). Adjusting chair timeout enforcement procedures for oppositional children. *Behavior Therapy, 21,* 257–271.

Rosenzweig, S. (1936). Some implicit common factors in diverse methods of psychotherapy. *American Journal of Orthopsychiatry, 6,* 412–415.

Rothbaum, B. O., Hodges, L., Smith, S., Lee, J. H., & Price, L. (2000). A controlled study of virtual reality exposure therapy for the fear of flying. *Journal of Consulting and Clinical Psychology, 68,* 1020–1026.

Saigh, P. A., Yule, W., & Indamar, S. C. (1996). Imaginal flooding of traumatized children and adolescents. *Journal of School Psychology, 34*(2), 163–183.

Serketich, W. J., & Dumas, J. E. (1996). The effectiveness of behavioral parent training to modify antisocial behavior in children: A meta-analysis. *Behavior Therapy, 27,* 171–186.

Shirk, S. R. & Russell, R. L. (1992). A reevaluation of estimates of child therapy effectiveness. *Journal of the American Academy of Child and Adolescent Psychiatry, 31*(4), 703–709.

Skinner, B. F. (1953). *Science and human behavior.* New York: Macmillan.

Smagner, J. P., & Sullivan, M. H. (2005). Investigating the effectiveness of behavioral parent training with involuntary clients in child welfare settings. *Research on Social Work Practice, 15*(6), 431–439.

Smith, M. L., Glass, G. V., & Miller, T. I. (1980). *The benefits of psychotherapy.* Baltimore: Johns Hopkins University Press.

Stokes, T. F., & Baer, D. M. (1977). An implicit technology of generalization. *Journal of Applied Behavior Analysis, 10,* 349–367.

Terrell, G., Durkin, K., & Wiesley, M. (1959). Social class and the nature of incentive in discrimination learning. *Journal of Abnormal and Social Psychology, 59,* 270–272.

Terrell, G., & Kennedy, W. A. (1957). Discrimination learning and transposition in children as a function of the nature of the reward. *Journal of Experimental Psychology, 53,* 257–260.

Terrell, G., & Ware, R. (1961). Role of the delay of reward in speed of size and form discrimination learning in children. *Child Development, 32,* 409–415.

Thorndike, E. L. (1898). Animal intelligence: An experimental study of the associative processes in animals. *Psychological Review Monographs, 8,* 1–109.

Thorpe, G. L., & Olson, S. L. (1997). *Behavior therapy: Concepts, procedures, and applications* (2nd ed.). Boston: Allyn & Bacon.

Tiano, J. D., & McNeil, C. B. (2005). The inclusion of fathers in behavioral parent training. *Child and Family Behavior Therapy, 27*(4), 1–28.

U.S. Department of Health and Human Services. (1999). *Mental health: A report of the surgeon general—Executive summary.* Rockville, MD: U.S. Department of Health and Human Services, Substance Abuse and Mental Health Services Administration, Center for Mental Health Services, National Institutes of Health, National Institute of Mental Health.

Vasta, R., & Novak, G. (1975). Acquisition of a language concept through simple modeling. *Psychological Reports, 36*(3), 807–816.

Velting, O. N., Setzer, N. J., & Albano, A. M. (2004). Update on and advances in assessment and cognitive-behavioral treatment of anxiety disorders in children and adolescents. *Professional Psychology: Research and Practice, 35*(1), 42–54.

Vidyasagar, P., & Michra, H. (1993). Effect of modeling on aggression. *Indian Journal of Clinical Psychology, 20,* 50–52.

Walker, E. C. (1979). Treatment of children's disorders by relaxation training: The poor man's biofeedback. *Journal of Clinical Child Psychology, 8*(1), 22–25.

Webster-Stratton, C. (1984). Randomized trial of two parent-training programs for families with conduct disordered children. *Journal of Consulting and Clinical Psychology, 52*(4), 666–678.

Weiss B., & Weisz, J. R. (1995). Relative effectiveness of behavioral versus nonbehavioral child psychotherapy. *Journal of Consulting and Clinical Psychology, 63*(2), 317–320.

Weisz, J. R., Weiss, B., Alicke, M. D., & Klotz, M. L. (1987). Effectiveness of psychotherapy with children and adolescents: A meta-analysis for clinicians. *Journal of Consulting and Clinical Psychology, 55,* 542–549.

Williams, M. A., & Gross, A. M. (1994). Behavior therapy. In V. B. Van Hasslet & Michel Hersen (Eds.), *Advanced abnormal psychology* (pp. 419–439). New York: Plenum Press.

Witryol, S. L., & Fischer, W. F. (1960). Scaling children's incentives by the method of paired comparison. *Psychological Reports, 7*, 471–474.

Wolpe, J. (1958). *Psychotherapy by reciprocal inhibition*. Stanford, CA: Stanford University Press.

Wolpe, J. (1969). *The practice of behavior therapy*. New York: Pergamon Press.

World Health Organization. (2001). *The world health report 2001—Mental health: New understanding, new hope*. Geneva, Switzerland: Author.

Wurtele, S. K., Marrs, S. R., & Miller-Perrin, C. L. (1987). Practice makes perfect? The role of participant modeling in sexual abuse prevention programs. *Journal of Consulting and Clinical Psychology, 55*(4), 599–602.

CHAPTER 6

The Role of Family in Treatment

ELIZABETH BRESTAN KNIGHT AND LORRAINE E. RIDGEWAY

"Who lives at home?" is a common intake assessment question. The answer to that question can vary widely, as modern families can be defined in a number of ways. According to census data, there were 72.5 million children under the age of 18 living in the United States in 2001 (U.S. Census Bureau, 2005). Seventy-one percent of the child population lived in two-parent households, 26% lived with a single parent, and 4% lived in households without a parent (U.S. Census Bureau, 2005). These data provide some information regarding the makeup of today's modern family; however, they do not provide a complete picture. Family structure can be influenced by a number of events, such as divorce, the death of a parent, or relocation away from extended family and community networks. The composition of a child's family can also change after the addition of new family members through remarriage, the blending of two families, a parent's cohabitation with an unmarried partner, the birth of a sibling, or the addition of an extended family member or friend to the residence. Through all of these potential life changes, the child's definition of family is subject to change.

In this chapter, we focus on some relevant aspects related to the inclusion of families in treatment. We address the role of family throughout the therapy process, including the decision to seek treatment, the intake assessment, conducting child-focused treatment, and ending services. The purpose of the chapter is to highlight our view that the family should be an integral part of most cognitive-behavioral therapies targeting child emotional and behavioral problems. To begin, however, a few of the terms that we use in this chapter require definition. Throughout the chapter we use the term "child" and "children" to refer to any child or adolescent under the age of 18. We use the term "parent" and "caregiver" interchangeably to refer to an adult who is responsible for the child's care and well-being. Finally, although we recognize that there is a long tradition of therapy in which the focus is the entire family system (Haley, 1963; Minuchin, 1974; Nichols & Schwartz, 2004), "therapy" and "treatment" refer to empirically based, cognitive-behavioral therapies (CBTs) targeting child disorders.

Clinicians working with families often encounter a great deal of variation in the family structure of parents and children presenting for treatment. For example, although a majority of the U.S. child population lives in a household with two parents, these individuals can be more specifically described as biological parents, stepparents, adoptive parents, or foster parents (U.S. Census Bureau, 2005). Adoptive parents and foster parents can have a kinship relationship (e.g., grandparent, aunt, uncle), or they may be of no relation to the child. The presence of additional family members can also vary greatly. Some households are multigenerational, in that extended family members and/or grandparents live in the same home (Santisteban & Mitrani, 2003). Single parents may have a live-in romantic partner who is not discussed during the intake assessment (Boyd-Franklin, 2003). Additionally, clinicians may need to incorporate a kinship network or members of a church family into therapy sessions or treatment planning (Boyd-Franklin, 2003). In short, a child's understanding of his or her family should determine who is invited to therapy sessions.

Having a large network of individuals associated with the child can be an asset to the family because their help can be enlisted in the therapeutic process. For example, family members can help to cue the child to use coping skills in the home environment or help to support a parent who is starting a new discipline program. However, there is also the possibility that important people in the child's life may have differing views about the utility of therapy and whether the child has a problem that needs to be addressed. This can be a challenge to the treatment process, but it is important for the therapist to understand who the child interacts with daily, how these individuals relate to one another, and how these family members may influence the child's functioning (Boyd-Franklin, 2003; Santisteban & Mitrani, 2003).

A change in the unique constellation of individuals within the family can influence treatment planning and treatment goals. For example, in family reunification cases, the clinician's goal will likely be to help the child adjust to a new living situation with biological parents after spending time in foster care. Stepfamilies may request help in establishing a behavior management program for a newly blended family of adolescents. A child whose parent has recently died may be referred for grief counseling. Foster parents or adoptive parents may request assistance in establishing a relationship with a new child in the home. In all of these examples, characteristics of the family system would influence treatment goals in concert with the presenting problems of the child. As such, it is crucial for clinicians to examine the clinic-referred child's family context.

The child's family is an important part of his or her world. One way to conceptualize this world is to consider the broader social context of the child's environment. According to Bronfenbrenner's (1979) ecological theory of development, each individual lives within multiple circles of influence. These circles of influence can be conceptualized as nesting structures, with larger structures incorporating smaller structures. Because children typically develop emotional and behavioral problems in the context of their environment (e.g., home, school, and neighborhood), clinicians must consider the broader context in these bidirectional circles to understand a child's current level of development and psychopathology.

Microsystems include the immediate settings in which the child operates. Typically, the child has daily contact with individuals and entities in these microsystems; however, CBTs targeting child behavioral and emotional problems often include no more than one or two microsystems from this ecological level. For example, most clinicians initially focus on the family microsystem, which can include the child's siblings, the child's caregivers, extended family living within the household, and the child. The child's psychopathology can be considered to exist within the family microsystem, as the problems related to the child's diagnosis likely affect the entire family in some way (Kazak, Rourke, & Crump, 2003). Subsystems important to the treatment process also exist within each microsystem, including the marital relationship, sibling relationships, and interactions between parents and the clinic-referred child. An infant or very young child may have a limited number of microsystems; however, older children can be members of several microsystems, including school, peers, after school programs, day care, the neighborhood, church, and even the mental health setting where the family seeks treatment. Thus, as clinicians, we attempt to establish a new microsystem for the child within which we attempt to make changes.

The next circle in the child's environment is the *mesosystem,* which includes interactions between different *microsystems.* For example, parents attending a parent-teacher conference, a family therapy session at the psychology clinic, the family's involvement in church activities, or an extended visit from out-of-town grandparents are all examples of mesosystem interactions. Understanding the way that entities within the mesosystem interact is crucial for treatment because the size and influence of the family may best be described here. It is also important for clinicians to consider how the interactions within the mesosystem impact the child and the child's presenting problem. For children living in isolated households, mesosystem interactions may be limited. In these situations, the lack of a support network for isolated caregivers may have a negative influence on the child (Wahler & Afton, 1980). Alternatively, some children may have an extended group of individuals from the community (e.g., church family, nonrelative kinship network in the neighborhood) who are considered family (Gushue, Greenan, & Brazaitis, 2005). The social support that can result from the community operating as family can serve as a buffer for children and has been reported as a strength for African American families in particular (Boyd-Franklin, 2003). However, clinicians should be cautious about overgeneralizations (e.g., some aspects of a large family network can be experienced as negative) and evaluate the unique aspects of the mesosystem for every child presenting for treatment (Santisteban & Mitrani, 2003).

The next structure in Bronfenbrenner's (1979) ecological theory is the *exosystem,* which includes a member of the child's microsystem (e.g., a parent or a sibling) and an outside organization (e.g., parent's workplace, sibling's peer group), but not the child directly. When considering the exosystem, the clinician is mindful of the indirect influence on the child of larger entities, such as the parent's workplace or the parent's social network. For example, a parent may experience a great deal of stress from his or her workplace and as a result have less patience with the clinic-referred child during home discipline situations. Helping the parent to understand the source of stress in his or her life and providing information on ways to manage this workplace stress would be important for the treatment of this family (Kazdin, 1995).

Finally, the *macrosystem* includes the influence of cultural values and attitudes of the family's social environment on the child. Clinicians typically do not include these entities as a focus of CBT, but in some situations it can be helpful to address them with the family. In our work with physically abusive families, it is often useful to discuss the current mainstream U.S. cultural views toward corporal punishment. Not surprisingly, we frequently find a discrepancy between the parent's view on corporal punishment and the stance of Child Protective Services (CPS). Ultimately, we have found it productive for the therapeutic process to discuss the potential end result of this macrosystem-level disparity for the child (i.e., a substantiated report of physical abuse). Robbins et al. (2003) described another macrosystem-level issue encountered in their work with Hispanic youth: the family's perception that immigrant parents are of lower status if they do not speak the dominant culture's language. Clearly, both of these macrosystem-level influences on family functioning and perceptions would be important to address in treatment.

Bronfenbrenner's (1979) theory can serve as a helpful rubric for clinicians to consider when conceptualizing a child's presenting problem and the role of the family and community in the development and maintenance of child symptoms. Indeed, it is important for the clinician to consider the context the child lives in, how these "circles of influence" may serve to support or challenge the child's functioning, how an intervention could best target the child's problems, and who should be included in this intervention. Throughout the rest of this chapter, we address various microsystem- and mesosystem-level issues that are important to consider during CBT treatment for children.

PARENT-CHILD MICROSYSTEM ISSUES

Within the parent-child microsystem, family characteristics may contribute to the development of the child's presenting problem (Goodman & Gotlib, 1999). For example, it has long been hypothesized that parents influence the symptomatology of children through social learning history (Patterson, 1982), and a growing literature describes the family factors related to child anxiety (Wood, McLeod, Sigman, Hwang, & Chu, 2003), disruptive behavior disorders (Kazdin, 1995), and child depression (Hammen & Rudolph, 2003).

Mash and Wolfe (2005) note that in some families, parents exhibit behaviors (e.g., argumentative or aggressive) that resemble those their children display. Parents typically serve as the most salient role model in their child's life; children observe how the parent behaves, expresses affect, and perceives the world. Children may later use the same thoughts, behavior, and affect to respond to their world. In fact, research suggests that problems such as child aggression and anxiety may actually be enhanced by interactions with the family (Barrett, Rapee, Dadds, & Ryan, 1996).

Although parent variables have been implicated in the development of child psychopathology, research also supports a bidirectional model in which the parent and child influence each other (Kendall & Ollendick, 2004; Kendall & Suveg, 2006). For example, a poor fit between child and parent temperament may result in a pattern of maladaptive interactions that culminates in poor child outcomes. In such instances, the fit between parent and child may contribute in meaningful ways to child psychopathology (e.g., Oppositional Defiant Disorder), and the interaction between the parent and child may need to be targeted in therapy.

Research on the relation between parent and child psychopathology has relied on mothers almost exclusively (Phares & Compas, 1992; Phares, Fields, Kamboukos, & Lopez, 2005; Phares, Lopez, Fields, Kamboukos, & Duhig, 2005; Silverstein & Phares, 1996; Zimmerman, Salem, & Notaro, 2000). However, the role of fathers in the development of psychopathology has received increased attention in recent years (for a review, see Connell & Goodman, 2002). Research suggests that fathers have a significant influence on their child's long-term adjustment and that a father's presence or absence within the family changes the quality of the mother-child relationship (Belsky, 1981; Hops et al., 1987; Lamb & Lewis, 2004). Although preliminary evidence suggests that paternal involvement can enhance treatment outcomes for children with Oppositional Defiant Disorder (e.g., Bagner & Eyberg, 2003; Webster-Stratton, 1985), this has yet to be empirically tested for most childhood disorders.

As discussed throughout the chapters in this volume, a number of empirically based treatments (EBTs) have been evaluated for a wide range of childhood disorders. However, randomized controlled studies have not been conducted to determine the optimal level of involvement for fathers, mothers, clinic-referred children, and additional microsystem-level individuals when utilizing EBTs. For example, Barmish and Kendall (2005) found that family-based treatment outcome studies for child anxiety typically included only parents and the identified child as participants, rather than additional family members. Barmish and Kendall also found substantial variability across studies in the description of the participating parents and the nature of their involvement in treatment. Because this lack of information regarding family and extrafamilial participation is consistent across treatments for other child disorders, the extent to which family or extended family should be involved in child-focused CBT is currently unknown.

SEEKING TREATMENT

Clinic Referral

Children typically do not refer themselves to treatment. Rather, some adult in the child's environment made an appraisal of the child's functioning and determined that something was "not right." Typically, teachers, physicians, CPS workers, or parents refer children for therapy (Weisz & Hawley, 1998). The role that these microsystem-level individuals play in the therapy process varies with the nature of the child's problem. For example, teachers may be included in treatment because the child exhibits classroom behavior problems that are inhibiting his or her ability to learn. Physicians and psychologists often work in tandem to address problems related to pediatric disorders such as asthma (McQuaid & Walders, 2003), diabetes (Wysocki, Greco, & Buckloh, 2003), or cancer (Vannatta & Gerhardt, 2003). Additionally, in-home case managers may be enlisted to help generalize behavioral family treatment to the home setting for CPS referrals (Chaffin et al., 2004). With the rare exception of self-referred adolescents who seek treatment independent of caregivers, parents typically decide whether the family (or any other outside individuals) will participate in therapy. On the whole, the circumstances surrounding child referrals appear quite distinct from that of adult clients, who often initiate and pay for their own treatment. Although there are several avenues that may lead to the initiation of therapeutic services for children, there are also many factors that may prevent a child from receiving intervention for a psychological problem.

Barriers to Service Delivery for Children

Sadly, many children who are in need of mental health services do not receive them. It has been estimated that as many as 50% of youth with emotional or behavioral disturbances do not receive treatment (Costello et al., 1998; Sturm, Ringel, & Andreyeva, 2003). Although more community-based services are available to families than ever before, certain factors may still preclude families from seeking treatment. Some aspects of this breakdown in mental health service delivery represent systemic problems such as a dearth of local child-oriented clinicians (Romer & McIntosh, 2005), long waiting lists, and the absence of state-funded clinics (Hoagwood, 2005). These systemic barriers are beyond the control of parents; however, several family-specific barriers can influence treatment delivery as well.

One family-specific barrier to help-seeking behavior is caregiver perceptions of treatment (McCabe, Yeh, Garland, Lau, & Chavez, 2005). Empirically based treatments have been criticized for their adherence to a manualized approach and the perceived lack of individual flexibility in their treatment process (Ollendick, 1999; Ollendick, King, & Chorpita, 2006). Additionally, parents may display resistance to treatment techniques and discontinue treatment if the therapeutic approach is not consistent with their expectations (e.g., inclusion of parent homework, an emphasis on parent-child interaction rather than individual play therapy with the child, psychological intervention in lieu of drug therapy, or psychological intervention that includes drug therapy). Finally, families may terminate services because of poor rapport with the clinician (McCabe et al., 2005).

Another barrier to treatment concerns the ability of the parent or guardian to identify providers in the community. Caregivers may not know where to seek treatment for their child's problems, and they may not be aware of the services that are available for their child. This problem may be worse for recent immigrant families or caregivers confronted with a language barrier (McCabe et al., 2005). Given the number and diversity of helping professionals who might be engaged (e.g., licensed mental health counselors, marriage and family therapists, social workers, clinical psychologists, psychiatrists, school psychologists, clergy, and pediatricians), parents may be confused about where to seek services. Contributing to this confusion is the large number of agencies typically involved in mental health service delivery for children (e.g., community mental health clinics, the education system, the judicial system, psychiatry and primary care clinics; Hoagwood, 2005).

Some parents suffer from mental health problems that prevent them from seeking treatment for their child. Indeed, parent psychopathology appears to have a strong link to child psychopathology. Behavioral genetic evidence suggests a high level of heritability for a number of childhood disorders, such as Attention-Deficit/Hyperactivity Disorder, Obsessive-Compulsive Disorder, and depression (Goodman & Gotlib, 1999). Any one of these disorders—and associated shared environmental factors—could function as a service delivery barrier.

Financial barriers may also prevent a child from receiving therapy. Practically speaking, a child may not have insurance coverage, or the child's caregivers may not have funds to pay for therapy (Hoagwood, 2005). Additionally, parents with a low socioeconomic status (SES) may not have transportation to attend sessions or a flexible work schedule that will allow them to bring their child to therapy on a regular basis. Finally, low-SES parents may be unable to attend therapy sessions if they have multiple children and no means of securing child care for them.

Caregivers may postpone seeking treatment for their children because they have difficulty overcoming their apprehension about the stigma related to obtaining psychological services (Penn et al., 2005). Indeed, families across socioeconomic and cultural strata may decide not to seek treatment because of concerns about stigma or labeling. Although parents may be concerned about negative outcomes associated with forgoing treatment for the child, they may be more concerned about negative stereotypes associated with seeking help from a "shrink." Some parents may even fear negative feedback concerning their parenting practices. Parental fears about whether treatment confidentiality will be maintained has been cited as a particularly salient barrier for ethnic minority families (McCabe et al., 2005).

Finally, parents referred to community clinics may have low motivation to seek services because they were referred by an outside agency (i.e., school, the judicial system, or physician) and do not perceive the need for therapy (Weisz & Hawley, 1998). There may even be disagreement between caregivers about whether treatment is needed. If parents are not in agreement concerning whether to seek help for a child's problem, payment for services may become especially controversial in the family. Given the significant costs (e.g., copayments, travel, lost wages, child care) associated with therapy—even when therapy is covered by insurance or is provided free of charge—it is easy to see how the decision to seek treatment may itself become a source of parental conflict. Motivational interviewing may be one way to address the problem of low parental motivation for treatment (Miller & Rollnick, 2002). The use of motivational interviewing techniques is widespread in the substance abuse literature (e.g., Ahluwalia et al., 2006; Madson & Campbell, 2006; McCambridge & Strang, 2004), but their use with families and children is currently in its early stages (Chaffin et al., 2004).

We have now highlighted many of the systemic and family barriers that can prevent caregivers from seeking mental health services for their child. Any one of these factors may contribute to the undertreatment of youth, and, in reality, these family-based barriers are likely to interact in ways that are currently unknown. Yet despite the aforementioned barriers, many families *do* seek treatment for children with emotional, behavioral, and social problems. We now highlight important factors related to the inclusion of the family in assessment and treatment.

ASSESSMENT

Prior to beginning treatment, a thorough assessment should be conducted to determine the severity and nature of the child's problems. Although there has been an emphasis on EBTs for some time (Lonigan, Elbert, & Johnson, 1998), researchers have just begun to focus attention on developing empirically based assessment practices with children (Mash & Hunsley, 2005). A thorough assessment is the hallmark of most CBTs for children and is critical to understanding the presenting problem and its context. Baseline assessment information provides the basis for case conceptualization, permitting a better understanding of the presenting problem, the specific symptoms the child exhibits, factors contributing to the onset and maintenance of the child's difficulties, and specific child and family strengths. In addition, the initial assessment provides critical information for subsequent treatment decisions. For example, an understanding of the symptomatology, skill deficits, and other factors that influence the child's functioning should enhance decisions about what intervention to use, who needs to be included in the intervention, and how to determine if therapeutic techniques are producing change. In general, the consensus of most research-oriented practitioners suggests that a multimethod, multimodal approach to assessment is a best practice. In practical terms, this means the assessor will gather information from multiple people, across multiple domains, and in multiple formats (Mash & Terdal, 1997). Mash and Terdal also note that, in addition to including a multimethod, multiple informant approach, a sound behavioral assessment should recognize the importance of contextual variables, be an ongoing process, and lead to the development of an effective intervention approach.

CLINICAL INTERVIEW

The clinical interview is an important first step in the pretreatment assessment process. An accurate diagnosis typically requires input from the family because children are often poor reporters of their own behavior problems (Edelbrook, Costello, Dulcan, Kalas, & Conover, 1985; Fallon & Schwab-Stone, 1994; Schwab-Stone, Fallon, Briggs, & Crowther, 1994). Typically, children are interviewed, but the extent to which their contributions are useful tends to be a function of their developmental level. Very young children (i.e., 3 or 4 years old) or a children with severe developmental impairments can participate in the clinical interview, but generally do so on a limited basis. Though most adolescents participate in a clinical interview, they may have only limited information about early developmental or educational history and may be unwilling or unable to report on their present difficulties accurately. For example, research conducted on the Diagnostic Interview for Schedule for Children—Revised indicated that child reports, particularly at younger ages, were less reliable than parent reports across diagnostic categories in the *Diagnostic and Statistical Manual of Mental Disorders* (*DSM*; Fallon & Schwab-Stone, 1994; Schwab-Stone et al., 1994). In particular, children were less reliable when reporting on severity and duration of symptoms, unobservable behaviors, and externalizing behaviors. Research does suggest that children's accuracy and reliability increases with age (Edelbrook et al., 1985; Fallon & Schwab-Stone, 1994). However, even in studies that show children capable of providing valid information about their own behaviors, researchers suggest using this information as a valuable complement to information gathered from caretakers (Arseneault, Kim-Cohen, Taylor, Caspi, & Moffitt, 2005).

There are a number of interview techniques and schedules available to clinicians. They vary from structured *DSM*-based diagnostic interviews to semi-structured approaches designed to provide a flexible guide for the interview process (Sattler, 2002, pp. 1–37). Though a detailed discussion of available interview approaches is beyond the scope of this chapter, Sattler (2002, pp. 1–37, 2002, pp. 38–64) provides a thorough review of both structured and semi-structured approaches as well as guidelines for conducting the interview process with children and families. We direct the interested reader to his volume on behavioral and clinical assessment of children (Sattler, 2002) for more information.

As discussed earlier, the family's behaviors, attitudes, and perceptions may play a critical role in the development and maintenance of the presenting problem. For this reason, we recommend that the clinician focus on aspects related to the antecedents, behavior, and consequences (ABCs) of the child's problem during the clinical interview. Assessing these aspects of the presenting problem is the foundation for behavioral assessment and provides much of the information needed for planning clinical interventions (Mash & Terdal, 1997). The ABCs of the presenting problem can be considered part of its context. Typically, family members provide many of the antecedents and consequences that maintain and influence child behavior. By systematically assessing these contextual factors, the clinician can determine the optimal targets for intervention. For example, if a child's problem behavior involves anxious avoidance of a feared stimulus, and child avoidance behaviors are routinely reinforced by parent attention or removal of the feared stimulus, then the clinician will likely need to alter the parent's behavior to effectively reduce child avoidance.

During the clinical interview, the clinician should also address how family members view the client, their understanding of the presenting problem, their perceived role in the maintenance of the presenting problem, and their treatment expectations (Lochman, Powell, Whidby, & Fitzgerald, 2006). For example, if various members of the family have discrepant views regarding the nature of the presenting problem or the way therapy should address the presenting problem, the clinician may need to address these discrepancies before commencing treatment. Parent biases and expectations may be important to address in the clinical interview because the clinician may need to alter parental expectations of change, as well as assumptions about the nature of therapy sessions and who will be included in treatment.

The clinical interview is likely to be the initial point of in-depth contact between the clinician and the family. This first contact facilitates the development of the therapeutic relationship (Santisteban et al., 1996). Clinicians should view the clinical interview as an opportunity, not only to gather information, but also to lay the foundation for the therapeutic alliance. During the clinician's first contact with the family, many positive aspects of family functioning will likely emerge. It is important to acknowledge these positive interactions, perceptions, and attributes to foster the expectation that therapy will consist of a balance of "what they are doing right" and "what they are doing wrong."

PARENT RATING SCALES

There are a number of measures that can be used in the assessment of clinic-referred families. Many clinicians value paper-and-pencil measures as a component of their intake assessments. They are easy to administer and can provide a great deal of information in a short amount of time relative to other assessment methods. Self-report measures are often completed by child clients, and there are various measures designed expressly for this purpose. Though child self-report measures are a critical component of any pretreatment analysis, they should not be the only source of assessment information. Parents, caregivers, and other important people considered part of the child's family should be asked to complete assessment measures as well. In fact, paper-and-pencil questionnaires may be the only feasible way to gather information from some people in the child's environment. For example, a child may spend a great deal of time with his or her grandparents. Though the grandparents are an integral part of the child's family and might provide invaluable information to the clinician, they may not be able to attend sessions or the pretreatment assessment. As such, the clinician could gather family information through questionnaires that he or she might not otherwise obtain.

One basic construct that is important to assess during an intake assessment is the parent's view of the severity and frequency of the child's behavioral, emotional, and social problems. A number of such parent-report measures are available for use, including the Behavior Assessment System for Children, second edition (BASC-2; Reynolds & Kamphaus, 2004), the Child Behavior Checklist (Achenbach, 1991), and the Eyberg Child Behavior Inventory (ECBI; Eyberg & Pincus, 1999). All three measures provide detailed information about a wide range of potential problem areas, and all are well-established, reliable, and valid measures. Understanding the parent's view of the child's difficulties can help guide treatment in a number of ways. Primarily, these measures serve as a source of information regarding parent perceptions of the normative or relative frequency of the child's behavior, provide targets for intervention, and offer a means to track treatment progress.

Some parent report measures also provide information concerning what problems are likely to be most important. For example, the ECBI allows parents to report about the frequency of a given behavior as well as whether they consider it a problem. A parent may report that fighting occurs only sometimes, yet is considered a problem, whereas dawdling at the table may occur always but is not considered a problem. Knowing the most common and most problematic behaviors can provide excellent guidance concerning treatment targets. In addition, information gathered from parent rating scales can reveal potential discrepancies between the parent's view of and expectations about the child's behavior and what should be expected given what is known about normative child development. Once a clinician knows where discrepancies exist, he or she can begin to address them in therapy.

Several rating scales are available to provide information regarding caregiver perceptions of other treatment-related constructs. For example, there are well-researched measures to address the caregiver's parenting-related stress (Parenting Stress Index; Abidin, 1995), perception of parent-child violence (Parent-Child Conflict Tactics Scale; Straus, Hamby, Finkelhor, Moore, & Runyan, 1998), and parenting locus of control (Parental Locus of Control; Campis, Lyman, & Prentice-Dunn, 1986). There are also promising measures designed to assess parents' tolerance of their child's behavior (Child Rearing Inventory; Brestan, Eyberg, Algina, Johnson, & Boggs, 2003), report of negative and positive parenting practices (Parenting Perceptions Inventory; Hazzard, Christensen, & Margolin, 1983), motivation for treatment (Readiness, Efficacy, Attributions, Defensiveness, and Importance Questionnaire; Brestan, Ondersma, Simpson, & Gurwitch, 1999; Butcher & Niec, 2006), and parenting stage of change (Parent Readiness for Change Scale; Butcher & Niec, 2006; Ondersma, 1999). Parents' level of stress, locus of control, and parent-child conflict have all been linked to treatment outcomes (Hagekull, Bohlin, & Hammarberg, 2001; Mouton & Tuma, 1988; Roberts, Joe, & Rowe-Hallbert, 1992; Romano, Tremblay, Boulerice, & Swisher, 2005). In addition, researchers suggest that expectations regarding child behavior are related to lowered rates of child maltreatment, reduced parenting stress, and better child outcomes (Reich, 2005). By assessing these parenting domains, the clinician will have a better understanding of contextual factors that may need to be addressed in the treatment process.

One factor that may need to be addressed prior to beginning a planned intervention is parent motivation to change. The concept of readiness for change, based on the stages of change model (McConnaughy, Prochaska, & Velicer, 1983), has previously been evaluated in relation to treatment outcomes for adults (Principe, Marci, & Glick, 2006). Two parent-focused measures of this construct, the Parent Readiness for Change Scale and the Readiness, Efficacy, Attributions, Defensiveness, and Importance Questionnaire, are currently available, and initial research has addressed their psychometric properties (Butcher & Niec, 2006). Preliminary research also indicates that parents' readiness for change may be related to treatment outcome and attrition from behavioral parent training (Butcher & Niec, 2006). The rationale for administering these measures during a pretreatment assessment is to evaluate whether clinic-referred parents are highly motivated for treatment. These highly motivated parents may require a very different initial treatment approach relative to parents who are looking for someone to "fix" their child (Lochman et al., 2006).

In all, paper-and-pencil measures are valuable sources of clinical assessment data because they provide information regarding caregiver perceptions about the child's problem. Once integrated, these data can be used to develop hypotheses about the nature of the child's problems and to determine if there are discrepant views about the child's functioning. Where discrepancies exist, authors have occasionally questioned the validity of behavior ratings, but lack of concordance is not necessarily a reflection of low accuracy or bias. Instead, the consensus appears to be that rating discrepancies are equally likely, if not more likely, to reflect cross-setting variation in child behavior (Christensen, Margolin, & Sullaway, 1992; De Los Reyes & Kazdin, 2005; Gross, Fogg, Garvey, & Julion, 2004; Lee, Elliott, & Barbour, 1994; Thuppal, Carlson, Sprafkin, & Gadow, 2002).

Behavior Observations Assessments that include multimethod, multiobserver data are considered to be a rich source of clinical information. Behavioral observations may add unique information to the evaluation process that enhances the social validity of the assessment (Sattler, 2002, pp. 83–119). Family observations conducted by the clinician can provide a crucial third-party perspective. Though rating scales are convenient, children may be poor historians, and parent self-report concerning parenting practices may be biased. Indeed, although it may not require much additional time to conduct a clinic-based family observation, these data may provide the clearest view of parent-child interactions, the power structure and alliances within the family, and family communication patterns (Nelson, Finch, & Ghee, 2006).

Observations can be unstructured ("Please play with your child for the next 10 minutes") or conducted using a structured sequence of tasks and a detailed coding system. Coding systems have been used for a number of child problem behaviors; however, they have been used most commonly with children with Oppositional Defiant Disorder, Attention-Deficit/Hyperactivity Disorder, and anxiety problems. For all of these diagnoses it is helpful to observe the child with at least one parent to evaluate their interactions. The clinician may also observe the dyad and look specifically for symptoms that will aid in differential diagnosis and treatment (e.g., the child refuses to stay in the room with the parent and will not return when the parent requests the child to do so). In the case of a noncompliant child, the clinician may wish to observe parent behaviors that evoke or otherwise contribute to problem behavior (e.g., issuing repeated commands before the child has the chance to comply and then failing to acknowledge when the child obeys some of the commands). Ultimately, the maladaptive child and parent behaviors observed during this assessment can serve as the basis for a treatment plan and can provide the family with concrete goals as they progress through treatment.

The Dyadic Parent-Child Interaction Coding System (DPICS) is one example of a well-validated behavioral coding system for parent-child observations (Eyberg, Nelson, Duke, & Boggs, 2005). It was developed to be used by clinicians and researchers engaged in the treatment and assessment of children with disruptive behavior disorders and their parents. The DPICS includes parent and child categories such as verbalizations (behavior descriptions, labeled praises), vocalizations (whining, yelling), and motor behavior (positive physical touch). It has strong evidence of interrater reliability, discriminative validity (Aragona & Eyberg, 1981; Bessmer, Brestan, & Eyberg, 2007; Borrego, Timmer, Urquiza, & Follette, 2004; Forster, Eyberg, & Burns, 1990), and convergent validity with measures of parenting stress and parent reports of child behavior problems (Bessmer et al., 2007). The DPICS has also been found to be sensitive to treatment changes (Boggs, McDiarmid, Eyberg, & Stevens, 2004; Eisenstadt, Eyberg, McNeil, Newcomb, & Funderburk, 1993; Eyberg et al., 2001;

McNeil, Capage, Bahl, & Blanc, 1999; Nixon, Sweeney, Erickson, & Touyz, 2003; Schuhmann, Foote, Eyberg, Boggs, & Algina, 1998; Webster-Stratton, Reid, & Hammond, 2004) and to discriminate between clinic-referred and nonreferred dyads for mothers and fathers (Bessmer et al., 2007; Brestan, Foote, & Eyberg, 2007).

One aspect of the DPICS that has been found to discriminate physically abusive and nonabusive parent-child dyads was the presence of laughter, with dyads having a history of physical abuse exhibiting significantly less laughter (Deskins, 2005). Consistent with this finding, Lochman et al. (2006) suggest conducting a behaviorally based parent-child interaction observation of conduct disordered children and their parents to assess the warmth and humor (or lack thereof) of the parent-child interaction. Although the research version of the DPICS is a fairly complex coding system to learn, the newly revised clinical coding system is quite user-friendly (Eyberg et al., 2005).

Behavior observations such as behavioral avoidance tasks (BATs) can provide valuable assessment data for anxiety referrals (Kendall & Suveg, 2006; Silverman & Ollendick, 2005). Those that include family members can provide the clinician with valuable information regarding the child's anxiety-related behavior, the processes maintaining the anxiety-related behavior, and potential targets for behavioral intervention at both the individual and the family level. The primary benefit of BATs is that they can be used to provide information about the child's behavior when contact with a feared stimulus is accomplished in an active (the child is moving toward the object) or passive (the object is moving toward the child) manner. Baldwin and Dadds (this volume) suggest that including parents in a BAT observation can allow the clinician to observe patterns of interaction and parent behaviors that reinforce the child's avoidance of a feared stimulus. One negative aspect of the BATs is that there are many different systems in existence, and, unlike coding systems for child disruptive behavior, there are relatively few normative data to support their use (Mori & Armendariz, 2001).

Assessment data obtained from behavioral observations has been cited as an important contribution to the treatment of family problems (Nichols & Schwartz, 2004). Observational data complement most CBTs because they provide a point of reference for evaluating problem severity at pretreatment, as well as a means of assessing response to treatment and treatment outcome.

SPECIAL ISSUES IN FAMILY ASSESSMENT: CHILD MALTREATMENT

Additional measures and methods may be needed in the assessment of families with a history of suspected or indicated child maltreatment. By its very nature, child maltreatment involves a maladaptive dyadic interaction between a parent and one or more children in a family.

As such, an assessment for potential child maltreatment requires the involvement of the family. In these cases, the caretaker suspected of abuse will be a primary target of assessment and intervention rather than just an ancillary source of information and support for the child client.

According to Gershater-Molko, Lutzker, and Sherman (2003), a comprehensive assessment for child maltreatment should take a developmental-ecological approach, where child maltreatment is seen as occurring in the larger developmental, familial, and social context in which it occurs rather than just as a single incident between a parent and a child (Fantuzzo, McDermott, & Lutz, 1999; Stockhammer, Salzinger, Feldman, Mojica, & Primavera, 2001; Wolfe & McEachran, 1997). When assessing child maltreatment, the clinician needs to assess various aspects of both the child's and the parent's functioning and psychological adjustment, which can be done using standard assessment techniques that a clinician would use in any family assessment (e.g., structured diagnostic interviews, self-report forms such as the BASC or ECBI, and behavioral observations such as the DPICS). In addition, the clinician should assess family functioning. With regard to familial and social functioning, the most frequently cited targets for assessment are family stressors, marital and relationship functioning, social support, and living environment (Gershater-Molko & Lutzker, 1999; Hansen & MacMillan, 1990; Hansen, Sedlar, & Warner-Rogers, 1999; Wolfe & McEachran, 1997). Self-report measures such as the Conflict Tactics Scale-R, Parenting Stress Index, and the Social Support Questionnaire (Sarason, Levine, Basham, & Sarason, 1983) can provide the clinician with critical information regarding these constructs.

The Child Abuse Potential Inventory (CAP; Milner, 1986) is a well-researched, reliable, and valid measure used to differentiate families with a potential for physical child abuse from families without such risk (Feindler, Rathus, & Silver, 2003). However, due to the chance of both false-positive and false-negative identifications, the CAP should be used to complement other assessment measures rather than as the sole basis for classification (Milner, 1986; Milner & Murphy, 1995), although results from research regarding the use of the CAP as a measure of treatment change indicate that its use in this manner is questionable (Chaffin & Valle, 2003).

Assessment as an Ongoing Process

Most CBTs for child behavioral, emotional, and social problems are heavily assessment driven. As discussed previously, the initial assessment provides the clinician with information critical to case conceptualization and treatment planning. However, assessment in clinical practice with children and families should be seen as an ongoing process (Mash & Terdal, 1997). For this reason, clinicians should be prepared to collect assessment measures at intake and at regular intervals throughout treatment. In child- and family-targeted CBTs, assessment techniques should be employed to track treatment progress and guide the course of the intervention. For example, in treating children with externalizing disorders, we administer a measure of child behavior problems (the ECBI) to parents on a weekly basis. This allows us to track changes in parent perceptions of child behavior at each session. We can also track specific behaviors to determine when certain problem behaviors remit or when new problem behaviors appear. We also use the information gathered from parent report instruments and diagnostic checklists as collateral information when making decisions regarding readiness for treatment termination. Each clinician will need to determine which assessment techniques and measures are best suited to his or her particular client and family needs. Regardless of the methods and instruments used, assessment should be employed before, during, and upon completion of treatment.

INDIVIDUAL TREATMENT

Most of the EBTs for childhood and adolescent disorders are rooted in social learning theory and the cognitive-behavioral perspective. A common component across treatment protocols for child depression, anxiety, eating disorders, aggression, inattention and hyperactivity, and disruptive behavior is the inclusion of caregivers in the therapy process. It has been hypothesized that including family members in therapy is important for generalization of treatment effects to the home environment and improving treatment outcome through reinforcement and practice of skills. There is also research to support the notion that including parents in treatment is beneficial for the maintenance of treatment gains over time (Dadds, Heard, & Rapee, 1992; Eyberg, Edwards, Boggs, & Foote, 1998).

The state of EBTs for children has evolved since the *Journal of Clinical Child Psychology*'s special issue on "Empirically Supported Psychosocial Interventions for Children" was published in 1998 (Lonigan, Elbert, & Johnson, 1998). At that time, there were relatively few EBTs with a family focus available for child depression, adolescent depression, or child anxiety. In the area of child disruptive behavior disorders and Attention-Deficit/Hyperactivity Disorder, however, several parent-training protocols were found to have strong empirical support. Review of the current literature reveals that treatment outcome research has continued at a high rate since publication of the 1998 special issue, and many EBTs for children now include some aspect of family involvement (Kazdin & Weisz, 2003). It is beyond the scope of this chapter to review all of the EBTs for child psychopathology, but the interested reader has a number of resources and texts available for reference. In addition to this volume, which contains comprehensive chapters on all of the major childhood disorders, texts by Christophersen and Mortweet (2001) and Kazdin and Weisz should be considered excellent resources on the subject of empirically based child and adolescent treatments.

As of this writing, the update to the *Journal of Clinical Child Psychology*'s 1998 special issue is forthcoming (Silverman, 2006). Additionally, the interested reader is directed to the American Psychological Association's Division 53 web site (www.clinicalchildpsychology.org). This web site on EBTs is maintained by the Society of Clinical Child and Adolescent Psychology and contains a focus on the integration of research and practice (Silverman, 2006).

CONFIDENTIALITY WITH CHILDREN AND FAMILIES

Regardless of the type of presenting problem or the particular EBT chosen to address child symptomatology, providing specific guidelines to the family regarding confidentiality at the onset of treatment is crucial (American Psychological Association [APA], 2002; Health Insurance Portability and Accountability Act, 1996; Rae & Fournier, 1999). Confidentiality issues raised in clinical work with families and children are more complicated than for adults (Rae & Fournier, 1999). Children are typically not conferred the privilege of confidential communication in the context of therapy until they reach adolescence. Because state guidelines vary with regard to the age at which children gain the privilege of confidentiality, clinicians need to consult state laws and explain the limits to confidentiality to every child and parent seeking treatment. With very young children, and in cases where the parents are fully integrated into treatment, discussions about confidentiality may be relatively straightforward. However, when a clinician is working primarily with an older child, it is important to carefully explain the nature of confidentiality and any limits to it in language that the child and family can readily understand.

Some parents may accept child-clinician confidentiality even when the child is young and the clinician is not legally obligated to protect confidentiality. In other cases, parents may have great difficulty with the concept of client-therapist confidentiality and may demand detailed information about the content of therapy sessions involving the child. For example, confidentiality in sessions may become an especially important therapy issue when working with an enmeshed family where privacy rights are frequently tested and debated. In these situations, issues of confidentiality and family involvement must be treated delicately (Rae & Fournier, 1999).

Issues of confidentiality become especially important when working with adolescent clients as they may have difficulty establishing rapport with the therapist without an assurance of confidentiality (Rae & Fournier, 1999). As mentioned earlier, how clinicians handle confidentiality may be determined largely by the state in which they are practicing. For example, in the authors' practicing state of Alabama, children have the same rights to confidentiality as adults once they reach the age of 14. Thus, when we see a 14-year-old in therapy, we explain to the family that any information the adolescent reveals in therapy cannot be divulged without the client's permission. In fact, we need a release of information from the adolescent to call the adolescent's home and speak to his or her parent. This sometimes causes difficulty for parents, who may believe they are entitled to know what is going on in therapy, particularly as they typically pay for clinical services.

CONSENT FOR TREATMENT

Children and parents must also consent for treatment. With minor children, it is usually the guardian who must do so, as children are unable to legally consent to or refuse therapeutic services (Rae & Fournier, 1999). One of the most important ethical principles of therapy is that entering into services should be voluntary (APA, 2002; Rae & Fournier, 1999). Obviously, this will not always be the case when working with families, because children may be enrolled in treatment despite their wishes. Though not legally obligated to do so, we recommend that therapists gain child assent for services whenever possible, which is consistent with APA ethical guidelines. If a child is old enough to understand the process, we always ask permission to work with him or her and the family. In this way, we hope to foster a sense of involvement and let the child know that his or her views are important.

As a practical matter, when working with adolescents, both parents and adolescents must provide consent for treatment. Adolescents cannot be forced to participate in or attend therapy if they do not want to do so, and adolescents are sometimes inclined to view this situation as a way of gaining the upper hand, so to speak. Care must be taken to ensure that the adolescent's rights are protected without damaging potential alliances between the therapist and the adolescent or the family. In addition, families who are court-ordered for treatment or referred by a CPS caseworker present a unique challenge with regard to consent. Though informed consent is critical to ethical practice, families who are court-ordered for services may not be able legally to refuse to seek treatment. Even in these cases, however, it is generally recognized that a family cannot be forced to participate in any specific service, and if requested, the therapist should help the family find alternative sources of treatment. Explaining the family's rights at the outset may help assuage concerns with respect to involuntary services.

DEVELOPMENTAL CONSIDERATIONS

The role of the family in treatment often varies depending on the child's age, developmental stage, and presenting problem. As such, clinicians should be prepared to use developmentally sensitive techniques when engaging families in treatment.

Although it has been hypothesized that matching interventions to child or adolescent developmental level can result in more efficacious treatment outcomes for families, further research in this area is needed (Holmbeck, O'Mahar, Abad, Colder, & Updegrove, 2006). A general guideline for clinicians until more research is available would be to employ techniques that correspond with the child's (and parents'!) cognitive, social, emotional, and behavioral level. We recommend including an IQ screener (for older children, adolescents, and adults) and a test of receptive language (for young children) in the intake assessment to help determine the general cognitive development of the clinic-referred family.

Developmentally, young children lack the cognitive ability to independently implement changes in their environment. Very young children and children with developmental delays spend most of their time in the family context. For these reasons, parents may be present during most therapy sessions, or they may attend a concurrent session with a different therapist. Developmental milestones of concern for young children in treatment include learning to accept "no," compliance to parental directives, behavioral self-control, speech development, and toileting. Examples of EBTs with a high level of parent involvement and orientation toward these early developmental milestones include Eyberg's parent child interaction therapy (PCIT; Brinkmeyer & Eyberg, 2003; Hembree-Kigin & McNeil, 1995) and Webster-Stratton's The Incredible Years program (Webster-Stratton, 1992; Webster-Stratton & Reid, 2003).

Families of older children with emotional and/or behavioral problems may have less involvement in treatment but still be involved in an indirect manner. In these cases, older children would likely spend time in individual therapy learning skills (e.g., anger management or anxiety management skills) that they will implement themselves. Therapy sessions will likely target problems that the child encounters with developmental milestones such as relationships with peers and family, emotion regulation, participating in extracurricular activities, completion of chores, and academic functioning. Parents may be involved in a portion of the sessions to learn the coping skills assigned for homework practice. One example of a treatment oriented toward older children is Kendall's coping cat program (Kendall, 1992) in which parents are involved in a supportive role and meet with the therapist during the third session to work on treatment goals (Kendall & Suveg, 2006).

Treatments for adolescents typically require a different type of family involvement than for younger children. As mentioned previously, a parent's involvement in therapy with an adolescent will vary as a function of the parent's own willingness to participate in therapy and the adolescent's decision regarding his or her right to confidentiality within the therapeutic relationship. Notably, there is some research to suggest that relative to younger children, adolescents with anxiety problems have improved treatment outcomes when parents are *not* involved in their treatment (Barmish & Kendall, 2005). Because adolescents belong to more microsystems than younger children, their therapy typically involves the social contexts of school, work, and peers—in addition to the family. Developmental tasks that are especially important for adolescent adjustment include constructs such as social problem-solving skills, communication skills, and the development of autonomy.

Despite the frequency of severe psychopathology in adolescence, there are few EBTs to choose from for this developmental period. Unfortunately, treatment for adolescent psychological problems such as eating disorders and suicide currently lack empirical support, and the optimal inclusion of families in these treatments is unknown (Spirito & Esposito-Smythers, 2006; Weisz & Hawley, 2002; Wilfley, Passi, Cooperberg, & Stein,

2006). There are, however, a number of family-based EBTs for the treatment of adolescent substance abuse (for a review, see Lochman & van den Steenhoven, 2002).

CULTURAL CONSIDERATIONS

The United States is becoming increasingly more culturally diverse. It is predicted that by the year 2050, half of the U.S. population will consist of people of color (Hall, 1997). Given this prediction, the number of children from diverse racial and ethnic backgrounds presenting for psychological treatment will likely increase accordingly.

To truly consider a child's cultural framework, each "individual needs to be understood in the context of the family, and . . . the family in turn needs to be understood in the context of the culture" (Szapocznik & Kurtines, 1993, p. 400). It is important, then, for clinicians to have an awareness of the cultural variables that shape all families who seek psychological treatment. Typically, parents and children are shaped by multiple cultural forces, which, at a minimum, will include the family culture and the mainstream U.S. culture. Among immigrant families, racial and ethnic minority families, and biracial families, parents and children can be influenced by very different cultural forces as a function of the unique context (both time and place) in which these individuals have lived (Szapocznik & Kurtines, 1993). Ultimately, a complex clinical picture can emerge when intergenerational conflict along acculturation lines, disparities in cultural loyalties, and child psychopathology co-occur.

The ways culture influences treatment outcome are complex and, as yet, ill defined. Modification of the current child-focused EBTs available for clinical practice may be needed to treat culturally diverse families effectively. However, tailoring a family-based EBT must be done in a theoretically relevant and consistent way, and there are currently very few empirical studies evaluating the use of culturally modified EBTs (Christophersen & Mortweet, 2001). One promising exception is the Guiando a Ninos Activos (Guiding Active Children [GANA]) program, a treatment protocol adapted from PCIT for the treatment of Mexican American families with oppositional children. McCabe and colleagues (2005) provided a detailed description of the process by which they adapted PCIT for their population. However, because the results of this randomized study are pending, it is unclear whether the adaptations made to PCIT will result in significantly improved treatment outcomes.

For some cultural groups, culturally modified EBTs may have the same effectiveness as mainstream EBTs. However, some families may feel more comfortable with the therapy process of culturally modified EBTs—even if the treatment outcome is not significantly better. The problem is that we do not know which treatment modifications need to be made for which cultural groups. To complicate matters further, preliminary research suggests that as successive generations of families from specific cultural groups become more acculturated to the mainstream U.S. culture (or more bicultural in attitudes and functioning), different therapeutic techniques may be more effective than others (Santisteban et al., 1996). Research addressing this question will need to target factors related to acculturation and cultural worldview (e.g., collectivist versus individualist) as potential mediators of EBT effectiveness with different cultural groups.

Notably, one well-researched treatment approach exists for Hispanic youth. Brief strategic family therapy (BSFT) is an EBT that was developed by the University of Miami's Center for Family Studies (Robbins et al., 2003). The approach is unique in that it was developed for use with a specific minority cultural group as opposed to being a cultural modification of an existing EBT. The BSFT model was originally developed to provide a culturally appropriate treatment for behavior-disordered Hispanic youth; however, it has also been used with African American youth (Santisteban et al., 1997). As the name would imply, the focus of BSFT is on the entire family, with theoretical underpinnings stemming from the structural (Minuchin, 1974) and strategic (Haley, 1963) family therapy orientations. Although technically not a CBT, we have included the BSFT model here to serve as an example of a culturally sound treatment with ample empirical evidence to support its efficacy with youth ages 6 to 18 (Santisteban et al., 1997; Szapocznik, Rio, Murray, & Cohen, 1989).

Although the interface between family psychology and cross-cultural psychology is relatively new (Szapocznik & Kurtines, 1993), there are a few variables for clinicians to be mindful of when working with culturally diverse families. First, consistent with the APA (2002) Code of Ethics, in the absence of EBTs for multicultural groups, clinicians should use their clinical judgment to provide families with the most theoretically sound and culturally consistent intervention available. Second, clinicians need to be sensitive to the possibility that culture and demographics can play an important role in a child's definition of family—and who should be involved in the treatment process (Boyd-Franklin, 2003). Third, it will be important to assess the prevailing cultural norms for child internalizing and externalizing behavior from these family members (Christophersen & Mortweet, 2001). Fourth, among some cultures and minority ethnic groups there is often an attitude of keeping family business private. As a result, some families may prefer group therapy to individual therapy. Several researchers have found that immigrant families for whom English is a second language were more likely to participate in therapy if they were given the chance to enroll in group therapy rather than individual therapy (Cunningham, Bremner, & Boyle, 1995; Taylor & Biglan, 1998). Families from culturally diverse backgrounds, particularly those who are not native to the United States, may be better served by a group modality, particularly if such therapy is offered in the community where they live (Cunningham et al., 1995; Kazdin, 1997).

To work effectively with families, we recommend that clinicians strive to understand the unique belongingness that each family member will bring to therapy. Knowing a family's cultural background may aid in the conceptualization of the family problem and inform treatment format. However, racial and ethnic background should not be used as a shortcut to understanding the family, as perceptions within the family regarding the child's problem and the role of treatment may vary considerably. We also suggest that clinicians and clinical researchers continue to increase their multicultural competency by attending conference workshops and reading material related to this topic (e.g., Constantine & Sue, 2005).

FAMILY INVOLVEMENT IN TREATMENT

Often the therapist must choose the level of involvement that family members will have in the treatment process. The role of the family in treatment will likely depend on the therapist's orientation, the theoretical model used to treat the child, and the therapist's explanation to the family regarding their future role in the treatment. Kendall (2006) suggests that when delivering CBTs for children, child therapists should adopt the posture of serving as a coach to the child and family presenting for treatment. Indeed, a primary feature of CBT includes didactic training in needed skills (e.g., relaxation training for anxiety), followed by practice of those skills between therapy sessions. Adult clients and some adolescent clients are able to complete therapeutic tasks on their own. However, most children will need help to do so. In the authors' experience with behavior-disordered children, we often tell our clients' parents that they will be the most important agents of change and that we are there to help them become therapists for their children. Thus, from a CBT perspective, the therapist will likely need significant family involvement to effect change.

Parent involvement may change over the course of treatment. Indeed, Kendall (2006) makes the point that the role of parents in therapy can change over the weeks and months of therapy. It is possible, even, for a parent's role to change within a single session, depending on the subject matter covered. For example, it is quite common for a therapist to serve as a consultant for a learning disabilities case. In this role, the therapist may serve as an advocate for the family by attending meetings on the child's individual education plan or serving as a liaison between the family and the school. However, the parent may be the consultant to the therapist by providing information and opinions regarding the severity of the child's problem. At other points, the therapist and parent may engage in a working collaboration by developing treatment plans and working on the common goal of improving outcomes for the child in treatment. In this role, the therapist provides structure, guidance, and expertise to help the parent manage the child's behavior, but the parent assumes primary responsibility for change.

Finally, a parent may be a co-client with the child in therapy. This is quite common in cases when a child is referred for the treatment of a problem that is influenced by the parent's behavior. In such cases, the clinician's treatment goals may differ from the caregiver's expectations. Parents may expect to drop off their child, much like a car needing an oil change, but instead find themselves the focus of a parent-based therapy. If the parent prefers to leave the child with the therapist so that they can "talk about it" individually, the use of CBT techniques may be met with resistance. This could be damaging to the therapeutic relationship and may interfere with effective treatment. As most clinicians with a behavioral focus will attest, providing talk therapy alone is unlikely to produce change in many children's presenting problems. Rather, the parent must be involved in the therapy process itself to formulate a behavioral plan to address the presenting problem. Research supports this view in that family involvement in treatment has been found to produce better results than treating a child alone across a variety of child presenting problems (Bagner & Eyberg, 2003; Barmish & Kendall, 2005; Barrett, Dadds, & Rapee, 1996; Lochman et al., 2006).

Parents may also be co-clients in cases where they have deficits in the very skills the therapist is trying to teach the child. This can occur when the child's presenting problem mirrors some aspect of his or her parent. Because some parents are unaware of their role in the maintenance and development of problem behavior, psychoeducation could be incorporated into the treatment plan to help parents understand their role in the presenting problem. If the clinic-referred child is modeling dysfunctional parental behavior, the clinician may need to address parent behaviors in treatment as well. For example, a child who exhibits difficulties with anger control may have a parent with problems in the same domain (Leve, Kim, & Pears, 2005; Romano et al., 2005). Research indicates that parents of children who have aggressive behavior problems may have difficulties with social problem solving and cognitive distortions (Lochman et al., 2006). In these situations, Nelson et al. (2006) recommend that the therapist involve the aggressive parent in treatment by teaching him or her techniques that will need to be taught to the originally identified patient: the child. After teaching the aggressive parent the anger management skills needed to reduce the problem behavior, therapists can then educate the child about aggression: how it is triggered, the body's typical responses to provocation, and effective coping techniques.

SKILL ACQUISITION

When parents and other family members are involved in treatment, they are able to support the child's acquisition of skills. Because the social environment plays such a key role in shaping child behavior, clinicians must attempt to effect change in as many child microsystems as possible if therapeutic gains are to continue after the end of services. Perhaps no context is more salient for a child than the parent-child relationship.

Parents may need to learn the same skills as their children, not just because they lack the skills themselves, but also because they serve as the context in which the child client spends the majority of his or her time. Lochman et al. (2006) use the terms "cold" and "hot" processing to describe the ways skill acquisition can take place. Cold processing occurs when the child and parent are taught skills in session, and then goals are set with regard to those skills for the coming week. This model of teaching skills and then asking children and parents to practice those skills together is a common and useful therapeutic approach. Therapists typically see child clients for only 50 minutes each week. Although therapists have the opportunity to model coping skills and provide in vivo structuring to interpersonal interactions in session, parents are with their children many hours each day. Therefore, they can prove much more effective teachers of skills.

Most important, parents may have more opportunities to practice skills with their children in highly salient situations. Such situations provide for hot processing of skills, whereby instruction and practice take place in vivo (Lochman et al., 2006). Consider, for example, a child who is in treatment due to her lack of social skills. Her parents will have opportunities to supervise her in social settings playing with other children. They can then coach her in the use of appropriate skills taught in therapy. As she applies those skills to real-world situations in the moment, she is more likely to retain the very information her therapist would like her to know. Similarly, it may be much easier for a child to walk through steps for relaxation as a coping response to anger when he is in the therapy room and is not actively angry. However, when he goes home and gets into a fight with a sibling, he may have difficulty remembering and enacting those steps in the moment. If his parents were included in therapy sessions, they could assist him in implementing his newly learned skills when they are most needed.

Therapists can also work to provide opportunities for hot processing during therapy sessions. For example, the family could replay a problematic interaction in session with the clinician coaching the skills needed to address the problem. Clinicians are unlikely to have such opportunities for hot processing and in vivo learning for their child clients if they do not involve the child's family in treatment. Therefore, for many of the problems child clients face, it is best to include family members in therapy.

Family involvement in the treatment process is not limited to time spent in sessions. Due to the importance of hot processing opportunities, and the large amount of time most parents are with their children, homework is often a crucial part of CBT for children. Homework may include actual practice of skills taught in therapy, as with training for social, coping, problem-solving, and anger management skills. It may also include implementing therapeutic interventions, as with token economies or behavior charts. Regardless of the form it takes, homework is just that: work that parents do with their children at home. In this way, parents can serve as an extension of the therapist, helping the child to complete therapeutic activities and to practice skills outside of the therapy session. In our work with behavior disordered children, we often tell the parents that they are going to become therapists for their children, emphasizing their role as the vehicle of change in their children's lives.

It should be noted that the term "homework" may be aversive to some parents. They may associate homework with school, which may have negative connotations, especially for parents who had difficulties in school themselves. To be sensitive to the needs of the client, therapists may need to adjust their terminology accordingly. Some parents may find terms such as "weekly practice" more palatable, and so they may be more likely to comply with assignments. The same can be said for clinic-referred children, particularly those whose difficulties are school-related. Thus, clinicians should choose terminology wisely and with careful thought about client's needs and worldview.

In this section, we have outlined several ways that families may be involved in individual CBT. Individual therapy is costly, however, and some families may not be able to afford individual sessions with a psychologist. Attending a group program may be more cost-effective for them. In other situations, parents who are concerned about the stigma of receiving psychological intervention may feel more comfortable in a group situation. Next, we address the role of family in group treatments targeting emotional, behavioral, and social problems of childhood.

GROUP TREATMENT

Some CBTs can be offered either in an individual family or a group format. Often the children are seen in one group while parents participate in a concurrent group. In Kazdin and Weisz's (2003) compendium on EBTs for children, three treatment programs are described that involve seeing children and families in a group format. The adolescent coping with depression program (Clarke, DeBar, & Lewinsohn, 2003) includes concurrent groups for adolescents and parents. Adolescents participate in group therapy twice weekly for 8 weeks, while parents meet once weekly in a parallel group. Some sessions are conducted with parents and adolescents together to allow for practice of family problem-solving skills. Webster-Stratton's Incredible Years program involves therapist-administered group sessions for parents using videotaped vignettes (Webster-Stratton & Reid, 2003). Lochman, Barry, and Pardini's (2003) anger coping and coping power program includes parallel parent and child groups in which children learn coping and anger management skills while their parents are taught strategies for supporting the skills their children are learning.

Overall, research comparing group and individual treatments has found little to no difference in effectiveness between group and individual therapy. Group and individual treatments produce significantly better results than control groups, and both produce results similar to each other (for reviews, see McRoberts, Burlingame, & Hoag, 1998; Tillitski, 1990). Because there are a number of advantages and disadvantages to providing intervention in a group format, clinicians need to determine the best intervention modality for each unique family.

Researchers who favor the group format assert that it provides social support for families, provides the opportunity for seeing common experiences among group members (universality), results in a heightened sense of mastery due to group problem solving, and allows for a more cost-effective method of treatment delivery (Manassis et al., 2002). Others assert that many of these group benefits (i.e., mastery and universality) are not exclusive to the group format but also occur in individual treatment, albeit through different means (Kivlighan & Kivlighan, 2004). In addition, they argue that an individual approach allows therapists to tailor treatment to family needs. For example, focusing time on helping a parent who is depressed or addressing marital stressors would be more difficult in a group format of parent training, where the focus often is on helping a group of parents with behavior management issues and not on an individual parent's needs (Taylor & Biglan, 1998). Unfortunately, we know very little about the truth of such assertions and have little to no empirical data on which to base conclusions.

Different process routes could impact the effects of group and individual therapy for a specific child or family. When averaged across clients, there may be no differences between the two modalities. However, certain client, treatment, or therapist characteristics might differentially impact outcomes, or even adherence to treatment and treatment completion, for specific clients. For example, Manassis et al. (2002) found that socially anxious children made more treatment gains in individual therapy than in group therapy when the focus of treatment was on something other than social anxiety. In addition, there was a trend for greater improvement of depressive symptoms in individual than in group therapy. It is possible that individual therapy produces better outcomes than group therapy for depressed or socially anxious clients, particularly when these symptoms are not the primary aim of treatment.

Families with greater parent psychopathology or marital discord or more family stressors or child behavior problems have poorer treatment outcomes in general than do families without such problems. It is possible that such families might benefit from individual therapy, where the therapist would have more flexibility to focus on issues other than child behavior problems (Taylor & Biglan, 1998). However, families experiencing these stressors may have less time and monetary resources to avail themselves of multiple therapy services. Therefore, family resources (e.g., time, money) would have to be weighed against family needs for treatment to come to the best decision for a given family.

Parents with low social support and single parents tend to experience fewer gains with regard to child conduct problems than do parents with high social support or parents who have a partner at home (Taylor & Biglan, 1998). Group therapy for parents who are single and lack social support may be beneficial in that a social support network is readily available in fellow group members. Indeed, a preliminary case study reported that families involved in group PCIT developed a contact network whereby they called each other to check on progress, provide support, and problem-solve (Niec, Hemme, Yopp, & Brestan, 2005). Notably, these families created their phone buddy system without prompting from their therapists.

Although group treatment may be a good initial option for some isolated families, special attention should be given to at-risk and traditionally underserved populations, as many of the variables discussed earlier (single parents, parental dysfunction, lack of social support, low SES, high levels of child dysfunction) put families at risk for continuing and escalating problems that may require individual attention following group treatment.

ENDING SERVICES

Treatment services for children and families end for a variety of reasons. Treatment termination ideally takes place once treatment goals have been met. Unfortunately, therapy services are frequently terminated prematurely. In fact, attrition rates in therapy are often quite high. As many as 40% to 60% of child, adolescent, and family therapy clients drop out of services, often against the advice of their clinician (Kazdin, 2004). Many clients fail to return after the initial intake visit, and often dropout occurs before the third session. The issue may be even more complicated with child clients because most of the factors related to attrition are unrelated to the child client and outside of his or her control.

The reasons for attrition are likely as diverse and varied as the families we serve. Research shows that economically disadvantaged, single-parent, and socially isolated families tend to have poorer outcomes in treatment and higher attrition rates than families without these characteristics. Stress, a lack of support, a history of mistrust of the mental health field, lack of resources to pay for services, and a dearth of services in their communities may all be contributing factors (Snell-Johns, Mendez, & Smith, 2004).

Many research studies have included commonsense ways to keep families in treatment (see Snell-Johns et al., 2004, for a review). For example, according to Snell-Johns and colleagues, many effective treatments for children and families have offered child care, transportation, and low- or no-cost services to families in an effort to address issues such as economic disadvantage and lack of social support. In a group parent training program conducted by the present authors, we provided families with child care for all of their children, transportation if needed, dinner for the family, and free services in an effort to increase accessibility. Although these approaches have been included in well-researched treatments, their influence on attrition has not been studied.

Such is the case with many of the approaches used to address attrition. For example, Snell-Johns and colleagues (2004) note that providing in-home services may be a good way to help a family that has difficulty attending sessions in a clinic. A number of programs have provided such services very effectively, and with better results than treatment as usual. However, Snell-Johns et al. point out that these programs are typically very comprehensive, and we still do not know enough about the specific effects of providing services in the home relative to the effects of all other program characteristics.

One approach to reducing attrition that has been well-studied is the use of telephone contact (see Snell-Johns et al., 2004, for a review). A number of studies have demonstrated that simply calling a family prior to their first visit, or between weekly visits, increases the likelihood that the family will attend the next session and will complete therapy. Szapocznik et al. (1988) found that calling the family prior to their first visit to problem-solve any existing issues that might make it difficult for them to attend the first session significantly increased attendance and decreased attrition. Although there are many strategies currently in use to keep families in treatment, something as simple as a telephone call may be the best way to maintain a therapeutic connection with families.

As clinicians, we need to find the approach(es) that work best for each family. This requires communicating with parents about any obstacles they see to their completing therapy. We have to be willing to work with families to overcome barriers, let them know that we are genuinely concerned about addressing such issues, and do what we can to keep that thread of connection. It also requires flexibility and a willingness to think outside the box. As we have discovered in our own clinical experience, sometimes it might even require a very large box of corn dogs and a few gallons of Kool-Aid!

For those families who stay in therapy, how does the clinician determine the optimal time to terminate services? The APA (2002) Ethics Code states that therapy services should be terminated when the client no longer needs services, is not likely to benefit further, or is being harmed by services. Deciding when one of these situations applies is not necessarily an easy matter. The decision to terminate services will likely be based on a number of factors, including attainment of treatment goals, current child and family symptomatology, and whether the child meets the diagnostic criteria for a disorder. As discussed in previous sections, CBTs are assessment-driven. Assessment during the course of treatment allows the clinician to track family progress and may help to determine when treatment termination may be warranted. Posttreatment assessment helps to establish when treatment goals have been met and when the presenting problem has remitted. For example, PCIT carries with it specific mastery criteria for continuing from one phase of treatment to another and for terminating therapy (Eyberg et al., 2005; Hembree-Kigin & McNeil, 1995). Sessions of PCIT continue until parents and children have met those goals. Mash (1998) concludes that it is important to assess not only quantitative symptom reduction, but also the magnitude and quality of symptom reduction, improvements in functioning, and subjective feelings of satisfaction with treatment outcomes. Ideally, the decision to terminate treatment should be a collaborative one made between the clinician and family.

The therapist should take the family's level of satisfaction with outcomes into account during the decision-making process. Assessing treatment satisfaction provides a measure of social validity for a given intervention (Dudley, Melvin, Williams, Tonge, & King, 2005; Mash & Terdal, 1997). There are formal means of assessing treatment satisfaction (measures) and informal means (the family verbally expresses satisfaction with treatment). When assessing satisfaction with treatment, it may be important to gather information regarding both the child client's and the parents' views about treatment. Our search for treatment satisfaction measures yielded only one measure designed for general use with children and families (Client Satisfaction Questionnaire; Copeland, Koeske, & Greeno, 2004; Shapiro, Welker, & Jacobson, 1997). There is a dearth of well-researched measures for use with parents and children. Measures of parent satisfaction for specific treatments or problem areas are available. For example, the Therapy Attitude Inventory (Eyberg, 1993; Eyberg & Johnson, 1974) was developed for use with behavioral parent training programs for child externalizing disorders, and research has demonstrated promising evidence for its reliability and validity (Brestan, Jacobs, Rayfield, & Eyberg, 1999; Eyberg, 1993). On the whole, however, research regarding psychometrics and the utility of such measures across therapeutic interventions is lacking. Much more research is needed regarding the assessment of treatment satisfaction and its relationship to the process of therapy with children and families.

SUMMARY

Understanding the context in which families live is an extremely important aspect of clinical practice. It is one thing to work with a parent and child on a list of house rules that includes the rule "No leaving the yard." It is quite another thing, however, to consider this rule after discovering that the family lives on a busy street with drug activity at the end of the block. Clinicians should strive to understand the family context and the client's worldview whenever possible. This will help to put the parents' concerns into perspective. Understanding the family context also allows clinicians to conceptualize the child client's presenting problem, access potential environmental strengths, and decide on the most appropriate intervention.

Given the number of interventions that are currently available to treat the various disorders of childhood, there has never been a better time to be a child clinician! In particular, the volume of treatment outcome research that has been conducted since the 1998 Task Force on Empirically Supported Treatments (Lonigan, Elbert, & Johnson, 1998) is truly inspiring. Though knowledge regarding the types of treatments that are effective with children continues to grow, the field is still in its early stages and much remains to be discovered concerning the complexities involved in clinical work with children and families.

It is our hope that the role of family in treatment will continue to be a focus of clinical research in the area of child-focused EBTs. We concur with Kendall (2006) that characteristics such as the child's developmental level and presenting problem should be addressed by this line of research. More research is also needed to examine the optimal role of family members in EBTs, the effects of various levels of involvement for family members, and the role of family members other than parents (i.e., siblings, grandparents, kinship networks) in therapy. In the absence of this information, we suggest that clinicians strive to use empirically informed treatments whenever possible. This is especially true in the multicultural arena.

We urge clinical researchers to continue their investigation into the role of the family in child-focused CBT. We need to move beyond the discussion of which treatment packages work best to treat child psychopathology and address the question of who should be included in treatment and how these individuals should be involved.

REFERENCES

Abidin, R. R. (1995). *Parenting Stress Index (PSI) manual* (3rd ed.). Charlottesville, VA: Pediatric Psychology Press.

Achenbach, T. M. (1991). *Manual for the Child Behavior Checklist and 1991 profile.* Burlington: University of Vermont, Department of Psychiatry.

Ahluwalia, J. S., Okuyemi, K., Nollen, N., Choi, W. S., Kaur, H., Pulvers, K., et al. (2006). The effects of nicotine gum and counseling among African American light smokers: A 2 x 2 factorial design. *Addiction, 101,* 883–891.

American Psychological Association. (2002). Ethical principles of psychologists and code of conduct. *American Psychologist, 57,* 1060–1073.

Aragona, J. A., & Eyberg, S. M. (1981). Neglected children: Mother's report of child behavior problems and observed verbal behavior. *Child Development, 52,* 596–602.

Arsenault, L., Kim-Cohen, J., Taylor, A., Caspi, A., & Moffitt, T. E. (2005). Psychometric evaluation of 5- and 7-year-old children's self-reports of conduct problems. *Journal of Abnormal Child Psychology, 33,* 537–550.

Bagner, D., & Eyberg, S. M. (2003). Father involvement in parent training: When does it matter? *Journal of Clinical Child and Adolescent Psychology, 32,* 599–605.

Barmish, A. J., & Kendall, P. C. (2005). Should parents be co-clients in cognitive-behavioral therapy for anxious youth? *Journal of Clinical Child and Adolescent Psychology, 34,* 569–581.

Barrett, P. M., Dadds, M. R., & Rapee, R. M. (1996). Family treatment of childhood anxiety: A controlled trial. *Journal of Consulting and Clinical Psychology, 64*, 333–342.

Barrett, P. M., Rapee, R. M., Dadds, M. M., & Ryan, S. M. (1996). Family enhancement of cognitive style in anxious and aggressive children. *Journal of Abnormal Child Psychology, 24*, 187–203.

Belsky, J. (1981). Early human experience: A family perspective. *Developmental Psychology, 17*, 3–23.

Bessmer, J. L., Brestan, E. V., & Eyberg, S. M. (2007). *The Dyadic Parent-Child Interaction Coding System II (DPICS II): Reliability and validity with mother-child dyads.* Manuscript submitted for publication.

Boggs, S., McDiarmid, M. D., Eyberg, S. M., & Stevens, G. (2004, August). *Efficacy of parent-child interaction therapy: Report of a randomized trial with short-term maintenance.* Paper presented at the annual meeting of the American Psychological Association, Honolulu, HI.

Borrego, J., Jr., Timmer, S. G., Urquiza, A. J., & Follette, W. C. (2004). Physically abusive mothers' responses following episodes of child noncompliance and compliance. *Journal of Consulting and Clinical Psychology, 72*, 897–903.

Boyd-Franklin, N. (2003). *Black families in therapy* (2nd ed.). New York: Guilford Press.

Brestan, E. V., Eyberg, S. M., Algina, J., Johnson, S. B., & Boggs, S. R. (2003). How annoying is it? Defining parental tolerance for child misbehavior. *Child and Family Behavior Therapy, 25*, 1–15.

Brestan, E. V., Foote, R. C., & Eyberg, S. M. (2007). *The Dyadic Parent-Child Interaction Coding System II (DPICS II): Reliability and validity with father-child dyads.* Manuscript submitted for publication.

Brestan, E. V., Jacobs, J. R., Rayfield, A. D., & Eyberg, S. M. (1999). A consumer satisfaction measure for parent-child treatments and its relation to measures of child behavior change. *Behavior Therapy, 30*, 17–30.

Brestan, E. V., Ondersma, S. J., Simpson, S. M., & Gurwitch, R. H. (1999, April). *Application of stage of change theory to parenting behavior: Validating the Parent Readiness for Change Scale.* Poster presented at the 7th Florida Conference on Child Health Psychology, Gainesville.

Brinkmeyer, M. Y., & Eyberg, S. M. (2003). Parent-child interaction therapy for oppositional children. In A. E. Kazdin & J. R. Weisz (Eds.), *Evidence-based psychotherapies for children and adolescents* (pp. 204–223). New York: Guilford Press.

Bronfenbrenner, U. (1979). *The ecology of human development: Experiments by nature and design.* Cambridge, MA: Harvard University Press.

Butcher, J. L., & Niec, L. N. (2006). *Measuring the "fix my child" attitude: Validity of the READI, a measure of parents' motivation for change.* Manuscript submitted for publication.

Campis, L. K., Lyman, R. D., & Prentice-Dunn, S. (1986). The Parental Locus of Control Scale: Development and validation. *Journal of Clinical Child Psychology, 15*, 260–267.

Chaffin, M., Silovsky, J. F., Funderburk, B., Valle, L. A., Brestan, E. V., Balachova, T., et al. (2004). Parent-child interaction therapy with physically abusive parents: Efficacy for reducing future abuse reports. *Journal of Consulting and Clinical Psychology, 72*, 500–510.

Chaffin, M., & Valle, A. (2003). Dynamic prediction characteristics of the Child Abuse Potential Inventory. *Child Abuse and Neglect, 27*, 463–481.

Christensen, A., Margolin, G., & Sullaway, M. (1992). Interparental agreement on child behavior problems. *Psychological Assessment, 4*, 419–425.

Christophersen, E. R., & Mortweet, S. L. (2001). *Treatments that work with children: Empirically supported strategies for managing childhood problems.* Washington, DC: American Psychological Association.

Clarke, G. N., DeBar, L. L., & Lewinsohn, P. M. (2003). Cognitive-behavioral group treatment for adolescent depression. In A. E. Kazdin & J. R. Weisz (Eds.), *Evidence-based psychotherapies for children and adolescents* (pp. 120–134). New York: Guilford Press.

Connell, A. M., & Goodman, S. H. (2002). The association between psychopathology in fathers versus mothers and children's internalizing and externalizing behavior problems: A meta-analysis. *Psychological Bulletin, 128,* 746–773

Constantine, M. G., & Sue, D. W. (2005). *Strategies for building multicultural competence in mental health and educational settings.* Hoboken, NJ: Wiley.

Copeland, V. C., Koeske, G., & Greeno, C. G. (2004). Child and mother Client Satisfaction Questionnaire scores regarding mental health services: Race, age, and gender correlates. *Research on Social Work Practice, 14,* 434–442.

Costello, E. J., Burns, B. J., Costello, A. J., Edelbrock, G., Dulcan, M., & Brent, D. (1998). Service utilization and psychiatric diagnosis in pediatric primary care: The role of the gatekeeper. *Pediatrics, 82,* 435–441.

Cunningham, C. E., Bremner, R., & Boyle, M. (1995). Large group community-based parenting programs for families of preschoolers at risk for disruptive behavior disorders: Utilization, cost effectiveness, and outcome. *Journal of Child Psychology and Psychiatry, 36,* 1141–1159.

Dadds, M. R., Heard, P. M., & Rapee, R. M. (1992). The role of family intervention in the treatment of child anxiety disorders: Some preliminary findings. *Behavior Change, 9,* 171–177.

De Los Reyes, A., & Kazdin, A. E. (2005). Informant discrepancies in the assessment of childhood psychopathology: A critical review, theoretical framework, and recommendations for further study. *Psychological Bulletin, 131,* 483–509.

Deskins, M. M. (2005). The Dyadic Parent-Child Interaction Coding System II: Reliability and validity with school-aged dyads. *Dissertation Abstracts International, 66,* 2302B.

Dudley, A. L., Melvin, G. A., Williams, N. J., Tonge, B. J., & King, N. J. (2005). Investigation of consumer satisfaction with cognitive-behavior therapy and sertraline in the treatment of adolescent depression. *Australian and New Zealand Journal of Psychiatry, 39,* 500–506.

Edelbrook, C., Costello, A. J., Dulcan, M. K., Kalas, R., & Conover, N. C. (1985). Age differences in the reliability of the psychiatric interview of the child. *Child Development, 56,* 265–275.

Eisenstadt, T. H., Eyberg, S., McNeil, S. B., Newcomb, K., & Funderburk, B. (1993). Parent-child interaction therapy with behavior problem children: Relative effectiveness of two stages and overall treatment outcome. *Journal of Clinical Child Psychology, 22,* 42–51.

Eyberg, S. (1993). Consumer satisfaction measures for assessing parent training programs. In L. VandeCreek, S. Knapp, & T. L. Jackson (Eds.), *Innovations in clinical practice: Vol. 12. A source book* (pp. 377–382). Sarasota, FL: Professional Resource Press/Professional Resource Exchange.

Eyberg, S. M., Edwards, D., Boggs, S. R., & Foote, R. (1998). Maintaining the treatment effects of parental training: The role of booster sessions and other maintenance strategies. *Clinical Psychology: Science and Practice, 5,* 544–554.

Eyberg, S. M., Funderburk, B. W., Hembree-Kigin, T. L., McNeil, C. B., Querido, J. G., & Hood, K. K. (2001). Parent-child interaction therapy with behavior problem children: One and two year maintenance of treatment effects in the family. *Child and Family Behavior Therapy, 23,* 1–20.

Eyberg, S. M., & Johnson, S. M. (1974). Multiple assessment of behavior modification with families: Effects of contingency contracting and order of treated problems. *Journal of Consulting and Clinical Psychology, 42,* 594–606.

Eyberg, S. M., Nelson, M. M., Duke, M., & Boggs, S. R. (2005). *Manual for the Dyadic Parent-Child Interaction Coding System* (3rd ed.). Retrieved June 19, 2007, from the University of Florida, Parent-Child Interaction Therapy web site, www.pcit.org.

Eyberg, S. M., & Pincus, D. (1999). *Eyberg Child Behavior Inventory and Sutter-Eyberg Student Behavior Inventory: Professional manual*. Odessa, FL: Psychological Assessment Resources.

Fallon, T., & Schwab-Stone, M. (1994). Determinants of reliability in psychiatric surveys of children aged 6–12. *Journal of Child Psychology and Psychiatry, 38*, 1391–1408.

Fantuzzo, J., McDermott, P., & Lutz, M. N. (1999). Clinical issues in the assessment of family violence involving children. In R. T. Ammerman & M. Hersen (Eds.), *Assessment of family violence: A clinical and legal sourcebook* (2nd ed., pp. 10–23). New York: Wiley.

Feindler, E. L., Rathus, J. H., & Silver, L. B. (2003). *Assessment of family violence*. Washington, DC: American Psychological Association.

Forster, A. A., Eyberg, S. M., & Burns, G. L. (1990). Assessing the verbal behavior of conduct problem children during mother-child interactions: A preliminary investigation. *Child and Family Behavior Therapy, 12*, 13–22.

Gershater-Molko, R. M., & Lutzker, J. R. (1999). Child neglect. In R. T. Ammerman & M. Hersen (Eds.), *Assessment of family violence: A clinical and legal sourcebook* (2nd ed., pp. 157–183). New York: Wiley.

Gershater-Molko, R. M., Lutzker, J. R., & Sherman, J. A. (2003). Assessing child neglect. *Aggression and Violent Behavior, 8*, 563–585.

Goodman, S. H., & Gotlib, I. H. (1999). Risk for psychopathology in the children of depressed mothers: A developmental model for understanding mechanisms of transmission. *Psychological Review, 106*, 458–490.

Gross, D., Fogg, L., Garvey, C., & Julion, W. (2004). Behavior problems in young children: An analysis of cross-informant agreements and disagreements. *Research in Nursing and Health, 27*, 413–425.

Gushue, G. V., Greenan, D. E., & Brazaitis, S. J. (2005). Using the multicultural guidelines in couples and family counseling. In M. G. Constantine & D. W. Sue (Eds.), *Strategies for building multicultural competence in mental health and educational settings* (pp. 56–72). Hoboken, NJ: Wiley.

Hagekull, B., Bohlin, G., & Hammarberg, A. (2001). The role of perceived control in child development: A longitudinal study. *International Journal of Behavioral Development, 25*, 429–437.

Hall, C. C. I. (1997). Cultural malpractice: The growing obsolescence of psychology with the changing U.S. population. *American Psychologist, 52*, 642–651.

Hammen, C., & Rudolph, K. D. (2003). Childhood mood disorders. In E. J. Mash & R. A. Barkley (Eds.), *Child psychopathology* (2nd ed., pp. 233–278). New York: Guilford Press.

Hansen, D. J., & MacMillan, V. M. (1990). Behavioral assessment of child-abusive and neglectful families. *Behavior Modification, 14*, 255–278.

Hansen, D. J., Sedlar, G., & Warner-Rogers, J. E. (1999). Child physical abuse. In R. T. Ammerman & M. Hersen (Eds.), *Assessment of family violence: A clinical and legal sourcebook* (2nd ed., pp. 127–156). New York: Wiley.

Haley, J. (1963). *Strategies of psychotherapy*. New York: Grune & Stratton.

Hazzard, A., Christensen, A., & Margolin, G. (1983). Children's perceptions of parental behaviors. *Journal of Abnormal Child Psychology, 11*, 49–59.

Health Insurance Portability and Accountability Act of 1996, Pub. L. No. 104-191, 104th Cong., 2nd Sess. (1996).

Hembree-Kigin, T., & McNeil, C. (1995). *Parent-child interaction therapy*. New York: Plenum Press.

Hoagwood, K. (2005). The research, policy, and practice context for delivery of evidence-based mental health treatment for adolescents: A systems perspective. In D. L. Evans, E. B. Foa, R. E. Gur, H. Hendin, C. P. O'Brien, M. E. P. Seligman, et al. (Eds.), *Treating and preventing adolescent mental health disorders: What we know and what we don't know* (pp. 546–560). New York: Oxford University Press.

Holmbeck, G. N., O'Mahar, K., Abad, M., Colder, C., & Updegrove, A. (2006). Cognitive-behavioral therapy with adolescents: Guides from developmental psychology. In P. C. Kendall (Ed.), *Child and adolescent therapy: Cognitive-behavioral procedures* (3rd ed., pp. 419–464). New York: Guilford Press.

Hops, H., Biglan, A., Sherman, L., Arthur, J., Friedman, L., & Osteeen, V. (1987). Home observations of family interactions of depressed women. *Journal of Consulting and Clinical Psychology, 55,* 341–346.

Kazak, A. E., Rourke, M. T., & Crump, T. A. (2003). Families and other systems in pediatric psychology. In M. C. Roberts (Ed.), *Handbook of pediatric psychology* (3rd ed., pp. 159–175). New York: Guilford Press.

Kazdin, A. E. (1995). *Conduct disorder in childhood and adolescence* (2nd ed.). Thousand Oaks, CA: Sage.

Kazdin, A. E. (1997). Parent management training: Evidence, outcomes, and issues. *Journal of the American Academy of Child and Adolescent Psychiatry, 36,* 1349–1356.

Kazdin, A. E. (2004). Psychotherapy for children and adolescents. In M. J. Lambert (Ed.), *Bergin and Garfield's handbook of psychotherapy and behavior change* (5th ed., pp. 543–589). Hoboken, NJ: Wiley.

Kazdin, A. E., & Weisz, J. R. (Eds.). (2003). *Evidence-based psychotherapies for children and adolescents.* New York: Guilford Press.

Kendall, P. C. (1992). *Coping cat workbook.* Ardmore, PA: Workbook Publishing.

Kendall, P. C. (2006). Guiding theory for therapy with children and adolescents. In P. C. Kendall (Ed.), *Child and adolescent therapy* (3rd ed., pp. 1–30). New York: Guilford Press.

Kendall, P. C., & Ollendick, T. H. (2004). Setting the research and practice agenda for anxiety in children and adolescence: A topic comes of age. *Cognitive and Behavioral Practice, 11,* 65–74.

Kendall, P. C., & Suveg, C. (2006). Treating anxiety disorders in youth. In P. C. Kendall (Ed.), *Child and adolescent therapy* (3rd ed., pp. 243–293). New York: Guilford Press.

Kivlighan, D. M., & Kivlighan, M. C. (2004). Counselor intentions in individual and group treatment. *Journal of Counseling Psychology, 51,* 347–353.

Lamb, M. E., & Lewis, C. (2004). The development and significance of father-child relationships in two-parent families. In M. E. Lamb (Ed.), *The role of the father in child development* (pp. 272–306). Hoboken, NJ: Wiley.

Lee, S. W., Elliott, J., & Barbour, J. (1994). A comparison of cross-informant behavior ratings in school-based diagnosis. *Behavioral Disorders, 19,* 87–97.

Leve, L. D., Kim, H. K., & Pears, K. C. (2005). Childhood temperament and family environment as predictors of internalizing and externalizing trajectories from ages 5 to 17. *Journal of Abnormal Child Psychology, 33,* 505–520.

Lochman, J. E., Barry, T. D., & Pardini, D. A. (2003). Anger control training for aggressive youth. In A. E. Kazdin & J. R. Weisz (Eds.), *Evidence-based psychotherapies for children and adolescents* (pp. 263–281). New York: Guilford Press.

Lochman, J. E., Powell, N. R., Whidby, J. M., & Fitzgerald, D. P. (2006). Aggressive children: Cognitive-behavioral assessment and treatment. In P. C. Kendall (Ed.), *Child and adolescent therapy* (3rd ed., pp. 33–81). New York: Guilford Press.

Lochman, J. E., & van den Steenhoven, A. (2002). Family-based approaches to substance abuse prevention. *Journal of Primary Prevention, 23,* 49–114.

Lonigan, C. J., Elbert, J. C., & Johnson, S. B. (1998). Empirically supported psychosocial interventions for children: An overview. *Journal of Clinical Child Psychology, 27,* 138–145.

Madson, M. B., & Campbell, T. C. (2006). Measures of fidelity in motivational enhancement: A systemic review. *Journal of Substance Abuse Treatment, 31,* 67–73.

Manassis, K., Mendlowitz, S. L., Scapillato, D., Avery, D., Fiksenbaum, L., Freire, M., et al. (2002). Group and individual cognitive-behavioral therapy for childhood anxiety disorders: A randomized trial. *Journal of the American Academy of Child and Adolescent Psychiatry, 41,* 1423–1430.

Mash, E. J. (1998). Treatment of child and family disturbance: A behavioral-systems perspective. In E. J. Mash & R. A. Barkley (Eds.), *Treatment of childhood disorders* (2nd ed., pp. 3–51). New York: Guilford Press.

Mash, E. J., & Hunsley, J. (2005). Evidence-based assessment of child and adolescent disorders: Issues and challenges. *Journal of Clinical Child and Adolescent Psychology, 34,* 362–379.

Mash, E. J., & Terdal, L. G. (1997). Assessment of child and family disturbance: A behavioral-systems approach. In E. J. Mash & L. G. Terdal (Eds.), *Assessment of childhood disorders* (3rd ed., pp. 3–68). New York: Guilford Press.

Mash, E. J., & Wolfe, D. A. (2005). *Abnormal child psychology* (3rd ed.) Belmont, CA: Thomson Wadsworth.

McCabe, K. M., Yeh, M., Garland, A. F., Lau, A. S., & Chavez, G. (2005). The GANA program: A tailoring approach to adapting parent child interaction therapy for Mexican Americans. *Education and Treatment of Children, 28,* 111–129.

McCambridge, J., & Strang, J. (2004). The efficacy of single-session motivational interviewing in reducing drug consumption and perceptions of drug-related risk and harm among young people: Results from a multi-site cluster randomized trial. *Addiction, 99,* 39–52.

McConnaughy, E. A., Prochaska, J. O., & Velicer, J. O. (1983). Stages of change in psychotherapy: Measurement and sample profiles. *Psychotherapy: Theory, Research and Practice, 20,* 368–375.

McNeil, C. B., Capage, L. C., Bahl, A., & Blanc, H. (1999). Importance of early intervention for disruptive behavior problems: Comparison of treatment and waitlist-control groups. *Early Education and Development, 10,* 445–454.

McQuaid, E. L., & Walders, N. (2003). Pediatric asthma. In M. C. Roberts (Ed.), *Handbook of pediatric psychology* (3rd ed., pp. 269–285). New York: Guilford Press.

McRoberts, C., Burlingame, G. M., & Hoag, M. J. (1998). Comparative efficacy of individual and group psychotherapy: A meta-analytic perspective. *Group Dynamics: Theory, Research, and Practice, 2,* 101–117.

Miller, W. R., & Rollnick, S. (2002). *Motivational interviewing: Preparing people for change* (2nd ed.). New York: Guilford Press.

Milner, J. S. (1986). *The Child Abuse Potential Inventory: Manual* (2nd ed.). Webster, NC: Psytec.

Milner, J. S., & Murphy, W. D. (1995). Assessment of child physical and sexual abuse offenders. *Family Relations, 44,* 478–488.

Minuchin, S. (1974). *Families and family therapy.* Cambridge, MA: Harvard University Press.

Mori, L. T., & Armendariz, G. M. (2001). Analogue assessment of child behavior problems. *Psychological Assessment, 13,* 36–45.

Mouton, P. Y., & Tuma, J. M. (1988). Stress, locus of control, and role satisfaction in clinic and control mothers. *Journal of Clinical Child Psychology, 17,* 217–224.

Nelson, W. M., Finch, A. J., & Ghee, A. C. (2006). Anger management with children and adolescents: Cognitive-behavioral therapy. In P. C. Kendall (Ed.), *Child and adolescent therapy* (3rd ed., pp. 114–165). New York: Guilford Press.

Nichols, M. P., & Schwartz, R. C. (2004). *Family therapy concepts and methods* (6th ed.). Boston: Pearson.

Niec, L. N., Hemme, J. M., Yopp, J. M., & Brestan, E. V. (2005). Parent-child interaction therapy: The rewards and challenges of a group format. *Cognitive and Behavioral Science, 12,* 113–125.

Nixon, R., Sweeney, L., Erickson, D., & Touyz, S. (2003). Parent-child interaction therapy: A comparison of standard and abbreviated treatments for oppositional defiant preschoolers. *Journal of Consulting and Clinical Psychology, 71,* 251–260.

Ollendick, T. H. (1999). Empirically supported treatments: Promises and pitfalls. *Clinical Psychologist, 52*, 1–3.

Ollendick, T. H., King, N. J., & Chorpita, B. F. (2006). Empirically supported treatments for children and adolescents. In P. C. Kendall (Ed.), *Child and adolescent therapy: Cognitive-behavioral procedures* (3rd ed., pp. 492–520). New York: Guilford Press.

Ondersma, S. J. (1999). *The Parent Readiness for Change Scale (PRFCS).* Unpublished manuscript.

Patterson, G. R. (1982). *Coercive family process.* Eugene, OR: Castalia.

Penn, D. L., Judge, A., Jamieson, P., Garczynski, J., Hennessy, M., & Romer, D. (2005). Stigma. In D. L. Evans, E. B. Foa, R. E. Gur, H. Hendin, C. P. O'Brien, M. E. P. Seligman, et al. (Eds.), *Treating and preventing adolescent mental health disorders: What we know and what we don't know* (pp. 532–543). New York: Oxford University Press.

Phares, V., & Compas, B. E. (1992). The role of fathers in child and adolescent psychopathology: Make room for Daddy. *Psychological Bulletin, 111*, 387–412.

Phares, V., Fields, S., Kamboukos, D., & Lopez, E. (2005). Still looking for Poppa. *American Psychologist, 60*, 735–736.

Phares, V., Lopez, E., Fields, S., Kamboukos, D., & Duhig, A. M. (2005). Are fathers involved in pediatric psychology research and treatment? *Journal of Pediatric Psychology, 30*, 631–643.

Principe, J. M., Marci, C. D., & Glick, D. M. (2006). The relationship among patient contemplation, early alliance, and continuation in psychotherapy. *Psychotherapy: Theory, Research, Practice, Training, 43*, 238–243.

Rae, W. A., & Fournier, C. J. (1999). Ethical and legal issues in the treatment of children and families. In S. W. Russ & T. H. Ollendick (Eds.), *Handbook of psychotherapies with children and families* (pp. 67–83). New York: Kluwer Academic/Plenum Press.

Reich, S. (2005). What do mothers know? Maternal knowledge of child development. *Infant Mental Health Journal, 26*, 143–156.

Reynolds, C. R., & Kamphaus, R. W. (2004). *Behavior Assessment System for Children: Manual* (2nd ed.). Circle Pines, MN: American Guidance Service.

Robbins, M. S., Szapocznik, J., Santisteban, D. A., Hervis, O. E., Mitrani, V. B., & Schwartz, S. J. (2003). Brief strategic family therapy for Hispanic youth. In A. E. Kazdin & J. R. Weisz (Eds.), *Evidence-based psychotherapies for children and adolescents* (pp. 407–424). New York: Guilford Press.

Roberts, M. W., Joe, V. C., & Rowe-Hallbert, A. (1992). Oppositional child behavior and parental locus of control. *Journal of Clinical Child Psychology, 21*, 170–177.

Romano, E., Tremblay, R. E., Boulerice, B., & Swisher, R. (2005). Multilevel correlates of childhood physical aggression and prosocial behavior. *Journal of Abnormal Child Psychology, 33*, 565–578.

Romer, D., & McIntosh, M. (2005). The role of primary care physicians in detection and treatment of adolescent mental health problems. In D. L. Evans, E. B. Foa, R. E. Gur, H. Hendin, C. P. O'Brien, M. E. P. Seligman, et al. (Eds.), *Treating and preventing adolescent mental health disorders: What we know and what we don't know* (pp. 579–595). New York: Oxford University Press.

Santisteban, D. A., Coatsworth, J. D., Perez-Vidal, A., Mitrani, V., Jean-Gilles, M., & Szapocznik, J. (1997). Brief structural/strategic family therapy with African American and Hispanic high-risk youth. *Journal of Community Psychology, 25*, 453–471.

Santisteban, D. A., & Mitrani, V. B. (2003). The influence of acculturation processes on the family. In K. M. Chun, P. B. Organista, & G. Marin (Eds.), *Acculturation: Advances in theory, measurement, and applied research* (pp. 121–135). Washington, DC: American Psychological Association.

Santisteban, D. A., Szapocznik, J., Perez-Vidal, A., Kurtines, W. M., Murray, E. J., & LaPerriere A. (1996). Efficacy of intervention for engaging youth and families into treatment and some variables that may contribute to differential effectiveness. *Journal of Family Psychology, 10,* 35–44.

Sarason, I. G., Levine, H. M., Basham, R. B., & Sarason, B. R. (1983). Assessing social support: The Social Support Questionnaire. *Journal of Personality and Social Psychology, 44,* 127–139.

Sattler, J. M. (2002). *Assessment of children: Behavioral and clinical applications* (4th ed.). La Mesa, CA: Author.

Schuhmann, E., Foote, R., Eyberg, S. M., Boggs, S., & Algina, J. (1998). Parent-child interaction therapy: Interim report of a randomized trial with short-term maintenance. *Journal of Clinical Child Psychology, 27,* 34–45.

Schwab-Stone, M., Fallon, T., Briggs, M., & Crowther, B. (1994). Reliability of diagnostic reporting for children aged 6–11 years: A test-retest study of the Diagnostic Interview Schedule for Children—Revised. *American Journal of Psychiatry, 151,* 1048–1051.

Shapiro, J. P., Welker, C. J., & Jacobson, B. J. (1997). The Youth Client Satisfaction Questionnaire: Development, construct validation, and factor structure. *Journal of Clinical Child Psychology, 26,* 87–98.

Silverman, W. K. (2006). Nothing is as practical as a good theory: A mantra for our efforts to disseminate evidence-based practice. *In Balance: Society of Clinical Child and Adolescent Psychology Newsletter, 21,* 1.

Silverman, W. K., & Ollendick, T. H. (2005). Evidence-based assessment of anxiety and its disorders in children and adolescents. *Journal of Clinical Child and Adolescent Psychology, 34,* 380–411.

Silverstein, L. B., & Phares, V. (1996). Expanding the parenting paradigm: An examination of dissertation research 1986–1994. *Psychology of Women Quarterly, 20,* 39–53.

Snell-Johns, J., Mendez, J. L., & Smith, B. H. (2004). Evidence-based solutions for overcoming access barriers, decreasing attrition, and promoting change with underserved families. *Journal of Family Psychology, 18,* 19–35.

Spirito, A., & Esposito-Smythers, C. (2006). Addressing adolescent suicidal behavior: Cognitive-behavioral strategies. In P. C. Kendall (Ed.), *Child and adolescent therapy: Cognitive-behavioral procedures* (3rd ed., pp. 217–242). New York: Guilford Press.

Stockhammer, T. F., Salzinger, S., Feldman, R. S., Mojica, E., & Primavera, L. H. (2001). Assessment of the effects of physical child abuse within an ecological framework: Measurement issues. *Journal of Community Psychology, 29,* 319–344.

Straus, M. A., Hamby, S., Finkelhor, D., Moore, D., & Runyan, D. (1998). Identification of child maltreatment with the Parent-Child Conflict Tactics Scales: Development and psychometric data for a national sample of American parents. *Child Abuse and Neglect, 22,* 249–270.

Sturm, R., Ringel, J. S., & Andreyeva, T. (2003). Geographic disparities in children's mental health care. *Pediatrics, 112,* 308–315.

Szapocznik, J., & Kurtines, W. M. (1993). Family psychology and cultural diversity: Opportunities for theory, research, and application. *American Psychologist, 48,* 400–407.

Szapocznik, J., Perez-Vidal, A. P., Brickman, A., Foote, F., Santisteban, D., Hervis, O., et al. (1988). Engaging adolescent drug abusers and their families in treatment: A strategic structural systems approach. *Journal of Consulting and Clinical Psychology, 56,* 552–557.

Szapocznik, J., Rio, A., Murray, E., & Cohen, R. (1989). Structural family versus psychodynamic child therapy for problematic Hispanic boys. *Journal of Consulting and Clinical Psychology, 57,* 571–578.

Taylor, T. K., & Biglan, A. (1998). Behavioral family interventions for improving child-rearing: A review of the literature for clinicians and policy makers. *Clinical Child and Family Psychology Review, 1,* 41–60.

Thuppal, M., Carlson, G. A., Sprafkin, J., & Gadow, K. D. (2002). Correspondence between adolescent report, parent report, and teacher report of manic symptoms. *Journal of Child and Adolescent Psychopharmacology, 12,* 27–35.

Tillitski, C. J. (1990). A meta-analysis of estimated effect sizes for group versus individual versus control treatments. *International Journal of Group Psychotherapy, 40,* 215–224.

U.S. Census Bureau. (2005). *Living arrangements of children: 2001* (U.S. Census Bureau Publication No. P70-104). Washington, DC: Author.

Vannatta, K., & Gerhardt, C. A. (2003). Pediatric oncology: Psychosocial outcomes for children and families. In M. C. Roberts (Ed.), *Handbook of pediatric psychology* (3rd ed., pp. 342–357). New York: Guilford Press.

Wahler, R. G., & Afton, A. D. (1980). Attentional processes in insular and noninsular mothers: Some differences in their summary reports about child problem behaviors. *Child Behavior Therapy, 2,* 25–41.

Webster-Stratton, C. (1985). The effects of father involvement in parent training for conduct problem children. *Journal of Child Psychology and Psychiatry, 26,* 801–810.

Webster-Stratton, C. (1992). *The Incredible Years: A trouble-shooting guide for parents of children aged 3–8.* Toronto: Umbrella Press.

Webster-Stratton, C., & Reid, M. J. (2003). The Incredible Years parent, teachers, and children training series: A multifaceted treatment approach for young children with conduct problems. In A. E. Kazdin & J. R. Weisz (Eds.), *Evidence-based psychotherapies for children and adolescents* (pp. 224–240). New York: Guilford Press.

Webster-Stratton, C., Reid, M. J., & Hammond, M. (2004). Treating children with early-onset conduct problems: Intervention outcomes for parent, child, and teacher training. *Journal of Clinical Child and Adolescent Psychology, 33,* 105–124.

Weisz, J. R., & Hawley, K. M. (1998). Finding, evaluating, refining, and applying empirically supported treatments for children and adolescents. *Journal of Clinical Child Psychology, 27,* 206–216.

Weisz, J. R., & Hawley, K. M. (2002). Developmental factors in the treatment of adolescents. *Journal of Consulting and Clinical Psychology, 70,* 21–43.

Wilfley, D. E., Passi, V. A., Cooperberg, J., & Stein, R. I. (2006). Cognitive-behavioral therapy for youth with eating disorders and obesity. In P. C. Kendall (Ed.), *Child and adolescent therapy* (3rd ed., pp. 322–355). New York: Guilford Press.

Wolfe, D. A., & McEachran, A. (1997). Child physical abuse and neglect. In E. J. Mash & L. G. Terdal (Eds.), *Assessment of child disorders* (3rd ed., pp. 523–568). New York: Guilford Press.

Wood, J. J., McLeod, B. D., Sigman, M., Hwang, W., & Chu, B. C. (2003). Parenting and childhood anxiety: Theory, empirical findings, and future directions. *Journal of Child Psychology and Psychiatry, 44,* 134–151.

Wysocki, T., Greco, P., & Buckloh, L. M. (2003). Childhood diabetes in psychological context. In M. C. Roberts (Ed.), *Handbook of pediatric psychology* (3rd ed., pp. 304–320). New York: Guilford Press.

Zimmerman, M. A., Salem, D. A., & Notaro, P. C. (2000). Make room for Daddy II: The positive effects of fathers' role in adolescent development. In R. D. Taylor & M. C. Wang (Eds.), *Resilience across contexts: Family, work, culture, and community* (pp. 233–253). Mahwah, NJ: Erlbaum.

CHAPTER 7

Medical and
Pharmacological Issues

SCOTT H. KOLLINS AND JOSHUA M. LANGBERG

The use of pharmacological interventions for child and adolescent behavioral and emotional disorders has increased substantially in recent years (Olfson, Marcus, Weissman, & Jensen, 2002; Raghavan et al., 2005; Thomas, Conrad, Casler, & Goodman, 2006). Although much attention has focused on the increased use of stimulant drugs to treat Attention-Deficit/Hyperactivity Disorder (ADHD), increases in other classes of drugs (e.g., antidepressants, antipsychotics) have also been reported (Hunkeler et al., 2005; Olfson et al., 2002; Zito et al., 2000, 2002).

Given the rising prevalence of medication use for behavioral and emotional difficulties in youth, it is critical for psychologists and other nonmedical professionals who work with these patients to have a good understanding of a number of basic issues pertaining to pharmacological treatment. Medication use can influence both assessment and ongoing psychological treatment for a range of difficulties. The purpose of this chapter is to highlight the pharmacological treatment of child and adolescent behavioral disorders with an emphasis on how this form of intervention can be integrated with psychological assessment and treatment. For ease of presentation, throughout the chapter we refer to psychological or behavioral disorders as "psychiatric disorders" and refer to specific diagnoses (e.g., ADHD, depression) by name.

This chapter examines the kinds of medication most often used to treat child psychiatric disorders, reviews basic principles of psychopharmacology, and considers how medication use can be integrated into broader comprehensive assessment and treatment plans.

MEDICATIONS USED TO TREAT CHILD AND ADOLESCENT BEHAVIOR DISORDERS

Many medications used to treat psychiatric disorders in children and adolescents are not specifically approved for such use by the U.S. Food and Drug Administration (FDA). Thus, we focus our discussion on medications that have been empirically

159

evaluated, with special attention devoted to those compounds that have not yet been approved for use with children and/or adolescents by the FDA. Comprehensive reviews of this topic are available in other sources (Brown & Sammons, 2002; Wilens, 2004). This review of psychopharmacological treatments is organized by the disorders they are most commonly used to treat, focusing on ADHD, mood disorders, and anxiety disorders.

Pharmacotherapy for Attention-Deficit/Hyperactivity Disorder

Among children, few disorders are more closely associated with pharmacotherapy than ADHD. Medications used to treat this common disorder fall generally into two classes: stimulants and nonstimulants. The stimulants are so named because of their excitatory effects on the central nervous system (CNS), and the term "nonstimulant" is used to describe a more diverse set of compounds whose mechanisms of action vary.

Stimulant Drugs　The two drugs most frequently used to treat ADHD are methylphenidate and amphetamine. Methylphenidate acts in the CNS primarily by blocking the dopamine transporter; amphetamine acts by facilitating presynaptic release of dopamine. The net result for both drugs is an increase in dopaminergic activity, primarily in areas of the brain that are associated with attention and inhibitory processes, which are thought to function abnormally in diagnosed individuals (Pliszka, 2005; Sagvolden, Johansen, Aase, & Russell, 2005). Methylphenidate and amphetamine are the active ingredients in the majority of FDA-approved medications for ADHD. Methylphenidate-based products include (in alphabetical order) Concerta, Daytrana, Focalin, Metadate CD, Ritalin, and Ritalin LA. Amphetamine products include Adderall, Adderall XR, and Dexedrine. Because the active compound is similar for these products, the primary manner in which the products differ is the way the drug is delivered. Indeed, the past decade has seen a dramatic increase in the number of delivery options, most of which have been developed to allow for once-daily dosing. Products that permit once-daily dosing (e.g., Adderall, Ritalin LA) were developed because both methylphenidate and amphetamine are relatively short-acting stimulants, with durations of action ranging from 4 to 8 hours. Consequently, to provide symptom relief for extended periods (e.g., a full school day), short-acting stimulants such as Ritalin had to be dispensed two or even three times daily. Since the mid-1990s, however, delivery systems that allow for a more gradual, extended release of medication have been developed and marketed with great commercial success under many of the earlier referenced product labels.

Stimulant treatment of ADHD has been a mainstay of child psychiatry for decades, with the first controlled clinical trials involving methylphenidate published in the early 1960s. Since that time, several thousand studies have documented the efficacy of these drugs for reducing symptoms of inattention, hyperactivity, and impulsivity (Conners, 2002). To date, there are no comparative studies that demonstrate the superiority of any one stimulant product over another, and the selection of a product for any particular child will depend on his or her special needs and response to medications (Brown et al., 2005).

Although the efficacy of stimulant medication for treating ADHD is well-established, there is more debate over the potential adverse effects of the medication. In fact, concerns over stimulant safety have resulted in considerable controversy in the field. Stimulant drugs do result in a number of common side effects that occur in a minority of patients; these include insomnia, appetite suppression, and rebound behavioral effects when the medication wears off. However, these side effects tend to be mild to moderate in severity and tend to diminish after taking the medication for some time. More significant concern has been aroused by infrequent but severe side effects such as growth suppression (Pliszka, Matthews, Braslow, & Watson, 2006; Poulton, 2005), cardiac problems ("Debate over Warnings for ADHD Stimulants," 2006; Nissen, 2006; Rappley, Moore, & Dokken, 2006; Wooltorton, 2006), and even cytotoxicity (El-Zein et al., 2005, 2006; Preston et al., 2005).

Another controversial issue is the extent to which stimulant drug treatment for ADHD might increase the risk for substance abuse among these vulnerable patients. Because of their stimulant properties, both methylphenidate and amphetamine are considered to have high abuse potential (Kollins, MacDonald, & Rush, 2001), although clinical and experimental evidence suggests that patients themselves are less likely to find the effects of the drugs euphorogenic (Fredericks & Kollins, 2004; MacDonald Fredericks & Kollins, 2005). Nevertheless, these compounds have increasingly been shown to be widely misused (McCabe, Knight, Teter, & Wechsler, 2005; McCabe, Teter, & Boyd, 2004), which has caused additional concern among prescribers. In general, there appears to be consensus that additional research is needed to clarify the potentially negative effects of stimulant medications, but the risk:benefit associated with their use is still supported by a large number of well-controlled studies documenting their safety and efficacy when used as prescribed.

Nonstimulant Drugs   A number of nonstimulant drugs have been evaluated for the treatment of ADHD, most of which have yielded less robust effects than stimulants. The only FDA-approved nonstimulant product for the treatment of ADHD is Strattera, whose generic name is atomoxetine. This product, along with Adderall XR, is one of only two products with FDA approval for adults. Atomoxetine works by selectively inhibiting the norepinephrine transporter, thus facilitating norepinephrine transmission, which plays a role in the regulation of attentional and inhibitory processes (Arnsten & Li, 2005).

Although the evidence base for atomoxetine in treating ADHD is not nearly as extensive as for the stimulants (the drug was approved in late 2002), the existing data suggest that the drug is quite effective in reducing the symptoms associated with ADHD. Although overall effect sizes for atomoxetine tend to be smaller than those reported in trials of stimulants, it is difficult to predict how any individuals will respond; this drug has been found to be superior to placebo in a number of clinical trials (Brown et al., 2005; Steinhoff, 2004).

Atomoxetine's side effect profile is different from that of stimulants, with upset stomach, nausea, and sleepiness commonly reported. With respect to safety, the FDA has required the manufacturers of Straterra to include a warning on the label that the drug may increase suicidal thinking and behavior in some patients. This warning was issued after a review of available data suggesting that a very small (less than 0.5%) of patients reported these kinds of thoughts compared to no reports in patients taking placebo. As noted with stimulants, however, the overall risk:benefit ratio for atomoxetine is favorable, and the drug represents an acceptable alternative to stimulant medication in the treatment of ADHD.

A number of other nonstimulant products have been evaluated for the treatment of ADHD, some of which are described in more detail in subsequent sections.

However, we will focus less on these products, as none has been formally approved by the FDA for treatment of ADHD. The other nonstimulant drugs include both tricyclic and selective serotonin reuptake inhibiting antidepressants, the novel antidepressant buproprion, monoamine oxidase inhibitors, and antihypertensive agents (Spencer, Biederman, Wilens, & Faraone, 2002). It is worth noting that the wakefulness-promoting agent modafinil (to be marketed under the trade name Sparlon) is likely to be approved for use with ADHD by the time of publication of this volume and has been shown to have efficacy at least as high as that of atomoxetine (Biederman et al., 2006; Greenhill et al., 2006; Swanson et al., 2006).

PHARMACOTHERAPY FOR MOOD DISORDERS

In contrast to the decades of research and clinical work on ADHD medications, much less work has been done to evaluate pharmacotherapy for mood disorders in children (including both depression and Bipolar Disorder), despite the fact that these difficulties affect a substantial number of youth. In fact, prior to 1997, no study had been conducted that demonstrated the superiority of a medication over placebo for the treatment of childhood depression, although since that time, the number of pediatric patients enrolled in clinical trials for depression has increased 10-fold (Cheung, Emslie, & Mayes, 2006). In spite of the significant increase in research into the pharmacotherapy of childhood mood disorders, only one compound, fluoxetine (Prozac), has received FDA approval for the treatment of depression or Bipolar Disorder. The following briefly reviews two classes of drugs that have been studied: antidepressant medications and so-called mood stabilizers.

Antidepressant Medications Antidepressant medications can be divided into several different classes: tricyclics (desipramine, imipramine, nortriptyline), selective serotonin reuptake inhibitors (SSRIs; fluoxetine [Prozac], citalopram [Celexa], escitalopram [Lexapro], paroxetine [Paxil], sertraline [Zoloft]), and selective norepinephrine reuptake inhibitors (SNRIs; mirtazapine [Remeron], nefazadone [Serzone], venlafaxine [Effexor]).

It is well-accepted that tricyclic antidepressant medications fare no better than placebo for treating depression or Bipolar Disorder in children (Cheung et al., 2006; Wagner & Ambrosini, 2001). Among studies conducted with SSRIs and SNRIs, only fluoxetine has shown a consistent pattern of positive results compared to placebo. The most recent study, funded by the National Institute of Mental Health and conducted in 13 sites across the country, reported that fluoxetine resulted in significant improvement in depression in 61% of patients, compared to only 35% for those receiving placebo. Importantly, this study also found that an even greater proportion of children and adolescents (71%) improved when receiving a combination of fluoxetine and psychotherapy (March et al., 2004). Studies with other SSRIs and SNRIs have reported inconsistent results, with some showing improvement and others failing to find significant results (Cheung et al., 2006).

As with all drugs, SSRIs carry with them certain safety concerns that must be evaluated relative to their potential benefits. For fluoxetine, the most commonly reported side effects in clinical trials are nervousness, insomnia, and anxiety. It should be noted, however, that the rates of discontinuation due to side effects (an index of the treatment-emergent rate of side effects) in studies of fluoxetine and other SSRIs often do not exceed those of patients taking placebo (Emslie et al., 2002).

One specific safety concern that bears explicit comment regards the potential for increased suicidal ideation and behavior in children and adolescents who receive antidepressant medication. In October 2004, the FDA required all manufacturers of SSRIs to add a black-box warning to the labels for these products indicating this potential risk. This action was taken after a review of available clinical trial data (published and unpublished) that suggested a small increase in suicidality among children and teens. Given the elevated suicide risk associated with a diagnosis of depression, some researchers have called attention to the challenges inherent in interpreting these kinds of data. Nevertheless, clinicians should be ever mindful of the need to closely monitor the use of these products in youth to ensure that suicidal behavior does not emerge.

Mood Stabilizers   The prevalence and phenomenology of Bipolar Disorder in children, especially young children, is a topic of considerable debate, especially the extent to which it is mistaken for or comorbid with ADHD (Wozniak, 2005). Because of the historical view that Bipolar Disorder was relatively rare in children, there are currently no approved medications for the treatment of children younger than 12. Several forms of the standard mood stabilizer, lithium, have been approved for use to treat Bipolar Disorder in older children. Because there has been so much controversy over the clinical features of Bipolar Disorder, particularly in young children, experts in the area have convened to publish guidelines for conducting clinical trials with this population (Carlson et al., 2003). Lithium and valproic acid are regarded as first-line treatments for children with Bipolar Disorder, largely because these have been considered first-line treatments with adults. However, more recently, some have advocated the use of other kinds of agents, particularly atypical antipsychotics, such as risperidone, aripiprazole, and quetiapine, as they have been shown to have some efficacy (Danielyan & Kowatch, 2005). Given the limitations of the research literature and the lack of any FDA-approved options, the most conservative conclusion to be drawn about the pharmacological treatment of Bipolar Disorder in children is that additional research needs to be done, and both traditional mood stabilizers (lithium) and newer agents may be promising new approaches.

PHARMACOTHERAPY FOR ANXIETY PROBLEMS

Anxiety disorders comprise a cluster of diagnoses, including specific phobias, Generalized Anxiety Disorder, Separation Anxiety Disorder, Obsessive-Compulsive Disorder (OCD), Panic Disorder, and Posttraumatic Stress Disorder. Collectively, these disorders represent a significant proportion of mental health referrals for children and adolescents. Substantial evidence supports the use of nonpharmacological interventions for the treatment of the whole range of anxiety disorders in children; these are reviewed elsewhere in this volume (see Baldwin & Dadds, this volume). Our emphasis is on those psychopharmacological interventions that have garnered empirical support.

There are currently three medications that have been approved for the treatment of OCD in children and adolescents: clomipramine (Anafranil; approved for children ages 10 and older), fluvoxamine (Luvox; approved for children ages 8 and older), and sertraline (Zoloft; approved for children ages 6 and older). Additionally, the medication doxepin (Sinequan) is approved for the treatment of anxiety disorders in general in children ages 12 and older.

It is important to note that although medication treatment for anxiety disorders in children has been shown to be superior to placebo, the combination of medication and cognitive behavioral treatment (CBT) has been shown to be the most effective approach. For example, in the recently completed Pediatric OCD Treatment Study (POTS), 53% of children receiving a combination of sertraline and CBT showed a clinically significant response, compared to CBT alone (40%), sertraline alone (21.4%), or placebo (3.6%). The difference between combined treatment and CBT was not statistically significant, but the difference between combined treatment and sertraline was significant (TEAM, 2004).

The safety profile of medications used to treat anxiety disorders in children and adolescents is similar to those medications used to treat depression, since the drugs are generally in similar classes. One exception is the use of clomipramine, which is a tricyclic antidepressant and, as such, carries some additional safety concerns, including possible cardiovascular effects (Wilens et al., 1996).

SUMMARY

A wide range of medications are used to treat children and adolescents with psychiatric disorders, although only a handful have undergone the kinds of rigorous empirical assessment required to obtain FDA approval. Mental health professionals who work with children and adolescents need to be aware of the evidence base for the use of these medications to provide balanced and useful information to parents. The foregoing section has attempted to highlight the data on the most common disorders in childhood. The review is necessarily truncated and does not include discussion of medications used to treat other problems, such as psychotic disorders, aggression, and enuresis. Interested readers should consult Brown and Sammons (2002) or Wilens (2004).

BASIC PRINCIPLES OF PSYCHOPHARMACOLOGY

In addition to a solid understanding of the medications most commonly used to treat psychiatric disorders and the evidence supporting their efficacy and safety, it is critical for clinicians to familiarize themselves with the basic principles governing how drugs work in the body. This information can help inform assessment and treatment planning. The purpose of this section is to review several basic principles of psychopharmacology, the study of the psychological and behavioral effects of drugs. Our review of basic pharmacology concerns itself with (a) the clinical effects versus the side effects of medication, (b) the dose-response relation, (c) drug half-life, and (d) peak effects.

CLINICAL EFFECTS VERSUS SIDE EFFECTS

When medication is used to treat a psychiatric disorder, the goal is to achieve a clinical effect. That is, the drug should reduce impairment and suffering, typically by reducing the behavior and emotional problems that are causing difficulty in a person's life. If possible, the medication should also promote the individual's adaptive effectiveness, such as school functioning, peer acceptance, and family functioning. Because the drugs we reviewed previously act in the CNS, they have the potential to influence all aspects of mood and behavioral functioning, as well as a range of psychological processes, including attention, concentration, sensation, perception, and motivation.

Furthermore, it is well established that any neurotransmitter system targeted by a psychoactive drug is likely to exert effects on multiple aspects of cognition, mood, and behavior. Because these systems may be responsible for more than one kind of functioning, their use can result in some effects that are not of clinical interest and may even be unpleasant or unwanted. For example, as discussed previously, stimulant drugs used for treating ADHD are thought to be effective because they alter the functioning of the neurotransmitters norepinephrine and dopamine, which are associated with such processes as attention and concentration. However, these neurotransmitters are also associated with elevated arousal elsewhere in the CNS. Consequently, in addition to the clinical effects of improving concentration and attention, these drugs may increase blood pressure and heart rate, increase respiration, decrease appetite, and disrupt sleep patterns in some individuals. Part of the successful management of any behavioral or psychological problem through medication use is to balance the beneficial clinical effects of the medication with the potential side effects.

THE DOSE-RESPONSE RELATION

It is a basic principle of pharmacology that the effects of a drug (a *response* of some sort that is related to behavior change) are systematically related to the amount of the drug (the *dose*) that is in the body. This relation is described as the dose-response function and can be graphically displayed to show the effects of different doses of a drug on some aspect of behavior. One important aspect of the dose-response function is that there is considerable variability, both across children and even within the same child, with respect to the manner in which doses influence different areas of functioning (i.e., academic, social, emotional; Douglas, Barr, Desilets, & Sherman, 1995; Sprague & Sleator, 1977; Tannock, Schachar, Carr, & Logan, 1989). This basic principle of psychopharmacology underscores the need for individualized assessment of drug effects.

Another important feature of the dose-response relation to consider is that it is not always a linear function. In other words, it is not true that if a small dose of a drug is moderately effective in managing some problem behavior, a larger dose will always be better. The way different children respond to medication may result in very different dose-response profiles. The response of individual children to varying doses of a drug can be categorized in at least four ways: (1) Behavioral improvement is related to stepwise increases in dose; (2) behavioral improvement is subject to a threshold effect at a moderate or high dose; (3) behavioral improvement reaches a peak at a moderate dose and shows a decrease at higher doses; or (4) behavioral improvement is inconsistent across doses (Rapport, DuPaul, Stoner, & Jones, 1986). These patterns of responding are illustrated in Figure 7.1, which also shows how the dose-response relationship can be graphically presented.

Figure 7.1 also highlights the necessity of examining several different doses of medication to conclusively determine which dose is optimal for managing a specific behavioral problem. For example, if a clinician prescribed only a relatively high dose of medication to the child in Panel C without also evaluating other doses, he or she may erroneously conclude that the medication was not effective, as this particular dose had little effect. Similarly, prescribing only a low dose to this child would not have much effect. Only by examining different doses in comparison to one another can a physician confidently determine which dose is the most effective for managing a behavior problem.

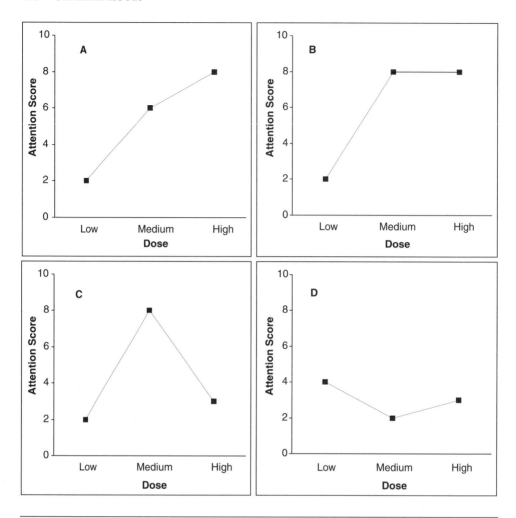

Figure 7.1 Different dose-response patterns for several different doses of a drug. Scores on a rating of attention (higher = better) are plotted as a function of drug dose.

HALF-LIFE

Another related pharmacological principle is that drugs are broken down and eliminated from the body over a particular time course, and as this happens, there is less drug available in the system to influence behavior across the time period. Because the effects of a drug are related to the amount of the drug in the body, it follows that the faster the drug is broken down and eliminated from the body, the shorter the length of time the drug will exert its effects. The rate at which different drugs are broken down and eliminated from the body is described generally as the *half-life* of a medication. This term is used to describe the time it takes to eliminate half of a drug from the body (hence the term half-life). For example, the half-life of normally administered immediate-release methylphenidate is 2 to 3 hours. This means that it takes between 2 and 3 hours for half of an initial dose to be eliminated from the body. This also means that 4 to 6 hours after taking a dose of methylphenidate, only 25% is left in the body:

50% of the drug is left after the first 2 to 3 hours and 50% of 50% (25%) is left after another 2 to 3 hours. With respect to stimulant drugs used to treat ADHD, it is relevant to note that the newer long-acting formulations discussed earlier are designed to deliver the drug more slowly across the course of a day. As such, even though the active ingredient is still the same, the effective half-life of the medication is extended since the total dose of the drug does not start to be metabolized until later in the day. The result is that the overall duration of action is longer.

The half-lives of other drugs can be much longer. For example, fluoxetine and other SSRIs have half-lives of 1 to 4 *days*. This means that, especially if such medication is administered on a daily basis, it takes much longer for the drug to be completely eliminated from the body. Conversely, it also means that it may take several days (or weeks) for a drug to reach therapeutic levels in the body. For example, suppose that a drug has a half-life of 1 day (24 hours) and a dose of 10 mg is prescribed, once daily. On the second day, 5 mg remains in the body, and this is added to that day's additional 10 mg dose. On the third day, 2.5 mg of the original dose, plus 5 mg of the second dose, plus 10 mg of that day's dose remain in the body, for a total of 17.5 mg. This regimen may be continued until a certain level of the drug in the body is reached, at which time the dosing regimen may be altered to maintain this level.

One might ask why not just administer a larger dose all at once? In general, this may not be possible with some drugs due to potentially problematic side effects of large doses given in one administration. In any case, an understanding of the concept of the half-life of drugs is important to help caregivers understand the dosing regimen prescribed by their physician. Further, this information may be helpful in determining whether changes or aberrations in behavior or other functioning of a child are likely due to drug effects or other factors.

The half-life of a given medication may vary somewhat across individuals. For example, as noted previously, the average half-life of methylphenidate is between 2 and 3 hours. For a child at the lower end of the range (half-life = 2 hours), only 25% of the medication would remain 4 hours after a dose. By contrast, a child at the upper end of the range (half-life = 3 hours) would not eliminate that much of the medication until 6 hours after the initial dose. These differences may require different dosing regimens for different children to attain maximum clinical efficacy. The former child may benefit from doses administered every 4 hours, whereas the latter child may benefit from a more delayed regimen. Of course, as noted previously, the best way to determine the best dosing schedule is to conduct an individualized medication assessment.

PEAK EFFECTS

The final basic principle of psychopharmacology is that drugs (especially stimulants) often exert their optimal clinical effects at a point well after administration. This time point is often referred to as the time of *peak effects* and, because it is related to the concept of half-life, varies significantly across drugs. For example, the peak effects for standard formulations of methylphenidate usually occur 1.5 to 2 hours after administration. This means that although beneficial effects may be observed sooner, the maximal effect of the drug is not likely to occur until later, and the effects after that time period may begin to diminish. The newer formulations of stimulant drugs used to treat ADHD provide an extended duration of peak effects. For example, Concerta, a methylphenidate-based product, was designed to mimic 3-times a day dosing and thus results in peak plasma concentrations (and corresponding peak behavioral effects) that last much longer than standard formulations of methylphenidate (Swanson et al., 2003).

Understanding when different drugs exert their peak effects can provide valuable information to clinicians, parents, and teachers who are administering or overseeing the use of the drug. For example, a child whose attention and concentration deficits are most apparent in a math class just before lunch might not benefit from a dose of standard Ritalin that is administered 4 or 5 hours earlier at breakfast since the peak effects of the medication will likely occur 1.5 to 2 hours after administration. The relevance of how peak effects and pharmacokinetics more broadly affect functioning was demonstrated in a recent study comparing two extended-release methylphenidate products (Concerta and Metadate) in an analogue classroom setting. This study found that when controlling for overall daily dose of the drug, the subtle differences in delivery systems of the two products resulted in significant behavioral differences throughout the course of the day (Swanson et al., 2004).

An important caveat to these principles of psychopharmacology is that the patterns of side effects, dose-response functions, half-lives, and peak effects are not uniform across individuals. In fact, even within the same individual, considerable variation is possible. For example, as noted previously, the specific behavior under study influences the relation between the amount of the drug and the extent of behavior change (the dose-response relation). Similarly, factors such as the presence of other prescription or over-the-counter medications, recent meals, and sleep patterns may all influence the half-life and/or peak effects of drugs within the same child. These characteristics of drug effects underscore two important facts, discussed later in the chapter. First, the only way to confidently determine the specific effects of a drug for any given child is to conduct a carefully controlled medication assessment. Second, generally speaking, drugs affect individuals in different ways. This principle of psychopharmacology is important to keep in mind as it can influence the expectations of important individuals who interact with a medicated child, such as parents and teachers. For example, a teacher may observe that some children in the class respond favorably to a particular stimulant treatment regimen but see few benefits for other children prescribed the same medication.

Understanding these basic principles of psychopharmacology, specifically as they pertain to individual (or multiple) medications that children might be receiving, should enhance the clinician's ability to inform clients about how pharmacological interventions can complement other treatment modalities. The remainder of this chapter focuses on research examining the utility of combining pharmacological and psychosocial treatments for psychiatric disorders among children and adolescents.

CLINICAL ISSUES RELEVANT TO THE PHARMACOLOGICAL TREATMENT OF CHILDHOOD PSYCHIATRIC DISORDERS

With the dramatic increase in the prevalence of psychotropic medications for all ages and for most childhood mental health disorders, it is imperative that clinicians develop an understanding of the efficacy, side effects, mechanisms of change, and compliance and safety issues associated with psychotropic medications. Documented increases in polypharmacy necessitates that clinicians have information about multiple medications to make informed treatment decisions (dosReis et al., 2005). Because the majority of children and adolescents are prescribed psychotropic medications by primary care pediatricians (DeLeon & Wiggins, 1996), clinicians are commonly asked to perform service coordination duties. Although coordination of services may be viewed as an extra burden, it provides knowledgeable clinicians with the opportunity to increase the efficacy and safety with which psychotropic medications are utilized, which in turn can increase the efficacy of the overall treatment plan (Brown & Sammons, 2002).

MEDICATION AND PSYCHOTHERAPY: COMBINED TREATMENT

Large-scale randomized clinical trials have now been completed for three of the most commonly occurring childhood and adolescent disorders: ADHD, Major Depressive Disorder, and OCD. A fourth large study, the Child and Adolescent Anxiety Multimodal Study, was ongoing at the time this chapter was written and is not discussed in detail (see Compton et al., 2004, for a review of CBT for anxiety disorders).

The Multimodal Treatment Study (MTA) was the first major multisite clinical trial and examined the relative efficacy of medication alone (stimulants), behavioral intervention alone, combined medication and behavioral intervention, and treatment as usual community care for the treatment of children with ADHD (Arnold et al., 1997; Greenhill et al., 1996; MTA Cooperative Group, 1999). The Treatment for Adolescents with Depression Study (TADS) utilized a similar study design to compare the benefits of medication alone (fluoxetine), cognitive-behavioral therapy alone, a combination of medication and CBT, and a medication placebo for adolescents diagnosed with Major Depressive Disorder (March et al., 2004). Finally, the Pediatric OCD Treatment Study (POTS) compared the effects of CBT alone, sertraline alone, and the combination of the two (TEAM, 2004). These large multisite trials were designed and funded primarily to provide information for clinicians about the type of treatment or combination of treatments that most effectively treat major childhood disorders. While there continues to be much discussion surrounding the findings of these studies, a number of critical points can be gleaned from this research that have significant implications for clinicians working with children and adolescents. The remainder of this section focuses primarily on how the results of these large multimodal trials can be used to inform and guide the evidence-based treatment of children and adolescents.

Taken as a whole, the results of the MTA, TADS, and POTS studies support the assertion that the combination of behavioral or psychosocial treatment plus medication produces improvements above what medication or psychotherapy alone can provide. In the MTA, 68% of children who received combination treatment were rated in the normal range on a measure of ADHD symptoms as compared to 56% for medication management alone, 34% for behavioral treatment alone, and 25% for community control after completing 14 months of active treatment. Although the difference between the combined group and the medication management group did not attain statistical significance for the primary outcome measure of ADHD symptoms (Conners et al., 2001; MTA Cooperative Group, 1999), a secondary analysis that combined outcomes across different domains of functioning reported statistical superiority for the combination group (Conners et al., 2001). In addition, the average daily dose of medication for MTA participants receiving combined treatment was significantly lower than the average daily dose for participants in the medication alone group (Vitiello et al., 2001). This is an important finding since, as described previously, the negative side effects associated with medications may be more likely to occur at higher doses.

In the TADS, adolescents who received both fluoxetine and CBT exhibited a significantly greater decline in symptoms of depression as compared to adolescents receiving fluoxetine or CBT alone. Participants who received the combination of fluoxetine and CBT also reported the greatest decrease in clinically significant suicidal thinking (March et al., 2004).

Finally, as described previously, the POTS reported that a combination of CBT and sertraline was most effective at reducing OCD symptoms in children ages 7 through 17. Moreover, in this study, clinical remission (a secondary outcome measure) was highest in the combination group (53.6%), compared to the CBT alone (39.3%) and the sertraline alone (21.4%) groups. Importantly, the combined and CBT groups did not differ from one another statistically, but were both superior to sertraline alone (TEAM, 2004).

COLLABORATION

These groundbreaking studies demonstrate that optimal evidence-based mental health care can be provided only through collaboration between disciplines—specifically, care providers who can administer both medication and some form of psychosocial treatment. As the data from these large, multisite trials demonstrate, the combination of medication and therapy is currently the most effective form of treatment for children and adolescents. Accordingly, if psychiatrists, pediatricians, and clinicians are not working together, then children and adolescents are likely to be receiving less than optimal care. Developing a comprehensive treatment plan that includes strategies for coordinating medication management with psychotherapy will improve outcomes and decrease the safety risks associated with some medications. Unfortunately, in the context of standard mental health care, this kind of collaboration presents significant challenges.

Although there are many barriers to the delivery of optimal mental health care for children and adolescents, two are emphasized and briefly discussed here: (1) the lack of access to appropriate psychological treatment and (2) the limitations of primary care providers for managing medication in an empirical manner.

Service Availability   The first issue surrounding the delivery of optimal care to youth with psychiatric disorders is the relative lack of services available to the majority of children (Ringeisen, Oliver, & Menvielle, 2002). The multisite studies discussed earlier have been critiqued on the grounds that the interventions tested in these trials are likely to be available only in university settings, and then, usually in the context of funded clinical research. In other words, the availability of these services in many, if not most, communities across the United States (and elsewhere) is limited. Moreover, in the settings where such comprehensive services are offered, they are likely to be cost-prohibitive to all but those with the highest socioeconomic status or those with the most comprehensive health care insurance. Consequently, we may have the necessary tools to reduce the suffering associated with childhood psychiatric disorders, but we lack the infrastructure to deliver evidence-based interventions. Unfortunately, the literature offers little guidance concerning how to address this issue. The best recommendations at present are for mental health care providers to become well-versed in evidence-based treatments for children with psychiatric disorders and to strive to identify and implement multidisciplinary treatments in their communities. Current work funded by the National Institutes of Health and other entities emphasizes the dissemination of empirically based treatment services. Hopefully this research will lead to advances in the care of vulnerable patient populations.

Medication Management   A second issue pertaining to the management of psychiatric disorders in childhood is the feasibility of providing optimal pharmacological treatment for children in the context of primary care. As discussed previously, there is substantial evidence for the efficacy of a range of pharmacological interventions in the treatment of childhood psychiatric disorders. However, the manner in which the medications are prescribed in these clinical trials often differs dramatically from how medications are prescribed in clinical practice. The MTA ADHD study offers an excellent example of this disconnect. Recall that the children assigned to the medication management group fared better than any other group with respect to reduction of core ADHD symptoms. Recall also that the worst-faring group was the one referred into the community (i.e., routine care). The important point here is that of those children in the routine care group, the vast majority received medication only. Why the difference between stimulant treatment in the study group and the community? Although a number of explanations may apply, one of the most striking is that participants in the study group met with their physician at least monthly, and when they did, the prescribing practices were governed by a rigorous algorithm for medication management that relied on objective input from parents and teachers to guide decisions about dose changes. This finding highlights the importance of using objective data, preferably from multiple sources, to guide medication use. Unfortunately, the resources (i.e., time, staff) required to support this kind of assessment and treatment monitoring may be beyond the capacity of primary care providers (i.e., pediatricians and family practice physicians), who write the majority of prescriptions for children with psychiatric disorders.

The challenges facing stimulant treatment, though unfortunate for patients, may provide an excellent opportunity for other mental health professionals (e.g., psychologists) to contribute to the enhancement of treatment outcomes in the community. Psychologists whose training emphasizes the objective assessment of behavior could be called on to work closely with prescribers to conduct the kind of careful medication titration that has been shown to be most effective in clinical trials. There is currently federally funded research ongoing to explore other, more cost-effective approaches for disseminating the titration algorithms from the MTA study to clinical practice. Although the emphasis here has been on the barriers to optimal medication management in children with ADHD, the principles of careful objective assessment and outcome tracking are likely to be applicable to all areas of child and adolescent psychopharmacology.

SUMMARY

Although not necessarily ubiquitous, the use of pharmacological agents for treating childhood psychiatric disorders has been increasing rapidly. Many nonmedical professionals have watched these trends with dismay, and there is considerable controversy over the appropriateness of such widespread medication use in young people. Nevertheless, pharmacological treatments for certain childhood and adolescent disorders have considerable empirical support. Familiarity with the literature in this area along with certain key principles of psychopharmacology is essential for mental health workers to provide and coordinate the best possible care for those youth suffering from psychiatric conditions. Equally important is evidence that supports the use of nonpharmacological interventions in addition to and, in some cases, prior to the prescription of medication. Clearly, in the treatment of psychiatric conditions affecting youth, there are important roles to be played by a variety of disciplines, including psychiatrists, psychologists, and other mental health professionals.

REFERENCES

Arnold, L. E., Abikoff, H. B., Cantwell, D. P., Conners, C. K., Elliott, G., Greenhill, L. L., et al. (1997). National Institute of Mental Health Collaborative Multimodal Treatment Study of Children with ADHD (the MTA): Design challenges and choices. *Archives of General Psychiatry, 54*(9), 865–870.

Arnsten, A. F., & Li, B. M. (2005). Neurobiology of executive functions: Catecholamine influences on prefrontal cortical functions. *Biological Psychiatry, 57*(11), 1377–1384.

Biederman, J., Swanson, J. M., Wigal, S. B., Boellner, S. W., Earl, C. Q., & Lopez, F. A. (2006). A comparison of once-daily and divided doses of modafinil in children with attention-deficit/hyperactivity disorder: A randomized, double-blind, and placebo-controlled study. *Journal of Clinical Psychiatry, 67*(5), 727–735.

Brown, R. T., Amler, R. W., Freeman, W. S., Perrin, J. M., Stein, M. T., Feldman, H. M., et al. (2005). Treatment of attention-deficit/hyperactivity disorder: Overview of the evidence. *Pediatrics, 115*(6), e749–e757.

Brown, R. T., & Sammons, M. T. (2002). Pediatric psychopharmacology: A review of new developments and recent research. *Professional Psychology: Research and Practice, 33*(2), 135–147.

Carlson, G. A., Jensen, P. S., Findling, R. L., Meyer, R. E., Calabrese, J., DelBello, M. P., et al. (2003). Methodological issues and controversies in clinical trials with child and adolescent patients with bipolar disorder: Report of a consensus conference. *Journal of Child and Adolescent Psychopharmacology, 13*(1), 13–27.

Cheung, A. H., Emslie, G. J., & Mayes, T. L. (2006). The use of antidepressants to treat depression in children and adolescents. *Canadian Medical Association Journal, 174*(2), 193–200.

Compton, S. N., March, J. S., Brent, D., Albano, A. M., Weersing, R., & Curry, J. (2004). Cognitive-behavioral psychotherapy for anxiety and depressive disorders in children and adolescents: An evidence-based medicine review. *Journal of the American Academy of Child and Adolescent Psychiatry, 43*(8), 930–959.

Conners, C. K. (2002). Forty years of methylphenidate treatment in attention-deficit/hyperactivity disorder. *Journal of Attention Disorders, 6*(Suppl. 1), S17–S30.

Conners, C. K., Epstein, J. N., March, J. S., Angold, A., Wells, K. C., Klaric, J., et al. (2001). Multimodal treatment of ADHD in the MTA: An alternative outcome analysis. *Journal of the American Academy of Child and Adolescent Psychiatry, 40*(2), 159–167.

Danielyan, A., & Kowatch, R. A. (2005). Management options for bipolar disorder in children and adolescents. *Pediatric Drugs, 7*(5), 277–294.

Debate over warnings for ADHD stimulants. (2006). *Child Health Alert, 24*, 1.

DeLeon, P. H., & Wiggins, J. G., Jr. (1996). Prescription privileges for psychologists. *American Psychologist, 51*(3), 225–229.

dosReis, S., Zito, J. M., Safer, D. J., Gardner, J. F., Puccia, K. B., & Owens, P. L. (2005). Multiple psychotropic medication use for youths: A two-state comparison. *Journal of Child and Adolescent Psychopharmacology, 15*(1), 68–77.

Douglas, V. I., Barr, R. G., Desilets, J., & Sherman, E. (1995). Do high doses of stimulants impair flexible thinking in attention-deficit hyperactivity disorder? *Journal of the American Academy of Child and Adolescent Psychiatry, 34*(7), 877–885.

El-Zein, R. A., Abdel-Rahman, S. Z., Hay, M. J., Lopez, M. S., Bondy, M. L., Morris, D. L., et al. (2005). Cytogenetic effects in children treated with methylphenidate. *Cancer Letters, 230*(2), 284–291.

El-Zein, R. A., Hay, M. J., Lopez, M. S., Bondy, M. L., Morris, D. L., Legator, M. S., et al. (2006). Response to comments on "Cytogenetic effects in children treated with methylphenidate" by El-Zein et al. *Cancer Letters, 231*(1), 146–148.

Emslie, G. J., Heiligenstein, J. H., Wagner, K. D., Hoog, S. L., Ernest, D. E., Brown, E., et al. (2002). Fluoxetine for acute treatment of depression in children and adolescents: A placebo-controlled, randomized clinical trial. *Journal of the American Academy of Child and Adolescent Psychiatry, 41*(10), 1205–1215.

Fredericks, E. M., & Kollins, S. H. (2004). Assessing methylphenidate preference in ADHD patients using a choice procedure. *Psychopharmacology, 175*(4), 391–398.

Greenhill, L. L., Abikoff, H. B., Arnold, L. E., Cantwell, D. P., Conners, C. K., Elliott, G., et al. (1996). Medication treatment strategies in the MTA study: Relevance to clinicians and researchers. *Journal of the American Academy of Child and Adolescent Psychiatry, 35*(10), 1304–1313.

Greenhill, L. L., Biederman, J., Boellner, S. W., Rugino, T. A., Sangal, R. B., Earl, C. Q., et al. (2006). A randomized, double-blind, placebo-controlled study of modafinil film-coated tablets in children and adolescents with attention-deficit/hyperactivity disorder. *Journal of the American Academy of Child and Adolescent Psychiatry, 45*(5), 503–511.

Hunkeler, E. M., Fireman, B., Lee, J., Diamond, R., Hamilton, J., He, C. X., et al. (2005). Trends in use of antidepressants, lithium, and anticonvulsants in Kaiser Permanente-insured youths, 1994–2003. *Journal of Child and Adolescent Psychopharmacology, 15*(1), 26–37.

Kollins, S. H., MacDonald, E. K., & Rush, C. R. (2001). Assessing the abuse potential of methylphenidate in nonhuman and human subjects: A review. *Pharmacology, Biochemistry, and Behavior, 68*(3), 611–627.

MacDonald Fredericks, E., & Kollins, S. H. (2005). A pilot study of methylphenidate preference assessment in children diagnosed with attention-deficit/hyperactivity disorder. *Journal of Child and Adolescent Psychopharmacology, 15*(5), 729–741.

March, J., Silva, S., Petrycki, S., Curry, J., Wells, K., Fairbank, J., et al. (2004). Fluoxetine, cognitive-behavioral therapy, and their combination for adolescents with depression: Treatment for Adolescents with Depression Study (TADS) randomized controlled trial. *Journal of the American Medical Association, 292*(7), 807–820.

McCabe, S. E., Knight, J. R., Teter, C. J., & Wechsler, H. (2005). Non-medical use of prescription stimulants among U.S. college students: Prevalence and correlates from a national survey. *Addiction, 100*(1), 96–106.

McCabe, S. E., Teter, C. J., & Boyd, C. J. (2004). The use, misuse, and diversion of prescription stimulants among middle and high school students. *Substance Use and Misuse, 39*(7), 1095–1116.

MTA Cooperative Group. (1999). Multimodal Treatment Study of Children with ADHD: A 14-month randomized clinical trial of treatment strategies for attention-deficit/hyperactivity disorder. *Archives of General Psychiatry, 56*(12), 1073–1086.

Nissen, S. E. (2006). ADHD drugs and cardiovascular risk. *New England Journal of Medicine, 354*(14), 1445–1448.

Olfson, M., Marcus, S. C., Weissman, M. M., & Jensen, P. S. (2002). National trends in the use of psychotropic medications by children. *Journal of the American Academy of Child and Adolescent Psychiatry, 41*(5), 514–521.

Pliszka, S. R. (2005). The neuropsychopharmacology of attention-deficit/hyperactivity disorder. *Biological Psychiatry, 57*(11), 1385–1390.

Pliszka, S. R., Matthews, T. L., Braslow, K. J., & Watson, M. A. (2006). Comparative effects of methylphenidate and mixed salts amphetamine on height and weight in children with attention-deficit/hyperactivity disorder. *Journal of the American Academy of Child and Adolescent Psychiatry, 45*(5), 520–526.

Poulton, A. (2005). Growth on stimulant medication: Clarifying the confusion. A review. *Archives of Disease in Childhood, 90*(8), 801–806.

Preston, R. J., Kollins, S. H., Swanson, J. M., Greenhill, L. L., Wigal, T., Elliott, G. R., et al. (2005). Comments on "Cytogenetic effects in children treated with methylphenidate" by El-Zein et al. *Cancer Letters, 230*(2), 292–294.

Raghavan, R., Zima, B. T., Andersen, R. M., Leibowitz, A. A., Schuster, M. A., & Landsverk, J. (2005). Psychotropic medication use in a national probability sample of children in the child welfare system. *Journal of Child and Adolescent Psychopharmacology, 15*(1), 97–106.

Rappley, M. D., Moore, J. W., & Dokken, D. (2006). ADHD drugs and cardiovascular risk. *New England Journal of Medicine, 354*(21), 2296–2298.

Rapport, M. D., DuPaul, G. J., Stoner, G., & Jones, T. J. (1986). Comparing classroom and clinic measures of attention deficit disorder: Differential, idiosyncratic, and dose-response effects of methylphenidate. *Journal of Consulting and Clinical Psychology, 54*(3), 334–341.

Ringeisen, H., Oliver, K. A., & Menvielle, E. (2002). Recognition and treatment of mental disorders in children: Considerations for pediatric health systems. *Pediatric Drugs, 4*(11), 697–703.

Sagvolden, T., Johansen, E. B., Aase, H., & Russell, V. A. (2005). A dynamic developmental theory of attention-deficit/hyperactivity disorder (ADHD) predominantly hyperactive/impulsive and combined subtypes. *Behavioral and Brain Sciences, 28*(3), 397–419; discussion 419–368.

Spencer, T. J., Biederman, J., Wilens, T. E., & Faraone, S. V. (2002). Novel treatments for attention-deficit/hyperactivity disorder in children. *Journal of Clinical Psychiatry, 63*(Suppl. 12), 16–22.

Sprague, R. L., & Sleator, E. K. (1977). Methylphenidate in hyperkinetic children: Differences in dose effects on learning and social behavior. *Science, 198*(4323), 1274–1276.

Steinhoff, K. W. (2004). Attention-deficit/hyperactivity disorder: Medication treatment-dosing and duration of action. *American Journal of Managed Care, 10*(Suppl. 4), S99–S106.

Swanson, J. M., Greenhill, L. L., Lopez, F. A., Sedillo, A., Earl, C. Q., Jiang, J. G., et al. (2006). Modafinil film-coated tablets in children and adolescents with attention-deficit/hyperactivity disorder: Results of a randomized, double-blind, placebo-controlled, fixed-dose study followed by abrupt discontinuation. *Journal of Clinical Psychiatry, 67*(1), 137–147.

Swanson, J., Gupta, S., Lam, A., Shoulson, I., Lerner, M., Modi, N., et al. (2003). Development of a new once-a-day formulation of methylphenidate for the treatment of attention-deficit/hyperactivity disorder: Proof-of-concept and proof-of-product studies. *Archives of General Psychiatry, 60*(2), 204–211.

Swanson, J. M., Wigal, S. B., Wigal, T., Sonuga-Barke, E., Greenhill, L. L., Biederman, J., et al. (2004). A comparison of once-daily extended-release methylphenidate formulations in children with attention-deficit/hyperactivity disorder in the laboratory school (the Comacs Study). *Pediatrics, 113*(3, Pt. 1), e206–e216.

Tannock, R., Schachar, R. J., Carr, R. P., & Logan, G. D. (1989). Dose-response effects of methylphenidate on academic performance and overt behavior in hyperactive children. *Pediatrics, 84*(4), 648–657.

TEAM (2004). Cognitive-behavior therapy, sertraline, and their combination for children and adolescents with obsessive-compulsive disorder: The Pediatric OCD Treatment Study (POTS) randomized controlled trial. *Journal of the American Medical Association, 292*(16), 1969–1976.

Thomas, C. P., Conrad, P., Casler, R., & Goodman, E. (2006). Trends in the use of psychotropic medications among adolescents, 1994 to 2001. *Psychiatric Services, 57*(1), 63–69.

Vitiello, B., Severe, J. B., Greenhill, L. L., Arnold, L. E., Abikoff, H. B., Bukstein, O. G., et al. (2001). Methylphenidate dosage for children with ADHD over time under controlled conditions: Lessons from the MTA. *Journal of the American Academy of Child and Adolescent Psychiatry, 40*(2), 188–196.

Wagner, K. D., & Ambrosini, P. J. (2001). Childhood depression: Pharmacological therapy/ treatment (pharmacotherapy of childhood depression). *Journal of Clinical Child Psychology, 30*(1), 88–97.

Wilens, T. E. (2004). *Straight talk about psychiatric medications for kids.* New York: Guilford Press.

Wilens, T. E., Biederman, J., Baldessarini, R. J., Geller, B., Schleifer, D., Spencer, T. J., et al. (1996). Cardiovascular effects of therapeutic doses of tricyclic antidepressants in children and adolescents. *Journal of the American Academy of Child and Adolescent Psychiatry, 35*(11), 1491–1501.

Wooltorton, E. (2006). Medications for attention deficit hyperactivity disorder: Cardiovascular concerns. *Canadian Medical Association Journal, 175*(1), 29.

Wozniak, J. (2005). Recognizing and managing bipolar disorder in children. *Journal of Clinical Psychiatry, 66*(Suppl. 1), 18–23.

Zito, J. M., Safer, D. J., dosReis, S., Gardner, J. F., Boles, M., & Lynch, F. (2000). Trends in the prescribing of psychotropic medications to preschoolers. *Journal of the American Medical Association, 283*(8), 1025–1030.

Zito, J. M., Safer, D. J., dosReis, S., Gardner, J. F., Soeken, K., Boles, M., et al. (2002). Rising prevalence of antidepressants among U.S. youths. *Pediatrics, 109*(5), 721–727.

CHAPTER 8

Ethical Issues

IAN M. EVANS

The translation of clinical assessment, through to a formulation of the child client's needs, and from thence to treatment planning and delivery is a complex clinical judgment task (Evans & Litz, 1987; Evans & Wilson, 1983). As such, it involves more than simply administering psychometrically sound instruments and implementing evidence-based techniques. It involves societal standards and expectations, implicit professional assumptions and personal biases, and values. This is the stuff of ethics. Case conceptualization, the link between assessment and treatment, requires ethical decision making according to propriety, context, and acceptability of professional actions, including acceptability to children.

The greater the likelihood that case conceptualization will lead to treatments that will make a difference in children's lives, the more important must be the professional desire to do the right thing. Many years ago, I attended a public lecture on the University of Hawaii campus by the famous maverick psychiatrist Thomas Szasz. He made the wry comment that "consulting a psychiatrist is like calling in a TV repairman because you don't like the program you're watching." It was a clever line, made all the more pleasing because he was challenging the disease model of his own medical profession (see, e.g., Albee & Joffe, 2004). Whether it is psychiatry or clinical psychology, mental health services or education, behavior therapy or cognitive therapy, the issue has haunted professional practice ever since we had medications, institutions, and management techniques powerful enough to actually influence behavior and seriously threaten individual autonomy (Evans, 1997). Behavior therapy, therefore, has always had to confront the same value questions: Is this a problem, and for whom? Should it be changed? Should any means be used to change it?

These questions have practical relevance to any assessment, conceptualization, and ultimate treatment decisions. They have special ethical relevance whenever the target individual is a child, because, unlike an adult, child clients cannot answer any of these questions for themselves. Children also typically are limited in two critical ways: They cannot easily refuse to be assessed and treated, and, conversely, they cannot usually advocate for themselves or personally request an intervention. Even when adolescents have confidential access to mental health professionals, such as school counselors, they prefer to discuss their problems with peers. Young people rarely contribute directly to the formulation of their own clinical case, although they could and probably should.

As I shall endeavor to show, concerns related to these three questions have been addressed thoughtfully over the recent history of cognitive-behavior therapy (see also Evans, Scotti, & Hawkins, 1999). But, as basic concerns become clarified, new dilemmas and issues are raised. This is the challenge of ethics: It is always possible to go beyond the fundamentals to new standards, clearer values, and deeper insights. To illustrate how ethical debate and controversy keep upping the professional ante, this chapter discusses each of the three base questions in turn. It then examines three additional implications for professional decision making and planning that have not been central to the literature on behavioral case conceptualization in the past, but that are implicit in all thoughtful and responsible clinical practice: the role of culture, children's human and civil rights, and the status of children in society. Hopefully, it will be seen that these bigger issues closely parallel the more familiar clinical decisions regarding whether, how, and for whom behavior should be changed. The overriding question is whether what we do professionally is in the best interests of the child, and children in general.

IS THIS BEHAVIOR A PROBLEM, AND FOR WHOM?

Throughout this volume, my fellow authors describe with assurance the nature of different syndromes, how they may be recognized, and their estimated prevalence. Behavior theory, however, has always asserted that a wide range of individual actions can occur in many situations, and that what makes them pathological (change-worthy) are certain dimensions of the actions, rather than their form or topography. Thus, for example, many children will react with withdrawal, hesitancy, and increased autonomic arousal at the sight of a large dog. What features of this reaction might allow us to judge it as phobic? Intensity might be one, as would difficulty in calming the child by verbal reassurance that the dog was harmless. Another important dimension might be the range of dog-related stimuli that could be expected to produce a fear response of a given intensity: matters of size, breed, whether on a leash, and whether it is wagging its tail or flattening its ears. All of these stimuli provide differential information about threat to a typical child, but not to one we might describe as phobic. Of central importance, too, is the degree to which the child's fear reaction interferes with everyday activities such as walking to school, playing in the park, visiting relatives with a dog, or, best of all, the pleasure of having a dog of one's own. As another example, any child might refuse to eat something; what makes this refusal anorexia is related to frequency, persistence, appealingness of the food, relationship to current level of hunger, secondary consequences such as severe weight loss, and so on.

ADULT PERCEPTIONS

All this seems nice and sensible, but it is largely neglected in the literature, since once the judgment is made that behavior of a certain topography is a problem, the verbal label (diagnosis) largely controls professional behavior. It is also of concern that the recent literature has tended to ignore the orthodox behavioral interpretation rather than confirm or disconfirm it. Thus, there may truly be very different properties (different forms) that distinguish between natural avoidance of threat and phobic anxiety, or between refusing food one does not like and anorexic starvation. Yet few have taken up the challenge of clarifying these distinctions. And thus it is today possible that a syndrome can be defined, measured, and discussed clinically as an entity, without clear assurance that this thing is a "thing" for reasons any more fundamental than social labeling (social constructionism).

The more benign and less controversial side of this perspective is that even if a behavior, or pattern of behavior, is truly identifiable as a syndrome (a meaningful entity), the degree of concern that it should engender is still related to social and environmental contexts. Activity becomes hyperactivity at some level of intensity, but becomes a problem only in contexts where inhibited, self-managed behavior is valued by adults. This much is very widely accepted and understood. A pattern of behavior that fits textbook descriptions of a syndrome like a glove is still only a problem if someone says it is. In adult mental health services, persons themselves are likely to identify their problem and relate it to the experience of distress (even if some of that distress is engendered by other people's complaints, say, that of a spouse or work colleagues). However, with children, it is usually adults who define the pattern as a problem. Sometimes this definition is based on a judgment that the child is distressed ("It is a concern that my child seems so uncomfortable around his peers"), and sometimes it is based on the adult's experience of being distressed ("It worries me that my child doesn't seem to have friends"). Sometimes it is based on adult criteria that are irrelevant to children and youth. For example, in research on school dropout prevention, high school students who hardly ever attend school may be identified as dropouts and show up as a statistic but do not consider themselves dropouts because they have plans to return. Other students who physically attend school perceive themselves as dropouts because they are disengaged and have plans to leave (Evans, Cicchelli, Cohen, & Shapiro, 1995).

SOCIAL CONSTRUCTIONISM

A reader might be willing to go along with this argument thus far but balk at some of the logical consequences. Perhaps the most important is the conclusion that no child behavior is problematic unless it is perceived as a problem by someone in authority. It would further follow that any valid measure of clinical improvement can be an assessment only of whether that perception has changed. There is a strong and weak form of this assumption. The weak form is that problem behavior can be objectively measured on a dimension of severity, but the meaning of that severity, or its ability to be tolerated, will be a social judgment. The strong form, however, is that although there may be objective measures of a behavior's intensity or frequency, its meaning is strictly a social, subjective judgment.

The difference between the two forms of the assumption can be illustrated by a rating scale such as the Child Behavior Checklist (CBCL; Achenbach & Edelbrock, 1983). The weak version is that the rating by a parent that the child exhibits certain characteristics is valid and objective, but that the weight we should afford that rating is subjective. The strong version is that the weight implicitly afforded the items is subjective, and thus the rating itself is a measure of the rater's perception, not reality. It would also follow that the more there is emotional involvement by raters in what they are rating, and the more likely what they are rating will be used to make a clinical judgment, the more likely it is that the strong version will be true. In other words, parents can objectively record the caloric intake of a healthy child about whom they have no concerns, but cannot be expected to provide an objective rating of anorexia in a child who has been hospitalized for serious malnourishment.

Another logical corollary of the social judgment argument is that there is no such thing as a true improvement in a clinically defined pattern, only a reduction in complaints about it. This was an argument made very forcefully and effectively by the late Don Baer (1990), who simply pointed out that a problem has been "cured" when no one complains about it any more. Our task as clinicians is to stop the complaining. And *that* is not such a silly idea. We might well spend time trying to reassure parents that a behavior is typical, that Johnny will grow out of it (that it is their hang-up about cleanliness that determines their child's messiness; their need for compliance that makes a child disobedient; their need for control that makes a child defiant; their need for order that makes a child overactive, and so on). One might also suggest meeting the complainant halfway by facilitating some small measure of change. The clinician's implicit message to the parent is: "In exchange for your being more accommodating, I will make sure that the frequency/level/intensity of your child's distressing pattern of behavior is noticeably decreased." "Noticeably" is the operative word here, because as clinicians, we frequently encounter evidence of improvement according to our good records and observations, only to find it has been discounted by a parent or teacher who perceives no change (see, e.g., Reitman, Murphy, Hupp, & O'Callaghan, 2004). When that happens, we have further evidence that the problem is, at least partially, an adult construction. These constructions are strongly influenced by adult expectations of how children should behave during different stages of development, as well as the degree to which parents believe they have the authority and right to make decisions for their children—especially adolescents—regarding dress, music, sexuality, and substance use.

Sometimes the meaning ascribed to behavior can be viewed by parents as "needed"; that is to say, it serves some emotional function for them. The parents' needs are being met by virtue of their having a child with pathology. It is therefore a valuable part of any diagnostic interview with parents to try to ascertain the function of the child's problem for them—for their relationship, their self-image, or their family dynamics. Occasionally in clinical and educational settings, we encounter a particularly difficult issue around discordant adult concerns. This is when a behavior that we as professionals might consider quite typical, developmentally appropriate, or of minor importance is judged by a parent or teacher to be highly aversive and undesirable. The behavior of the child somehow elicits a negative reaction from the adult that reflects that adult's previous learning history. The range and causes of such negative reactions are extremely broad. They vary from moral outrage related to the adult's religious beliefs, through simple dislikes and attitudes (e.g., cannot tolerate dirt, or has anxiety about expressions of aggression), to vulnerabilities related to adult needs (perhaps for affection, respect, or control).

Somewhat more rarely, the adult's excessive response to minor and normal childhood activities is a reflection of a very serious clinical disorder, those that would be defined by labels such as Borderline Personality Disorder (BPD), depression, or Schizophrenia. It is easy to see how a mother with BPD might interpret unrelated child behavior as rejection, a depressed teacher might be irritated by a child's attempt at humor, and a father with Schizophrenia and paranoid delusions could react with suspicion and anger to a child's innocent mistake. If the complaining adult has a diagnosed mental health disorder, it is much easier to appreciate how his or her pathology is distorting his or her perception of the child (and there are good interventions to help parents in the psychiatric system to better understand their reactions and to help children recognize that their parent's response is itself a symptom). When, however, the parent has a similar but subclinical cognitive distortion, it is much harder to acknowledge that the behavioral description may be as much a reflection of the parent's cognitive and emotional errors (irrational thinking) as the child's deviance.

WHO IS THE CLIENT?

The ethical dilemma this common assessment and conceptualization problem represents is that of deciding who the client is. In principle, if the clinician takes the view that the referring parent is the client, it would not matter how appropriate or inappropriate one thought the requested behavior change to be; one would simply devise a plan to achieve it. If, on the other hand, one takes the view that the child is the client— your responsibility regardless of who is asking for or paying for your professional service—then you might focus your planning on strategies to alter parental attitudes and values. Neither focus is satisfactory. Over the years, clinical behavior therapists have come to recognize that the "Who is your client?" question is not well formulated. The clinician always has multiple responsibilities. The referred child is perhaps the foremost responsibility, in terms of protection, safety, and upholding standards of normative development, both absolute and within a given culture. Yet there is also responsibility to the adult: The clinician has a duty to help the adult acquire adaptive behavioral patterns and standards that will promote long-term acceptance of and love for the child. And there is responsibility to the society that empowers our professional status and its institutions: representing the need to uphold the principles of the school or the values and standards of the local community.

Simple measures of child behavior change (treatment outcome), particularly if based on adult ratings, cannot come close to measuring whether these responsibilities have been successfully discharged. Thus, for practicing child clinicians, the measurement standard for an acceptable empirical study, such as improvement in CBCL score, is substantially below the standard required for ethical practice. This is one reason more and more formulaic outcome studies say less and less to practicing clinicians (cf. Waehler, Kalodner, Wampold, & Lichtenberg, 2000)—an ethical and professional challenge that the research community must take much more seriously if scientific inquiry is expected to raise ethical standards of practice and significantly improve children's quality of life.

SHOULD BEHAVIOR BE CHANGED?

At first blush, it would seem that this question is inversely connected to the previous one. Surely, if a behavior is not a problem, then there is no need to change it, and if it is a problem, then there is a professional obligation to do something about it. If the problematic element of the behavior is in the distorted perceptions or emotions of the complaining adult, then it is the perception, not the behavior, that needs to be changed. To start with the easier, default option, let us reformulate the question as "Should *this* behavior be changed?" Such a question was asked very early on in behavior therapy. Among the first authors to do so were Winett and Winkler (1972), whose paper, subtitled "Be Still, Be Quiet, Be Docile," addressed their concern that classroom interventions for disruptive behavior tended to emphasize children keeping their bottoms on their seats and not shouting out, instead of focusing on learning goals and social outcomes and encouraging active, engaged, and lively classroom participation. Another important paper with the same general theme was written by Hawkins (1975) and entitled "Who Decided *That* Was the Problem?" In that classic paper, Hawkins dealt with the fact that many child clients whose behavior was being reported as successfully modified in the clinical research literature typically had multiple issues, and yet only one or two behaviors were targeted for intervention. The issue of disagreement among child, parent, and therapist has continued to pose clinical dilemmas (Hawley & Weisz, 2003).

Selecting Treatment Goals (Targets)

Assuming that all child clients have a variety of needs, and assuming that a clinician can work systematically on only one or two at a time, how are we to prioritize and select an intervention target according to ethical, clinical, and rational (empirical) criteria? Although the answer appears less than clear-cut, there has emerged within the child behavior therapy literature a certain consensus regarding how to prioritize, which depends considerably on the client and family or teacher circumstances (Voeltz, Evans, Derer, & Hanashiro, 1983). The judgment boils down to maximizing our influence while minimizing harm to the child. For instance, with parents who might be skeptical regarding the value of treatment at all, an intervention with a high probability of early success might be tried first. If the child is a danger to self or others, then that behavior should be targeted, unless it is so rare and inaccessible that there would be value in modifying some other behavior that might lead to a reduction in the more serious but more remote target. All other things being equal, the clinician might be wise to target the behavior found most annoying by others, especially parents, even if it is not by some criteria the most clinically serious of the difficulties. The value of that criterion is that it may be more likely to encourage active positive engagement in the procedure by parents. Because the risk of physical abuse is so high in developed countries, the goal of keeping a child safe is maximized by addressing behaviors that caregivers find highly aversive. The same consideration applies to school settings, where particular patterns of behavior may be aversive to teachers and result in expulsion. Finally, there would be value in targeting those behaviors that are likely to generalize to other contexts and be most useful for the child client in a wide variety of settings.

Those of us who became interested in behavioral interrelationships suggested refining these practical criteria still further (Evans, Meyer, Kurkjian, & Kishi, 1988). If we knew, for example, the prerequisite behaviors for social and academic success at school, then those would be good behaviors on which to focus. Here Staats's (1975) concept of basic behavioral repertoires (BBRs) has been of enormous usefulness to clinicians making these complex judgments. As individual repertoires are always highly complex and behaviors always interrelated, the insight that some behaviors are the independent (causal) variables for other behaviors is hugely significant. Staats and his research group gave many examples of BBRs, especially in the verbal-cognitive area, where it is particularly obvious that behavioral development is hierarchical, with future development dependent on the acquisition of earlier skills and competencies.

The only real difficulty with this approach turns out to be quite a major one: No one has really established systematically what all of these core prerequisite skills are across a wide variety of relevant domains. Wahler (1975) used to talk about "keystone" behaviors and documented one: skills in solitary play or the lack thereof that seemed to underlie or support a whole raft of negative, disruptive, and irritating behaviors in children. Promising though this was, the concept never really amounted to much. Fortunately, one can say that the idea is still alive in the procedure known as pivotal response training, which is a key behavioral strategy for children with autism (Koegel & Koegel, 2006). Pivotal skills are like keystone behaviors; they are the ones that are useful for learning any new skill and functionally useful in a wide variety of settings. The idea is somewhat like learning to learn: Do we want to help our child clients solve a particular problem, or do we want them to learn problem-solving skills? Can we focus attention on skills that show a person how to learn? This is particularly useful for children with intellectual disability, who by definition show less incidental learning than other children. It is reminiscent of the old adage "Give a man a fish and he'll eat for a day; teach him how to fish and he'll feed his family for life"—or, as I saw recently on a T-shirt in Buffalo, New York, "Teach a man to fish and he'll sit in a boat and drink beer all day." Which leads me nicely to the topic of unintended consequences.

UNINTENDED CONSEQUENCES

The discussion of response relationships thus far has important practical implications for selecting and prioritizing intervention targets but is only peripherally an ethical dilemma. It becomes a major ethical concern, however, if the relationships among behaviors in the repertoire result in an unanticipated change in other behaviors. Although originally thought to be a fiction of psychoanalysis, we know now that symptom substitution (negative side effects of treatment) is commonplace rather than rare (Voeltz & Evans, 1982). A related threat is if the changed behavior makes it harder for the child to gain acceptance in his or her social system—family and community. A major part of assessment and case conceptualization is to try to ensure that the intervention will not be iatrogenic (have unintended negative consequences). These consequences can occur in a variety of forms. The most obvious is that the clinical treatment of children often emphasizes eliminating, reducing, or in some way decreasing a behavior, activity, or symptom. Some behaviors, however, may in fact be beneficial to the child: indicating a need, promoting autonomy, or communicating a deeper distress. In fact, the very term "symptom" conveys the implication that the real problem is deeper and more complex, and the target behavior, whether anxiety, depression, noncompliance, or eating disorder, is merely indicative of some more serious systemic dysfunction.

Even when the intervention focuses on the development of new and, hopefully, constructive (Evans, 1993) skills for children (problem solving, self-management, emotion regulation are popular choices), it is necessary to consider whether these are acceptable within the peer culture. Children and adolescents are particularly susceptible to peer criticism and rejection. Fitting in (even if it is in a counterculture group) is important. Observing or at least talking to the client's peer group will ensure that the selection of targets and the methods of their attainment are not totally out of place. Simply being in special education or receiving mental health services is stigmatizing for children in many communities. Intervention design needs to be sensitive to the importance of keeping professional efforts as naturalistic as possible (Evans & Berryman, 1995).

Judgment regarding what behavior to change may also be overly influenced by the availability of established or empirically supported interventions. In a study conducted many years ago on clinicians' judgments about which of a variety of possible behaviors should be targeted, we noted that behavioral clinicians tended to select those problems for which there were well-established intervention procedures (e.g., enuresis) rather than those for which formal treatment procedures did not really exist at that time (e.g., sibling rivalry; Wilson & Evans, 1983). It is the old story that if all you have is a hammer, everything looks like a nail.

SHOULD ANY MEANS BE USED TO CHANGE BEHAVIORS OF CONCERN?

Once this question is asked explicitly as an ethical question, the importance of the matter for professional judgment becomes very obvious. Are all intervention plans equally acceptable? Wolf (1978, p. 207) posed the question "Do the participants, care-givers and other consumers consider the treatment procedures acceptable?" as one of the three judgments required to establish what he termed "social validity." Since then there have been numerous studies in which stakeholders have been asked to rate the acceptability of different treatment strategies (e.g., Hunsley, 1992; Kazdin, 1980). How-ever, interventions cannot be judged in the abstract—in the absence of knowledge of the circumstances and of the alternatives. Certain rules of thumb can be inferred from community standards and social expectations, for instance the concept that the least intrusive intervention should be attempted before a more invasive one is adopted (Meyer & Evans, 1989). Nevertheless, at the level of the individual client, treatment acceptability is no more than an extension of the principle of informed consent.

INFORMED CONSENT

Parents who are more self-confident, less anxious, better educated, and from higher socioeconomic groups are more likely to raise doubts about their child's participating in a research protocol or subjected to a treatment plan (Rothmier, Lasley, & Shapiro, 2003). Although most parents are likely to have the best interests of their child at heart, this cannot be relied on when they have been stressed and challenged by their child's behavior. When disruptive or aggressive behavior is itself a consequence of lax discipline or overprotection, the difficulty of introducing boundaries, rules, and fair but consistent consequences is considerable. To observe this dynamic in action, one only has to watch *Supernanny* on television. With considerable skill, Supernanny Jo Frost implements standard, evidence-based contingency management procedures, as well as a heavy emphasis on creating alternative positive activity structures. Physical punishment is not permitted. Parents often show resistance that might have been overcome had the rationale for the procedures been fully discussed; however, perhaps the advantage of being a nanny rather than a psychologist is that one can impose rules and lay down the law (Frost, 2006).

To what extent should a child be able to participate in a treatment decision, since these involve both choice of target and choice of intervention method? With adults, and hopefully adolescents, it is common practice for the psychologist to explain his or her conceptualization to the client as a rationale for the intervention plan. There are many good behavioral reasons for this. It allows for some degree of checking the face validity of one's interpretation. It establishes the professional relationship as a problem-solving partnership. It provides insight and a principled basis for the treatment procedures recommended. These same advantages are not as easily achieved with child clients, yet they are equally desirable. A child who understands, agrees with, and consents to a treatment plan and its goals is more likely to collaborate, engage with therapy, and learn generalizable skills. Informed consent is the bedrock of ethical practice.

With children, however, there are obvious cognitive limitations to meaningful consent. In terms of assent to research participation, studies show that children younger than about 9 years really cannot sufficiently understand the conditions, the potential for harm, or even their right to refuse, as opposed to please (Ondrusek, Abramovitch, Pencharz, & Koren, 1998). The concept of choice is itself culturally determined: highly valued in the United States, much less so in other parts of the world. The Afrocentric emphasis on destiny, for example, as well as economic conditions means that freedom of choice is unimportant compared to freedom from want (Mbigi & Maree, 1995). The right of children to choose is also tempered in Western societies by assumptions regarding children's ability to comprehend what might be good for them as a long-term prospect. For example, in 1999 the English high court overruled a 15-year-old girl's decision to refuse a heart transplant (Dyer, 1999).

TREATMENT CONTEXTS

Empirically supported intervention strategies, even those that meet the ethical standards of appropriateness discussed, are always implemented within a service context. Sometimes this is an inpatient facility, sometimes a mental health or correctional outpatient setting, sometimes a school or community program, and sometimes simply a family or other nonprofessional context. Whatever the context, it behooves the clinician implementing the focused protocol to ensure that the general setting not only supports the principles of the intervention, but is itself in keeping with the values and principles of the specific treatment. There is scant ethical justification for conducting an anger management program for young offenders, for example, if the correctional facility in which they are incarcerated does not meet the same therapeutic standard.

Formal literature on treatment contexts is scarce, although much can be inferred from other sources. There are anecdotal reports of the difficulties encountered by clinicians attempting to gain full compliance from those responsible for implementing children's intervention plans. But even if the staff of an agency or institution (including nonprofessional staff, such as family members) carry out the intervention exactly as designed, there is no a guarantee that the many unspecified features of the milieu will be commensurate with the goals of the intervention. The potentially negative effects of institutional regimes have been known for some time (e.g., Hobbs, 1975). It is easy to imagine the ethical concerns that arise from poorly trained and overstressed staff, the influence of equally disturbed or delinquent peers, or the stigma associated with certain institutions or special classes. While individual clinicians designing individual treatments may not have much power and influence in large bureaucratic organizations, there is clearly a professional opportunity, when designing the intervention, to both model and specify standards of care for children that go beyond the specifics of the treatment plan. We have an ethical obligation to attend to such elements.

Let us consider one example. Our research group has been examining the emotional climate of the classrooms in which intervention plans for disruptive behavior were being implemented (Harvey & Evans, 2003). It became apparent during this research that some teachers were able to create classroom climates that included elements similar to the positive emotion coaching environments that Gottman, Katz, and Hooven (1997) have described in parents. Some were not. In classrooms with positive emotional climates, it was relatively easy to implement positive intervention plans. Although we are presenting these observations as illustrative of the need for a positive context for specific treatments, it seems equally likely that positive treatments are not implemented with integrity if the adults in the setting are the ones directly responsible for carrying out the designed program. Ever since the pioneering work of Wahler (1980) with socially unsupported single mothers, we have known that behavioral interventions cannot actually be carried out correctly by intervention agents who are not able or willing to carry out the procedures in accordance with the general principles on which the treatment was based.

There has been much recent work on the importance of treatment integrity, a concept first articulated by Yeaton and Sechrest (1981). If I might coin the phrase "context integrity," it will be seen that there is, as yet, no formal procedure for judging the extent to which the treatment setting meets the requirements of the principles and methods underlying the specific treatment protocol. Some clinical researchers have begun to recognize that an evidence-based intervention cannot improve practices that are favorable to children unless the capacity of the institutional context (such as a school) is given equal attention (Ervin, Schaughency, Matthews, Goodman, & McGlinchey, 2006). This will be an important area for future research that is driven by ethical, not just methodological, guidelines.

THE ROLE OF CULTURE

The demographics of evidence-based clinical services in the *public* domain in developed countries typically mean that the professional is middle class and White (or a member of the majority group), and the clients and their families are poor, less well educated, and members of a minority or a migrant group. Culturally sensitive or culturally competent clinical practice with children usually means, therefore, that members of a dominant and probably privileged majority are aware of special needs, practices, or considerations that pertain to a client and his or her family from a minority group. Ethical practitioners will also be aware that clients from minority groups are not homogeneous. Sensitivities of this kind are very important, but they slightly miss the point related to equity and justice. Ethical professional practice with children requires the clinician to understand his or her own culture and not assume that it represents some basic standard or core values against which other groups can be evaluated or judged. Thus, we might readily find in the American literature on cognitive-behavioral therapy with children examples of how an intervention might be adjusted to mesh more readily with the needs of an immigrant Latino family or an African American family. Yet one would be hard-pressed to find empirical literature on African American professional practices that has been adapted for White American families.

Among the various ethical challenges that this state of affairs engenders is the issue of maintaining a power differential in which the metacommunication from the clinician in the dominant group is "You [the family and the child] need to be more like me. And because I am sensitive to cultural differences, I will help you and make it easier for you to achieve this." America is an amazingly diverse country, and not simply along ethnic lines, but in terms of lifestyle, religion, regional loyalty, social class, country of origin, and many other dimensions. Thus, it is important to understand individual and group diversity. For example, the reader could likely review all the chapters in this volume and pick out the content where it is clear that the authors are considering their topic through a lens other than mainstream American culture. You will probably not find a great many examples. Of course, it is reasonable to argue that this is an American book written largely by mainstream American authors, and yet the clinicians who are going to use the information are going to have to use it largely with people considerably different from themselves. This is not a criticism of the chapters or their excellent authors, but emphasizes for readers that ethical practice will be up to them—they will not obtain direct guidance from the empirical literature published in the journals and texts of the dominant group. Nezu (2005) has made a compelling argument that experiencing diversity in our daily lives will be necessary for professionals to move beyond basic cultural competence goals.

CULTURE-FAIR CONCEPTUALIZATIONS

The categorization and labeling of children is a highly political process with many negative consequences for children that generally outweigh the possible professional advantages of having a shared diagnostic system (Hobbs, 1975). The great advantage of a behavioral or psychological model of problematic behavior in children has been that it allows for the understanding of processes of influence and learning history and how these interact with developmental change and current social context (including racism) to generate the conditions that might benefit from professional intervention. This advantage is lost in the use of disease-analogy labels. Within the cognitive-behavioral tradition there has been greater attention to fixed diagnostic categories because the empirically supported treatment movement has become so dependent on manualized treatment packages designed for specific diagnostic entities.

In contrast, case conceptualization models implicitly include causal variables that embrace cultural differences and allow for some consideration of communities' histories of disadvantage, such as poverty and colonialism (Matthews, 1997). They allow inclusion of broad principles, such as what it means to be an illegal immigrant family, a refugee, or a member of an ethnic minority. Because the case conceptualization model seeks to understand proximal and distal influences, it might assess the availability of social support but recognize that this might come from an extended rather than a nuclear family, from a religious group, or from a collectivist rather than an individualistic value system (Tanaka-Matsumi, Seiden, & Lam, 1996).

Just as we have criteria for what constitutes an adequate assessment instrument according to psychometric standards, it is possible to conduct a "cultural audit" of a case conceptualization. Evans and Paewai (1999) proposed some strategies for validating a professional case formulation in the context of a cultural partnership in which the minority and majority cultures have standards of equity derived from a historical treaty. The Treaty of Waitangi, signed in 1840 and given modern legal status in New Zealand in the 1970s, guarantees certain rights to the indigenous Māori people that can be translated into professional mandates. Thus the right to self-determination might translate to the right for the case conceptualization for a Māori child to be conducted by a Māori clinician in a Māori-managed service. If that is not currently feasible, the treaty's provision of an equal partnership would encourage assessment and treatment planning to be carried out in collaboration with cultural guardians.

CHILDREN'S HUMAN RIGHTS

In 1989, the United Nations General Assembly adopted the *UN Convention on the Rights of the Child,* although not all nations have ratified it. The 54 articles that define the basic human rights of every child can be divided into broad categories, but these rights are considered indivisible. This holistic approach emphasizes the right to survival; for children to develop to their fullest potential; to protection from abuse, exploitation, and other harmful influences; and to participate fully in family, cultural, and social life. The core underlying principles are nondiscrimination (and across today's fractious world we might think specifically of gender discrimination), placing priority on the best interests of the child, the right to survive and develop, and respect for the views of the child. Psychologists might also note the rights to access public education and to basic literacy.

Protection from Physical Punishment

The International Committee monitoring the Convention has recommended that all forms of physical punishment be proscribed, which often runs counter to community and cultural standards. The cultural sensitivities advocated in the previous section cannot translate to acceptance of practices that we as professionals judge to be undesirable, even if they are traditional, commonplace, or tolerated in some cultural contexts—some Pacific Island communities constituting one such example (Kapavalu, 1993).

Consider, as a more explicit example, the death early in 2006 of 4-year-old Sean Paddock, allegedly caused by his mother using "corporal chastisement" techniques she had learned about from the web site of an evangelical minister and his wife, Michael and Debi Pearl (Locke, 2006). The Pearls' book, *To Train Up a Child*, their newsletter—distributed widely to parents—and their web site, www.nogreaterjoy.org, contain extensive recommendations regarding chastisement. For example, they recommend for a 6-month-old baby that parents "swat the offending hand with a little instrument (light wooden spoon, rubber spatula, flexible tubing less than a quarter inch in diameter, or any instrument that will cause an unpleasant sting without leaving any marks)" (Pearl, 2006, p. 3).

Respect for fundamentalist Christian congregations as a cultural group should not inhibit child psychologists from challenging such advice on the basis of evidence (Gershoff, 2002). However, when working individually with families likely to use spanking or more severe violence to discipline their child, it is useful to consider that favorable attitudes toward corporal punishment can be connected to literal interpretation of the Bible (Wiehe, 1990). Changing parental beliefs about punishment may require a focus on explaining its harmful and ineffectual nature, rather than advocating other, more positive strategies (Robinson, Funk, Beth, & Bush, 2005). This is because, as Robinson and his colleagues found, many defenders of corporal punishment see it as similar to bad-tasting medicine—unpleasant but necessary. Given our considerable professional understanding of ways to influence and support people like Sean Paddock's mother, it can be asserted that we have an ethical obligation to study both effective positive interventions and strategies for disseminating them and educating the public. Programs such as Triple P (Positive Parenting Program; Sanders, 1999) have achieved outstanding success in the use of marketing-style dissemination techniques without loss of professional and empirical fidelity.

Placing Interventions in the Context of Children's Rights

As our methods of intervention improve, it will be a challenge to demonstrate the generality of these approaches. An interesting comparison has been made between research demonstrating the efficacy of a procedure in controlled lab or research-intensive clinical settings, and research that demonstrates the effectiveness of the procedure in more typical settings with clinicians different from those invested individuals who designed and implemented the original procedure. In assessment, similar distinctions are made between the formal psychometrics of an instrument or measurement technique and its clinical utility. The latter refers to the value of the instrument for making meaningful clinical decisions (Nelson-Gray, 2003). In the future, there will be a new level or standard for both assessments and interventions. Beyond effectiveness will be the requirement to demonstrate transportability (Herschell, McNeil, & McNeil, 2004), the chances that the method will be used where it is most needed (uptake) and be modified to accommodate those with the greatest needs. Beyond clinical utility will be the requirement to demonstrate that an assessment strategy allows the highest priority cases to be targeted and treated.

These sorts of ideas are commonplace in international development aid and in public health. Clean drinking water, good quality seed, accessible contraception, prenatal clinics, and breast-feeding are not rocket science, although they are based on sound scientific, empirically validated fundamentals. If assessment procedures and treatments have merit, the core idea would surely be transferable to wider client groups, and it may soon be recognized as an ethical obligation to contribute at this level as well. There is, after all, something rather perverse about treatment programs designed to help obese and overweight children in developed countries, while in developing countries similar aged children are dying of starvation. Both cases are examples of malnutrition, and some similar elements can be discerned in both, such as barriers to obtaining healthy food. An observation such as this is not in any way intended to suggest that programs for obese children in Western industrialized countries are unethical. The individual overweight child in Houston, Liverpool, or Auckland is distressed and likely to benefit greatly from a good program. In fact, we could just about guarantee successful intervention for any such child given our current techniques. Adhering to a higher ethical standard would suggest that we spend less time refining those techniques in minor ways (since the core elements are well understood) and more time ensuring that they can be taken up by less sophisticated clinical services in the poorer suburbs of Texas, England, and New Zealand. This is not some radical critique of Western plenty (though one could certainly make such a critique; see, e.g., Pettifor, 2006), but an ethical standard that proposes that considerations of transportability of methods might be as important as conventional standards of empirical validity.

Another way to present this argument from the ethical perspective is to reexamine the concept of effectiveness as one of outcome equity. When clinical researchers talk about an effectiveness study, there is usually a presumption that the outcome evaluation will take place in a typical clinical setting, or a cluster of facilities. But do we have any real understanding of how disparate such services are across communities, regions, and nations? It seems likely that there are in most basic services large differences in resources, staff competencies, and many other variables, depending on whether the services are in rural, inner-city, or other locations, or have access to consultants in universities, medical schools, VA hospitals, and so on. Consider the analogy with international studies of children's reading, mathematics, and science achievement. Based on the Organization for Economic Cooperation and Development's (2001) *Program for International Student Assessment*, it is possible not only to estimate international levels of literacy achievement (e.g., high in New Zealand,

Finland, and Canada), but also to examine variability within those scores. Low variation means high equity (in countries like Korea, Spain, Mexico, and Japan). Clearly, in clinical contexts, although outcomes are much harder to standardize than for educational achievement, our ethical goals should be to obtain not only positive outcomes, but positive outcomes across the prevalent treatment settings and agencies. Equitable clinical outcomes for interventions should be a new standard, combining effectiveness, uptake, and cultural applicability (including dependency on only local, not special, resources).

CHILDREN'S STATUS IN SOCIETY

Societies have always differed in the degree to which children are considered adult possessions, should be submissive, or are held responsible for their actions (Benedict, 1938). It is beyond the scope of this chapter to examine the complex legal issues surrounding different communities' assumptions regarding the ages at which children are deemed competent to stand trial, to make decisions independent of parental authority, or to exercise choice. Drinking age, voting age, driving age, consent to sex, and right to privacy in medical treatments (such as abortion) all differ within and across nations and reflect considerable emotional and legal ambiguity for adult societies. Koocher and Keith-Spiegel (1990) have provided a clear and very useful guide to these issues for clinicians in the United States, which is recommended reading. What I will touch upon are the ethical dilemmas posed by common practices in assessment, conceptualization, and treatment within the general cognitive-behavioral paradigm.

AUTONOMY AND INDEPENDENCE

An important principle that translates into an ethical concern is that of autonomy and societal perceptions of when a young person is able to be independent and think independently. Decisions about independence, sexual freedom, drinking age, and similar concerns interact with clinical needs more than we might realize when thinking only within the confines of our own cultural experience, which includes generational changes and differences. In the United States there is a premium placed on children behaving responsibly, based on self-motivation and self-guidance (Bear, Manning, & Izard, 2006). Clinicians, therefore, have to be mindful of interventions relying primarily on rules, rewards, and punishments that foster obedience and compliance.

It is generally accepted that parents have a right to control and manage their children, and in some cultures and jurisdictions in the United States, parents are held accountable for their children's lack of school attendance and criminal conduct. At the same time, children are afforded a certain level of societal protection, largely because of society's overriding interest in whether children become productive citizens and recognition that some parents fail to meet basic standards of care. When designing an intervention that requires parents to alter their behavior management strategies, clinicians are confronted with a clash of subtle and often unrecognized assumptions about parental versus child competence and rights. These considerations are not spelled out in parenting manuals and child management protocols, and it is often up to the clinician to ensure that interventions are appropriate for the cultural group and the specific expectations of individual families.

PERCEPTIONS OF VULNERABILITY AND SOCIAL BENEFIT

Perhaps the most important ethical principle relates to the value that is placed on a child as a vulnerable individual. The role of the family as a unit to promote positive development is an area for which international understandings vary considerably. The catchphrase (originally from African communities) "It takes a whole village to raise a child" has been adopted as a leftist political and social slogan in the United States, where it implies that responsibility for children must be shared beyond the family. This may mean that in the development of intervention plans it can be expected that a wide range of individuals may have a role and a function in supporting positive behavior. Again, this has been a well-understood concept in behavioral work, perhaps best illustrated by the pioneering studies of Tharp and Wetzel (1969). Recognizing that to bring about meaningful change in the behavior of young people at risk it would be necessary to locate those individuals who had some degree of influence over the target child, Tharp and Wetzel thus sought out "behavior change agents," who might be defined as those individuals who had access to rewards or rewarding experiences that were meaningful to (functioned as reinforcers for) the children designated as clients.

Until recently, behavioral clinicians have not had to worry too much about how our work contributes to the general social good. Audits of a given nation's progress on major indicators of children's status and progress in society have, happily, never been one of the outcome variables for which clinicians feel responsible. However, as behavior theory and principles have begun to extend beyond the individual case to more general areas of prevention, to population-based intervention design and community change, some of these issues and concerns are beginning to creep into clinical consciousness. Case conceptualization, as we have seen, has the enormous advantage of allowing for ever-broadening circles of influence affecting the child, from family, to school, to neighborhood, to community, to society. The brilliant work of Bronfenbrenner in the 1970s was always seen as highly compatible with clinical work in the cognitive-behavioral tradition, as well as family systems concepts. A number of treatment strategies have explicitly identified these circles of influence, a good example being multisystemic therapy (Henggeler, Schoenwald, Borduin, Rowland, & Cunningham, 1998).

Despite these areas of compatibility, it would not be fair to professionals working at the clinical level to be held accountable for broader societal problems. We would all agree that a fundamental human right for children is to be protected against violence, physical aggression, and sexual abuse. However, the clinician working with abusive fathers cannot be expected to answer to a United Nations committee concerned about the level of violent deaths of children in a given country. Yet it may be that the links between the general human rights of children and individual clinical activities could be better spelled out to the benefit of children overall and individual child clients in particular.

THE UNIFORMITY DILEMMA

As cognitive-behavioral interventions become more stylized (follow a set manual or protocol), so their potential for large-scale prevention initiatives or interventions at the population level becomes more appealing and more plausible. Inevitably, such programs are conducted with the most worthy intentions. Nevertheless, there is always the possibility that the standards of behavior and personality style generally valued in a given culture may not be suitable for all children. It is usually accepted without question that programs are good if they focus on such outcomes as preventing suicide, school dropout, and anxiety (especially social anxiety and shyness) and promoting healthy weight and being outgoing. Yet even with such apparently desirable outcomes, there is the risk of reducing individual variability and diversity of experience. Clinicians willingly encouraging programs such as these might see the dilemma more clearly when confronting other programs that are popular among conservatives, such as just saying no to drugs or preventing sexually transmitted disease through total abstinence.

Large-scale prevention programs present a variety of ethical dilemmas. Typically, it is not really possible to obtain informed consent. The program is generally a skill-building program designed to enhance social skills, emotion regulation, self-control, study habits, and reasoning or problem-solving skills. However, there may be differential abilities and opportunities to acquire these skills, thus differentially advantaging some children over others. (Of course, that would nullify the argument regarding the danger of creating greater uniformity among children.) When presented as a curricular activity for schools or after school programs, such programs often have catchy, upbeat names that disguise the true intent and nature of the program. If not genuinely available for all children, such programs carry a likelihood of stigmatizing children who are considered at risk for poor social and educational outcomes. In a similar way, many such programs rely on more capable peers as models, coaches, mentors, or ambassadors; this further differentiates the successful, competent, and confident children from the others.

I am not arguing that large-scale intervention or prevention programs are inherently unethical. But I do wish to alert the reader to the ethical challenges they present that need to be considered. If choice and autonomy are general values, then children in a given society need to have the right to choose to be moody, angry, lonely, or rebellious or to waste their time playing video games. Usually children do not choose to be these things; instead, they are imposed by circumstances far beyond their control. Programs might be considered to have an ethical edge if their universality is designed to reduce bullying, gossiping, text-taunting, teasing, and name-calling, which are all procedures imposed by a majority or more powerful group to control the individual and reduce individuality. Tolerance training, antidiscrimination, and celebration, or at least acceptance of individual differences, might prove to be the elements of a skill-building program that has indisputable ethical standing.

PROFESSIONAL ETHICS AND SOCIETAL PERCEPTIONS OF CHILDHOOD

Fisher (2003) has suggested that there are virtues that correspond to the five major broad principles of the American Psychological Association's Ethics Code. Prudence and honesty are highly valued virtues in scientific work. Compassion, fairness, and conscientiousness are important in service provision. Integrity and respectfulness are key virtues for individual clinical work. No one principle or related virtue is more important than any other; the challenge always arises when principles are in opposition. Emphasis on scientific integrity—a hallmark of cognitive-behavior therapy—cannot result in subordination of values relating to the special needs of children and recognition of the broader societal pressures that they face.

It is irresponsible to suggest to clinicians that the only ethical practice is the implementation of empirically supported treatments—at least until the rigor of those treatment outcome studies is greatly improved. Good treatment outcome studies reporting effect size do not include equity evaluations and only now have begun to require reporting on the likelihood of treatment dropout (noncompletion), relapse, and failure. Individual clinicians need to make adjustments to programs and protocols according to cultural conditions and available resources. The individual clinician with the individual child (and that is not the only or even the best way to apply clinical knowledge) cannot be satisfied with numerical abstractions such as effect size. Treatments need to be modified and refined until a good outcome is achieved; that is the essence of the experimental analysis of the single case.

Many ethical practices have been developed to protect vulnerable clients from professional exploitation. Conflicts of interest arise unwittingly because of the power differential between the professional clinician and the client. When children and families live in circumstances of social disadvantage, such as poverty, autonomy and fairness are even more at risk (Prilleltensky, 2003). Ironically, as treatments become more effective, so the inequities of power differentials become potentially more damaging. It is always important in treatment design to strive to promote independence, to remove barriers to personal agency, choice, and new opportunities, and to foster self-management. Cultural differences in values around these constructs may mean that these goals apply to how communities can become less socially toxic environments for raising children (Garbarino, 1995).

SUMMARY

I have attempted to highlight some of the more salient issues and to suggest ways in which professional virtues are connected to the complexity of clinical judgment. I believe the strategies known loosely as behavioral assessment provide a solid foundation for this interplay between values and decisions. Assessment that is defined merely by psychometric standards—that are considered measures of some psychological phenomenon—do not lead readily to treatment. They would do so if their primary purpose was to establish a diagnosis and if there were standardized protocols for treating each diagnostic condition. However, neither of those conditions has been shown to be robust. Diagnosis is best achieved by matching symptoms to criteria. And although empirically supported treatments are usually keyed to specific syndromes, the variability within a syndrome and the likelihood of "comorbidity" of problem domains has meant that generic, highly manualized treatment protocols have not fared well in terms of clinical utility (Barlow, 1981). Case conceptualization, on the other hand, provides the kinds of causal networks that allow for the formulation of a treatment plan, and good assessment helps to elucidate the factors that contribute to and maintain the problem.

The primary message conveyed here is that ethical issues, broadly interpreted as values relating to children and their circumstances, are of direct relevance in mapping out causal influences. It has been said in science that there is nothing as practical as a good theory; here I have tried to demonstrate to the reader that there is nothing as practical as sound ethics. Being ethical means wanting to do the right thing because it is right. Our practices are right if they help us to understand and appreciate children, their potential, and the diverse contexts of their lives.

REFERENCES

Achenbach, T. M., & Edelbrock, C. (1983). *Manual for the Child Behavior Checklist and Revised Child Behavior Profile.* Burlington: University of Vermont, Department of Psychiatry.

Albee, G. W., & Joffe, J. M. (2004). Mental illness is NOT "an illness like any other." *Journal of Primary Prevention, 24,* 419–436.

Baer, D. M. (1990). Exploring the controlling conditions of importance. *Behavior Analyst, 13,* 183–186.

Barlow, D. H. (1981). On the relation of clinical research to clinical practice: Current issues, new directions. *Journal of Consulting and Clinical Psychology, 49,* 147–155.

Bear, G. G., Manning, M. A., & Izard, C. E. (2006). Responsible behavior: The importance of social cognition and emotion. *School Psychology Quarterly, 18,* 140–157.

Benedict, R. (1938). Continuities and discontinuities in cultural conditioning. *Psychiatry, 1,* 161–167.

Dyer, C. (1999). English teenager given heart transplant against her will. *British Medical Journal, 319,* 209.

Ervin, R. A., Schaughency, E., Matthews, A., Goodman, S. D., & McGlinchey, M. T. (2006). Primary and secondary prevention of behavior difficulties: Developing a data-informed problem-solving model to guide decision making at a school-wide level. *Psychology in the Schools, 44,* 7–18.

Evans, I. M. (1993). Constructional perspectives in clinical assessment. *Psychological Assessment, 5,* 264–272.

Evans, I. M. (1997). The effect of values on scientific and clinical judgment in behavior therapy. *Behavior Therapy, 28,* 483–493.

Evans, I. M., & Berryman, J. S. (1995). Naturalistic strategies for modifying and preventing challenging behaviors. In W. W. Woolcock & J. W. Domaracki (Eds.), *Instructional strategies in the community: A resource guide for community instruction for persons with disabilities* (pp. 157–184). Austin, TX: ProEd.

Evans, I. M., Cicchelli, T., Cohen, M., & Shapiro, N. (Eds.). (1995). *Staying in school: Partnerships for educational change.* Baltimore: Paul H. Brookes.

Evans, I. M., & Litz, B. T. (1987). Behavioral assessment: A new theoretical foundation for clinical measurement and evaluation. In H. J. Eysenck & I. Martin (Eds.), *Theoretical foundations of behavior therapy* (pp. 331–351). New York: Plenum Press.

Evans, I. M., Meyer, L. M., Kurkjian, J. A., & Kishi, G. S. (1988). An evaluation of behavioral interrelationships in child behavior therapy. In J. C. Witt, S. N. Elliott, & F. N. Gresham (Eds.), *Handbook of behavior therapy in education* (pp. 189–215). New York: Plenum Press.

Evans, I. M., & Paewai, M. K. (1999). Functional analysis in a bicultural context. *Behavior Change, 16,* 20–36.

Evans, I. M., Scotti, J. R., & Hawkins, R. P. (1999). Understanding where we are going by looking at where we have been. In J. R. Scotti & L. H. Meyer (Eds.), *Behavioral intervention: Principles, models, and practices* (pp. 3–23). Baltimore: Paul H. Brookes.

Evans, I. M., & Wilson, F. E. (1983). Behavioral assessment as decision making: A theoretical analysis. In M. Rosenbaum, C. M. Franks, & Y. Jaffe (Eds.), *Perspectives on behavior therapy in the eighties* (pp. 35–53). New York: Springer.

Fisher, C. B. (2003). *Decoding the Ethics Code: A practical guide for psychologists.* Thousand Oaks, CA: Sage.

Frost, J. (2006). *Ask Supernanny: What every parent wants to know.* London: Hodder and Stoughton.

Garbarino, J. (1995). *Raising children in a socially toxic environment.* San Francisco: Jossey-Bass.

Gershoff, E. T. (2002). Corporal punishment by parents and associated child behaviors and experiences: A meta-analytic and theoretical review. *Psychological Bulletin, 128,* 539–579.

Gottman, J. M., Katz, L. F., & Hooven, C. (1997). *Meta-emotion: How families communicate emotionally.* Hillsdale, NJ: Erlbaum.

Harvey, S., & Evans, I. M. (2003). Understanding the emotional environment of the classroom. In D. Fraser & R. Openshaw (Eds.), *Informing our practice* (pp. 182–195). Palmerston North, New Zealand: Kanuka Grove Press.

Hawkins, R. P. (1975). Who decided *that* was the problem? Two stages of responsibility for applied behavior analysts. In W. S. Wood (Ed.), *Issues in evaluating behavior modification* (pp. 195–214). Champaign, IL: Research Press.

Hawley, K. M., & Weisz, J. R. (2003). Child, parent, and therapist (dis)agreement on target problems in outpatient therapy: The therapist's dilemma and its implications. *Journal of Consulting and Clinical Psychology, 71,* 62–70.

Henggeler, S. W., Schoenwald, S. K., Borduin, C. M., Rowland, M. D., & Cunningham, P. B. (1998). *Multisystemic treatment of antisocial behavior in children and adolescents.* New York: Guilford Press.

Herschell, A. D., McNeil, C. B., & McNeil, D. W. (2004). Clinical child psychology's progress in disseminating empirically supported treatments. *Clinical Psychology: Science and Practice, 11,* 267–288.

Hobbs, N. (1975). *The futures of children.* San Francisco: Jossey-Bass.

Hunsley, J. (1992). Development of the Treatment Acceptability Questionnaire. *Journal of Psychopathology and Behavioral Assessment, 14,* 55–64.

Kapavalu, H. (1993). Dealing with the dark side in the ethnography of childhood: Child punishment in Tonga. *Oceania, 63,* 29–36.

Kazdin, A. E. (1980). Acceptability of alternative treatments for deviant child behavior. *Journal of Applied Behavior Analysis, 13,* 259–273.

Koegel, R. L., & Koegel, L. K. (2006). *Pivotal response treatments for autism: Communication, social, and academic development.* Baltimore: Paul H. Brookes.

Koocher, G. P., & Keith-Spiegel, P. C. (1990). *Children, ethics, and the law: Professional issues and cases.* Lincoln: University of Nebraska Press.

Locke, M. (2006). *Dead child's mom sought discipline tips.* Retrieved June 17, 2006, from http://www.newsobserver.com/102/story/418676.html.

Matthews, A. K. (1997). A guide to case conceptualization and treatment planning with minority group clients. *Behavior Therapist, 20,* 35–39.

Mbigi, L., & Maree, J. (1995). *Ubuntu: The spirit of African transformation management.* Randburg, South Africa: Knowledge Resources.

Meyer, L. H., & Evans, I. M. (1989). *Non-aversive intervention for behavior problems: A manual for home and community.* Baltimore: Paul H. Brookes.

Nelson-Gray, R. O. (2003). Treatment utility of psychological assessment. *Psychological Assessment, 15,* 521–531.

Nezu, A. M. (2005). Beyond cultural competence: Human diversity and the appositeness of asseverative goals. *Clinical Psychology: Science and Practice, 12,* 19–32.

Ondrusek, N., Abramovitch, R., Pencharz, P., & Koren, G. (1998). Empirical examination of the ability of children to consent to clinical research. *Journal of Medical Ethics, 24,* 158–165.

Organization for Economic Cooperation and Development. (2001). *Knowledge and skills for life: First results from the OECD Program for International Student Assessment (PISA).* Paris: Author.

Pearl, M. (2006 June). *Too young to spank?* Retrieved June 17, 2006, from http://www.nogreaterjoy.org/index/TheRod.

Pettifor, A. (2006). *The coming first world debt crisis.* Basingstoke, UK: Palgrave Macmillan.

Prilleltensky, I. (2003). Poverty and power. In S. C. Carr & T. S. Sloan (Eds.), *Poverty and psychology: From global perspective to local practice* (pp. 19–44). New York: Kluwer Academic.

Reitman, D., Murphy, M. A., Hupp, S. D. A., & O'Callaghan, P. M. (2004). Behavior change and perceptions of change: Evaluating the effectiveness of a token economy. *Child and Family Behavior Therapy, 26,* 17–36.

Robinson, D. H., Funk, D. C., Beth, A., & Bush, A. M. (2005). Changing beliefs about corporal punishment: Increasing knowledge about ineffectiveness to build more consistent moral and informational beliefs. *Journal of Behavioral Education, 14,* 117–139.

Rothmier, J. D., Lasley, M. V., & Shapiro, G. G. (2003). Factors influencing parental consent in pediatric clinical research. *Pediatrics, 111,* 1037–1041.

Sanders, M. R. (1999). Triple P—Positive Parenting Program: Towards an empirically validated multilevel parenting and family support strategy for the prevention of behavioral and emotional problems in children. *Clinical Child and Family Psychology Review, 2,* 71–90.

Staats, A. W. (1975). *Social behaviorism.* Homewood, IL: Dorsey Press.

Tanaka-Matsumi, J., Seiden, D. Y., & Lam, K. N. (1996). The Culturally Informed Functional Assessment (CIFA) interview: A strategy for cross-cultural behavioral practice. *Cognitive and Behavioral Practice, 3,* 215–233.

Tharp, R. G., & Wetzel, R. J. (1969). *Behavior modification in the natural environment.* New York: Academic Press.

Voeltz, L. M., & Evans, I. M. (1982). The assessment of behavioral interrelationships in child behavior therapy. *Behavioral Assessment, 4,* 131–165.

Voeltz, L. M., Evans, I. M., Derer, K. R., & Hanashiro, R. (1983). Targeting excess behavior for change: A clinical decision model for selecting priority goals in educational contexts. *Child and Family Behavior Therapy, 5,* 17–35.

Waehler, C. A., Kalodner, C. R., Wampold, B. E., & Lichtenberg, J. W. (2000). Empirically supported treatment (ESTs) in perspective: Implications for counselling psychology training. *Counseling Psychologist, 28,* 657–671.

Wahler, R. G. (1975). Some structural aspects of deviant child behavior. *Journal of Applied Behavior Analysis, 8,* 27–42.

Wahler, R. G. (1980). The insular mother: Her problems in parent-child treatment. *Journal of Applied Behavior Analysis, 13,* 207–219.

Wiehe, V. R. (1990). Religious influence on parental attitudes toward the use of corporal punishment. *Journal of Family Violence, 5,* 173–186.

Wilson, F. E., & Evans, I. M. (1983). The reliability of target behavior selection in behavioral assessment. *Behavioral Assessment, 5,* 33–54.

Winett, R. A., & Winkler, R. C. (1972). Current behavior modification in the classroom: Be still, be quiet, be docile. *Journal of Applied Behavior Analysis, 5,* 499–504.

Wolf , M. M. (1978). Social validity: The case for subjective measurement or how applied behavior analysis is finding its heart. *Journal of Applied Behavior Analysis, 11,* 203–215.

Yeaton, W. H., & Sechrest, L. (1981). Critical dimensions in the choice and maintenance of successful treatment: Strength, integrity, and effectiveness. *Journal of Consulting and Clinical Psychology, 49,* 156–167.

PART II

ASSESSMENT, CONCEPTUALIZATION, AND TREATMENT OF SPECIFIC DISORDERS

CHAPTER 9

Depressive Disorders

BENJAMIN L. HANKIN, KATHRYN E. GRANT, CATHERINE CHEELEY,
EMILY WETTER, FARAHNAZ K. FARAHMAND,
AND ROBERT I. WESTERHOLM

D epression is a prototypical multifactorial disorder that profoundly affects individuals' emotions, thoughts, sense of self, behaviors, interpersonal relations, physical functioning, biological processes, work productivity, and overall life satisfaction. In addition, depression is one of the most commonly occurring of the major psychiatric disorders—indeed, it has been called the "common cold" of mental illness (Gotlib & Hammen, 2002). Given the multiple effects that depression has and its common occurrence, it has been ranked the fourth leading cause of disability and premature death worldwide (Murray & Lopez, 1996).

It is now recognized that depression over the life span typically has its origins in adolescence. For that reason, this chapter focuses on several main issues concerning depression in children and adolescents (for reviews of these topics in adults, see Gotlib & Hammen, 2002): definition and description, diagnosis and assessment, potential etiological influences and hypothesized causes, and behavioral and pharmacological interventions. After reviewing these central issues, we present a case description, including history, assessment, conceptualization, and treatment factors and considerations, and final recommendations to students and clinicians.

DESCRIPTION, DIAGNOSIS, AND ASSESSMENT ISSUES IN DEPRESSION

According to the official psychiatric classification system, the *Diagnostic and Statistical Manual of Mental Disorders*, fourth edition, text revision (*DSM IV-TR*; American Psychiatric Association, 2000), an episode of Major Depression can be diagnosed with the same symptoms in childhood and adolescence as in adulthood (e.g., sleep changes, appetite changes, feelings of worthlessness, concentration difficulties), except that irritability can be applied as a mood symptom along with depressed, sad mood and anhedonia (loss of pleasure) in youth. *DSM-IV-TR* states that dysthymia in youth has the same symptom profile as in adults, but there is a minimum 1-year duration in youth compared with 2 years in adulthood. Although some research investigates Major Depressive Disorder separately from Dysthymic Disorder, most studies either combine them or focus on depressive symptoms more broadly. For these reasons, this chapter reviews research on childhood depression in general, rather than specific work involving Major Depressive Disorder or Dysthymic Disorder, unless otherwise noted.

Although there is substantial evidence that depressed children and adolescents can be identified using *DSM* criteria, there is also evidence that the syndrome and predominant symptoms of depression may differ as a function of age and development. Developmental differences in depression may be present because (a) younger children may not have developed the requisite cognitive, social, emotional, or biological capacities to experience certain typical adult depressive symptoms, and/or (b) the causes and/or consequences of depression may change across developmental periods (Cicchetti & Toth, 1998; Weiss & Garber, 2003). Very young children, especially preschoolers, tend not to report depressed mood or hopelessness and are more likely to describe somatic symptoms of depression. They are also more likely to "look depressed" (G. A. Carlson & Kashani, 1988; Kovacs, 1996; Ryan, Puig-Antich, Ambrosini, & Rabinovich, 1987; Weiss & Garber, 2003). Other symptoms, such as anhedonia and psychomotor retardation, become more prevalent with the transition from childhood into adolescence. These findings suggest the importance of using measures of depression that were developed for children and adolescents rather than relying solely on measures that represent downward extensions of measures developed for adults. Measures developed specifically for children and adolescents are also more likely to provide normative data for parallel parent and teacher versions, which is useful for evaluating the relative severity of symptoms (Rudolph & Lambert, in press). See Rudolph and Lambert for a review of assessment measures developed for children and adolescents.

Another issue in the definition and classification of depression, which has important implications for assessment, is whether the latent structure of depression is best considered a category or a dimension. When viewed dimensionally, depression is said to differ quantitatively by degree (i.e., individuals are more or less depressed). When viewed categorically, depression is said to differ from healthy functioning in a qualitatively distinct way, such that individuals may be identified as either depressed or not. For the most part, research shows that the structure of depression is dimensional in children and adolescents (Hankin, Fraley, Lahey, & Waldman, 2005) and adults (e.g., A. M. Ruscio & Ruscio, 2002; J. Ruscio & Ruscio, 2000). Thus, there is no discrete separation between youth diagnosed with depression and those experiencing subclinical depression (i.e., children and adolescents with fewer than the required number of symptoms for an official diagnosis).

Even though the evidence reveals that depression in children, adolescents, and adults is continuously or dimensionally distributed, in practice, clinical decision making is discrete (e.g., depressed/not depressed) and often driven by third-party payment. Thus, in the same way that cutoffs are employed to diagnose high blood pressure and obesity (other continuously distributed health problems), discrete cut points (e.g., > 5 out of 9 symptoms according to *DSM-IV-TR*) are imposed on the diagnosis of depression. Along with identifying a discrete number of *DSM*-defined symptoms of depression, clinicians must also establish clinically significant impairment or distress (e.g., harmful dysfunction; Wakefield, 1992) and a minimum time frame (2 weeks).

The various assessment tools used to measure and diagnose depression range from methods that assess depressed mood and depressed syndrome using dimensional scales to qualitative assessments of depressive disorder (Compas, Ey, & Grant, 1993). Depressed mood refers to the affective state of depression (i.e., sadness or irritability). No other symptoms or time frame are required to accompany the definition of depressed mood. Depressed syndrome is an internally consistent clustering of symptoms that are theoretically or empirically determined (e.g., depressed mood, loss of interest, changes in appetite or eating, changes in sleeping, difficulty concentrating, low self-esteem).

Assessing depressed mood can be accomplished in many ways, such as simply asking the youth how sad, depressed, or down he or she feels, having the child draw a face that characterizes his or her mood (e.g., Feeling Faces Chart; Friedberg & McClure, 2002, p. 83), or requesting that the youth describe his or her level of depressed mood using a Likert scale. To assess the depressed syndrome, there are brief, reliable, valid, and well-normed questionnaires (for more information on depression rating scales, see Brooks & Kutcher, 2001; Rudolph & Lambert, in press) that can be completed in a short time by the adolescent. Widely used examples of such assessments are the Children's Depression Inventory (CDI; Kovacs, 2003), the Mood and Feeling Questionnaire (Angold, Costello, Messer, & Pickles, 1995), the Reynolds Child Depression Scale (RCDS) and the Reynolds Adolescent Depression Scale (RADS; Reynolds, 1987, 1989), and the Youth Self-Report (YSR; Achenbach, Dumenci, & Rescorla, 2003). The parent-version of the Achenbach scale is often used in conjunction with the YSR (i.e., Child Behavior Checklist [CBCL]; Achenbach et al., 2003). Although syndromes are typically assessed using dimensional scales, most syndrome measures have established clinical cut points based on normative data to distinguish youth most likely to need clinical attention.

To render a diagnosis of depression, clinical rating scales (e.g., Children's Depression Rating Scale: Poznanski, Cook, & Carroll, 1979) or semi-structured interviews (e.g., Schedule for Affective Disorders and Schizophrenia in School Age Children [K-SADS]: Chambers, 1985; Child and Adolescent Psychiatric Assessment: Angold et al., 1995) are typically used, often in combination. With these methods, a trained professional interviews the adolescent and often a parent to determine the number of symptoms present, the duration and severity of the symptoms, and the degree of impairment or distress experienced by the child (see Rudolph & Lambert, in press, for a review of methods for diagnosing depression in children and adolescents).

The purpose of the assessment should dictate the type of measures used. In clinical practice, it is advisable to include dimensional measures to assess the degree to which the child's or adolescent's self-report differs from age- and gender-matched normative samples. Some measures (e.g., CDI, RADS, RCDS) are specific to depression and serve as reliable initial screens for depressive disorder. Other, broader scales (e.g., YSR, CBCL) are less useful for assessing symptoms that map onto *DSM* criteria for mood disorders but offer the advantage of assessing a range of other forms of psychopathology. Given high rates of comorbidity, such information is essential for effective treatment planning (Rudolph & Lambert, in press). To fully establish a diagnosis of depression, many sources recommend that clinicians begin by administering a broad clinical interview and a self-report measure (e.g., the CDI or the YSR or CBCL) as part of a general screening. If the youth scores above the empirical cut point on a depression-related subscale or depressive symptoms are noted in general clinical interviews, the child can be evaluated further with additional, more thorough diagnostic assessments.

Although research on childhood depression, diagnosis, and assessment has increased greatly over the past 20 years, Rudolph and Lambert (in press) have identified several very significant gaps in the literature. First, although gathering information from multiple sources is recommended, and there is evidence that each provides unique information, there are few guidelines for integrating them. Much more research is needed to establish the incremental validity of assessment measures in relation to each other. Second, the extent to which various measures are responsive to change in depressive symptoms is unknown. This is especially important for determining the effectiveness of treatments and is complicated by the fact that depression has been found to remit naturally over time. Third, it remains unclear whether measures of depression are invariant across various demographic variables, including age, sex, race and ethnicity, and culture. For example, there is emerging evidence suggesting that the most commonly used measures of depression are not invariant across either ethnicity or age.

One of the most striking issues confronting the field is the continuing lack of consensus on a definition of childhood depression. Although taxonomic analysis of depression definitions and assessment strategies (e.g., Compas et al., 1993) suggest ways in which mood, syndrome, and disorder conceptualizations are interrelated, the truth is that many of the measures that fall into these categories differ widely from one another. For example, there is substantial variability in items. Some of the most widely used measures combine symptoms of anxiety and depression (e.g., YSR), and others include subscales that assess interpersonal problems (e.g., CDI) or derive their content directly from the *DSM* (e.g., K-SADS). Such variability also includes variability on whether the measure is dimensional or categorical and whether it was developed empirically on children and adolescents or developed as a downward extension from theoretically based adult measures.

EPIDEMIOLOGY OF DEPRESSION

The prevalence rate of depression has been examined in many studies with different age groups and with different methods and samples. In this brief review of the literature, community samples are emphasized for estimating prevalence rates of depression because samples drawn from psychiatric clinics may be biased in various ways (e.g., actively seeking treatment, exhibiting greater severity, and revealing higher comorbidity), and these biases can inflate artificially the prevalence rates of depression.

Cross-sectional studies based on adolescent self-report indicate that between 20% and 50% (Kessler, Avenevoli, & Merikangas, 2001; Petersen et al., 1993) of adolescents report significant levels of depressive symptoms. Prospective longitudinal studies of self-reported depressive symptoms show that average levels of depressive mood and symptoms rise substantially, from relatively low levels in childhood to much higher levels starting in middle adolescence (Cole, Martin, Peeke, Seroczynski, & Fier, 1999; Ge, Lorenz, Conger, & Elder, 1994; Wade, Cairney, & Pevalin, 2002; Wichstrom, 1999). These elevated rates of depressed mood or symptoms indicate more than just benign adolescent "moodiness" or "turmoil," but rather represent a substantial risk for later clinically significant depressive disorder (Pine, Cohen, Cohen, & Brook, 1999) and impaired functioning (Gotlib, Lewinsohn, & Seeley, 1995).

Cross-sectional studies of clinical levels of a diagnosis of depression show that the rates of depression are generally low in children and increase to near adult prevalence levels in adolescence. The lifetime prevalence rate of depression among preadolescent school-age children is less than 3% (Cohen, Cohen, Kasen, & Velez, 1993; Costello et al., 1996). Rates of depression among adolescents are generally comparable to those observed among adults: 14% lifetime prevalence for Major Depression and 11% lifetime prevalence for minor depression (Kessler et al., 1994). For comparison purposes, the lifetime prevalence of Major Depressive Disorder for 18- to 29-year-olds was 16.6% in the most recent large-scale epidemiological study (Kessler et al., 2005). Consistent with these cross-sectional findings, various prospective, community-based studies (Cohen et al., 1993; Costello, Mustillo, Erkanli, Keeler, & Angold, 2003; Hankin et al., 1998; Reinherz, Giaconia, Lefkowitz, & Pakiz, 1993) reveal a pattern in which low rates of clinical depression in childhood (e.g., 1% to 3%) increase dramatically in middle to late adolescence, when they reach rates observed throughout adulthood (up to 17%). Indeed, one of these longitudinal studies (Hankin et al., 1998) revealed a sixfold increase in rates of depression from early adolescence (3% prevalence at age 15) to the end of adolescence (17% at age 18).

As noted at the beginning of this chapter, most individuals experience their first depression sometime during adolescence. In a recent prospective follow-back study, Kim-Cohen et al. (2003) examined what percentage of adults from an entire birth cohort of individuals, which has been followed for 26 years, had experienced an episode of depression during childhood or adolescence. They found that of the adults who had experienced a depressive disorder by age 26, the vast majority (75%) had already had a previous depressive disorder in childhood or adolescence, whereas only 25% of the sample that had a lifetime diagnosis of depression had experienced onset of depression in adulthood (ages 21–26). Similar results have been reported in other large-scale, prospective community studies (e.g., Lewinsohn, Rohde, Seeley, Klein, & Gotlib, 2000). However, in contrast to these findings, Kessler and colleagues (2005) found that most adults with a psychiatric disorder (e.g., anxiety disorder, conduct problems) had experienced symptoms prior to age 14, but the average age of onset for depression was 30 years old. The reasons for the discrepancy between the recent, large-scale epidemiological study by Kessler and the other studies in terms of age of onset for first depressions are unclear. There are differences in study design and method: Kessler and colleagues had adults retrospectively recall depression onset dates, whereas the studies with adolescent onset (e.g., Kim-Cohen et al., 2003; Lewinsohn et al., 2000) prospectively followed youth from adolescence through adulthood. This latter method with prospective follow-ups is considered more reliable and valid than retrospective recall.

Twice as many adult women as men are depressed. This sex difference emerges between childhood and early adolescence and lasts throughout adulthood. Approximately 25% to 40% of adolescent girls exhibit high levels of depressed mood, compared with 20% to 35% of adolescent boys (Petersen et al., 1993). More girls than boys report depression starting in early adolescence, around the ages of 12 and 13 (Angold, Erkanli, Silberg, Eaves, & Costello, 2002; Ge et al., 1994; Twenge & Nolen-Hoeksema, 2002; Wade et al., 2002; Wichstrom, 1999). Longitudinal studies investigating the emergence of the sex difference at the level of depressive disorder find the same pattern: More girls than boys begin to become clinically depressed after age 12 to 13 (Costello et al., 2003; Hankin et al., 1998; Reinherz et al., 1993; Weissman, Warner, Wickramaratne, Moreau, & Olfson, 1997). Finally, the female preponderance in depression remains at this 2:1 female-to-male ratio from adolescence throughout most of adulthood (i.e., until old age; Hankin & Abramson, 1999).

Pubertal development and timing have been studied in relation to the sex difference in adolescent depression. Angold and colleagues (Angold, Costello, & Worthman, 1998) found the sex difference in depression diverged at Tanner Stage III and was a better predictor than age alone. Moreover, girls who started puberty earlier than their peers were more likely to become depressed (Ge, Conger, & Elder, 1996, 2001; Graber, Lewinsohn, Seeley, & Brooks-Gunn, 1997). Thus, sex, age, and pubertal development may represent risk factors to be considered in the conceptualization and assessment process.

CONTINUITY AND RECURRENCE OF DEPRESSION OVER THE LIFE COURSE

As suggested by this longitudinal epidemiological data, depressed mood during childhood carries risk for development of depressive disorder in adulthood. One prospective community study found that teacher reports at age 6 and youths' self-reports at age 9 of anxious or depressive symptoms predicted occurrence of Major Depressive Disorder at age 21 (Reinherz, Giaconia, Hauf, Wasserman, & Paradis, 2000). There is even stronger continuity for depression from adolescence into adulthood (Hankin et al., 1998; Lewinsohn, Allen, Seeley, & Gotlib, 1999; Pine et al., 1999; Pine, Cohen, Gurley, Brook, & Ma, 1998; Weissman et al., 1997). Although it appears obvious and it has been asserted repeatedly that early-onset depression predicts greater continuity of depression in adulthood, the story of continuity in depression over the life span is not so clear. There is confusion over the definition and operationalization of "early onset" that has led to the inaccurate assumption that both child- and adolescent-onset depressions are continuous with depression in adulthood. Evidence suggests strongly that there is heterogeneity of juvenile depression, such that depression with onset prior to puberty appears to follow a different course and to be etiologically distinct from depression that begins in adolescence (Harrington, Fudge, Rutter, Pickles, & Hill, 1990; Silberg et al., 1999; Thapar & McGuffin, 1997; Weissman et al., 1999). This is consistent with the notion that there are important developmental differences (e.g., symptoms and potential causes) between depression that arises during childhood and depression that develops in adolescence or adulthood (Duggal, Carlson, Sroufe, & Egeland, 2001; Jaffee et al., 2002). Unfortunately, few studies have actually assessed continuity of depression from childhood to adulthood; most of the prospective community studies providing evidence for continuity begin in adolescence. Additional research is needed to examine the full course of prepubertal, or child-onset, depression through adolescence and into adulthood.

Depression is a chronic, recurrent disorder. Approximately 50% of adults with a diagnosis of depression will experience a recurrence within 2 years, over 80% within 5 to 7 years, and individuals who have had more than 3 lifetimes episodes of depression are particularly likely to have another recurrence (Belsher & Costello, 1988; Judd, 1997; Solomon, Haaga, & Arnow, 2001). Moreover, once adults have had multiple recurrences, their time to experience the next recurrence decreases with each additional recurrence. Approximately 40% of youth will have another depressive episode in 3 to 5 years after their initial onset (Lewinsohn, Clarke, Seeley, & Rohde, 1994; Rao, Hammen, & Daley, 1991).

COMORBIDITY

Understanding the pattern of comorbidity of depression with other disorders is vital for accurate diagnosis, assessment, and treatment. Depression typically co-occurs with other disorders (especially anxiety and disruptive behavioral disorders) during childhood and adolescence. Angold and colleagues (Angold, Costello, & Erkanli, 1999) showed that depression is associated at greater than chance levels with anxiety disorders (median odds ratio = 8.2), Conduct and Oppositional Defiant Disorder (median odds ratio = 6.6), and Attention-Deficit/Hyperactivity Disorder (median odds ratio = 5.5).

Developmental patterns of sequential comorbidity have also been discovered. Children and early adolescents are more likely to have a co-occurring diagnosis of Separation Anxiety Disorder and depression, whereas older adolescents are more likely to exhibit comorbid eating disorders and substance use problems. Elevations in symptoms of or a diagnosis of anxiety often precedes the development of depressive symptoms or disorder (Avenevoli, Stolar, Li, Dierker, & Ries Merikangas, 2001; Cohen et al., 1993; Cole, Peeke, Martin, Truglio, & Seroczynski, 1998; Kim-Cohen et al., 2003; Pine et al., 1998; Reinherz et al., 1993). Externalizing behaviors also tend to predict later depressive symptoms, whereas depressive symptoms do not predict later externalizing behaviors (Curran & Bollen, 2001; Kim-Cohen et al., 2003).

CONCEPTUALIZING THE DEVELOPMENT OF DEPRESSION

This section reviews various hypothesized and empirically supported causes of depression in children and adolescents. We emphasize a vulnerability-stress framework, in which recent stressful events trigger an underlying predisposition, as one of the most promising approaches for understanding the ontogeny of depression (Hankin & Abela, 2005b). First, we consider and review the role of life events as stressors, and then we review various depression vulnerabilities (e.g., genetics, parenting, peers). We review these vulnerabilities separately, although it is important to highlight that it is unlikely that any single vulnerability or etiological framework (e.g., biological, interpersonal, cognitive, emotional, personality) will provide a necessary and sufficient causal explanation for the development of depression because depression is a prototypic multifactorial syndrome. Instead, it is most likely that a developmentally sensitive, integrative theoretical model can and should combine these disparate depression vulnerabilities and stressors into a coherent vulnerability-stress model of depression (for examples, see Garber & Horowitz, 2002; Goodyer, 2001; Hammen & Rudolph, 2003; Hankin & Abramson, 2001). As such, a comprehensive assessment and conceptualization needs to consider the many processes, mechanisms, and risk factors that contribute to depression.

LIFE EVENTS AND STRESSORS

In the broadest sense, causal risk factors for depression are either environmentally or genetically based. The environmental risk factor that has received the greatest research attention and support is exposure to stressful life experiences. Grant and colleagues (2003) proposed that stress be defined as *environmental events or chronic conditions that objectively threaten the physical and/or psychological health or well-being of individuals of a particular age in a particular society.*

In spite of growing recognition that a stressor should be defined as an event or circumstance that is "objectively threatening" (i.e., independent raters can agree it poses a threat to the average child), only the most labor-intensive narrative interviews are capable of assessing such threat. Such methods use situational information to rate how stressful events would be for the average individual in a particular set of circumstances (Brown & Harris, 1978; Hammen, 2005). Given the time demands and costs associated with administering such measures, they have been used by fewer than 2% of researchers (Grant, Compas, Thurm, McMahon, & Gipson, 2004). Most researchers use stress checklists, which are problematic because they assess a limited range of events and are not equipped to account for differences in the meaning of events across different contexts (e.g., the item "death of a grandparent" has a different meaning for a youth who never met that grandparent than it has for a youth who was raised by that grandparent; Hammen & Rudolph, 2003).

Grant and colleagues (2004) have argued the need for an empirically based measure that incorporates the sophistication of stress interviews into usable checklists, so that researchers can measure stressors comprehensively, accurately, and consistently across studies. Such a measure could be used as a screening device for more intensive interviews (when those are deemed warranted) and could serve as the foundation for a stressor classification system or taxonomy that is analogous to classification systems for child and adolescent psychopathology (Grant et al., 2003).

In spite of measurement problems in stress research, there is substantial evidence that stressors contribute to the development of depressive symptoms across the life span (Brown & Harris, 1989; Goodyer, 2001; Grant et al., 2004; Meyer, Chrousos, & Gold, 2001; Monroe & Simons, 1991). Almost all individuals (up to 80%) with a depressive disorder have encountered at least one significant negative life event in the month prior to the onset of depression (Goodyer, 2001; Hammen, 2005). Additionally, longitudinal studies have discovered that experiencing stressors precedes the initial elevation, recurrence, and exacerbation of depression (e.g., Ge et al., 2001; Goodyer, Herbert, Tamplin, & Altham, 2000; Grant et al., 2004).

Ge and colleagues (1994) have found evidence for a rise in the number of uncontrollable negative life events starting after age 13. They also found that this increasing trajectory in stressors closely paralleled the rise in depressive symptoms in their adolescent sample (Ge et al., 1994). Thus, the fact that stressors appear to be on an increasing trajectory from late childhood into adolescence provides a potential explanation for why the levels of depression rise throughout adolescence. The increasing trajectory of stressors begins around puberty, which is a transitional period in development, and transitions frequently are associated with additional increases in stress (Caspi & Moffitt, 1991; Ge et al., 2001; Graber, Brooks-Gunn, & Petersen, 1996). Further, there is some evidence that adolescent girls exhibit a significantly greater increase in stressors after age 13 than do boys (Ge et al., 1994; Rudolph & Hammen, 1999), and this developmental time line for the sex difference in stressors matches the emergence of the sex difference in depression. Indeed, girls' increased experience of stressors, particularly interpersonal stressors, has been found to partly explain why girls are more depressed than boys (Hankin, Mermelstein, & Roesch, 2007). In addition to the stress exposure perspective (that stressors contribute to depression), a complementary perspective suggests that the stress-depression relationship is a bidirectional process. The stress generation hypothesis (Hammen, 1991) suggests that because of personality characteristics or behaviors related to depression, some individuals generate stressful circumstances, and these can then lead to further increases in depression. Recent multiwave longitudinal studies provide the strongest support to date for the stress generation hypothesis. In a three-wave, 1-year longitudinal study of adolescents (8th- and 10th-graders), Hankin Abramson, Miller, and Haeffel (2004) found that depressive symptoms at one time point predicted later increases in objectively assessed stressors at the following time point and that stressors at the same time point were concurrently associated with depressive symptoms. Similar results were obtained in a 10-wave 1-year longitudinal study of children (ages 6–14) of affectively ill parents (Abela, Nueslovici, & Chan, 2004): A bidirectional relationship was found between negative events and increases in depressive symptoms. Finally, a recent multiwave study found support for both stress exposure and stress generation hypotheses in two different samples of children and adolescents (Cole, Nolen-Hoeksema, Girgus, & Paul, 2006), suggesting that the relationship between stress and depression is reciprocal. It is clear that not everyone who experiences negative life events becomes depressed. Although the majority of those individuals who are significantly depressed encountered at least one major negative life event prior to the onset of the depression, only 20% to 50% of individuals who experience severe, major negative life events develop clinically significant levels of depression (e.g., Goodyer et al., 2000; Lewinsohn, Roberts, Seeley, & Rohde, 1994). So negative events typically interact with other risk factors to predict depression.

GENETIC INFLUENCES

Behavior genetic studies with children and adolescents have found depression to be moderately heritable (for reviews, see Rice, Harold, & Thapar, 2002b; Sullivan, Neale, & Kendler, 2000). Heritability estimates for parents' rating of youths' depressive symptoms are modest to high (range 30% to 80%), whereas these genetic estimates are lower for youths' own ratings of their depressive symptoms (range 15% to 80%, 35% average; Rice et al., 2002b). Reasons for this discrepancy have not yet been determined. Evidence from twin research also suggests that depressive symptoms are heritable starting in adolescence (after age 11) and continuing throughout adulthood, whereas shared common family environment, but not genetic factors, is linked with depression in childhood before age 11 (Rice, Harold, & Thapar, 2002a). The extent to which this pattern might explain the stronger continuity between adolescent (relative to child) depression and depression in adulthood has not yet been explored.

The liability to experience negative events also appears to be partially heritable (Thapar, Harold, & McGuffin, 1998). A longitudinal twin study (Silberg et al., 1999) found that genetic liability increased the risk for depression and experiencing stressors for girls after, but not before, puberty. Thus, stressors may serve as mediators of genetic risk (Rice, Harold, & Thapar, 2003).

More commonly, however, genetic risk and stressful experiences have been found to interact with one another to predict depression. The most specific evidence to date for a gene-environment interaction comes from molecular genetic studies with adults that include assessments of environmental stressors (Caspi et al., 2003; Grabe et al., 2004; Kaufman et al., 2004; Kendler, Kuhn, Vittum, Prescott, & Riley, 2005; but see Gillespie, Whitfield, Williams, Heath, & Martin, 2005, for failure to replicate). These studies have found that a functional polymorphism in the promoter region of the serotonin transporter (5-HTT) interacts with the occurrence of stressors over time in adulthood to predict the onset of depression. Specifically, those individuals who had one or two copies of the short allele form of 5-HTT (the genetic vulnerability) and encountered more stressors over time experienced the greatest incidence of depression. In the only genetic X stress study to date with an adolescent sample, the short form 5HTTLPR interacted with stressors to predict youth-rated depressive symptoms cross-sectionally among 12- to 17-year-old girls, but not boys (Eley et al., 2004).

Despite the general consensus across the adult molecular genetic studies, there is one interesting inconsistency in results. Most studies in this area found that adults who experienced more severe stress and have the short 5-HTT allele were the most likely to develop depression. In contrast, Kendler and colleagues (2005) found that smaller stressors, or minor hassles, interacted with the genetic risk of having a short 5-HTT allele to predict depression, whereas experiencing more severe stress directly contributed to depression regardless of genetic risk.

Problems with current stress measurement strategies may contribute to these apparent inconsistencies. Almost all of the studies (e.g., Caspi et al., 2003) used self-report checklists to assess major negative life events. And, stressful life event checklists often confound major and minor events due to insufficient provision of contextual information (i.e., checklist events that appear to be major events turn out to be minor events when probed during intensive follow-up interviews; Dohrenwend, 2006).

Thus, this pattern of results might not be as inconsistent as it first appears. Major events may predict depression directly, perhaps through the development of negative cognitive mediators. Minor events may interact with cognitive vulnerability that developed in response to severe stressors or was already present in those at genetic risk for depression. Additional research is needed to test these hypotheses.

We believe that keeping abreast of progress in the fields of molecular genetics and gene-environment interactions will be crucial in the upcoming years (e.g., see Moffitt, Caspi, & Rutter, 2006).

Temperament

One mechanism through which genetic risk for depression may be transmitted across generations is the genetic transmission of temperament (Compas, Connor-Smith, & Jaser, 2004; Hankin & Abramson, 2001). Temperament refers to individual emotional and behavioral tendencies that appear early in life, are stable across time and situations, and have a biological basis (Rothbart & Bates, 1998). These traits are at least moderately heritable (Plomin & Caspi, 1999). Moreover, several longitudinal studies indicate that temperament and emotionality, measured in childhood, predict the later development of depressive disorders (Krueger, 1999; Lonigan, Phillips, & Hooe, 2003; Newman, Caspi, Moffitt, & Silva, 1997; van Os, Jones, Lewis, Wadsworth, & Murray, 1997).

Numerous theories have been proposed to explain the development and structure of temperament (e.g., Clark & Watson, 1991; Kagan, 1998; Kagan, Reznick, & Gibbons, 1989; Phillips, Lonigan, Driscoll, & Hooe, 2002; Rothbart, Ahadi, Hersey, & Fisher, 2001; Thomas & Chess, 1985; Thomas, Chess, Birch, Hertzig, & Korn, 1963). Temperamental characteristics, such as negative emotionality, positive emotionality, and physiological overarousal, in turn, have been linked to depression. Nonetheless, little is known about the processes by which temperament may lead to depression. In one of the few studies to address this question Hankin (2005b) showed that initial levels of negative and positive emotionality predicted the occurrence of additional stressors over 4 prospective waves (in 6th–10th-graders), and these stressors explained the prospective association between baseline negative and positive emotionality and later elevations in depressive symptoms over time. Thus, in this study, temperament traits conferred vulnerability to depression through stress generation. Additional studies, such as this one, are needed (a) to examine the processes through which temperament characteristics may lead to depressive symptoms and (b) to further our understanding of the interrelationships among risk factors for depression. For example, it is likely that other vulnerabilities (e.g., cognitive, interpersonal) interact with these increased stressors to augment the generated stressors and depression association (e.g., see Hankin & Abramson, 2001).

PARENTAL ISSUES AND INFLUENCES

Given evidence for the heritability of depression, it is not surprising that parental depression is one of the strongest predictors of depression in youth (Beardslee, Versage, & Gladstone, 1998). Not only are the children of depressed parents up to 6 times more likely to develop depression (Kessler, 2002) and experience earlier onset of depressive episodes than the children of nondepressed parents (Lewinsohn & Essau, 2002), but these children also experience higher rates of other internalizing disorders, externalizing disorders, and problems in school, social deficits, and low self-esteem (Goodman & Gotlib, 1999).

There is also evidence of processes through which parental depression contributes to depression in offspring that go beyond genetics and nongenetic biological mechanisms (e.g., dysregulation of the child's neuroregulatory systems while in utero). Two, in particular, have received considerable research attention: (1) increased exposure to stressors in families in which a parent is depressed and (2) disruptions to parent-child attachment (Goodman & Gotlib, 1999).

The children of depressed parents are exposed to a greater number of stressors than children of nondepressed parents (Adrian & Hammen, 1993). These stressors can include increased marital conflict (Cummings & Davies, 2002; Goodman & Gotlib, 1999; Olsson, Nordstrom, Arinell, & von Knorring, 1999), poor parenting behaviors (Lovejoy, Graczyk, O'Hare, & Neuman, 2000), and an increased need for the child to assume the role of caretaker or comforter for the depressed parent (Radke-Yarrow, Zahn-Waxler, Richardson, & Susman, 1994). Thus, increased exposure to stressors represents one mechanism through which depression is transmitted from parent to child.

A second, related mechanism is disruptions in parent-child attachment. Depression may interfere with parents' ability to provide their children with the warmth, consistency, and sensitivity necessary for the development of a secure attachment (Ainsworth, Blehar, Waters, & Wall, 1978; Bowlby, 1980; V. Carlson, Cicchetti, Barnett, & Braunwald, 1989; West, Spreng, Rose, & Adam, 1999). Insecure attachment patterns (e.g., high avoidance and anxiety) have been posited to serve as vulnerability factors for a diversity of psychological problems, including depression (Davila, Ramsay, Stroud, & Steinberg, 2005), and several cross-sectional studies have demonstrated that attachment insecurity is associated with depressive symptoms in adolescent samples (e.g., Armsden, McCauley, Greenberg, & Burke, 1990; Muris, Meesters, van Melick, & Zwambag, 2001; West et al., 1999). In one of the few prospective studies in this area, Hammen and colleagues (1995) reported that attachment insecurity was associated with increases in depressive symptoms over a 1-year longitudinal follow-up (among female high school seniors), especially in the context of interpersonal stress. More recently, results from a multiwave longitudinal study (Abela et al., 2005) showed that children who exhibited high levels of negative attachment patterns reported greater elevations in depressive symptoms following elevations in their parent's level of depressive symptoms.

Peer Influences and Interpersonal Vulnerabilities

An additional interpersonal mechanism through which youth depression may develop is negative relationships outside the home. For example, poor attachments to parents may result in negative internal working models of relationships with others (Ainsworth et al., 1978; Bowlby, 1980), which may negatively influence a young person's ability to develop stable connections with peers. There has been little research investigating such links (Abela et al., 2005; Hammen et al., 1995; Stice, Ragen, & Randall, 2004), but there is ample evidence that interpersonal problems are associated with depression (Cumsille & Epstein, 1994; Garber, Little, Hilsman, & Weaver, 1998; Kashani, Suarez, Jones, & Reid, 1999; Klein, Lewinsohn, & Seeley, 1997; Marcotte, Fortin, Potvin, & Papillon, 2002; Sheeber, Hops, Alpert, Davis, & Andrews, 1997).

Interpersonal theories of depression (e.g., Joiner & Coyne, 1999) posit that social impairment contributes to the development of depression (for a review, see Rudolph & Asher, 2000). In support of these theories, studies have found that depressed adolescents often engage in excessive reassurance seeking from peers (Abela et al., 2005; Joiner, Metalsky, Gencoz, & Gencoz, 2001; Prinstein, Borelli, Cheah, Simon, & Aikins, 2005) and demonstrate interpersonal dependency (Blatt & Zuroff, 1992).

Excessive reassurance seeking is defined as "a relatively stable tendency to excessively and persistently seek assurances from others that one is loveable and worthy, regardless of whether such assurance has already been provided" (Joiner, Katz, & Lew, 1999, p. 270). Cross-sectional studies show that higher levels of reassurance seeking are associated with higher levels of depressive symptoms in both child and early adolescent populations (Abela et al., 2005; Joiner, 1999). Similarly, youth psychiatric inpatients with a primary diagnosis of a depressive disorder have been found to exhibit higher levels of reassurance seeking than those with a primary diagnosis of an externalizing or anxiety disorder (Joiner et al., 2001). High levels of reassurance seeking also have been found to predict clinically significant depressive episodes in children and early adolescents exhibiting an insecure attachment style to their parents (Abela et al., 2005).

Although Abela and colleagues (2005) have reported negative effects associated with reassurance seeking in younger samples, results from a recent prospective study suggest that reassurance seeking may serve as a vulnerability factor to depression only starting in early adolescence (Abela, Zuroff, Ho, Adams, & Hankin, 2006). These authors speculate that reassurance seeking may be more normative and perhaps even adaptive in children, whereas in adolescence it interferes with developmental tasks associated with autonomy and societal expectations for self-sufficiency.

Interpersonal dependency is an exaggerated need for relatedness and a desire to be in direct, immediate contact with close others (e.g., parents, peers). Cross-sectional studies show that higher levels of dependency are associated with higher levels of depressive symptoms in adolescents but not children (Abela, Taxel, & Sakellaropoulo, in press; Abela & Taylor, 2003; Fichman, Koestner, & Zuroff, 1994; Luthar & Blatt, 1993). However, prospective studies have failed to find a relationship between dependency and increases in depressive symptoms over time (Abela, Taxel, et al., in press; Abela & Taylor, 2003).

Research investigating the temporal association between peer relationship problems and depression indicates a reciprocal relationship between them (Gotlib & Hammen, 1992; Joiner, Coyne, & Blalock, 1999; Prinstein et al., 2005; for a review, see Hammen & Rudolph, 2003). For example, interpersonal deficits and lack of social support can lead to symptoms of depression, and in turn, depressive symptoms can lead to problems in peer relationships and social withdrawal. Interestingly, Stice and colleagues (2004) have shown that adolescents' perceptions of low *parental* support predicted future depression, whereas initial depression predicted decreased *peer* support.

There is also evidence of age and sex influences on interpersonal relationships and risk for depression. The transition into adolescence is characterized by increases in peer contact, heightened importance placed on close friendships and support from peers, and greater autonomy from parents (Parker, Rubin, Price, & DeRosier, 1995; Rose & Rudolph, 2006). As the importance of positive peer relationships increases during the transition into adolescence, deficits in interpersonal skills become more apparent and can increase vulnerability to depression (for a review, see Rudolph & Asher, 2000). This appears to be particularly true for girls. For example, girls who engaged in excessive reassurance seeking and had poor peer relationships were particularly likely to exhibit greater depression over time (Prinstein et al., 2005).

PHYSICAL FACTORS: BIOLOGICAL VULNERABILITY

Biological markers of depression likely represent proximal manifestations of more distal genetic and/or environmental risk factors. Evidence of physically observable risk factors for depression has emerged for adults, but the evidence of such markers for adolescents is less conclusive (for reviews, see Kaufman, Martin, King, & Charney, 2001; Thase, Jindal, & Howland, 2002). For example, there is evidence of dysregulation of the human stress response (i.e., abnormalities in the hypothalamic-pituitary-adrenal [HPA] axis) in depressed adults (Gold, Goodwin, & Chrousos, 1988; Meyer et al., 2001). But results of studies conducted with youth have been inconsistent (Dahl, Kaufman, Ryan, & Perel, 1992; Ryan, 1998). This may reflect the fact that the brain and neuroregulatory processes are not fully developed in children and adolescents (Kaufman et al., 2001; Rudolph, Hammen, & Daley, in press; Thase et al., 2002).

Some research with depressed children (e.g., Meyer et al., 2001), however, has revealed blunted growth hormone (GH) secretion in response to pharmacological challenges. Also, Birmaher et al. (2000) have found that offspring of depressed parents, who were at high risk for depression but had not yet experienced clinical depression, exhibited reduced GH response. Such studies suggest that GH response may index a biological vulnerability for depression in youth.

Research with adults also has established that there is reduced blood flow and metabolism in the frontal and prefrontal cortex of depressed individuals (Rudolph et al., in press; Tomarken & Keener, 1998). Davidson and colleagues (Davidson, Pizzagalli, Nitschke, & Putnam, 2002) have theorized that underactivation of this area of the brain represents an underactivation of the approach system, which is associated with reduced engagement with the environment and reduced experience of pleasure. Limited investigation of this area has occurred with adolescents (Kaufman et al., 2001), but some studies have shown that child (Tomarken, Simien, & Garber, 1994) and infant (Dawson, Frey, Panagiotides, & Osterling, 1997) offspring of depressed mothers, who are at high risk for depression but not yet depressed, displayed left frontal underactivity.

Such biological markers are likely genetically based, at least in part (Davidson et al., 2002). There is also evidence that early exposure to stressful life experiences predicts biological abnormalities (i.e., in the HPA axis) consistent with those associated with depression (for reviews, see Goodman, 2002; Heim & Nemeroff, 2001). Thus, both genetic and environmental causes may lead to biological markers associated with depression.

COGNITIVE VULNERABILITY

Cognitive vulnerability represents another proximal risk factor for depression that likely results from more distal genetic or environmentally based causal processes. Three cognitive vulnerability factors have received the most attention: (1) negative inferential styles about causes of events, consequences, and the self (Abramson, Metalsky, & Alloy, 1989); (2) dysfunctional attitudes (Beck, 1987); and (3) the tendency to ruminate in response to depressed mood (Nolen-Hoeksema & Morrow, 1991).

A person with a negative inferential style is likely to attribute negative events to global and stable causes, to catastrophize the consequences of negative events, and to view himself or herself as flawed or deficient following negative events. An individual with dysfunctional attitudes is likely to think his or her self-worth hinges on being perfect or receiving approval from others. Rumination describes the cognitive process in which mildly dysphoric individuals focus on the meanings and implications of their depressed mood and, as a result, develop enduring and severe depressive symptoms.

Prospective research with adolescents has established each of these cognitive risk factors as predictors of depression in youth (Hankin, Abramson, & Siler, 2001; Lewinsohn, Joiner, & Rohde, 2001; Park, Goodyer, & Teasdale, 2004; Southall & Roberts, 2002). For example, Hankin and Roesch (2005) have shown that each of these cognitive vulnerabilities interacts with stressors to prospectively predict depressive symptom trajectories in adolescence (6th–10th graders). In addition, Abela and colleagues (2005) have reported that negative cognitions were associated with increased depression for youth whose parents had recently demonstrated an increase in depressive symptoms.

Some researchers have argued that cognitive vulnerability to depression emerges only during the transition from late childhood to early adolescence, when children acquire the ability to engage in abstract reasoning and formal operational thought (Cole & Turner, 1993; Nolen-Hoeksema, Girgus, & Seligman, 1992; Turner & Cole, 1994; for discussion, see Gibb, Coles, & Heimberg, 2005; Hankin & Abela, 2005a). But studies have shown that cognitive vulnerability interacts with stressors to predict depression in young children as well (e.g., Hankin & Abela, 2005a).

Another developmental hypothesis that has garnered initial support is that some cognitive vulnerabilities in childhood exist and can be measured reliably and validly, but these cognitive risks have not yet consolidated into stable, trait like negative thinking patterns. Prospective, multiwave research with youth in early, middle, and late adolescence (Hankin, 2005b; Hankin, Fraley, & Abela, 2005) lends initial support to this hypothesis. Youths' negative thinking patterns, specifically negative inferential styles and dysfunctional attitudes, were not very stable in middle adolescence (6th–8th grades), but exhibited relative stability consistent with personality traits starting in middle adolescence (9th–10th grades) through late adolescence. Also supportive of this theory is a recent quantitative review of cognitive risk factors for depression in children and adolescents (Lakdawalla, Hankin, & Mermelstein, 2006) that found that cognitive vulnerabilities interacted with stress to predict prospective elevations of depression across ages, with stronger effects in adolescence than in childhood.

The available evidence fairly consistently shows that cognitive vulnerabilities confer risk to depression in youth, especially under conditions of high stress, but less is known about the origins of these depressogenic thinking patterns and their relation to other risk factors for depression (e.g., Lau & Eley, 2006; Lau, Rijsdijk, & Elay, 2006). Remaining questions include the following: Are there ways in which genetic risk for depression might be cognitively mediated? Might this help explain the findings that both genetic influences and cognitive risk factors are stronger in adolescents than in children? Are particular temperaments associated with the tendency to view others and the world in a particular way? Do youth learn negative views of the world through experiences with stressful life events or parental modeling or negative environmental feedback from parents and/or peers (Rudolph et al., in press; for a review of social learning theories of the development of negative cognitions, see Garber & Martin, 2002)? Do biological and cognitive processes represent the same entity viewed from different vantage points (i.e., are biological markers the physical representation of particular ways of thinking), or does one risk factor lead to another. Much additional research is needed to answer these questions. Understanding the ways in which various risk factors are interconnected will be helpful for assessment, conceptualization, and treatment of depression.

SUMMARY OF CONCEPTUALIZATION APPROACHES AND IMPLICATIONS FOR ASSESSMENT

In sum, numerous risk factors for adolescent depression have been identified. At the broadest level, each of these factors emanate from genetic or environmental influences (e.g., fateful adversity), or the interplay among nature and nurture (cf., Moffitt et al., 2006). Beyond those broad distinctions, there are numerous specific markers that are likely to be influenced both by nature and nurture, including exposure to specific stressful life experiences, temperament, parental depression, family and peer relationships, biological markers, and cognitive risk factors. An important area for future research is investigation of the ways these risk factors are interrelated.

Numerous broad conceptual models have been developed positing particular associations among genetic, stressful life experience, interpersonal process, and cognitive process factors (for examples, see Garber & Horowitz, 2002; Goodyer, 2001; Hammen & Rudolph, 2003; Hankin & Abramson, 2001). But much work remains to fully understand the ways these variables work together to predict depression. For example, it is unclear to what extent particular risk factors (e.g., biological risk factors and cognitive risk factors) temporally represent a single mechanism viewed from multiple vantage points and to what extent they represent sequences of mechanisms that are causally related.

With regard to assessment, it is clear that some risk factors for depression are more pertinent to available treatment methods. For example, well-established treatments of depression (see later discussion) target cognitive and interpersonal processes, so assessment of such risk factors is especially useful for guiding treatment. Assessment of stressful life events is also useful, as such events may be implicated in the development of particular cognitive patterns that serve to predict, exacerbate, or maintain depressive symptoms. Assessment of parental history of depression is also likely to help inform case conceptualization and provide clinicians with meaningful information about possible etiological factors associated with the adolescent's diagnosis. Although less frequently used in clinical assessment, measures of temperament should be considered as they may help conceptualize the links among various interrelated risk factors in a case. Finally, although medications that act directly on the brain represent commonly prescribed treatments, assessment of biological markers of depression has not yet been linked in meaningful ways to such treatments; thus, at the present time, their use in clinical assessment is limited.

TREATMENT FOR CHILD AND ADOLESCENT DEPRESSION

Broadly considered, intervention includes treatment of youth diagnosed with depression as well as prevention prior to onset of depression. Many studies have evaluated treatment (for reviews, see Clarke, DeBar, & Lewinsohn, 2003; Evans et al., 2005; Weersing & Brent, 2003) and prevention (for reviews, see Evans et al., 2005) programs for adolescent depression. Our review focuses on treatments that have been investigated sufficiently to be considered empirically based therapies. In particular, we review results of the largest randomized clinical trial to date to treat adolescent depression, the Treatment of Adolescent Depression Study ("Fluoxetine, Cognitive-Behavioral Therapy, and Their Combination for Adolescents with Depression: Treatment for Adolescents with Depression Study [TADS] Randomized Controlled Trial," 2004) and two recent meta-analyses of prevention studies for adolescent depression (Horowitz & Garber, in press; Merry, McDowell, Hetrick, Bir, & Muller, 2004).

Many individual, moderately sized treatment studies have shown that depression in adolescents can be ameliorated through individual psychotherapies, such as cognitive-behavioral therapy (CBT) or interpersonal psychotherapy, and antidepressants, such as selective serotonin reuptake inhibitors (Evans et al., 2005). Consistent with these smaller studies, the recently completed TADS trial ("Fluoxetine, Cognitive-Behavioral Therapy, and Their Combination for Adolescents with Depression: Treatment for Adolescents with Depression Study [TADS] Randomized Controlled Trial," 2004) showed that moderate to severe clinical depression in adolescence can be treated most efficaciously by the combination of antidepressants (fluoxetine in TADS) and CBT (71% response rate versus 34.8% response for placebo). This combination was also the most efficacious in reducing suicidality. No suicides occurred in the TADS trial, which was completed prior to the FDA's warning in 2004 on use of antidepressant medications in youth. The combination of fluoxetine with CBT was better than use of fluoxetine alone (71% response rate versus 60.6%), whereas results with CBT alone were not significantly different from pill placebo (43.2% response rate versus 34.8%). Taking both risk and benefit into account, it presently appears that the combination of fluoxetine with CBT is the superior short-term treatment for adolescent clinical depression.

Likewise, many moderately sized prevention trials have been completed, and the results have been mixed. Most of the prevention studies have used CBT-based approaches to attempt to reduce the onset of depression in youth. One meta-analysis of studies with youth (ages 5–19; Merry et al., 2004) showed that psychological preventions were effective when aimed at targeted, or at-risk, youth, whereas universal prevention programs were not effective. Consistent with this, a second recent meta-analysis (Horowitz & Garber, in press) concluded that selective prevention efforts are moderately effective immediately and in the short long term (6-month follow-ups), whereas universal programs are not. Horowitz and Garber suggest that selective prevention programs that are aimed at mildly depressed youth or those with elevated risk profiles (e.g., cognitive vulnerably to depression) are most accurately described as treatment rather than prevention. As such, these meta-analytic reviews of the prevention literature dovetail nicely with the primary depression treatment literature in demonstrating that effective treatments (e.g., CBT, interpersonal therapy) do exist for children and adolescents.

Case Description

To illustrate the ways that current knowledge related to conceptualization, assessment, and treatment of depression can be used in clinical work, a case presentation is provided. This case presentation represents the combined therapy experiences of two adolescents diagnosed with depression.

Presentation

R. is a 13-year-old Hispanic girl in foster care who was referred for therapy by her foster mother due to ongoing emotional and peer relational problems. R. presented with depressed mood, anxiety, low self-esteem, and suicidal ideation. She was attractive, slightly overweight, and was dressed and groomed appropriately for her age. She was a bright individual and was eager to connect with others. R. was talented artistically, wrote poetry, sang in the choir, and danced. At the time of intake, she was in her first foster care placement and had been living with her foster family for approximately 1 year. R. attended a public school in a large metropolitan city. She was in a regular eighth-grade classroom and received no specialized services within school. Despite her emotional and peer relational difficulties, R. did not exhibit academic difficulties.

Presenting Complaints

R reported that she was "going through depression" and that she'd been feeling very sad for approximately the past 9 months. In addition to her depressed mood, she stated that she often feels nervous and that she thinks she's "not as good as [her] peers." Her anxiety usually manifested itself in the evening with feelings of nervousness and apprehension about interacting with peers in school the following day. She reported that she resorted to walking around her block on a nightly basis (during the school week) to try to soothe her nerves and decrease her concurrent physical restlessness so that she could sleep at night. Additionally, in the mornings before school, she felt stomach pains, headaches, and tension in her neck and shoulders.

R.'s low self-esteem resulted in repeated reassurance seeking from others, which often turned away peers and confirmed her unfavorable view of herself. She denied actively trying to harm or kill herself, but she admitted that she often thought about death and had made a suicidal gesture with a sharp object approximately 6 months before presenting for the evaluation.

History

Because R.'s biological mother and father separated before she was born, R. was initially raised solely by her biological mother. However, her biological mother's chronic and recurring substance use problems eventually resulted in her being unable to care for R. At the age of 7, R. was placed in the custody of her biological father, with whom she had had very little previous contact. R. reported that her biological father maintained an emotional distance during the entirety of her placement, but that he was able to provide for her material needs.

(continued)

When R. was 11, her father sexually molested her on two separate occasions. R. initially kept the abuse secret for fear of her father's retaliation and because she thought no one would believe her. She eventually reported the sexual abuse and was subsequently removed from her father's home. Soon thereafter, at the age of 12, R. was placed into foster care.

Assessment

The Youth Self Report (YSR), Child Behavior Checklist (CBCL), and Teacher Report Form (TRF) were administered to assess a broad range of psychological symptoms across three different informants: child, parent, and teacher, respectively. R. scored in the clinical range for both anxious-depressed and somatic symptoms across all three reporters.

The Children's Depression Inventory (CDI) was used to assess R.'s self-reported symptoms of depression. She scored in the subclinical range for Total Depression and Negative Mood and reported clinically significant levels of Negative Self-Esteem.

Given R.'s scores on the Achenbach measures and the CDI, the Schedule for Affective Disorders and Schizophrenia for School-age Children (K-SADS) was used to assess for specific depressive diagnoses as well as possible Posttraumatic Stress Disorder (PTSD) symptoms related to the sexual abuse. R. met criteria for Dysthymic Disorder and endorsed subclinical symptoms of PTSD related to sexual abuse.

Case Conceptualization

Although it could not fully be established, there may have been a genetic basis to R.'s depression. Her biological mother's substance abuse may have been comorbid with depression. R.'s mother may have used alcohol as a form of self-medication in an attempt to alleviate her depressed mood. In addition to this potential genetic predisposition, R. may have been exposed to environmental risks linked to parental depression, such as family adversity and problematic parenting styles. As a result, she may have learned maladaptive ways of viewing herself and her world. The history of loss and disrupted attachment, as well as betrayal in an intimate relationship (i.e., sexual abuse), may have contributed to a belief that she was not lovable or valuable and placed her at risk for excessive reassurance seeking and interpersonal dependence (for evidence that maltreatment contributes to formation of cognitive vulnerabilities, see Gibb, 2002; Gibb & Alloy, 2006; Hankin, 2005a).

As she became an adolescent, peer relationships became more important for R., and she was exposed to interpersonal stressors that activated maladaptive cognitive patterns associated with low self-esteem. Interpersonal stressors also activated her tendency toward excessive reassurance seeking and interpersonal dependence, which served to exacerbate her interpersonal problems. Societal pressures to meet a thin ideal coupled with her larger body size further hurt her self-esteem. This effect was worsened by an overly critical foster father, who complained that she ate too much. R. also used a ruminative coping style in response to interpersonal difficulties, which served to exacerbate and prolong her symptoms of depression.

Overview of Treatment Plan

To address all of R.'s presenting problems, it was necessary to implement a multifaceted and collaborative treatment plan. Cognitive-behavioral therapy (CBT) was utilized to address the negative cognitions related to R.'s past losses and abuse. Interpersonal therapy was also incorporated to strengthen her social skills and ability to relate to others. Additionally, relaxation techniques (i.e., gradual muscle relaxation and deep/diaphragmatic breathing) were implemented to reduce R.'s anxiety and somatic complaints. Family sessions were held once a month, in addition to R.'s weekly individual sessions, to (a) provide support to her foster parents in order to maintain her placement and reduce further losses and breaks in attachment and (b) to involve them as partners in the therapy. Finally, it was necessary to collaborate with both a psychiatrist to prescribe medication for R.'s depressive symptoms and school personnel to assess R.'s progress in that context and to enlist school staff as additional partners.

Course of Treatment and Assessment of Progress and Complicating Factors, Including Managed Care Considerations

The first complicating factor was the termination of R.'s first foster care placement. R.'s first foster family had limited financial resources and two children of their own. The foster mother was warm and engaging and participated in treatment. However, the foster father rarely came to family sessions and was frequently critical of R. when he was in attendance. He described her as "eating [them] out of house and home." After approximately 3 months of treatment, R.'s foster placement fell apart. According to her foster mother, her marriage was in trouble and she had to choose between R. and her husband. Strategies for handling this significant disruption included (a) advocating for a new foster home placement as soon as possible, (b) developing a relationship with the new foster family, and (c) working with the first foster mother to develop a plan for maintaining contact with R. and for reducing the negative attributions associated with this event.

Fortunately, R. was immediately placed in another foster home that included a warm and engaging mother and her teenage daughter. The new foster mother was bright and successful in her nursing career and reported that she was very committed to R. She was also willing to become involved immediately in R.'s treatment. In addition, the former foster mother demonstrated a commitment to R. and maintained regular contact with her. Thanks to the strengths of these families, R. connected quickly to her new foster family and maintained a strong connection with her former foster mother.

A second treatment complication was R.'s medication noncompliance. Although R. and her new foster mother reported willingness to use medication to treat her depression, R. frequently did not take the required dose, providing numerous reasons (e.g., forgetfulness, nausea, feeling embarrassed and different from her peers) for not taking her medication on a regular basis. Strategies to address noncompliance included (a) additional psychoeducation, such as the provision of statistics of the number of youth affected by depression and prescribed medication; (b) in-session rehearsal of behavioral and cognitive strategies for

(continued)

remembering to take the medication; (c) problem solving around specific concerns; and (d) rewards for consistent medication compliance. These strategies proved effective and R. became compliant with her medication.

A third treatment complication involved treatment constraints imposed by managed care. The utilization management component of managed care coordinates how much or how long care is given, as well as the type and level of care. The purpose is to ensure care is delivered cost-effectively and at the right level and doesn't use unnecessary resources. R.'s insurance was provided through her foster mother's work by a health maintenance organization (HMO). This is the most restrictive type of managed care benefit plan. R.'s foster mother's HMO initially allowed reimbursement for assessment, medication management, and five sessions of therapy. Fortunately, educating the managed care provider about R.'s history and the progress of her current treatment as well as strongly advocating for the importance of continued therapy proved successful in changing the provider's mind, and additional sessions were approved.

As therapy progressed, R. was responsive to the skills and techniques implemented in both CBT and interpersonal therapy. For example, she began using physical activity as an alternative to rumination. She reported that the release of energy helped relieve anxiety and tension the night before and the morning of school and contributed to a more positive body image. She also became more involved in activities related to her artistic and academic strengths, which appeared to improve her self-esteem and provided opportunities to make new friends. As she developed confidence and practiced her interpersonal skills, she became more independent in her relationships and less likely to seek reassurance. After 6 months, the YSR and CDI were readministered. Her scores had dropped into the subclinical range for anxiety-depression, somatic complaints, and low self-esteem.

Unfortunately, approximately 11 months into treatment, a final treatment complication occurred. During the year she was in treatment, R. fell in love for the first time and began dating a boy from her school. After they had been dating for approximately 9 months, R.'s boyfriend began spending time with another girl. This caused R. to become jealous and distressed. She began to doubt his commitment to her and she began to ruminate about aspects of herself that she viewed as inferior to the other girl. R. sought excessive reassurance from her boyfriend and became more dependent on him. Eventually, she discovered that he was sexually involved with the other girl, and when she confronted him, he broke off their relationship. This intimate betrayal triggered her former loss-related maladaptive cognitive patterns, and R. once again began to view herself as unlovable and critically flawed.

After this negative event and its cognitive and emotional sequelae, R.'s attendance at therapy became erratic. But, rather than admit she was struggling, R. created various positive excuses for why she was unable to attend therapy (e.g., a special recital, a leadership camp). It was only after speaking with her foster mother that it became clear that R.'s gains from therapy had drastically deteriorated. Her foster mother reported that R. was no longer obeying her or taking her medication, was skipping school, missing her curfew, and running away. Unfortunately, this led R.'s foster mother to decide that she would not keep R. in her home. Within a few months, the foster mother returned R. to the care of the Department of Children and Family Services. Soon thereafter, R. was moved to a group home in another part of the state.

Follow-Up

Because R. was moved to another part of the state, it was difficult to maintain contact with her. But efforts were made to find her another provider and to give that provider a summary of R.'s previous treatment. In addition, R. was encouraged to stay in touch with her former therapist to preserve that attachment. The therapist encouraged both foster mothers to stay in touch with R. in hopes that those relationships might be preserved.

TREATMENT IMPLICATIONS AND RECOMMENDATIONS TO CLINICIANS AND STUDENTS

It is useful for a clinician to develop a comprehensive and integrative case conceptualization in hopes of avoiding repetition of the causal factors that may have contributed to the client's presenting problem. In this case, some of the primary causal factors appear to include the losses, attachment problems, and betrayals that R. experienced earlier in her life. When her boyfriend's betrayal and the loss of that relationship reactivated those deep vulnerabilities, the gains that had been made in treatment were not enough to protect her from her old maladaptive thinking and interpersonal relationship patterns. Although it may not have been possible to alter the outcome of her romantic relationship, a different treatment approach might have prevented the loss of the second foster care placement, which, ultimately, may have been more damaging than the loss of her boyfriend.

In retrospect, the factors that contributed to R.'s problems warranted a higher priority on family therapy earlier in the course of treatment. Although family sessions were conducted once a month, it probably would have been beneficial to make family therapy the foundation of R.'s treatment. Utilizing this treatment strategy would have increased the therapist's capacity to monitor the foster mother's investment in R., provide her with more psychoeducation about the ways R.'s issues might play out in the home, and better enlist her assistance in helping R. cope with issues at school. In such a model, cognitive-behavioral and interpersonal therapy strategies would be taught in the family context. Although this might have initially lessened the cognitive and interpersonal progress that R. made through individual therapy, the long-term gains would likely have been more beneficial.

In conclusion, this case highlights some caveats that are likely to be true for all cases. In particular, it illustrates the importance of conducting a thorough assessment to develop a strong case conceptualization. This conceptualization should include an understanding of distal factors (e.g., a history of loss, disrupted attachments, and betrayal) that contributed to the onset of depression as well as proximal factors that may mediate the effect of those distal factors or serve to maintain current depressive symptoms (e.g., negative attributions, rumination, interpersonal processes). It also underscores the importance of utilizing that conceptualization to develop a comprehensive treatment plan that addresses each of these factors.

SUMMARY

Depression is a prevalent mental illness with significant developmental, emotional, educational, interpersonal, and economic costs. As depression tends to develop during adolescence and often is a recurrent disorder, it is important that appropriate assessment and conceptualization be conducted so that efficacious, empirically based treatments can be used to help those youth who are depressed. This chapter has provided a brief review of the description, diagnosis and assessment, etiological issues important in conceptualization, and empirically based interventions in child and adolescent depression, and has included a case with history, presenting complaints, case conceptualization, and treatment recommendations in hopes that up-to-date knowledge can be used by students and clinicians to decrease the enormous individual and global burdens of depression.

REFERENCES

Abela, J. R. Z., Hankin, B. L., Haigh, E. A. P., Adams, P., Vinokuroff, T., & Trayhern, L. (2005). Interpersonal vulnerability to depression in high-risk children: The role of insecure attachment and reassurance seeking. *Journal of Clinical Child and Adolescent Psychology, 34*(1), 182–192.

Abela, J. R. Z., Nueslovici, J. N., & Chan, C. (2004, August). *A multi-wave longitudinal study of the transactional relations between depressive symptoms, hopelessness, and stress in high-risk youth.* Paper presented at the annual convention of the Canadian Association for Child and Adolescent Psychiatry, Montreal, Quebec, Canada.

Abela, J. R. Z., Taxel, E., & Sakellaropoulo, M. (in press). Integrating two subtypes of depression: Psychodynamic theory and its relation to hopelessness depression in schoolchildren. *Journal of Early Adolescence.*

Abela, J. R. Z., & Taylor, G. V. (2003). Specific vulnerability to depressive mood reactions in schoolchildren: The moderating role of self-esteem. *Journal of Clinical Child and Adolescent Psychology, 32*(3), 408–418.

Abela, J. R. Z., Zuroff, D. C., Ho, R., Adams, P., & Hankin, B. L. (2006). Excessive Reassurance seeking, hassles, and depressive symptoms in children of affectively-ill parents: A multi-wave longitudinal study. *Journal of Abnormal Child Psychology, 34*, 171–188.

Abramson, L. Y., Metalsky, G. I., & Alloy, L. B. (1989). Hopelessness depression: A theory-based subtype of depression. *Psychological Review, 96*(2), 358–372.

Achenbach, T. M., Dumenci, L., & Rescorla, L. A. (2003). DSM-oriented and empirically based approaches to constructing scales from the same item pools. *Journal of Clinical Child and Adolescent Psychology, 32*(3), 328–340.

Adrian, C., & Hammen, C. (1993). Stress exposure and stress generation in children of depressed mothers. *Journal of Consulting and Clinical Psychology, 61*(2), 354–359.

Ainsworth, M. S., Blehar, M. C., Waters, E., & Wall, S. (1978). *Patterns of attachment: A psychological study of the Strange Situation.* Hillsdale, NJ: Erlbaum.

American Psychiatric Association. (2000). *Diagnostic and statistical manual of mental disorders* (4th ed., text rev.). Washington, DC: Author.

Angold, A., Costello, E. J., & Erkanli, A. (1999). Comorbidity. *Journal of Child Psychology and Psychiatry and Allied Disciplines, 40*, 57–87.

Angold, A., Costello, E. J., Messer, S. C., & Pickles, A. (1995). Development of a short questionnaire for use in epidemiological studies of depression in children and adolescents. *International Journal of Methods in Psychiatric Research, 5*(4), 237–249.

Angold, A., Costello, E. J., & Worthman, C. M. (1998). Puberty and depression: The roles of age, pubertal status, and pubertal timing. *Psychological Medicine, 28*(1), 51–61.

Angold, A., Erkanli, A., Silberg, J., Eaves, L., & Costello, E. J. (2002). Depression scale scores in 8- to 17-year-olds: Effects of age and gender. *Journal of Child Psychology and Psychiatry, 43*(8), 1052–1063.

Armsden, G. C., McCauley, E., Greenberg, M. T., & Burke, P. M. (1990). Parent and peer attachment in early adolescent depression. *Journal of Abnormal Child Psychology, 18*(6), 683–697.

Avenevoli, S., Stolar, M., Li, J., Dierker, L., & Ries Merikangas, K. (2001). Comorbidity of depression in children and adolescents: Models and evidence from a prospective high-risk family study. *Biological Psychiatry, 49*(12), 1071–1081.

Beardslee, W. R., Versage, E. M., & Gladstone, T. R. G. (1998). Children of affectively ill parents: A review of the past 10 years. *Journal of the American Academy of Child and Adolescent Psychiatry, 37*(11), 1134–1141.

Beck, A. T. (1987). Cognitive models of depression. *Journal of Cognitive Psychotherapy, 1*(1), 5–37.

Belsher, G., & Costello, C. G. (1988). Relapse after recovery from unipolar depression: A critical review. *Psychological Bulletin, 104*(1), 84–96.

Birmaher, B., Dahl, R. E., Williamson, D. E., Perel, J. M., Brent, D. A., Axelson, D. A., et al. (2000). Growth hormone secretion in children and adolescents at high risk for major depressive disorder. *Archives of General Psychiatry, 57*, 867–872.

Blatt, S. J., & Zuroff, D. C. (1992). Interpersonal relatedness and self-definition: Two prototypes for depression. *Clinical Psychology Review, 12*(5), 527–562.

Bowlby, J. (1980). *Attachment and loss.* New York: Basic Books.

Brooks, S. J., & Kutcher, S. (2001). Diagnosis and measurement of adolescent depression: A review of commonly utilized instruments. *Journal of Child and Adolescent Psychopharmacology, 11*(4), 341–376.

Brown, G. W. & Harris, T. (1978). Social origins of depression: A reply. *Psychological Medicine, 8*(4), 577–588.

Brown, G. W., & Harris, T. O. (1989). Depression. In G. W. Brown & T. O. Harris (Eds.), *Life events and illness* (pp. 49–93). New York: Guilford Press.

Carlson, G. A., & Kashani, J. H. (1988). Phenomenology of major depression from childhood through adulthood: Analysis of three studies. *American Journal of Psychiatry, 145*(10), 1222–1225.

Carlson, V., Cicchetti, D., Barnett, D., & Braunwald, K. (1989). Disorganized/disoriented attachment relationships in maltreated infants. *Developmental Psychology, 25*(4), 525–531.

Caspi, A., & Moffitt, T. E. (1991). Individual differences are accentuated during periods of social change: The sample case of girls at puberty. *Journal of Personality and Social Psychology, 61*(1), 157–168.

Caspi, A., Sugden, K., Moffitt, T. E., Taylor, A., Craig, I. W., Harrington, H., et al. (2003). Influence of life stress on depression: Moderation by a polymorphism in the 5-HTT gene. *Science, 301*(5631), 386–389.

Chambers, W. J. (1985). The assessment of affective disorders in children and adolescents by semistructured interview: Test-retest reliability of the Schedule for Affective Disorders and Schizophrenia for School-Age Children, present episode version. *Archives of General Psychiatry, 42*(7), 696–702.

Cicchetti, D., & Toth, S. L. (1998). The development of depression in children and adolescents. *American Psychologist, 53*(2), 221–241.

Clark, L. A., & Watson, D. (1991). General affective dispositions in physical and psychological health. In C. R. Snyder & D. R. Forsyth (Eds.), *Handbook of social and clinical psychology: The health perspective* (pp. 221–245). Elmsford, NY: Pergamon Press.

Clarke, G. N., DeBar, L. L., & Lewinsohn, P. M. (2003). Cognitive-behavioral group treatment for adolescent depression. In A. E. Kazdin (Ed.), *Evidence-based psychotherapies for children and adolescents* (pp. 120–134). New York: Guilford Press.

Cohen, P., Cohen, J., Kasen, S., & Velez, C. N. (1993). An epidemiological study of disorders in late childhood and adolescence: Pt. I. Age- and gender-specific prevalence. *Journal of Child Psychology and Psychiatry, 34*(6), 851–867.

Cole, D. A., Martin, J. M., Peeke, L. A., Seroczynski, A. D., & Fier, J. (1999). Children's over- and underestimation of academic competence: A longitudinal study of gender differences, depression, and anxiety. *Child Development, 70*(2), 459–473.

Cole, D. A., Nolen-Hoeksema, S. K., Girgus, J., & Paul, G. (2006). Stress exposure and stress generation in child and adolescent depression: A latent trait-state-error approach to longitudinal analyses. *Journal of Abnormal Psychology, 115*(1), 40–51.

Cole, D. A., Peeke, L. G., Martin, J. M., Truglio, R., & Seroczynski, A. D. (1998). A longitudinal look at the relation between depression and anxiety in children and adolescents. *Journal of Consulting and Clinical Psychology, 66*(3), 451–460.

Cole, D. A., & Turner, J. E. (1993). Models of cognitive mediation and moderation in child depression. *Journal of Abnormal Psychology, 102*(2), 271–281.

Compas, B. E., Connor-Smith, J., & Jaser, S. S. (2004). Temperament, stress reactivity, and coping: Implications for depression in childhood and adolescence. *Journal of Clinical Child and Adolescent Psychology, 33*(1), 21–31.

Compas, B. E., Ey, S., & Grant, K. E. (1993). Taxonomy, assessment, and diagnosis of depression during adolescence. *Psychological Bulletin, 129*, 323–344.

Costello, E. J., Angold, A., Burns, B. J., Erkanli, A., Stangl, D. K., & Tweed, D. L. (1996). The Great Smoky Mountains Study of youth: Functional impairment and serious emotional disturbance. *Archives of General Psychiatry, 53*(12), 1137–1143.

Costello, E. J., Mustillo, S., Erkanli, A., Keeler, G., & Angold, A. (2003). Prevalence and development of psychiatric disorders in childhood and adolescence. *Archives of General Psychiatry, 60*(8), 837–844.

Cummings, M. E., & Davies, P. T. (2002). Effects of marital conflict on children: Recent advances and emerging themes in process-oriented research. *Journal of Child Psychology and Psychiatry, 43*(1), 31–63.

Cumsille, P. E., & Epstein, N. (1994). Family cohesion, family adaptability, social support, and adolescent depressive symptoms in outpatient clinic families. *Journal of Family Psychology, 8*(2), 202–214.

Curran, P. J., & Bollen, K. A. (2001). The best of both worlds: Combining autoregressive and latent curve models. In L. M. Collins & A. G. Sayer (Eds.), *New methods for the analysis of change* (pp. 107–135). Washington, DC: American Psychological Association.

Dahl, R. E., Kaufman, J., Ryan, N. D., & Perel, J. M. (1992). The dexamethasone suppression test in children and adolescents: A review and a controlled study. *Biological Psychiatry, 32*(2), 109–126.

Davidson, R. J., Pizzagalli, D., Nitschke, J. B., & Putnam, K. (2002). Depression: Perspectives from affective neuroscience. *Annual Review of Psychology, 53*, 545–574.

Davila, J., Ramsay, M., Stroud, C. B., & Steinberg, S. J. (2005). Attachment as vulnerability to the development of psychopathology. In B. L. Hankin & J. R. Z. Abela (Eds.), *Development of psychopathology: A vulnerability-stress perspective* (pp. 215–242). Thousand Oaks, CA: Sage.

Dawson, G., Frey, K., Panagiotides, H., & Osterling, J. (1997). Infants of depressed mothers exhibit atypical frontal brain activity: A replication and extension of previous findings. *Journal of Child Psychology and Psychiatry, 38*(2), 179–186.

Dohrenwend, B. P. (2006). Inventorying stressful life events as risk factors for psychopathology: Toward resolution of the problem of intracategory variability. *Psychological Bulletin, 132,* 477–495.

Duggal, S., Carlson, E. A., Sroufe, L. A., & Egeland, B. (2001). Depressive symptomatology in childhood and adolescence. *Development and Psychopathology, 13*(1), 143–164.

Eley, T. C., Sugden, K., Corsico, A., Gregory, A. M., Sham, P., McGuffin, P., et al. (2004). Gene-environment interaction analysis of serotonin system markers with adolescent depression. *Molecular Psychiatry, 9*(10), 908–915.

Evans, D. L., Foa, E. B., Gur, R. E., Hendin, H., O'Brien, C. P., Seligman, M. E. P., et al. (2005). *Treating and preventing adolescent mental health disorders.* Oxford: Oxford University Press.

Fichman, L., Koestner, R., & Zuroff, D. C. (1994). Depressive styles in adolescence: Assessment, relation to social functioning, and developmental trends. *Journal of Youth and Adolescence, 23*(3), 315–330.

Fluoxetine, cognitive-behavioral therapy, and their combination for adolescents with depression: Treatment for Adolescents with Depression Study (TADS) randomized controlled trial. (2004). *Journal of the American Medical Association, 292*(7), 807–820.

Friedberg, R. D., & McClure, J. M. (2002). *Clinical practice of cognitive therapy with children and adolescents: The nuts and bolts.* New York: Guilford Press.

Garber, J., & Horowitz, J. L. (2002). Depression in children. In I. H. Gotlib & C. L. Hammen (Eds.), *Handbook of depression* (pp. 510–540). New York: Guilford Press.

Garber, J., Little, S., Hilsman, R., & Weaver, K. R. (1998). Family predictors of suicidal symptoms in young adolescents. *Journal of Adolescence, 21*(4), 445–457.

Garber, J., & Martin, N. C. (2002). Negative cognitions in offspring of depressed parents: Mechanisms of risk. In S. H. Goodman & I. H. Gotlib (Eds.), *Children of depressed parents: Mechanisms of risk and implications for treatment* (pp. 121–153). Washington, DC: American Psychological Association.

Ge, X., Conger, R. D., & Elder, G. H. J. (1996). Coming of age too early: Pubertal influences on girls' vulnerability to psychological distress. *Child Development, 67*(6), 3386–3400.

Ge, X., Conger, R. D., & Elder, G. H. J. (2001). Pubertal transition, stressful life events, and the emergence of gender differences in adolescent depressive symptoms. *Developmental Psychology, 37*(3), 404–417.

Ge, X., Lorenz, F. O., Conger, R. D., & Elder, G. H. (1994). Trajectories of stressful life events and depressive symptoms during adolescence. *Developmental Psychology, 30*(4), 467–483.

Gibb, B. E. (2002). Childhood maltreatment and negative cognitive styles: A quantitative and qualitative review. *Clinical Psychology Review, 22*(2), 223–246.

Gibb, B. E. & Alloy, L. B. (2006). A prospective test of the hopelessness theory of depression in children. *Journal of Clinical Child and Adolescent Psychology, 35*(2), 264–274.

Gibb, B. E., Coles, M. E., & Heimberg, R. G. (2005). Differentiating symptoms of social anxiety and depression in adults with social anxiety disorder. *Journal of Behavior Therapy and Experimental Psychiatry, 36*(2), 99–109.

Gillespie, N. A., Whitfield, J. B., Williams, B., Heath, A. C., & Martin, N. G. (2005). The relationship between stressful life events, the serotonin transporter (5-HTTLPR) genotype and major depression. *Psychological Medicine, 35,* 101–111.

Gold, P. W., Goodwin, F. K., & Chrousos, G. P. (1988). Clinical and biochemical manifestations of depression: Relations to the neurobiology of stress. *New England Journal of Medicine, 319*(6), 348–353.

Goodman, S. (2002). Depression and early life experiences. In I. H. Gotlib & C. Hammen (Eds.), *Handbook of depression* (pp. 245–267). New York: Guilford Press.

Goodman, S. H., & Gotlib, I. H. (1999). Risk for psychopathology in the children of depressed mothers: A developmental model for understanding mechanisms of transmission. *Psychological Review, 106*(3), 458–490.

Goodyer, I. M. (2001). Life events: Their nature and effects. In I. M. Goodyer (Ed.), *Depressed child and adolescent* (2nd ed., pp. 204–232). New York: Cambridge University Press.

Goodyer, I. M., Herbert, J., Tamplin, A., & Altham, P. M. E. (2000). Recent life events, cortisol, dehydroepiandrosterone and the onset of major depression in high-risk adolescents. *British Journal of Psychiatry, 177*, 499–504.

Gotlib, I. H., & Hammen, C. L. (1992). Psychological aspects of depression: Toward a cognitive-interpersonal integration. Oxford: Wiley.

Gotlib, I. H., & Hammen, C. (Eds.). (2002). *Handbook of depression* (2nd ed.). New York: Guilford Press.

Gotlib, I. H., Lewinsohn, P. M., & Seeley, J. R. (1995). Symptoms versus a diagnosis of depression: Differences in psychosocial functioning. *Journal of Consulting and Clinical Psychology, 63*(1), 90–100.

Grabe, H. J., Lange, M., Volzke, H., Lucht, M., Freyberger, H. J., John, U., et al. (2004). Mental and physical distress is modulated by a polymorphism in the 5-HT transporter gene interacting with social stressors and chronic disease burden. *Molecular Psychiatry, 10*, 220–224.

Graber, J. A., Brooks-Gunn, J., & Petersen, A. C. (1996). *Transitions through adolescence: Interpersonal domains and context.* Hillsdale, NJ: Erlbaum.

Graber, J. A., Lewinsohn, P. M., Seeley, J. R., & Brooks-Gunn, J. (1997). Is psychopathology associated with the timing of pubertal development? *Journal of the American Academy of Child and Adolescent Psychiatry, 36*(12), 1768–1776.

Grant, K. E., Compas, B. E., Stuhlmacher, A. F., Thurm, A. E., McMahon, S. D., & Halpert, J. A. (2003). Stressors and child and adolescent psychopathology: Moving from markers to mechanisms of risk. *Psychological Bulletin, 129*(3), 447–466.

Grant, K. E., Compas, B. E., Thurm, A. E., McMahon, S. D., & Gipson, P. (2004). Stressors and child and adolescent psychopathology: Measurement issues and prospective effects. *Journal of Clinical Child and Adolescent Psychology, 33*, 412–425.

Hammen, C. (1991). Generation of stress in the course of unipolar depression. *Journal of Abnormal Psychology, 100*(4), 555–561.

Hammen, C. (2005). Stress and depression. *Annual Review of Clinical Psychology, 1*(1), 293–319.

Hammen, C. L., Burge, D., Daley, S. E., Davila, J., Paley, B., & Rudolph, K. D. (1995). Interpersonal attachment cognitions and prediction of symptomatic responses to interpersonal stress. *Journal of Abnormal Psychology, 104*, 436–443.

Hammen, C., & Rudolph, K. D. (2003). Childhood mood disorders. In E. J. Mash & R. A. Barkley (Eds.), *Child psychopathology* (2nd ed., pp. 233–278). New York: Guilford Press.

Hankin, B. L. (2005a). Childhood maltreatment and psychopathology: Prospective tests of attachment, cognitive vulnerability, and stress as mediating processes. *Cognitive Therapy and Research, 29*(6), 645–671.

Hankin, B. L. (2005b, November). *Stability of cognitive vulnerabilities to depression in youth: An examination of the trait-structure in a multi-wave longitudinal study.* Paper presented at the Association for Behavioral and Cognitive Therapies, Washington, DC.

Hankin, B. L., & Abela, J. R. Z. (2005a). Depression from childhood through adolescence and adulthood: A developmental vulnerability-stress perspective. In B. L. Hankin & J. R. Z. Abela (Eds.), *Development of psychopathology: A vulnerability-stress perspective* (pp. 245–288). Thousand Oaks, CA: Sage.

Hankin, B. L., & Abela, J. R. Z. (2005b). *Development of psychopathology: A vulnerability-stress perspective.* Thousand Oaks, CA: Sage.

Hankin, B. L., & Abramson, L. Y. (1999). Development of gender differences in depression: Description and possible explanations. *Annals of Medicine, 31*(6), 372–379.

Hankin, B. L., & Abramson, L. Y. (2001). Development of gender differences in depression: An elaborated cognitive vulnerability-transactional stress theory. *Psychological Bulletin, 127*(6), 773–796.

Hankin, B. L., Abramson, L. Y., Miller, N., & Haeffel, G. J. (2004). Cognitive vulnerability-stress theories of depression: Examining affective specificity in the prediction of depression versus anxiety in three prospective studies. *Cognitive Therapy and Research, 28*(3), 309–345.

Hankin, B. L., Abramson, L. Y., Moffitt, T. E., Silva, P. A., McGee, R., & Angell, K. E. (1998). Development of depression from preadolescence to young adulthood: Emerging gender differences in a 10-year longitudinal study. *Journal of Abnormal Psychology, 107*(1), 128–140.

Hankin, B. L., Abramson, L. Y., & Siler, M. (2001). A prospective test of the hopelessness theory of depression in adolescence. *Cognitive Therapy and Research, 25*(5), 607–632.

Hankin, B. L., Fraley, R. C., & Abela, J. R. Z. (2005). Daily depression and cognitions about stress: Evidence for a trait-like depressogenic cognitive style and the prediction of depressive symptoms trajectories in a prospective daily diary study. *Journal of Personality and Social Psychology, 88,* 673–685.

Hankin, B. L., Fraley, R. C., Lahey, B. B., & Waldman, I. D. (2005). Is depression best viewed as a continuum or discrete category? A taxometric analysis of childhood and adolescent depression in a population-based sample. *Journal of Abnormal Psychology, 114*(1), 96–110.

Hankin, B. L., Mermelstein, R., & Roesch, L. (2007). Sex differences in adolescent depression: Stress exposure and reactivity. *Child Development, 78,* 279–295.

Hankin, B. L., & Roesch, L. (2005, April). *Cognitive vulnerabilities to depression and stress: General and specific predictors of psychopathology in youth.* Paper presented at the Society for Research in Child Development, Atlanta, GA.

Harrington, R., Fudge, H., Rutter, M., Pickles, A., & Hill, J. (1990). Adult outcomes of childhood and adolescent depression: Pt. I. Psychiatric status. *Archives of General Psychiatry, 47,* 465–473.

Heim, C., & Nemeroff, C. B. (2001). The role of childhood trauma in the neurobiology of mood and anxiety disorders: Preclinical and clinical studies. *Biological Psychiatry, 49,* 1023–1039.

Horowitz, J. L., & Garber, J. (in press). The prevention of depressive symptoms in children and adolescents: A meta-analytic review. *Journal of Consulting and Clinical Psychology.*

Jaffee, S. R., Moffitt, T. E., Caspi, A., Fombonne, E., Poulton, R., & Martin, J. (2002). Differences in early childhood risk factors for juvenile-onset and adult-onset depression. *Archives of General Psychiatry, 59*(3), 215–222.

Joiner, T. E. J. (1999). A test of interpersonal theory of depression in youth psychiatric inpatients. *Journal of Abnormal Child Psychology, 27,* 77–85.

Joiner, T. E., & Coyne, J. C. (Eds.). (1999). *The interactional nature of depression: Advances in interpersonal approaches.* Washington, DC: American Psychological Association.

Joiner, T. E., Coyne, J. C., & Blalock, J. (1999). On the interpersonal nature of depression: Overview and synthesis. In T. Joiner & J. C. Coyne (Eds.), *The interactional nature of depression: Advances in interpersonal approaches.* (pp. 3–19). Washington, DC: American Psychological Association.

Joiner, T. E., Katz, J., & Lew, A. (1999). Harbingers of depressotypic reassurance seeking: Negative life events, increased anxiety, and decreased self-esteem. *Personality and Social Psychology Bulletin, 25*(5), 630–637.

Joiner, T. E., Metalsky, G. I., Gencoz, F., & Gencoz, T. (2001). The relative specificity of excessive reassurance-seeking to depressive symptoms and diagnoses among clinical samples of adults and youth. *Journal of Psychopathology and Behavioral Assessment, 23*(1), 35–41.

Judd, L. L. (1997). The clinical course of unipolar major depressive disorders. *Archives of General Psychiatry, 54*(11), 989–991.

Kagan, J. (1998). Biology and the child. In W. Damon & N. Eisenberg (Eds.), *Handbook of child psychology* (5th ed., pp. 177–235). New York: Wiley.

Kagan, J., Reznick, S. J., & Gibbons, J. (1989). Inhibited and uninhibited types of children. *Child Development, 60*(4), 838–845.

Kashani, J. H., Suarez, L., Jones, M. R., & Reid, J. C. (1999). Perceived family characteristic differences between depressed and anxious children and adolescents. *Journal of Affective Disorders, 52*(1/3), 269–274.

Kaufman, J., Martin, A. S., King, R. A., & Charney, D. (2001). Are child-, adolescent-, and adult-onset depression one and the same disorder? *Biological Psychiatry, 49*(12), 980–1001.

Kaufman, J., Yang, B.-Z., Douglas-Palumberi, H., Houshyar, S., Lipschitz, D., Krystal, J. H., et al. (2004). Social supports and serotonin transporter gene moderate depression in maltreated children. *Proceedings of the National Academy of Sciences, USA, 101,* 17316–17321.

Kendler, K. S., Kuhn, J. W., Vittum, J., Prescott, C. A., & Riley, B. (2005). The interaction of stressful life events and a serotonin transporter polymorphism in the prediction of episodes of major depression. *Archives of General Psychiatry, 62*(5), 529–535.

Kessler, R. C. (2002). Epidemiology of depression. In I. H. Gotlib & C. L. Hammen (Eds.), *Handbook of depression* (pp. 23–42). New York: Guilford Press.

Kessler, R. C., Avenevoli, S., & Merikangas, K. R. (2001). Mood disorders in children and adolescents: An epidemiologic perspective. *Biological Psychiatry, 49*(12), 1002–1014.

Kessler, R. C., Berglund, P., Demler, O., Jin, R., Merikangas, K. R., & Walters, E. E. (2005). Lifetime prevalence and age-of-onset distributions of DSM-IV disorders in the National Comorbidity Survey replication. *Archives of General Psychiatry, 62,* 593–602.

Kessler, R. C., McGonagle, K. A., Zhao, S., Nelson, C. B., Hughes, M., Eshleman, S., et al. (1994). Lifetime and 12-month prevalence of DSM-III-R psychiatric disorders in the United States: Results from the National Comorbidity Survey. *Archives of General Psychiatry, 51,* 8–19.

Kim-Cohen, J., Caspi, A., Moffitt, T. E., Harrington, H., Milne, B. J., & Poulton, R. (2003). Prior juvenile diagnoses in adults with mental disorder: Developmental follow-back of a prospective-longitudinal cohort. *Archives of General Psychiatry, 60*(7), 709–717.

Klein, D. N., Lewinsohn, P. M., & Seeley, J. R. (1997). Psychosocial characteristics of adolescents with a past history of dysthymic disorder: Comparison with adolescents with past histories of major depressive and non-affective disorders, and never mentally ill controls. *Journal of Affective Disorders, 42*(2), 127–135.

Kovacs, M. (1996). Presentation and course of major depressive disorder during childhood and later years of the life span. *Journal of the American Academy of Child and Adolescent Psychiatry, 35*(6), 705–715.

Kovacs, M. (2003). *Children's Depression Inventory: Technical manual.* Toronto: Multi-Health Systems.

Krueger, R. F. (1999). Personality traits in late adolescence predict mental disorders in early adulthood: A prospective-epidemiological study. *Journal of Personality, 67*(1), 39–65.

Lakdawalla, Z., Hankin, B. L., & Mermelstein, R. (2006). *Cognitive vulnerabilities to depression: A conceptual and quantitative review.* Manuscript submitted for publication.

Lau, J. Y. F. & Eley, T. C. (2006). A cognitive-behavioral genetic approach to emotional development in childhood and adolescence. In T. Canli (Ed.), *Biology of personality and individual differences* (pp. 335–352). New York: Guilford Press.

Lau, J. Y. F, Rijsdijk, F., & Eley, T. C. (2006). I think, therefore I am: A twin study of attributional style in adolescents. *Journal of Child Psychology and Psychiatry, 47*(7), 696–703.

Lewinsohn, P. M., Allen, N. B., Seeley, J. R., & Gotlib, I. H. (1999). First onset versus recurrence of depression: Differential processes of psychosocial risk. *Journal of Abnormal Psychology, 108*(3), 483–489.

Lewinsohn, P. M., Clarke, G. N., Seeley, J. R., & Rohde, P. (1994). Major depression in community adolescents: Age at onset, episode duration, and time to recurrence. *Journal of the American Academy of Child and Adolescent Psychiatry, 33*(6), 809–818.

Lewinsohn, P. M., & Essau, C. A. (2002). Depression in adolescents. In I. H. Gotlib & C. L. Hammen (Eds.), *Handbook of depression* (pp. 541–559). New York: Guilford Press.

Lewinsohn, P. M., Joiner, T. E. J., & Rohde, P. (2001). Evaluation of cognitive diathesis-stress models in predicting major depressive disorder in adolescents. *Journal of Abnormal Psychology, 110*(2), 203–215.

Lewinsohn, P. M., Roberts, R. E., Seeley, J. R., & Rohde, P. (1994). Adolescent psychopathology: Pt. II. Psychosocial risk factors for depression. *Journal of Abnormal Psychology, 103*(2), 302–315.

Lewinsohn, P. M., Rohde, P., Seeley, J. R., Klein, D. N., & Gotlib, I. H. (2000). Natural course of adolescent major depressive disorder in a community sample: Predictors of recurrence in young adults. *American Journal of Psychiatry, 157*(10), 1584–1591.

Lonigan, C. J., Phillips, B. M., & Hooe, E. S. (2003). Relations of positive and negative affectivity to anxiety and depression in children: Evidence from a latent variable longitudinal study. *Journal of Consulting and Clinical Psychology, 71*(3), 465–481.

Lovejoy, M. C., Graczyk, P. A., O'Hare, E., & Neuman, G. (2000). Maternal depression and parenting behavior: A meta-analytic review. *Clinical Psychology Review, 30*(5), 561–592.

Luthar, S. S., & Blatt, S. J. (1993). Dependent and self-critical depressive experiences among inner-city adolescents. *Journal of Personality, 61*(3), 365–386.

Marcotte, D., Fortin, L., Potvin, P., & Papillon, M. (2002). Gender differences in depressive symptoms during adolescence: Role of gender-typed characteristics, self-esteem, body image, stressful life events, and pubertal status. *Journal of Emotional and Behavioral Disorders, 10*(1), 29–42.

Merry, S., McDowell, H., Hetrick, S., Bir, J., & Muller, N. (2004). Psychological and/or educational interventions for the prevention of depression in children and adolescents. *Cochrane Review* (2), 1–104.

Meyer, S. E., Chrousos, G. P., & Gold, P. W. (2001). Major depression and the stress system: A life span perspective. *Development and Psychopathology, 13*(3), 565–580.

Moffitt, T. E., Caspi, A., & Rutter, M. (2006). Measured gene-environment interactions in psychopathology: Concepts, research strategies, and implications for research, intervention, and public understanding of genetics. *Perspectives on Psychological Science, 1*, 5–27.

Monroe, S. M., & Simons, A. D. (1991). Diathesis-stress theories in the context of life stress research: Implications for the depressive disorders. *Psychological Bulletin, 110*, 406–425.

Muris, P., Meesters, C., van Melick, M., & Zwambag, L. (2001). Self-reported attachment style, attachment quality, and symptoms of anxiety and depression in young adolescents. *Personality and Individual Differences, 30*(5), 809–818.

Murray, C. J. L., & Lopez, A. D. (1996). *The global burden of disease*. Cambridge, MA: Harvard University Press.

Newman, D. L., Caspi, A., Moffitt, T. E., Silva, P. A. (1997). Antecedents of adult interpersonal functioning: Effects of individual differences in age 3 temperament. *Developmental Psychology, 33*(2), 206–217.

Nolen-Hoeksema, S., Girgus, J. S., & Seligman, M. E. (1992). Predictors and consequences of childhood depressive symptoms: A 5-year longitudinal study. *Journal of Abnormal Psychology, 101*(3), 405–422.

Nolen-Hoeksema, S., & Morrow, J. (1991). A prospective study of depression and posttraumatic stress symptoms after a natural disaster: The 1989 Loma Prieta earthquake. *Journal of Personality and Social Psychology, 61*(1), 115–121.

Olsson, G. I., Nordstrom, M.-L., Arinell, H., & von Knorring, A.-L. (1999). Adolescent depression: Social network and family climate—A case-control study. *Journal of Child Psychology and Psychiatry, 40*(2), 227–237.

Park, R. J., Goodyer, I. M., & Teasdale, J. D. (2004). Effects of induced rumination and distraction on mood and overgeneral autobiographical memory in adolescent major depressive disorder and controls. *Journal of Child Psychology and Psychiatry, 45*(5), 996–1006.

Parker, J. G., Rubin, K. H., Price, J. M., & DeRosier, M. E. (1995). Peer relationships, child development, and adjustment: A developmental psychopathology perspective. In D. Cicchetti & D. J. Cohen (Eds.), *Developmental psychopathology: Vol. 2. Risk, disorder, and adaptation* (pp. 96–161). Oxford: Wiley.

Petersen, A. C., Compas, B. E., Brooks-Gunn, J., Stemmler, M., Ey, S., & Grant, K. E. (1993). Depression in adolescence. *American Psychologist, 48*(2), 155–168.

Phillips, B. M., Lonigan, C. J., Driscoll, K., & Hooe, E. S. (2002). Positive and negative affectivity in children: A multitrait-multimethod investigation. *Journal of Clinical Child and Adolescent Psychology, 31*(4), 465–479.

Pine, D. S., Cohen, E., Cohen, P., & Brook, J. (1999). Adolescent depressive symptoms as predictors of adult depression: Moodiness or mood disorder? *American Journal of Psychiatry, 156*(1), 133–135.

Pine, D. S., Cohen, P., Gurley, D., Brook, J., & Ma, Y. (1998). The risk for early-adulthood anxiety and depressive disorders in adolescents with anxiety and depressive disorders. *Archives of General Psychiatry, 55*(1), 56–64.

Plomin, R., & Caspi, A. (1999). Behavioral genetics and personality. In L. A. E. Pervin & O. P. John (Eds.), *Handbook of personality: Theory and research* (2nd ed., pp. 251–276). New York: Guilford Press.

Poznanski, E. O., Cook, S. C., & Carroll, B. J. (1979). A depression rating scale for children. *Pediatrics, 64*, 442–450.

Prinstein, M. J., Borelli, J. L., Cheah, C. S., Simon, V. A., & Aikins, J. W. (2005). Adolescent girls' interpersonal vulnerability to depressive symptoms: A longitudinal examination of reassurance-seeking and peer relationships. *Journal of Abnormal Psychology, 114*(4), 676–688.

Radke-Yarrow, M., Zahn-Waxler, C., Richardson, D. T., & Susman, A. (1994). Caring behavior in children of clinically depressed and well mothers. *Child Development, 65*(5), 1405–1414.

Rao, U., Hammen, C., & Daley, S. E. (1991). Continuity of depression during the transition to adulthood: A 5-year longitudinal study of young women. *Journal of the American Academy of Child and Adolescent Psychiatry, 38*, 908–915.

Reinherz, H. Z., Giaconia, R. M., Hauf, A. M. C., Wasserman, M. S., & Paradis, A. D. (2000). General and specific childhood risk factors for depression and drug disorders by early adulthood. *Journal of the American Academy of Child and Adolescent Psychiatry, 39*(2), 223–231.

Reinherz, H. Z., Giaconia, R. M., Lefkowitz, E. S., & Pakiz, B. (1993). Prevalence of psychiatric disorders in a community population of older adolescents. *Journal of the American Academy of Child and Adolescent Psychiatry, 32*(2), 369–377.

Reynolds, W. M. (1987). *Reynolds Adolescent Depression Scale: Professional manual.* Odessa, FL: Psychological Assessment Resources.

Reynolds, W. M. (1989). *Reynolds Child Depression Scale: Professional manual.* Odessa, FL: Psychological Assessment Resources.

Rice, F., Harold, G. T., & Thapar, A. (2002a). Assessing the effects of age, sex and shared environment on the genetic aetiology of depression in childhood and adolescence. *Journal of Child Psychology and Psychiatry, 43*(8), 1039–1051.

Rice, F., Harold, G. T., & Thapar, A. (2002b). The genetic aetiology of childhood depression: A review. *Journal of Child Psychology and Psychiatry, 43*(1), 65–79.

Rice, F., Harold, G. T., & Thapar, A. (2003). Negative life events as an account of age-related differences in the genetic aetiology of depression in childhood and adolescence. *Journal of Child Psychology and Psychiatry, 44*, 977–987.

Rose, A. J., & Rudolph, K. D. (2006). A review of sex differences in peer relationship processes: Potential trade-offs for the emotional and behavioral development of girls and boys. *Psychological Bulletin, 132*(1), 98–131.

Rothbart, M. K., Ahadi, S. A., Hersey, K. L., & Fisher, P. (2001). Investigations of temperament at 3 to 7 years: The Children's Behavior Questionnaire. *Child Development, 72*(5), 1394–1408.

Rothbart, M. K., & Bates, J. E. (1998). Temperament. In W. Damon & N. Eisenberg (Eds.), *Handbook of child psychology* (5th ed., pp. 105–176). New York: Wiley.

Rudolph, K. D., & Asher, S. R. (2000). Adaptation and maladaptation in the peer system: Developmental processes and outcomes. In A. J. Sameroff, M. Lewis, & S. M. Miller (Eds.), *Handbook of developmental psychopathology* (2nd ed., pp. 157–175). Dordrecht, The Netherlands: Kluwer Academic.

Rudolph, K. D., & Hammen, C. (1999). Age and gender as determinants of stress exposure, generation, and reactions in youngsters: A transactional perspective. *Child Development, 70*(3), 660–677.

Rudolph, K. D., Hammen, C., & Daley, S. E. (in press). Mood disorders. In E. J. Mash & D. A. Wolfe (Eds.), *Behavioral and emotional disorders in adolescence.* New York: Guilford Press.

Rudolph, K. D., & Lambert, S. F. (in press). Assessment of child and adolescent depression. In E. J. Mash & R. A. Barkley (Eds.), *Assessment of childhood disorders* (4th ed.). New York: Guilford Press.

Ruscio, A. M., & Ruscio, J. (2002). The latent structure of analogue depression: Should the Beck Depression Inventory be used to classify groups? *Psychological Assessment, 14*(2), 135–145.

Ruscio, J., & Ruscio, A. M. (2000). Informing the continuity controversy: A taxometric analysis of depression. *Journal of Abnormal Psychology, 109*(3), 473–487.

Ryan, N. D. (1998). Psychoneuroendocrinology of children and adolescents. *Psychiatric Clinics of North America, 21*(2), 435–441.

Ryan, N. D., Puig-Antich, J., Ambrosini, P., & Rabinovich, H. (1987). The clinical picture of major depression in children and adolescents. *Archives of General Psychiatry, 44*(10), 854–861.

Sheeber, L., Hops, H., Alpert, A., Davis, B., & Andrews, J. (1997). Family support and conflict: Prospective relations to adolescent depression. *Journal of Abnormal Child Psychology, 25*(4), 333–344.

Silberg, J. L., Pickles, A., Rutter, M., Hewitt, J., Simonoff, E., Maes, H., et al. (1999). The influence of genetic factors and life stress on depression among adolescent girls. *Archives of General Psychiatry, 56*(3), 225–232.

Solomon, A., Haaga, D. A. F., & Arnow, B. A. (2001). Is clinical depression distinct from subthreshold depressive symptoms? A review of the continuity issue in depression research. *Journal of Nervous and Mental Diseases, 189*(8), 498–506.

Southall, D., & Roberts, J. E. (2002). Attributional style and self-esteem in vulnerability to adolescent depressive symptoms following life stress: A 14-week prospective study. *Cognitive Therapy and Research, 26*(5), 563–579.

Stice, E., Ragen, J., & Randall, P. (2004). Prospective relations between social support and depression: Differential direction of effects for parent and peer support? *Journal of Abnormal Psychology, 113*(1), 155–159.

Sullivan, P. F., Neale, M. C., & Kendler, K. S. (2000). Genetic epidemiology of major depression: Review and meta-analysis. *American Journal of Psychiatry, 157*(10), 1552–1562.

Thapar, A., Harold, G., & McGuffin, P. (1998). Life events and depressive symptoms in childhood: Shared genes or shared adversity? A research note. *Journal of Child Psychology and Psychiatry, 39*(8), 1153–1158.

Thapar, A. & McGuffin, P. Anxiety and depressive symptoms in childhood: A genetic study of comorbidity. *Journal of Child Psychology and Psychiatry, 38*(6), 651–656.

Thase, M. E., Jindal, R., & Howland, R. H. (2002). Biological aspects of depression. In I. H. Gotlib & C. L. Hammen (Eds.), *Handbook of depression* (pp. 192–218). New York: Guilford Press.

Thomas, A., & Chess, S. (1985). Genesis and evolution of behavioral disorders: From infancy to early adult life. *Annual Progress in Child Psychiatry and Child Development, 1985,* 140–158.

Thomas, A., Chess, S., Birch, H. G., Hertzig, M. E., & Korn, S. (1963). *Behavioral individuality in early childhood.* Oxford: New York University Press.

Tomarken, A. J., & Keener, A. D. (1998). Frontal brain asymmetry and depression: A self-regulatory perspective. *Cognition and Emotion, 12*(3), 387–420.

Tomarken, A. J., Simien, C., & Garber, J. (1994). Resting frontal brain asymmetry discriminates adolescent children of depressed mothers from low risk controls. *Psychophysiology, 3,* 97–98.

Turner, J. E., & Cole, D. A. (1994). Development differences in cognitive diatheses for child depression. *Journal of Abnormal Child Psychology, 22*(1), 15–32.

Twenge, J. M., & Nolen-Hoeksema, S. (2002). Age, gender, race, socioeconomic status, and birth cohort difference on the children's depression inventory: A meta-analysis. *Journal of Abnormal Psychology, 111*(4), 578–588.

van Os, J., Jones, P., Lewis, G., Wadsworth, M., & Murray, R. (1997). Developmental precursors of affective illness in a general population birth cohort. *Archives of General Psychiatry, 54*(7), 625–631.

Wade, T. J., Cairney, J., & Pevalin, D. J. (2002). Emergence of gender differences in depression during adolescence: National panel results from three countries. *Journal of the American Academy of Child and Adolescent Psychiatry, 41*(2), 190–198.

Wakefield, J. C. (1992). Disorder as harmful dysfunction: A conceptual critique of DSM-III-TR's definition of mental disorder. *Psychological Review, 99*(2), 232–247.

Weersing, V. R., & Brent, D. A. (2003). Cognitive-behavioral therapy for adolescent depression: Comparative efficacy, mediation, moderation, and effectiveness. In A. E. Kazdin (Ed.), *Evidence-based psychotherapies for children and adolescents* (pp. 135–147). New York: Guilford Press.

Weiss, B., & Garber, J. (2003). Developmental differences in the phenomenology of depression. *Development and Psychopathology, 15*(2), 403–430.

Weissman, M. M., Warner, V., Wickramaratne, P., Moreau, D., & Olfson, M. (1997). Offspring of depressed parents: 10 years later. *Archives of General Psychiatry, 54*(10), 932–940.

West, M., Spreng, S. W., Rose, S. M., & Adam, K. S. (1999). Relationship between attachment-felt security and history of suicidal behaviors in clinical adolescents. *Canadian Journal of Psychiatry, 44*(6), 578–582.

Wichstrom, L. (1999). The emergence of gender difference in depressed mood during adolescence: The role of intensified gender socialization. *Developmental Psychology, 35*(1), 232–245.

CHAPTER 10

Anxiety Disorders

JENNIFER S. BALDWIN AND MARK R. DADDS

DESCRIPTION OF THE DISORDER

Anxiety is a term that describes normal feelings children experience when they perceive threat or danger. In times of real danger, anxiety is adaptive and short-lived. In contrast, anxiety disorders are characterized by irrational fears or worries that cause significant interference and/or distress in a child's life. According to self-reports using community samples, anxiety disorders are the most common childhood emotional disorders, with childhood prevalence rates ranging from 10% to 21% (E. J. Costello, Mustillo, Erkanli, Keeler, & Angold, 2003; Kim-Cohen et al., 2003). Despite their high prevalence, many children's anxiety problems go untreated (Vasey & Dadds, 2001). Various explanations have been put forward to account for lower rates of referral for child anxiety problems, including parent difficulties in detecting internalizing symptoms and the potentially lower salience of anxiety problems relative to externalizing problems (Mash & Wolfe, 2005).

Anxiety is a multifaceted phenomenon that includes behavioral, cognitive, and physical symptoms. Physical symptoms can include increased heart rate, sweating, dry mouth, nausea, fatigue, and heart palpitations (Barrios & Hartmann, 1997). The behavioral symptom most associated with anxiety disorders is avoidance of situations and is a critical factor in the maintenance of anxiety problems. Other behavioral manifestations include muscle tension, fidgeting, nail biting, stuttering, restlessness, avoidance of eye contact, compulsions, crying, twitching, and maintaining close physical proximity to caregivers (Barrios & Hartmann, 1997). Cognitive symptoms can include difficulty concentrating, self-consciousness, obsessions, thoughts of incompetence, thoughts of going crazy or dying, thoughts of harm befalling caregivers, and thoughts of appearing foolish (Barrios & Hartmann, 1997; Dadds & Barrett, 2001).

Across development, there are changes in the nature of children's fears. Fears of loud noises, strangers, and separation from caregivers are common during infancy. Fears of animals, the dark, and imaginary creatures develop during the preschool years and may give rise to fears of social and performance evaluation during middle childhood. Fears of negative evaluation and fears about the future and other abstract worries emerge during adolescence. The onset of anxiety disorders parallels the emergence of fears in children across development. Whereas separation anxiety can begin as early as preschool, Social Phobia and generalized anxiety do not peak until late childhood. In contrast, Panic Disorder is uncommon in childhood and may not begin until late adolescence or early adulthood. Gender differences in rates of anxiety disorders are found across childhood, adolescence, and adulthood. From age 6, and throughout life, girls experience anxiety disorders at twice the rate of boys (Roza, Hofstra, van der Ende, & Verhulst, 2003).

Findings regarding the long-term outcome of anxiety problems in children are controversial. Keller, Lavori, Wunder, Beardslee, and Schwarts (1992) found that in a sample of children ages 6 to 19 years, the average duration of an anxiety disorder was 4 years. It was estimated that approximately 50% of those with anxiety disorders would still have the disorder 8 years later (Keller et al., 1992). In contrast, other studies have found the durability of anxiety problems in children to be quite variable over shorter time periods (e.g., Last, Perrin, Hersen, & Kazdin, 1996; Poulton et al., 1997).

Several classification schemes have been developed to categorize childhood problems (e.g., *International Statistical Classification of Diseases* [*ICD-10*]: World Health Organization, 1994; *Diagnostic and Statistical Manual of Mental Disorders* [*DSM-IV*]: American Psychiatric Association, 1994). The main categories of anxiety disorders from the *DSM-IV* are described next.

Separation Anxiety Disorder (SAD) is characterized by developmentally inappropriate and persistent fear that something will happen to the child's attachment figures or that something will happen to the child that will separate him or her from his or her attachment figures. Common features of its presentation include avoidance behaviors, refusal to attend school, sleeping in the parents' bed, fear of the dark, reluctance to be involved in peer activities, and excessive questioning about parent schedules. It is the most common anxiety disorder in childhood and has the earliest average age of onset (7 years). Separation Anxiety Disorder commonly co-occurs with Generalized Anxiety Disorder (GAD; Last et al., 1996), specific phobias, and depression.

Social Phobia involves a marked and persistent fear of embarrassment, humiliation, and fear of negative evaluations by others in social situations (Kashdan & Herbert, 2001). Typically, the feared social or performance situations are avoided, but sometimes they are endured with great distress. Due to social fears being a common and transitory fear during later childhood and adolescence, symptoms must have persisted for 6 months for a diagnosis to be given (American Psychiatric Association, 1994). There can be marked differences in the way Social Phobia is manifested in children and adolescents as compared to adults. For instance, whereas adults may experience panic attacks in feared social situations, children may express their anxiety through crying, freezing, irritability (Albano, 1995), and somatic symptoms (Faust & Forehand, 1994). Furthermore, children may not recognize that their fear of social situations is unreasonable and excessive (American Psychiatric Association, 1994). Adolescents with Social Phobia may present with problems such as fighting, truancy (Davidson, Hughes, George, & Blazer, 1993), substance abuse (DeWit, MacDonald, & Offord, 1999), and depression.

Selective mutism is considered an extreme form of Social Phobia that typically occurs before the age of 5 years but is very rare (Anstendig, 1999). Children with selective mutism fail to speak in situations in which speaking is expected (e.g., school), despite speaking in other situations (American Psychiatric Association, 1994).

Specific Phobia is characterized by an extreme fear of objects or situations that do not pose a real threat (N. J. King, Hamilton, & Ollendick, 1988). As with Social Phobia, children may not recognize that their fear is excessive or unreasonable (American Psychiatric Association, 1994). Although Specific Phobia can be comorbid with other anxiety disorders, very few children are referred for treatment exclusively for Specific Phobia.

Generalized Anxiety Disorder involves excessive and uncontrollable anxiety or worry about past or future events (Masi, Mucci, Favilla, Romano, & Poli, 1999). It is characterized by self-doubt, muscle tension, sleep disturbance, irritability, and a lack of energy (American Psychiatric Association, 1994). Children with GAD are often described as perfectionistic, and they typically seek constant approval and reassurance about their performance and other worries (Silverman & Ginsburg, 1995). The content of their worries typically concerns competence and performance in several areas (e.g., school, sport) but may also include worrying about catastrophic events (e.g., terrorism, earthquakes; American Psychiatric Association, 1994). In children, GAD commonly co-occurs with other anxiety disorders and depression. The average age of onset is 10 to 14 years (Albano, Chorpita, & Barlow, 2003).

Obsessive-Compulsive Disorder (OCD) involves obsessions (repeated, intrusive, and unwanted thoughts or images) that cause anxiety, usually accompanied by compulsions (repetitive behaviors or mental acts) that represent attempts to alleviate the anxiety (R. A. King, Leonard, & March, 1998). The most common obsessions in children and adolescents are fear of contamination, fear of harm to self or to others, concerns relating to symmetry and exactness, and preoccupation with sexual or religious themes. The most common compulsions include excessive washing and cleaning, checking, counting, repeating, touching, and arranging. Children are more likely to engage in their compulsive rituals at home than in other settings (American Psychiatric Association, 1994), and children may also draw family members into their compulsions (e.g., insisting that their parents do or say things "just right"). In contrast to adults with OCD, children may not recognize that their obsessions and compulsions are unreasonable (American Psychiatric Association, 1994). Obsessive-Compulsive Disorder can co-occur with tic disorders, disruptive behavior disorders, learning disorders, impulse control disorders (e.g., Trichotillomania), and other anxiety disorders. The average age of onset of OCD in children is 9 to 12 years, with about 2% to 3% of children being affected by the condition (Hanna, 1995; Piacentini & Graae, 1997). Children who develop OCD at a younger age (6–10 years) tend to have a family history of OCD (Swedo, Rapoport, Leonard, Lenane, & Cheslow, 1989).

Panic Disorder is diagnosed when there are recurrent unexpected panic attacks, apprehension about future attacks, fears regarding the consequences of panic attacks (e.g., going crazy), or a significant change in behavior due to the attacks (American Psychiatric Association, 1994). Panic attacks are discrete periods in which there is a sudden onset of fear and discomfort that involves feelings of impending doom or a need to escape. Panic attacks are usually accompanied by physical and cognitive symptoms that are involved in the fight-flight response: palpitations, shortness of breath, feeling dizzy, trembling, derealization, depersonalization, and fears of dying or going crazy (American Psychiatric Association, 1994). Secondary to Panic Disorder, Agoraphobia may develop, which involves anxiety or avoidance of situations from which escape may be difficult or help may not be available should a panic attack occur (e.g., crowds, buses, trains, elevators; Ollendick, 1998). Panic attacks are very uncommon in young children, and the typical age of onset for the first panic attack is

15 to 19 years (Von Korff, Eaton, & Keyl, 1985). The time of onset of panic attacks has been linked to the period following puberty (Hayward, Killen, Wilson, & Hammer, 1997), and they are no longer thought to be related to children's lacking the cognitive ability to make catastrophic interpretations (e.g., feelings of derealization means "I am going crazy"; Mattis & Ollendick, 1997; Nelles & Barlow, 1988). Many adolescents may experience isolated panic attacks, but few actually develop Panic Disorder. Panic Disorder in adolescents may be comorbid with other anxiety disorders and depression.

Comorbidity between anxiety disorders in children is high; an estimated 50% of children with one anxiety disorder meet criteria for an additional anxiety disorder (Anderson, 1994). This is partly due to the high symptom overlap among the anxiety disorders, which can contribute to diagnostic uncertainty (Labellarte, Ginsburg, Walkup, & Riddle, 1999). School refusal can be related to many anxiety disorders, such as SAD, Social Phobia, and GAD (Last & Strauss, 1990). Posttraumatic Stress Disorder has many characteristics of an anxiety disorder and is discussed in detail in Chapter 11 of this volume.

DIAGNOSIS AND ASSESSMENT

The diagnosis and assessment of anxiety problems in children can be difficult and differs from the approach taken with adults. Whereas adults possess the language skills to describe their internal world and their subjective experience of anxiety, children are still developing the language necessary to describe their internal states. Assessment strategies with children must take into account their developmental age and their level of language acquisition. In addition, whereas most adults are seeking help for their anxiety, children often arrive at clinics because of parental concerns. Thus, children may not feel comfortable acknowledging anxiety problems, and social desirability must be taken into account in children's self-reports.

Given these problems, the assessment of anxiety disorders in children and adolescents should incorporate multiple informants (e.g., parent, child, teacher), multiple methods (e.g., interviews, observations, rating scales), and multiple situations (e.g., home, school) to obtain a complete picture of the problem.

In addition to assessing areas such as developmental history, medical history, school history, social history, and family psychiatric history, which are relevant to all childhood problems, the specific factors listed in Table 10.1 may be relevant in determining the development and conceptualization of the anxiety problem. Assessment methods may include combinations of structured clinical interviews, behavioral observations, self-report measures, and psychophysiological measures.

Structured clinical interviews can be of use where determining the reliability of a specific anxiety diagnosis is of primary interest. The structured format allows for greater objectivity than a clinical interview and allows for the tracking and monitoring of specific symptoms over time and across settings (March & Albano, 1998). The most commonly used structured interview for specifically assessing anxiety disorders is the Anxiety Disorders Interview Schedule for *DSM-IV*, Child Version (ADIS-IV-C; Silverman & Albano, 1996). The ADIS-IV-C consists of separate child and parent interview schedules, which are generally appropriate for 6- to 17-year-olds. Interrater reliability and test-retest reliability have been shown to be good to excellent across anxiety diagnoses, with younger children as reliable reporters as older children (Silverman, Saavedra, & Pina, 2001). Other structured interview schedules that are available

Table 10.1

General Factors That May Contribute to the Etiology and Maintenance of Childhood
Anxiety Problems

Factors	*Questions to Consider*
Physiological factors	What are the physical and somatic symptoms (e.g., muscle tension, nausea) associated with avoidance? Are there any medical or drug factors playing a role?
Temperamental factors	Is there a family history of anxiety or other psychiatric problems? How would the parent describe the child's ability to confront new situations and people from a young age?
Social learning factors	What stressful events might have precipitated the onset of the problem? What conditioning experiences might have occurred with previously neutral stimuli (e.g., school, dogs, dentist)? Who might be modeling and reinforcing avoidant and anxious responding in the child?
Cognitive factors	Is the child overly alert to threat cues in the environment? What is the child's view of his or her competencies and ability to overcome adversity? What are the child's underlying beliefs about the problem?
Social skills	Does the child have age-appropriate verbal and nonverbal social skills? Does the child have close friendships with same-age peers?
Family factors	What is the extent of the anxiety problems in other family members? Does the family foster independence in the child and provide warmth and stability?

Note: From "Practitioner Review: Psychological Management of Anxiety Disorders in Childhood," by M. R. Dadds and P. M. Barrett, 2001. *Journal of Child Psychology and Psychiatry, 42*, pp. 999–1011. Adapted with permission.

include the Diagnostic Interview Schedule for Children (A. J. Costello, Edelbrock, Dulcan, Kalas, & Klaric, 1984), the Diagnostic Interview Schedule for Children & Adolescents (Herjanic & Reich, 1982), and the Schedule of Affective Disorders and Schizophrenia for School-Age Children (Chambers et al., 1985).

The Children's Yale-Brown Obsessive Compulsive Scale (Scahill et al., 1997) is a semi-structured interview that guides clinicians in the detailed analysis of patterns of obsessions and compulsions that may be present. In semi-structured formats, clinicians can exercise their judgment in tailoring the interviewing strategy to the age and developmental level of the child and to exploring particular symptoms in greater depth.

Behavioral observations range from self-monitoring activities completed by parents and children to clinician-rated observation methods (March & Albano, 1998). Parents may be asked to keep a diary of times when their child becomes anxious (or avoidant) and to note specific details of the situation, what the parents' response was to the behavior, and the outcome. This type of monitoring activity can provide valuable information regarding the factors maintaining the child's anxiety. Depending on cognitive ability, adolescents may be able to complete feelings diaries, where they note situations, thoughts, and behaviors associated with anxious or stressed feelings. This personal material can then be integrated into the cognitive challenge components of treatment. An indirect measure of fear and anxiety to threat-related stimuli is the behavioral avoidance and approach test (BAT). The BAT can be tailored to the specific feared stimulus of interest, and several measures of approach and distress can be taken (Dadds, Rapee, & Barrett, 1994). For example, an adolescent with Panic Disorder with Agoraphobia who fears being in elevators could be asked to approach (and get into) an elevator under controlled conditions. A range of measures, including proximity to the elevator, time spent in the elevator, and ratings of subjective units of distress (SUDs), can be taken. Following the BAT, the adolescent could be asked to recall specific thoughts or images that occurred during the task. An adolescent's refusal to attempt the BAT may provide important information regarding his or her tolerance of distress and the extent of avoidance (March & Albano, 1998). In some cases, it may be useful to include parents in the BAT procedure to observe parent-child interactions that may be reinforcing avoidance patterns. Recent innovative uses of BATs include using them to measure height phobia in a virtual reality environment, where participants rated their SUDs for each floor of a virtual glass elevator (Ressler et al., 2004).

A variety of self-report measures are available for use with children and parents. The primary measures that are used in clinical work include the Revised Children's Manifest Anxiety Scale (RCMAS; Reynolds & Paget, 1981), the Spence Children's Anxiety Scale (SCAS; Spence, 1998), the SCARED-R (Muris, Merckelbach, Schmidt, & Mayer, 1999), the Fear Survey Schedule for Children Revised (Ollendick, Matson, & Helsel, 1985), the modified State-Trait Anxiety Inventory for Children (J. E. Fox & Houston, 1983) and the Multidimensional Anxiety Scale for Children (MASC; March, Parker, Sullivan, Stallings, & Conners, 1997). The SCAS is the only measure that is based on current *DSM* categories. Although most measures are considered to have good internal consistency and reliability, some measures have demonstrated poor discriminant validity (Perrin & Last, 1992). In particular, the RCMAS cannot discriminate between anxious children and children with other clinical conditions. Thus, many measures may tap anxiety in children, but few can ensure that the anxiety is attributable to an anxiety disorder. The MASC, an empirically derived measure, has demonstrated satisfactory discriminant validity. The MASC has discriminated between anxious youths and youths with Attention-Deficit/Hyperactivity Disorder, with an overall classification rate of 71% and a false-positive rate of 33% (March et al., 1999). Typically, there is poor agreement between parent and child reports of anxiety in both clinical and community samples (Vance et al., 2002). This underlines the importance of using self-report measures in the context of a thorough multimodal assessment.

Psychophysiological measures such as galvanic skin response and heart rate monitoring are one approach to quantifying the role of physiological symptoms in the etiology of anxiety. Some studies suggest that elevated heart rate during stressful situations without habituation may be a biological marker of an inhibited temperament (Beidel, 1991). Psychophysiological measures are rarely used in clinical practice, however, due to difficulties in interpreting the data and the expertise required to administer the measures (N. J. King, Ollendick, & Murphy, 1997).

When diagnosing an anxiety disorder, it is important to consider whether anxiety is a functional response to a real threat faced by a child. For instance, if a child is experiencing real threats to safety and security, such as abandonment, abuse, and bullying, then diagnosing the child with anxiety would not be appropriate. Furthermore, it is important to consider the developmental appropriateness of the anxiety concerns of the child. For instance, nighttime fears may be considered developmentally appropriate in preschool children but become less developmentally congruent as children progress through middle childhood (March & Albano, 1998). The diagnostic formulation should include the particular *DSM* or *ICD* anxiety diagnosis as well as any comorbidities, with specifiers regarding relationship factors and cultural factors within the family. Measures that assess multiple domains of the child's adjustment, such as the Child Behavior Checklist (Achenbach & Edelbrock, 1993), which has formats for parents, teachers, and youths, are particularly useful in screening for comorbidities.

CONCEPTUALIZATION

Several integrated models of anxiety have emerged that aid in the conceptualization of anxiety problems (e.g., Vasey & Dadds, 2001). Here we examine each of the components of these models in turn.

DEVELOPMENTAL ISSUES

Fears and anxieties need to be interpreted according to the developmental age of the child. For example, fears of separation from a caregiver are common in infancy and should not be considered abnormal. However, when separation anxiety persists beyond infancy and causes significant interference in a child's school or social life, then the fear may be considered excessive. Social fears are common in middle childhood, but social fearfulness and avoidance is considered deviant by later childhood. Thus, what we expect children to be able to master changes across development and parallels the ages of onset of anxiety disorders.

Most young children exhibit normal age-dependent obsessive-compulsive behaviors. These take the form of ritualistic and repetitive behaviors such as bedtime rituals, preferences for symmetry and exactness, and rigid likes and dislikes. These rituals help give children a sense of mastery and control over their environment and typically disappear by middle childhood. When distinguishing between normal obsessive-compulsive behaviors as part of development and OCD, it is important to consider the timing, content, and severity of the obsessive-compulsive behaviors.

Children's ability to describe their fears and worries changes across development according to their language acquisition. In infancy and early childhood, parent reports of anxiety are relied on exclusively; during middle and late childhood, children are able to provide verbal reports of their own anxiety.

LEARNING AND MODELING

Children can acquire fears and anxieties via a number of learning pathways. Rachman (1978) described three pathways to fear: direct conditioning, vicarious learning, and transmission of information. Modern learning theory perspectives build on Rachman's original theory by considering the impact of temperament influences, contextual variables, prior experiences, postevent variables, and preparedness of the fear (see Mineka & Zinbarg, 2006). We now outline the role each pathway may play in the development of anxiety problems in children.

Children can acquire fears and anxieties via direct classical conditioning processes. For instance, children's first experiences with novel situations (e.g., dentist, doctor, animals, injury, and being lost) may be quite aversive and precede the development of clinical anxiety problems. However, children who have had several nontraumatic encounters with a novel situation are less likely to develop a fear of that situation following a traumatic encounter (Mineka & Zinbarg, 2006). Children do not tend to develop fears of any random object; certain fears are seen as "prepared," as they are very easily acquired (Ohman & Mineka, 2001). Thus, children are more likely to develop fears of snakes, heights, or water than modern-day threats such as guns or cars (Mineka & Zinbarg, 2006).

Avoidant responding in children can contribute to the maintenance of anxiety problems in children via conditioning influences (Ollendick, Vasey, & King, 2001). Escape from a situation that is associated with anxiety leads to feelings of relief, which serve as a reinforcer of the avoidant behavior. Furthermore, avoidance can also prevent mastery of normal developmental challenges, which increases the likelihood of related problems and the persistence of anxiety. That is, through avoidance, a child can have limited contact with social and academic contexts, leading to incompetence (Ollendick et al., 2001). A child's incompetence in these areas, coupled with anxiety regarding performance, increases the likelihood that anxious children will be rejected or fail in these contexts. This serves to further reinforce avoidant and anxious responding in the future.

In addition to direct aversive conditioning, indirect, vicarious learning of fears may also occur. In particular, social learning processes in families can influence children's responses to novel situations via modeling, information, and reinforcement (Dadds, Davey, & Field, 2001). Parents' avoidant or anxious reactions to threat stimuli (e.g., separation, dental visits, medical procedures) are a major source of learning of fear in young children (e.g., Lumley, Melamed, & Abeles, 1993). Families that are enmeshed and are characterized by anxiety may expose children to more information about threat-related stimuli and more modeling of poor coping responses (Dadds et al., 2001). Families can also communicate information that causes children to reevaluate a situation as more fearful than previously experienced (Davey, 1997). Maternal overprotection is related to childhood anxiety (Rapee, 1997) and is best described by the parent who is hypervigilant, discourages independent behavior, and is highly controlling (Thomasgard & Metz, 1999). This may convey to a child that there is an imminent threat or danger and may prevent a child from developing his or her own coping strategies (Rapee, 1997).

Family environments may provide opportunities for the modeling of anxious behaviors, such as shyness and low sociability. Adults with Social Phobia recall their families trying to isolate them from normal social experiences (Bruch, 1989; Bruch & Heimberg, 1994). Barrett, Dadds, Rapee, and Ryan (1996) found that parents of anxious children encouraged their children to respond avoidantly in situations where there was an ambiguous threat. In some cases, parents of anxious children were observed to keep prompting until the child proposed a more avoidant plan (Dadds, Barrett, Rapee, & Ryan, 1996). Thus, parents of anxious children may model avoidant responses toward ambiguous threats and fail to teach their children effective coping responses.

However, not every child who has experienced a traumatic event or has witnessed avoidant responding will develop an anxiety problem. One source of individual differences, given exposure to some of the influences noted earlier, is the temperament factor known as behavioral inhibition (see section on Genetic Influences). Recently, researchers have been investigating how learned fear responses might be lessened or controlled in the treatment of anxiety disorders. The processes of extinction, reconsolidation of emotional learning, emotion regulation, and the relevant neural structures appear to be some of the most promising areas for future research (see review in Phelps & LeDoux, 2005).

PARENTAL ISSUES

Anxiety tends to run in families, with children who are anxious often having a parent who also has an anxiety disorder. Although children in such families may have a genetic predisposition to develop anxiety, learning influences such as modeling, transmission of information, and parenting style are also factors of influence (see previous section). Furthermore, an insecure attachment may develop between a parent and child, which places the child at increased risk of developing an anxiety disorder.

Attachment theory proposes that the bond formed between children and their parents early in life influences how children will interact with people, novel situations, and objects throughout their life (Bowlby, 1971). Insecure attachment between mother and child may be a risk factor for the development of anxiety in childhood (Bernstein, Borchardt, & Perwien, 1996). Insecure attachments include avoidant (e.g., avoiding intimate contact with parent) and anxious/ambivalent styles (e.g., clinging to parent, high distress at separation, lack of independent exploration). In a comprehensive longitudinal study, attachment style was measured at 12 months with the Strange Situation test, followed by an interview-based assessment of anxiety disorders at 17 years (Warren, Huston, Egeland, & Sroufe, 1997). Infants who were anxiously or ambivalently attached were more likely to develop anxiety disorders during childhood and adolescence than securely attached infants (Warren et al., 1997).

Attachment processes may interact with temperament tendencies (e.g., behavioral inhibition; see section on Genetic Influences) and coercive operant cycles in the development of anxiety disorders. Following from the model of coercive operant parenting developed in studies of oppositional behavior (Patterson, 1982), Dadds and Roth (2001) proposed that inhibited children and their parents may become locked in an anxious-coercive cycle that escalates the child's anxious responding. Specifically, children who have an anxious temperament are likely to regularly seek comfort from and proximity to the parent, which is given in the short term. However, at some point, the demands may exceed the parent's comfort level, and the parent is driven into a more rejecting stance in an effort to encourage independence. Research by N. A. Fox and Calkins (1993) demonstrated that a rejecting stance toward a child with an anxious temperament is likely to escalate a child's demands for comfort and proximity. If the parent acquiesces, the child's escalation is reinforced by regaining the parent's attention and comfort, and the parent's behavior is reinforced by the termination of the child's demands. This is the beginning of a cycle of child demanding and fearfulness and parent rejection and acquiescence. As these cycles repeat, the attachment between parent and child becomes insecure, and social learning processes ensure that the cycle becomes self-perpetuating. Thus, the interaction of child temperament, parent-child attachment, and social learning processes may help to maintain anxiety problems.

LIFE EVENTS

Stressful life events have been shown to be associated with the development of anxiety disorders in children. Early childhood bereavement, parental divorce, and long-term separation from the mother have been associated with the development of anxiety

(Goodyer, 1990; Goodyer & Altham, 1991). Dollinger, O'Donnell, and Staley (1984) found that children had increased levels of anxiety disorders following natural disasters such as earthquakes and bushfires. However, stressful life events cannot provide a full account of the development of anxiety disorders in children. They appear to be neither necessary nor sufficient for anxiety disorders to occur. For instance, many children survive trauma without developing clinically significant anxiety problems, and some children with anxiety disorders do not experience increased exposure to stressful life events (Goodyer, Wright, & Altham, 1990). Furthermore, stressful life events do not provide a specific pathway to anxiety, as they tend to occur before the onset of most psychiatric disorders and physical illnesses (Goodyer, 1990).

Most of the impact of stressful life events on the development of anxiety occurs via altered parent-child relationships in interaction with the child's temperament (Dadds & Barrett, 2001). For instance, the impact of divorce on children's mental health may occur through changes to routine, breakdown in parent-child communication, and changes to child-rearing practices (Emery, 1982). McFarlane (1987) found that posttraumatic symptoms in children following a fire were best predicted by mothers who exhibited anxious and overprotective behavior after the event. Furthermore, the amount of distress children display during painful medical procedures is strongly influenced by whether a parent engages in distress-promoting behaviors (e.g., excessive reassurance) during the procedure (Salmon & Pereira, 2002).

GENETIC INFLUENCES

Genetic studies suggest that a risk factor for developing anxiety disorders is temperament qualities that are inherited (DiLalla, Kagan, & Reznick, 1994). Behavioral inhibition (BI; Kagan, Reznick, & Snidman, 1988) is an inborn quality that is associated with a risk of developing anxiety disorders. It is defined as a marked restraint or fearfulness often shown from 2 years of age toward unfamiliar people, situations, or events. In a review of studies of BI and later psychopathology, Hirshfeld-Becker et al. (2003) found that BI in toddlerhood posed an increased risk for later anxiety disorders, particularly Social Anxiety Disorder. However, anxiety disorders are not an inevitable outcome of BI (Prior, Smart, Sanson, & Oberklaid, 2000), and the developmental trajectory may depend on the family environment in which the child is raised. Mash and Wolfe (2005) argue that parents who are overprotective may shield their children from stressful life experiences, experiences that would help them confront their fears. Kagan, Snidman, Arcus, and Reznick (1994) found that highly reactive infants whose mothers focused on setting limits and not just soothing showed less distress and inhibition at follow-up observations.

Approximately one-third of the variance in anxiety disorders in children can be accounted for by genetic contributions, according to child-based twin studies (Eley, 2001). However, the genetic risk factors may also be common to the development of depression in children. In her review of genetic influences on anxiety in children, Eley found that there was a greater genetic contribution to anxiety for females than males and that this contribution may increase with age. Genetic influences vary across different anxiety domains, with the highest heritability estimates for obsessive-compulsive behaviors and shyness and inhibition (Eley et al., 2003). Although a disposition toward becoming anxious is mostly inherited, studies of monozygotic twin pairs suggest that they do not have the same types of anxiety disorders, implicating a role for nonshared environmental influences. Shared environmental influences are thought to play a greater role in the development of separation anxiety and specific phobias, implicating the role of parental and family factors (e.g., Eley et al., 2003; Muris & Merckelbach, 2001).

Peer Influences

Peer relationships are a unique influence on children and provide opportunities for learning specific social skills that cannot be learned through interaction with adults. Children who are anxious and avoid social situations are limiting their opportunities to master the social skills necessary to make and keep friendships. The continuation of avoidance behaviors over long periods of time makes the child's fears of social rejection and failure more likely to be realized (Kashdan & Herbert, 2001). Withdrawn children begin to be identified by their peers as shy and withdrawn, and rejected by them, from about the second grade (Rubin, 1993). By early adolescence, they feel lonely, rejected, and more incompetent in social interactions than their nonanxious peers (Rubin, Chen, & Hymel, 1993). Thus, anxiety, avoidance, and cognitive biases may be perpetuated while social skills fail to develop.

The nature of the social skills deficits changes across development. During primary school, withdrawn children are less able to understand others' perspectives (LeMare & Rubin, 1987). In middle to late childhood, these children show deficits in conflict resolution and negotiation strategies and are more likely to be unassertive in dealing with these dilemmas (Rubin, Daniels, & Bream, 1984). On the odd occasion when withdrawn children are assertive, peers tend not to comply with their directives (Stewart & Rubin, 1995).

Peer relationship difficulties may be associated with the development of different types of anxiety disorders in children, but particularly Social Anxiety Disorder. Children who are neglected or rejected by their peers report the highest levels of social anxiety (Inderbitzen, Walters, & Bukowski, 1997), and peer acceptance and social anxiety have been found to be inversely related to one another in children and adolescents (e.g., La Greca & Lopez, 1998; La Greca & Stone, 1993).

Physical Factors Affecting Behavior

A variety of medical conditions can cause symptoms of anxiety, including generalized anxiety, panic attacks, and obsessions or compulsions. The general medical conditions can include endocrine conditions (e.g., hypoglycemic episodes, hyperthyroidism, pheochromocytoma), cardiovascular conditions (e.g., cardiac arrhythmias, pulmonary embolism, congestive heart failure), respiratory conditions (e.g., pneumonia, hyperventilation), metabolic conditions (e.g., vitamin B12 deficiency, porphyria), and neurological conditions (e.g., seizure, migraine, neoplasms, encephalitis; American Psychiatric Association, 1994; Bernstein & Kinlan, 1997). In considering the potential role of a medical condition in the etiology of an anxiety disorder, several factors are important. Typically, there is a temporal association between the onset, worsening, or amelioration of the medical condition and the anxiety symptoms (American Psychiatric Association, 1994). Furthermore, it is worthwhile considering the entire picture of the anxiety presentation and whether there are any atypical features present that may implicate a medical cause. For example, acute onset of obsessive-compulsive symptoms in young children can be caused by a condition known as pediatric autoimmune neuropsychiatric disorders associated with streptococcal infections (Kim et al.,

2004). This form of OCD is characterized by neurological abnormalities (e.g., choreiform movements, motoric hyperactivity), and the onset of symptoms is temporally related to the streptococcal infection (American Psychiatric Association, 1994).

DRUGS AFFECTING BEHAVIOR

Medications that may evoke symptoms of anxiety in children include antihistamines, antiasthmatics, sympathomimetics, steroids, haloperidol, pimozide, selective serotonin reuptake inhibitors (SSRIs), and antipsychotics (Bernstein & Kinlan, 1997). Anxiety symptoms can also occur during substance intoxication or withdrawal. Substances that may cause anxiety symptoms during intoxication include alcohol, amphetamines, caffeine, cannabis, cocaine, hallucinogens, inhalants, and phencyclidine (American Psychiatric Association, 1994). Substances that may cause anxiety symptoms during withdrawal include alcohol, cocaine, sedatives, hypnotics, and anxiolytics (American Psychiatric Association, 1994). However, the persistence of symptoms of anxiety beyond the phases of intoxication and withdrawal, or the presence of premorbid anxiety problems, may indicate a primary anxiety disorder.

CULTURAL AND DIVERSITY ISSUES

Although research into the effects of ethnocultural factors on the development of anxiety disorders in children and adolescents is limited, some research has shown differences in the rates of specific anxiety disorders experienced across different ethnic groups. For instance, Hawaiian children show rates of OCD that are twice as high as other ethnic groups (Guerrero et al., 2003). Hispanic children have higher rates of SAD than do White children, and Hispanic parents rate their children as more fearful (Ginsburg & Silverman, 1996). The authors argue that this can be explained by the importance placed on family interdependence in the Hispanic culture, in contrast with the independence valued in White culture. Similarly, Native Hawaiians score higher on a measure of separation anxiety than Whites, Japanese Americans, and Filipino Americans (Austin & Chorpita, 2004).

Culturally mediated beliefs, traditions, and practices surrounding children are thought to play a role in the kind of anxiety problems they display and how these are viewed by significant others. Cultures that assign greater negative attributions and shame to norm violations in interpersonal settings will show higher rates of social anxiety (Austin & Chorpita, 2004). For instance, Chinese Americans show higher rates of social anxiety than Native Hawaiians and Whites (Austin & Chorpita, 2004). In cultures that value inhibition, compliance, and obedience (e.g., China, Nigeria), children and adolescents show higher rates of safety and social-evaluative fears than children from Australia and the United States (Ollendick, Yang, King, Dong, & Akande, 1996). Similarly, Thai children display more symptoms of anxiety (such as somatic complaints and shyness) than American children (Weisz, Weiss, Suwanlert, & Chaiyasit, 2003).

In considering the role of cultural factors in a particular child anxiety case, it is useful to consider the behavior + lens principle, described by Weisz et al. (2003). This principle suggests that child psychopathology is a mixture of child behavior and the lens through which a child's behavior is viewed by individuals in the child's culture. Both the child's behavior and the lens can be influenced by cultural factors.

BEHAVIORAL TREATMENT

Behavioral treatment approaches have their historical roots in case studies such as that of "Little Albert" (Watson & Rayner, 1920) and "Little Peter" (Jones, 1924) that highlighted the role of learning in the development of anxiety disorders. Since that time, researchers have examined the efficacy of various treatment approaches using methods such as case study reports and randomized controlled trials of manualized treatments. A range of different therapeutic techniques are used, including psycho-education, social learning techniques, social skills training, parent-child relationship work, cognitive skills training, school interventions, self-rewarding, and reduction of arousal skills (see Table 10.2). Next, we describe the general aspects of cognitive-behavioral treatment (CBT) for anxiety disorders as well as intervention techniques relevant to specific anxiety disorders (e.g., OCD).

One of the first clinical trials evaluating behavioral treatment with adolescents for school phobia was conducted in the mid-1980s (Blagg & Yule, 1984). Results suggested that behavioral therapy was significantly more effective in returning adolescents to school than hospitalization or home tutoring. Later, work by Kendall and colleagues (e.g., Kendall, 1994; Kendall et al., 1997) examined the effectiveness of a manualized CBT program to treat a mixed group of anxious children. They evaluated the efficacy of a 16-session individual CBT treatment program with 47 9- to 13-year-olds with GAD, SAD, or Social Phobia. The individual treatment package, known as Coping Cat, had children develop an individualized FEAR plan: *F* for feeling good by learning to relax; *E* for expecting good versus bad things to happen through positive self-talk; *A* for actions and attitudes that can help children face fears; and *R* for rewards for efforts to overcome fears. Kendall found that 64% of treated children no longer met criteria for their primary anxiety disorder, compared to 5% in the wait-list condition.

Table 10.2

The Range of Anxiety Techniques Available in Working with Children and Families

Treatment Categories	Examples of Techniques
Psychoeducation	Education regarding the nature of anxiety and adaptive and nonadaptive anxiety responses; identify thoughts and feelings
Reducing physiological arousal	Relaxation; breathing retraining
Cognitive skills	Identify and change anxious thoughts; attention to nonthreat stimuli; develop positive expectancies; self-reinforcement for success
Social skills training	Rehearsal of verbal and nonverbal social skills; assertiveness training
Social learning	Graded exposure; modeling; positive reinforcement for nonavoidant coping
Family interventions	Training parents as models of courage and social competence; reinforcement strategies training and dealing with reassurance seeking; communication and problem-solving training
School interventions	Programs to facilitate positive peer relations; gradual school reentry (for school refusal)
Relapse prevention	Review skills; identify high-risk situations and strategies to address these situations; identify future goals

Significant improvements, as noted on parent reports, child reports, and behavioral observation measures for treated children, were maintained at 1-year follow-up. Subsequent studies utilizing the Coping Cat program have replicated these findings (e.g., Kendall et al., 1997). Treatment gains were still maintained an average of 3.5 years after treatment (Kendall & Southam-Gerow, 1996). However, approximately 40% of treated children still met criteria for an anxiety disorder following treatment.

Due to the role of parent-child relationship problems, parental psychopathology, and direct parental influences on child coping, several researchers have added family-based interventions to Kendall's program to improve outcomes. For example, Barrett, Dadds, and Rapee (1996) compared an individual CBT intervention with a family-based CBT intervention for children ages 9 to 14 years with a mixture of anxiety presentations. The family component focused on teaching parents child management skills to deal with their child's anxiety (reinforcement skills, planned ignoring) and teaching parents what the children were learning in their individual sessions so that parents could model and encourage the practice of skills outside of sessions. The program also taught parents how they could use the same skills to manage their own anxiety. The combined treatment led to greater improvements at the conclusion of therapy and at 1-year follow-up: 88% of children in the combined treatment no longer had a *DSM-III-R* anxiety diagnosis, compared with 61% in the CBT-only group and 26% in the wait-list condition.

Barrett (1998) demonstrated that family-based CBT could also be effectively delivered in a group format, thus reducing the costs of intervention. Mendlowitz et al. (1999) also examined the efficacy of a parent component delivered in a group format with children ages 7 to 14 with a *DSM-IV* anxiety diagnosis. Children in all treatment groups showed improvements on measures of anxious and depressive symptomatology, with greater improvement where concurrent parent involvement in therapy occurred. Spence, Donovan, and Brechman-Toussaint (2000) compared individual CBT with family-based CBT for socially phobic adolescents. Adolescents in both treatments improved, with a nonsignificant trend toward family treatment being superior to individual treatment.

While most family interventions focus on providing parents with the skills to manage their child's anxiety, Cobham, Dadds, and Spence (1998) evaluated treatment where the focus of the family intervention was on managing parent anxiety. Sixty-seven children ages 7 to 14 years were assigned to either a CBT group treatment program or a CBT group treatment with a parental anxiety management (PAM) component. Results indicated that combined CBT and PAM led to superior reductions in child anxiety levels compared to CBT alone, but only when the parents were anxious. This study indicates that high parental anxiety is a risk factor for poorer treatment outcomes for anxious children, and that specifically addressing the parent's own anxiety can reduce its negative impact on treatment outcome.

As previously mentioned, group therapy has been studied as a cost-effective way of delivering treatment to a large number of anxious children and their families. Although most research supports the equivalence of individual and group-delivered treatments, some research suggests that individual therapy may be superior for some children. For example, Manassis et al. (2002) found that highly socially anxious children in individual treatment made greater gains than in the group treatment. School-based interventions for the prevention of anxiety disorders in children and adolescents have also been shown to be effective when directed toward large groups of children (Dadds et al., 1999).

Research by Silverman et al. (1999) challenged the notion that there is an active component in CBT that leads to recovery. They compared an exposure-based contingency management condition (CM), exposure-based self-control condition (SC), and an education support control condition (ES) for the treatment of children with specific phobias. According to parent report and child report measures, equivalent therapeutic change was seen in all three conditions. However, more children were diagnosis-free on the ADIS in the SC condition than either the CM or ES conditions. Furthermore, the ES condition gave information about CBT, which families may have been able to utilize to their child's benefit. Thus, further research is needed before conclusions can be drawn about the active components of CBT treatments for anxiety.

In sum, CBT is recognized as an effective treatment for a variety of anxiety presentations and age groups when compared to wait-list controls. Both individual and group programs are helpful for at least 60% of children and adolescents, and in most cases, the benefits last for several years after treatment. However, further research is needed to determine whether CBT interventions are more effective than non-CBT treatments. Adding a family-based component to treatment appears to improve outcome. The involvement of the family may be particularly important for younger children and when parents are also anxious. Hudson's (2005) review of CBT for anxious youth identified several factors that are predictive of outcome. Although not always consistent across studies, some predictors of poorer outcome with CBT include older children, males, children with depressive symptoms, children who are less involved later in therapy (perhaps during the critical stage of exposure), children from families with parental psychopathology (anxiety, depression, hostility, and paranoia), and higher levels of family dysfunction and stress. Few studies have examined the critical components of treatment that lead to change. There is some emerging evidence to suggest that gradual exposure is a critical ingredient in therapy and that providing skills to the child, such as cognitive restructuring and self-rewarding prior to exposure, is particularly beneficial (Hudson, 2005).

Treatments for OCD are increasingly emphasizing the role of the family, especially for young children. The main CBT treatment for OCD involves exposure and response prevention; that is, children are exposed to their worst fears gradually, while not engaging in their rituals (March, Frances, Kahn, & Carpenter, 1997). Barrett, Healy-Farrell, and March (2004) randomly allocated 77 children and adolescents with OCD to individual cognitive-behavioral family therapy (CBFT), group CBFT, or a wait-list control condition. Parent sessions focused on "psychoeducation, problem-solving skills, and strategies to reduce parental involvement in the child's symptoms, along with encouraging family support of home-based exposure and response prevention trials" (Barrett et al., 2004, p. 52). Significant improvement occurred in OCD diagnostic status and severity across both individual and group CBFT, with no significant differences between these conditions, and gains being maintained at 6-month follow-up. There were no significant changes across measures for the wait-list condition. Thus, CBFT was effectively administered in a group format for child OCD.

Hayward et al. (2000) evaluated the efficacy of a group CBT treatment for female adolescents with Social Phobia and its effect on depression. Adolescents were assigned to a 16-week group treatment ($n = 12$) or no treatment ($n = 23$). Posttreatment, fewer adolescents met criteria for Social Phobia than adolescents in the no-treatment group. However, these differences disappeared at 1-year follow-up. The study also found that adolescents in the treated group had a lower incidence of Major Depression than adolescents in the no-treatment group. This suggests that treating adolescents for

Social Phobia with a cognitive-behavioral treatment program may reduce their levels of depression.

School interventions may need to be developed when anxiety-related disorders such as school refusal begin to affect children's school adjustment. There are three main categories of school refusers: phobic, anxious-depressed, and separation-anxious (N. J. King & Bernstein, 2001). Research suggests that CBT strategies used with children, parents, and teachers are effective in returning children to school and reducing children's anxious and depressive symptoms (e.g., Heyne et al., 2002; N. J. King et al., 1998). In particular, child treatment consists of rapport building, coping skills (e.g., relaxation) training, self-talk, assertiveness, self-reward, and exposure to feared situations. Sessions with parents and teachers consist of training in behavioral management techniques (e.g., differential attention, contingency management procedures, reinforcement for positive coping behaviors). However, as with CBT for anxiety disorders in general, the specific components of therapy that lead to therapeutic change remain largely unknown (see Last, Hansen, & Franco, 1998).

MEDICAL TREATMENT

Medications are not considered a first-line treatment for anxiety disorders in children and adolescents. Pharmacological interventions are likely to be considered as an adjunct to cognitive-behavioral therapies in older children and adolescents who are demonstrating severe anxiety symptoms and where disturbance to daily functioning is high (e.g., chronic avoidance of school). Research findings on the effectiveness of various medications are difficult to interpret due to methodological problems such as the presence or absence of various concurrent therapies (e.g., CBT, psychodynamic therapy; Kearney & Silverman, 1998). In a well-designed study with school refusers, a combination of imipramine and CBT was shown to be more effective in improving school attendance in anxious-depressed adolescents than was a placebo and CBT (Bernstein et al., 2000).

The pharmacotherapy agents that are used to treat anxiety in children and adolescents can be divided into three categories: tricyclic antidepressants (TCAs), SSRIs, and anxiolytics. The TCAs can produce severe side effects, including cardiac changes, which require close monitoring, and thus TCAs are not considered a treatment of choice (Velosa & Riddle, 2000). The SSRIs include fluoxetine and fluvoxamine, and in comparison to TCAs produce much fewer side effects. They have been used to treat the entire spectrum of anxiety conditions, including GAD, Social Phobia, SAD (Birmaher et al., 1994), and selective mutism (Dummit, Klein, Tancer, Asche, & Martin, 1996), with varying levels of success. The SSRIs are often used in conjunction with CBT in the treatment of pediatric OCD (March, Frances, et al., 1997).

The anxiolytic benzodiazepines can be used to treat Panic Disorder in adolescents (Bernstein et al., 1996). Bernstein and Kinlan (1997) recommend that benzodiazepines be used only in the short-term with children due to the potential for tolerance and dependence. In adults, benzodiazepines may hinder the effectiveness of CBT. Marks et al. (1993) found that the use of alprazolam during exposure in adults with Panic Disorder inhibited the maintenance of gains in the long term. More research is needed on the effectiveness of medications alone and in combination with CBT before definitive practice guidelines can be given.

Recent research suggests that extinction of fear can be aided by the use of D-cycloserine (DCS), which acts on the NMDA glutamatergic receptor in the brain.

Ressler et al. (2004) conducted a randomized controlled trial of different amounts of DCS (high, low, placebo) given to height phobics before sessions of virtual reality therapy for their fear. Although DCS did not demonstrate an anxiolytic effect for the first session of therapy, for all future sessions and follow-up, patients who had taken DCS showed a reduced fear of heights compared with those who took a placebo. Perhaps one future for medical adjuncts to therapy lies in the area of medications that act as learning enhancements for psychological interventions.

Case Description

Case Introduction

Peta, an 8-year-old girl, lived with her parents, Liza (32 years) and David (42 years). Two older stepsiblings from her father's first marriage had recently left home. These included an older brother, Thomas, age 19, and an older sister, Megan, age 20. The parents were of Anglo-Irish working-class origins, and the father currently worked as a bus driver. The mother was engaged in home duties and worked part time in a cafeteria. Extended family living in the same city included a maternal grandmother, whom Peta had regular contact with, and a maternal uncle, who was hospitalized.

Both maternal and paternal sides of the family had a clear history of psychopathology. The uncle's hospitalization was a result of chronic Schizophrenia, and the maternal grandmother had a history of depression and compulsive checking behavior. The maternal grandfather, deceased at the time of the referral, had a history of alcohol abuse and, according to Liza, physically and sexually abused her throughout her childhood. David reported that his father also abused alcohol and rarely lived in the family home due to a strong predilection for aimless wandering. During his times in the home, he was violent toward his wife and the children. David's mother also appeared to be disturbed, although it was difficult to discern the exact nature of the problem from David's descriptions ("She had a screw loose"). It appeared that she was verbally and physically abusive of David, greatly favoring David's older sister. David's son by his first marriage and Peta's stepbrother, Thomas, had a history of severe conduct and learning problems that had resulted in school failure and expulsion and repeated trouble with the police.

David and Liza reported that their marriage had been unstable and that at times in the past, David had been physically violent. However, both were able to speak openly about their past and future and expressed optimism that recent improvements in their relationship would continue to grow. David presented as a generally happy and talkative man with no obvious psychopathology or distress. He had a history of osteoarthritis and heart disease, the latter having required a period of hospitalization approximately 4 years prior to referral. Peta was frightened by her father's heart problems and aware of their serious nature.

Liza presented as mildly anxious, with a history of recurrent dysthymia. She had poor self-esteem, and this was reinforced by the power structure of the

(continued)

family, in which David made the decisions and afforded her little respect. Over the past 8 years, Liza had immersed herself in the care and upbringing of Peta as a way of undoing the painful memories of her own childhood and to prove to herself that she could achieve something worthwhile.

Presenting Complaints

Peta presented as a slender, pretty, and intelligent 8-year-old girl. She spoke happily and confidently to the therapist and appeared quite comfortable about disclosing the details of her fears and anxieties. At times, however, she would become visibly anxious while discussing her family, wringing and clasping her hands, frowning and shuffling about. The main problems she reported were (a) her need to go back and check the school classroom while leaving school for the day; she said she was scared that her things might be taken away or thrown out; (b) fear that her mother or father might not return from work one day; and (c) fear that some of her things in her bedroom may be (accidentally) thrown out with the garbage. Liza and David both agreed that their daughter's checking behavior was the main problem. However, they were also concerned that Peta was becoming increasingly irritable, noncompliant, and aggressive with her mother. During daily activities such as getting dressed for school, arguments between Peta and her mother were becoming increasingly frequent, and many would culminate in Peta having a temper tantrum and repeatedly accusing her mother of not loving her. The father reported no such problems.

Peta was generally well adjusted at school and had a number of friends there and in the home neighborhood. Several times over the prior month, she had reported hearing a mature female voice quietly calling "Peta, come here," when no one had called. Since an early age, Peta had an imaginary friend whom she would play with and talk to, even in front of other people. She was fully aware that this friend existed in her imagination only.

The parents had vastly different interpretations of Peta's problems. For David, it was simply a matter of lack of discipline from his wife. He felt that Peta was becoming out of control because his wife was unable to discipline her effectively. Liza, aware that both her family and her husband's family had a history of mental illness, was scared that Peta was showing the first signs of Schizophrenia. In particular, Liza said that Peta sometimes reminded her of her brother, who had been diagnosed with Schizophrenia.

History

Peta was an unplanned, but wanted, child. The birth was complicated by fetal and maternal distress, with subsequent cesarean delivery. Apart from some mild asthma, Peta developed into a healthy and happy baby. During middle childhood in the few years prior to referral, however, Peta suffered a number of losses. First, her older brother and sister both moved out of the family home. She was quite upset about this as she was very close to both. Next, she experienced the loss of her grandfather, to whom she was quite close. Her parents reported that Peta's grandmother began teasing Peta about the possibility that others in the family could die soon as well. For example, it was reported that the grandmother would constantly remind Peta of her father's heart condition and that her mother could die any night while working late at the cafeteria.

Next, Peta had to separate from her third-grade teacher, to whom she was extremely attached. At the time of separation and transition into the fourth grade, the teacher had become ill and virtually disappeared from Peta's life. The parents reported that Peta would cry at night about not seeing this teacher, expressing constant fears that the teacher was either dead or dying. Soon after, Peta's mother returned to work in a job that demanded working late at night. Peta found this stressful and would follow her mother out to her car, visibly distressed and asking her not to go. Over these 2 years, Peta had also suffered the loss of three pet cats. All were killed in traffic accidents outside the family home.

According to her parents, the first sign that anything was wrong came shortly after the death of the first two cats and her grandfather. She became more anxious than usual, fearful of her parents leaving her, expressing fear that she or her parents might die, and intermittently accusing her parents of not loving her. Soon afterward, the separation from her third-grade teacher occurred, another cat died, and her mother returned to work. Against this backdrop of loss in Peta's life, there appears to be a particular event that triggered the actual checking behavior. Her performance of daily chores was suffering; in particular, she was refusing to clean up her room. One weekend, her father, frustrated at the state of her room and tired of the constant battles to get her to clean it up, took matters into his own hands. In the space of an hour he had removed everything from her room that he did not consider necessary. Peta had become hysterical during the cleaning, but she was unable to stop him. The parents reported that her checking of the garbage began the next day and the checking of her school possessions began the next week.

These problems had persisted at a reasonably stable level since that time, with the exception of some recent improvement due to the parents seeking help from a clinical psychologist in private practice. The psychologist had recommended a reward system focusing on checking after school, and this had led to some improvements (checking had reduced from an estimated mean of 5 down to 2 or 3 checks per afternoon). However, the parents had found the cost of this practitioner to be beyond their means and had asked their physician to refer them to a less costly clinic.

Assessment

As a general measure of Peta's functioning, we asked both parents to complete the Revised Problem Behavior Checklist (Quay & Petersen, 1983). The overall levels of disturbed behavior were not in the clinical range for either parent; however, scores on items measuring anxiety were elevated, confirming the interview data that Peta was experiencing distressing levels of anxiety. There was no evidence that Peta was suffering any signs of depression, according to parental report on the Bellevue Index of Depression (Petti, 1978) or Peta's self-report on the Child Depression Inventory (Kovacs & Beck, 1977). Although the mother reported a history of dysthymia, her score on the Beck Index of Depression (Beck,

(continued)

Ward, Mendelsonn, Mock, & Erbough, 1961) showed no indication that she was currently depressed. Both parents scored in the normal range on the Spanier Dyadic Adjustment Scale (Spanier, 1976), indicating no major marital problems. However, scores on the Parent Problems Checklist (Dadds & Powell, 1991) indicated that David and Liza had considerable problems acting as a team in their parenting duties and that fights would often occur over the best way to handle Peta.

Case Conceptualization

Using *DSM-IV* criteria, Peta was diagnosed with OCD, with both obsessions and compulsions being present. It is important to consider Peta's overall adjustment in relation to the degree of stress she had experienced in the prior 2 years. First, it is clear that the obsessive-compulsive behavior was not severely debilitating; she was still coping well at school, she had good peer relations, and she showed no other emotional or behavioral problems apart from the OCD. Second, when one considers the nature of the stress Peta had experienced, the form of the OCD seems understandable. That is, the obsessions and compulsions were, to a large extent, realistic in that they represented her attempts to find stability and consistency in an unpredictable environment.

Peta's problems appear to be a result of genetic vulnerability mixed with environmental stress. Both sides of her family lineage have a history of Schizophrenia, substance abuse, and general conflict. Her mother's side also has a history of OCD. Given this history, it is important to consider that Peta's current problem may be a precursor to more serious psychiatric problems in the future. There are also protective factors present in this case: Peta's high level of intelligence (as shown by her ability to carry out treatment, her verbal skills, and reports from her teachers), her excellent social skills and social adjustment, and her parents' motivation to rectify and improve both their marriage and their daughter's problems.

In terms of the specific nature of Peta's obsessive thoughts and compulsions, a social learning conceptualization offered the most parsimonious account and clearest directions for treatment. These factors may be very different from the factors that were associated with the onset of the disorder. For example, a therapist might consider that the loss of significant others was the original reason that Peta began obsessing and ritualizing, and thus focus on helping Peta to resolve her feelings about the losses. On the contrary, it is likely that the problem behavior, once established, is now being maintained by different factors. We hypothesized that social learning and cognitive factors were maintaining the problem.

For Peta, thoughts of important objects and people had taken on aversive qualities; that is, they produced unpleasant arousal. Upon having these thoughts, she experienced increased muscle tension, shortness of breath, a sick feeling in the stomach, thoughts of loss and separation, and general feelings that some impending disaster was just around the corner. Having no other way of relieving these feelings, she would attempt to reassure herself that the content of the thought was not true—that is, that no loss had occurred. This would temporarily reduce the anxiety until the thought would occur again.

Thus, thoughts of her schoolbooks, her possessions, and her parents going to work had become conditioned stimuli, capable of producing severe arousal (conditioned response) because of their association with various unconditioned stimuli (death, separation from loved ones, family violence). Engaging in ritualization could temporarily reduce her arousal level; thus, ritualization was being negatively reinforced by the reduction in anxiety it produced. Further, ritualization has another insidious effect on obsessive thoughts: It prevents the conditioned aversiveness of the thoughts from undergoing extinction. That is, the rituals remove both the obsessive thoughts and the arousal. Specifically, because the thoughts are never experienced in the absence of arousal, no extinction can occur. In parallel with these conditioned effects, the anxious person increasingly allocates attentional resources to the detection of threat in the environment. For Peta, any signal of separation or removal thus became a potentially threatening cue (conditioned stimulus) for anxiety.

Interpersonally, we can also see a number of processes that were helping to maintain the problem. Inadvertently, her parents were reinforcing the problem behavior. When another person displays unusual, inappropriate, or aberrant behavior, his or her normal behavior becomes less salient. Peta's parents were worried about her checking behavior and were constantly on the lookout for it. When anxiety-related behaviors occurred, they would immediately attend to her and employ various strategies in an attempt to stop her. Their responses ranged from chastising her to comforting her. When she was not ritualizing, her parents tended to ignore her in an effort to avoid upsetting the temporary cessation of rituals. For example, when leaving for work, if Liza noticed that Peta was calm, she would try to sneak out without her noticing. In response, Peta became more vigilant. Thus, Peta's anxiety and ritualization were positively reinforced, with parental attention increasingly contingent on the display of these behaviors. Conversely, behaviors other than ritualizing and verbalizing fears were effectively on an extinction schedule.

Finally, it is quite possible that some of Peta's behaviors may have been learned, and were being maintained, by direct observation of other family members. In particular, it is possible that she was imitating some of her grandmother's checking behaviors.

The conceptualization of Peta's problem emphasized three components: conditioning and cognitive processes, reinforcement contingencies provided by her parents, and broader imitation and stress coming from the extended family. Thus, the treatment we proposed to the parents was multiphasic, having various components that targeted each of the suspected causal factors in sequence.

Course of Treatment and Assessment of Progress

1. Conditioning and Cognitive Processes

The aim of this component was to decondition the various stimuli that had taken on the potential to cause distress. We wanted Peta to be able to think about and experience such things as leaving school, her mother going to work, the garbage being thrown out, and so on, without her ritualizing and without experiencing distress. To achieve this, we used a simple exposure and response

(*continued*)

prevention procedure. In preparation, Peta was trained to let her body relax and engage in a preplanned self-talk script as a way of controlling her anxiety and not ritualizing. She invented the script, which, set in the form of a short poem, focused on feeling strong and confident.

First, we rehearsed the use of these coping skills during our clinic sessions. The therapist would ask Peta to deliberately think of a "yucky" thought (the hypothesized conditioned stimuli) about losing something important. As Peta's anxiety would start to rise, the therapist would then instruct her to engage in the coping procedure until the anxiety abated. Peta learned how to do this quite quickly and effectively, so, next, she was instructed to use the procedure whenever she felt increased anxiety climbing and the need to check.

To help Peta counter her hypervigilance to threat cues in the environment, she was instructed to notice and list "happy, positive, and friendly" things that she could attend to when she felt she was at especially high risk for becoming anxious. For example, during the walk from the school to her mother's car, Peta was increasingly able to attend to the presence of some friends, her mother's reassuring company, and that she was soon going to be able to play with her toys at home rather than focus on the possibility of her books being removed.

2. Parental Contingency Training

While Peta was being trained to implement the coping strategy, her parents were taught the basic behavior management skills of reinforcement and extinction. This included training them to provide effective praise contingent upon Peta's not checking, and to "actively ignore" (provide immediate attention to appropriate behavior immediately following extinction of undesirable actions) checking behavior. Because Peta was becoming increasingly aggressive with her mother and because her parents would often use verbal and physical threats in their interactions with her, her parents were instructed to increase the use of praise and active ignoring in their general interactions with Peta.

To accomplish these training goals, we provided the parents with written materials, the therapist modeled the use of the procedures, and then the parents rehearsed them while the therapist provided feedback. This continued until the parents could demonstrate use of effective praise and ignore repetitive complaining while the therapist acted as Peta.

3. Modeling and General Stress Effects

There was evidence that Peta's grandmother was suffering some form of OCD that included checking behavior. Further, it appeared that she was teasing Peta about death and loss by repeatedly pointing out, for example, that her parents could die at any time. This behavior obviously constitutes severe emotional abuse of a vulnerable child. Unfortunately, the grandmother refused to be seen by the therapist, even though the approach made to her emphasized that her help and expertise were needed to help Peta. Thus, there appeared to be no alternative but to advise the parents to restrict the grandmother's access to Peta to structured visits when another adult was present.

Finally, there remained the issue of the general family conflict and how Peta would cope with any future loss. Sensitive to the fact that we had advised the parents to deliberately ignore checking behavior, we were concerned that Peta was left with no method for discussing and solving emotional problems with her intimates. Thus, the parents were advised to regularly take time (approximately twice a week) to sit with Peta at bedtime and encourage her to talk openly and, if possible, find solutions to her fears and problems. The parents were briefly trained to actively listen and encourage exploration and problem solving rather than be directive with Peta.

In this case, we agreed to begin treatment by training Peta in the coping strategy and the parents in the contingency management skills as the first treatment component, in parallel. Thus, the weekly sessions were divided into 30 minutes spent with Peta, 30 minutes with the parents, followed by 15 minutes with everyone together to review how everything was going. Measures of checking behavior were to be the main criteria for determining treatment effectiveness. The target behaviors were defined as follows:

1. School checking—Peta returns or attempts to return to classroom after leaving the building after school is dismissed. The number of times was to be recorded.
2. Garbage checking—Peta either checks through or attempts to check through the garbage or makes a comment to her parents about the possibility of one or more of her possessions being in the garbage. Because this behavior was sometimes happening many times each day, we decided to score only "yes" (the behavior occurred that day) or "no" (the behavior did not occur that day).
3. Checking on parents—Peta moves into vicinity of parents, in the home, with no other purpose than to check on their presence, or she expresses concern that one or both of them may leave or die. This was scored "yes" or "no" for each day.
4. Overall happiness—At the end of the day, an estimate of how happy Peta had been that day was to be recorded using a 5-point scale: 1 = extremely unhappy to 5 = extremely happy.

These measures were completed by both Peta and her mother. Figure 10.1 shows the effects of treatment on measures of checking and general happiness according to Peta and her mother, respectively. First, it is clear from the similarity of the two profiles that Peta and Liza agreed moderately well on the frequency of checking and on Peta's general level of happiness. The only obvious exception to this is the frequency of school checking, for which Peta reported higher frequencies due to some checking occurring prior to her mother's arriving at the school.

Complicating Factors

During the first phase of intervention, checking on the garbage reduced to zero and stayed at that level. School checking and checking on parents both showed minor improvements over baseline frequencies; however, they stabilized without ever reducing to zero rate. It was decided that a more intensive intervention was required, and the therapist set about discussing different

(continued)

strategies with Peta and her parents. Everyone agreed that Peta was working very hard and had made substantial improvements. However, at times she would be distracted or temporarily lose motivation and become engrossed in an obsessive thought. Thus, we decided that a more intensive incentive would help to increase the salience of the program.

In the next phase of treatment, a contingency management program was established using a "differential reinforcement of zero rates" (DRO) system. Using DRO, the periods in which the problem behavior is likely to occur are divided into a number of short intervals. Whenever the child abstains from engaging in the problem behavior for the length of the interval, the predetermined reward is given. This occurs for each interval, and rewards are accrued hierarchically. For example, for the problem of checking on parents, the times at which Peta was at home were divided into a series of 1-hour intervals. Each hour without checking was rewarded with a happy face placed on a publicly displayed poster, a small amount of money, a hug, and verbal praise. Happy faces could be saved up and, at Peta's discretion, could be traded for a range of other rewards that had been agreed upon during the design of the token system. Figure 10.1 shows that the implementation of this system was associated with a reduction to zero in checking in both school and home environments.

Clinical experience has shown that it is usually much more difficult to phase out a contingency management system than it is to start one. Thus, fading of the system began after day 6, with the length of the intervals, the type of rewards, and the amount of independent self-monitoring of Peta's behavior all varying over the next few weeks. Peta was actively involved in the design of this phase, and she fully comprehended the need for her to be able to avoid checking without artificial prompts. From Figure 10.1 it can be seen that her checking behavior remained at zero until the system was phased out in the final stage of therapy.

Figure 10.1 also shows daily happiness ratings made by both Peta and her mother. It is clear that treatment was associated with a small but consistent improvement in Peta's overall mood.

Managed Care Considerations

Managed care was not considered in this case.

Follow-Up

Unfortunately, a maintenance program could not be built into treatment because the family moved to another state a few weeks after treatment ended. Thus, the follow-up assessment was limited to telephone calls. The parents indicated that Peta had shown no signs of checking or ritualization at 5 months following termination.

Treatment Implications of the Case

A cognitive-behavioral conceptualization and treatment of an 8-year-old child with OCD was described. The approach was useful in formulating a plan that is practical and easily understandable to children, parents, and clinicians alike. This approach allows the clinician to assess the idiosyncrasies of each particular case and then design

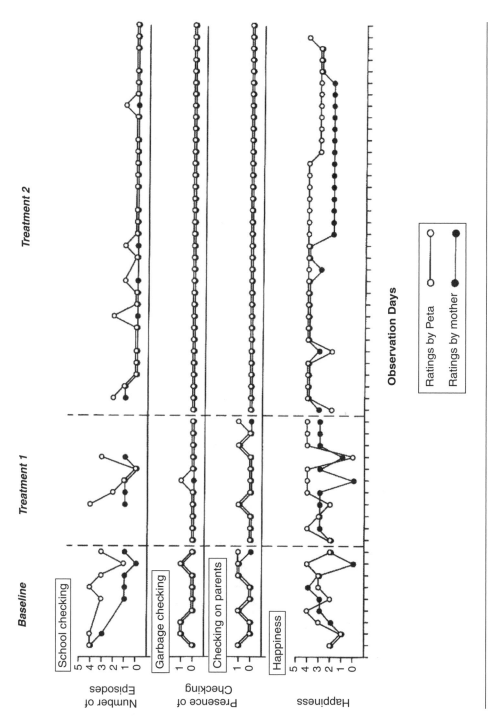

Figure 10.1 Ratings on four measures for baseline, treatment 1, and treatment 2.

a treatment program that incorporates those idiosyncrasies. For example, although the type of attention that a child's compulsive behavior will attract from parents and siblings will differ from family to family, that attention and its effects on the child will still follow the general laws of reinforcement. We also saw how the social learning approach alerted the therapist to influences of the broader family context through general stress and modeling and imitation processes.

RECOMMENDATIONS TO CLINICIANS

The approach taken in this case is not without limitations. For severe cases of OCD, more intensive and structured interventions may be needed. For example, where the patient or the family is less compliant with therapeutic instructions or the rituals are so severe that the patient cannot resist them, medication or hospitalization may be required in the short term.

With OCD, the main thrust of therapeutic success usually comes from altering the rituals and then targeting the obsessional thinking. Patients who are predominantly obsessional and do not have marked rituals are difficult to treat with behavioral methods.

RECOMMENDATIONS TO STUDENTS

The treatment plan described earlier specifies the content of therapy. Just as important is the process by which a therapeutic plan is implemented, especially when treatment involves the cooperation of multiple parties, such as therapists, children, parents, and teachers. The method used in Peta's case has been comprehensively described by Sanders and Dadds (1993). This approach emphasizes the team aspects of the intervention: that parents and child(ren) are afforded equal status with the therapist and that all information and psychological knowledge is shared equally among the group. Assessment information and the treatment plan are discussed, formulated, and openly agreed upon as a team before any action is taken.

REFERENCES

Achenbach, T. M., & Edelbrock, C. (1983). *Manual for the Child Behavior Checklist and Revised Child Behavior Profile* (2nd ed.). Burlington: University of Vermont, Department of Psychiatry.

Albano, A. M. (1995). Treatment of social anxiety in adolescents. *Cognitive and Behavioral Practice, 2,* 271–298.

Albano, A. M., Chorpita, B. F., & Barlow, D. H. (2003). Childhood anxiety disorders. In E. J. Mash & R. A. Barkley (Eds.), *Child psychopathology* (2nd ed., pp. 279–329). New York: Guilford Press.

American Psychiatric Association. (1994). *Diagnostic and statistical manual of mental disorders* (4th ed.). Washington, DC: Author.

Anderson, J. C. (1994). Epidemiological issues. In T. H. Ollendick, N. J. King, & W. Yule (Eds.), *International handbook of phobic and anxiety disorders in children and adolescents* (pp. 43–66). New York: Plenum Press.

Anstendig, K. D. (1999). Is selective mutism an anxiety disorder? *Journal of Anxiety Disorders, 13,* 417–434.

Austin, A. A., & Chorpita, B. F. (2004). Temperament, anxiety, and depression: Comparisons across five ethnic groups of children. *Journal of Clinical Child and Adolescent Psychology, 33,* 216–226.

Barrett, P. M. (1998). Evaluation of cognitive-behavioral group treatments for childhood anxiety disorders. *Journal of Clinical Child Psychology, 27*(4), 459–468.

Barrett, P. M., Dadds, M. R., & Rapee, R. M. (1996). Family treatment of childhood anxiety: A controlled trial. *Journal of Consulting and Clinical Psychology, 64*, 333–342.

Barrett, P. M., Dadds, M. R., Rapee, R. M., & Ryan, S. (1996). Family enhancement of cognitive styles in anxious and aggressive children: The FEAR effect. *Journal of Abnormal Child Psychology, 24*, 187–203.

Barrett, P. M., Healy-Farrell, L., & March, J. S. (2004). Cognitive-behavioral family treatment of childhood obsessive-compulsive disorder: A controlled trial. *Journal of the American Academy of Child and Adolescent Psychiatry, 43*(1), 46–62.

Barrios, B. A., & Hartmann, D. P. (1997). Fears and anxieties. In E. J. Mash & L. G. Terdal (Eds.), *Assessment of childhood disorders* (3rd ed., pp. 230–327). New York: Guilford Press.

Beck, A. T., Ward, C. H., Mendelsonn, M., Mock, J., & Erbough, J. (1961). An inventory for measuring depression. *Archives of General Psychiatry, 41*, 561–571.

Beidel, D. C. (1991). Social phobia and overanxious disorder in school-age children. *Journal of the American Academy of Child Psychiatry, 30*, 545–552.

Bernstein, G. A, Borchardt, C. M., & Perwien, A. R. (1996). Anxiety disorders in children and adolescents: A review of the past 10 years. *Journal of the American Academy of Child and Adolescent Psychiatry, 35*, 1110–1119.

Bernstein, G. A., Borchardt, C. M., Perwien, A. R., Crosby, R. D., Kushner, M. G., Thuras, P. D., et al. (2000). Imipramine plus cognitive-behavioral therapy in the treatment of school refusal. *Journal of the American Academy of Child and Adolescent Psychiatry, 39*(3), 276–283.

Bernstein, G. A., & Kinlan, J. (1997). Summary of the practice parameters for the assessment and treatment of children and adolescents with anxiety disorders. *Journal of the American Academy of Child and Adolescent Psychiatry, 36*, 1639–1641.

Birmaher, B., Waterman, G. S., Ryan, N., Cully, M., Balach, L., Ingram, J., et al. (1994). Fluoxetine for childhood anxiety disorders. *Journal of the American Academy of Child and Adolescent Psychiatry, 33*, 993–999.

Blagg, N. R., & Yule, W. (1984). The behavioral treatment of school refusal: A comparative study. *Behavior Research and Therapy, 22*, 119–127.

Bowlby, J. (1971). *Attachment and loss: Vol. 1. Attachment.* Harmondsworth, England: Penguin.

Bruch, M. A. (1989). Familial and developmental antecedents of social phobia: Issues and findings. *Clinical Psychology Review, 9*(1), 37–47.

Bruch, M. A., & Heimberg, R. G. (1994). Differences in perceptions of parental and personal characteristics between generalized and nongeneralized social phobics. *Journal of Anxiety Disorders, 8*(2), 155–168.

Chambers, W. J., Puig-Antich, J., Hirsch, M., Paez, P., Ambrosini, P. J., & Tabrizi, M. A. (1985). The assessment of affective disorders in children and adolescents by semistructured interview: Test-retest reliability of the Schedule for Affective Disorders and Schizophrenia for school-age children, present episode. *Archives of General Psychiatry, 42*, 696–702.

Cobham, V. E., Dadds, M. R., & Spence, S. H. (1998). The role of parental anxiety in the treatment of childhood anxiety. *Journal of Consulting and Clinical Psychology, 66*(6), 893–905.

Costello, A. J., Edelbrock, C. S., Dulcan, M. K., Kalas, R., & Klaric, S. H. (1984). *Development and testing of the NIMH Diagnostic Interview Schedule for Children on a clinical population: Final report* (Contract RFP-DB-81–0027). Rockville, MD: Center for Epidemiological Studies, National Institute of Mental Health.

Costello, E. J., Mustillo, S., Erkanli, A., Keeler, G., & Angold, A. (2003). Prevalence and development of psychiatric disorders in childhood and adolescence. *Archives of General Psychiatry, 60*, 837–844.

Dadds, M. R., & Barrett, P. M. (2001). Practitioner review: Psychological management of anxiety disorders in childhood. *Journal of Child Psychology and Psychiatry, 42,* 999–1011.

Dadds, M. R., Barrett, P. M., Rapee, R. M., & Ryan, S. (1996). Family process and child anxiety and aggression: An observational analysis. *Journal of Abnormal Child Psychology. 24,* 715–734.

Dadds, M. R., Davey, G. C. L., & Field, A. P. (2001). Developmental aspects of conditioning processes in anxiety disorders. In M. Vasey & M. R. Dadds (Eds.), *Developmental psychopathology of anxiety* (pp. 205–230). New York: Oxford University Press.

Dadds, M. R., Holland, D. E., Laurens, K. R., Mullins, M., Barrett, P. M., & Spence, S. H. (1999). Early intervention and prevention of anxiety disorders: Results at 2-year follow-up. *Journal of Consulting and Clinical Psychology, 67,* 145–150.

Dadds, M. R., & Powell, M. B. (1991). The relationship of interparental conflict and global marital adjustment to aggression, anxiety and immaturity in aggressive and nonclinic children. *Journal of Abnormal Child Psychology, 19,* 553–568.

Dadds, M. R., Rapee, R. M., & Barrett, P. M. (1994). Behavioral observation. In T. H. Ollendick, N. J. King, & W. Yule (Eds.), *International handbook of phobic and anxiety disorders in children and adolescents* (pp. 349–364). New York: Plenum Press.

Dadds, M. R., & Roth, J. H. (2001). Family processes in the development of anxiety problems. In M. Vasey & M. R. Dadds (Eds.), *Developmental psychopathology of anxiety* (pp. 278–303). New York: Oxford University Press.

Davey, G. C. L. (1997). A conditional model of phobias. In G. C. L. Davey (Ed.), *Phobias: A handbook of theory, research, and treatment* (pp. 301–322). Chichester, England: Wiley.

Davidson, J. R. T., Hughes, D. C., George, L. K., & Blazer, D. G. (1993). The epidemiology of social phobia: Findings from the Duke Epidemiological Catchment Area Study. *Psychological Medicine, 23,* 709–718.

DeWit, D. J., MacDonald, K., & Offord, D. R. (1999). Childhood stress and symptoms of drug dependence in adolescence and early adulthood: Social phobia as a mediator. *American Journal of Orthopsychiatry, 69,* 61–72.

DiLalla, L. F., Kagan, J., & Reznick, J. S. (1994). Genetic etiology of behavioral inhibition among 2-year-old children. *Infant Behavior and Development, 17,* 405–412.

Dollinger, S. J., O'Donnell, J. P., & Staley, A. A. (1984). Lightning-strike disaster: Effects on children's fears and worries. *Journal of Consulting and Clinical Psychology, 52,* 1028–1038.

Dummit, E., Klein, R., Tancer, N., Asche, B., & Martin, J. (1996). Fluoxetine treatment of children with selective mutism: An open trial. *Journal of the American Academy of Child and Adolescent Psychiatry, 35,* 615–621.

Eley, T. (2001). Genetic influences. In M. Vasey & M. R. Dadds (Eds.), *Developmental psychopathology of anxiety* (pp. 45–59). New York: Oxford University Press.

Eley, T. C., Bolton, D., O'Connor, T. G., Perrin, S., Smith, P., & Plomin, R. (2003). A twin study of anxiety-related behaviors in pre-school children. *Journal of Child Psychology and Psychiatry, 44,* 945–960.

Emery, R. E. (1982). Interparental conflict and the children of divorce and discord. *Psychological Bulletin, 9,* 310–330.

Faust, J., & Forehand, R. (1994). Adolescents' physical complaints as a function of anxiety due to familial and peer stress: A causal model. *Journal of Anxiety Disorders, 8,* 139–153.

Fox, J. E., & Houston, B. K. (1983). Distinguishing between cognitive and somatic trait and state anxiety in children. *Journal of Personality and Social Psychology, 45,* 862–870.

Fox, N. A., & Calkins, S. D. (1993). Social withdrawal: Interactions among temperament, attachment, and regulation. In K. H. Rubin & J. B. Asendorph (Eds.), *Social withdrawal, inhibition and shyness in childhood* (pp. 81–100). Hillsdale, NJ: Erlbaum.

Ginsburg, G. S., & Silverman, W. K. (1996). Phobic and anxiety disorders in Hispanic and Caucasian youth. *Journal of Anxiety Disorders, 10,* 517–528.

Goodyer, I. M. (1990). Family relationships, life events and childhood psychopathology. *Journal of Child Psychology and Psychiatry and Allied Disciplines, 31*(1), 161–192.

Goodyer, I. M., & Altham, P. M. (1991). Lifetime exit events and recent social and family adversities in anxious and depressed school-aged children. *Journal of Affective Disorders, 21,* 219–228.

Goodyer, I. M., Wright, C., & Altham, P. M. (1990). The friendships and recent life events of anxious and depressed school-aged children. *British Journal of Psychiatry, 156,* 689–698.

Guerrero, A. P. S., Hishinuma, E. S., Andrade, N. N., Bell, C. K., Kurahara, D. K., Lee, T. G., et al. (2003). Demographic and clinical characteristics of adolescents in Hawaii with obsessive-compulsive disorder. *Archives of Pediatric Adolescent Medicine, 157,* 665–670.

Hanna, G. (1995). Demographic and clinical features of obsessive-compulsive disorder in children and adolescents. *Journal of the American Academy of Child and Adolescent Psychiatry, 34,* 19–27.

Hayward, C., Killen, J. D., Wilson, D. M., & Hammer, L. D. (1997). Psychiatric risk associated with early puberty in adolescent girls. *Journal of the American Academy of Child and Adolescent Psychiatry, 36,* 255–262.

Hayward, C., Varady, S., Albano, A. M., Thienemann, M., Henderson, L., & Schatzberg, A. F. (2000). Cognitive-behavioral group therapy for social phobia in female adolescents: Results of a pilot study. *Journal of the American Academy of Child and Adolescent Psychiatry, 39*(6), 721–726.

Herjanic, B., & Reich, W. (1982). Development of a structured psychiatric interview for children: Agreement between child and parent on individual symptoms. *Journal of Abnormal Child Psychology, 10,* 307–324.

Heyne, D., King, N., Tonge, B., Rollings, S., Young, D., Pritchard, M., et al. (2002). Evaluation of child therapy and caregiver training in the treatment of school refusal. *Journal of the American Academy of Child and Adolescent Psychiatry, 41,* 687–695.

Hirshfeld-Becker, D. R., Biederman, J., Calltharp, S., Rosenbaum, E. D., Faraone, S. V., & Rosenbaum, J. F. (2003). Behavioral inhibition and disinhibition as hypothesized precursors to psychopathology: Implications for pediatric bipolar disorder. *Biological Psychiatry, 53,* 985–999.

Hudson, J. L. (2005). Efficacy of cognitive-behavioral therapy for children and adolescents with anxiety disorders. *Behavior Change, 22*(2), 55–70.

Inderbitzen, H. M., Walters, K. S., & Bukowski, A. L. (1997). The role of social anxiety in adolescent peer relations: Differences among sociometric status groups and rejected subgroups. *Journal of Clinical Child Psychology, 26,* 338–348.

Jones, M. C. (1924). A laboratory study of fear: The case of Peter. *Journal of General Psychology, 31,* 308–315.

Kagan, J., Reznick, J. S., & Snidman, N. (1988). Biological bases of childhood shyness. *Science, 240,* 167–171.

Kagan, J., Snidman, N., Arcus, D., & Reznick, S. J. (1994). *Galen's prophecy: Temperament in human nature.* New York: Basic Books.

Kashdan, T. B., & Herbert, J. D. (2001). Social anxiety disorder in childhood and adolescence: Current status and future directions. *Clinical Child and Family Psychology Review, 4*(1), 37–61.

Kearney, C. A., & Silverman, W. K. (1998). A critical review of pharmacotherapy for youth with anxiety disorders: Things are not as they seem. *Journal of Anxiety Disorders, 12*(2), 83–102.

Keller, M. B., Lavori, P., Wunder, J., Beardslee, W. R., & Schwarts, C. E. (1992). Chronic course of anxiety disorders in children and adolescents. *Journal of the American Academy of Child and Adolescent Psychiatry, 31,* 595–599.

Kendall, P. C. (1994). Treating anxiety disorders in children: Results of a randomized clinical trial. *Journal of Consulting and Clinical Psychology, 62*(1), 100–110.

Kendall, P. C., Flannery-Schroeder, E., Panichelli-Mindel, S. M., Southam-Gerow, M., Henin, A., & Warman, M. (1997). Therapy for youths with anxiety disorders: A second randomized clinical trial. *Journal of Consulting and Clinical Psychology, 65*(3), 366–380.

Kendall, P. C., & Southam-Gerow, M. (1996). Long-term follow-up of a CBT for anxiety-disordered youth. *Journal of Consulting and Clinical Psychology, 64*(4), 724–730.

Kim, S. W., Grant, J. E., Kim, S. I., Swanson, T. A., Bernstein, G. A., Jaszcz, W. B., et al. (2004). A possible association of recurrent streptococcal infections and acute onset of obsessive-compulsive disorder. *Journal of Neuropsychiatry and Clinical Neurosciences, 16*(3), 252–260.

Kim-Cohen, J., Caspi, A., Moffitt, T. E., Harrington, H., Milne, B. J., & Poulton, R. (2003). Prior juvenile diagnoses in adults with mental disorder: Developmental follow-back of a prospective-longitudinal cohort. *Archives of General Psychiatry, 60,* 709–717.

King, N. J., & Bernstein, G. (2001). School refusal in children and adolescents: A review of the past 10 years. *Journal of the American Academy of Child and Adolescent Psychiatry, 40,* 197–205.

King, N. J., Hamilton, D. I., & Ollendick, T. H. (1988). *Children's phobias: A behavioral perspective.* Chichester, England: Wiley.

King, N. J., Ollendick, T. H., & Murphy, G. C. (1997). Assessment of childhood phobias. *Clinical Psychology Review, 17*(7), 667–687.

King, N. J., Tonge, B. J., Heyne, D., Pritchard, M., Rollings, S., Young, D., et al. (1998). Cognitive-behavioral treatment of school-refusing children: A controlled evaluation. *Journal of the American Academy of Child and Adolescent Psychiatry, 37,* 395–403.

King, R. A., Leonard, H., & March, J. (1998). Practice parameters for the assessment and treatment of children and adolescents with obsessive-compulsive disorder. *Journal of the American Academy of Child and Adolescent Psychiatry, 37*(Suppl. 10), 27S–45S.

Kovacs, M., & Beck, A. T. (1977). An empirical clinical approach toward a definition of child depression. In J. G. Schulterbrandt & A. Raskin (Eds.), *Depression in children: Diagnosis, treatment and conceptual models* (pp. 1–25). New York: Raven Press.

Labellarte, M. J., Ginsburg, G. S., Walkup, J. T., & Riddle, M. A. (1999). The treatment of anxiety disorders in children and adolescents. *Biological Psychiatry, 46,* 1567–1578.

La Greca, A. M., & Lopez, N. (1998). Social anxiety among adolescents: Linkages with peer relations and friendships. *Journal of Abnormal Child Psychology, 26,* 83–94.

La Greca, A. M., & Stone, W. L. (1993). Social Anxiety Scale for Children—Revised: Factor structure and concurrent validity. *Journal of Clinical Child Psychology, 22,* 17–27.

Last, C. G., Hansen, C., & Franco, N. (1998). Cognitive-behavioral treatment of school phobia. *Journal of the American Academy of Child and Adolescent Psychiatry, 37,* 404–411.

Last, C. G., Perrin, S., Hersen, M., & Kazdin, A. E. (1996). A prospective study of childhood anxiety disorders. *Journal of the American Academy of Child and Adolescent Psychiatry, 35,* 1502–1510.

Last, C. G., & Strauss, C. C. (1990). School refusal in anxiety-disordered children and adolescents. *Journal of the American Academy of Child and Adolescent Psychiatry, 29*(1), 31–35.

LeMare, L. J., & Rubin, K. H. (1990). Perspective taking and peer interaction: Structural and developmental analyses. *Child Development, 58*(2), 306–315.

Lumley, M. A., Melamed, B. G., & Abeles, L. A. (1993). Predicting children's presurgical anxiety and subsequent behavior changes. *Journal of Pediatric Psychology, 18*(4), 481–497.

Manassis, K., Mendlowitz, S. L., Scapillato, D., Avery, D., Fiksenbaum, L., Freire, M., et al. (2002). Group and individual cognitive-behavioral therapy for childhood anxiety disorders: A randomized trial. *Journal of the American Academy of Child and Adolescent Psychiatry, 41,* 1423–1430.

March, J. S., & Albano, A. M. (1998). New developments in assessing pediatric anxiety disorders. *Advances in Clinical Child Psychology, 20,* 213–241.

March, J. S., Conners, C., Arnold, G., Epstein, J., Parker, J., Hinshaw, S., et al. (1999). Multidimensional Anxiety Scale for Children (MASC): Confirmatory factor analysis in a pediatric ADHD sample. *Journal of Attention Disorders, 3*(2), 85–89.

March, J. S., Frances, A., Kahn, D. A., & Carpenter D. (1997). Expert consensus guidelines: Treatment of obsessive-compulsive disorder. *Journal of Clinical Psychiatry, 58*(Suppl. 4), 1–72.

March, J. S., Parker, J., Sullivan, K., Stallings, P., & Conners, C. K. (1997). Multidimensional Anxiety Scale for Children (MASC): Factor structure, reliability, and validity. *Journal of the American Academy of Child and Adolescent Psychiatry, 36*(4), 554–565.

Marks, I. M., Swinson, R. P., Basoglu, M., Kuch, K., Noshirvani, H., O'Sullivan, G., et al. (1993). Alprazolam and exposure alone and combined in panic disorder with agoraphobia: A controlled study in London and Toronto. *British Journal of Psychiatry, 162,* 776–787.

Mash, E. J., & Wolfe, D. A. (2005). *Abnormal child psychology* (3rd ed.). Belmont, CA: Wadsworth/Thomson Learning.

Masi, G., Mucci, M., Favilla, L., Romano, R., & Poli, P. (1999). Symptomology and comorbidity of GAD in children and adolescents. *Comprehensive Psychiatry, 40,* 210–215.

Mattis, S. G., & Ollendick, T. H. (1997). Children's cognitive responses to the somatic symptoms of panic. *Journal of Abnormal Child Psychology, 25,* 47–57.

McFarlane, A. C. (1987). Posttraumatic phenomena in a longitudinal study of children following a natural disaster. *Journal of the American Academy of Child and Adolescent Psychiatry, 26,* 764–769.

Mendlowitz, S. L., Manassis, K., Bradley, S., Scapillato, D., Miezitis, S., & Shaw, B. F. (1999). Cognitive-behavioral group treatments in childhood anxiety disorders: The role of parental involvement. *Journal of the American Academy of Child and Adolescent Psychiatry, 38,* 1223–1229.

Mineka, S., & Zinbarg, R. (2006). A contemporary learning theory perspective on the etiology of anxiety disorders: It's not what you thought it was. *American Psychologist, 61,* 10–26.

Muris, P., & Merckelbach, H. (2001). The etiology of childhood specific phobia: A multifactorial model. In M. Vasey & M. R. Dadds (Eds.), *Developmental psychopathology of anxiety* (pp. 355–385). New York: Oxford University Press.

Muris, P., Merckelbach, H., Schmidt, H., & Mayer, B. (1999). The revised version of the Screen for Child Anxiety Related Emotional Disorders (SCARED-R). *Personality and Individual Differences, 26,* 99–112.

Nelles, W. B., & Barlow, D. H. (1988). Do children panic? *Clinical Psychology Review, 8,* 359–372.

Ohman, A., & Mineka, S. (2001). Fears, phobias, and preparedness: Toward an evolved module of fear learning. *Psychological Review, 108,* 483–522.

Ollendick, T. H. (1998). Panic disorder in children and adolescents: New developments, new directions. *Journal of Clinical Child Psychology, 27,* 234–245.

Ollendick, T. H., Matson, J. L., & Helsel, W. J. (1985). Fears in children and adolescents: Normative data. *Behavior Research and Therapy, 23,* 465–467.

Ollendick, T. H., Vasey, M. W., & King, N. J. (2001). Operant conditioning influences in childhood anxiety. In M. W. Vasey & M. R. Dadds (Eds.), *Developmental psychopathology of anxiety* (pp. 231–252). New York: Oxford University Press.

Ollendick, T. H., Yang, B., King, N. J., Dong, Q., & Akande, A. (1996). Fears in American, Australian, Chinese, and Nigerian children and adolescents: A cross-cultural study. *Journal of Child Psychology and Psychiatry, 37*, 213–220.

Patterson, G. R. (1982). *Coercive family process.* Eugene, OR: Castalia Press.

Perrin, S., & Last, C. (1992). Do childhood anxiety measures measure anxiety? *Journal of Abnormal Child Psychology, 20*, 567–578.

Petti, T. A. (1978). Depression in hospitalized psychiatry patients: Approaches to measuring depression. *Journal of the American Academy of Child Psychiatry, 22*, 11–21.

Phelps, E. A., & LeDoux, J. E. (2005). Contributions of the amygdala to emotion processing: From animal models to human behavior. *Neuron, 48*(2), 175–187.

Piacentini, J., & Graae, F. (1997). Childhood OCD. In E. Hollander & D. Stein (Eds.), *Obsessive-compulsive disorders: Diagnosis, etiology, treatment* (pp. 23–46). New York: Marcel Dekker.

Poulton, R., Trainor, P., Stanton, W., McGee, R., Davies, S., & Silva, P. A. (1997). The (in)stability of adolescent fears. *Behavior Research and Therapy, 35*(2), 159–163.

Prior, M., Smart, D., Sanson, A., & Oberklaid, F. (2000). Does shy-inhibited temperament in childhood lead to anxiety problems in adolescence? *Journal of the American Academy of Child and Adolescent Psychiatry, 39*, 461–468.

Quay, H. C., & Petersen, D. R. (1983). *The Revised Behavior Problem Checklist.* Miami, FL: University of Miami.

Rachman, S. (1978). *Fear and courage.* San Francisco: Freeman.

Rapee, R. M. (1997). Potential role of child rearing practices in the development of anxiety and depression. *Clinical Psychology Review, 17*, 47–67.

Ressler, K. J., Rothbaum, B. O., Tannenbaum, L., Anderson, P., Graap, K., Zimand, E., et al. (2004). Cognitive enhancers as adjuncts to psychotherapy: Use of D-cycloserine in phobic individuals to facilitate extinction of fear. *Archives of General Psychiatry, 61*, 1136–1144.

Reynolds, C. R., & Paget, K. D. (1981). Factor analysis of the revised Children's Manifest Anxiety Scale for Blacks, males, and females with national innovative sample. *Journal of Consulting and Clinical Psychology, 49*, 352–359.

Roza, S. J., Hofstra, M. B., van der Ende, J., & Verhulst, F. C. (2003). Stable prediction of mood and anxiety disorders based on behavioral and emotional problems in childhood: A 14-year follow-up during childhood, adolescence, and young adulthood. *American Journal of Psychiatry, 160*(12), 2116–2121.

Rubin, K. H. (1993). The Waterloo Longitudinal Project: Correlates and consequences of social withdrawal from childhood to adolescence. In K. H. Rubin & J. B. Asendorph (Eds.), *Social withdrawal, inhibition, and shyness in childhood* (pp. 291–314). Hillsdale, NJ: Erlbaum.

Rubin, K. H., Chen, X., & Hymel, S. (1993). The socio-emotional characteristics of aggressive and withdrawn children. *Merrill-Palmer Quarterly, 39*, 518–534.

Rubin, K. H., Daniels, T., & Bream, L. (1984). Social isolation and social problem solving: A longitudinal study. *Journal of Consulting and Clinical Psychology, 52*, 17–25.

Salmon, K., & Pereira, J. K. (2002). Predicting children's response to an invasive medical investigation: The influence of effortful control and parent behavior. *Journal of Pediatric Psychology, 27*, 227.

Sanders, M. R., & Dadds, M. R. (1993). *Behavioral family intervention.* New York: Allyn & Bacon.

Scahill, L., Riddle, M., McSwiggin-Hardin, M., Ort, S. I., King, R. A., Goodman, W. K., et al. (1997). Children's Yale-Brown Obsessive Compulsive Scale: Reliability and validity. *Journal of the American Academy of Child and Adolescent Psychiatry, 36*, 844–852.

Silverman, W. K., & Albano, A. M. (1996). *Anxiety Disorders Interview Schedule for DSM-IV: Child version.* San Antonio, TX: Psychological Corporation.

Silverman, W. K., & Ginsburg, C. S. (1995). Specific phobia and generalized anxiety disorder. In J. S. March (Ed.), *Anxiety disorders in children and adolescents* (pp. 151–180). New York: Guilford Press.

Silverman, W. K., Kurtines, W. M., Ginsburg, G. S., Weems, C. F., Rabian, B., & Serafini, L. T. (1999). Contingency management, self-control, and education support in the treatment of childhood phobic disorders: A randomized clinical trial. *Journal of Consulting and Clinical Psychology, 67*(5), 675–687.

Silverman, W. K., Saavedra, L. M., & Pina, A. A. (2001). Test-retest reliability of anxiety symptoms and diagnoses with Anxiety Disorders Interview Schedule for DSM-IV: Child and parent versions. *Journal of the American Academy of Child and Adolescent Psychiatry, 40*(8), 937–944.

Spanier, G. B. (1976). Measuring dyadic adjustment. *Journal of Marriage and the Family, 38,* 15–28.

Spence, S. H. (1998). A measure of anxiety symptoms among children. *Behavior Research and Therapy, 36*(5), 545–566.

Spence, S. H., Donovan, C., & Brechman-Toussaint, M. (2000). The treatment of childhood social phobia: The effectiveness of a social skills training-based, cognitive-behavioral intervention, with and without parental involvement. *Journal of Child Psychology and Psychiatry and Allied Disciplines, 41,* 713–726.

Stewart, S. L., & Rubin, K. H. (1995). The social problem-solving skills of anxious-children. *Development and Psychopathology, 7,* 323–336.

Swedo, S. E., Rapoport, J. L., Leonard, H., Lenane, M., & Cheslow, D. (1989). Obsessive-compulsive disorder in children and adolescents: Clinical phenomenology of 70 consecutive cases. *Archives of General Psychiatry, 46,* 335–341.

Thomasgard, M., & Metz, W. P. (1999). Parent-child relationship disorders: What do the Child Vulnerability Scale and the Parent Protection Scale measure? *Clinical Pediatrics, 38,* 347–354.

Vance, A., Costin, J., Barnett, R., Luk, E., Maruff, P., & Tonge, B. (2002). Characteristics of parent and child-reported anxiety in psychostimulant medication naïve, clinically referred children with attention deficit hyperactivity disorder, combined type (ADHD-CT). *Australian and New Zealand Journal of Psychiatry, 36,* 234–239.

Vasey, M. W., & Dadds, M. R. (2001). *Developmental psychopathology of anxiety.* New York: Oxford University Press.

Velosa, J. F., & Riddle, M. A. (2000). Pharmacologic treatment of anxiety disorders in children and adolescents. *Child and Adolescent Psychiatric Clinics of North America, 9*(1), 119–133.

Von Korff, M., Eaton, W. W., & Keyl, P. M. (1985). The epidemiology of panic attacks and panic disorder: Results of three community surveys. *American Journal of Epidemiology, 122,* 970–981.

Warren, S. L., Huston, L., Egeland, B., & Sroufe, L. A. (1997). Child and adolescent anxiety disorders and early adjustment. *Journal of the American Academy of Child and Adolescent Psychiatry, 36*(5), 637–644.

Watson, J. B., & Rayner, R. (1920). Conditioned emotional reactions. *Journal of Experimental Psychology, 3,* 1.

Weisz, J. R., Weiss, B., Suwanlert, S., & Chaiyasit, W. (2003). Syndromal structure of psychopathology in children Thailand and the United States. *Journal of Consulting and Clinical Psychology, 71,* 375–385.

World Health Organization. (1994). International statistical classification of diseases and related health problems—10th revision. Geneva, Switzerland: Author.

CHAPTER 11

Posttraumatic Stress Disorder

ABBY H. FRIEDMAN, SARAH B. STEVENS, AND TRACY L. MORRIS

Unfortunately, traumatic events are common occurrences in the lives of individuals. Hurricane Katrina, the terrorist strikes of September 11, 2001, and the war in Iraq highlight the presence and impact of trauma on individuals and groups. Under some circumstances, the experience of a traumatic event can lead to a diagnosis of Posttraumatic Stress Disorder (PTSD), characterized by avoidance, numbing, and increased arousal to trauma-related stimuli. Though the diagnosis of PTSD was first described in the third edition of the *Diagnostic and Statistical Manual of Mental Disorders* (*DSM-III*; American Psychiatric Association, 1980), traumatic stress has been observed throughout the ages. Previous descriptions of "war neurosis," "shell shock" and "battle fatigue" were common in the lexicon of the armed forces following battles and other military efforts. Likewise, symptoms similar to the diagnostic criteria for PTSD have been detailed by Samuel Pepys, Charles Dickens, and Sigmund Freud.

According to the current edition of the *DSM*, the *DSM-IV-TR* (American Psychiatric Association, 2000), Criterion A for PTSD specifies that an individual *must experience or witness a traumatic event or events that involve actual or threatened death or physical injury to self or others.* Additionally, the person must experience intense fear, helplessness, or horror. Importantly, the *DSM* notes that children and adolescents may experience and express distress in a markedly different manner than adults, including the expression of distress through disorganized or agitated behavior. J. R. Davidson and Foa (1991) have described Criterion A as the "gatekeeper" of the PTSD diagnosis. A diagnosis of PTSD cannot be made without exposure to a traumatic event. Pfefferbaum (2005) provided a review of Criterion A events in children and adolescents, including natural events (hurricanes, tornadoes, and floods), illnesses, and man-made events (criminal acts, accidents, and war). There also is evidence suggesting an association between media coverage of violence and terrorism and PTSD (Pfefferbaum et al., 1999; Schuster et al., 2001).

In addition to the Criterion A event, a diagnosis of PTSD requires the presence of three core symptom clusters (i.e., reexperiencing symptoms, avoidance, and arousal). Reexperiencing symptoms (Criterion B) are persistent memories and images of the

264

event(s). These may take the form of dreams, thoughts, images, or flashbacks. Children, in particular, may be prone to recurrent nightmares, play reenacting, or distress at cues of the traumatic events (Donnelly & Amaya-Jackson, 2002; Scheeringa & Zeanah, 1995). For example, a child who experienced a motor vehicle crash may have frequent nightmares about the accident, become distressed at the sight of the car or location of the accident, or engage in play in which the accident is reenacted with toy cars.

Avoidance (Criterion C) is closely linked with reexperiencing symptoms, in that the individual persistently avoids certain stimuli associated with the trauma or has difficulty recalling aspects of the event. This avoidance extends to thoughts, feelings, and memories of the event(s). It is common for children and adolescents who have experienced trauma to display blunted affect, detachment, or numbing toward regular activities. It is important to note that a child's age and developmental level may affect the amount of information that the child is able to recall or recount. Some children may refuse to acknowledge the trauma at all. Older children or adolescents may express a sense of a foreshortened future, in which they have difficulty imagining an extended life.

Arousal (Criterion D) is commonly found in children and adolescents who have experienced trauma. Children may experience sleep disturbance, anger outbursts, and difficulty concentrating as a result of the trauma; likewise, somatic complaints, such as stomach pain and headaches, are often reported by younger children who may be unable to verbalize their cognitive distress. In addition to these difficulties, children may experience hypervigilance, a heightened attention toward environmental stimuli, appearing on guard or hyperactive, particularly in situations that are reminders of the traumatic event. They also may show an exaggerated startle response. These symptoms must be present for at least a month and must cause clinically significant distress.

EPIDEMIOLOGY AND ETIOLOGY

The prevalence of traumatic events and PTSD in adult populations has been examined through a variety of investigations. In a telephone survey of approximately 4,000 adult women, Resnick, Kilpatrick, Dansky, Saunders, and Best (1993) estimated that the lifetime prevalence rates for exposure to a traumatic event for women in the United States was close to 70%, with one third of the participants reporting sexual and/or physical assault and one half reporting multiple incidents of trauma. Breslau, Davis, Andreski, and Peterson (1991) and Norris (1992) found similar prevalence rates in community samples of adults, ranging from 40% to 70%. Resnick et al. reported population rates of lifetime PTSD ranging from 18% (those who experienced any trauma) to 38% (those who experienced physical assault); individuals exposed to crime were at a higher risk for developing PTSD. Fewer studies have examined prevalence rates of PTSD in children and adolescents. Giaconia et al. (1995) found that over 40% of adolescents had experienced at least one traumatic event by the age of 18, and lifetime prevalence rates of PTSD in children and adolescents have ranged from 3% (e.g., Garrison et al., 1995) to 8% (e.g., Cuffe et al., 1998).

Though comprehensive data on rates of PTSD among children is limited, a body of literature exists on the consequences of *specific* traumatic events, particularly natural disasters. Lonigan, Anthony, and Shannon (1998) assessed posttraumatic symptoms among children in Charleston, South Carolina, following Hurricane Hugo and found that 5.5% of their sample met criteria for PTSD and that prevalence rates increased as level of exposure increased. Russoniello et al. (2002) examined PTSD symptoms in children 6 months after Hurricane Floyd and found that 95% of the children surveyed experienced at least one symptom of PTSD, with 71% experiencing moderate to severe symptoms. The link between natural disasters and PTSD symptoms in children is well-established and has been demonstrated across several studies (e.g., Hsu, Chong, & Yang, 2002; McDermott, Lee, & Judd, 2005; Shannon & Lonigan, 1994; Vernberg, La Greca, Silverman, & Prinstein, 1996).

Several studies have examined the effects of illness and natural death on children and adolescents. Mintzer et al. (2005) found that 16% of adolescents who had undergone recent organ transplantation met full symptom criteria for PTSD, with an additional 14% meeting partial criteria. Taïeb, Moro, Baubet, Revah-Lévy, and Flament (2003) conducted a review of studies of childhood cancer and found that 2% to 20% of survivors met criteria for PTSD. Posttraumatic stress symptoms also have been found in children who have undergone bone marrow transplantation (Stuber, Nader, & Yasuda, 1991) and children who have sustained orthopedic injuries (Starr et al., 2004). In addition to personal illness, McClatchey and Vonk (2005) found that two-thirds of children who had experienced the sudden death of a family member had moderate to severe levels of PTSD symptoms. Parental death, in particular, has been linked to PTSD symptoms in children (Stoppelbein & Greening, 2000).

Motor vehicle crashes also have been implicated in the development of PTSD in children, particularly car and bus crashes (Keppel-Benson, Ollendick, & Benson, 2002; Landolt, Vollrath, Timm, Gnehm, & Sennhauser, 2005; Stallard, Salter, & Velleman, 2004; Zink & McCain, 2003). By far the most well-researched events with respect to PTSD and children are violent and criminal acts, such as sexual and physical abuse (Ackerman, Newton, McPherson, Jones, & Dykman, 1998; Deblinger, McLeer, & Atkins, 1989; Kiser, Heston, & Millsap, 1991; Linning, & Kearney, 2004; Runyon, Deblinger, Ryan, & Thakkar-Kolar, 2004), witnessing domestic violence (Jarvis, Gordon, & Novaco, 2005; Levendosky, Huth-Bocks, Semel, & Shapiro, 2002; Mertin & Mohr, 2002; Silva & Alpert, 2000), and community violence (Buka, Stichick, Birdthistle, & Earls, 2001; Horowitz, McKay, & Marshall, 2005; Pynoos & Nader, 1988).

DIAGNOSIS AND ASSESSMENT

Given the different developmental and social levels of children who have been exposed to traumatic events, assessing these symptoms in an appropriate and sensitive manner is paramount.

STRUCTURED INTERVIEWS

Seen as the gold standard with respect to assessment and diagnosis, structured and semi-structured interviews based on diagnostic criteria are highly beneficial to a complete understanding of PTSD symptomatology and degree of functional impairment related to traumatic events. In addition to interviewing the child regarding his or her symptoms, many structured interviews also have a parent or caregiver version in order to gain a comprehensive understanding of the behaviors and symptoms that children and adolescents may be experiencing. Despite the time-consuming nature of the assessment, interviews provide a thorough evaluation of symptoms.

The Anxiety Disorders Interview Schedule for Children (ADIS-IV-C/P; Albano & Silverman, 1996) is a structured interview specifically designed to assess anxiety disorders in children and adolescents. The ADIS-IV-C/P is a modification of the Anxiety Disorders Interview Schedule (ADIS), a structured interview designed to assess psychological disorders in adults. The ADIS-IV-C/P is based on diagnostic criteria from the *DSM-IV* and provides a comprehensive and logical structure to the assessment of anxiety disorders in children and adolescents. Clinicians and researchers can use the ADIS-IV-C/P to examine both child and parent perceptions of presenting symptoms, as well as the functions and patterns of anxious behavior. In addition to anxiety disorders, the ADIS-IV-C/P also includes sections for mood, externalizing, and other disorders, yielding a broad evaluation of diagnostic status. Kappa coefficients for the child and parent versions of the ADIS-IV ranged from good to excellent (.63 to .88), and test-retest reliability also fell in the excellent range (Silverman, Saavedra, & Pina, 2001). The Diagnostic Interview for Children and Adolescents (DICA; Earls, Smith, & Reich, 1988) assesses PTSD symptoms as well as other *DSM* diagnoses and can also be used as a semi-structured interview. Reich (2000) found variable test-retest reliability, ranging from fair ($\kappa = .23$) to excellent ($\kappa = .96$), and Yasik et al. (2001) reported an overall kappa of .94 for the DICA PTSD module. The Schedule for Affective Disorders and Schizophrenia for Children PTSD scale (K-SADS; Kaufman, Birmaher, & Brent, 1997) is a semi-structured interview based on *DSM* criteria; the PTSD module was found to have kappas of .67 for present diagnosis and .60 for lifetime diagnosis. The Diagnostic Interview Schedule for Children (Shaffer, Fisher, & Dulcan, 1996) is a highly structured interview also based on *DSM* criteria. Jensen (1995) reported moderate to excellent test-retest reliability, though the author noted higher kappa ranges for clinic populations (.38 to .86) as compared to community samples (.00 to .66). The Clinician Administered PTSD Scale for Children and Adolescents (CAPS-CA; Nader & Fairbanks, 1994) is a developmentally sensitive structured interview similar to the adult CAPS, which assesses the *DSM* PTSD symptom clusters. To date, no studies have examined the psychometrics of the CAPS-CA; however, the adult version of the instrument appears to have strong test-retest reliability (.77 to .96) and high convergent validity with the Structured Clinical Interview for the *DSM-IV*.

SELF-REPORT MEASURES

For school-age children and adolescents, self-report measures also may be used to supplement information gained through structured interviews, as well as provide information about therapeutic change. The Children's Impact of Traumatic Events Scale—Revised (CITES-R; Wolfe, Gentile, Michienzi, & Sas, 1991) is a 78-item Likert scale designed to assess the impact of trauma in children ages 8 to 16. However, the internal consistency averaged a relatively low .64, and correlations with other self-report measures were modest (Chaffina & Shultz, 2001). The Children's PTSD Inventory (Saigh et al., 2000) is a 43-item inventory based on *DSM-IV* criteria designed for 7- to 18-year-olds. The measure has demonstrated excellent internal consistency ($\alpha = .95$), high test-retest reliability ($\kappa = .87$), and excellent interrater reliability ($\kappa = .98$).

The Children's Posttraumatic Stress Reaction Index (CPTS-RI; Frederick, 1985) is a 20-item instrument based on *DSM-III* criteria used with children ages 8 and up. According to Nader, Pynoos, Fairbanks, and Frederick (1990), the CPTS-RI has been shown to have good internal consistency ($\kappa = .78$ to .83), as well as excellent interrater reliability (.94), and excellent interitem agreement ($\kappa = .88$). The Child PTSD Symptom Scale (Foa, Johnson, Feeny, & Treadwell, 2001) measures symptoms found in the clusters of the *DSM-IV* PTSD diagnosis, as well as functional impairment. The measure was found to have high internal consistency ($\alpha = .70$ to $.89$) as well as strong convergent validity with the CPTS-RI (Foa et al., 2001). The Trauma Symptom Checklist for Children (TSCC; Briere, 1996) is a 54-item report of symptoms associated with traumatic stress used with children and adolescents ages 8 to 16. The measure also contains two validity indices to assess under- and overreporting and has demonstrated high internal consistency ($\alpha = .82$ to $.89$). The TSCC has also been highly correlated with other measures of PTSD and related symptomatology, including the CITES-R (.60), Children's Depression Inventory (.45 to .73), and CBCL (.21 to .68).

Children and adolescents who have experienced traumatic events may also exhibit comorbid disorders, such as depression and other anxiety disorders, and may be more likely than controls to report somatic complaints. As such, it may be beneficial to collect self-report information with respect to such commonly co-occurring symptoms. Measures of child depression (e.g., Children's Depression Inventory; Kovacs, 1992), general anxiety (e.g., Multidimensional Anxiety Scale for Children; March, Parker, Sullivan, & Stallings, 1997), and broadband measures (e.g., Youth Self Report; Achenbach, 1991) often are helpful adjuncts to specific measures of PTSD symptomatology.

REPORT BY OTHERS

Information from caregivers and teachers may be used to supplement data obtained from children themselves. Many of the structured interviews listed earlier include parent versions to assess the diagnosis of PTSD (CAPS-CA, K-SADS, ADIS-IV-C/P). Several questionnaire measures have been created to obtain parent and teacher reports of child PTSD symptoms. The Parent-Report of Posttraumatic Symptoms (Greenwald & Rubin, 1999) is a 30-item report that is similar to the child report version and asks parents to rate symptoms of PTSD in their child on a 3-point scale. The PTSD Checklist— Parent Report (Ford et al., 2000) is another measure of child symptomatology based on parent report. In addition, broadband measures of child functioning may be completed by parents or teachers (e.g., Child Behavior Checklist [CBCL]: Achenbach & Rescorla, 2001; Behavioral Assessment System for Children: Kamphaus, Reynolds, & Hatcher, 1999).

Observational assessment of children may also prove helpful in evaluating PTSD, particularly with regard to play activities. The *DSM-IV* authors note that children may engage in repetitive play that demonstrates themes or highlights certain aspects of the traumatic event. For example, a child involved in a motor vehicle accident may repeatedly crash toy cars or blocks together or pretend that an ambulance is coming. Parents, caregivers, and teachers may be particularly likely to report these kinds of repetitive play activities, as they often occur at home, school, or in private areas.

CONCEPTUALIZATION

PEER INFLUENCES

Social relationships play an important role in child development (e.g., Ladd & Troop-Gordon, 2003). Children who have experienced traumatic events may have difficulty with social functioning as a result of trauma symptoms, both in childhood and in later life. In an overview of PTSD literature, Yule (2001) found that children often withdraw from peers and family members following traumatic events and may experience difficulty in social functioning as a result of avoidance and shame. Giaconia et al. (1995)

examined social functioning at age 18 and found that children who had PTSD had significantly higher levels of interpersonal problems compared with those who had not experienced a traumatic event and those who had experienced a traumatic event but had not developed PTSD. These results were consistent with those found by J. R. Davidson, Hughes, and Blazer (1991), in which participants reported lower levels of subjective social support.

Bolton et al. (2004) found that effects of trauma on psychosocial functioning are mediated by psychopathology, with comorbid Major Depressive Disorder being associated with more difficulty in interpersonal relationships. Pynoos et al. (2004) examined group dynamics following traumatization and found that individuals who have experienced traumatic events may have difficulty identifying with those who have not experienced such an event, thus polarizing the individual. This polarization may have a significant impact on the social connectedness of the individual; children who experience traumatic events may feel that they are somehow different and thus begin to separate or de-identify with friends. In the case of children who had been victimized at day care, the children had difficulty identifying with children of similar ages who were not victimized, including their own siblings. There also is evidence suggesting that trauma in childhood and young adulthood can have ramifications in later life. Colman and Widom (2004) examined the effect of child abuse on adult relationships and found that victims of abuse reported higher rates of divorce, unfaithful sexual behavior, and cohabitation than controls. They were also twice as likely to leave their romantic partner.

There is evidence to suggest that PTSD may sometimes be a consequence of peer victimization. Lev-Wiese, Nuttman-Schwartz, and Sternberg (2006) examined peer rejection during childhood and adolescence and found that a third of participants reported experiencing social peer rejection and rated this rejection as their most traumatizing event. The isolation felt by these young adults contributed significantly to reports of PTSD symptomatology.

PARENTAL VARIABLES

Children are often with their parents at the time of a traumatic incident, and thus their parents also may suffer from PTSD. Research has shown that PTSD in children and adolescents is related to the severity of parental PTSD symptoms (e.g., Schreier, Ladakakos, Morabito, Chapman, & Knudson, 2005). Kilic, Ozguven, and Sayil (2003) demonstrated that child PTSD severity was related to parental PTSD severity in families exposed to an earthquake in Turkey and that family functioning was negatively impacted by PTSD symptomatology. Pretrauma parental psychopathology also has been associated with the development of PTSD in children and adolescents (e.g., Green et al., 1991).

Only limited research has evaluated the relation between parental modeling and PTSD. Studies have demonstrated that children's self-report of anxiety is related to how frequently parents express anxiety and fear (e.g., Gerull & Rapee, 2002; Muris, Steerneman, Merckelbach, & Meesters, 1996). Thus, children may imitate their parents' anxious behavior in response to traumatic situations, putting them at greater risk of developing PTSD. These studies point to the importance of targeting parents immediately after traumatic incidents for prevention and intervention. Additional research is needed concerning the effects of prevention and intervention programs delivered immediately after traumatic events.

Developmental Factors

Developmental factors play an integral role in understanding PTSD in children and adolescents. Posttraumatic reactions are a result of the interaction between various developmental factors and aspects of the trauma.

Age Age plays a role in determining how a child processes, copes with, and reacts to a traumatic event (e.g., Kaplow, Dodge, Amaya-Jackson, & Saxe, 2005; Stallard, Velleman, Langsford, & Baldwin, 2001). Younger children are more likely to exhibit avoidant behavior and repetitive play representative of trauma-related stimuli, and nightmares (see Pfefferbaum, 1997, for a review; Yule, Perrin, & Smith, 1999). Older children and adolescents are more likely to experience dissociative and reexperiencing symptoms, comorbid depression, and substance use (e.g., Carrion, Weems, Ray, & Reiss, 2002; Kilpatrick et al., 2003). Coping skills become more advanced with age, with adolescents demonstrating more adaptive coping than younger children (e.g., Fields & Prinz, 1997). Age also plays a role in determining risk of exposure to trauma. For example, school-age children and adolescents are more likely to be exposed to violence than infants and younger children (e.g., Pynoos, 1994).

Risk Factors Risk factors for the development of PTSD in children and adolescents include variables specific to the trauma, child, and family. Aspects of family functioning, parental psychopathology, and parental PTSD are discussed in detail in the section on Parental Variables. Specific to the trauma, the closer one is physically and emotionally (e.g., loss of loved ones), the greater the risk of developing PTSD (e.g., Pfefferbaum, 1997). Recent studies on the September 11th attacks demonstrated that greater physical and emotional proximity were related to higher probability of children developing PTSD (e.g., Brown & Goodman, 2005; Hoven et al., 2004).

Trauma-Related Variables Related to proximity is the severity or intensity of exposure to the trauma. Lonigan and Shannon (1994) demonstrated that children's reports of trauma severity were predictive of PTSD symptom severity. Further, Carlson and Dalenberg (2000) found that three aspects of an event increase the likelihood that it will elicit traumatic symptoms: lack of controllability, negative valence, and suddenness. Animal and human research has shown that distress is more likely when the organism has limited control over the situation (Abramson, Seligman, & Teasdale, 1978; Foa, Zinbarg, & Rothbaum, 1992). Likewise, an event is more likely to be perceived as negative, and to elicit fear, if it involves physical or emotional pain, injury, or death. The timing of an event is also salient, as events that occur suddenly may be more overwhelming than those that happen gradually. Further, Rojas and Pappagallo (2004) reviewed evidence suggesting that man-made traumas (e.g., kidnapping, torture, rape) result in higher rates of PTSD in children and adolescents than do natural traumas (e.g., earthquakes, hurricanes, tornadoes).

Pretrauma Variables Longitudinal studies have shown that children with preexisting psychological disorders are more likely to develop PTSD following exposure to traumatic events (e.g., Boney-McCoy & Finkelhor, 1996). For example, pretrauma anxiety disorders have been found to predict PTSD in children and adolescents (e.g., Saxe et al., 2005; Silva et al., 2000). With respect to sex, several studies have shown greater prevalence rates of PTSD for girls compared to boys (e.g., Groome & Soureti, 2004; Stallard et al., 2004). Inconsistent findings have been reported regarding ethnicity. Some studies have demonstrated statistically significant differences in prevalence rates of PTSD across children of different ethnic groups (e.g., La Greca, Silverman, Vernberg, & Prinstein, 1996), but other studies have found no such differences (e.g., Abram et al., 2004; Mintzer et al., 2005). Cross-study differences in how ethnicity, race, and culture are defined may account for inconsistent results.

Protective Factors   Although a traumatic experience is a necessary criterion, it is not sufficient for meeting diagnostic criteria for PTSD. Often, children are exposed to potentially traumatic events yet do not develop PTSD (see Silva & Kessler, 2004, for a review). Studies have demonstrated that children with strong social support (e.g., La Greca et al., 1996), positive parental figures (e.g., Punamaki, Quota, & El Sarraj, 2001), high intelligence (e.g., Quota, El-Sarraj, & Punamaki, 2001), and strong community support (e.g., Scott, Knoth, Beltran-Quiones, & Gomez, 2003) are less likely to develop PTSD. Overall, research has indicated that it is a combination of factors, rather than a single variable, that protects children and adolescents from developing PTSD (e.g., Freitas & Downey, 1998). Such research suggests a diathesis-stress pathway for resiliency: Protective factors and risk factors interact to determine the child's response to trauma. Research on resiliency to PTSD is a relatively new area, and further longitudinal and large group studies are warranted.

PHYSICAL FACTORS AFFECTING BEHAVIOR

Anxiety disorders in general are linked to a variety of health issues. Diagnostic criteria for anxiety disorders include physical symptoms and sensations, such as rapid heart beat, blushing, sweating, chest pains, dizziness or faintness, nausea, restlessness, and irritability. Research suggests that anxiety disorders in general, and the physiological symptoms underlying PTSD in particular, may further serve to exacerbate symptoms of PTSD. Symptoms such as increased heart rate, trembling and shaking, dizziness, and shortness of breath may influence sleep disturbance, concentration, and hypervigilance, leading to a vicious cycle of arousal and heightened distress (Falsetti & Resnick, 1997; Foa, Steketee, & Rothbaum, 1989).

There is considerable evidence suggesting that PTSD and trauma may adversely affect the physical health of individuals. Giaconia et al. (1995) found that adolescents with PTSD were 5 times more likely to rate their physical health as fair or poor compared to individuals who had not experienced a trauma. Likewise, individuals who had experienced a trauma but did not meet criteria for PTSD were twice as likely to rate their health as fair or poor. Adolescents with PTSD were 6 times more likely to have taken 3 or more sick days per month in the past year than individuals who had not experienced a trauma. Diagnoses of PTSD also were related to suicidality, with adolescents meeting criteria for PTSD being almost 11 times more likely to have attempted suicide than nontraumatized individuals.

Several studies have examined the effect of childhood trauma on physical health in adulthood. Farley and Patsalides (2001) found that women who had been physically and sexually abused as children were significantly more likely to endorse chronic problems in cardiovascular, immune, musculoskeletal, neurologic, reproductive, dermatologic, and urinary health than individuals in the matched control group. They also used significantly more prescription medications, visited medical clinics more, and endorsed more physical symptoms overall. A strong positive correlation was found between PTSD severity and physical symptoms. Similarly, Cloitre, Cohen, Edelman, and Han (2001) found that among women traumatized in childhood, PTSD was a significant predictor of lower perceived health, and trauma exposure was a predictor of medical distress.

Much of the effect of PTSD and trauma on physical health must be extrapolated from adult literature, as fewer studies have examined specific health impacts in childhood. In a clinical study, Koss, Woodruff, and Koss (1990) found that women who had been victimized visited medical professionals twice as much as nonvictimized women. Sutherland, Bybee, and Sullivan (1998) found that women who had been victims of violent crime were more likely to endorse chronic pain and somatic symptoms without medical cause, such as headaches and muscle aches. Although victimized women may be more likely to report physical health concerns, Robohm and Buttenheim (1996) found that they were less likely to have gynecological exams, which may adversely affect physical and reproductive health. This underutilization may be related to avoidance of stimuli associated with the trauma. Woods and Wineman (2004) found that only violent trauma contributed to long-term health outcomes in women, as women who reported nonviolent trauma were less likely to report physical problems.

Though a variety of research has shown that physical health in adulthood can be affected by trauma and PTSD in childhood, there is still a need to examine the effects of traumatic events, and PTSD in particular, on the physical health of children. Further prospective and longitudinal studies are needed to examine the changes in health status following a traumatic event, as well as whether therapeutic interventions ameliorate future health concerns.

DRUGS AFFECTING BEHAVIOR

PTSD is highly comorbid with substance use disorders, and though the child and adolescent literature is more limited than the adult literature, several large studies have highlighted this association. Giaconia et al. (2000) conducted a cross-sectional analysis of longitudinal data and found that adolescents with substance use disorders were significantly more likely to have experienced a Criterion A event and were 3 times more likely to meet a diagnosis of PTSD than those without a substance use disorder. Acierno et al. (2000) found that girls who had been sexually assaulted, physically assaulted, or witnessed domestic violence were twice as likely to smoke cigarettes. Using data collected from the national survey of adolescents, Kilpatrick et al. (2003) reported that traumatic events, particularly those involving interpersonal violence, were highly predictive of substance use disorders, even after controlling for family history.

Though some cursory links among trauma, PTSD, and substance use in childhood have been found, further research is needed to fully explore the impact of traumatic events on substance use and abuse. Longitudinal research may provide a greater understanding of the prevalence and function of substance use in children and adolescents with PTSD. Future studies should examine the development of substance use behaviors following a traumatic event to determine whether specific factors, such as type of trauma, social support, or comorbid disorders, are related to substance use and abuse.

GENETIC INFLUENCES

Recent studies have demonstrated that neurochemical, biological, and genetic factors play a role in the development of PTSD (see Yehuda, 1999, for a review). Twin studies have shed some light on the role of genetics. As much as 30% of the variance in PTSD symptoms may be accounted for by shared genetics in monozygotic twins (e.g., Stein, Jang, Taylor, Vernon, & Livesley, 2002; True, Rice, Eisen, & Heath, 1993). Further, studies have shown that Holocaust survivors with PTSD are more likely than Holocaust survivors who do not have PTSD to have children who develop PTSD following exposure to a trauma (e.g., Yehuda, Schmeidler, Giller, Siever, & Binder-Byrnes, 1998). It is exceedingly difficult to determine whether these findings are primarily a function of genetic variation, environmental variation, or a combination of these factors. For example, if genetic variation alone were responsible for the expression of the disorder, a 100% concordance rate would be expected for monozygotic twins (raised apart) following exposure to a traumatic event. However, as perfect concordance has yet to be observed in studies of PTSD, future studies of the etiology and course of the disorder will likely need to include both genetic and environmental variables.

LEARNING AND MODELING

Mowrer's (1947, 1960) two-factor learning theory has been invoked to describe the etiology of PTSD for several decades. The two factors include elements of both classical (respondent) and instrumental (operant) conditioning. The classical conditioning account begins with a neutral stimulus (e.g., an intersection). When the intersection is paired with screeching tires (an unconditioned stimulus, or generically, a loud sound that requires no previous conditioning to elicit arousal and fear) and is capable of eliciting conditioned arousal and fear (e.g., a pounding heart) even in the absence of screeching tires, a fear response or conditioned emotional response is the result. Research on classical conditioning has demonstrated that under most circumstances, the neutral stimulus must be paired with the conditioned stimulus repeatedly to reliably elicit the conditioned response. Mowrer acknowledged that the aversive nature of fear may motivate humans to behave in various ways to avoid such aversive states. The second factor in the theory, instrumental conditioning, plays a role in maintaining avoidant behavior. Mower suggested that behaviors that produce escape and avoidance are likely to be reinforcing (repeated) because they eliminate or prevent one from experiencing fear. A more thorough discussion of learning principles in the conceptualization of PTSD may be found in Freeman and Morris (1999).

CULTURAL AND DIVERSITY ISSUES

Cross-Cultural Research   Although PTSD has been observed across the globe, there is evidence suggesting that responses to disaster and other stressors may differ across cultures (Lechat, 1990). Many studies have focused on trauma related to natural disasters, such as earthquakes in Mexico, Japan, and China (de la Fuente, 1990; Joh, 1997; Zhang & Zhang, 1991), floods in Puerto Rico (Canino, Bravo, Rubio-Stipec, & Woodbury, 1990), and volcanic eruptions and earthquakes in Peru (Lima, Santacruz, Lozano, & Chavez, 1990). Other studies have examined the effects of violent crime and war. Some PTSD-like syndromes have been demonstrated in refugee populations from Vietnam (Mollica, Poole, Son, Murray, & Tor, 1997) and Palestine (Thabet &

Vostanis, 1999). Ahmad, Sundelin-Wahlsten, Sofi, Qahar, and von Knorring (2000) created a cross-cultural semi-structured interview to assess PTSD in a variety of populations. The Posttraumatic Stress Symptoms for Children was validated on child populations drawn from Iraq and Kurdistan and Sweden, and satisfactory levels of internal consistency, and excellent sensitivity and specificity were reported.

Multicultural Research   Most studies of PTSD have been conducted with predominantly European American samples. Only recently have we begun to examine the effects of traumatic events on multiethnic populations. Most of the available research on PTSD in diverse populations focuses on the effects of natural disaster. Following Hurricane Andrew in Florida, several investigations examined differential associations of race and ethnicity on PTSD symptoms. Garrison et al. (1995) obtained information from Hispanic, African American, and European American adolescents and found that, though the rates of PTSD symptoms were higher among minority individuals, differences were not statistically significant. Vernberg et al. (1996) also examined a multiethnic population. Although group differences were not initially apparent, follow-up assessment revealed that African American and Hispanic ethnicity were associated with higher levels of posttraumatic symptoms. It is anticipated that research on Hurricanes Katrina and Rita and other 2004 and 2005 storms will improve our understanding of the relation between ethnicity and PTSD.

Diversity also includes sexual orientation. Gay, lesbian, and bisexual individuals are at higher risk for hate crimes than heterosexuals and may also be victims of homophobia. According to the 1984 Gay and Lesbian Task Force report (National Gay and Lesbian Task Force, 1984) 19% of gay men and women had experienced a physical assault due to their sexual orientation, and 44% had been threatened with violence. Perhaps no incident has highlighted this issue more than the murder of Matthew Shepard, a gay teenager in Wyoming. Given the sensitive nature of questions regarding hate crimes, and antigay crimes in particular, Rayburn, Earleywine, and Davison (2003) used an unmatched count technique and reported that individuals admitted to engaging in higher levels of antigay hate crimes than had previously been reported; 5% of participants reported getting into a physical fight with a person due to sexual orientation, and 35% reported damaging the property of a gay individual. Bradford and Ryan (1988) found that 52% of lesbians reported verbal attacks regarding their sexual orientation, and 6% reported physical attacks. In a qualitative study, Noelle (2002) examined the impact of the Matthew Shepard murder on members of the gay, lesbian, and bisexual community and found that these individuals felt more unsafe and worried about their own physical safety in light of the event.

BEHAVIORAL TREATMENT

Controlled studies of treatments for PTSD in children and adolescents are a relatively recent development in the field. Research has indicated that interventions with exposure-based components are most effective (e.g., Smith, Perrin, & Yule, 1999). Exposure involves presentation of feared trauma-related stimuli, with the goal of habituation and a reduction in anxiety symptoms. Interested readers are referred to recent reviews of exposure-based treatments for PTSD in children and adolescents, including Ruggiero, Morris, and Scotti (2001) and Feeny, Foa, Treadwell, and March (2004).

Exposure-Based Procedures

In vivo exposure involves repeated exposure to actual trauma-related stimuli; imaginal exposure involves retelling or depicting (e.g., drawing) aspects of traumatic situations. Exposure often takes place in a gradual or hierarchical fashion, with the least feared situations presented first, and followed by repeated exposure until habituation. Following a decrease in anxiety and distress in the presence of each stimulus, the next feared stimulus in the hierarchy is presented. Few large group studies have been conducted specifically on in vivo and imaginal exposure therapies for PTSD.

Several large group studies have investigated the efficacy of PTSD treatment packages, which include imaginal and in vivo treatment components; however, in the absence of dismantling or component analysis studies, it is impossible to determine whether exposure or other aspects of the treatment package are responsible for positive treatment outcomes (e.g., Deblinger, Lippmann, & Steer, 1996; Deblinger, Steer, & Lippmann, 1999). In a small-N study, Albano, Miller, Cote, and Barlow (1997) used gradual imaginal and in vivo exposure presented in hierarchical fashion with a 6-year-old child who was attacked by a dog and her 7-year-old brother who witnessed the incident. Following treatment, the children no longer met criteria for PTSD, providing support for graduated exposure in reducing symptoms of PTSD in children and adolescents.

Flooding is prolonged or extended exposure to trauma-related stimuli that is usually presented during one session with the goal of habituation and anxiety symptom reduction. Rather than one session a week, flooding usually consists of prolonged consecutive sessions over a week-long or 10-day period. Because the nature of trauma-relevant stimuli makes it difficult to use in vivo flooding, imagery is often used during exposure sessions. Several clinical trials have demonstrated the efficacy of flooding for treating adults with PTSD (e.g., Foa, Rothbaum, Riggs, & Murdock, 1991; Keane, Fairbank, Caddell, & Zimmering, 1989; Marks, Lovell, Noshirvani, Livanou, & Thrasher, 1998). To date, no clinical trials or large group studies have been published on the efficacy of flooding for PTSD in children and adolescents. A number of case studies, however, have demonstrated that flooding may be an effective method for treating PTSD in children and adolescents who have experienced war-related trauma (e.g., Saigh, 1987a, 1987b, 1987c, 1989) and chemical disasters (e.g., Yule, 1998). These studies have demonstrated positive effects of flooding on PTSD symptoms. As the ability to generalize results from single-case designs is limited, larger group studies are necessary to further elucidate the efficacy of flooding for treating PTSD in children and adolescents.

Anxiety Management Training

Anxiety management training (AMT) was originally developed to reduce and manage stress (e.g., Veronen & Kilpatrick, 1982) and was later modified and empirically validated for reducing symptoms of anxiety in trauma victims (e.g., Foa et al., 1991, 1999). The AMT methods used to teach anxiety reduction include cognitive restructuring, relaxation training, biofeedback, and social skills training (e.g., Feeny et al., 2004; Meadows & Foa, 2000). Recent clinical trials have demonstrated positive treatment outcomes for the use of AMT for adults with PTSD (e.g., Foa et al., 1999; Pantalon & Motta, 1998). However, only one study has evaluated the efficacy of AMT for children with PTSD. Farrell, Hains, and Davies (1998) delivered 10 sessions of AMT to four children who had been sexually abused. The treatment sessions consisted of psycho-education, relaxation training, self-monitoring, cognitive restructuring, and exposure. All four children experienced decreases in PTSD symptoms according to self-report measures. These preliminary findings must be interpreted with caution given the small sample size. Additional studies are needed to replicate these promising results.

Eye Movement Desensitization and Reprocessing

Eye movement desensitization and reprocessing (EMDR) was developed by Shapiro (1995) and involves having clients imagine trauma-related stimuli while tracking the therapist's finger rapidly back and forth with their eyes. This method has been theorized to include both exposure and cognitive restructuring components. Findings have been somewhat controversial. Some studies have demonstrated positive treatment outcomes, but studies on EMDR for adults have shown a lack of support for the rapid eye movement component of the treatment (e.g., P. R. Davidson & Parker, 2001). One well-controlled clinical trial on EMDR was conducted with 32 children who met criteria for PTSD and demonstrated a reduction in anxiety and depressive symptoms, both immediately and 6 months following treatment (Chemtob, Nakashima, & Carlson, 2002). Studies by Oras, Cancela de Ezpeleta, and Ahmad (2004) and Puffer, Greenwald, and Elrod (1998) also have demonstrated reductions in PTSD symptoms for children treated with EMDR, though these studies were flawed (e.g., small samples, poor treatment integrity, no randomization to treatment or control groups). Future large-scale, well-controlled studies are needed to compare imaginal or in vivo exposure to EMDR for PTSD in children and adolescents. Of particular interest is whether EMDR represents an improvement over other exposure-based treatments and, specifically, the extent to which rapid eye movements are necessary to produce positive outcomes.

Parent Training

Aggressive, noncompliant, and defiant behavior commonly accompanies PTSD in children and adolescents and should be addressed in treatment with parents and other caregivers (e.g., Vogel & Vernberg, 1993). Although many well-controlled treatment studies have included parent training components, none has isolated these aspects to determine how effective behavioral management is for reducing anxiety and PTSD symptoms (e.g., March, Amaya-Jackson, Murray, & Schulte, 1998).

Child-Parent Therapy: Abuse-Related

A limited number of studies have examined the effect of behavioral treatment on the parent-child relationship following trauma, and those that have done so have focused primarily on trauma resulting from physical or sexual abuse. In such studies, reductions in PTSD symptoms and improvements in the parent-child relationship have been demonstrated (e.g., Cohen, Deblinger, Mannarino, & Steer, 2004; Cohen, Mannarino, & Knudsen, 2005; Deblinger et al., 1996, 1999; King et al., 2000; Trowell et al., 2002). The treatment packages evaluated in these investigations included one or more of the following treatment components: AMT, exposure, psychoeducation, coping skills, and parent training in behavioral management. Taken together, these studies have demonstrated behavioral treatment packages to be effective methods for reducing PTSD symptoms in children and adolescents with abuse-related trauma histories. Future studies should focus on investigating the efficacy of individual treatment components.

GROUP TREATMENTS

Group treatments may be especially beneficial for children and adolescents with PTSD and may allow clinicians to target large groups of individuals in crisis situations (see Feeny et al., 2004, for a review). Several well-controlled studies have been conducted on the efficacy of group-based behavioral treatments for PTSD in children and adolescents (e.g., Chemtob et al., 2002; Ehntholt, Smith, & Yule, 2005; Goenjian et al., 1997; March et al., 1998; B. D. Stein et al., 2003). Group interventions have largely been delivered in school settings. Despite several differences in treatments and methodology, all treatments contained one or more of the following components: psychoeducation, relaxation training, anger management, and exposure. Ehntholt et al. administered six sessions of a cognitive-behavioral therapy package to 26 children who had experienced war-related traumas. A wait-listed control group consisted of 11 children. Following treatment, children in the treatment group exhibited lower PTSD severity and fewer behavioral problems. Treatment gains were not maintained, however, at a 2-month follow-up assessment. Chemtob et al. assessed children exposed to Hurricane Iniki for PTSD: 248 second- to sixth-graders were randomly assigned to a manual-based individual or group treatment. Both groups evidenced a reduction in PTSD symptoms at treatment completion and 1 year following treatment. Children enrolled in the group treatment were more likely to complete treatment. Following an earthquake, 64 sixth- and seventh-graders participated in a study of an exposure-based intervention for PTSD 1.5 years after a magnitude 6.9 quake in Armenia (Goenjian et al., 1997). Thirty-five students from two schools received treatment, and 29 students from two other schools acted as controls. The treatment group received four group therapy sessions and approximately two additional individual therapy sessions over a 3-week period. Treatment group participants experienced a reduction in PTSD symptoms immediately following and 18 months after treatment. Taken together, these studies suggest that group-delivered behavioral treatments are effective for reducing symptoms of PTSD in children and adolescents.

MEDICAL TREATMENTS

PHARMACOTHERAPY

A number of open and clinical trials have been conducted on pharmacological interventions for PTSD in adults (for a review, see Marmar, Neylan, & Schoenfeld, 2002). Research on pharmacological interventions for PTSD in children (e.g., Donnelly, Amaya-Jackson, & March, 1999) has been much more limited. A small number of case studies and open trials have demonstrated reductions in PTSD symptoms over 8- to 24-week periods for children and adolescents on selective serotonin reuptake inhibitors (e.g., Seedat et al., 2002), tricyclic antidepressants (e.g., Robert, Blakeney, Villarreal, & Rosenberg, 1999), antipsychotics (e.g., Stathis, Martin, & McKenna, 2005), and beta blockers (e.g., Pitman et al., 2002). Although these medications may be beneficial for reducing symptoms of PTSD in children and adolescents, there also are several potential negative side effects to consider, including impaired daily functioning, drug interactions, and sedation (e.g., Efron & Oberklaid, 2003). Many pharmacological treatments for PTSD in children and adolescents have not yet been subjected to clinical trials and are not approved for use by the U.S. Food and Drug Administration.

It is important to note that many children who experience a trauma seek medical attention and receive services for PTSD from medical personnel. Despite a lack of clinical trials on the efficacy of pharmacological treatments for PTSD in children, one study demonstrated that as many as 95% of medical personnel prescribe medications to treat the disorder in children and adolescents (Cohen, Mannarino, & Rogal, 2001). Clinical trials are needed to evaluate the efficacy of pharmacological treatments for PTSD in children and adolescents. Further, longitudinal studies are needed to determine the long-term effects of such pharmacological interventions, and comparison studies are needed to evaluate the relative merit of pharmacological, behavioral, and combined treatment approaches.

Case Description

Background

Noah was a 12-year-old boy who lived with his foster parents and two other foster boys (ages 7 and 9 years). Noah resided with his biological mother and four younger half-siblings through age 10, at which time he was placed in the care of his biological father due to physical abuse, sexual abuse, and neglect in his mother's home. Following termination of his mother's parental rights, two of Noah's half-siblings were placed with their paternal grandmother; the other pair was placed in foster care and subsequently adopted. Approximately 18 months after placement with his father, Noah was removed from the home due to physical abuse and placed in foster care. At the time of intake, proceedings were under way to terminate his father's parental rights.

Noah's mother had an extensive history with social services. She gave birth to Noah, her first child, at age 16. She did not complete high school, nor had she ever obtained paid employment. Her romantic relationships were characterized as unstable and chaotic; her five children had been fathered by four men, none of whom she married. Prior to termination of her parental rights, she had been referred for mental health and parent education services. The case record indicated a history of polysubstance dependence, Major Depression, and Histrionic Personality Disorder. She was minimally cooperative with initial treatment efforts and later refused to participate in court-ordered family service recommendations. Noah's father had been involved with the juvenile justice system for antisocial behavior, including burglary and weapons possession, and had received court-ordered treatment for alcohol and cocaine abuse. At the time his son was placed in his care, he reportedly had maintained stable employment and sobriety for the previous 5 years.

Presenting Complaint

The case was referred through a consulting arrangement with a county Children and Youth Services (CYS) agency. Noah's caseworker was concerned that he was exhibiting problems related to his history of abuse and requested an evaluation to assist with recommendations for potential adoptive placement.

Noah's stature was small for his age. He was well groomed and appropriately dressed. He was soft-spoken and made minimal eye contact. He was cooperative with the examiner, responding to direct questions, but engaged in little spontaneous discussion. Noah's foster parents were interviewed separately. They reported that Noah had few friends and had difficulty getting along with his foster siblings. They stated that at times he appeared quite fearful and at other times extremely irritable and aggressive. Noah's grades in school were average to above average. He declined participation in all extracurricular opportunities, and his foster parents were growing increasingly concerned about his social isolation.

History

Due to the absence of direct information from his biological parents, Noah's history was obtained primarily through review of his CYS case file. Available medical reports indicated that his birth was uncomplicated and developmental milestones were met within normal limits. The CYS agency first became involved when Noah was an infant, due to reports from neighbors of deplorable housing conditions and suspected neglect. Over the years, CYS received several additional reports of suspected physical abuse and neglect. The majority of abuse reports were not substantiated, but concerns regarding housing conditions and Noah's mother's ability to parent her growing family necessitated the development of a family service plan and continued monitoring by CYS.

When Noah was 10 years old, the police were called to his home in response to a domestic disturbance. Upon arrival, the police found Noah's mother and her boyfriend embroiled in a violent physical battle. Noah's mother had returned home that evening and walked in on her boyfriend forcing Noah to perform oral sex. The two adults were taken to the police station, and CYS was called to take custody of the children. Subsequent medical evaluation indicated that Noah had been sodomized (likely on multiple occasions due to the extent of scarring) and tested positive for gonorrhea and chlamydia. X-rays also indicated a history of multiple fractures of both arms, for which previous medical treatment had not been obtained. Noah was seen by a crisis counselor, but the recommendation for further psychological treatment was not pursued once he moved from a temporary foster placement to his biological father's home.

Noah's father reported that his son was a "sissy" and he wished he would act more like a man. Noah frequently failed to meet his father's expectations, and the two frequently argued over chores. Noah did not get along well with his father's girlfriend or her three children who were living in the home. Noah's teachers observed bruising of his arms and face on several occasions, but when they inquired he shrugged it off as the result of accidents, such as falling off his bike. Six months prior to the most recent referral for services, Noah was absent from school for several days. Upon his return, he appeared to have difficulty using his right arm and appeared to be in pain. School officials made a report of suspected abuse to CYS. Noah's father and his girlfriend were interviewed, and

(continued)

the girlfriend acknowledged that Noah had been beaten by his father—but that it was justified, as Noah was a difficult child. Noah was placed in foster care. His father expressed no desire to have him return home and refused to participate in a family reunification plan. Given the state of affairs and pending criminal charges against Noah's father, CYS initiated proceedings to terminate parental rights and make Noah available for potential adoption.

Assessment

The Child Behavior Checklist (Achenbach, 1991) was completed by Noah's foster parents. Noah's Internalizing Behavior Scale score was in the clinical range, as were related subscales. No significant elevations were obtained for Externalizing Behavior.

Noah completed several self-report measures, including the Children's Depression Inventory (Kovacs, 1992), Multidimensional Anxiety Scale for Children (March et al., 1997), and Trauma Symptom Checklist for Children (Briere, 1996). The scores on each of these measures indicated that Noah was experiencing substantial arousal, fear, and social withdrawal.

In addition to questionnaires, the Anxiety Disorders Interview Schedule for Children (Albano & Silverman, 1996) was administered separately to Noah and his foster parents. Both sets of interviews indicated that Noah met criteria for PTSD. He was also experiencing substantial depression and social anxiety that appeared to stem from his abuse experiences.

Course of Treatment

As Noah was initially reserved and reluctant to discuss the details of his abuse history and current symptoms, considerable time was devoted to the establishment of rapport. Noah was seen weekly in 50-minute sessions. The first four sessions were devoted to establishing the parameters of the therapeutic relationship and facilitating free verbal exchange. Noah gradually became more comfortable discussing his thoughts, feelings, and behaviors with the therapist. He revealed that he had been plagued by nightmares for as long as he could remember and that during the day images of past beatings and forced sexual activity frequently interfered with his ability to concentrate. He worried that other children could tell he was "different" and would think he was gay, weak, or bad if they knew what had happened to him. He worried he would never have a girlfriend. He was embarrassed by being in foster care and ashamed of the mixed feelings he harbored about his biological parents.

Nineteen individual treatment sessions were conducted using a combination of anxiety management and exposure-based approaches. Anxiety management encompassed several empirically supported cognitive-behavioral strategies, including relaxation training, cognitive restructuring, and social skills training (Deblinger & Heflin, 1996; March et al., 1998). Treatment also incorporated graduated exposure to imaginal and in vivo stimuli (with a series of hierarchies constructed from Noah's reported fears). Imaginal exposure was used to address specific abuse-related stimuli, such as intrusive recollections of forced sexual activity, and in vivo exposure was used to address fears related to social interaction with adults and peers.

Concurrent with Noah's individual sessions focusing on exposure and anxiety management, eight biweekly sessions were held with Noah's foster parents focusing on contingency management and behavioral activation. A point system was implemented to facilitate Noah's compliance with household chores (goals were met within the second week of implementation and maintained throughout). To address concerns related to Noah's social isolation, his foster parents were coached to facilitate social activity. First, the foster family increased their rate of joint activities (preparing meals together, playing board games, fishing). Later, the foster father offered to coach Noah, his foster siblings, and several neighborhood children in playing softball. Eventually, with modeling and encouragement of his foster parents, Noah began to spontaneously invite peers to age-appropriate activities.

Approximately 6 months after the initial intake, treatment was terminated by joint agreement. Noah, his foster parents, and his caseworker all reported that they were pleased with the outcome and did not deem further treatment necessary at that time. Self- and parent report questionnaires were readministered during a termination session, and all scores had fallen to within normal limits.

Follow-Up

An advantage of consultancy arrangements with CYS is that ongoing social service involvement may provide therapists with follow-up information, which may not always be available through traditional outpatient therapy settings. One year after treatment termination, Noah continued to reside with his foster parents, who were taking steps to make the placement permanent. He was doing well in school (with all grades well above average), had made several friends, was participating in several extracurricular activities, and had taken his first girlfriend to a school dance. Though it is unreasonable to expect that the events of his early childhood have left no mark, there is every indication that with the support of his new family, Noah has a bright future ahead.

SUMMARY

Posttraumatic Stress Disorder is characterized by avoidance, numbing, and increased arousal to trauma-related stimuli. To qualify for a diagnosis, the individual must have been exposed to a traumatic event that involved actual or threatened death or serious injury and a clear threat to one's physical integrity. In children, the experience of intense fear can be inferred from disorganized or agitated behavior. Persistent reexperience of the traumatic event via intrusive distressing recollections or, in young children, via repetitive play is likely. Many children with PTSD also report recurrent distressing dreams or frightening dreams without recognizable content. In older children, dissociative flashback episodes may be experienced, whereas in young children, trauma-specific reenactment may occur. Intense psychological distress and persistent avoidance of internal or external cues that symbolize or resemble aspects of the traumatic event are also characteristic of PTSD. Numbing of general responsiveness (not present before the trauma), trauma-specific memory loss, diminished interest in activities, and hypervigilance are among a range of other possible symptoms. Finally,

PTSD symptoms must cause "clinically significant distress" or impairment in social, occupational, or other important areas of functioning and persist for at least 1 month.

Cognitive-behavioral conceptualizations of PTSD have emphasized that individuals have varying degrees of vulnerability to the development of PTSD symptoms, but certain characteristics of the trauma experience increase the risk of developing the full syndrome. Specifically, the intensity and frequency of exposure and proximity to the stimulus seem to be among the most prominent environmental factors influencing the onset of the disorder. Research exploring resiliency or protective factors for PTSD (e.g., social support, intelligence) are relatively new, and further longitudinal and large group studies are warranted.

Much has been learned about child and adolescent PTSD in the past quarter-century. Treatment packages for PTSD have included combinations of exposure, psychoeducation, coping skills, and parent-focused behavioral management training. Taken together, studies have demonstrated efficacy in reducing PTSD symptoms in children and adolescents with abuse-related trauma histories. Although pharmacotherapy for PTSD among children and adolescents may be common, the evidence base for such practices appears to be rather limited. Future studies should focus on investigating the efficacy of individual treatment components as well as examining the transportability of these interventions. Recent disasters and large-scale traumatic events have provided opportunities to learn more about how we react to trauma but have also revealed the limitations of our existing knowledge.

REFERENCES

Abram, K. M., Teplin, L. A., Charles, D. R., Longsworth, S. L., McLelland, G. M., & Dulcan, M. K. (2004). Posttraumatic stress disorder and trauma in youth in juvenile detention. *Archives of General Psychiatry, 61,* 403–410.

Abramson, L. Y., Seligman, M. E., & Teasdale, J. D. (1978). Learned helplessness in humans: Critique and reformulation. *Journal of Abnormal Psychology, 87,* 49–74.

Achenbach, T. M. (1991). *Child Behavior Checklist for ages 4–18.* Burlington: University of Vermont.

Achenbach, T. M., & Rescorla, L. A. (2001). *Manual for ASEBA school-age forms and profiles.* Burlington: University of Vermont, Research Center for Children, Youth, and Families.

Acierno, R., Kilpatrick, D. G., Resnick, H., Saunders, B., de Arellano, M., & Best, C. L. (2000). Assault, PTSD, family substance use, and depression as risk factors for cigarette use in youth: Findings from the national survey of adolescents. *Journal of Traumatic Stress, 13,* 381–397.

Ackerman, P. T., Newton, J. E. O., McPherson, W. B., Jones, J. G., & Dykman, R. A. (1998). Prevalence of posttraumatic stress disorder and other psychiatric diagnoses in three groups of abused children (sexual, physical, and both). *Child Abuse and Neglect, 22,* 759–774.

Ahmad, A., Sundelin-Wahlsten, V., Sofi, M. A., Qahar, J. A., & von Knorring, A. L. (2000). Reliability and validity of a child-specific cross-cultural instrument for assessing posttraumatic stress disorder. *European Child and Adolescent Psychiatry, 9,* 285–294.

Albano, A. M., Miller, P. P., Cote, G., & Barlow, D. H. (1997). Behavioral assessment and treatment of PTSD in prepubertal children: Attention to developmental factors and innovative strategies in the case study of a family. *Cognitive and Behavioral Practice, 4,* 245–262.

Albano, A. M., & Silverman, W. (1996). *Anxiety Disorders Interview Schedule for DSM-IV: Child version.* San Antonio, TX: Psychological Corporation.

American Psychiatric Association. (1980). *Diagnostic and statistical manual of mental disorders* (3rd ed.). Washington, DC: Author.

American Psychiatric Association. (2000). *Diagnostic and statistical manual of mental disorders* (4th ed., text rev.). Washington, DC: Author.

Bolton, D., Hill, J., O'Ryan, D., Udwin, O., Boyle, S., & Yule, W. (2004). Long-term effects of psychological trauma on psychosocial functioning. *Journal of Child Psychology and Psychiatry, 45,* 1007–1014.

Boney-McCoy, S., & Finkelhor, D. (1996). Is youth victimization related to trauma symptoms and depression after controlling for prior symptoms and family relationships? A longitudinal, prospective study. *Journal of Consulting and Clinical Psychology, 64,* 1406–1416.

Bradford, J. B., & Ryan, C. (1988). *National lesbian health care survey: Final report.* Washington, DC: National Lesbian and Gay Health Foundation.

Breslau, N., Davis, G. C., Andreski, P., & Peterson, E. (1991). Traumatic events and posttraumatic stress disorder in an urban population of young adults. *Archives of General Psychiatry, 48,* 216–222.

Briere, J. (1996). Treatment outcome research with abused children. *Child Maltreatment, 1,* 348–352.

Brown, E. J., & Goodman, R. F. (2005). Childhood traumatic grief: An exploration of the construct in children bereaved on September 11. *Journal of Clinical Child and Adolescent Psychology, 34,* 248–259.

Buka, S. L., Stichick, T. L., Birdthistle, I., & Earls, F. J. (2001). Youth exposure to violence: Prevalence, risks, and consequences. *American Journal of Orthopsychiatry, 71,* 298–310.

Canino, G. J., Bravo, M., Rubio-Stipec, M., & Woodbury, M. (1990). The impact of disaster on mental health: Prospective and retrospective analyses. *International Journal of Intercultural Relations, 22,* 431–452.

Carlson, E. B., & Dalenberg, C. J. (2000). A conceptual framework for the impact of traumatic experiences. *Trauma, Violence, and Abuse, 1,* 4–28.

Carrion, V. G., Weems, C. F., Ray, R., & Reiss, A. L. (2002). Toward an empirical definition of pediatric PTSD: The phenomenology of PTSD symptoms in youth. *Journal of the American Academy of Child and Adolescent Psychiatry, 41,* 166–173.

Chaffina, M., & Shultz, S. (2001). Psychometric evaluation of the Children's Impact of Traumatic Events Scale - Revised. *Child Abuse and Neglect, 25,* 401–411.

Chemtob, C. M., Nakashima, J., & Carlson, J. G. (2002). Brief treatment for elementary school children with disaster-related posttraumatic stress disorder: A field study. *Journal of Clinical Psychology, 58,* 99–112.

Cloitre, M., Cohen, L. R., Edelman, R. E., & Han, H. (2001). Posttraumatic stress disorder and extent of trauma exposure as correlates of medical problems and perceived health among women with childhood abuse. *Women and Health, 34,* 1–17.

Cohen, J. A., Deblinger, E., Mannarino, A. P., & Steer, R. A. (2004). A multisite randomized controlled trial for children with sexual abuse-related PTSD symptoms. *Journal of the American Academy of Child and Adolescent Psychiatry, 43,* 393–402.

Cohen, J. A., Mannarino, A. P., & Knudsen, K. (2005). Treating sexually abused children: 1 year follow-up of a randomized controlled trial. *Child Abuse and Neglect, 29,* 135–145.

Cohen, J. A., Mannarino, A. P., & Rogal, S. (2001). Treatment practices for childhood posttraumatic stress disorder. *Child Abuse and Neglect, 25,* 123–135.

Colman, R. A., & Widom, C. S. (2004). Childhood abuse and neglect and adult relationships: A prospective study. *Child Abuse and Neglect, 28,* 1133–1151.

Cuffe, S. P., Addy, C. L., Garrison, C. Z., Waller, J. L., Jackson, K. L., McKeown, R. E., et al. (1998). Prevalence of PTSD in a community sample of older adolescents. *Journal of the American Academy of Child and Adolescent Psychiatry, 37,* 147–205.

Davidson, J. R., & Foa, E. B. (1991). Diagnostic issues in posttraumatic stress disorder: Considerations of the DSM-IV. *Journal of Abnormal Psychology, 100,* 346–355.

Davidson, J. R., Hughes, D., & Blazer, D. G. (1991). Post-traumatic stress disorder in the community: An epidemiological study. *Psychological Medicine, 21,* 713–721.

Davidson, P. R., & Parker, K. H. (2001). Eye movement desensitization and reprocessing (EMDR): A meta-analysis. *Journal of Consulting and Clinical Psychology, 69,* 305–316.

Deblinger, E., & Heflin, A. H. (1996). *Treating sexually abused children and their nonoffending parents: A cognitive behavioral approach.* Thousand Oaks, CA: Sage.

Deblinger, E., Lippmann, J., & Steer, R. (1996). Sexually abused children suffering posttraumatic stress symptoms: Initial treatment outcome findings. *Child Maltreatment, 1,* 310–321.

Deblinger, E., McLeer, S. V., & Atkins, M. S. (1989). Posttraumatic stress in sexually abused, physically abused, and non-abused children. *Child Abuse and Neglect, 13,* 403–408.

Deblinger, E., Steer, R. A., & Lippmann, J. (1999). Two-year follow-up study of cognitive behavioral therapy for sexually abused children suffering posttraumatic stress symptoms. *Child Abuse and Neglect, 23,* 1371–1378.

de la Fuente, R. (1990). The mental health consequences of the 1985 earthquakes in Mexico. *International Journal of Mental Health, 19,* 21–29.

Donnelly, C. L., & Amaya-Jackson, L. (2002). Post-traumatic stress disorder in children and adolescents. *Pediatric Drugs, 4,* 159–170.

Donnelly, C. L., Amaya-Jackson, L., & March, J. S. (1999). Psychopharmacology of pediatric posttraumatic stress disorder. *Journal of Child and Adolescent Psychopharmacology, 9,* 203–220.

Earls, F., Smith, E., & Reich, W. (1988). Investigating psychopathological consequences of a disaster in children: A pilot study incorporating a structure diagnostic interview. *Journal of the American Academy of Child and Adolescent Psychiatry, 27,* 90–95.

Efron, D., & Oberklaid, F. (2003). Psychotropic medication for children: The pediatrician's dilemma. *Journal of Pediatrics and Child Health, 39,* 509–510.

Ehntholt, K. A., Smith, P. A., & Yule, W. (2005). School-based cognitive behavioral therapy group intervention for refugee children who have experienced war-related trauma. *Clinical Child Psychology and Psychiatry, 10,* 235–250.

Falsetti, S. A., & Resnick, H. S. (1997). Frequency and severity of panic attack symptoms in a treatment seeking sample of trauma victims. *Journal of Traumatic Stress, 10,* 683–689.

Farley, M., & Patsalides, B. M. (2001). Physical symptoms, posttraumatic stress disorder, and healthcare utilization of women with and without childhood physical and sexual abuse. *Psychological Reports, 89,* 595–606.

Farrell, S. P., Hains, A. A., & Davies, W. H. (1998). Cognitive behavioral interventions for sexually abused children exhibiting PTSD symptomatology. *Behavior Therapy, 29,* 241–255.

Feeny, N. C., Foa, E. B., Treadwell, K. R. H., & March, J. (2004). Posttraumatic stress disorder in youth: A critical review of the cognitive and behavioral treatment outcome literature. *Professional Psychology: Research and Practice, 35,* 466–476.

Fields, L., & Prinz, R. J. (1997). Coping and adjustment during childhood and adolescence. *Clinical Psychology Review, 17,* 937–976.

Foa, E. B., Dancu, C. V., Hembree, E. A., Jaycox, L. H., Meadows, E. A., & Street, G. P. (1999). A comparison of exposure therapy, stress inoculation training, and their combination for reducing posttraumatic stress disorder in female assault victims. *Journal of Consulting and Clinical Psychology, 67,* 194–200.

Foa, E. B., Johnson, K. M., Feeny, N. C., & Treadwell, K. R. H. (2001). The Child PTSD Symptom Scale: A preliminary examination of its psychometric properties. *Journal of Clinical Child Psychology, 30,* 376–384.

Foa, E. B., Rothbaum, B. O., Riggs, D. S., & Murdock, T. B. (1991). Treatment of posttraumatic stress disorder in rape victims: A comparison between cognitive-behavioral procedures and counseling. *Journal of Consulting and Clinical Psychology, 59,* 715–723.

Foa, E. B., Steketee, G., & Rothbaum, B. O. (1989). Behavioral/cognitive conceptualizations of post traumatic stress disorder. *Behavior Therapy, 20,* 155–176.

Foa, E. B., Zinbarg, R., & Rothbaum, B. O. (1992). Uncontrollability and unpredictability in post-traumatic stress disorder: An animal model. *Psychological Bulletin, 112,* 218–238.

Ford, J. D., Racusin, R., Ellis, C. G., Daviss, W. B., Reiser, J., Fleischer, A., et al. (2000). Child maltreatment, other trauma exposure, and posttraumatic symptomatology among children with oppositional defiant and attention deficit hyperactivity disorders. *Child Maltreatment, 5,* 205–218.

Frederick, C. (1985). Selected foci in the spectrum of post traumatic stress disorders. In L. J. Murphy (Ed.), *Perspectives on disaster recovery* (pp. 110–130). East Norwalk, CT: Appleton-Century-Crofts.

Freeman, K. A., & Morris, T. L. (1999). Explaining the effects of child sexual abuse: A behavior analytic conceptualization. *Journal of Child Sexual Abuse, 7,* 3–21.

Freitas, A. L., & Downey, G. (1998). Resiliency: A dynamic perspective. *International Journal of Behavioral Development, 22,* 263–285.

Garrison, C. Z., Bryant, E., Add, C. L., Spurrier, P. G., Freedy, J. R., & Kilpatrick, D. G. (1995). Posttraumatic stress disorder in adolescents after Hurricane Andrew. *Journal of the American Academy of Child and Adolescent Psychiatry, 34,* 1193–1201.

Gerull, F. C., & Rapee, R. M. (2002). Mother knows best: Effects of maternal modeling on the acquisition of fear and avoidance behavior in toddlers. *Behavior Research and Therapy, 40,* 279–288.

Giaconia, R. M., Reinherz, H. Z., Hauf, A. C., Paradis, A. D., Wasserman, M. S., & Langhammer, D. M. (2000). Comorbidity of substance use and post-traumatic stress disorders in a community sample of adolescents. *American Journal of Orthopsychiatry, 70,* 253–262.

Giaconia, R. M., Reinherz, H. Z., Silverman, A. B., Pakiz, B., Frost, A. K., & Cohen, E. (1995). Traumas and posttraumatic stress disorder in a community population of older adolescents. *Journal of the American Academy of Child and Adolescent Psychiatry, 34,* 1369–1380.

Goenjian, A. K., Karayan, I., Pynoos, R. S., Minassian, D., Najarian, L. M., Steinberg, A. M., et al. (1997). Outcome of psychotherapy among early adolescents after trauma. *American Journal of Psychiatry, 154,* 536–542.

Green, B. L., Korol, M., Grace, M. C., Vary, M. G., Leonard, A. C., Gleser, G. C., et al. (1991). Children and disaster: Age, gender, and parental effects on PTSD symptoms. *Journal of the American Academy of Child and Adolescent Psychiatry, 30,* 945–951.

Greenwald, R., & Rubin, A. (1999). Assessment of posttraumatic symptoms on children: Development and preliminary validation of parent and child scales. *Research on Social Work Practice, 9,* 61–76.

Groome, D., & Soureti, A. (2004). Post-traumatic stress disorder and anxiety symptoms in children exposed to the 1999 Greek earthquake. *British Journal of Psychology, 95,* 387–397.

Horowitz, K., McKay, M., & Marshall, R. (2005). Community violence and urban families: Experiences, effects, and directions for intervention. *American Journal of Orthopsychiatry, 75,* 356–368.

Hoven, C. W., Duarte, C. S., Ping, W., Erickson, E. A., Musa, G. J., & Mandell, D. J. (2004). Exposure to trauma and separation anxiety in children after the WTC attack. *Applied Developmental Science, 4,* 172–183.

Hsu, C., Chong, M., & Yang, P. (2002). Posttraumatic stress disorder among adolescent earthquake victims in Taiwan. *Journal of the American Academy of Child and Adolescent Psychiatry, 41,* 875–881.

Jarvis, K., Gordon, E., & Novaco, R. (2005). Psychological distress of children and mothers in domestic violence emergency shelters. *Journal of Family Violence, 20,* 389–402.

Jensen, P. (1995). Test-retest reliability of the Diagnostic Interview Schedule for Children (DISC 2.1): Parent, child, and combined algorithms. *Archives of General Psychiatry, 52,* 61–71.

Joh, H. (1997). Disaster stress of the 1995 Kobe earthquake. *Japan Psychologica: An International Journal of Psychology in the Orient, 40,* 192–200.

Kamphaus, R. W., Reynolds, C. R., & Hatcher, N. M. (1999). Treatment planning and evaluation with the BASC: The Behavior Assessment System for Children. In M. E. Maruish & N. J. Mahwah (Eds.), *The use of psychological testing for treatment planning and outcomes assessment* (2nd ed., pp. 563-597). Hillsdale, NJ: Erlbaum.

Kaplow, J. B., Dodge, K. A., Amaya-Jackson, L., & Saxe, G. N. (2005). Pathways to PTSD: Pt. II. Sexually abused children. *American Journal of Psychiatry, 162,* 1305–1310.

Kaufman, J., Birmaher, B., & Brent, D. (1997). Schedule for Affective Disorders and Schizophrenia for School-Age Children—Present and lifetime version (K-SADS-PL): Initial reliability and validity data. *Journal of the American Academy of Child and Adolescent Psychiatry, 36,* 980–988.

Keane, T. M., Fairbank, J. A., Caddell, J. M., & Zimering, R. T. (1989). Implosive (flooding) therapy reduces symptoms of PTSD in Vietnam combat veterans. *Behavior Therapy, 20,* 245–260.

Keppel-Benson, J. M., Ollendick, T. H., & Benson, M. J. (2002). Posttraumatic stress in children following motor vehicle accidents. *Journal of Child Psychology and Psychiatry and Allied Disciplines, 43,* 203–213.

Kilic, E. Z., Ozguven, H. D., & Sayil, I. (2003). The psychological effects of parental mental health on children experiencing disaster: The experience of Bolu earthquake in Turkey. *Family Process, 42,* 485–495.

Kilpatrick, D. G., Ruggiero, K. J., Acierno, R., Saunders, B. E., Resnick, H. S., & Best, C. L. (2003). Violence and risk of PTSD, major depression, substance abuse/dependence and comorbidity: Results from the national survey of adolescents. *Journal of Consulting and Clinical Psychology, 71,* 692–693.

King, N. J., Tonge, B. J., Mullen, P., Myerson, N., Heyne, D., Rollings, S., et al. (2000). Treating sexually abused children with post-traumatic stress symptoms: A randomized clinical trial. *Journal of the American Academy of Child and Adolescent Psychiatry, 39,* 1347–1355.

Kiser, L. J., Heston, J., & Millsap, P. A. (1991). Physical and sexual abuse in childhood: Relationship with post-traumatic stress disorder. *Journal of the American Academy of Child and Adolescent Psychiatry, 30,* 776–783.

Koss, M. P., Woodruff, W. J., & Koss, P. G. (1990). Relation of criminal victimization to health perceptions among women medical patients. *Journal of Consulting and Clinical Psychology, 58,* 147–152.

Kovacs, M. (1992). *Children's Depression Inventory.* North Tonawanda, NY: Multi-Health Systems.

Ladd, G. W., & Troop-Gordon, W. (2003). The role of chronic peer difficulties in the development of children's psychological adjustment problems. *Child Development, 74,* 1344–1367.

La Greca, A. M., Silverman, W. K., Vernberg, E. M., & Prinstein, M. J. (1996). Symptoms of posttraumatic stress in children after Hurricane Andrew: A prospective study. *Journal of Consulting and Clinical Psychology, 64,* 712–723.

Landolt, M. A., Vollrath, M., Timm, K., Gnehm, H. E., & Sennhauser, F. H. (2005). Predicting posttraumatic stress symptoms in children after road traffic accidents. *Journal of the American Academy of Child and Adolescent Psychiatry, 44,* 1276–1283.

Lechat, M. F. (1990). The public health dimensions of disasters. *International Journal of Mental Health, 19,* 70–79.

Levendosky, A. A., Huth-Bocks, A. C., Semel, M. A., & Shapiro, D. L. (2002). Trauma symptoms in preschool-age children exposed to domestic violence. *Journal of Interpersonal Violence, 17,* 150–165.

Lev-Wiesel, R., Nuttman-Schwartz, O., & Sternberg, R. (2006). Peer rejection during adolescence: Psychological long-term effects—A brief report. *Journal of Loss and Trauma, 11,* 131–142.

Lima, B. R., Santacruz, H., Lozano, J., & Chavez, H. (1990). Disasters and mental health: Experience in Colombia and Ecuador and its relevance for primary care in mental health in Latin America. *International Journal of Mental Health, 19,* 3–20.

Linning, L. M., & Kearney, C. A. (2004). Post-traumatic stress disorder in maltreated youth: A study of diagnostic comorbidity and child factors. *Journal of Interpersonal Violence, 19,* 1087–1101.

Lonigan, C. J., Anthony, J. L., & Shannon, M. P. (1998). Diagnostic efficacy of posttraumatic symptoms in children exposed to disaster. *Journal of Clinical Child Psychology, 27,* 255–267.

Lonigan, C. J., & Shannon, M. P. (1994). Children exposed to disaster II: Risk factors for the development of post-traumatic symptomatology. *Journal of the American Academy of Child and Adolescent Psychiatry, 33,* 94–107.

March, J. S., Amaya-Jackson, L., Murray, M. C., & Schulte, A. (1998). Cognitive-behavioral psychotherapy for children and adolescents with post-traumatic stress disorder following a single-incident stressor. *Journal of the American Academy of Child and Adolescent Psychiatry, 37,* 585–593.

March, J. S., Parker, J. D. A., Sullivan, K., & Stallings, P. (1997). Multidimensional Anxiety Scale for Children (MASC): Factor structure, reliability, and validity. *Journal of the American Academy of Child and Adolescent Psychiatry, 36,* 554–566.

Marks, I., Lovell, K., Noshirvani, H., Livanou, M., & Thrasher, S. (1998). Treatment of post-traumatic stress disorder by exposure and/or cognitive restructuring. *Archives of General Psychiatry, 55,* 317–325.

Marmar, C. R., Neylan, T. C., & Schoenfeld, F. B. (2002). New directions in the pharmacotherapy of posttraumatic stress disorder. *Psychiatric Quarterly, 73,* 259–270.

McClatchey, R. S., & Vonk, M. E. (2005). An exploratory study of posttraumatic stress disorder symptoms among bereaved children. *Omega: Journal of Death and Dying, 51,* 285–300.

McDermott, B. M., Lee, E. M., & Judd, M. (2005). Posttraumatic stress disorder and general psychopathology in children and adolescents following a wildfire disaster. *Canadian Journal of Psychiatry, 50,* 137–143.

Meadows, E. A., & Foa, E. B. (2000). Cognitive behavioral treatment for PTSD. In A. Y. Shalev, R. Yehuda, & A. C. McFarlance (Eds.), *International handbook of human response to trauma* (pp. 337–346). Dordrecht, The Netherlands: Kluwer Academic.

Mertin, P., & Mohr, P. B. (2002). Incidence and correlates of posttrauma symptoms in children from backgrounds of domestic violence. *Violence and Victims, 17,* 555–567.

Mintzer, L. L., Stuber, M. L., Seacord, D., Castaneda, M., Mesrkhani, V., & Glover, D. (2005). Traumatic stress symptoms in adolescent organ transplant recipients. *Pediatrics, 115,* 1640–1644.

Mollica, R. F., Poole, C., Son, L., Murray, C. C., & Tor, S. (1997). Effects of war trauma on Cambodian refugee adolescents' functional health and mental health status. *Journal of the American Academy of Child and Adolescent Psychiatry, 36,* 1098–1106.

Mowrer, O. H. (1947). On the dual nature of learning: A reinterpretation of "conditioning" and "problem-solving." *Harvard Educational Review, 17,* 102–148.

Mowrer, O. H. (1960). *Learning theory and behavior.* New York: Wiley.

Muris, P., Steerneman, P., Merckelbach, H., & Meesters, C. (1996). The role of parental fearfulness and modeling in children's fear. *Behavior Research and Therapy, 34,* 265–268.

Nader, K. O., & Fairbanks, L. A. (1994). The suppression of reexperiencing: Impulse control and somatic symptoms in children following traumatic exposure. *Anxiety, Stress and Coping: An International Journal, 7,* 229–239.

Nader, K. O., Pynoos, R. S., Fairbanks, L., & Frederick, C. (1990). Childhood PTSD reactions one year after a sniper attack. *American Journal of Psychiatry, 147,* 1526–1530.

National Gay and Lesbian Task Force. (1984). *Task force report on anti-LGBT violence and victimization.*

Noelle, M. (2002). The ripple effect of the Matthew Shepard murder. *American Behavioral Scientist, 46,* 27–50.

Norris, F. H. (1992). Epidemiology of trauma: Frequency and impact of different potentially traumatic events on different demographic groups. *Journal of Consulting and Clinical Psychology, 60,* 409–418.

Oras, R., Cancela de Ezpeleta, S., & Ahmad, A. (2004). Treatment of traumatized refugee children with eye movement desensitization and reprocessing in a psychodynamic context. *Nordic Journal of Psychiatry, 58,* 199–203.

Pantalon, M. V., & Motta, R. W. (1998). Effectiveness of anxiety management training in the treatment of posttraumatic stress disorder: A preliminary report. *Journal of Behavior Therapy and Experimental Psychiatry, 29,* 21–29.

Pfefferbaum, B. (1997). Posttraumatic stress disorder in children: A review of the past 10 years. *Journal of the American Academy of Child and Adolescent Psychiatry, 36,* 1503–1511.

Pfefferbaum, B. (2005). Aspects of exposure in childhood trauma: The stressor criterion. *Journal of Trauma and Dissociation, 6,* 17–26.

Pfefferbaum, B., Nixon, S. J., Krug, R. S., Tivis, R. D., Moore, V. L., Brown, J. M., et al. (1999). Clinical needs assessment of middle and high school students following the 1995 Oklahoma City bombing. *American Journal of Psychiatry, 156,* 1069–1074.

Pitman, R. K., Sanders, K. M., Zusman, R. M., Healy, A. R., Cheema, F., Lasko, N. B., et al. (2002). Pilot study of secondary prevention of posttraumatic stress disorder with propranolol. *Biological Psychiatry, 51,* 189–192.

Puffer, M. K., Greenwald, R., & Elrod, D. E. (1998). A single session EMDR study with twenty traumatized children and adolescents. *Electronic Journal of Traumatology, 3*(Article 6). Available from http://www.fsu.edu/~trauma/v3i2art6.html.

Punamaki, R., Quota, S., & El-Sarraj, E. (2001). Resiliency factors predicting psychological adjustment after political violence among Palestinian children. *International Journal of Behavioral Development, 25,* 256–267.

Pynoos, R. S. (1994). Traumatic stress and developmental psychopathology in children and adolescents. In R. S. Pynoos (Ed.), *Posttraumatic stress disorder: A clinical review* (pp. 65–98). Baltimore: Siridian Press.

Pynoos, R. S., & Nader, K. (1988). Psychological first aid and treatment approach to children exposed to community violence: Research implications. *Journal of Traumatic Stress, 1,* 445–473.

Pynoos, R. S., Steinberg, A. M., Dyb, G., Goenjian, A. K., Chen, S.-H., & Brymer, M. J. (2004). Reverberations of danger, trauma, and PTSD on group dynamics. In B. Sklarew, S. W. Twemlow, & S. M. Wilkinson (Eds.), *Analysts in the trenches: Streets, schools, war zones* (pp. 10–22). Hillsdale, NJ: Analytic Press.

Quota, S., El-Sarraj, E., & Punamaki, R. L. (2001). Mental flexibility as resiliency factor among children exposed to political violence. *International Journal of Psychology, 36,* 1–7.

Rayburn, N. R., Earleywine, M., & Davison, G. C. (2003). An investigation of base rates of anti-gay hate crimes using the unmatched-count technique. *Journal of Aggression, Maltreatment, and Trauma, 6,* 137–150.

Reich, W. (2000). Diagnostic Interview for Children and Adolescents (DICA). *Journal of the American Academy of Child and Adolescent Psychiatry, 39,* 59.

Resnick, H. S., Kilpatrick, D. G., Dansky, B. S., Saunders, B. E., & Best, C. L. (1993). Prevalence of civilian trauma and posttraumatic stress disorder in a representative national sample of women. *Journal of Consulting and Clinical Psychology, 61,* 984–991.

Robert, R., Blakeney, P. E., Villarreal, C., & Rosenberg, L. (1999). Imipramine treatment in pediatric burn patients with symptoms of acute stress disorder: A pilot study. *Journal of the American Academy of Child and Adolescent Psychiatry, 38,* 873–882.

Robohm, J. S., & Buttenheim, M. (1996). The gynecological care experience of adult survivors of childhood sexual abuse. *Women and Health, 24,* 59–76.

Rojas, V. M., & Pappagallo, M. (2004). Risk factors for PTSD in children and adolescents. In R. R. Silva (Ed.), *Posttraumatic stress disorders in children and adolescents: Handbook* (pp. 38–59). New York: Norton.

Ruggiero, K. J., Morris, T. L., & Scotti, J. R. (2001). Treatment for children with posttraumatic stress disorder: Current status and future directions. *Clinical Psychology, Science, and Practice, 8,* 210–227.

Runyon, M. K., Deblinger, E., Ryan, E. E., & Thakkar-Kolar, R. (2004). An overview of child physical abuse. *Trauma, Violence, and Abuse, 5,* 65–85.

Russoniello, C. V., Skalko, T. K., O'Brien, K., McGhee, S. A., Bingham-Alexander, D., & Beatley, J. (2002). Childhood posttraumatic stress disorder and efforts to cope after Hurricane Floyd. *Behavioral Medicine, 28,* 61–71.

Saigh, P. A. (1987a). In vitro flooding of an adolescent's posttraumatic stress disorder. *Journal Clinical Child Psychology, 16,* 147–150.

Saigh, P. A. (1987b). In vitro flooding of childhood posttraumatic stress disorder. *School Psychology Review, 16,* 203–211.

Saigh, P. A. (1987c). In vitro flooding of childhood posttraumatic stress disorders: A systematic replication. *Professional School Psychology, 2,* 135–146.

Saigh, P. A. (1989). The use of an in vitro flooding package in the treatment of traumatized adolescents. *Developmental and Behavioral Pediatrics, 10,* 17–21.

Saigh, P. A., Yasik, A. E., Oberfield, R. A., Green, B. L., Halamandaris, P. V., Rubenstein, H., et al. (2000). Children's PTSD Inventory: Development and reliability. *Journal of Traumatic Stress, 13,* 369–380.

Saxe, G. N., Stoddard, F., Hall, E., Chawla, N., Lopez, C., Sheridan, R., et al. (2005). Pathways to PTSD: Pt. I. Children with burns. *American Journal of Psychiatry, 162,* 1299–1304.

Scheeringa, M. S., & Zeanah, C. H. (1995). Two approaches to the diagnosis of posttraumatic stress disorder in infancy and early childhood. *Journal of the American Academy of Child and Adolescent Psychiatry, 34,* 191–201.

Schreier, H., Ladakakos, C., Morabito, D., Chapman, L., & Knudson, M. M. (2005). Posttraumatic stress symptoms in children after mild to moderate pediatric trauma: A longitudinal examination of symptom prevalence, correlates, and parent-child symptom reporting. *Journal of Trauma, 58,* 353–363.

Schuster, M. A., Stein, D. B., Jaycox, L. H., Collins, R. L., Marshall, G. N., Elliott, M. N., et al. (2001). A national survey of stress reactions after the September 11, 2001 terrorist attacks. *New England Journal of Medicine, 345,* 1185–1192.

Scott, R. L., Knoth, R. L., Beltran-Quiones, M., & Gomez, N. (2003). Assessment of psychological functioning in adolescent earthquake victims in Colombia using the MMPI-A. *Journal of Traumatic Stress, 16,* 49–57.

Seedat, S., Stein, D. J., Ziervogel, C., Middleton, T., Kaminer, D., Emsley, R. A., et al. (2002). Comparison of response to a selective serotonin reuptake inhibitor in children, adolescents, and adults with posttraumatic stress disorder. *Journal of Child and Adolescent Psychopharmacology, 12,* 37–46.

Shaffer, D., Fisher, P., & Dulcan, M. K. (1996). The NIMH Diagnostic Interview Schedule for Children version 2.3 (DISC-2.3): Description, acceptability, prevalence rates, and performance in the MECA study. *Journal of the American Academy of Child and Adolescent Psychiatry, 35,* 865–877.

Shannon, M. P., & Lonigan, C. J. (1994). Children exposed to disaster: Epidemiology of posttraumatic symptoms and symptom profiles. *Journal of the American Academy of Child and Adolescent Psychiatry, 33,* 80–94.

Shapiro, F. (1995). *Eye movement desensitization and reprocessing: Basic principles, protocols, and procedures.* New York: Guilford Press.

Silva, R. R., & Alpert, M. (2000). Stress and vulnerability to posttraumatic stress disorder in children and adolescents. *American Journal of Psychiatry, 157,* 1229–1235.

Silva, R. R., Alpert, M., Munoz, D. M., Singh, S., Matzner, F., & Dummit, S. (2000). Stress and vulnerability to posttraumatic stress disorder in children and adolescents. *American Journal of Psychiatry, 157,* 1229–1235.

Silva, R. R., & Kessler, L. (2004). Resiliency and vulnerability factors in childhood PTSD. In R. R. Silva (Ed.), *Posttraumatic stress disorders in children and adolescents: Handbook* (pp. 18–37). New York: Norton.

Silverman, W., Saavedra, L., & Pina, A. (2001). Test-retest reliability of anxiety symptoms and diagnoses with the Anxiety Disorders Interview Schedule for DSM-IV: Child and parent versions. *Journal of the American Academy of Child and Adolescent Psychiatry, 40,* 937–944.

Smith, P., Perrin, S., & Yule, W. (1999). Cognitive behavior therapy for post traumatic stress disorder. *Child Psychology and Psychiatry Review, 4,* 177–182.

Stallard, P., Salter, E., & Velleman, R. (2004). Posttraumatic stress disorder following road traffic accidents: A second prospective study. *European Child and Adolescent Psychiatry, 13,* 172–178.

Stallard, P., Velleman, R., Langsford, J., & Baldwin, S. (2001). Coping and psychological distress in children involved in road traffic accidents. *British Journal of Clinical Psychology, 40,* 197–208.

Starr, A. J., Smith, W. R., Frawley, W. H., Borer, D. S., Morgan, S. J., Reinert, C. M., et al. (2004). Symptoms of posttraumatic stress disorder after orthopaedic trauma. *Journal of Bone and Joint Surgery, 86,* 1115–1121.

Stathis, S., Martin, G., & McKenna, J. G. (2005). A preliminary case series on the use of quetiapine for posttraumatic stress disorder in juveniles within a youth detention center. *Journal of Clinical Psychopharmacology, 25,* 539–544.

Stein, B. D., Jaycox, L. H., Kataoka, S. H., Wong, M., Tu, W., Elliot, M. N., et al. (2003). A mental health intervention for school children exposed to violence. *Journal of the American Medical Association, 290,* 603–611.

Stein, M. B., Jang, K. L., Taylor, S., Vernon, P. A., & Livesley, J. (2002). Genetic and environmental influences on trauma exposure and posttraumatic stress disorder symptoms: A twin study. *American Journal of Psychiatry, 159,* 1675–1681.

Stoppelbein, L., & Greening, L. (2000). Posttraumatic stress symptoms in parentally bereaved children and adolescents. *Journal of the American Academy of Child and Adolescent Psychiatry, 39,* 1112–1120.

Stuber, M. L., Nader, K., & Yasuda, P. (1991). Stress responses after pediatric bone marrow transplantation: Preliminary results of a prospective longitudinal study. *Journal of the American Academy of Child and Adolescent Psychiatry, 30,* 952–957.

Sutherland, C., Bybee, D., & Sullivan, C. (1998). The long-term effects of battering on women's health. *Women's Health Research and Gender Behavior Policy, 4,* 41–70.

Taïeb, O., Moro, M. R., Baubet, T., Revah-Lévy, A., & Flament, M. F. (2003). Posttraumatic stress symptoms after childhood cancer. *European Child and Adolescent Psychiatry, 12,* 255–264.

Thabet, A. A. M., & Vostanis, P. (1999). Post-traumatic stress reactions in children of war. *Journal of Child Psychology and Psychiatry, 40,* 385–391.

Trowell, J., Kolvin, I., Weeramanthri, T., Sadowski, H., Berelowitz, M., & Galsser, D. (2002). Psychotherapy for sexually abused girls: Psychopathological outcome findings and patterns of change. *British Journal of Psychiatry, 160,* 234–246.

True, W. R., Rice, J., Eisen, S. A., & Heath, A. C. (1993). A twin study of genetic and environmental contributions to liability for posttraumatic stress symptoms. *Archives of General Psychiatry, 50,* 257–264.

Vernberg, E. M., La Greca, A. M., Silverman, W. K., & Prinstein, M. J. (1996). Prediction of posttraumatic stress symptoms in children after Hurricane Andrew. *Journal of Abnormal Psychology, 105,* 237–248.

Veronen, L. J., & Kilpatrick, D. G. (1982, April). *Stress inoculation training for victims of rape: Efficacy and differential findings.* Paper presented at the 16th annual convention of the Association for the Advancement of Behavior Therapy, Los Angeles.

Vogel, J. M., & Vernberg, E. M. (1993). Task force: Pt. 1. Children's psychological response to disaster. *Journal of Clinical Child Psychology, 4,* 464–485.

Wolfe, V. V., Gentile, C., Michienzi, T., & Sas, L. (1991). The Children's Impact of Traumatic Events Scale: A measure of post-sexual abuse PTSD symptoms. *Behavioral Assessment, 13,* 359–383.

Woods, S. J., & Wineman, N. M. (2004). Trauma, posttraumatic stress disorder symptom clusters, and physical health symptoms in postabused women. *Archives of Psychiatric Nursing, 18,* 26–34.

Yasik, A. E., Saigh, P. A., Oberfield, R. A., Green, B. L., Halamandaris, P., & McHugh, M. (2001). The validity of the Children's PTSD Inventory. *Journal of Traumatic Stress, 14,* 81–95.

Yehuda, R. (1999). Biological factors associated with susceptibility to posttraumatic stress disorder. *Canadian Journal of Psychiatry, 44,* 34–39.

Yehuda, R., Schmeidler, J., Giller, E. L., Siever, L. J., & Binder-Byrnes, K. (1998). Relationship between posttraumatic stress disorder characteristics of Holocaust survivors and their adult offspring. *American Journal of Psychiatry, 155,* 841–843.

Yule, W. (1998). Posttraumatic stress disorder in children and its treatment. In T. W. Miller (Ed.), *Children of trauma: Stressful life events and their effects on children and adolescents* (pp. 219–243). Madison, CT: International Universities Press.

Yule, W. (2001). Posttraumatic stress disorder in the general population and in children. *Journal of Clinical Psychiatry, 62,* 23–28.

Yule, W., Perrin, S., & Smith, P. (1999). Post-traumatic stress reactions in children and adolescents. In W. Yule (Ed.), *Post-traumatic stress disorders: Concepts and therapy* (pp. 25–50). New York: Wiley.

Zhang, H., & Zhang, Y. (1991). Psychological consequences of earthquake disaster survivors. *International Journal of Psychology, 26,* 613–621.

Zink, K. A., & McCain, G. C. (2003). Posttraumatic stress disorder in children and adolescents with motor vehicle-related injuries. *Journal for Specialists in Pediatric Nursing, 8,* 99–107.

CHAPTER 12

Oppositional Defiant and Conduct Disorders

LEE KERN AND TALIDA STATE

DESCRIPTION OF THE DISORDERS

It is not uncommon for children to periodically engage in behaviors that are disruptive or oppositional in nature. In fact, such behaviors are observed at a relatively higher rate among preschool-age children and adolescents. At times, however, the behaviors persist, become unmanageable by others, and impair typical functioning at home or school. When this occurs, the clinical criteria for a diagnosis of Oppositional Defiant Disorder (ODD) or Conduct Disorder (CD) may be met. These disorders are characterized by a constellation of behaviors that range from acts of hostility and defiance to major violations of social norms and the rights of others. Although the *Diagnostic and Statistical Manual of Mental Disorders,* fourth edition, text revision (*DSM-IV-TR;* American Psychiatric Association, 2000) describes ODD and CD as distinct disorders, the high probability that children diagnosed with CD were previously diagnosed with ODD dictates that we consider these syndromes jointly in this chapter (see Mash & Wolfe, 2005).

To meet *DSM-IV-TR* diagnostic criteria, a child or adolescent must frequently engage in at least four behaviors that are negative, hostile or defiant. Specific behaviors and key features of the disorder are listed in Table 12.1. In addition, diagnosis requires that children and adolescents experience significant impairment in social or academic areas as a result of the behaviors.

To receive a diagnosis of ODD, behaviors must be chronic and persist for a period of at least 6 months. Thus, isolated incidents of defiance are not characteristic of the disorder. Indeed, many of the behaviors seen in ODD routinely occur among typical children and adolescents. Only when the frequency of the behaviors is excessive, particularly when compared with same-age peers of equivalent developmental level, is the diagnosis appropriate.

Conduct Disorder is characterized by more extreme violations of social norms than ODD. According to *DSM-IV-TR* criteria, there are four main categories of CD: aggression toward people or animals, destruction of property, deceitfulness or theft,

Table 12.1
Behavioral Characteristics of Oppositional Defiant Disorder

Key Features	Behavior
Negativistic, hostile, and defiant behavior	Often loses temper
	Often argues with adults
	Often actively defies or refuses to comply with adults' requests or rules
	Often deliberately annoys people
	Often blames others for his or her mistakes or misbehavior
	Is often touchy or easily annoyed by others
	Is often angry and resentful
	Is often spiteful or vindictive

and serious violations of rules. The following behaviors fall under aggression toward people or animals: (a) bullying, threatening, or intimidating; (b) initiating physical fights; (c) using a weapon; (d) physical cruelty to people; (e) physical cruelty to animals; (f) stealing while confronting a victim; and (g) forcible sexual activity. Destruction of property is composed of firesetting or deliberate property destruction. Deceitfulness or theft includes (a) breaking into another's house, building, or car; (b) lying with a deviant purpose; or (c) stealing property of value without victim confrontation. Serious rule violations are defined as (a) staying out at night without parental permission, beginning before age 13; (b) running away from home overnight; and (c) school truancy, beginning before age 13. More specific information is provided in Table 12.2.

To be diagnosed with CD, at least three of the behaviors listed in Table 12.2 must have been present during a 12-month period prior to diagnosis, and at least one in the previous 6 months. Typically, the behaviors occur across home, school, and community settings.

There are two subtypes of CD, depending on the age of onset. Childhood-onset CD is diagnosed if at least one of the behaviors needed for diagnosis occurs prior to 10 years of age. Adolescent-onset CD is diagnosed thereafter. Aggressive behavior toward others and problems with peer interactions are typical of individuals with an earlier age of onset. Generally, fewer aggressive behaviors and peer problems occur with the later onset, and problems are less likely to persist into adulthood.

Conduct Disorder is also classified according to three levels of severity. Mild CD describes behaviors that cause relatively minor harm to others, such as lying, being truant from school, or staying out after dark without parent permission. Moderate CD indicates intermediate levels of problem behaviors, such as vandalism or shoplifting. Severe CD is distinguished by the considerable harm the behaviors inflict on others; behaviors seen in this category include use of a weapon, breaking and entering, and forcible sexual acts.

A meta-analysis conducted by Frick and colleagues (1993) of over 60 factor analyses found both an overt-covert dimension and a destructive-nondestructive dimension of CD. Overt behaviors are those that are socially evident; covert behaviors are secretive and not readily observed by others. Destructive behaviors are physically damaging to another person or property, in contrast to nondestructive behaviors that produce no physical harm or damage. Behaviors characteristic of CD fall into one of four

Table 12.2

Behavioral Characteristics of Conduct Disorder

Key Features	Behavior	Examples
Aggression toward people and animals	Bullies, threatens, or intimidates	Repeatedly telling peers they will be hurt
	Initiates physical fights	Picking fights after school with others
	Has used a weapon that can cause serious physical harm	Using bat, brick, broken bottle, knife, or gun against another
	Has been physically cruel to people	Pinching or scratching sibling, attacking a peer
	Has been physically cruel to animals	Torturing an animal
	Has stolen while also confronting a victim	Mugging, purse snatching, extortion, armed robbery
	Has forced someone into sexual activity	Engaging in sexual assault, rape
Destruction of property	Has deliberately engaged in firesetting	Setting fire to a building with the intention of causing serious damage
	Has deliberately destroyed others' property (other than firesetting)	Smashing car windows, vandalism
Deceitfulness or theft	Has broken into someone else's house, building, or car	Breaking and entering
	Lies to obtain goods or favors or to avoid obligations	Cons others for own self-interest; lies to avoid debts
	Has stolen items of nontrivial value without confronting a victim	Shoplifting, check forging
Serious violations of rules	Stays out at night despite parental prohibitions, beginning before age 13	Refusing to return home late at night, after parent curfew
	Has run away from parental or parental-surrogate home	Running away overnight at least twice, or once without returning for a lengthy period
	Is often truant from school, beginning before age 13	Refusing to attend school without legitimate excuse for absence

dimensions. For example, aggressive behaviors lie within the overt-destructive dimension; oppositional behaviors are consistent with the overt-nondestructive dimension; violations of property represent the covert-destructive dimension; and browsing an adult entertainment website might fall within the covert-nondestructive dimension. These dimensions bear resemblance to the legal distinctions between violent offenses, property offenses, and status offenses.

Conduct problems characteristic of ODD and CD represent the most common referrals for mental health services for children. In a recent review of epidemiological studies on ODD and CD conducted between 1997 and 2001, Maughan, Rowe, Messer, Goodman, and Meltzer (2004) found prevalence rates of ODD ranging from 1.9% to 13.3% for boys and 1.0% to 9.4% for girls; prevalence rates for CD ranged from 1.7% to 14% for boys and 0.6% to 8% for girls. The significant variability in prevalence rates can be attributed to a number of factors, including the age of the population sampled and type of informant (Essau, 2003). For instance, parent reports and adolescent self-reports of the presence and severity of symptoms differ substantially, depending on symptoms considered. Also, *DSM* diagnostic criteria periodically change. For example, the most recent change in *DSM* criteria have resulted in a reduction in the CD incidence rate. By contrast, prevalence rates increase when latent symptoms are considered in addition to symptoms that are present at the time of diagnosis. Finally, different prevalence rates emerge in different settings, with public school programs for children with emotional and behavioral disorders reporting a higher prevalence of CD than alcohol and drug services, juvenile justice, mental health, or child welfare programs.

DIAGNOSIS AND ASSESSMENT

Differential diagnosis of both ODD and CD is difficult for a number of reasons. First, behaviors consistent with these disorders are not uncommon among typically developing children and adolescents. Diagnosis depends on the severity and persistence of behaviors as well as the extent to which they interfere with typical functioning. As a result, the criteria for diagnosis lack specificity. Second, there is considerable overlap in the behaviors meeting diagnostic criteria for a number of disorders delineated by the *DSM-IV*. For example, children may fail to follow directions because of hearing loss or language comprehension problems, which could be mistaken for oppositional behavior. Likewise, children with mood and psychotic disorders may engage in oppositional behaviors. As a rule, ODD and CD are not diagnosed if associated behaviors occur only during the course of another disorder. Third, psychiatric disorders can, and often do, co-occur. Most commonly, ODD co-occurs (i.e., is comorbid) with Attention-Deficit/Hyperactivity Disorder (ADHD) and mood disorders (e.g., depression).

For the reasons already described, accurate diagnosis should involve a multi-method approach to assessment, which can serve several purposes (McMahon & Frick, 2005). First, as noted, assessments generate information that can lead to or rule out a given diagnostic label (i.e., differential diagnosis). Second, assessment results can contribute to the development of an intervention plan. Third, periodic and recurring assessments can be used to evaluate the ongoing effectiveness of intervention strategies. In addition to multiple methods of assessment, multiple informants increase assessment reliability and offer a richer collection of perspectives, particularly when informants interact with the child in diverse settings.

There are four broad approaches to the assessment of ODD and CD. Interviews are commonly conducted with parents, other adults (e.g., teachers), and sometimes the children themselves, particularly if they are older. An interview should identify the specific problem behaviors and determine their history, duration, and intensity. Interviews may be either structured or unstructured. Structured interviews are generally more reliable for diagnostic purposes. Two commonly used structured interviews are the Diagnostic Interview Schedule for Children-IV (Shaffer, Fisher, Lucas, Dulcan,

& Schwab-Stone, 2000) and the Diagnostic Interview for Children and Adolescents (Reich, 2000). These interviews, available in child, parent, and teacher versions, are directly linked to the *DSM-IV* criteria for diagnosis of ODD and CD. Less structured interviews may also be used and, if conducted properly, can be useful for intervention planning and development. For example, less structured functional or behavioral interviews make it possible to determine the environmental conditions associated with occurrences (and nonoccurrences) of problem behaviors, which can be used to generate intervention strategies.

Although interviews can produce a wealth of valuable information, an individual's recollection of past events may be subject to bias, and some parents may even exaggerate their child's symptoms to obtain services. In addition, research suggests that symptom reporting declines as the structured interviews progress (Jensen, Wantanabe, & Richters, 1999). For these and other reasons, interviews are best used in conjunction with other assessment strategies.

A second approach to assessment is to obtain behavioral ratings. Rating scales differ from interviews in that they permit statistical comparisons that allow the examiner to determine the extent to which perceptions of a particular child's behaviors differ from perceptions of the behavior of children of similar age and same sex. The Behavioral Assessment System for Children (Reynolds & Kamphaus, 2004) is an example of a rating scale that assesses behavior problems consistent with ODD and CD, such as aggression, oppositional behavior, lying, and stealing. Other commonly used measures are the Achenbach System of Empirically Based Assessment (Achenbach & Rescorla, 2001), the Conners Rating Scales (Conners, 1997), the Early Childhood Inventory-4 (Sprafkin & Gadow, 1996), and the Revised Behavior Problem Checklist (Quay & Peterson, 1996). Both parent and teacher forms of the all of these rating scales are available, and child forms are available of all but the Revised Behavior Problem Checklist.

A third method of assessment is direct observation. Observations are most useful when they are conducted in natural settings, such as a child's school, home, or community, rather than a contrived setting such as a clinic, where children's behavior may be atypical. Direct observations can confirm the presence of behaviors associated with ODD or CD that are identified using pencil-and-paper or interview methods. In addition, more detailed information about environmental events that precede and follow incidents of problem behavior can be gathered, leading more directly to interventions. Finally, data regarding the frequency, duration, or intensity of behaviors can be collected pre- and postintervention to determine intervention effectiveness. A limitation of this method of assessment is that reactivity may occur. Specifically, children may behave in an atypical fashion when they become aware of being observed. Another limitation is that low-frequency or covert behaviors particularly common in CD, such as theft, property destruction, and curfew violations, are unlikely to be observed.

A final assessment strategy is record review. Many agencies, such as schools, law enforcement, and child protection services, collect information about occurrences of youth behavior problems. These records may assist in diagnosis by providing data about the frequency, duration, and intensity of behavior. The reports also can be used to validate information gathered during parent and teacher interviews. On occasion, this information may also be useful for intervention development. For example, school incident records may document that low-intensity, high-frequency aggression is most likely to occur during unstructured recess, providing important information about when to provide additional staff support or training.

CONCEPTUALIZATION

Underlying our conceptualization of ODD and CD is the notion that mental health outcomes reflect a complex interaction between biological and psychological factors, including external influences arising from environmental events. According to this perspective, certain personal characteristics, such as genetic vulnerability, may increase the likelihood that a child will be diagnosed with a particular disorder. However, the ways individual characteristics and environmental variables interact to produce ODD and CD are not well understood (Burke, Loeber, & Birmaher, 2002). The relation between these factors and the development of ODD and CD is further complicated by their frequent co-occurrence with other psychiatric conditions, such as ADHD, which may exacerbate symptoms. Researchers are just beginning to unravel the ways multiple disorders influence each other. The following sections offer a tentative discussion of some of the most compelling explanations of the emergence and maintenance of ODD and CD.

DEVELOPMENTAL ISSUES

Oppositional and defiant behaviors are a part of typical development in children and adolescents. Most, if not all, children are oppositional from time to time, disobeying adults, arguing, talking back, or even engaging in tantrums and destructive behaviors. These types of behavior typically abate. As noted, it is only when they are excessive and persist for periods of time greater than is typical for children of the same age and developmental level that they become a serious concern. When this happens, the behaviors begin to interfere with the child's learning, school adjustment, and social life.

Adolescence is a transitional period marked by physical and psychological changes. It is not uncommon for teenagers to question adult rules, expectations, and authority. However, when adolescents are disruptive and destructive, committing acts of aggression, truancy, lying, theft, or vandalism, a diagnosis of CD may be warranted. As suggested previously, a hallmark of the diagnosis is that these individuals often express little or no concern for the basic rights of others.

A number of theories have attempted to explain the pathways that lead from developmentally normative behaviors to persistent patterns of highly problematic behaviors. It is generally the case that less severe symptoms precede those that are more severe. Research by Speltz, McClellan, DeKlyen, and Jones (1999) found that ODD present in the preschool period places one at higher risk of developing CD in adolescence, especially when co-occurring with ADHD. Furthermore, many authors have hypothesized that problem behaviors of children and adolescents who later develop ODD begin in the toddler years (Keathley, 1995; Wahler, 1994). According to these accounts children experience difficulties learning to become autonomous and separating from emotional attachments with their parents. In struggling to keep their parents' attention, children exhibit behaviors that are perceived as problematic and are inadvertently reinforced. Although developmental factors obviously play an important role in the emergence and course of ODD and CD, once early behavior problems begin, environmental factors play a significant role in whether they will continue.

Learning and Modeling

Although research derived from learning theory has not tended to emphasize diagnostic status, decades of research has demonstrated that learning plays a considerable role in the development of behavior problems characteristic of ODD and CD. The family environment is considered particularly important for learning the negotiation and problem-solving skills that will be needed in future social interactions. For example, Martin (1981) emphasized the importance of early interactions between mother and child. Martin speculated that an irritable and demanding child coupled with an inconsistent or laissez-fare parenting style were antecedents of early coercive child behavior cycles. Mothers who were responsive and attentive to their children's needs were better able to establish a balance of power and control over their child and, as a result, had more compliant children. Conversely, children of uninvolved mothers were forced to become increasingly coercive during their first 3 years of life.

Building on the work of Martin (1981) and others in the social learning tradition, Patterson and his colleagues at the Oregon Social Learning Center (see Patterson, Reid, & Dishion, 1992) have offered one of the most compelling models of antisocial behavior to date. In a widely cited paper, Patterson, De Baryshe, and Ramsey (1989) argued that early manifestations of child behavior problems could result in the development of coercive interaction patterns in parent-child dyads. The conditioning process begins with the child's display of challenging and aversive behaviors (e.g., whining, arguing, or even physical aggression). Unskilled disciplinary tactics employed by the parent are thought to result in escalation of the intensity of the child's aversive behavior. If, following this escalation, the parent gives in or terminates demands for compliance, the child's antisocial behavior is reinforced. For example, when asked to pick up toys, a young child may tantrum and hit her mother. To terminate such unpleasant problem behavior, her mother may withdraw the request to clean up. In this way, the aggression and tantrum have been inadvertently reinforced by the parent (i.e., under similar circumstances the probability of aggression and tantrums is increased). With sufficient repetition, this pattern of interaction becomes coercive—the child has learned that antisocial behavior is likely to produce something desirable or facilitate escape from something undesirable—and the parent learns that by giving in, he or she can effectively terminate problem behaviors.

In a longitudinal study, Patterson, Capaldi, and Bank (1991) extended their earlier work, concluding that families often provide direct reinforcement of problem behaviors as well as expose children to antisocial behavior. Early manifestations of child problem behavior may be a result of parental responses and vice versa, producing escalating cycles of problem behavior. Through a process akin to shaping, periodic efforts by the parent to reassert control may actually increase the intensity of child antisocial behavior over time. Ultimately, children raised in these environments begin to exhibit coercive, antisocial behavior in other settings, such as school; this is thought to result in social problems and school failure (Patterson et al., 1992).

Many authors have emphasized the importance of the mutual influences the parent and child exert on one another (see Maccoby & Martin, 1983). For example, nonresponsive mothers are indifferent to and ignore their infant's cries, need for contact comfort, and efforts to establish proximity. Individual differences in infants, such as the rate and intensity of their demands, will also play a role in influencing maternal responses. That is, the more demanding the infant, the more avoidant the mother can become, rejecting the child's attempts at interaction.

Given training in antisocial behavior in the home environment, problem behavior may begin to appear in other settings. Children entering school for the first time often have limited experience interacting with same-age peers. Lacking the skills to negotiate conflict in socially appropriate ways, the child may engage in inappropriate behaviors, such as aggression. For example, when demanding that a peer share a toy, the child may strike the peer, causing the peer to surrender the object, inadvertently teaching the child that hitting is an effective way to obtain desired items. Likewise, in an effort to maintain an orderly classroom, teachers may directly reinforce problem behaviors by withdrawing demands when confronted by a child's challenging behavior. Moving beyond a direct contingency analysis, Bandura (1975) argued that children learn inappropriate behaviors by observing others engage in those behaviors, either directly or through avenues such as the media. Accordingly, when parents engage in antisocial or aggressive behaviors, children model those behaviors. For example, children may use the same aggressive tactics as their parents when dealing with others. Modeling of antisocial behavior also plays an important role in the development of antisocial behavior as conceptualized by Patterson and his colleagues (see Patterson et al., 1992).

PARENTAL ISSUES

An extensive body of literature has examined the influence of a child's family context on the development of ODD and CD. Specifically, researchers have focused on identifying characteristics of parents and families of children with ODD and CD that set them apart from parents and families of unaffected children. Research has consistently linked various dimensions of family functioning and parental characteristics to behavior problems. Variables found to be predictors of ODD and CD include low socioeconomic status (SES), parental psychopathology, parental criminality, parent-child interactions, and parental age.

Low SES has been frequently investigated as a potential risk factor for ODD and CD. For example, in a study examining the prevalence of CD, Cohen et al. (1993) concluded that higher rates of CD occur in children and adolescents residing in impoverished neighborhoods. These findings were replicated by Leventhal and Brooks-Gunn (2000), who found that low SES played a large role in externalizing problems in children. The relationship has been attributed to a variety of factors, including fewer educational, medical, and community resources, a higher rate of criminality and antisocial behaviors, substance abuse, and the presence of deviant groups in low-SES and urban neighborhoods. As a consequence, children growing up in impoverished areas are exposed to fewer protective factors that would reduce the risk of developing ODD and CD.

Parental psychopathology is another risk factor for disruptive behavior. Numerous studies have substantiated a link between parent and child dysfunction. In a study by Garbarino (2000), both parental ADHD status and parental psychopathology were positively correlated with children's development of CD. Higher rates of maternal antisocial behavior, histrionic behavior, and disturbed adjustment were found in mothers of children with CD (Lahey, Russo, Walker, & Piacentini, 1989), and maternal mood disorders and anxiety disorders have been associated with higher rates of ADHD and comorbid ODD/CD (Chronis et al., 2003). Paternal Antisocial Personality Disorder was also found to significantly predict comorbid CD among children with ADHD (Pfiffner, McBurnett, Rathouz, & Judice, 2005).

Specific forms of parental psychopathology, such as parent antisocial behavior, have been found to predict child antisocial behavior. Moreover, poor parenting practices appear to be repeated across generations (Capaldi, Pears, Patterson, & Owen, 2003; Smith & Farrington, 2004). Parent discipline tactics that are either very permissive or overcontrolling can lead to a variety of psychopathological symptoms in children. Studies have shown that children with ODD and CD often come from families characterized by poor supervision, ineffective and inconsistent parenting, frequent use of negative and harsh discipline, rigid and inflexible relationships, and a parental lack of interest and positive involvement in the child's life (Hollenstein, Granic, Stoolmiller, & Snyder, 2004; Pfiffner et al., 2005).

Another variable associated with an increased rate of both ODD and CD is parental substance and alcohol abuse (Loeber, Green, Keenan, & Lahey, 1995). Parental stimulant and cocaine dependence as well as alcohol abuse have been associated with a higher rate of ADHD and ODD/CD (Chronis et al., 2003).

LIFE EVENTS

Children with ODD and CD often experience multiple stressors in their lives, such as parental marital discord and divorce, death, or exposure to traumatic events. The specific ways these events impact the course of these disorders is still unclear. It is believed that such events can set the stage for the emergence of problem behaviors or can aggravate already present symptoms.

The role of marital discord and divorce on children's development has been the focus of extensive research. Meta-analyses by Amato and Keith (1991) and Amato (2001) indicated that children with divorced parents exhibited more behavioral and emotional problems, were generally more poorly behaved, and experienced more difficulties with interpersonal relationships compared to children who experienced parental death and those who lived in two-parent families. The mechanism through which divorce affects children, however, is unclear. Although it has been hypothesized that economic hardship resulting from lower income and fewer resources in a single-parent household might account for child behavior problems, Amato and colleagues concluded that there is weak support for this theory. Instead, it appears that marital distress can lead to frequent disagreements over child-rearing practices, damage to the parenting alliance, and inconsistent discipline practices (Jouriles et al., 1991). This is supported by research indicating that children in two-parent families with high marital discord exhibit considerably lower levels of well-being when compared to children in two-parent or divorced families with low levels of conflict (Amato, 2001; Amato & Keith, 1991).

The relationship between exposure to traumatic events and the occurrence of problem behaviors also has been explored. The clearest evidence indicates that being the victim of trauma in the form of assault, family and community violence, and sexual abuse is predictive of an ODD diagnosis (Ford et al., 1999). No such association has been found between events such as accidents, disasters, or illness and ODD. Although it is likely that exposure to a variety of stressful life events may contribute to the risk for ODD and CD in children, research has not delineated a clear path between them. Also, it is possible that ODD and CD in children and adolescents can increase the chance of stressful life events, rather than vice versa, given the presence of antisocial behaviors that characterize these disorders.

GENETIC INFLUENCES

As with other problems appearing in childhood and adolescence, evidence suggests that genetic and environmental factors interact to produce antisocial and aggressive behaviors, but these behaviors emerge only under environmental conditions in which they are supported or reinforced. Evidence for the role of genetics comes primarily from family, twin, and adoption studies. Studies of twins typically compare the rate of antisocial behaviors among monozygotic (MZ) or identical twins, sharing 100% of their genetic material, and dizygotic (DZ) or fraternal twins, who share only 50% of their genetic makeup. Higher rates of ODD or CD in MZ twins, relative to DZ twins, suggest stronger genetic influence on variation in the trait or characteristic. Similarly, adoption studies examine similarities between children who are adopted at birth (or at a very young age) and their biological and adoptive parents. For example, in a review of 12 twin and adoption studies focused on antisocial behavior, Mason and Frick (1994) found medium to large effect sizes in studies examining genetic influences. In these studies, approximately 50% of the variance in measures of antisocial behavior was attributed to genetic factors, with significantly larger estimates found for severe forms of antisocial behavior.

DiLalla (2002) reviewed family, twin, and adoption studies on offender behaviors. This review indicated that the presence of criminal behavior in both biological and adoptive parents increased the risk of criminality in children, supporting the role of environmental factors. Thus, they concluded that genetic influences did not fully explain the presence of criminal behavior. In an earlier review of six twin studies, DiLalla and Gottesman (1989) found high concordance for delinquency between both MZ (87%) and DZ (72%) twins. They concluded that these data offered additional support for an environmental, rather than genetic, etiology, at least for delinquent behavior.

Slutske, Cronk, and Nabors-Oberg (2003) analyzed seven behavioral genetic twin studies, conducted between 1995 and 2002, that focused on CD. The studies produced surprisingly divergent heritability estimates, ranging from as low as 7% to as high as 69%. The authors pointed to the complexity of such analyses and suggested that the variability may be explained by factors such as sex, age, or different CD subtypes. For example, research by Taylor, Iacono, and McGue (2000) suggests that environment may have a larger impact on antisocial and aggressive behavior as children age. Their findings indicated a greater genetic influence for early-onset delinquency compared to late-onset type; in part, this was attributed to the influence of peers on late-onset delinquency.

Collectively, these findings underscore the difficulty of determining the role of genetics in ODD and CD. One commonly cited problem is that twin studies do not control for similarity of environments and, on the other hand, that significant environmental differences exist between twins raised in the same family (i.e., nonshared environmental influences). In the past decade, twin research has become more refined, independently examining both shared family environmental factors, such as parent SES and parent psychopathology, and nonshared environmental factors, such as life events, peer influence, and different rearing practices. Another limitation common to both twin and adoption studies on antisocial behavior is the heavy reliance on parent report (DiLalla, 2002) in the majority of studies.

PEER INFLUENCES

Research concerning the influence of peer relations on development of ODD and CD has also been mixed. It was long held that children who engage in aggressive and antisocial behaviors are rejected by their peers (Dishion, French, & Patterson, 1995). Indeed, for many children with ODD and CD diagnoses, peer rejection may very well be common. Typically, antisocial children progress from early rejection by prosocial peers to later affiliation with deviant peer groups. The combination of peer rejection and association with deviant group places children and adolescents at greater risk for ODD and CD (Rutter, Giller, & Hagell, 1998).

Recent research, however, has identified subgroups of aggressive children who are not rejected by their peers (Adler & Adler, 1995, 1996). In fact, in some cases, aggressive behaviors function to establish dominance and social superiority over one's peers. Further, studies of social networks indicate that some aggressive children hold central positions within their peer groups and are considered among the most popular students in their class (e.g., T. W. Farmer, Farmer, & Gut, 1999). In sum, rejected or not, peer interactions tend to reinforce aggression and problem behavior (Atlas & Peplar, 1998). Peer affiliation and social position appear to play important roles in the development and maintenance of ODD and CD behaviors.

PHYSICAL FACTORS AFFECTING BEHAVIOR

Many studies have explored the potential link between physical factors and behaviors consistent with ODD and CD. To date, however, the research is far from conclusive. Although studies have determined that specific brain injuries, such as frontal lobe damage, are associated with aggressive dyscontrol (Brower & Price, 2001), there is no research suggesting that any specific injury reliably predicts aggressive and antisocial behavior.

Among young children, biological risk factors have received the most attention, and research has explored prenatal problems, early developmental exposure to toxins (e.g., cigarette smoke), physical damage to brain structures, atypical glucose metabolism, and underarousal. In a comprehensive review of this literature, Burke et al. (2002) concluded that there is no empirical evidence that implicates biological factors in the etiology of disruptive behavior disorders.

In addition to the aforementioned factors, a substantial literature has examined the role of neurotransmitters and neurochemicals in impulse control and aggression. The findings, however, have been mixed and also complicated by confounding variables. For example, Dabbs and Morris (1990) found that testosterone was associated with antisocial behavior, but the relation was moderated by socioeconomic status (SES). That is, although they found an association between testosterone levels and antisocial behavior, the correlation was not strong among higher SES subjects. Thus, it appears that the role of physical factors, if any, must be understood in relation to interactions between other environmental and sociological variables.

DRUGS AFFECTING BEHAVIOR

Substance abuse has been shown to be a primary factor influencing the emergence and development of ODD and CD. Several studies have documented a strong association between CD and substance abuse. Data from the National Longitudinal Youth Survey, summarized by Windle (1997), indicated that early adolescent antisocial behavior is a significant predictor of substance abuse, specifically alcohol-related problems, in late adolescence. Similarly, data from the Ontario Child Health Study (Boyle & Offord, 1991) indicated that CD was strongly associated with the use of tobacco, alcohol, marijuana, and hard drugs, according to adolescent self-report. This relationship also appears to extend to parental drug use. For example, Clark, Parker, and Lynch (1999) found that paternal substance use predisposed boys to increased antisocial disorders, and antisocial behavior disorders later led to substance-related problems in early adolescence.

The direction of the relationship between ODD/CD and substance use is unclear, but most likely is reciprocal. That is, substance abuse may precede, co-occur, or follow behavior problems characteristic of ODD and CD. Regardless, substance abuse exacerbates the problems associated with the disorders. It is of particular concern among adolescents, placing them at greater risk for delinquency and recidivism. Further, adolescents with CD who also abuse substances often develop more serious diagnoses, such as adult Antisocial Personality Disorder.

Cultural and Diversity Issues

Cultural and diversity issues play a role in many aspects of ODD and CD, including assessment and diagnosis, intervention, and interpretation of risk factors. Recent work has revealed that ethnic minorities are likely to be overidentified with disruptive behavior problems. Clearly, bias at least partly accounts for this fact. To illustrate, using vignettes of symptoms of ODD for African American, Caucasian, and racially unspecified children, Day (2002) examined rates of diagnosis, as well as confidence in their accuracy. The vignette describing an African American child received significantly more diagnoses of ODD compared to the other two groups, with clinicians also expressing more confidence in the diagnosis.

Another area of research has examined whether different parenting practices across cultural groups may influence the rate of ODD and CD. For example, given that physical punishment has been linked to higher levels of externalizing and aggressive behaviors in children, Deater-Deckard, Dodge, Bates, and Pettit (1996) compared this relationship across two different ethnic groups: European Americans and African Americans from a broad range of socioeconomic levels. Their findings suggested that the link between physical punishment as a disciplinary procedure and development of aggression in children may be culture-specific. That is, increased physical punishment was associated with higher levels of externalizing and aggressive behavior, but only for European American children. There were no significant correlations between physical discipline and externalizing behaviors for African American children. The findings of Deater-Deckard et al. were recently replicated (Lansford, Deater-Deckard, Dodge, Bates, & Pettit, 2004). Children's perception of discipline may play an important mediating role. According to Rohner, Kean, and Cournoyer (1991), parental use of physical discipline was predictive of future child maladjustment only when children equated it with parental rejection. This is consistent with research by Lansford et al. (2005), who examined cultural context as a moderator between physical discipline and children's adjustment. After interviewing 336 mother-child dyads from China, India, Italy, Kenya, the Philippines, and Thailand, they concluded that the perceived cultural normativeness or acceptability of physical discipline, particularly children's perceptions, moderated the association between this form of discipline and child aggression.

Cross-cultural studies also have examined and compared the prevalence of ODD and CD among ethnic groups living in and outside of the United States. Bird et al. (2001) studied Puerto Rican families residing on the island and Hispanics, African Americans, and Caucasians residing in the mainland United States. Their findings suggested lower rates of antisocial behavior among children residing in Puerto Rico compared with other ethnic subgroups residing in United States. This was the case in spite of the lower SES of the Puerto Rican sample.

Taken together, the available data indicate that many factors may account for the differences in prevalence rates across cultural groups, including cultural bias, perceptions of discipline, and family attachments. Caution must be exercised when interpreting parental behavior in a cultural context. Notwithstanding the importance of cultivating a richer understanding of cultural differences and community norms, practitioners must also carefully weigh the extent to which a given child-rearing practice may present an immediate danger to the health and welfare of a child.

BEHAVIORAL TREATMENT

A considerable evidence base suggests that behavioral interventions can effectively reduce behavior problems associated with CD and ODD (e.g., Webster-Stratton, Reid, & Hammond, 2004). Research also indicates that, rather than arbitrarily selecting an intervention, outcomes can be enhanced when selection is linked to the function or purpose the behavior serves for the individual (e.g., Newcomer & Lewis, 2004). That is, CD and ODD behaviors influence, and are influenced by, environmental events. Environmental events that precede problem behavior are referred to as antecedents. Consequences, by contrast, follow problem behaviors and may well maintain their occurrence. Assuming that the antecedents and consequences of antisocial behavior can be identified, interventions can be individually tailored to modify them. To isolate antecedents and consequences associated with problem behavior, practitioners rely on a method termed *functional behavioral assessment*. Functional behavioral assessment defines a process of gathering the information necessary to develop hypotheses specifying antecedents and consequences surrounding the problem behavior.

There are two basic approaches for gathering functional assessment information (Kern, O'Neill, & Starosta, 2005). The first approach uses *indirect methods*, so named because they rely on an individual's recall about past events. Interviews are the most common indirect method (Kern, Hilt, & Gresham, 2004). At a minimum, interviews should solicit information about the topography of problem behavior and frequency of occurrence. Interviews should also elucidate distal variables contributing to the behavior (e.g., skills deficits, risk factors), antecedent events, and potential sources of reinforcement. Interviews are best administered to adults most familiar with the child. Interviews administered to the child or adolescent may provide vital information about covert behaviors (e.g., stealing; e.g., Kern, Dunlap, Clarke, & Childs, 1994).

Record review is another source of indirect information. Records are routinely kept by agencies and individuals involved in the child's care, including mental health providers, psychiatrists and psychologists, schools, medical providers, and juvenile courts. Record review may reveal patterns of events related to problem behavior. For example, school records may reveal a history of school failure, indicated by poor grades or low standardized test scores, which may be related to patterns of school truancy. Likewise, psychiatric records sometimes point to traumatic events or recurring risk factors that are associated with aggressive behaviors, such as incarceration of a parent. Some functional information may also be gleaned from permanent products data. For example, disciplinary referrals, crisis intervention logs, and suspension reports can help to detect patterns of problem behaviors (e.g., difficulty in a particular class, fights with a certain peer). Finally, records sometimes describe past interventions and may inform current behavioral and pharmacological interventions.

The second approach to gathering functional assessment information is *direct methods.* Direct methods document problem behavior and associated events at the time they occur. In addition to documenting the behavior, it is critical to code environmental events occurring just prior to the behavior (antecedent events) and following the problem behavior (consequences). For instance, a behavior specialist might document the time of day that a student engaged in an aggressive episode, the activity or events taking place just prior to the aggression, the individual to whom the aggression was directed, and the consequences applied following the aggression.

Many formats have been used to conduct behavioral observations. Perhaps the most common tool is the ABC chart. This is simply a sheet of paper divided into three columns to document antecedents (A), behaviors (B), and consequences (C). Other assessment tools that may be used in functional assessments include the Functional Assessment Observation, checklists, scatter plots, and schedule analyses (described in Kern et al., 2005).

When conducting a functional assessment of children diagnosed with ODD and CD, it is generally prudent to employ multiple strategies of data gathering, including both direct and indirect methods. Multiple methods are employed to enable the clinician to assess the extent to which the information converges around a given functional hypothesis. Also, because children spend time in multiple settings, including home, school, and community, assessment and intervention efforts should involve persons from all of these contexts.

After indirect and direct assessment is complete, functional hypotheses are formulated. These statements provide a summary of the information collected by describing relevant (a) setting events, (b) antecedents, (c) the behavior, and (d) the presumed function the behavior serves. Most important, functional hypotheses serve as a link between the assessment and intervention plan (i.e., behavior support plan). By explicating the likely relations between environmental events and the problem behavior, they implicate classes of interventions most likely to be effective.

Several guidelines are useful for developing functional hypotheses. First, they should emerge from the data. Rather than being speculative, or diagnosis-driven, functional hypotheses are derived directly from data obtained from the child and those who interact with him or her most frequently. Functional assessments should also lead to interventions that clearly specify events that can be changed. For example, the observation that tantrums and subsequent suspensions are associated with the presentation of difficult class work suggests a number of possible intervention strategies, such as altering the type or amount of work assigned. By contrast, explanations that appeal to physiological states (e.g., excessive anger) do not facilitate an understanding of the events that play a role in triggering or maintaining the behavior and thus are not useful in a behavioral analysis. Again, functional assessments must yield intervention targets that can be manipulated.

Functional hypotheses generally appear in a format that sequentially lists the antecedent, the behavior, and the presumed function. An example of a functional hypothesis is *When parental attention is limited at home (antecedent), Ali steals items from her mother and distributes them at school (behavior) to obtain attention (function).* Another example is *When Ramón is asked to complete a difficult assignment (antecedent), he refuses to comply (behavior) to escape the work (function)*.

Distal or remote events can also influence the appearance of problem behavior. For instance, problems with a peer at a previous time, punishment by a parent the night before, or a fight on the morning school bus may play a role in the later occurrence of problem behavior. Unfortunately, because their relationship to problem behavior is not readily apparent, distal events are often overlooked. In addition, it is often difficult to document or track the occurrence of such events. Still, whenever relevant, remote or prior historical factors should be considered and included in a functional assessment.

After developing functional hypotheses, related interventions can be selected. Comprehensive intervention plans include four components. The first component is antecedent or setting event interventions. The purpose of this category of interventions is to prevent problem behaviors. To do so, antecedent events that evoke problem behavior are either eliminated or modified in some way. For example, in one of the previous examples, it was concluded that the absence of parental attention was an antecedent for Ali's stealing, which functioned to produce attention from others. In this case, Ali's single mother worked two jobs and often had to work overtime to provide for her family. Consequently, Ali was frequently home alone. Thus, an antecedent intervention was introduced where Ali's grandmother stopped by each morning to help her prepare for school. In addition, she enrolled in an after school sports program and then went directly to a neighbor's house, where she spent the evening until her mother returned from work.

There are numerous evidence-based antecedent interventions (see Kern, Choutka, & Sokol, 2002, for a review). For behaviors that serve the function of escaping from a task or activity, interventions include reducing the difficulty level of the task, offering a choice of tasks or choices embedded within a task, prepracticing difficult or new work, providing opportunities for periodic breaks, increasing preferred or interesting tasks and assignments, assuring that activities are functional or meaningful, and interspersing easy tasks among lengthy or more difficult tasks. For behaviors that function to get attention, adult or peer attention can be scheduled in some systematic way. For example, at school a counselor can check in with a student periodically throughout the school day. Peer attention can be arranged by organizing peer tutoring or cooperative learning experiences. Problem behaviors that produce access to activities or preferred items can be addressed by scheduling predictable access to the item or activity or providing warnings about when access to the item or activity will end.

The second component of a comprehensive intervention plan is alternative skill instruction. This involves teaching socially acceptable alternatives to engaging in problem behavior. Instruction may pertain to academic or social skill deficits. For example, because students with ODD and CD typically lag behind their peers academically (e.g., Nelson, Benner, Lane, & Smith, 2004), problem behaviors may result from academic difficulties. In fact, studies focused on interventions to improve academic skills have demonstrated collateral reductions in behavior problems (Sutherland & Wehby, 2001).

Likewise, interventions may target teaching appropriate social behaviors to replace problem behaviors that occur in the context of social interactions. For example, Kern, Ringdahl, Hilt, and Sterling-Turner (2001) determined that the function of aggressive behavior exhibited by a young boy with ODD was to obtain preferred toys. Intervention involved instruction to request access to a toy in a socially appropriate way. In addition, the child was taught to self-monitor his appropriate requests to share toys during play situations. The intervention successfully increased appropriate requesting and eliminated problem behavior.

The third component of an intervention plan is consequence strategies. This group of intervention strategies delineates how others will respond should problem behaviors occur. Consequences should be linked to behavioral function in a way that will not reinforce the problem behavior. Specifically, parents and teachers may develop uniform responses to problem behavior that are irrelevant or even contraindicated given the probable function of the behavior. For example, a parent may send an adolescent to her room when she begins arguing about requests to perform her household chores. Such a consequence may inadvertently reinforce arguing because the likely purpose or function of the arguing was to delay performance of chores or to escape from the task entirely. An effective consequence for arguing in this situation must ensure that arguing does *not* allow the child to escape task completion.

When selecting consequences for problem behavior, several additional guidelines should be considered. First, consequences sometimes escalate problem behavior, particularly with children and adolescents with ODD and CD. It is important to select a consequence that is likely to reduce future occurrences of the problem behavior while also minimizing the likelihood that immediate escalations will occur. Second, consequences that are natural or logical have a greater long-term impact than arbitrary and unrelated consequences. For example, repayment for property that an individual destroys is more natural and logical than removing privileges. Finally, whenever possible, responses that teach alternative appropriate behavior may encourage that behavior in the future. For instance, prompting an adolescent to negotiate or asking a child to brainstorm solutions to a problem allows him or her to practice more adaptive responses when confronted with similar challenges in the future.

The final intervention component is lifestyle changes. This group of interventions is the least empirically tested, and their role and impact is not fully understood, particularly with individuals with ODD and CD. Still, this important area should not be overlooked. Lifestyle interventions attempt to enhance the individual's quality of life. There is ample evidence that serious problem behaviors, including those associated with ODD and CD, are much more frequent when youth experience multiple risk factors (Mash & Wolfe, 2005). Although they come in many forms, risk factors common among this population include incarceration of a parent, lack of parental supervision, and parental drug and alcohol use. Because of the pervasive impact these types of events have on the lives of children and adolescents, it is critical to attempt to address them in some way. Although ideally risk factors should be eliminated, this often is not possible. Lifestyle interventions focus on reducing or ameliorating the impact that risk factors have on children. For example, identifying an adult mentor who is a positive role model with whom the student can spend time and in whom the student can confide may reduce the impact of an adverse family environment. Arranging for meaningful and enjoyable activities, such as participating on a sports team or taking music lessons, could also enhance an individual's general satisfaction with life and help mitigate other risk factors.

Successful outcomes are most readily accomplished when interventions are implemented across home, school, and community settings. When services are provided within multiple systems of care (e.g., mental health, juvenile justice, special education, medical), as is frequently the case for with individuals with ODD and CD, careful collaboration and coordination is necessary. Comprehensive interventions that are implemented in a coordinated manner can result in powerful and enduring changes.

MEDICAL TREATMENT

Pharmacological interventions are infrequently considered as a first-choice treatment for children and adolescents with ODD and CD. When medication is prescribed, it is usually in conjunction with psychosocial interventions. Although several medications have been evaluated, none has been demonstrated to be consistently effective in treating ODD and CD. Most often, medication is prescribed when ODD and CD occur with other disorders, such as ADHD or mood disorders.

Several reviews shed light on the use and effectiveness of medications for ODD and CD. In 1997, Steiner and Dunne summarized interventions for CD and concluded that there were no adequate controlled studies focusing on the efficacy of medication for individuals with CD and comorbid disorders. Farley, Adams, Lutton, and Scoville (2005) studied evidence-based treatments for ODD in preadolescents, concluding that no studies addressed the efficacy of medication for this age group diagnosed with ODD alone. Most of the research has investigated the efficacy of medication for children with ODD and comorbid ADHD. E. M. Z. Farmer, Compton, Burns, and Robertson (2002) reviewed interventions for childhood externalizing behavior disorders, particularly ODD/CD and ADHD. Although medium to large effect size changes were found, the medications were evaluated across very short periods of time. Together, these studies concluded that parent education and behavioral intervention produced the most positive outcomes for disruptive behavior disorders, whereas medication had an effect mostly on symptoms of ADHD.

A few recent studies have focused on risperidone for treating children with disruptive behavior disorders, primarily ODD, CD, and ADHD. Aman, Binder, and Turgay (2004) found that children receiving risperidone had clinically and statistically significant reductions in disruptive and hyperactive behaviors when compared to children receiving a placebo, with or without the concomitant use of psychostimulants. Again, however, the co-occurrence of ADHD makes it difficult to determine the effectiveness of the medication for ODD and CD alone.

In a larger, cross-cultural study including 32 sites in 12 countries across Europe, North America, and southern Africa, Croonenberghs, Fegert, Findling, De Smet, and Van Dongen (2005) reported that risperidone significantly reduced the severity of disruptive behavior, with few side effects. These authors concluded that additional research is needed to define the best pharmacological treatment for CD, but there is growing international consensus that risperidone is currently a first choice of medication for children with CD. At the same time, agreement continues that medication should be considered a supplement to enhance the effects of psychosocial interventions.

Case Description

To illustrate the nature and course of ODD/CD, along with assessment and intervention efforts, let us introduce Simeon. Simeon is a 12-year-old boy who attends his local public middle school. He is an only child and lives with his mother, Ms. Shores, who is divorced from his father. His mother recently sought assistance from a regional mental health clinic due to Simeon's escalating problem behaviors. Several serious issues at school and home heightened his mother's interest in accessing services. Simeon was recently suspended from school for threatening a peer with a tool during shop class. A parent-teacher meeting revealed that Simeon regularly bullied and attempted to intimidate his peers. He also was involved in several fights during the present school year on his way home from school. In addition, he refused to complete schoolwork and often disrespected his teachers. At home, Simeon had frequent "temper tantrums." During one tantrum, he smashed a window in his bedroom, and during another he broke several dishes.

The presence of behavior problems was not new to Simeon's mother. Minor behavior problems emerged around age 2. At that time, his parents described him as irritable and moody. Although he was frequently noncompliant, his parents sometimes could persuade him to follow requests by threatening to take away toys, activities, or privileges. At other times, they simply found it too draining to persist. Ms. Shores reported that Simeon's behavior problems escalated around age 4. This coincided with his father's increasing use of illegal drugs. Ms. Shores indicated that she was often preoccupied with her husband's drug problems, which sometimes included physical abuse toward her and Simeon. They divorced when Simeon was 6 years old. Following the divorce, Ms. Shores and Simeon moved to an apartment.

When Simeon entered school, his teachers noted that he was slow to complete assignments. As he graduated to the early elementary grades, slow assignment completion evolved into active refusal to initiate many academic activities. At the same time, his teachers noted increasing problems in peer interaction. Simeon's behavior toward his classmates was demanding and demeaning, and they began to actively reject him. He was unable to form any close friendships. When Simeon turned 8 years old, he was labeled by the school as having an emotional/behavioral disorder and began to receive school-based services.

The mental health facility where Simeon's family recently sought services embarked on a multimethod assessment. They began by conducting an informal interview with Simeon's parents, followed by a more formal interview (the Diagnostic Interview Schedule for Children-IV), which was administered to Simeon and his parents. Simeon, his parents, and his special education teacher also completed a rating scale, the Behavioral Assessment System for Children. To supplement the interview and rating scale information, direct observations were conducted at home and school. A functional assessment was also conducted, which included a review of records documenting behavioral incidents at school, as well as prior evaluations submitted by his family.

Collectively, the information obtained indicated that Simeon met the criteria for Conduct Disorder based on the presence of aggression toward people (bullying, intimidating, fighting) and destruction of property. Indeed, the rating scales indicated that his aggression exceeded the 90th percentile for boys of his age. A number of additional findings emerged from the assessment. First, educational assessments indicated that Simeon was functioning far below grade level in all academic areas. He was reading at the third-grade level and his math performance was at the fourth-grade level. Direct observations conducted at school indicated that most of Simeon's aggression and other problem behaviors

(continued)

occurred during academic activities. He also become aggressive during nonacademic activities (e.g., lunch, gym). Most of his aggression was directed toward a particular group of peers who taunted him and appeared to enjoy seeing him become upset.

Historical information suggested that Simeon was moody and temperamental at a very young age. His unwillingness to follow his parents' requests was reinforced when they failed to persist. Thus, at a young age he began to learn that problem behaviors allowed him to avoid doing things he did not want to do. This inconsistent approach to discipline probably exacerbated his problem behaviors. His growing pattern of aggressive behavior was most likely aggravated by his father's erratic conduct and violent behavior toward him and his mother. Simultaneously, Simeon's need for attention may have been ignored because of his mother's preoccupation with her husband's problems.

Simeon entered school without academic readiness skills. His early social adjustment at school entry was difficult. As an only child who experienced only limited peer contact prior to school entry, he was unable to successfully negotiate social situations. Throughout his school years, he continued to fall further behind, both academically and socially. He continued to employ aggressive behavior to escape from difficult work and unpleasant social interactions.

Intervention for Simeon focused on both home and school settings. The goal of his intervention was to teach him alternatives to aggression and problem behavior, improve his academic skills, and develop his appropriate social skills. At school, Simeon's teacher introduced the antecedent intervention of making certain that all academic assignments were matched to his skill level. In addition, specific, individualized, intensive skill instruction was scheduled during the school day and for 30 minutes after school to improve Simeon's reading and math fluency. A home program was developed for extra academic practice in the evenings. Simeon's mother was taught to use simple strategies, such as repeated readings, for 15 to 20 minutes nightly. To address problem behaviors that occurred during academics, Simeon was taught to recognize when he was feeling angry or frustrated using an emotion thermometer corresponding to high, moderate, and low levels of anger and frustration. Throughout the day, and particularly when his teacher noticed that he appeared to be getting upset, Simeon was prompted to label how he felt on the thermometer. Simultaneously, he was encouraged to engage in the socially appropriate replacement behavior of displaying a card on his desk indicating that he needed assistance with his work.

To address Simeon's peer problems, he was asked to select a peer with whom he would be comfortable practicing social skills. His selected peer, Terrance, agreed to discuss and role-play appropriate behavior based on scenarios the teacher had observed posed problems for Simeon. In addition, Terrance agreed to quietly remind Simeon of appropriate behaviors and responses during naturalistic situations. Simeon's gym teacher also began a positive peer reporting program, whereby students were rewarded for commenting on one another's appropriate behavior.

A counselor from the mental health clinic developed an intervention for the home. A schedule was developed to increase consistency in Simeon's home routine. The schedule allotted time on a daily basis for academic skill practice and homework, chores, and joint pleasurable activities with his mother. A corresponding incentive system was developed to reward Simeon with points for completing academic activities and chores and refraining from inappropriate behavior. Simeon's mother was encouraged to regularly acknowledge his appropriate behavior and schedule special outings when he earned a preplanned number of points.

Simeon's teacher and mother monitored his progress by noting the frequency of his problem behaviors both before and after the intervention was initiated. The data collected indicated that Simeon made slow but steady progress with continued implementation of the intervention strategies. After 6 months, problem behaviors were infrequent and were limited to minor events, such as complaining about a chore or academic task.

One complicating factor in Simeon's ongoing progress was his father's involvement. Throughout the first year of the plan, Simeon's father was incarcerated and had no contact with him. His incarceration ended the following year, and Simeon began to spend weekends and occasionally longer periods of time with him. His mother noticed that this coincided with an increase in problem behaviors in her presence. Simeon began to balk at completing homework and academics. Simeon's father agreed to use the schedule and incentive system when Simeon was with him. The consistency of chores and academic expectations, coupled with rewards for acceptable behavior, quickly resolved the problem.

The success of the intervention for Simeon can be attributed to its reliance on assessment information, implementation across settings, and consistent follow-through over time. The assessment information facilitated an identification of the underlying issues that contributed to Simeon's problem behavior, such as poor academic skills and inappropriate responses to difficult assignments and peer conflict. Armed with this information, the intervention plan directly targeted these problems by making environmental modifications (i.e., decreasing work difficulty), teaching appropriate behaviors (i.e., ways to get assistance) to replace problem behaviors, and remediating skill deficits. Further, introducing intervention across settings assured that plans were in place to address problem behaviors wherever they occurred. Consistency was enhanced when Simeon's mother and father both implemented the same intervention plan. Finally, sustained implementation of the plan assured continued progress, which was documented through ongoing data collection.

SUMMARY

Clinicians are advised to consider several issues when developing and implementing comprehensive interventions for children with ODD and CD. First, the underlying reasons or functions for behavior problems, particularly in older children and adolescents, may not be readily apparent. At times, assessments may be lengthy and require an analysis of data patterns and the convergence of information from multiple sources to arrive at reasonable hypotheses. In addition, problem behaviors that are not readily observable, such as those distinctive of CD (e.g., stealing, firesetting), may require soliciting information directly from students to fully understand variables related to the behavior. Whenever possible, behavioral assessment should be considered an ongoing process. As treatment progress is evaluated, intervention components are added or modified to increase the response to intervention. Second, interventions do not always result in immediate behavioral change, as Simeon's case illustrates. This is particularly so with older children who have long histories of reinforcement for problem behaviors. Also, in the case of skill deficits, such as academic and social problems, learning new behaviors takes time. It is important to persist, especially when behavior is changing in the desired direction. Finally, a team approach to intervention enhances the likelihood that intervention will be acceptable to all parties and will be implemented across settings.

Students should be aware that children and adolescents with ODD and CD often present myriad complex issues that include family problems, life events, academic challenges, and social difficulties. Unraveling these issues and determining the focus of intervention is a difficult process that can challenge even the most seasoned professional. Intervention for children and adolescents is also complicated by the fact that parents with significant problems, such as depression or drug dependence, often find it difficult to consistently implement interventions with their children. In such situations, multiple systems of care must be coordinated to maximize therapeutic outcomes.

REFERENCES

Achenbach, T. M., & Rescorla, L. A. (2001). *Manual for the ASEBA school-age forms and profiles.* Burlington: University of Vermont, Research Center for Children, Youth, and Families.

Adler, P. A., & Adler, P. (1995). Dynamics of inclusion and exclusion in preadolescent cliques. *Social Psychology Quarterly, 58,* 145–162.

Adler, P. A., & Adler, P. (1996). Preadolescent clique stratification and the hierarchy of identity. *Sociological Inquiry, 66,* 111–142.

Aman, M. G., Binder, C., & Turgay, A. (2004). Risperidone effects in the presence/absence of psychostimulant medicine in children with ADHD, other disruptive behavior disorders, and subaverage IQ. *Journal of Child and Adolescent Psychopharmacology, 14*(2), 243–254.

Amato, P. R. (2001). Children of divorce in the 1990s: An update of the Amato and Keith (1991) meta-analysis. *Journal of Family Psychology, 15*(3), 355–370.

Amato, P. R., & Keith, B. (1991). Parental divorce and the well being of children: A meta-analysis. *Psychological Bulletin, 110*(1), 26–46.

American Psychiatric Association. (2000). *Diagnostic and statistical manual of mental disorders* (4th ed., text rev.). Washington, DC: Author.

Atlas, R. S., & Peplar, D. J. (1998). Observations of bullying in the classroom. *Journal of Educational Research, 92,* 86–99.

Bandura, A. (1975). *Social learning and personality development.* New York: Holt, Rinehart and Winston.

Bird, B. J., Canino, G. J., Davies, M., Zhang, H., Ramirez, R., & Lahey, B. B. (2001). Prevalence and correlates of antisocial behaviors among three ethnic groups: Statistical data included. *Journal of Abnormal Child Psychology, 29*(6), 465–478.

Boyle, M., & Offord, D. R. (1991). Psychiatric disorder and substance use in adolescence. *Canadian Journal of Psychiatry, 36*(10), 699–705.

Brower, M. C., & Price, B. H. (2001). Neuropsychiatry of frontal lobe dysfunction in violent and criminal behavior: A critical review. *Journal of Neurology, Neurosurgery, and Psychiatry, 71*(6), 720–726.

Burke, J. D., Loeber, R., & Birmaher, B. (2002). Oppositional defiant and conduct disorder: Pt. II. A review of the past 10 years. *Journal of the American Academy of Child and Adolescent Psychiatry, 41*(11), 1275–1293.

Capaldi, D. M., Pears, K. C., Patterson, G. R., & Owen, L. D. (2003). Continuity of parenting practices across generations in an at-risk sample: A prospective comparison of direct and mediated associations. *Journal of Abnormal Child Psychology, 31*(2), 127–142.

Chronis, A. M., Lahey, B. B., Pelham, W. E., Kipp, H. L., Baumann, B. L., & Lee, S. S. (2003). Psychopathology and substance abuse in parents of young children with attention-deficit/hyperactivity disorder. *Journal of the American Academy of Child and Adolescent Psychiatry, 42*(12), 1424–1432.

Clark, D. B., Parker, A. M., & Lynch, K. G. (1999). Psychopathology and substance-related problems during early adolescence: A survival analysis. *Journal of Clinical Child Psychology, 28*(3), 333–341.

Cohen, P., Cohen, J., Kasen, S., Velez, C. N., Hartmark, C., Johnson, J., et al. (1993). An epidemiological study of disorders in late childhood and adolescence: Pt. I. Age- and gender-specific prevalence. *Journal of Child Psychology and Psychiatry, 34*(6), 851–867.

Conners, C. K. (1997). *Conners Rating Scales—Revised manual.* New York: Multi-Health Systems.

Croonenberghs, J., Fegert, J. M., Findling, R. L., De Smet, G., & Van Dongen, S. (2005). Risperidone in children with disruptive behavior disorders and subaverage intelligence: A 1-year, open-label study of 504 patients. *Journal of the American Academy of Child and Adolescent Psychiatry, 44*(1), 64–72.

Dabbs, J. M., & Morris, R. (1990). Testosterone, social class, and antisocial behavior in a sample of 4,462 men. *Psychological Science, 1*(3), 209–211.

Day, J. (2002). *The effect of race on the diagnosis of oppositional defiant disorder.* IL. (ERIC Document Reproduction Service No. ED470718). Information Analyses, Research Reports.

Deater-Deckard, K., Dodge, K. A., Bates, J. E., & Pettit, G. S. (1996). Physical discipline among African American and European American mothers: Links to children's externalizing behaviors. *Developmental Psychology, 32*(6), 1065–1072.

DiLalla, L. F. (2002). Behavior genetics of aggression in children: Review and future directions. *Developmental Review, 22*(4), 593–622.

DiLalla, L. F., & Gottesman, I. I. (1989). Heterogeneity of causes for delinquency and criminality: Lifespan perspectives. *Development and Psychopathology, 1*(4), 339–349.

Dishion, T. J., French, D. C., & Patterson, G. R. (1995). The development and ecology of antisocial behavior. In D. Cicchetti & D. J. Cohen (Eds.), *Developmental psychopathology: Vol. 2. Risk, disorder, and adaptation* (pp. 421–471). New York: Wiley.

Essau, C. A. (2003). Epidemiology and comorbidity. In C. A. Essau (Ed.), *Conduct and oppositional defiant disorders* (pp. 33–59). Mahwah, NJ: Erlbaum.

Farley, S. E., Adams, J. S., Lutton, M. E., & Scoville, C. (2005). What are effective treatments for oppositional and defiant behaviors in preadolescents? *Journal of Family Practice, 54*(2), 162–165.

Farmer, E. M. Z., Compton, S. N., Burns, J. B., & Robertson, E. (2002). Review of the evidence base for treatment of childhood psychopathology: Externalizing disorders. *Impact of childhood psychopathology interventions on subsequent substance abuse* [Special issue]. *Journal of Consulting and Clinical Psychology, 70*(6), 1267–1302.

Farmer, T. W., Farmer, E. M. Z., & Gut, D. M. (1999). Implications of social development research for school-based interventions for aggressive youth with EBD. *Journal of Emotional and Behavioral Disorders, 7,* 130–136.

Ford, J. D., Racusin, R., Daviss, W. B., Ellis, C. G., Thomas, J., Rogers, K., et al. (1999). Trauma exposure among children with oppositional defiant disorder and attention deficit-hyperactivity disorder. *Journal of Consulting and Clinical Psychology, 67*(5), 786–789.

Frick, P. J., Lahey, B. B., Loeber, R., Tannenaum, L. E., Van Horn, Y., Christ, M. A. G., et al. (1993). Oppositional defiant disorder and conduct disorder: A meta-analytic review of factor analyses and cross-validation in a clinic sample. *Clinical Psychology Review, 13,* 319–340.

Garbarino, J. (2000). Personality and environmental correlates of attachment styles in children with ADHD and/or conduct disorder. *Dissertation Abstracts International, 60*(9), 3543A.

Hollenstein, T., Granic, I., Stoolmiller, M., & Snyder, J. (2004). Rigidity in parent-child interactions and the development of externalizing and internalizing behavior in early childhood. *Journal of Abnormal Child Psychology, 32*(6), 595–607.

Jensen, P. S., Wantanabe, H. K., & Richters, J. E. (1999). Who's up first? Testing for order effects in structured interviews using a counterbalanced experimental design. *Journal of Abnormal Child Psychology, 27,* 439–445.

Jouriles, E. N., Murphy, C. M., Farris, A. M., Smith, D. A., Richters, J. E., & Waters, E. (1991). Marital adjustment, parental disagreements about child rearing, and behavior problems in boys: Increasing the specificity of the marital assessment. *Child Development, 62*(6), 1424–1433.

Keathley, M. E. A. (1995). The incapacity to be alone in conduct disordered boys. *Dissertation Abstracts International, 56*(4), 2331B.

Kern, L., Choutka, C. M., & Sokol, N. G. (2002). Assessment-based antecedent interventions used in natural settings to reduce challenging behavior: A review of the literature. *Education and Treatment of Children, 25,* 113–130.

Kern, L., Dunlap, G., Clarke, S., & Childs, K. E. (1994). Student-Assisted Functional Assessment Interview. *Diagnostique, 19,* 7–20.

Kern, L., Hilt, A. M., & Gresham, F. (2004). An evaluation of the functional behavioral assessment process used with students with or at risk for emotional and behavior disorders. *Education and Treatment of Children, 27,* 440–452.

Kern, L., O'Neill, R. E., & Starosta, K. (2005). Gathering functional assessment information. In L. M. Bambara & L. Kern (Eds.), *Individualized supports for students with problem behaviors* (pp. 129–164). New York: Guilford Press.

Kern, L., Ringdahl, J. E., Hilt, A., & Sterling-Turner, H. E. (2001). Linking self-management procedures to functional analysis results. *Behavioral Disorders, 26,* 214–226.

Lahey, B. B., Russo, M. F., Walker, J. L., & Piacentini, J. C. (1989). Personality characteristics of the mothers of children with disruptive behavior disorders. *Journal of Consulting and Clinical Psychology, 57*(4), 512–515.

Lansford, J. E., Chang, L., Dodge, K. A., Malone, P. S., Oburu, P., Palmérus, K., et al. (2005). Physical discipline and children's adjustment: Cultural normativeness as a moderator. *Child Development, 76*(6), 1234–1246.

Lansford, J. E., Deater-Deckard, K., Dodge, K. A., Bates, J. E., & Pettit, G. S. (2004). Ethnic differences in the link between physical discipline and later adolescent externalizing behaviors. *Journal of Child Psychology and Psychiatry, 45*(4), 801–812.

Leventhal, T., & Brooks-Gunn, J. (2000). The neighborhoods they live in: The effects of neighborhood residence on child and adolescent outcomes. *Psychological Bulletin, 126*(2), 309–337.

Loeber, R., Green, S. M., Keenan, K., & Lahey, B. B. (1995). Which boys will fare worse? Early predictors of the onset of conduct disorder in a 6-year longitudinal study. *Journal of the American Academy of Child and Adolescent Psychiatry, 34*(4), 499–509.

Maccoby, E. E., & Martin, J. A. (1983). Socialization in the context of the family: Parent-child interaction. In P. H. Mussen (Ed.), *Handbook of child psychology: Vol. IV. Socialization, personality, and social development* (4th ed., pp. 1–101). New York: Wiley.

Martin, J. (1981). A longitudinal study of the consequences of early mother-infant interaction: A microanalytic approach. *Monographs of the Society for Research in Child Development, 46*(3), 1–58.

Mash, E. J., & Wolfe, D. A. (2005). *Abnormal child psychology* (3rd ed.). Belmont, CA: Thompson/Wadsworth.

Mason, D. A., & Frick, P. J. (1994). The heritability of antisocial behavior: A meta-analysis of twin and adoption studies. *Journal of Psychopathology and Behavioral Assessment, 16*(4), 301–323.

Maughan, B., Rowe, R., Messer, J., Goodman, R., & Meltzer, H. (2004). Conduct disorder and oppositional defiant disorder in a national sample: Developmental epidemiology. *Journal of Child Psychology and Psychiatry, 45,* 609–619.

McMahon, R. J., & Frick, P. J. (2005). Evidence-based assessment of conduct problems in children and adolescents. *Journal of Clinical Child and Adolescent Psychology, 24,* 447–505.

Nelson, J. R., Benner, G. J., Lane, K. & Smith, B. W. (2004). Academic achievement of K-12 students with emotional and behavioral disorders. *Exceptional Children, 71*(1), 59–73.

Newcomer, L. L., & Lewis, T. J. (2004). Functional behavioral assessment: An investigation of assessment reliability and effectiveness of function-based interventions. *Journal of Emotional and Behavioral Disorders, 12,* 168–181.

Patterson, G. R., Capaldi, D., & Bank, L. (1991). An early starter model for predicting delinquency. In D. Pepler & K. H. Rubin (Eds.), *The development and treatment of childhood aggression* (pp. 139–168)). Hillsdale, NJ: Erlbaum.

Patterson, G. R., De Baryshe, B. D., & Ramsey, E. (1989). A developmental perspective on antisocial behavior. *American Psychologist, 44,* 329–335.

Patterson, G. R., Reid, J. R., & Dishion, T. J. (1992). *Antisocial boys.* Eugene, OR: Castalia.

Pfiffner, L. J., McBurnett, K., Rathouz, P. J., & Judice, S. (2005). Family correlates of oppositional and conduct disorders in children with attention deficit/hyperactivity disorder. *Journal of Abnormal Child Psychology, 33*(5), 551–563.

Quay, H. C., & Peterson, D. (1996). *Revised Behavior Problem Checklist, PAR edition: Professional manual.* Odessa, FL: Psychological Assessment Resources.

Reich, W. (2000). Diagnostic Interview for Children and Adolescents (DICA). *Journal of the American Academy of Children and Adolescent Psychiatry, 39,* 59–66.

Reynolds, C. R., & Kamphaus, K. W. (2004). *Behavioral Assessment System for Children* (2nd ed.). Circle Pines, MN: American Guidance Service.

Rohner, R. P., Kean, K. J., & Cournoyer, D. E. (1991). Effects of corporal punishment, perceived caretaker warmth, and cultural beliefs on the psychological adjustment of children in St. Kitts, West Indies. *Journal of Marriage and the Family, 53*(3), 681–693.

Rutter, M., Giller, H., & Hagell, A. (1998). *Antisocial behavior in young people.* Cambridge: Cambridge University Press.

Shaffer, D., Fisher, P., Lucas, C. P., Dulcan, M. K., & Schwab-Stone, M. E. (2000). NIMH Diagnostic Interview for Children, Version IV (NIMH DISC-IV): Description, differences from previous versions, and reliability of some common diagnoses. *Journal of the American Academy of Child and Adolescent Psychiatry, 39,* 28–38.

Slutske, W. S., Cronk, N. J., & Nabors-Oberg, R. E. (2003). Familial and genetic factors. In C. A. Essau (Ed.), *Conduct and oppositional defiant disorders: Epidemiology, risk factors, and treatment* (pp. 137–162). Hillsdale, NJ: Erlbaum.

Smith, C. A., & Farrington, D. P. (2004). Continuities in antisocial behavior and parenting across three generations. *Journal of Child Psychology and Psychiatry, 45*(2), 230–247.

Speltz, M. L., McClellan, J., DeKlyen, M., & Jones, K. (1999). Preschool boys with oppositional defiant disorder: Clinical presentation and diagnostic change. *Journal of the American Academy of Child and Adolescent Psychiatry, 38*(7), 838–845.

Sprafkin, J., & Gadow, K. D. (1996). *Early childhood symptom inventories.* Stony Brook, NY: Checkmate Plus.

Steiner, H., & Dunne, J. E. (1997). Summary of the practice parameters for the assessment and treatment of children and adolescents with conduct disorder. *Journal of the American Academy of Child and Adolescent Psychiatry, 36*(10), 1482–1485.

Sutherland, K. S., & Wehby, J. H. (2001). Exploring the relationship between increased opportunities to respond to academic requests and the academic and behavioral outcomes of students with EBD: A review. *Remedial and Special Education, 22*(3), 113–121.

Taylor, J. T., Iacono, W. G., & McGue, M. (2000). Evidence for a genetic etiology of early-onset delinquency. *Journal of Abnormal Psychology, 109,* 634–643.

Wahler, R. G. (1994). Child conduct problems: Disorders in conduct or social continuity? *Journal of Child and Family Studies, 3*(2), 143–156.

Webster-Stratton, C., Reid, M. J., & Hammond, M. (2004). Treating children with early-onset conduct problems: Intervention outcomes for parent, child, and teacher training. *Journal of Clinical Child and Adolescent Psychology, 33,* 105–124.

Windle, M. (1997). Mate similarity, heavy substance use and family history of problem drinking among young adult women. *Journal of Studies on Alcohol, 58*(6), 573–580.

CHAPTER 13

Learning, Motor, and Communication Disorders

T. STEUART WATSON, TONYA S. WATSON,
AND JENNIFER RET

LEARNING DISORDERS

DESCRIPTION OF THE DISORDER

Difficulties in learning encompass a wide range of problems, from children with severe cognitive deficits to those who are capable of learning at an adequate rate but fail to do so because of insufficient motivation or poor instruction. A learning *disorder* is usually synonymous with a learning *disability* because the individual's difficulties in learning are not due to general intellectual factors (i.e., overall cognitive ability) or because of inadequate reinforcement in the environment or inappropriate instruction (i.e., a performance deficit).

It is estimated that approximately 2% of schoolchildren in the United States meet diagnostic criteria for a learning disability (Swanson, 2005). Children diagnosed with learning disabilities comprise the largest subgroup of children placed in special education classes. According to the U.S. Office of Education (1977), four criteria must be met for a student to be identified with a learning disability (LD): (1) a discrepancy between aptitude and achievement; (2) manifested in one of seven basic academic domains; (3) not due to a sensory disorder, mental deficiency, inadequate or inappropriate instruction, linguistic diversity, emotional or behavioral problems, or economic disadvantage; and (4) the assumption that the learning problem is based *within* the individual (i.e., neurobiologically based). These criteria have strongly influenced the development of assessment and intervention methods for students with learning problems over the past 30 years. A detailed critical analysis of these criteria is beyond the scope of this chapter, but it should be noted that the existing data do not support the notion that adherence to the aforementioned criteria has improved outcomes for students with learning problems (Macmillan & Siperstein, 2002). The question that ultimately concerns most practitioners, teachers, and parents is *What sort of conceptualization is most likely to lead to improved outcomes?* Although the answer to this question is evolving, many authors have converged on the idea that learning disorders result from a mismatch between the student's abilities and the instructional environment. Because a given student's neurobiology cannot be precisely manipulated (at least not at present), mental health providers must be content with facilitating changes in the school and home environment. Over time, instructional manipulations that result in improved learning are retained, and others are discarded. This approach to assessment and intervention is called response to intervention (RTI) and is described later.

Diagnosis and Assessment

Consistent with the diagnostic approach outlined in the *Diagnostic and Statistical Manual of Mental Disorders* (*DSM-IV-TR*; American Psychiatric Association, 2000), most states use some type of discrepancy formula (i.e., difference between cognitive ability and achievement in one or more academic area) to formally identify a child with a learning disability. Although use of the discrepancy formula is not required by federal law, states turn to a discrepancy formula to regulate the number of children diagnosed as learning disabled. Hence, there is significant variability in discrepancy formulas for learning disabilities from state to state. It has been half-jokingly noted that some children are *cured* of their learning disability when they move from one state to another because a different discrepancy formula is used. Under the discrepancy formula, suspected cases of learning disability are evaluated based on the results of psychoeducational testing, including (at a minimum) a standardized measure of cognitive ability (e.g., Wechsler Intelligence Scale for Children, 4th edition [WISC-IV]: Wechsler, 2003) and a measure of achievement (e.g., Woodcock-Johnson Test of Achievement, 3rd edition: Woodcock, McGrew, & Mather, 2001). In some instances, tests measuring some aspect of cognitive processing are included to identify potential processing deficits that may be impact a student's ability to learn. According to the *DSM-IV*, specific forms of learning disability include Reading Disorder, Math Disorder, and the Disorders of Written Expression and their variants. In each instance, users of the *DSM* are instructed to diagnose learning disabilities when discrepancies between tests of overall cognitive ability and specific tests of achievement reach 15 points or greater (or approximately 1 standard deviation on conventional tests of achievement and intellectual ability). Additional criteria for diagnosis include functional impairment and ruling out differential diagnoses such as Pervasive Developmental Disorder or Mental Retardation.

Unfortunately, traditional measures of achievement and tests of cognitive processing have proven to be of little use for either diagnosis or treatment planning. Moreover, research has consistently failed to find an aptitude-by-treatment interaction. If the aforementioned assessment procedures and methodology are not useful for assisting with diagnosis or treatment design, what type of assessment procedures should be used to identify and assist children with learning problems? Over the past 10 years, brief academic assessment procedures, similar to those employed in functional behavior assessment, have been developed to identify children who are having difficulty in their curriculum and to identify instructional strategies that are most likely to be beneficial for that individual. This approach, also known as response to intervention, begins with a baseline measurement of the student's current level of academic responding to assist in identification of students with learning problems and for measuring changes in academic responding to different types of intervention (to assist in treatment planning). There are some excellent sources on implementing an RTI model (see Chidsey-Brown & Steege, 2005), and the professional literature is beginning to demonstrate the efficacy of the model (cf. Gresham, 2006). In addition, there has been a sharp increase in the use of curriculum-based measurement procedures and instruments, such as the Dynamic Indicators of Basic Early Literacy Skills. This instrument allows for the identification of students who are not learning in their current curriculum at a rate that is commensurate with others in their classroom, school, or district. Most important, if RTI is successful, individuals who are struggling and in need of remediation should be able to get help much more rapidly than in the past (Fuchs, 2002; Fuchs & Fuchs, 1997; Good, Gruba, & Kaminski, 2002).

CONCEPTUALIZATION

Developmental Issues   It has been estimated that roughly 5% of the general population would meet the diagnostic criteria for a learning disability (Lyon, 1996). It is a long-held belief that the prevalence rate for a learning disability diagnosis is higher for boys than for girls. Indeed, schools typically identify more boys as having a learning disability than girls. However, sex differences in the identification of LDs appear to be related to the rate of disruptive behavior displayed in the classroom by boys. In contrast to boys, girls with LDs seem less prone to disruptive behavior. Although it has typically been the case that 4 times as many males as females are diagnosed with learning problems (Shaywitz, Shaywitz, Fletcher, & Escobar, 1990), recent evidence suggests a more equal identification rate among males and females (Graziano, 2002). Longitudinal, epidemiological, and survey data suggest that boys and girls are similarly affected by reading disabilities (Flynn & Rahbar, 1994; Lyon, 1996).

There are a number of developmental issues that complicate the task of distinguishing learning problems from other problems or disorders. For instance, roughly 10% to 35% of children identified with a learning disability also have a comorbid diagnosis of Attention-Deficit/Hyperactivity Disorder (ADHD; Gresham, MacMillan, Bocian, Ward, & Forness, 1998). It is often difficult to determine if the relationship between LDs and ADHD is an artifact or the result of similar underlying biological or environmental factors.

Learning and Modeling   There is no evidence that, as a group, children identified as learning disabled learn differently from other children. The instructional strategies to which they best respond may be more idiosyncratic than for children not diagnosed with a learning disability, but the basic principles of learning remain the same. For instance, some children with a learning disability in reading (i.e., Reading Disorder) respond better to instructional techniques such as passage previewing than to repeated reading, and vice versa. Children without a learning disability in reading will typically learn to read regardless of the curriculum or particular strategies utilized by the classroom teacher (Tier I strategies). Children who are having difficulty learning to read or who are diagnosed with a LD in reading may require exposure to a variety of instructional strategies before a successful approach is identified. Importantly, the RTI model allows a practitioner to select the reading strategy most likely to result in learning for a particular student. Although it is never too late to seek help for a learning disability, early identification is important when seeking to ensure academic success. The longer one waits to intervene, the wider the gap between the student with a disability and his or her peers becomes. Children who struggle academically are also more likely to experience the negative sequelae associated with academic failure (e.g., teacher reprimands for incorrect work), poor social interactions, and impaired parent-child relations (e.g., arguments about inadequate performance or homework).

In terms of improving learning outcomes, there are three general principles that should be emphasized regardless of the chosen intervention. The first principle is the use of direct instruction, or directly teaching the skill that you want the student to learn (Kay, 2005; Rivera, Al-Otaiba, & Koorland, 2006). The second principle is strategy instruction, for example, teaching tool skills such as note taking or study skills (Belfiore & Hutchinson, 1998) or the use of a particular learning or cognitive strategy (Lau, 2006). The third principle is support from school and home. Specifically, parents must spend time at home reinforcing the skills and strategies taught at school. It is vitally important that the school and parents maintain close contact to evaluate the success (or failure) of current interventions and initiate any changes that need to be made with regard to educational programming. The school-home note is especially efficacious in helping parents and teacher communicate about homework assignments, school behavior, academic progress, and practice needs (Flynn, Kotkin, Brady, & Fine, 2003; Gable, 2002; McCain & Kelley, 1994).

Parental Issues   Children diagnosed with a learning disability are especially prone to behavior problems, particularly males, who are more likely to exhibit externalizing behaviors. In addition, parents of children diagnosed with a learning disability report greater levels of stress associated with parenting than parents whose children are not diagnosed with a LD. Furthermore, these parents attributed their stress in parenting to child-related characteristics (Baker & McCal, 1995). Other researchers have highlighted the difficulties associated with parenting a child with a learning disability and noted that many of the problems were related to negative experiences with the educational system and the parents' concern for their child's social well-being and future (Waggoner & Wilgosh, 1990).

Life Events   The role that specific life events may play in contributing to the development of learning disorders remains unclear. For instance, it has been suggested that otitis media with effusion (OME) may interfere with normal language development, particularly phonologic development, which, in turn, impacts the child's subsequent cognitive and academic functioning (Teele, Klein, Chase, Menyuk, & Rosner 1990). Recent research, however, indicates that the OME by itself probably does not play a significant role in hindering language development, but that hearing loss that occurs as a result of persistent OME may be related to delayed language development and subsequent learning problems (Miccio, Gallagher, Grossman, Yont, & Vernon-Feagans, 2001; Theodore, Bray, Kehle, & DioGuardi, 2006).

A number of other life events may result in learning problems or disorders. The major categories of these are physical trauma or traumatic brain injury, environmental toxins such as lead and mercury, malnourishment during either pregnancy or the early childhood years, oxygen deprivation, and childhood illness. All of these can result in mild to severe effects in terms of impacting learning (Graziano, 2002).

Genetic Influences   As with many other psychological disorders, the precise role that genetics plays in the development and maintenance of a learning disability is unclear. Researchers have relied on both family studies and twin studies in an attempt to understand the role that genetics plays in learning disorders. Pennington (1995), for instance, noted that children with severe reading disabilities were more likely to have a close family member with a similar disability than not. Likewise, DeFries et al. (1997) found greater similarities in reading disabilities among identical twins than fraternal twins, even when the identical twins were raised separately.

More recently, Shaywitz and Shaywitz (2003) has used functional magnetic resonance imaging to study the brain activity of individuals when they are reading. These studies have shown that there are differences in brain activity between children who are fluent readers and children who have difficulties with reading. For instance, children who have difficulty with reading or who are diagnosed with a learning disability in reading rely greatly on the *left interior front gyrus* and *the left parietotemporal area,* which are the parts of the brain that link letters with sounds and that help in decoding words, respectively. Children with reading difficulties also have difficulty accessing the portion of the brain that is responsible for integrating, storing, and retrieving words (left occipitotemporal area). Perhaps of greater interest are the findings of Aylward et al. (2003) and Shaywitz and Shaywitz (2003, 2004), who reported that physical changes occur as a result of academic interventions that improve reading skills. Thus, knowledge of the neurological aspects of reading helps in the conceptualizing and understanding reading problems. In principle, a better understanding of how successful reading interventions affect underlying brain function could one day result in enhancements to instructional practice.

Peer Influences   Although children diagnosed as LD do not differ in the number of friends they report compared to children without LD diagnoses, there do appear to be differences in the number of mutually reported friendships. That is, the peers of LD children are less likely to endorse a child with a learning disability as a friend than a child without a learning disability (Vaughn & Elbaum, 1999). A number of other consistent findings emerge regarding the relationship between children diagnosed as LD and their peers:

- LD children are less likely to be socially accepted and more likely to be rejected by their peers (Kavale & Forness, 1995; Swanson & Malone, 1992).
- LD children are more likely to be socially neglected (Wiener, 1987).
- The low peer acceptance of LD children is relatively stable over time (Bryan, 1976).
- The social status of LD children declines over the course of the academic year (Kuhne & Wiener, 2000).
- LD children who receive services in the general education classroom enjoy higher peer acceptance than those who are placed in resource, self-contained, or fully inclusive settings (Wiener & Tardif, 2004).

It has been also suggested that children with learning disabilities exhibit concurrent deficits in social skills, particularly in interpreting social cues from peers (Horowitz, 1981; Maheady & Sainato, 1986). If these deficits are combined with comorbid problems such as ADHD, ineffective parenting, language difficulties, or stressful family situations, the deficits in social skills may be exacerbated and lead to both internalizing (i.e., anxiety and depression) and externalizing (e.g., acting out, disrupting the classroom, disobeying rules) behavior problems (Wiener, 2004).

Drugs Affecting Behavior   Approximately 30% to 70% of children whose primary diagnosis is ADHD are concurrently diagnosed with a learning disability (DuPaul & Stoner, 1994; Mayes, Calhoun, & Crowell, 2000). In these cases, it is difficult to determine if the learning problem is due to the student's low rate of attention to instruction, low rate of task engagement, low rate of assignment completion, or some combination of all of these factors. Although various psychotropic medications may improve the symptoms associated with ADHD, concurrent improvements in academic performance are rare unless some aspect of the instructional environment has been modified. In addition, when there are other problems that coexist with the learning disability (e.g., self-injury, Obsessive-Compulsive Disorder, impulse control disorders, aggressive behavior), psychopharmacological agents may be used successfully to treat those conditions. However, the use of medication does not appear to have an impact on student learning unless the condition was interfering with the acquisition of material or the opportunity to respond during instruction.

Cultural and Diversity Issues   According to the National Center for Learning Disabilities (NCLD; 2006), race and ethnicity may be factors related to the development of a learning disability. In 2001, 1% of Caucasian children and 2.6% of non-Hispanic African American children were receiving special education because of learning disabilities. Although researchers have argued that this is the result of economic disadvantage the NCLD argues that LD is not the result of economic hardship. It is unclear why a particular racial or ethnic group would be more prone to developing a learning disorder. In terms of treatment, the literature does not support the hypothesis that ethnicity or sex influences the effectiveness of treatment.

Reid and Valle (2004) noted that culturally diverse parents are disproportionately adversely affected and disenfranchised by the LD label. Kalyanpur and Harry (2004) concurred with Reid and Valle and offered that the exclusion of parents from the critical discourse on LD and the perception of poor parenting practices among culturally diverse parents have contributed to the negative impact on these students and their families. The result of this negative impact, according to these authors, has been the exclusion of culturally diverse children from the mainstream of American educational practice.

PEDIATRIC MOTOR DISORDERS

Description of the Disorder

As defined by Delgado and Albright (2003, p. 1), pediatric motor disorders "involve a disturbance of central motor control that can be manifested in alterations of posture and movement." Movement disorders can be divided into two groups: hyperkinesias, which involve excesses of movement, and hypokinesias, which involve the paucity, loss, or limitation of movement (Fahn, Greene, Ford, & Bressman, 1998). The most common pediatric hyperkinesias are ataxia, chorea, dystonia, myoclonus, spasticity/ rigidity, and tremor, which are discussed later. The most frequently seen forms of pediatric hypokinesia are bradykinesia, meaning slow movement; akinesia, the transient loss of spontaneous movements; and spasticity, which is resistance to passive movement (Sanger, 2005). These different labels encompass a wide range of difficulties, including problems with completion of voluntary movements, the occurrence of involuntary movements that can be rapid or slow, short or long in duration and mild or strong in severity, and resistance to passive movement that might be initiated in the environment.

Hyperkinesias   Ataxia is characterized by poor coordination while attempting to perform voluntary movements. Movements often appear jerky or disjointed, and ataxia may be mistaken for simple clumsiness, inaccuracy, or instability (Sanger, 2005). Acute cerebellar ataxia is the form most commonly seen in children, and its onset often follows an infectious viral disease (usually chickenpox). It can affect the trunk (truncal ataxia) and the lower (gait ataxia) or upper (appendicular ataxia) extremities. Acute cerebellar ataxia may or may not subside on its own within a period of weeks or months; occasionally the condition will persist throughout life. Jerky eye movements (nystagmus) or jerky speech patterns (dysarthria) may occur in concert with the characteristic body movements. This disorder generally occurs in children under 3 years of age. If the condition persists for more than 3 months, or if it occurs in the absence of a virus, it is likely that other causes, such as genetics or neurological lesions or tumors, will need to be ruled out. One such genetic disorder with gait ataxia as its major feature is Angelman syndrome. Angelman syndrome is quite rare, with approximately 1,000 cases known to exist in the United States. The gait ataxia associated with Angelman syndrome is accompanied by functionally severe developmental delays, which are present by 6 to 12 months of age, speech impairment, and often tremor in the limbs. Ataxia-telangiectasia (also known as Louis-Bar syndrome) is also marked by an ataxic gait, deficiencies in the immune system such as chronic respiratory infections, late-onset developmental delays, and seizures.

Chorea (from the Greek word *khorcia*, meaning "dance") involves rapid, random, excessive, and often wildly exaggerated movements that seem to flow almost continuously from one body part to the next, which results in involuntary, completely unintentional movements. Often the affected individual appears extremely fidgety. However, in its most severe form, known as ballism (Greek word *ballismes*, meaning "jumping about"), chorea can cause limbs to flail about uncontrollably. Athetosis, characterized by slower, writhing and twisting movements, and choreoathetosis, which is somewhere between the sharp, rapid jerks of chorea and the slow movements of athetosis, are slight variations of this disorder (Sanger, 2005). In children, choreic movements are most commonly seen in cases of cerebral palsy (described later). Although this category is generally distinct from others on the pediatric motor disorders spectrum, there is some subjectivity when it comes to differentiating between the three subcategories, and further research is needed to make the distinction clear, if there should indeed be a distinction.

Dystonia is characterized by involuntary movements and/or muscle contractions that can be fleeting or sustained; these lead to twisting or repetitive motions, abnormal posturing, or some combination of these. Although this disorder is characterized by involuntary movements, these most often occur when the individual is in the midst of attempting a voluntary movement. That is, typically, the intended movement is made and an additional (unintended) movement of some proximal or distal part of the body is also made. Although the name dystonia implies that there is some abnormality in muscle tone, there usually is not. Often, a distinguishing feature of this particular motor disorder is that the dystonic movement in one part of the body is triggered by the movement of another part of the body. The two parts may be near each other (the foot and the leg) or on opposite sides of the body (the right hand and the left hand). The severity of the dystonic movement may worsen with stress or volatile emotional states. Another distinguishing feature of this disorder is the predictable nature of the contractions or movements; they lack the random, flowing quality of the movements associated with chorea. Yet another characteristic of dystonia is the ability of tactile or proprioceptive sensory tricks to diminish or ameliorate the involuntary movements. These usually involve touching the affected body part with the hand or fingers; the physiological mechanism of these sensory tricks is not well understood. Hallervorden-Spatz disease is a rare disorder characterized by dystonic movements, parkinsonism, and dementia that primarily affects children; typically the course is rapid, with death occurring prior to age 30 (Fahn et al., 1998).

The involuntary movements that characterize myoclonus are sudden, jolting, and very brief in topography (50–200 milliseconds; Delgado & Albright, 2003). The short duration of myoclonic contractions helps to distinguish this movement disorder from others. Myoclonus may be classified based on its clinical characteristics, distribution (focal, generalized, segmental, or multifocal), site of origin (cortical areas, subcortical areas, or the spinal cord), or its etiology. It can affect one or several distinct parts of the body (focal or multifocal), a portion of the body (segmental), or the whole body (generalized). It may occur as a single, unpredictable jerk or as repetitive, rhythmic movement. Although the movements are quick, like those associated with chorea, they do not have the quality of flowing from body part to body part. Rather, a series of very similar movements may occur in rapid succession repeatedly, or the jerking movement may occur only once. Common, mild forms of myoclonus include the hiccups and the sudden jerking movements that occasionally occur in normal people as they fall asleep (sometimes called "sleep starts"). *Reflex myoclonus* may be triggered by external stimuli of auditory, visual, or tactile modalities; *action myoclonus* is triggered by voluntary movements. The latter form can be extremely debilitating because it can interfere with normal daily activities where the myoclonus is produced by movements that are required of the activity or task.

Tremor is an involuntary oscillation of the muscles in the affected body part that results in a shaky appearance. It is often expressed in Hertz (the number of cycles per second). Tremors are generally subdivided into three phenomenological categories: (1) rest tremors, which occur when the body part is completely supported and at rest; (2) action tremors, which occur when the individual makes voluntary muscle movements; and (3) postural tremors, which occur when the afflicted person attempts to maintain a specific posture, such as holding the arms outstretched. Action tremors are further subdivided into categories according to the type of voluntary movement with which they are associated: (a) *Kinetic tremors* occur during any kind of directed action; (b) *intention* or*target tremors* are kinetic tremors that increase in severity as the affected body part reaches its target; (c) *isometric tremors* occur during muscular resistance (contraction without movement); and (d) *task- or position-specific tremors* occur almost exclusively during certain tasks that require high levels of coordination, such as writing. It is normal for people to experience tremors when they strenuously exert their muscles, for example when lifting or pushing a heavy object. It is the presence of tremor in the absence of resistance that may indicate pathology. A chronic, visible postural tremor known as essential tremor may be the most well-known form of this movement abnormality. About 20% of adult cases of essential tremor had an age of onset below 20 years (Koller, Silver, & Lieberman, 1994), and cases have been documented in children as young as 24 months (Bain et al., 1994). Tremor may occur in almost any part of the body, and it may appear suddenly or gradually worsen over time. Tremors often accompany ataxia, dystonia, and myoclonus, and in children, they may be caused by a number of genetic and/or neurological disorders.

Hypokinesias Bradykinesia literally means "slow movement." Voluntary movements made with the affected limb(s) are painstaking and protracted. The disorder can affect the entire body, half of the body, or a single limb. In any case, it is most obvious when the individual is asked to perform some rapid, repetitive movement such as curling the toes. Bradykinesia and akinesia (the loss of spontaneous movements) are included in a cluster of symptoms known as parkinsonism and are both familiar signs of Parkinson's disease. It is important to note that although Parkinson's disease is the most common cause of parkinsonism, it is not the only cause (Fahn et al., 1998). Parkinsonism can often have secondary causes, such as hydrocephalus, infection, or brain tumors (Fernandez-Alvarez & Aicardi, 2001). Because parkinsonism is the most common form of hypokinesia, the two terms are used interchangeably in many texts. This can become confusing for the reader because hypokinesia (decreased amplitude of movement) is sometimes even listed as another symptom of Parkinson's disease, along with muscular rigidity and resting tremor (described later).

Spasticity involves tense, involuntarily contracted muscles. In its most severe form, spasticity may affect a child even when he or she is not moving, causing rigid, fixed joints. It is similar, and often difficult to distinguish from, rigidity, which is an individual's resistance to passive movement by a stimulus in the environment or by another person. Rigidity generally does not affect voluntary movements directly, so it is not typically disabling on its own. However, in children, spasticity and rigidity are often accompanied by other motor problems that do impact the individual's ability to make voluntary movements. The most common cause of all movement disorders in childhood is cerebral palsy, a heterogeneous group of disorders caused by nonprogressive lesion(s) in the motor areas of the brain that can occur either in utero, during birth, or during the first 3 years of life as a result of infection or trauma. In its most common form (called spastic cerebral palsy), cerebral palsy is characterized by varying degrees of spasticity and/or rigidity, with the child exhibiting tense, contracted muscles that resist passive movement most or all of the time. Other forms may also be characterized by athetosis (termed athetoid or dyskinetic cerebral palsy), ataxia (ataxic cerebral palsy), or a mixture of various symptoms (mixed cerebral palsy). Cerebral palsy and cases of spasticity and rigidity (without cerebral palsy) can be generalized to include the entire body, or include only certain portions of the body. Bradykinesia and rigidity also appear in juvenile Huntington's disease, and although a severe chorea frequently accompanies adult-onset Huntington's disease, this phenomenon is far less common in children. In children and adults, the disease progresses slowly, beginning with minor movement difficulties that gradually worsen over time. The juvenile form, however, has a more rapid progression (Osborne, Munson, & Burman, 1982). Symptom onset may also include tremor, seizures, and loss of intellectual abilities. In adults, the disease also has a psychological component that frequently leads to dementia. In children, psychological symptoms often present in the form of conduct or behavior problems (Lenti & Bianchini, 1993).

DIAGNOSIS AND ASSESSMENT

To properly and accurately diagnose movement disorders, it is essential to directly observe the child with a suspected motor anomaly. Parents may be asked to videotape their children who are suspected of having motor problems so that a thorough record of the actual movements and any surrounding occurrences can be observed by the clinician. In the case of suspected hyperkinesias, one must determine whether the movements are actually (a) involuntary and (b) abnormal. It is possible that the movements may be compulsive in nature, in which case they are still considered voluntary. It may be that they simply are exaggerated gestures or mannerisms, which could be difficult to distinguish from involuntary movements, as in the case of children who have severe language problems. It is also possible that sustained, involuntarily contracted muscles could be a means for the individual to reduce pain in some chronic conditions. According to Fahn et al. (1998, p. 8), "As a general rule, abnormal, involuntary movements are exaggerated with anxiety and diminished during sleep." Although abnormal movements are often involuntary, many involuntary movements are not in the least abnormal. It is important to remember that automatic movements, such as breathing or walking around a familiar space in the dark, are not the same as involuntary movements. Automatic movements can be interrupted (at least for certain periods) as required. In the case of involuntary movements, however, this kind of control either requires great effort on the part of the individual or is altogether impossible (Fernandez-Alvarez & Aicardi, 2001).

Once the clinician has decided that the movements are indeed involuntary and abnormal, the next step is to describe them as completely and thoroughly as possible to determine which category they fit into best and whether they may be the product of some other disorder that is not related specifically to movement. The quality of the movements (rhythmicity, duration, speed), the pattern of movement, the suspected triggers(s), the amplitude of movements over long and short time periods (whether or not they have worsened with time), whether the movements can be ameliorated through sensory tricks or intention, and what other kinds of sensations accompany them are all important features to note. This information will also assist the clinician in selecting the most appropriate diagnosis from among the different categories of movement disorders that have a large number of overlapping symptoms, or in determining that the symptoms are due to some other medical condition. In either case, the detailed information may also provide clues about how to treat (or simply prevent the occurrence of) the problematic movements in the future. It is important to note that some of the symptoms that characterize these disorders are sometimes seen in the course of normal human development. However, the duration and severity of the problem will dictate whether a diagnosis is made. Because the source of movement disorders is often related to a neurological condition of the patient, it is critical that serious medical conditions that may need immediate treatment be considered in the process of diagnosing an individual with no known history of trauma or disease.

To effectively differentiate a suspected movement disorder from other problems that may also affect movement, such as epilepsy, further investigation into the individual's medical status is often necessary. A particular type of movement disorder, called paroxysmal disorders, which are characterized by intermittent periods of normal movement, is often initially misdiagnosed as epilepsy. To further complicate matters, many syndromes on the seizure disorder spectrum actually include myoclonus as a major feature (Aicardi, 1994). Because epilepsy and other seizure disorders have several unique features that are very rarely seen in the motor disorders described in this chapter, such as a pre-event aura, episodes of altered consciousness, and a unique postictal state, the presence (or absence) of these specific features is often used to rule out problems on the seizure spectrum. When these features cannot be reliably detected because of the age or cognitive status of the affected person, often an electroencephalogram is used to determine if any epileptiform activity is present during the actual movement. In addition, brain imaging techniques may be used to investigate the presence of structural abnormalities. Genetic testing is often also included in standard medical work-ups because every category of movement disorder has at least one heritable form.

Several rating scales have been developed to evaluate the specific characteristics associated with, or to gauge the severity of, particular motor problems (e.g., the Unified Parkinson's Disease Rating Scale, the Movement Assessment Battery for Children, the Griffith's Test, and the Burke-Fahn-Marsden Dystonia Rating Scale). The purpose of these scales has traditionally been to quantify the symptoms of a presenting problem rather than to make a precise diagnosis.

Although the causes of many of the motor disorders we have described are genetic or biological in nature (trauma, infection, etc.) and they therefore lend themselves to this system of differential diagnosis, it is important to note that there is some evidence for the existence of psychogenic movement disorders. These children present with symptoms that are nearly indistinguishable from the clinical clusters we have mentioned. Upon further investigation, however, genetic testing and/or imaging indicate no underlying physiological source for the anomalies. With inconsistent clinical features (i.e., presence of rigidity and spasticity but no brain lesions or neurological trauma), psychological treatment is often recommended to identify triggers (i.e., antecedents) that may occasion the movements (Fahn et al., 1998).

CONCEPTUALIZATION

Developmental Issues   Motor development has been defined as "the change in motor behavior across the life span and the processes which underlie these changes" (Clark & Whitall, 1989, p. 128). Early movements (often referred to as reflexes) are generally considered to be prewired because they are dependent on physiological and neurological maturation (Ames & Ilg, 1964, 1966), unlike more complex movements that are thought to be dependent on interaction with the environment (Malina, 1984; O'Brien, 1994; Thomas, 1984). Unlike movement disorders with an adult onset, childhood movement disorders are typically symptoms of other, underlying medical conditions (Sanger, 2003). In fact, there is a growing body of research that suggests that a number of different childhood disorders can present with movement-related symptomatology (e.g., Misbahuddin & Warner, 2001; West, Lockhart, O'Farrell, & Farrer, 2003). Sanger (2003, p. 529) posits that this similarity in the expression of symptoms when there is any injury to the motor systems of the brain may indicate the presence of a "final common pathway of motor disorders in which there is only a limited number of different characteristic deficits." Sanger also points out that the differences in epidemiology between adults and children are likely due to the varying impact of injury on the developing versus the nondeveloping brain. The process of development may result in the progression or alteration of symptoms. Unfortunately, there are few longitudinal studies that have sought to illuminate the effects of congenital disorders and pediatric injury on behavior and motor function in adulthood (Fernandez-Alvarez & Aicardi, 2001).

Learning and Modeling   Despite the dearth of longitudinal studies investigating the effects of motor disorders on adult quality of life, there is some evidence to suggest that early intervention efforts with preterm infants, most of whom are at high risk for developmental disorders, can have a significant impact on their developing motor skills (Morgan, Koch, Lee & Aldag, 1988; Ruiz, Le Fever, & Hakanson, 1981). A recent review of the literature identified several treatment regimens that, when performed prior to the premature infant's departure from the hospital, can have positive effects on motor development (Westrup, Bohm, Lagercrantz, & Stjernqvist, 2004). These programs attempt to stimulate the motor system while mimicking the conditions of the intrauterine environment. The primary example of this type of program is the Newborn Individualized Developmental Care and Assessment Program . Also identified as promising interventions were those that could be employed outside of the hospital and later on in development (through preschool), including specific programs for motor training that utilize treadmills or specific means for encouraging practice of the motor skill that is deficient. Many of these approaches are relatively recent innovations and require further investigation. They do, however, show promise for the remediation of specific motor skills (Blauw-Hospers & Hadders-Algra, 2005).

Parental Issues   There is some evidence to suggest that parents may have difficulty responding to the needs of their youngsters with movement disorders, especially if these disorders are present prior to the acquisition of language. The child's motoric responses may be inconsistent with or unrelated to the child's needs or desires, which may provide unreliable information to the caregiver and lead to misperceptions about the child's behavioral or cognitive status (Spiker, Boyce, & Boyce, 2002).

A recent Turkish study investigated the self-perceived quality of life of mothers caring for children diagnosed with moderate to severe cerebral palsy. These mothers tended to rate their quality of life lower in several domains, including emotional well-being, somatic symptomatology, social functioning, and vitality, than did the mothers of children having only minor health problems, such as cough, fever, or diarrhea. Although this study is somewhat limited by its correlational design and relatively small sample size (40 children with cerebral palsy, 44 control children), it nonetheless provides valuable information regarding the effects of caring for a child with a multifaceted neurological disorder that affects the ability to make voluntary movements. Because this study did not include children evidencing only the mild impairments associated with cerebral palsy, the relationship between the breadth and magnitude of deficits and parental quality of life is still somewhat unclear (Eker & Handan, 2004). In general, the extant research supports the hypothesis that parenting a child with a motor disorder is more stressful than parenting a child without a motor disorder (cf. Britner, Morog, Pianta, & Marvin, 2003; Nereo, Fee, & Hinton, 2003). It is unclear, however, if parenting is more stressful because the child has a disability with concurrent physical demands or because there are increased problem behaviors and difficulties in social interactions with peers.

In terms of intervention, it has been shown that parents can actually help to accelerate motor development in children with disabilities if they are (a) given the opportunity to become active participants and agents of change in their child's motor developmental programming and (b) given techniques to implement at home that are consistent with contemporary models of early motor learning (Mahoney & Perales, 2006).

Life Events   During adolescence, any number of problems may appear in the child with a motor disorder. For example, in the case of a child with cerebral palsy, it is not unusual for there to be a loss of skills during this period. Most often, the loss of skills is due to physical and psychogenic factors such as a large weight gain or a change in mental attitude regarding the evaluation of effort required to learn new skills (Leppert & Capute, 1996). These events may then exacerbate any preexisting negative self-perceptions, problems in peer relationships, and the desire to learn new motor patterns.

Genetic Influences   In the absence of trauma, there is almost certainly a genetic component to each of the motor disorders described. Although in many cases the pattern of inheritance is not yet completely understood, research is being conducted, especially in the area of Parkinson's disease, to isolate the genetic basis for various movement disorders. In addition to the strong evidence supporting a genetic component in parkinsonism, there also appear to be some predispositional markers for each of the diagnoses mentioned, including paroxysmal disorders (Fernandez-Alvarez & Aicardi, 2001).

Peer Influences   Unfortunately (but perhaps not surprisingly), studies have demonstrated that children who are enrolled in special education classes and/or who utilize special services at school are much more likely to be bullied by their peers than are typical students (O'Moore & Hillery, 1989; Whitney, Smith, & Thompson, 1994). In one such study, children attending an outpatient clinic for treatment of conditions associated with visible symptoms (e.g., motor and coordination problems) were twice as likely to report being bullied at school as children who attended the clinic for conditions that were not associated with such overt symptoms (e.g., headaches, asthma, abdominal pains; Dawkins, 1996). The author of this study concluded that special populations with physical disabilities that are readily apparent to peers and potential bullies ought to be afforded special protection and support while at school to avoid the potentially dangerous effects of bullying.

Physical Factors Affecting Behavior   One of the most obvious difficulties facing a child with a motor disorder is safely navigating the environment. Difficulty in climbing stairs, for example, or traversing any number of environmental barriers could contribute to the development of behavioral problems, particularly in younger children. Motor disorders that involve the oral musculature and that impact the child's ability to communicate clearly with peers and adults may also result in externalizing behavior problems and reliance on physical force to satisfy basic needs. In cases where normal feeding is impacted, children may exhibit noncompliant behavior at mealtime or may develop severely restricted food preferences based on what is easily eaten (Leppert & Capute, 1996). Problems at mealtime may then negatively affect the parent-child relationship. In fact, problems in feeding are one of the two most common antecedents for fatal child abuse among toddlers.

Drugs Affecting Behavior   In adults, levodopa is highly effective in reducing, and in many cases eliminating, the symptoms of parkinsonism. However, this drug has the potential to complicate treatment by inducing dystonic movements, especially when taken in high doses. Patients with mild parkinsonian symptoms are best treated with the lowest effective dose of levodopa, and in some cases, drug treatment may not be necessary at all. For children and adolescents, a number of medications may be used to reduce spasticity, among them diazepam, trihexyphenidyl HCL, and baclofen. Most physicians use considerable caution when prescribing these medications for children because of the many adverse side effects associated with them; the ones most likely to negatively impact a school-age child include sleepiness, sedation, and depression (Butler & Campbell, 2000).

Cultural and Diversity Issues   There is some evidence suggesting that ethnicity may play a role in the prevalence of motor disorders. Morton, Sharma, Nicholson, Broderick, and Poyser (2001) found that the rate of cerebral palsy in Pakistani children born of two Pakistani parents was 5 times higher than for Indian children born of two Indian parents. The rate of cerebral palsy was 4 times higher in mixed marriages (i.e., Pakistani and Indian) than in the Indian children and was roughly the same as with Pakistani children. The authors noted that these results may be due to the Pakistani cultural practice of consanguineous marriage.

Interestingly, there appear to be differences among various ethnic and cultural groups with respect to the acceptance of persons with disabilities. For instance, Germans were found to have the highest overall acceptance of people with disabilities, with the English second and Italians third. The least accepted among all ethnic groups were people with AIDS, mental retardation, psychiatric illness, and cerebral palsy.

Behavioral Treatment

There are only a few behavioral treatments available for movement-related symptoms. Spasticity, which is brought on by sensory stimulation or rapid movement, can sometimes be controlled by pushing weight onto the affected limb. For instance, if a spasm begins in the leg in response to a painful stimulus such as particularly restrictive clothing, standing up can sometimes break the cycle of the uncontrolled movement. Simply identifying the triggering stimulus and preventing exposure to it can also be a simple yet effective option for the control of spasms (Fahn et al., 1998).

Patients may receive treatment from occupational therapists to regain function after surgery or to learn to adapt the environment to meet their needs. They may work with physical therapists as a nonsurgical means of treatment for the disorder. Often these forms of therapy involve educating the patient about skills related to self-care and rehabilitation; many behavioral adaptations, such as exercise and recreational and work-related activities, are also taught (Shannon, 2003).

Medical Treatment

As mentioned earlier, a number of pharmacological agents are sometimes used to help control movements associated with motor disorders. Other medical approaches to treatment consist of physical and/or occupational therapy and strategic application of braces. Surgical interventions are also available, including tendon releases, tendon lengthenings, and bone procedures, but these are usually reserved for more severe cases of spasticity or uncontrolled movement. Another innovative intervention involves the use of botulinum A toxin, which can be injected into specific nerve groups to reduce spasticity with no general adverse effects on behavior noted (Albright, 2003). A more extreme surgery called selective dorsal rhizotomy requires surgeons to cut the neural connections between the spastic muscles and the spinal cord, which reduces the spasticity, but is irreversible and involves greater risks, including paralysis of unrelated muscles (McLaughlin et al., 2002).

PEDIATRIC COMMUNICATION DISORDERS

DESCRIPTION OF THE DISORDER

Communication disorders are the most widespread disabilities in early childhood and are characterized by difficulties in speech or language (Wetherby & Prizant, 1997). Although some communication disorders are not diagnosed until adulthood, the majority of individuals with communication difficulties seek treatment during childhood and adolescence. Although there is a wide range of possible communication disorders, the most commonly diagnosed in the pediatric population are articulation and stuttering. These two disorders are the focus of this section.

Articulation Disorder   Phonological disorder is a broad term referring to a group of language disorders that affect the ability to develop easily understood speech by the age of 4. Phonological disorders are sometimes also manifested in difficulty in reading and spelling. Articulation problems, a subset of phonological disorders, are the most common speech impairment and are characterized by errors in phonological production such that individuals with the disorder fail to form speech sounds correctly (Cohen, 2001). Sound omissions, substitutions, and distortions are the most common features of an articulation problem, as well as lisping and errors in the selection and ordering of sounds within syllables and words (i.e., *aks* instead of *ask*). In some instances, children with phonological disorders display concurrent difficulties with the proper use of grammar and syntax and word retrieval. Written language may also be negatively impacted by a phonological disorder (Bowen & Cupples, 1998).

The impact of the disorder on a child's speech intelligibility can range from having little or no effect to making speech completely incomprehensible. As intelligibility is impacted, the child may experience high levels of frustration and embarrassment as others react to the disorder evident in everyday speech (Cohen, 2001). Often, less severe forms of articulation difficulties may not be detected until the child enters preschool or another environment outside of the home and is found to be difficult to understand by persons outside of the immediate family.

Stuttering   Stuttering (also known as dysfluent speech or stammering) is characterized by the involuntary repetition of speech sounds, syllables, words, or phrases, prolongations of sounds, and/or hesitations in speech that impair its rhythmic quality (Gupta, 1999; Miltenberger & Woods, 1998; Schoenbordt, 2004). The presence and severity of stuttering varies from situation to situation and is often the most severe when special pressure (e.g., stress or anxiety) is placed on communication (e.g., giving a speech at school). It is usually not present, however, during oral reading, singing, or when talking to inanimate objects or pets. The most severe cases of stuttering involve noticeable tension and strain by the speaker, often including motor movements such as rapid eye blinking, tics, face or lip tremors, head jerking, exaggerated breathing movements, fist clenching, and overall slow speaking (American Psychiatric Association, 2000; Gupta, 1999).

Stuttering often develops gradually, as dysfluencies start with the repetition of initial consonants, first words of a phrase or sentence, or long words, and progressively become more frequent, often occurring at the most meaningful word or phrase in the utterance. Physiologically, stuttering is the result of a disruption of the airflow involved in speech production caused by tightening of the laryngeal muscles. Genetics are also believed to play a role in stuttering, although the exact influence is unclear. In addition, neurological connections to stuttering (e.g., problems with interhemispheric lateralization) have also been identified, although questions remain as to whether such links are a cause or an effect of stuttering (Miltenberger & Woods, 1998).

Diagnosis and Assessment

Early assessment of communication difficulties in children is critical due to the significant role that communication and language play in children's ability to form relationships, learn from social interactions, and gain independence as they mature (Wetherby & Prizant, 1997). Furthermore, although psychopathology has not been found to be more common in children who stutter, several other issues may arise that can impact the child. For example, teasing by peers can lead to social difficulties, aggressive behavior, antisocial behavior, increased anxiety, or dysphoria. Also, for fear of difficult speaking situations, the child may learn to avoid certain situations (Miltenberger & Woods, 1998). Early identification of communication disorders in children also aids in the prevention of academic and socioemotional difficulties that may develop during the initial school years as a result of impaired communication skills (Wetherby & Prizant, 1997).

Articulation Disorders   According to the *DSM-IV-TR* (American Psychiatric Association, 2000), an individual is diagnosed as having a phonological (articulation) disorder if the following criteria are met. First, the child must fail to use speech sounds that are appropriate for his or her age and dialect. This can include errors in sound production, use, representation, or organization. Second, the articulation difficulties interfere with academic or occupational achievement or social communication. Third, the difficulties are not the result of Mental Retardation, a speech-motor or sensory deficit, or environmental deprivation.

Articulation assessments typically include a hearing screening as well as informal procedures (e.g., physical examination of the mouth, tongue, lips, hard and soft palate, etc.; direct observation; speech sampling) and formal procedures such as standardized tests (Sunderland, 2004). Schoenbrodt (2004) recommends that assessments of articulation also include word and sentence productions representative of all speech sounds, as well as samples of conversational speech.

Stuttering   According to the *DSM-IV-TR* (American Psychiatric Association, 2000), an individual is diagnosed with stuttering if the following criteria are met. First, the child must display a disturbance in the fluency and time patterning of speech that is inappropriate for his or her age (e.g., frequent repetitions or prolongations of sounds or syllables). This can also include interjections, broken words (pauses within a word), audible or silent blocking (filled or unfilled pauses in speech), circumlocutions (word substitutions to avoid problematic words), and words produced with excessive physical tension. Second, the stuttering difficulties must interfere with academic or occupational achievement or social communication. Finally, the difficulties cannot be the result of a speech-motor or sensory deficit.

Stuttering should be assessed when it is first noticed that a child's speech does not meet the criteria for what is considered fluent speech (e.g., moves forward with ease, free of irregularities and pauses, appears effortless). Assessment of a fluency disorder by a speech-language pathologist (SLP) can include review of existing data, interviews with parents, teachers, and the student, direct observation in a variety of settings, speech sampling, and standardized tests (Sunderland, 2004).

CONCEPTUALIZATION

Developmental Issues   Intelligibility of speech is largely dependent on a normal developmental process. At 18 months of age, 25% of a child's speech is intelligible at 18 months. By 36 months, 75% to 100% of speech is intelligible. Articulation disorder has been found to be more prevalent in males, with approximately 3 times as many boys being affected as girls. Roughly 7% to 8% of children ages 5 years and older meet criteria for a diagnosis of phonological or articulation disorder (American Psychiatric Association, 2000; Shriberg & Kwiatkowski, 1994).

The onset of stuttering typically occurs between the ages of 2 and 7 years (peaking at 5 years old), with 98% of cases being reported before the age of 10. Stuttering is estimated to affect 1% of the population worldwide, with figures ranging from .03% to 2.1% in school-age children (Lue, 2001) and affecting approximately 5% of preschool-age children. In childhood, the male-to-female ratio of stuttering is approximately 3:1 (Miltenberger & Woods, 1998). In addition, individuals with stuttering have been found to display phonological disorder and expressive language disorder at a higher frequency than the general population (American Psychiatric Association, 2000).

Due to the fact that articulation is a skill that develops naturally with age, the majority of children are likely to experience difficulties with articulation that are considered common in normal development. However, when a child displays articulation difficulties beyond what is considered typical for his or her age or developmental level, a SLP should be contacted to determine if further assessment is needed (Sunderland, 2004). In children with mild or moderate forms of the disorder (not due to a medical condition), approximately 75% show spontaneous normalization by 6 years of age. Similarly, about 10% of people have stuttered at any time in their lives with sufficient severity to be classified as having a stuttering disorder (Miltenberger & Woods, 1998). Twenty-five percent of all children experience a normal stage of stuttering as they develop speech (with 4% having stuttering difficulties for 6 months or more; Lue, 2001).

Learning and Modeling   In the absence of physical problems (e.g., dental occlusions, cleft palate, cerebral palsy), mental retardation, or other obvious medical or neurological conditions, the most likely (and parsimonious) etiology of articulation problems is that the child has failed to learn the proper means of reproducing certain speech sounds. Thus, speech therapy for articulation problems focuses on teaching the oral movements that produce correct speech sounds.

An operant model can also be applied to the *etiology* of stuttering. For example, when parents or others notice a child's dysfluency, they may reprimand the child or respond in other ways that increase the child's anxiety or physiological arousal in speaking situations, such that the tension or arousal alone may serve to increase the frequency of stuttering. Also, stuttering may become negatively reinforced by the tension reduction in the vocal muscles (e.g., laryngeal muscles) that immediately follows the stutter, therefore increasing the likelihood of stuttering behavior as a means to achieve tension reduction during speech (Miltenberger & Woods, 1998).

In addition, the operant model can also be used to explain the *maintenance* of stuttering. Specifically, it is reasoned that if external contingencies (e.g., reinforcement and punishment) can increase or decrease fluency rates, then similar factors may also be maintaining stuttering behaviors. For example, stuttering may be reinforced by parents or others who complete the child's sentences, thus allowing the child to escape an aversive speaking situation. Social reinforcement (e.g., attention by parents or others to a child who stutters) should be considered in the maintenance of stuttering (Miltenberger & Woods, 1998).

Parental Issues   Although speech and language therapists play a key and primary role in remediating all types of communication disorders, parents also play a vital role in influencing the rate of therapeutic progress. Parents who implement strategies and prompts at home and who support the therapist's recommendations typically see faster progress in treatment. In addition, parents of children with communication disorders may develop anxiety regarding their child's social and communicative competency. In some cases, parents may begin to doubt their parenting skills because their child is not speaking clearly and, in the case of stuttering, may feel that the problem is being exacerbated by their parenting practices (Rustin, 1995).

Life Events   A number of life events may impact a child's ability to clearly articulate speech sounds. For instance, dental trauma can cause articulation errors, and severe malocclusions can prevent the child from making the correct lip or tongue movements (Witzel, 1996). In other cases, motor disorders such as cerebral palsy may be related to errors in articulation because of the lack of motor control over the oral musculature that produces speech sounds. It is not uncommon for there to also be problems in articulation with children who have a hearing impairment, either congenital or acquired, or in children with mental retardation.

The research regarding the role of trait anxiety in children who stutter is mixed; some studies have found a relationship between trait anxiety and stuttering, and others have not (Blood, Blood, Bennett, & Simpson, 1994; Craig, 1990; Woods, Miltenberer, & Flach, 1996). Relatedly, state (or situation-specific) anxiety seems to play a larger role in stuttering in that certain situations, such as speaking novel or difficult words, that can cause anxiety may result in an increase in the frequency of stuttering (Miltenberger & Woods, 1998).

Genetic Influences   A large percentage of speech problems occur because of difficulties coordinating the oral-motor muscles responsible for the production of speech sounds that provide speech sound articulation, fluency, and an individual's voice (Cohen, 2001). In some cases of articulation disorder, there is a clear association with hearing impairment (e.g., due to chronic otitis media with effusion), structural problems of the oral peripheral speech mechanism (e.g., cleft palate), neurological disorders (e.g., cerebral palsy), cognitive abilities (e.g., Mental Retardation), or psychosocial problems. However, in at least 3% of preschool children with articulation disorders, the cause is unknown and is therefore referred to as a functional or developmental disorder.

Familial clustering (Gupta, 1999) and twin studies (American Psychiatric Association, 2000) provide strong evidence for a genetic component in the development of stuttering. The risk of stuttering for first-degree biological relatives is more than 3 times the risk in the general population. For men who have a history of stuttering, it is estimated that approximately 10% of their daughters and 20% of their sons will also stutter. Also, the presence or family history of phonological disorder or expressive language disorder increases the likelihood of stuttering (American Psychiatric Association, 2000).

Peer Influences   Unfortunately, children with communication difficulties are viewed as less than competent by their peers and are more likely to experience social problems. Hall (1991) found that fourth- and sixth-grader with mild articulation problems were viewed more negatively by peers than children without articulation problems. Sadly, being excluded from social groups may inhibit the development of more proficient speech because of reduced opportunities to interact with fluent speakers and benefit from peer modeling.

Although peers may not play a role in the etiology of stuttering, they do seem to be aware of speech dysfluencies as young as 3 years of age. Vanryckeghem, Brutten, and Hernandez (2005) found that the speech-relevant self-concept among children ages 3 to 6 who stuttered was significantly lower than for same-age and same-sex peers who did not stutter. Because of their negative self-evaluation regarding their own speech, children who stutter may avoid speaking situations, thus exacerbating stuttering. Recent research continues to support earlier studies suggesting that children who stutter are more likely to be bullied by their peers and more likely to experience social rejection when compared to children who did not stutter (Davis, Howell, & Cooke, 2002).

Physical Factors Affecting Behavior   Children who have experienced a traumatic brain injury can suffer injuries to the structures of the brain involved in communication. Those areas crucial for the production of speech—specifically, the structures involved in the coordination of the phonation and articulation of speech—may be injured or damaged as the result of a traumatic brain injury, commonly resulting in dysarthric speech (e.g., slow speech accompanied by articulation difficulties) or dysfluent speech (i.e., stuttering). However, overall speech problems are less likely to occur than language problems for children who have suffered a traumatic brain injury (Schoenbrodt, 2004).

Articulation disorders are common in persons with cleft palates or a history of cleft palates or faulty velopharyngeal structure or function, and may also be the result of some dental irregularities. Articulation difficulties are common to those born with fetal alcohol syndrome as the result of structural abnormalities or the delayed development of one or more speech mechanisms. Stuttering is common in people with Down syndrome (Schoenbrodt, 2004).

Cultural and Diversity Issues   The American Psychiatric Association (2000) recommends that assessments of communication disorders must take into account the culture and language of the child. Brice (2001) warns that children who speak English as a second language or speak in a different dialect do not have a communication disorder simply because of their unique language or dialect. Brice recommends that to diagnose a child who is an English-language learner as having a communication disorder, the difficulties must be apparent in both languages or dialects.

Culturally based differences have been found regarding attitude toward speech disorders. For instance, people born outside of North America were more likely to associate speech disorders with emotional and psychological disturbance than people born in North America (Bebout & Arthur, 1992).

Cultural factors also play an important role in determining the cause and course of stuttering and therefore should be given substantial consideration. Experts believe stuttering is best viewed as a multidimensional disorder encompassing affective, behavioral, and cognitive domains (often referred to as the ABCs of stuttering), in which cultural factors have a great impact. Therefore, complete assessments must take into account the feelings and attitudes of the individual, especially those that may be culture-specific (Cooper & Cooper, 1998).

Behavioral Treatment

Many pediatric communication disorders show significant improvement with therapy led by a SLP. The goal of speech-language therapy is to instruct children on new techniques to help them overcome their difficulties (Brice, 2001). Interventions by a SLP for children with articulation difficulties initially focus on acquisition (i.e., teaching the child to physically produce the desired sound). Next, intervention will focus on generalization (i.e., having the child demonstrate correct articulation in a variety of contexts and settings, such as with and without a model by the SLP, the desired sound at the start of a word, and at the end of a word). Teachers and parents of a child with articulation difficulties are recommended to focus on the child's message instead of his or her errors and to notice and reinforce the child's improvements (Sunderland, 2004).

Significant improvements can also be made by children with stuttering difficulties through the interventions applied in speech therapy (Gupta, 1999). Present research suggests that recovery estimates range from 20% to 80% and that some diagnosed with stuttering also show spontaneous recovery (typically before 16 years of age; American Psychiatric Association, 2000).

The SLP begins a stuttering intervention by first increasing the child's awareness of any specific difficulties he or she is having (e.g., troublesome sounds) as well as any situations that have been observed to increase his or her difficulties speaking fluently (e.g., anxiety, stress; Sunderland, 2004). In a study by Wagaman, Miltenberger, and Arndorfer (1993), both children and their parents participated in awareness training as a component to stuttering treatment; specifically, they were instructed to identify all instances of stuttering by the child verbally or by raising their hand.

Next, the SLP instructs the child on a variety of strategies to assist in diminishing the disorder, including relaxation techniques (Sunderland, 2004). Wagaman et al. (1993) incorporated instruction of relaxation techniques (along with modeling diaphragmatic breathing) in treatment as well. This portion of treatment included teaching proper breathing techniques (e.g., lengthening the diaphragm during inhale and reducing it during exhale) to the children and their parents, instructing the children to speak during natural exhalations, and modeling how to monitor if this is being done correctly by placing a finger up to the mouth as they spoke (to feel the exhale of a breath), as well as instructing the children to stop speaking if they began to stutter and begin the relaxation techniques immediately.

In addition, interventions can include instructing parents and teachers to talk to children who stutter in a calm, slow, and relaxed manner, to respond after a 2- to 3-second pause after the child finishes speaking, and to avoid situations in which the child stutters (e.g., fatigue, stress, competition). Also, parents and teachers should make their best attempts to not interrupt the child while he or she is speaking and should focus on occasions where the child speaks fluently and apply praise and reinforcement as appropriate (Gupta, 1999). Praise applied during the social support phase was the third element of treatment by Wagaman et al. (1993, p. 54), which concluded the "simplified form of behavioral treatment for stuttering in children." Overall, this version of treatment was found to decrease the level of stuttering in all eight participants, was maintained through posttreatment (10 to 13 months later), and generalized outside of treatment for all participants.

Although SLP-guided interventions have been found to significantly impact stuttering in children, Brice (2001) adds that improvement does not always imply being cured. Gupta (1999) also notes that studies demonstrating the positive impact of speech therapy on stuttering are often confounded by natural remission, waxing and waning of the disorder, and relapse. Nonetheless, the importance of early referral for children with stuttering difficulties to a SLP is recognized (Sunderland, 2004).

MEDICAL TREATMENT

Articulation problems that occur as the result of a motor disorder, such as Parkinson's disease, may respond favorably to medication such as one that is levodopa-based (Goberman, Coelho, & Robb, 2005). However, because the articulation problems of children are usually not due to a physical disorder or disease process, medication is very rarely, if ever, used in treatment. For treating stuttering, three drugs have been shown to be effective: olanzapine (Lavid, Franklin, & Maguire, 1999; Maguire et al., 2004), haloperidol (Ludlow & Braun, 1993; Murray, Kelly, Campbell, & Stefanik, 1977), and risperidone (Maguire, Riley, Franklin, & Gottschalk, 2000). Given the side effects often associated with these medications, they should be used cautiously in children who stutter or perhaps when other, nonpharmacological interventions have not been effective.

Case Description

Case Introduction

Jann is a 10-year-old Caucasian female attending fifth grade in a middle-class suburban school district. She lives with her father, Karl, mother, Janeen, and 12-year-old brother, Travis. Her brother performs exceptionally well in school, earning straight A's. Jann is described by both parents as being socially outgoing, interested in arts and crafts, and working below her true academic potential.

Presenting Complaints

The primary problems, according to Jann's parents, are her difficulty with reading, spelling, and language-related subjects. In fact, her parents report that she is dyslexic and LD in reading. Jann reports that she does not enjoy reading and would rather spend her time playing outside, watching TV, and playing games with her brother. Jann is also described by her parents as being messy and disorganized. She has been receiving special education services for 1 year at her elementary school, with a diagnosis of LD in reading.

History

Jann's parents report that she met all developmental milestones within normal limits, including all aspects of language development (i.e., babbling, saying first words, putting two words together, and using sentences). She attended day care and preschool part time (3 days per week) and was enrolled in kindergarten at

(continued)

---

age 5. Her mother indicates that Jann was never as interested in academic-type tasks as either her brother or her peers, as she prefers more physical activities. Jann's grade reports and teacher notes reveal that she had difficulty in learning sound-symbol relationships and that she did not progress as rapidly as her peers in learning phonics or sight words. Jann's grades have been mostly B's and C's with an occasional A.

Jann's parents expressed concern to her teachers and school principal when Jann was in second grade regarding her difficulty and lack of enjoyment in reading. The school responded by saying that Jann was not sufficiently far behind her peers for a formal evaluation to be conducted. Her teacher indicated that she would provide Jann with extra help in reading. She also recommended to her parents some home instructional strategies (e.g., sounding out words, reading 20 minutes per day) and that private tutoring 2 to 3 days per week would be helpful. A tutor was hired and focused on using a phonics-based approach to teaching reading. For the past 2 years, Jann has been working with her tutor 2 days per week for 1 hour each session. By the end of second grade, Jann's parents were not satisfied with her progress in reading. They sought and obtained a private neuropsychological evaluation to determine if she met criteria for a learning disability, the results of which are detailed next.

Assessment

A licensed psychologist conducted a neuropsychological evaluation on Jann using the WISC-IV, the Woodcock-Johnson III Tests of Achievement, the Clinical Evaluation of Language Fundamentals-4, the Wide Range Assessment of Memory and Learning-2, the Beery Visual Motor Integration Test, the Conners Continuous Performance Test, and the Behavior Assessment System for Children (Parent Report, Teacher Report, and Self-Report). The results of this comprehensive battery of tests revealed low-average cognitive abilities (Full-Scale IQ was 92), average reading scores (Broad Reading was 90), low-average language scores (Core Language score was 84), average verbal and visual memory, low-average visual-motor integration skills, and average behavioral functioning. The only area where the psychologist identified potential problems was in impulsive responding and borderline inattention. Despite the consistency of all the test scores, the psychologist concluded that Jann presented the profile of a student with a learning disability in reading and further offered that a phonics-based approach, such as the Orton-Gillingham method, could be useful. This recommendation was offered apparently without consideration that Jann had been receiving tutoring using a phonics-based method for the past 2 years with limited success. The battery of tests administered to Jann is illustrative of the problems associated with using traditional psychoeducational evaluations for treatment planning. Unfortunately, no direct measure of reading performance was obtained, and the results of testing were of only limited utility for treatment planning.

Group achievement test scores provided by the school indicated that Jann was reading at about one grade level lower than her grade placement. When compared to her overall cognitive abilities, it appeared that Jann was reading at the level expected based on the traditional discrepancy formula for determining LD.

Case Conceptualization

Despite the somewhat ambiguous nature of the assessment results, Jann was brought by her parents to our academic clinic for assessment and treatment of reading problems. A thorough review was conducted of her developmental, medical, and social history, all of which were unremarkable. There were no medical conditions, such as otitis media with effusion, injuries or traumas, developmental difficulties or lags, or other factors that could be clearly linked to her current reading problems. In fact, Jann presented as a normal 10-year-old female based on her appearance, use of language, social skills, and style of dress. She presented as somewhat quiet at first, which was to be expected, but became quite talkative after her parents left the room.

Jann was first interviewed to determine her perception of her academic skills and to have her identify any areas of concern, academic or otherwise. She identified reading as being difficult for her and indicated that she would like to be a more fluent reader. She also indicated that she and her parents often argued about her academic progress and that they became frustrated when helping her read. Jann did not indicate any other problems either at school or home.

To obtain a direct measure of Jann's overall reading skills, we first asked her to read short passages (1–3 minutes) from library books that she brought from home and that were appropriate for her age and area of interest. We then had her read from selected passages from her curricular materials that required independent reading (e.g., social studies, science). Jann was timed so that we could compute a *words correct per minute* (WCPM) score as well as number of errors. We also noted the words on which she made errors and the type of errors made so that we could conduct an analysis of her typical error patterns. After Jann read three passages, some consistencies emerged across readings. First, Jann's oral reading rate and WCPM were commensurate with her grade placement. Second, she was not proficient at decoding unknown words. Third, she made substitutions of unknown words with known words that frequently altered the meaning of the sentence. Fourth, when she made an error or had difficulty reading a word, she either repeated a few words prior to the unknown word and continued reading or she reread the entire sentence. Finally, she lacked prosody in her reading.

Upon obtaining these data and considering her history of tutoring using a phonics-based approach, we decided that improving her sight word vocabulary might improve her reading fluency. To determine the most effective means of teaching sight words, we tested two instructional approaches based on SAFMEDS (**S**ay **A**ll **F**ast **M**inute **E**very **D**ay **S**huffled), a, precision teaching approach (). We printed words that she incorrectly identified from her reading passages on index cards, one word per card. We then randomly assigned 30 words to either a rapid condition (10 words), a slow condition (10 words), or a control condition (10 words). In the rapid condition, Jann was shown the word, which was correctly pronounced for her, and then she rapidly repeated

(continued)

the word 2 or 3 times. Thus, each word was presented for approximately 3 to 5 seconds. In the slow condition, the same basic procedure was implemented except that Jann was prompted to look carefully at the word, say it out loud, continue looking at it, and then say it several more times out loud. In the slow condition, each word was presented for approximately 10 seconds or longer. In the control condition, no instruction was given on the words. After all the words had been presented once according to these procedures, each word was again presented and Jann was prompted to say each word. Correctly pronounced words were placed in one pile and incorrect words were placed in a separate pile. Words from the incorrect pile were again instructed using the procedure for that condition. The instructional procedure was continued until all 10 words were correctly identified. The three primary dependent variables of interest were the number of words correctly pronounced on the first trial, the number of trials required for all 10 words to be correctly pronounced, and the amount of generalization from the index cards to the reading passages. A secondary variable of interest was the procedure that Jann identified as being the most preferred.

Our results were consistent with those of Watson and Ray (1997), who found that the rapid condition resulted in faster acquisition of target words and required less instructional time than the slow condition. In addition, generalization was 80% from the index cards to the reading passages. That is, 80% of the words correctly pronounced on the index cards were subsequently correctly pronounced when Jann read the word in context from her reading passage. Jann also reported that she liked the faster condition better.

The entire instructional sequence, from identifying mispronounced words to instruction and assessment, were modeled for Jann's parents and her tutor. Her parents were instructed to use this procedure 3 times per week, and her tutor was instructed to use it for all words incorrectly pronounced during their tutoring time. Both Jann's parents and her tutor were cautioned not to use a decoding or phonics-based approach to help Jann identify unknown words. An intervention script detailing each of the procedures was developed and given to her parents and tutor. In addition, a dot-to-dot reinforcement program was implemented whereby reinforcement was provided for complying and participating with the procedure and not for number of words pronounced correctly.

Course of Treatment and Assessment of Progress

Jann's parents and tutor were given monitoring sheets so that treatment integrity could be assessed and progress measured (Watson, 2004). For the first 4 weeks, we examined the data sheets and graphed Jann's progress on the three primary dependent variables. We also assessed Jann's WCPM and number of errors to determine if the procedure was increasing the number of words read correctly and reducing the number of errors made when reading text. Thereafter, a check was conducted every 2 to 4 weeks. The data indicated that Jann was becoming a more proficient reader (i.e., more words correct and fewer errors while maintaining generalization) but that prosody had not significantly improved. In addition, Jann's parents anecdotally reported that she was engaging in more spontaneous reading than before. Given the results, the next phase of treatment was to improve prosody.

Complicating Factors

The primary complicating factors in this type of intervention are (a) the integrity of the intervention process and (b) boredom with the procedure for Jann, her parents, and her tutor. We hoped that providing instructional scripts, training the parents and tutor in the intervention, monitoring the data sheets, and conducting follow-up assessments would help to promote treatment integrity. With regard to becoming bored with the intervention, we modeled using verbal reinforcement during the instructional procedure and implemented the dot-to-dot program for compliance rather than performance.

Follow-Up

Jann and her parents were called between visits to determine if there were any problems with implementation or motivation. We also assessed performance with reading probes approximately 1 time per month. We assessed WCPM, errors, generalization, and comprehension to make certain that the instructional procedure was continuing to be effective for Jann and that it was making a difference in her in-school academic performance (a social validity measure).

TREATMENT IMPLICATIONS OF THE CASE

Generally, phonics-based reading instruction is an effective means of remediating reading problems, particularly in the younger grades. However, this approach was not effective for Jann. Despite minimal progress using a phonics-based approach, Jann's school, her tutor, and the psychologist recommended that this approach be continued. A better approach would have been to utilize the RTI approach to develop an intervention strategy that was effective for Jann.

RECOMMENDATIONS FOR CLINICIANS

The utilization of an RTI strategy by school personnel might have eliminated the need for a referral to our clinic in the first place. That is, when Jann's reading problems first became apparent, an appropriate and empirically based instructional strategy may have resulted in more rapid improvements in her reading ability and fewer negative interactions between Jann and her parents concerning academic performance. Most typically, an RTI model would involve the use of multiple, empirically based reading strategies such as listening, passage previewing, repeated reading, and paired reading (Bonfiglio, Daly, Persampieri, & Andersen, 2006). Regardless of the strategies used in an RTI model for determining the most effective intervention, the basic procedures are the same: (a) comparison of 3 to 4 empirically derived interventions; (b) repeated, brief assessments; (c) a validation phase to demonstrate that the strategy that emerged as the most effective is resulting in changes in the dependent variables; (d) implementation of the chosen strategy with a high degree of integrity; and (e) efforts to ensure that the chosen strategy is resulting in meaningful academic changes for the individual (Gresham, 2006).

SUMMARY

Approximately 15% of students experience some type of academic difficulty, although they will never be diagnosed with a learning disorder. Parents and children are often acutely aware of academic problems even when they fall short of the criteria established for the diagnosis of a learning disorder. In the past, failure to qualify for a diagnosis or special educational placement would result in the denial of many special services or accommodations. Fortunately, many school districts are now adopting a model of academic intervention that does not require the student to fail. Under these models, teachers and parents can refer students for academic assessment and intervention *before* they fail and *before* the provision of a formal diagnosis. It is imperative that practitioners become familiar with models of brief academic assessment and response to intervention so that students who are experiencing academic difficulties can receive intervention when it can be of maximum benefit and long before students and their families experience the negative side effects of many years of academic failure.

REFERENCES

Aicardi, J. (1994). Syndromic classification in the management of childhood epilepsy. *Journal of Child Neurology, 9,* 14–8.

Albright, A. (2003). Neurosurgical treatment of spasticity and other pediatric movement disorders. *Journal of Child Neurology, 18,* 67–78.

American Psychiatric Association. (2000). *Diagnostic and statistical manual of mental disorders* (4th ed., text rev.). Washington, DC: Author.

Ames, L. B., & Ilg, F. (1964). The developmental point of view with special reference to the principle of neuromotor interweaving. *Journal of Genetic Psychology, 105,* 95–209.

Ames, L. B., & Ilg, F. (1966). Individuality in motor development. *Journal of the American Physical Therapy Association, 46,* 121–127.

Aylward, E. H., Richards, T. L., Berninger, V. W., Nagy, W. E., Field, K. M., Grimme, A. C., et al. (2003). Instructional treatment associated with changes in brain activation in children with dyslexia. *Neurology, 61,* 212–219.

Bain, P., Findley, L., Thompson, P., Gresty, M., Rothwell, J., Harding, A., et al. (1994). A study of hereditary essential tremor. *Brain: A Journal of Neurology, 117,* 805–824.

Baker, D. B., & McCal, K. (1995). Parenting stress in parents of children with attention-deficit hyperactivity disorder and parents of children with learning disabilities. *Journal of Child and Family Studies, 4,* 57–68.

Bebout, L., & Arthur, B. (1992). Cross-cultural attitudes toward speech disorders. *Journal of Speech and Hearing Research, 35,* 45–52.

Belfiore, P. J., & Hutchinson, J. M. (1998). Enhancing academic achievement through related routines: A functional approach. In T. S. Watson & F. M. Gresham (Eds.), *Handbook of child behavior therapy* (pp. 83–97). New York: Plenum Press.

Blauw-Hospers, C. H., & Hadders-Algra, M. (2005). A systematic review of the effects of early intervention on motor development. *Developmental Medicine and Child Neurology, 47,* 421–432.

Blood, G. W., Blood, I. M., Bennett, S., & Simpson, K. C. (1994). Subjective anxiety measurements and cortisol responses in adults who stutter. *Journal of Speech and Hearing Research, 37*, 760–768.

Bonfiglio, C. M., Daly, E. J., Persampieri, M., & Andersen, M. (2006). An experimental analysis of the effects of reading interventions in a small group reading instruction context. *Journal of Behavioral Education, 15*, 93–109.

Bowen, C., & Cupples, L. (1998). A tested phonological therapy in practice. *Child Language Teaching and Therapy, 14*, 29–50.

Brice, A. (2001). *The ERIC Clearinghouse on disabilities and gifted education (ERIC EC): Children with communication disorders: Update 2001.* Retrieved September 16, 2006, from http://www.ericec.org/digests/e617.html.

Britner, P. A., Morog, M. A., Pianta, R. C., & Marvin, R. S. (2003). Stress and coping: A comparison of self-report measures of functioning in families of young children with cerebral palsy or no medical diagnosis. *Journal of Child and Family Studies, 12*, 335–348.

Bryan, T. (1976). Peer popularity of learning disabled children: A replication. *Journal of Learning Disabilities, 9*, 307–311.

Butler, C., & Campbell, S. (2000). Evidence of the effects of intrathecal baclofen for spastic and dystonic cerebral palsy. *Developmental Medicine and Child Neurology, 42*, 634–645.

Chidsey-Brown, R., & Steege, M. W. (2005). *Response to intervention: Principles and strategies for effective practice.* New York: Guilford Press.

Clark, J., & Whitall, J. (1989). Changing locomotion patterns: From walking to skipping. In M. Woollacott & A. Shumway-Cooke (Eds.), *Development of posture and gait across the life span* (pp. 128–151). Columbia: University of South Carolina Press.

Cohen, N. J. (2001). *Language impairment and psychopathology in infants, children, and adolescents.* Thousand Oaks, CA: Sage.

Cooper, E. B., & Cooper, C. S. (1998). Multicultural considerations in the assessment and treatment of stuttering. In D. E. Battle (Ed.), *Communication disorders in multicultural populations* (2nd ed., pp. 247–275). Boston: Butterworth-Heinemann.

Craig, A. (1990). An investigation into the relationship between anxiety and stuttering. *Journal of Speech and Hearing Disorders, 55*, 290–294.

Davis, S., Howell, P., & Cooke, F. (2002). Sociodynamic relationships between children who stutter and their non-stuttering classmates. *Journal of Child Psychology and Psychiatry, 43*, 939–947.

Dawkins, J. L. (1996). Bullying, physical disability, and the pediatric patient. *Developmental Medicine and Child Neurology, 38*, 603–612.

DeFries, J. C., Filipek, P. A., Fulker, D. W., Olson, R. K., Pennington, B. F., Smith, S. D., et al. (1997). Colorado Learning Disabilities Research Center. *Learning Disability Quarterly, 7–8*, 19.

Delgado, M. R., & Albright, A. L. (2003). Movement disorders in children: Definitions, classifications, and grading systems. *Journal of Child Neurology, 18*, S1–S8.

DuPaul, G. J., & Stoner, G. D. (1994). *ADHD in the schools: Assessment and intervention strategies.* New York: Guilford Press.

Eker, L., & Handan, T. E. (2004). An evaluation of quality of life of mothers of children with cerebral palsy. *Disability and Rehabilitation, 26*, 1354–1359.

Fahn, S., Greene, P., Ford, B., & Bressman, S. (1998). *Handbook of movement disorders.* Philadelphia: Current Medicine.

Fernandez-Alvarez, E., & Aicardi, J. (2001). *Movement disorders in children.* London: Mac Keith Press.

Flynn, D., Kotkin, R. A., Brady, J., & Fine, A. H. (2003). Implementing school-home collaborative treatment plans: Best practices in school-home based interventions. In A. H. Fine & R. A.

Kotkin (Eds.), *The therapist's guide to learning and attention disorders* (pp. 211–236). San Diego, CA: Academic Press.

Flynn, J. M., & Rahbar, M. H. (1994). Prevalence of reading failure in boys compared with girls. *Psychology in the Schools, 31*, 66–71.

Fuchs, L. (2002). Three conceptualizations of "treatment" in a response-to-intervention framework for LD identification. In R. Bradley, L. Danielson, & D. Hallahan (Eds.), *Learning disabilities: Research to practice* (pp. 521–529). Mahwah, NJ: Erlbaum.

Fuchs, L., & Fuchs, D. (1997). Use of curriculum-based measurement in identifying students with disabilities. *Focus on Exceptional Children, 30*, 1–16.

Gable, L. F. (2002). The efficacy of a school-home note intervention using Internet communication for decreasing inappropriate classroom behaviors of secondary level students (Doctoral dissertation, Mississippi State University, 2002). *Dissertation Abstracts International, 63*, 496.

Goberman, A. M., Coelho, C. A., & Robb, M. P. (2005). Prosodic characteristics of Parkinsonian speech: The effect of levodopa-based medication. *Journal of Medical Speech-Language Pathology, 13*, 51–68.

Good, R., Gruba, J., & Kaminski, R. (2002). Best practices in using Dynamic Indicators of Basic Early Literacy Skills (DIBELS) in an outcome-driven model. In A. Thomas & J. Grimes (Eds.), *Best practices in school psychology: Pt. IV* (pp. 611–649). Bethesda, MD: National Association of School Psychologists.

Graziano, A. M. (2002). *Developmental disabilities: Introduction to a diverse field.* Needham Heights, MA: Allyn & Bacon.

Gresham, F. M. (2006). Response to intervention. In G. G. Bear & K. M. Minke (Eds.), *Children's needs: Pt. III. Development, prevention, and intervention* (pp. 525–540). Bethesda, MD: National Association of School Psychologists.

Gresham, F. M., MacMillan, D. L., Bocian, K. M., Ward, S. L., & Forness, S. R. (1998). Comorbidity of hyperactivity-impulsivity-inattention and conduct problems: Risk factors in social, affective, and academic domains. *Journal of Abnormal Child Psychology, 26*, 393–406.

Gupta, V. B. (1999). *Manual of developmental and behavioral problems in children.* New York: Dekker.

Hall, B. C. (1991). Attitudes of fourth and sixth graders toward peers with mild articulation disorders. *Language, Speech, and Hearing Services in Schools, 22*, 334–340.

Horowitz, E. C. (1981). Popularity, de-centering ability, and role-taking skills in learning disabled and normal children. *Learning Disability Quarterly, 4*, 23–30.

Kalyanpur, M., & Harry, B. (2004). Impact of the social construction of LD on culturally diverse families: A response to Reid and Valle. *Journal of Learning Disabilities, 37*, 530–533.

Kavale, K. A., & Forness, S. R. (1995). Social skill deficits and training: A meta-analysis of the research in learning disabilities. *Advances in Learning and Behavioral Disabilities, 9*, 119–160.

Kay, S. (2005). The effects of a parent delivered direct instruction reading curriculum on the early literacy skills of first grade children (Doctoral dissertation, University of Massachusetts, Amherst, 2005). *Dissertation Abstracts International, 66*, 489.

Koller, W., Silver, D., & Lieberman, A. (1994). An algorithm for the management of Parkinson's disease. *Neurology, 44*, 1–52.

Kuhne, M., & Wiener, J. (2000). Stability of social status of children with and without learning disabilities. *Learning Disability Quarterly, 23*, 64–75.

Lau, K. L. (2006). Implementing strategy instruction in Chinese language classes: A school-based Chinese reading strategy instruction program. *Educational Research, 48*, 195–209.

Lavid, N., Franklin, D. L., & Maguire, G. A. (1999). Management of child and adolescent stuttering with olanzapine: Three case reports. *Annals of Clinical Psychiatry, 11*, 233–236.

Lenti, C., & Bianchini, E. (1993). Neuropsychological and neuroradiological study of a case of early-onset Huntington's chorea. *Developmental Medicine and Child Neurology, 35,* 1007–1010.

Leppert, M. O., & Capute, A. J. (1996). Cerebral palsy and associated dysfunction. In R. A. Haslam & P. J. Valetutti (Eds.), *Medical problems in the classroom: The teacher's role in diagnosis and management* (pp. 341–359). Austin, TX: ProEd.

Ludlow, C. L., & Braun, A. (1993). Research evaluating the use of neuropharmacological agents for treating stuttering: Possibilities and problems. *Journal of Fluency Disorders, 18,* 169–182.

Lue, M. S. (2001). *A survey of communication disorders for the classroom teacher.* Boston: Allyn & Bacon.

Lyon, G. R. (1996). Learning disabilities. *Special Education for Students with Learning Disabilities, 6,* 54–76.

Macmillan, D. L., & Siperstein, G. N. (2002). Learning disabilities as operationally defined as schools. In R. Bradley, L. Danielson, & D. P. Hallahan (Eds.), *Identification of learning disabilities: Research to practice* (pp. 287–333). Mahwah, NJ: Erlbaum.

Maguire, G. A., Riley, G. D., Franklin, D. L., & Gottschalk, L. A. (2000). Risperidone in the treatment of stuttering. *Journal of Clinical Psychopharmacology, 20,* 479–482.

Maguire, G. A., Riley, G. D., Franklin, D. L., Maguire, M. E., Nguyen, C. T., & Brojeni, P. H. (2004). Olanzapine in the treatment of developmental stuttering: A double-blind, placebo-controlled trial. *Annals of Clinical Psychiatry, 16,* 63–67.

Maheady, L., & Sainato, D. (1986). Learning-disabled students' perceptions of social events. In S. J. Ceci (Ed.), *Handbook of cognitive, social, and neuropsychological aspects of learning disabilities* (pp. 381–402). Hillsdale, NJ: Erlbaum.

Mahoney, G., & Perales, F. (2006). The role of parents in early motor intervention. *Down Syndrome: Research and Practice, 10*(2), 67–73.

Malina, R. M. (1984). Physical growth and maturation. In J. R. Thomas (Ed.), *Development during childhood and adolescence* (pp. 2–26). Minneapolis, MN: Burgess.

Mayes, S. D., Calhoun, S. L., & Crowell, E. W. (2000). Learning disabilities and ADHD: Overlapping spectrum disorders. *Journal of Learning Disabilities, 33,* 417–424.

McCain, A. P., & Kelley, M. L. (1994). Improving classroom performance in underachieving preadolescents: The additive effects of response cost to a school-home note system. *Child and Family Behavior Therapy, 16,* 27–41.

McLaughlin, J., Bjornson, K., Temkin, N., Steinbok, P., Wright, V., Reiner, A., et al. (2002). Selective dorsal rhizotomy: Meta-analysis of three randomized controlled trials. *Developmental Medicine and Child Neurology, 44,* 17–25.

Miccio, A. W., Gallagher, E., Grossman, C. B., Yont, K. M., & Vernon-Feagans, L. (2001). Influence of chronic otitis media on phonological acquisition. *Clinical Linguistics and Phonetics, 15,* 47–51.

Miltenberger, R. G., & Woods, D. W. (1998). Speech dysfluencies. In T. S. Watson & F. M. Gresham (Eds.), *Handbook of child behavior therapy* (pp. 127–142). New York: Plenum Press.

Misbahuddin, A., & Warner, T. (2001). Dystonia: An update on genetics and treatment. *Current Opinion in Neurology, 14,* 471–475.

Morgan, A., Koch, V., Lee, V., & Aldag, J. (1988). Neonatal Neurobehavioral Examination: A new instrument for quantitative analysis of neonatal neurological status. *Physical Therapy, 68,* 1352–1358.

Morton, R., Sharma, V., Nicholson, J., Broderick, M., & Poyser, J. (2002). Disability in children from different ethnic populations. *Child: Care, Health, and Development, 28,* 87–93.

Murray, T. J., Kelly, P., Campbell, L., & Stefanik, K. (1977). Haloperidol in the treatment of stuttering. *British Journal of Psychiatry, 130*, 370–373.

National Center for Learning Disabilities. (2006). *LD at a glance.* Retrieved September 19, 2006, from http://www.ncld.org/index.php.

Nereo, N. E., Fee, R. J., & Hinton, V. J. (2003). Parental stress in mothers of boys with Duchenne muscular dystrophy. *Journal of Pediatric Psychology, 28*, 473–484.

O'Brien, C. C. (1994). Motor development and learning and children. In G. Boulton-Lewis & D. Catherwood (Eds.), *The early years* (pp. 145–185). Victoria: Australian Council for Educational Research.

O'Moore, A. & Hillery, B. (1989). Bullying in Dublin schools. *Irish Journal of Psychology, 10*, 426–441.

Osborne, J., Munson, P., & Burman, D. (1982). Huntington's chorea: Report of 3 cases and review of the literature. *Archives of Disease in Childhood, 57*, 99–103.

Pennington, B. (1995). Genetics of learning disabilities. *Journal of Child Neurology, 10*(Suppl. 1), S69–S77.

Reid, D. K., & Valle, J. W. (2004). The discursive practice of LD: Implications for instruction and parent-school relations. *Journal of Learning Disabilities, 37*, 466–481.

Rivera, M. O., Al-Otaiba, S., & Koorland, M. A. (2006). Reading instruction for students with emotional and behavioral disorders and at risk of antisocial behaviors in primary grades: Review of literature. *Behavioral Disorders, 31*, 323–337.

Ruiz, M., Le Fever, J., & Hakanson, D. (1981). Early development of infants of birth weight less than 1,000 grams with reference to mechanical ventilation in newborn period. *Pediatrics, 68*, 330–335.

Rustin, L. (1995). Parents and families of children with communication disorders. *Folia Phoniatrica et Logopaedica, 47*, 123–129.

Sanger, T. D. (2003). Pediatric movement disorders. *Current Opinion in Neurology, 16*, 529–535.

Sanger, T. D. (2005, January 28). *Pediatric movement disorders.* Retrieved October 1, 2005, from http://www.mdvu.org/library/pediatric.

Schoenbrodt, L. (2004). *Childhood communication disorders: Organic bases.* Clifton Park, NY: Thomson/Delmar Learning.

Shannon, J. B. (2003). *Movement disorders sourcebook.* Detroit, MI: Omnigraphics.

Shaywitz, S. E., & Shaywitz, B. A. (2003). Neurobiological indices of dyslexia. In H. L. Swanson, K. R. Harris, & S. Graham (Eds.), *Handbook of learning disabilities* (pp. 514–531). New York: Guilford Press.

Shaywitz, S. E., & Shaywtiz, B. A. (2004). Neurobiologic basis for reading and reading disability. In P. McCardle & V. Chhabra (Eds.), *The voice of evidence in reading research* (pp. 417–442). Baltimore: Paul H. Brookes.

Shaywitz, S. E., Shaywitz, B. A., Fletcher, J. M., & Escobar, M. D. (1990). Prevalence of reading disability in boys and girls: Results of the Connecticut longitudinal study. *Journal of the American Medical Association, 264*, 998–1002.

Shriberg, L. D., & Kwiatkowski, J. (1994). Developmental phonological disorders: Pt. I. A clinical profile. *Journal of Speech and Hearing Research, 37*, 1100–1126.

Singer, H. (1986). Tardive dyskinesia: A concern for the pediatrician. *Pediatrics, 77*, 553–556.

Spiker, D., Boyce, G., & Boyce, L. (2002). Parent-child interactions when young children have disabilities. In L. Glidden (Ed.), *International review of research in mental retardation* (Vol. 25, pp. 35–70). San Diego: Academic Press.

Sunderland, L. C. (2004). Speech, language, and audiology services in public schools. *Intervention in School and Clinic, 39*, 209–217.

Swanson, H. L. (2005). Working memory, intelligence, and learning disabilities. In O. Wilhelm, & R. W. Engle (Eds.), *Handbook of understanding and measuring intelligence* (pp. 409–429). Thousand Oaks, CA: Sage.

Swanson, H. L., & Malone, S. (1992). Social skills and learning disabilities: A meta-analysis of the literature. *School Psychology Review, 21,* 427–443.

Teele, D. W., Klein, J. O., Chase, C., Menyuk, P., & Rosner, B. A. (1990). Otitis media in infancy and intellectual ability, school achievement, speech, and language at age 7 years. Greater Boston Otitis Media Study Group. *Journal of Infectious Diseases, 162,* 685–694.

Theodore, L. A., Bray, M. A., Kehle, T. J., & DioGuardi, R. J. (2006). Language-related disorders in childhood. In L. Phelps (Ed.), *Chronic health-related disorders in children: Collaborative medical and psychoeducational interventions* (pp. 139–155). Washington, DC: American Psychological Association.

Thomas, J. R. (1984). Children's motor skill development. In J. R. Thomas (Ed.), *Development during childhood and adolescence* (pp. 91–104). Minneapolis, MN: Burgess.

U.S. Office of Education (1977). Assistance to states for education for handicapped children: Procedures for evaluating specific learning disabilities. *Federal Register, 42,* G1082–G1085.

Vanryckeghem, M., Brutten, G. J., & Hernandez, L. M. (2005). A comparative investigation of the speech-associated attitude of preschool and kindergarten children who do and do not stutter. *Journal of Fluency Disorders, 30,* 307–318.

Vaughn, S., & Elbaum, B. (1999). The self-concept and friendships of students with learning disabilities: A developmental perspective. In R. Gallimore (Ed.), *Developmental perspectives with high incidence disabilities* (pp. 81–107). Mahwah, NJ: Erlbaum.

Wagaman, J. R., Miltenberger, R. G., & Arndorfer, R. E. (1993). Analysis of a simplified treatment for stuttering in children. *Journal of Applied Behavior Analysis, 26,* 53–61.

Waggoner, K., & Wilgosh, L. (1990). Concerns of families of children with learning disabilities. *Journal of Learning Disabilities, 23,* 97–98, 113.

Watson, T. S. (2004). Treatment integrity. In T. S. Watson & C. H. Skinner (Eds.), *Encyclopedia of school psychology* (pp. 356–358). New York: Kluwer Press.

Watson, T. S., & Ray, K. P. (1997). The effects of different units of measurement on instructional decision making. *School Psychology Quarterly, 12,* 42–53.

Wechsler, D. (2003). *Wechsler Intelligence Scale for Children* (WISC-IV, 4th ed.). San Antonio, TX: Harcourt.

West, A. B., Lockhart, P. J., O'Farell, C., & Farrer, M. J. (2003). Identification of a novel gene linked to Parkinsons via a bi-directional promoter. *Journal of Molecular Biology, 326,* 11–19.

Westrup, B., Bohm, B., Lagercrantz, H., & Stjernqvist, K. (2004). Preschool outcome in children born very prematurely and cared for according to the Newborn Individualized Developmental Care and Assessment Program (NIDCAP). *Acta Paediatrica, 93,* 498–507.

Wetherby, A. M., & Prizant, B. M. (1997). Speech, language, and communication disorders in young children. In J. D. Noshpitz, S. Greenspan, S. Wieder, & J. Osofsky (Eds.), *Handbook of child and adolescent psychiatry* (Vol. 1, pp. 473–491). New York: Wiley.

Whitney, I., Smith, P. K., & Thompson, D. (1994). Bullying and children with special educational needs. In P. K. Smith & S. Sharp (Eds.), *School bullying: Insights and perspectives* (pp. 213–240). New York: Routledge.

Wiener, J. (1987). Peer status of learning disabled children and adolescents: A review of the literature. *Learning Disabilities Research, 2,* 62–69.

Wiener, J. (2004). Do peer relationships foster behavioral adjustment in children with learning disabilities? *Learning Disability Quarterly, 27,* 21–30.

Wiener, J., & Tardif, C. (2004). Social and emotional functioning of children with learning disabilities: Does special education placement make a difference? *Learning Disabilities Research and Practice, 19,* 20–33.

Witzel, M. A. (1996). Communication disorders associated with medical problems. In R. H. A. Haslam & P. J. Velletutti (Eds.), *Medical problems in the classroom: The teacher's role in diagnosis and management* (3rd ed., pp. 209–246). Austin, TX: ProEd.

Woodcock, R. W., McGrew, K. S., & Mather, N. (2001). *Woodcock-Johnson III Tests of Achievement.* Itasca, IL: Riverside.

Woods, D. W., Miltenberger, R. G., & Flach, A. D. (1996). Habits, tics, and stuttering: Prevalence and relation to anxiety and somatic awareness. *Behavior Modification, 20,* 216–225.

CHAPTER 14

Attention-Deficit/Hyperactivity Disorder

MARK D. RAPPORT, MICHAEL J. KOFLER, R. MATT ALDERSON,
AND JOSEPH S. RAIKER

Attention-Deficit/Hyperactivity Disorder (ADHD) is a complex, chronic, and potentially debilitating disorder of brain, behavior, and development that affects between 3% and 7% of school-age children, or approximately 1.1 to 2.5 million children between 5 and 13 years of age in the United States, based on recent census estimates (U.S. Census Bureau, 2005). Accumulating evidence suggests that the core symptoms of ADHD—inattentiveness, severe impulsivity (both behavioral and cognitive), and overactivity—reflect dysfunction or dysregulation of cerebellar-striatal/adrenergic-prefrontal circuitry (Castellanos, 2001).

Near-, intermediate-, and long-term studies reveal a rather bleak picture of adverse outcomes associated with ADHD, ranging from scholastic underachievement and school failure to dysfunctional interpersonal and employment-related relationships. An overwhelming majority (>90%) of children with ADHD perform poorly in school and underachieve scholastically (i.e., 10 to 15 point deficits on standardized academic achievement batteries)—a fact highlighted by the estimated 10% to 70% with comorbid learning disabilities in reading, spelling, math, or handwriting (Barkley, 2006). They make more failing grades, have lower grade point averages (1.7 vs. 2.6), and are retained (42% vs. 13%), suspended (60% vs. 19%), and expelled (14% vs. 6%) more often from school relative to typically developing peers. An alarming 23% (3% to 7% prevalence estimates = 249,000 to 581,002) to 32% (3% to 7% prevalence estimates = 346,436 to 808,351) of children with ADHD fail to complete high school (for details, see Barkley, Fischer, Smallish, & Fletcher, 2006; Mannuzza, Klein, Bessler, Malloy, & LaPadula, 1993), which translates into significantly fewer entering (22% vs. 77%) and completing (5% vs. 35%) college.

The elevated risk for adverse outcomes associated with ADHD continues throughout late adolescence. Those diagnosed with the disorder are sexually active at an earlier age, with a higher number of sexual partners, and are less likely to use contraceptives relative to their peers—a collective set of behaviors that increases their risk for teenage pregnancy and contracting sexually transmitted diseases. The inattentive and impulsive components of the disorder also contribute to their poor driving records. They receive more speeding citations (4–5 vs. 1–2) and are involved in and at fault for more vehicular accidents (26% vs. 9% involved in 3 or more crashes) relative to same-age control children, particularly those causing serious injury (60% vs. 17%). Their poorer overall driving skills are highlighted by significantly higher rates of license suspensions and revocations (32% vs. 4%) relative to same-age peers (Barkley, 2006).

The impairing nature of the disorder continues into adulthood for many individuals. A surprising 90% of children previously diagnosed with ADHD are gainfully employed by their late 20s to early 30s; however, their overall socioeconomic status is significantly lower relative to controls followed over the same time frame (Manuzza et al., 1993). Moreover, young adults with ADHD are more likely to be fired from their job (55% vs. 23%), change jobs more frequently (2.6 vs. 1.3), evince more ADHD symptoms on the job, and earn lower employee work performance ratings relative to peers. Approximately 66% of those diagnosed with ADHD during childhood continue to experience significant symptoms of the disorder as adults, and some meet diagnostic criteria for Antisocial (11%–21%), Histrionic (12%), Passive Aggressive (18%), and Borderline (14%) Personality Disorder. The increased risk associated with the development of comorbid personality disorders in adulthood, however, appears to be conveyed by elevated Conduct Disorder (CD) symptoms during childhood and/or the expression of CD problems during adolescence.

Attention-Deficit/Hyperactivity Disorder is a controversial clinical disorder and is difficult to diagnose for several reasons. One of the core symptom clusters used to define the disorder—attentional problems—has poor specificity and occurs with high frequency in many other childhood disorders. Many of the disorder's core and secondary symptoms represent dimensional variants of normal temperament, and ADHD is presumed to reflect diverse factors or pathways that result in a similar developmental outcome, a phenomenon termed *equifinality*.

Despite the abundance of assessment instruments available today, none are uniquely sensitive and valid for diagnosing ADHD. This situation is due to two intertwined factors: the introduction of ADHD as a diagnostic category prior to developing appropriate tools to measure its core features and the failure to scrutinize core deficits or features of the disorder and their underlying assumptions prior to designing assessment instruments. The initial section on current assessment strategies highlights these issues, and the conceptualization section provides a detailed discussion of theoretical issues underlying the design of clinical assessment measures for ADHD. The ensuing two sections examine empirically based treatments for ADHD, followed by a detailed case description that illustrates the major topical issues discussed throughout the chapter.

ASSESSMENT

OVERVIEW

Expert guidelines in psychiatry (McClellan & Werry, 2000) and psychology (Barkley, 2006) recommend that a qualified clinician conduct a comprehensive diagnostic evaluation utilizing multiple assessment instruments. These range from subjective measures such as ratings scales and clinical interviews to increasingly objective measures such as direct observation and sophisticated actigraphs. Aside from the handful of small *n* and uncontrolled case studies, self-report and self-monitoring instruments have been confined to assessing treatment-emergent effects (i.e., side effect rating scales) and co-occurring symptomatology (e.g., self-report depression and anxiety inventories) in ADHD. Clinicians interested in these specialty instruments can find detailed discussions throughout this book and elsewhere (cf. Mash & Terdal, 1997). The diagnostic process must also include a careful review of psychoeducational test data and the child's social-developmental, medical, educational, psychiatric, familial, and treatment histories, as discussed in the following sections.

Historical Information

Obtaining detailed and accurate historical information is essential to the assessment of ADHD. Information obtained concerning the onset, course, and duration of behavioral and emotional problems is one of the most valid means of separating ADHD from other childhood disorders, following the early methods of defining clinical syndromes used by Hippocrates (i.e., recognizing patterns or clusters of symptoms). A child with a relatively benign history of behavioral and academic problems, for example, whose academic performance is compromised beginning in fifth grade accompanied by an acute onset of behavioral and/or emotional difficulties, is unlikely to have ADHD based on our knowledge of the disorder. Alternative candidates, such as affective disorders, anxiety disorders, early-onset Schizophrenia, or abrupt environmental change represent more likely alternatives to explain the difficulties. Table 14.1 provides an overview of the differences in onset, course, and duration of problematic symptoms in childhood-onset disorders.

Questions concerning pre-, pari-, and postnatal development, early or continued ingestion of alcohol, drugs, and other toxins, length and course of pregnancy, delivery and birth complications, Apgar scores, and other information relevant to the child's early development are outlined in the University of Central Florida Children's Learning Clinic-IV (CLC-IV) clinical intake form shown in Table 14.2 (also available in pdf version from the author). The rationale for including this information derives from research suggesting slight elevations in pregnancy complications and physical abnormalities, general health problems, allergies, and accidental injuries and poisonings in children with ADHD (for a review, see Rapport, Timko, & Wolfe, 2006).

Detailed medical, educational, and child and family psychiatric, social, and developmental histories are required. Obtained historical information contributes to the diagnostic process by providing converging evidence of occurrences common to children with ADHD. For example, family psychiatric histories typically reflect a higher prevalence of ADHD in first-degree biological relatives of children with ADHD (25% to 37% average risk), particularly in fathers (44%) and brothers (39%; Biederman, Faraone, Keenan, Knee, & Tsuang, 1990).

The educational history associated with ADHD is typically characterized by an early onset and gradual worsening of behavioral, emotional, and academic difficulties. Teachers often invoke the term *immaturity* when describing 4- to 5-year-old children with ADHD. A laundry list of pejorative characteristics that reflect gradually impairing levels of inattentiveness, impulsivity-hyperactivity, and general classroom

Table 14.1
Onset, Course, and Duration of Major Clinical Disorders of Childhood

Clinical Disorder	Onset[a,b,c]	Course	Duration
Disruptive Behavior Disorders			
Attention-Deficit/Hyperactivity Disorder (ADHD)[g]	3.5[b]	Chronic	Adolescence–lifelong
Conduct Disorder (CD)	<10[c]	Variable	Adulthood[d]
	<16[c]	Variable	Early adulthood
Oppositional Defiant Disorder (ODD)	<8[c]	Variable	Remits or antecedent to CD
Pervasive Developmental Disorders			
Asperger's Disorder	3–6[c]	Chronic	Lifelong
Autistic Disorder[e]	<3[b]	Chronic	Lifelong
Childhood Disintegrative Disorder[e]	3–4[b] or [c]	Chronic	Lifelong
Rett's Disorder[e]	1–2 & <4[c]	Chronic	Lifelong or fatal
Mood Disorders			
Major Depressive Disorder[f]	5–19[b] or [c]	Variable	Remits or variable
Dysthymic Disorder	8.5[c]	Variable	Remits or variable
Manic Episode (In context of Bipolar Disorder)	5–14	Variable	Lifelong
Anxiety Disorders			
Acute Stress Disorder	Any age[h]	1 month	2 days to 1 month
Obsessive-Compulsive Disorder[i]	6–15(m)[c]	Chronic	Lifelong
	20–29(f)[c]	Chronic	Lifelong
Posttraumatic Stress Disorder	Acute or Delayed[h]	Variable Variable	2 months to 2 years
Separation Anxiety Disorder[l]	9–13[b]or[c]	Variable	2 years–adolescence
Social Phobia[l]	Mid-teens[b] or [c]	Chronic	Remits by adulthood
Specific Phobia[j,l]	7–12[b] or [c]	Variable	Remits by adolescence
Other Clinical Disorders			
Tourette's Disorder	7[c]	Variable	Lifelong
Early-Onset Schizophrenia[l]	5–11[b] or [c]	Variable	Lifelong

[a]Age of onset indicates age in years at which symptoms are most frequently first reported in children; [b]Acute onset; [c]Insidious onset; [d]At risk for Antisocial Personality Disorder and Substance Abuse Disorder as adults; [e]Typically associated with mental retardation; [f] typically associated with an anxiety disorder; [g]Frequently associated with Conduct Disorder; [h]Onset immediately following a traumatic event; [i]Commonly associated with depression, other anxiety disorders, and/or Tourette's; [j]Slightly higher rates in females and dependent on the type of phobia; [k]Significantly higher number of males versus females prior to age 10; [l]Frequently continuous with adult anxiety disorder.

From "Treating Children with Attention-Deficit/Hyperactivity Disorder (ADHD)" (pp. 65–107), by M. D. Rapport, in *Handbook of Psychological Treatment Protocols for Children and Adolescents,* V. B. Van Hasselt and M. Hersen (Eds.), 1998, New York: Erlbaum. Adapted with permission.

disruptiveness replaces the immaturity adjective invoked during the first and second grades. Intellectual development frequently lags behind same-age peers by as much as 7 to 15 points on standardized intelligence tests, and academic functioning is nearly always impaired except in high IQ ADHD children. This constellation of chronic and worsening behavioral, cognitive, and emotional problems results in more failing

Table 14.2
Children's Learning Clinic-IV Clinical Intake Form

Child's Name_____DOB_____Age_____

PREGNANCY

Prenatal history:

Planned_____Smoking_____ETOH_____Medications_____
_____Vitamins_____Other substances_____
(**Note:** Specify type, amount/dosage or number, and duration for each category)

Parinatal history:

Full term/other_____Medical complications (e.g., preeclampsia)_____
_____

Labor_____Delivery (e.g., natural, induced, C-section)_____
Delivery complications_____

Postnatal history:

APGAR score_____Height_____Weight_____Complications_____
_____Hospital stay_____

DEVELOPMENTAL HISTORY

Early temperament (describe child's reaction/interaction with caregivers and environment including eye contact, ability to be comforted, use and reaction to gestures, social bonding)_____
_____
Early development problems (e.g., colic, eating difficulties, sleep problems)_____

Developmental Milestones (in months):

Roll over_____Sit up_____crawl_____1st steps unassisted_____
Independent walking_____First words_____3-word sentences_____Toilet training_____

MEDICAL HISTORY

Diseases/chronic infections/febrile illnesses_____
(**Note:** Describe history, treatment, and outcome for each incident)

Chronic ear infections (otitis media)_____
Hospitalizations/ER visits_____
Head injuries/loss of consciousness_____
Surgeries/sutures (event and number)_____
Broken bones/other medical problems_____
Allergies_____Accidental poisonings_____
Medications (current/past)_____
Other medical problems (e.g., seizures, hearing loss, vision problems)_____

Table 14.2

(*Continued*)

EDUCATIONAL HISTORY

Age (e.g., 4–5 Years)
School/facility_____Location_____
Teacher_____Grades/comments_____
Behavior_____
(**Note:** Complete above information for each grade/classroom placement)

Previous testing/assessments/special education staffing/placements_____
_____

Suspensions/expulsions/school-initiated punishments (include age/grade, event, outcome)
_____

SOCIAL FUNCTIONING

Peer relationships (friends—younger/older preference, home/school)_____
_____
Organized sports/activities (e.g., soccer, baseball, swimming, Scouts, karate)_____
_____
Other preferred activities (e.g., hobbies, computer/video games, art, music, bicycling,
skateboarding, water sports)_____
Family relationships (with parents, siblings, other family members)_____
_____

FAMILY HISTORY

Paternal
Siblings_____
Parents_____
Grandparents_____

Maternal
Siblings_____
Parents_____
Grandparents_____

(**Note:** Describe all serious medical and psychiatric problems/diagnoses; include probes for
school failure, learning problems, suicidal behavior/depression, anxiety, substance abuse, and
treatments for unknown diagnoses.)

grades and grades failed, culminating in a 10 to 30 point lag on standardized academic
achievement tests (Barkley, DuPaul, & McMurray, 1990).

Methods and assessment tools used in clinic, laboratory, and classroom settings
to diagnose children with ADHD are reviewed in the ensuing sections, emphasizing
their incremental validity for rendering diagnostic decisions.

CHECKLISTS AND RATING SCALES

Behavior checklists and rating scales play a prominent role in assessing children with ADHD. They serve as an important source of information concerning a child's behavior in different settings, how others judge behavior, and the extent to which behavior deviates from age- and sex-related norms. Information gleaned from rating scales contributes to the diagnostic process, and several scales serve as treatment efficacy measures. Specific psychometric properties of commonly used rating scales are provided in Table 14.3.

Limitations common to most rating scales include their reliance on subjective judgments and multiple threats to internal validity. These include halo effects, response bias, intensity and immediacy effects, and rater expectation bias (Harris & Lahey, 1982; McClellen & Werry, 2000). The underlying assumptions that Likert rating formats (e.g., 0–3 symptom severity rating) reflect interval level measurement and that all behavioral and emotional problems should be equally weighted (i.e., count equally toward a total score when endorsed at the same level) represent additional psychometric challenges to clinical rating scales.

Checklists and rating scales reviewed next are listed under *broad-band* and *narrow-band* categories. This distinction represents differences in scale development and the breadth of behavioral-emotional problems assessed by the instruments.

Broad-Band Rating Scales   Broad-band rating scales provide for a rapid screening of the most common child clinical disorders and allow clinicians to compare obtained profile scores to scores based on sex and developmentally appropriate behavior. The severity of ADHD symptoms can be assessed, and patterns or presence of more general psychopathological dysfunction can be documented. Screening for other potential diagnoses is important for two reasons: Attentional difficulties are common to most child clinical disorders, and ADHD is highly comorbid with other disorders, particularly learning disabilities, Oppositional-Defiant Disorder, and Conduct Disorder. Converging evidence also indicates that ADHD without the presence of other disorders may be associated with a different developmental outcome (Fergusson, Lynskey, & Horwood, 1997; Rapport, Scanlan, & Denney, 1999).

Characteristics and psychometric properties of available broad-band rating scales are provided in Table 14.3. Most scales report separate sex norms for children ages 6 to 18, with some scales reporting norms for children as young as 2 years (e.g., CBCL, BASC-2). Scales that do not provide separate norms for boys and girls must be administered with caution, because sex differences in behavioral and cognitive symptoms are well documented in the literature. All scales use a Likert-type endorsement format, with response options indicating either frequency or severity of behavior. Completion time for scales is generally between 10 and 20 minutes, but may vary based on the respondent's reading level. The number of scale items ranges from 27–28 for the short forms of the Conners teacher and parent rating scales, respectively, to 160 for the parent version of the new Behavior Assessment System for Children, second edition (BASC-2). Scales with too few items may fail to assess important aspects of behavior, but increasing the number of items is beneficial only to the extent that added items are not redundant with existing items, as indicated by overly high internal consistency. Internal consistency estimates and test-retest reliability metrics are within recommended ranges for the broad-band scales listed in Table 14.3.

Table 14.3

Broadband and *DSM-IV* Rating Scales Used in Childhood Assessment of ADHD

Scale	No. of Items	Item Type	Comp. Time	T-R	Int. Con. (alpha)	Validity Evidence			Norms			Publisher/Cost
						Conv/Div	Criterion	ROM	Age	Sex	Rating Period	
Broadband Scales												
BASC-2 Reynolds & Kamphaus, 2002	P 134–160 T 100–139	0–3 freq.	10–20	(1–10 wk) .65–.92 (7 mo.) .69	.72–.95 .73–.97	CBCL Attention (.66) Conners Parent (.71) Conners Teacher Inattention (.81) TRF Attention (.76)	BGD: With and without CD, behavior disorder, depression, emotional disturbance, ADHD, LD, Mild MR, and Autism.	N/A	2–21	Y	NR	American Guidance Services, Inc. Complete kit: $360/$500 (w/ or w/o software; manual, 25 of each form type, 25 DO forms) From 25 @ $30
CBCL Achenbach & Rescorla, 2001 Rater: Parent	118	0–2 freq.	15–20	(1 wk) .80–.94 (3 mo) M = .84	.63–.67	93 items identical b/t CBCL & TRF See manual for detailed validity information.	Discriminant analysis (referred vs. nonreferred: 80–88% correctly identified) BGD: ADHD v. non-ADHD, LD	No sig. correlation with actometer (Aronen, Fjällberg, Paavonen, & Soininen, 2002)	2–18	Y	past 6 mo.	ASEBA Complete computer scoring kit: $325 (manual, software, 50 CBCL, TRF, & YSR forms) Forms 50 @ $25 (any type)

Psychometric Properties

Measure / Author / Rater	N	Score range	Admin time				Discriminant		Age		Time frame	Cost
CBCL-TRF Achenbach & Rescorla, 2001 Rater: Teacher	118	0–2 freq.	15–20	.72–.95	(2 wk) .60–.96 (2 mo) .63–.88	Factor scores "correlate well" with equiv. CTRS scales Sig. corr. b/t scores and direct observations	Discriminant analysis (referred vs. nonreferred): 74–80% correctly identified BGD: ADHD vs. non-ADHD, LD	NR	5–18	Y	Past 2 mo.	see CBCL
CBRF-A Van Egeren, Frank, & Paul, 1999 Inpatient only	65	0–3 sev.	NR	NR	(2 wk) .63–.76 (3 wk) .38 (OA)	Overactivity Scale with: CBCL: .23–.28 (Externalizing, Aggressive Behavior) –.21 (Internalizing)	Overactivity scale did not predict length of hospital stay	NR	3–17	N	8-hour shift	Author Cost: NR
CBRSC Neeper, Lahey, & Frick, 1990 Rater: Teacher	70	0–5 freq.	10–15	Published norms based on earlier 81-item test—NR for available scale					6–14	Y	NR	Harcourt Assessment, Inc. Complete kit: $133 (contents unspecified) Forms: $29 (# unspecified)

(continued)

Table 14.3
(Continued)

Scale		No. of Items	Item Type	Comp. Time	T-R	Int. Con. (alpha)	Conv/Div	Criterion	ROM	Age	Sex	Rating Period	Publisher/Cost
CRS-R Conners, Sitarenios, Parker, & Epstein, 1998	Long P	80	0–3 (not at all true to very much true)	15–20	(6–8 wk) .47–.85	.73–.94 .77–.96	Long: Short: .95–1.00 P:T: .12–.55 CDI:	BGD: ADHD v. non-ADHD, emotional problems Sensitivity (.78–.92)	CPT: r = .33–.44	3–17	Y	Last month	Pearson Assessments Complete kit: $255 (manual, 25 of each form type) Forms: 25 @ $37/$40 (long/short)
Rater: Parent, Teacher	T	59			.47–.88	.86–.94	.40–.82 (teacher) .36–.79 (parent)	Specificity (.91–.94)					
Self-report and ADHD *DSM-IV* Scale also available	Short P	25			.89–96	.88–.95		PPP (.85–1.0)					
	T	27			.72–.92			NPP (.21–.61)					
CSI-4 Gadow & Sprafkin, 1994, 2002 Screens for *DSM* Disorders including ADHD	P	77	0–3 freq.	10–20	(2 wk) .66–.88 (P & T)	.74–.94 (both)	ADHD-HI & (C) vs: TRF-Externalizing: .69 (.53) IOWA-Conners-IO: .70 (.83)	ADHD category (6 studies): Mean sensitivity: .64 (.87 if using either teacher or parent) Mean specificity: .77 (.62 if using either teacher or parent)		3–18	Y	"Overall bx"	Checkmate Plus, Inc. Complete kit: $98/$358 (w/ or w/o software; manuals, 25 each form, plus scoring sheets, profiles) Forms: 50 @ $32
	T	99											

Instrument	Rater	N	Response	Time (min)						Age			Publisher/Cost
DSMD Naglieri, LeBuffe, & Pfeiffer, 1994 No attention subscale		111	1–5 freq.	15–20	.73–.94	.90–.95	CBCL Attention Subscale: .50	65–90% correctly classified across disorders	N/A	5–18	Y	NR	PAR. Inc. Complete kit: $260 (manual, 25 each child and adolescent forms) Forms: 25 @ $85
MCBC Sines, 1986/1988 Activity level scale	Parent	77	T–F	10–15	(ukn) .49–.78	.58–.83	NR	NR	NR	9–14	Y	NR	Author: Cost: NR
	Teacher	68			NR	NR							
PBQ Behar & Stringfield, 1974		30	0–2 freq.	5–10	(3–4 mo.) .60–.94	NR	Sig. corr. w/DO of clsrm bx & interactions	BGD: Normal vs. hyperactive, emotionally disturbed preschool children	NR	3–6	NR	NR	Author: Cost: NR
RBPC Quay & Peterson, 1993		89	0–3 sever.	15–20	(2 mo.) .49–.83	.73–.94	Original BPS: .63–97 CBCL: .43–.92 among alike scales ME not sig. correlated with DO of gross motor activity (r = 00; N = 34)	Discriminate clinical from nonclinical groups of children	NR	5–18	N	NR	PAR, Inc. Complete kit: $182 (manual, 50 forms & profile sheets) Forms: 25 @ $58 Software: $318

(continued)

Table 14.3
(*Continued*)

| | | | | | | Psychometric Properties | | | | | | |
| | | | | | | Validity Evidence | | | Norms | | | |
Scale	No. of Items	Item Type	Comp. Time	T-R	Int. Con. (alpha)	Conv/Div	Criterion	ROM	Age	Sex	Rating Period	Publisher/Cost
Stand-alone scales												
WWPARS Werry, 1968 Rater: Parent	22	0–2 freq.	5	NR	NR	WWPARS rating at age 4.5 sig. related to CPRS rating at 6.5 years (Campbell et al., 1978)	Predicted some improvements in mother-child interactions in response to stimulant meds in hyperactive children (Barkley & Cunningham, 1979)	Actometer M = .65 Range: .24 (classroom) to .77 (woodshop); .67 during gym	2–9, N = 140	NR	NR	Free online
DSM-IV scales												
ACTeRS Ullmann, Sleator, & Sprague, 2000 — Teacher	24	1–5 freq.	5–15	(2 wk) .68–.78	.92–.97	CPRS (.78–.90)	Hyperactivity scores medication sensitive in ADHD students; BGD: ADHD/non-ADHD	NR	5–14	N	NR	MetriTech, Inc. Complete kit: $62 (manual + 50 forms; parent OR teacher) Forms: 50 @ $43
Parent	25				.78–.96	CBCL (.80–.81)						

360

Instrument	Rater	Items	Response scale	Admin. time	Test-retest	Internal consistency	Correlations	Validity	Age range	Normed	Time frame	Publisher / Cost
ADDES-3 McCarney, 2004	Home	46	0–5 freq.	12–15	(ukn) .87+	.99	Unavailable from publisher		5–18	Y	NR	Hawthorne Educational Services, Inc. Complete kit: $232; Forms: 50 @ $35 (either version); Software: $35
	School	60										
ADHD-SC-4 Gadow & Sprafkin, 1997	Parent	50	0–4 freq.	NR	(6 wk) .75–.82	.93–.95	CBCL (.48–.81) TRF (.45–.88)	NR — Sensitivity .81–.85 Specificity .57–.94	3–18	Y	NR	PAR, Inc. Complete kit: $69 (manual, 25 each version, scoring sheets); Forms: 50 @ $30
	Teacher				.70–.89	.92–.95		Sensitivity .61–.89 Specificity .57–.94				
ADHD-IV DuPaul, Power, Anastopoulos, & Reid, 1998	Home	18	0–3 freq.	10	(4 wk) .78–.86	.86–.92	CPRS-R: .10–.80 CRTS-R: .12–.41 ADHD Bx Code: .25–.26 AES: .36	Sensitivity .72–.84 Specificity .49–.86 PPP .54–.78 NPP .81–.81 BGD: ADHD-I, ADHD-C, and controls (parent and teacher)	5–18	Y	Last 6 mo.	Guilford Publications, Inc. Complete kit: $42 (book, manual, scale); Forms: photocopiable
	School				.88–.90	.88–.96						
ADHD-SRS Holland, Gimpel, & Merrell, 1998 Rater: Parent, teacher (same form; separate norms provided)		56	0–4 freq.	10–15	(2 wk) .93–.98	.92–.99	ADDES: .80–.95 CTRS: .64–.97 (like scales) ADHD-IV: .89–.93	NR — BGD: ADHD vs. non-ADHD	5–18	Y	NR	Wide Range, Inc. Complete kit: $85 (manual, 25 forms); Forms: 25 @ $38

(continued)

Table 14.3
(Continued)

| | | | | | | Psychometric Properties | | | | | | |
| | | | | | | Validity Evidence | | | Norms | | | |
Scale	No. of Items	Item Type	Comp. Time	T-R	Int. Con. (alpha)	Conv/Div	Criterion	ROM	Age	Sex	Rating Period	Publisher/Cost
ADHDT Gilliam, 1995 Rater: Parent or Teacher	36	0–2 sev.	5–10	(1 wk) .85–.94 (2 wk) .85–.92	.91–.97	Compared to 7 other tests used to dx ADHD or bx concerns: "satisfactory" CTRS: .53–.72 ADDES-S: –.81 to –.88 ACTeRS: –.71 to –.78	BGD: ADHD vs. non-ADHD True positives/ negatives: 92% False positives: 7.7%	NR	3–23	Y	NR	Pro-Ed, Inc Complete kit: $110 (manual, 50 summary/ response forms) Forms: 50 @ $50
BADDS	50		10–20	(ukn.) .61–.93	.73–.89				3–18	Y	NR	Hawthorne Educational Services, Inc. Complete kit: $350/$195 (w/ or w/o software; manual, 5 of each form) Forms: 25 @ $59

BASC-M Kamphaus & Reynolds, 1998	Parent	47	0–3 freq.	5–10	(2–8 wk) .57–.90	.64–.83	CBCL: –.68 to .79	BGD: ADHD vs. non-ADHD & ADHD-I vs. ADHD-C (both versions)	*NR*	4–18	Y	*NR*	American Guidance Services, Inc. Complete kit: $129 (manual, 25 each form, scoring template) Forms: 25 @ $32
	Teacher				.72–.93	.78–.93	CTRS-R (–.36 to .62)						
BHSQ-R DuPaul & Barkley, 1992	Home and School versions	20	9-point scale	5–10	(ukn.) .60–.89	.64–.66							Guilford Publications, Inc. Complete kit: $33 (book, manual, scale) Forms: photocopiable
CAAS Lambert, Hartsough, & Sandoval, 1990 Rater: Teacher or parent	Home	31	1–4 freq.	2–5	(3 yr) .32–.44	.75–.81	*NR*	*NR*	*NR*	5–13	*NR*	*NR*	American Guidance Services, Inc. Complete kit: $155 (manual, 25 each form, scoring profile) Forms: 25 @ $50
	School				.40–.82	.78–.94							

(*continued*)

Table 14.3
(Continued)

Scale		No. of Items	Item Type	Comp. Time	T-R	Int. Con. (alpha)	Conv/Div	Criterion	ROM	Age	Sex	Rating Period	Publisher/Cost
								Validity Evidence		**Norms**			
													Psychometric Properties
ECADDES McCarney & Johnson, 1995	Home	50	0–4 freq.	12–15	(1 mo.) .82–.89	.87–.97	CPRS-R: .41–.71 ADHDT: .46–.81	BGD: ADHD vs. non-ADHD	NR	2–6	Y	NR	Hawthorne Educational Services, Inc. Complete kit: $162 (technical and intervention manuals, parent's guide, 50 school, home, & *DSM-IV* forms) Forms: $35 per 50 forms (home or school); $22 per 50 *DSM-IV*
	School	56			.90–.98								
NICHQ VAS Wolraich et al., 1998/2003	P ⎯⎯ T	0–3 freq.	10–15	N/R	.90–.92	DISC-IV (.79)	BGD: ADHD vs. non-ADHD	N/R	5–12	N	6 mo.	NICHQ Free online: http:// www.nichq.org

S-ADHD-RS Spadafore & Spadafore, 1997 Rater: Teacher	50	0–4 freq.	10	(2 wk – 1 mo.) .88–.90	NR	NR	Correctly identified: 50/50 ADHD Incorrectly identified 2/50 non-ADHD as ADHD	NR	5–19	Y	NR	Complete kit: $80 (manual, 25 scoring protocols, 25 observation forms, 25 med tracking forms) Forms: 25 @ $25
SNAP-IV Swanson, 1992 Rater: Teacher or parent (same form)	90	0–3 freq.	10–15	(2 wk) .70–.90	.90+	NR	NR	NR	NR	Y	NR	Form and scoring guidelines are free online: http://www.adhd.net

ACTeRS = ADHD Comprehensive Teacher Rating Scale; ADDES-2 = Attention Deficit Disorders Evaluation Scale—Second Edition; ADDES-S = Attention Deficit Disorders Evaluation Scale—Secondary-Age Student; ADHD-IV = ADHD Rating Scale-IV; ADHD-SC-4 = ADHD Symptom Checklist—*DSM-IV* Edition; ADHD-SRS = ADHD Symptoms Rating Scale; ADHDT = ADHD Test; BADDS = Brown Attention Deficit Disorder Scale; BASC = Behavior Assessment System for Children; BASC-M = Behavior Assessment System for Children—Monitor for ADHD; BGD = Between-group differences; BHSQ-R = Barkley Home Situations Questionnaire—Revised; CADS = Conners' ADHD/DSM-IV Scales; CAAS = Children's Attention and Adjustment Survey; CBCL = Child Behavior Checklist; CBRF-A = Child Behavior Rating Form—Abbreviated; CBRSC = Comprehensive Behavior Rating Scale for Children; CDI = Children's Depression Inventory; CPRS-R = Conners' Parent Rating Scale—Revised; CPT = Continuous Performance Test; CRS-R = Conners' Rating Scales—Revised; CSI-4 = Child Symptom Inventory—Fourth Edition; CTRS = Conners' Teacher Rating Scale—Revised; ECADDES = Early Childhood Attention Deficit Disorders Evaluation Scale; M = Mean; MCBC = Missouri Children's Behavior Checklist; NICHQ VAS = National Institute for Children's Healthcare Quality Vanderbilt Assessment Scale; NPP = Negative Predictive Power; P = Parent; PBQ = Preschool Behavior Questionnaire; PPP = Positive Predictive Power; RBPC = Revised Behavior Problem Checklist; S-ADHD-RS = Spadafore ADHD Rating Scale; SNAP-IV = Swanson, Nolan, & Pelham Rating Scale—Version IV; T = Teacher; TRF = Teacher Report Form; WWPARS = Werry-Weiss-Peters Activity Rating Scale.

Note: Pricing information obtained from publishers' websites, accessed February, 2006.

Convergent and criterion validity data are available for many of the broad-band scales, providing inchoate evidence that the scales measure what they purport to measure. Validity evidence is generally limited to comparisons with other existing rating scales (which may be inflated due to shared source and item variance) and the scale's ability to statistically discriminate between ADHD and non-ADHD groups. The Achenbach (CBCL/TRF), Conners, and Child Symptom Inventory (CSI-IV) are exceptions, with recent versions demonstrating moderate to high *sensitivity* and *specificity* (the probability that a symptom is or is not present, given that a child has ADHD). Clinicians, however, are more interested in *positive* and *negative predictive power*—that is, the probability that a child does or does not have ADHD, given the presence of particular symptoms. The Conners and Achenbach parent and teacher rating scales (see Table 14.3) report moderate to high positive predictive power and low to moderate negative predictive power. Scale costs vary by test and publisher and are not necessarily correlated with scale quality.

Most broad- and narrow-band rating scales have not been compared to more objective measures such as precision actigraphs or direct observations of classroom behavior. The few studies that have examined these relationships tend to provide discouraging results. For example, Aronen and colleagues (2002) compared CBCL parent ratings of hyperactivity with high-precision actigraph measurements of activity level and failed to find a significant correlation. A similar study revealed that, when measured by step counter, nearly 64% of children rated as clinically hyperactive were less active than the most active child rated normal by the teacher (Tryon & Pinto, 1994).

Narrow-Band Rating Scales   In contrast to broad-band scales, which are typically used early in the assessment process to quickly screen for several of the most common childhood disorders, narrow-band scales generally provide greater depth and breadth of specific symptoms relevant to situational characteristics associated with ADHD. Age and sex norms are available for some but not all scales—a serious limitation considering the well-documented developmental and sex differences in children's attention and activity level. Completing narrow-band scales typically requires significantly less time relative to broad-band scales because they are more focused and contain fewer items. Reliability and validity evidence is generally adequate when available, and these values are subject to the same concerns described in the section on broad-band scales. For example, the new ADDES-3 reports an internal consistency of .99, which indicates significant redundancy in the items and suggests that a shorter version of the scale could decrease administration time without negatively impacting reliability and validity. Emerging evidence suggests that scales with fewer items may also be equally sensitive for detecting treatment effects compared to longer rating scales.

Scale costs vary by test and publisher; however, there is no clear relationship between cost and diagnostic utility. Most scales require an initial investment, ranging from $33 to $350, for a starter kit containing the test manual and a requisite of forms. Additional packages cost between $30 and $59 for 25 to 50 forms. Two of the narrow-band scales, the ADHD-IV and the Barkley Home Situations Questionnaire (BHSQ), allow the user to freely photocopy the scale for unlimited use. One scale, the National Initiative for Children's Healthcare Quality Vanderbilt Assessment Scale (NICHQ VARS), is free online. Normative data and reliability and validity evidence for the parent version of this scale are based on a relatively small sample.

STRUCTURED/SEMI-STRUCTURED CLINICAL INTERVIEWS

Overview The distinction between structured and semi-structured interviews lies in the degree of freedom granted to the clinician to stray from a given script and ask open-ended, probing questions in response to symptom endorsements made by the interviewee. Rutter and Graham (1968) are credited with pioneering the development and use of structured and semi-structured clinical interviews to aid clinical judgment. The development of these schedules represents the recognition of both the questionable reliability and validity of unaided clinical interviews and the frequent disagreement between parent and child reports of symptom endorsement and severity. To illustrate the potential problems associated with unaided diagnosis, consider the seminal study by Sleator and Ullmann (1981), which found that nearly 80% of children meeting formal diagnostic criteria for ADHD were misdiagnosed by their primary pediatricians. At 3-year follow-up, these children were no different from children correctly diagnosed with respect to continuing behavior problems, poor grades, and medication status. The fact that most children with ADHD fail to exhibit signs of hyperactivity in an office setting contributed to the high rate of misdiagnosis, and highlights the need for reliable and valid instruments for assessing childhood disorders in general, and ADHD in particular.

Structured and semi-structured clinical interviews result in decreased error compared to unstructured clinical interviews, both errors arising from internal (e.g., differential training level of clinicians, clinician biases) and external (e.g., discrepancies between informants) sources. Using the Hippocratic model, clinical diagnosis is based on the recognition of specific clusters of symptoms that characterize a particular disorder. Children with ADHD historically are poor informants, regarding both the presence and the severity of problematic symptoms. Information must thus be obtained from adult informants who are familiar with the child (e.g., parent or guardian, teachers).

Clinical Interviews Semi-structured clinical interviews provide unique information beyond the data gained from rating scales. They are currently the only assessment option that allows the clinician to probe for the onset, course, and duration of endorsed symptoms—a necessity for differential diagnosis—and are currently considered the gold standard for ADHD assessment and diagnosis. Strong convergent and discriminant validity is reported for most of the available semi-structured interviews, and test-retest reliability suggests stability of diagnosis over 1 to 3 years in clinical samples (Pelham, Fabiano, & Massetti, 2005). High sensitivity and specificity are typically reported for the semi-structured interviews, with only limited information available pertaining to positive (PPP) and negative (NPP) predictive power. The lack of PPP and NPP metrics is due in part to the use of semi-structured clinical interviews as the gold standard from which the predictive power of other measures (e.g., rating scales) is established.

Semi-structured clinical interviews typically require between 1 and 2 hours to complete, depending on a range of factors. These include the clinician's experience, the informant's ability to remain focused and recall historical information, and the severity, range, and duration of presenting problems (see Table 14.4). The time investment limits their practicality for repeated use (e.g., for assessing treatment effects). Financial investment varies significantly across interview schedules. Some are free and

Table 14.4
Clinical Child Diagnostic Interviews

Measures	Age Range	Time (min.)	Test-Retest (Kappa)	Symptom History	Disorders Considered	Scoring Format	Instrument Cost	Training Required
Structured Interviews								
Diagnostic Interview Schedule for Children-IV (DISC-IV)	6–17 (P) 9–17 (C)	90–120 (P) 45–90 (C)	0.79 (P) 0.42 (C)	4 weeks/ 12 months	All major Dx	Y/N	$150– $2,000	2–3 day training module
Diagnostic Interview for Children and Adolescents-IV (DICA-IV)	6–17	60–120	NR (P) 0.32 (C) 0.59 (A)	4 weeks/ 12 months	All major Dx	Y/N	$1,000	2–4 weeks
Children's Interview for Psychiatric Syndromes (CHiPS)	6–18	40	0.4	NR	All major Dx	Y/N	$115	NDR
Semi-structured Interviews								
Schedule for Affective Disorders and Schizophrenia for School-Age Children (K-SADS)	6–17	30–90	0.63	6 months/ Lifetime	All major Dx	0–3	Free online	CTR
Semi-structured Clinical Interview for Children and Adolescents (SCICA)	13–18	60–90	0.57 (Attention problems scale)	NR	Does not correspond with *DSM-IV*		$110–$295 $25 for 50	NDR
Child and Adolescent Psychiatric Assessment (CAPA)	9–17	20–210 M=66 (P) 22–150 M=59 (C)	NR for ADHD 0.55 for CD	3 months	All major Dx	0–3	$600 + $2,000 Fixed costs	BA
Interview Schedule for Children and Adolescents (ISCA)	8–17	120–150 (P) 45–90 (C)	Between 0.64 and 1.0	NR	All major Dx	0–3		CTR

Note: Properties are equivalent for parent and child/adolescent version unless otherwise indicated. A = Adolescent; BA = Bachelor's-level training; C = Child; CTR = Clinical training required; DX = Diagnosis; NDR = No degree requirements; P = Parent; NR = Not reported.

available online (e.g., K-SADS), whereas others have an initial cost of $600 in addition to $2,000 fixed training costs (e.g., CAPA). All but one of the semi-structured interviews covers all major *DSM-IV* diagnoses for school-age children through age 18. Some of the semi-structured interviews provide separate versions for parents, children, and adolescents. None of the available semi-structured interviews include a teacher version. Clinicians must use other instruments to obtain school-related information for purposes of establishing impairment across multiple settings.

The Child and Adolescent Psychiatric Assessment (CAPA) appears to be the most extensively developed of the clinical interviews, but requires up to 2 weeks of classroom instruction and an additional 1 to 2 weeks of practice to acquire the necessary certification (Angold & Costello, 2000). This training is estimated to cost $600, and there is an additional fixed cost of $2,000, which may limit widespread usage among clinicians, especially when schedules such as the K-SADS demonstrate adequate reliability and validity and are available online at no cost. The CAPA, however, may be superior to other available schedules due to several excellent features. The instrument provides for an intensity rating that varies by three symptom groupings: intrapsychic phenomena such as worrying, qualitatively different symptoms such as psychosis, and conduct disturbances. Training and coding are based on a detailed glossary, and thoroughly investigated symptoms are matched to appropriate glossary definitions and levels of severity. Formal rules are provided for the use of screening, mandatory, and discretionary questions.

The Diagnostic Interview for Children and Adolescents, *DSM-IV* edition, provides separate versions for children (ages 6–12) and adolescents (13–18) based on field testing of interview questions with different age, sex, and ethnic groups. Two to four weeks of training, at a cost of approximately $1,000, is required to reach the desired level of competence. The duration of training is based on clinician experience and includes topics such as age-appropriate probe questions and maintaining a child's interest through techniques such as tone of voice and appropriate nonverbal gestures. Reliability estimates corroborate research findings indicating that children are less reliable reporters of externalizing symptoms but more reliable reporters on internalizing symptoms relative to their parents. Computer versions are available, but initial research suggests poor reliability compared to the standard interview format.

The Kiddie Schedule for Affective Disorders and Schizophrenia (K-SADS) is currently the most widely used semi-structured clinical interview. The Present-Lifetime (PL) version collects information from the parent regarding current symptomatology as well as symptomatology at its most frequent and severe levels in the past. A separate interview is conducted with the child, and a third pair of ratings is generated based on integration of the parent and child reports with historical information and other data (e.g., rating scales). The K-SADS-PL focuses on chronology, treatment, impairment, and severity of symptoms. The initial screening interview consists of 82 items covering all major *DSM-IV* diagnostic categories. Cutoff scores are used to determine the need to administer the in-depth supplementary sections available for each diagnostic category, thus shortening administration time by allowing the clinician to skip supplementary sections based on negative endorsement of key screening questions. Interrater reliability estimates for the K-SADS are among the highest of any of the semi-structured clinical interviews. Extensive knowledge of diagnostic and symptom subtleties is required owing to lack of formal training requirements, and clinicians must evoke clinician judgment to interject noncued verbal probes to clarify informant responses and elicit examples of problematic behavioral and emotional symptoms.

OBSERVATION METHODS

Natural Settings A recent meta-analytic review found that independent observations of on-task behavior in natural classroom settings resulted in statistically significant differences between ADHD and typically developing peer groups in 27 of 29 studies. After correcting for study methodology, best case estimation indicated that children with ADHD were on task in the classroom an average of 75% of the time across studies compared with 88% for typically developing children (Kofler, Rapport, & Alderson, in press). Direct observations are often considered the gold standard for experimental and outcome research; however, their use in clinical assessment is limited by several factors. No two research teams or commercially available observation systems define attention in exactly the same way, and research indicates that differences in observational schema can produce widely discrepant results in collected data.

Commercially available observation systems shown in Table 14.5 are available for school-age children and typically require between 10 and 30 minutes of observation. Multiple days of observation are required to produce representative and reliable data. Many systems offer software versions of their product, allowing the clinician to record behavior directly onto a personal digital assistant (PDA) or laptop computer. Although direct observations by independent observers can provide more objective and valid data than any of the other assessment methods discussed here, their relatively high temporal cost coupled with the general lack of norms suggests that their usefulness may be limited to situations where large discrepancies exist between teacher, parent, and other informant reports.

Relatively low-cost observations can be completed by classroom teachers. For example, desk checks ("Is the child prepared for class?"), teacher records of verbally intrusive behavior, and the percentage of daily academic assignments completed correctly discriminate between groups of children with and without ADHD (Pelham et al., 2005). These methods have the potential for objectivity that characterizes the independent observation methodologies, but they await critical evaluation to determine their utility for rendering diagnostic judgments at the individual level.

LABORATORY TASKS

A comprehensive review of laboratory- and clinic-based neuropsychological, cognitive, and behavioral tests, tasks, and experimental paradigms by Rapport, Chung, Shore, Denney, and Isaacs (2000) found that only five of 56 currently used measures reliably distinguished ADHD from non-ADHD groups. These tasks differ from unreliable measures in several important ways. Reliable tasks require recognition or recall memory of relevant stimuli, more rapid processing (measured in milliseconds or seconds for reliable tasks, versus minutes for most unreliable tasks), and place greater demands on phonological or visuospatial working memory compared to unreliable tasks. Specific tasks are not reviewed because none of them currently have diagnostically relevant psychometric properties (e.g., sensitivity, specificity, PPP, or NPP), most

Table 14.5
Mechanical and Observational Assessment Tools

Instrument/Distributor	Age Range	Recording Length	Norms	Software Available	Cost
Mechanical					
Actigraphs	Any	22 days per 32 Kilobytes of memory	N	Y	Starter: $1,000+ (w/ necessary software and reader interface); $500–$2,000 for each additional actigraph
Ambulatory monitoring MiniMitter MTI, Inc.					
Actometers[a] Model 108 Engineering Department Times Industries, Waterbury, CT 06720	Any	Variable	N	Y[b]	NR
Pedometers (available at sporting goods stores)	Any	Range: 99,999 steps (~5.25 miles) to 1,000 miles	N		
Stand-alone				N	$10–$40
With data downloadable to PC				Y	$125–$400+
Direct Observations					
ADHD BCS Barkley, 1990	NR	15 min.	N	N	NR
AET-SSBD Sopris West	School age	15 min.	Y	N	Kit: $108 (includes all 3 parts of SSBD)

(continued)

Table 14.5
(Continued)

Instrument/Distributor	Age Range	Recording Length	Norms	Software Available	Cost
ADHD-SOC Checkmate Plus, Ltd.	School age	16 min.	N	N	Kit: $25
BASC-2 SOS AGS, Inc.	School age	15 min.	N	Y	25 forms @ $33
BOSS Harcourt Assessment	School age	15 min.	N	Y	Kit: $120
COC Abikoff, 1977/1980	School age	32 min.	N	N	NR
DOF ASEBA	5–14	10 min.	Y	Y	50 forms @ $25
SECOS Saudargas, 1997	Grades 1–5	20 min.	Y	N	
Noldus Observer Noldus Information Technology	Any	Variable	N	Y	Observer Basic 5.0 $1,795 Observer Video Pro 5.0 $5,850

AET-SSBD = Academic Engaged Time Code of the SSBD; BCS = Behavior Coding System; BOSS = Behavioral Observation of Students in Schools; COC = Classroom Observation Code; DOF = Direct Observation Form; SECOS = State-Event Classroom Observation System; SOC = School Observation Code; SOS = Student Observation System. [a]Many studies report either using the Kaulins and Willis actometers (no longer manufactured) or enlisting a jeweler to modify a self-winding wristwatch as described by Schulman and Reisman (1959). [b]Eaton, McKeen, and Saudino (1996) provide SAS syntax for performing group-level data analysis based upon actometer readings.

are relatively insensitive to between-dose medication effects, and none provides incremental validity above classroom observations, rating scales, and academic efficiency measures.

SUMMARY

A chief role of behavioral assessment is the identification of prominent behavioral, cognitive, affective, and physical signs and symptoms in the individual. Obtained information is used to formulate an initial diagnosis, select and evaluate response to treatment, and in some cases, portend long-term outcome. The complexity and multifaceted nature of ADHD, which includes broad-based behavioral and cognitive domains, eludes facile efforts at clarification and measurement. Many areas of dysfunction are apparent only under certain environmental conditions or situations (Douglas, 1988; Whalen & Henker, 1985). To complicate matters, children with ADHD frequently exhibit an inconsistent pattern of deficits from day to day, even when tasks and other parameters are constant. This phenomenon occurs in both field and highly controlled laboratory settings, to the dismay of researchers and clinicians alike (for reviews, see Castellanos et al., 2005; Rapport, 1990).

Eliciting information from single sources and limiting or relying exclusively on certain types of information to diagnose ADHD results in a high rate of misidentified cases. A desirable evaluation for children suspected of ADHD includes comprehensive history taking, parent (and, when appropriate, child) clinical interview, review of teacher and parent broad- and narrow-band rating scale data, psychoeducational test data, and behavioral observation. Direct observation of children functioning in an academic setting can be extraordinarily helpful, but is usually not feasible owing to time and cost constraints. By-products of the child's behavior in educational settings (i.e., permanent products), such as academic completion rates, may address this void (Pelham et al., 2005). Auxiliary neurocognitive assessment, coupled with behavioral observation during testing, provides valuable information but awaits psychometric validation. Objective measures of activity level, such as actigraphs, represent the sine qua non of behavioral assessment but are too costly for many clinical settings.

CONCEPTUALIZATION

DSM-IV CLINICAL MODEL

The appropriate design of assessment instruments for diagnosing children with ADHD and assessing treatment outcome rests on correctly specifying the core deficits associated with the disorder. Elucidation of core deficits, central processes, and the means by which these cause ADHD behavior problems inform us about the types (and content) of instruments to develop that will enable valid measurement. When developing neurocognitive instruments, hypothesized underlying mechanisms and processes guide the researcher in the design and manipulation of task parameters thought to challenge suspected systems.

Figure 14.1 illustrates the implicit and explicit causal assumptions underlying the current *Diagnostic and Statistical Manual of Mental Disorders* (*DSM-IV-TR*; American Psychiatric Association, 2000) clinical model of ADHD. It presumes that biological influences (e.g., genetics, pre-, pari-, postnatal insults) give rise to individual differences in the functional properties of neurobiological systems (e.g.,

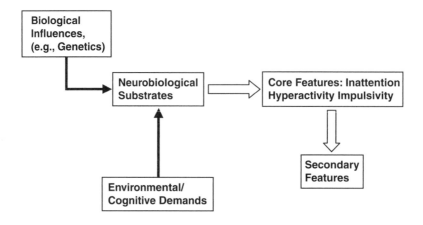

Figure 14.1 A visual schematic of the *DSM-IV* conceptual model of ADHD.

dopaminergic-noradrenergic neurotransmission in the frontal-striatal-cerebellar regions) that are etiologically responsible for the core psychological (i.e., cognitive and behavioral) features of ADHD. The *DSM-IV* clinical model conceptualizes inattention and hyperactivity-impulsivity as the core features of the disorder, and related behavioral and emotional problems as causal by-products of core symptoms. For example, academic underachievement represents a causal consequence of broader, more primary features of the disorder, such as chronic inattention and hyperactivity; children who cannot sit in their seat and pay attention are unable to complete academic assignments. Other secondary features common to ADHD, such as inadequate social skills and peer relationships, low frustration tolerance, and strained family relationships, are also by-products of core behavioral and cognitive influences to the extent that children rely on them for successful execution. Empirical validation of core processes can proceed at multiple levels but must eventually entail careful manipulation of discrete independent variables and observation of their effects to understand how underlying mechanisms and processes transcend to behavioral characteristics of ADHD.

ALTERNATIVE CONCEPTUAL MODELS

Theories of ADHD evolved from implied brain damage (Strauss & Lehtinen, 1947) and dysfunction (Cruickshank & Dolphin, 1951; Strauss & Kephart, 1955) to single-construct theories of sustained attention (Douglas, 1972), deficient rule-governed behavior (Barkley, 1989), cognitive-energetic dysregulation (Sergeant, Oosterlaan, & van der Meere, 1999), and delay aversion (Sonuga-Barke, 2002). Reviews of these models and their underlying psychological and neurobiological constructs and etiological factors are available (cf. Barkley, 2006; Castellanos & Tannock, 2002). Recent conceptualizations of ADHD include a comprehensive theory with behavioral inhibition as its core component, and an alternative model that postulates working memory dysfunction as a candidate endophenotype.

Behavioral Inhibition   The most contemporary and ambitious theory of ADHD was proposed in 1997 by Dr. Russell Barkley, building on earlier theoretical models of behavioral inhibition derived from Gray's (1982) theory of brain-behavior processes, wherein an underactive behavioral inhibition system fails to provide sufficient anxiety and fearfulness, resulting in the initiation or continuation of unwanted behavior (Quay, 1997). The central feature of the disorder is a developmental delay in behavioral inhibition. Disruption of this system affects children's ability to inhibit (a) previously reinforced behavior or responses, (b) ongoing behavior that should be stopped to permit consideration of more appropriate or adaptive responses, and (c) attention to task-irrelevant events (e.g., distractions). Poorly developed and inefficiently modulated behavioral inhibition processes subsequently impact the use and control of four higher order executive functions—working memory, internalization of speech/verbal working memory, self-regulation of affect/motivation/arousal, and reconstitution—that are necessary to direct and regulate the motor system and guide and provide control over current and future behavior (see Figure 14.2). Collectively, these deficiencies are causally related to the broad range of impairments observed in individuals with ADHD (for a comprehensive discussion, see Barkley, 2006).

Empirical evidence of executive function deficits in children with ADHD is incontrovertible (Willcutt, Doyle, Nigg, Faraone, & Pennington, 2005), providing strong support for the central portion of Barkley's (1997) model. Laboratory-based studies examining two of the hypothesized behavioral inhibition (BI) deficits by means of the stop-signal task, however, have produced mixed results. Recent meta-analytic reviews examining these studies suggest that previously reported BI differences between children with ADHD and normally developing controls appear to be due to deficiencies in central processing and attention rather than deficient behavioral inhibition (Alderson, Rapport, & Kofler, in press; Lijffijt, Kenemans, Verbaten, & van Engeland, 2005). Moreover, working memory's reliance on BI processes as a core executive function in the proposed model is difficult to defend because working memory processes must be invoked to evaluate stimuli (including situational cues) prior to the initiation of the inhibition process. Specifically, the central executive component of working memory regulates attentional resources, such as switching attention among competing stimuli, and phonological and visuospatial stimuli must be evaluated by working memory subsystems prior to BI activation. This suggests that behavioral inhibition is downstream of working memory processes. Competing models must recognize this conundrum and hypothesize a core role for working memory within a multilayered model.

Working Memory   Recent conceptual models emphasize an endophenotypic approach, recognizing the probable involvement of multiple systems and levels in the pathophysiology of ADHD. Endophenotypes involve heritable traits that vary quantitatively and index a child's probability for developing the disorder. They follow a causal developmental model perspective and attempt to link etiological factors (e.g., candidate genes) to putative brain differences or abnormalities (e.g., catecholaminergic dysregulation, striatal lesions, EEG theta excess) to candidate endophenotypes (e.g., working memory deficits) to behavioral outcomes (e.g., delay aversion, scholastic underachievement, inattentiveness, disorganization). Recent empirical findings concerning potential candidate genes, underlying neurobiology and physiology, cognitive impairments, and associated behavioral outcomes support a multilayered, integrated model of ADHD.

Extant research provides growing support for working memory (WM) dysfunction as a candidate endophenotype. A visual schematic of the model is shown

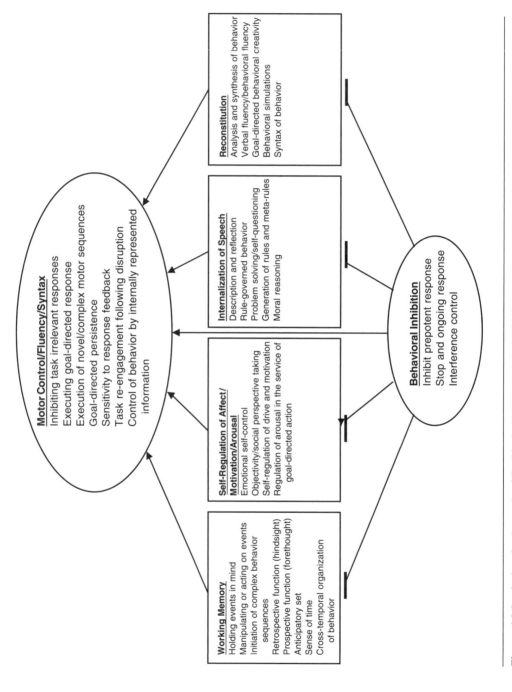

Figure 14.2 A visual schematic of Barkley's (1997) model of ADHD.

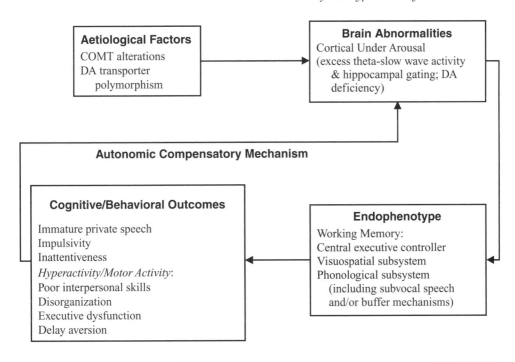

Figure 14.3   A visual schematic of Rapport et al.'s (2000) conceptual working memory model of ADHD. Biological influences underlie brain abnormalities (e.g., cortical underarousal) that adversely affect working memory processes and associated cognitive/behavioral outcomes.

in Figure 14.3. Hypothesized underlying etiological factors include alterations in catechol-O-methyl transferase (COMT) and genetic polymorphisms that influence dopaminergic and/or noradrenergic function (Castellanos & Tannock, 2002). These factors give rise to brain abnormalities, such as excess theta (slow wave, 4.0 to 7.5 hz) activity and decreased blood flow in frontal and prefrontal regions, which are associated with cortical underarousal during tasks that tax working memory processes. Motor movement serves three functions. The first is to increase *autonomic* arousal to help compensate for *cortical* underarousal (excess slow wave activity) while engaged in cognitive activities that rely on working memory. The second is to compensate for the rapid decline of WM representations by inputting new stimuli, which take the form of stimulation-seeking behavior. The third function of increased motor activity is to reduce the aversive nature of attending to tasks that tax working memory by means of escape behavior and, later, by means of avoidance behavior (e.g., out-of-seat behavior, behavior incompatible with homework completion). The three forms of motor activity vary significantly in topography and require sophisticated measurement to differentiate them from each other.

Evidence supporting the working memory model derives from multiple sources. Compelling evidence for heritability (reviewed later in the chapter) coupled with emerging evidence of cortical underarousal (including catecholaminergic dysregulation) in prefrontal regions provides an initial linkage of etiological factors and brain differences in ADHD (Beauchaine, Katkin, Strassberg, & Snarr, 2001; Ferguson & Pappas, 1979; Loo & Barkley, 2005). A central role for cortical hypoarousal as an underlying physiological process in ADHD is also demonstrated by studies reporting increased slow wave (theta) and decreased fast wave (beta) activity in children with ADHD while performing academic (Mann, Lubar, Zimmerman, Miller, & Muenchen, 1992) and cognitive (Clarke, Barry, McCarthy, & Selikowitz, 1998; El-Sayed, Larsson, Persson, & Rydelius, 2002) tasks.

A comprehensive model of ADHD must include a convincing account of the excessive motor activity observed in children with ADHD, a feat thus far unaccomplished by extant models. Hyperactivity is traditionally viewed as a core clinical feature and *ubiquitous*, rather than serving a functional role as hypothesized by the working memory model. The WM model postulates that challenges to WM subsystems (phonological and visuospatial) will evoke increased activity level to compensate for cortical underarousal until WM systems are overloaded. When this occurs, children shift from task engagement to escape behavior or vacillate between these two states. Measured activity level is likely to show an overall reduction and change in topography under these circumstances, as children seek to reduce the aversive nature of impinging task demands (e.g., out-of-seat behavior, seeking alternative stimuli).

A recent study illustrates the hypothesized causal relationship between working memory and children's activity level (Rapport, Timko, Kofler, & Alderson, 2005). Children with ADHD and age- and IQ-matched normally developing control children completed computer-administered phonological and visuospatial working memory tasks under varying set sizes (i.e., number of stimuli) in a counterbalanced order once per week across a 4-week time span. Activity level was measured using sophisticated actigraphs placed on both ankles. Both groups of children were significantly more active while completing working memory tasks relative to baseline periods, and motor activity increased linearly as a function of increasing working memory demands except under the largest set size. Control children continued to show increased activity level when administered the largest set size (i.e., 6 stimuli), whereas children with ADHD exhibited a decrease in measured motor activity coupled with an increase in escape behavior (e.g., out-of-seat behavior, looking away from the computer screen). These results suggest that increases in motor activity serve an important purpose for all children—it increases autonomic arousal to facilitate cognitive functioning. The finding that children with ADHD exhibit significantly higher levels of motor movement relative to controls suggests a compensatory process, wherein higher levels of motor input (i.e., autonomic arousal) are needed to help compensate for chronic cortical underarousal (i.e., excess theta–slow wave activity) when WM systems are overwhelmed. Children with ADHD, and potentially all children, engage in escape behavior when WM is overwhelmed. Collectively, the WM model poses serious challenges to the notion of ubiquitous, purposeless activity level in ADHD.

Other Conceptualization Factors and Variables

Findings from family and twin studies reviewed next, coupled with accumulating evidence for working memory as a candidate endophenotype, provide compelling evidence that the majority of variation in the behavioral traits constituting ADHD results from genetic factors. Other factors discussed—including developmental issues, learning and modeling, parenting style, life events, peer influences, and culture—are best viewed as influencing the extent and diversity of impairments rather than causing the impairments.

Genetic Influences   The field of behavior genetics is concerned with evaluating the extent to which behavioral similarities between individuals are correlated with degree of biological relationship. The strength of this relationship is quantified using heritability estimates derived from twin studies because these enable investigators to control for environmental influences that might otherwise confound genetic variation. Heritability refers to the proportion of phenotypic (i.e., observable) variation that is explained by genetic factors (i.e., after statistical control for environmental influences).

Studies employing behavioral genetic methodology provide compelling support for a heritable, biologically based etiology for ADHD. Most twin studies of ADHD have utilized scores on parental rating scales as dependent variables. Heritability estimates derived from these ratings indicate that approximately 65% of individual differences in attention are attributable to genetic variation (Gjone, Stevenson, & Sundet, 1996; Sherman, Iacono, & McGue, 1997). Similarly, 70% of individual differences in parent-rated impulsivity-hyperactivity are genetic in origin (Sherman et al., 1997; Silberg et al., 1996), and genetic differences account for 83% of observed variation in composite ratings of ADHD symptoms (Levy, Hay, McStephen, Wood, & Waldman, 1997; Nadder, Silberg, Eaves, Maes, & Meyer, 1998).

A small number of studies have computed heritability estimates based on discrete diagnostic categories derived from structured interviews or the application of cutoff scores to rating scales. The majority of these have used mothers as informants. The resulting heritability estimates have been very comparable to those based on continuous rating scale scores, ranging from .75 to .89 (Levy et al., 1997; Sherman et al., 1997; Thapar, Hervas, & McGuffin, 1995), with a median of .75. Thus, approximately 75% of observed variation in categorically diagnosed ADHD is genetically based. These data suggest that the heritability of ADHD is similar regardless of whether symptomatology is expressed categorically or in terms of continuous dimensions. This inference has been explicitly tested in two studies (Gjone et al., 1996; Levy et al., 1997). Both demonstrated that degree of heritability was constant across levels of symptomatic severity within their samples. These findings indicate that the features of ADHD are heritable and normally distributed in the population rather than representing a categorically distinct group.

Developmental Issues   Key developmental issues that contribute to the conceptual understanding of ADHD center on three interrelated questions: What is the normal developmental trajectory of children's motor activity? Is there evidence of heterotypic continuity in ADHD; that is, do the types and forms of behavior problems change over time? Are there significant, sex-related behavioral or cognitive differences in ADHD that merit scrutiny?

Motor behavior frequency and intensity show an upward trajectory in toddlers and early preschoolers, but the changes are less pronounced and slower relative to those observed during infancy. Development of gross and fine motor behavior dominates this period as children explore and interact with their environment and acquire myriad skills, ranging from using scissors and crayons to riding a tricycle. Environmental, and particularly setting, effects can significantly influence children's activity level at this time. Some children attend nursery schools and day care facilities, whereas others have limited access to playgroups and other children. The stability of children's activity level over this period is remarkable despite differences in context and environment. For example, the test-retest correlation for a sample of 129 boys and girls assessed at age 3 and again at age 4 was .44 and .43, respectively (Buss, Block, & Block, 1980). This finding indicates strong continuity in children's activity level at a time when development is proceeding rapidly.

The relationship between age and activity level changes rapidly in late preschool and early elementary school (age 5 to 10), but for the first time shows a *decline* after peaking at approximately 8 years of age (Eaton, McKeen, & Campbell, 2001). Children are expected to sit and engage in academic tasks and other cognitive activities for longer time intervals. Those able to do so are praised for their concentration abilities and tenacity, with accompanying high grades and test scores. Pejorative characteristics are conferred on those less able to regulate their activity level after entering elementary school; they are described as distractible, aggressive, restless, hyperactive, and impulsive. A majority of these children develop serious learning problems, make marginal or failing grades, exhibit a wide range of externalizing behavior problems, and experience impaired interpersonal relationships.

Evidence concerning the heterotypic continuity of ADHD is mixed. Symptoms of ADHD arise early in childhood; however, their presence does not necessarily portend a persistent pattern of ADHD beyond 3 years of age in an estimated 50% to 90% of children so characterized (Palfrey, Levine, Walker, & Sullivan, 1985). Continuation of early ADHD-like symptoms to 4 years of age, however, is highly predictive of clinical hyperactivity at 9 years of age (Campbell, 1990). Thus, the early onset, degree, and persistence of symptoms past 4 years of age is highly predictive of a clinical diagnosis (indicating continuing and worsening impairment) and continuing difficulties throughout adolescence and early adulthood. The stability of the diagnosis is also noteworthy. High percentages of children meeting formal diagnostic criteria in childhood continue to meet diagnostic criteria 8 to 10 years later as adolescents (70% to 80%: Barkley, Fischer, Edelbrock, & Smallish, 1990) and young adults (46% to 66%: Barkley, Fischer, Smallish, & Fletcher, 2002), although the level and topography of some core variables change with advancing age. Inattention problems tend to remain relatively stable between 7 and 11 years of age, whereas hyperactivity declines moderately (Hart, Lahey, Loeber, Applegate, & Frick, 1995). Fidgetiness tends to replace the excessive gross motor activity during adolescence, and most adolescents with ADHD report feeling more restless compared to age-matched controls (Weiss & Hechtman, 1993).

Sex predicts *DSM-IV* diagnostic subtype in many studies of children with ADHD, with females likely to exhibit more inattentive symptoms and males likely to display more hyperactive-impulsive behavior (Abikoff et al., 2002; Biederman & Faraone, 2004; Graetz, Sawyer, & Baghurst, 2005). These findings, however, may reflect differences in referral source. Few sex differences emerge in clinic-based samples, whereas lower levels of aggression and fewer internalizing symptoms are reported in community-based samples of girls relative to boys (Gaub & Carlson, 1997). Girls also appear to have a lower risk for comorbid externalizing disorders (ODD, CD) and depression than boys (Biederman et al., 2002).

Parental Factors   Considerable research has been devoted to studying parents of children with ADHD. Much of the early research focused on understanding whether there were particular parental attributes that contributed to the disorder's development, that is, whether parents were causally responsible for the myriad behavioral problems displayed by their children. Information gleaned from this research failed to support a causal role for faulty parenting.

Second-generation observational studies conducted in child research clinics generated considerably more information concerning the interactions of children with their parents. This advance was achieved by having parents and their children follow prearranged scripts, engage in games, participate in discussions, and attempt specific child management techniques under close observation. Collectively, these studies indicate that children with ADHD are more defiant and demanding, more talkative, more negative, and less likely to comply with parent requests. They also place heavier demands on their parents' attention and supervisory responsibilities due to their inability to play and work independently, and higher activity level relative to typically developing children (DuPaul, McGoey, Eckert, & VanBrakle, 2001). The collective result is a significantly higher level of intrafamily conflict.

Studies of specific styles and interaction patterns associated with parents of children with ADHD suggest a general parenting approach characterized by a more lax but overreactive, coercive, and acrimonious interaction pattern, coupled with higher levels of emotional expression and lower parenting efficacy. Mothers of ADHD children tend to be less responsive to their children's requests for attention, more negative and directing, and less rewarding of appropriate behavior relative to control families (DuPaul et al., 2001). This identified interaction and commanding style of child management by mothers of children with preschool hyperactivity is highly correlated with the persistence of ADHD symptomatology throughout childhood (Campbell, 1990). Barkley and Cunningham (1979) reported an interesting finding that supports the bidirectional and interactional, rather than causal, nature of parent–ADHD child interactions. Mothers of children with ADHD were significantly less controlling and more positive when their children were receiving psychostimulant treatment relative to no medication or placebo. This finding strongly suggests that the parents' negative reactions and aversive managerial style are elicited to a considerable degree by the overly demanding, noncompliant, impulsive, and defiant nature of their children.

Life Events and Physical Factors   Extant research is relatively consistent in demonstrating that children with ADHD—as a group—experience significantly more adverse life events compared to typically developing children. These findings contribute to the supposition that ADHD may reflect a broad spectrum of early insults that manifest themselves as a final common pathway.

A higher incidence of pre-, pari-, and postnatal incidents, as well as brain trauma—once considered idiopathic of ADHD—remains unproven based on systematic intake data collected in recent years. Research concerning other adverse life events, including general health problems, sleep disturbance, accidental injuries, minor physical anomalies, and motor coordination problems, suggests that they occur at higher rates in ADHD children relative to the general population.

A greater incidence of general health problems is common for children with ADHD, particularly allergies and recurring upper respiratory infections. Sleep disturbance is also common. An estimated 56% of children with ADHD experience difficulty falling asleep, and up to 39% experience sleep continuity disturbance, often beginning in infancy, based on parent report (Corkum, Tannock, & Moldofsky, 1998).

Accidental injuries are common in children with ADHD, and recent studies suggest that these are associated with their higher levels of hyperactivity and aggression. For example, a study of 10,394 British children reported that overactivity and aggression uniquely contributed to the incidence of accidental injuries in children with ADHD (Bijur, Golding, Haslum, & Kurzon, 1988); however, a recent study examining 6,000 children in England reported that hyperactivity alone predicted increased accidental injuries after controlling for demographic and socioeconomic factors (Lalloo, Sheiham, & Nazroo, 2003). Collectively, their higher rate of accidental injuries results in greater use of outpatient medical care facilities, particularly emergency medical services (Leibson, Katusic, Barbaresi, Falissard, & O'Brian, 2001), and are associated with 3 times the annual health costs of typical children (Swenson et al., 2003).

Children with ADHD experience significantly higher rates of motor coordination problems relative to typically developing children (Barkley, DuPaul, et al., 1990) and many meet diagnostic criteria for Developmental Coordination Disorder. Problems with gross motor coordination, motor overflow, sluggish gross motor movements, fine motor coordination (balance, paper mazes, handwriting), and motor preparedness (Oosterlaan & Sergeant, 1995) are the most commonly documented difficulties. A higher incidence of minor physical anomalies in ADHD is also common. These slight deviations in outward appearance (e.g., hair whorls on the back of the head, index finger longer than middle finger), however, are inconsistently related to behavior problems.

Peer Influences   The chronic and pervasive peer difficulties associated with ADHD are well documented. A majority of children with ADHD experience significant problems in social relationships with other children (Pelham & Bender, 1982). These findings are not particularly surprising given the core symptoms of the disorder (inattentive, impulsive, excessive motor activity) and broad range of expected impairments. Children with ADHD overwhelm peers with their unbridled enthusiasm and are viewed as overly talkative, loud, intrusive, domineering, impulsive, and emotionally reactive. Their inability to hold information sufficiently long to thoroughly process and use it for social interactions (i.e., working memory deficits) contributes to their preference for immediate gratification, deficient delay skills, difficulty understanding instructions and rules, immature speech, and verbal communication deficits. These deficient social and peer interaction patterns are so discerning that they are rejected by non-ADHD peers within 20 to 30 minutes, particularly children with ADHD who display higher levels of emotional reactivity, aggression, and sensation-seeking behavior (DuPaul et al., 2001; Mikami & Hinshaw, 2003). They also are more likely to bully and be bullied by other children relative to their peers (Unnever & Cornell, 2003). The collective impact of these behaviors, coupled with deficient knowledge concerning social interactions, portends poorly for the development of desired social interactions and relations throughout adolescence and into adulthood (Barkley et al., 2006). To make matters worse, they possess limited understanding or appreciation of their problems, which, in turn, contributes to an inflated perception of their abilities, accomplishments, and the extent to which others like them (Diener & Milich, 1997). Some peer interaction and social behaviors show moderate improvement with treatment; however, maintenance and generalization of treatment effects are the exception rather than the rule.

Cultural and Diversity Issues   ADHD prevalence rates for other countries are similar to U.S. averages when estimates are derived using identical diagnostic criteria (e.g., *DSM-III-R, DSM-IV*). U.S. estimates derived from studies published since 2000 typically range from 1.5% to 9.9% (mean = 7.7%), with higher estimates reported from studies using *DSM-IV* criteria (7.4% to 9.9%). The increase in prevalence rates over previous years may reflect increased awareness and improved diagnostic practices to some degree, but more likely represents changes in diagnostic subtyping, that is, the addition of *primarily inattentive* and *primarily hyperactive-impulsive* subtypes to the *combined* subtype.

Cultural and diversity factors play important roles in understanding ADHD because of their influence on observations, perceptions, and reports of child symptoms. For example, a study examining teacher perceptions found that Thai teachers reported higher rates of off-task behavior in same-age elementary school children relative to U.S. teachers. Direct observations of the children, however, showed the opposite result: U.S. children were off-task significantly more often than were Thai children (Weisz, Chaiyasit, Weiss, Eastman, & Jackson, 1995). Differences in child ratings also occur among teachers from mainland China, Hong Kong, and the United Kingdom (Alban-Metcalfe, Cheng-Lai, & Ma, 2002) and may reflect different expectations for children from different cultural backgrounds. de Ramirez and Shapiro (2005) reported an interesting example of this phenomenon. Hispanic teachers rated Hispanic children higher than Caucasian children on a hyperactivity-impulsivity scale, whereas Caucasian and Hispanic teacher ratings of Caucasian students were not significantly different. Mexican mothers are also less likely than both Mexican American and Puerto Rican mothers to report impulsive behavior in their children (Schmitz & Velez, 2003). Collectively, these findings suggest that differences in cultural expectations of children's behavior may significantly affect adult ratings and require due consideration when obtaining information from parents and teachers.

MEDICAL TREATMENT

Treatment of attention deficits traditionally involves using behavior or pharmacological therapy alone or in combination. Pharmacological interventions (particularly the psychostimulants), however, are considered more cost-effective and have the added benefit of affecting both behavioral and cognitive domains throughout the day without the specific programming and oversight required by behavior therapy. Table 14.6 displays the most frequently prescribed psychostimulants and their corresponding properties. A low dose is usually prescribed initially, with dosage gradually titrated upward on a biweekly basis until clinical improvement is optimized, while minimizing potential emergent symptoms. Second- and third-tier interventions typically include antidepressants, selective serotonin reuptake inhibitors (SSRIs), clonidine, and, less frequently, atypical antipsychotics for the treatment of highly aggressive children with ADHD. Combined regimens, such as stimulants and antidepressants, are prescribed with increasing frequency to treat the comorbid conditions (e.g., mood disturbance) that often accompany ADHD. Pemoline, once considered a viable treatment for ADHD, is rarely prescribed because of elevated risk for hepatic failure.

BASIC CLINICAL PROPERTIES AND PRESCRIPTION PRACTICES

Understanding the basic clinical properties of psychostimulants is essential for assessing outcome. Some physicians continue to prescribe psychostimulants based on children's body weight (i.e., on a mg/kg basis), despite compelling evidence that methylphenidate (MPH) dosage titrated to gross body weight or body mass is unrelated to treatment response (Rapport & Denney, 1997). This practice frequently results in overdosing low-weight and underdosing high-weight children. Knowledge of the behavioral time-response course of these agents is equally important because of the

Table 14.6

Prescription Psychostimulants for ADHD

	Generic Name	Brand Name	Dosing Schedule	Onset of Action	Peak Half-Life	Peak Behavioral Effect	Duration of Behavioral Effect
Extended Release	Mixed salts of amphetamine	Adderall XR	q A.M.	60–120 minutes	11–13 hours	Bimodal	10–12 hours
	Dexmethylphenidate hydrochloride	Focalin XR	q A.M.	60 minutes	2–4.5 hours	Bimodal	6–8 hours
	Methylphenidate hydrochloride	Concerta	q A.M.	30–120 minutes	3.5 hours	Bimodal	12 hours
	Methylphenidate transdermal system	Daytrana	q A.M.	60–120 minutes	1.4–4 hours	NA	12 hours
Intermediate Release	Methylphenidate hydrochloride	Metadate CD	q A.M.	30–120 minutes	6.8 hours	Bimodal	6–8 hours
		Metadate ER	q A.M.	60–90 minutes	NA	5 hours	4–8 hours
		Ritalin SR	b.i.d.	60–90 minutes	NA	5 hours	4–8 hours
		Ritalin LA	q A.M.	30–120 minutes	2.5 hours	Bimodal	6–8 hours
	Dextroamphetamine	Dexedrine Spansule	b.i.d.	60–90 minutes	12 hours	8 hours	6–8 hours
Immediate Release	Methylphenidate	Ritalin	b.i.d. to t.i.d.	20–60 minutes	2.8 hours	2 hours	3–6 hours
		Methylin	b.i.d. to t.i.d.	20–60 minutes	3 hours	2 hours	3–6 hours
	Dexmethylphenidate hydrochloride	Focalin	b.i.d. to t.i.d.	20–60 minutes	2.2 hours	2 hours	4 hours
	Mixed salts of amphetamine	Adderall	b.i.d. to t.i.d.	30–60 minutes	9.7–13.8 hours	1–2 hours	4–6 hours
	Dextroamphetamine	Dextrostat	b.i.d. to t.i.d.	20–60 minutes	10.25 hours	2 hours	4–6 hours
	Dexedrine	b.i.d. to t.i.d.	20–60 minutes	12 hours	3 hours	4–6 hours	

q A.M. = Once daily in the morning; b.i.d. = Twice a day; t.i.d. = Three times a day.

wide variation in onset and behavioral half-life among brands. As shown in Table 14.6, onset of medication effects varies between 20 and 120 minutes, and therapeutic effects last between 3 and 12 hours. Diminished therapeutic effectiveness occurs away from the peak time of behavioral effect. Outcome measures, including subjective teacher and parent verbal reports, may thus only partially reflect medication effects or not reflect them at all if based on inactive time parameters. Increasing the dosage does not remedy the problem; low and high doses of the same medicine have an identical behavioral half-life and time-response course. Moreover, it is important to consider the overlap of behavioral half-lives for each medicine to optimize treatment effects (i.e., a second dose must be administered before the behavioral effects associated with the first dose wear off). It is encouraging to note that most children who fail to benefit from a prescribed stimulant respond positively to an alternative formula. Finally, brand name mixtures (e.g., Ritalin) are typically more potent than generic medications (e.g., methylphenidate), and switching from the former to the latter may result in diminished therapeutic efficacy.

Dose-Response Effects

A large-scale observation study of 76 children with ADHD provides a representative précis of dose-response effects in natural classroom environments (Rapport, Denney, DuPaul, & Gardner, 1994). Children received each of four MPH doses and a placebo for 1 week in a counterbalanced order following baseline assessment. Attention (percent on-task), academic efficiency (percentage of assignments completed accurately), and classroom deportment (teacher ratings of behavior) all improved significantly with increasing MPH dose, as depicted in Figure 14.4. Collectively, these findings and those derived from experimental studies using sophisticated learning and cognitive paradigms (Rapport & Kelly, 1991) fail to support earlier views that cognitive function and behavior are optimized at low and high dosages, respectively (Sprague & Sleator, 1977).

Despite showing *statistically significant* effects for all dose levels relative to baseline and placebo, a more interesting question concerns the *clinical significance* of the results; that is, to what extent are treated children functioning like their typically developing classmates with respect to school performance and behavior? Conventional metrics (e.g., the reliable change index) address this question by quantifying the degree to which treated children's attention, academic efficiency, and classroom deportment are similar to classmate controls. Figure 14.5 reveals an interesting pattern of results. Attention and classroom deportment were either significantly improved or normalized in high percentages of children under active medication (76% to 94%), whereas only 53% showed this level of change in academic efficiency. These findings highlight the observation that improved attention and behavior do not necessarily translate into improved academic functioning for approximately half the children receiving psychostimulants. The findings also emphasize the need for auxiliary interventions (e.g., academic tutoring) and teacher rating scales that reflect improved adaptive functioning (e.g., the Academic Performance Rating Scale; DuPaul, Rapport, & Perriello, 1991). The *deceased person rule* is a useful guideline for determining a scale's validity for assessing adaptive functioning in children. If a deceased person can obtain a desirable score on the scale due solely to an absence of maladaptive behaviors (e.g., bothers others, easily distracted, acts like he's driven by a motor are endorsed as *not*

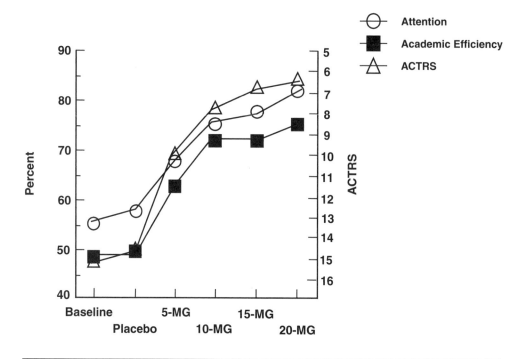

Figure 14.4 Mean group dose-response curves for three classroom measures. ACTRS = Abbreviated Conners Teacher Rating Scale. Upward movement on the ordinate indicates improvement. From "Attention Deficit Disorder and Methylphenidate: Normalization Rates, Clinical Effectiveness, and Response Prediction in 76 Children," by M. D. Rapport, C. B. Denney, G. J. DuPaul , and M. J. Gardner, 1994, *Journal of the American Academy of Child and Adolescent Psychiatry, 33*, pp. 882–893. Adapted with permission.

occurring), then it probably is not a good outcome measure for children (Rapport, 1993).

POTENTIAL EMERGENT EFFECTS

Side effects can and do occur with stimulant treatment, but most can be avoided or minimized with appropriate management. The most commonly reported side effects associated with psychostimulant treatment fall into one of three categories: cardiovascular effects (i.e., heart rate, blood pressure), physical effects (i.e., weight and growth), and physical and behavioral complaints. A recent review indicates that cardiovascular and physical effects associated with psychostimulant therapy are usually transient, dose-dependent, readily resolved by discontinuing therapy, and fail to remain significant in long-term follow-up studies (Rapport & Moffitt, 2002). Other common side effects, such as reduced appetite and associated weight loss (or the failure to make expected weight gains), can be minimized or eliminated by ingesting medication after rather than prior to meals. Clinical lore held that food reduced drug efficacy, but this has not held up to scientific scrutiny (Swanson, Sandman, Deutsch, & Baren, 1983). Physical and behavioral complaints frequently reported following psychostimulant treatment must be disentangled from the general discomfort reported by same-age

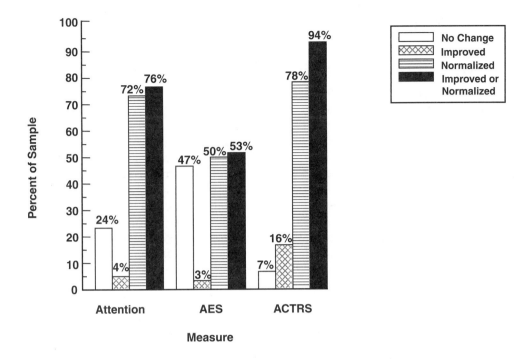

Figure 14.5 Clinical status of the group collapsed across methylphenidate dose conditions for three classroom measures. AES = Academic efficiency score; ACTRS = Abbreviated Conners Teacher Rating Scale. From "Attention Deficit Disorder and Methylphenidate: Normalization Rates, Clinical Effectiveness, and Response Prediction in 76 Children," by M. D. Rapport, C. B. Denney, G. J. DuPaul , and M. J. Gardner, 1994, *Journal of the American Academy of Child and Adolescent Psychiatry, 33,* pp. 882–893. Adapted with permission.

children not receiving medication. For example, high percentages of typically developing children report headaches, daily fatigue, sore muscles, and abdominal discomfort; children with clinical disorders other than ADHD report higher levels of these complaints in addition to stomach aches under no-medication conditions. Obtaining baseline measures of children's physical and behavioral complaints prior to initiating a medication protocol is necessary to sort out the extent to which effects are due to typical bodily complaints rather than medication.

BEHAVIORAL TREATMENT

Behavioral interventions designed to treat children with ADHD mainly focus on improving classroom functioning and parent-child interactions. Second-tier interventions ameliorate dysfunctional peer relationships and specific skill deficits by means of peer tutoring, group-level management techniques, mediation, and special skills training. The discussion in this section focuses exclusively on classroom interventions and parent training for two reasons: Poor academic functioning (including maladaptive behavior) is the chief complaint of parents and teachers leading to referral for a diagnostic evaluation, and auxiliary interventions are currently in a nascent developmental stage with limited empirical validation (for reviews, see Barkley, 2006; DuPaul & Stoner, 2003).

OVERVIEW OF CLASSROOM INTERVENTIONS

Early behavioral interventions focused on decreasing disruptive, maladaptive behavior in children with ADHD. The discovery that reducing disruptive behavior rarely translated into improved academic performance led to the abandonment of these interventions. This was an important finding, because academic achievement is one of the best predictors of a good prognosis and favorable long-term outcome in children. Accumulating research also revealed that behavioral interventions requiring teachers to deliver positive feedback (using verbal praise or by administering points, stars, or checks on a sheet containing descriptions of desirable behavior) were also less than ideal. The most pronounced shortcoming involved the excessive demands on teacher time relative to the large numbers of students in a typical classroom. A second criticism was that many children with ADHD tended to be drawn off-task by the delivery of positive feedback and experienced difficulty getting back on-task—an effect opposite of that intended by the intervention (Rapport, 1983).

Empirical studies examining the relative efficacy of behavioral interventions beginning in the early 1970s and continuing through the 1980s revealed an interesting finding. If the behavioral intervention directly targeted improved academic performance as its main goal (e.g., by making consequences specific for completing academic work successfully), disruptive behavior nearly always showed a concomitant decline in frequency. The procedure was coined the *incompatible response approach* (Allyon, Layman, & Kandel, 1975). It implied that increased academic performance was incompatible with disruptive conduct in the classroom and should be the primary target of intervention efforts.

During the 1980s and continuing to the present, the most successful classroom interventions followed this general principle and focused on developing incentive and/or feedback systems that directed children's attention to the completion of their school work. A combination of positive and mildly aversive corrective feedback delivered consistently, continuously, unemotionally, and with minimal delay worked optimally. This type of intervention relies on a behavioral principle termed *response cost*. Children earn points that can be traded for structured free time or specific classroom activities and lose points for not attending to their academic assignments (Rapport, Murphy, & Bailey, 1982).

RESPONSE COST INTERVENTIONS

The Attention Training System (ATS) is a prototypical example of a response cost intervention procedure for the classroom (see Figure 14.6). After receiving basic instructions, children earn 1 point per minute throughout the duration of the academic period. The ATS display window shows accumulated points.

The classroom teacher possesses a handheld remote-control device (see Figure 14.6) that is used anywhere within the classroom to control up to four student units. This allows the teacher to work with other students throughout the academic period, either in small groups or individually, while monitoring targeted children's behavior. The teacher continues with instructional activities so long as targeted students are appropriately engaged in academic activities, because the ATS automatically awards points on a 1-minute interval for remaining on task. This procedural component is

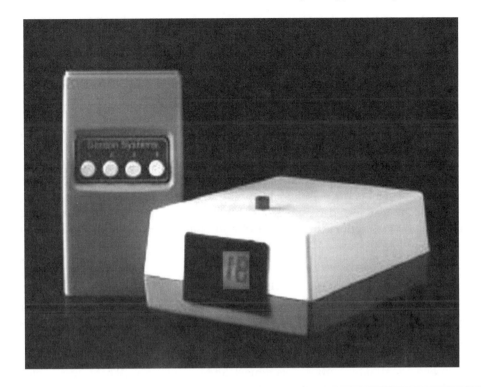

Figure 14.6 The Attentional Training System (ATS). Invented by M.D. Rapport (see Rapport, Murphy, & Bailey, 1982) for treating children with ADHD. Manufactured and distributed for commercial use by Gordon Systems, DeWitt, NY.

advantageous relative to traditional behavioral interventions for two reasons: It permits teachers to continue their ongoing instructional activities rather than stopping to deliver incentives to targeted students, and it avoids inadvertently drawing children with ADHD off-task by delivering incentives or verbal feedback.

The teacher activates the handheld held device by pushing a button on occasions when students are not attending to their assigned activities. The red dome on the student's desk module illuminates for 15 seconds and signals the child of an electronic point loss from his or her accumulated total due to off-task behavior. The teacher immediately returns to the ongoing instructional activity and checks the student's progress again in a minute or two. Earned points are recorded in an observation log at the conclusion of the academic period and exchanged for structured free-time activities later in the day (e.g., 15 points earns 15 free-time minutes). A leaner point-to-earned-free-time ratio (e.g., 2:1) is initiated after several weeks of successful classroom functioning. Dr. Mark D. Rapport invented and designed the original ATS, and Dr. Michael Gordon (Gordon Systems, DeWitt, NY: www.gsi-add.com) commercially developed and marketed the system.

Several variations of response cost interventions have been developed and examined empirically over the past decade. One alternative uses color-coded cards; students begin an academic period with a specific color card, which is replaced with a lower point value color card for classroom infractions. Card construction typically utilizes either a Velcro backing or paper pocket to facilitate visual display within the classroom. Accumulated earnings based on card colors are exchanged for desirable activities and privileges during the day based on preassigned point totals (Barkley et al., 1996).

Group format response cost interventions may be preferred in situations in which several or even most students in the classroom evince disruptive conduct and/or difficulties remaining on task. For example, the entire class can be awarded tokens such as poker chips at the beginning of an academic period (e.g., placed in a bowl or on a display board with Velcro), with each classroom infraction costing the students one chip. Chips remaining at the end of the period are cashed in for structured free-time activities. Group-level response cost may also be preferable to traditional token reinforcement systems for preschoolers owing to the reduced teacher demands. For example, teachers preferred a response cost intervention wherein students lost buttons from a chart for classroom infractions to a traditional token system that administered buttons for following rules (McGoey & DuPaul, 2000).

OTHER SCHOOL-BASED INTERVENTIONS

Varieties of behavioral procedures used in isolation, or as a comprehensive intervention component, prove effective for reducing discrete incidences of maladaptive behavior. These include time-out and carefully delivered reprimands and corrective statements. The maintenance and generalization of treatment effects—similar to other behavioral interventions—is nonexistent in most cases. That is, desirable behavioral effects are evidenced only while contingencies are actively employed; long-term maintenance of treatment effects has never been empirically demonstrated. The largest intervention study for children with ADHD conducted to date, the Multimodal Treatment Study, cogently illustrates this point. Children assigned to the comprehensive psychosocial treatment group participated in an 8-week summer treatment program and subsequently received ongoing teacher-administered behavioral interventions throughout the school year, with additional paraprofessional assistance for the initial 3 months. Poststudy results revealed that children were not significantly improved relative to a treatment-as-usual control group (i.e., a group receiving typical community-based services) and were significantly worse relative to a medication-only (psychostimulant) group (Jensen et al., 2001).

These findings are not particularly surprising given the suspected neurobiological nature of the disorder. They highlight the fact that extant interventions for ADHD are maintenance treatments that require continuous monitoring and adjustment to optimize effectiveness.

Recent efforts to improve the classroom functioning of children with ADHD focus on innovative instructional designs, computer-assisted instruction, and environmental management. The instructional design thrust focuses on altering aspects of academic tasks, such as the presentation format, types of materials, length, and timing, to better capture the child's attention and optimize learning time. Extant research indicates that stimulating tasks that can be completed within a brief time period and that vary the presentation format, interspersed with nonacademic assignments, are associated with improved attention and completion rates (for a review, see DuPaul & Stoner, 2003). Initial attempts to develop computer-assisted interventions for ADHD are promising but require replication with larger numbers of children for extended periods of time (e.g., an entire school year). Computer-based, comprehensive curriculums, all-day classroom management, and school-home communication programs have been proposed but unrealized to date (Rapport, 1998).

Attempts at environmental management date back to Cruickshank and Dolphin's (1951) initial attempt to isolate children with hyperactivity in three-sided cubicles to reduce stimulation based on the suspicion of a defective attentional filtering system. This practice continues today; children with ADHD are frequently placed away from other children and near the teacher's desk to minimize distraction. Extant research, however, has never consistently demonstrated that children with ADHD are more easily distracted than sex- and age-matched controls. In fact, a majority of studies specifically designed to study this phenomenon have failed to find significant between-group differences in distractibility (Kessler, 1980).

Home-based contingency management systems are widely used, wherein parents provide daily incentives or mild punishment based on children's behavior at school. This type of system usually entails children's receiving checkmarks, tokens, or other forms of visual feedback (e.g., daily ratings) throughout the school day following incidences or periods of appropriate behavior and/or academic accomplishment. Parents review a daily summary of the child's school day and mete out agreed upon consequences. These types of systems are noteworthy for increasing communication and feedback between school and home but have several inherent disadvantages and are generally less robust relative to school-based systems. The most significant disadvantage is the extended delay between the child's behavior (adaptive or maladaptive) and receipt of consequences. Temporal proximity is an important part of any behavioral reinforcement scheme, and particularly relevant for children with ADHD for several reasons. Children with ADHD typically exhibit poor delay skills and suboptimal working memory and organizational abilities (children fail to remember specifics about the day, and parents receive daily reports inconsistently). Extant research also convincingly demonstrates that immediate consequences are significantly more effective than delayed consequences for children with ADHD. Other disadvantages of home-based programs include the inability of many parents to provide consistent consequences and the negative emotional carryover effects associated with returning home to aversive reprimands in the context of an already strained parent-child relationship.

PARENT-CHILD INTERVENTIONS

Behavior management training is nearly always recommended for parents of children with ADHD. The reason is rather straightforward. Most parents have never received formal training in child development or child management unless they were raised in a large family or attended college and majored in psychology, child development, or education. As a result, most have only anecdotal information about normal development, and know even less about how to manage maladaptive behavior.

The thrust of behavior management programs is threefold. A first initiative is to educate parents concerning the use of effective behavior management techniques (e.g., reinforcement, time-out, extinction). Subsequent sessions focus on instructing parents in how to exploit this knowledge to decrease maladaptive and increase adaptive functioning throughout the day. The final stage focuses on teaching parents how to generalize this knowledge to different settings and situations and *preplan* for potentially aversive situations (e.g., extended car rides, grocery shopping). Considerable emphasis is placed on assigning homework tasks, preplanning for the upcoming week, and reviewing and suggesting strategic techniques for recent parent-child difficulties. Most comprehensive programs also emphasize implementing organizational techniques at home (making charts, arranging folders and backpacks, establishing a designated homework area and schedule) and teaching parents how to use constructive verbal communication techniques with their child. Collectively, parent behavioral management training is usually quite effective, but like other ADHD interventions, is a maintenance treatment that requires ongoing adjustments and continuous effort. Detailed behavior management programs are available from several sources (e.g., Barkley, 2006).

Case Description

Case Introduction

Sean was a 10-year-old male referred by a rural school system for a comprehensive clinical diagnostic evaluation and second opinion. He was previously seen by a licensed clinical psychologist, who concluded that he met diagnostic criteria for ADHD based on parent and teacher rating scales, a 50-minute parent interview, a brief interview with the child, and the absence of anxiety based on a normed child anxiety rating scale. Sean's parents requested special accommodations by the school to address their son's chronic and worsening difficulties. The school system sought to ensure that the ADHD diagnosis was accurate before scheduling an Individualized Educational Assessment Plan (IEP) meeting to determine appropriate educational goals, interventions to accomplish these goals, and assessment procedures.

Presenting Complaints

Sean's parents reported chronic and worsening school difficulties. Attending school each day was becoming increasingly problematic "because of his ADHD." Discussions with school personnel indicated that Sean was experiencing difficulties in multiple areas of functioning. His ability to pay attention was variable; he could pay attention for extended time intervals some days, yet appeared highly distractible and unfocused on other days. Sean's gross motor activity level was equally perplexing. The classroom teacher reported that he was usually able to sit and stay in his seat without signs of excessive motor activity, but became fidgety and even hyperactive at other times. Sean had no close friends in school and only one or two in his neighborhood despite the availability of children his age in both settings. He frequently came to school late and ate lunch by himself in the school cafeteria. Peer relationships were mixed: He appeared to interact well with other children but characteristically elected to avoid companionship.

History

Historical review of records indicated long-standing difficulties at home and in school, despite above-average intelligence. School problems included attentional difficulties, impulsivity, and sporadic hyperactivity. Records also indicated difficulties with peer relationships, poor organization skills, difficulties completing academic assignments on a routine basis, and a growing dislike for school.

Assessment

Teacher and Parent Ratings Scales

Broad- (CBCL, TRF, CSI) and narrow-band (ADHD Rating Scale) rating scales completed by the classroom teacher and parents revealed a mixed pattern of results. Teacher ratings for the TRF adaptive functioning indices indicated above-average learning and school performance but below-average functioning in areas related to happiness and effort. Internalizing dimension TRF scores were moderately elevated, indicating possible anxiety and social withdrawal. Externalizing dimension scores were moderately elevated for inattentiveness and hyperactivity. The *DSM* clinical syndrome scale scores were elevated for ADHD and anxiety disorder.

Parent endorsements were between 1.5 and 2 standard deviations above the mean for ADHD-related symptoms (inattention, impulsivity-hyperactivity) based on age and sex norms. The Externalizing broad-band scale was significantly elevated due to endorsement of ADHD, ODD, and CD behavior problems. The CSI was significantly elevated for symptoms related to ADHD, but also included endorsements of behavioral and emotional problems related to Generalized Anxiety Disorder, Separation Anxiety Disorder, and specific phobias. Collectively, parent and teacher ratings presented a mixed picture of ADHD-like symptoms (primarily by parent endorsement) and anxiety symptoms.

Behavioral Assessment: Classroom Observations

Unobtrusive classroom observations were scheduled to obtain information concerning Sean's ability to pay attention, complete academic assignments, and participate in classroom discussions and peer interactions. Sean and two typically developing male classmates were observed over a 2-day period as an initial step to minimize reactivity. Sean was unacquainted with the consulting clinical psychologist.

Behavioral observations from the Direct Observation Form (Achenbach & Edelbrock, 1986) revealed a mixed and variable pattern of syndrome scale scores. The Withdrawn-Inattentive and Hyperactive scales were moderately elevated for some observation intervals, but within the normal range for other recording periods. Observations of on-task behavior ranged from 40% to 100% across the 2 days. Written narratives revealed that Sean could read at his desk for 30 contiguous minutes, complete a reading assignment without difficulty, and occasionally volunteer to answer questions posed by the classroom teacher. On other occasions, the teacher needed to prompt him to pay attention. Sean worked cooperatively with other children during small group work. He requested to go to the bathroom on several occasions during both observation days, which the teacher attributed to excessive water consumption due to the high elevation, low humidity climate.

(continued)

Behavioral Assessment: Playground and Lunchroom Observations

Observations of Sean's behavior on the school's playground were recorded using the ADHD School Observation Code (Gadow, Sprafkin, & Nolan, 1996) for approximately 30 minutes per day over a 2-day time span. The instrument was developed particularly for observations of children with externalizing disorders in school settings. Results revealed no incidences of physical aggression, noncompliance, or verbal aggression, and lower than normal appropriate social behavior.

Sean sat near, but not next to, other children while eating lunch in the cafeteria. He ate slowly, picked at his food, and appeared ensconced in thought throughout the lunch period. Collectively, behavioral observations failed to show the elevations for aggressive behavior, noncompliance, and inappropriate social behavior typically reported for children with ADHD.

Psychoeducational Assessment

The Wechsler Intelligence Scale for Children—Revised results revealed that Sean's intellectual abilities were within the very superior range, with no significant discrepancies noted in higher order factor scores or individual subtests except for coding and digit span, which were moderately lower. The Kaufman Test of Educational Achievement (Kaufman & Kaufman, 1983) results revealed above-grade and -age expectancy achievement in mathematical applications (98th percentile) and computation (77th percentile) and reading comprehension (99th percentile) and decoding (63rd percentile). Spelling achievement was average and below expectancy based on assessed intelligence. Observations of his behavior during the assessment yielded an erratic pattern. He demonstrated excellent concentration and low motor activity throughout most of the assessment, but exhibited excessive motor activity and moderate agitation during several timed tests.

Semi-Structured Clinical Interview

The K-SADS was administered separately to Sean and his parents. Parents endorsed all items relevant to ADHD, with an early onset and continuing, worsening course. ODD items were also endorsed with high frequency, with onset at 7 years and a progressive, worsening course. Separation anxiety criteria were fully met, but follow-up probes indicated that Sean did not complain of somatic symptoms prior to school days or experience other common symptoms of Separation Anxiety Disorder while attending school. Several panic attack symptoms were endorsed (shortness of breath, accelerated heart rate, occasional trembling and shakiness, feelings of unreality), but a negative history of discrete episodes of spontaneous panic attacks was reported. Evidence for Simple and Social Phobia was negative except for airplanes (related to a fear of dying). Review of generalized anxiety symptoms yielded endorsements of most items. No evidence of other disorders, including mood and thought disturbance, was revealed. Overall, Sean's parents described him as a "worrier" with multiple fears and concerns.

The child interview was remarkable. Sean admitted experiencing some difficulties with concentration and completing academic assignments, but denied other symptoms characteristic of ADHD, mood disorders, thought disorders, CD, ODD (except for arguing with and disobeying parents), Posttraumatic Stress Disorder, and other anxiety disorders until reviewing obsessive-compulsive symptoms. He described a chronic and worsening history of obsessional thinking, particularly thoughts concerning contamination, and, to a lesser extent, "getting things right." Symptom onset coincided with an outbreak of body warts that required careful hygiene and regular washing at 7 to 7.5 years of age.

Sean currently washes his hands between 20 and 30 times daily after touching various objects or thinking about germs. Morning and nighttime rituals are laborious and complex and accompanied by excessive worry concerning whether the ritual—particularly morning bathing—was performed correctly. Myriad other rituals were detailed, such as not permitting his silverware to touch anything off his plate, having his parents wrap his lunch in a prescribed manner to avoid contamination, checking under tables at restaurants for gum, and touching one hand or foot an equal number of times while avoiding sidewalk cracks.

Sean's symptoms were particularly disabling at school. He feels clean for approximately .5 hours before requesting a bathroom break to wash his hands. His inconsistent completion of in-seat academic assignments and sporadic hyperactivity reflects his obsessional thinking that things must be exactly right and completed in a prescribed manner. For example, he checks and rechecks math problems for correctness, frequently beginning with the first problem even if he has completed a full page of problems. He also flips back to previously read pages to check whether he missed reading a word. These checking behaviors interfere with his ability to complete in-class assignments and tests. He becomes highly anxious that he won't be able to complete the task in time, is forced to abandon his checking rituals, and rushes through the remainder of the assignment or test. Other Obsessive-Compulsive Disorder (OCD) symptoms accounted for parent-endorsed behavioral difficulties; for example, his inability to stay at a friend's house overnight was related to his need to engage in daily rituals and the potential for embarrassment rather than separation fears.

Case Conceptualization

The onset, course, and duration of behavioral and academic problems were consistent with ADHD. Teacher scale endorsements suggested the presence of ADHD, anxiety, and affective disturbance problems. Parent ratings, coupled with parent clinical interview data, revealed a pattern of overendorsed clinical symptomatology; epidemiological evidence indicates an extremely low probability for greater than three co-occurring clinical disorders in a child. Parental overendorsement frequently signifies parental psychopathology. Behavioral observations produced a mixed pattern of results: Sean's concentration, reflective problem solving approach, and tenacity were exceptional for a 10-year-old boy, but deteriorated under particular timed test situations. This pattern is characteristic of anxiety rather than ADHD. A diagnostic picture of OCD was crystallized following the child clinical interview, and highlights the fact that children are often the most salient source for examining internalizing problems. Sean's parents had no idea of the intrusive nature or impairing extent of his illness.

(continued)

Course of Treatment, Assessment of Progress, Complicating Factors, and Follow-Up

Additional assessments were undertaken to detail the full range of Sean's obsessive-compulsive clinical features using highly specialized OCD instruments (e.g., Yale-Brown Obsessive Compulsive Scale). A full clinical report, coupled with a recommendation for cognitive behavior therapy, was forwarded to the school board. Appropriate treatment facilities were unavailable in Sean's community, and the school system paid for in-patient treatment at an out-of-state psychiatric hospital. Sean and his family relocated following his discharge from the hospital to enable him to receive booster therapy sessions, which are nearly always required for severe OCD. As a result, follow-up care consisted of ensuring that appropriate clinical information was forwarded to the new treatment facility and helping the parents locate an appropriate treatment facility.

TREATMENT IMPLICATIONS OF THE CASE

The described case highlights the need to conduct a comprehensive diagnostic assessment for referred children. Empirically supported treatments present the sine qua non for children with OCD but must often be modified to account for the unique features of the child's presentation and other living situations. Weekly monitoring of OCD symptoms using psychometrically sound instruments is recommended.

RECOMMENDATIONS FOR CLINICIANS

Most practicing clinical psychologists will be unable to conduct direct observations of referred children owing to practice and reimbursement limitations. The described case, however, highlights the importance of obtaining information from multiple sources, including a semi-structured interview with the child. Cover all sections in the basic interview, rather than bypassing sections based on the child's clinical presentation or parent report. No one in Sean's life had any suspicions concerning his OCD symptoms, nor the impairing nature of the disorder.

RECOMMENDATIONS FOR STUDENTS

Students interested in child psychopathology must develop competency with a wide range of clinical assessment instruments. Some training programs do not mandate learning how to conduct structured and semi-structured clinical interviews with children, and others fail to teach students how to ask questions, probe responses, or use examples appropriate for children of different ages, sexes, and cultural backgrounds. It is incumbent upon you to learn these techniques from appropriate workshops and training sites to the greatest extent possible.

SUMMARY

Misdiagnosis and overdiagnosis of ADHD has increased exponentially in recent years due to myriad factors. Among the most influential are the nonpathognomic nature of

ADHD symptoms (e.g., inattention), unrealistic time constraints permitted for conducting a comprehensive diagnostic evaluation, and an overreliance on rating scales and nonstandardized clinical office interviews. Evidence-based diagnostic practice procedures, whereby valid information is obtained from multiple sources pertaining to a child's past and current functioning, are recommended to yield incremental benefit for clinical psychology practice.

REFERENCES

Abikoff, H., Gittelman-Klein, R., & Klein, R. (1977). Validation of a classroom observation code for hyperactive children. *Journal of Counseling and Clinical Psychology, 45,* 772–783.

Abikoff, H., Gittelman, R., & Klein, R. (1980). Classroom observation code for hyperactive children: A replication of validity. *Journal of Counseling and Clinical Psychology, 5,* 555–565.

Abikoff, H., Jensen, P. S., Arnold, L. L., Hoza, B., Hechtman, L., Pollack, S., et al. (2002). Observed classroom behavior of children with ADHD: Relationship to gender and comorbidity. *Journal of Abnormal Child Psychology, 30,* 349–359.

Achenbach, T. M., & Edelbrock, C. S. (1986). Empirically based assessment of the behavioral/emotional problems of 2- and 3-year-old children. *Journal of Abnormal Child Psychology, 15,* 629–650.

Achenbach, T. M., & Rescorla, L. A. (2001). *Manual for the ASEBA School-Age Forms & Profiles.* Burlington, VT: University of Vermont Research Center for Children, Youth, & Families.

Alban-Metcalfe, J., Cheng-Lai, A., & Ma, T. (2002). Teacher and student teacher ratings of attention-deficit/hyperactivity disorder in three cultural settings. *International Journal of Disability, Development, and Education, 49,* 281–299.

Alderson, R. M., Rapport, M. D., & Kofler, M. J. (in press). *Attention-deficit/hyperactivity disorder and stop-signal behavioral inhibition: A meta-analytic review of the stop-signal paradigm.* Manuscript under review.

Allyon, T., Layman, D., & Kandel, H. (1975). A behavioral-educational alternative to drug control of hyperactive children. *Journal of Applied Behavior Analysis, 8,* 137–146.

American Psychiatric Association. (2000). *Diagnostic and statistical manual of mental disorders* (4th ed., text rev.). Washington, DC: Author.

Angold, A., & Costello, E. J. (2000). Child and Adolescent Psychiatric Assessment (CAPA). *Journal of the American Academy of Child and Adolescent Psychiatry, 39,* 39–48.

Aronen, E. T., Fjällberg, M., Paavonen, E. J., & Soininen, M. (2002). Day length associates with activity level in children living at 60 degrees North. *Child Psychiatry and Human Development, 32,* 217–226.

Barkley, R. A. (1989). The problem of stimulus control and rule-governed behavior in children with attention deficit disorder with hyperactivity. In L. M. Bloomingdale & J. M. Swanson (Eds.), *Attention deficit disorder* (Vol. 4, pp. 203–234). New York: Pergamon Press.

Barkley, R. A. (1990). *Attention-deficit hyperactivity disorder: A handbook for diagnosis and treatment.* New York: Guilford Press.

Barkley, R. A. (1997). Behavioral inhibition, sustained attention, and executive function: Constructing a unifying theory of ADHD. *Psychological Bulletin, 121,* 65–94.

Barkley, R. A. (2006). *Attention-deficit hyperactivity disorder: A handbook for diagnosis and treatment* (3rd ed.). New York: Guilford Press.

Barkley, R. A., & Cunningham, C. E. (1979). The effects of methylphenidate on the mother-child interactions of hyperactive children. *Archives of General Psychiatry, 36,* 201–208.

Barkley, R. A., DuPaul, G. J., & McMurray, M. B. (1990). A comprehensive evaluation of attention deficit disorder with and without hyperactivity. *Journal of Consulting and Clinical Psychology, 58,* 775–789.

Barkley, R. A., Fischer, M., Edelbrock, C. S., & Smallish, L. (1990). The adolescent outcome of hyperactive children diagnosed by research criteria: Pt. I. An 8-year prospective follow-up study. *Journal of the American Academy of Child and Adolescent Psychiatry, 29,* 546–557.

Barkley, R. A., Fischer, M., Smallish, L., & Fletcher, K. (2002). The persistence of attention-deficit/hyperactivity disorder into young adulthood as a function of reporting source and definition of disorder. *Journal of Abnormal Psychology, 111,* 279–289.

Barkley, R. A., Fischer, M., Smallish, L., & Fletcher, K. (2006). Young adult outcome of hyperactive children: Adaptive functioning in major life activities. *Journal of the American Academy of Child and Adolescent Psychiatry, 45,* 192–202.

Barkley, R. A., Murphy, K. R., & O'Connell, T. (2005). Effects of two doses of methylphenidate on simulator driving performance in adults with attention deficit hyperactivity disorder. *Journal of Safety Research, 36,* 121–131.

Barkley, R. A., Shelton, T. L., Crosswait, C., Moorehouse, M., Fletcher, K., Barrett, S., et al. (1996). Preliminary findings of an early intervention program for aggressive hyperactive children. *Annals of the New York Academy of Sciences, 794,* 277–289.

Beauchaine, T. P., Katkin, E. S., Strassberg, Z., & Snarr, J. (2001). Disinhibitory psychopathology in male adolescents: Discriminating conduct disorder from attention-deficit/hyperactivity disorder through concurrent assessment of multiple autonomic states. *Journal of Abnormal Psychology, 110*(4), 610–624.

Behar, L. & Stringfield, S. (1974). A behavior rating scale for the preschool child. *Developmental Psychology, 10,* 601–610.

Biederman, J., & Faraone, S. V. (2004). Massachusetts General Hospital studies of gender influences on attention-deficit/hyperactivity disorder in youths and relatives. *Psychiatric Clinics of North America, 27,* 225–232.

Biederman, J., Faraone, S. V., Keenan, K., Knee, D., & Tsuang, M. T. (1990). Family-genetic and psychosocial risk factors in DSM-III attention deficit disorder. *Journal of the American Academy of Child and Adolescent Psychiatry, 29,* 526–533.

Biederman, J., Mick, M., Faraone, S. V., Braaten, E., Doyle, A., Spencer, T., et al. (2002). Influence of gender on attention deficit hyperactivity disorder in children referred to a psychiatric clinic. *American Journal of Psychiatry, 159,* 36–42.

Bijur, P., Golding, J., Haslum, M., & Kurzon, M. (1988). Behavioral predictors of injury in school-age children. *American Journal of Diseases in Children, 142,* 1307–1312.

Buss, D. M., Block, J. H., & Block, J. (1980). Preschool activity level: Personality correlates and developmental implications. *Child Development, 51,* 401–408.

Campbell, S. B. (1990). *Behavior problems in preschool children.* New York: Guilford Press.

Castellanos, F. X. (2001). Neuroimaging studies of ADHD. In M. V. Solanto, A. F. T. Arnsten, & F. X. Castellanos (Eds.), *Stimulant drugs and ADHD: Basic and clinical neuroscience* (pp. 243–258). New York: Oxford University Press.

Castellanos, F. X., Sonuga-Barke, E. J., Scheres, A., Di Martino, A., Hyde, C., & Walters, J. R. (2005). Varieties of attention-deficit/hyperactivity disorder-related intra-individual variability. *Biological Psychiatry, 57,* 1416–1423.

Castellanos, F. X., & Tannock, R. (2002). Neuroscience of attention-deficit/hyperactivity disorder: The search for endophenotypes. *Nature Reviews Neuroscience, 3,* 617–628.

Clarke, A. R., Barry, R. J., McCarthy, R., & Selikowitz, M. (1998). EEG analysis in attention deficit hyperactivity disorder: A comparative study of two subtypes. *Psychiatry Research, 81,* 19–29.

Conners, C. K., Sitarenios, G., Parker, J. D. A., & Epstein, J. N. (1998). Revision and restandard-ization of the Conners Teacher Rating Scale (CTRS-R): Factor structure, reliability, and criterion validity. *Journal of Abnormal Child Psychology, 26,* 279–291.

Corkum, P., Tannock, R., & Moldofsky, H. (1998). Sleep disturbances in children with attention-deficit/hyperactivity. *Journal of the American Academy of Child and Adolescent Psychiatry, 37,* 637–646.

Cruickshank, W. M., & Dolphin, J. E. (1951). The educational implications of psychological studies of cerebral palsied children. *Exceptional Children, 18,* 3–11.

de Ramirez, R., & Shapiro, E. S. (2005). Effects of student ethnicity on judgments of ADHD symptoms among Hispanic and White teachers. *School Psychology Quarterly, 20,* 268–287.

Diener, M. B., & Milich, R. (1997). Effects of positive feedback on the social interactions of boys with attention deficit hyperactivity disorder: A test of the self-protective hypothesis. *Journal of Clinical Child Psychology, 26,* 256–265.

Douglas, V. I. (1972). Stop, look, and listen: The problem of sustained attention and impulse control in hyperactive and normal children. *Canadian Journal of Behavioral Science, 4,* 259–282.

Douglas, V. I. (1988). Cognitive deficits in children with attention deficit disorder with hyperac-tivity. In L. M. Bloomingdale & J. Sergeant (Eds.), *Attention deficit disorder: Criteria, cognition, intervention* (pp. 65–82). New York: Pergamon Press.

DuPaul, G. J., & Barkley, R. A. (1992). Situational variability of attention problems: Psychometric properties of the Revised Home and School Situations Questionnaires. *Journal of Clinical Child Psychology, 21,* 178–188.

DuPaul, G. J., McGoey, K. E., Eckert, T., & VanBrakle, J. (2001). Preschool children with attention-deficit/hyperactivity disorder: Impairments in behavioral, social, and school functioning. *Journal of the American Academy of Child and Adolescent Psychiatry, 40,* 508–515.

DuPaul, G. J., Power, T. J., Anastopoulos, A. D., & Reid, R. (1998). *The ADHD Rating Scale-IV: Checklists, norms, and clinical interpretation.* New York: Guilford.

DuPaul, G. J., Rapport, M. D., & Perriello, L. M. (1991). Teacher ratings of academic skills: The development of the Academic Performance Rating Scale. *School Psychology Review, 20,* 284–300.

DuPaul, G. J., & Stoner, G. (2003). *ADHD in the school: Assessment and intervention strategies* (2nd ed.). New York: Guilford Press.

Eaton, W. O., McKeen, N. A., & Campbell, D. W. (2001). The waxing and waning of movement: Implications for psychological development. *Developmental Review, 21,* 205–223.

Eaton, W. O., McKeen, N. A., & Saudino, K. J. (1996). Measuring human individual differences in general motor activity with actometers. In K. P. Ossenkopp, M. Kavaliers, & P. R. Sanberg (Eds.), *Measuring Movement and Locomotion: From Invertebrates to Humans* (pp. 79–92). Austin, TX: R. G. Landes Co.

El-Sayed, E., Larsson, J. O., Persson, H. E., & Rydelius, P. A. (2002). Altered cortical activity in children with attention-deficit/hyperactivity disorder during attentional load task. *Journal of the American Academy of Child and Adolescent Psychiatry, 41*(7), 811–819.

Ferguson, H. B., & Pappas, B. A. (1979). Evaluation of psychophysiological, neurochemical, and animal models of hyperactivity. In R. L. Trites (Ed.), *Hyperactivity in children.* Baltimore: University Park Press.

Fergusson, D. M., Lynskey, M. T., & Horwood, L. J. (1997). Attentional difficulties in middle childhood and psychosocial outcomes in young adulthood. *Journal of Child Psychology and Psychiatry, 38,* 633–644.

Gadow, K. D., & Sprafkin, J. (1997). *Child symptom inventory 4: Norms manual.* Stony Brook, NY: Checkmate Plus.

Gadow, K. D. & Sprafkin, J. (2002). Child Symptom Inventory 4: Screening and Norms Manual. Stony Brook, NY: Checkmate Plus.

Gadow, K. D., Sprafkin, J., & Nolan, E. E. (1996). *Attention Deficit Hyperactivity Disorder School Observation Code*. Stony Brook, NY: Checkmate Plus.

Gaub, M., & Carlson, C. (1997). Gender differences in ADHD: A meta-analysis and critical review. *Journal of the American Academy of Child and Adolescent Psychiatry, 36*(8),1036–1045.

Gilliam, J. E. (1995). Examiners manual for the Attention-Deficit/Hyperactivity Disorder Test: A method for identifying individuals with ADHD. Austin, TX: Pro-Ed.

Gjone, H., Stevenson, J., & Sundet, J. M. (1996). Genetic influence on parent-reported attention-related problems in a Norwegian general population twin sample. *Journal of the American Academy of Child and Adolescent Psychiatry, 35*, 599–596.

Graetz, B. W., Sawyer, M. G., & Baghurst, P. (2005). Gender differences among children with DSM-IV ADHD in Australia. *Journal of the American Academy of Child and Adolescent Psychiatry, 44*, 159–168.

Gray, J. A. (1982). *The neuropsychology of anxiety*. New York: Oxford University Press.

Harris, F. C., & Lahey, B. B. (1982). Recording system bias in direct observational methodology: A review and critical analysis of factors causing inaccurate coding behavior. *Clinical Psychology Review, 2*, 539–556.

Hart, E. L., Lahey, B. B., Loeber, R., Applegate, B., & Frick, P. J. (1995). Developmental changes in attention-deficit hyperactivity disorder in boys: A 4-year longitudinal study. *Journal of Abnormal Child Psychology, 23*, 729–750.

Holland, M. L., Gimpel, G. A., & Merrell, K. W. (1998). Innovations in assessing ADHD: Development, psychometric properties, and factor structure of the ADHD Symptoms Rating Scale (ADHD-SRS). *Journal of Psychopathology & Behavioral Assessment, 20*, 307–332.

Jensen, P. S., Hinshaw, S. P., Swanson, J. M., Greenhill, L. L., Connors, C. K., Arnold, L. E., et al. (2001). Findings from the NIMH Multimodal Treatment Study of ADHD (MTA): Implications and applications for primary care providers. *Journal of Developmental and Behavioral Pediatrics, 22*, 60–73.

Kamphaus, R. W. & Reynolds, C. R. (1998). BASC monitor for ADHD manual and software guide. American Guidance Service, Inc.: Circle Pines, Minnesota.

Kaufman, A. S., & Kaufman, N. L. (1983). *Kaufman Assessment Battery for Children*. Circle Pines, MN: American Guidance Services.

Kessler, J. W. (1980). History of minimal brain dysfunction. In H. Rie & E. Rie (Eds.), *Handbook of minimal brain dysfunction: A critical review*. New York: Wiley.

Kofler, M. J., Rapport, M. D., & Alderson, R. M. (in press). Classroom Inattention in ADHD: A Meta-analytic Review of Off-task Behavior Rates. *The Journal of Child Psychology and Psychiatry and Allied Disciplines*.

Lalloo, R., Sheiham, A., & Nazroo, J. Y. (2003). Behavioral characteristics and accidents: Findings from the Health Survey for England. *Accident Analysis and Prevention, 35*, 661–667.

Lambert, N., Hartsough, C., & Sandoval, J. (1990). Manual for the Children's Attention and Adjustment Survey. Circle Pines, MN: American Guidance Service.

Leibson, C. L., Katusic, S. K., Barbaresi, W. J., Falissard, B., & O'Brian, P. C. (2001). Use and cost of medical care for children and adolescents with and without attention-deficit/hyperactivity disorder. *Journal of the American Medical Association, 285*, 60–66.

Levy, F., Hay, D. A., McStephen, M., Wood, C., & Waldman, I. (1997). Attention-deficit hyperactivity disorder: A category or a continuum? Genetic analysis of a large-scale twin study. *Journal of the American Academy of Child and Adolescent Psychiatry, 36*, 737–744.

Lijffijt, M., Kenemans, L., Verbaten, M. N., & van Engeland, H. (2005). A meta-analytic review of stopping performance in attention-deficit/hyperactivity disorder: Deficient inhibitory motor control? *Journal of Abnormal Psychology, 114*(2), 216–222.

Loo, S. K., & Barkley, R. A. (2005). Clinical utility of EEG in attention deficit hyperactivity disorder. *Applied Developmental Neuropsychology, 12*(2), 64–76.

Mann, C. A., Lubar, J. F., Zimmerman, A. W., Miller, C. A., & Muenchen, R. A. (1992). Quantitative analysis of EEG in boys with attention-deficit hyperactivity disorder: Controlled study with clinical implications. *Pediatric Neurology, 8*, 30–36.

Mannuzza, S., Klein, R. G., Bessler, A., Malloy, P., & LaPadula, M. (1993). Adult outcome of hyperactive boys: Educational achievement, occupational rank, and psychiatric status. *Archives of General Psychiatry, 50*, 565–576.

Mash, E. J., & Terdal, L. G. (1997). *Assessment of childhood disorders* (3rd ed.). New York: Guilford Press.

McCarney, S. B. (2004). *Attention Deficit Disorders Evaluation Scale-Third Edition (ADDES-3).* Columbia, MO: Hawthorne Educational Services.

McCarney, S. B., & Johnson, N. W. (1995). Early Childhood Attention Deficit Disorders Intervention Manual. Columbia, MO: Hawthorne Educational Services, Inc.

McClellan, J. M., & Werry, J. S. (2000). Research psychiatric diagnostic interviews for children and adolescents. *Journal of the American Academy of Child and Adolescent Psychiatry, 39*, 19–27.

McGoey, K. E., & DuPaul, G. J. (2000). Total reinforcement and response cost procedures: Reducing the disruptive behavior of preschool children with attention-deficit/hyperactivity disorder. *School Psychology Quarterly, 15*, 330–343.

Mikami, A. Y., & Hinshaw, S. P. (2003). Buffers of peer rejection among girls with and without ADHD: The role of popularity with adults and goal-directed solitary play. *Journal of Abnormal Child Psychology, 31*, 381–397.

Nadder, T. S., Silberg, J. L., Eaves, L. J., Maes, H. H., & Meyer, J. M. (1998). Genetic effects on ADHD symptomatology in 7- to 13-year-old twins: Results from a telephone survey. *Behavior Genetics, 28*, 83–99.

Naglieri, J., LeBuffe, P., & Pfeiffer, S. I. (1994). Devereux Scales of Mental Disorders. San Antonio, TX: The Psychological Corporation.

Neeper, R., Lahey, B. B., & Frick, P. J. (1990). Manual for the Comprehensive Behavior Rating Scale for Children (CBRSC). San Antonio, Texas: Psychological Corporation.

Oosterlaan, J., & Sergeant, J. A. (1995). Response choice and inhibition in ADHD, anxious, and aggressive children: The relationship between S-R compatibility and stop signal task. In J. A. Sergeant (Ed.), *Eunethydis: European approaches to hyperkinetic disorder* (pp. 225–240). Amsterdam: University of Amsterdam Press.

Palfrey, J. S., Levine, M. D., Walker, D. K., & Sullivan, M. (1985). The emergence of attention deficits in early childhood: A prospective study. *Journal of Developmental and Behavioral Pediatrics, 6*, 339–348.

Pelham, W. E., & Bender, M. E. (1982). Peer relationships in hyperactive children: Description and treatment. In K. D. Gadow & I. Bialer (Eds.), *Advances in learning and behavioral disabilities* (Vol. 1, pp. 365–436). Greenwich, CT: JAI Press.

Pelham, W. E., Fabiano, G. A., & Massetti, G. M. (2005). Evidence-based assessment of attention deficit hyperactivity disorder in children and adolescents. *Journal of Clinical Child and Adolescent Psychology, 34*, 449–476.

Quay, H. C. (1997). Inhibition and attention deficit hyperactivity disorder. *Journal of Abnormal Child Psychology, 25*, 7–13.

Quay, H. C., & Peterson, D. R. (1993). The Revised Behavior Problem Checklist: Manual. Odessa, FL: Psychological Assessment Resources.

Rapport, M. D. (1983). Attention deficit disorder with hyperactivity: Critical treatment parameters and their application in applied outcome research. In M. Hersen, R. Eisler, & P. Miller (Eds.), *Progress in behavior modification* (pp. 219–298). New York: Academic Press.

Rapport, M. D. (1993). Attention deficit hyperactivity disorder. In T. H. Ollendick & M. Hersen (Eds.), *Handbook of child and adolescent assessment* (pp. 269–291). Newton, MA: Allyn & Bacon.

Rapport, M. D. (1998). Treating children with attention-deficit/hyperactivity disorder (ADHD). In V. B. Van Hasselt & M. Hersen (Eds.), *Handbook of psychological treatment protocols for children and adolescents* (pp. 65–107). New York: Erlbaum.

Rapport, M. D. (1990). Controlled studies of the effects of psychostimulants on children's functioning in clinic and classroom settings. In C. K. Conners & M. Kinsbourne (Eds.), *Attention deficit hyperactivity disorder* (pp. 77–111). Munich, Germany: Medizin Verlag Munchen.

Rapport, M. D., Chung, K., Shore, G., Denney, C. B., & Isaacs, P. (2000). Upgrading the science and technology of assessment and diagnosis: Laboratory and clinic-based assessment of children with ADHD. *Journal of Clinical Child Psychology, 29,* 555–568.

Rapport, M. D., & Denney, C. (1997). Titrating methylphenidate in children with attention-deficit/hyperactivity disorder: Is body mass predictive of clinical response? *Journal of the American Academy of Child and Adolescent Psychiatry, 36,* 523–530.

Rapport, M. D., Denney, C. B., DuPaul, G. J., & Gardner, M. J. (1994). Attention deficit disorder and methylphenidate: Normalization rates, clinical effectiveness, and response prediction in 76 children. *Journal of the American Academy of Child and Adolescent Psychiatry, 33,* 882–893.

Rapport, M. D., & Kelly, K. L. (1991). Psychostimulant effects on learning and cognitive function: Findings and implications for children with attention deficit hyperactivity disorder. *Clinical Psychology Review, 11,* 61–92.

Rapport, M. D., & Moffitt, C. (2002). Attention deficit/hyperactivity disorder and methylphenidate: A review of height/weight, cardiovascular and somatic complaint side effects. *Clinical Psychology Review, 22*(8), 1107–1131.

Rapport, M. D., Murphy, A., & Bailey, J. S. (1982). Ritalin versus response cost in the control of hyperactive children: A within-subject comparison. *Journal of Applied Behavior Analysis, 15,* 20–31.

Rapport, M. D., Scanlan, S. W., & Denney, C. B. (1999). Attention-deficit/hyperactivity disorder and scholastic achievement: A model of dual developmental pathways. *Journal of Child Psychology and Psychiatry, 40,* 1169–1183.

Rapport, M. D., Timko, T., Kofler, M., & Alderson, R. M. (2005). Hyperactivity: A core deficit or byproduct of working memory deficiency? Paper presented in the symposium entitled, Attentional Processes in ADHD: Findings from Laboratory and Field Investigations at the American Psychological Association Annual Conference. Washington, DC.

Rapport, M. D., Timko, T. M., Jr., & Wolfe, R. (2006). Attention-deficit/hyperactivity disorder. In M. Hersen (Ed.), *Clinician's handbook of child behavioral assessment* (pp. 401–435). New York: Elsevier Academic Press.

Reynolds, C., & Kamphaus, R. (2001). *Behavioral Assessment System for Children- 2.* Circle Pines, MN: American Guidance Service.

Rutter, M., & Graham, P. (1968). The reliability and validity of the psychiatric assessment of the child: Pt. II. Interview with the parent. *British Journal of Psychiatry, 114,* 581–592.

Saudargas, R. A. (1997). State-Event Classroom Observation System (SECOS). Observation manual. University of Tennessee. Knoxvllle.

Schmitz, M. F., & Velez, M. (2003). Latino cultural differences in maternal assessments of attention-deficit/hyperactivity symptoms in children. *Hispanic Journal of Behavioral Sciences, 25,* 110–122.

Sergeant, J. A., Oosterlaan, J., & van der Meere, J. (1999). Information processing and energetic factors in attention-deficit/hyperactivity disorder. In H. C. Quay & A. E. Hogan (Eds.), *Handbook of disruptive behavior disorders* (pp. 75–104). Dordrecht, The Netherlands: Kluwer Academic.

Sherman, D. K., Iacono, W. G., & McGue, M. K. (1997). Attention-deficit hyperactivity disorder dimension: A twin study of inattention and impulsivity-hyperactivity. *Journal of the American Academy of Child and Adolescent Psychiatry, 36,* 745–753.

Silberg, J., Rutter, M., Meyer, J., Maes, H., Hewitt, J., Simonoff, E., et al. (1996). Genetic and environmental influences on the covariation between hyperactivity and conduct disturbance in juvenile twins. *Journal of Child Psychology and Psychiatry, 37,* 803–816.

Sines, J. O. (1986). Normative data for the revised Missouri children's behavior checklist – Parent form (MCBC-P). *Journal of Abnormal Child Psychology, 14,* 89-94.

Sines, J. O. (1988). Teachers' norms and teacher-parent agreement on the Missouri Children's Behavior Checklist. *Journal of School Psychology, 26,* 413–416.

Sleator, E. K., & Ullmann, R. K. (1981). Can the physician diagnose hyperactivity in the office? *Pediatrics, 67,* 13–17.

Sonuga-Barke, E. J. S. (2002). Psychological heterogeneity in AD/HD: A dual pathway model of behavior and cognition. *Behavioral Brain Research, 130*(1/2), 29–36.

Spadafore, G. L. & Spadafore, S. J (1997). *Spadafore attention deficit hyperactivity disorder rating scale.* Novato, CA: Academic Therapy Publications.

Sprague, R. L., & Sleator, E. K. (1977). Methylphenidate in hyperkinetic children: Differences in dose effects on learning and social behavior. *Science, 198*(4323), 1274–1276.

Strauss, A. A., & Kephart, N. C. (1955). *Psychopathology and education of the brain-injured child: Vol. II. Progress in theory and clinic.* New York: Grune & Stratton.

Strauss, A. A., & Lehtinen, L. E. (1947). *Psychopathology and education of the brain-injured child.* New York: Grune & Stratton.

Swanson, J. M. (1992). *School-based assessments and interventions for ADD students.* Irvine, CA: K.C. Publications.

Swanson, J. M., Sandman, C. A., Deutsch, C., & Baren, M. (1983). Methylphenidate hydrochloride given with or before breakfast: Pt. I. Behavioral, cognitive, and electrophysiological effects. *Pediatrics, 72,* 49–55.

Swenson, A. R., Birnbaum, H. G., Secnik, K., Marynchenko, M., Greenberg, P., & Claxton, A. (2003). Attention-deficit/hyperactivity disorder: Increased costs for patients and their families. *Journal of the American Academy of Child and Adolescent Psychiatry, 42,* 1415–1423.

Thapar, A., Hervas, A., & McGuffin, P. (1995). Childhood hyperactivity scores are highly heritable and show sibling competition effects: Twin study evidence. *Behavior Genetics, 25*(6), 537–544.

Tryon, W. W., & Pinto, L. P. (1994). Comparing activity measurements and ratings. *Behavior Modification, 18,* 251–261.

Ullmann, R.K., Sleator, E.K., & Sprague, R.L. (2000). ACTeRS teacher and parent forms manual. Champaign, IL: Metritech, Inc.

U.S. Census Bureau. (2005). *Annual estimates of the population by sex and 5-year age groups for the United States: April 1, 2000 to July 1, 2005 (NC-EST2005–01).* Retrieved June 2, 2006, from http://www.census.gov.

Unnever, J. D., & Cornell, D. G. (2003). Bullying, self-control, and ADHD. *Journal of Interpersonal Violence, 18,* 129–147.

van Egeren, L. A., Frank, S. J., & Paul, J. S. (1999). Daily behavior ratings among children and adolescent inpatients: The abbreviated child behavior rating form. *Journal of the American Academy of Child and Adolescent Psychiatry, 38,* 1417–1425.

Weiss, G., & Hechtman, L. (1993). *Hyperactive children growing up* (2nd ed.). New York: Guilford Press.

Weisz, J. R., Chaiyasit, W., Weiss, B., Eastman, K. L., & Jackson, E. W. (1995). A multimethod study of problem behavior among Thai and American children in school: Teacher reports versus direct observations. *Child Development, 66,* 402–415.

Werry, J. S. (1968). Developmental hyperactivity. *Pediatric Clinics of North America, 15,* 581–599.

Whalen, C. K., & Henker, B. (1985). The social worlds of hyperactivity (ADDH) children. *Clinical Psychology Review, 5,* 447–478.

Willcutt, E. G., Doyle, A. E., Nigg, J. T., Faraone, S. V., & Pennington, B. F. (2005). Validity of the executive function theory of attention-deficit/hyperactivity disorder: A meta-analytic review. *Biological Psychiatry, 57*(11), 1336–1346.

Wolraich, M. L., Hannah, J. N., Baumgaertel, A., & Feurer, I. D. (1998). Examination of DSM-IV criteria for attention deficit/hyperactivity disorder in a county-wide sample. *Journal of Developmental and Behavioral Pediatrics, 19,* 162–168.

Wolraich, M. L., Lambert, E. W., Baumgaertel, A., Garcia-Tornel, S., Feurer, I. D., Bickman, L., & Doffing, M. A. (2003). Teachers' screening for attention deficit/hyperactivity disorder: comparing multinational samples on teacher ratings of ADHD. *Journal of Abnormal Child Psychology, 31,* 445–455

CHAPTER 15

Early-Onset Schizophrenia

IAN KODISH AND JON McCLELLAN

Schizophrenia is a relatively common and often disabling chronic mental illness characterized by impairments in thought process, affect, and social function. Approximately 1% of the worldwide population is affected in their lifetime, resulting in tremendous societal costs and personal suffering. Symptoms such as distressing hallucinations, delusions or paranoia typically emerge in early adulthood and demand medical treatment. Early-onset Schizophrenia (EOS), defined as onset prior to age 18 years, is diagnosed using the same standardized criteria as for adults. Schizophrenia in children and adolescents exhibits clinical and biological continuity with the adult-onset form (Nicolson, Lenane, Hamburger, et al., 2000).

CLINICAL PRESENTATION

EPIDEMIOLOGY

Most epidemiological surveys of childhood psychiatric disorders have not addressed Schizophrenia. In the general population, the peak ages of onset of Schizophrenia range from 15 to 30 years (Mueser & McGurk, 2004). Approximately one-third of individuals with Schizophrenia have their first psychotic episode prior to age 20. Childhood-onset Schizophrenia (COS), defined as onset prior to age 13, is rare, with prevalence estimates of approximately 1 in 10,000. The rates of Schizophrenia in the general population are relatively equivalent between the sexes, although males may be slightly more affected and exhibit more debilitating deficits with lower remission rates. Males also tend to be affected several years prior to females, and perhaps because of this, in EOS boys outnumber girls more than 2 to 1 (American Academy of Child and Adolescent Psychiatry [AACAP], 2001).

SYMPTOMATOLOGY AND COURSE OF ILLNESS

Symptoms of Schizophrenia are broadly characterized into positive and negative. Positive symptoms tend to include behavioral overexpressions, such as florid hallucinations, fixed delusional beliefs, and nonlinear thought processes, whereas negative symptoms tend to be deficits, including emotional blunting, anergy, asociality, and paucity of speech or thought (American Psychiatric Association, 1997). Early-onset Schizophrenia tends to be associated with hallucinations, thought disorder, and flat affect. Systematic delusions are less common in this age group (Green, Padron-Gayol, Hardesty, & Bassiri, 1992; Russell, Bott, & Sammons, 1989; Werry, McClellan, & Chard, 1991). Systemized delusions require more advanced cognitive and abstract abilities; thus the differences in symptom presentation are likely developmental and can change over time as the individual matures. Youth with EOS demonstrate significant communication deficits, with loose associations, illogical thinking, and impaired discourse skills, while incoherence and poverty of speech are less often a problem (Caplan, 1994).

The clinical course of Schizophrenia tends to exhibit phasic changes that vary in severity and quality and show significant individual variability (AACAP, 2001). Although not associated with the marked shifts in functioning between remission and relapse that is characteristic of mood disorders, Schizophrenia can nevertheless be classified into prodromal, acute, recovery, residual, and chronic phases based on symptom presentation and treatment response. In the weeks to years prior to clinical diagnosis, most patients exhibit prodromal features, including mild positive symptoms (illusions, magical thinking), evolving mood symptoms (dysphoria, irritability), cognitive difficulties, and social withdrawal. Youth, especially children who tend to display a more insidious onset, may exhibit subtle mood and anxiety symptoms, increased idiosyncratic or bizarre preoccupations, and occasionally more disruptive behaviors or conduct problems that can complicate diagnosis.

The acute phase of Schizophrenia is defined by deterioration of functioning and increasing predominance of hallucinations, delusions, and disorganized speech or behaviors. This phase generally lasts 1 to 6 months, depending on treatment response, and is commonly the stage when patients receive attention by professional clinicians due to increasingly apparent distress and gross functional impairment. Treatment of acute psychosis exacerbation commonly includes antipsychotic medication. Patients tend to respond to initial treatment with significant improvement in psychotic symptoms. Nevertheless, continued impairment, particularly due to negative symptoms, is often evident. This recovery phase is often characterized by improving positive symptoms, with more persistent problems with flat affect, anergia, and social withdrawal. Some patients will experience a postschizophrenic depression.

If treatment is effective, youth with EOS may have prolonged periods between acute phases with little impairment due to positive symptoms, classified as a residual phase. Prodromal and residual phases may each exhibit a lower intensity or frequency of subtle psychotic symptoms, although most patients with residual illness continue to suffer from deficits associated with negative symptoms. Some youth with EOS will experience subsequent acute episodes despite adequate treatment (Ropcke & Eggers, 2005). These episodes tend to be associated with a greater proportion of negative symptoms, which can be increasingly difficult to treat (Remschmidt, 2002). Longitudinal studies show variable levels of disability and exacerbations of acute episodes (J. R. Asarnow, Tompson, & Goldstein, 1994; J. M. McClellan, Werry, & Ham, 1993). Youth with EOS frequently exhibit moderate to severe impairment across their life span (Eggers & Bunk, 1997; Hollis, 2000; Jarbin, Ott, & Von Knorring, 2003; J. M. McClellan et al., 1993; Ropcke & Eggers, 2005). When followed into adulthood, children with EOS demonstrated greater social deficits and lower levels of employment, and were less likely to live independently, even relative to those with other serious childhood psychiatric disorders (Hollis, 2000; Jarbin et al., 2003).

Predictors of a more positive outcome include higher cognitive ability, treatment responsivity, and adequacy of therapeutic resources (Remschmidt, Martin, Schulz, Gutenbrunner, & Fleischhaker, 1991). A poorer prognosis is predicted by a family history of nonaffective psychosis, low premorbid functioning, insidious onset, diagnosis prior to adolescence, low intellectual functioning, severe symptoms during acute phases, and higher rates of negative symptoms (Fleischhaker et al., 2005; Jarbin et al., 2003; Maziade et al., 1996; Ropcke & Eggers, 2005; Rutter, Kim-Cohen, & Maughan, 2006). There is evidence in adults that early effective treatment improves outcome, with some patients experiencing a substantial reduction of psychotic symptoms (Harrow, Grossman, Jobe, & Herbener, 2005). Therefore, establishing a clearer understanding of the early manifestations of Schizophrenia is of prime importance for early recognition, accurate diagnosis, and effective treatment.

PREMORBID FUNCTIONING

The onset of EOS tends to be insidious, especially for those with COS. The associated cognitive and behavioral impairments are thought to reflect progressive alterations in neurodevelopmental trajectories. Increasing evidence points to subtle abnormalities emerging in childhood, even when clinical onset occurs later in adulthood (Rutter et al., 2006). A longitudinal study of adults with Schizophrenia revealed stable impairments in receptive language and early motor development as early as 1 year of life (Isohanni, Murray, Jokelainen, Croudace, & Jones, 2004). Similarly, blind retrospective ratings of childhood home movies revealed differences in socioemotional features and motor coordination among children who subsequently developed EOS (Walker, Grimes, Davis, & Smith, 1993). In a longitudinal study, self-reported psychoticlike symptoms at age 11 predicted increased risk for Schizophrenia Spectrum Disorder by age 26 (M. Cannon et al., 2002; Poulton et al., 2000).

The majority of children with EOS exhibit premorbid abnormalities, including social withdrawal and isolation, disruptive behavioral disorders, developmental delays, and speech and language difficulties (AACAP, 2001). An earlier age of onset is thought to be associated with more dramatic impairments (Biswas, Malhotra, Malhotra, & Gupta, 2006; Hollis, 1995; Vourdas, Pipe, Corrigall, & Frangou, 2003). Longitudinal studies investigating illness course indicate that both premorbid impairments in social functioning and an insidious nature of onset are strong predictors of poorer clinical outcome (Fleischhaker et al., 2005; Ropcke & Eggers, 2005).

NEUROCOGNITIVE DEFICITS

Studies of neuropsychological functioning in EOS suggest that impairments in social functioning and disordered thought processes are paralleled by deficits in cognitive abilities. Similar to findings in adults, EOS is associated with deficits in multiple cognitive domains, including poorer performance on tasks of working memory and other executive functions (Rhinewine et al., 2005). Children with Schizophrenia selectively demonstrate significant impairments in a task that demands executive functioning to control saccadic eye movements (Ross, Heinlein, Zerbe, & Radant, 2005). When compared to youths with bipolar illness, who also exhibit some deficits in memory and sustained effort, youths with Schizophrenia tend to exhibit greater global deficits and impairments on delayed recall tasks, where information must be held on-line and applied to changing task demands (J. McClellan, Prezbindowski, Breiger, & McCurry, 2004). Similar deficits in working memory and executive functioning have been demonstrated in healthy first-degree relatives of COS probands, suggesting trait loading of underlying genetic vulnerability (Gochman et al., 2004).

Several studies have also demonstrated that the degree of global cognitive impairment in EOS is related to negative symptom severity (Rhinewine et al., 2005). These generalized cognitive deficits have also been reported in studies of antipsychotic-naive patients (Oie, Sunde, & Rund, 1999) and are common to patients with onset in childhood or adolescence (Kumra, Giedd, et al., 2000; Rhinewine et al., 2005). A large population study of adults with Schizophrenia revealed that younger age of onset is associated with selectively greater impairments in verbal learning and memory (Tuulio-Henriksson, Partonen, Suvisaari, Haukka, & Lonnqvist, 2004). Early-onset Schizophrenia also has been linked to higher rates of premorbid speech and language impairments (Nicolson, Lenane, Singaracharlu, et al., 2000). However, it is important to recognize that there is no specific neuropsychological profile diagnostic for Schizophrenia (Kumra, Wiggs, et al., 2000; J. McClellan et al., 2004).

Premorbid cognitive functioning tends to be lower in youth with Schizophrenia, and the normal developmental course of enhanced intellectual maturity through adolescence appears to be compromised. A large historical cohort study of adults with Schizophrenia revealed that IQ at age 17 is significantly less than that predicted by language functions at ages 6 to 8 in subjects who subsequently developed Schizophrenia compared those who remained healthy in later life or subsequently suffered from a different psychiatric illness (Reichenberg et al., 2005). This developmental progression in cognitive impairments was also demonstrated by a cross-sectional study of adolescents with Schizophrenia, who exhibited significant attentional impairments at all ages, yet also showed gradually increasing impairments on the more difficult tasks between ages 10 and 20 (Thaden et al., 2006). Alternatively, other evidence suggests that much of the decline in intellectual functioning in COS is restricted to early in the illness, with subsequent stabilization (Gochman et al., 2005).

Neuropsychological impairments in Schizophrenia are seen in other clinically relevant modalities, including those related to emotional recognition. Adults with Schizophrenia are less accurate at ascribing appropriate labels to emotional faces compared to healthy controls, which likely contributes to impairments in social communication and adjustment (Schneider et al., 2006). Lower performance on affect perception tests has been associated with increased bizarre behavior, psychotic symptoms, and some negative symptoms (Addington & Addington, 1998; Kohler, Bilker, Hagendoorn, Gur, & Gur, 2000; Poole, Tobias, & Vinogradov, 2000). Neuroimaging studies further suggest that impaired and inefficient neural networks may underlie these emotional processing difficulties, as patients with Schizophrenia failed to gradually habituate the activation of hippocampal structures despite equivalent initial responses to happy or sad faces (Holt et al., 2005). In line with impairments in the processing of environmental cues, patients of all ages with Schizophrenia show deficits in olfactory identification, and poorer discrimination was associated with more negative symptoms (Corcoran et al., 2005). Interestingly, previous studies have revealed a strong correlation between olfactory processing ability and measures of social drive, suggesting that asociality and other negative symptoms may have neurobiological relevance to impaired olfactory processing (Malaspina & Coleman, 2003).

DIAGNOSIS AND ASSESSMENT

Although a diagnosis of Schizophrenia in children and adolescents is defined by the same standardized criteria used for adults, accurate assessment is often complicated by unique developmental concerns and requires a thorough diagnostic evaluation. Evaluation in youth often involves sorting through a complicated array of clinical and social data. Clinical presentations and symptom assessment are confounded by normative developmental factors. Misdiagnosis is common, particularly at the time of onset (Carlson, 1990; J. McClellan & McCurry, 1998; J. M. McClellan et al., 1993). Many youth first diagnosed with Schizophrenia have different psychiatric disorders at follow-up in outcome studies, including Bipolar Disorder (Werry et al., 1991) and other psychotic mood disorders (Calderoni et al., 2001), as well as personality disorders (Thomsen, 1996). The vast majority of youth referred to a national study did not have the disorder upon stricter review, but instead displayed a heterogeneous mixture of developmental delays, mood lability, and subclinical psychotic symptoms (McKenna et al., 1994). Misdiagnosis may result from significant overlap between presenting symptoms of Schizophrenia and psychotic mood disorder (AACAP, 1998). The initial diagnosis is often made by clinicians unfamiliar with EOS and carries a number of important implications in terms of stigma, prognosis, and treatment. The high rate of comorbid disorders in EOS (Russell et al., 1989) also contributes to diagnostic difficulties and the importance of longitudinal assessment.

Furthermore, most children who report hallucinations do not meet criteria for Schizophrenia, and many will not even have a psychotic disorder (Del Beccaro, Burke, & McCauley, 1988). Normative childhood experiences, including overactive imaginations and vivid fantasies, can be misinterpreted as psychosis. Distinguishing between formal thought disorder and developmental disorders impairing speech and language function can be a challenge (Caplan, 1994). Further complicating matters is the fact that youth with histories of maltreatment report psychoticlike experiences that may represent traumatic memories or dissociative symptoms (Hlastala & McClellan, 2005; Shevlin, Dorahy, & Adamson, 2007). Thus, expertise in childhood psychopathology and experience in interpreting reports of psychotic symptoms in youth are important prerequisite skills for clinicians evaluating youth referred for possible psychosis.

DIAGNOSTIC CRITERIA AND SYMPTOM PRESENTATION

Diagnosis of EOS is made by criteria outlined in the *Diagnostic and Statistical Manual of Mental Disorders* (*DSM-IV*-TR) or the *International Classification of Diseases* (*ICD-10*; see Tables 15.1 and 15.2). Agreement between these two diagnostic systems appears to be high in adolescents (Armenteros et al., 1995). Psychotic symptoms (e.g., hallucinations, delusions, and significantly disorganized behavior) are the hallmark of Schizophrenia. The *DSM-IV-TR* duration criterion requires that evidence of the illness must be present for at least a 6-month period, unless remission has occurred with treatment. Untreated acute psychotic symptoms, including significant negative symptoms, must persist for at least 1 month to meet diagnostic criteria. Greater sensitivity is noted with auditory hallucinations that include a running commentary on a patient's behaviors or bizarre delusions beyond the realm of possibility. Reports vary as to whether the paranoid subtype (Eggers, 1978) or the undifferentiated subtype (J. M. McClellan et al., 1993; Werry et al., 1991) is more common in EOS. Because symptoms

Table 15.1

DSM-IV-TR Diagnostic Criteria for Schizophrenia

A. *Characteristic Symptoms:* At least two of the following are needed, each present for a significant period of time during a 1-month period:

   1. Delusions
   2. Hallucinations
   3. Disorganized speech
   4. Grossly disorganized or catatonic behavior
   5. Negative symptoms (i.e., affective flattening, alogia, or avolition)

   Note: Only one symptom is required if delusions are bizarre or hallucinations include a voice providing a running commentary on the person's actions or thoughts, or two or more voices are conversing with each other.

B. *Social/Occupational Dysfunction:* For a significant portion of the time since onset of the disturbance, one or more major areas of functioning, such as work, interpersonal relations, or self-care, are markedly below the level achieved before onset (or, in EOS, failure to achieve expected level of social, academic, or occupational achievement).

C. *Duration:* Continuous signs must persist for at least 6 months, with at least 1 month of symptoms (or less, if successfully treated) that meet Criterion A (i.e., active-phase symptoms), and may include periods of prodromal or residual symptoms. During these periods, the signs of the disturbance may be manifested solely by negative symptoms or two or more symptoms listed in Criterion A present in an attenuated form (e.g., odd beliefs, unusual perceptual experiences).

D. *Schizoaffective and Mood Disorder Exclusion:* These must have been ruled out because either (1) no Major Depressive, Manic, or Mixed Episodes have occurred concurrently with the active-phase symptoms or (2) if mood episodes have occurred concurrently with the active-phase symptoms, their duration has been brief relative to the total duration of the active and residual periods.

E. *Substance/General Medical Condition Exclusion:* The disturbance is not due to the direct physiological effects of drugs of abuse, medications, or a general medical condition.

F. *Relationship to Pervasive Developmental Disorder:* If there is a history of Autistic Disorder or another Pervasive Developmental Disorder, the additional diagnosis of Schizophrenia is made only if prominent delusions or hallucinations are also present for at least a month (or less, if successfully treated).

From *Diagnostic and Statistical Manual of Mental Disorders* (4th ed., text rev.), by the American Psychiatric Association, 2000, Washington, DC: Author. Adapted with permission.

can change dramatically throughout the course of treatment, it is not clear whether these subtypes represent truly distinct clinical or biological entities in youth (AACAP, 2001). Importantly, symptoms must also result in functional impairments, which in children can include failure to meet developmental expectations in social functioning or academic achievement. Impairments tend to be pervasive rather than limited to specific situations, and although functioning improves with treatment, deficits are often chronic and may not return to premorbid levels (APA, 2000).

Hallucinations are most commonly auditory in nature, experienced as voices separate from thoughts (APA, 2000). This can be difficult to assess in children, who often have fantasy play that includes fictitious dialogue. True psychotic symptoms must therefore be differentiated from reports of psychoticlike phenomena due to overactive imaginations, developmental impairments resulting in idiosyncratic thinking, or

Table 15.2
ICD-10 Description of Schizophrenia

The schizophrenic disorders are characterized in general by fundamental and characteristic distortions of thinking and perception and by inappropriate or blunted affect. Although there are no pathognomonic symptoms, the most important psychopathological phenomena include thought manipulation or broadcasting, delusions of control, or delusional perception. Other phenomena that must be present with other symptoms include hallucinatory voices giving running commentary, discussing the patient, or emanating from his or her body; persistent bizarre delusions; persistent hallucinations with overvalued ideas; breaks in thought process; negative symptoms; and behavioral impairments.

The diagnosis of Schizophrenia should not be made in the presence of extensive depressive or manic symptoms unless it is clear that schizophrenic symptoms antedated the affective disturbance. Nor should Schizophrenia be diagnosed in the presence of overt brain disease or during states of drug intoxication or withdrawal. Diagnosis is also excluded if criteria are met for:

1. Acute Schizophrenia-like disorder, symptoms persisting for less than 1 month
2. Schizoaffective Disorder, mixed type
3. Schizotypal Disorder

From *The ICD-10 Classification of Mental and Behavioral Disorders: Clinical Descriptions and Diagnostic Guidelines,* by the World Health Organization, 1992, Geneva, Switzerland: Author. Adapted with permission.

psychological coping responses to traumatic events. Hallucinations that occur during moving religious experiences or associated with sleep are also considered to be normal in children and adults.

Hallucinations can also be olfactory or tactile in nature, which may raise suspicion for alternative etiologies such as seizure disorder or toxic ingestion. Increased clinical concern is also given to patients with command auditory hallucinations and minimal insight, resulting in a greater likelihood to behaviorally respond to suggestions driven by psychotic thinking. Although clinical treatment can significantly improve the course of symptoms, cases that remit before 6 months may raise questions of diagnostic accuracy, as negative symptoms such as lack of social interest usually persist.

Other psychotic phenomena include strange and unrealistic beliefs that do not accord with one's life experience and culture. These delusions may be persecutory (e.g., being followed by the FBI), referent (e.g., certainty that the television is communicating a special message), grandiose (e.g., a belief that one possesses supernatural powers), somatic (e.g., a belief that one suffers from a terminal illness, despite medical evidence to the contrary), or religious (e.g., a belief that one is a religious prophet). Delusions may also involve thought withdrawal or insertion, or beliefs of being controlled by an outside force.

Disorganized speech, another core symptom, is characterized by inappropriate pauses or loose associations with frequent, sudden, or apparently unrelated changes in the conversation. Patients with Schizophrenia often provide oblique responses to questions, and the tangential flow of discourse can be a significant obstacle to defining the full scope of delusional beliefs and recent clinical course. Disorganized speech is often matched by disorganized behavior, with impairments in sustaining goal-oriented activities or requirements of daily living, such as hygiene. Disorganized thinking and behavior can result in significant medical consequences, including accidental injury, excessive ingestion of water, or even aberrant body temperatures due to inappropriate dress. Indeed, the risk of suicide or accidental death directly due to behaviors caused by psychotic thinking in EOS appears to be at least 5% (Eggers, 1978; Werry et al., 1991).

Negative symptoms refer to a variety of deficits, including avolition, affective flattening, and alogia. These are commonly demonstrated by a history of social isolation and lack of interest in previously enjoyable activities. Limited eye contact, blank stares, or psychomotor blunting of body language are indicative of affective flattening. Negative symptoms can be difficult to differentiate from depression. Antipsychotic medications can further contribute to narrowing the range of emotional expression, placing greater emphasis on course and associated symptoms.

Differential Diagnosis

Differentiating EOS from other psychiatric or neurological illnesses can be a challenge. A thorough review of presenting symptoms, premorbid functioning, symptom course, and family history will improve accuracy of diagnosis. Clinicians should adhere to standardized diagnostic criteria and ideally be familiar with pediatric presentation and normal development.

Organic Psychosis   Psychotic symptoms can emanate from nonpsychiatric medical syndromes. Delirium, which presents as a gross disruption in thinking and perceptions, is also typically characterized by waxing and waning symptoms and fluctuating levels of consciousness. Delirium may arise from any number of medical conditions, including infection, metabolic disorders, intoxication or withdrawal states, or encephalopathies. Seizure disorders may induce psychotic perceptions or bizarre behavior. Infections of the CNS or lesions such as brain tumors or head trauma often require urgent treatment; thus accurate diagnosis is imperative. Other metabolic, immune, or neurological disorders, including lipid storage diseases, endocrinopathies, Wilson's disease, and HIV, may also exhibit psychotic symptoms.

Probably the most important condition to assess is acute intoxication and substance abuse. Use of illicit substances, including stimulants, inhalants, and hallucinogens, can present as acute psychosis. This can be complicated to differentiate because many individuals with Schizophrenia have comorbid substance abuse, with some studies in adolescents suggesting rates as high as 50% (Hsiao & McClellan, in press; J. McClellan & McCurry, 1998). A substance-induced psychotic episode is generally expected to remit after a period of abstinence. Alternatively, illicit substances will exacerbate symptoms of Schizophrenia, but evidence of the illness will persist during periods of abstinence. However, some studies suggest that Schizophrenia may result from an interaction between an underlying vulnerability and exposure to substance use, including cannabis (Maki et al., 2005).

A thorough initial diagnostic assessment includes appropriate pediatric and neurological evaluations. Laboratory and neuroimaging procedures cannot be used to make a diagnosis of Schizophrenia. However, these tests are important for ruling out complicating medical conditions, assessing basic health, and establishing a baseline for medication monitoring. Initial laboratory tests to be considered include blood counts, serum chemistries, thyroid functions, urinalysis, and toxicology screens. The use of atypical antipsychotics requires the monitoring of metabolic functions, including glucose and serum lipid levels. Chromosomal analysis may also be indicated for patients with clinical features suggestive of a developmental syndrome, as several are associated with increased risk for psychosis.

Psychotic Mood Disorders Differentiating EOS from mood disorders in youth can be quite difficult, as both disorders commonly present with a variety of overlapping affective and psychotic symptoms. Mania in teenagers is often associated with hallucinations, delusions, and thought disorder (Pavuluri, Herbener, & Sweeney, 2004). Historically, studies found that approximately half of adolescents with Bipolar Disorder were originally misdiagnosed as having Schizophrenia (Calderoni et al., 2001; Carlson, 1990; Werry et al., 1991). With greater clinical awareness, differential diagnosis appears to be improving, although distinguishing acute psychotic mania from acute Schizophrenia remains a challenge, particularly when restricted to cross-sectional clinical data (Carlson, Bromet, & Sievers, 2000). Furthermore, negative symptoms in adolescents with Schizophrenia can be mistaken for depression, and psychotic depression can itself present with mood-congruent or -incongruent psychotic features (AACAP, 1998). Longitudinal assessment and retrospective evaluation of the temporal overlap of mood episodes and psychotic symptoms are critical to accurate diagnosis.

Schizoaffective Disorder is diagnosed when criteria for both mood disorder and Schizophrenia are met, episodes of psychosis occur independently of mood episodes, and the mood episodes are present for a substantial portion of the course of illness. Youth with Schizoaffective Disorder may have a particularly debilitating form of illness, given impairments in both thought and mood. However, this disorder has not been well studied in juveniles (Eggers, 1989). Furthermore, the application of the diagnosis may be variably applied in community settings, including being used to describe youth with significant mood and behavioral dysregulation that report atypical psychotic symptoms related to histories of trauma (J. M. McClellan & Hamilton, 2006).

Atypical Psychotic Symptoms Reports of atypical psychoticlike phenomena are characterized qualitatively by greatly detailed symptom reports suggestive of fantasy or overinterpretation of nonpsychotic mental processes. Some symptoms exhibit situational specificity, such as coincidence with attention-seeking behaviors or aggressive outbursts (Hlastala & McClellan, 2005; Hornstein & Putnam, 1992; J. McClellan & McCurry, 1999; J. M. McClellan et al., 1993). By definition, youth reporting atypical psychotic symptoms have lower rates of negative symptoms, bizarre behaviors, and thought disorder; otherwise they would be diagnosed with Schizophrenia (Hlastala & McClellan, 2005). Such symptom reports can represent posttraumatic stress phenomena, factitious or conversion disorders, personality disorders, or developmental delays. These issues can interfere with the accurate reporting of internal experiences and result in misinterpretations or misrepresentations of questions during clinical interviews. Moreover, these symptom reports can be reinforced by well-meaning caretakers or clinicians.

Youth with conduct or other nonpsychotic emotional disorders and histories of trauma may report psychoticlike symptoms and receive inappropriate Schizophrenia spectrum diagnoses (J. M. McClellan & Hamilton, 2006). These youth typically present with behavioral and emotional dysregulation. The psychoticlike symptoms mirror those seen in adults with borderline personality and may represent dissociative or anxiety-driven phenomena characterized by excessive ruminative worry, depersonalization, or derealization (Altman, Collins, & Mundy, 1997; J. McClellan, McCurry, Snell, & DuBose, 1999). In the absence of overt psychotic behavior, a pattern of chaotic, inconsistent relationships and problems with emotional dys-regulation points more toward behavioral or personality disorder, even if some positive symptoms are reported (Lofgren, Bemporad, King, Lindem, & O'Driscoll, 1991; J. McClellan & McCurry, 1998; Thomsen, 1996).

Finally, it is important to recognize that a history of maltreatment does not rule out Schizophrenia. Some youth with EOS have trauma histories (Hlastala & McClellan, 2005). A careful assessment of abuse histories is an important part of any pediatric psychiatric evaluation.

Obsessive-Compulsive Disorder   Features of Obsessive-Compulsive Disorder (OCD) include anxiety-driven symptoms, which may be associated with elaborate beliefs that drive maladaptive behavioral patterns. For example, youth with OCD may have thoughts that some harm may come to them or their parents if a ritual is not performed. However, individuals with OCD, especially older children and ado-lescents, typically recognize their symptoms as irrational and products of their own thinking. Psychosis is characterized by poor insight, with beliefs that hallucinations and delusions occur independently of one's own cognitive processes.

Autism and Pervasive Developmental Disorder   Autistic Spectrum Disorders are distinguished from Schizophrenia by the absence or transitory nature of psychotic symptoms. Autism and COS used to be considered the same illness until seminal studies demonstrated that the two were distinct in regard to age of onset, course, and family history (Kolvin, 1971; Rutter, 1972).

However, the combination of cognitive deficits and social disinterest associated with Pervasive Developmental Disorder (PDD) can be difficult to distinguish from the negative symptoms and premorbid states of Schizophrenia. Furthermore, some youth with EOS first present as having PDD (Volkmar & Cohen, 1991; Volkmar, Cohen, Hoshino, Rende, & Paul, 1988). Patients with COS and comorbid PDD exhibit greater cortical gray matter reductions and greater incidence of autism in siblings, suggesting that comorbidity confers greater susceptibility to regressive brain changes and that both illnesses may involve related underlying risks (Sporn et al., 2004).

Diagnostic Challenges   The accurate assessment of EOS can be aided by a num-ber of procedures to inform diagnosis and aid in treatment planning. These include multi-informant interviews, structured interview tools, symptom rating scales, record review, and longitudinal data afforded by serial mental status examinations and be-havioral checklists. The initial interviews with the child, caregivers, teachers, and other relevant adults provide rich and ecologically valid data. Youth with EOS can generally describe relevant aspects of their psychotic symptoms, although many may be too disorganized or confused to provide accurate details or relevant history, result-ing in great reliance on collateral information.

In general, psychotic symptoms are confusing to the individual and experienced as distressing external phenomena beyond their control. The more detailed, organized, or ego-syntonic the symptom reports, the less likely are such symptoms to represent true psychosis (Reimherr & McClellan, 2004). In evaluating children younger than 12, the clinician must ensure that the child understands the context of the question, and that developmental considerations are taken into account. Beyond a positive response to suggestive questions, psychosis represents an impairment in thought process and typically includes associated symptoms, including disorganized thinking and behavior, and a deterioration in functioning. Without such symptoms, the validity of psychoticlike symptom reports in children should be carefully scrutinized.

Involving parents or caregivers in assessment is particularly important when gathering information about developmental, psychological, medical, and family psychiatric history. A fuller picture of functioning will come from interviews with other therapists and medical providers; involving teachers early in assessment and treatment planning will inform optimal academic, behavioral, and social interventions. Record review is an informative, and often neglected, assessment tool. Attention should be placed on identifying a pattern of declining functioning and a prodromal phase of illness. All school-age children also have an academic record that provides a measure of academic and, often, social and emotional functioning (e.g., class participation style, discipline record, social difficulties) that can be quite extensive for those who have already qualified for special education services. When prior information and relatives or caretakers are unavailable, diagnosis must initially be driven by careful observation in private and group settings, noting positive and negative symptoms as well as disorganization in speech and behavior. Finally, due to familial associations, assessment of family psychiatric history is important and may offer diagnostic clues.

Diagnoses made in clinical settings are notorious for being unreliable (J. M. McClellan & Werry, 2000), yet evidence suggests that the diagnostic accuracy of EOS can be substantially improved through the use of structured diagnostic interviews (Carlson et al., 2000). Although well-designed diagnostic instruments are available, most are used only in epidemiological and clinical research (J. M. McClellan & Werry, 2000). Clinician-based structured interview tools provide guidelines for the diagnostic interview while allowing for clinician probes, rewording of items, and clinical judgment to influence the evaluation. Therefore, it is important for the clinicians administering the interview to be familiar with EOS, in addition to broader issues relating to developmental psychopathology in children.

Observation and serial mental status examination are essential components of a comprehensive evaluation in EOS. Observation in the child's natural environments (e.g., school, home) is informative. Behavioral checklists can also provide a useful method for screening children at risk for psychotic disorders, measuring social and emotional functioning, and assessing comorbid conditions. Impairments in attention, problem solving, abstract reasoning, and memory functioning may indicate the need for further neuropsychological assessment. Clinical status can also be tracked by symptom rating scales. Most instruments assessing psychosis were designed for adults (e.g., Positive and Negative Syndrome Scale for Schizophrenia, Scale for the Assessment of Positive Symptoms). However, most studies with children and adolescents have modified adult measures for use with EOS.

CONCEPTUALIZATION

DEVELOPMENTAL ISSUES

Understanding the clinical impact of Schizophrenia involves recognizing alterations in the developmental course of numerous aspects of functioning: social and emotional functioning, intellectual capacities, and brain development. Developmental factors in EOS may be of particular importance due to the tremendous neuroplasticity and associated anatomical refinements that are coincident with growth and cognitive maturation throughout childhood. Deviations in the trajectory of these refinements are thought to contribute to impaired plasticity, excessive cortical reductions, and altered neuronal circuitry, eventually manifesting as clinical symptoms.

Specific concerns related to development in EOS include ever-changing roles within educational and family systems and evolving conceptions of self and associated sense of independence. Schizophrenia can impair a child's ability to navigate these developmental challenges and create unique demands for more developmentally sensitive treatment resources. Fortunately, the neuroplasticity underlying brain maturation and adaptation to environmental forces is thought to exhibit redundancies to normalize neurodevelopment and inhibit aberrant processes, which may otherwise result in psychopathology. This notion is described by viewing developmental trajectory as progressing on a grooved canal whose course is initially defined by genetic forces and early neuroanatomical substrates. Over time, both genetic expression and experiential forces influence the direction of the developmental trajectory, either through canalizing processes directing toward the normative pathway and buffering against psychopathology or through adverse influences that can push the trajectory beyond the threshold for psychopathology (Grossman et al., 2003; Waddington et al., 1999). Endogenous developmental processes are therefore continually interacting with experiential factors to refine brain function and structure (Greenough, Black, & Wallace, 1987). In patients with EOS, this dynamic process continues in the context of various vulnerabilities to illness, leading to the expression of psychosis in a heterogeneous fashion (Waddington, Scully, Quinn, Meagher, & Morgan, 2001). Subsequent episodes are similarly influenced by the unique timing and quality of an individual's developmental experiences, yet patients may exhibit a clinical pattern that can be increasingly difficult to alter.

Schizophrenia is generally viewed as a neurodevelopmental disorder whereby genetic and environmental risk factors interact to disrupt normal neurodevelopmental processes, the results of which are the clinical manifestations of the illness. Early neurodevelopmental insults are implicated in the etiology of Schizophrenia, as suggested by an association with perinatal complications and minor physical anomalies (Waddington et al., 1999). Postmortem studies also reveal evidence for abnormalities in neuronal circuit formation, with abnormal anatomical distributions suggesting impaired patterns of neuronal migration or elimination (Akbarian et al., 1996; D. A. Lewis & Levitt, 2002). Subtle premorbid abnormalities likely represent early neuropathological manifestations of the disorder.

An appreciation of normative brain development is required to understand aberrant processes associated with Schizophrenia. Primate brain development proceeds in a pattern of programmed synaptic overproduction and subsequent elimination to establish increasingly specialized functional networks. This developmental pruning pattern has been demonstrated in longitudinal neuroimaging studies, in addition to studies examining cross-sectional postmortem synaptic measures (Gogtay, Giedd, et al., 2004; Huttenlocher, 1979). These maturational refinements generally proceed from subcortical brain regions to cortical regions with increasingly demanding integrative functions, which also tend to be more advanced from an evolutionary perspective (Toga, Thompson, & Sowell, 2006). Higher order association cortices exhibit anatomical maturation only after lower order somatosensory and visual cortices, as might be expected given their role in integrating information from widespread brain regions (Gogtay, Giedd, et al., 2004). Quantitative synaptic studies also reveal that while primary visual and sensorimotor cortices begin the course of dramatic synaptic pruning early in childhood, the highly integrative prefrontal cortex continues to elaborate synaptic contacts until adolescence, when programmed reductions are thought to refine circuits (Gogtay, Giedd, et al., 2004; Huttenlocher & Dabholkar, 1997). This frontalization of regional refinements is thought to contribute to the maturation of cognitive skills regulated by progressively integrative regions, as even within prefrontal cortex, dorsolateral prefrontal and orbitofrontal regions that regulate complex working memory and emotional processing, are refined last (Toga et al., 2006). The function of neurons in the highly integrative prefrontal cortex is also reflected in their size, as the complexity of information processing associated with each brain region correlates with the amount of dendritic and synaptic elaborations on excitatory neurons (Elston, Benavides-Piccione, & DeFelipe, 2001).

Multiple lines of evidence suggest that normal brain development is disrupted in Schizophrenia. Significant neuroanatomical reductions in multiple brain regions are apparent at first diagnosis, regardless of age (Frazier et al., 1996; Lim et al., 1996; Rapoport, Addington, Frangou, & Psych, 2005; Thompson et al., 2001). The most consistent neuroanatomical findings in Schizophrenia are increased volumes of lateral ventricles and reductions in hippocampus, thalamus, and frontal lobe volumes (Mehler & Warnke, 2002; Rapoport et al., 1997).

Longitudinal MRI studies have further indicated that whereas the rate of regional gray matter loss in healthy children and adolescents averages 1% to 2% per year in parietal cortices, and even less in other regions, patients with COS showed a more rapid progressive loss, approaching 3% to 4% per year in some regions (Thompson et al., 2001). This dramatic course of atrophy also exhibited an anatomical pattern, with early parietal impairments followed by ventral spread to temporal lobes, sensorimotor cortices, and prefrontal regions. Disturbances in the developmental tuning of cortical refinements could therefore contribute to progressive functional impairments and herald clinical onset of the disease, regardless of age. Because children with transient psychosis and behavioral problems do not appear to exhibit these differences, despite receiving similar medication as the COS group, these multifocal volumetric reductions are thought to directly reflect Schizophrenia pathology rather than a broader consequence of psychosis (Gogtay, Sporn, et al., 2004).

There may be some regional specificity to the volumetric reductions in COS, with significant loss of medial prefrontal gray matter but much less progressive loss of the neighboring anterior cingulate cortex (Vidal et al., 2006). This distinction may be a result of the functional or developmental differences between regions, including variations in myelination. The organization of myelinated fiber bundles in the left anterior cingulate region exhibited disruptions that tended to progress over time and were not associated with duration of psychosis. These findings build on previous work revealing subtle anatomical abnormalities in frontal glial elements in patients with Schizophrenia (Bartzokis, 2002; Davis et al., 2003; Uranova et al., 2001).

Interestingly, regional brain maturation is associated with progressive increases in cortical myelination well into adulthood (Toga et al., 2006). Maturation of brain function is a dynamic process of progressive and regressive changes in multiple neuronal elements and cellular types, which function to adaptively refine neural networks (Greenough et al., 1987; Grossman et al., 2003). Alterations in this developmental course as a consequence of Schizophrenia must therefore also entail both neurodevelopmental and neurodegenerative components, preventing simple classification in one of these descriptive categories (Waddington et al., 2001). Similarly, the mechanism by which reductions in cortical synaptic material contributes to cognitive function or clinical impairments is not clear. Some studies suggest that prefrontal reductions are associated with greater symptom severity in Schizophrenia (T. D. Cannon et al., 2002; Gur et al., 2000; Staal et al., 2001; Wible et al., 2001), but a consistent correlation between anatomical pathology and clinical impairments is lacking. Surprisingly, one study of COS demonstrated cortical reductions that were associated with symptom improvement (Vidal et al., 2006). This finding has also been reported in some studies of adults with Schizophrenia (DeLisi, Sakuma, Ge, & Kushner, 1998; Gur et al., 1998). Despite dramatic progressive cortical reductions, no relationship with cognitive ability was seen in a cohort of patients after the onset of COS, as intellectual functioning remained relatively stable (Gochman et al., 2005). Evidence generally supports the notion, however, that symptoms of Schizophrenia emerge at one point on a developmental path, after significant alterations in neuroanatomical connectivity have been at work for some time. Abnormalities in the regulation of programmed synaptic refinements in Schizophrenia are thought to contribute to impairments in plasticity and cognitive functioning, which become most clearly manifest in the complex integrative regions of the brain and the functions they serve.

LEARNING AND MODELING

Symptoms of Schizophrenia are thought to reflect neurophysiological impairments that can be affected by a variety of experiential factors. Despite significant behavioral abnormalities, patients with EOS are not thought to exhibit symptoms as a result of modeling by others. In fact, patients display idiosyncracies that fall outside cultural norms and thereby help identify illness. Patients further demonstrate deficits in role-play tasks thought to be associated with several facets of cognitive dysfunction, suggesting that they may not be able to appropriately model behavior even when specifically directed to do so (Cohen, Forbes, Mann, & Blanchard, 2006).

Studies examining the aberrant learning processes in Schizophrenia reveal that under mild task demands, patients are able to perform adequately using greater energy in brain regions thought to contribute to task performance, suggesting inefficient neuronal processing (Callicott et al., 2003). When task difficulty is increased, however, patients with Schizophrenia are no longer able to meet processing demands and exhibit significant encoding deficits compared to normal controls, likely contributing to impairments in a wide range of cognitive tasks (Cairo, Woodward, & Ngan, 2006). Impairments in verbal learning and memory are specifically thought to contribute to idiosyncratic thinking and bizarre beliefs, resulting in greater disorganization and impaired reality testing (Subotnik et al., 2006).

Deficits also apply to procedural learning, including visuomotor learning using prism visual adaptation tasks. Adults with Schizophrenia demonstrate impairments in adapting appropriately to changing patterns of distortion in visual stimuli, suggesting compromised neuroplasticity and inaccurate adaptation to changing perceptual feedback (Bigelow et al., 2006). While these procedural learning deficits are independent of conscious awareness, patients also demonstrated significant differences in other complex appraisal tasks, such as rating their confidence in the accuracy of their responses during various memory tasks. Despite exhibiting similar performance as normal controls, an OCD cohort, and a cohort with Posttraumatic Stress Disorder (PTSD), patients with Schizophrenia reported greater confidence in wrong responses and lower confidence in correct responses. These metamemory deficits suggest that individuals with Schizophrenia make strong inferences from relatively little external evidence, which may lead to inaccurate cognitive assessments of the environment and contribute to delusional schemas (Moritz, Woodward, & Chen, 2006).

PARENTAL ISSUES

Family responsiveness was falsely indicted as an etiological factor in Schizophrenia for some time. Focus on parenting style led to the notion of the schizophrenogenic mother, whose habit of placing the child in impossible binds resulted in chronic psychotic behavior. Fortunately, subsequent investigation of etiological factors has shifted away from blaming parents.

Although families should not be blamed for their child's illness, their involvement in treatment remains important. Studies examining the impact of family on the course of Schizophrenia in adults in the 1970s revealed worse outcomes in patients with families demonstrating high levels of criticism, emotional overinvolvement, or hostility (Wearden, Tarrier, Barrowclough, Zastowny, & Rahill, 2000). This affective style was described as high in expressed emotion (EE) and, when exhibited by family members toward patients hospitalized for Schizophrenia, was a robust predictor of future relapse (Butzlaff & Hooley, 1998). This supported the notion that despite neurobiological abnormalities, the environmental milieu is a significant factor in illness progression and led to therapeutics efforts to improve the emotional climate of affected families. Further research suggests high emotional expressivity may be a response by caring relatives of patients with more severe mental illness, who may therefore be more likely to exhibit strong emotional responses to escalating psychotic behaviors (Hooley & Campbell, 2002). Thus, high EE may not be causal, but reactive.

More recent work focuses on family factors that can exert a helpful impact on the course of the illness. The converse of the negative consequences of high EE suggests that families with low EE may buffer the consequences of Schizophrenia and enable improved adjustment and functional recovery, preventing future hospitalizations. For instance, the amount of positive remarks from caregivers at baseline is associated with significant improvement in negative symptoms and social functioning at 3-month follow-up (O'Brien et al., 2006). Furthermore, higher measures of warmth in a household are associated with lower relapse rates and improved social functioning in patients discharged from inpatient hospitalizations (Bertrando et al., 1992; Ivanovic, Vuletic, & Bebbington, 1994). Research also suggests that among parents who do not exhibit emotional overinvolvement, improved clinical outcome was associated with lower attribution of symptom controllability, presumably placing less blame on the patient for expressing symptoms (Lopez et al., 2004).

Studies examining differences in how patients interpret the behavior of relatives further suggest that the effect of interaction style may be unique to familial norms and that favorable outcome is not strictly associated with the adherence to a universally appropriate set of behaviors. Interestingly, in African American families, high EE does not appear to be a predictor of relapse. Opposite of Caucasian households, high levels of critical and intrusive behavior are associated with better outcome over a 2 year period (Rosenfarb, Bellack, & Aziz, 2006). The authors suggest that family style affects how the same behaviors are interpreted, either as distressing violations or as expressions of caring concern, and that supportive treatment interventions must be tailored to the specific dynamics of each family.

Parents of children with EOS function as a crucial link to therapeutic intervention and should be supported with education on the nature of the illness. Minimizing barriers to appropriate treatment is essential. Emotional support must also be available to parents, who are understandably reluctant to accept the notion that their child is diagnosed with a potentially debilitating mental illness. Parents are also frequently frustrated with the mental health system for a variety of reasons. They have commonly experienced significant diagnostic variability by multiple clinicians, resulting in frequent adjustments of medication regimens and the need to manage associated side effects. They may face enormous financial burdens. The time and stress of the illness impacts time spent with other family members. Parents function as the child's primary advocate and need to be supported and empowered to facilitate that role.

LIFE EVENTS

As Schizophrenia is thought to involve both genetic and environmental factors that interactively contribute to illness, many conceptualize this process by a diathesis-stress model; that is, patients with Schizophrenia are thought to have an increased vulnerability to illness (diathesis), which becomes unmasked by future adverse experience (stress; Tsuang, 2000). A variety of early neurodevelopmental insults are associated with significantly increased risk of Schizophrenia, including prenatal complications, history of maternal influenza during pregnancy, and growing up during periods of severe famine. These risks may be separate from, or mediated by, underlying genetic risks. Although these associations may not be the same in EOS (Ordonez et al., 2005), the underlying vulnerability to neurodevelopmental trauma is likely similar.

Other experiential factors that have been identified as risk factors relate to social adversity, yet many question whether the downward social drift of patients debilitated by mental illness is the force behind the association. A population study from Sweden, however, found that exposure to several adverse social factors in childhood were independently associated with future risk of developing Schizophrenia, with greater risk for increasing numbers of exposures (Wicks, Hjern, Gunnell, Lewis, & Dalman, 2005). Struggling to cope with adversity is likely a source of significant ongoing stress for patients, which may further contribute to clinical deterioration and increase vulnerability to subsequent events. Longitudinal studies have indicated that the period preceding psychotic exacerbation is associated with experiencing more major life events beyond one's control (Ventura, Nuechterlein, Lukoff, & Hardesty, 1989), and even the amount of minor hassles can directly predict symptom exacerbation (Norman & Malla, 2001). This raises concern that patients with Schizophrenia are at increased vulnerability due to limited social supports and coping abilities, and several studies further indicate more ratings of negative life events in patients with Schizophrenia (Bebbington, 1987). However, not all have replicated this finding (Gureje & Adewunmi, 1988). One study found lower rates of all types of life events in patients with Schizophrenia, suggesting experiential deprivation instead of stress overload as a contributory factor. The results further indicated that patients appraised their life events as significantly less controllable and less well-managed than nonschizophrenic participants (Horan et al., 2005). Other studies suggest that recent significant life events may carry a greater contribution to acute episodes earlier in the course of the illness (Castine, Meador-Woodruff, & Dalack, 1998), perhaps before more consistent behavioral repertoires develop.

The effect of trauma may also be responsible for other factors thought to be associated with clinical course, such as parental rearing style (Bak et al., 2005). In line with early vulnerability to experiential factors, hallucinatory symptoms and high scores on the Schizophrenia scale of the Minnesota Multiphasic Personality Inventory exhibit a strong association with childhood trauma (Read, van Os, Morrison, & Ross, 2005). Furthermore, children exposed to multiple types and more severe abuse exhibit a dose-response effect with respect to hallucinatory symptom severity (Shevlin et al., 2007). A cohort study of COS, however, did not find an association between history of traumatic experiences and earlier onset of symptoms (Nicolson, Lenane, Hamburger, et al., 2000). The appearance of hallucinatory symptoms following traumatic experiences may be a manifestation of dissociative coping responses. This is an important diagnostic issue, particularly in children. As noted earlier, youth reporting atypical psychotic symptoms that lacked overt signs of psychosis had a much higher rate of abuse and PTSD compared to those diagnosed with EOS (Hlastala & McClellan, 2005). Although Schizophrenia is not commonly thought to result directly from traumatic experiences, minimizing significant stressors in the lives of patients makes sense clinically and may decrease associated morbidity and mortality. Indeed, despite reporting a similar number of negative life events, adolescents with Schizophrenia who engaged in suicidal behavior reported a greater proportion of their life events as negative (Fennig, Horesh, Aloni, Apter, & Weizman, 2005). This indicates that perception of events may be an important influence on behavioral outcomes, and recent research has aimed at identifying perceived stressors in patients' lives during times of discharge, when they exhibit the greatest frequency of suicidal acts (Kimhy, Harkavy-Friedman, & Nelson, 2004).

GENETIC INFLUENCES

Schizophrenia is generally thought to stem from early vulnerability to altered neuronal circuitry through development. Genetic factors are likely a major source of this vulnerability. Schizophrenia is highly familial, although the majority of cases are sporadic (i.e., no immediate first-degree relative with the illness). Monozygotic twins are discordant for Schizophrenia 50% of the time. The broad heritability of Schizophrenia is estimated at 85% (Craddock, O'Donovan, & Owen, 2006). Importantly, experiential factors contributing to Schizophrenia symptoms may not be independent from genetic programming, as experience-induced alterations in brain structure and function are driven by induced activation of genes and the proteins they express.

The most common interpretation of the current neurobiological and genetic Schizophrenia literature is that the illness is the sum result of different susceptibility genes. This is the common gene, common variant model. In this model, each susceptibility allele is presumed common, yet carries a relatively small degree of risk. The combination of risk variants plus environmental factors results in this illness. This notion is consistent with the finding that relatives of patients with Schizophrenia are at higher risk for other psychotic and psychiatric disorders and may share a number of putative susceptibility genes that confer cumulative vulnerability to various traits of psychiatric illness. However, to date there are no identified common gene variants definitively linked with the disorder.

Another model, the common disease, rare variant hypothesis, suggests that rare large-effect mutations result in the illness (J. M. McClellan, Susser, & King, 2007). In this model, the illness in most affected individuals and families is caused by different mutations. Thus, a large number of genes, each with a very large number of potential disease-causing mutations, are responsible for the illness. Both models are under study and may not be mutually exclusive.

With its associated high premorbid abnormalities, COS might have a greater genetic liability. Whereas relatives of children with COS may have similar rates of Schizophrenia and Schizoaffective Disorder as seen in adults (Nicolson & Rapoport, 1999), studies report more severe premorbid neurodevelopmental abnormalities and a higher rate of familial Schizophrenia Spectrum Disorders in COS (R. F. Asarnow, 1999; Nicolson et al., 2003; Nicolson, Lenane, Hamburger, et al., 2000). This is consistent with greater familial diathesis even if symptoms are not severe enough to warrant a diagnosis of Schizophrenia, a trend further supported by the Helsinki High-Risk Study of mothers with Schizophrenia Spectrum Disorders diagnosed before 1975 (Niemi, Suvisaari, Haukka, & Lonnqvist, 2005). Children at increased familial risk of Schizophrenia exhibited more emotional symptoms, more social inhibition, and more neurological soft signs than controls, and severe neurological symptoms and preschool deficits in social adjustment predicted future diagnosis of Schizophrenia Spectrum Disorders.

Although no one genetic lesion has been identified as responsible for Schizophrenia, recent advances in genetic mapping and linkage analyses have identified several candidates for susceptibility genes. The complexity of genetic expression and post-translational modification are further complicated by developmental and regional alterations in expression patterns, making identification of the site and timing of abnormal expression extremely difficult. Recently, strategies to reveal susceptibility genes have attempted to bridge the gap between genes and clinical phenotypes by identifying endophenotypes, various biological expressions that can be identified premorbidly and are highly associated with genetic vulnerability to Schizophrenia. Genetic heterogeneity, however, is a significant challenge to these approaches.

Recent meta-analyses have identified approximately a dozen loci as likely sites of susceptibility genes in Schizophrenia, and most are thought to contribute to impaired neurotransmission or altered expression of plasticity-related proteins (Badner & Gershon, 2002; C. M. Lewis et al., 2003).

Candidate genes have been suggested in several of these regions, including dysbindin on 6p22, neuregulin on 8p22, *G72* on 13q34, *COMT* on 22q11, *PRODH* on 22q11, *RGS4* on 1q21, *DISC1* on 1q42, and *GRM3* on 7q21 (Harrison & Weinberger, 2005). Each of these genes is biologically plausible. However, for each candidate gene, both positive and negative associations have been reported; strengths of effects are generally weak; the specific allele or haplotype associated with the illness varies across studies; and definitive causative mutations for the most part have not been identified.

PEER INFLUENCES

Research on attachment patterns has stressed the importance of nurturing relationships in many developmental domains. Adolescence has been viewed as a critical window of vulnerability for clinical pathology in Schizophrenia. From a neurodevelopmental perspective, highly integrative regions continue to undergo significant refinements during adolescence, which may tax vulnerable circuits, contributing to progressive impairments in cognitive processing and eventual expression of psychosis (D. A. Lewis, 1997). Clinically, patients commonly exhibit increasing degrees of social withdrawal in association with other negative symptoms, further depriving individuals of relational cues and essential interactive feedback. Lacking the appropriate relational support, individuals become reliant on their own interpretation of their symptomatology, which can itself become increasingly confounded by impairments in higher cognitive functions. Particularly in EOS, early behaviors commonly include idiosyncrasies that tend to further distance youth from their peers. These factors likely contribute to findings of intellectual impairments in youth with EOS, who exhibit their greatest impairments in global cognitive deficits and social knowledge (J. McClellan et al., 2004).

Children in psychiatric clinics who were subsequently found to develop Schizophrenia later in life exhibited relationship difficulties with peers and abnormal suspiciousness (M. Cannon et al., 2001). These developmental deficits are consistent with adult research findings of impaired identification of emotional content in facial expressions, particularly in patients with more severe symptoms (Kohler et al., 2000). These patients are thus deprived of social interaction and impaired in regard to processing requirements to appropriately interpret subtle social cues. With compounding developmental expectations throughout childhood, EOS is likely associated with increased vulnerability to experiential neglect. Clinical treatment in EOS therefore strives to return children to normative environments to reestablish peer relationships and encourage social reintegration.

PHYSICAL FACTORS AFFECTING BEHAVIOR

Psychosis is associated with many medical conditions that impair cortical processing, and ruling out these conditions during initial assessments can be critical, not only for appropriate diagnosis and treatment, but also because several of these conditions are potentially life-threatening. Psychiatry consultants in hospital settings commonly encounter delirium in adults and children, which can result in acute perceptual disturbances and disorientation, typically with extreme variations in levels of consciousness. Delirium is also associated with significantly increased mortality in hospitalized adults and children, with younger patients exhibiting more impairments in attention, often in the setting of fever, severe burns, or intensive care (Turkel & Tavare, 2003). The treatment of delirium usually focuses on alleviating the underlying illness, along with pharmacotherapy using low-dose but high-frequency antipsychotics, based on response.

Mental status changes are also common in patients who suffer brain insults, either infectious, cancerous, vascular, or traumatic in nature. Meningitis and encephalitis are life-threatening conditions that can cause autonomic instability and death unless treated appropriately. Vascular thrombosis or hemorrhage can result from abnormalities in clotting, lipid metabolism, or blunt trauma, and elicit symptoms of psychosis that may be confused with primary psychiatric illness. These conditions highlight the importance of thorough medical evaluations when indicated, particularly on first presentation of psychosis.

Seizure disorders can also include symptoms of perceptual disturbances, commonly marked by gustatory or olfactory hallucinations rather than the auditory nature of most hallucinations in Schizophrenia. The nature of hallucinations can also be a clue in other conditions, as lesions in occipital regions can result in visual hallucinations, most commonly of simple figures or shapes; although delirium is also associated with a preference for visual hallucinations, these hallucinations tend to be more complex and associated with other perceptual abnormalities. Furthermore, the events are typically episodic, coinciding with seizure activity or postictal states.

Drugs Affecting Behavior

Both prescription and illicit drugs can elicit psychotic symptoms that may resemble Schizophrenia. Among drugs of abuse, those with hallucinogenic properties such as LSD, mushrooms, peyote, psilocybin, and cannabis can result in immediate perceptual disturbances that tend to normalize shortly after the acute experience. Cannabis, however, may be a significant independent risk factor for Schizophrenia (Maki et al., 2005). Amphetamine and other stimulants such as PCP and cocaine can also result in hallucinatory experiences that may be quite disturbing. Some agents may be associated with chronic impairment, particularly methamphetamine. Symptoms in patients exhibiting chronic impairments in the context of significant drug use are often indistinguishable from Schizophrenia. Because it is often impossible to determine if they would have developed the disorder in the absence of a history of drug abuse, assessment relies more heavily on premorbid functioning.

Several medical therapies are also associated with greater risk for psychosis, including corticosteroids, anesthetics, anticholinergics, and antihistamines. Amphetamines used to treat attention-deficit syndromes have been associated with psychosis, particularly when patients surreptitiously take higher doses. This raises important concerns for treating children who exhibit disruptive behaviors with these agents (Schaeffer & Ross, 2002). Children with Schizophrenia Spectrum Disorders may be at increased vulnerability to the neurophysiological effects of stimulants (Lieberman, Kane, & Alvir, 1987). Careful clinical review and monitoring are therefore essential in this population, in addition to future long-term clinical studies.

Cultural and Diversity Issues

Several studies have identified cultural differences with clinical implications for treating psychiatric illness, including the very nature of how emotions are expressed and recognized (Ekman et al., 1987; Marsh, Elfenbein, & Ambady, 2003). A greater understanding of how these factors contribute to symptoms of Schizophrenia will enhance diagnostic accuracy and improve treatments. One international study found that across cultures, patients with Schizophrenia exhibit poorer performance on facial emotion discrimination tasks, and patients and normal controls within the Indian cohorts scored lower than either of their American or German counterparts, suggesting an interaction between cultural factors and expression of symptoms (Habel et al., 2000).

Even within the culturally diverse American society, factors associated with group norms can similarly interact with clinical course and treatment efforts. Among patients diagnosed with Schizophrenia or Schizoaffective Disorder, those of Latino or African American descent scored lower on perception of emotion tasks than those of Euro-American ancestry. These findings persisted after adjusting for neurocognitive and symptom level and further support an association between emotional perception and functional outcomes in Schizophrenia. These findings also emphasize the importance of tailoring treatment to relevant ethnocultural factors (Kee, Green, Mintz, & Brekke, 2003; Pinkham, Penn, Perkins, & Lieberman, 2003).

Cultural factors also have implications on the interpretation of symptoms and thus diagnosis. Delusional beliefs and hallucinatory experiences in the context of religious rituals may be interpreted differently based on cultural perspective. Diagnostic assessment must therefore include the identification of precipitating events and the associated environmental context, as well as temporal pattern. In addition, research investigating cultural factors may be confounded by differential treatment practices. In general, however, the prevailing values of a given culture are thought to shape the content of delusions rather than cause them (Draguns & Tanaka-Matsumi, 2003), and prevalence rates of Schizophrenia are thought to be similar in diverse regions of the world.

Cultural factors may influence intellectual and emotional maturation. One area of interest is the association between immigration status and Schizophrenia. First-generation migrants are at greater risk for Schizophrenia, and an even greater risk is seen in second-generation subjects with one or more parents born in another country (Cantor-Graae & Selten, 2005). First- and second-generation migrants from developing countries also exhibited higher rates of Schizophrenia as a group than those from developed countries. This suggests that cultural adversity can contribute to the risk for Schizophrenia, and that mismatch between cultural heritage and current environment may be a significant factor.

Growing up in an urban environment also has been identified as an important risk factor, even after controlling for socioeconomic status, drug use, air pollution, and obstetric complications (Spauwen, Krabbendam, Lieb, Wittchen, & van Os, 2004; van Os, Pedersen, & Mortensen, 2004). It has been suggested that the sheer complexity and greater degrees of freedom inherent in navigating the urban environment, similar to juggling diverse cultural roles, may contribute to functional impairments and increased vulnerability to psychotic disorders such as Schizophrenia.

BEHAVIORAL TREATMENT

Treatment for EOS is generally directed at the profound impairments in cognitive, social, and behavioral functioning. Interventions have been developed to address specific impairments as well as to accomplish the general goal of reintegrating patients into their natural communities. The treatment of EOS demands comprehensive evaluation and a developmentally sensitive approach. Pharmacotherapy is the primary mode of treatment, but compliance can be problematic (Sarti & Cournos, 1990). Behavioral treatments are increasingly employed to reduce symptoms and improve quality of life. Most studies have been restricted to adults with the disorder. Psychosocial treatment strategies aimed at juveniles commonly draw from evidence in adults and have been generally classified into individual psychotherapy, family-based interventions, cognitive remediation, specific skills training, and assertive community treatment.

Youth with Schizophrenia appear to benefit from interventions that offer tailored support and education through individual therapy. For adults with Schizophrenia, cognitive-behavioral therapy that focuses on identifying and challenging the patterns of thoughts and emotional processes related to psychosis has demonstrated enduring effects on symptom severity and adherence to treatment (Pilling et al., 2002). These therapies can be adapted for youth as long as developmental considerations are taken into account.

Family interventions may be more appropriate targets of psychosocial treatments for youth. In adults, family interventions improve treatment compliance and prevent psychotic relapses and associated hospital admissions (Huxley, Rendall, & Sederer, 2000; Pilling et al., 2002). Youth with Schizophrenia are more likely than adults to reside with their families and further depend on the family system for support. Despite differential intensity of services and variety in the targets of specific interventions (behavioral, psychoeducational, or supportive), studies comparing various family interventions demonstrate minimal differences (Bustillo, Lauriello, Horan, & Keith, 2001; Schooler et al., 1997; Zastowny, Lehman, Cole, & Kane, 1992). Most also exhibit enduring results (Glynn, Cohen, Dixon, & Niv, 2006; Mueser, Bond, Drake, & Resnick, 1998; Tarrier, Barrowclough, Porceddu, & Fitzpatrick, 1994).

There is one study of family interventions in EOS. Standard pharmacotherapy and hospitalization were compared to similar treatment augmented with three phases of family interventions lasting 2 years, including problem-solving sessions, parent seminars, and coordination of wider educational networks (Rund, 1994). Although clinical outcomes of relapse rates and global functioning scores were improved in the family intervention group, the relapse rates 2 years after treatment remained high, supporting greater severity of illness in EOS. Nevertheless, subjects with poor premorbid functioning exhibited the greatest benefit from family psychoeducation, and the interventional programs were more cost-effective than traditional treatments.

Cognitive rehabilitation treatments have focused on improving neuropsychological deficits associated with Schizophrenia, specifically targeting attention, planning, and memory. Rehabilitation efforts in juveniles have not been well studied, but could be designed based on similar neuropsychological deficits as in adults and evidence for declining intellectual functioning early in the course of the illness (Gochman et al., 2005). Studies with adults, however, do not support the efficacy of cognitive remediation approaches (Pilling et al., 2002), and improvement is likely restricted to specific cognitive abilities that were targeted rather than global functioning (Wykes & van der Gaag, 2001).

Treatment efforts to increase illness education are also common during hospitalization and thought to be essential for treatment compliance. Yet, similar to cognitive rehabilitation, studies reveal that though educational intervention improves knowledge of the specific illness topics discussed, it does not improve social functioning or relapse risk. Incorporating behavioral components related to pharmacologic treatment into educational programs appears to provide greater improvements in medication adherence than strictly educational strategies (Mueser et al., 1998; Zygmunt, Olfson, Boyer, & Mechanic, 2002).

Skills training curricula have been designed to address impairments in functioning in patients with Schizophrenia, specifically targeting social deficits through improving interpersonal skills. Skills training typically emphasizes behavioral rehearsal; breaking skills into manageable steps, modeling skills, and providing opportunities for practice, and finally, providing feedback on performance accompanied by positive reinforcement. Training focuses on a variety of skills, including medication management, personal hygiene, recreation, food preparation, and money management. Although a review recently determined that skills training does not appear to reduce symptoms or prevent relapse, it has been associated with improved skills within the practiced domain, and positively affects patient satisfaction, role functioning, and self-efficacy (Bellack, Dickinson, Morris, & Tenhula, 2005). Acquired skills may not translate to improved community functioning, but they may be effective at reducing social anxiety and improving assertiveness skills.

Because of the importance of reintegrating patients into the community, youth with Schizophrenia demand intensive case management supports. Models for comprehensive treatments for adults with Schizophrenia are attempting to enhance coordination of providers and community services. Assertive community treatments have made significant reductions in inpatient hospital care, improved housing stability, and may be particularly effective for patients with severe illness at high risk for relapse (Essock & Kontos, 1995; Lehman, 1998).

Despite the lack of controlled studies in EOS, youth with Schizophrenia are expected to benefit from a multimodal intervention strategy, using individual, family, or group therapies as adjuncts to pharmacotherapy. These should be tailored to the developmental needs of each patient based on emotional and cognitive maturity. A significant focus should be given to family support due to the tremendous impact of EOS on family functioning. Comprehensive services for EOS should include crisis intervention and in-home services, and the option for day treatment or partial hospitalization. Engaging in comprehensive treatment strategies also serves to maintain consistent therapeutic relationships, thus helping to monitor and promote treatment compliance.

MEDICAL TREATMENT

The efficacy of antipsychotic medications in the treatment of adults with Schizophrenia is well established (Lehman et al., 2004). Numerous controlled trials have demonstrated the effectiveness of typical and atypical antipsychotics, with improvements in overall functioning, reductions in psychotic symptoms, and decreased likelihood for relapse. Treatment guidelines for EOS are based primarily on the adult literature, with antipsychotics recommended as first-line therapy. Unfortunately, as of yet, there are very few studies examining the efficacy of antipsychotics on children and adolescents. Even less in known about the long-term side effects of these agents or their impact on neurodevelopment.

For youth with EOS, relapses are highly associated with treatment noncompliance, and many will require maintenance treatment throughout life. Treatment of initial episodes is typically recommended for at least 6 to 12 months to reduce the likelihood for relapse. Longer courses of treatment are recommended for those with positive family histories or recurrent psychotic episodes (AACAP, 2001). Long-term treatment is thought to reduce the frequency and intensity of subsequent acute episodes, and limit the morbidity due to associated impairments in social, emotional, and cognitive functioning.

Atypical antipsychotics are generally considered the first choice of treatment due to decreased risk of dyskinesias and extrapyramidal motor symptoms and greater clinical effectiveness for reducing negative symptoms (Kelleher, Centorrino, Albert, & Baldessarini, 2002). However, in adults, the Clinical Antipsychotic Trials of Intervention Effectiveness (CATIE; Lieberman et al., 2005) raises questions about the long-term effectiveness and tolerability of antipsychotic medications for Schizophrenia, and the superiority of atypical agents. The CATIE study compared four atypical agents, olanzapine, quetiapine, risperidone, and ziprasidone and one traditional neuroleptic, perphenazine, in 1,493 adults with chronic Schizophrenia, across 57 U.S. sites. Most patients (74%) discontinued their study medication before completing 18 months of treatment. Treatment was maintained longer with olanzapine in comparison to risperidone and quetiapine, but not in comparison to perphenazine or ziprasidone. Olanzapine was more often discontinued due to weight gain and metabolic changes. Perphenzine had the highest rate of discontinuation secondary to extrapyramidal symptoms. Thus, CATIE suggests that, at least with perphenazine, rates of discontinuation between atypical and traditional agents are similar. In addition, the long-term tolerability, efficacy, and compliance with antipsychotic agents are clearly concerns for individuals with chronic Schizophrenia.

Controlled trials of typical antipsychotic agents for EOS support the effectiveness of haloperidol (Spencer, Kafantaris, Padron-Gayol, Rosenberg, & Campbell, 1992), loxapine (Pool, Bloom, Mielke, Roniger, & Gallant, 1976), thioridazine, and thiothixene (Realmuto, Erickson, Yellin, Hopwood, & Greenberg, 1984). Unfortunately, side effects were extremely common, with extrapyramidal symptoms and sedation prevailing. Furthermore, a substantial number of youth did not exhibit significant symptom improvement. Although long-term use in children has not been studied, youth appear to experience the same kind of side effects as adults, including concerns about cardiac repolarization prolongation and hyperprolactinemia due to potent dopamine blockade (Campbell, 1999; Holzer & Eap, 2006).

Although atypical antipsychotic medications are widely used in juveniles, there are few controlled trials for EOS. Side effects associated with these agents include impaired glucose metabolism, cardiac arrhythmias, hyperlipidemia, and sedation. Clozapine exhibited greater clinical benefit than haloperidol in adolescents with treatment-refractory COS, but was also associated with greater sedation, weight gain, sialorrhea, and acute neutropenia (Kumra et al., 1996). Clozapine is generally considered a second-line agent given concerns over its side effect profile. The Treatment of Adolescents with Psychosis Study (TAPS) compared olanzapine, risperidone, and haloperidol in youths with more broadly defined psychotic disorders, using a randomized controlled design (Sikich, Hamer, Bashford, Sheitman, & Lieberman, 2004). In TAPS, youths maintained treatment on olanzapine significantly longer than the other two agents. Children and adolescents appear to be at higher risk of extrapyramidal symptoms and weight gain than reported in adult studies (Sikich et al., 2004).

Otherwise, support for commonly used atypical agents is primarily based on case reports, open-label trials, and the adult literature. Risperidone (Armenteros, Whitaker, Welikson, Stedge, & Gorman, 1997; Grcevich, Findling, Rowane, Friedman, & Schulz, 1996; Simeon, Carrey, Wiggins, Milin, & Hosenbocus, 1995; and olanzapine (Findling et al., 2003; Kumra et al., 1998) have been reported to be helpful for positive and negative symptoms in children and adolescents with Schizophrenia. Sedation and weight gain tend to be problematic, however, and some reports suggest an increased risk for insulin resistance and diabetes with olanzapine (Sernyak, Gulanski, & Rosenheck, 2005). Quetiapine is less studied, but has been shown to be effective in treating youth who have failed prior atypical antipsychotics (Healy, Subotsky, & Pipe, 1999; Szigethy, Brent, & Findling, 1998). Problems with weight gain and sedation are also noted. Ziprazidone is an atypical agent that appears to produce less weight gain. To date there are no published trials evaluating its effectiveness and safety in EOS.

Finally, aripiprazole is the most recent antipsychotic released for treatment of Schizophrenia. In adults, the agent is associated with fewer side effects (Goodnick & Jerry, 2002). This medicine is thought to exhibit unique properties through its partial agonist effect on D2 receptors and less affinity for histaminergic and muscarinic receptors, which are thought to contribute to the weight gain associated with other agents. Other pharmacologic interventions currently in development are thought to similarly exhibit partial agonism of various receptors, and are increasingly based on targets identified through genetic linkage data and clinical endophenotypes exhibited in Schizophrenia (Marek & Merchant, 2005).

General procedures for the use of medication in treating EOS are available to help guide clinical practice (AACAP, 2001). The choice of agent in the acute phase should be based on any history of treatment in the patient or their relatives, the side effect profile of each medicine, and, often, practical considerations of delivery options and insurance coverage. Individual responses can be quite variable, with immediate effects likely due to sedation. A trial of at least 4 to 6 weeks is needed before determining effectiveness. Interestingly, the lag time between when these medications act on their target receptors, transporters, and synaptic enzymes and the time of therapeutic benefit suggests that the clinical improvements reflect a gradual compensatory response within the circuitry regulated by these targets, as opposed to the immediate pharmacological response. Rapid increases in dose can result in greater likelihood of side effects and increased use of high doses that generally do not hasten recovery. If clinical utility has not been demonstrated after 6 weeks of treatment, another agent should be selected. Clozapine is generally reserved for treatment-refractory cases after failure of two other agents has been demonstrated. However, its use may be gaining favor due to continued evidence of clinical benefit in treatment-resistant adult patients (McEvoy et al., 2006).

As acute psychotic symptoms respond to medication therapy, patients will commonly exhibit persistence of confusion, disorganization, or dysphoria. Additional improvement is often noted for 6 to 12 months following the initiation of treatment. Decreases in dosage may be indicated when side effects become problematic or negative symptoms worsen, as may occur when high doses are used to control initial psychotic symptoms. Most patients with EOS require long-term pharmacological therapy, even during residual phases. In adults with Schizophrenia, relapse rates over 1 year are significantly lower in those continuing treatment (Lehman et al., 2004). Over 5 years, 80% of adults will exhibit at least one relapse. This risk is significantly decreased with maintenance therapy (Robinson et al., 1999).

Patients should maintain regular physician contact, at least monthly, in order to adequately monitor symptom course, side effects, and compliance. Adjustments in medications should be gradual, reserved for significant side effects or changes in symptom severity. Side effects remain a significant obstacle in treatment of youth with Schizophrenia, even with atypical agents (Armenteros & Davies, 2006; Correll et al., 2006). As rare patients may not exhibit a relapse, a medication-free trial may be considered in newly diagnosed patients who are symptom-free for 6 to 12 months, provided close monitoring and follow-up are available in case of clinical deterioration. Indeed, one study of COS found that 23% of subjects were diagnosed with illnesses other than Schizophrenia after a 4-week period without medications (Kumra et al., 1999).

Case Description

The patient, Doug, a Caucasian teenage boy, began experiencing a significant change in his behavior at age 14 years. In the 6 months before being referred for mental health treatment, Doug began to display increasing difficulties with concentration. He also became less interested in spending time with acquaintances, and was more easily upset over situations that he found frustrating or

(continued)

anxiety-provoking. Prior to developing these symptoms, Doug was described as being a loner. He never had many friends and tended to play by himself. As a younger child he saw a counselor for concerns over social isolation. He was a below average student, although his IQ was in the normal range. His teachers and parents were concerned that he was underperforming academically. His language function was intact. He did not have significant problems with his behavior, other than occasional arguing and defiance. He was mostly characterized as being shy or odd.

As he entered ninth grade, his difficulties progressed. He stopped completing his schoolwork. He became more withdrawn and began reporting unusual beliefs. He felt that other students were watching him with cameras, and posting the photos on the Internet. He would stare into space for hours, oblivious to what others around him were doing. He became religiously preoccupied, engaging in angry diatribes about sinners and God's will. It became increasingly difficult for his family to engage him in conversation. He became more isolated, refusing to leave his room or go to school. He was described as emotionally flat and distant. Finally, Doug ran away from home and was picked up by the police. He was taken to a local emergency room and admitted to a psychiatric hospital for involuntary treatment.

During the initial hospitalization, Doug was diagnosed with Psychosis, NOS and briefly stabilized on risperidone. His involuntary period of treatment ended, and he was discharged home to his family. He soon stopped taking his medication because he felt his treating psychiatrist was a demon and was trying to poison him.

Doug lived at home with both parents and an older brother. His parents were college-educated and worked during the day. Religion was important to the family, although Doug's unusual religious beliefs were quite different from the views of other family members. His parents also expressed concern over using medications and the potential for side effects. Thus, although they were supportive of Doug's being in treatment, they had trouble strictly reinforcing medication compliance. They also worried that his illness was due to his diet, and hoped his symptoms would resolve with prayer.

As a 15-year-old, Doug was hospitalized again for ongoing psychotic symptoms and treatment noncompliance. At that time he was reporting auditory hallucinations, mind reading, paranoia, and beliefs regarding religious symbolism. In response to his internal stimuli, he began mumbling almost constantly. He feared that doctors and family members were trying to harm him. He demonstrated new bizarre behaviors, including threatening aggression and urinating in his room. His thinking was confused and perseverative. He had no insight into his illness, and felt the entire hospitalization was a plot.

A standardized diagnostic assessment was performed, using the KID-SCID (Matzner, Silva, Silvan, Chowdhury, & Nastasi, 1997), a semi-structured diagnostic interview based on the Structured Interview for *DSM-IV* (SCID; First, Gibbon, Spitzer, & Williams, 1996). The KID-SCID includes modules that assess childhood psychiatric disorders, plus the mood, psychosis, and substance abuse modules found in the adult version. A diagnosis of Schizophrenia was made. There was no reported history of substance use.

A neuropsychological evaluation was completed. His cognitive functioning was in the normal range. However, his responses to questions were slow. He demonstrated difficulties with verbal reasoning and problem-solving. He also underwent a thorough medical evaluation to rule out any underlying organic conditions causing his psychotic symptoms. His serum chemistries, blood counts, thyroid function, and ceruloplasm were within normal limits. He had a negative toxicology screen. He had a normal electroencephalogram and brain MRI scan.

During the hospitalization, he had trials of ziprasidone, aripiprazole, and quetiapine. Doug was noncompliant with ziprasidone, partly due to suspicions this medicine was poisonous. Aripiprazole was started, with an eventual dose of 20 mg per day. However, he developed symptoms of akathisia, so he was switched to quetiapine. He made some improvement on this agent, with a final dose of 800 mg per day. Divalproex was added to the quetiapine for concerns over agitation and irritability. Unfortunately, although his thinking was significantly improved from the time of admission, he remained quite delusional, with ongoing hallucinations and poor insight. He constantly paced the unit, asking visiting adults to let him leave. He also consistently denied any need for treatment and stated he would stop taking his medications upon discharge.

Because of these clinical concerns, Doug was transferred to a long-term residential unit for extended care. He continued to demonstrate significant psychotic symptoms. Therefore, quetiapine was cross-tapered with olanzapine. He was maintained on olanzapine 20 mg per day for 10 weeks without much improvement. As he continued to display significant psychotic symptoms with intermittent mood symptoms, the divalproex was stopped without any notable change.

Based on the failure of multiple adequate trials of antipsychotic agents, a trial of clozapine was initiated. His blood counts were monitored per the clozapine protocol. This dosage was increased slowly over 3 months to a high dose of 650 mg per day. Doug often experienced sedation with dosage increases. His blood counts were mostly within normal limits, although there were occasions when the dose needed to be held for a low absolute neutrophil count. Fortunately, his counts always normalized within 24 hours, and serum chemistries and metabolic functions remained within normal limits.

Doug improved substantially on clozapine, with less idiosyncratic and disorganized behavior. At times he still reported delusional beliefs. He also continued to demonstrate a great deal of pacing, social isolation, and flat affect. However, he was able to attend a specialized school program, interact superficially with peers and staff in therapeutic activities, and accompany his family home on passes.

His parents participated in psychoeducation meetings and parent support groups. The focus in therapy was helping them cope with their grief over Doug's illness and changing expectations given the impact of illness on his life and theirs. There was also a great deal of effort spent on community planning. Working with the family, a special education program was established in Doug's local school. Medication therapy was arranged through a community mental health center that was familiar with using clozapine. The parents also worked to arrange

(*continued*)

afterschool activities through their church. Finally, the parents became involved with a statewide parent advocacy program for mental health.

After a 9-month hospitalization, Doug was discharged home to community care. He continues on his clozapine and is going to school. The family continues to work with community providers on medication management, behavioral strategies, and functional supports. They are beginning to look ahead toward the time that Doug will turn 18 and will transition into adult services.

Treatment Implications of the Case

This case demonstrates the gradual decline in functioning commonly seen in youth with EOS. Doug's increasingly idiosyncratic behavior and social withdrawal were paralleled by an increasingly disorganized thought process, resulting in greater functional impairments. He was highly suspicious of any treatments, particularly medications. This case stresses the need for thorough medical evaluations, thoughtful pharmacotherapy strategies, appropriate monitoring of side effects, and family interventions. Fortunately, Doug eventually responded to antipsychotic treatment and inpatient hospitalization and has been able to appropriately transition back to the care of his family and participate in school and community resources.

SUMMARY

Schizophrenia is a relatively common and often disabling chronic mental illness characterized by impairments in thought process, affect, and social function. Early-onset Schizophrenia, defined as onset prior to age 18, is diagnosed using the same standardized criteria as for adults. Childhood-onset Schizophrenia, defined as onset prior to age 13, is quite rare, occurring at a rate of 1 in 10,000 persons. Although a diagnosis of Schizophrenia for children and adolescents is made using the same criteria used for adults, accurate assessment is often complicated by unique developmental concerns, and requires a thorough diagnostic evaluation. Evaluation in youth often involves sorting through a complicated array of clinical and social data. Clinical presentations and symptom assessment are confounded by normative developmental factors. Misdiagnosis is common and may result from significant overlap between presenting symptoms of Schizophrenia and psychotic mood disorder (AACAP, 1998). In the absence of care, individuals diagnosed with EOS typically experience a gradual decline in functioning that results in increasingly idiosyncratic behavior, disorganized thought, withdrawal, and significant functional impairment. Best practice recommendations for the care of individuals diagnosed with EOS typically blend supportive community and family-based approaches with appropriately monitored antipsychotic treatment. Multiple medication trials are often needed before an appropriate pharmacotherapy can be identified for a given individual, and medication adherence is a significant challenge to successful intervention. Thorough medical evaluations, thoughtful pharmacotherapy strategies, appropriate monitoring of side effects, and family interventions (as well as inpatient hospitalization, when necessary) appear to maximize the functional capabilities of persons diagnosed with EOS and greatly enhance their quality of life.

REFERENCES

Addington, J., & Addington, D. (1998). Facial affect recognition and information processing in schizophrenia and bipolar disorder. *Schizophrenia Research, 32*(3), 171–181.

Akbarian, S., Kim, J. J., Potkin, S. G., Hetrick, W. P., Bunney, W. E., Jr., & Jones, E. G. (1996). Maldistribution of interstitial neurons in prefrontal white matter of the brains of schizophrenic patients. *Archives of General Psychiatry, 53*(5), 425–436.

Altman, H., Collins, M., & Mundy, P. (1997). Subclinical hallucinations and delusions in nonpsychotic adolescents. *Journal of Child Psychology and Psychiatry, 38*(4), 413–420.

American Academy of Child and Adolescent Psychiatry. (1998). Practice parameter for the assessment and treatment of children and adolescents with depressive disorders. *Journal of the American Academy of Child and Adolescent Psychiatry, 37,* 63–83.

American Academy of Child and Adolescent Psychiatry. (2001). Practice parameter for the assessment and treatment of children and adolescents with schizophrenia. *Journal of the American Academy of Child and Adolescent Psychiatry, 40*(Suppl. 7), S4–S23.

American Psychiatric Association. (1997). Practice guideline for the treatment of patients with schizophrenia. *American Journal of Psychiatry, 154*(Suppl. 4), 1–63.

American Psychiatric Association. (2000). *Diagnostic and statistical manual of mental disorders* (4th ed., text rev.). Washington, DC: Author.

Armenteros, J. L., & Davies, M. (2006). Antipsychotics in early onset schizophrenia: Systematic review and meta-analysis. *European Child and Adolescent Psychiatry, 15*(3), 141–148.

Armenteros, J. L., Fennelly, B. W., Hallin, A., Adams, P. B., Pomerantz, P., Michell, M., et al. (1995). Schizophrenia in hospitalized adolescents: Clinical diagnosis, DSM-III-R, DSM-IV, and ICD-10 criteria. *Psychopharmacology Bulletin, 31*(2), 383–387.

Armenteros, J. L., Whitaker, A. H., Welikson, M., Stedge, D. J., & Gorman, J. (1997). Risperidone in adolescents with schizophrenia: an open pilot study. *Journal of the American Academy of Child and Adolescent Psychiatry, 36*(5), 694–700.

Asarnow, J. R., Tompson, M. C., & Goldstein, M. J. (1994). Childhood-onset schizophrenia: A follow-up study. *Schizophrenia Bulletin, 20*(4), 599–617.

Asarnow, R. F. (1999). Neurocognitive impairments in schizophrenia: A piece of the epigenetic puzzle. *European Child and Adolescent Psychiatry, 8*(Suppl. 1), 5–8.

Badner, J. A., & Gershon, E. S. (2002). Meta-analysis of whole-genome linkage scans of bipolar disorder and schizophrenia. *Molecular Psychiatry, 7*(4), 405–411.

Bak, M., Krabbendam, L., Janssen, I., de Graaf, R., Vollebergh, W., & van Os, J. (2005). Early trauma may increase the risk for psychotic experiences by impacting on emotional response and perception of control. *Acta Psychiatrica Scandinavica, 112*(5), 360–366.

Bartzokis, G. (2002). Schizophrenia: Breakdown in the well-regulated lifelong process of brain development and maturation. *Neuropsychopharmacology, 27*(4), 672–683.

Bebbington, P. E. (1987). Life events in schizophrenia: The WHO collaborative study. *Social Psychiatry, 22*(4), 179–180.

Bellack, A. S., Dickinson, D., Morris, S. E., & Tenhula, W. N. (2005). The development of a computer-assisted cognitive remediation program for patients with schizophrenia. *Israel Journal of Psychiatry and Related Sciences, 42*(1), 5–14.

Bertrando, P., Beltz, J., Bressi, C., Clerici, M., Farma, T., Invernizzi, G., et al. (1992). Expressed emotion and schizophrenia in Italy: A study of an urban population. *British Journal of Psychiatry, 161,* 223–229.

Bigelow, N. O., Turner, B. M., Andreasen, N. C., Paulsen, J. S., O'Leary, D., S., & Ho, B. C. (2006). Prism adaptation in schizophrenia. *Brain and Cognition, 61*(3), 235–242.

Biswas, P., Malhotra, S., Malhotra, A., & Gupta, N. (2006). Comparative study of neuropsychological correlates in schizophrenia with onset in childhood, adolescence and adulthood. *European Child and Adolescent Psychiatry, 15*(6), 360–366.

Bustillo, J., Lauriello, J., Horan, W., & Keith, S. (2001). The psychosocial treatment of schizophrenia: An update. *American Journal of Psychiatry, 158*(2), 163–175.

Butzlaff, R. L., & Hooley, J. M. (1998). Expressed emotion and psychiatric relapse: A meta-analysis. *Archives of General Psychiatry, 55*(6), 547–552.

Cairo, T. A., Woodward, T. S., & Ngan, E. T. (2006). Decreased encoding efficiency in schizophrenia. *Biological Psychiatry, 59*(8), 740–746.

Calderoni, D., Wudarsky, M., Bhangoo, R., Dell, M. L., Nicolson, R., Hamburger, S. D., et al. (2001). Differentiating childhood-onset schizophrenia from psychotic mood disorders. *Journal of the American Academy of Child and Adolescent Psychiatry, 40*(10), 1190–1196.

Callicott, J. H., Mattay, V. S., Verchinski, B. A., Marenco, S., Egan, M. F., & Weinberger, D. R. (2003). Complexity of prefrontal cortical dysfunction in schizophrenia: More than up or down. *American Journal of Psychiatry, 160*(12), 2209–2215.

Campbell, M. (1999). Risperidone-induced tardive dyskinesia in first-episode psychotic patients. *Journal of Clinical Psychopharmacology, 19*(3), 276–277.

Cannon, M., Caspi, A., Moffitt, T. E., Harrington, H., Taylor, A., Murray, R. M., et al. (2002). Evidence for early-childhood, pan-developmental impairment specific to schizophreniform disorder: Results from a longitudinal birth cohort. *Archives of General Psychiatry, 59*(5), 449–456.

Cannon, M., Walsh, E., Hollis, C., Kargin, M., Taylor, E., Murray, R. M., et al. (2001). Predictors of later schizophrenia and affective psychosis among attendees at a child psychiatry department. *British Journal of Psychiatry, 178*, 420–426.

Cannon, T. D., Thompson, P. M., van Erp, T. G., Toga, A. W., Poutanen, V. P., Huttunen, M., et al. (2002). Cortex mapping reveals regionally specific patterns of genetic and disease-specific gray-matter deficits in twins discordant for schizophrenia. *Proceedings of the National Academy of Sciences, USA, 99*(5), 3228–3233.

Cantor-Graae, E., & Selten, J. P. (2005). Schizophrenia and migration: A meta-analysis and review. *American Journal of Psychiatry, 162*(1), 12–24.

Caplan, R. (1994). Thought disorder in childhood. *Journal of the American Academy of Child and Adolescent Psychiatry, 33*(5), 605–615.

Carlson, G. A. (1990). Child and adolescent mania: Diagnostic considerations. *Journal of Child Psychology and Psychiatry, 31*(3), 331–341.

Carlson, G. A., Bromet, E. J., & Sievers, S. (2000). Phenomenology and outcome of subjects with early- and adult-onset psychotic mania. *American Journal of Psychiatry, 157*(2), 213–219.

Castine, M. R., Meador-Woodruff, J. H., & Dalack, G. W. (1998). The role of life events in onset and recurrent episodes of schizophrenia and schizoaffective disorder. *Journal of Psychiatric Research, 32*(5), 283–288.

Cohen, A. S., Forbes, C. B., Mann, M. C., & Blanchard, J. J. (2006). Specific cognitive deficits and differential domains of social functioning impairment in schizophrenia. *Schizophrenia Research, 81*(2/3), 227–238.

Corcoran, C., Whitaker, A., Coleman, E., Fried, J., Feldman, J., Goudsmit, N., et al. (2005). Olfactory deficits, cognition and negative symptoms in early onset psychosis. *Schizophrenia Research, 80*(2/3), 283–293.

Correll, C. U., Penzner, J. B., Parikh, U. H., Mughal, T., Javed, T., Carbon, M., et al. (2006). Recognizing and monitoring adverse events of second-generation antipsychotics in children and adolescents. *Child and Adolescent Psychiatric Clinics of North America, 15*(1), 177–206.

Craddock, N., O'Donovan, M. C., & Owen, M. J. (2006). Genes for schizophrenia and bipolar disorder? Implications for psychiatric nosology. *Schizophrenia Bulletin, 32*(1), 9–16.

Davis, K. L., Stewart, D. G., Friedman, J. I., Buchsbaum, M., Harvey, P. D., Hof, P. R., et al. (2003). White matter changes in schizophrenia: Evidence for myelin-related dysfunction. *Archives of General Psychiatry, 60*(5), 443–456.

Del Beccaro, M. A., Burke, P., & McCauley, E. (1988). Hallucinations in children: A follow-up study. *Journal of the American Academy of Child and Adolescent Psychiatry, 27*(4), 462–465.

DeLisi, L. E., Sakuma, M., Ge, S., & Kushner, M. (1998). Association of brain structural change with the heterogeneous course of schizophrenia from early childhood through 5 years subsequent to a first hospitalization. *Psychiatry Research, 84*(2/3), 75–88.

Draguns, J. G., & Tanaka-Matsumi, J. (2003). Assessment of psychopathology across and within cultures: Issues and findings. *Behavior Research and Therapy, 41*(7), 755–776.

Eggers, C. (1978). Course and prognosis of childhood schizophrenia. *Journal of Autism and Childhood Schizophrenia, 8*(1), 21–36.

Eggers, C. (1989). Schizo-affective psychosis in childhood: A follow-up study. *Journal of Autism and Childhood Schizophrenia, 19*, 327–334.

Eggers, C., & Bunk, D. (1997). The long-term course of childhood-onset schizophrenia: A 42-year follow-up. *Schizophrenia Bulletin, 23*(1), 105–117.

Ekman, P., Friesen, W. V., O'Sullivan, M., Chan, A., Diacoyanni-Tarlatzis, I., Heider, K., et al. (1987). Universals and cultural differences in the judgments of facial expressions of emotion. *Journal of Personality and Social Psychology, 53*(4), 712–717.

Elston, G. N., Benavides-Piccione, R., & DeFelipe, J. (2001). The pyramidal cell in cognition: A comparative study in human and monkey. *Journal of Neuroscience, 21*(17), RC163.

Essock, S. M., & Kontos, N. (1995). Implementing assertive community treatment teams. *Psychiatric Services, 46*(7), 679–683.

Fennig, S., Horesh, N., Aloni, D., Apter, A., & Weizman, A. (2005). Life events and suicidality in adolescents with schizophrenia. *European Child and Adolescent Psychiatry, 14*(8), 454–460.

Findling, R. L., McNamara, N. K., Youngstrom, E. A., Branicky, L. A., Demeter, C. A., & Schulz, S. C. (2003). A prospective, open-label trial of olanzapine in adolescents with schizophrenia. *Journal of the American Academy of Child and Adolescent Psychiatry, 42*(2), 170–175.

First, M. B., Gibbon, M., Spitzer, R. L., & Williams, J. B. W. (1996). *User's guide for the Structured Clinical Interview for DSM-IV Axis I Disorders: Research version.* New York: Biometrics Research.

Fleischhaker, C., Schulz, E., Tepper, K., Martin, M., Hennighausen, K., & Remschmidt, H. (2005). Long-term course of adolescent schizophrenia. *Schizophrenia Bulletin, 31*(3), 769–780.

Frazier, J. A., Giedd, J. N., Hamburger, S. D., Albus, K. E., Kaysen, D., Vaituzis, A. C., et al. (1996). Brain anatomic magnetic resonance imaging in childhood-onset schizophrenia. *Archives of General Psychiatry, 53*(7), 617–624.

Glynn, S. M., Cohen, A. N., Dixon, L. B., & Niv, N. (2006). The potential impact of the recovery movement on family interventions for schizophrenia: Opportunities and obstacles. *Schizophrenia Bulletin, 32*(3), 451–463.

Gochman, P. A., Greenstein, D., Sporn, A., Gogtay, N., Keller, B., Shaw, P., et al. (2005). IQ stabilization in childhood-onset schizophrenia. *Schizophrenia Research, 77*(2/3), 271–277.

Gochman, P. A., Greenstein, D., Sporn, A., Gogtay, N., Nicolson, R., Keller, A., et al. (2004). Childhood onset schizophrenia: Familial neurocognitive measures. *Schizophrenia Research, 71*(1), 43–47.

Gogtay, N., Giedd, J. N., Lusk, L., Hayashi, K. M., Greenstein, D., Vaituzis, A. C., et al. (2004). Dynamic mapping of human cortical development during childhood through early adulthood. *Proceedings of the National Academy of Sciences, USA, 101*(21), 8174–8179.

Gogtay, N., Sporn, A., Clasen, L. S., Nugent, T. F., III, Greenstein, D., Nicolson, R., et al. (2004). Comparison of progressive cortical gray matter loss in childhood-onset schizophrenia with that in childhood-onset atypical psychoses. *Archives of General Psychiatry, 61*(1), 17–22.

Goodnick, P. J., & Jerry, J. M. (2002). Aripiprazole: Profile on efficacy and safety. *Expert Opinion on Pharmacotherapy, 3*(12), 1773–1781.

Grcevich S. J., Findling, R. L., Rowane, W. A., Friedman, L., & Schulz, S. C. (1996). Risperidone in the treatment of children and adolescents with schizophrenia: A retrospective study. *Journal of Child and Adolescent Psychopharmacology, 6*(4), 251–257.

Green, W. H., Padron-Gayol, M., Hardesty, A. S., & Bassiri, M. (1992). Schizophrenia with childhood onset: A phenomenological study of 38 cases. *Journal of the American Academy of Child and Adolescent Psychiatry, 31*(5), 968–976.

Greenough, W. T., Black, J. E., & Wallace, C. S. (1987). Experience and brain development. *Child Development, 58*(3), 539–559.

Grossman, A. W., Churchill, J. D., McKinney, B. C., Kodish, I. M., Otte, S. L., & Greenough, W. T. (2003). Experience effects on brain development: Possible contributions to psychopathology. *Journal of Child Psychology and Psychiatry, 44*(1), 33–63.

Gur, R. E., Cowell, P. E., Latshaw, A., Turetsky, B. I., Grossman, R. I., Arnold, S. E., et al. (2000). Reduced dorsal and orbital prefrontal gray matter volumes in schizophrenia. *Archives of General Psychiatry, 57*(8), 761–768.

Gur, R. E., Cowell, P., Turetsky, B. I., Gallacher, F., Cannon, T., Bilker, W., et al. (1998). A follow-up magnetic resonance imaging study of schizophrenia: Relationship of neuroanatomical changes to clinical and neurobehavioral measures. *Archives of General Psychiatry, 55*(2), 145–152.

Gureje, O., & Adewunmi, A. (1988). Life events and schizophrenia in Nigerians: A controlled investigation. *British Journal of Psychiatry, 153*, 367–375.

Habel, U., Gur, R. C., Mandal, M. K., Salloum, J. B., Gur, R. E., & Schneider, F. (2000). Emotional processing in schizophrenia across cultures: Standardized measures of discrimination and experience. *Schizophrenia Research, 42*(1), 57–66.

Harrison, P. J., & Weinberger, D. R. (2005). Schizophrenia genes, gene expression, and neuropathology: On the matter of their convergence. *Molecular Psychiatry, 10*(1), 40–68; image 45.

Harrow, M., Grossman, L. S., Jobe, T. H., & Herbener, E. S. (2005). Do patients with schizophrenia ever show periods of recovery? A 15-year multi-follow-up study. *Schizophrenia Bulletin, 31*(3), 723–734.

Healy, E., Subotsky, F., & Pipe, R. (1999). Quetiapine in adolescent psychosis. *Journal of the American Academy of Child and Adolescent Psychiatry, 38*(11), 1329.

Hlastala, S. A., & McClellan, J. (2005). Phenomenology and diagnostic stability of youths with atypical psychotic symptoms. *Journal of Child and Adolescent Psychopharmacology, 15*(3), 497–509.

Hollis, C. (1995). Child and adolescent (juvenile onset) schizophrenia: A case control study of premorbid developmental impairments. *British Journal of Psychiatry, 166*(4), 489–495.

Hollis, C. (2000). Adult outcomes of child- and adolescent-onset schizophrenia: Diagnostic stability and predictive validity. *American Journal of Psychiatry, 157*(10), 1652–1659.

Holt, D. J., Weiss, A. P., Rauch, S. L., Wright, C. I., Zalesak, M., Goff, D. C., et al. (2005). Sustained activation of the hippocampus in response to fearful faces in schizophrenia. *Biological Psychiatry, 57*(9), 1011–1019.

Holzer, L., & Eap, C. B. (2006). Risperidone-induced symptomatic hyperprolactinaemia in adolescents. *Journal of Clinical Psychopharmacology, 26*(2), 167–171.

Hooley, J. M., & Campbell, C. (2002). Control and controllability: Beliefs and behavior in high and low expressed emotion relatives. *Psychological Medicine, 32*(6), 1091–1099.

Horan, W. P., Ventura, J., Nuechterlein, K. H., Subotnik, K. L., Hwang, S. S., & Mintz, J. (2005). Stressful life events in recent-onset schizophrenia: Reduced frequencies and altered subjective appraisals. *Schizophrenia Research, 75*(2/3), 363–374.

Hornstein, N. L., & Putnam, F. W. (1992). Clinical phenomenology of child and adolescent dissociative disorders. *Journal of the American Academy of Child and Adolescent Psychiatry, 31*(6), 1077–1085.

Hsiao, R., & McClellan, J. (in press). Substance abuse in early onset psychotic disorders. *Journal of Dual Diagnosis.*

Huttenlocher, P. R. (1979). Synaptic density in human frontal cortex: Developmental changes and effects of aging. *Brain Research, 163*(2), 195–205.

Huttenlocher, P. R., & Dabholkar, A. S. (1997). Regional differences in synaptogenesis in human cerebral cortex. *Journal of Comparative Neurology, 387*(2), 167–178.

Huxley, N. A., Rendall, M., & Sederer, L. (2000). Psychosocial treatments in schizophrenia: A review of the past 20 years. *Journal of Nervous and Mental Diseases, 188*(4), 187–201.

Isohanni, M., Murray, G. K., Jokelainen, J., Croudace, T., & Jones, P. B. (2004). The persistence of developmental markers in childhood and adolescence and risk for schizophrenic psychoses in adult life: A 34-year follow-up of the northern Finland 1966 birth cohort. *Schizophrenia Research, 71*(2/3), 213–225.

Ivanovic, M., Vuletic, Z., & Bebbington, P. (1994). Expressed emotion in the families of patients with schizophrenia and its influence on the course of illness. *Social Psychiatry and Psychiatric Epidemiology, 29*(2), 61–65.

Jarbin, H., Ott, Y., & Von Knorring, A. L. (2003). Adult outcome of social function in adolescent-onset schizophrenia and affective psychosis. *Journal of the American Academy of Child and Adolescent Psychiatry, 42*(2), 176–183.

Kee, K. S., Green, M. F., Mintz, J., & Brekke, J. S. (2003). Is emotion processing a predictor of functional outcome in schizophrenia? *Schizophrenia Bulletin, 29*(3), 487–497.

Kelleher, J. P., Centorrino, F., Albert, M. J., & Baldessarini, R. J. (2002). Advances in atypical antipsychotics for the treatment of schizophrenia: New formulations and new agents. *CNS Drugs, 16*(4), 249–261.

Kimhy, D., Harkavy-Friedman, J. M., & Nelson, E. A. (2004). Identifying life stressors of patients with schizophrenia at hospital discharge. *Psychiatric Services, 55*(12), 1444–1445.

Kohler, C. G., Bilker, W., Hagendoorn, M., Gur, R. E., & Gur, R. C. (2000). Emotion recognition deficit in schizophrenia: Association with symptomatology and cognition. *Biological Psychiatry, 48*(2), 127–136.

Kolvin, I. (1971). Studies in the childhood psychoses: Pt. I. Diagnostic criteria and classification. *British Journal of Psychiatry, 118*(545), 381–384.

Kumra, S., Briguglio, C., Lenane, M., Goldhar, L., Bedwell, J., Venuchekov, J., et al. (1999). Including children and adolescents with schizophrenia in medication-free research. *American Journal of Psychiatry, 156*(7), 1065–1068.

Kumra, S., Frazier, J. A., Jacobsen, L. K., McKenna, K., Gordon, C. T., Lenane, M. C., et al. (1996). Childhood-onset schizophrenia: A double-blind clozapine-haloperidol comparison. *Archives of General Psychiatry, 53*(12), 1090–1097.

Kumra, S., Giedd, J. N., Vaituzis, A. C., Jacobsen, L. K., McKenna, K., Bedwell, J., et al. (2000). Childhood-onset psychotic disorders: Magnetic resonance imaging of volumetric differences in brain structure. *American Journal of Psychiatry, 157*(9), 1467–1474.

Kumra, S., Jacobsen, L. K., Lenane, M., Karp, B. I., Frazier, J. A., Smith, A. K., et al. (1998). Childhood-onset schizophrenia: An open-label study of olanzapine in adolescents. *Journal of the American Academy of Child and Adolescent Psychiatry, 37*(4), 377–385.

Kumra, S., Wiggs, E., Bedwell, J., Smith, A. K., Arling, E., Albus, K., et al. (2000). Neuropsychological deficits in pediatric patients with childhood-onset schizophrenia and psychotic disorder not otherwise specified. *Schizophrenia Research, 42*(2), 135–144.

Lehman, A. F. (1998). Public health policy, community services, and outcomes for patients with schizophrenia. *Psychiatric Clinics of North America, 21*(1), 221–231.

Lehman, A. F., Lieberman, J. A., Dixon, L. B., McGlashan, T. H., Miller, A. L., Perkins, D. O., et al. (2004). Practice guideline for the treatment of patients with schizophrenia (2nd ed.). *American Journal of Psychiatry, 161*(Suppl. 2), 1–56.

Lewis, C. M., Levinson, D. F., Wise, L. H., DeLisi, L. E., Straub, R. E., Hovatta, I., et al. (2003). Genome scan meta-analysis of schizophrenia and bipolar disorder: Pt. II. Schizophrenia. *American Journal of Human Genetics, 73*(1), 34–48.

Lewis, D. A. (1997). Development of the prefrontal cortex during adolescence: Insights into vulnerable neural circuits in schizophrenia. *Neuropsychopharmacology, 16*(6), 385–398.

Lewis, D. A., & Levitt, P. (2002). Schizophrenia as a disorder of neurodevelopment. *Annual Review of Neuroscience, 25*, 409–432.

Lieberman, J. A., Kane, J. M., & Alvir, J. (1987). Provocative tests with psychostimulant drugs in schizophrenia. *Psychopharmacology, 91*(4), 415–433.

Lieberman, J. A., Stroup, T. S., McEvoy, J. P., Swartz, M. S., Rosenheck, R. A., Perkins, D. O., et al. (2005). Effectiveness of antipsychotic drugs in patients with chronic schizophrenia. *New England Journal of Medicine, 353*(12), 1209–1223.

Lim, K. O., Harris, D., Beal, M., Hoff, A. L., Minn, K., Csernansky, J. G., et al. (1996). Gray matter deficits in young onset schizophrenia are independent of age of onset. *Biological Psychiatry, 40*(1), 4–13.

Lofgren, D. P., Bemporad, J., King, J., Lindem, K., & O'Driscoll, G. (1991). A prospective follow-up study of so-called borderline children. *American Journal of Psychiatry, 148*(11), 1541–1547.

Lopez, S. R., Hipke, K. N., Polo, A. J., Jenkins, J. H., Karno, M., Vaughn, C., et al. (2004). Ethnicity, expressed emotion, attributions, and course of schizophrenia: Family warmth matters. *Journal of Abnormal Psychology, 113*(3), 428–439.

Maki, P., Veijola, J., Jones, P. B., Murray, G. K., Koponen, H., Tienari, P., et al. (2005). Predictors of schizophrenia: A review. *British Medical Bulletin, 73–74*, 1–15.

Malaspina, D., & Coleman, E. (2003). Olfaction and social drive in schizophrenia. *Archives of General Psychiatry, 60*(6), 578–584.

Marek, G., & Merchant, K. (2005). Developing therapeutics for schizophrenia and other psychotic disorders. *NeuroRx: Journal of the American Society for Experimental NeuroTherapeutics, 2*(4), 579–589.

Marsh, A. A., Elfenbein, H. A., & Ambady, N. (2003). Nonverbal "accents": Cultural differences in facial expressions of emotion. *Psychological Science, 14*(4), 373–376.

Matzner, F., Silva, R., Silvan, M., Chowdhury, M., & Nastasi, L. (1997, May). *Preliminary test-retest reliability of the KID-SCID.* Paper presented at the meeting of the American Psychiatric Association Scientific Proceedings, San Diego, CA.

Maziade, M., Gingras, N., Rodrigue, C., Bouchard, S., Cardinal, A., Gauthier, B., et al. (1996). Long-term stability of diagnosis and symptom dimensions in a systematic sample of patients with onset of schizophrenia in childhood and early adolescence: Pt. I. Nosology, sex and age of onset. *British Journal of Psychiatry, 169*(3), 361–370.

McClellan, J., & McCurry, C. (1998). Neurodevelopmental pathways in schizophrenia. *Seminars in Clinical Neuropsychiatry, 3*(4), 320–332.

McClellan, J., & McCurry, C. (1999). Early onset psychotic disorders: Diagnostic stability and clinical characteristics. *European Child and Adolescent Psychiatry, 8*(Suppl. 1), 13–19.

McClellan, J., McCurry, C., Snell, J., & DuBose, A. (1999). Early-onset psychotic disorders: Course and outcome over a 2-year period. *Journal of the American Academy of Child and Adolescent Psychiatry, 38*(11), 1380–1388.

McClellan, J., Prezbindowski, A., Breiger, D., & McCurry, C. (2004). Neuropsychological functioning in early onset psychotic disorders. *Schizophrenia Research, 68*(1), 21–26.

McClellan, J. M., & Hamilton, J. D. (2006). An evidence-based approach to an adolescent with emotional and behavioral dysregulation. *Journal of the American Academy of Child and Adolescent Psychiatry, 45*(4), 489–493.

McClellan, J. M., Susser, E., & King, M. C. (2007). Schizophrenia: a common disease caused by multiple rare alleles. *British Journal of Psychiatry, 190*, 194-199.

McClellan, J. M., & Werry, J. S. (2000). Introduction: Research psychiatric diagnostic interviews for children and adolescents. *Journal of the American Academy of Child and Adolescent Psychiatry, 39*(1), 19–27.

McClellan, J. M., Werry, J. S., & Ham, M. (1993). A follow-up study of early onset psychosis: Comparison between outcome diagnoses of schizophrenia, mood disorders, and personality disorders. *Journal of Autism and Developmental Disorders, 23*(2), 243–262.

McEvoy, J. P., Lieberman, J. A., Stroup, T. S., Davis, S. M., Meltzer, H. Y., Rosenheck, R. A., et al. (2006). Effectiveness of clozapine versus olanzapine, quetiapine, and risperidone in patients with chronic schizophrenia who did not respond to prior atypical antipsychotic treatment. *American Journal of Psychiatry, 163*(4), 600–610.

McKenna, K., Gordon, C. T., Lenane, M., Kaysen, D., Fahey, K., & Rapoport, J. L. (1994). Looking for childhood-onset schizophrenia: The first 71 cases screened. *Journal of the American Academy of Child and Adolescent Psychiatry, 33*(5), 636–644.

Mehler, C., & Warnke, A. (2002). Structural brain abnormalities specific to childhood-onset schizophrenia identified by neuroimaging techniques. *Journal of Neural Transmission, 109*(2), 219–234.

Moritz, S., Woodward, T. S., & Chen, E. (2006). Investigation of metamemory dysfunctions in first-episode schizophrenia. *Schizophrenia Research, 81*(2/3), 247–252.

Mueser, K. T., Bond, G. R., Drake, R. E., & Resnick, S. G. (1998). Models of community care for severe mental illness: A review of research on case management. *Schizophrenia Bulletin, 24*(1), 37–74.

Mueser, K. T., & McGurk, S. R. (2004). Schizophrenia. *Lancet, 363*(9426), 2063–2072.

Nicolson, R., Brookner, F. B., Lenane, M., Gochman, P., Ingraham, L. J., Egan, M. F., et al. (2003). Parental schizophrenia spectrum disorders in childhood-onset and adult-onset schizophrenia. *American Journal of Psychiatry, 160*(3), 490–495.

Nicolson, R., Lenane, M., Hamburger, S. D., Fernandez, T., Bedwell, J., & Rapoport, J. L. (2000). Lessons from childhood-onset schizophrenia. *Brain Research Reviews, 31*(2/3), 147–156.

Nicolson, R., Lenane, M., Singaracharlu, S., Malaspina, D., Giedd, J. N., Hamburger, S. D., et al. (2000). Premorbid speech and language impairments in childhood-onset schizophrenia: Association with risk factors. *American Journal of Psychiatry, 157*(5), 794–800.

Nicolson, R., & Rapoport, J. L. (1999). Childhood-onset schizophrenia: Rare but worth studying. *Biological Psychiatry, 46*(10), 1418–1428.

Niemi, L. T., Suvisaari, J. M., Haukka, J. K., & Lonnqvist, J. K. (2005). Childhood predictors of future psychiatric morbidity in offspring of mothers with psychotic disorder: Results from the Helsinki High-Risk Study. *British Journal of Psychiatry, 186*, 108–114.

Norman, R. M., & Malla, A. K. (2001). Family history of schizophrenia and the relationship of stress to symptoms: Preliminary findings. *Australian and New Zealand Journal of Psychiatry, 35*(2), 217–223.

O'Brien, M. P., Gordon, J. L., Bearden, C. E., Lopez, S. R., Kopelowicz, A., & Cannon, T. D. (2006). Positive family environment predicts improvement in symptoms and social functioning among adolescents at imminent risk for onset of psychosis. *Schizophrenia Research, 81*(2/3), 269–275.

Oie, M., Sunde, K., & Rund, B. R. (1999). Contrasts in memory functions between adolescents with schizophrenia or ADHD. *Neuropsychologia, 37*(12), 1351–1358.

Ordonez, A. E., Bobb, A., Greenstein, D., Baker, N., Sporn, A., Lenane, M., et al. (2005). Lack of evidence for elevated obstetric complications in childhood onset schizophrenia. *Biological Psychiatry, 58*(1), 10–15.

Pavuluri, M. N., Herbener, E. S., & Sweeney, J. A. (2004). Psychotic symptoms in pediatric bipolar disorder. *Journal of Affective Disorders, 80*(1), 19–28.

Pilling, S., Bebbington, P., Kuipers, E., Garety, P., Geddes, J., Orbach, G., et al. (2002). Psychological treatments in schizophrenia: Pt. I. Meta-analysis of family intervention and cognitive behavior therapy. *Psychological Medicine, 32*(5), 763–782.

Pinkham, A. E., Penn, D. L., Perkins, D. O., & Lieberman, J. (2003). Implications for the neural basis of social cognition for the study of schizophrenia. *American Journal of Psychiatry, 160*(5), 815–824.

Pool, D., Bloom, W., Mielke, D. H., Roniger, J. J., Jr., & Gallant, D. M. (1976). A controlled evaluation of loxitane in 75 adolescent schizophrenic patients. *Current Therapeutic Research, 19*(1), 99–104.

Poole, J. H., Tobias, F. C., & Vinogradov, S. (2000). The functional relevance of affect recognition errors in schizophrenia. *Journal of the International Neuropsychological Society, 6*(6), 649–658.

Poulton, R., Caspi, A., Moffitt, T. E., Cannon, M., Murray, R., & Harrington, H. (2000). Children's self-reported psychotic symptoms and adult schizophreniform disorder: A 15-year longitudinal study. *Archives of General Psychiatry, 57*(11), 1053–1058.

Rapoport, J. L., Addington, A. M., Frangou, S., & Psych, M. R. (2005). The neurodevelopmental model of schizophrenia: Update 2005. *Molecular Psychiatry, 10*(5), 434–449.

Rapoport, J. L., Giedd, J., Kumra, S., Jacobsen, L., Smith, A., Lee, P., et al. (1997). Childhood-onset schizophrenia. Progressive ventricular change during adolescence. *Archives of General Psychiatry, 54*(10), 897–903.

Read, J., van Os, J., Morrison, A. P., & Ross, C. A. (2005). Childhood trauma, psychosis, and schizophrenia: A literature review with theoretical and clinical implications. *Acta Psychiatrica Scandinavica, 112*(5), 330–350.

Realmuto, G. M., Erickson, W. D., Yellin, A. M., Hopwood, J. H., & Greenberg, L. M. (1984). Clinical comparison of thiothixene and thioridazine in schizophrenic adolescents. *American Journal of Psychiatry, 141*(3), 440–442.

Reichenberg, A., Weiser, M., Rapp, M. A., Rabinowitz, J., Caspi, A., Schmeidler, J., et al. (2005). Elaboration on premorbid intellectual performance in schizophrenia: Premorbid intellectual decline and risk for schizophrenia. *Archives of General Psychiatry, 62*(12), 1297–1304.

Reimherr, J. P., & McClellan, J. M. (2004). Diagnostic challenges in children and adolescents with psychotic disorders. *Journal of Clinical Psychiatry, 65*(Suppl. 6), 5–11.

Remschmidt, H. (2002). Early-onset schizophrenia as a progressive-deteriorating developmental disorder: Evidence from child psychiatry. *Journal of Neural Transmission, 109*(1), 101–117.

Remschmidt, H., Martin, M., Schulz, E., Gutenbrunner, C., & Fleischhaker, C. (1991). The concept of positive and negative schizophrenia in child and adolescent psychiatry. In A. Marneros, N. C. Andreasen, & M. T. Tsuang (Eds.), *Positive versus negative schizophrenia* (pp. 219–242). Berlin, Germany: Springer-Verlag.

Rhinewine, J. P., Lencz, T., Thaden, E. P., Cervellione, K. L., Burdick, K. E., Henderson, I., et al. (2005). Neurocognitive profile in adolescents with early-onset schizophrenia: Clinical correlates. *Biological Psychiatry, 58*(9), 705–712.

Robinson, D., Woerner, M. G., Alvir, J. M., Bilder, R., Goldman, R., Geisler, S., et al. (1999). Predictors of relapse following response from a first episode of schizophrenia or schizoaffective disorder. *Archives of General Psychiatry, 56*(3), 241–247.

Ropcke, B., & Eggers, C. (2005). Early-onset schizophrenia: A 15-year follow-up. *European Child and Adolescent Psychiatry, 14*(6), 341–350.

Rosenfarb, I. S., Bellack, A. S., & Aziz, N. (2006). Family interactions and the course of schizophrenia in African American and White patients. *Journal of Abnormal Psychology, 115*(1), 112–120.

Ross, R. G., Heinlein, S., Zerbe, G. O., & Radant, A. (2005). Saccadic eye movement task identifies cognitive deficits in children with schizophrenia, but not in unaffected child relatives. *Journal of Child Psychology and Psychiatry, 46*(12), 1354–1362.

Rund, B. R. (1994). Cognitive dysfunctions and psychosocial treatment of schizophrenics: Research of the past and perspectives on the future. *Acta Psychiatrica Scandinavica, 384*(Suppl.), 9–16.

Russell, A. T., Bott, L., & Sammons, C. (1989). The phenomenology of schizophrenia occurring in childhood. *Journal of the American Academy of Child and Adolescent Psychiatry, 28*(3), 399–407.

Rutter, M. (1972). Childhood schizophrenia reconsidered. *Journal of Autism and Childhood Schizophrenia, 2*(4), 315–337.

Rutter, M., Kim-Cohen, J., & Maughan, B. (2006). Continuities and discontinuities in psychopathology between childhood and adult life. *Journal of Child Psychology and Psychiatry, 47*(3/4), 276–295.

Sarti, P., & Cournos, F. (1990). Medication and psychotherapy in the treatment of chronic schizophrenia. *Psychiatric Clinics of North America, 13*(2), 215–228.

Schaeffer, J. L., & Ross, R. G. (2002). Childhood-onset schizophrenia: Premorbid and prodromal diagnostic and treatment histories. *Journal of the American Academy of Child and Adolescent Psychiatry, 41*(5), 538–545.

Schneider, F., Gur, R. C., Koch, K., Backes, V., Amunts, K., Shah, N. J., et al. (2006). Impairment in the specificity of emotion processing in schizophrenia. *American Journal of Psychiatry, 163*(3), 442–447.

Schooler, N. R., Keith, S. J., Severe, J. B., Matthews, S. M., Bellack, A. S., Glick, I. D., et al. (1997). Relapse and rehospitalization during maintenance treatment of schizophrenia: The effects of dose reduction and family treatment. *Archives of General Psychiatry, 54*(5), 453–463.

Sernyak, M. J., Gulanski, B., & Rosenheck, R. (2005). Undiagnosed hyperglycemia in patients treated with atypical antipsychotics. *Journal of Clinical Psychiatry, 66*(11), 1463–1467.

Shevlin, M., Dorahy, M., & Adamson, G. (2007). Childhood traumas and hallucinations: An analysis of the National Comorbidity Survey. *Journal of Psychiatric Research, 41*(3/4), 222–228.

Sikich, L., Hamer, R. M., Bashford, R. A., Sheitman, B. B., & Lieberman, J. A. (2004). A pilot study of risperidone, olanzapine, and haloperidol in psychotic youth: A double-blind, randomized, 8-week trial. *Neuropsychopharmacology, 29*(1), 133–145.

Simeon, J. G., Carrey, N. J., Wiggins, D. M., Milin, R. P., & Hosenbocus, S. N. (1995) Risperidone effects in treatment-resistant adolescents: Preliminary case reports. *Journal of Child and Adolescent Psychopharmacology, 5*(1), 69–79.

Spauwen, J., Krabbendam, L., Lieb, R., Wittchen, H. U., & van Os, J. (2004). Does urbanicity shift the population expression of psychosis? *Journal of Psychiatric Research, 38*(6), 613–618.

Spencer, E. K., Kafantaris, V., Padron-Gayol, M. V., Rosenberg, C. R., & Campbell, M. (1992). Haloperidol in schizophrenic children: Early findings from a study in progress. *Psychopharmacology Bulletin, 28*(2), 183–186.

Sporn, A. L., Addington, A. M., Gogtay, N., Ordonez, A. E., Gornick, M., Clasen, L., et al. (2004). Pervasive developmental disorder and childhood-onset schizophrenia: Comorbid disorder or a phenotypic variant of a very early onset illness? *Biological Psychiatry, 55*(10), 989–994.

Staal, W. G., Hulshoff Pol, H. E., Schnack, H. G., van Haren, N. E., Seifert, N., & Kahn, R. S. (2001). Structural brain abnormalities in chronic schizophrenia at the extremes of the outcome spectrum. *American Journal of Psychiatry, 158*(7), 1140–1142.

Subotnik, K. L., Nuechterlein, K. H., Green, M. F., Horan, W. P., Nienow, T. M., Ventura, J., et al. (2006). Neurocognitive and social cognitive correlates of formal thought disorder in schizophrenia patients. *Schizophrenia Research, 85*(1/3), 84–95.

Szigethy, E., Brent, S., & Findling, R. L. (1998). Quetiapine for refractory schizophrenia. *Journal of the American Academy of Child and Adolescent Psychiatry, 37*(11), 1127–1128.

Tarrier, N., Barrowclough, C., Porceddu, K., & Fitzpatrick, E. (1994). The Salford Family Intervention Project: Relapse rates of schizophrenia at 5 and 8 years. *British Journal of Psychiatry, 165*(6), 829–832.

Thaden, E., Rhinewine, J. P., Lencz, T., Kester, H., Cervellione, K. L., Henderson, I., et al. (2006). Early-onset schizophrenia is associated with impaired adolescent development of attentional capacity using the identical pairs continuous performance test. *Schizophrenia Research, 81*(2/3), 157–166.

Thompson, P. M., Vidal, C., Giedd, J. N., Gochman, P., Blumenthal, J., Nicolson, R., et al. (2001). Mapping adolescent brain change reveals dynamic wave of accelerated gray matter loss in very early-onset schizophrenia. *Proceedings of the National Academy of Sciences, USA, 98*(20), 11650–11655.

Thomsen, P. H. (1996). Schizophrenia with childhood and adolescent onset: A nationwide register-based study. *Acta Psychiatrica Scandinavica, 94*(3), 187–193.

Toga, A. W., Thompson, P. M., & Sowell, E. R. (2006). Mapping brain maturation. *Trends in Neurosciences, 29*(3), 148–159.

Tsuang, M. (2000). Schizophrenia: Genes and environment. *Biological Psychiatry, 47*(3), 210–220.

Turkel, S. B., & Tavare, C. J. (2003). Delirium in children and adolescents. *Journal of Neuropsychiatry and Clinical Neurosciences, 15*(4), 431–435.

Tuulio-Henriksson, A., Partonen, T., Suvisaari, J., Haukka, J., & Lonnqvist, J. (2004). Age at onset and cognitive functioning in schizophrenia. *British Journal of Psychiatry, 185*, 215–219.

Uranova, N., Orlovskaya, D., Vikhreva, O., Zimina, I., Kolomeets, N., Vostrikov, V., et al. (2001). Electron microscopy of oligodendroglia in severe mental illness. *Brain Research Bulletin, 55*(5), 597–610.

van Os, J., Pedersen, C. B., & Mortensen, P. B. (2004). Confirmation of synergy between urbanicity and familial liability in the causation of psychosis. *American Journal of Psychiatry, 161*(12), 2312–2314.

Ventura, J., Nuechterlein, K. H., Lukoff, D., & Hardesty, J. P. (1989). A prospective study of stressful life events and schizophrenic relapse. *Journal of Abnormal Psychology, 98*(4), 407–411.

Vidal, C. N., Rapoport, J. L., Hayashi, K. M., Geaga, J. A., Sui, Y., McLemore, L. E., et al. (2006). Dynamically spreading frontal and cingulate deficits mapped in adolescents with schizophrenia. *Archives of General Psychiatry, 63*(1), 25–34.

Volkmar, F. R., & Cohen, D. J. (1991). Comorbid association of autism and schizophrenia. *American Journal of Psychiatry, 148*(12), 1705–1707.

Volkmar, F. R., Cohen, D. J., Hoshino, Y., Rende, R. D., & Paul, R. (1988). Phenomenology and classification of the childhood psychoses. *Psychological Medicine, 18*(1), 191–201.

Vourdas, A., Pipe, R., Corrigall, R., & Frangou, S. (2003). Increased developmental deviance and premorbid dysfunction in early onset schizophrenia. *Schizophrenia Research, 62*(1/2), 13–22.

Waddington, J. L., Lane, A., Scully, P., Meagher, D., Quinn, J., Larkin, C., et al. (1999). Early cerebro-craniofacial dysmorphogenesis in schizophrenia: A lifetime trajectory model from neurodevelopmental basis to "neuroprogressive" process. *Journal of Psychiatric Research, 33*(6), 477–489.

Waddington, J. L., Scully, P. J., Quinn, J. F., Meagher, D. J., & Morgan, M. G. (2001). The origin and course of schizophrenia: Implications for clinical practice. *Journal of Psychiatric Practice, 7*(4), 247–252.

Walker, E. F., Grimes, K. E., Davis, D. M., & Smith, A. J. (1993). Childhood precursors of schizophrenia: Facial expressions of emotion. *American Journal of Psychiatry, 150*(11), 1654–1660.

Wearden, A. J., Tarrier, N., Barrowclough, C., Zastowny, T. R., & Rahill, A. A. (2000). A review of expressed emotion research in health care. *Clinical Psychology Review, 20*(5), 633–666.

Werry, J. S., McClellan, J. M., & Chard, L. (1991). Childhood and adolescent schizophrenic, bipolar, and schizoaffective disorders: A clinical and outcome study. *Journal of the American Academy of Child and Adolescent Psychiatry, 30*(3), 457–465.

Wible, C. G., Anderson, J., Shenton, M. E., Kricun, A., Hirayasu, Y., Tanaka, S., et al. (2001). Prefrontal cortex, negative symptoms, and schizophrenia: An MRI study. *Psychiatry Research, 108*(2), 65–78.

Wicks, S., Hjern, A., Gunnell, D., Lewis, G., & Dalman, C. (2005). Social adversity in childhood and the risk of developing psychosis: A national cohort study. *American Journal of Psychiatry, 162*(9), 1652–1657.

World Health Organization. (1992). *The ICD-10 classification of mental and behavioral disorders: Clinical descriptions and diagnostic guidelines.* Geneva, Switzerland: Author.

Wykes, T., & van der Gaag, M. (2001). Is it time to develop a new cognitive therapy for psychosis: Cognitive remediation therapy (CRT)? *Clinical Psychology Review, 21*(8), 1227–1256.

Zastowny, T. R., Lehman, A. F., Cole, R. E., & Kane, C. (1992). Family management of schizophrenia: A comparison of behavioral and supportive family treatment. *Psychiatric Quarterly, 63*(2), 159–186.

Zygmunt, A., Olfson, M., Boyer, C. A., & Mechanic, D. (2002). Interventions to improve medication adherence in schizophrenia. *American Journal of Psychiatry, 159*(10), 1653–1664.

CHAPTER 16

Substance Use Disorders

ERIC F. WAGNER AND ASHLEY AUSTIN

DESCRIPTION OF THE DISORDER

Adolescent substance use is a highly prevalent behavior. Three out of every four high school seniors have tried alcohol, and half have tried at least one illicit drug (Johnston, O'Malley, Bachman, & Schulenberg, 2006). The Monitoring the Future Study, which is conducted annually by researchers at the Survey Research Center of the University of Michigan, reveals that 75.1% of 12th-graders have consumed alcohol, 57.5% have been drunk, and 50.4% have tried an illicit substance (usually, but not always, marijuana). When asked about substance use over the past 12 months, 68.6% reported drinking one or more times, 47.7% reported having been drunk one or more times, and 38.4% reported using an illicit drug one or more times. When asked about past month substance use, 47% of seniors reported drinking one or more times, 30.2% reported having been drunk one or more times, and 23.1% reported using an illicit drug one or more times. Corresponding data collected from 8th- and 10th-graders confirm that substance use is inversely correlated with age. Nonetheless, drinking and drug use are remarkably common even among younger teens; for example, 33.9% of 8th-graders and 56.7% of 10th-graders reported drinking alcohol during the past year.

Despite legal sanctions for substance use, such behavior (and especially alcohol use) is statistically normative. The reality of widespread use of substances by teens has complicated attempts to develop consistent diagnostic criteria capable of distinguishing adolescent substance use from problem substance use. Experts do not agree on the necessary and sufficient criteria for diagnosing a substance use disorder in a teenager (Hays & Ellickson, 1996). Clinicians often turn to the *Diagnostic and Statistical Manual of Mental Disorders*, fourth edition, text revision (*DSM-IV-TR*; American Psychiatric Association, 2000) for guidance concerning whether an adolescent has a substance use problem. For *DSM* purposes, the key diagnostic distinction pertains to whether the problem is characterized as abuse or dependence. Based on the *DSM*, a 14-year-old girl would receive a substance *abuse* disorder diagnosis if she engaged in any of the following four behaviors: (1) recurrent substance use resulting in a failure to fulfill major role obligations at work, school, or home; (2) recurrent substance use in situations in which it is physically hazardous; (3) recurrent substance-related legal problems; and (4) continued substance use despite having persistent or recurrent social or interpersonal problems caused or exacerbated by the effects of the substance. She would instead receive a substance *dependence* diagnosis if, during the past year, she demonstrated three or more of the following seven symptoms: (1) tolerance to the effects of a substance, as defined by either (a) a need for markedly increased amounts of the substance to achieve intoxication or desired effect or (b) markedly diminished effect with continued use of the same amount of the substance; (2) withdrawal, as defined by either (a) withdrawal syndrome in the absence of substance consumption or (b) using the substance to relieve or avoid withdrawal symptoms; (3) using larger amounts of the substance or using the substance for a longer period than intended; (4) a persistent desire or unsuccessful efforts to cut down or control substance use; (5) a great deal of time spent in activities necessary to obtain the substance, use the substance, or recover from its effects; (6) important social, occupational, or recreational activities given up or reduced because of substance use; and (7) continued substance use despite knowledge of having a persistent or recurrent physical or psychological problem likely to have been caused or exacerbated by drinking.

Although most of the *DSM-IV* substance use disorders (SUDs) diagnostic criteria are (a) face valid and (b) significantly and positively correlated with one another, the extent to which the designated symptoms and syndromes (i.e., abuse versus dependence) are developmentally appropriate representations of teen substance use problems remains unknown. The fundamental appropriateness of the *DSM-IV* criteria for estimating alcohol (and other drug) problems among youth has been called into question (e.g., see S. L. Bailey, Martin, Lynch, & Pollock, 2000; Chung et al., 2000; Martin & Winters, 1998; Wagner, Lloyd, & Gil, 2002). Multiple concerns have been voiced, including (a) a lack of knowledge about the overall validity of the diagnostic criteria for adolescents; (b) the fact that several symptoms are very rare among adolescents with substance use problems (e.g., withdrawal, substance-related medical problems); (c) the fact that some symptoms do not appear to distinguish adolescents with and without substance use problems (e.g., tolerance to the effects of alcohol); and (d) the fact that some symptoms tend to occur only in particular teenage subgroups (e.g., older conduct-disordered males are much more likely to demonstrate hazardous use and legal problems; Martin & Winters, 1998). A further limitation of the *DSM-IV* is the absence of criteria concerning the frequency or quantity of consumption; in the *DSM-IV* diagnostic scheme, it is possible for an adolescent to drink frequently (or in large quantities) yet not cross the threshold necessary for receiving a diagnosis.

With respect to the frequency and quantity of substance use behavior, it is important to stress that even infrequent and light alcohol or other drug use may increase a teenager's risk for car accidents, unwanted or unprotected sexual encounters, and violent interpersonal exchanges. That said, there is little doubt that teenagers who use alcohol or other drugs often and in large quantities are the teenagers most likely to suffer the types of negative consequences associated with the emergence of substance use problems. Moreover, few would dispute that daily or near daily use of alcohol or other drugs by an adolescent represents compulsive substance use, a widely validated, primary indicator of substance use problems.

Accurate measurement of the frequency and quantity of adolescent substance use is a concern, as many teens may have many reasons to underreport or deny involvement with substances. Collateral reporters (e.g., parents, siblings, friends) are an alternative, but these informants typically and significantly underestimate teen substance use, as they have limited opportunities to observe it (Engels, van der Vorst, Deković & Meeus, 2006). Moreover, diagnostic cutoffs based exclusively on the frequency or quantity of use are problematic. If the cutoff for abuse is set too low, normative users might be erroneously labeled as substance abusing, a label with potentially profound and enduring negative consequences for its carrier. If the cut-off for abuse is set too high, adolescents with real problems related to their use of alcohol or drugs will not obtain the treatment they need. Already, only 1 out of every 10 adolescents with a substance use problem receives treatment (H. W. Clark, Horton, Dennis, & Babor, 2002; Dennis, Dawud-Noursi, Muck, & McDermeit, 2003). Setting inappropriately high diagnostic cutoffs will worsen the problem. Given the limitations of use frequency and quantity diagnostic criteria, most clinicians naturally take into account both use patterns and negative consequences resulting from use in making determinations of SUDs among teenagers. Negative consequences are in fact the only type of diagnostic criteria on which adolescent substance use experts agree (Hays & Ellickson, 1996), though it is important to remember that definitions of negative consequences must be developmentally meaningful (e.g., has your substance use caused problems like breaking curfew? making excuses to parents? skipping school?).

To summarize, a big issue in the adolescent substance use field is distinguishing normative use from problematic use. Research and clinical experience has indicated that an adolescent with substance use problems will:

- Meet one or more of 10 of the 11 symptoms associated with *DSM-IV*-defined substance abuse and dependence (i.e., with the caveat that the tolerance symptom be disqualified from consideration, as has been recommended by Chung et al., 2000).
- Be using substances more frequently and in larger amounts than expected given the teenager's chronological age and sex.
- Have endured undeniably undesirable consequences from his or her use of alcohol or other drugs.

DIAGNOSIS AND ASSESSMENT

Much of current practice in adolescent substance abuse treatment relies on the time-tested techniques and philosophies of adult substance abuse treatment. It is important to recognize that inherent in these approaches are assumptions that may not match the developmental realities of children and adolescents. Compared to adults with alcohol or drug problems, teenage substance abusers have:

- A briefer history of use.
- More episodic use.
- Fewer consequences of protracted use.
- Experience with a greater number and variety of substances.
- Ongoing and rapid developmental changes.
- Less intragroup developmental homogeneity.
- Greater risk for co-occurring problems.
- Developmental transitions that dramatically alter substance use trajectories.

These developmentally specific characteristics of adolescent substance use problems speak to the need to diagnose and assess substance use problems in a developmentally appropriate manner. As reviewed earlier, use of the *DSM-IV* criteria is commonplace despite ongoing debate as to their developmental appropriateness. Most clinicians use *DSM-IV*-based assessment and diagnostic approaches in part because they help in making a well-rounded and well-reasoned clinical judgment about an adolescent's substance use. There is wide consensus that the etiology of adolescent substance use problems involves complex interactions among developmental, biological, psychological, and social phenomena. Thus, to the extent possible, diagnosis and assessment should consider all of these dimensions. Furthermore, to the extent possible, assessment should rely on multiple information sources, including self-reports, parents' and teachers' reports, psychometric testing, observation of the teenager's behavior, and drug screening tests. The bottom line here is that collecting data from multiple sources will enhance the accuracy of diagnosis. In regard to content areas, recommended practice in conducting an adolescent substance abuse assessment is to collect data across the following domains: (a) substance use itself; (b) psychiatric morbidity and its temporal relation to substance use and use problems; (c) cognitive processes, especially neuropsychological functioning; (d) family relations and home environment; and (e) interpersonal skills. Certain areas of a teenager's life may be especially likely to be affected by substance use. In that regard, assessment should attend to the following areas: (a) school or vocational adjustment, (b) recreation and leisure activities, (c) personality characteristics, (d) friends, (e) trouble with the law, and (f) physical health and somatic concerns.

The numerous advantages of a valid, standardized, and clinically relevant assessment of adolescent substance use problems are well known (e.g., see Winters, Latimer, & Stinchfield, 1999). Effective clinical assessments aid clinical decision making, are insulated against clinician biases and inconsistencies, and provide a lingua franca for the field. Some good examples of standardized and clinically valid instruments are the Personal Experiences Inventory (Winters et al., 1999), the Drug Use Screening Inventory (Tarter & Hegedus, 1991), the Customary Drinking and Drug Use Record (Brown et al., 1998), the Teen-Addiction Severity Index (Kaminer, Wagner, Plummer, & Seifer, 1993), and the Global Appraisal of Individual Needs (Dennis, Funk, Godley, Godley, & Waldron, 2004). All of these measures share one important feature: They focus on behaviors, contexts, and lifestyle choices salient to adolescence.

A good assessment typically begins with a short interview with the adolescent and his or her parents about the presenting problem. Rather than focus on the specifics of the frequency, type, or quantity of substance use (this will come later), discussion should address the negative consequences or "bad things" that have accompanied the teen's use of substances. Adolescents and their parents often have differing opinions on such matters; such contradictions should be identified for the clients without siding with the adolescent or the parents. A meeting with the teenager or parents alone also can be helpful, but only after issues related to confidentiality are discussed and understood by all parties. Next, a comprehensive and standardized adolescent substance abuse assessment is performed, using an instrument like those described earlier. Finally, the clinician provides feedback about assessment results, which is a great opportunity for solidifying a working alliance with clients. Miller and Rollnick's (2002) motivational interviewing approach can be especially helpful in this regard.

CONCEPTUALIZATION

Developmental Issues

Adolescent substance abuse treatment approaches rely heavily on the time-tested techniques and philosophies of adult substance abuse treatment (Wagner, 2003; Wagner & Kassel, 1995). However, both clinicians and researchers have begun to challenge the developmental congruence of adult-derived methods and techniques. On multiple clinically relevant accounts, adolescent substance abusers are different from adult substance abusers. Add to this the normative developmental differences between adolescents and adults, and the potential limitations of adult-derived treatment approaches come into focus. Most clinicians and researchers agree that to be maximally effective, adolescent substance abuse treatment must take into account such developmental realities. For example, substance abusing teenagers show wide divergence in developmental status, the anticipated effects and consequences of alcohol and drug use, the social and emotional contexts of use, and the risk factors contributing to the onset and trajectory of use (Wagner & Kassel, 1995). Although little researched, individual differences that vary with developmental status may causally contribute to long-term differences in treatment response (Brown, 1993, 2004; Wagner, 2003).

Learning and Modeling

Conceptualizations of substance use behaviors have been greatly influenced by cognitive and social learning theories. Bandura's (1997, 1999) distinction between outcome expectancies and self-efficacy expectations has been particularly influential. According to Bandura (1977), outcome expectancy is one's belief that a particular behavior (e.g., substance use) will lead to certain positive outcomes, and self-efficacy expectations reflect one's confidence in the ability to successfully carry out the behavior. According to this theory, the probability of substance use is a result of the reciprocal influence of outcome expectations and self-efficacy expectations (Niaura, 2000). Studies have demonstrated that outcome expectancies can influence the actual behavioral effects of alcohol. Specifically, when outcome expectations are positive, alcohol consumption may have particularly rewarding consequences (Marlatt & Rohsenow, 1980).

Because outcome expectancies appear to play an important role in the behavioral consequences of substance use, it is important to understand how these expectations are formed. According to cognitive social learning theory (CSLT), developing outcome and efficacy expectations is not limited to direct experience, but can be learned through numerous channels, including observations of others engaging in a substance use and verbal discussions about substance use (Niaura, 2000). Research conducted with a group of 12- to 14-year-old nondrinkers confirmed that well-developed alcohol expectancies exist prior to the time youth begin to drink (Christiansen, Goldman, & Inn, 1982). It was suggested that these expectancy factors were learned through family, peer associations, the media, and witnessing drinking by other individuals. In fact, research consistently demonstrates that peer, sibling, and parental modeling of substance use behaviors contribute to adolescent substance use (Hawkins, Catalano, & Miller, 1992). The Christiansen et al. study also found that outcome expectancy factors became more specific and firmly established with age and drinking experience.

Several studies have found that the substance-related outcome expectancies held by adolescents are overwhelmingly positive (i.e., enhanced sex, power, and stress reduction; see Brown, Goldman, Inn, & Anderson, 1980; Christiansen et al., 1982). Thus, the preconditions for positive reinforcement of substance use are present before most individuals ever use substances. While it appears that adolescents have general expectations about substance use in advance of actual use, these expectations are adjusted and refined based on direct substance use experience. If initial substance use experiences are positive, then expectancies become increasingly positive. If the experiences are associated with negative consequences, then the previously held positive expectancies are replaced with increasingly negative expectancies (i.e., increased aggression, loss of control, impaired behavioral functioning).

The second part of the CSLT model concerns the influence of self-efficacy expectations on substance use behavior. According to CSLT, efficacy expectations are considered to have a primary predictive role in explaining all effortful behavior (Niaura, 2000). However, it is important to understand that self-efficacy is not a global concept. Instead, self-efficacy is hypothesized to vary across behavior domains (Brandon, Herzog, Irvin, & Gwaltney, 2004). In the domain of substance abuse, self-efficacy expectations relate primarily to one's beliefs about whether one has the necessary coping skills to deal with life events. Social learning theorists propose that efficacy expectations about general coping skills are critical to initial decisions to use as well as whether patterns of substance use will be normal or problematic (Abrams & Niaura, 1987). Furthermore, according to Bandura (1997), perceived self-efficacy in one's ability to resist using substances affects every phase of addiction: (a) initiating and achieving changes in substance use behaviors, (b) rebounding from relapse, and (c) long-term maintenance of abstinence. Specifically, research with adults suggests that individuals with high self-efficacy are more likely to successfully quit using substances without treatment (Carey & Carey, 1993), remain in treatment longer (DiClemente & Hughes, 1990), demonstrate greater mastery of the self-control and self-regulatory skills taught in treatment that are associated with posttreatment success (Sitharthan & Kavanaugh, 1990; Stephens, Wertz, & Roffman, 1995), and be at lower risk for relapse posttreatment (Bandura, 1997; Marlatt, Baer, & Quigley, 1995). In short, CSLT posits that the process by which individuals learn both to use and to stop using alcohol and other substances is an ongoing dynamic interchange between outcome expectancies and self-efficacy expectancies that develop from both direct and indirect experiences with substance use.

PARENTAL ISSUES

Parental substance use and parenting practices are important predictors of adolescent substance use. Research findings consistently illustrate the influence of parent behavior on subsequent substance use among adolescents. Children of parents with SUDs are at increased risk for early use of alcohol and tobacco, as well as problem use of alcohol and marijuana (D. B. Clark, Cornelius, Kirisci, & Tarter, 2005; D. B. Clark, Parker, & Lynch, 1999). There are several factors associated with parental alcohol and illicit drug use that may escalate an adolescent's risk for developing substance use problems, including (a) the increased availability of alcohol or drugs in the home, (b) parents modeling substance use behaviors, (c) parents conveying a supportive attitude regarding the use of alcohol or drugs, and (d) the increased likelihood of ineffective parenting practices while under the influence of drugs or alcohol (Clayton, 1992; Hawkins et al., 1992). In addition to parental substance use, inappropriate disciplinary practices such as lax supervision and excessively severe or inconsistent discipline place youth at greater risk for substance use and delinquency (Baumrind, 1991), as does insufficient parent involvement and support (Baumrind, 1991; Hawkins et al., 1992). Moreover, in families characterized by a high level of conflict, adolescents are at an increased risk for early initiation of substance use and the development of substance use problems (Hawkins et al., 1992; Kaminer, 1994).

In contrast to the deleterious impact of poor parenting practices on adolescent substance involvement, recent research indicates that supportive parenting practices may have a protective influence on adolescent substance use behaviors. A meta-analysis of studies examining the relation between adolescent alcohol consumption and family factors indicated that adolescent alcohol use was inversely related to family support (Foxcroft & Lowe, 1991). Additionally, Marshal and Chassin (2000) found that among adolescent females, perceptions of high levels of parental support had a positive influence on drinking behavior compared to those girls who perceived low levels of parental support. Averna and Hesselbrock (2001) found that higher perceived social support from family was associated with a later onset of marijuana use and less marijuana and tobacco use among adolescents. Similarly, among teens with alcohol using parents, only those with low parental support demonstrated an increase in symptoms related to alcohol use (Urberg, Goldstein, & Toro, 2005). A study conducted by Getz and Bray (2005) suggests that mothers' monitoring of adolescent activities and peers may protect against heavy alcohol use. Likewise, Wood, Read, Mitchell, and Brand (2004) found that among recent high school graduates, higher levels of perceived parental involvement were negatively associated with peer influence and alcohol use and related problems. Finally, a positive family milieu has been shown to reduce the risk of adolescent substance use and abuse even when multiple risk factors are present (Vega & Gil, 1998).

It is clear that parental substance use and parenting practices are important predictors of substance involvement among adolescents; it is less clear whether these factors serve a primary predictive role. Some researchers suggest that parenting plays a moderating role in adolescent substance use behaviors. Specifically, parenting and family factors are predictive of the types of peers with whom an adolescent chooses to associate, as well as the relative influence of these peer networks on adolescent substance use behavior (Marshal & Chassin, 2000; Urberg et al., 2005).

Peer Influences

Empirical research consistently demonstrates that associating with alcohol and drug using peers is among the strongest predictors of teen substance involvement (Barnes & Welte, 1986; Nash, McQueen, & Bray, 2005; Urberg et al., 2005). In a recent study, peer substance use and peer approval of substance use were identified as stronger predictors of adolescent substance use behaviors than most other psychosocial factors, including family factors (Nash et al., 2005). In particular, having close, supportive relationships with substance using peers appears to place teens at increased risk for greater substance use (Averna & Hesselbrock, 2001; Urberg et al., 2005; Wills, Resko, Ainette, & Mendoza, 2004). In a study examining the progression of substance use symptoms among adolescents, Urberg and colleagues found that peer drinking was not related to teen alcohol use problems when perceived peer support was low; however, when perceived peer support was high, adolescent alcohol abuse and dependency symptoms were significantly correlated with peer drinking. Similarly, perceived peer support was positively associated with frequency of alcohol use (Averna &

Hesselbrock, 2001). Moreover, the influence of peer support on adolescent substance use behaviors appears to persist through both early and middle adolescence (Wills et al., 2004).

There are two important aspects of peer influence that appear to impact adolescent substance use behavior: active social influences (e.g., explicit offers to use a substance) and passive social influences (perception and interpretation of substance use and re-inforcement of others; Wood et al., 2004; Wood, Read, Palfai, & Stevenson, 2001). In a sample of recent high school graduates, both active and passive peer influences were associated with heavy episodic drinking and with alcohol-related negative consequences (Wood et al., 2004). However, researchers caution that findings related to the importance of peer influence on adolescent substance use behavior may be misleading (Urberg, Luo, Pilgrim, & Degirmencioglu, 2003). Similarities found between adolescent and peer substance use may be a function of peer selection processes. Specifically, substance using adolescents may select peer networks with similar attitudes and behaviors toward substance use. Indeed, children and early adolescents select friends based on shared characteristics (i.e., deviant behavior, family problems, poor academic performance) associated with subsequent substance use (Oetting & Beauvais, 1987).

In addition to the initiation of substance use and the development of substance use problems, associating with substance using peers has been linked to poor treatment response and outcome among adolescents with substance use problems. Jainchill, Hawke, De Leon, and Yagelka (2000) and Latimer, Winters, Stinchfield, and Traver (2000) found that among youth who receive treatment for substance use problems, associating with deviant peers is linked to poor substance use outcomes at 12 months posttreatment. Similarly, Stinchfield, and Winters (2003) found that peer substance use was associated with poorer substance use outcomes at both 6 and 12 months post-treatment for boys who received hospital-based treatment and at 6 months posttreatment for girls. Furthermore, among clinical samples of adolescents with substance use problems, social pressure related to spending time with substance using peers post-treatment was identified as the primary predictor of relapse to substance use (Brown, Vik, & Creamer, 1989). Although the underlying mechanisms associated with peer influence are not fully understood, it is evident that peer relationships are important contributors to adolescent substance use behaviors, including initiation and continuation of substance use, the development of problematic use patterns, response to treatment, and recovery from substance use problems.

LIFE EVENTS

A link between the use of alcohol and other substances and stressful life events has been clearly demonstrated in multiple studies conducted with both adolescents and adults. A large body of research addresses the relationship between childhood abuse and the development of substance use problems. Although the relationship appears to be complex, several reviews of empirical research find support for the association between childhood abuse and later substance use (see Beitchman et al., 1992; Kaplan, Pelcovitz, & Labruna, 1999; Widom, Weiler, & Cottler, 1999). The influence of childhood victimization on substance use appears to be particularly strong when the abuse is sexual (J. A. Bailey & McCloskey, 2005; Kilpatrick et al., 2000). In the study conducted by Kilpatrick et al., findings indicated that among a household probability sample of adolescents, those who reported sexual assault in the year prior to the study were 2.4 times more likely to report alcohol abuse, 1.6 times more likely to report marijuana use, and 2.6 times more likely to report other drug use than adolescents who reported no past year history of sexual assault. Similarly, J. A. Bailey and McCloskey found that among a sample of female adolescents, childhood sexual abuse was correlated with later substance use. In both cases, the relation between substance use and child sexual assault persisted when controlling for other forms of childhood abuse. As of yet, the pathway from childhood abuse to later substance use problems has not been empirically substantiated; however, there are several theoretically supported models (e.g., depressive self-concept and behavioral undercontrol) that are gaining empirical support (J. A. Bailey & McCloskey, 2005).

In addition to the influence of childhood abuse on substance use problems, a growing body of literature has illustrated the importance of other stressors and, in particular, the cumulative effect of these stressors in predicting later substance use problems (Newcomb, Huba, & Bentler, 1986; Turner & Lloyd, 1995, 2003). Based on a 20-item list of lifetime traumas, Turner and Lloyd (1995) found a significant relationship between the number of traumas experienced before age 18 and later substance abuse or dependence. Similarly, a study conducted by Newcomb and colleagues found that among adolescents, the sum of stressful life events experienced in the 6 months prior to the study was positively associated with alcohol and other drug use. More recently, in a study examining exposure to stressful life experiences among non-Hispanic White, African American, foreign-born Hispanic, and U.S.-born Hispanic young adults (ages 19–21), researchers found that increased exposure to adverse life events (lifetime cumulative adversity) was significantly associated with an increased risk for substance dependence for each of the ethnic groups (Turner & Lloyd, 2003). Interestingly, in addition to cumulative risk, findings from this research support the influence of both distal and proximal stressful life events on risk for substance dependence.

As childhood trauma has been one of the most widely researched traumatic life events among adolescents, there is a considerable body of evidence supporting the influence of child victimization, specifically sexual abuse, on subsequent adolescent substance use. In addition, a growing body of research indicates that what may be exceptionally significant in accounting for substance use and the development of substance use problems among adolescents is the cumulative effect of life stressors that occur during childhood and adolescence.

GENETIC INFLUENCES

A central goal of adolescent substance use research is to understand the role of genetic influences on the onset of substance use and the development of SUDs in adolescents. Human genetic studies have identified specific regions on chromosomes that are associated with an increased risk for alcohol dependence (Foroud et al., 2000). Specifically, research conducted by the Collaborative Study on the Genetics of Alcoholism has identified specific genes (GABRA2 and GABRA3) that influence the risk for alcoholism (Edenberg & Kranzler, 2005). Additionally, research has identified alcohol metabolizing enzymes that provide protective effects against the development of alcohol problems in specific populations (Oroszi & Goldman, 2004). Differences in 5-HTTLPR, the serotonin transporter gene promoter, has been associated with Type II alcoholism (Hallikainen et al., 1999; Sander et al., 1998). It is important to acknowledge that the majority of studies of genes related to alcohol use have been conducted with adults, and it remains unclear how these genetic influences affect adolescent alcohol use and disorders.

It is becoming increasingly clear that genetic factors play a fundamental role in the development of alcohol use problems, yet mounting evidence underscores the importance of the interplay between genes and environment, particularly during the developmental stages of adolescence (Rose & Dick, 2004–2005). One of the most effective methods for examining the influence of genetic and environmental influences on alcohol use and the development of alcohol use problems during adolescence has been longitudinal studies of adolescent twins. One major finding from these types of studies is that environmental factors play a more salient role in the initiation of alcohol use than do genetic factors (Hopfer, Crowley, & Hewitt, 2003; Rhee et al., 2003; Rose & Dick, 2004–2005). However, genetic influences become increasingly important, and environmental influences become decreasingly important, when adolescents move from early, experimental alcohol use to more established drinking patterns (Rose & Dick, 2004–2005). These findings are similar to results obtained by Rhee and colleagues indicating that problem alcohol use was highly attributable to genetic factors.

In sum, emerging research illustrates how complex interactions between genetic predisposition and myriad environmental factors interact to influence alcohol use behaviors among adults and adolescents. The relationship between genetics and environment is particularly complicated in the context of constant developmental change that marks adolescence. Ongoing research in genetics should ultimately clarify the relative importance of different factors.

Physical Factors Affecting Behavior: Psychiatric Comorbidity

It has become increasingly apparent that psychiatric comorbidity is one of the most salient issues affecting the course and treatment of adolescent substance use problems. A review of community studies of substance use and other psychiatric disorders among adolescents revealed consistently high rates of comorbidity across studies (Armstrong & Costello, 2002). In a study of high school students, Lewinsohn, Hops, Roberts, Seeley, and Andrews (1993) found that the lifetime comorbidity rate for youth with SUDs was over 60%, whereas it was only 30% for youth without a SUD diagnosis. Similarly, Kandel et al. (1999) found the rates of comorbidity among heavy alcohol or drug using youth were nearly 3 times the comorbidity rates of youth who did not use alcohol or drugs.

The findings from community samples support research conducted with clinical samples of adolescents, which suggest that a majority of adolescents with SUDs meet diagnostic criteria for at least one other psychiatric disorder (Office of Applied Studies, 2003). The psychiatric disorders that most commonly co-occur in treated populations of adolescents with substance use problems are Conduct Disorder (32% to 59%) and mood disorders (35% to 61%; Wise, Cuffe, & Fischer, 2001). Anxiety disorders, Attention-Deficit/Hyperactivity Disorder (ADHD), and disruptive behavior disorders are also highly correlated with substance use problems in adolescents (Lewinsohn et al., 1993; Wise et al., 2001).

Although directionality of the relationship between SUDs and comorbid psychiatric disorders remains unclear (Kandel et al., 1997), it is evident that substance abusing adolescents with comorbid psychopathology use substances earlier, with greater frequency, and more chronically than substance abusing adolescents with no comorbidity (Greenbaum, Prange, Friedman, & Silver, 1991; Miller-Johnson, Lochman, Coie,

Terry, & Hyman, 1998). Moreover, recent research suggests that psychiatric comorbidity may negatively impact treatment response and outcome among adolescents with substance use problems. In particular, a number of studies indicate that externalizing disorders are associated with poor treatment response, retention, and outcomes among adolescents with substance use problems (Galaif, Hser, Grella, & Joshi, 2001; Kaminer, Tarter, Bukstein, & Kabene, 1992; Rounds-Bryant & Staab, 2001; Wise et al., 2001). The presence of Conduct Disorder was associated with regular posttreatment marijuana use in a study of 1,094 youth in outpatient, residential, and inpatient substance abuse treatment programs (Rounds-Bryant & Staab, 2001). Additionally, in a study conducted by Wise et al., substance abusing adolescents diagnosed with disruptive disorders had less success in a residential treatment program than their counterparts without a comorbid disruptive disorder. Likewise, a diagnosis of Conduct Disorder was positively correlated with treatment dropout among dually diagnosed youth in a residential program (Kaminer et al., 1992) as well as among youth in both the outpatient and residential programs in the Drug Abuse Treatment Outcome Studies for Adolescents (Galaif et al., 2001).

It is evident that the presence of co-occurring externalizing disorders impedes successful treatment of substance abuse problems among adolescents. However, findings about the influence of internalizing disorders such as mood disorders, adjustment disorders, and anxiety disorders on treatment-related outcomes are ambiguous. Kaminer et al. (1992) found that mood disorders and adjustment disorders were more prevalent among treatment completers than noncompleters in a sample of adolescents receiving inpatient substance abuse treatment. Likewise, the presence of internalizing disorders such as anxiety and depression was associated with higher rates of treatment completion for males in outpatient treatment (Friedman & Glickman, 1986). Similar findings were obtained by Blood and Cornwall (1994) in a study that examined treatment completion rates for youth receiving inpatient and day treatment services. In this study, high scores on the Internalizing scale from the Youth Self Report predicted treatment completion. In contrast, Fiegelman (1987) found that the presence of moderate to severe depressive symptomatology was associated with high rates of dropout from a day treatment program. Additionally, Dobkin, Chabot, Maliantovitch, and Craig (1998) found that depression and anxiety were associated with poorer treatment response among adolescents participating in an inpatient substance abuse treatment program. A comparison of substance abusers with no comorbidity, with comorbid externalizing disorders, and with comorbid internalizing and externalizing disorders revealed that the youth with no comorbidity had the best substance use outcomes at both the 6- and 12-months posttreatment (Rowe, Liddle, Greenbaum, & Henderson, 2004). In light of research illustrating the significant effect of co-occurring psychiatric disorders on each phase of adolescent substance use, it is evident that comorbidity is among the most compelling and challenging issues facing researchers and treatment providers in the area of adolescent substance use problems.

CULTURAL AND DIVERSITY ISSUES

Although teen alcohol and other drug involvement cuts across racial and ethnic lines, research consistently reveals that drug and alcohol use patterns are distinct for youth of different racial and ethnic backgrounds (Johnston et al., 2006; Office of Applied Studies, 2003; Warheit, Vega, Khoury, Gil, & Elfenbein, 1996). With the exception of marijuana, African American youth consistently demonstrate the lowest prevalence rates for alcohol and other substances, and non-Hispanic Whites have the highest rates of use for most substances. In contrast, the prevalence of substance use among Hispanic youth remains much less clear. Monitoring the Future (Johnston et al., 2006) results suggest that substance use among Hispanic teens is more similar to rates of use among non-Hispanic White youth, but the National Survey on Drug Use and Health (Substance Abuse and Mental Health Services Administration, 2006) findings indicate that rates of reported use among Hispanic teens are more similar to rates of their African American counterparts. In addition to racial and ethnic differences in substance use initiation, the prevalence of SUDs among adolescents also varies across racial and ethnic groups (Turner & Gil, 2002; Wagner et al., 2002). Research consistently indicates that non-Hispanic White youth have the highest rates of SUDs, and African American youth have the lowest. In general, rates of SUDs among Hispanic youth tend to fall between rates of non-Hispanic White and African American youth, and there are significant differences in rates of SUDs between foreign-born and U.S.-born Hispanic adolescents.

Different findings for Hispanic adolescents across studies may reflect the heterogeneity of Hispanic adolescents across the United States and may represent within-group differences associated with nativity, geography, and acculturation. Specifically, Vega, Gil, and Kolody (2002) indicate that by measuring U.S.-born and foreign-born Hispanics together, important subgroup differences in substance use go unnoticed. Studies that do examine substance use trends among subgroups of Hispanic adolescents consistently identify significant subgroup differences (Office of Applied Studies, 2002; Vega & Gil, 1998; Warheit et al., 1996). These studies indicate that reported substance use varies for Hispanic adolescents of different nationalities, as well as for immigrant versus U.S.-born Hispanic youth. According to the NSDUH , there were differences in reported adolescent substance use across Hispanic subgroups (Mexican, Puerto Rican, Central and South American, Cuban;, This is further supported by findings indicating that Cuban adolescents had higher reported substance use prevalence rates than Nicaraguan adolescents (Warheit et al., 1996). These findings should be interpreted with caution, as substance use differences among subgroups of Hispanic youth may reflect differences in geography or acculturation rather than nationality (Warheit & Gil, 1998; Warheit et al., 1996). For example, a study evaluating substance use patterns among Hispanic adolescents in different geographical regions of the United States found divergent trends across states (Vega et al., 2002). However, it has been suggested that the differences in substance use among Hispanic adolescents may be a function of acculturation level rather than nationality (Warheit et al., 1996). The potential importance of acculturation in onset and patterns of substance use has been demonstrated with both Hispanic adults (Vega, Alderete, Kolody, & Aguilar-Gaxiola, 1998) and adolescents (Warheit & Gil, 1998). For example, in a study examining lifetime use of cigarettes, alcohol, marijuana, and other drugs among multiethnic adolescent males, Warheit and Gil found statistically significant differences between U.S.-born Hispanics and foreign-born Hispanics for reported cigarette use, alcohol use, and marijuana use. In all instances, reported substance use was greater among U.S.-born Hispanic youth than their foreign-born counterparts, suggesting the potentially important influence of acculturation on the initiation of substance use among Hispanic adolescents.

To better understand substance use and the development of SUDs among ethnic minority youth, it is necessary to examine the factors associated with substance use among teens from different racial and ethnic groups. Risk and protective factors relevant to adolescent substance use have been classified by Hawkins and colleagues (1992) into two primary groups: (1) individual and interpersonal (e.g., personal characteristics and interpersonal relationships) risk factors and (2) contextual (e.g., societal and cultural) risk factors. The differential impact of these factors on the development of substance use problems among ethnic minority youth remains unclear. However, emerging research suggests that adolescent exposure and vulnerability to risk factors varies substantially across racial and ethnic groups (Gil, Vega, & Turner, 2002; Maddahian, Newcomb, & Bentler, 1988; Vega, Zimmerman, Warheit, Apospori, & Gil, 1993; Wallace & Muroff, 2002). Specifically, African American youth appear to be exposed to more contextual (Gil et al., 2002; Wallace & Muroff, 2002) and psychosocial risk factors, including exposure to major and traumatic life events (Gil et al., 2002; Turner & Lloyd, 2003). In contrast, non-Hispanic White youth seem to have greater exposure to individual and interpersonal risk factors (Maddahian et al., 1988; Wallace & Muroff, 2002). Among Hispanic adolescents, specific cultural factors (e.g., acculturation, nativity) may influence substance use, creating potentially important within-Hispanic-group differences in risks for substance use (Vega et al., 1998).

In addition, findings reveal that the cumulative effect of exposure to risk factors varies significantly across racial and ethnic groups of adolescents. While the cumulative effect of exposure to risk factors seems to be highly associated with substance use behaviors among non-Hispanic White and Hispanic youth, this relationship is much weaker for African American adolescents (Gil et al., 2002; Maddahian et al., 1988; Turner & Lloyd, 2003). A better understanding of the specific factors, including cultural factors, related to substance use behaviors among ethnically diverse groups of adolescents is a necessary step toward ensuring the development and delivery of culturally relevant substance abuse treatment.

BEHAVIORAL TREATMENT

The most common and most researched behavioral treatment models for adolescent substance use problems are the cognitive-behavioral therapies (CBT). There are variations across CBTs in the specifics of implementation, but the models share a general conceptual basis (i.e., the social learning perspective) and a set of techniques. As noted by Waldron and Kaminer (2004) in their informative review of CBTs for treating adolescent alcohol and drug use problems, cognitive-behavioral models conceptualize substance use as a learned behavior initiated and maintained by environmental factors. As a result, the circumstances surrounding drug or alcohol use, such as the setting, time, and place, are emphasized. These circumstances are used to conduct a functional analysis of substance use, with explicit attention to the antecedents and consequences (positive and negative) of alcohol and other drug use. Once the contingencies of substance use are identified, clients are trained in methods for managing urges and cravings and resisting use; these methods include a range of techniques from different learning perspectives (e.g., behavioral self-control, reinforcing alternative behaviors that compete with substance use, stress and temptation coping-skills training).

Operant models emphasize that the antecedents and consequences of substance use play an important role in contemporary CBTs for alcohol and drug use problems. Most CBTs also acknowledge the short- and long-term reinforcing potential of the physiological effects related to alcohol and drug ingestion. Treatment strategies derived exclusively from an operant model (e.g., contingency management; see

Ledgerwood & Petry, 2006; Petry et al., 2006) have shown considerable promise in treating drug problems for adults and have the potential to be effective in treating substance problems for teens. Broad CBT models assume that alcohol and drug use is influenced by operant factors such as social reinforcement and the direct experience of substance use as rewarding or punishing. However, contemporary CBT models increasingly incorporate concepts from social learning and social cognitive models such as the observation and imitation of models (e.g., peers, parents, siblings), cognitive expectancies concerning the effects of substance use, and self-efficacy about one's ability to successfully manage temptations to use.

Although there is variation among CBTs in the specifics of implementation, Waldron and Kaminer (2004) point out that most CBTs for substance use problems include the following components: (a) self-monitoring, (b) avoidance of stimulus cues, (c) altering reinforcement contingencies, and (d) coping-skills training to manage and resist urges to use. Moreover, CBTs often include training in additional substance use and life skills areas such as drug and alcohol refusal skills, communication and assertiveness, problem solving, mood regulation, and relapse prevention. Finally, CBTs characteristically rely on therapeutic techniques, including the use of modeling, behavior rehearsal, feedback, and homework assignments.

Despite key differences in design and methodology across empirical studies of the effectiveness of CBTs for treating adolescent substance use problems, Waldron and Kaminer (2004) conclude that existing research provides consistent evidence that both individual and group CBT produce significant and clinically meaningful reductions in teenage substance use. Despite ongoing controversy concerning potential iatrogenic effects of group therapy for problem youth (see Macgowan & Wagner, 2005), Waldron and Kaminer found no evidence that group CBT was less effective (or produced more untoward effects) than individual CBT. These authors suggest the following future research directions for CBTs for adolescent substance use problems: (a) the improvement of short- and long-term outcomes, (b) the enhancement of treatment motivation and engagement, and (c) the identification of mechanisms and processes associated with treatment response.

MEDICAL TREATMENT

The pharmacological treatment of SUDs has been a relatively neglected area of treatment research among adolescents with substance use problems; still, the use of medication to treat this population has increased over the last decade (Cornelius, Clark, Bukstein, & Salloum, 2005). Emerging research suggests that pharmacotherapy may indeed be an important aspect of treatment for specific subgroups of individuals with SUDs. One subgroup of adolescents who may benefit from pharmacotherapy are those with co-occurring psychiatric and substance use problems. As recognition about the high prevalence of comorbidity among youth with substance use problems increases, so does the importance of identifying effective interventions to treat the complex issues associated with having both substance use and psychiatric problems. Only recently have researchers begun to examine whether medications that have been effective in treating specific psychiatric disorders among children and adolescents will produce similar benefits when used to treat youth with comorbid psychiatric disorders and SUDs.

A comprehensive review conducted by Cornelius and colleagues (2005) describes the state of research examining pharmacological treatments for the psychiatric disorders most common during childhood and adolescence. Findings from two open-label studies indicate that the FDA-approved selective serotonin reuptake inhibitor antidepressant fluoxetine was associated with successful outcomes (decreased depressive symptoms and decreased alcohol use) among youth with co-occurring Major Depression and alcohol use disorders (Cornelius et al., 2001; Riggs, Mikulich, Coffman, & Crowley, 1997). Another study examined the influence of a stimulant medication among a sample of teens with ADHD and a SUD. Results indicated a decrease in ADHD symptomology but no significant changes in substance use behavior among teens taking the medication compared to a placebo control group (Riggs, Mikulich, & Hall, 2001). Unfortunately, to date there are no other controlled studies examining pharmacotherapy for dually diagnosed youth with ADHD and a SUD, so it is not possible to draw conclusions about the efficacy of such treatments. Moreover, there are no published studies examining the influence of medication on changes in substance use among youth evidencing some of the most prevalent forms of psychiatric comorbidity: co-occurring Conduct Disorder and a SUD and co-occurring anxiety and a SUD (Cornelius et al., 2005). However, because of the high prevalence of comorbidity among adolescents with substance use problems and the paucity of efficacious treatments for these youth, research in the area of pharmacotherapy is becoming increasingly consequential.

Historically, pharmacological interventions for adults have targeted four specific aspects of substance abuse treatment: (1) creating an aversive reaction to the abused substance, (2) substituting a medication for the abused substance, (3) blocking the positive effects of the abused substance, and (4) relieving the symptoms of withdrawal and craving (Kaminer, 1995). Although there is considerably less research examining the use of pharmacotherapy employing these strategies for treating SUDs among adolescents, existing studies suggest the potential utility of such interventions for treating adolescents who are dependent on heroin and other opioids (Marsch et al., 2005). A recent randomized clinical trial examined the differential influence of buprenorphine and clonidine on treatment retention and outcome among a sample of opioid-dependent adolescents participating in a behavioral therapy program based on the community reinforcement approach (Marsch et al., 2005). Study findings indicate that combining buprenorphine and behavioral therapy was significantly more efficacious in treating this population than was a combination of behavioral therapy and clonidine. Youth receiving the buprenorphine had higher rates of treatment retention and demonstrated greater rates of abstinence from opioids than their counterparts. Moreover, youth who were given buprenorphine were overwhelmingly more likely to initiate participation in an aftercare program where naltrexone was provided for relapse prevention.

In contrast, other pharmacological interventions associated with adolescent treatment are marked by a lack of supporting evidence and often controversy. For example, Kaminer (1995) indicates that using the medication disulfiram as an aversive therapy to prevent alcohol consumption is a common form of pharmacotherapy among adults but is often viewed as unethical when proposed to treat adolescents with alcohol use problems. Because evidence supporting the efficacy of disulfiram use in adults is moderate and the use of negative reinforcement or aversive therapies with children or adolescents is controversial, Kaminer suggests that it is highly unlikely that aversive pharmacotherapies such as disulfiram will be used regularly with alcohol-dependent adolescents. Moreover, although methadone maintenance is a common treatment for opioid dependence among adults, it is rare among adolescents

(Kaminer, 1995). This may be a result of strict guidelines for adolescents seeking this form of treatment. Guidelines indicate that any person under age 18 must have an official consent signed by a legal guardian and two documented attempts at short-term detoxification or drug-free treatment; in addition, a program physician must document that the youth is physiologically dependent on narcotic drugs (Kaminer, 1995).

It is evident that there remains a dearth of efficacious pharmacotherapies for adolescents with SUDs. However, the advancement of pharmacological research among adolescents with substance use problems is critical to efforts aimed at identifying potentially efficacious treatment options to address the complex needs of the most challenging subgroups of substance abusing adolescents: teens with comorbid psychiatric disorders and SUDs, and opioid- and other drug-dependent teens.

Finally, it is worth considering how the message "Stop taking the drugs that you like; instead, take the ones that we prescribe" may be interpreted by adolescents. Adolescents are quite sensitive and reactive when they detect such inconsistencies in authority figures' messages. Psychopharmacological interventions might be helpful in some cases, but it is important that the underlying rationale and behavioral targets of any prescribed medication be explained to the adolescent in the most developmentally sensitive manner possible.

Case Description

Case Introduction

Andrés, a 16-year-old Hispanic male, had just been expelled from the 11th grade when he was referred to the Alcohol Treatment Targeting Adolescents in Need (ATTAIN) program. This is a five-session cognitive-behavioral and motivational enhancement treatment program being investigated in a grant funded by the National Institute of Alcohol Abuse and Alcoholism (R01 AA12180, PI Wagner). Andrés was court-mandated to treatment after being arrested on charges of possession of marijuana with intent to sell. At the time of his initial assessment, he described himself as a U.S.-born Hispanic White and was living with his mother and father, both of whom were born in Ecuador. He described his family as "a little religious" and reported that they attended services weekly. Additional family activities included "watching television together" and "going out to eat."

Presenting Complaints

When asked about his presenting complaints, Andrés and his mother recalled his arrest, stating that he was charged with intent to sell because of the large amount of marijuana he was carrying. He reported regular and considerable involvement with both alcohol and marijuana use, though he noted that he had begun to prefer using alcohol following his arrest. The primary negative consequences he reported in relation to his substance use were his expulsion, his arrest, and not having enough money because he spent it on alcohol and marijuana. When asked to describe the pros of his substance use, he reported, "I don't

(continued)

have to deal with my problems or pay attention," and "It helps me calm down and relax." He added, "I don't go out of my way for school. I just don't care about it. But, in my house, like let's say I get mad at my dad, and we end up fighting or something, and my friends are there, or I just call them up and say, 'Hey come pick me up.' And we hang out at his house and just drink or something and I don't pay attention. I just start talking to my friends."

History

The referral to ATTAIN was not Andrés's first experience in the juvenile justice system. In the year prior to his referral, he reported that he spent 5 days in secure detention, although he did not specify the circumstances surrounding the detainment. Andrés indicated that he had had no previous counseling for substance use or mental health problems. He also reported that both of his parents had used alcohol, tobacco, and marijuana in the past, although he denied that they used any other substances. He added that this alleged use had never caused problems for the family. He stated that he first used alcohol on his own at age 12, first used marijuana at age 14, and had tried cocaine once in the past year but did not like it. He denied involvement with any other substances, including tobacco. His current substance use pattern, which involved using alcohol or marijuana on most days of the week, had been established for approximately 1 year.

Assessment

Andrés's first appointment with ATTAIN consisted of an evaluation session. He arrived at the assessment session with his mother so that she, as his legal guardian, would be able to sign the consent forms necessary to admit him into the program and provide her perspective on Andrés's problems. At the start of the session, issues related to confidentiality, the right to withdraw from the program, and voluntary consent were discussed and agreed upon. The exceptions to confidentiality were identified as risk of harm to self or others, someone potentially harming him (e.g., physical or sexual abuse), or an adult placing him in situations in which he is under pressure to use alcohol or other drugs. Using the procedures and instruments described earlier in the Diagnosis and Assessment section, the clinician obtained information from Andrés and his mother about psychiatric symptomatology (including depression and suicidality), substance use, involvement with the juvenile justice system, family dynamics, peer relations, social support, cognitive functioning, and demographics. Andrés was asked extensive questions about psychiatric symptomatology to ensure that he was not in any danger or in need of more intensive treatment. He denied symptoms of depression and suicidality. The only *DSM-IV* disorders for which he met diagnostic criteria were Psychoactive Substance Dependence (Marijuana), Psychoactive Substance Dependence (Alcohol), and Conduct Disorder.

Case Conceptualization

Consistent with the CBT tenets underlying the ATTAIN program, Andrés's alcohol and marijuana use problems were conceptualized as arising from a complex interplay of social and historical influences. Based on findings from the assessment and Andrés's self-report, the social influence of peers appeared to be of particular importance in determining his substance use behavior. In the client's own words, "My dad thinks and my mom says, 'Why don't you start hanging out with the kids that you grew up with since elementary (school),' but [what my parents don't know is] they all ended up to be messed up kids. They're druggies, or they're in jail, or they're dead. My social life, though, everyone I know smokes. So if I go to school, everyone is there smoking a blunt." To address the range of factors influencing his substance use, standard CBT therapeutic techniques such as functional analysis, decisional balance exercises (i.e., weighing the pros and cons of using and not using), behavior rehearsal, feedback, and homework assignments were employed.

Course of Treatment and Assessment of Progress

Andrés attended ATTAIN sessions regularly and completed the treatment program's five sessions in a timely manner. At his request, two additional meetings with the therapist took place to revisit and review material from the initial five sessions. Because it derives from an NIAAA-funded randomized clinical trial, the ATTAIN treatment is manualized, although there is considerable room for the individualization of treatment in response to the client's presenting problems and clinical needs. The session-by-session format of the ATTAIN program is presented in Table 16.1.

Assessment of Andrés's progress was made by measuring his substance use before, during, and after treatment.

Table 16.2 presents a summary of his alcohol use data (the substance he described currently using most often), which demonstrate that he benefited considerably from his involvement in the program.

Complicating Factors (Including Medical Management)

As mentioned in the discussion of psychiatric comorbidity, the presence of co-occurring psychiatric and substance use disorders among adolescents represents a significant challenge to efforts aimed at providing effective substance abuse treatment. In particular, externalizing disorders such as Conduct Disorder are consistently associated with poor treatment response, retention, and outcomes among adolescents with substance use problems (Galaif et al., 2001; Kaminer et al., 1992; Rounds-Bryant & Staab, 2001; Wise et al., 2001). It is estimated that 22% to 82% of teens with substance use problems have at least one additional psychiatric diagnosis (Office of Applied Studies, 2003). The most common co-occurring psychiatric disorders among treatment samples of adolescents with substance use problems are Conduct Disorder (32% to 59%) and mood disorders (35% to 61%; Wise et al., 2001). As such, psychiatric comorbidity is the norm rather than the exception among substance abusing teens in treatment. This is particularly concerning because of the dearth of empirical support for efficacious interventions targeting dually diagnosed adolescents (Cornelius et al., 2005). As a result, co-occurring psychiatric disorders (and their clinical management) represent a key complicating factor in attempts to treat adolescent substance use problems.

(continued)

Table 16.1
MSSession Content of the ATTAIN Program

Session 1
Things That Are Important to Me: Exercise to identify personal priorities.
Decision to Change: Decisional balance exercise to identify the good and not so good things about using and not using.[a]
Goals for Change Questionnaire: Exercise to identify how important making a change in substance use is and self-efficacy about making these changes.[a]
Session Check-In: Self-monitoring exercise allowing for functional analysis of substance use behavior during the week. Weekly goal for change is identified.[b]
Personalized Feedback Summaries: Norm-based feedback on client's substance use level based on time line follow-back assessment information.

Session 2
Brief Situational Confidence Questionnaire (profile review): Profile regarding self-confidence not to use in high-risk situations.
Triggers/High-Risk Exercise: Exercise to identify personal antecedents and consequences for use.
Options and Actions Plan: Development of plan to manage substance use in high-risk situations.
Climbing Mount Success: Graphic to accompany discussion of challenges regarding making changes in substance use.
Where Are You Now Scale: Question to evaluate client perception of severity of substance use problems; compared with response at time of assessment.[a]

Session 3
Feeling Badly If You Slip: Relapse prevention exercise to manage slips in attempts to change substance use behavior.
Communication Skills, Rights, and Practicing Better Communication: Exercises to teach general and specific aspects of effective communication.
Change Plan Worksheet: Exercise to teach how to identify a specific problem to work on and define steps for constructively addressing the problem.

Session 4
Brief Situational Confidence Questionnaire: Completion of second questionnaire about situational drug use patterns; profile reviewed in Session 5.[a]
General Causes of Stress: Exercise identifying specific sources of stress.
Coping with Stress/Stress Prevention: Information on stress management.
Future Goals: Identification of 1-month, 1-year, and 5-year goals for substance use reduction and general life goals.

Session 5
Decision to Change: Decisional balance exercise completed in the 1st session revisited and discussed.[a]
Brief Situational Confidence Questionnaire Profile Review: Comparison of situational drug use profiles at assessment and time of the 4th session.[a]
Goals for Change: Exercise to identify how important making a change in use is and self-efficacy about making changes.[a]
Where Are You Now Scale: Question to measure client's perception of the severity of his or her substance use problem; compared with 2 previous responses[a]
Support Strategy: Listing of social supports that can help to maintain changes.
Resources for Support: Information about other substance use treatment.

[a]Completed several times and responses compared at different points in the program.
[b]Completed in each session.

Table 16.2
Andrés's Substance Use before, during, and after ATTAIN Participation

Maximum Number of Drinks per Drinking Day

Pretreatment	21
Posttreatment	19
3-month follow-up	4
6-month follow-up	5

Longest Period of Continuous Abstinence (Days in 90-Day Span)

Pretreatment	34
Posttreatment	37
3-month follow-up	53
6-month follow-up	62

Average Number of Drinks per Drinking Day

Pretreatment	8.7
Posttreatment	11.3
3-month follow-up	2.0
6-month follow-up	4.3

Percentage of All Days Drinking Occurred (90-Day Span)

Pretreatment	13.3
Posttreatment	4.0
3-month follow-up	3.2
6-month follow-up	1.8

Managed Care Considerations

From the managed care perspective, important considerations include (a) appropriate diagnostic labeling, (b) appropriate intensity of care (i.e., outpatient, partial hospital, inpatient), and (c) appropriate duration of care. At present, there is no consensus among adolescent treatment experts in regard to any of these considerations. While adolescents must receive diagnoses in order to receive services under managed care, substance use diagnoses and diagnosis for related problems can have long-term, serious consequences. Thus, it is recommended that assessment and treatment services, when provided under the managed care system, adhere as closely as possible to current best practices.

Follow-Up

The literature indicates that 50% of teenagers treated for substance use problems will relapse within 3 months of the completion of treatment, and 66% will relapse within 6 months of the completion of treatment (Brown, Mott, & Myers, 1990; Brown et al., 1989; Latimer, Newcomb, Winters, & Stinchfield, 2000). Although treatment can be effective for teenagers with substance use problems, relapse rates remain high, with most treated adolescents returning to alcohol or other drug use between 3 and 6 months after the completion of treatment. Thus, it is recommended that follow-up contact with adolescents treated for substance use problems extend to at least 6 months posttreatment. Moreover, Brown and colleagues (1989, 1990) have found that for teens who do relapse, exposure to alcohol and other drug use in their posttreatment social environment and

(continued)

lack of involvement in self-help groups are key determinants of use. Again, this speaks to the need for long-term follow-up care, as well as the importance of the posttreatment environment in determining the course of posttreatment substance use trajectories.

SUMMARY

This chapter has reviewed some of the key issues and concerns relating to the assessment, conceptualization, and treatment of adolescents with alcohol and other drug use problems. Most adolescents will have some experience with alcohol or other drug use, and most of those who use will not develop *DSM-IV*-defined psychoactive substance use disorders. Unfortunately, some teenagers who use alcohol or other drugs will end up demonstrating significant (and diagnosable) problems related to their substance involvement. At present there is limited consensus on how best to distinguish a teen substance user from a teen substance abuser. Historically, attempts to assess, conceptualize, and treat teens with substance use problems have relied on approaches originally designed for use with adult substance abusers; understandably, the developmental appropriateness of these approaches has been called into question. Fortunately, the past decade has seen a dramatic increase in the availability of developmentally informed assessment and intervention methods for addressing adolescent substance use problems. Among those methods with the greatest empirical support are cognitive-behavioral therapies. Ongoing research involving adolescents with SUDs should permit more definitive statements about the efficacy of CBT for this population in the very near future.

REFERENCES

Abrams, D. B., & Niaura, R. S. (1987). Social learning theory. In H. T. Blane & K. E. Leonard (Eds.), *Psychological theories of drinking and alcoholism* (pp. 131–178). New York: Guilford Press.

American Psychiatric Association. (2000). *Diagnostic and statistical manual of mental disorders* (4th ed., text rev.). Washington, DC: Author.

Armstrong, T. D., & Costello, E. J. (2002). Community studies on adolescent substance use, abuse, or dependence and psychiatric comorbidity. *Journal of Consulting and Clinical Psychology, 70*(6), 1224–1239.

Averna, S., & Hesselbrock, V. (2001). The relationship of perceived social support to substance use in offspring of alcoholics. *Addictive Behaviors, 26,* 363–374.

Bailey, J. A., & McCloskey, L. A. (2005). Pathways to adolescent substance use among sexually abused girls. *Journal of Abnormal Child Psychology, 33*(1), 39–53.

Bailey, S. L., Martin, C. S., Lynch, K. G., & Pollock, N. K. (2000). Reliability and concurrent validity of DSM-IV subclinical symptom ratings for alcohol use disorders among adolescents. *Alcoholism: Clinical and Experimental Research, 24,* 1795–1802.

Bandura, A. (1977). Self-efficacy: Toward a unified theory of behavioral change. *Psychological Bulletin, 84,* 191–215.

Bandura, A. (1997). *Self-efficacy: The exercise of control.* New York: Freeman.

Bandura, A. (1999). A sociocognitive analysis of substance abuse: An agentic perspective. *Psychological Science, 10*(3), 214–217.

Barnes, G. M., & Welte, J. W. (1986). Adolescent alcohol abuse: Subgroup differences and relationships to other problem behaviors. *Journal of Adolescent Research, 1,* 79–94.

Baumrind, D. (1991). The influence of parenting style on adolescent competence and substance use. *Journal of Early Adolescence, 11,* 56–95.

Beitchman, J. H., Zucker, K. J., Hood, J. E., daCosta, G. A., Ackman, D., & Cassavia, E. (1992). A review of the long-term effects of child sexual abuse. *Child Abuse and Neglect, 16,* 101–118.

Blood, L., & Cornwall, A. (1994). Pretreatment variables that predict completion of an adolescent substance abuse treatment program. *Journal of Nervous and Mental Diseases, 182*(1), 14–19.

Brandon, T. H., Herzog, T. A., Irvin, J. E., & Gwailtney, C. J. (2004). Cognitive and social learning models of drug dependence: Implications for the assessment of tobacco dependence in adolescents. *Addiction, 99*(Suppl. 1), 51–77.

Brown, S. A. (1993). Recovery patterns in adolescent substance abuse. In J. S. Baer, G. A. Marlatt, & R. J. McMahon (Eds.), *Addictive behaviors across the life span* (pp. 160–183). Newbury Park, CA: Sage.

Brown, S. A. (2004). Measuring youth outcomes from alcohol and drug treatment [Review on conceptual, design and measurement issues critical in optimizing the study of treatment outcomes for alcohol and drug abusing youths]. *Addiction, 99*(Suppl. 2), 38–46.

Brown, S. A., Goldman, M. S., Inn, A., & Anderson, L. R. (1980). Expectations of reinforcement from alcohol: Their domain and relation to drinking patterns. *Journal of Consulting and Clinical Psychology, 48,* 419–426.

Brown, S. A., Mott, M. A., & Myers, M. G. (1990). Adolescent alcohol and drug treatment outcome. In R. R. Watson (Ed.), *Drug and alcohol abuse prevention, drug and alcohol abuse reviews* (pp. 373–403). Clifton, NJ: Humana.

Brown, S. A., Myers, M. G., Lippke, L., Tapert, S. F., Steward, D. G., & Vik, P. W. (1998). Psychometric evaluation of the Customary Drinking and Drug Use Record (CDDR): A measure of adolescent alcohol and drug involvement. *Journal of Studies on Alcohol, 59,* 427–438.

Brown, S. A., Vik, P. W., & Creamer, V. A. (1989). Characteristics of relapse following adolescent substance abuse treatment. *Addictive Behaviors, 14,* 291–300.

Carey, K. B., & Carey, M. P. (1993). Changes in self-efficacy resulting from unaided attempts to quit smoking. *Psychology of Addictive Behaviors, 7,* 219–224.

Christiansen, B. A., Goldman, M. S., & Inn, A. (1982). Development of alcohol-related expectancies in adolescents: Separating pharmacological from social-learning influences. *Journal of Consulting and Clinical Psychology, 50*(3), 336–344.

Chung, T., Colby, S. M., Barnett, N. P., Rohsenow, J., Spirito, A., & Monti, P. M. (2000). Screening adolescents for problem drinking: Performance of brief screens against DSM-IV alcohol diagnoses. *Journal of Studies on Alcohol, 61,* 579–587.

Clark, D. B., Cornelius, J. R., Kirisci, L., & Tarter, R. E. (2004). Childhood risk categories for substance involvement: A general liability typology. *Drug and Alcohol Dependence, 77,* 13–21.

Clark, D. B., Parker, A. M., & Lynch, K. G. (1999). Psychopathology, substance use, and substance related problems. *Journal of Clinical Child Psychology, 28,* 333–341.

Clark, H. W., Horton, A. M., Dennis, M., & Babor, T. F. (2002). Moving from research to practice just in time: The treatment of cannabis use disorders comes of age. *Addiction, 97*(Suppl. 1), 1–3.

Clayton, R. R. (1992). Transitions in drug use: Risk and protective factors. In M. Glantz & R. Pickens (Eds.), *Vulnerability to drug abuse* (pp. 15–51). Washington, DC: American Psychological Association.

Cornelius, J. R., Bukstein, O. G., Birmaher, B., Salloum, I. M., Lynch, K., Pollock, N. K., et al. (2001). Fluoxetine in adolescents with major depression and an alcohol use disorder: An open label trial. *Addictive Behaviors, 26,* 735–739.

Cornelius, J. R., Clark, D. B., Bukstein, O. G., & Salloum, I. M. (2005). Treatment of co-occurring alcohol, drug, and psychiatric disorders. In M. Galanter (Ed.), *Recent developments in alcoholism: Vol. 17. Alcohol problems in adolescents and young adults—Epidemiology, neurobiology, prevention, treatment* (pp. 349–365). New York: Kluwer Academic/Plenum Press.

Dennis, M., Dawud-Noursi, S., Muck, R. D., & McDermeit, M. (2003). The need for developing and evaluating adolescent treatment models. In S. J. Stevens & A. R. Morral (Eds.), *Adolescent substance abuse treatment in the United States: Exemplary models from a national evaluation study* (pp. 3–34). New York: Haworth Press.

Dennis, M. L., Funk, R., Godley, S. H., Godley, M. D., & Waldron, H. (2004). Cross-validation of the alcohol and cannabis use measures in the Global Appraisal of Individual Needs (GAIN) and Timeline Followback (TLFB; Form 90) among adolescents in substance abuse treatment. *Addiction, 99*(Suppl. 2), 120–128.

DiClemente, C. C., & Hughes, S. O. (1990). Stages of change profiles in outpatient alcoholism treatment. *Journal of Substance Abuse, 2*, 217–235.

Dobkin, P. L., Chabot, L., Maliantovitch, K., & Craig, W. (1998). Predictors of outcome in drug treatment of adolescent inpatients. *Psychological Reports, 83*(1), 175–186.

Edenberg, H. J., & Kranzler, H. R. (2005). The contribution of genetics to addiction therapy approaches. *Pharmacology and Therapeutics, 108*(1), 86–93.

Engels, R. C, van der Vorst, H., Deković, M., & Meeus, W. (2007). Correspondence in collateral and self-reports on alcohol consumption: A within-family analysis. *Addictive Behaviors, 32*, 1016–1030.

Fiegelman, W. (1987). Day-care treatment for multiple drug abusing adolescents: Social factors linked with completing treatment. *Journal of Psychoactive Drugs, 19*(4), 335–344.

Foroud, T., Edenberg, H. J., Goate, A., Rice, J., Flury, L., Koller, D. L., et al. (2000). Alcoholism susceptibility loci: Confirmation studies in a replicate sample and further mapping. *Alcoholism: Clinical and Experimental Research, 24*, 933–945.

Foxcroft, D. R., & Lowe, G. (1991). Adolescent drinking behavior and family socialization factors: A meta-analysis. *Journal of Adolescence, 14*(3), 255–273.

Friedman, A. S., & Glickman, N. W. (1986). Program characteristics for successful treatment of adolescent drug abuse. *Journal of Nervous and Mental Diseases, 174*(11), 669–679.

Galaif, E. R., Hser, Y. I., Grella, C. E., & Joshi, V. (2001). Prospective risk factors and treatment outcomes among adolescents in DATOS-A. *Journal of Adolescent Research, 16*(6), 661–678.

Getz, J. G., & Bray, J. H. (2005). Predicting heavy alcohol use among adolescents. *American Journal of Orthopsychiatry, 75*(1), 102–116.

Gil, A. G., Vega, W. A., & Turner, R. J. (2002). Early and mid-adolescence risk factors for later substance abuse by African Americans and European Americans. *Public Health Report, 117*(S1), S15–S29.

Greenbaum, P. E., Prange, M. E., Friedman, R. M., & Silver, S. E. (1991). Substance abuse prevalence and comorbidity with other psychiatric disorders among adolescents with severe emotional disturbances. *Journal of the American Academy of Child and Adolescent Psychiatry, 30*, 575–583.

Hallikainen, T., Saito, T., Lachman, H. M., Volavka, J., Pohjalainen, T., Ryynanen, O. P., et al. (1999). Association between low activity serotonin transporter promoter genotype and early onset alcoholism with habitual impulsive violent behavior. *Molecular Psychiatry, 4*, 385–388.

Hawkins, J. D., Catalano, R. F., & Miller, J. Y. (1992). Risk and protective factors for alcohol and other drug problems in adolescence and early adulthood: Implications for substance abuse prevention. *Psychological Bulletin, 112*(1), 64–105.

Hays, R. D., & Ellickson, P. L. (1996). What is adolescent alcohol misuse in the United States according to the experts? *Alcohol and Alcoholism, 31*, 297–303.

Hopfer, C. J., Crowley, T. J., & Hewitt, J. K. (2003). Review of twin and adoption studies of adolescent substance use. *Journal of the American Academy of Child and Adolescent Psychiatry, 42,* 710–719.

Jainchill, N., Hawke, J., De Leon, G., & Yagelka, J. (2000). Adolescents in therapeutic communities: One-year posttreatment outcomes. *Journal of Psychoactive Drugs, 32*(1), 81–94.

Johnston, L. D., O'Malley, P. M., Bachman, J. G., & Schulenberg, J. E. (2006). *Monitoring the Future national survey results on drug use, 1975–2005: Vol. I: Secondary school students* (NIH Publication No. 06-5883). Bethesda, MD: National Institute on Drug Abuse.

Kaminer, Y. (1994). *Adolescent substance abuse: A comprehensive guide to theory and practice.* New York: Plenum Press.

Kaminer, Y. (1995). Issues in the pharmacological treatment of adolescent substance abuse. *Journal of Child and Adolescent Psychopharmacology, 5*(2), 93–106.

Kaminer, Y., Tarter, R. E., Bukstein, O. G., & Kabene, M. (1992). Comparison between treatment completers and noncompleters among dually diagnosed substance-abusing adolescents. *Journal of the American Academy of Child and Adolescent Psychiatry, 31*(6), 1046–1049.

Kaminer, Y., Wagner, E., Plummer, B., & Seifer, R. (1993). Validation of the Teen Addiction Severity Index (T-ASI): Preliminary findings. *American Journal on Addictions, 2,* 250–254.

Kandel, D. B., Johnson, J. G., Bird, H. R., Canino, G., Goodman, S. H., Lahey, B. B., et al. (1997). Psychiatric disorders associated with substance use among children and adolescents: Findings from the Methods for the Epidemiology of Child and Adolescent Disorders (MECA) Study. *Journal of Abnormal Child Psychology, 25*(2), 121–132.

Kandel, D. B., Johnson, J. G., Bird, H. R., Weissman, M. M., Goodman, S. H., Lahey, B. B., et al. (1999). Psychiatric comorbidity among adolescents with substance use disorders: Findings from the MECA study. *Journal of the American Academy of Child and Adolescent Psychiatry, 38,* 693–699.

Kaplan, S. J., Pelcovitz, D., & Labruna, V. (1999). Child and adolescent abuse and neglect research: A review of the past 10 years. *Journal of the American Academy of Child and Adolescent Psychiatry, 8,* 1214–1222.

Kilpatrick, D. G., Acierno, R., Saunders, B. E., Resnick, H. S., Best, C. L., & Schnurr, P. P. (2000). Risk factors for adolescent substance abuse and dependence: Data from a national sample. *Journal of Consulting and Clinical Psychology, 68,* 19–30.

Latimer, W. W., Newcomb, M., Winters, K. C., & Stinchfield, R. D. (2000). Adolescent substance abuse treatment outcome: The role of substance abuse problem severity, psychosocial, and treatment factors. *Journal of Consulting and Clinical Psychology, 68,* 684–696.

Latimer, W. W., Winters, K. C., Stinchfield, R., & Traver, R. E. (2000). Demographic, individual, and interpersonal predictors of adolescent alcohol and marijuana use following treatment. *Psychology of Addictive Behaviors, 14*(2), 162–173.

Ledgerwood, D., & Petry, N. (2006). Does contingency management affect motivation to change substance use? *Drug and Alcohol Dependence, 83,* 65–72.

Lewinsohn, P. M., Hops, H., Roberts, R. E., Seeley, J. R., & Andrews, J. A. (1993). Adolescent psychopathology: Pt. I. *Journal of Abnormal Psychology, 102,* 133–144.

Macgowan, M. J., & Wagner, E. F. (2005). Iatrogenic effects of group treatment on adolescents with conduct and substance use problems: A review of the literature and a presentation of a model. *Journal of Evidence Based Social Work, 2,* 79–90.

Maddahian, E., Newcomb, M. D., & Bentler, P. M. (1988). Risk factors for substance use: Ethnic differences among adolescents. *Journal of Substance Abuse, 1,* 11–23.

Marlatt, G. A., Baer, J. S., & Quigley, L. A. (1995). Self-efficacy and addictive behavior. In A. Bandura (Ed.), *Self-efficacy in changing societies* (pp. 289–315). New York: Cambridge University Press.

Marlatt, G. A., & Rohsenow, D. J. (1980). Cognitive processes in alcohol use: Expectancy and the balanced placebo design. In K. N. Mello (Ed.), *Advances in substance abuse: Behavioral and biology research* (pp. 159–199). Greenwich, CT: JAI Press.

Marsch, L. A., Bickel, W. K., Badger, G. J., Stothart, M. E., Quesnel, K. J., Stanger, C., et al. (2005). Comparison of pharmacological treatments for opioid-dependent adolescents. *Archives of General Psychiatry, 62,* 1157–1164.

Marshal, M. P., & Chassin, L. (2000). Peer influence on adolescent alcohol use: The moderating role of parental support and discipline. *Applied Developmental Science, 4,* 80–88.

Martin, C. S., & Winters, K. C. (1998). Diagnosis and assessment of alcohol use disorders among adolescents. *Alcohol Health and Research World, 22,* 95–105.

Miller, W. R., & Rollnick, S. (Eds.). (2002). *Motivational interviewing: Preparing people for change* (2nd ed.). New York: Guilford Press.

Miller-Johnson, S., Lochman, J. E., Coie, J. D., Terry, R., & Hyman, C. (1998). Comorbidity of conduct and depressive problems at sixth grade: Substance use outcomes across adolescence. *Journal of Abnormal Child Psychology, 26*(3), 221–232.

Nash, S. G., McQueen, A., & Bray, J. H. (2005). Pathways to adolescent alcohol use: Family environment, peer influence, and parental expectations. *Journal of Adolescent Health, 37,* 19–28.

Newcomb, M. D., Huba, G. J., & Bentler, P. M. (1986). Life change events among adolescents: An empirical consideration of some methodological issues. *Journal of Nervous and Mental Diseases, 174*(5), 280–289.

Niaura, R. (2000). Cognitive social learning and related perspectives on drug craving. *Addiction, 95*(Suppl. 2), S155–S163.

Oetting, E. R., & Beauvais, F. (1987). Peer cluster theory, socialization, characteristics, and adolescent drug use: A path analysis. *Journal of Counseling Psychology, 34,* 205–213.

Office of Applied Studies. (2002). *Youth marijuana admissions by race and ethnicity.* Retrieved March 28, 2004, from http://www.oas.samhsa.gov.

Office of Applied Studies. (2003). *National Survey on Drug Use and Health (NSDUH).* Retrieved March 28, 2003, from http://www.samsha.org.

Oroszi, G., & Goldman, D. (2004). Alcoholism: Genes and mechanisms. *Pharmacogenomics, 5*(8), 1037–1048.

Petry, N., Alessi, S., Carroll, K., Hanson, T., MacKinnon, S., Rounsaville, B., et al. (2006). Contingency management treatments: Reinforcing abstinence versus adherence with goal-related activities. *Journal of Consulting and Clinical Psychology, 74,* 592–601.

Rhee, S. H., Hewitt, J. K., Young, S. E., Corley, R. P., Crowley, T. J., & Stallings, M. C. (2003). Genetic and environmental influences on substance initiation, use, and problem use in adolescents. *Archives of General Psychiatry, 60,* 1256–1264.

Riggs, P. D., Mikulich, S. K., Coffman, L. M., & Crowley, T. J. (1997). Fluoxetine in drug-dependent delinquents with major depression: An open trial. *Journal of Child and Adolescent Psychopharmacology, 7,* 87–95.

Riggs, P. D., Mikulich, S. K., & Hall, S. (2001, June). Effects of pemoline on ADHD, antisocial behaviors, and substance use in adolescents with conduct disorder and substance use disorder. Paper presented at the 63rd annual scientific meeting of the College on Problems of Drug Dependence, Scottsdale, AZ.

Rose, R. J., & Dick, D. M. (2004–2005). Gene-environment interplay in adolescent drinking behavior. *Adolescent Research and Health, 28*(4), 222–229.

Rounds-Bryant, J. L., & Staab, J. (2001). Patient characteristics and treatment outcomes for African-American, Hispanic, and White adolescents in DATOS-A. *Journal of Adolescent Research, 16,* 624–641.

Rowe, C. L., Liddle, H. A., Greenbaum, P. E., & Henderson, C. E. (2004). Impact of psychiatric comorbidity on treatment of adolescent drug abusers. *Journal of Substance Abuse Treatment, 26*, 129–140.

Sander, T., Harms, H., Dufeu, P., Kuhn, S., Hoehe, M., Lesch, K. P., et al. (1998). Serotonin transporter gene variants in alcohol-dependent subjects with dissocial personality disorder. *Biological Psychiatry, 43*, 908–912.

Sitharthan, T., & Kavanaugh, D. J. (1990). Role of self-efficacy in predicting outcomes from a programme for controlled drinking. *Drug and Alcohol Dependence, 27*, 87–94.

Stephens, R. S., Wertz, J. S., & Roffman, R. A. (1995). Self-efficacy and marijuana cessation: A construct validity analysis. *Journal of Consulting and Clinical Psychology, 63*, 1022–1031.

Stinchfield, R., & Winters, K. C. (2003). Predicting adolescent drug abuse treatment outcome with the Personal Experience Inventory (PEI). *Journal of Child and Adolescent Substance, 13*(2), 103–120.

Substance Abuse and Mental Health Services Administration. (2006). *Results from the 2005 National Survey on Drug Use and Health: National Findings* (Office of Applied Studies, NSDUH Series H-30, DHHS Publication No. SMA 06-4194). Rockville, MD: Author.

Tarter, R., & Hegedus, A. M. (1991). The Drug Use Screening Inventory: Its applications in the evaluation and treatment of alcohol and other drug abuse. *Alcohol Health and Research World, 15*, 65–75.

Turner, R. J., & Gil, A. G. (2002). Psychiatric and substance use disorders in south Florida: Racial/ethnic and gender contrasts in a young adult cohort. *Archives of General Psychiatry, 59*, 43–50.

Turner, R. J., & Lloyd, D. A. (1995). Lifetime traumas and mental health: The significance of cumulative adversity. *Journal of Health and Social Behavior, 36*(4), 360–376.

Turner, R. J., & Lloyd, D. A. (2003). Cumulative adversity and drug dependence in young adults: Racial/ethnic contrasts. *Addiction, 98*, 305–315.

Urberg, K., Goldstein, M. S., & Toro, P. A. (2005). Supportive relationships as a moderator of the effects of parent and peer drinking on adolescent drinking. *Journal of Research on Adolescence, 15*(1), 1–19.

Urberg, K. A., Luo, Q., Pilgrim, C., & Degirmencioglu, S. M. (2003). A two-stage model of peer influence in adolescent substance use: Individual and relationship-specific differences in susceptibility to influence. *Addictive Behaviors, 28*, 1243–1256.

Vega, W. A., Alderete, E., Kolody, B., & Aguilar-Gaxiola, S. (1998). Illicit drug use among Mexicans and Mexican Americans in California: The effects of gender and acculturation. *Addiction, 93*(12), 1839–1850.

Vega, W. A., & Gil, A. G. (1998). *Drug use and ethnicity in early adolescence.* New York: Plenum Press.

Vega, W. A., Gil, A. G., & Kolody, B. (2002). What do we know about Latino drug use? Methodological evaluation of state databases. *Hispanic Journal of Behavioral Sciences, 24*(4), 395–408.

Vega, W. A., Zimmerman, R. S., Warheit, G. J., Apospori, E., & Gil, A. G. (1993). Risk factors for early adolescent drug use in four ethnic and racial groups. *American Journal of Public Health, 83*, 185–189.

Wagner, E. F. (2003). Conceptualizing alcohol treatment research for Hispanic/Latino adolescents. *Alcoholism: Clinical and Experimental Research, 27*, 1349–1352.

Wagner, E. F., & Kassel, J. D. (1995). Substance use and abuse. In R. T. Ammerman & M. Hersen (Eds.), *Handbook of child behavior therapy in the psychiatric setting* (pp. 367–388). New York: Wiley.

Wagner, E. F., Lloyd, D. A., & Gil, A. G. (2002). Racial/ethnic and gender differences in the incidence and onset age of DSM-IV alcohol use disorder symptoms among adolescents. *Journal of Studies on Alcohol, 63,* 609–619.

Waldron, H., & Kaminer, Y. (2004). On the learning curve: Cognitive behavioral therapies for adolescent substance abuse. *Addiction, 99*(Suppl. 2), 93–105.

Wallace, J. M., & Muroff, J. R. (2002). Preventing substance abuse among African American children and youth: Race differences in risk factor exposure and vulnerability. *Journal of Primary Prevention, 22*(3), 235–261.

Warheit, G. J., & Gil, A. G. (1998). Substance use and other social deviance. In W. A. Vega & A. G. Gil (Eds.), *Drug use and ethnicity in early adolescence* (pp. 37–68). New York: Plenum Press.

Warheit, G. J., Vega, W. A., Khoury, E. L., Gil, A. A., & Elfenbein, P. H. (1996). A comparative analysis of cigarette, alcohol, and illicit drug use among an ethnically diverse sample of Hispanic, African-American, and non-Hispanic White adolescents. *Journal of Drug Issues, 26*(4), 901–922.

Widom, C. S., Weiler, B. L., & Cottler, L. B. (1999). Childhood victimization and drug abuse: A comparison of prospective and retrospective findings. *Journal of Consulting and Clinical Psychology, 67*(6), 867–880.

Wills, T. A., Resko, J. A., Ainette, M. G., & Mendoza, D. (2004). Role of parent support and peer support in adolescent substance use: A test of mediated effects. *Psychology of Addictive Behaviors, 18*(2), 122–134.

Winters, K. C., Latimer, W. W., & Stinchfield, R. D. (1999). Assessing adolescent drug use with the Personal Experience Inventory. In M. E. Maruish (Ed.), *The use of psychological testing for treatment planning and outcomes assessment* (2nd ed., pp. 599–630). Mahwah, NJ: Erlbaum.

Wise, B. K., Cuffe, S. P., & Fischer, T. (2001). Dual diagnosis and successful participation of adolescents in substance abuse treatment. *Journal of Substance Abuse Treatment, 21,* 161–165.

Wood, M. D., Read, J. P., Mitchell, R. E., & Brand, N. H. (2004). Do parents still matter? Parent and peer influences on alcohol involvement among recent high school graduates. *Psychology of Addictive Behaviors, 18*(1), 19–30.

Wood, M. D., Read, J. P., Palfai, T., & Stevenson, J. (2001). Social influences and alcohol use and misuse among college students: The mediational role of alcohol outcome expectancies. *Journal of Studies on Alcohol, 63,* 32–43.

PART III

SPECIAL POPULATIONS AND ISSUES

CHAPTER 17

Neglected, Physically Abused, and Sexually Abused Children

JAN FAUST, SARA CHAPMAN, AND LINDSAY M. STEWART

DESCRIPTION OF THE DISORDER

BACKGROUND ON MALTREATMENT AND ABUSE

C hild abuse and maltreatment is a phenomenon that has been occurring for hundreds of years. Although the rate of victimization and the number of victims have been slowly decreasing in recent years, the National Child Abuse and Neglect Data System (NCANDS), maintained by the U.S. Department of Health and Human Services (USDHHS), reports that an estimated 872,000 children and adolescents in the United States were either abused or neglected in 2004 (the most recently available statistics, USDHHS, 2004). An estimated 1,490 children were killed as a result of abuse or maltreatment (USDHHS, Administration on Child, Youth, and Families 2006).

Precise, reliable, and functional definitions are essential to the prevention, detection, reporting, and treatment of child abuse and maltreatment. However, despite numerous debates in the literature, there is currently a lack of consensus regarding how to define these concepts (Cicchetti & Lynch, 1995). There appears to be a lack of consensus among numerous professionals as to which parenting practices are intolerable and unsafe and whether the definition of maltreatment should be consistent across multiple professions for clinical, scientific, and legal purposes. As a result, definitions of child abuse and neglect often differ according to state law and/or the views of different professional groups (Child Welfare Information Gateway, 2006a). We believe that greater cross-state consensus is desirable and, for the purposes of this chapter, offer operational definitions of each form of child maltreatment. These definitions are derived from the most frequently cited literature and law available. When necessary, we use the term *child maltreatment* to broadly invoke all forms of abuse, including neglect, physical abuse, sexual abuse, and emotional abuse (Child Welfare Information Gateway, 2006a).

Definitions of Maltreatment and Abuse

Neglect can be characterized as a failure to provide for the child's physical, emotional, developmental, medical, or educational needs (Child Welfare Information Gateway, 2006a). Physical neglect may include the refusal of or delay in seeking health care for a child, abandonment, inadequate supervision, refusal to allow a runaway to return home, and expulsion from the home. Emotional neglect includes marked inattention to the child's needs for affection, refusal or failure to provide needed psychological care, spousal abuse in the child's presence, parental drug use in the child's presence, and failure to prohibit drug or alcohol use by the child. Of the three types of neglect, emotional neglect is often the most difficult to define. Educational neglect involves allowing chronic truancy, failure to enroll a child of mandatory age in school (usually before 16 years of age), and/or failure to attend to special educational needs (American Humane Association, 2004). It is vital to take into consideration the cultural values and standards of care when making a determination of child neglect. One should keep in mind that failure to provide may be a result of economic deprivation (Children's Defense Fund, 2005). However, when the cultural milieu conflicts with the legal definition, the law prevails over culture and the state is required to intervene.

Physical abuse is defined as multiple acts of aggression that either inflict harm to or endanger the physical well-being of the child. Examples include hitting, burning, punching, biting, kicking, and shaking. These actions may be intentional or unintentional, such as the use of corporal punishment (Child Welfare Information Gateway, 2006b). The results of physical punishment are classified on a continuum of severity. For example, bruises are deemed minor injuries, whereas burns are viewed as more severe (D. Wolfe, 1999). Again, definitions of physical abuse can vary among states (Child Welfare Information Gateway, 2006b).

Sexual abuse includes behaviors such as fondling a child's genitals, having a child touch an adult's genitals, masturbating in front of a child, and engaging in intercourse with a child. In addition, sexual abuse may take the form of exposing children to pornographic materials and deliberately exposing a child to sexual acts. Commercial exploitation through the production of pornographic materials and prostitution or solicitation of a child for sexual purposes are also considered sexual abuse (Child Welfare Information Gateway, 2006b). It is believed that sexual abuse cases are underreported, as secrecy is often a key feature of such circumstances and a "conspiracy of silence" is employed (Haugaard, 2000).

Emotional or psychological abuse includes acts or omissions by the parents or caregivers that have caused, or could cause, serious behavioral, cognitive, emotional, or mental disorders (American Humane Association, 2004). For example, parents may use extreme forms of punishment, such as locking a child in a closet for extended periods or leaving a small child alone all day while the parent goes to work. Emotional abuse also includes verbal threats and degradation, such as name-calling and belittling (American Humane Association, 2004). In many cases, emotional abuse coexists with other forms of abuse and neglect, and it is sometimes confused with them.

In this chapter, we present recent statistics on the prevalence of child abuse and maltreatment, as well as the many factors that must be considered when clinicians attempt to assess, diagnose, conceptualize, and treat children and adolescents who have been exposed to neglect and sexual and/or physical abuse.

OUTCOMES ASSOCIATED WITH CHILDHOOD ABUSE AND MALTREATMENT

The effect of abuse on the child is the result of action or neglect committed by an adult or other individual rather than a specific form of child psychopathology; thus, maltreatment is not included as a diagnosable disorder in the *Diagnostic and Statistical Manual of Mental Disorders*, fourth edition, text revision (*DSM-IV-TR*; American Psychiatric Association, 2000). Instead, the *DSM-IV-TR* includes child maltreatment in the category "other conditions that may be a focus of clinical attention" (e.g., V Codes). When the focus of assessment or treatment involves severe maltreatment of a child, the appropriate V Code is identified and recorded on Axis I. For example, diagnostic codes 999.54, 999.53, and 999.52 are used to indicate that the presenting problem is the physical abuse, sexual abuse, and neglect of a child, respectively (American Psychiatric Association, 2000). However, if a child is suffering from another clinical disorder on Axis I, such as Posttraumatic Stress Disorder (PTSD), then the maltreatment would be noted on Axis IV (psychosocial and environmental problems). The clinician should make sure to note the abuse on either Axis I or IV as a history of or ongoing maltreatment; the distinction can have a powerful influence on assessment, diagnosis, prognosis, and treatment of the child's condition.

CHILD ABUSE, MALTREATMENT, AND POSTTRAUMATIC STRESS DISORDER

Systematic efforts to understand and treat the reactions of war veterans following exposure to traumatic experiences on the battlefield contributed significantly to our present conceptualization of PTSD. More recently, it has been acknowledged that PTSD can develop following other extreme stressors, such as sexual assault (Rothbaum, Foa, & Riggs, 1992), natural disasters (La Greca, Silverman, Vernberg, & Prinstein, 1996), terrorism (Calderoni, Alderman, Silver, & Bauman, 2006), severe car accidents (Jaspers, 1998), and exposure to community violence (Fitzpatrick & Boldizar, 1993). Early conceptualizations of trauma suggested that some underlying vulnerability within the individual accounted for such responses (McKeever & Huff, 2003). More recently, however, it has been observed that PTSD is one of the few diagnoses in our nosological system in which the etiology, or cause, of the psychological problems is known. That is, PTSD responses are due to trauma. Further, although PTSD was once conceptualized as an adult disorder, it is now accepted that children and adolescents may also develop PTSD. DeBellis (1997) argues that the experience of early maltreatment, including neglect, sexual abuse, and physical abuse, may be one of most common causes of PTSD in children. This notion is consistent with the finding that sexual and physical abuse, as well as neglect, experienced in childhood contribute to increased risk of developing PTSD, even when other risk factors are controlled (Widom, 1999). The effects of maltreatment and abuse on children's psychological adjustment may be long-lasting. For instance, Famularo, Fenton, Augustyn, and Zuckerman (1996) examined children who had just been removed from their parents' custody following maltreatment and found that 62% of these children experienced PTSD; however, 32.7% of the sample continued to meet diagnostic criteria for PTSD 2 years after the initial diagnosis. There is also evidence that younger children are more vulnerable to developing PTSD following maltreatment experiences (Famularo, Fentin, Kinscherff, Ayoud, & Barnum, 1993). Thus, due to the developmental status of the child, and possibly factors such as the inability to understand, verbalize, and process the trauma, very young children are especially susceptible to the deleterious effects of traumatic experiences such as maltreatment and abuse.

OTHER PSYCHOLOGICAL OUTCOMES ASSOCIATED WITH CHILD ABUSE AND MALTREATMENT

Clinicians who aim to understand and treat maltreated and abused children will find that diagnosing and conceptualizing maltreatment-related problems is challenging. Children are apt to display many different responses following the trauma of maltreatment and abuse, and many intra- and interindividual factors must be considered in understanding children's adjustment to these experiences. Not all children who experience sexual abuse, physical abuse, and/or neglect develop symptoms of post-traumatic stress. Instead, children with abuse and maltreatment histories may present with other problematic reactions, such as disruptive behavior disorders and depression (Famularo, Kinscherff, & Fenton, 1992) and or even suicidality (Bergen, Martin, Richardson, Allison, & Roeger, 2003). Younger children who experience trauma may present with attention difficulties, impaired concentration, and hyperactivity, thus closely mimicking the presentation of children with Attention-Deficit/Hyperactivity Disorder.

As suggested earlier, there is some evidence that reactions to trauma vary by child age and developmental level (Fletcher, 1996a). Very young and preverbal children's responses to trauma may include developmental regression, increased number and severity of fears, greater demands for closeness, and repetitive play of traumatic content. Alternatively, older children may cope via repeating the story verbally, acting out behaviorally, or exhibiting somatic symptoms (Kruczek & Salsman, 2006; Pfefferbaum et al., 1999). Kruczek and Salsman noted that older adolescents may rely more on peer support, engage in denial or avoidance, or may develop conduct problems, including defiance and rule-breaking behaviors in response to abuse or maltreatment. Some children, particularly those with excellent support systems and those who have already had the opportunity to process the trauma, may not present with any symptoms of psychopathology (Putnam, 2003). It is important to note that lack of overt symptomatology does not always imply healthy adjustment; children who use denial and avoidance to cope with the trauma may not present with psychopathology when assessed via standardized measures (Cohen, 1998).

FAMILY AND ENVIRONMENTAL CONSIDERATIONS IN ABUSE AND MALTREATMENT

Child abuse and maltreatment may arise from problems in the child's family environment, such as lack of parental supervision, blurred boundaries in the family, and parental psychopathology. Such issues are discussed in the Conceptualization section of this chapter. Disclosure of the abuse may itself have a pervasive effect on the child's environment and subsequent adjustment. Thus, one particularly important issue to consider when allegations of abuse or maltreatment arise is that there is often a significant and immediate deleterious impact on the child and his or her family. For example, allegations of abuse, even if unfounded, are stigmatizing to the child and family. In addition, when allegations of abuse or maltreatment surface, the child and his or her siblings may be removed from the home. Alternatively, the offending parents may be removed from the home, and if allegations of abuse or maltreatment are substantiated, the parents may face imprisonment. When these situations occur, the child may experience guilt that he or she caused the parents to be removed from the home and family, as well as negativity from other family members who resent the child's having caused the parents' removal. In addition, a parent's removal from the home may have significant financial repercussions, such as having to sell a primary residence, moving, and new school placements. Further, in the absence of the alleged maltreating parent, the other parent may face greater parental and financial responsibilities, which could compromise that parent's ability to support the abused child in a positive way. This lack of support can have a further deleterious impact on the abused child.

Accurate diagnoses for children exposed to trauma and maltreatment are critical; the case conceptualization, treatment plan, and integration are unique to each abused child. Even within a particular diagnostic category, such as PTSD, symptom presentation can vary widely, and resulting impairments in academic, social, and other important areas of functioning may differ markedly from patient to patient.

Further adding to the complexity of children's responses to abuse and maltreatment is the notion that many risk and protective factors influence not only immediate psychological adjustment to trauma, but also treatment response and the maintenance of symptoms over time. For instance, variables such as previous trauma exposure, family environment factors, peer and family support, and coping skills are just a few of the factors that must be considered when assessing and treating children with neglect or sexual and/or physical abuse experiences. In addition, unique aspects of the trauma, such as severity, duration, frequency, age of onset, and even perpetrator characteristics, may influence children's psychological adjustment. There is some evidence to suggest that the child victim's relationship to the perpetrator may influence psychological adjustment. More specifically, the closer the child's relationship to the perpetrator, the more negative the outcomes (Trickett, Noll, Reiffman, & Putnam, 2001). Alternatively, it may be that the relationship of the perpetrator to the child influences the type of problems that result. For example, one recent study found that adolescents who were assaulted by nonstrangers were more likely to develop PTSD than those assaulted by nonrelational strangers, whereas those children assaulted by acquaintances or strangers were more likely to develop behavioral problems, such as delinquency, than incest survivors (Lawyer, Ruggerio, Resnick, Kilpatrick, & Saunders, 2006) Finally, some researchers have argued that the more sustained and pervasive the abuse, the worse the outcome for children. For example, Garnefski and Diekstra (1997) found that when compared to children with a history of sexual abuse only, children who reportedly experienced both sexual and physical abuse displayed more emotional problems, aggressive behavior, and suicidal ideation or attempts.

In this chapter, although we place particular emphasis on PTSD, as it is one of the most common psychological outcomes following exposure to abuse and maltreatment in children, clinicians working with this population must recognize that a wide variety of psychological sequelae may result from such experiences.

PREVALENCE OF CHILD AND ADOLESCENT MALTREATMENT

Federal legislation, specifically the Child Abuse Prevention and Treatment Act of 1974 and later the Keeping Children and Families Safe Act of 2003, has established a general definition for child abuse and neglect. According to this definition, child abuse and neglect is conceptualized as "any recent act or failure to act on the part of a parent or caretaker, which results in death, serious physical or emotional harm, sexual abuse or exploitation; or, an act of failure to act which represents an imminent risk of serious harm" to a child under age 18. Since the establishment of this definition, all states have enacted laws prohibiting the maltreatment of children. However, when examining prevalence rates, one of the most prominent issues is the lack of consensus about how to define abuse and maltreatment. This inconsistency is due, in part, to the fact that most states recognize four types of maltreatment (neglect and physical, sexual, and emotional abuse) and that the specific criteria used to define these forms of maltreatment vary from state to state. This variability subsequently impacts reported prevalence rates of abuse and maltreatment. Even where definitional consensus has emerged, prevalence rates may still vary because federal and state agencies and private organizations use different methods to collect and analyze the data (American Humane Association, 2004).

The underreporting of abuse or lack of verified findings is another problem confronting researchers and policy makers and appears to be caused by multiple factors. For example, in the case of childhood sexual abuse, there typically are few obvious outward signs of abuse, or the child may have been threatened by the perpetrator not to disclose the abuse (Center for the Prevention of Child Abuse of Dutchess County, 2006). Though current prevalence rates are likely underestimates, data obtained from the NCANDS still indicate that 872,000 children in the United States were victims of abuse and neglect in 2004 (USDHHS, Administration on Child, Youth, and Families, 2006).

The number of confirmed reports of abuse and maltreatment pales in comparison to the actual number of NCANDS referrals for suspected abuse and maltreatment, which exceeded 3.5 million in 2004. Perhaps even more concerning is the fact that many children are victims of multiple types of abuse. Researchers have estimated that between 50% and 81% of maltreated children experience multiple types of abuse (Garnefski & Diekstra, 1997).

Prevalence by Type of Maltreatment or Abuse

Child sexual abuse occurs across all ethnic and socioeconomic groups (Finkelhor, 1993). Data from the NCANDS (USDHHS, 2003) for 2001 indicate that approximately 9.6% of confirmed child abuse and neglect cases involved sexual abuse of some type. The most recent estimate from the NCANDS database (USDHHS, 2004) found that 9.7% of cases of abuse or maltreatment involved sexual abuse. In the child sexual abuse literature, estimates of prevalence vary tremendously, depending on the definitions and methods researchers use (Hunter, 2006). For example, different estimates of prevalence are obtained when the sexual abuse is limited to contact (e.g., fondling, penetration) versus noncontact (e.g., exposure to explicit materials; Gorey & Leslie, 2001) forms of abuse. By contrast, Epstein and Bottoms (1998) found that 17% of a sample of 1,712 college students surveyed reported experiencing sexual abuse as a minor, which would suggest that prevalence could be higher than previously thought. Children may choose not to disclose the abuse for fear of negative reactions from others (e.g., disbelief or shame; see Arata, 1998; Berliner & Conte, 1995) or fears arising from perpetrator threats or concerns about removal from the home (Arata, 1998).

Data from the NCANDS (USDHHS, 2004) suggest that of the 872,000 confirmed cases of abuse reported in 2004, 17% experienced physical abuse. Physical abuse prevalence estimates are complicated by the very fine line that exists between corporal punishment, other forms of harsh discipline, and physical abuse. The lack of clear definition may lead to gross underestimation of incidents of physical abuse.

Specifically, many more instances of physical abuse are reported than are accepted or verified because they do not meet certain state-specified criteria for physical abuse. For instance, in the state of Florida, hitting is not considered abuse when it involves an open hand (as opposed to a fist), and it is acceptable to spank a child with a belt, so long as the buckle of the belt is not used. Although Florida Statute 415 delineates that physical abuse constitutes abuse when an object is utilized, the nonbuckle end of a belt is an acceptable form of discipline according to the state reporting agency (suggesting that even parameters of the state law tend to drift over time). Further, in many states, physical abuse such as hitting must lead to observable outcomes (marks, bruises, burns) before the case will be accepted, investigated, or verified by state personnel. Thus, so long as there is no physical evidence, theoretically a parent may hit a child repeatedly without fear of prosecution. Additionally, children who are repeatedly abused in this way may come to view the abuse as normative and cease reporting it to others. It may be argued that such repeated exposure to corporal punishment constitutes psychological maltreatment, but child protective services very often do not consider it as such.

CULTURE, ETHNICITY, AND SOCIOECONOMIC STATUS

Despite the strong emotional impact and heightened public awareness concerning sexual and physical abuse, they are far less common than child neglect or emotional abuse. Of the 872,000 children found to be victims of abuse and maltreatment in 2004, approximately 62.4% were neglected by parents or caretakers, Poverty is the most noted and persistent risk factor for abuse (Bethea, 1999; Children's Defense Fund, 2005). Children who experience neglect are particularly likely to come from families of lower socioeconomic status (SES), and lower SES families are more likely to be ethnic monitories (Sedlak & Broadhurst, 1996). The Children's Defense Fund reported that children who live in families with annual income less than $15,000 are 22 times more likely to be abused or neglected than children living in families with annual income of $30,000 or more. Such stark socioeconomic realities are also reflected in the broadest indicators of abuse and neglect.

As might be expected given the relationship between poverty and neglect, the impact of low SES on risk of maltreatment does not apply uniformly. For example, Putnam (2003) reports that SES has much less of an influence on risk for child sexual abuse than other forms of maltreatment. Interestingly, although children of different ethnicities generally experience similar rates of sexual abuse, recent evidence suggests that ethnicity may affect how children express their symptoms. For instance, Shaw, Lewis, Loeb, Roasdo, and Rodriguez (2001) found that Hispanic girls have more emotional and behavioral problems following experiences of sexual abuse than Caucasian and African American girls.

INTERACTION OF SEX AND AGE IN THE RISK FOR ABUSE AND MALTREATMENT

Child abuse and maltreatment are not bound by age, yet NCANDS (USDHHS, 2004) data suggest an inverse relationship between the child's age and rate of victimization. Generally, as the child's age increases, the likelihood of victimization decreases. However, research also suggests that the likelihood of certain types of maltreatment changes over time (Sedlak & Broadhurst, 1996). Younger children, who need the most supervision and parental care, are more likely to be victims of abuse, particularly neglect, than any other age group. For example, in 2004, children younger than 1 year constituted 10.3% of all victims of abuse and maltreatment (USDHHS, Administration on Child, Youth, and Families, 2006). Sedlak and Broadhurst report that toddlers, preschoolers, and young adolescents are the most common victims of physical and emotional abuse. Physical injury appears most likely when children are between the ages of 12 and 17, which D. Wolfe (1999) attributes to parent-teen conflict. Some researchers argue that sexual abuse begins much earlier, at approximately 3 years of age, a time at which children are especially vulnerable (Sedlak & Broadhurst, 1996). However, other researchers (see Finkelhor, 1993) have found that the risk of sexual abuse increases as the child ages. This is consistent with data obtained by the USDHHS (1998), which revealed that 36% of sexual abuse cases occur to children ages 12 and older, while younger age groups comprised much smaller percentages of cases. Some researchers argue for a sex-by-age interaction when assessing risk for sexual abuse, such that the risk for sexual abuse in girls may begin earlier and last longer than the risk for boys (Putnam, 2003).

Although some authors report nonsignificant interactions among sex, prevalence, and type of abuse, Tolin and Foa (2002) found that girls are at greater risk of sexual abuse, and boys are at greater risk of physical assault. Several additional studies support the notion of a sex-by-type-of-abuse interaction. For instance, in the case of sexual abuse, girls constitute approximately 80% of reported cases (USDHHS, 2003). Boney-McCoy and Finkelhor (1995) also found that female adolescents are more likely than male adolescents to experience sexual assault, and female adolescents may be more vulnerable to PTSD (Cuffe, Addy, & Garrison, 1998).

Contextual variables associated with sexual abuse also differ for boys and girls. For example, boys are more likely to be abused by male nonfamily members (teachers, soccer coaches, scout leaders, etc.), whereas girls are more likely to be abused by male family members. However, in general, both boys and girls are more likely to be abused by someone they know and trust versus a stranger (Berliner & Elliott, 2002; Finkelhor, 1995; USDHHS, Administration on Child, Youth, and Families, 2006).

Fatalities Resulting from Abuse and Maltreatment

Child abuse and neglect may have even more serious consequences than the development of mental health problems. According to the NCANDS (USDHHS, 2004), a reported 1,490 children died as a result of maltreatment in 2004, and more than 75% of these deaths were determined to have been caused by parents. While 35.5% of these deaths were due to neglect, 33% of the fatalities were due to multiple types of maltreatment, and 81% occurred in children younger than 4 years.

Perpetrators of Child Abuse and Maltreatment

Of the 872,000 children who experienced maltreatment during 2004, 78.5% were abused by a parent (USDHHS, Administration on Child, Youth, and Families, 2006). In this same sample, there were more female perpetrators of maltreatment and abuse than males: 58% versus 42%, respectively. Eighty-four percent of all child victims in this sample were abused by a parent, acting alone or with another person; mothers acting alone were twice as likely to be the perpetrator of abuse than fathers acting alone (USDHHS, Administration on Child, Youth, and Families, 2006). In addition,

18.3% of children who experienced maltreatment were found to be abused by both parents (USDHHS, Administration on Child, Youth, and Families, 2006).

Although parents, and other individuals, such as neighbors or friends, may perpetrate abuse against a child, the type of abuse committed appears to vary according to the perpetrator's relationship to the child. More specifically, when parents are perpetrators of maltreatment, they are more likely to commit neglect than sexual or physical abuse; the opposite is true for nonparent perpetrators (USDHHS, Administration on Child, Youth, and Families, 2006).

ASSESSMENT AND DIAGNOSIS

ASSESSMENT OF CHILD MALTREATMENT

As with conventional Axis I clinical disorders affecting children, the assessment of child maltreatment is a multifaceted process, and clinicians should be prepared to comprehensively assess the family, family-based and individual stressors, and relationship quality. Role clarification—simply identifying the client (i.e., the parents, child, or entire family)—is a daunting task. Helfer (1997) regards building rapport, be it with reluctant parents or mistrustful children, as yet another assessment barrier. The sheer complexity of the assessment presents significant challenges even for experienced child clinicians.

Clinicians should strive to create an environment that is supportive, nurturing, and free of judgment or blame (Helfer, 1997). To maximize the likelihood that a parent will provide factual information about maltreatment, try to be as empathic and understanding as possible. Being empathic does not mean that the clinician condones all parent actions; rather, the clinician should attempt to become fully cognizant of the circumstances surrounding the alleged maltreatment and other factors that may have contributed to the situation. For example, telling parents that you understand that raising a child can sometimes be frustrating gives credence to their emotional reaction without conveying approval of a physical assault on a child. Clinicians should be aware that abusive parents may not display emotions overtly in the interview, and the absence of strong affect may be due to denial of the abuse. Moreover, whether guilty of abuse or not, all parents in such situations face stressors that include possible separation from their child and concerns about losing the love of their offspring.

Clinicians assessing child maltreatment should be prepared to work with individuals that may present with complex and intense emotional behavior that may include anxiety reactions, such as PTSD symptomatology, and depression. Externalizing behaviors may be observed with child clients. Due to the nature of maltreatment cases, children often experience some sense of loss. Therefore, it is helpful for the clinician to be familiar with the stages of the grieving process (denial, anger, blame, bargaining, depression, and acceptance) that often accompany the experience of abuse (Helfer, 1997). Whatever the emotional climate of the interview, clinicians should strive to remain open and direct in their interview tactics.

Evaluating the family is a critical component in the assessment of child maltreatment. Often, a team of professionals (medical doctors, psychologists, social workers, etc.) is required to coordinate their activities and work cooperatively. This cooperation facilitates a more thorough assessment of the circumstances surrounding the abuse, as child maltreatment may indicate a breakdown in the family's infrastructure. In the case of physical abuse, medical doctors will be of great value as they are able to assess the physical injuries and the implications of such abuse. Abuse-related injuries should be assessed in terms of the child's age, as well as the type and severity of the injury (or injuries). The severity often indicates the degree of control the parent had over his or her actions and emotions. Typically, the more severe an injury is, the less safe the child is returning to that environment. Furthermore, a bizarre injury could indicate serious psychopathology of the abuser (Seagull, 1997). The age of the child is also a vital component, especially in the case of neglect. Younger children, who have limited means to care for themselves and are more vulnerable, are often a higher safety risk than older children (USDHHS, Administration on Child, Youth, and Families, 2006).

The role of the psychologist or mental health worker is central to the assessment of maltreatment. Through psychological testing and clinical interviews, the psychologist will be able to assess if the parent or child has significant cognitive limitations or suffers from a mental disorder. The role of the psychologist is also key in sexual abuse cases, as physical evidence may or may not be available at the initial assessment immediately following the abuse disclosure. In such cases, the clinical interview is a vital tool for gathering information about the victim's experience (Seagull, 1997).

Evaluating the child is another key component in the assessment of child maltreatment. Similar to working with children in other areas, the clinician should take into consideration the child's age and developmental level and adapt clinical techniques to elicit the most accurate information possible about the abuse or neglect. Studies have shown that children who are maltreated often suffer from a delay in social, cognitive, emotional, and language developmental abilities (D. Wolfe, 1999). It is not clear if these deficits are a consequence or a contributing factor to maltreatment (Seagull, 1997). According to the USDHHS, Administration on Children, Youth, and Families (2003), children who are developmentally delayed or have physical disabilities may be at a higher risk of abuse or neglect as they are more vulnerable and more challenging to care for in some situations. It would be wise for the clinician to utilize a variety of sources when determining the developmental level of the child. Direct observation, collateral reports from parents and teachers, and measures with psychometric integrity may all yield information regarding the state of the child.

Utilizing the school as a resource in evaluating maltreated children and their family can prove invaluable. For example, the clinician should inquire about the child's attendance at school as this information may give help to verify or disconfirm allegations of abuse or neglect. Children who are being physically abused may not be sent to school after an incident to prevent others from reporting obvious physical injury. Moreover, the very definition of neglect includes parents who do not provide educational support for their children; thus children who are often truant might be regarded as at higher risk of being neglected. Predictably, a large number of unexcused absences is closely linked to low achievement (Seagull, 1997).

When working with a child, the clinician should conduct the interview in a setting away from the parents. Such an arrangement maximizes the child's comfort in discussing the abuse or neglect. The clinician should keep in mind that specific questions are generally considered more appropriate for young children, but that the younger the child, the longer it may take to develop rapport. The use of open-ended questions is generally considered more acceptable for older children. The clinician's overall focus should be on gathering information about the child's environment *from the child's perspective.* Asking the child about discipline methods used and the rules of the house will give insight to the structure, or lack thereof, in the living environment (Seagull, 1997). Finally, clinicians should pay careful attention to the child's behavior (i.e., how easily the child leaves the parent, psychomotor behaviors, etc.) during the interview, including parent-child interactions.

Working with victims of sexual abuse requires the clinician to approach the interview in a unique fashion. First, victims of sexual abuse may not fully disclose details about the abuse in one or two sessions. The clinician must be patient and use empathy when working with this type of client. Studies have shown that when children are ready to discuss the incident, younger children are often very accurate in their accounts of sexual abuse (Orbach & Lamb, 1999). To help elicit factual information, Goodman and Bottom (1993) suggest that clinicians utilize statements such as "Tell me about what really happened." Over the years, interviews utilizing anatomically correct dolls have been conducted to facilitate the elicitation of information. There is mixed opinion regarding the utility of such interviews. Some authors discount the information gleaned due to concerns about bias (Ceci & Bruck, 1995). Other professionals claim, based on developmental considerations, that the dolls are necessary to cue recall of the traumatic event (Everson & Boat, 1994).

Finally, clinicians should be aware of the emotions frequently displayed by children: fear, guilt, anger, and depression. Children are often fearful of the consequences from reporting abuse to a professional. For example, a child may fear that he or she will be placed in a foster home and treated badly. A child might also be concerned that the abuse report will lead someone else to be harmed (Seagull, 1997). In cases of child abuse, it has been reported that a perpetrator will sometimes threaten to kill a family member if the child tells someone about the abuse. Children who disclose sexual abuse might also feel guilt for "telling the secret." Children may also be less likely to disclose the abuse when the abuse is especially severe or perpetrated by family members (Arata, 1998). Some children are led to believe that the abuse was their fault, a tactic used by some perpetrators (Seagull, 1997). Asking questions such as "Why do you think this happened?" might help feelings of guilt surface and allow the client and therapist to process this emotion. Past literature suggests that feelings of guilt may serve as a defense mechanism against anxiety for clients (Gardner, 1970). By focusing on guilt and accepting ownership of the abuse, the client does not have to worry about the unpredictable and uncontrollable environment in which he or she lives. In regard to anger, maltreated children tend to show heightened levels of aggression compared to nonmaltreated children (Dutton, 1999). Furthermore, antisocial behaviors and hyperactivity may appear elevated in children who suffer from abuse or neglect (Hildyard & Wolfe, 2002). Under these circumstances, the clinician should assess what makes the child angry and what the consequences are for acting out. Depression is another emotional reaction frequently displayed by victims of maltreatment (Werleke & Wolfe, 2003). Although it is unclear if depression is a contributing factor or a result of the maltreatment, the clinician should be prepared to help the child process the depression. Furthermore, it should be noted that these emotions (fear, guilt, anger, depression) are frequently intertwined.

Other aspects of the child's environment may also play a role in his or her functioning. For example, mothers who are depressed and emotionally unavailable may become hostile toward the child (Seagull, 1997). When the child is unable to form a secure attachment to the parent, feelings of anger, guilt, and depression may result.

SPECIFIC METHODS IN ASSESSING CHILD MALTREATMENT AND TRAUMA RESPONSES

Over the years, there have been a number of measures (e.g., semi-structured interviews, behavioral rating scales, direct observation, and self-reports) developed to assess child maltreatment. Although many measures have been offered, many are of unknown value in the assessment of child maltreatment.

Physical Abuse   A clinician should assess both physical and behavioral indicators when determining if physical abuse is occurring. A child who is being physically abused may present with unexplained bruises, burns, cuts, bites, broken bones, swelling, or black eyes. There may also be evidence of delayed or inappropriate treatment for injuries. Typically, when asked about the physical injuries, children will have bizarre explanations or may say they don't remember how the injuries occurred. In addition, their recounting of the events may not be consistent when they repeat it across caregivers (e.g., between teacher and therapist). Additionally, the clinician should assess if the child appears to be moving uncomfortably as a result of injuries and listen for any complaints of soreness or excessive somatic symptoms a child might be experiencing as a result of the abuse (National Children's Advocacy Center, n.d.).

In terms of behavioral indicators, a child who is self-destructive, aggressive, or withdrawn to an extreme degree may be displaying a consequence of abuse (Chalk, Gibbons, & Scarupa, 2002; National Center for Children's Advocacy, n.d.). Physically abused children may be absent from school often, as the caregiver does not want anyone to see the physical signs of abuse. Similarly, a child who arrives at school early or stays late to avoid going home may be experiencing abuse at home. Children who wear clothing inappropriate for the setting or weather may be covering up evidence of physical abuse (National Children's Advocacy Center, n.d.).

A parent's (or other caregiver's) behavior may also be indicative of abuse occurring at home. Similar to the child, if the parent provides an unreasonable, conflicting, or unconvincing explanation for the child's injuries, the clinician should consider the possibility of abuse occurring. Again, the clinician should assess the discipline methods used at home as well as the parent's own abuse history. The clinician should evaluate how the parent describes the child. For instance, if the child is referred to as "evil" or is similarly negatively regarded, the clinician should further explore the parent-child relationship and attachment status (Child Welfare Information Gateway, 2006a). Observation of the child's response to the caregiver's behavior in the treatment room is also important. For example, should the child flinch when a parent waves an innocuous hand while providing an explanation to the evaluator or cower in another part of the room when the parent moves less subtly, the interviewer should be suspicious of physical abuse.

To supplement the interview and other accounts of the abusive events, rating scales are sometimes administered. The Child Abuse Potential Inventory (Milner, 1986) was developed as a screen for physical abuse. Although it is completed by the caregiver, the measure yields information about both child and parenting behaviors to determine risk of physical abuse. This measure yields 10 factor scores for both child and parenting domains. It has solid internal consistency, reliability, and validity data. It is one of the few instruments available that presents information about classification errors. Neither false negatives nor false positives are desirable, but the author is to be commended for presenting information about the classification power of the instrument. The Child Abuse Potential Inventory is one of the most widely accepted in forensic settings (e.g., custody evaluations). Another popular rating scale, the Parenting Stress Index (Abidin, 1995), was developed to assess at-risk children and their parents who may need assistance in their parenting practices. The measure was designed to evaluate stress in parent-child systems and assist in the determination of maladaptive parenting. Normative data were gathered from a nonrandomized and stratified sample, but the measure has been shown to have solid psychometric properties in a variety of settings. The Parenting Stress Index is also commonly used in forensic settings.

Emotional Abuse   Emotional abuse is often hard to prove, but direct observation of parent-child interactions often are useful in making such determinations. For example, in emotional abuse cases, the parent may put down the child through name-calling or insults. The caregiver may use isolation, rejection, humiliation, terrorization, or corruption, or ignore the child as other methods of abuse. Reports by the child that he or she does not feel attached to the parent may be a cause for concern. Victims of this type of abuse may display delays in either emotional or physical development. Severely emotionally abused victims may display behaviors such as rocking, biting, sucking, or head banging. Older children, especially adolescents, may engage in delinquent behavior or substance use. Changes in sleeping patterns, extreme acting-out or inhibition patterns, or parenting other children may also be observed (National Children's Advocacy Center, n.d.).

Sexual Abuse   Sexual abuse may result from touching (intercourse, fondling, molesting, oral sex) or nontouching (pornography, exposure, obscene language). As a result, there are a variety of symptoms that a victim may display. Regarding physical signs, a victim may complain of pain, swelling, or itching in the genital area; have difficulty walking or standing; become pregnant; develop a venereal disease; or have frequent urinary or yeast infections (National Children's Advocacy Center, n.d.).

In terms of behavioral symptoms, a child may report nightmares or engage in play that is repetitive or reveals aspects of the abuse. At school, a child may refuse to change for gym or participate in physical activities. Victims of sexual abuse often will adjust their role in the family and might become overly protective of their siblings. Children and adolescents who display a great deal of insight and knowledge about sexual activity at a premature age or who engage in inappropriate sexual play may also be victims of sexual abuse. As a result of the abuse, victims may be wary of close physical relationships (National Children's Advocacy Center, n.d.).

Parent behavior may also be indicative of sexual abuse. Parents' attempts to isolate the child from others, extreme overprotectiveness, and highly restrictive limitations on social interaction may warrant a high level of concern. Sexually abusive parents or caregivers are often jealous of other members of the family (Child Welfare Information Gateway, 2006a). Howes, Cicchetti, Toth, and Rogosch (2000) found that even after a perpetrator is removed from the family, the effects of sexual abuse continue to negatively impact family functioning. Consequently, clinicians should be careful to assess current family structure and to ensure that abuse is not ongoing (Child Welfare Information Gateway, 2006a).

With respect to specific measures in the assessment of sexual abuse, the Child Sexual Behavior Inventory (Friedrich, 1997) measures behavior indicative of sexual victimization for individuals from 2 to 12 years of age. The measure classifies children's sexual behavior into nine domains. Although the accuracy (sensitivity) of abused and nonabused children ranges from 68% to 83%, there are many false positives and false negatives; hence it is imperative to use additional sources of information when making a determination of child sexual abuse.

Another form of assessment for sexually abused children is the use of anatomically correct dolls presented in interview format. As stated earlier, the use of these dolls has been controversial. In a recent study, Thierry, Lamb, Orbach, and Pipe (2005) found that the dolls did not enhance the amount of detail when children responded to open-ended questions. When direct questions were asked (as in structured interviews), younger children were more likely to reenact with the dolls, whereas the older children were more likely to verbalize. Most important, the younger children were more likely to play with the dolls in a suggestive manner and to contradict information previously presented without the dolls. Older children were more consistent in their disclosures (Thierry et al., 2005)

Over the years, many professionals have encouraged the use of drawings in the assessment of sexual abuse, often without regard to the psychometric integrity of this evaluative technique. Van Hutton (1994) attempted to develop a quantitative scoring system for the House-Tree-Person and the Draw-A-Person tests, but so far there are limited psychometric data to support the integrity of this measure. Most clinicians regard drawings as useful for developing rapport and perhaps in facilitating the disclosure of sensitive information during the interview.

Neglect   Neglect includes such actions as abandoning the child and extreme inattention to the child. For instance, if there appears to be a consistent lack of supervision or the child has unattended medical needs, neglect may be occurring at home. Likewise, a neglected child may be frequently hungry or have inadequate nutrition. A clinician can assess the child's hygiene and dress to determine if these are inappropriate or inadequate, both of which are signs of child neglect (National Children's Advocacy Center, n.d.).

Collateral reports from the child's teacher may help the clinician clarify if neglect is occurring. For instance, if a child lacks proper nutrition or is frequently hungry, he or she may try to steal or beg food from other students at school. Likewise, victims of neglect may fall asleep in class or display fatigue. Children who display extreme loneliness or desire lots of affection may also be displaying the effects of neglect. As with other forms of abuse, a child who engages in self-destructive behavior, is frequently absent or tardy to school, or drops out of school may be neglected. Children who report that a parent is often absent from home reveal evidence of neglect (National Children's Advocacy Center, n.d.).

Parents who are neglect their child may present as apathetic or depressed. Additional signs of parental neglect include indifference toward the child, irrational or bizarre behaviors, and alcohol or drug abuse. A clinician should also assess the parents' expectations of the child, as neglectful parents are often unrealistic in terms of the child's capabilities (Child Welfare Information Gateway, 2006a). There are no specific measures of neglect. Some assessment strategies include neglect as part of the evaluation, such as the Checklist for Child Abuse Evaluation (Petty, 1990), which assesses all forms of neglect; however, this assessment lacks psychometrics.

DIAGNOSIS AND ASSESSMENT OF PTSD

With respect to the impact of maltreatment on children, we have focused primarily on the assessment, diagnosis, conceptualization, and treatment of PTSD, as it is one of the most common outcomes seen in children exposed to neglect, physical abuse, and sexual abuse. However, children's responses to trauma are determined by the complex interaction of many factors, and as a result, clinicians must be aware that children with a history of abuse may demonstrate a variety of other problematic reactions, including aggressiveness, school refusal, depression, and withdrawal from family and peers. Consequently, the assessment of child exposure to maltreatment must also include a thorough evaluation for co-occurring conditions such as PTSD and clinical depression.

A diagnosis of PTSD is made in accordance with criteria set forth in *DSM-IV* (American Psychiatric Association, 2000). Structured and unstructured clinical interviews and paper-and-pencil questionnaires are the backbone of the assessment protocol, but other methods are also available to help the clinician assess for trauma exposure and other symptoms of psychopathology. However, many measures used in child research and clinical settings require a greater than average amount of clinical judgment when determining the validity of the assessment data. For example, many sexually abused children appear to have no symptoms when assessed with questionnaires.

The Kiddie Schedule for Affective Disorders and Schizophrenia for School-Age Children (K-SADS) is among the best known semi-structured interviews and is used to assess lifetime and current episodes of psychiatric disorders in children ages 6 to 18. The interview is administered to children and their parents and assesses both the presence and severity of symptoms (Ambrosini, 2000). The K-SADS is compatible with criteria used for diagnosis of psychopathology in *DSM-IV,* including PTSD. The K-SADS must be administered by trained clinicians and contains multiple skip-out sections, which allows for shorter administration time (Ambrosini, 2000). Another useful interview is the Childhood PTSD Interview—Child version and Childhood PTSD Interview—Parent version (Fletcher, 1996b). The target population is children 7 to 18 years of age. These measures are structured interviews that ask children or parents to identify specific traumatic events. In addition to PTSD symptoms, the interviews also assess for the presence of symptoms or behaviors that might be expected among individuals who have experienced maltreatment, including anxiety, depression, dissociation, omens, survivor guilt, self-blame, denial, self-destructive behavior, changes in eating behavior, antisocial behavior, and risk taking (Carlson, 1997).

Among the self-report instruments, one of the most commonly employed is the Trauma Symptom Checklist for Children (TSCC; Briere, 1996). The measure assesses underresponsivity, hyperresponsivity, anxiety, depression, anger, posttraumatic stress, dissociation, and sexual concerns. A version of the TSSC can be obtained without the inclusion of sexual items. Although the TSSC has been used extensively in research, it would benefit from better norms and additional validation studies.

Another option, Pearlman's (2003) Trauma and Attachment Belief Scale, assesses self safety, other safety, self-trust, self-esteem, self-control, and other control. The measure was developed to assess beliefs related to the effects of trauma for all forms of victimization; there are two versions, one for ages 9–18 years and one for 17 to 78. The measure is normed and has good internal consistency and reliability. Unfortunately, it has not yet been shown to reliably discriminate between traumatized and nontraumatized individuals.

A sexual abuse–specific scale that has been widely used is the Children's Impact of Traumatic Events Scale—Revised (V. V. Wolfe, Gentile, Michienzi, Sas, & Wolfe, 1991). This is a 78-item measure intended to assess the impact of sexual abuse on children between the ages of 8 and 16 years. It includes four dimensions (PTSD symptoms, Social Reactions, Attributional Style, and Eroticism) and 11 subscales. Children respond on a 3-point ("very true," "somewhat true," "not true") Likert scale. Overall, the reliability (coefficient alpha) of this measure was a modest .69 across the 11 subscales.

CONCEPTUALIZATION

The most prominent conceptualizations of child PTSD are primarily associated with the cognitive-behavioral model. Although initially derived from adult populations with trauma exposure, the model has been extended to explain the development of maltreatment-related PTSD in children. Foa, Rothbaum, Riggs, and Murdock's (1991) cognitive-behavioral model of PTSD includes the theoretical principles of learning theory and cognitive information processing. On the learning theory side, the model reflects the influence of both classical and operant conditioning. Classical conditioning theory suggests that initially neutral trauma stimuli become associated with trauma via temporal association with the innately fear-provoking, traumatic event (unconditioned stimuli: US). Thus, previously neutral stimuli (NS) become conditioned stimuli (CS), and thereby serve to elicit the PTSD or fear response. For example, if the child experiences physical abuse (US) while in the presence of a previously neutral odor, such as a perfume or cologne (NS), that odor then becomes associated with the traumatic experience; when subsequent exposure to that odor produces the PTSD fear reaction, it has become a conditioned response (CR). It is often the case that multiple neutral stimuli (e.g., odors, sights, sounds) become associated with the unconditioned stimulus (trauma) as well as other conditioned responses. Thus, because generalization of the fear response is common, children with PTSD may respond with anxiety and physiological arousal to a multitude of stimuli.

The operant conditioning aspect of this model suggests that children successfully learn to avoid the trauma-related stimuli, as this lessens their anxiety and other negative responses associated with such triggers. That is, because avoidance results in reduced anxiety, it becomes reinforcing; consequently, the child will avoid situations, conversations, activities, thoughts, and feelings related to the trauma. Some features of PTSD that are unique to this disorder (i.e., dissociation and exaggerated startle response) could be related to the way the child interprets and integrates the trauma and associated stimuli, as well as the extent to which the child believes he or she can control trauma-related cues. Thus, children's perceptions of the trauma may influence their trauma responses and feelings of fear (Faust, 2000). Data suggesting that perceived threat of harm during a trauma is a better predictor PTSD than actual threat underscore the importance of children's perceptions of trauma in case formulation.

Research has found that children who are abused by family members are more likely to experience PTSD than children who are abused by extrafamilial individuals. Such a finding can be explained by cognitive behavioral models of PTSD. In general, when children experience abuse, they are likely to develop conditioned fear responses to a variety of environmental stimuli. When abuse occurs in the child's home and is perpetrated by a family member or caretaker, the feared stimuli acquired through association, which serve to influence the child's perceived threat of harm, are likely to include aspects of the home environment (Faust, 2000). Hence, because children may be less able to avoid trauma-related triggers when they occur in the home, avoidance behaviors may not be possible; consequently, anxiety in response to cues actually increases (Faust, 2000). In addition, familial abuse may result in the development of vulnerability and feeling of helplessness, which may place the child at risk for future victimization (Boney-McCoy & Finkelhor, 1995). Childhood neglect, physical abuse, and sexual abuse may all contribute to maladaptive cognitions, and both abuse and distorted thinking theoretically may lead to increased risk for PTSD later in development (McKeever & Huff, 2003). Children with a history of abuse may exhibit a hostile attributional bias and learned helplessness. Thus, abuse in childhood increases the risk for later trauma, as well as maladaptive thinking, which may contribute to the development of PTSD (McFarlane, 1999).

Finally, the importance of mediating and moderating variables with respect to the origins of child maltreatment and the development of trauma symptoms must be considered. For example, developmental factors, such as the child's age, as well as social support, parenting, and family-related variables, play an integral role in child maltreatment and traumatic stress. In addition, many current conceptualizations of child psychopathology resulting from abuse have focused on life events, genetic vulnerabilities, and risk and protective factors in the child's life.

The following is an overview of the factors commonly considered in conceptualizations of both child maltreatment and childhood PTSD.

DEVELOPMENTAL ISSUES

Early Trauma Exposure   Perhaps one of the most troubling findings in the child-trauma literature is that younger children may be more vulnerable to the effects of trauma exposure than older children or adults (Fletcher, 1996a). For example, Davidson and Smith (1990) reported that trauma exposure occurring before age 11 is more likely to result in the development of PTSD than trauma experienced in later childhood, and early stress in infants, in the form of separation from caregivers, is a risk factor for developing more chronic responses to later trauma and stress (Breslau, Davis, Andreski, & Peterson, 1991). In addition, Faust and Stewart (in press) discovered that the earlier the trauma exposure occurred in children's development, the more serious the resulting psychopathology. More specifically, sexually abused children who exhibited psychotic symptoms were found to have experienced the onset of abuse at a mean age of 4 years and 8 months, whereas those children who displayed PTSD symptoms first experienced sexual abuse at a mean age of 7 years and 9 months. There are several reasons why early trauma exposure might result in more deleterious outcomes than trauma exposure that occurs later in life. When faced with such adverse events as maltreatment and abuse, not only is children's psychological development (e.g., self-control, attachment, self-esteem) hindered, but impairments in other domains (D. Wolfe, 1999), such as social, cognitive, and intellectual development, may also result.

Attachment and Interactions with Caregivers   From the very beginning of life, a caregiver's interaction with the child provides the groundwork for future development, especially relationship formation. Thus, it is not surprising that abuse or neglect can specifically hinder the child-caregiver relationship (Anderson & Alexander, 2005). Infants with caregivers who are accepting and responsive become securely attached; infants whose caregivers respond in a rejecting, inconsistent, or abusive manner may become insecurely attached. Evidence suggests that both infants maltreated by their parents and children who experience sexual and physical abuse are likely to display disorganized attachment patterns to caregivers (Barnett, Ganiban, & Cicchetti, 1999; Lyons-Ruth & Jacobvitz, 1999). Some researchers argue that early experiences between the child and his or her caregivers influence not only attachment, but also the child's ability to cope with later trauma experiences (Cassidy & Mohr, 2001).

Children with abuse histories often hail from families with high levels of conflict and cohesion, suggesting that boundary violations may be a problem in these families. Children who do not learn to trust miss important socialization opportunities, and those who do not receive affection or nurturance from others are at a higher risk for developing emotional and behavioral problems in the future (D. Wolfe, 1999). Furthermore, children in these situations have difficulty maintaining a healthy and positive reciprocal relationship with the caregiver. Whereas children who are not victims of maltreatment are likely to be securely attached to caregivers, a victim of childhood maltreatment often forms an insecure-disorganized attachment to caregivers (van IJzendoorn, Schuengel, & Bakermans-Kranenburg, 1999). Moreover, van IJzendoorn and colleagues reported in a meta-analysis that children who displayed disorganized attachments were more likely to display difficulties with social skills and externalizing behaviors, as reported by teachers and parents, and were at an increase risk of displaying dissociative symptoms and having internalizing difficulties.

Emotional Regulation   Emotions play a pivotal role in the development of a child. Emotional regulation is defined as the ability to modulate or control the intensity and expression of feelings and impulses, especially in an adaptive manner (Cicchetti, Ganiban, & Barnett, 1990; Maughan & Cicchetti, 2002). Emotions are essential, as they serve as a monitoring and warning system for the detection of threats in the environment (D. Wolfe, 1999). Unfortunately, due to the turmoil typically found in the maltreated child's environment, victims often have difficulty learning to interpret and label their emotions (Shipman, Zeman, Penza, & Champion, 2000). Studies have shown that maltreating parents tend to show more negative emotions (Herrenkohl, Herrenkohl, Egolf, & Wu, 1991; Lyons-Ruth, Connell, Zoll, & Stahl, 1987) and fewer positive emotions than nonmaltreating parents (Bugenthal, Blue, & Lewis, 1990; Burgess & Conger, 1978; Kavanagh, Youngblade, Reid, & Fagot, 1988). Furthermore, emotional affective expressions that represent distress, such as crying, may trigger avoidance, disappointment, rejection, or abuse on the caregiver's behalf (Klorman, Cicchetti, Thatcher, & Ison, 2003; Pollak, Cicchetti, Hornung, & Reed, 2000). Children reared under these conditions apparently learn to inhibit or use minimal facial expressions, in particular anger (Pollak & Sinha, 2002). Thus, the emotion regulation strategies utilized by children can be directly influenced by their environment, including the experience of maltreatment (Shipman & Zeman, 2001). Interestingly, it has been found that preschool children who have experienced abuse or neglect are more likely to home in on anger and threat-related signals given by another person (e.g., a facial expression) versus other expressed emotions (Pollak et al., 2000).

Learning and Education   Until recently, few studies assessed the neuropsychological functioning of children exposed to trauma, and thus, little was known about how abuse, maltreatment, and PTSD influenced children's cognitive functioning and academic performance and achievement. Additionally, studies attempting to understand the influence of child abuse and maltreatment on cognitive functioning and academic performance are often confounded by the presence of psychopathology and other factors affecting the child, such as family conflict. In addition, preexisting academic difficulties have been shown to heighten risk for PTSD (Silverman & La Greca, 2002).Thus, it is often difficult to determine whether resulting impairments in cognitive functioning are due to the abuse and maltreatment specifically, the child's symptomatology, or a combination of such variables. Nevertheless, some researchers (i.e., Kruczek & Salsman, 2006) have argued that traumatic experiences, including abuse and maltreatment, have the potential to negatively affect academic achievement.

One of the first studies to assess cognitive functioning in children with PTSD reported decreased performance in the domains of attention, abstract reasoning, and executive functioning (Beers & De Bellis, 2002). Specifically, when compared to control children with no history of trauma exposure or PTSD, children with maltreatment-related PTSD were found to exhibit greater susceptibility to distraction, greater impulsivity, and more errors on tasks of sustained attention. After corrections to control for statistical errors, PTSD subjects did not perform differently from control children on tasks tapping memory and learning, language, visual-spatial abilities, or motor skills. However, in their discussion of results, Beers and De Bellis noted that because they did not include a group of maltreated children without PTSD, it remained unclear whether such impairments were due to maltreatment alone or the presence of PTSD.

Although some studies of children with trauma exposure and PTSD do not report memory problems similar to those seen in the adult literature (Palmer et al., 1999), some studies have found evidence of such deficits. For example, Moradi, Doost, Taghavi, Yule, and Dalgleish (1999) used the Rivermead Behavioral Memory Test to assess cognitive functioning in children (ages 11–17); they reported that children with PTSD, regardless of symptom severity, displayed poorer general memory and reading performance relative to nontraumatized controls. Furthermore, they suggest that child and adolescent memory and reading performance may be influenced by the intrusive avoidance and/or hyperarousal characteristic of PTSD, resulting in impairments in academic functioning.

One recent study sought to partial out the confounding effects of psychopathology on cognitive functioning in abused and maltreated children. Saigh, Yasik, Oberfield, Halamandaris, and Bremner (2006) compared scores obtained from the Wechsler Intelligence Scale for Children, third edition, in three groups of children: children with trauma exposure and PTSD, children with trauma exposure without PTSD, and a control group of children with no history of trauma exposure or PTSD. Researchers reported that children with PTSD had significantly lower Full-Scale IQs, mostly due to their significantly lower performance on measures of verbal intelligence, and 40% of this group reported academic impairments after exposure to the traumatic event. More specifically, these children showed lower mean scores on the Vocabulary, Similarities, and Comprehension subscales. Trauma-exposed children without PTSD did not show such impairments in intellectual performance, and only 10% of this group reported impaired academic functioning after trauma exposure. No differences between the three groups of children were noted in Performance IQ. Thus, it is not mere exposure to extreme stressors that influences academic functioning, but rather the presence of PTSD symptoms (Saigh, Mroueh, & Bremner, 1997). This is consistent with the finding that adolescent girls who met diagnostic criteria for PTSD were significantly more likely to fail a class or grade and be suspended from school than girls with subclinical or no PTSD symptoms (Lipschitz, Rasmusson, Anyan, Cromwell, & Southwick, 2000).

One important outcome of impaired cognitive functioning in children with PTSD and maltreatment and abuse histories is the resulting impact on academic achievement. Shonk and Cicchetti (2001) reported that when compared to a control group of nonmaltreated children, maltreated children (ages 5–12 years) were rated by their teachers as having lower levels of academic engagement, as reflected by lack of persistence in and avoidance of challenging tasks, and overreliance on teacher feedback and support. These authors suggest that maltreatment negatively affects children's individual competencies, which leads to higher rates of poor academic achievement and behavioral problems and an increased likelihood of dropout and other negative outcomes.

Kendall-Tackett and Eckenrode (1996) examined the influence of neglect, neglect with other forms of abuse, and no history of maltreatment or abuse on children's academic achievement and behavior in children who were in kindergarten through 12th grade. These authors found that neglected children performed more poorly on academic and behavioral measures in almost every category, including receiving lower grades and more suspensions and disciplinary referrals, and being at risk for retention (Kendall-Tackett & Eckenrode, 1996). Another study found that when compared to children without PTSD, children with PTSD exhibited more hyperactive and impulsive behaviors in the classroom, such as difficulty staying in their seats, acting before thinking, and exhibiting distractive behaviors (Warnygora, 2005).

PARENT AND FAMILY ENVIRONMENT ISSUES

Research has suggested that parenting styles, attitudes toward the child, and parent-child relationships may be linked to the likelihood of maltreatment. From a developmental perspective, parenting styles focus on two key child-rearing dimensions: degree of parental sensitivity and the degree of parental demand. Parental demand is the amount of control the parent tries to exert over the child; parental responsiveness is the extent to which parent-child interactions (both positive and negative) are either child-focused or parent-focused (Baumrind, 1971; Maccoby & Martin, 1983). When examining the interaction between parental demand and responsiveness, four parenting styles emerge: authoritative, authoritarian, indulgent, and neglecting. Research suggests that abusive parents are more likely than nonabusive parents to use an authoritarian style of parenting (LaRose & Wolfe, 1987). Authoritarian parents are demanding of their children and reject or are unresponsive to the child's needs. Similar to authoritarian parents, neglecting parents are unresponsive to the child's needs; however, unlike their authoritarian counterparts, neglecting parents are undemanding of their children (Baumrind, 1971; D. Wolfe, 1999).

Overall, research suggests that maltreating parents often do not encourage the development of the child's autonomy. Instead, the parent sets up a lifestyle in which the parent and the child are isolated. Numerous studies have shown that abusive parents are less responsive, affectionate, playful, and supportive than nonabusive parents. In addition, abusive parents tend to have less enjoyable interactions with their child. Negative interactions are frequently reciprocated with increasingly negative exchanges between the child and parent more often than is true with nonabusive parents and their children. Furthermore, the literature suggests that abusive parents are less satisfied with their children and view parenting as more difficult and unenjoyable. Abusive parents are also more likely to employ controlling discipline techniques, such as punishment, threats, and coercion (cf. Cicchetti & Lynch, 1995). Consequently, the same parent is less likely to use reasoning or affection when disciplining the child, and the type of punishment appears to be conditional on the child's behavior (presumably setting the stage for escalation of violence).

Most models of child psychopathology emphasize the transactional nature of relationships, positing that while an abusive environment affects the child, the child in turn exerts his or her own influence on the environment. Children of abusive mothers tend to be more noncompliant than children of nonabusive mothers (Koenig, Cicchetti, & Rogosch, 2000), but the relationship is likely reciprocal and cyclical. That is, perceived noncompliance by the mother leads to more abuse, which in turn leads to more acting-out and defiance by the child. Interestingly, abusive parents seem to have unrealistic expectations about child development (Cicchetti & Lynch, 1995). For example, when compared to nonabusive parents, abusive parents are more likely to report higher levels of externalizing problems, which may reflect the abusive parent's lower tolerance for or tendency to be reactive to disruptive or acting-out behaviors (Mash, Johnson, & Kovitz, 1983). Thus, abusive parents are more likely to perceive their child as displaying externalizing behaviors (Lau, Valeri, & McCarty, 2006). In the case of an infant, an abusive parent tends to be more hostile and controlling than a nonabusive parent (Cicchetti & Lynch, 1995). As a result of the mother's hostility, the infant may not bond with her and may be more difficult to tend to and soothe, leading to frustration on the part of the parent.

In families with maltreating parents, the children sometimes trade roles with the caregiver and become "parentified" (Howes & Cicchetti, 1993). In another example of reciprocal relationships, the nonoffending mother's relationship to her child is detached and/or conflictual, and decreased emotional closeness between mother and child may place the child as risk for maltreatment and abuse (Lipovsky, Saunders, & Hanson, 1992; Paveza, 1988). Additionally, children in such a relationship may feel their mother does not protect them from the abuse, leading to greater conflict.

Several family environment variables may increase the risk for maltreatment and abuse. For instance, numerous reports indicate that when child sexual abuse occurs, it usually does so in the context of a variety of other family stressors (Nash et al, 1993). Variables significantly associated with the risk of abuse and maltreatment include parental mental illness, domestic violence, substance use by caregivers, and family income at or below the poverty level (Walrath, Ybarra, Sheenan, Holden, & Burns, 2006). In addition, the absence of one or both parents (Finkelhor, 1993) as well as family isolation, frequent moves, and maternal sexual abuse combined with maternal drug use (McCloskey & Bailey, 2000) are significantly related to increased risk of sexual abuse in preadolescent girls.

A number of family variables have been identified in the families of children with PTSD. Studies have highlighted lack of family support, parent and family disorganization, and family conflict in the development and maintenance of PTSD. Faust and Norman-Scott (2000), for example, found that the greater the family conflict and the more impaired the family organization, the more severe the PTSD response in sexually abused children. In addition, the expression of PTSD symptoms has been noted to be influenced by maternal adjustment and level of family cohesiveness, support, and conflict (e.g., Runyon, Faust, Kenny, & Kelly, 1997).

GENETIC INFLUENCES

There is some evidence to support the intergenerational transmission of child abuse. That is, although abuse per se is not genetic, parents or others who abuse children are more likely to have been abused themselves as children. For example, early reports by Faller (1989) suggested that 59% of mothers and 53% of fathers of sexually abused children were themselves victims of child sexual abuse. This may be due in part to factors that allow the abuse to occur (lack of boundaries, adequate supervision, etc.), not what is actually transmitted from generation to generation. More specifically, when looking at the intergenerational nature of sexual abuse, children are at increased risk for sexual abuse when their parent has been abused, but the abused parent may not even be the one who commits the abuse. For example, McCloskey and Bailey (2000) found that in a sample of 179 preadolescent girls, those girls whose mothers were sexually abused in childhood were 3.6 times more likely to also be sexually abused by their father or stepfather when compared to girls whose mothers had not been sexually abused. But, once again, the abuse may be a function of environmental experience rather than genetic transmission.

Evidence supporting a genetic component of PTSD has been found in both twin studies and intergenerational research on families (Broekman, Olff, & Boer, 2007). One potential confound in genetics research on PTSD is that criteria for diagnosis require the presence of an external traumatic event. In some cases, an individual may carry a genetic vulnerability for PTSD, but if he or she is not exposed to trauma, the person cannot be easily differentiated from family members who do not possess the vulnerability (Segman & Shalev, 2003). In addition, True and Lyons (1999) report that genetic contribution to risk for developing PTSD is partially shared with the overall risk for exposure to traumatic events. Thus, genetic vulnerability to PTSD may also confer a general increased risk for certain types of trauma exposure. For example, one twin study found that exposure to violent crimes was influenced by both genetic and environmental factors, whereas exposure to natural disasters is influenced only by environmental (and not genetic) components (Stein, Jang, Taylor, Vernon, & Livesley, 2002). Also, genetic factors may vary in the extent to which they explain variance in different symptoms of PTSD (True & Lyons, 1999).

PEER INFLUENCES

Although peers do not cause maltreatment, it is important to note the effect that abuse or neglect can have on peer relationships. Deficits in emotional regulation can result in deficits in social awareness and peer acceptance. For example, it has been noted that children with physical abuse histories or those having witnessed domestic violence between parents are more likely to be both physically and verbally aggressive toward their peers (Kaplan, Pelcovitz, & Labruna, 1999). Children who have been unable to manage their emotions are more likely to have maladaptive interactions with peers and dating partners (Rogosch, Cicchetti, & Aber, 1995).

Starting in the preschool years, children who fail to learn sensitivity and empathy will have more difficulty initiating and maintaining positive, reciprocal peer relationships. In an early study by Main and George (1985), none of the abused toddlers studied showed concern while witnessing another toddler who was in distress (crying). On the other hand, the nonabused toddlers expressed concern one-third of the time. When the abused toddlers did confront their distressed peer, it was with anger, fear, or physical attack. Studies have shown that victims of physical abuse are less likely to notice the distress of others, possibly as a result of their own abuse experiences. In a study of 16 school-age children, Parker and Herrera (1996) found that interactions between abused children and their friends involved less intimacy and more conflict than for nonabused children.

Social support may moderate the relationship between child abuse and maltreatment and children's adjustment. The experience of abuse and maltreatment may impair children's social functioning, thus resulting in difficulty obtaining social support, which would otherwise serve as a buffer against poor outcomes. For instance, using a teacher rating scale of children's classroom behavior, Warnygora (2005) found that children with PTSD were less able to develop and maintain appropriate relationships with peers. In addition, children who are abused or maltreated may not seek out needed social support or peer contacts due to coping methods such as avoidance. One recent study found that sexually abused adolescents were less likely to use support-seeking coping strategies and more likely to use avoidance coping (Bal, Crombez, & Van Oost & Debourdeaudhuij, 2003). These authors explained their findings by citing the work of Ackerman, Newton, McPherson, Jones, and Dykman, (1998), who posited that adolescents may avoid support-seeking coping methods, as such interactions may cause them to reexperience the trauma.

Cultural and Diversity Issues

Cultural and diversity issues are two critical concepts that must be taken into account when discussing child abuse and maltreatment. Due to the lack of consensus among professionals with respect to definitions of abuse and other unresolved political issues, the relationship between culture, diversity, and maltreatment has not been clearly delineated in the literature. Even so, child maltreatment is a worldwide phenomenon and affects millions of children each year (World Health Organization, 2006).

As stated previously in this chapter, definitions of child abuse and maltreatment in the United States vary according to state law. Taking into consideration worldwide child-rearing practices, research has failed to identify a universally acceptable child-rearing strategy. One must give credence to the social and historical context of the child-rearing practices in which the child abuse or maltreatment is currently occurring (Korbin, 1997). Notably, it is often the dominant culture within a given context that determines what behaviors (i.e., parenting practices) are socially acceptable. Thus, it is often the case that what is acceptable parenting practice in one group is looked down upon by another group. In the United States, for example, cultural orientation often conflicts with state and federal laws, resulting in much confusion, anger, and distress among those families who favor the use of physical discipline (perhaps the norm in their country of origin) and who are subsequently reported to the state's child protective services.

Numerous authors have presented definitions of child maltreatment that are culturally inclusive. Finkelhor and Korbin (1988) suggested that child maltreatment must include behaviors that are proscribed, preventable, and proximate; Starr (1988) extends the definition to include cultural and societal standards in which an act is judged from the cultural context. Taking into account the cultural and societal standards is important, as child-rearing practices that can cause harm or injury to a child without malicious intent are generally not classified as maltreatment.

Although PTSD has been found in all cultural groups, some evidence suggests that certain cultural, racial, and ethnic groups may be more susceptible to developing PTSD in response to trauma. Rabalais, Ruggerio, and Scotti (2002) found that, when compared to Caucasian youth, African American and Hispanic youth have an increased risk of developing PTSD following trauma, and they are less likely to experience reductions in symptoms over time. Kruczek and Salsman (2006) suggest that poverty, the unavailability of social support, and the history of oppression may explain the increased risk of PTSD in minority groups.

One other important issue with respect to culture is that children of different racial, ethnic, and cultural groups may be exposed to different types of trauma. For instance, whereas research on trauma exposure in children and adolescents in the United States primarily focuses on abuse, maltreatment, and community and domestic violence, research on child and adolescent trauma exposure in other cultures is more likely to focus on terrorism, civil war, and natural disasters. Researchers investigating PTSD in children of other cultures have assessed the influence of traumatic events such as the tsunami on Southeast Asian children, war on Cambodian refugees (Sack, Clarke, & Seeley, 1996), and earthquakes on Armenian children (Goenjian et al., 1995).

BEHAVIORAL TREATMENT

Despite decades of research on the efficacy of treatments for adults with PTSD, similar research with children has, until recently, been quite limited. Over the past decade, some researchers have begun to examine the efficacy of cognitive-behavior therapy (CBT) for abused and maltreated children with, and without, PTSD. There is now evidence to suggest that such cognitive-behavioral treatments, which are similar to those used with adult trauma populations, may be effective in the treatment of children who have been neglected or abused.

TREATMENT OF SEXUAL ABUSE

One promising intervention for children with sexual abuse is trauma-focused cognitive-behavioral therapy (TF-CBT). According to Cohen, Deblinger, Mannarino, and Steer (2004), TF-CBT consists of feeling identification, stress inoculation techniques, graduated exposure exercises to facilitate the direct discussion of the abuse, cognitive processing of the abuse, integrating the experience into the child's view of self and world, and an education component focused on healthy sexuality and safety skill building. When the model is used with adults as caretakers of abused children, a parent training component is added.

In a recent study of 82 sexually abused children and their caretakers, Cohen, Mannarino, and Knudsen (2005) found that TF-CBT was more efficacious than nondirective, supportive therapy in alleviating symptoms. Over the course a year, children receiving TF-CBT showed decreased sexual concerns and significant improvements in depressive and anxiety symptoms, including PTSD, as measured by the TSCC (Briere, 1996). In a large-scale, multisite study, Cohen et al. (2004) randomly assigned 229 children to received either TF-CBT or child-centered therapy. They found that children receiving TF-CBT showed significant improvements in PTSD, depressive and behavioral symptoms, and decreased attributions related to the abuse and feelings of shame.

There is also some evidence suggesting that TF-CBT may have long-lasting effects on PTSD symptom reduction. For instance, Deblinger, Steer, and Lippman (1999) studied 100 children with a history positive for sexual abuse who were randomly assigned to receive one of three conditions: TF-CBT for the child only, TF-CBT for both parent and child, or TF-CBT for parents. When compared to a group of sexually abused children receiving standard community care, the authors found that children who received TF-CBT (both with and without their caretakers) showed significant reductions in PTSD symptoms. Furthermore, both children receiving TF-CBT with their parents and those whose parents received TF-CBT alone showed significant improvements in self-reported depression on parent ratings of behavioral problems. Such findings were maintained at 1-year follow-up.

Cognitive-behavioral approaches to the treatment of PTSD may be effective for even very young children. In their sample of preschool children with a history of sexual abuse, Cohen and Mannarino (1996, 1997) found that those children receiving TF-CBT showed greater PTSD symptom improvement than children in the nondirective supportive therapy group. In another study, sexually abused children ages 2 to 8 who experienced TF-CBT in a group format showed improvements in maternal abuse-specific distress and body safety skills when compared to children who received supportive group counseling (Deblinger Stauffer, & Steer, 2001)

COGNITIVE-BEHAVIORAL THERAPY FOR PTSD

Cognitive-behavioral treatments of PTSD in children are similar to those used with adults in that they generally rely on systematic desensitization to target any stimuli that elicit a fear response, thereby desensitizing the individual to the cues and extinguishing the anxiety response (Faust, 2000). In practice, systematic desensitization via exposure to real or imaginary stimuli is combined with relaxation techniques; in theory, systematic desensitization works because of reciprocal inhibition: One simply cannot be relaxed and anxious at the same time. Thus, when children are not allowed to escape or avoid the anxiety aroused by trauma-related cues, and instead must resort to adaptive coping strategies (i.e., relaxation techniques), the associations between the trauma-related stimuli and fear are extinguished (Faust, 2000).

Cognitive-behavioral therapies for child PTSD typically include three components. Treatment helps the child to develop adaptive coping responses, which reduce anxiety and extinguish the association between trauma-related cues, the fear responses, and the reinforcing nature of avoidance behaviors. To build healthier coping responses, the child learns relaxation techniques such as diaphragmatic breathing and progressive muscle relaxation (PMR). In addition, the therapist facilitates the development of adaptive coping by teaching the child to recognize, question, and replace distorted thoughts and self-statements with more positive ones (Faust, 2000). Progressive muscle relaxation involves having the child tense and relax various muscles, which enables the child to recognize and differentiate between tense and calm feelings. Although original models of PMR, such as Jacobson's method, are useful, several approaches have been developed specifically for use with child populations. Some relaxation methods, such as Koeppen's (1993), attach imagery to the procedure. For instance, the child is told not just to make a fist, but to imagine he or she is squeezing a lemon and making juice. The use of imagery in conjunction with relaxation training may be especially useful in younger children, as it allows them to more fully understand the process and remain actively engaged. When children have achieved full body relaxation, additional imaging techniques can be used to help them build a safe, peaceful scene to attach to their newly relaxed state. Instructing children to imagine themselves walking down 10 steps, each step allowing them to become more and more relaxed, will help to facilitate the transition from total body relaxation to their imaginary safe scene. After they have "descended" the steps and their imaginary scene is discussed in detail, the therapist instructs the children to climb back up the steps in their imagination. At each step on the way up, the children are told that they are becoming more alert, but that they will maintain their sense of relaxation and calmness.

It is extremely important that the child successfully masters the relaxation procedures prior to addressing the hierarchy, as talking about feared situations in the absence of positive coping strategies (relaxation and imagery) is likely to cause the child considerable anxiety (Faust, 2000). In practice, it is both common and helpful for the therapist to record the relaxation procedure on cassette or CD and instruct the child to practice at home daily, as this reinforces the acquisition of new skills. After the child demonstrates successful use of the relaxation procedures, the therapist facilitates the second aspect of cognitive-behavioral interventions for PTSD by helping the child to develop a fear hierarchy. There are two classes of stimuli included on the hierarchy: those that are directly feared and those that are avoided due to fear. Because the child may be unable or unwilling to provide enough detail due to avoidance, a separate fear hierarchy should be developed with the child's caretakers (and eventually integrated with the child's hierarchy), as they are often able to clarify or provide additional information. Each hierarchy item should be rated independently by child and caretaker with respect to level of fear. It has been the case in our clinic that sometimes the feared stimuli are so extensive, or there are so many (seemingly unrelated) fears, that adjunctive hierarchies must be developed. Finally, the therapist instructs the child and parent, independently, to rate each item based on the child's degree of fearfulness.

After the hierarchy is constructed, systematic desensitization is used. The therapist creates exposure to the feared stimuli by describing each item on the hierarchy in detail, typically in order from least to most anxiety- or avoidance-provoking. As the therapist speaks, the children are instructed to imagine the feared stimuli and utilize their relaxation skills when they become afraid. The therapist should instruct the children that, should their fear become too overwhelming, they may raise a finger to signal this anxiety to the therapist. After exposure to an item on the hierarchy, the children are asked to rate their degree of fear or anxiety on a scale of 1 to 5. Older children may rank their fear using a wider scale (i.e., 1 to 8 or 1 to 10). Only after the children have achieved a degree of fearfulness equivalent to a score of 1 does the therapist move on to the next item on the hierarchy. The process is repeated as needed.

The third component of CBT for children with PTSD is parent education and training. Research suggests that this aspect of treatment may be especially important in child maltreatment populations. For instance, Deblinger et al. (2001) found that in a sample of sexually abused children, those whose parents received TF-CBT (with or without their children) reported fewer depressive symptoms. In addition, these parents reported fewer behavioral problems in their children, and the effects were maintained for 2 years following the intervention. In traditional CBT, parents are encouraged to reinforce their child's acquisition of adaptive coping skills, such as relaxation and positive self statements. Behavioral management techniques may help parents to recognize, reward, and therefore increase adaptive behavior. Parents may also be taught differential reinforcement techniques, emphasizing the importance of rewarding the child for adaptive behaviors (e.g., use of coping skills) and extinguishing (ignoring) maladaptive, regressive behaviors (e.g., whining) that are common among children with PTSD.

Case Description

Identifying and Referral Information

Anna was an 11-year-old Caucasian female who was referred for treatment due to trauma-related symptoms stemming from several episodes of molestation by her sixth-grade history teacher. Anna was having difficulties sleeping, relocating frequently to the family room couch. She said she had a number of nightmares with themes of abduction and persecution. Anna's mother stated that Anna was an affable child, but she was withdrawing from people, particularly men. Although an excellent student, Anna went from a "mostly A's" to failing a number of her classes. She said she "did not have the energy" to complete her homework assignments and was no longer motivated to study for tests and quizzes. She reported a loss of desire to attend her martial arts classes, where she excelled as a third-degree black belt. She had been interested in applying for a special magnet school geared toward law and criminal justice; however, she was no longer motivated to complete the application process. Furthermore, though desiring to choose a career in constitutional law, which blended her love of history and political science, she no longer had "any idea of what [she] wished to be when [she] grew up." Her mother noted that Anna was not eating and that she was "supersensitive," crying often with little apparent provocation. She had also begun to argue more frequently with her younger sister. Both Anna and her mother denied the presence of suicidal ideation. Anna and her mother identified the onset of many of the symptoms as roughly corresponding to the time of the first episode of molestation, or about 4 months prior to treatment.

Background of Presenting Problem

Anna's history teacher, Mr. James, had identified Anna and two other female children as his "class leaders." Such designation carried with it much social privilege, as the role was coveted by many children since Mr. James identified these

(continued)

children as exceptional. Mr. James allowed the girls to lead class discussions, assist in the grading of papers, and stay after school to clean dry-erase boards and similar classroom activities. Anna said that on several occasions, Mr. James would bring cupcakes and other treats, reserving them for Anna at day's end. She said that during these times she was alone with Mr. James, and he would lean up against her and place his hands under her shirt or down her pants to fondle her. These activities were initially reported by Anna's closest friend to the guidance counselor, who in turn informed Anna's parents. Mr. James was immediately placed on administrative leave. It should be noted that Mr. James had two children of his own, and his wife taught at a different school in the same school district.

Other Relevant History

Anna's parents never married and lived separately for the majority of Anna's life. Her mother retained primary custody of Anna; however, Anna shared an abundance of time with her father since he either took her to school or picked her up every day. In addition, Anna and her father were involved in martial arts together, and they belonged to several museums and historical societies. Anna was the only product of this union; her father did not have other children. However, Anna did have a maternal half-sister, Catherine, who was 4 years younger (7 years old at the time of intake). Although Anna's mother and Catherine's father never married or lived together, they engaged in a long-term dating relationship that continued throughout Anna's treatment. Interviews revealed a significant amount of conflict among all three adults in Anna's life.

Diagnosis and Conceptualization

Anna's symptoms met criteria for both Major Depressive Disorder and PTSD. In addition, her responses on the TSCC (Briere, 1996) and Children's Depression Inventory (Kovacs, 1992) resulted in clinically significant elevations and thus were areas of concern. One of the most salient features of her PTSD presentation was avoidance of stimuli that reminded her of the abusive events. So disruptive was the avoidance that Anna would avoid a specific wing of the school building. Taking the circuitous route necessary to avoid the classroom ultimately resulted in multiple school detentions for tardiness. Indeed, as Anna walked the halls of the school, she reportedly became extremely anxious, even though Mr. James was incarcerated. Her avoidance of specific areas of the building reduced her anxiety (negative reinforcement). In addition, Anna was unwilling to open her yearbook for fear of seeing Mr. James's picture. Again, avoidance of the yearbook successfully terminated anxiety arising from stimuli that could potentially remind her of her abuse. Anna was also extremely fearful of seeing Mr. James, since she was scheduled to testify at his trial. In addition to the symptoms described earlier, Anna also experienced guilt about the losses suffered by Mr. James and his family due to his loss of a job and potential long-term incarceration. She experienced cognitive distortions that contributed to the maintenance of the PTSD and depressive symptomatology. Taken together, it was apparent that Anna suffered multiple PTSD symptoms that interfered significantly with her everyday functioning; she also experienced a significant loss of self-efficacy and depressive symptoms. It was determined that it would be best to treat the PTSD and depression simultaneously.

Treatment

As stated previously, PTSD treatments derive from both classical and operant conditioning, as well as CBT. To counter conditioned fear and avoidance responses, Anna was treated via systematic desensitization and cognitive restructuring; these efforts were supplemented by instruction in and reinforcement of adaptive coping skills. During intake, the therapist met separately with Anna and her parents and obtained background information about the presenting problem and detailed information regarding the sexual assault. The therapist also had access to police reports and child protective services reports. After the intake was completed, the therapist spent several sessions establishing rapport, with an emphasis on developing a warm and trusting relationship. Once this was established, the therapist had Anna describe her most relaxing and safe environment, her safe image. Anna's safe image involved lying on the couch in the living room, with the ceiling fan blowing gently over her while she watched two of her favorite television comedies. In this scene she imagined cuddling with her favorite blanket that had calico cats crocheted onto it; she also imagined that she was alone in the dim living room (far away from her "annoying baby sister"). She said she liked to imagine the sound of the ceiling fan gently whirring in the background.

After the scene was developed, Anna was instructed in PMR techniques; the conclusion of the exercise involved the therapist's introduction of Anna's safe, relaxing imagery. After in-session practice, Anna was sent home with the taped relaxation protocol to practice prior to the subsequent session. After she could relax herself with relative ease, the therapist had her develop a fear hierarchy, which she expanded based on input from her parents, the police, and the child protective services worker. In this way, Anna was not overly exposed to the feared stimuli while developing the hierarchy. Anna also was avoidant in her provision of details regarding her molestation, so having the additional information was imperative for effective utilization of the imaginal desensitization procedure. Although mostly imaginal, some of the stimuli utilized were quasi in vivo, such as a videotape and pictures from the Anna's yearbook. A secondary hierarchy was added over the course of treatment that was prospective in nature. Specifically, Anna developed a fear hierarchy involving the impending trial of Mr. James, which included items such as seeing Mr. James and his family at the courthouse as well as being asked to recall very private aspects of the molestation in the courtroom with others present. Each item on the hierarchy was gradually introduced, from the least to the most feared.

Anna was also instructed in diaphragmatic breathing and identifying cognitive distortions, including the belief that she was responsible for the abuse. Her parents were then educated in how to best aid Anna in dealing with the issue of responsibility. For example, Anna's parents asked her why she did not tell them of the molestation, implying that Anna was responsible for the continued abuse

(continued)

and responsible for her own protection. Anna's parents were able to understand how such questions could make Anna feel guilty and responsible for her own abuse. In addition, Anna was able to challenge the cognitive distortion that "had [she] been a better student, perhaps Mr. James would not have molested [her]." Ultimately, she was able to tell herself that it is adults' responsibility to protect children, even though she liked the attention, treats, and privileges Mr. James bestowed on her.

Finally, Anna's parents were instructed in how to use behavioral contracting to enhance her motivation to participate in treatment (e.g., listen to the relaxation tape and engage in the new coping strategies), should this be necessary. However, because Anna was, in fact, highly motivated to participate in her treatment, her parents did not need to employ a formal behavioral contract. Instead, her father provided frequent verbal praise and communicated his pride in her strength and perseverance. Anna's parents were instructed in the importance of minimizing their family conflict and were provided with specific instruction in communication and problem solving.

With respect to prevention, Anna and her parents, in separate sessions, were given safety training to assist the family in preventing retraumatization and abuse. This is very important because children and adults who are sexually assaulted are at an increased risk of repeated episodes of abuse. The safety training also included the identification of "good touches and bad touches" (in a developmentally appropriate manner) and instruction in safety planning, assertiveness, and communication skills.

Response to Treatment and Prognosis

Anna was seen for treatment for approximately 6 months. Although she no longer met diagnostic criteria for either PTSD or Major Depressive Disorder after approximately 4.5 months, she continued in treatment for an additional 6 weeks during Mr. James's trial. Anna was given a miniature calico glass cat to hold in her hand while providing testimony to prompt her in the utilization of relaxation skills. She was able to provide clear, consistent testimony, and her recall was not impaired by anxiety. Mr. James was convicted of Anna's molestation. The therapist met with Anna after the trial to evaluate whether she continued to feel guilt regarding Mr. James's adjudication. Consistent with grief-processing theory, Anna's use of adaptive cognitive self statements appeared to facilitate a transition from guilt to (appropriate) anger. For example, instead of telling herself that she was hurting Mr. James by testifying against him, she was able to recognize and subsequently tell herself that he had hurt *her,* and as an adult caring for children he had the obligation to protect her. By termination, Anna was able to enjoy the life of a typical middle school student, including reading her yearbook without hesitation, reviewing school videos without worrying that Mr. James was also in the films, and walking freely throughout school grounds without anxiety and avoidance. Anna became an A student once again and completed the first draft of the magnet school application on her own initiative. She also suggested that she and her father attend a regional father-daughter competition in their martial arts specialty. It was evident that she had renewed interest in the activities that previously brought her much joy. Anna's parents noticed that her tearfulness and sensitivity had also diminished significantly, and though she continued to argue with her sister, the chronic irritability was absent. Anna's mother stated that the sibling arguments appeared to revolve around typical sister disagreements.

Anna's nightmares ceased fairly quickly after beginning desensitization procedures, as did her sleep disruption. The only time she relocated to the couch was on weekends, when she would sneak out of her room while the others were sleeping to watch reruns of her favorite television show.

Epilogue

Recently Anna stopped by the therapist's office. Treatment had been terminated 5 years earlier. Anna is currently a junior in high school at the magnet program to which she applied. She is a junior instructor in martial arts at a martial arts school, president of the Political Science Honor Society, and a member of the National Junior Honor Society. She has three close female friends and dates a boy whom she met at the beginning of her junior year. Anna said she was looking forward to going to college, hoping that she would be accepted at a university in New England. In addition, she said she would like to attend law school but was leaning more toward international law instead of constitutional law. She had also become fluent in French and Spanish.

Anna's father stated that she is close with both her parents and has a more amicable relationship with her younger sister, Catherine. He noted that Anna had taken Catherine "under her wing, like a big sister."

SUMMARY

Child abuse and maltreatment is a phenomenon that has been occurring for hundreds of years and is still all too common in today's society. Although the rate of victimization and number of victims have been slowly decreasing, in 2004 nearly 900,000 children and adolescents in the United States were abused or neglected, and almost 1,500 children were killed (USDHHS, Administration on Child, Youth, and Families, 2006).

Despite a surge in interest in child maltreatment, there is a lack of consensus regarding how to define it, and this has negatively impacted efforts to facilitate detection and reporting. As with conventional Axis I clinical disorders affecting children, the assessment of child maltreatment is a multifaceted process, and clinicians should be prepared to comprehensively assess the family, family-based and individual stressors, and relationship quality, in addition to standard features of clinical child assessment for common forms of psychopathology. The sheer complexity of assessment remains daunting even for experienced child clinicians. Building rapport, whether with abusive parents or mistrustful children and adolescents, is also extremely challenging (Helfer, 1997). As with other child disorders, CBT models of PTSD and trauma are presently very influential. Foa et al.'s (1991) cognitive-behavioral model of PTSD, for example, combines elements of both learning and cognitive information-processing paradigms. Despite decades of research on the efficacy of treatments for adults with PTSD, similar research with children has, until recently, been limited. Fortunately,

CBT treatments developed for adult trauma populations also appear to be effective with maltreated children and adolescents.

REFERENCES

Abidin, R. R. (1995). *Parenting Stress Index* (3rd ed.). Odessa, FL: Psychological Assessment Resources.

Ackerman, P. T., Newton, J. E. O., McPherson, W. B., Jones, J. G., & Dykman, R. A. (1998). Prevalence of posttraumatic stress disorder and other psychiatric diagnoses in three groups of abused children (sexual, physical, and both). *Child Abuse and Neglect, 22,* 759–774.

Ambrosini, M. D. (2000). Historical development and present status of the Schedule for Affective Disorders and Schizophrenia for School Age Children (K-SADS). *Journal of the American Academy of Child and Adolescent Psychiatry, 39,* 49–58.

American Humane Association. (2004). *Fact sheet: Child abuse and neglect in America— What the data say.* Retrieved November, 21, 2006, from http://www.americanhumane. org/site/PageServer?pagename=nr_fact_sheets_childabusedata.

American Psychiatric Association. (2000). *Diagnostic and statistical manual of mental disorders* (4th ed., text rev.). Washington, DC: Author.

Anderson, C. L., & Alexander, P. C. (2005). The effects of abuse on children's development: An attachment perspective. In P. Forrest Talley (Ed.), *Handbook for the treatment of abused and neglected children* (pp. 3–24). Binghamton, NY: Haworth Press.

Arata, C. M. (1998). To tell or not to tell: Current functioning of child sexual abuse survivors who disclosed their victimization. *Child Maltreatment: Journal of the American Professional Society on the Abuse of Children, 3,* 63–71.

Bal, S., Crombez, G., Van Oost, P., & Debourdeaudhuij, I. (2003). The role of social support in well being and coping with self-reported stressful events in adolescents. *Child Abuse and Neglect, 27,* 1377–1395.

Barnett, D., Ganiban, J., & Cicchetti, D. (1999). Maltreatment, negative expressivity, and the development of Type D attachments from 12 to 24 months of age. *Monographs of the Society for Research in Child Development, 64*(3), 97–118.

Baumrind, D. (1971). Current patterns of parental authority. *Developmental Psychology Monographs, 4*(1, Pt. 2).

Beers, S. R., & De Bellis, M. S. (2002). Neuropsychological functioning in children with maltreatment related PTSD. *American Journal of Psychiatry, 159,* 483–485.

Bergen, H. A., Marin, G. G., Richardson, A. S., Allison, S., & Roeger, L. (2003). Sexual abuse and suicidal behavior: A model constructed from a large community sample of adolescents. *Journal of the American Academy of Child and Adolescent Psychiatry, 42,* 1301–1309.

Berliner, L., & Conte, J. R. (1995). The effects of disclosure and intervention on sexually abused children. *Child Neglect and Abuse, 19,* 371–384.

Berliner, L., & Elliott, D. M. (2002). Sexual abuse of children. In J. E. B. Myers, L. Berliner, J. Briere, C. T. Hendrix, C. Jenny, et al. (Eds.), *The APASC handbook on child maltreatment* (2nd ed., pp. 55–78). Thousand Oaks, CA: Sage.

Bethea, L. (1999). Primary prevention of child abuse. *American Family Physician, 56,* 1577–1590.

Boney-McCoy, S., & Finkelhor, D. (1995). Psychosocial sequelae of violent victimization in a national youth sample. *Journal of Consulting and Clinical Psychology, 63,* 726–736.

Breslau, N., Davis, G. C., Andreski, M. A., & Peterson, E. (1991). Traumatic events and posttraumatic stress disorder in an urban population of young adults. *Archives of General Psychiatry, 48,* 216–222.

Briere, J. (1996). *Professional manual for the Trauma Symptom Checklist for Children.* Odessa, FL: Psychological Assessment Resources.

Broekman, B. F. P., Olff, M., & Boer, F. (2007). The genetic background to PTSD. *Neuroscience and Biobehavioral Reviews, 31,* 348–362.

Bugenthal, D. B., Blue, J., & Lewis, J. (1990). Caregiver beliefs and dysphoric affect directed to difficult children. *Developmental Psychology, 26,* 631–638.

Burgess, R., & Conger, R. (1978). Family interaction in abusive, neglectful and normal families. *Child Development, 49,* 1163–1173.

Calderoni, M. E., Alderman, E. M., Silver, E. J., & Bauman, L. J. (2006). The mental health impact of 9/11 on inner-city high school students 20-miles north of Ground Zero. *Journal of Adolescent Health, 39,* 57–65.

Carlson, E. B. (1997). *Trauma assessment.* New York: Guilford Press.

Cassidy, J., & Mohr, J. J. (2001). Unsolvable fear, trauma, and psychopathology: Theory, research, and clinical considerations related to disorganized attachment across the lifespan. *Clinical Psychology: Science and Practice, 8,* 275–298.

Ceci, S., & Bruck, M. (1995). *Jeopardy in the courtroom: A scientific analysis of children's testimony.* Washington, DC: American Psychological Association.

Center for the Prevention of Child Abuse of Dutchess County. (2006). *Handbook for parents.* Retrieved November 15, 2006, from http://www.child-abuse-prevention.org/handbook_parents.shtml.

Chalk, R., Gibbons, A., & Scarupa, H. J. (2002). *The multiple dimensions of child abuse and neglect: New insights into an old problem.* Washington, DC: Child Trends. Retrieved April 27, 2006, from www.childtrends.org/Files/ChildAbuseRB.pdf.

Child Abuse Prevention and Treatment Act if 1974 (Publication No. 93-247, 88 Stat 4, codified as amended at 42 USC SS 5101–5106). Available from http://www.acf.hhs.gov/programs/cb/laws_policies/policy/im/2003/im0304a.pdf.

Children's Defense Fund. (2005). *The state of America's children.* Washington, DC: Author.

Child Welfare Information Gateway. (2006a). *Recognizing child abuse and neglect: Signs and symptoms.* Retrieved November 13, 2006, from http://www.childwelfare.gov/pubs/factsheets/signs.cfm.

Child Welfare Information Gateway. (2006b). *What is child abuse and neglect?* Retrieved November 13, 2006, from http://www.childwelfare.gov/pubs/factsheets/whatiscan.cfm.

Cicchetti, D., Ganiban, J., & Barnett, D. (1990). Contributions from the study of high risk populations to understanding the development of emotion regulation. In K. Dode & J. Garber (Eds.), *The development of emotion regulation* (pp. 1–54). New York: Cambridge University Press.

Cicchetti, D., & Lynch, M. (1995). Failures in the expectcable environment and their impact on individual development: The case of child maltreatment. In D. Cicchetti & D. J. Cohen (Eds.), *Developmental psychopathology: Vol. 2. Risk, disorder and adaptation* (pp. 32–71). Oxford, England: Wiley.

Cohen, J. A. (1998). Practice parameters for the assessment and treatment of children with posttraumatic stress disorder. *Journal of the American Academy of Child and Adolescent Psychiatry, 35,* 4s-26s.

Cohen, J. A., Deblinger, E., Mannarino, A. P., & Steer, R. A. (2004). A multisite, randomized controlled trail for children with sexual abuse-related PTSD symptoms. *Journal of the American Academy of Child and Adolescent Psychiatry, 43,* 393–402.

Cohen, J. A., & Mannarino, A. P. (1996). A treatment study for sexually abused preschool children: Initial findings. *Journal of the American Academy of Child and Adolescent Psychiatry, 35,* 42–50.

Cohen, J. A., & Mannarino, A. P. (1997). A treatment study for sexually abused preschool children: Outcome during 1-year follow-up. *Journal of the American Academy of Child and Adolescent Psychiatry, 36,* 1228–1235.

Cohen, J. A., Mannarino, A. P., & Knudsen, K. K. (2005). Treating sexually abused children: 1 year follow up of a randomized controlled trial. *Child Neglect and Abuse, 29*(2), 135–145.

Cuffe, S. P., Addy, C. L., & Garrison, C. Z. (1998). Prevalence of PTSD in a community sample of older adolescents. *Journal of the American Academy of Child and Adolescent Psychiatry, 37*(2), 147–154.

Davidson, S., & Smith, R. (1990). Traumatic experiences in psychiatric outpatients. *Journal of Traumatic Stress Studies, 3,* 459–475.

DeBellis, M. D. (1997). Posttraumatic stress disorder and acute stress disorder. In R. T. Ammerman & M. Hersen (Eds.), *Handbook of prevention and treatment with children and adolescents* (pp. 455–494). New York: Wiley.

Deblinger, E., Stauffer, L. B., & Steer, R. A. (2001). Comparative efficacies of supportive and cognitive behavioral group therapies for young children who have been sexually abused and their non offending mothers. *Child Maltreatment, 6,* 332–343.

Deblinger, E., Steer, R. A., & Lippman, J. (1999). Two-year follow-up study of cognitive behavioral therapy for sexually abused children suffering post-traumatic stress symptoms. *Child Abuse and Neglect, 23,* 1371–1378.

Dutton, D. G. (1999). Traumatic origins of intimate rage. *Aggression and Violent Behavior, 4,* 431–447.

Epstein, M. A., & Bottoms, B. L. (1998). Memories of childhood sexual abuse: A survey of adults. *Child Abuse and Neglect, 22,* 1217–1238.

Everson, M. D., & Boat, B. W. (1994). Putting the anatomical doll controversy in perspective: An examination of major doll uses and related criticisms. *Child Abuse and Neglect, 18,* 113–129.

Faller, K. C. (1989). Why sexual abuse: An exploration of the intergenerational hypothesis. *Child Abuse and Neglect, 13,* 543–548.

Famularo, R., Fenton, T., Augustyn, M., & Zuckerman, B. (1996). Persistence of pediatric posttraumatic stress disorder after two years. *Child Abuse and Neglect, 20,* 1245–1248.

Famularo, R., Fenton, T., Kinscherff, R., Ayoub, C., & Barnum, R. (1993). Maternal and child post-traumatic stress disorder in cases of child maltreatment. *Child Abuse and Neglect, 18,* 27–36.

Famularo, R. A., Kinscherff, R. T., & Fenton T. (1992). Psychiatric diagnoses of maltreated children. *Journal of the American Academy of Child and Adolescent Psychiatry, 31,* 863–867.

Faust, J. (2000). Integration of family and cognitive behavioral therapy for treating sexually abused children. *Cognitive and Behavioral Practice, 73,* 361–368.

Faust, J., & Norman-Scott, H. (2000, August). *Risk and protective factors in the trauma response to childhood sexual abuse trauma.* Paper presented at the annual meeting of the Association for the Advancement of Behavior Therapy, New Orleans, LA.

Faust, J., & Stewart, L. M. (in press). Impact of child abuse timing and family environment on psychosis. *Journal of Trauma.*

Finkelhor, D. (1993). Epidemiological factors in the clinical identification of child sexual abuse [Special issue]. *Child Abuse and Neglect: Clinical Recognitions of Sexually Abused Children, 17,* 67–70.

Finkelhor, D. (1995). The victimization of children: A developmental perspective. *American Journal of Orthopsychiatry, 65,* 177–193.

Finkelhor, D., & Korbin, J. (1988). Child abuse as an international issue. *Child Abuse and Neglect, 11*(3), 397–407.

Fitzpatrick, K. M., & Boldizar, J. P. (1993). The prevalence and consequences of exposure to community violence among African American youth. *Journal of the American Academy of Child and Adolescent Psychiatry, 32,* 424–430.

Fletcher, K. E. (1992). *When bad things happen.* Worcester: University of Massachusetts Medical Center.

Fletcher, K. E. (1996a). Child posttraumatic stress disorder. In E. J. Mash & R. A. Barkely (Eds.), *Child psychopathology* (pp. 242–276). New York: Guilford Press.

Fletcher, K. E. (1996b, July). *Preliminary psychometrics of four new measures of childhood PTSD.* Paper presented at the International Research Conference on Trauma and Memory, Durham, NH.

Foa, E. B., Rothbaum, B. O., Riggs, D. S., & Murdock, T. B. (1991). Treatment of posttraumatic stress disorder in rape victims: A comparisons between cognitive behavioral procedures and counseling. *Journal of Consulting and Clinical Psychology, 59,* 715–723.

Friedrich, W. (1997). *Child Sexual Behavior Inventory.* Odessa, FL: Psychological Assessment Resources.

Gardner, R. A. (1970). The use of guilt as a defense against anxiety. *Psychoanalytic Review, 57*(1), 124–136.

Garnefski, N., & Diekstra, R. F. W. (1997). Comorbidity of behavioral, emotional, and cognitive problems in adolescence. *Journal of Youth and Adolescence, 26,* 321–338.

Goenjian, A. K., Pynoos, R. S., Steinberg, A. M., Najarian, L. M., Asarnow, J. R., & Karayan, I., et al. (1995). Psychiatric comorbidity in children after the 1988 earthquake in Armenia. *Journal of the American Academy of Child and Adolescent Psychiatry, 34,* 1174–1184.

Goodman, G. S., & Bottom, B. L. (1993). *Child victims, child witnesses: Understanding and improving testimony.* New York: Guilford Press.

Gorey, K. M., & Leslie, D. R. (2001). Working toward a valid prevalence estimate of child sexual abuse: A reply to Bolen and Scannapieco. *Social Science Review, 75*(1), 151–158.

Haugaard, J. J. (2000). The challenge of defining child sexual abuse. *American Psychologist, 55,* 1036–1039.

Helfer, M. E. (1997). Communication in the therapeutic relationship: Concepts, strategies, and skills. In M. E. Helfer, R. S. Kemp, & R. D. Krugman (Eds.), *The battered child* (pp. 107–119). Chicago: University of Chicago Press.

Herrenkohl, R. C., Herrenkohl, E. C., Egolf, B. P., & Wu, P. (1991). The developmental consequences of child abuse: The Lehigh Longitudinal Study. In R. H. Starr & D. A. Wolfe (Eds.), *The effects of child abuse and neglect* (pp. 57–81). New York: Guilford Press.

Hildyard, K. L., & Wolfe, D. A. (2002). Child neglect: Developmental issues and outcomes. *Child Abuse and Neglect, 26,* 679–695.

Howes, P. W., & Cicchetti, D. (1993). A family/relational perspective on maltreating families: Parallel processes across systems and social policy implications. In D. Cicchetti & S. L. Toth (Eds.), *Child abuse, child development, and social policy* (pp. 399–438). Norwood, NJ: Ablex.

Howes, P. W., Cicchetti, D. D., Toth, S. L., & Rogosch, F. A. (2000). Affective, organizational, and relational characteristics of maltreating families: A system's perspective. *Journal of Family Psychology, 14,* 95–110.

Hunter, S. V. (2006). Understanding the complexity of child sexual abuse: A review of the literature with implications for family counseling. *Family Journal: Counseling and Therapy for Couples and Families, 14,* 349–358.

Jaspers, J. P. C. (1998). Whiplash and posttraumatic stress disorder. *Disability and Rehabilitation: An International Multidisciplinary Journal, 20,* 397–404.

Kaplan, S. J., Pelcovitz, D., & Labruna, V. (1999). Child and adolescent abuse and neglect research: A review of the past 10 years: Pt. I. Physical and emotional abuse and neglect. *Journal of the American Academy of Child and Adolescent Psychiatry, 38*(10), 1214–1222.

Kavanagh, K., Youngblade, L., Reid, J., & Fagot, B. (1988). Interactions between children and abusive versus control parents. *Journal of Clinical Child Psychology, 17,* 137–142.

Keeping Children and Families Safe Act of 2003. (Publication No. 108-36). Available from http://www.acf.hhs.gov/programs/cb/laws_policies/policy/im/2003/im0304a.pdf.

Kendall-Tackett, K. A., & Eckenrode, J. (1996). The effects of neglect on academic achievement and disciplinary problems: A developmental perspective. *Child Abuse and Neglect, 20,* 161–169.

Klorman, R., Cicchetti, D., Thatcher, J. E., & Ison, J. R. (2003). Acoustic startle in maltreated children. *Journal of Abnormal Child Psychology, 31*(4), 359–370.

Koenig, A. L., Cicchetti, D., & Rogosch, F. A. (2000). Child compliance/noncompliance and maternal contributors to internalization in maltreating and nonmaltreating dyads. *Child Development, 71*(4), 1018–1032.

Koeppen, A. S. (1993). Relaxation training for children. In C. E. Schaefer & D. M. Cangelosi (Eds.), *Play therapy techniques* (pp. 237–243). Laham, MD: Jason Avonson.

Korbin, J. (1997). Culture and child maltreatment. In M. E. Helfer, R. S. Kemp, & R. D. Krugman (Eds.), *The battered child* (pp. 107–119). Chicago: University of Chicago Press.

Kovacs, M. (1992). *Professional manual for the Children's Depression Inventory (CDI).* North Towanda, NY: Multi Health Systems.

Kruczek, T., & Salsman, J. (2006). Prevention and treatment of posttraumatic stress disorder in the school setting. *Psychology in the Schools, 43,* 461–470.

La Greca, A. M., Silverman, W. K., Vernberg, E. M., & Prinstein, M. J. (1996). Symptoms of posttraumatic stress disorder in children after Hurricane Andrew: A prospective study. *Journal of Consulting and Clinical Psychology, 64,* 712–723.

LaRose, L., & Wolfe, D. A. (1987). Psychological characteristics of parents who abuse or neglect their children. In B. B. Lahey & A. E. Kazdin (Eds.), *Advances in clinical child psychology* (Vol. 10, pp. 55–97). New York: Plenum Press.

Lau, A. S., Valeri, S. M., & McCarty, C. A. (2006). Abusive parents' reports of child behavior problems: Relationship to observed parent-child interactions. *Child Abuse and Neglect, 30*(6), 639–655.

Lawyer, S. R., Ruggerio, K. J., Resnick, H. S., Kilpatrick, D. G., & Saunders, B. E. (2006). Mental health correlates of the victim perpetrator relationship among interpersonally victimized adolescents. *Journal of Interpersonal Violence, 21,* 1333–1353.

Lipovsky, J. A., Saunders, B. E., & Hanson, R. F. (1992). Parent-child relationships of victims and siblings in incest families. *Journal of Child Sexual Abuse, 1,* 35–49.

Lipschitz, D. S., Rasmusson, A. M., Anyan, W., Cromwell, P., & Southwick, S. (2000). Clinical and functioning correlates of posttraumatic stress disorder in urban adolescent girls at a primary care clinic. *Journal of the American Academy of Child and Adolescent Psychiatry, 39,* 1104–1111.

Lyons-Ruth, K., Connell, D., Zoll, D., & Stahl, J. (1987). Infants at social risk: Relations among infant maltreatment, maternal behavior, and infant attachment behavior. *Developmental Psychology, 23,* 223–232.

Lyons-Ruth, K., & Jacobvitz, D. (1999). Attachment disorganization: Unresolved loss, relational violence, and lapses in behavioral and attentional strategies. In J. Cassidy & P. R. Shaver (Eds.), *Handbook of attachment: Theory, research, and clinical applications* (pp. 520–554). New York: Guilford Press.

Maccoby, E. E., & Martin, J. A. (1983). Socialization in the context of the family: Parent-child interaction. In P. H. Mussen (Ed.), *Handbook of child psychology* (4th ed., pp. 1–101). New York: Wiley.

Main, M., & George, C. (1985). Responses of abused and disadvantaged toddlers to distress in agemates: A study in the daycare setting. *Developmental Psychology, 21,* 407–412.

Mash, J. E., Johnson, C., & & Kovitz, K. (1983). A comparison of the mother-child interactions of physically abused and nonabused children during play and task situations. *Journal of Clinical Psychology, 12,* 337–346.

Maughan, A., & Cicchetti, D. (2002). Impact of child maltreatment and interpersonal adult violence on children's emotion regulation abilities and socioemotional adjustment. *Child, Development, 73*, 1525–1542.

McCloskey, L. A., & Bailey, J. A. (2000). The intergenerational transmission of risk for child sexual abuse. *Journal of Interpersonal Violence, 15*, 1019–136.

McFarlane, A. C. (1999). Risk factors for the acute biological and psychological response to trauma. In R. Yehuda (Ed.), *Risk factors for posttraumatic stress disorder* (pp. 163–190). Washington, DC: American Psychiatric Press.

McKeever, V. M., & Huff, M. E. (2003). A diathesis stress model of posttraumatic stress disorder: Ecological, biological, and residual stress pathways. *Review of General Psychology, 7*, 237–250.

Milner, J. S. (1986). *Child Abuse Potential Inventory.* Webster, NC: Psytec.

Moradi, A. R., Doost, H. T. N., Taghavi, M. R., Yule, W., & Dalgleish, T. (1999). Everyday memory deficits in children and adolescents with PTSD: Performance on the Rivermead Behavioural Memory Test. *Journal of Child Psychology and Psychiatry, 40*, 357–361.

Nash, M. R., Hulsey, T. L., Sexton, M. C., Harralson, T. L., Lambert, W., & Lynch, G. V. (1993). Adult psychopathology associated with a history of childhood sexual abuse: A psychoanalytic perspective. In J. M. Masling & R. F. Bornstein (Eds.), *Psychoanalytic perspectives on psychopathology: Vol. 4. Empirical studies of psychoanalytic theories* (pp. 111–137). Washington, DC: American Psychological Association.

National Children's Advocacy Center. (n.d.). *Physical and behavioral indicators of abuse.* Retrieved November 13, 2006, from http://www.nationalcac.org/families/for_workers/abuse_indicators.html.

Orbach, Y., & Lamb, M. E. (1999). Assessing the accuracy of a child's account of sexual abuse: A case study. *Child Abuse and Neglect, 23*(1), 91–98.

Palmer, L. K., Franz, C. E., Armsworth, N., Swank, P., Copley, J. V., & Bush, C. A. (1999). Neuropsychological sequelae of chronically psychologically traumatized children: Specific findings in memory and higher cognitive functions. In V. L. Banyard (Ed.), *Trauma and memory* (pp. 229–244). Thousand Oaks, CA: Sage.

Parker, J. G., & Herrera, C. (1996). Interpersonal processes in friendship: A comparison of maltreated and nonmaltreated children's experiences. *Developmental Psychology, 32*, 1025–1038.

Paveza, G. J. (1988). Risk factors in father-daughter child sexual abuse: A case control study. *Journal of Interpersonal Violence, 3*, 290–306.

Pearlman, L. (2003). *Trauma and Attachment Belief Scale.* Los Angeles: Western Psychiatric Services.

Petty, J. (1990). *Checklist for Child Abuse Evaluation.* Odessa, FL: Psychological Assessment Resources.

Pfefferbaum, B., Nixon, S., Tucker, P. M., Tivis, R. D., Moore, V. L., Gurwitch, R. H., et al. (1999). Posttraumatic stress responses in bereaved children after the Oklahoma City bombing. *Journal of the American Academy of Child and Adolescent Psychiatry, 38*, 1372–1379.

Pollak, S. D., Cicchetti, D., Hornung, K., & Reed, A. (2000). Recognizing emotion in faces: Developmental effects of child abuse and neglect. *Developmental Psychology, 36*, 679–688.

Pollak, S., & Sinha, P. (2002). Effects of early experience on children's recognition of facial displays of emotion. *Developmental Psychology, 38*(5), 784–791.

Putnam, F. W. (2003). Ten-year research update review: Child sexual abuse. *Journal of the American Academy of Child and Adolescent Psychiatry, 42*, 269–278.

Rabalais, A. E., Ruggerio, K. J., & Scotti, J. R. (2002). Multicultural issues in the response of children to disasters. In A. M. La Greca, W. K. Silverman, E. M. Vernberg, & M. C. Roberts (Eds.), *Helping children cope with disasters and terrorism* (pp. 73–99). Washington, DC: American Psychological Association.

Rogosch, F. A., Cicchetti, D., & Aber, J. L. (1995). The role of child maltreatment in early devi- ations in cognitive and affective processing abilities and later peer relationship problems. *Development and Psychopathology, 7,* 591–609.

Rothbaum, B. O., Foa, E. B., & Riggs, D. S. (1992). A prospective examination of post-traumatic stress disorder in rape victims. *Journal of Traumatic Stress, 5*(3), 455–475.

Runyon, M., Faust, F., Kenny, M., & Kelly, D. (1997, August). *Maternal depression and child's perception of the family environment as predictors of post trauma symptomatology in abused children.* Paper presented at the annual meeting of the American Psychological Association, Chicago.

Sack, W. H., Clarke, G. N., & Seeley, J. (1996). Multiple forms of stress in Cambodian adolescent refugees. *Child Development, 67,* 106–116.

Saigh, P., A., Mroueh, M., & Bremner, J. K. (1997). Scholastic impairments among traumatized children. *Behaviour Research and Therapy, 35,* 429–436.

Saigh, P. A., Yasik, A. E., Oberfield, R. A., Halamandaris, P. V., & Bremner, J. D. (2006). The intellectual performance of traumatized children and adolescents with or without posttraumatic stress disorder. *Journal of Abnormal Psychology, 115,* 332–340.

Seagull, E. W. (1997). Family assessment. In M. E. Helfer, R. S. Kemp, & R. D. Krugman (Eds.), *The battered child* (pp. 150–174). Chicago: University of Chicago Press.

Sedlak, A. J., & Broadhurst, D. D. (1996). *Third national incidence study of child abuse and neglect: Final report.* Washington, DC: U.S. Department of Health and Human Services.

Segman, R. H., & Shalev, A. Y. (2003). Genetics of posttraumatic stress disorder. *CNS Spectrums, 8,* 693–698.

Shaw, J., Lewis, J., Loeb, A., Rosado, J., & Rodriguez, R. (2001). A comparison of Hispanic and African-American sexually abused girls and their families. *Child Abuse and Neglect, 25,* 1363–1379.

Shipman, K. L., & Zeman, J. (2001). Socialization of children's emotion regulation in mother-child dyads: A developmental psychopathology perspective. *Development and Psychopathology, 13,* 317–336.

Shipman, K. L., Zeman, J., Penza, S., & Champion, K. (2000). Emotion management skills in sexually maltreated and nonmaltreated girls: A developmental psychopathology perspective. *Development and Psychopathology, 12,* 47–62.

Shonk, S. M., & Cicchetti, D. (2001). Maltreatment, competency deficits, and risk for academic and behavioral maladjustment. *Developmental Psychology, 37,* 3–17.

Silverman, W. K., & La Greca, A. M. (2002). Children experiencing disasters: Definitions, reactions, and predictors of outcomes. In A. M. La Greca, W. K. Silverman, M. Vernberg, & M. C. Roberts (Eds.), *Helping children cope with disasters and terrorism* (pp. 11–22). Washington, DC: American Psychological Association.

Starr, R. H. (Ed.). (1988). *Child abuse prediction: Policy implications.* Cambridge, MA: Ballinger.

Stein, M. B., Jang, K. L., Taylor, S., Vernon, P. A., & Livesley, W. J. (2002). Genetic and envi- ronmental influences on trauma exposure and posttraumatic stress disorder symptoms: A twin study. *American Journal of Psychiatry, 159,* 1675–1681.

Thierry, K., Lamb, M., Orbach, Y., & Pipe, M. (2005). Developmental differences in the function and use of anatomical dolls during interviews with alleged sexual abuse victims. *Journal of Consulting and Clinical Psychology, 73*(6), 1125–1134.

Tolin, D. F., & Foa, E. B. (2002). Gender and PTSD: A cognitive model. In R. Kimerling, P. Ouimette, & J. Wolfe (Eds.), *Gender and PTSD* (pp. 76–97). New York: Guilford Press.

Trickett, P., Noll, J., Reiffman, A., & Putnam, F. (2001). Variants of intrafamilial sexual abuse experiences: Implications for short- and long-term development. *Development and Psychopathology, 13,* 1001–1019.

True, W. R., & Lyons, M. J. (1999). Genetic risk factors for PTSD: A twin study. In R. Yehuda (Ed.), *Risk factors for posttraumatic stress disorder* (pp. 61–78). Washington, DC: American Psychiatric Association.

U.S. Department of Health and Human Services. (1998). *Child maltreatment 1996: Reports from the states to the National Child Abuse and Neglect Data System.* Washington, DC: U.S. Government Printing Office.

U.S. Department of Health and Human Services, Administration on Children, Youth, and Families. (2003). *Emerging practices in the prevention of child abuse and neglect.* Washington, DC: U.S. Government Printing Office.

U.S. Department of Health and Human Services, Administration on Child, Youth, and Families. (2006). *Child maltreatment 2004.* Washington, DC: U.S. Government Printing Office.

Van Hutton, V. (1994). *HTP and DAP as measures in children: A quantitative scoring system.* Odessa, FL: Psychological Assessment Resources.

van IJzendoorn, M. H., Schuengel, C., & Bakermans-Kranenburg, M. J. (1999). Disorganized attachment in early childhood: Meta-analysis of precursors, concomitants, and sequelae. *Development and Psychopathology, 11,* 225–249.

Walrath, C. M., Ybarra, M. L., Sheenan, A. K., Holden, E. W., & Burns, B. J. (2006). Impact of maltreatment of children serviced in community mental health programs. *Journal of Emotional and Behavioral Disorders, 14,* 143–156.

Warnygora, N. R. (2005). Evaluating the behavioral and neuropsychological differences of children with and without posttraumatic stress disorder utilizing a teacher rating scale. *Dissertation Abstracts International, 65,* 6705B–6907B.

Werleke, C., & Wolfe, D. A. (2003). Child maltreatment. In E. J. Mash & R. A. Barkley (Eds.), *Child psychopathology* (2nd ed., pp. 632–684). New York: Guilford Press.

Widom, C. S. (1999). Post traumatic stress disorder in abused and neglected children grown up. *American Journal of Psychiatry, 156,* 1223–1229.

Wolfe, D. (1999). *Child abuse: Vol. 10. Implications for child development and psychopathology* (2nd ed.). Thousand Oaks, CA: Sage.

Wolfe, V. V., Gentile, C., Michienzi, T., Sas, L., & Wolfe, D. (1991). Children's Impact of Traumatic Events Scale: A measure of post-sexual abuse PTSD symptoms. *Behavioral Assessment, 13*(4), 359–383.

World Health Organization. (2006). *Preventing child maltreatment: A guide to taking action and generating evidence.* Geneva, Switzerland: Author.

CHAPTER 18

Neurologically Impaired Children

CHARLES J. GOLDEN

DESCRIPTION OF THE DISORDER

Neurological impairment in children covers a wide range of disorders whose psychological and cognitive impact range from minimal or nonexistent to complete inability to function at any level. The impact of these numerous disorders is further complicated by the time at which the child's disorder occurs and the nature of the specific disorder. The reaction of the child's brain can be ameliorated by plasticity (the ability of the brain to reorganize after a brain injury), but this is affected by the age of the child and the nature of the specific disorders, with localized disorders in the youngest children most likely to show reorganization.

If this chapter had been written when the author was a graduate student in the early 1970s, the areas considered for inclusion would have been much more limited. Over the past 3 decades, it has been recognized that many (if not all) of the disorders that arise in early childhood or adolescence may have a neurological root, including many of the traditional mental health disorders, such as anxiety and depression. Thus, current neuropsychological work is not limited to traditional disorders such as head trauma and cerebral palsy. Contemporary neuropsychology now encompasses the full range of childhood disorders traditionally seen in mental health, psychiatric, educational, and neurological settings. Further, it has been recognized that disorders such as cancer and kidney disorders—even when the brain is not directly involved—can affect short- and long-term brain development, resulting in learning, cognitive, and emotional problems that are not simply reactions to chronic illness.

The scope of neuropsychological research is expanding. The current chapter is limited to those disorders most associated with neurological insults and disorders rather than such disorders as anxiety, which are described elsewhere in this volume. In addition, neurological disorders discussed in this chapter are limited to those directly affecting the brain. A wide range of neurological disorders also affect the spinal cord and the peripheral nervous system and have dramatic impacts on psychological and physical functioning, yet largely spare cognitive function. Finally, this discussion emphasizes those disorders and conditions having the largest impact on cognitive functioning, broadly conceived as deficits in learning, memory, intelligence, attention, and executive functions.

Even a cursory evaluation of the literature reveals numerous conditions that may lead to cognitive impairment beginning in the developing fetus. These conditions may result from genetic, infectious, or environmental factors and include a wide variety of primarily motor disorders that often have cognitive effects, such as general movement disorders (Dewey & Bottos, 2004; McMahon, Filloux, Ashworth, & Jensen, 2002) and cerebral palsy (Blondis, 2004; Fennell & Dikel, 2001; Tran, Gray, & O'Callaghan, 2005). Prematurity is a condition frequently associated with neurodevelopmental problems or neurological damage (Dammann & Leviton, 2004; Foulder-Hughes & Cooke, 2003; Hagberg & Jacobsson, 2005; Luciana, 2003; Nosarti, Rifkin, & Robin, 2003; Sesma & Georgieff, 2003). The associated problems of low birth weight and small size have also been implicated as causal factors (Frisk, Amsel, & Whyte, 2002; Ment et al., 2003; Peterson & Ment, 2001; Taylor, Minich, Klein, & Hack, 2004; Woodward, Mogridge, Wells, & Inder, 2004), along with exposure to alcohol and other substances (Aucott, Donohue, Atkins, & Allen, 2002; Morrow et al., 2001), and such conditions as prenatal trauma, maternal diabetes, and hypoxia (DeBoer, Wewerka, Bauer, Georgieff, & Nelson, 2005; Jiang, Yin, Shao, & Wilkinson, 2004; Lee et al., 2005; Robinson, 2005; Scher, Redline, & Bangert, 2002). Genetic disorders may arise from myriad problems, such as Lesch-Nyhan, sickle cell disease, autism, Tourette's, Fragile X syndrome, and Down syndrome (Trisomy 21; Coleman, 2005; Schatz & Buzan, 2006; Schatz, Finke, & Roberts, 2004; Verte, Geurts, Roeyers, Oosterlaan, & Sergeant, 2005; Visser, Schretlen, Harris, & Jinnah, 2005).

Postbirth, a whole range of disorders may cause neurological damage. These commonly include vascular disorders (Hetherington, Tuff, Anderson, Miles, & DeVeber, 2005; Hurvitz, Warschausky, Berg, Tsai, & Roth, 2004; Kirkham & Hogan, 2004; Max, 2004), trauma (Barlow, Thompson, Johnson, & Minns, 2004; Eilander, Wijnen, Scheirs, deKort, & Prevo, 2005; Ettaro, Berger, & Songer, 2004; King, MacKay, & Simick, 2003; Lazoritz & Palusci, 2001; Makaroff & Putnam, 2003; Middleton, 2001; Reichert & Schmidt, 2001; Savage, Depompei, Tyler, & Lash, 2005; Yuma, Maxson, & Brown, 2006), childhood cancer (Mulhern & Butler, 2004), near-drowning (Hughes et al., 2002), infections of the central nervous system (Anderson, Anderson, Grimwood, & Nolan, 2004; Carter, Neville, & Newton, 2003; Schmidt et al., 2006), HIV/AIDS (Mitchell, 2001; Smith, Martin, & Wolters, 2004), tumors (Fuemmeler, Elkin, & Mullins, 2002), organ transplants (Rodrigue, Gonzalez-Peralta, & Langham, 2004), and neurosurgery for epilepsy, tumors, and other conditions (Aarsen, Van Dongen, Paquier, Van Mourik, & Catsman-Berrevoets, 2004; deBode, Firestine, Mathern, & Dobkin, 2005; Pataraia et al., 2005).

DIAGNOSIS AND ASSESSMENT

Diagnoses typically derive either from the *Diagnostic and Statistical Manual of Mental Disorders*, fourth edition, text revision (*DSM-IV-TR*), which focuses on the types of emotional, cognitive, and behavioral symptoms shown, or from neurological diagnoses, which generally focus on etiology, except for conditions where the etiology is unknown. The *DSM-IV* diagnoses are discussed first.

DSM-IV DISORDERS

The *DSM-IV* diagnoses generally offer weak coverage of the neurological disorders and their subsequent impairment in children. Diagnoses are often very general and in many cases nonspecific, so that children with very different etiologies and symptoms may be grouped together in a single category. In many of the cases, disorders that arise from nonneurological causes are lumped together with those arising from neurological disorders. The result is confusion and poor diagnostic practices.

Mental Retardation   The most well-known of the potentially neurologically based disorders is Mental Retardation (MR). The *DSM-IV* requires an IQ of 70 or below, along with concurrent impairments in two of the following areas of adaptive functioning: self-care, home living, social and interpersonal skills, use of community resources, self-direction, functional academic skills, work, leisure, health, and safety. The age of onset must be before 18 years, so it is possible to be born with MR or to develop normally and then acquire it through injury or disease.

The areas impaired will vary widely from person to person, depending on the etiology and the degree of mental retardation. Mental Retardation is divided into five levels: mild, with an IQ from 50–55 to 70; moderate, with an IQ from 35–40 to 50–55; severe, with an IQ from 20–25 to 35–40; profound, with an IQ below 20–25; and unspecified, where the person is for some reason untestable (e.g., has aphasia or paralysis) but where MR is presumed based on other evidence. In outpatient practice, nearly all diagnoses of MR fall into the mild range.

Not all cases of MR are presumed to be caused by neurologic damage. By definition, approximately 2.5% of the population will have normal brains but be at the lowest end of the IQ curve and thus be diagnosed with MR. However, MR in practice occurs in at least 5% of the population, suggesting that at least half of all individuals diagnosed with MR have a brain injury or brain disorder. Nearly all cases below mild MR fall into this latter group, as do a large percentage of those with mild MR. It has also been argued that all MR has a neurological etiology, but this has yet to be demonstrated by objective tests.

Mental Retardation can arise from numerous neurological disorders. These include trauma and stroke (as long as they occur before age 18). Children who are born with MR may have had a stroke in the prenatal or perinatal period or suffered trauma. They may have been exposed to drugs or alcohol as fetuses, or exposed to any of a wide range of chemicals or substances that can interfere with brain development. Children with cerebral palsy may or may not have MR, depending on the extent and location of their brain injury.

Disorders that solely involve the motor tracks of the brain may leave cognition intact. However, these cases may be diagnosed as MR because of an inability to develop motor speech or to do tasks normally associated with early childhood development. In such cases, a careful consideration of the extent and location of any brain impairment is necessary in making a correct diagnosis, usually based on neuroradiological rather than psychological data.

On the other hand, brain impairment that involves only the more complex areas of the brain may result in normal early development that stalls out in elementary school, when the child fails to make normal progress. Such children may be tested at normal levels but see their IQ decline as they get older because the lack of ongoing brain development makes it impossible for them to keep up with peers. Such children may be misdiagnosed as "unmotivated" or "depressed" or given another psychological diagnosis when the neurodevelopmental disorder is the real primary diagnosis.

Learning Disorders   Learning disorders have become a primary area of both research (e.g., Downie, Frisk, & Jakobson, 2005; Golden, Zillmer, & Spiers, 1992; Simon, Bearden, McGinn, & Zackai, 2005; Woodrich, Kaplan, & Deering, 2006) and practice. The learning disorders in the *DSM-IV* include disorders of reading, mathematics, written expression, and those "not otherwise specified." All of the disorders are primarily characterized by a discrepancy between intelligence and educational level and actual skills, which interfere with academic achievement or daily living skills related to the area of the disorder. Such disorders also must have a cognitive etiology and not be due to peripheral sensory injury (deafness, blindness, lack of sensation) or motor disorders (paralysis, lack of coordination). Learning disabilities are not diagnosed when the disability is primarily the result of environmental deprivation (e.g., lack of education) or a refusal to study or learn.

READING DISORDER   Often referred to as dyslexia, Reading Disorder involves a discrepancy between reading skills and intelligence. Neuropsychologically, the disorder is thought to be primarily related to injuries in the posterior aspects of the left hemisphere, usually in the temporal, parietal, or occipital areas of the brain. The left temporal-occipital area is often referred to as the "reading" area of the brain. Although this is a gross oversimplification of the complex brain processes involved in reading, this name reflects the importance of the temporal-occipital junction where sounds and visual symbols are integrated in the young child. There is some evidence that injuries to the right hemisphere may slow acquisition of these skills, which may appear similar to a Reading Disorder but improve over time (see the section on Conceptualization for more detail).

MATHEMATICS DISORDER   Often referred to in neuropsychology as dyscalculia, Mathematics Disorder involves a similar discrepancy between mathematical abilities and intelligence. This disorder is more complex than reading because it involves not only performing mathematical calculations, but also reading and writing mathematical symbols and utilizing mathematical concepts and procedures in both verbal and nonverbal applications.

The most basic form of mathematical disorder, where the individual is unable to understand or manipulate basic mathematical symbols, is generally seen as a parietal-occipital disorder that involves both spatial concepts and visual recognition and analysis. The right hemisphere plays a larger role than in reading because of the spatial nature of many mathematical computations. Luria (1973) argues that these primary mathematical skills are the domain of the left hemisphere when dealing with basic calculations, but he does not address this issue with children. More complex verbal problem solving generally involves both hemispheres of the brain, including the anterior as well as posterior cognitive areas.

WRITING DISORDER   Referred to as dysgraphia, Disorder of Written Expression involves a discrepancy between written skills and intelligence. This may be reflected in the inability of the individual to write letters correctly (despite the absence of motor or sensory problems) or may involve spelling or grammar skills. The act of writing is generally centered in the temporal-parietal area opposite the hand one writes with (usually the left hemisphere). Interestingly, forcing a left-handed child to write with his or her right hand, as is seen in some settings, may force the left hemisphere to take over functions more naturally assumed by the right hemisphere. More complex writing tasks such as grammar and spelling may also be mediated at the temporal-occipital-parietal junction, particularly in an area called the angular gyrus. Writing as a whole is a complex process that involves many brain areas as well as environmental factors such as practice.

Expressive Language Disorder   This disorder involves expressive language skills substantially below expectations based on nonverbal measures of intelligence and/or receptive language skills. These disorders can be the result of injuries to the peripheral or central motor system with no associated cognitive deficits, or may be part of a larger language problem arising from injuries to the general area of the anterior cortex known as Broca's area. This disorder may include obvious motor problems or even paralysis, but may also be reflected in word-finding problems, telegraphic speech, mutism, word substitutions for similar sounds, word-sound simplifications, and a range of other related deficits. In older children, rapid onset of these problems may be observed after a trauma or stroke. This may occur in younger children as well. However, problems found among younger children are likely to arise from multiple brain areas and thus are more difficult to discuss in terms of a specific neurophysiological etiology.

Mixed Receptive-Expressive Language Disorder   The main feature of this disorder is the presence of both receptive and expressive language problems when compared to nonverbal tests of functioning. Neuropsychologically, these disorders are thought to arise from brain injury or the failure of brain development in the dominant (usually left) hemisphere of the brain. However, all cases of brain injury to the left hemisphere do not result in such problems; it depends on etiology (this disorder is more likely to be present after cerebrovascular problems and as a result of neurodevelopmental genetic disorders) as well as the timing and specificity of the injury. Early, more focal injuries are more likely to show compensation (plasticity) by the brain in such a manner as to limit or even eliminate any symptoms (Golden et al., 1992).

Phonological Disorder   Phonological disorders involve problems in producing or using sounds. This may include substitution of sounds for one another, omissions of sounds, or similar problems. Such individuals generally sound distinctly different from children of the same age and dialect and sociocultural background. This disorder may be developmental and disappear over time, may reflect peripheral damage to the auditory or motor speech system, or may reflect brain defects as a result of injury or genetics—again, primarily in the dominant hemisphere speech areas. When the result of actual brain defects, these disorders will generally persist into later years but are responsive to therapy. The severity of the condition can vary widely. When a brain defect is involved, cognitive deficits are more likely as well, which is not the case with the peripheral motor or auditory etiologies.

Hyperactivity   Diverse theories exist on the etiology of hyperactivity (see Golden & Anderson, 1979). The two major theories involve the arousal and attention functions of the reticular activating system (RAS). Basically, one theory argues that hyperactivity is the result of overarousal caused by a dysfunction in this area of the brain. The overarousal makes the child hyperresponsive and unable to control an attentional process, just like an infant in the early months of life. In the case of the hyperactive child, a decrease in this stimulus-bound behavior, which usually accompanies maturation of the brain, never takes place. The alternative theory argues just the opposite: that the hyperactive child is underaroused. This results in a state of stimulus deprivation which the child finds unpleasant. As a consequence, the child attempts to increase stimulation of the brain in the only way he or she knows how: by increased motor behavior and attention to high-level stimuli, thereby increasing motor sensory feedback.

Both theories have strong adherents, and both can be justified on the basis of some available evidence (Golden & Anderson, 1979). It is possible that both are correct; some children may show different types of hyperactivity, despite the fact that the overt behavior is similar. One hypothesized difference between these children would exist, however, in the first 2 years of life. We would expect the overaroused child to be fussy, be difficult to put to sleep, have difficulty in establishing long sleep periods, and generally be overreactive. On the other hand, the underaroused child might resist going to sleep but would sleep well after falling asleep. Indeed, the child might even seem somewhat lethargic and may be referred to as a "good" (meaning quiet) baby. In general, children with both types of history may be found in the hyperactive population.

Another discriminator may be response to medication. When exposed to a stimulant, the overaroused child might get much worse, whereas the underaroused child might be expected to get better (although dosage may play an important role in each case). Because there are hyperactive children who respond in both ways (as well as not at all), this evidence suggests the possibility of two forms of neuropsychological hyperactivity.

In general, a review of the literature is of little help in deciding which theory is correct (Golden & Anderson, 1979). One problem is that if there are two or more forms of hyperactivity, these forms have been mixed in most research, causing contradictory results and inadequate conclusions. Until this issue is addressed more directly, it is unlikely that any substantive progress in this area will be made.

Another important issue in the development of childhood hyperactivity is the question of time of injury. Rutter (1980) presented evidence that children with injuries after age 2 or 3 do not develop hyperactivity at a rate higher than that of a normal control population. His studies indicated that a separate form of hyperactivity did exist, however, that appeared to result from injuries before birth or very early in life and that might have an organic basis. Thus the type of hyperactivity discussed here may occur only in very early injuries, whereas later forms are caused by emotional or other neuropsychological problems.

Autistic Disorder   Autistic Disorder is characterized by impaired development in social interaction skills and in both verbal and nonverbal communication skills. There is also a restriction of interests and activities. Autism may range from the extremely severe case, which may be accompanied by Mental Retardation and other neurological problems, to milder cases where intelligence may be normal. Autism is assumed to start before 36 months of age. It has been hypothesized that this disorder may also reflect injury to the subcortical reticular areas of the brain. This disorder may appear on the extreme ends of the continuum of the arousal disorders seen in hyperactivity. Arousal may be at such a high level as to make it impossible for the child to make sense of reality. Such a problem may also cause stimulation to actually be painful or unpleasant to the child, resulting in withdrawal and isolative behavior. On the other hand, arousal may be so low that even hyperactive behavior is insufficient to allow the child any normal contact with the world. The child may produce behavior designed to intensify stimulus input even more (such as head banging) or withdraw into an inner world cut off from the reality of the situation. Either of these mechanisms can be invoked to explain the symptoms of some children.

In some cases there is etiology involving a clear precipitating event (e.g., meningitis); in other cases there is no clear cause. In the latter case, there may of course be a precipitant that was simply not recognized because of inadequate history or evaluation, or because it is so subtle that current evaluation techniques cannot detect the problems.

Asperger's Disorder   Asperger's Disorder is characterized by problems in social interactions and restricted interests and activities, but does not include the communication problems seen in autism. Asperger's neuropsychological etiology is unclear. Such individuals will have normal or above-average intelligence and often do well on a variety of neuropsychological tests. Interestingly, when tested, such children may perform similarly to individuals with nonverbal learning deficits, demonstrating problems with visual-spatial skills, problems with complex motor skills, and problems with nonverbal executive tasks. This pattern is suggestive of possible injury to the nondominant hemisphere, but the disorder is not as clear-cut as would be seen in a childhood stroke. Specifically, the problems appear to lie in the integrative functions of the nondominant hemisphere. More research on the development of Asperger's is needed, but there is a strong belief that most, if not all, cases reflect a neurologic disorder.

Dementia   At one time, the definition of Dementia was limited to adults who suffered brain injury or disease. However, the *DSM-IV* allows for Dementia to be diagnosed in childhood and adolescence. Diagnosis of this condition is generally limited to children who have shown normal development up until a head trauma, infarct, disease, or other neurological disorder causes a marked decline in memory and/or cognitive problems. (This is different from Childhood Disintegrative Disorder, which is not assumed to have a neurological etiology, but which will result in similar behavior.) Dementias are classified by their etiology (e.g., dementia secondary to head injury).

In reality, dementias will have very different presentations across clients, their only commonalities being the presence of a neurological cause, memory problems, and cognitive problems. Cognitive problems may include such diverse areas as attention (e.g., Anderson, Godber, Smibert, Weiskop, & Ekert, 2004), intelligence (e.g., Bava, Ballantyne, & Trauner, 2005), inhibition (e.g., Christ, White, Brunstrom, & Abrams, 2003), academic skills (e.g., Downie et al., 2005), executive skills (e.g., Powell & Voeller, 2004), and visuospatial skills (e.g., Simon et al., 2005). The presentations differ as much as the full range of brain disorders seen in the general population. The disorder may be classified by etiology (when known) or as "not otherwise specified" when the etiology is unclear.

Cognitive Disorder   Cognitive Disorder is similar to Dementia in many ways, with extensive overlap and similarity between the symptoms of each disorder. However, cognitive disorder does not meet the full criteria for a diagnosis of Dementia. In many cases, the requirement of a significant memory disorder is lacking, with the major problems being cognitive in nature and following the same general areas as discussed in the previous paragraph. Cognitive Disorder generally will not be diagnosed if all of the symptoms can be accounted for by mental retardation, learning problem, or one of the communication disorders preciously discussed. However, when the criteria for those disorders is not met or the problems range beyond what would normally be seen in those disorders, then Cognitive Disorder can be diagnosed. It is not unusual to see this diagnosis as the only *DSM-IV* diagnosis in a brain injured child who has clear cognitive problem but who cannot meet the strict criteria of the other disorders. The disorder may be classified by etiology (when known) or as "not otherwise specified" when the etiology is unclear. There is no breakdown by type or nature of the Cognitive Disorder.

NEUROLOGICAL DISORDERS

Neurological conceptualization of the childhood disorders focuses, as noted earlier, on etiology rather than behavioral impact. Thus, the neurological diagnosis tells us more about how the condition came about than the specific cognitive and behavioral problems. The most frequent causes of childhood disorders are genetic disorders, stroke (both before and after birth), head trauma (both before and after birth), metabolic disorders that affect the brain, cancer of the blood or cancer in the brain, meningitis, encephalitis, other infections, pediatric AIDS, generalized infections of the body, idiopathic epilepsy, epilepsy associated with another neurological disorder, in utero and later exposure to drugs, alcohol, heavy metals, and other substances that impact brain development, hypoxia, near-drowning, respiratory distress, and failure of any major organ system. It is not within the scope of this chapter to examine each of these in detail, but they can be found described in standard pediatric neurology texts.

ASSESSMENT

In the case of all these disorders, a physician's assessment is necessary to identify medically treatable conditions. Beyond that, there is a need for a comprehensive neuropsychological evaluation, which often needs to be repeated as the child develops or the disorder progresses. The time for reevaluations varies by condition and situation and typically ranges from 1 to 5 years between evaluations.

A comprehensive evaluation will differ in terms of specific tests by the age and the specific neurological condition involved. However, the areas that need evaluation are similar across disorders, although the emphasis on each area will differ depending on the specific disorder and the reason for the examination. These areas include:

- *Motor function:* This includes both fine and gross motor functioning. Psychological testing traditionally focuses on fine motor control which can be measured through construction type tests (such as Block Design or drawing tests). Gross motor skills are less well evaluated although they can be observed during testing including such functions as walking. Motor skills should be evaluated for each side of the body independently as well as for bilateral function.
- *Tactile functions:* These include the ability to feel touch and pressure and to recognize objects with touch. Subtests of the Halstead-Reitan and Luria-Nebraska provide basic evaluations of these skills. Tactile skills, like motor skills, should be evaluated for each side of the body independently as well as for bilateral function.

- *Language functions:* Evaluation for language happens both in the course of giving any test (following and responding to questions) or conducting any interview. They are also specifically evaluated in verbal tests from intelligence and memory exams as well as tests of academic function. Language is complex and much can be learned from a qualitative analysis of spontaneous language and responses to test and interview questions rather than relying on test scores alone. Areas of concern include both expressive language (the ability to speak and communicate) and receptive language (the ability to understand.) In children with brain injury, there is often the need for the services of a speech and language pathologist in addition to the evaluations done by psychologists.

- *Academic functions:* Comprehensive evaluations of reading, writing, and mathematical skills are generally a routine part of these evaluations for school age children. A number of comprehensive tests exist for these evaluations which can be part of a school evaluation as well. The exams need to include overall achievement as well as an analysis of those basic skills which underlie each area.

- *Visual and visuospatial skills:* These areas include an analysis of basic visual skills (such as object recognition) along with the relationship between objects spatially. More complex tests include visual reasoning and identification of patterns within visual stimuli as well as complex spatial relationships. More basic skill evaluations can include visual field evaluations, although these are more often done as part of an opthamological or optometric evaluation.

- *Auditory skills:* These begin with the ability to hear sounds and words in each ear and to break down and analyzed those skills. The evaluation should usually be accompanied by an audiological examination. Verbal receptive skills are further evaluated in the language analysis, but generally additional tests are necessary to look at more complex analysis of nonverbal sounds, which include tone, rhythm, pattern, and nonverbal sound recognition.

- *Memory functions:* Both verbal and nonverbal memory functions are usually analyzed. Memory may be broken down into short term working memory (less than a second), immediate (several seconds to a minute), delayed (twenty minutes or more), and long term (days or weeks or years). In general, short-term, immediate, and delayed memory are evaluated routinely, while long term memory is generally assessed via tests of knowledge or events.

- *Intelligence:* Higher level verbal and nonverbal skills should be routinely evaluated. These include such tasks as comprehension tests, similarities, abstractive skills, problem solving, and pattern analysis. These are typically evaluated by standard comprehensive intelligence exams.

- *Executive skills:* These are evaluated in older children and adolescents, examining the ability to learn from experience, complex problem solving, hypothesis testing, flexibility, insight, and abstract analysis. These are among the most difficult skills to evaluate, requiring special tests like the Category Test, Wisconsin Card Sort Test, Tower of Hanoi, and others (Golden et al., 1992).

- *Attentional abilities:* The basic ability to maintain attention over time is an essential part of most evaluations as deficits in this area will impact many of the other areas of evaluation. While tests like Digit Symbol or Digit Span measure a limited form of attention, sustained attention can be assessed with computerized tests like the Connors Continuous Performance Test (Connors & MHS staff, 2000).

CONCEPTUALIZATION

Widely divergent theories have come to a consensus concerning a simple fact; almost all behavior, and certainly all behavior we consider important to being human, is mediated through the brain. While it does not follow that all behavioral dysfunction is caused by brain dysfunction or abnormality, it does force us to take a closer look at the important interaction between individuals' environments and the processing of information gathered from the environment in the central nervous system.

It is important to recognize that there is no single "organic brain syndrome"; virtually any symptom of abnormal behavior that one can name can arise, under the proper circumstances and with the proper injury, from a dysfunction of the brain. Thus, the focus changes from looking at the occasional brain-injured child with "classic" symptoms to an attempt to understand the way in which the brain works, the ways in which it may become dysfunctional, and the ways in which many forms of abnormal behavior in the child, adolescent, and adult arise from brain damage.

Two theories, with minor changes, have dominated the field through most of its history. First, *localizationism* suggests that each area of the brain has a specific function. Injuries to these areas result in specific and predictable symptoms. If a child has the specific symptoms, then the area of the brain injury is known. By contrast, *equipotentism* assumes that higher-level abilities (those which are neither fundamentally motor nor sensory in nature) are a result of the brain as a whole, with problems similar regardless of the specific location of the "association" areas which are injured. Differences in symptoms reflect degree of damage rather than location.

Most models of brain function, rehabilitation, and assessment utilize assumptions derived from of one of the above theories, though these underlying theoretical assumptions are not always acknowledged. Classic descriptions of "the brain-damaged child" include attentional deficits, emotional lability, coordination difficulties, and poor academic functioning. Though never explicitly stated, such a description implies that all brain-damaged children are alike, regardless of the localization of their injury. For example, the notion that the brain is functionally homogeneous reflects equipotential thinking.

Neither equipotentiality nor the localizationist model have enjoyed universal acceptance. Many modern theorists have begun to question the assumptions underlying both of them. For example, localizationist theory has been criticized since many clinical and experimental cases have been observed with lesions in a specific area which are not accompanied by the symptoms predicted by localizationist theory. In other cases, a specific area may be intact but the patient still shows symptoms associated with insult or injury to that area. Equipotentiality theory has similar problems. Some small lesions result in extensive deficits, whereas some large lesions produce relatively few problems in comparison.

LURIA'S ALTERNATIVE

The evidence in regard to the inadequacies of both the localizationist and equipotential approach to brain-behavior relationships has resulted in a growing exploration of alternatives to these basic theories. Probably the most comprehensive and well-known alternative was postulated by the Soviet neuropsychologist A. R. Luria. Luria, in his extensive publications, noted that any alternative theory must do three things: (1) explain the data that fit the localizationist hypothesis; (2) explain the data that support the equipotential hypothesis; and (3) explain the data inconsistent with one or both theories. (See Luria, 1973, for the most basic introduction to his theory, or Golden et al., 1992, for an introduction to Luria's thinking.)

Luria developed a set of alternative hypotheses to describe brain function. The most basic and important concept in this theory is that of the *functional* system. A functional system is probably best explained by first looking to the operation of the rest of the human body (Mecacci, 1979). Mecacci suggests that the function of a brain system is similar to the function of other systems, such as the digestive system. For example, if we were to remove the stomach from a person, we would find that digestion had stopped in that person. Using the same techniques as employed by localizationist research, we would then conclude that the stomach is the digestion center of the body.

It is clear that the assignment of digestive function to the stomach alone is a fallacious assumption. Although the stomach plays a specific role in digestion, it is not solely responsible for that process. If the rest of the digestive system were removed, the stomach would not be able to carry on digestion by itself. The brain, Luria (1973) suggests, operates in a similar manner. Each area of the brain can operate only in conjunction with other areas of the brain to produce a behavior. No area of the brain is singly responsible for any voluntary human behavior. However, just as the stomach plays a specific role in the digestive system, each area of the brain plays a specific role in behavior. The assumption that functional systems produce behavior is consistent, to some degree, with both the equipotential and localization theories. Like the equipotential theory, Luria regards behavior as the result of an interaction of many areas of the brain. Like the localizationist theory, Luria assigns a specific role to each area of the brain.

However, Luria's theory has clear disagreements with both the localization and the equipotentiality approaches. Luria assumed that only specific parts, not all parts of the brain, combine to produce behavior. Furthermore, there is no equipotentiality of brain tissue. Brain tissue is conceptualized as being specialized both psychologically and physiologically. Localizationist assumptions of centers for specific observable behaviors contradict this theory. Behavior is conceived of as being a function of systems of brain areas rather than unitary specific areas. A given behavior will be impaired when any part of the functional system responsible for the behavior is impaired. Thus, for example, some individuals without injury to the "reading center" still are unable to learn to read if there is damage to any of a number of parts of the functional system for reading.

Some additional assumptions are needed to account for all observations. The most important of these is the concept of *alternative* functional systems. This concept suggests that a given behavior may be produced by more than one functional system. In more colloquial terms, there is more than one way to "skin a cat"—and more than one way to engage in most behaviors. This principle both accounts for the lack of expected deficits in some patients and explains many cases of spontaneous recovery of behavior despite permanent damage to the brain. (Cases of recovery after temporary damage need not be explained by this assumption.) Recovery can take place in several ways. In some cases, higher level brain skills can compensate for lower level skills. For example, an adult with a partial deficit in auditory discrimination may compensate by using lip reading to supplement his or her ability to decode spoken language and use the context of the talk to decipher further words or phrases which were not understood. Under informal conditions, it may be impossible to notice any deficit in such individuals.

Recovery can be enhanced by supplementing higher level with lower level skills. For example, a person may lose the ability to generate problem-solving strategies after certain injuries. By teaching this person a concrete approach to problems that requires no independent generation of a problem-solving strategy this deficit can be minimized. Finally, the role of the injured area may be assumed by other areas of the brain. The brain, under the right conditions, is indeed plastic and the normal organization of skills is not absolute. In addition, by changing the nature of the task (e.g., by changing the composition of the functional system used to complete a task), we can change the location of information processing. This might involve using another input or output modality, or changing the verbal or nonverbal emphasis of the information transmitted to the patient.

Luria's theory, based on these assumptions, is attractive in that it can explain nearly all the observations which have been made of brain injured patients, regardless of the approach used to generate that information. However, it remains a theoretical model, and while consistent with current data, it is not necessarily superior to earlier models of brain-behavior relations. There is still much we do not understand about the operation of the brain. Indeed, despite our growing sophistication, we remain relatively primitive in our analysis of brain-behavior relationships.

Like localization theories, Luria assigns specific functions to each of the areas of the brain, with this assignment based on both physiological data and psychological observations. Each area in turn participates in functional systems. An area can be involved in any number of functional systems, depending on the importance of the discrete skill mediated by that area. The multiple functional role of each area of the brain is referred to as pluripotentiality. An area can thus be involved in relatively few or many behaviors.

The specific areas involved in a behavior depend upon how the behavior has been taught (Luria, 1973). The person taught a phonetic approach to reading does not use the same functional systems for reading as the sight reader. As a consequence, we can never assume that because overt behaviors are similar the underlying functional systems are the same. Indeed, such assumptions about equivalence of underlying functional systems are a major error even in many theories that are outwardly consistent with Luria's basic conceptions. Thus a test administered to a child as a measure of specific neuropsychological skills may not, in fact, measure what we assume it does. This can lead to significant misunderstandings about the neuropsychological basis of a behavior and to inappropriate treatment or rehabilitative programs.

To understand further functional systems, we must have some recognition of the basic skills required for any given functional system. Luria divides the brain into three basic units. Two of these units are further subdivided into more distinctive areas. Each of these units is involved in all behavior without exception, although the relative contribution of each unit will vary with the behavior. Similarly, the role of specific areas within each unit will vary with every behavior. The three units can be described as Arousal and Attention Processes (Unit I), Sensory Reception and Integration, (Unit II) and Motor Execution, Planning, and Evaluation, (Unit III).

FIRST UNIT

The Arousal Unit (Unit I) consists of those parts of the brain identified as the Reticular Activating System (RAS). This system is a collection of diffuse intertwined structures which act to raise or lower cortical arousal. The structure itself extends from the pons and medulla through the thalamus to the cortex. The system is absolutely necessary for survival and behavior, since without arousal the cortex is unable to respond to incoming stimuli. Disorders of the RAS can vary in the extreme, from narcolepsy (chronic, pathological sleep) to insomnia. In addition to its role in arousal, the RAS is also responsible for the filtering of input, especially from those senses which are always "on" (tactile/kinesthetic, auditory). This prevents the cortex from being flooded with constant, irrelevant stimuli which can interfere with cognitive processing. Thus this system plays an important role in focusing attention, concentration, and similar tasks.

SECOND UNIT

The second unit is the sensory reception and integration unit. This unit is responsible for most early life learning skills, as well as for many of the abilities tapped by tests of intelligence for young children. The second unit can be subdivided into three types of areas: primary, secondary, and tertiary. The primary areas act as sensory reception areas. Of all of the areas of the cortex, this area is the most "hard wired," meaning that the functions of the primary areas and the connections within the area are largely predetermined by genetics. In the primary areas, input is received on a general "point-to point" basis from the appropriate sensory organs. It is at this stage as well that initial cortical integration of the material occurs. In the second unit, there are three primary areas, each devoted to a specific sense. The auditory primary area is in the temporal lobe; the visual primary area is in the occipital lobe; and the tactile/kinesthetic primary area is in the parietal lobe. There is little difference in the primary areas of the two hemispheres. Destruction of both primary areas for a given modality results in such conditions as cortical blindness or cortical deafness.

There is a secondary area corresponding to each of the primary areas of the second unit. It is the role of the secondary area to analyze and integrate the information received at the primary areas. Thus the acoustic secondary area (in the temporal lobe) is responsible for analyzing sounds, organizing them into phonemes, pitch, tone, rhythm, and so on. The secondary visual area (in the occipital lobe) does the analogous task for vision, differentiating foreground from background, detecting movement, analyzing color, shape, and form, and so on. The secondary tactile area (in the parietal lobe) will analyze direction, strength, localization of touch, movement of muscles and joints, and so on.

The secondary areas of the second unit process information sequentially. This allows us to be aware of stimulus changes (e.g., detect movement) and to link events temporally. This is an important function. For example, in the case of speech, phonemes must be sequentially linked in order to form words and sentences. Injuries to the secondary area generally will first affect the sequential nature of the analysis. For example, a person may be able to understand two but not three phonemes in a row, after a partial injury to the auditory secondary area. An individual may only be able to examine one object at a time, or one word (or letter) at a time in injuries to the secondary visual area. Injuries to the secondary parietal area will not impair sensation, but may inhibit two-point discrimination, detection of direction of movement, or recognition of shapes or letters traced on the skin.

At the secondary level there is a greater differentiation of function between the parts of the second unit in the left and right hemispheres. The left hemisphere (in most individuals) predominates in the analysis of verbal, overlearned material while the right hemisphere predominates in the analysis of nonverbal material, especially spatial relationships and musical skills. However, it should be recognized that both hemispheres play a role in most behaviors.

Thus there are linguistic skills mediated by the right hemisphere [as in the recognition of long, complex words and the perception and retention of consonant sounds (Luria, 1973) and the left hemisphere is capable of some spatial analysis (as in recognition of familiar figures). Indeed for many behaviors there is an interaction between the hemispheres that is necessary for efficient behavior. Physiologically, there are large tracts in the brain (chiefly the corpus callosum) the purpose of which is the integration and coordination of behavior between the hemispheres.

Another way of looking at right-left hemisphere differences is in terms of how overlearned material may be. In the case of music, for example, primary musical interpretation is usually localized in the right hemisphere. However, in accomplished musicians such skills may be localized more in the left hemisphere. Similarly, verbal skills, when not overlearned, require extensive right hemispheric input to analyze unfamiliar sounds (when first learning speech or in learning a foreign language later in life), to analyze squiggles which eventually become overlearned letters and numbers, and to analyze the spatial movements necessary to write, which begins as a simple right hemisphere copying task. Thus the stage at which one is in learning a given type of material may strongly influence the brain areas across the hemispheres that are primarily involved in those behaviors. For children, where little information has been overlearned, the right hemisphere will play a much larger role than in the adolescent or adult.

The tertiary level of the second unit, located primarily in the parietal lobe of the two hemispheres, is responsible for cross-modal integration and simultaneous (as opposed to sequential) analysis of input from the sensory modalities. This simultaneous integration across sense modalities complements the sequential analysis of the secondary units. However, these areas are also capable of sequential analysis of material that is initially integrated. The tertiary parietal areas play a primary role in many of the tasks commonly subsumed under "intelligence." Auditory-visual integration is necessary for reading, whereas auditory-tactile integration is necessary for writing. Arithmetic, as well as body location in space and visual-spatial skills, depends upon visual-tactile integration. Grammatical skills, syntax, abstractions, logical analysis, understanding of prepositions, spatial rotation, angle determination, and stereognosis are just a few of the skills mediated by the tertiary parietal area (Luria, 1980). Indeed, with only a few exceptions, all of the skills measured on the Weschler Intelligence Scale for Children (WISC) are mediated by the tertiary area of the second unit.

There is increasing hemispheric differentiation of tasks at the tertiary level of the second unit. The left hemisphere is largely responsible for reading, writing, and the understanding of arithmetic symbols and processes. Grammar, syntax, and other language related skills are generally left hemisphere. The left tertiary area also is involved in the reproduction of complex figures, especially in the reproduction of details (rather than major outlines). The right hemisphere is responsible for visual-spatial relationship of parts, the spatial nature of arithmetic (such as borrowing or carrying over), verbal-spatial skills, facial recognition, recognition of emotional (nonverbal) facial and postural reactions, and the analysis of unusual or unknown pictures.

THIRD UNIT

The primary area of the third unit is the motor output area of the brain. Commands are sent from this area (through the motor tracts of the brain) to the specific muscles needed to perform any given behavioral act (including speech functions). The secondary area of the third unit is responsible for organizing the sequence of motor acts. Whereas the primary areas send individual commands, the secondary areas must organize and sequence the temporal pattern of movement.

These two areas do not function independently. For motor movements to take place, there must be adequate information available on muscle and joint status (kinesthetic and proprioceptive feedback). To allow for this, there are multiple connections between the motor and tactile primary areas and between the motor and tactile secondary areas. In addition, 20% of the cells in the primary motor area are tactile cells and 20% of the cells in the primary tactile area are motor cells (Luria, 1980). Thus these areas interact on a behavioral level. Developmentally, these areas also tend to develop in tandem (i.e., the two primary areas and the two secondary areas develop in about the same time, in the absence of injury). Coordination with both the visual and auditory-sensory areas is also necessary for accurate motor movement (Luria, 1980).

The functions of the tertiary area of the third unit, most commonly called the prefrontal lobes, are in many ways dramatically different from the functions of the primary and secondary areas. The tertiary area of the third unit of the brain represents the highest level of development of the mammalian brain. The major tasks of this area can be described as follows: planning (decision making), evaluation, temporal continuity, impulse and emotional control (delay of gratification), focusing of attention, and flexibility (creativity).

The planning function is unquestionably central to human behavior. The prefrontal lobes receive information from the tertiary area of the second (sensory) unit, as well as from the emotional (limbic) system and the first unit. They proceed to analyze this information, and then plan behavioral reactions. This function allows one to respond rationally to environmental changes and demands according to sensory input and past experience. This function is especially important for long range planning, rather than the short term "reactions" which dominate behavior in most animals as well as children. This ability is closely related to the skill of delaying gratification (without external reward or restraint) and impulse control (again, without external restraint or reward), two more important functions of the prefrontal lobes (Golden et al., 1992). As the prefrontal lobes develop, they assume dominance over the first unit of the brain (RAS). The prefrontal tertiary areas thereafter direct attentional focus and have direct connections with the subcortical areas, so that the level of arousal may be consciously modulated.

Another major function of the frontal lobes is evaluative skills. The frontal lobes must evaluate whether a person's behavior is consistent with long term goals and plans, much as the secondary (premotor) area monitors behavior to ensure that short term motor goals are accomplished (e.g., walking across a room or communicating specific information). Evaluative skills, when intact in injured people, can be a source of depression. These individuals continue to exercise the capacity to recognize when they are unable to formulate or put long-term plans into action.

Since many of the skills mediated by the tertiary frontal lobe area can be subsumed under the word "maturity," it is difficult to be sure if one is seeing a frontal lobe deficit or immaturity due to environmental training in children and adolescents. Thus it may be late adolescence or young adulthood before the behavioral pattern of such a deficit is clearly discriminable from childishness, juvenile delinquency, or psychiatric disorders common to the adolescent period.

DEVELOPMENTAL ISSUES

In adult neuropsychology, all the units of the brain are theoretically fully functioning before the onset of a given disorder. Thus all one has to do is identify deficits in order to identify brain injury (assuming a normal environment). However, child neuropsychology presents a unique challenge because the child is developing and changing. All skills do not exist at any given age. Thus it is of no concern to anyone that a 6-month-old does not speak. Such an infant is not expected to talk. The major problem that developmental change causes in neuropsychological evaluation is the need to be able to identify, for a given child, what skills should exist. This is further complicated by the fact that children develop neurologically at different rates, making dubious any set list of expected skills. At any given age, lack of some skills might be considered sure signs of brain damage and lack of other skills might be considered normal, whereas still others may be seen as indicating dysfunction. To complicate matters even further, this neurological growth must interact with an appropriate environment: if one is raised only by monks who never speak, one will never learn to speak.

Given this situation, it is absolutely critical for anyone wishing to understand child neuropsychology to be aware of the developmental sequences likely to be reflected in children. In general, there are two major types of theories to describe neurodevelopmental processes (Golden et al., 1992). The first assumes that the child's brain is the equal of the adult's brain-it is capable of all skills and skill levels but must develop sequentially, with quantitative gains being made as the child grows older. Thus at 3 years a child can finger tap 12 times, at 4 years 16 times, and so on, until one reaches adult speeds. Similarly, the young child is viewed as having all essential problem-solving skills: only the complexity, speed, and other related dimensions with which the child can successfully cope change with age.

Other theories assume that there are distinct neurodevelopmental periods in which *qualitative* rather than just quantitative changes in skills occur. Thus one is not able to use certain problem strategies appropriately until a certain stage is reached. This type of theory is very similar to developmental theories advocated by Piaget and Vygotsky (Luria, 1980).

It is this latter type of theory on which the following discussion is based. It is assumed that certain skills are more developmentally advanced than others and that the child cannot learn them until that neurological stage is reached. Thus if frontal lobe skills do not develop until age 12, it is senseless to include a test of frontal lobe abilities in a battery designed for the 8-year-old. Although the child may give an answer, its correctness or incorrectness will not measure frontal lobe activity because that area is not contributing to the child's behavioral processing at that age.

In the present context, neurological development is seen as the end product of several factors: myelinization, dendritic growth, growth of cell bodies, establishment of pathways among neurons, and other related physical and biochemical events. All of these processes are necessary for complete neurological development but none alone is sufficient. Thus there is at present no known one-to-one relationship between periods of physical growth in the brain (such as myelinization) and psychological maturation. Any such relationship that exists remains poorly understood. As a result, times for various developmental periods given here are based on behavioral rather than physiological observations. As such, they are subject to change as our understanding increases and are not to be seen as rigid or essential to the basic theory.

In addition to the necessary physiological substrate, there is also an environmental requirement before behavior emerges. Thus at any level above the basic primary sensory and motor skills, physiological maturation serves only as a potential basis for the emergence of skills mediated by that area. Without the appropriate experience, the abilities will not develop. Thus although the secondary visual area (and the eye itself) can differentiate red from blue, one will not give import to these differences unless one is taught to distinguish them. This is true of all the skills that are mediated by secondary or tertiary levels of the brain. In the following discussion, for the sake of simplicity, normal environmental experience will be assumed.

Finally, it needs to be recognized that as a child passes through developmental stages, the nature of functional systems underlying a behavior changes. Even though the child may have the same behavior at 5 that the adolescent has at 19, the way in which the brain processes the information for that behavior and executes the behavior is quite likely to be different. If we were to give the same test to both the 5- and the 19-year-old, we cannot assume that we are measuring the same skills or the same underlying processes. Nor can we test the child at age 5 to predict a skill that does not develop until age 8 or 13. Since the child has not passed through the developmental stage required for the emergence of the more sophisticated behavior, our "information" on the skill at age 5 is essentially meaningless. This phenomenon particularly explains why IQs for adolescents cannot be predicted reliably at early ages: the areas necessary for that later "IQ" are not yet developed in the young child. The development of the brain can be separated into five stages: (1) development of the First Unit; (2) development of the primary motor and sensory areas; (3) development of secondary motor and sensory areas; (4) development of the tertiary areas of the Second Unit (parietal lobe); and (5) development of the tertiary areas of the Third Unit (prefrontal lobes).

Stage 1

The most basic part of the brain clearly lies in the RAS and related structures. This system is in general developed by birth and certainly fully operational by 12 months after conception. The neuropsychologist, in working with infants, should be clearly aware that the development of this unit depends upon time since conception, not since birth. We cannot expect a premature infant born at 6 months after conception to show behavior that we see in a full term baby. Before development of this system, we would expect the child to show disorders of arousal and attention relative to the full term baby, although such deficits need not be permanent if the problem is developmental and not related to brain dysfunction.

The RAS is particularly sensitive to damage during the time it is being formed. While we need not concern ourselves with more severe disorders (which often lead to death or severe retardation), disorders of attention/filtering appear to be much more likely in injuries prior to 12 months after conception. Indeed, Rutter and his associates found that head injuries in childhood after this period produce no unusual attention deficits (Rutter, 1980). His data suggest that the only true physiological hyperactivity is caused by these early injuries. Later hyperactivity may then be related to emotional/environmental factors rather than to brain damage. Taken together, these data suggest that children with acquired brain damage, contrary to clinical lore, should not necessarily be more active, or have greater difficulty with concentration than their normal peers.

After this initial period, injuries to the RAS appear to result more often in disorders of consciousness (coma, stupor, etc.) rather than disorders of attention (the direction of conscious activity toward specific and appropriate stimuli). Injuries to the nearby limbic system may cause emotional disorders which simulate hyperactivity to some degree. These disturbances are qualitatively different from true attention disorders and are more stress and anxiety related. (Later, similar behavior can be created by frontal lobe dysfunction, but not until Stage 5.)

Stage 2

Stage 2 of neurological development proceeds concurrently with Stage 1 development. Stage 2 involves the primary areas of the brain in the Second Unit and the Third Unit. Unlike the secondary and tertiary areas, the "wiring" of the primary areas is built in, not the result of environmental interaction. Generally, this area is fully operational by 12 months after conception similar to the timing in Unit 1.

During the early part of life, cortical response to the outside world is "dominated" by these primary areas. Built into these areas are basic motor behaviors-for example, crying, grasping,-and basic sensory behaviors-depth discrimination, recognition of high pitched voices, and so on. All of these behaviors are genetically "built-in," and all appear to have (or have had- such as the Moro response) some definite survival function. In general these behaviors last only as long as the primary areas dominate cortical functioning. As secondary areas take over, these more primitive behaviors become quiescent. For example, a baby may be able to make a differential response to certain sounds as an infant but, if not taught the differential response on a secondary level, will be unable to make the discrimination at age 3.

Depending upon the age and extent of injury, children respond differently to damage to the primary areas of the cortex. If the injury occurs early- before birth or shortly thereafter- the complete destruction of sensory primary area can be compensated for by the primary area in the opposite hemisphere. This, of course, applies only to unilateral injuries. For example, a child might be born partially paralyzed on one side of the body because of primary level injuries. But if the child is seen at age 5, there may be no residual behavioral sequelae-the child has apparently normal motor and sensory function. If the injury occurs early enough, no deficit may be seen even at birth. One child seen by this author was born without a right hemisphere, yet showed no motor, tactile, visual, or auditory deficits of any kind. Caution should be exercised when generalizing, however. Injuries must be of a certain size (severity) and must include certain areas for this takeover to occur. Moreover, many motor deficits and sensory deficits arise from injuries to places other than the four primary areas.

Injuries after this period are more serious, but many can be compensated for by the brain. Thus loss of a primary auditory area on one side will result in a higher threshold of hearing but otherwise not interfere with day to day life. Loss of the primary visual areas will cause the loss of half the eye fields, which can be compensated partially by eye movement. Motor loss can cause hemiplegia, but with proper therapy and exercise some control can be regained. Bilateral injuries are much more serious. These can cause deafness, blindness, or paralysis. Partial injuries produce some fraction of the above results depending upon their seriousness.

Stage 3

This stage begins concomitant with the first two stages but extends through about age 5. Secondary level discriminations begin to develop as soon as the adequate attentional focus of Stage 1 and the capacity to relay information from the primary areas to secondary levels are adequate. Such behaviors as fear of strangers mark the emergence of significant secondary visual discriminations, whereas such behaviors as differential responses to a particular woman's voice as opposed to other female voices mark auditory development. Eye-hand coordination, crawling, early walking, and so on, mark secondary motor milestones.

The secondary areas are highly related to the concept of dominance. It is at this level of the brain that we see the first significant differentiation of the brain into "verbal" and "nonverbal" hemispheres. However, the brain is not committed to the left hemisphere as verbal until the development of the secondary areas is markedly advanced. This occurs at about age 2, or, more precisely, when the child develops consistent verbal skills. Injuries to the left hemisphere prior to this time will result in much less deficit than injuries after this time. In general, injuries prior to 2 years will result in switch of dominance for verbal skills to the right hemisphere. The earlier this occurs the better and more complete the transfer. After age 2 some transfer may occur, but this is usually minimal. The results of injuries incurred subsequent to 2 years of age begin to resemble the results of adult injuries more and more. Thus there appears to be a critical period in which these unilateral injuries are minimized; thereafter, they are much more serious. Such "plasticity" mechanisms do not apply when the injury is diffuse.

This plasticity of the brain does not appear to occur with small injuries- only when significant injury occurs to secondary areas is plasticity observed. As a consequence, we have the paradox that a small injury at birth may produce no less deficit than larger injuries and, in some cases, have greater effects on later behavior. During the first 5 years of life, the secondary areas are the primary sites of learning in the human cortex. This age limit, like others in this chapter, is only approximate. There are extensive individual differences. During this period, the child's primary and most important learning occurs within single modalities rather than between them. Cross-modality learning at this stage does not represent integrative learning but rather rote memory. The child learning to read at this level must memorize the letter or word-sound combinations. The visual symbol for a word lacks meaning for the young child except through its association with the spoken word. Thus the child must say the word to understand it, or repeat the phonemes in an attempt to integrate the sounds and recognize the word. It is not surprising that countries such as the Soviet Union, which emphasize early reading, teach by rote repetition until the lesson is learned. It is not until Stage 4 that the child is capable of true, integrative cross-modality learning.

STAGE 4

Stage 4 is concerned primarily with the tertiary area of the second unit, located primarily in the parietal lobe. This area, along with the prefrontal lobes of Stage 5, represents the most advanced parts of the human brain. More of the human brain is devoted to tertiary, integrative areas than is the brain of any other animal (Luria, 1980).

The parietal tertiary area is responsible for efficient performance in most major educational skills: reading, writing, arithmetic, grammar, syntax, drawing, logic, analogies, naming, categorizing, dimensionality, and other similar skills. Not surprisingly, most major IQ tests tap skills related to this tertiary unit.

The tertiary parietal area is not psychologically active until about age 5 to 8. As a result, the effect of earlier injuries to the tertiary area may not be observable until ages 8 to 12. Therefore, if a child has an injury limited to this area at age 2 one might conclude that at age 3 the child is normal and unharmed, only to discover that at age 10 the child has serious learning impairments. This consideration is extremely important in legal cases or situations in which one is asked to predict future behavior. It is essentially impossible to do better than actuarial data in predicting whether a 4-year-old will later have tertiary level problems (except, of course, in cases where brain damage in other areas is already obvious). Neither a young normal child nor a young child with a discrete tertiary parietal injury will be able to complete tasks requiring development of this area. Failure to perform such tasks successfully subsequent to brain damage is meaningless, for the normal child will fail as well. In cases where the injury is limited to the tertiary injuries, real prediction is impossible at the earlier ages.

STAGE 5

During this final stage of brain development, the prefrontal (tertiary) areas of the third unit develop. In general, this development does not begin until the child reaches 10 to 12 years old, and may continue into the earlier twenties. The age of onset of development in this period varies significantly across children. Initiation of development is often related to the onset of puberty but may precede or lag behind this event.

During this stage, many of the behaviors we associate with maturity begin to develop. Individuals with injuries to these areas do not necessarily show any decrease on intelligence tests, which focus on skills in the Second Unit and the primary and secondary areas of the Third Unit. During this stage such skills as inhibition of impulses, inhibition of response to outside distractors, inhibition of emotional impulses, and organization and planning for the future take place. The ability to evaluate one's behavior fully is developed, as is the ability to develop higher levels of moral and ethical control. Sophistication in the interpretation of complex and abstract events is increased, especially in the areas of analyzing emotional cues and interpersonal interactions. Without these areas, as we shall see, severe behavioral disorders may develop.

In adolescents, the effects of prefrontal injuries are of major concern since this area is the primary area of brain development during the adolescent period. It has long been recognized that in some children with apparent or known brain injury there is recovery at about the time of adolescence or shortly thereafter. In these cases it is hypothesized that the development of an intact prefrontal area serves to compensate for previously existing deficits. Thus the hyperactive child, as he or she matures, may demonstrate greater cortical activity in general and of the prefrontal area in particular. In the case of the learning-disabled child, the higher levels of brain function allow the child to substitute alternate functional systems for the more basic skills which are impaired. In other cases, of course, the prefrontal lobes are not able to do this because of insufficient development or the seriousness of the deficit. In some cases a dysfunctional prefrontal area can actually intensify the seriousness of the deficits, in addition to ameliorating problems.

As noted earlier, one of the primary functions of the prefrontal lobe is inhibition over the lower emotional and arousal centers of the brain, as well as the ability to inhibit one's response to impulses. Failure of adequate prefrontal development results in the failure to establish these skills. In essence, the child fails to show normal maturational growth and the failure to develop autonomous self-control. Rather than resulting in behavioral regression, the child reaches a plateau at the developmental level of an 8- or 9-year-old. This becomes especially serious as the child matures physically. Behavior that can be controlled or tolerated in a younger child is neither tolerable, since the adolescent is more dangerous, nor as controllable. Deficits of this kind are not unusual among impulsive children who may be disruptive in school and eventually classified as "juvenile delinquent." These children may also show disorders in their ability to appreciate consequences, to plan for the future, and to evaluate their own behavior effectively. Drug use and alcohol use may be common because of lack of judgment and impulsivity, and the ease with which their behavior can be modified by strong outside influence (e.g., peer pressure) whether good or bad. Early drug or alcohol use can lead to greater impairment as these substances further interfere with brain function. These deficits can lead to later adult disorders, such as schizophrenia or manic depressive disease.

Developmental Lag   Up until now we have discussed brain function and development as if all delays were indicative of developmental problems. This, of course, is not always the case. Development of a brain area in a given child may simply be slower than in other children. Indeed, statistically speaking, half of all children must develop slower than the other half, while 10% of normal children will develop slower than the other 90%. In other words, whatever criteria we set for development, there will always be slow children. In these children, deficits similar to the ones we have described will develop but eventually disappear as the child matures. It is impossible to predict which child will eventually spontaneously develop normal behavior, and which child may need special intervention. This produces a strong tendency to overdiagnose serious problems when, in fact, the child in question is demonstrating a transient developmental lag that will remit with further development. Indeed, over the past century and especially the past 3 decades, we have steadily increased our expectations regarding what a child should be able to do at a given age. Concomitant with this has been an increase in the number of "exceptional" children. It is likely that higher expectations partially account for the increasing number of children who "need" special help. Greater needs for special education are unlikely to be the result of broad changes in brain development, which has probably not noticeably changed over the past several thousand years.

LEARNING AND MODELING

By definition, neurological disorders do not arise as a function of learning or modeling. However, children with neurological problems are capable of learning new behaviors from others. This is often a negative factor: children placed with other children who have neurological disorders may learn new and inappropriate behaviors from these children. In addition, parents may expect less of the neurologically impaired child. Thus, they will not try to shape the child's behavior in the same way as one shapes the behavior of a "normal" child because of lower expectations. While it is true that many neurologically impaired children may learn slower, they are in most cases capable of learning. Thus, it is important to have expectations for these children that take into account their difficulties and limitations, but which do not discount their ability to learn and behave in appropriate ways. One may not be able to make the paralyzed child walk, but we can teach the child not to drive a motorized wheelchair into other people. The child with head trauma may be impulsive, but can still be taught to act more appropriately and to limit the impact of their impulsivity on others.

PARENTAL ISSUES

As with learning, parents do not cause brain injury (with the exception of abuse and exposure disorders). The major parenting issues involve expectations and the desire to protect the child. As noted in the learning section, reasonable expectations are necessary so that children are taught appropriate behaviors.

The desire to protect the child, while natural, often leads to over-protection. For example, if a child has difficultly dressing, the overprotective parent may dress them rather than watch them struggle and become frustrated. If they are clumsy in sports, the parent may withdraw them from such activities. If school is difficult, the parent may help the child get excused from difficult tasks. The difficulty here is the same as with learning expectations: there is a need to balance the child's impairments against the flexibility and plasticity of the brain as discussed previously. Thus, parents need to encourage children to always grow and develop skills and never make the assumption that further development is impossible. Such development may be slow, but the child's brain needs continued stimulation to develop at whatever rate it is capable of attaining.

LIFE EVENTS

Although we are born with a general brain organization, the specifics of that organization depend on interaction with the environment, especially in the tertiary and secondary areas, which are responsible for most voluntary, intelligent behavior. As a result, deficits may exist simply because one has never been taught the skill. While this is generally recognized for more complex behaviors like reading, Luria's work stresses that this is true for such simple secondary discriminations as distinguishing one phoneme from another, or perceiving the curvature of a line. As a result, there is no such thing as a culture-free test within this system. There are no experiences common to all people, no matter how "basic" they may be within a given culture. As a result, neuropsychological tests may yield either grossly or subtly different results in different populations, both within and between major cultural groups. This is especially serious in children, and such factors must be taken into account before one infers brain dysfunction.

The second important variable is the multidetermination of behavior. Behavior occurs as it does for a wide variety of reasons in addition to brain function: experience (as described above), emotional factors, reinforcement history, motivation, cooperation, biological status, sleep status, strength, peripheral sensory and motor factors, presence of drugs or medicines in the body, nutrition, blood oxygen levels, and so on. Rarely is there a behavior whose etiology lies solely on the realm of a neuropsychological deficit. In some cases, these other factors may exaggerate the severity of the deficit, in others it may attenuate the severity of the deficit. In either case, these factors must be considered in studying the individual.

Finally, we must recognize the role of functional autonomy. As used here, this concept suggests that while a behavior may initially have emerged because of a physiological dysfunction, it may continue long after the physiological cause has disappeared. In such cases, the behavior is said to have become "functionally autonomous." For example, the hyperactive child may mature (cognitively) to a stage where hyperactivity is no longer necessary, but the behavior continues since it is the only way the child knows to get attention, to control his or her teachers, and to influence matters at home. Another child may be neurologically capable of reading on par with a 10- or 12-year-old, but be so convinced that this is impossible that the child engages in behavior that makes learning impossible (One such child told me he didn't have time to study the "kid's stuff" that 6-year-olds studied.) This is of course related to the concept of the self-fulfilling prophecy; once we have decided we are unable to learn something, it is quite unlikely that the material will be learned. As a consequence, a continuing deficit may not necessarily be an indication of permanent brain injury, especially when, for example, the "reading deficit" is not accompanied by other basic skill deficits that would be expected if a part of the functional system for reading had been injured.

GENETIC INFLUENCES

Genetic influences play a major role in many neurological disorders, although the extent of those roles in each disorder is not always well established. Some disorders, like head trauma or heavy metal poisoning, clearly appear to be solely the result of the environment. Others, like Down's Syndrome, have clear and well documented genetic etiologies. Most fall somewhere in between these extremes.

PEER INFLUENCES

Unlike many other disorders discussed in this book, the primary features of neurological disorders are not considered to be influenced by peers. However, as with parental influences, the behavioral expression of the disorder is affected by the client's interactions with the social and physical environment. Of special concern in peer relationships, is self-esteem. Neurologically disordered children are often seen as "odd" and may be ostracized or made fun of by peers. Such behavior can strongly affect the child's perception of themselves and lead to other psychological disorders such as depression or anxiety. Indeed, because of the presence of brain injury, many children may be more susceptible to the development of these disorders.

In some cases, neurological problems may lead to extreme attempts to fit in, usually through misbehavior or identification with fringe peer elements when this is possible. Children with brain disorders may have very poor judgment and may be easily pressured into dangerous or illegal activities. These children may also be more prone to victimized sexually. However, due to the wide range of differences in the expression of these disorders, the vulnerability of any given child must be determined on a case-by-case basis. Striking a balance between protecting the neurologically impaired child and promoting experiences that could enhance their independence in adolescence and adulthood is likely to be challenging to even the most informed parent-clinician team.

DRUGS AFFECTING BEHAVIOR

Illicit and legal drugs (like alcohol or prescription drugs) may have unexpected or exaggerated effects in this population due to the interaction with compromised brain function. The impact of disinhibitory and stimulant drugs may be extreme, leading to additional behavioral abnormalities. Similarly, CNS depressants may result in excessive decline in cognitive skills and arousal levels. The impact however will differ with the nature, extent, and etiology of the neurological disorder.

CULTURAL AND DIVERSITY ISSUES

Neurological disorders affect all people regardless of cultural and diversity backgrounds, with similar impacts in terms of behavior and changes in cognition. Cultural groups will vary in terms of the tolerance they have for specific symptoms which develop, however research on neurological disorders and culture or diversity other than gender is very limited.

BEHAVIORAL TREATMENT

Noncognitive behavioral approaches can be very effective in the neurologically impaired child when properly aimed at the functional level and skills of the child. This requires a thorough understanding of the cognitive/developmental level of the child which will frequently be inconsistent with chronological age and physical appearance. Behavioral intervention should be straight forward and concrete and not demand cognitive analysis and discrimination which is impaired by the brain dysfunction. In addition, speed of learning may be slower than expected and the impact of inconsistency in the execution of behavioral plans may have an exaggerated negative impact on the results. A lack of patience, lack of consistency, lack of immediacy, and too much complexity in plans are the most common problems when working with this population. Most often problems are due to an overestimation of the cognitive skills possessed by the neurologically impaired child.

MEDICAL TREATMENT

Medical assessment and treatment are essential in the treatment of the neurologically impaired child. However, the necessary treatment varies extensively with the specific etiology of the neurological impairment.

Case Study

Given the wide diversity of children with neurological disorders, presenting a case description which is useful or representative of the process is difficult. Rather than pick a more severe and obvious case, a milder case which is typical of many which raise more questions than can be answered was selected.

The client is a 15-year-old single, left-handed, Hispanic male. He was referred for learning problems. He developed normally until age 2 when he stopped speaking after a head trauma following an automobile accident in which he was a passenger. After being hospitalized for 5 days, he was placed in individual speech therapy, which the client participated in twice weekly for a couple of years. This helped the client become more able to articulate simple words, although he spoke with a lisp. Subsequently, he was placed in a "Pre-K Handicap Program" that was comprised of children categorized as being mildly to moderately learning disabled. Conversational abilities were not developed to a level commensurate with his chronological age until sometime after the second grade.

In elementary school, the school-based assessments revealed difficulties in the areas of verbal articulation and processing abilities. He required approximately 15 to 20 minutes additional time to complete assignments when compared to his peers. There was also a history of reading comprehension and mathematics problems. The client reported he frequently met with his teachers after regular class hours to obtain individual assistance with mathematics. Additional accommodations reportedly included extra time on tests. Despite this, scores on standardized tests were very poor.

He received a comprehensive test battery which included the WISC-III, the Woodcock Johnson Tests of Cognitive Ability—Third Edition (Extended Scale), the WRAML, the Woodcock Johnson Tests of Achievement—Third Edition (Extended Scale), the Nelson Denny Reading Comprehension Test (NDRT), the Key Math Test-Revised, the Conners' Continuous Performance Test II (CPT-II), the Wisconsin Card Sorting Test (WCST), the Category Test, Finger Tapping, the Tactual Performance Test (TPT), the Trail Making Test A & B, the Stroop Color-Word Test, the Test of Memory and Malingering (TOMM), and the MMPI-A (Adolescent version).

The client's overall intellectual functioning was average compared to same-age peers. Verbal and nonverbal skills are evenly developed. Memory scores were in the average range compared to same-age peers. Auditory and visual delay scores were slightly lower than expected. He demonstrated a weakness in processing speed. Achievement scores were in the average range, with weakness in the area of math fluency, math calculation skills, and broad math. In speeded reading on the NDRT, he scored one standard deviation below his intelligence scores, achieving only a seventh grade level of reading. On the Key Math Test-Revised, his scores were all below average and below his current grade level, one standard deviation below his IQ. On the CPT-II, his performance was in the normal range overall. His performances on tests of executive function were all in the normal range as were basic measures of motor skills. However, he had significant difficulty on the Tactual Performance Test. This test is used to assess sensory and motor function, including recognition of three-dimensional shapes by touch, spatial-motor problem solving, and memory for tactile and spatial information. The client is blindfolded and asked to place blocks of various shapes into corresponding slots in a board as quickly as possible. He had difficulty learning tactile stimuli and their respective locations over trials with the performance on his nondominant hand worse than his dominant hand performance. He was able to remember the shapes after the exam was over, but had difficulty with their location. There was no evidence of expressive or receptive speech problems. The MMPI-A showed a single elevation on Scale 9 (Hypomania). The TOMM was normal.

This case raises several issues. First, his head injury occurred many years before the current comprehensive examination, making a cause-effect relationship difficult to establish. While he initially had clear speech regression, those problems disappeared over the years, resulting in an average IQ, but slowness in both math and reading comprehension tasks. Neither math nor reading could be established as impaired early in development (e.g., age 2) since they no age appropriate tasks existed for these skill areas. Thus, we do not know what their later development would be. In addition, we do not know if the current IQ is lower than it would have been if the injury had not occurred. There are no significant variations among the subtests, an indicator often not seen in early childhood injuries (as opposed to adult or adolescent injuries). Problems with TPT performance suggest some sensory processing problems, however.

Overall, his performance during the evaluation revealed generally average skills except in the areas of reading and math, especially when tested under speeded conditions. However, these skills are only one standard deviation below his IQ and the local schools require a 1.5 standard deviation difference to establish a learning disability. He did not show any executive skill deficits which occur frequently with childhood injuries. Since he did not qualify for a learning disorder or Dementia (memory was normal), a Cognitive Disorder was considered. This is a difficult diagnosis since it depends on whether one assumes the problem in speedily responding to academic tasks was due to the head injury or simply would have happened anyway. While no definitive answer is possible, it was decided since there was clear evidence of a significant head injury, that the results were more likely to reflect the residual impact of the head injury rather than a natural variation. As such, he was diagnosed with Cognitive Disorder due to Head Injury. Additional testing time for the standardized testing in the school environment (e.g., Stanford Achievement Test) was recommended (50%). This recommendation, like many in this area, would be implemented in the broader school system rather than being implemented by the examiners.

SUMMARY

Neurological impairment in children covers a wide range of disorders whose psychological and cognitive impact range from minimal or nonexistent to complete inability to function at any level. Over the past 3 decades, it has been recognized that many (if not all) of the disorders which arise in early childhood or adolescence may have a neurological root, including many of the traditional "mental health" disorders like anxiety and depression. Thus, current neuropsychological work is not limited to traditional disorders like head trauma or cerebral palsy and thus contemporary neuropsychology now extends to the full range of childhood disorders. This chapter has concerned itself primarily with those disorders most associated with neurological insults and in particular, those which directly affect the brain functions, broadly conceived as deficits in learning, memory, intelligence, attention, and executive functions. Luria's (1973, 1980) concept of the *functional system* remains an important heuristic for organizing neuropsychological data, guiding case formulation, and developing treatment recommendations.

Noncognitive behavioral approaches can be very effective in the neurologically impaired child when properly aimed at the functional level and skills of the child. Behavioral interventions that do not demand cognitive analysis and discrimination (which is often impaired by the brain dysfunction) should be emphasized. Inconsistency in the execution of behavioral plans and overestimation of the neurologically impaired child's cognitive skills are among the most serious threats to successful intervention. Medical assessment and treatment are essential for neurologically impaired children, but the intensity of treatment varies extensively with the etiology of the neurological impairment.

REFERENCES

Aarsen, F., Van Dongen, H., Paquier, P., Van Mourik, M., & Catsman-Berrevoets, C. (2004). Long-term sequelae in children after cerebellar astrocytoma surgery. *Neurology, 62*, 1311–1316.

Anderson, V., Anderson, P., Grimwood, K., & Nolan, T. (2004). Cognitive and executive function 12 years after childhood bacterial meningitis: Effect of acute neurologic complications and age of onset. *Journal of Pediatric Psychology, 29*, 67–81.

Anderson, V., Godber, T., Smibert, E., Weiskop, S., & Ekert, H. (2004). Impairments of attention following treatment with cranial irradiation and chemotherapy in children. *Journal of Clinical and Experimental Neuropsychology, 26*, 684–697.

Aucott, S., Donohue, P., Atkins, E., & Allen, M. (2002). Neurodevelopmental care in the NICU. *Mental Retardation and Developmental Disabilities Research Reviews, 8*, 298–308.

Barlow, K., Thompson, E., Johnson, D., & Minns, R. (2004). The neurological outcome of non-accidental head injury. *Pediatric Rehabilitation, 7*, 195–203.

Bava, S., Ballantyne, A., & Trauner, D. (2005). Disparity of verbal and performance IQ following early bilateral brain damage. *Cognitive and Behavioral Neurology, 18*, 163–170.

Blondis, T. (2004). Neurodevelopmental motor disorders: Cerebral palsy and neuromuscular diseases. In D. Dewey & D. Tupper (Eds.), *The science and practice of neuropsychology: Developmental motor disorders—A neuropsychological perspective* (pp. 113–136). New York: Guilford Press.

Carter, J., Neville, B., & Newton, C. (2003). Neuro-cognitive impairment following acquired central nervous system infections in childhood: A systematic review. *Brain Research Reviews, 43*, 57–69.

Christ, S., White, D., Brunstrom, J., & Abrams, R. (2003). Inhibitory control following perinatal brain injury. *Neuropsychology, 17*, 171–178.

Coleman, M. (2005). Other neurological signs and symptoms in autism. In M. Coleman (Ed.), *The neurology of autism* (pp. 101–118). New York: Oxford University Press.

Connors, K., & MHS staff. (2000). Connors Continuous Performance Test II. North Tonawanda, NY: MHS.

Dammann, O., & Leviton, A. (2004). Inflammatory brain damage in preterm newborns: Dry numbers, wet lab, and causal inferences. *Early Human Development, 79,* 1–15.

deBode, S., Firestine, A., Mathern, G., & Dobkin, B. (2005). Residual motor control and cortical representations of function following hemispherectomy: Effects of etiology. *Journal of Child Neurology, 20,* 64–75.

DeBoer, T., Wewerka, S., Bauer, P., Georgieff, M., & Nelson, C. (2005). Explicit memory performance in infants of diabetic mothers at 1 year of age. *Developmental Medicine Camp: Child Neurology, 47,* 525–531.

Dewey, D., & Bottos, S. (2004). Neuroimaging of developmental motor disorders. In D. Dewey & D. Tupper (Eds.), *The science and practice of neuropsychology: Developmental motor disorders—A neuropsychological perspective* (pp. 26–43). New York: Guilford Press.

Downie, A., Frisk, V., & Jakobson, L. (2005). The impact of periventricular brain injury on reading and spelling abilities in the late elementary and adolescent years. *Child Neuropsychology, 11,* 479–495.

Eilander, H., Wijnen, V., Scheirs, J., deKort, P., & Prevo, A. (2005). Children and young adults in a prolonged unconscious stated due to severe brain injury: Outcome after an early intensive neurorehabilitation programme. *Brain Injury, 19,* 425–436.

Ettaro, L., Berger, R., & Songer, T. (2004). Abusive head trauma in young children: Characteristics and medical charges in a hospitalized population. *Child Abuse Camp: Neglect, 28,* 1099–1111.

Fennell, E., & Dikel, T. (2001). Cognitive and neuropsychological functioning in children with cerebral palsy. *Journal of Child Neurology, 16,* 58–63.

Foulder-Hughes, L., & Cooke, R. (2003). Do mainstream schoolchildren who were born preterm have motor problems? *British Journal of Occupational Therapy, 66,* 9–16.

Frisk, V., Amsel, R., & Whyte, H. (2002). The importance of head growth patterns in predicting the cognitive abilities and literacy skills of small-for-gestational-age children. *Developmental Neuropsychology, 22,* 565–593.

Fuemmeler, B., Elkin, T., & Mullins, L. (2002). Survivors of childhood brain tumors: Behavioral, emotional, and social adjustment. *Clinical Psychology Review, 22,* 547–586.

Golden, C. J., & Anderson, S. S. (1979). *Learning disabilities and brain dysfunction.* Springfield, IL: Charles C Thomas.

Golden, C. J., Zillmer, E., & Spiers, M. (1992). *Neuropsychological assessment and rehabilitation.* Springfield, IL: Charles C Thomas.

Hagberg, H., & Jacobsson, B. (2005). Brain injury in preterm infants: What can the obstetrician do? *Early Human Development, 81,* 231–235.

Hetherington, R., Tuff, L., Anderson, P., Miles, B., & DeVeber, G. (2005). Short-term intellectual outcome after arterial ischemic stroke and sinovenous thrombosis in childhood and infancy. *Journal of Child Neurology, 20,* 553–559.

Hughes, S., Nilsson, D., Boyer, R., Bolte, R., Hoffman, R., Lewine, J., et al. (2002). Neurodevelopmental outcome for extended cold water drowning: A longitudinal case study. *Journal of the International Neuropsychological Society, 8,* 588–595.

Hurvitz, E., Warschausky, S., Berg, M., Tsai, S., & Roth, E. (2004). Long-term functional outcome of pediatric stroke survivors. *Topics in Stroke Rehabilitation, 11,* 51–59.

Jiang, Z., Yin, R., Shao, X., & Wilkinson, A. (2004). Brain-stem auditory impairment during the neonatal period in term infants after asphyxia: Dynamic changes in brain-stem auditory evoked response to clicks of different rates. *Clinical Neurophysiology, 115,* 1605–1615.

King, W., MacKay, M., & Simick, A. (2003). Shaken baby syndrome in Canada: Clinical characteristics and outcomes of hospital cases. *Canadian Medical Association Journal, 168,* 155–159.

Kirkham, F., & Hogan, A. (2004). Risk factors for arterial ischemic stroke in childhood. *CNS Spectrums, 9,* 451–464.

Lazoritz, S., & Palusci, V. (2001). *Shaken baby syndrome: A multidisciplinary approach*. Binghamton, NY: Haworth Press.

Lee, J., Croen, L., Backstrand, K., Yoshida, C., Henning, L., Lindan, C., et al. (2005). Maternal and infant characteristics associated with perinatal arterial stroke in the infant. *Journal of the American Medical Association, 293*, 723–729.

Luciana, M. (2003). Cognitive development in children born preterm: Implications for theories of brain plasticity following early injury. *Development and Psychopathology, 15*, 1017–1047.

Luria, A. R. (1973). *The working brain*. New York: Basic Books.

Luria, A. R. (1980). *Higher cortical functions in man*. New York: Basic Books.

Makaroff, K., & Putnam, F. (2003). Outcomes of infants and children with inflicted traumatic brain injury. *Developmental Medicine Camp: Child Neurology, 45*, 497–502.

Max, J. (2004). Effect of side of lesion on neuropsychological performance in childhood stroke. *Journal of the International Neuropsychological Society, 10*, 698–708.

McMahon, W., Filloux, F., Ashworth, J., & Jensen, J. (2002). Movement disorders in children and adolescents. *Neurologic Clinics, 20*, 1101–1124.

Mecacci, L. (1979). *Brain and history: The relationship between neuropsychology and psychology in Soviet research*. New York: Brunner/Mazel.

Ment, L., Vohr, B., Allan, W., Katz, K., Schneider, K., Westerveld, M., et al. (2003). Change in cognitive function over time in very low-birth-weight infants. *Journal of the American Medical Association, 289*, 705–711.

Middleton, J. (2001). Practitioner review: Psychological sequelae of head injury in children and adolescents. *Journal of Child Psychology and Psychiatry, 42*, 165–180.

Mitchell, W. (2001). Neurological and developmental effects of HIV and AIDS in children and adolescents. *Mental Retardation and Developmental Disabilities Research Reviews, 7*, 211–216.

Morrow, C., Bandstra, E., Anthony, J., Ofir, A., Xue, L., & Reyes, M. (2001). Influence of prenatal cocaine exposure on full-term infant neurobehavioral functioning. *Neurotoxicology and Teratology, 23*, 533–544.

Mulhern, R., & Butler, R. (2004). Neurocognitive sequelae of childhood cancers and their treatment. *Pediatric Rehabilitation, 7*, 1–14.

Nosarti, C., Rifkin, L., & Murray, R. (2003). The neurodevelopmental consequences of very preterm birth: Brain plasticity and its limits. In D. Cicchetti & E. Walker (Eds.), *Neurodevelopmental mechanisms in psychopathology* (pp. 34–61). New York: Cambridge University Press.

Pataraia, E., Billingsley-Marshall, R., Castillo, E., Breier, J., Simos, P., Sarkari, S., et al. (2005). Organization of receptive language-specific cortex before and after left temporal lobectomy. *Neurology, 64*, 481–487.

Peterson, B., & Ment, L. (2001). Response: Abnormal cognition and behavior in preterm neonates linked to smaller brain volumes. *Trends in Neurosciences, 24*, 131–132.

Powell, K., & Voeller, K. (2004). Prefrontal executive function syndromes in children. *Journal of Child Neurology, 19*, 785–797.

Reichert, L., & Schmidt, M. (2001). Neurologic sequelae of shaken baby syndrome. In S. Lazoritz & V. Palusci (Eds.), *Shaken baby syndrome: A multidisciplinary approach* (pp. 79–99). Binghamtom, NY: Haworth Press.

Robinson, S. (2005). Systemic prenatal insults disrupt telencephalon development: Implications for potential interventions. *Epilepsy Camp: Behavior, 7*, 345–363.

Rodrigue, J., Gonzalez-Peralta, R., & Langham, M. (2004). Solid organ transplantation. In R. Brown (Ed.), *Handbook of pediatric psychology in school settings* (pp. 679–699). Mahwah, NJ: Erlbaum.

Rutter, M. (1980, September). *Childhood disorders.* Unpublished speech to the Conference on the Hyperactive Child, Omaha, NE.

Savage, R., Depompei, R., Tyler, J., & Lash, M. (2005). Pediatric traumatic brain injury: A review of pertinent issues. *Pediatric Rehabilitation, 8,* 92–103.

Schatz, J., & Buzan, R. (2006). Decreased corpus callosum size in sickle cell disease: Relationship with cerebral infarcts and cognitive functioning. *Journal of the International Neuropsychological Society, 12,* 24–33.

Schatz, J., Finke, R., & Roberts, C. (2004). Interactions of biomedical and environmental risk factors for cognitive development: A preliminary study of sickle cell disease. *Journal of Developmental Camp: Behavioral Pediatrics, 25,* 303–310.

Scher, M., Redline, R., & Bangert, B. (2002). Delayed onset of status epilepticus after transient asphyxia in an asymptomatic full-term neonate. *Journal of Child Neurology, 17,* 780–783.

Schmidt, H., Heimann, B., Djukic, M., Mazurek, C., Fels, C., Wallesch, C., et al. (2006). Neuropsychological sequelae of bacterial and viral meningitis. *Brain: A Journal of Neurology, 129,* 333–345.

Sesma, H., & Georgieff, M. (2003). The effect of adverse intrauterine and newborn environments on cognitive development: The experiences of premature delivery and diabetes during pregnancy. *Development and Psychopathology, 15,* 991–1015.

Simon, T., Bearden, C., McGinn, D., & Zackai, E. (2005). Visuospatial and numerical cognitive deficits in children with chromosome 22Q11.2 deletion syndrome. *Cortex, 41,* 145–155.

Smith, R., Martin, S., & Wolters, P. (2004). Pediatric and adolescent HIV/AIDS. In R. Brown (Ed.), *Handbook of pediatric psychology in school settings* (pp. 195–220). Mahwah, NJ: Erlbaum.

Taylor, H., Minich, N., Klein, N., & Hack, M. (2004). Longitudinal outcomes of very low birth weight: Neuropsychological findings. *Journal of the International Neuropsychological Society, 10,* 149–163.

Tran, U., Gray, P., & O'Callaghan, M. (2005). Neonatal antecedents for cerebral palsy in extremely preterm babies and interaction with maternal factors. *Early Human Development, 81,* 555–561.

Verte, S., Guerts, H., Roeyers, H., Oosterlaan, J., & Sergeant, J. (2005). Executive functioning in children with autism and Tourette syndrome. *Development and Psychopathology, 17,* 415–445.

Visser, J., Schretlen, D., Harris, J., & Jinnah, H. (2005). Lesch-nyhan disease. In S. Goldstein & C. Reynolds (Eds.), *Handbook of neurodevelopmental and genetic disorders in adults* (pp. 410–438). New York: Guilford Press.

Woodrich, D., Kaplan, A., & Deering, W. (2006). Children with epilepsy in school: Special service usage and assessment practices. *Psychology in Schools, 43,* 169–180.

Woodward, L., Mogridge, N., Wells, S., & Inder, E. (2004). Can neurobehavioral examination predict the presence of cerebral injury in the very low birth weight infant? *Journal of Developmental Camp: Behavioral Pediatrics, 25,* 326–334.

Yuma, P., Maxson, R., & Brown, D. (2006). All-terrain vehicles and children: History, injury burden, and prevention strategies. *Journal of Pediatric Health Care, 20,* 67–70.

CHAPTER 19

Habit Disorders

DOUGLAS WOODS, CHRISTOPHER A. FLESSNER,
AND CHRISTINE A. CONELEA

T his chapter provides a comprehensive review of the assessment, conceptualization, and treatment of children and adolescents (hereafter referred to as children)
with habit disorders. The chapter has three primary goals. The first is to describe
habit disorders, their diagnosis, and assessment. The second is to highlight the empirical basis for several important factors in the conceptualization of habit disorders (e.g.,
developmental issues, learning and modeling, genetic influences). The third goal is to
examine research demonstrating empirical support for both behavioral and medical
treatments for habit disorders and illustrate these data with a case description.

DESCRIPTION OF THE DISORDER

"Habit disorders" is an umbrella term that presently includes tic disorders (TDs) and
a host of body-focused behaviors (Teng, Woods, Twohig, & Marcks, 2002) such as
trichotillomania (TTM), nail biting, skin picking (SP), and bruxism (teeth grinding).
These disorders are all topographically distinct, and their etiological and functional
similarities are unclear. However, habit disorders are, by definition, repetitive and
relatively stable and result in negative physical and/or social consequences for the
individual. Recently, there has been an influx of empirical research examining the assessment, phenomenology, functional impact, and treatment of these behavior problems (Flessner et al., 2005; Flessner & Woods, in press; Wilhelm et al., 2003; Woods,
Wetterneck, & Flessner, 2006). Based on the extant research, this chapter examines the
three most impairing habit disorders: TTM, SP, and TDs.

TRICHOTILLOMANIA

Trichotillomania is characterized by the recurrent pulling out of one's hair, resulting
in noticeable hair loss. The pulling must be accompanied by an increasing sense of
tension prior to or while attempting to resist pulling and a feeling of gratification,
relief, or pleasure following pulling. The behavior must cause clinically significant

542

impairment or distress in day-to-day functioning and must not be better accounted for by another mental health condition (American Psychiatric Association, 2000). Despite these diagnostic criteria, many researchers and clinicians continue to confer a diagnosis of TTM in the absence of reported tension prior to and/or relief following pulling (Diefenbach, Tolin, Crocetto, Maltby, & Hannan, 2005; Watson & Allen, 1993; Watson, Dittmer, & Ray, 2000). To date, research has yet to examine whether differences (e.g., pulling severity, impact from pulling) exist between persons meeting full diagnostic criteria for TTM and those denying the presence of tension prior to and/or relief after pulling.

Depending on the size and age of the sample, age of onset typically ranges from 9 to 14 years (Christenson, Mackenzie, & Mitchell, 1991; L. J. Cohen et al., 1995; King et al., 1995; Reeve, Bernstein, & Christenson, 1992; Woods et al., 2006), although research has shown that hair pulling can begin as young as 18 months (Watson et al., 2000; Wright & Holmes, 2003). Hair may be pulled from any part of the body capable of growing hair (e.g., scalp, eyebrows, eyelashes, pubic area), but very young children (e.g., toddlers) typically pull from the scalp (L. J. Cohen et al., 1995; Wright & Holmes, 2003). Research suggests that hair pulling may wax (intensify) and wane (diminish) throughout the course of the disorder (du Toit, van Kradenburg, Niehaus, & Stein, 2001). Approximately 0.6% of the population meet full diagnostic criteria for TTM (Christenson, Pyle, & Mitchell, 1991), but research using more liberal diagnostic criteria (e.g., absence of tension prior to and/or relief after pulling) suggests that TTM occurs in 1% to 5% of the population (Graber & Arndt, 1993). The prevalence of TTM in childhood is unclear, although some believe the disorder is more prevalent in children than in adults (Mehregan, 1970). Trichotillomania is more prevalent in females, although the female-to-male ratio may be lower in children (L. J. Cohen et al., 1995).

Research examining the phenomenology of TTM suggests that at least two dimensions of pulling may exist (Christenson & Mackenzie, 1994; Christenson, Mackenzie, & Mitchell, 1991; Diefenbach, Mouton-Odum, & Stanley, 2002; du Toit et al., 2001). Christenson and Mackenzie referred to these dimensions as "automatic" and "focused" pulling. Automatic pulling is characterized by pulling that occurs primarily out of one's awareness (e.g., pulling while watching television, reading a book, listening to the radio), where the individual is frequently unaware that pulling has occurred until a later time (e.g., he or she sees hair on his or her lap). Focused pulling is characterized by pulling with an almost compulsive quality and involves pulling in response to a negative emotion (e.g., anxiety, stress, anger) or an intense thought or urge. Focused pulling may represent an attempt to decrease negative affect (e.g., anxiety, specific cognitions; Begotka, Woods, & Wetterneck, 2004; Woods et al., 2006). Researchers have suggested that focused and automatic pulling may require different interventions (Franklin, Tolin, & Diefenbach, 2006; Woods et al., 2006).

Most research has examined dimensions of pulling only in adults. It remains unclear to what extent these dimensions are applicable to children. For example, Reeve et al. (1992) found that none of 10 children assessed in their study reported pulling of a compulsive nature, suggesting that children either do not experience or may be unable to identify focused pulling. These results have led to the suggestion that the onset of focused pulling may follow a developmental trend.

Although hair loss is an obvious side effect of TTM, a significant number of individuals with TTM also bite, chew on, and occasionally swallow their hair (Woods,

Friman, & Teng, 2001). Swallowing one's hair (trichophagia) rarely results in hairballs, or trichobezoars, which is a serious health threat and can require surgery. Individuals with TTM may also experience repetitive strain injuries such as carpal tunnel syndrome (O'Sullivan, Keuthen, Jenike, & Gumley, 1996) and dental erosion from biting hair (Christenson & Mansueto, 1999).

There are both physical and psychological consequences associated with hair pulling. Individuals with TTM are likely to have comorbid diagnoses, with mood and anxiety disorders being the most common (Christenson, Mackenzie, et al., 1991; L. J. Cohen et al., 1995; Diefenbach et al., 2002; Schlosser, Black, Blum, & Goldstein, 1994). Christenson and colleagues assessed 60 adults with TTM and found that 55% met diagnostic criteria for Major Depression, and 15% met diagnostic criteria for Obsessive-Compulsive Disorder (OCD). In a subsequent study evaluating 123 chronic hair pullers, L. J. Cohen and colleagues found similarly high rates of Anxiety Disorder (15%), depression (14%), and OCD (13%).

As stated earlier, there is little research on children with TTM. Nevertheless, Reeve and colleagues (1992) found that 70% of children with TTM had at least one additional psychiatric diagnosis, with Overanxious Disorder and Dysthymia being the most common. Subsequent research has found similar rates of anxiety and mood disorders in children (King et al., 1995). Unfortunately, there is a profound lack of data examining comorbid concerns in very young children (e.g., below 6 years of age; Wright & Holmes, 2003). Nevertheless, Wright and Holmes found that the parents of infants who pulled their hair reported increased levels of anxiety in their children.

Skin Picking

Currently, SP has no specific diagnostic classification in the *Diagnostic and Statistical Manual of Mental Disorders* (*DSM-IV-TR*; American Psychiatric Association, 2000). As a result, most researchers define SP as recurrent picking accompanied by visible tissue damage, which results in significant distress and/or functional impairment (e.g., Bohne, Wilhelm, Keuthen, Baer, & Jenike, 2002; Keuthen et al., 2000; Teng et al., 2002; Wilhelm et al., 1999). Research suggests an age of onset between 12 and 16 years (Flessner & Woods, in press; Simeon et al., 1997; Wilhelm et al., 1999), with evidence indicating that picking may wax and wane throughout an individual's lifetime and may coincide with the menstrual cycle for some women (approximately 44%; Wilhelm et al., 1999). Skin picking can occur on nearly all body surfaces, but most commonly occurs on the face (Arnold, Auchenbach, & McElroy, 2001; Wilhelm et al., 1999). The relative prevalence of SP ranges from 2% in dermatology clinics to 3.8% to 4.6% in college students (Arnold et al., 2001; Bohne et al., 2002; Keuthen et al., 2000) and occurs more commonly in females than males (Bohne et al., 2002; Simeon et al., 1997). A lack of data exists regarding prevalence and sex differences in children.

Phenomenological research suggests that SP may reduce discomfort, tension, or some other negative feeling or state (Keuthen et al., 2000; Simeon et al., 1997), findings similar to those in adults with TTM (Begotka et al., 2004). In a recent study of 21 individuals with SP and 68 individuals with TTM, Lochner, Simeon, Niehaus, and Stein (2002) showed that the two groups were similar on demographic characteristics, psychiatric comorbidity, and personality dimensions. However, research has yet to examine whether the focused and automatic dimensions of TTM can be extended to SP, and research has yet to examine similarities and differences between childhood TTM and SP.

Neziroglu and Mancebo (2001) examined a number of physical consequences that can develop as a result of SP, including permanent disfigurement, soreness, bleeding, and possible infections. Flessner and Woods (in press) recruited skin pickers using an Internet-based survey and found that 85% of respondents engaged in behaviors to conceal the effects of SP, including wearing makeup and using specific hairstyles or clothing. In addition, 29% ($n = 27$) reported spending more than 15 minutes per day covering the effects of SP.

Comorbid psychiatric diagnoses, including alcohol abuse and dependence, OCD, Generalized Anxiety Disorder, and mild to moderate levels of depression and/or anxiety frequently have been found in persons who pick their skin (Arnold et al., 1998; M. R. Bloch, Elliot, Thompson, & Koran, 2001; Calikusu, Yucel, Poiat, & Baykal, 2003; Flessner & Woods, in press; Keuthen et al., 2000; Simeon et al., 1997; Wilhelm et al., 1999). Arnold and colleagues found that 12% ($n = 4$) of their sample of skin pickers reported suicidal ideation because of picking-related problems. Unfortunately, a lack of data exists examining comorbid concerns in children.

TIC DISORDERS

Tics are "sudden, rapid, recurrent, nonrhythmic, stereotyped motor movements or vocalizations" (American Psychiatric Association, 2000, p. 108). Although four categories of TDs exist, Chronic Motor or Vocal Tic Disorders (CTDs) and Tourette's syndrome (TS) are the most frequently studied. Single or multiple motor or vocal tics, but not both, which persist for at least 1 year characterize CTDs, and multiple motor tics and one or more vocal tics that persist for at least 1 year characterize TS. Both require onset before age 18 (American Psychiatric Association, 2000).

For most children, tics begin between the ages of 5 and 7 (Findley, 2001) and wax and wane over the course of the disorder (B. S. Peterson & Leckman, 1998). Research suggests that approximately 0.8% of the population suffer from motor tics and 0.5% suffer from vocal tics (Khalifa & Knorring, 2003). Although tics in children are quite common, prevalence estimates for TS range from about 0.04% to 3.0% (American Psychiatric Association, 2000; Hornsey, Banerjee, Zeitlan, & Robertson, 2001; Khalifa & Knorring, 2003; Mason, Banerjee, Eapen, Zeitlin, & Robertson, 1998). Tic Disorders are more common in males.

Many individuals with TDs report experiencing "premonitory urges." The premonitory urge is often described as an aversive itching, tickling, or tense sensation or as a mental awareness in the area of the body where a tic is about to occur (Leckman, King, & Cohen, 1999; Leckman, Peterson, Pauls, & Cohen, 1997; Leckman, Walker, & Cohen, 1993). Tics usually result in a temporary lessening or elimination of the urge. Research suggests that as many as 93% of persons diagnosed with a TD may experiencing some form of urge, feeling, or "need" to engage in a tic (Leckman et al., 1993), which may help to explain the perceived "voluntary" nature of tics reported by some individuals (Leckman et al., 1997). Although typically experienced by older children and adults (e.g., 10 years or older), children as young as 7 may report experiencing such urges (Leckman et al., 1999), and more recent research further supports the idea that the urge is present but not well formed in younger children (Woods, Piacentini, Himle, & Chang, 2005).

Individuals diagnosed with TDs can suffer a variety of negative physical consequences which are most often associated with the topography of the tic (Woods, Friman, et al., 2001). For example, tics involving repetitive lip or cheek biting can result in oral inflammation or infection, and tics directed toward the self can result in abrasions and fractures. When the tic involves the eyes, serious ocular injury can result (e.g., blindness from detached retina; Leckman et al., 1999). To date, there is no documented evidence suggesting physical consequences from vocal tics.

Perhaps the greatest concern for individuals diagnosed with a TD is the presence of comorbid psychiatric diagnoses (D. J. Cohen, Friedhoff, Leckman, & Chase, 1992; Gadow, Nolan, Sprafkin, & Schwartz, 2002). Research suggests that as many as 95% of individuals diagnosed with a TD meet diagnostic criteria for another psychiatric condition (Coffey, Biederman, Smoller, et al., 2000), with Attention-Deficit/Hyperactivity Disorder (ADHD; Cohen et al., 1992; Comings & Comings, 1985) and OCD (D. J. Cohen, Friedhoff, et al., 1992; Comings & Comings, 1985) representing the most frequently diagnosed comorbid concerns. In addition, research has suggested elevated rates of mood and anxiety disorders in TD populations (e.g., depression, social phobia, and Overanxious Disorder; Carter, Pauls, Leckman, & Cohen, 1994; Coffey, Biederman, Geller, et al., 2000; Mason et al., 1998; Spencer, Biederman, Harding, Wilens, & Faraone, 1995). Children diagnosed with TDs also have increased rates of disruptive behavior problems (e.g., Conduct and Oppositional Defiant Disorder; Coffey, Biederman, Geller, et al., 2000; Kadesjo & Gillberg, 2000; Mason et al., 1998; Spencer et al., 1995) and learning disorders (e.g., dyslexia; Carter et al., 1994; Kadesjo & Gillberg, 2000).

DIAGNOSIS AND ASSESSMENT

Although a number of strategies exist for the diagnosis and assessment of habit disorders in adults, substantially fewer options are available for children. We describe the available structured and unstructured diagnostic interviews for each of the disorders, followed by available dimensional measures of symptom severity. Finally, we discuss functional assessment strategies that can be broadly applied across all habit disorders.

Because no specific diagnostic criteria exist for SP, structured and unstructured interviews have not yet been developed. However, a number of structured interviews exist for TDs and TTM, and all children with habit disorders should be thoroughly assessed for co-occurring conditions. In our clinic, this is typically achieved through use of the National Institute of Mental Health's Diagnostic Interview Schedule for Children, Version IV (NIMH DISC-IV; Shaffer, Fisher, Lucas, Dulcan, & Schwab-Stone, 2000). The DISC consists of both parent (DISC-P) and child (DISC-Y) versions, and data from these interviews can be interpreted either together or separately. Both interviews have demonstrated good temporal stability in clinical samples (k = 0.43–0.96 and 0.25–0.92, respectively), and past versions of the DISC have demonstrated moderate to very good concurrent validity and good to excellent sensitivity to the diagnosis of uncommon psychiatric disorders.

An alternative to the more comprehensive structured interviews is the Trichotillomania Diagnostic Interview (TDI; Rothbaum & Ninan, 1994). The TDI provides a standardized assessment instrument for the diagnosis of TTM. The TDI includes a 3-point clinician-rated scale (threshold, subthreshold, and below threshold) for each of several questions designed to assess diagnostic criteria for TTM set forth by the *DSM*. Although providing an efficient formal assessment of TTM, the reliability and validity of the TDI for use with either children or adults have yet to be examined, and the instrument should be approached with caution.

In addition to diagnostic interviews, researchers and clinicians frequently employ the Yale Global Tic Severity Scale (YGTSS; Leckman et al., 1989) or the National Institute of Mental Health Trichotillomania Impairment Scale (NIMH-TIS; Swedo et al., 1989) as dimensional measures for the assessment of tic and TTM severity, respectively. The YGTSS is a semi-structured interview completed by the clinician, which is designed to measure the severity of a TD across several domains of severity, including tic number, frequency, complexity, intensity, and the amount of interference produced. The YGTSS has demonstrated adequate to excellent internal consistency, fair to excellent temporal stability across motor, vocal, and total tic scores, strong convergent validity, and adequate to strong discriminant validity (Leckman et al., 1989; Storch et al., 2005). The NIMH-TIS provides a single impairment rating (ranging from $0 = $ no impairment to $10 = $ severe impairment) completed by a clinician based on the damage resulting from pulling, time spent pulling or concealing damage to the area, and the individual's ability to control his or her hair pulling. The NIMH-TIS has shown minimally acceptable ($r = 0.71$; Stanley, Breckenridge, Snyder, & Novry, 1999) to excellent ($r = 0.94$; Crocetto, Diefenbach, Tolin, & Maltby, 2003) interrater reliability, and good to very good concurrent validity with hair damage ($r = 0.77$) and TTM severity. However, caution should be exercised when using this instrument because it has yet to be validated for use with children.

Self-report instruments are also available to aid in the assessment of TTM and SP severity. The Massachusetts General Hospital Hairpulling Scale (MGH-HS; Keuthen et al., 1995) is a 7-item self-report instrument designed to assess hair pulling severity (actual pulling, urge to pull, and distress from pulling) over the past week. Similarly, the Skin Picking Scale (SPS; Keuthen et al., 2001) is a 6-item self-report scale designed to assess the severity of SP (frequency and intensity of urges, time spent picking, interference, distress, and avoidance due to picking). Both the SPS and MGH-HS have demonstrated good psychometric properties for the assessment of picking and pulling severity in adults, respectively (Diefenbach, Tolin, Crocetto, et al., 2005; Keuthen et al., 2001; O'Sullivan et al., 1995). However, neither scale has been validated for use with children. As a result, caution should be exercised when interpreting severity ratings obtained from these instruments (Keuthen et al., 2001).

To aid in the identification and assessment of premonitory urges for children with TDs, Woods and colleagues (2005) developed the Premonitory Urge for Tics Scale (PUTS). The PUTS is a 9-item self-report scale designed to assess tic-related premonitory urges; higher scores indicate greater awareness of these urges. Woods and colleagues found that the PUTS demonstrated good psychometric properties for children 10 years or older but these were unacceptable for children younger than 10 years. Therefore, caution should be exercised when interpreting results from the PUTS for younger children.

In addition to these diagnostic and symptom severity measures, data should be collected about family health history, treatment history, and the social and/or physical consequences (e.g., teasing from peers, scars resulting from picking/pulling) associated with pulling, picking, or tics. We also recommend a thorough functional assessment of each repetitive behavior. Antecedents and consequences of the behavior should be carefully investigated, with the goal of isolating the specific behavioral functions maintaining the repetitive behavior. Functional assessment is considered an essential feature of contemporary interventions for children and adolescents with habit disorders.

CONCEPTUALIZATION

The conceptualization process requires the synthesis of information obtained via a variety of assessment strategies (e.g., structured, semi-structured, and informal interviews, self-report measures, functional assessment). Although many variables can influence the conceptualization process, this section highlights several important examples, including developmental issues, learning and modeling, parental issues, life events, genetic influences, peer influences, physical factors affecting behavior, drugs affecting behavior, and cultural and diversity issues.

DEVELOPMENTAL ISSUES

Hair pulling occurring in early childhood generally begins in the absence of significant environmental changes, is of short duration, and remits without intervention or with simple interventions (Miltenberger, Rapp, & Long, 2001). Miltenberger and colleagues have suggested that the shorter course of hair pulling in young children may be accounted for by the presence of a change agent, specifically a parent, who is able to implement a behavioral intervention consistently. In one of the few studies focusing on early-onset hair pulling, Wright and Holmes (2003) described the characteristics of 10 toddlers with hair pulling. Wright and Holmes reported that all children pulled exclusively from the scalp and commonly displayed anxiety (per parental report and clinical observation). In addition, pulling typically occurred during times of separation, boredom, fatigue, and stress. The authors noted that a TTM diagnosis is rarely made for toddlers and preschool children, given the difficulty of assessing *DSM* criteria regarding tension prior to and gratification following pulling. Other research has reported similar difficulties in both children and adults (King et al., 1995). In contrast, hair pulling beginning in adolescence or lasting for more than 6 months is generally characterized by a chronic course and tends to be more resistant to treatment (Chang, Lee, Chiang, & Lu, 1991; Winchel, 1992).

Data on the developmental course of SP are scarce. Koblenzer (1987) reported that severe SP was not related to age, although subsequent research has reported peaks ranging from the early 20s to between the ages of 30 and 45 (Bohne et al., 2002). The duration of severe SP has been reported to be an average of 21 years (Wilhelm et al., 1999).

The onset of tics usually occurs in the first decade of life, typically between the ages of 5 and 7 (Bornstein, Stefl, & Hammond, 1990; Leckman et al., 1999). Transient Tic Disorder remits by adolescence for the majority of children (B. S. Peterson, Pine, Cohen, & Brook, 2001). It is thought that about 5% to 24% of those with Transient Tic Disorder develop CTD or TS (D. J. Cohen, Riddle, & Leckman, 1992), although this progression has not been confirmed in longitudinal research (Glaros & Epkins, 2003).

In early childhood, motor tics of the face, eyes, and head are typically the first to emerge, followed by tics that emerge in a head-down direction (Leckman et al., 1999). Simple motor tics, such as brief movements, usually appear prior to complex motor tics, such as sequences of movements. Phonic tics typically appear after the onset of motor tics, and simple phonic tics, such as throat clearing or sniffling precedes complex phonic tics, such as words or phrases (Leckman et al., 1999). Worst-ever tic severity has been reported to occur at an average age of 10.6 years, and about 85% of adolescents experience a reduction in tic symptoms (M. H. Bloch et al., 2006). By adulthood, tic severity usually stabilizes, and tics tend to be less variable and occur during times of increased emotionality and fatigue (Leckman, Bloch, King, & Scahill, 2006).

Learning and Modeling

Behavioral conceptualizations of habit disorders have explained their development and maintenance in terms of classical and operant conditioning. Mansueto, Stemberger, Thomas, and Golomb (1997) described such a model for TTM. According to their conceptualization, internal and/or external stimuli develop the capacity to elicit the urge to pull through classical conditioning. For example, a child may pull hair in the presence of a given affective state or environmental setting. Over time, through classical conditioning, those stimuli may elicit the urge to pull. Similarly, in other habit disorders, internal and external stimuli may become paired with the behavior and thus elicit the urge to engage in the behavior.

Operant conditioning is also thought to play a role in habit disorders. Reinforcing consequences of a habit may include dissipation of the urge, social comfort or attention, or removal from an undesirable situation (such as completing chores or school assignments). In TTM, reinforcing consequences may include relief from stress, thoughts, or unwanted emotions, acquisition of a particular type of hair or hair root, or tactile stimulation from postpulling hair manipulation. Aversive consequences may also follow the performance of a habit. These consequences include physical sensations (e.g., pain), negative social reactions (e.g., ridicule or chastisement), or undesirable emotional states (e.g., depressed mood). Though speculative, the habit sequence may end when aversive stimulation becomes more salient than reinforcing stimulation.

Research in the area of habit disorders has also examined the impact of modeling. Reeve et al. (1992) obtained general psychological profiles of the parents of 10 children with TTM and reported symptoms related to anxiety and depression in 30% ($n = 3$) of these parents. Given the seemingly high rates of anxiety and affective symptoms observed, the authors speculated that parental anxiety contributes to the development of anxious behaviors in children. Relatedly, Woods, Watson, Wolfe, Twohig, and Friman (2001) found that talking about tics increased vocal tics in two boys with TS, suggesting that tics may be reactive to social attention.

Parental Issues

Parenting practices can potentially impact the development and maintenance of habit disorders. For example, if a child is ridiculed or chastised by peers following a tic, the child may withdraw from future social contact (Leckman & Cohen, 1999a). Parents may subsequently seek to protect their child by allowing or encouraging the child to avoid situations where ridicule or discomfort may occur. Although these efforts may be well-intentioned, such parental responses could increase feelings of shame and avoidance and increase avoidance behavior. By contrast, some parents may punish or blame their children for having tics. Parental criticism could increase child stress and anxiety and potentially exacerbate symptoms. Although some parents decide to keep their child uninformed about the condition (presumably to prevent social isolation), it is generally beneficial for parents to be accepting of the disorder and involve the child in treatment decisions should the need for treatment arise. As Leckman and Cohen note, children who adjust well to TDs tend to have families that do not treat the child as sick or vulnerable, but instead keep their child in the mainstream as much as possible, offer empathic support, and model assertive behavior.

LIFE EVENTS

Various life events and environmental factors have been implicated in the etiology and maintenance of habit disorders. In a group of 11 children with TTM, 45% described a significant life event that was associated with the onset of hair pulling (Hanna, 1997). Similarly, Reeve and colleagues (1992) found that children with TTM identified an average of 3.3 significant life events (as measured by the Life Events Checklist) occurring in the year prior to their evaluation as part of the study.

Although there has not yet been a systematic investigation of events associated with the onset of TTM, several factors have been described in the literature. These factors include psychosocial stressors within the family (e.g., separation from parents, divorce, death or illness of a loved one, moving to a new residence; Christenson & Mansueto, 1999; Hanna, 1997; Wright & Holmes, 2003), academic stressors (e.g., poor academic performance), and childhood illness or injury to the scalp or hair (Christenson & Mansueto, 1999). Childhood trauma and early physical and/or sexual abuse have also been associated with TTM onset (Lochner et al., 2002), but there is some disagreement regarding the relationship between sexual abuse and TTM, as the incidence of childhood sexual abuse in those with TTM has not been found to differ from the incidence in the general population (Christenson & Mansueto, 1999). However, Christenson (1995) did find that early-onset hair pulling was associated with higher incidences of physical and sexual abuse than later-onset TTM.

Relatively little research has examined the impact of specific life events on the exacerbation of SP. However, extant research does suggest that SP can be triggered by various emotions (e.g., stress, anxiety), cutaneous stimuli (e.g., infections, scabs), specific situations (e.g., reading or watching television), or by the desire to improve one's appearance (Bohne et al., 2002). However, additional research is necessary to further evaluate the influence of these stimuli on SP.

Several environmental factors are thought to mediate the expression of tics. Perinatal risk factors, such as hypoxic insults (e.g., maternal smoking), severe morning sickness during the first trimester, and maternal stress during pregnancy, have been associated with TDs and are thought to be related to the development of neural circuits involved in TS (Leckman & Cohen, 1999b). Silva, Munoz, Barickman, and Friedhoff (1995) found that events that made the child upset or anxious (e.g., arguments with family, beginning a new school, year), emotional trauma and fatigue, watching television, being alone, and being in a social gathering were most commonly associated with tic exacerbation. B. S. Peterson and colleagues (1999) later noted that any life event causing stress can produce symptom exacerbation (e.g., conflict, physical illness, death, or divorce).

GENETIC INFLUENCES

Given the similarities in the phenomenology, course, comorbidity, treatment response, and family history of TTM, SP, and TDs, these disorders have been conceptualized as being part of an obsessive-compulsive spectrum; as a result, they are thought to have some shared genetic and biological components (Bohne, Keuthen, & Wilhelm, 2005). Research on the genetics of specific habit disorders has begun to explore the genetic underpinnings of TTM and TDs; however, the literature on the genetics of SP remains sparse.

Although a specific gene for TTM has not been found, there is evidence to suggest an increased prevalence of TTM and other psychiatric disorders in the first-degree relatives of those diagnosed with TTM. L. J. Cohen et al. (1995) surveyed 123 people who pull hair and found that 3% of participants' family members had been formally diagnosed with TTM. The most common disorders among family members included substance abuse (29%), depressive disorders (20%), and anxiety disorders (10%). Other research has found similar results (Schlosser et al., 1994). King et al. (1995) examined the prevalence of hair pulling, tics, obsessive-compulsive symptoms, and pathological grooming behaviors among the parents of 15 children who pulled hair and found that 20% had parents with a history of pathological grooming behaviors and 53% had parents with OCD or obsessive-compulsive symptoms.

Tourette's syndrome and CTDs have been consistently demonstrated to be heritable in twin and family studies, which have shown that the risk for TS among relatives of a proband ranges from 9.8% to 15%, and from 15% to 20% for other TDs, rates that are significantly higher than among the general population (Pauls, 2002). Segregation analyses have for the most part provided support for the hypothesis that major genes are involved in the transmission and expression of tic disorders (Eapen, Pauls, & Robertson, 1993; Pauls & Leckman, 1986), although there is evidence to suggest that the genetic mechanism underlying tic disorders is complex and likely involves several different genes (Walkup et al., 1996). Genetic linkage and association studies have been conducted in an effort to localize and characterize the genes involved in the expression of TDs. Recent research examining the Slit- and Trk-like 1 gene has found that sequence variants in the gene are associated with TS (Abelson et al., 2005).

Peer Influences

Children exhibiting habit disorders may be alienated or socially rejected from their peers, which may in turn lead to the exacerbation of these behaviors or potentially to the later development of other psychiatric conditions (Greene, Biederman, Faraone, Sienna, & Garcia-Jetton, 1997). Boudjouk, Woods, Miltenberger, and Long (2000) assessed peer perceptions of adolescents with tics and TTM to determine if the presentation of habit disorders results in negative social evaluations. Fifty-one eighth-graders viewed and rated videos of actors either engaging or not engaging in habit behaviors, and results indicated that actors who pulled their hair or exhibited tics were perceived as less socially acceptable. These findings supported previous research by Woods, Fuqua, and Outman (1999), who found that increased severity and frequency of habit behaviors led to decreased social acceptability and that men with habits were rated as less socially acceptable than women with habits.

In addition to difficulties with social acceptability, individuals with habit disorders also suffer from peer relationship problems. Studies have suggested that people with TDs have difficulty making and keeping friends (Bawden, Stokes, Camfield, Camfield, & Salisbury, 1998; Hubka, Fulton, Shady, Champion, & Wand, 1988), are more withdrawn and less popular than their peers (Stokes, Bawden, Camfield, Backman, & Dooley, 1991), and experience difficulty with dating situations and marriage (A. K. Shapiro, Shapiro, & Wayne, 1972). Many people with TDs have comorbid psychiatric conditions, such as ADHD and OCD, and some research suggests that these conditions significantly contribute to the social problems faced by those with TDs (Bawden et al., 1998; Carter et al., 2000).

Research on quality-of-life issues has revealed that many people with TTM report refraining from intimate relationships, close relationships, group activities, and social events due to hair pulling (Diefenbach, Tolin, Hannan, Crocetto, & Worhunsky, 2005; Wetterneck, Woods, Norberg, & Begotka, 2006). Skin picking has also been found to engender negative social consequences, such as avoidance of social situations where others may notice skin damage (Flessner & Woods, in press; Neziroglu & Mancebo, 2001).

Physical Factors Affecting Behavior

Hair loss may result from several medical conditions, including male-pattern baldness, alopecia areata, chronic discoid lupus erythematosus, folliculitis decalvans, lichen planopilaris, alopecia mucinosa, and pseudopelade (American Psychiatric Association, 2000). These conditions should be considered when making a diagnosis of TTM, especially if the individual denies hair pulling. In addition, a scalp biopsy by a dermatologist can confirm a diagnosis of TTM if needed (Christenson & Mackenzie, 1994). Relatedly, habitual SP must also be distinguished from SP better accounted for by a medical or dermatological condition, such as itch-provoking neurodermatitis, psoriasis, leukemia, or diabetes mellitus (Bohne et al., 2002).

Tics or tic like movements can accompany a number of medical conditions, including stroke, Huntington's disease, Wilson's disease, Syndenham's chorea, Lesch-Nyhan syndrome, multiple sclerosis, postviral encephalitis, head injury, and muscle spasms (American Psychiatric Association, 2000). Differential diagnostic considerations that should be taken into account include family and medical history as well as the morphology, rhythm, and modifying influences on movements (American Psychiatric Association, 2000). Additional features that are characteristic of tics include temporary suppressibility of the movement, variability in the location of the movement, diminishment of the movement during sleep, and the presence of a premonitory urge (Towbin, Peterson, Cohen, & Leckman, 1999).

Streptococcal and viral infections have also been implicated in habit and obsessive-compulsive spectrum disorders in what has been called pediatric autoimmune neuropsychiatric disorders associated with streptococcal infections (Snider & Swedo, 2004). In a subgroup of children with tics, streptococcal infections are thought to stimulate an abnormal immune response in which antineuronal antibodies are produced and interfere with the neurons of the basal ganglia (Snider & Swedo, 2004). However, some argue against this hypothesis, noting that increases in tics during infection may be a result of a nonspecific stress response. Furthermore, antineuronal antibodies have not been found in many people with TDs and have yet to be correlated with symptom severity (Findley, 2001). Whether tics actually increase in response to strep infections remains hotly debated.

Drugs Affecting Behavior

Tics and TTM have sometimes been associated with stimulant use. Indeed, psychostimulants have facilitative effects on the transmission of dopamine and serotonin, neurotransmitters that have been implicated in TTM, tics, and OCD (Martin, Scahill, Vitulano, & King, 1998). Tics have been reported to be caused or exacerbated by the stimulant medications used to treat ADHD, such as methylphenidate, dextroamphetamine, pemoline, and atomoxetine (Ledbetter, 2005; Varley, Vincent,

Varley, & Calderon, 2001). Despite these reports, placebo-controlled studies examining the impact of methylphenidate and atomoxetine have found that these stimulants do not significantly induce or exacerbate tics (Allen et al., 2005; Palumbo, Spencer, Lynch, Co-Chien, & Faraone, 2004). The onset or exacerbation of TTM symptoms has previously been reported following treatment with methylphenidate for ADHD (Martin et al., 1998). However, this effect was observed only for boys, which the authors attributed to an increased likelihood of exposure to stimulants among males rather than a specific gender difference. The relationship between stimulants and TTM symptoms remains unclear, as no placebo-controlled studies have been conducted examining this issue.

CULTURAL AND DIVERSITY ISSUES

A study by Neal-Barnett, Ward-Brown, Mitchell, and Krownapple (2000) found that 55% of hair care professionals reported having African American customers who engaged in chronic hair pulling. However, McCarley, Spirrison, and Ceminsky (2002) surveyed college students and found that prevalence rates of TTM do not appear to differ between Caucasians and African Americans. In addition, they found that more African Americans than non–African Americans reported pulling in response to itchy and inflamed skin and feeling pleasure or relief as a consequence of pulling. Another prevalence study did not find differences between the prevalence rates of TTM in Israeli Jewish adolescents and college students in the United States (King et al., 1995).

Given that a common motivation for SP is the desire to improve one's appearance, Bohne et al. (2002) speculated that differential cultural emphasis on physical appearance may impact SP in different cultures. In the only known cross-cultural examination of chronic SP, Bohne and colleagues investigated SP in a sample of 133 German college students and found that the prevalence of SP tends to be stable across German and American cultures.

In a review of the English-language literature on TS, Staley, Wand, and Shady (1997) found that the demographics, family history, comorbidity, clinical features and treatment outcome of TS do not differ across various cultures. However, Gadow and colleagues (2002) found that young African American children (in comparison to young Caucasian children) may experience more severe symptoms of TDs. Mathews and colleagues (2001) examined the perception of TDs in Costa Rica and found that many people denied that their tics caused distress or impairment, even when objective evidence suggested that they did. The authors noted that in Costa Rica and other Latin American countries, tics are thought to represent bad habits that are under voluntary control rather than physical symptoms.

BEHAVIORAL TREATMENT

Several behavioral treatments have been used to treat habit disorders, including habit reversal (HR; Azrin & Nunn, 1973; Rapp, Miltenberger, Long, Elliot, & Lumley, 1998; Woods, Miltenberger, & Lumley, 1996), contingency management (Barrett, 1962; Corte, Wolf, & Locke, 1971; Watson & Sterling, 1998), function-based treatments (Deaver, Miltenberger, & Stricker, 2001; Miltenberger, Long, Rapp, Lumley, & Elliott, 1998), and cognitive-behavioral procedures (Deckersbach, Wilhelm, Keuthen, Baer, & Jenkie, 2002; Mansueto, Golomb, Thomas, & Stemberger, 1999). Among the behavioral interventions, HR has demonstrated the strongest empirical support (Elliott & Fuqua,

2000; Friman, Finney, & Christophersen, 1984) and is designated a "probably effica-cious" treatment for habit disorders (Chambless & Ollendick, 2001). In addition, HR has demonstrated efficacy for both adults and children for the treatment of a variety of habit disorders, including tics (Wilhelm et al., 2003), hair pulling (Azrin, Nunn, & Franz, 1980), and SP (Teng, Woods, & Twohig, 2006).

Habit reversal was originally developed by Azrin and Nunn (1973) as a multicom-ponent package for the treatment of tics and nervous habits. Since its inception, the specific components of HR have been modified to some extent. Most researchers to-day utilize a simplified HR procedure (hereafter referred to simply as HR), including awareness training, competing response training, and social support (Miltenberger, 2001; Woods, 2001). This simplified HR procedure has been shown to be equally ef-fective to the original procedure (Miltenberger, Fuqua, & McKinley, 1985).

During awareness training, the client is required to describe the target behavior and detect instances of the behavior (i.e., either simulated or actual behavior). The client then practices detecting the antecedents to the target behavior (e.g., premoni-tory urges, muscle tension, prehabit motor movements), and the therapist helps the client identify environmental stimuli (e.g., settings) that are likely to elicit the target behavior. Competing response training involves teaching the client to engage in a competing behavior contingent on the target behavior or early warning signs. The competing response must meet three criteria. It must be (1) physically incompatible with the target behavior (i.e., produces isometric tensing of the muscles involved in the habit movement), (2) socially inconspicuous, and (3) held for 1 minute contingent on the target behavior or early warning sign or until the urge to do the tic, pulling, or picking dissipates. Subsequent research has suggested that the competing response need not be topographically dissimilar from the target behavior (Sharenow, Fuqua, & Miltenberger, 1989; Woods, Murray, & Fuqua, 1999), but physical incompatibility is still routinely emphasized. The social support component consists of having friends and/or family members praise the client when he or she notices the client correctly engaging in the competing response. In addition, the person reminds the client to use the competing response when the client fails to detect and correctly implement the competing response contingent on an occurrence of SP, hair pulling, or the tic.

Components have also been added to HR (Piacentini & Chang, 2005). Given that habit behaviors tend to increase during times of anxiety and stress, anxiety manage-ment techniques such as deep breathing, imagery, and progressive muscle relaxation are sometimes used (A. A. Peterson, Campise, & Azrin, 1994). Operant techniques, such as contingency management, have also been added to HR (A. A. Peterson et al., 1994). When a clear functional relationship between the target behavior and environ-mental contingencies can be observed, operant techniques may be implemented to reinforce times when the target behavior is absent (Watson & Sterling, 1998). Support for HR has been found, but the generalizabilty and durability of these techniques is unclear (Piacentini & Chang, 2005). For children receiving HR, treatment may be intensive. Therefore, behavioral reward systems may be used to boost motivation and treatment compliance. Cognitive strategies have been used to help children recognize and label tic urges (Piacentini & Chang, 2005).

In TTM and SP, therapists may implement emotion-regulation techniques or cog-nitive restructuring to target thoughts, emotions, or imagery that may occur before, during, or after occurrences of the target behavior (Deckersbach et al., 2002; Keuthen, Aronowitz, Badenoch, & Wilhelm, 1999). Given recent research suggesting that the relationship between private events and pulling behavior is mediated by experiential avoidance (Begotka et al., 2004), acceptance-based approaches, such as combined habit reversal and acceptance and commitment therapy, have also been used to treat TTM (Woods et al., 2006).

MEDICAL TREATMENT

Several different pharmacological interventions have been used to target habit disorders, although few of these medications have been empirically tested in populations of children. Swedo et al. (1989) compared clomipramine to desipramine in a double-blind crossover study of TTM and found significant improvement with clomipramine. Ninan, Rothbaum, Marsteller, Knight, and Eccard (2000) found statistically significant reductions in pulling for a group receiving cognitive-behavior therapy plus HR, but neither the group receiving clomipramine nor pill placebo showed significant improvement. Trials of selective serotonin reuptake inhibitors (SSRIs), such as fluoxetine, have also been conducted and yielded mixed results. Although two placebo-controlled studies have shown negative results (Christenson, Mackenzie, Mitchell, & Callies, 1991; Streichenwein & Thornby, 1995), other research has shown positive results (Benarroche, 1991; Koran, Ringold, & Hewlett, 1992).

The medications most commonly used to treat TDs are dopamine antagonists (Carpenter, Leckman, Scahill, & McDougle, 1999). Typical neuroleptics that are prescribed for TDs include haloperidol (Haldol) and pimozide (Orap). Haloperidol has been reported to reduce tic symptoms in 70% to 80% of those receiving the drug, although numerous side effects are associated with the drug, and only 20% to 30% of people can tolerate it long term (Erenberg, Cruse, & Rothner, 1987). Side effects include fatigue, weight gain, dysphoria, Parkinsonian symptoms, akathisia, and cognitive dulling (Carpenter et al., 1999). Pimozide has been shown to be as effective as haloperidol for reduction of tics in double-blind studies (E. S. Shapiro et al., 1989), but it is currently only FDA-approved for treatment-refractory TS (Carpenter et al., 1999).

Atypical neuroleptics that can be prescribed for treatment of tic symptoms include risperidone (Risperdal), clozapine (Clozaril), and olanzapine (Zyprexa). Atypical neuroleptics are generally as effective as typical neuroleptics but pose a reduced risk of side effects such as tardive dyskinesia, acute extrapyramidal symptoms, and neuroleptic malignant syndrome (Watson, Howell, & Smith, 2001). Olanzapine has been reported to reduce tic symptoms in children (Semerci, 2000), although it may also be associated with tardive movement disorders (Dunayevich & Strakowski, 1999). Lombroso et al. (1995) found that risperidone improved tic severity for children in an open-label trial, and clozapine has been suggested to be a useful alternative for uncomplicated tic symptoms (Carpenter et al., 1999).

Alpha-adrenergic receptor agonists, such as clonidine and guanfacine, are also commonly prescribed for tic symptoms. Clonidine has been shown to be effective for reducing tic symptoms in some people (Leckman et al., 1991), although it does not benefit all people. Clonidine is associated with benign side effects, and research suggests that it is more effective in reducing motor tics than phonic tics (Leckman et al., 1991). Guanfacine has been shown to be effective in the treatment of ADHD and comorbid TS (Chappell et al., 1995). In comparison to clonidine, guanfacine does not cause as much sedation or hypotension (Balldin, Berggren, Eriksson, Lindstedt, & Sundkler, 1993).

Research on the pharmacological treatment of SP is limited but generally supports the efficacy of SSRIs (Arnold et al., 2001). For example, Arnold and colleagues (1999) examined the use of fluvoxamine in 14 females with SP. Among the 7 participants who completed the study, significant reductions in picking-related behaviors were found. Other medical treatments for SP that have shown some efficacy in case reports include clomipramine, naltrexone, primozide (Arnold et al., 2001), olanzapine (Christensen, 2004), and clonidine (Symons, Thompson, & Realmuto, 2004).

Case Description

Case Introduction

Adam is a 10-year-old boy living with his biological parents and younger sister. He is a fifth-grader at a local public school. He was accompanied to the clinic by his parents, who were present for the entire interview.

Maternal and paternal family history was positive for a variety of mental health concerns. Adam's mother reported that she had been diagnosed with OCD approximately 5 years prior and has seen a psychologist sporadically since that time. Adam's father reported subtle facial movements and rapid eye-blinking sporadically as a child but denied any additional mental health concerns. Additional family history revealed several persons with anxiety and mood disorder diagnoses on Adam's mother's side of the family, including an aunt (mother's biological sister) diagnosed with Generalized Anxiety Disorder, uncle (mother's biological brother) diagnosed with TS, and grandmother (mother's biological mother) diagnosed with OCD. Family history also revealed a diagnosis of ADHD on the father's side of the family (father's biological brother).

Adam's parents reported generally good communication between themselves and their children but noted that Adam frequently behaves inappropriately at school and at home, which sometimes makes communication difficult. Per parent and teacher report, Adam gets along well with children at school. However, his teacher noted that he frequently displays problems paying attention in class and impatience during class activities and often gets out of his seat during class exercises. During the interview, Adam displayed problems maintaining attention during questioning, frequently got out of his seat to play on the chalkboard located in the room, and repeatedly interrupted his parents while they answered questions. When Adam was able to sit still and answer questions, he appeared to answer questions openly and honestly. His parents denied developmental delays or medical concerns and reported that Adam was not currently taking medication.

Presenting Complaints

Adam and his parents were referred to our clinic due to several, apparently involuntary motor and vocal movements Adam was exhibiting. Adam and his parents described three motor tics: eye-blinking (blinking of both eyes repeatedly for 4 to 5 seconds), head-jerking (movement of his head forward, followed by a sudden and violent jerk of his head backward), and abdominal tensing (contraction of abdominal muscles for periods of 8 to 10 seconds). In addition to these motor tics, Adam also exhibited several vocal tics, including coughing, throat clearing, and sniffing.

In addition to Adam's motor and vocal tics, his parents also reported several behavioral problems both at home and school. Specifically, they reported that he is "always on the go" and seldom pays attention either during classes or to his parents at home. For example, Adam's teacher reported that he gets out of his seat at least 1 or 2 times during math and English classes and frequently "stares blankly" during these classes. In relation to this latter point, Adam frequently exhibits trouble recording and turning in his homework assignments at school. As a result, he is performing poorly in several classes (failing mathematics, spelling, and English). However, he is currently receiving above-average grades, B's, in both science and social studies (two classes he reportedly enjoys). Adam's parents reported similar disruptive behavior at home but no additional behavioral problems.

History

Adam's tics first began at approximately 7 years of age (3 years prior to the current assessment) but were subtle and noticeable only to close family members. Adam's mother reported that eye-blinking was the first tic she and her husband noticed, which was soon followed by frequent sniffing and coughing. His parents subsequently brought him to their pediatrician, who suggested that Adam was likely suffering from allergies. However, allergy medication proved unsuccessful. Upon further examination, the pediatrician suggested that Adam may be suffering from a TD and suggested talking with a neurologist. The neurologist referred the family to us for a psychosocial tic evaluation.

Adam's parents reported that he had displayed problems with inattention and hyperactivity/impulsivity since he was 4 or 5 years old. Although he has behaved in this manner for several years, his behavioral problems reportedly became more severe after leaving his old school (a parochial school) and entering a new school (a public school). His trouble recording and completing schoolwork has been present for several years as well, but until recently had never resulted in failing grades. His parents reported that his previous school had been more vigilant about his behavior problems but that his current school did not seem to work with Adam one-on-one as frequently. His parents reported trying several reward programs (e.g., earning stickers for completion of school tasks) to increase homework compliance but with only limited success.

Assessment

To provide a more comprehensive assessment of Adam's tics, a functional assessment was conducted as part of Adam's initial clinical interview. Results of the functional assessment (per parent and child report) revealed that increased tic activity was associated with not getting his way at home, difficult schoolwork, and the anticipation of events such as upcoming baseball practice and going out to dinner at favorite restaurant. To aid in Adam's case conceptualization, information was also requested from Adam's teacher (via written report), who reported that she noticed tics more frequently during math and English classes (in comparison to other periods throughout the day). She reported that she often asked Adam if he is all right (after he has had a bout of coughing or throat

(continued)

clearing) and frequently lets him leave the room (discontinue his assignment for a short time) to "collect himself" prior to completing his work. Adam's parents report engaging in similar behavior at home.

Adam reports that he often has a "funny feeling" in his throat before he begins to clear his throat. He noted that the feelings get stronger and stronger until he feels that he "has to tic." After clearing his throat, he reports, the feelings subside for a short period of time (i.e., a few minutes) but always return. He denied any sensations preceding other tics.

Adam and his parents were also asked to complete several self-report measures. These measures included the Multidimensional Anxiety Scale for Children (MASC; March, Parker, Sullivan, Stallings, & Conners, 1997) and several measures assessing attention problems via parent, child, and teacher reports. Results revealed elevated levels of anxiety (in comparison to other children Adam's age) and substantially elevated levels of inattention and hyperactivity/impulsivity. These elevated levels of disruptive behavior were supported by parent and teacher report, although Adam reported no such problems in either domain. Several additional self-report measures supported these findings.

In addition to completing the functional assessment and self-report measures, Adam and his parents were administered the DISC and the YGTSS. Results from the DISC confirmed a diagnosis of TS and suggested a secondary diagnosis of ADHD, combined type. Although Adam has demonstrated difficulty in math classes for several years and reported elevated levels of anxiety (per MASC report), the current assessment was unable to confirm a math learning disability and was unable to obtain corroborating evidence from parents or teachers regarding an anxiety disorder diagnosis. Information obtained via clinical interview, functional assessment, and self-report measures supported these diagnoses. Results from the YGTSS revealed a score of 45, indicating moderate tic severity.

Case Conceptualization

Adam is a 10-year-old boy referred to our clinic over concerns regarding a possible TD and disruptive behavior both at school and at home. Both Adam and his parents reported several motor (eye-blinking, abdominal tensing, and head jerking) and vocal (sniffing, coughing, and throat clearing) tics. These tics began around 7 years of age but have become both more frequent and severe since Adam started attending his current school almost 1.5 years ago. In addition, Adam's parents and teachers reported substantial problems with inattention and hyperactivity both at home and school. Although Adam's disruptive behavior has been present for several years, his behavior has become increasingly more difficult since beginning a new school last year. Specifically, Adam has been failing to complete school assignments and is failing several of his classes.

Course of Treatment and Assessment Progress

Based on our case conceptualization, several treatment recommendations were offered: possible referral to a psychiatrist for medication in conjunction with cognitive-behavior therapy (CBT; behavior modification, including token economy and time-out; training in problem-solving strategies; interpersonal problem solving, etc.) to treat ADHD symptoms. Progressive muscle relaxation (PMR) was suggested to reduce Adam's anxiety. In addition, HR (Azrin & Nunn, 1973) was recommended to reduce the frequency and severity of Adam's tics. Adam's parents were advised to institute a reward program for completion of homework assignments. Although a similar strategy had been tried previously with limited success, it was thought that a reward program may prove more efficacious with more rigorous implementation of contingency management procedures.

Adam and his parents worked collaboratively with the clinician to establish a reward program to aid in completion of homework at school. Adam earned one checkmark for each day his teacher signed a small 3 × 5 card indicating that he had accurately and completely finished all homework assigned the previous day. Upon collecting five checkmarks, Adam was allowed his choice of rewards (e.g., one extra hour of video games over the weekend, $5, or dinner at one of Adam's five favorite restaurants in town).

Based on discussion with Adam and his family, CBT (including PMR) for Adam's ADHD and anxiety symptoms was implemented prior to addressing the TD. After approximately 3 months of CBT and PMR, Adam's parents reported significant reductions in disruptive behavior both at home and at school, and Adam reported decreases in his overall level of anxiety. As a result, of Adam's progress, he and his family expressed interest in learning HR procedures to reduce the frequency and severity of Adam's tics.

Because Adam's head-jerking tic bothered him the most, HR (awareness training, competing response training, and social support) was implemented first for that tic. He was taught strategies for increasing awareness of his tic and was subsequently provided with a competing response (tensing of his neck muscles) to be used contingent upon his head-jerking tic or its warning signs (tingling feeling in his neck). Adam's parents were subsequently instructed to provide praise when he completed his exercises properly and reminders (e.g., "Don't forget to use your exercises") when Adam forgot to use his exercises. During subsequent sessions, we discussed Adam's progress, reviewed strategies for continuing his exposure exercises, and implemented HR for subsequent tics.

After approximately 5 months of therapy, Adam's disruptive behavior and overall level of anxiety continued to diminish. Although he continued to exhibit mild to moderate levels of inattention and impulsivity at home and school, his parents were enthusiastic about the progress he had made thus far. In addition, Adam's YGTSS scores decreased from 45 (moderate tic severity) to 25 (mild tic severity). Upon termination, Adam's parents reported that his grades had improved and he was now receiving passing marks (C's and B's) in all of his classes.

Complicating Factors

Adam's parents expressed concerns that Adam would not complete assignments during our therapy sessions. As a result, a reward program was instituted for completing homework assigned during therapy sessions. As noted, Adam earned one checkmark for successful completion of therapy assignments, which

(continued)

were later added to his total for successful completion of school assignments. With the additional incentive to actively participate, Adam regularly completed therapy assignments.

Managed Case Considerations

As this intervention was conducted in the context of an university-based outpatient clinic, managed care considerations were not heavily weighed in this case. Nevertheless, it is unlikely that the treatment described here would be problematic for most managed care providers. Habit reversal treatments are time-limited and empirically supported and outcomes can be readily documented. Consequently, the type of treatment described in this chapter conforms well to increasingly stringent demands for accountability in outpatient clinical practice.

Follow-Up

After treatment termination (approximately 5 months after our first session), follow-up contact was made once every 6 weeks (via telephone) for the next 6 months to examine Adam's continued progress. During our final conversation, Adam and his parents reported continued improvement in his behavior and he had earned B's on his most recent report card. Although he was periodically observed to employ his newly acquired CBT skills, his parents reported that his tics occurred so infrequently that Adam rarely had cause to utilize or practice his competing response.

TREATMENT IMPLICATIONS OF THE CASE

A cognitive-behavioral case conceptualization of a young child diagnosed with TS, ADHD, and elevated anxiety was described. This approach was useful in formulating a treatment strategy that was understandable and acceptable to both Adam and his parents. Although some components of CBT (e.g., problem-solving strategies) may have been difficult for Adam to understand initially, he and his parents had few problems utilizing the techniques once learned. In addition, Adam's case highlights the importance of a thorough functional and diagnostic assessment and how using such data can lay the foundation for a successful short-term, empirically supported intervention.

RECOMMENDATIONS TO CLINICIANS

In comparison to other psychiatric disorders such as depression and OCD, TS occurs relatively infrequently. In addition, few clinicians have a thorough understanding of the factors influencing tics and efficacious treatment approaches for the treatment of TS and other TDs. As a result, it is of great importance that clinicians remember the tenants of the scientist-practitioner model. That is, clinicians must work to integrate findings from empirical research into their clinical practice. Perhaps most important, clinicians naive to the treatment of TDs or unfamiliar with the growing research literature concerning TDs are best served by referring their clients to neurologists, psychiatrists, and psychologists (or other mental health professionals) in the community with more experience in this specialized area.

RECOMMENDATIONS TO STUDENTS

One of the most important aspects of the therapeutic process is the development of a solid case conceptualization. The development of a comprehensive case conceptualization involves the integration of assessment information and findings from previous research within the framework of the individual child. Failure to integrate these two separate (yet related) areas can be detrimental to not only the conceptualization of the child's case, but also to the efficacy of subsequent treatment strategies and techniques.

SUMMARY

This chapter has provided a comprehensive review of the assessment, conceptualization, and treatment of children and adolescents with habit disorders. Habit disorders include several topographically distinct behaviors with unclear etiological and functional similarities, including tic disorders, trichotillomania, nail biting, skin picking, and bruxism. Recently, there has been an influx of empirical research examining the assessment, phenomenology, and treatment of these behavior problems.

Although a number of strategies exist for the diagnosis and assessment of habit disorders in adults, substantially fewer options are available for children. Assessment methods include the usual staples of behavioral assessment: interviews; broad- and narrow-band, multi-informant rating scales; self-reports (where appropriate); and especially self-monitoring. In addition to diagnostic and symptom severity measures, data should be collected about family health history, treatment history, and the social and/or physical consequences (e.g., teasing from peers, scars resulting from picking or pulling) associated with pulling, picking, or tics. We also recommend a thorough functional assessment of each habit. The various antecedents and consequences of the habit should be carefully investigated, with the goal of isolating the specific behavioral functions maintaining the behavior. Functional assessment is considered an essential feature of contemporary interventions for children and adolescents with habit disorders.

The behavioral conceptualization process requires the synthesis of information obtained through a variety of assessment strategies, and clinicians should draw broadly on information that can contribute to a functional assessment. Indeed, in addition to inquiring about antecedents and consequences, a thorough functional behavioral assessment may require information about child development, modeling, parenting practices, life events, peer influences, and cultural influences.

Several different pharmacological interventions have been proposed for habit disorders, although few have been empirically tested with children or adolescents. Among the existing behavioral interventions, habit reversal treatment has garnered the strongest empirical support. Habit reversal has demonstrated efficacy for both adults and children for the treatment of a variety of habit disorders, including tics (Wilhelm et al., 2003), hair pulling (Azrin et al., 1980), and skin picking (Teng et al., 2006). Importantly, HR has been designated a "probably efficacious" treatment for habit disorders (Chambless & Ollendick, 2001). As clinicians work to integrate findings from empirical research into their clinical practice, it is important that those naive to the treatment of habit disorders work closely with neurologists, psychiatrists, and psychologists (or other mental health professionals) with more experience in this specialized area.

REFERENCES

Abelson, J. F., Kwan, K. Y., O'Roak, B. J., Baek, D. Y., Stillman, A. A., Morgan, T. M., et al. (2005). Sequence variants in SLITRK1 are associated with Tourette's syndrome. *Science, 310,* 317–320.

Allen, A. J., Kurlan, R. M., Gilbert, D. L., Coffey, B. J., Linder, S. L., Lewis, D. W., et al. (2005). Atomoxetine treatment in children and adolescents with ADHD and comorbid tic disorders. *Neurology, 65,* 1941–1949.

American Psychiatric Association. (2000). *Diagnostic and statistical manual of mental disorders* (4th ed., text rev.). Washington, DC: Author.

Arnold, L. M., Auchenbach, M. B., & McElroy, S. L. (2001). Psychogenic excoriation: Clinical feature, proposed diagnostic criteria, epidemiology and approaches to treatment. *CNS Drugs, 15,* 351–159.

Arnold, L. M., McElroy, S. L., Mutasim, D. F., Dwight, M. M., Lamerson, C. L., & Morris, E. M. (1998). Characteristics of 34 adults with psychogenic excoriation. *Journal of Clinical Psychiatry, 59,* 509–514.

Arnold, L. M., Mutasim, D. F., Dwight, M. M., Lamerson, C. L., Morris, E. M., & McElroy, S. L. (1999). An open clinical trial of fluvoxamine treatment of psychogenic excoriation. *Journal of Clinical Psychopharmacology, 19,* 15–18.

Azrin, N. H., & Nunn, R. G. (1973). Habit reversal: A method of eliminating nervous habits and tics. *Behavior Research and Therapy, 11,* 619–628.

Azrin, N. H., Nunn, R. G., & Franz, S. E. (1980). Treatment of hair pulling (trichotillomania): A comparative study of habit reversal and negative practice training. *Journal of Behavior Therapy and Experimental Psychiatry, 11,* 13–20.

Balldin, J., Berggren, U., Eriksson, E., Lindstedt, G., & Sundkler, A. (1993). Guanfacine as an alpha-2-agonist inducer of growth hormone secretion: A comparison with clonidine. *Psychoneuroendocrinology, 18,* 45–55.

Barrett, B. H. (1962). Reduction in rate of multiple tics by free operant conditioning methods. *Journal of Nervous and Mental Diseases, 7,* 187–195.

Bawden, H. N., Stokes, A., Camfield, C. S., Camfield, P. R., & Salisbury, S. (1998). Peer relationship problems in children with Tourette's disorder and diabetes mellitus. *Journal of Child Psychology and Psychiatry, 39*(5), 663–668.

Begotka, A. M., Woods, D. W., & Wetterneck, C. T. (2004). The relationship between experiential avoidance and the severity of trichotillomania in a nonreferred sample. *Journal of Behavior Therapy and Experimental Psychiatry, 35,* 17–24.

Benarroche, C. L. (1991, May). *Trichotillomania symptoms and fluoxetine response.* Paper presented at the 143rd annual meeting of the American Psychiatric Association, New Orleans, LA.

Bloch, M. H., Peterson, B. S., Scahill, L., Otka, J., Katsovich, L., Zhang, H., et al. (2006). Adulthood outcome of tic and obsessive-compulsive severity in children with Tourette syndrome. *Archives of Pediatrics and Adolescent Medicine, 160,* 65–69.

Bloch, M. R., Elliott, M., Thompson, H., & Koran, L. M. (2001). Fluoxetine in pathological skin picking. *Psychosomatics, 42,* 314–318.

Bohne, A., Keuthen, N., & Wilhelm, S. (2005). Pathologic hair pulling, skin picking, and nail biting. *Annals of Clinical Psychology, 17,* 227–232.

Bohne, A., Wilhelm, S., Keuthen, N. J., Baer, L., & Jenike, M. A. (2002). Skin picking in German students: Prevalence, phenomenology, and associated characteristics. *Behavior Modification, 26,* 320–339.

Bornstein, R. A., Stefl, M. E., & Hammond, L. (1990). A survey of Tourette syndrome patients and their families: The 1987 Ohio Tourette Survey. *Journal of Neuropsychiatry & Clinical Neurosciences, 2,* 275–281.

Boudjouk, P. J., Woods, D. W., Miltenberger, R. G., & Long, E. S. (2000). Negative peer evaluation in adolescents: Effects of tic disorders and trichotillomania. *Child and Family Behavior Therapy, 22,* 17–28.

Calikusu, C., Yucel, B., Poiat, A., & Baykal, C. (2003). The relation of psychogenic excoriation with psychiatric disorders: A comparative study. *Comprehensive Psychiatry, 44,* 256–261.

Carpenter, L. L., Leckman, J. F., Scahill, L., & McDougle, C. J. (1999). Pharmacological and other somatic approaches to treatment. In J. F. Leckman & D. J. Cohen (Eds.), *Tourette's syndrome tics, obsessions, compulsions: Developmental psychopathology and clinical care* (pp. 370–398). New York: Wiley.

Carter, A. S., O'Donnell, D. A., Schultz, R. T., Scahill, L., Leckman, J. F., & Pauls, D. L. (2000). Social and emotional adjustment in children affected with Gilles de la Tourette's syndrome: Associations with ADHD and family functioning. *Journal of Child Psychology and Psychiatry, 33,* 377–385.

Carter, A. S., Pauls, D. L., Leckman, J. F., & Cohen, D. J. (1994). A prospective longitudinal study of Gilles de la Tourette syndrome. *Journal of the American Academy of Child and Adolescent Psychiatry, 33*(3), 377–385.

Chambless, D. L., & Ollendick, T. H. (2001). Empirically supported psychological interventions: Controversies and evidence. *Annual Review of Psychology, 52,* 685–716.

Chang, C. H., Lee, M. B., Chiang, Y. C., & Lu, Y. C. (1991). Trichotillomania: A clinical study of 36 patients. *Journal of the Formosan Medical Association, 90,* 176–180.

Chappell, P. B., Riddle, M. A., Scahill, L., Lynch, K. A., Schultz, R., Arnsten, A., et al. (1995). Guanfacine treatment of comorbid attention-deficit hyperactivity disorder in Tourette's syndrome: Preliminary clinical experience. *Journal of the American Academy of Child and Adolescent Psychiatry, 34,* 1140–1146.

Christensen, R. C. (2004). Olanzapine augmentation of fluoxetine in the treatment of pathological skin picking. *Canadian Journal of Psychiatry, 49,* 788–789.

Christenson, G. A. (1995). Trichotillomania-from prevalence to comorbidity. *Psychiatric Times, 12,* 44–48.

Christenson, G. A., & Mackenzie, T. B. (1994). Trichotillomania. In M. Hersen & R. T. Ammerman (Eds.), *Handbook of prescriptive treatment for adults* (pp. 217–235). New York: Plenum Press.

Christenson, G. A., Mackenzie, T. B., & Mitchell, J. E. (1991). Characteristics of 60 adult chronic hair pullers. *American Journal of Psychiatry, 148,* 365–370.

Christenson, G. A., Mackenzie, T. B., Mitchell, J. E., & Callies, A. L. (1991). A placebo-controlled, double-blind crossover study of fluoxetine in trichotillomania. *American Journal of Psychiatry, 148,* 1566–1571.

Christenson, G. A., & Mansueto, C. S. (1999). Trichotillomania: Descriptive characteristics and phenomenology. In D. J. Stein, G. A. Christenson, & E. Hollander (Eds.), *Trichotillomania* (pp. 1–42). Washington, DC: American Psychiatric Press

Christenson, G. A., Pyle, R. A., & Mitchell, J. E. (1991). Estimated lifetime prevalence of trichotillomania in college students. *Journal of Clinical Psychiatry, 52,* 415–417.

Coffey, B. A., Biederman, J., Geller, D. A., Spencer, T. J., Kim, G. S., Bellordre, C. A., et al. (2000). Distinguishing illness severity from tic severity in children and adolescents with Tourette's disorder. *Journal of the American Academy of Child and Adolescent Psychiatry, 39,* 556–561.

Coffey, B. A., Biederman, J., Smoller, J. W., Geller, D. A., Sarin, P., Schwartz, S., et al. (2000). Anxiety disorders and tic severity in juveniles with Tourette's disorder. *Journal of the American Academy of Child and Adolescent Psychiatry, 39,* 562–568.

Cohen, D. J., Friedhoff, A. J., Leckman, J. F., & Chase, T. N. (1992). Tourette syndrome: Extending basic research to clinical care. In T. N. Chase, A. J. Friedhoff, & D. J. Cohen (Eds.), *Advances in Neurology* (pp. 341–362). New York: Raven Press.

Cohen, D. J., Riddle, M. A., & Leckman, J. F. (1992). Pharmacotherapy of Tourette's syndrome and associated disorders. *Psychiatric Clinics of North America, 15,* 109–129.

Cohen, L. J., Stein, D. J., Simeon, D., Spadaccini, E., Rosen, J., Aronowitz, B., et al. (1995). Clinical profile, comorbidity, and treatment history in 123 hair pullers: A survey study. *Journal of Clinical Psychiatry, 56,* 319–326.

Comings, D. E., & Comings, B. G. (1985). Tourette syndrome: Clinical and psychological aspects of 250 cases. *American Journal of Human Genetics, 37,* 435–450.

Corte, H. E., Wolf, M. M., & Locke, B. J. (1971). A comparison of procedures for eliminating self-injurious behavior of retarded adolescents. *Journal of Applied Behavior Analysis, 4,* 201–213.

Crocetto, J. S., Diefenbach, G. J., Tolin, D. F., & Maltby, N. (2003, November). *Self-report and clinician-rated hairpulling scales: A psychometric evaluation.* Poster presented at the 37th annual meeting of the Association of the Advancement of Behavior Therapy, Boston.

Deaver, C. M., Miltenberger, R. G., & Stricker, J. M. (2001). Functional analysis and treatment of hair twirling in a young child. *Journal of Applied Behavior Analysis, 34,* 535–538.

Deckersbach, T., Wilhelm, S., Keuthen, N. J., Baer, L., & Jenkie, M. A. (2002). Cognitive-behavior therapy for self-injurious skin picking: A case series. *Behavior Modification, 26,* 361–377.

Diefenbach, G. J., Mouton-Odum, S., & Stanley, M. A. (2002). Affective correlates of trichotillomania. *Behavior Research and Therapy, 40,* 1305–1315.

Diefenbach, G. J., Tolin, D. F., Crocetto, J., Maltby, N., & Hannan, S. (2005). Assessment of trichotillomania: A psychometric evaluation of hair-pulling scale. *Journal of Psychopathology and Behavioral Assessment, 27,* 169–178.

Diefenbach, G. J., Tolin, D. F., Hannan, S., Crocetto, J., & Worhunsky, P. (2005). Trichotillomania: Impact on psychosocial functioning and quality of life. *Behavior Research and Therapy, 43,* 869–884.

Dunayevich, E., & Strakowski, S. M. (1999). Olanzapine-induced tardive dystonia. *American Journal of Psychiatry, 156,* 662.

du Toit, P. L., van Kradenburg, J., Niehaus, D. J. H., & Stein, D. J. (2001). Characteristics and phenomenology of hair-pulling: An exploration of subtypes. *Comprehensive Psychiatry, 42,* 247–256.

Eapen, V., Pauls, D. L., & Robertson, M. M. (1993). Evidence for autosomal dominant transmission in Tourette's syndrome—United Kingdom Cohort Study. *British Journal of Psychiatry, 162,* 593–596.

Elliott, A. J., & Fuqua, R. W. (2000). Trichotillomania: Conceptualization, measurement, and treatment. *Behavior Therapy, 31,* 529–545.

Erenberg, G., Cruse, R. P., & Rothner, A. D. (1987). The natural history of Tourette syndrome: A follow-up study. *Annals of Neurology, 22,* 383–385.

Findley, D. B. (2001). Characteristics of tic disorders. In D. W. Woods & R. G. Miltenberger (Eds.), *Tic disorders, trichotillomania, and other repetitive behavior disorders: Behavioral approaches to analysis and treatment* (pp. 53–72). Boston: Kluwer Academic.

Flessner, C. A., Miltenberger, R. G., Egemo, K., Kelso, P., Jostad, C., Johnson, B., et al. (2005). An evaluation of the social support component of simplified habit reversal for the treatment of nail biting. *Behavior Therapy, 36,* 35–42.

Flessner, C. A., & Woods, D. W. (in press). Phenomenological characteristics, social problems, and economic impact associated with skin picking (SP) and problem skin picking (PSP). *Behavior Modification.*

Franklin, M. E., Tolin, D. F., & Diefenbach, D. (2006). Trichotillomania. In E. Hollander & D. J. Stein (Eds.), *Clinical manual of impulse control disorders* (pp. 149–173). Washington, DC: American Psychiatric Publishing.

Friman, P. C., Finney, J. W., & Christophersen, E. R. (1984). Behavioral treatment of trichotillomania: An evaluative review. *Behavior Therapy, 15,* 249–265.

Gadow, K. D., Nolan, E. E., Sprafkin, J., & Schwartz, J. (2002). Tics and comorbidity in children and adolescents. *Developmental Medicine and Child Neurology, 44,* 330–338.

Glaros, A. G., & Epkins, C. C. (2003). Habit disorders: Bruxism, trichotillomania, and tics. In M. C. Roberts (Ed.), *Handbook of pediatric psychology* (3rd ed., pp. 561–577). New York: Guilford Press.

Graber, J., & Arndt, W. B. (1993). Trichotillomania. *Comprehensive Psychiatry, 34,* 340–346.

Greene, R. W., Biederman, J., Faraone, S. V., Sienna, M., & Garcia-Jetton, J. (1997). Adolescent outcome of boys with attention-deficit/hyperactivity disorder and social disability: Results from a 4 year longitudinal follow-up study. *Journal of Consulting and Clinical Psychology, 65,* 758–767.

Hanna, G. L. (1997). Trichotillomania and related disorders in children and adolescents. *Child Psychiatry and Human Development, 27,* 255–268.

Hornsey, H., Banerjee, S., Zeitlin, H., & Robertson, M. (2001). The prevalence of Tourette syndrome in 13- and 14-year-olds in mainstream schools. *Journal of Child Psychotherapy and Psychiatry, 42,* 1035–1039.

Hubka, G. B., Fulton, W. A., Shady, G. A., Champion, L. M., & Wand, R. (1988). Tourette syndrome: Impact on Canadian family functioning. *Neuroscience and Biobehavioral Reviews, 12,* 259–261.

Kadesjo, B., & Gillberg, C. (2000). Tourette's disorder: Epidemiology and comorbidity in primary school children. *Journal of the American Academy of Child and Adolescent Psychiatry, 39,* 548–555.

Keuthen, N. J., Aronowitz, B., Badenoch, J., & Wilhelm, S. (1999). Behavioral treatment for trichotillomania. In D. J. Stein, G. A. Christenson, & E. Hollander (Eds.), *Trichotillomania* (pp. 147–166). Washington, DC: American Psychiatric Association.

Keuthen, N. J., Deckersbach, T., Wilhelm, S., Hale, E., Fraim, C., Baer, L., et al. (2000). Repetitive skin-picking in a student population and comparison with a sample of self-injurious skinpickers. *Psychosomatics, 41,* 210–215.

Keuthen, N. J., O'Sullivan, R. L., Ricciardi, J. N., Shera, D., Savage, C. R., Borgmann, A. S., et al. (1995). Massachusetts General Hospital (MGH) Hairpulling Scale: Pt. 1. Development and factor analysis. *Psychotherapy and Psychosomatics, 64,* 141–145.

Keuthen, N. J., Wilhelm, S., Deckersbach, T., Engelhard, I. M., Forker, A. E., Baer, L., et al. (2001). Skin Picking Scale: Scale construction and psychometric analysis. *Journal of Psychosomatic Research, 50,* 337–341.

Khalifa, N., & Knorring, A. (2003). Prevalence of tic disorders and Tourette syndrome in a Swedish population. *Developmental Medicine and Child Neurology, 45,* 315–319.

King, R. A., Scahill, L., Vitulano, L. A., Schwab-Stone, M., Tercyak, K. P., & Riddle, M. A. (1995). Childhood trichotillomania: Clinical phenomenology, comorbidity, and family genetics. *Journal of the American Academy of Child and Adolescent Psychiatry, 34,* 1451–1459.

Koblenzer, C. S. (1987). *Psychocutaneous disease.* Orlando, FL: Grune & Stratton.

Koran, L. M., Ringold, A., & Hewlett, W. (1992). Fluoxetine for trichotillomania: An open clinical trial. *Psychopharmacological Bulletin, 28,* 145–149.

Leckman, J. F., Bloch, M. H., King, R. A., & Scahill, L. (2006). Phenomenology of tics and natural history of tic disorders. In J. T. Walkup, J. W. Mink, & P. J. Hollenbeck (Eds.), *Advances in neurology* (Vol. 99, pp. 1–16). Philadelphia: Lippincott Williams & Williams.

Leckman, J. F., & Cohen, D. J. (1999a). Beyond the diagnosis: Darwinian perspectives on pathways to successful adaptation. In J. F. Leckman & D. J. Cohen (Eds.), *Tourette's syndrome: Tics, obsessions, compulsions* (pp. 140–154). New York: Wiley.

Leckman, J. F., & Cohen, D. J. (1999b). Evolving models of pathogenesis. In J. F. Leckman & D. J. Cohen (Eds.), *Tourette's syndrome: Tics, obsessions, compulsions* (pp. 155–176). New York: Wiley.

Leckman, J. F., Hardin, M. T., Riddle, M. A., Stevenson, J., Ort, S. I., & Cohen, D. J. (1991). Clonidine treatment of Gilles de la Tourette's syndrome. *Archives of General Psychiatry, 48,* 324–328.

Leckman, J. F., King, R. A., & Cohen, D. J. (1999). Tics and tic disorders. In J. F. Leckman & D. J. Cohen (Eds.), *Tourette's syndrome: Tics, obsessions, compulsions* (pp. 23–42). New York: Wiley.

Leckman, J. F., Peterson, B. S., Pauls, D. L., & Cohen, D. J. (1997). Tic disorders. *Psychiatric Clinics of North America, 20,* 839–861.

Leckman, J. F., Riddle, M. A., Hardin, M. T., Ort, S. I., Swartz, K. L., Stevenson, J., et al. (1989). Yale Global Tic Severity Scale: Initial testing of a clinician-rated scale of tic severity. *Journal of the American Academy of Child and Adolescent Psychiatry, 28,* 566–573.

Leckman, J. F., Walker, D. E., & Cohen, D. J. (1993). Premonitory urges in Tourette's syndrome. *American Journal of Psychiatry, 151,* 98–102.

Ledbetter, M. (2005). Atomoxetine use associated with onset of a motor tic. *Journal of Child and Adolescent Psychopharmacology, 15,* 331–333.

Lochner, C., Simeon, D., Niehaus, D. J. H., & Stein, D. J. (2002). Trichotillomania and skin-picking: A phenomenological comparison. *Depression and Anxiety, 15,* 83–86.

Lombroso, P. J., Scahill, L. D., King, R. A., Lynch, K. A., Chappel, P. B., Peterson, B. S., et al. (1995). Risperidone treatment of children and adolescents with chronic tic disorders: A preliminary report. *Journal of the American Academy of Child and Adolescent Psychiatry, 34,* 1147–1152.

Mansueto, C. S., Golomb, R. G., Thomas, A. M., & Stemberger, R. M. T., (1999). A comprehensive model for the behavioral treatment of trichotillomania. *Cognitive and Behavioral Practice, 6,* 23–43.

Mansueto, C. S., Stemberger, R. M. T., Thomas, A. M. T., & Golomb, R. G. (1997). Trichotillomania: A comprehensive behavioral model. *Clinical Psychology Review, 17,* 567–577.

March, J. S., Parker, J., Sullivan, K., Stallings, P., & Conners, C. K. (1997). Multidimensional Anxiety Scale for Children (MASC): Factor structure, reliability, and validity. *Journal of the American Academy of Child and Adolescent Psychiatry, 36,* 554–565.

Martin, A., Scahill, L., Vitulano, L., & King, R. A. (1998). Stimulant use and trichotillomania. *Journal of the American Academy of Child and Adolescent Psychiatry, 37,* 249–250.

Mason, A., Banerjee, S., Eapen, V., Zeitlin, H., & Robertson, M. M. (1998). The prevalence of Tourette syndrome in a mainstream school population. *Developmental Medicine and Child Neurology, 40,* 292–296.

Mathews, C. A., Amighetti, L. D. H., Lowe, T. L., van de Wetering, B. J. M., Freimer, N. B., & Reus, V. I. (2001). Cultural influences on diagnosis and perception of Tourette syndrome in Costa Rica. *Journal of the American Academy of Child and Adolescent Psychiatry, 40,* 456–463.

McCarley, N. G., Spirrison, C. L., & Ceminsky, J. L. (2002). Hair pulling behavior reported by African American and non-African American college students. *Journal of Psychopathology and Behavioral Assessment, 24,* 139–144.

Mehregan, A. M. (1970). Trichotillomania. *Archives of Dermatology, 102,* 129–133.

Miltenberger, R. G. (2001). Habit reversal treatment manual for trichotillomania. In D. W. Woods & R. G. Miltenberger (Eds.), *Tic disorders, trichotillomania, and other repetitive behavior disorders: Behavior approaches to analysis and treatment* (pp. 171–196). Boston: Kluwer Academic.

Miltenberger, R. G., Fuqua, R. W., & McKinley, T. (1985). Habit reversal with muscle tics: Replication and component analysis. *Behavior Therapy, 16,* 39–50.

Miltenberger, R. G., Long, E. S., Rapp, J. T., Lumley, V., & Elliott, A. J. (1998). Evaluating the function of hair pulling: A preliminary investigation. *Behavior Therapy, 29,* 211–219.

Miltenberger, R. G., Rapp, J. T., & Long, E. S. (2001). Characteristics of trichotillomania. In D. W. Woods & R. G. Miltenberger (Eds.), *Tic disorders, trichotillomania, and other repetitive behavior disorders: Behavioral approaches to analysis and treatment* (pp. 133–150). Boston: Kluwer Academic.

Neal-Barnett, A. M., Ward-Brown, B. J., Mitchell, M., & Krownapple, M. (2000). Hair-pulling in African-Americans—Only your hairdresser knows for sure: An exploratory study. *Cultural Diversity and Ethnic Minority Psychology, 6,* 352–362.

Neziroglu, F., & Mancebo, M. (2001). Skin picking as a form of self-injurious behavior. *Psychiatric Annals, 31,* 549–555.

Ninan, P. T., Rothbaum, B. O., Marsteller, F. A., Knight, B. T., & Eccard, M. B. (2000). A placebo-controlled trial of cognitive-behavior therapy and clomipramine in trichotillomania. *Journal of Clinical Psychology, 61,* 47–50.

O'Sullivan, R. L., Keuthen, N. J., Hayday, C. F., Ricciardi, J. N., Buttolph, M. L., Jenike, M. A., et al. (1995). Massachusetts General Hospital Hairpulling Scale: Pt. 2. Reliability and validity. *Psychotherapy Psychosomatics, 64,* 146–148.

O'Sullivan, R. L., Keuthen, N. J., Jenike, M. A., & Gumley, G. (1996). Trichotillomania and carpal tunnel syndrome. *Journal of Clinical Psychiatry, 57,* 174.

Palumbo, D., Spencer, T., Lynch, J., Co-Chien, H., & Faraone, S. V. (2004). Emergence of tics in children with ADHD: Impact of once-daily OROS®methylphenidate therapy. *Journal of Child and Adolescent Psychopharmacology, 14,* 185–194.

Pauls, D. L. (2002). An update on the genetics of Gilles de la Tourette syndrome. *Journal of Psychosomatic Research, 55,* 7–12.

Pauls, D. L., & Leckman, J. F. (1986). The inheritance of Gilles de la Tourette's syndrome and associated behaviors: Evidence for autosomal dominant transmission. *New England Journal of Medicine, 315,* 993–997.

Peterson, A. A., Campise, R. L., & Azrin, N. H. (1994). Behavioral and pharmacological treatments for tic and habit disorders: A review. *Journal of Developmental and Behavioral Pediatrics, 15,* 430–441.

Peterson, B. S., & Leckman, J. F. (1998). The temporal dynamic of Gilles de la Tourette syndrome. *Biological Psychiatry, 44,* 1337–1348.

Peterson, B. S., Leckman, J. F., Lombroso, P., Zhang, H., Lynch, K., Carter, A. S., et al. (1999). Environmental risk and protective factors. In J. F. Leckman & D. J. Cohen (Eds.), *Tourette's syndrome: Tics, obsessions, compulsions* (pp. 23–42). New York: Wiley.

Peterson, B. S., Pine, D. S., Cohen, P., & Brook, J. S. (2001). Prospective, longitudinal study of tic, obsessive-compulsive, and attention-deficit/hyperactivity disorders in an epidemiological sample. *Journal of the American Academy of Child and Adolescent Psychiatry, 40,* 685–695.

Piacentini, J., & Chang, S. (2005). Habit reversal training for tic disorders in children and adolescents. *Behavior Modification, 29,* 803–822.

Rapp, J. S., Miltenberger, R. G., Long, E. S., Elliott, A. J., & Lumley, V. A. (1998). Simplified habit reversal treatment for chronic hair pulling in three pre adolescents: A clinical replication with direct observation. *Journal of Applied Behavior Analysis, 31,* 229–302.

Reeve, E. A., Bernstein, G. A., & Christenson, G. A. (1992). Clinical characteristics and psychiatric comorbidity in children with trichotillomania. *Journal of the American Academy of Child and Adolescent Psychiatry, 31,* 132–138.

Rothbaum, B. O., & Ninan, P. T. (1994). The assessment of trichotillomania. *Behavior Therapy and Research, 32,* 651–662.

Schlosser, S., Black, D. W., Blum, N., & Goldstein, R. B. (1994). The demography, phenomenology, and family history of 22 persons with compulsive hair pulling. *Annals of Clinical Psychiatry, 6*, 147–152.

Semerci, Z. B. (2000). Olanzapine in Tourette's disorder. *Journal of the American Academy of Child and Adolescent Psychiatry, 39*, 140.

Shaffer, D., Fisher, P., Lucas, C. P., Dulcan, M. K., & Schwab-Stone, M. E. (2000). NIMH Diagnostic Interview Schedule for Children Version IV (NIMH DISC IV): Description, differences from previous versions, and reliability of some common diagnoses. *Journal of the American Academy of Child and Adolescent Psychiatry, 39*, 28–38.

Shapiro, A. K., Shapiro, E., & Wayne, H. (1972). Birth, developmental, and family histories and demographic information in Tourette's syndrome. *Journal of Nervous and Mental Diseases, 155*, 335–344.

Shapiro, E. S., Shapiro, A. K., Fulop, G., Hubbard, M., Mandeli, J., Nordlie, J., et al. (1989). Controlled study of haloperidol, pimozide, and placebo for the treatment of GTS. *Archives of General Psychiatry, 46*, 722–730.

Sharenow, E. L., Fuqua, R. W., & Miltenberger, R. G. (1989). The treatment of muscle tics with dissimilar competing response practice. *Journal of Applied Behavior Analysis, 22*, 35–42.

Silva, R. R., Munoz, D. M., Barickman, J., & Friedhoff, A. J. (1995). Environmental factors and related fluctuation of symptoms in children and adolescents with Tourette's disorder. *Journal of Child Psychology and Psychiatry, 36*, 305–312.

Simeon, D., Stein, D. J., Gross, S., Islam, N., Schmeidler, J., & Hollander, E. (1997). A double-blind trial of fluoxetine in pathologic skin picking. *Journal of Clinical Psychiatry, 58*, 341–347.

Snider, L. A., & Swedo, S. E. (2004). PANDAS: Current status and directions for research. *Molecular Psychiatry, 9*, 900–907.

Spencer, T., Biederman, J., Harding, M., Wilens, T., & Faraone, S. (1995). The relationship between tic disorders and Tourette's syndrome revisited. *Journal of the American Academy of Child and Adolescent Psychiatry, 34*, 1133–1139.

Staley, D., Wand, R., & Shady, G. (1997). Tourette disorder: A cross-cultural review. *Comprehensive Psychiatry, 38*, 6–16.

Stanley, M. A., Breckenridge, J. K., Snyder, A. G., & Novry, D. M. (1999). Clinician-rated measures of hair pulling: A preliminary psychometric evaluation. *Journal of Psychopathology and Behavioral Assessment, 21*, 157–170.

Stokes, A., Bawden, H. N., Camfield, P. R., Backman, J. E., & Dooley, J. M. (1991). Peer problems in Tourette's disorder. *Pediatrics, 87*(6), 936–942.

Storch, E. A., Murphy, T. K., Geffken, G. R., Sajid, M., Allen, P., Robertsi, J. W., et al. (2005). Reliability and validity of the Yale Global Tic Severity Scale. *Psychological Assessment, 17*, 486–491.

Streichenwein, S. M., & Thornby, J. I. (1995). A long-term, double-blind, placebo-controlled crossover trial of the efficacy of fluoxetine for trichotillomania. *American Journal of Psychiatry, 152*, 1192–1196.

Swedo, S. E., Leonard, H. L., Rapoport, J. L., Lenane, M. C., Goldberger, E. L., & Cheslow, D. L. (1989). A double-blind comparison of clomipramine and desipramine in the treatment of trichotillomania (hair pulling). *New England Journal of Medicine, 321*, 497–501.

Symons, F. J., Thompson, A., & Realmuto, G. (2004). Clonidine for self-injurious behavior. *Journal of the American Academy of Child and Adolescent Psychiatry, 43*, 1324–1325.

Teng, E. J., Woods, D. W., & Twohig, M. P. (2006). Habit reversal as a treatment for chronic skin picking: A pilot investigation. *Behavior Modification, 30*, 411–422.

Teng, E. J., Woods, D. W., Twohig, M. P., & Marcks, B. A. (2002). Body-focused repetitive behavior problems: Prevalence in a non-referred population and differences in perceived somatic activity. *Behavior Modification, 26,* 340–360.

Towbin, K. E., Peterson, B. S., Cohen, D. J., & Leckman, J. F. (1999). In J. F. Leckman & D. J. Cohen (Eds.), *Tourette's syndrome: Tics, obsessions, compulsions* (pp. 118–139). New York: Wiley.

Varley, C. K., Vincent, J., Varley, P., & Calderon, R. (2001). Emergence of tics in children with attention deficit hyperactivity disorder treated with stimulant medications. *Comprehensive Psychiatry, 42,* 228–233.

Walkup, J. T., LaBuda, M. C., Singer, H. S., Brown, J., Riddle, M. A., & Hruko, O. (1996). Family study and segregation analysis of Tourette syndrome: Evidence for a mixed model of inheritance. *American Journal of Human Genetics, 59,* 684–683.

Watson, T. S., & Allen, K. D. (1993). Elimination of thumb-sucking as a treatment for severe trichotillomania. *Journal of the American Academy of Child and Adolescent Psychiatry, 32,* 830–835.

Watson, T. S., Dittmer, K. I., & Ray, K. P. (2000). Treating trichotillomania in a toddler: Variations on effective treatments. *Child and Family Behavior Therapy, 22,* 29–40.

Watson, T. S., Howell, L. A., & Smith, S. L. (2001). Behavioral interventions for tic disorders. In D. W. Woods & R. G. Miltenberger (Eds.), *Tic disorders, trichotillomania, and other repetitive behavior disorders: Behavioral approaches to analysis and treatment* (pp. 73–95). Boston: Kluwer Academic.

Watson, T. S., & Sterling, H. E. (1998). Brief functional analysis and treatment of a vocal tic. *Journal of Applied Behavior Analysis, 31,* 471–474.

Wetterneck, C. T., Woods, D. W., Norberg, M. M., & Begotka, A. M. (2006). The social and economic impact of trichotillomania: Results from two nonreferred samples. *Behavioral Interventions, 21,* 97–109.

Wilhelm, S., Deckersbach, T., Coffey, B. J., Bohne, A., Peterson, A. L., & Baer, L. (2003). Habit reversal versus supportive psychotherapy for Tourette's disorder: A randomized controlled trial. *American Journal of Psychiatry, 160,* 1175–1177.

Wilhelm, S., Keuthen, N. J., Deckersbach, T., Engelhard, I. M., Forker, A. E., Baer, L. et al. (1999). Self-injurious skin picking: Clinical characteristics and comorbidity. *Journal of Clinical Psychiatry, 60,* 454–459.

Winchel, R. M. (1992). Trichotillomania: Presentation and treatment. *Psychiatric Annals, 22,* 84–89.

Woods, D. W. (2001). Habit reversal treatment manual for tic disorders. In D. W. Woods & R. G. Miltenberger (Eds.), *Tic disorders, trichotillomania, and other repetitive behavior disorders: Behavior approaches to analysis and treatment* (pp. 73–96). Boston: Kluwer Academic.

Woods, D. W., Friman, P. C., & Teng, E. J. (2001). Physical and social impairments in persons with repetitive behavior disorders. In D. W. Woods & R. G. Miltenberger (Eds.), *Tic disorders, trichotillomania, and other repetitive behavior disorders: Behavioral approaches to analysis and treatment* (pp. 33–51). Boston: Kluwer Academic.

Woods, D. W., Fuqua, R. W., & Outman, R. C. (1999). Evaluating the social acceptability of persons with habit disorders: The effects of topography, frequency, and gender manipulation. *Journal of Psychopathology and Behavioral Assessment, 21,* 1–18.

Woods, D. W., Miltenberger, R. G., & Lumley, V. A. (1996). Sequential application of major habit-reversal components to treat motor tics in children. *Journal of Applied Behavior Analysis, 29,* 483–493.

Woods, D. W., Murray, L. K., & Fuqua, R. W. (1999). Comparing the effectiveness of similar and dissimilar competing responses in evaluating the habit reversal treatment for oral-digital habits in children. *Journal of Behavior Therapy and Experimental Psychiatry, 30,* 289–300.

Woods, D. W., Piacentini, J., Himle, M. B., & Chang, S. (2005). Premonitory Urge for Tics Scale (PUTS): Initial psychometric results and examination of the premonitory urge phenomenon in youths with tic disorders. *Journal of Developmental and Behavioral Pediatrics, 26,* 397–403.

Woods, D. W., Watson, T. S., Wolfe, E., Twohig, M. P., & Friman, P. C. (2001). Analyzing the influence of tic-related talk on vocal and motor tics in children with Tourette's syndrome. *Journal of Applied Behavior Analysis, 34,* 353–356.

Woods, D. W., Wetterneck, C. T., & Flessner, C. A. (2006). A controlled evaluation of acceptance and commitment therapy plus habit reversal as a treatment for trichotillomania. *Behavior Research and Therapy, 44,* 639–656.

Wright, H. H., & Holmes, G. R. (2003). Trichotillomania (hair pulling) in toddlers. *Psychological Reports, 92,* 231–233.

CHAPTER 20

Juvenile Firesetting

TIMOTHY R. STICKLE AND LAURIE B. KAUFMAN

DESCRIPTION OF THE DISORDER

Intentional firesetting by children and adolescents is a serious problem resulting in dozens of deaths, serious injuries, and more than $300 million in property damage yearly, in addition to other serious consequences for children, families, and communities (Federal Bureau of Investigation [FBI], 1996; Federal Emergency Management Agency, 1997; Kolko & Kazdin, 1986; Stickle & Blechman, 2002).

Prevalence of juvenile firesetting is difficult to determine, in part because many fires go undetected or unreported (Kafry, 1980). In the United States, children and adolescents set the majority of reported fires, are arrested for arson more than for any other crime (Garry, 1997), and account for over half of all arson arrests (FBI, 1996). Firesetting has the highest rate of juvenile involvement of all crimes on the FBI index of the most serious crimes (FBI, 1996; National Fire Protection Association, 2001).

Past estimates of prevalence appear to have been strongly influenced by elevated base rates of firesetting behavior among clinically referred and incarcerated youth (Dadds & Fraser, 2006; Lowenstein, 2001). Estimates in normative, community samples in the United States and Australia suggest prevalence rates of fire play and firesetting ranging from 0% to 3% in young boys and girls not referred for treatment (ages 4–6), to about 6% to 7% in nonreferred boys ages 7 to 13 (Achenbach, 1991a; Dadds & Fraser, 2006). These estimates are considerably lower than those in clinical and adjudicated samples, which are typically between about 20% and 50% (e.g., Kolko & Kazdin, 1988; Stickle & Blechman, 2002).

Although juvenile firesetting is exhibited across the developmental spectrum from early childhood through adolescence, persistent, intentional firesetting appears to be most commonly seen in boys also exhibiting other antisocial behaviors (Dadds & Fraser, 2006; Forehand, Wierson, Frame, Kempton, & Armistead, 1991; Kolko & Kazdin, 1986; Stickle & Blechman, 2002). Although in some clinical samples nearly all children exhibit an interest in fire and over 50% of these children admit to experimenting with fire (e.g., Doherty, 2002; Kolko & Kazdin, 1986; Sharp, Blaakman, Cole, & Cole, 2006), normative sampling suggests considerably lower occurrence in the general population. Nevertheless, in troubled youth, experimenting with fire is prevalent enough that some authors argue assessment of firesetting behaviors should be a standard part of clinical intakes even for children with seemingly unrelated problems (e.g., Sharp et al., 2006).

It should be said from the outset that psychological conceptualizations of firesetting among youth have tended to be oversimplified until fairly recently. This oversimplification has generally taken two forms. Early psychological accounts of juvenile firesetting suggested that the behavior represented a unique type of pathology, which was usually labeled pyromania. According to this psychoanalytically derived conceptualization of firesetting, a youth set fires because he or she (but usually he) found fire arousing, usually sexually (e.g., Simmel, 1949). Empirical evidence provides no support for the central tenets of this conceptualization. Controlled study of individuals who set fires indicates no sexual arousal to firesetting among arsonists (Quinsey, Chaplin, & Upfold, 1989). Findings from Quinsey et al. and other controlled studies suggest that if what is known as pyromania exists at all, it is likely rare. Cumulative negative findings about such presumed associations have led some authors to refer to pyromania as a "diagnosis in search of a disorder" (Geller, Erlen, & Pinkus, 1986).

A second type of misleading psychological account also developed through clinical observation of youth who set fires, and was then generalized from a few individuals to the population of firesetting youth. That is, clinical observation of a few clinically referred and troubled youth led some to conclude that, among other things, a so-called ego triad of behaviors—firesetting, enuresis, and cruelty to animals—is an identifiable syndrome indicative of severe, persistent, violent pathology. Although each of these behaviors may, in fact, be associated with severe problems, controlled studies have failed to support that these particular behaviors co-occur systematically or are indicative of a specific psychological profile (Slavkin, 2001). Cruelty to animals, though, has been found to be associated with psychopathic traits in youth (Dadds, Whiting, & Hawes, 2006). Additionally, cruelty, psychopathic traits, and firesetting separately and together appear to be markers of more severe conduct problems when observed in children and adolescents who also show other conduct problems and antisocial behavior (Dadds et al., 2006; Frick, Stickle, Dandreaux, Farrell, & Kimonis, 2005; Stickle & Blechman, 2002).

In addition to psychological accounts of firesetting, it is also important to note that firesetting has long been of interest to a variety of disciplines. Extensive work and interest in juvenile firesetting takes place among fire service professionals and fire service organizations, law enforcement, and public policy groups, as well as among psychologists and other mental health professionals. To some extent, these groups and their associated literatures have been separate. Recently, there have been systematic attempts to synthesize the knowledge base across disciplines (e.g., Kolko, 2002; Putnam & Kirkpatrick, 2005).

Contemporary conceptualizations of juvenile firesetting indicate that both fire play, typically defined as experimentation with fire, and repeat firesetting are predictive of greater risk for continued firesetting (e.g., Kolko & Kazdin, 1988). Importantly, reliable data indicate that boys who exhibit conduct problems and intentionally set fires are responsible for the majority of intentionally set fires (e.g., Dadds et al., 2006; Kolko, Kazdin, & Meyer, 1985; Sakheim & Osborn, 1999). Although other factors are found to be related to firesetting in some individuals, previous fire setting, age of the child, other conduct problems, and, to a lesser extent, other mental health problems such as depression and anxiety (e.g., for girls who set fires) confer increased risk for repeat firesetting. Relevant findings and their implications are discussed in more detail in the remainder of the chapter.

DIAGNOSIS AND ASSESSMENT

Diagnosis of firesetting appears straightforward. That is, the act of firesetting is discrete and its consequences are readily observable. However, firesetting itself is typically covert, making it difficult to be certain of a particular child's involvement in setting fires that are not in locations obviously linked to the child, such as the home. Additionally, because behavior patterns, age, and related problems in youth who set fires are heterogeneous, assessment of severity and risk of continued firesetting and comorbid problems is extremely challenging.

The primary emphasis of this chapter is on mental health contexts for conceptualization, assessment, and treatment of juvenile firesetting. Therefore, the recommendations in this section are specific to these contexts. For recommendations and tools for assessment in fire service and law enforcement contexts, see Kolko (2002).

Two primary areas of assessment are discussed here. The overall process in a mental health context should include the principles and practices of evidence-based assessment for children and adolescents. That is, the assessment procedures and instruments should (a) begin with broad-band assessment and move to narrow-band assessment as specific problems and syndromes are indicated; (b) incorporate and be appropriate to the developmental level of the youth; (c) assess differing developmental pathways to particular problems (e.g., age of onset for Conduct Disorder); (d) have established psychometric properties; (e) have empirical support for their intended use; (f) be comprehensive (i.e., include cognitive, behavioral, emotional, and contextual factors), and (g) use multiple assessment measures and multiple sources of information (e.g., youth, parent, teacher, behavioral observation; Kamphaus & Frick, 2002; Mash & Hunsley, 2005b; McMahon & Frick, 2005). Additionally, firesetting-specific behavior should be assessed and incorporated into the comprehensive assessment once broad-band assessments have been completed. It is essential to embed assessment of fire interest and firesetting in comprehensive assessment because the presence of conduct problems or other mental health problems directly affects both understanding of the risks for firesetting and intervention strategies.

Firesetting is not a typical presenting problem in mental health settings; children who set fires are more often referred to fire service organizations (Pierce & Hardesty, 1997). Additionally, mental health professionals often consider treatment of firesetting to be outside their area of knowledge and competency. When firesetting is a presenting or co-occurring problem, the opportunity to prevent serious damage and injury should spur mental health professionals to directly address this behavior. Additionally, when firesetting accompanies serious behavioral and emotional difficulties, behaviorally oriented mental health professionals are arguably the professionals best equipped to intervene. The guidelines and recommendations provided here are aimed at outlining a framework and specific tools to encourage mental health professionals to assess and treat youth and families presenting with firesetting as either one of several problems or as a primary problem.

As noted, the clinical presentation and risk factors associated with firesetting are heterogeneous. As a result, data are lacking to support the reliability, validity, and clinical utility of proposed types and profiles of firesetters (see later in the chapter for details). The principles of assessment listed earlier provide a systematic framework for identifying, ruling in, and ruling out risk factors. The principles should also help clinicians to conceptualize other areas of concern, evaluate the risk of recurrent firesetting, and establish priorities for intervention.

A complete review of all relevant measures, research on related problems, and evidence-based assessment is beyond the scope of this chapter. For more comprehensive treatments, see other chapters in this volume addressing general issues in assessment and those for specific problems and disorders that accompany firesetting in particular cases. Additionally, more in-depth coverage of evidence-based assessment for children and adolescents is provided in a special section of the September 2005 issue of the *Journal of Clinical Child and Adolescent Psychology* (Mash & Hunsley, 2005a). We focus primarily on assessment of the firesetting behavior and its incorporation into a broad-based clinical child assessment process. The procedure and the principles noted earlier are briefly outlined and then applied in a case example to illustrate the recommended process. The particular assessment tools discussed were selected because they are widely available and have established reliability and validity for assessment and diagnosis in mental health settings. In many cases, other measures may be available that have comparable data supporting their use and can be used with similar results.

Assessment

Similar to recommendations for evidence-based assessment of conduct problems, a primary goal of assessment of firesetting youth should be to systematically evaluate the number, types, and severity of problems (McMahon & Frick, 2005), to make an additional determination of the most urgent intervention targets, and to assess impairment in functioning resulting from each problem. This process should include either established structured diagnostic interviews such as the Diagnostic Interview Schedule for Children (Shaffer, Fisher, Lucas, Dulcan, & Schwab-Stone, 2000) or comprehensive behavior checklists such as the youth, parent, and teacher versions of the Achenbach System of Empirically Based Assessment (Achenbach & Rescorla, 2001).

Additionally, mental health, medical, and criminal history of the youth and family members should be included. These histories provide the basis for assessing multiple risk factors such as age of onset of problems, duration of problems, potential genetic vulnerabilities, and temperamental vulnerabilities.

Results from broad-band assessments should be used to identify areas and problems needing more in-depth assessment. Follow-up narrow-band assessments target domains that are frequently implicated as problems for firesetting youth. Of particular importance in the conduct problem domain are research findings indicating that destructive behaviors are related to the presence of more varied conduct problems. A greater number and more varied range of conduct problems predict poorer long-term outcomes (Loeber et al., 1993). Additionally, the presence of significant conduct problems increases risk for Attention-Deficit/Hyperactivity Disorder (ADHD), learning problems and academic difficulties, substance abuse, anxiety, and depression (McMahon & Frick, 2005). The co-occurrence of anxiety and depression with conduct problems is especially likely for girls (Loeber & Keenan, 1994). Although anxiety and depression have less frequently been associated with firesetting in research samples, this is probably because most firesetting, and therefore most research on firesetting, involves boys.

Narrow-band assessment of conduct problems should include assessment of differing developmental pathways to Conduct Disorder. For example, an earlier age of onset (i.e., by age 10) predicts higher risk for Conduct Disorder. Noncompliance, for example, appears early in the conduct problem pathway and reduction of noncompliance can reduce risk for additional problems (McMahon & Frick, 2005).

Accumulating evidence suggests that within the early-onset conduct problem group, an impulsive conduct problem pathway and a second pathway characterized by callous and unemotional traits, similar to traits associated with adult psychopathy, can be identified (see e.g., Frick & Ellis, 1999; Stickle & Frick, 2002). The latter pathway has been associated with increased destructiveness and cruelty, which appear to be associated with severity and persistence of conduct problems (Frick et al., 2005) and with greater risk for continued firesetting (Dadds & Fraser, 2006). Such distinctions also have implications for intervention strategies, as youth with callous and unemotional traits show less impulsivity and poorer response to punishments than do other conduct problem youth (Hawes & Dadds, 2005; Stickle & Frick, 2002).

Assessment of family context should be included in any assessment where firesetting problems exist. In particular, research on both firesetting (e.g., Kolko & Kazdin, 1990; McCarty, McMahon, & the Conduct Problems Prevention Research Group, 2005) and conduct problems suggests that harsh, inconsistent, and lax discipline and low parental involvement are related to these problems (Reid, Patterson, & Snyder, 2002). Measures such as the Alabama Parenting Questionnaire (Frick, 1991) and observations of parent-child interaction (e.g., Child's Game/Parent's Game; see McMahon & Forehand, 2003), may provide useful information in this domain. Results from the overall assessment will guide establishment of priorities for initial treatment strategies and targets for ongoing intervention.

CONCEPTUALIZATION

Juvenile firesetting varies in onset, duration, frequency, and severity as a function of many child and family characteristics and experience with fire (e.g., Kolko & Kazdin, 1986). However, there are few risk factors that have been shown to be unique to the onset of firesetting above and beyond the risk of onset of conduct problems generally. Several theorized typologies of firesetting youth have been proposed; however, there is little empirical evidence to support such typologies based on characteristics and motivations for the firesetting (Kolko, 2002; Sharp et al., 2006). Therefore, juvenile firesetting is discussed here in terms of the predictive characteristics of children, their families, and their experiences with fire.

CHILD CHARACTERISTICS

Boys, children from single-parent homes, and children who have been abused are more likely to set fires than children who do not meet any of these criteria (McCarty et al., 2005). Juvenile firesetting is also related to sets of cognitive and behavioral characteristics of children. In clinical samples, firesetting youth exhibit greater deficits in social adjustment, including inappropriate expressions of anger and ineffective handling of social problems, compared to nonfiresetting youth (Kolko & Kazdin, 1986). Juvenile firesetting may also occur in the context of larger life events that the child is unable to respond to appropriately, such as the birth of a new sibling or family disruption (Kolko & Kazdin, 1986). As noted, youth who set fires are likely to exhibit other covert antisocial behaviors such as property destruction and stealing (Kolko & Kazdin, 1986) and aggressive and oppositional behaviors (McCarty & McMahon, 2005; Stickle & Blechman, 2002).

As with parents of children with conduct problems, parents of firesetting youth appear less warm and more harsh and use less effective discipline, monitor less, and supervise their children more loosely than parents of children without conduct problems. Compared to children without conduct problems, firesetting youth are more likely to live in single-parent homes with absent fathers, have mothers with higher rates of depression, and have a history of abuse (Kazdin & Kolko, 1986; Kolko & Kazdin, 1986; McCarty et al., 2005). Additionally, parents of firesetting youth are more likely to have a current or past mental illness and conflict between the mother and her partner than either parents of children with other conduct problems or children without conduct problems (Kazdin & Kolko, 1986). Not only do some parent characteristics differentiate firesetters from nonfiresetters, but they also appear to differentiate children who continue setting fires from those who desist. In general, children who continue setting fires after early childhood are more likely to have parents with the aforementioned parenting deficits and mental health and interpersonal problems (McCarty et al., 2005).

Parenting deficits and parent psychopathology influence children's social-cognitive processing deficits and stress, and are also related to inadequate parental monitoring of children's unstructured, unsupervised time with peers. As children become adolescents, peers become the primary source of exposure to firesetting and access to flammable materials (Pinsonneault, 2002a). In addition, peers are a source of exposure and encouragement for substance use. Although there is an absence of research examining the effect of drug use on juvenile firesetting, it seems likely that it is one of many factors, including pressure from peers to start fires, that increases disinhibition and the likelihood of firesetting in already vulnerable youth.

Research findings provide more evidence for environmental influence on firesetting (e.g., from early learning experiences to peers) than for heredity factors. Although there is no research specifically on genetic influence on juvenile firesetting, generally research on conduct problems suggests different pathways to aggressive and nonaggressive (i.e., overt and covert) behaviors (e.g., Eley, Lichtenstein, & Moffitt, 2003; Tuvblad, Eley, & Lichtenstein, 2005). Twin studies suggest that aggressive behaviors are more influenced by heredity and more stable through adolescence, whereas nonaggressive behaviors, including firesetting, are more influenced by environment and decrease from childhood to adolescence. It is also possible that the relationship between genetic influences and firesetting is indirect and could be mediated by sociocognitive abilities or emotion regulation skills. Taken together, empirical evidence suggests that juvenile firesetting is a serious and, at times, persistent behavior pattern that is related to children's social, cognitive, and behavioral deficits. The genesis of early firesetting behavior appears to be influenced by children's early fire experiences, poor parental monitoring, and ineffective parental discipline and supervision.

BEHAVIORAL TREATMENT

Juvenile firesetting is frequently associated with conduct problems, and firesetting behavior appears to share much in common with other conduct problems. Therefore, treatment for firesetting tends to include many components common to effective treatments for conduct problems: a cognitive-behavioral focus, parent involvement, and the involvement of community organizations. Treatments for juvenile firesetting, however, include an additional component that addresses the unique features of firesetting: children's curiosity about fire and the damage fire can do. Treatments that combine cognitive-behavioral child therapy and parent management training with fire safety education are usually needed to address juvenile firesetting. Collaboration between mental health services and community fire services are an important and underutilized strategy. The importance of this collaboration is underscored by data indicating that fire departments are often the first to come into contact with firesetting youth (Kolko, 2002; Pierce & Hardesty, 1997). Furthermore, many firesetting youth are referred for fire education or restitution and not mental health services, even if they exhibit significant psychopathology (Pierce & Hardesty, 1997).

The most effective interventions for juvenile firesetting are usually those that integrate mental health and fire services. Specifically, combining empirically supported psychological treatments designed for families of children with conduct problems and empirically supported fire safety education programs most effectively reduces firesetting (Adler, Nunn, Northam, Lebnan, & Ross, 1994; Henderson, MacKay, & Peterson-Badali, 2006; Kolko, 1996).

It is also worth noting that there are several widely used but ineffective treatments that should be avoided. For example, the use of threats and warnings about the potential dangers of fire, such as describing or having the child view injury to persons or property, is ineffective. Satiation, which typically involves having the child light matches for long periods of time, may have negative effects, as evidence indicates that repeat firesetting increases children's feelings of control over fire (Sharp et al., 2006).

PARENT MANAGEMENT TRAINING AND COGNITIVE-BEHAVIORAL THERAPY

The two psychological treatments found to be most effective in reducing conduct problems and firesetting are parent management training (PMT; Frick, 1998; Kazdin, 2005; Kolko, 2001; McMahon & Forehand, 2003) and cognitive-behavioral therapy (CBT) for children and adolescents (Kazdin, 2003). There is strong evidence that PMT and child CBT together significantly reduce conduct problems (Kazdin, 2003). There is also evidence that PMT and CBT together lead to significant decreases in firesetting and match play in a sample of firesetting youth (Kolko, 2001).

Reducing firesetting requires effective monitoring and discipline and reinforcement of alternative behaviors, which are consistent deficits in parents of firesetting youth. Parent management training is a set of interventions that addresses parents' expectations and behaviors to modify children's oppositional or aggressive behaviors. Sessions and homework focus on changing parental behaviors to make parents more consistent with each other, more positive in interacting with children, and more effective in disciplining their children.

When implemented correctly, PMT teaches parents to increase children's prosocial behaviors through positive contingencies such as positive interactions with parents and decrease inappropriate behaviors through the use of consistent, effective, noncoercive discipline strategies and parental monitoring. A typical PMT treatment protocol lasts approximately 12 weeks (e.g., Brinkmeyer & Eyberg, 2003; McMahon & Forehand, 2003; Patterson & Forgatch, 2005; Webster-Stratton & Reid, 2003). Even simple behavioral interventions with parents, however, can have substantial results.

For example, parents who attended a 35-minute session teaching them to child-proof their home and monitor their children were almost 5 times less likely to experience a fire at the hands of their children (McConnell, Dwyer, & Leeming, 1996).

Changing parent behaviors and parent-child interactions is consistently demonstrated as a key to addressing conduct problems. This same approach is particularly important for firesetting youth, given high rates of parental psychopathology and relationship dysfunction (Kazdin & Kolko, 1986). Parent management training addresses many parenting behaviors affected by parent psychopathology and psychosocial stressors, but parents with severe psychopathology or marital dysfunction may also need to be referred for individual or couples therapy.

In addition to changing parent behaviors and parent-child interactions, CBT can teach children skills to decrease their own conduct problem behaviors (Frick, 1998; Kazdin, 2003; Lochman, Barry, & Pardini, 2003; Sharp et al., 2006). For firesetting specifically, skill training typically focuses on changing the context in which children's firesetting occurs and enhancing their repertoire of appropriate behaviors (Kolko, 2001). For example, children learn to identify the antecedents of setting fires, such as feelings of loneliness or boredom or interpersonal conflicts. They learn to problem-solve by evaluating the risks and benefits of firesetting and identifying alternative behaviors, including self-instruction, interpersonal conflict resolution, and increased prosocial activities.

PSYCHOEDUCATIONAL INTERVENTION

Parent management training and CBT are designed to decrease children's conduct problems and firesetting by increasing parent effectiveness, improving the quality of the parent-child interaction, and enhancing children's problem-solving skills. In addition to these psychological treatments, reducing juvenile firesetting may also require fire safety education. Children who set fires exhibit greater curiosity about fire, more family interest in fire and exposure to people who smoke, and more knowledge about materials that burn, but less competence with fire than nonfiresetters (Kolko, Wilcox, Nishi-Strattner, & Kopet, 2002). Effective fire safety education programs include both cognitive, fire science components, such as knowledge of how fires start, and competence, fire safety components, such as how to escape a burning house (Kolko, 2001; Pinsonneault, 2002b).

Because children under the age of 10 are responsible for nearly half of all juvenile-set fires, including a high proportion of fire fatalities (Sharp et al., 2006), research on effective fire safety education has focused almost exclusively on 3- to 10-year-old children (e.g., Adler et al., 1994; Kolko, 1988; Kolko & Kazdin, 1986; Kolko, Watson, & Faust, 1991; McConnell, Leeming, & Dwyer, 1996; Sharp et al., 2006). This research converges on evidence that effective fire safety education programs with children ages 3 to 13 lead to increased knowledge of fire safety and prevention (Sharp et al., 2006), decreased interest in fire-related stimuli, and decreased involvement with fire (Adler et al., 1994; Kolko, 2001; Kolko et al., 1991). Even children as young as 3 are able to gain significant knowledge from fire safety education programs (McConnell, Dwyer, et al., 1996). The structured teaching of factual information about fires and what to do to prevent or escape fires seems to be a key component of effective programs. Interventions that involve just a visit with firefighters or to fire stations or discussions about the dangers of fire have been shown to be ineffective (Kolko, 2001; Kolko et al., 1991).

The choice of a fire safety intervention depends on the age and fire safety knowledge of the child and the child's home environment. Information about the child and family can be obtained through an evaluation prior to treatment conceptualization. A home visit that includes checking for smoke detectors and the presence of a fire safety plan may greatly reduce serious injury or damage from a fire (Doherty, 2002).

Generally, preschool and elementary school children tend to benefit from highly structured education programs that focus on fire safety rules and emphasize practicing rules and skills at home with parents. Preadolescent and early adolescent children tend to benefit from educational programs that take into account their more developed cognitive and motor skills and incorporates a more thorough understanding of fire and more complex safety planning (Pinsonneault, Richardson, & Pinsonneault, 2002).

COMMUNITY-BASED TREATMENT

Research on juvenile firesetting is making clear that the most effective treatments frequently combine mental health and fire service components (Henderson et al., 2006; Kolko, 2001). Interventions that involve parents and children in the psychological treatments utilizing PMT and CBT with empirically based fire safety education effectively reduce firesetting and behaviors associated with firesetting. With a serious yet covert pattern of behaviors such as juvenile firesetting, increased involvement of multiple community agencies should be the aim. Community-based, multidisciplinary teams that include representatives from mental health, human services, law enforcement, and fire service may be able to more effectively increase public awareness and increase the prevention of fires (Sharp et al., 2006), refer firesetters to appropriate interventions, and better implement treatment across settings (Kolko, 1996). There have been few program evaluations of multidisciplinary interventions for firesetting specifically. However, extensive research on multisystemic therapy for children and adolescents with conduct problems and severe antisocial behavior demonstrate that incorporating children's families, peers, schools, mental health professionals, and community organizations into treatment has been successful for children and adolescents with severe conduct problems (e.g., Henggler, Schoenwald, Borduin, Rowland, & Cunningham, 1998). Based on research on conduct problems, it is also clear that the more severe and chronic behaviors are, the greater the need for multidisciplinary community services.

MEDICAL TREATMENT

No medication has been tested in controlled studies or approved for use with firesetting or for conduct problems. However, there is a high rate of comorbidity between conduct problems and ADHD. In one longitudinal, national, multisite study of ADHD, 30% of the children with ADHD also exhibited conduct problems such as Oppositional Defiant Disorder or Conduct Disorder (MTA Cooperative Group, 2001). If a child or adolescent who sets fires also meets criteria for ADHD, effective treatments include not only psychological treatment but also stimulant medications.

Case Description

Introduction

Jeff, an 11-year-old boy, and his mother, Vicki, presented to the child and family treatment unit at a community mental health center as a walk-in intake appointment. Vicki and Jeff's father, Ronnie, were divorced 2 years earlier, and contact between Jeff and his father was inconsistent and sporadic. Also living in the household was Jeff's sister, Molly, age 14.

Presenting Complaints

A firesetting incident in which Jeff set a vacant lot ablaze while playing with matches and incendiary materials (leaves, sticks) led to the appointment. The fire was characterized by both Jeff and Vicki as a result of his curiosity about burning the materials that quickly got out of control. The family extinguished the fire with hoses, and no damage to buildings or persons was incurred. Although the fire worried Vicki and angered Jeff's father, a number of other concerns were evident through the course of the intake interview.

The primary concerns expressed by Vicki were Jeff's social withdrawal, school problems (falling grades, but not failing), conflict between Jeff and his mother, an apparent indifference to his father, arguing and conflict with his sister, lying about small things (where he was, homework), and general noncompliance with basic rules and requests. In a follow-up interview, the primary concern expressed by Ronnie was Jeff's noncompliance.

Assessment was conducted across 4 appointments in a 2-week period with mother, father, and Jeff. Assessment covered the presenting complaints, history of the problems, and family medical, mental health, and legal history. Additionally, a series of structured assessments moving from broad band to narrow band were administered.

Broad-Band Assessment

A Child Behavior Checklists (CBCL; Achenbach, 1991a) was completed by each parent; results indicated a clinical range of problems for the Withdrawn subscale, borderline clinical elevations for the Aggressive Behavior subscale, and clinical elevation on Academic Problems. The endorsed items from the Aggressive subscale were those indicating primarily noncompliant and oppositional behavior (stubborn, argues, etc.). Serious aggressive behaviors were not endorsed.[*] Jeff's teacher also completed the Teacher's Report Form (TRF; Achenbach, 1991b), which reports on the same behaviors as the CBCL, and showed borderline clinical elevations for Academic Problems and the Withdrawn subscale. Jeff completed the Youth Self-Report (YSR; Achenbach, 1991c) and showed borderline clinical elevation on the Anxious/Depressed subscale, endorsing items indicating feeling lonely, fear of doing something bad, poor schoolwork, and worry.

Areas of concern identified in the semi-structured interview were consistent with those endorsed on the CBCL, TRF, and YSR. Additionally, Vicki expressed concern about whether Jeff was depressed. Although such an account could not be immediately ruled out, neither her description of his behavior and moods nor the behavior checklists supported a diagnosis of Major Depression. Specifically, the interview with Jeff suggested that he felt isolated and angry with his father for canceling activities and that much of his behavior was aimed at getting his father's attention or retaliating for perceived rejection by his father. A telephone interview with Jeff's teacher, in conjunction with a review of Jeff's academic history, showed no evidence of cognitive impairment or learning problems. Jeff had been a good student prior to his parents' divorce, and his academic problems appeared to be a consequence of a change in his behavior resulting in a large number of incomplete assignments and to inattention in class. Previous achievement testing showed consistent above-average abilities in all academic areas.

The semi-structured interview also indicated that his parents had inconsistent household rules and that parental expectations differed between the two households, that there was conflict between the divorced parents about parenting, and that there was periodic comparison between the two children. Molly was invariably portrayed as compliant and causing no problems; she earned good grades and voiced criticisms of her brother that were consistent with her parents' views. Family history included anxiety and possibly depression among immediate family members and antisocial behavior among more distant family members.

Narrow-Band Assessment

More focused assessment to clarify the primary problems examined Oppositional Defiant Disorder and Conduct Disorder symptoms and related behaviors, firesetting, evidence of depression and anxiety, and more in-depth assessment of parenting for each parent. First, a series of behavioral assessment tools was administered. Jeff completed the Children's Firesetting Interview (Kolko & Kazdin, 1989b), Children's Depression Inventory (Kovacs, 1982), the Revised Child Manifest Anxiety Scale (Reynolds, 1985), and the Self-Report of Delinquency (Elliott & Ageton, 1980). Parents were administered the fire-specific portions of the Firesetting Risk Interview (Kolko & Kazdin, 1989a) and the Alabama Parenting Questionnaire (APQ; Shelton, Frick, & Wooton, 1996).

Results of these assessments indicated some elevated worry and elevated oppositional and defiant symptoms, consistent with previous broad-band assessments, and no evidence of significant depression. The firesetting interviews indicated that Jeff's knowledge of fire safety was somewhat low (e.g., understanding how to respond to fire). The notable fire-specific information, however, was that Jeff's previous fire-related incidents had been in the context of unsupervised time following conflict with one or both of his parents. The APQ results indicated both inconsistent discipline and a lack of positive discipline practices.

Case Conceptualization

Among the primary presenting concerns, firesetting, withdrawn behavior, and noncompliance were supported as the initial focus of treatment following assessment. Jeff's problem behaviors were exhibited primarily in the home, and to a lesser extent at school. Functional assessment suggested that both the noncompliance and the firesetting occurred in the context of family conflict, problems

(continued)

with parent-child interaction, and inconsistent parental discipline. Because of the variety of symptoms and family history, Jeff appeared to be at risk for developing more severe conduct problems, worsening school problems, and depression if current problems were not resolved. Additional firesetting and other destructive behavior were also risks unless improved problem-solving strategies for Jeff and increased consistency in parenting were implemented.

The initial treatment plan combined parent management training, based on the Parents and Adolescents Living Together approach (Patterson & Forgatch, 1987, 1989), to increase compliance, consistency in rules, consistency in consequences, and positive interactions and improve parental monitoring, with individual cognitive-behavioral therapy for Jeff focusing on firesetting and problem-solving skills training (PSST; Kazdin, Esveldt-Dawson, French, & Unis, 1987).

Parent management training covered teaching compliance, using requests that work, monitoring and tracking, teaching through encouragement, setting up contingencies, discipline, communication, and problem solving. Problem-solving skills training covered the following problem-solving steps: (a) What am I supposed to do? (b) What are the possibilities? (c) Concentrate, (d) Choose a Solution, and (e) How did it Work?

Course of Treatment

The first session with Jeff's parents focused on an explanation of the relationship between Jeff's undesirable and noncompliant behaviors and their parenting practices. Consistent with PMT guidelines, Jeff's parents were educated about the consequences of their actions and instructed on how to begin compliance tracking. This session concluded with a homework assignment; each parent was asked to write down house rules for their separate households and to record the situations that were most consistently associated with noncompliance. They were asked not to share this information with each other or with Jeff. Each family member was to also write down on separate slips of paper one or two rules that would make him or her happier as a family member. These slips were all placed in a box to be opened and discussed at a later time.

In the first session of PSST with Jeff, he was taught the steps listed earlier and provided with concrete examples so that the strategies could be recalled and used outside of session and without adult prompting. The steps were discussed in general terms and also applied specifically to possible firesetting. Because firesetting is a low-frequency behavior (generally, and for Jeff in particular), application to incidents involving fire was considered a low probability. Applying the problem-solving skills to fire-specific content was especially important for Jeff given the results of the functional assessment indicating that firesetting was triggered by situations comparable to more frequent problem behaviors. Jeff was also given homework to identify situations, thoughts, and feelings that prompted frustration and in which he had conflict with his parents.

Subsequent individual sessions focused on applying the problem-solving steps in board games during sessions and to past and anticipated situations at home and school. That is, the therapist and Jeff tracked these situations and his responses and worked toward increased application of problem-solving skills in day-to-day interactions. As described in the following paragraph, after the initial six sessions, this approach was combined with contingencies established with his parents, and Jeff received a variety of rewards for using these skills. Jeff's homework assignments were paced to match skills his parents were developing in PMT sessions. After the fifth individual session, Jeff, his parents, and his teacher reported improvements in his approach to problems. The next two sessions were spent dividing time between continued problem solving on general issues and fire safety education. Because the major firesetting event had been recent, the focus of these sessions was on antecedent events, Jeff's responses, and applying skills to his responses. Additionally, fire safety education materials were adapted from the "Learn Not to Burn" curriculum (National Fire Protection Association, 1979) to increase his knowledge of fire science (e.g., What is fire? How does it work?) and fire safety (rules, fire hazards).

After the initial PMT session, the focus for the next four sessions shifted to teaching the importance of how requests are made, reducing the number of requests, monitoring and tracking conflicts and interactions, increasing positive interactions and setting up a series of reward systems (point charts and prize boxes for points earned). Rewards were earned for compliance with requests (within 15 seconds), completed chores, and using targeted skills.

The next four PMT sessions were devoted to discipline and communication. In particular, Ronnie worked on smaller punishments for infractions as he tended to imposed severe punishments, and Vicki worked on increasing consistency in responding to infractions. A particular focus of this work was in helping these parents acknowledge that they were attempting to compensate for what they each saw as shortcomings in the other's parenting. Ronnie thought Vicki was too lax and Vicki thought Ronnie too harsh in responding to Jeff's behavior. As they each focused on how to improve their own parenting, they achieved consistency, Jeff's behavior improved, and they diminished their attempts to compensate for the other parent.

Treatment was terminated with a final family session after 10 PMT sessions and 10 individual CBT sessions. At termination, there had been no additional firesetting incidents, Jeff's compliance had increased to acceptable levels, his school work was improving, and he was no longer in the clinical range on any rating scales. Although conflict with his sister continued, Vicki and Ronnie had begun to intervene with Molly to reduce aversive interactions with Jeff. Routine 3- and 6-month follow-up contacts indicated that progress had been maintained and Jeff's withdrawn behavior had continued to decline.

---

*The 1991 forms (Achenbach, 1991a, 1991b, 1991c) were used (prior to publication of the newer forms), and *DSM*-oriented scales are not available for this version of the CBCL and companion forms. Thus, the endorsed items were consistent with Oppositional Defiant Disorder, but the scale and norms were not intended to make *DSM* diagnoses.

Treatment Implications

The relatively positive outcome of this case suggests several principles that may be applied to firesetting in youth. Existing evidence-based treatments for Oppositional

Defiant Disorder and Conduct Disorder can be adapted for treatment of juvenile firesetting. In particular, the context of firesetting behavior should be incorporated into treatment. Specifically, PMT and CBT are the most effective treatments for these problems and should be the treatments of choice. The case presented here is an example of a moderately troubled young man at risk for more serious dysfunction. In more severe cases, principles and practices of multisystemic therapy should also be incorporated. Although firesetting is a serious, dangerous, and frightening behavior, behavioral and cognitive-behavioral clinicians are equipped to treat firesetting and its typical accompanying problems.

RECOMMENDATIONS TO CLINICIANS AND STUDENTS

Evidence-based cognitive and behavioral therapies are changing. Early evidence-based treatments were based on the application of specific procedures and protocols to a variety of cases with similar problems. Treatments are evolving so that they incorporate principles of treatments and principles of change to sets of problems. This emphasis on principles blends research on effective treatments with core principles of cognitive and behavioral change. Firesetting is an example of a challenging, low-frequency behavior that has been the subject of few, problem-specific intervention studies.

Most clinicians do not treat firesetting, and there are few well-established treatment protocols to guide clinical practice for this problem. As this case illustrates, however, the principles of evidence-based treatments can be successfully applied to such cases. It is our hope that clinicians will increasingly emphasize evidence-based principles in treatment of unusual problems and in the treatment of children, adolescents, and families with multiple complex problems.

SUMMARY

Intentional firesetting by children and adolescents is a serious problem resulting in dozens of deaths, serious injuries, and more than $300 million in property damage yearly. The diagnosis of firesetting appears straightforward, but the behavior is typically covert and difficult to observe directly. Indeed, the behavior patterns, age, and problems of youth who set fires are heterogeneous, so assessment of the risk of continued firesetting and comorbid problems is extremely difficult.

Contemporary conceptualizations and research on juvenile firesetting indicate that both fire play and repeat firesetting are predictive of continued firesetting (e.g., Kolko & Kazdin, 1988). Moreover, boys who exhibit conduct problems and intentionally set fires are responsible for the majority of intentionally set fires (e.g., Dadds et al., 2006; Kolko, Kazdin, & Meyer, 1985; Sakheim & Osborn, 1999). Because juveniles that engage in firesetting share many attributes with conduct disordered youth, interventions for firesetters include many components common to effective treatments for conduct problems, such as a cognitive-behavioral focus, parent involvement, the involvement of community organizations, and fire safety and educational components. Collaboration between mental health services and community fire services are an important and underutilized strategy. The importance of this collaboration is underscored by data indicating that fire departments are often the first to come into contact with firesetting youth (Kolko, 2002; Pierce & Hardesty, 1997). The most effective interventions for juvenile firesetting are usually those that integrate mental health and fire services.

REFERENCES

Achenbach, T. M. (1991a). *Manual for the Child Behavior Checklist/4–18 and 1991 profile.* Burlington: University of Vermont, Department of Psychiatry.

Achenbach, T. M. (1991b). *Manual for the Teacher's Report Form and 1991 profile.* Burlington: University of Vermont, Department of Psychiatry.

Achenbach, T. M. (1991c). *Manual for the Youth Self-Report and 1991 profile.* Burlington: University of Vermont, Department of Psychiatry.

Achenbach, T. M., & Rescorla, L. A. (2001). *Manual for the ASEBA school-age forms and profiles.* Burlington: University of Vermont, Research Center for Children, Youth, and Families.

Adler, R., Nunn, R., Northam, E., Lebnan, V., & Ross, R. (1994). Secondary prevention of childhood firesetting. *Journal of the American Academy of Child and Adolescent Psychiatry, 33*(8), 1194–1202.

Brinkmeyer, M. Y., & Eyberg, S. M. (2003). Parent-child interaction therapy for oppositional children. In A. E. Kazdin & J. R. Weisz (Eds.), *Evidence-based psychotherapies for children and adolescents* (pp. 204–223). New York: Guilford Press.

Dadds, M. R., & Fraser, J. A. (2006). Fire interest, fire setting and psychopathology in Australian children: A normative study. *Australian and New Zealand Journal of Psychiatry, 40,* 581–586.

Dadds, M. R., Whiting, C., & Hawes, D. J. (2006). Associations among cruelty to animals, family conflict, and psychopathic traits in childhood. *International Journal of Interpersonal Violence, 21,* 411–429.

Doherty, J. (2002). Parent and community fire education: Integrating awareness in public education programs. In D. Kolko (Ed.), *Handbook on firesetting in children and youth* (pp. 283–303). Amsterdam: Academic Press.

Eley, T. C., Lichtenstein, P., & Moffitt, T. E. (2003). A longitudinal behavioral genetic analysis of the etiology of aggressive and nonaggressive antisocial behavior. *Development and Psychopathology, 15,* 383–402.

Elliott, D. S., & Ageton, S. (1980). Reconciling ethnicity and class differences in self-reported and official estimates of delinquency. *American Sociological Review, 45* (1), 95–110.

Federal Bureau of Investigation. (1996). *Crime in the United States.* Washington, DC: U.S. Government Printing Office.

Federal Emergency Management Agency. (1997). *Fire in the United States: 1985–1994* (9th ed.). Washington, DC: U.S. Fire Administration.

Forehand, R., Wierson, M., Frame, C. L., Kempton, T., & Armistead, L. (1991). Juvenile firesetting: A unique syndrome or an advanced level of antisocial behavior? *Behavior Research and Therapy, 29,* 125–128.

Frick, P. J. (1991). *The Alabama Parenting Questionnaire.* Unpublished instrument, University of Alabama.

Frick, P. J. (1998). Conduct disorders. In T. H. Ollendick & M. Hersen (Eds.), *Handbook of child psychopathology* (3rd ed., pp. 213–238). New York: Plenum Press.

Frick, P. J., & Ellis, M. (1999). Callous-unemotional traits and subtypes of conduct disorder. *Clinical Child and Family Psychology Review, 2*(3), 149–168.

Frick, P. J., Stickle, T. R., Dandreaux, D. M., Farrell, J. M., & Kimonis, E. R. (2005). Callous-unemotional traits in predicting the severity and stability of conduct problems and delinquency. *Journal of Abnormal Child Psychology, 33*(4), 471–487.

Garry, E. M. (1997). *Juvenile firesetting and arson* (OJJDP Fact Sheet #51). Washington, D.C.: U.S. Department of Justice.

Geller, J. L., Erlen, J., & Pinkus, R. L. (1986). A historical appraisal of America's experience with pyromania: A diagnosis in search of a disorder. *International Journal of Law and Psychiatry, 9*, 201–229.

Hawes, D. J., & Dadds, M. R. (2005). The treatment of conduct problems in children with callous-unemotional traits. *Journal of Consulting and Clinical Psychology, 73*(4), 37–741.

Henderson, J. L., MacKay, S., & Peterson-Badali, M. (2006). Closing the research-practice gap: Factors affecting adoption and implementation of a children's mental health program. *Journal of Clinical Child and Adolescent Psychology, 35*(1), 2–12.

Henggler, S. W., Schoenwald, S. K., Borduin, C. M., Rowland, M. D., & Cunningham, P. B. (1998). *Multisystemic treatment of antisocial behavior in children and adolescents.* New York: Guilford Press.

Kafry, D. (1980). Playing with matches: Children and fire. In D. Canter (Ed.), *Fires and human behavior* (pp. 47–61). New York: Wiley.

Kamphaus, R. W., & Frick, P. J. (2002). *Clinical assessment of child and adolescent personality and behavior* (2nd ed.). Boston: Pearson.

Kazdin, A. E. (2003). Problem-solving skills training and parent management training for conduct disorder. In A. E. Kazdin & J. R. Weisz (Eds.), *Evidence-based psychotherapies for children and adolescents* (pp. 241–262). New York: Guilford Press.

Kazdin, A. E. (2005). Evidence-based assessment for children and adolescents: Issues in measurement development and clinical application. *Journal of Clinical Child and Adolescent Psychology, 34*, 548–558.

Kazdin, A. E., Esveldt-Dawson, K., French, N. H., & Unis, A. S. (1987). Problem-solving skills training and relationship therapy in the treatment of antisocial child behavior. *Journal of Consulting and Clinical Psychology, 55*, 76–85.

Kazdin, A. E., & Kolko, D. J. (1986). Parent psychopathology and family functioning among childhood firesetters. *Journal of Abnormal Child Psychology, 14*(2), 315–329.

Kolko, D. J. (1988). Community interventions for juvenile firesetters: A survey of two national programs. *Hospital and Community Psychiatry, 39*(9), 973–979.

Kolko, D. J. (1996). Education and counseling for child firesetters: A comparison of skills training programs with standard practice. In E. D. Hibbs & P. S. Jensen (Eds.), *Psychosocial treatments of child and adolescent disorders: Empirically-based strategies for clinicians* (pp. 409–433). Washington, DC: American Psychological Association.

Kolko, D. J. (2001). Efficacy of cognitive-behavioral treatment and fire safety education for children who set fires: Initial and follow-up outcomes. *Journal of Child Psychology and Psychiatry, 42*(3), 359–369.

Kolko, D. J. (2002). Child, parent, and family treatment: Cognitive-behavioral interventions. In D. Kolko (Ed.), *Handbook on firesetting in children and youth* (pp. 305–336). Amsterdam: Academic Press.

Kolko, D. J., & Kazdin, A. E. (1986). A conceptualization of firesetting in children and adolescents. *Journal of Abnormal Child Psychology, 14*, 49–61.

Kolko, D. J., & Kazdin, A. E. (1988). Prevalence of firesetting and related behaviors among child psychiatric patients. *Journal of Consulting and Clinical Psychology, 56*(4), 628–630.

Kolko, D. J., & Kazdin, A. E. (1989a). Assessment of dimensions of childhood firesetting among patients and nonpatients: The Firesetting Risk Interview. *Journal of Abnormal Child Psychology, 17*(2), 157–176.

Kolko, D. J., & Kazdin, A. E. (1989b). The Children's Firesetting Interview with psychiatrically referred and nonreferred children. *Journal of Abnormal Child Psychology, 17*(6), 609–624.

Kolko, D. J., & Kazdin, A. E. (1990). Matchplay and firesetting in children: Relationship to parent, marital, and family dysfunction. *Journal of Clinical Child Psychology, 19*(3), 229–238.

Kolko, D. J., Kazdin, A. E., & Meyer, E. C. (1985). Aggression and psychopathology in childhood firesetters: Parent and child reports. *Journal of Consulting and Clinical Psychology, 53*(5), 377–385.

Kolko, D. J., Watson, S., & Faust, J. (1991). Fire safety/prevention skills training to reduce involvement with fire in young psychiatric inpatients: Preliminary findings. *Behavior Therapy, 22*, 269–284.

Kolko, D. J., Wilcox, D. K., Nishi-Strattner, L., & Kopet, T. (2002). Clinical assessment of juvenile firesetters and their families: Tools and tips. In D. J. Kolko (Ed.), *Handbook on firesetting in children and youth* (pp. 177–217). Amsterdam: Academic Press.

Kovacs, M. (1982). *Children's Depression Inventory (CDI).* North Tonawanda, NY: Multi-Health Systems.

Lochman, J. E., Barry, T. D., & Pardini, D. A. (2003). Anger control training for aggressive youth. In A. E. Kazdin & J. R. Weisz (Eds.), *Evidence-based psychotherapies for children and adolescents* (pp. 263–281). New York: Guilford Press.

Loeber, R., & Keenan, K. (1994). Interaction between conduct disorder and its comorbid conditions: Effects of age and gender. *Clinical Psychology Review, 14*, 497–523.

Loeber, R., Wung, P., Keenan, K., Giroux, B., Stouthamer-Loeber, M., Van Kammen, W. B., et al. (1993). Developmental pathways in disruptive child behavior. *Development and Psychopathology, 5*, 101–131.

Lowenstein, L. F. (2001). Recent research into arson (1992–2000): Incidence, causes and associated features, predictions, comparative studies, and prevention and treatment. *Police Journal, 74*, 108–119.

Mash, E. J., & Hunsley, J. (Eds.) (2005a). Developing guidelines for the evidence-based assessment of child and adolescent disorders (Special section). *Journal of Clinical Child and Adolescent Psychology, 34* (3).

Mash, E. J., & Hunsley, J. (2005b). Evidence-based assessment of child and adolescent disorders: Issues and challenges. *Journal of Clinical Child and Adolescent Psychology, 34*, 362–379.

McCarty, C. A., McMahon, R. J., & the Conduct Problems Prevention Research Group. (2005). Domains of risk in the developmental continuity of fire setting. *Behavior Therapy, 36*, 185–195.

McConnell, A. F., Dwyer, W. O., & Leeming, F. C. (1996). A behavioral approach to reducing fires in public housing. *Journal of Community Psychology, 24*(3), 201–212.

McConnell, A. F., Leeming, F. C., & Dwyer, W. O. (1996). Evaluation of a fire-safety training program for preschool children. *Journal of Community Psychology, 24*(3), 213–227.

McMahon, R. J., & Forehand, R. L. (2003). *Helping the noncompliant child* (2nd ed.). New York: Guilford Press.

McMahon, R. J., & Frick, P. J. (2005). Evidence-based assessment of conduct problems in children and adolescents. *Journal of Clinical Child and Adolescent Psychology, 34*, 477–505.

MTA Cooperative Group. (2001). ADHD comorbidity findings from the MTA study: Comparing comorbid subgroups. *American Journal of Child and Adolescent Psychiatry, 40*(2), 147–158.

National Fire Protection Association. (1979). *Learn not to burn curriculum.* Quincy, MA: Author.

National Fire Protection Association. (2001). *U.S. arson trends and patterns.* Quincy, MA: NFPA Fire Analysis and Research.

Patterson, G. R., & Forgatch, M. S. (1987). *Parents and adolescents living together: Part 1.* Eugene, OR: Castalia.

Patterson, G. R., & Forgatch, M. S. (1989). *Parents and adolescents living together: Part 2.* Eugene, OR: Castalia.

Patterson, G. R., & Forgatch, M. S. (2005). *Parents and Adolescents: Living Together, Part 1: The Basics, 2nd Ed.* Champaign, IL: Research Press.

Pierce, J. L., & Hardesty, V. A. (1997). Non-referral of psychopathological child firesetters to mental health services. *Journal of Clinical Psychology, 53*(4), 349–350.

Pinsonneault, I. L. (2002a). Developmental perspectives on children and fire. In D. Kolko (Ed.), *Handbook on firesetting in children and youth* (pp. 261–282). Amsterdam: Academic Press.

Pinsonneault, I. L. (2002b). Fire safety education and skills training. In D. Kolko (Ed.), *Handbook on firesetting in children and youth* (pp. 219–237). Amsterdam: Academic Press.

Pinsonneault, I. L., Richardson, J. P., & Pinsoneault, J. (2002). Three models of educational interventions for child and adolescent firesetters. In D. Kolko (Ed.), *Handbook on firesetting in children and youth* (pp. 261–282). Amsterdam: Academic Press.

Putnam, C. T., & Kirkpatrick, J. T. (2005). Juvenile firesetting: A research overview (NCJ 207606) Washington, DC: U.S. Department of Justice.

Quinsey, V. L., Chaplin, T. C., & Upfold, D. (1989). Arsonists and sexual arousal to fire setting: Correlation unsupported. *Journal of Behavior Therapy and Experimental Psychiatry, 3*, 203–209.

Reid, J. B., Patterson, G. R., & Snyder, J. (2002). *Antisocial behavior in children and adolescents: A developmental analysis and model for intervention.* Washington, DC: American Psychological Association.

Reynolds, C. R. (1985). *Revised Children's Manifest Anxiety Scale (RCMAS).* Los Angeles: Western Psychological Services.

Sakheim, G. A., & Osborn, E. (1999). Severe vs. nonsevere firesetters revisited. *Child Welfare League of America, 78*(4), 411–434.

Shaffer, D., Fisher, P. W., Lucas, C. P., Dulcan, M. K., & Schwab-Stone, M. E. (2000). NIMH Diagnostic Interview Schedule for Children, version, I. V. Description, differences from previous versions, and reliability of some common diagnoses. *Journal of the American Academy of Child and Adolescent Psychiatry, 39*, 29–38.

Sharp, D. L., Blaakman, S. W., Cole, E. C., & Cole, R. E. (2006). Evidence-based multidisciplinary strategies for working with children who set fires. *American Psychiatric Nurses Association, 11*(6), 329–337.

Shelton, K. K., Frick, P. J., & Wootton, J. (1996). Assessment of parenting practices in families of elementary school-age children. *Journal of Clinical Child Psychology, 25*, 317–329.

Simmel, E. (1949). Incendiarism. In *Searchlights on delinquency* (pp. 90–101). New York: International Universities Press.

Slavkin, M. L. (2001). Enuresis, firesetting, and cruelty to animals: Does the ego triad show predictive validity? *Adolescence, 36*, 461–466.

Stickle, T. R., & Blechman, E. A. (2002). Aggression and fire: Antisocial behavior in firesetting and nonfiresetting juvenile offenders. *Journal of Psychopathology and Behavioral Assessment, 24*, 177–193.

Stickle, T. R., & Frick, P. J. (2002). Developmental pathways to severe antisocial behavior: Interventions for youth with callous-unemotional traits. *Expert Review of Neurotherapeutics, 2*, 511–522.

Tuvblad, C., Eley, T. C., & Lichtenstein, P. (2005). The development of antisocial behaviour from childhood to adolescence: A longitudinal twin study. *European Child and Adolescent Psychiatry, 14*(4), 216–225.

Webster-Stratton, C., & Reid, M. J. (2003). The Incredible Years parents, teachers, and children training series. In A. E. Kazdin & J. R. Weisz (Eds.), *Evidence-based psychotherapies for children and adolescents* (pp. 224–240). New York: Guilford Press.

CHAPTER 21

Encopresis and Enuresis

PATRICK C. FRIMAN

This chapter discusses the two most commonly occurring elimination disorders affecting children: functional encopresis (FE) and nocturnal enuresis (NE). The structure for each section is virtually identical: (a) a description of the disorders with information on diagnosis and assessment; (b) conceptualizations of the disorders discussed in terms of development, learning and modeling, parental issues, life events, genetic influences, peer influences, physical factors affecting behavior, drugs affecting behavior, and cultural and diversity issues; (c) behavioral treatment; (d) medical treatment; and (e) a case description. Because of space limitations, the section on enuresis is confined to the nocturnal type (NE), which is by far the most prevalent.

FUNCTIONAL ENCOPRESIS

DESCRIPTION AND DIAGNOSIS

Functional encopresis involves fecal soiling into or onto a surface inappropriate for that purpose. The definition of FE from the *Diagnostic and Statistical Manual of Mental Disorders* (*DSM-IV*; American Psychiatric Association, 1994) lists four criteria for FE: (1) repeated passage of feces into inappropriate places, whether involuntary or intentional; (2) at least one such event a month for at least 3 months; (3) chronological age is at least 4 years (or equivalent developmental level); and (4) the behavior is not due exclusively to the direct physiological effects of a substance or a general medical condition except through a mechanism involving constipation. The *DSM-IV* subdivides FE in two ways. The first involves typing in terms of the history of continence. The "primary type" includes children who have not exhibited fecal continence, and the "secondary type" includes children who have been completely continent for a period of time. The second involves typing in terms of constipation. By far the most common type involves FE with constipation and overflow incontinence. Cases of this type present with evidence of constipation, obtained either through the case history or upon medical exam. A much less common type is the converse of the first, FE without constipation and overflow incontinence. Cases of this type present with no evidence of constipation. Approximately 3% of the general pediatric population are reported to be encopretic, and between 80% and 95% of encopretic children seen by primary care physicians present with a history of fecal retention and/or constipation (Hatch, 1988; Partin, Hamill, Fischel, & Partin, 1992).

ASSESSMENT

The initiation of the assessment should include a "go no further with treatment" maxim until the child has received a medical evaluation. One fundamental reason for this is the rare but real possibility of organic disease (discussed further later in the chapter). Another is the very serious problem of excessive waste accumulating in an organ with a finite amount of space. An unfortunately all too frequent presenting problem in medical clinics is encopretic children who have been in extended therapy with nonmedical professionals whose initial evaluation did not include referral for a medical evaluation and whose treatment did not address known causes of FE (e.g., diet, behavior, constipation). As result, the children's colonic systems can become painfully and dangerously distended, sometimes to the point of being life-threatening (e.g., McGuire, Rothenberg, & Tyler, 1983).

Levine (1975) reported on 102 children with FE who were seen in a general pediatric outpatient clinic. Of these children, 81 were found to have stool impaction at the time of the first visit. Of these 81 children, 39 were treated for constipation in infancy. As an aside, this fact by itself seriously undermines any general discussion of a psychosocial etiology for FE. In most cases, the parents need to be assured that their child's FE is not their fault and is not caused by a psychological disturbance. The medical examination can contribute substantially to this assurance. The physician will typically take a thorough medical, dietary, and bowel history. In addition, an abdominal examination and rectal examination are often necessary to check for either large amounts of stool or very dry stool in the rectal vault and to check for poor sphincter tone. Approximately 70% of constipation can be determined on physical exam; 90% is apparent from viewing a KUB (Barr, Levine, Wilkinson, & Mulvihill, 1979), which is a plain abdominal film (focused on the kidney, ureter, and bladder, hence KUB). The KUB can be especially helpful in determining FE when a fecal mass is not detected during a physical exam or when working with difficult-to-treat children, such as those who refuse a rectal exam or are obese (Loening-Baucke, 1996).

Some medical conditions (e.g., Hirschsprung's disease), if identified, may preclude referral to a behavioral practitioner. Levine (1981) provides an excellent tabular comparison for the clinician to use in differentiating FE from Hirschsprung's disease (the most common organic cause for bowel dysfunction that is present from birth on). Additionally, the absence of weight gain in a child who is below the growth curve for weight may be suggestive of one of the variety of malabsorption syndromes that are known to be present in a small percentage of children (cf. Barr et al., 1979).

CONCEPTUALIZATION

Developmental Issues The attainment of full continence is a developmental milestone; thus, FE itself is a developmental issue. In children with general developmental disabilities, the attainment of continence is almost always delayed, although authoritative epidemiological research on the extent of those delays in that population is unavailable. Early descriptive studies describe developmental delay, mental retardation, and/or neurological impairment as a factor in up to 30% of cases of FE (Wright,

Schaefer, & Solomons, 1979). Beyond possible correlations with learning disability, no research has demonstrated that FE in typically developing children is associated with delays in specific areas of development other than delayed continence.

Historically, the development of FE was believed to be the result of psychopathological processes, particularly in the areas of behavioral and personality disturbance (e.g., Wright et al., 1979). Yet at least three early studies and one recent study have failed to confirm this position (Cox, Morris, Borowitz, & Sutphen, 2002; Friman, Mathews, Finney, & Christophersen, 1988; Gabel, Hegedus, Wald, Chandra, & Chaponis, 1986; Loening-Baucke, Cruikshank, & Savage, 1987). Three studies found levels of behavioral problems that were higher than those of nonclinical samples, but two of these found that problems in an encopretic sample were significantly lower than those in a clinical sample (Gabel et al., 1986; Loening-Baucke et al., 1987). One study found no difference between nonclinical and encopretic samples (Friman et al., 1988). All four studies found clinically significant levels of behavior problems in a subsample of the children with FE ranging from 18% (Friman et al., 1988) to 21% (Loening-Baucke et al., 1987). Thus, as a group phenomenon, the development of FE cannot be traced to psychopathological variables. And the research on positive behavioral changes following successful treatment suggests that elevated psychological problems, when present, may be more of a consequence than a cause of FE (Levine, Mazonson, & Bakow, 1980; Young, Brennen, Baker, & Baker, 1995). Yet there are several caveats to this conclusion.

For example, encopretic children with elevated psychological problems are also at risk for treatment failure (Levine & Bakow, 1976; Stark, Spirito, Lewis, & Hart, 1990). This risk may be related to treatment resistance because a cardinal constituent of any set of child behavior problems is noncompliance. Because of the physiology of fecal elimination, delays in toileting resulting from resistance can lead to stool retention (see section on Physical Factors Influencing Behavior). Early papers sketching the functional position on FE, as well as current literature reviews on delayed toilet training, argue that when children are predisposed to constipation, opposition to training can devolve delayed toilet training into chronic FE (Christophersen & Friman, 2004; Levine, 1982; Levine & Bakow, 1976).

The most recent research involving developmental implications has explored this argument by focusing on delayed toilet training, or resistance to it, rather than FE itself. Constipation is a factor in up to 95% of encopretic children (Hatch, 1988; Partin et al., 1992). In simple terms, constipation is a collective term for the delayed transit of waste through the alimentary system. A recent study shows that it is significantly more present in children who resist fecal continence training (Blum, Taubman, & Osborne, 1997). A subsequent study attempted to determine the functional subcomponents of toilet training resistance and whether they were associated with constipation. The study investigated the relationship between general oppositional behavior, difficult temperament, and child resistance to fecal continence training. The study used a semi-structured interview and a specific task (room cleanup) to explore oppositional behaviors and a standardized instrument to explore temperament. The results showed no differences in oppositional behavior between children resisting toilet training and those who were fully trained. There was a trend toward a significant elevation ($p = .068$) in temperamental difficulties in the children resisting toilet training (Blum, Taubman, & Nemeth, 2004). A follow-up study investigated a relationship between "stubbornness," a colloquial term for a cluster of temperamentally relevant behaviors, and pediatric constipation. The primary finding was that children exhibiting constipation also exhibited significantly more stubbornness in general and toileting-related stubbornness in particular.

Learning and Modeling   All toileting-relevant behavior occurs in a learning context, and all family members and peers who exhibit such behavior in the presence of an encopretic child serve as possible models. Historically, early unpleasant toileting experiences were thought to determine personality and behavior (Freud, 2000/1905). Although no actual research confirmed or even supported this perspective, vestiges of this position remain operative to this day (Friman, 2002). The problem with the position is its association with psychodynamic theory. The predicate for the initial position involved infant sexuality (Freud, 2000/1905), and as the position evolved, a sexualized perspective on toilet training and incontinence remained (e.g., Aruffo, Ibarra, & Strupp, 2000; Sperling, 1994). In fact, without actually marshaling any empirical evidence, the *DSM-IV* description of FE without constipation includes an association with anal masturbation (American Psychiatric Association, 1994). The limited evidence in support of the psychodynamic perspective notwithstanding, the Freudian position that early experiences can influence subsequent behavior patterns is abundantly documented and appears particularly relevant to FE. The process by which this influence occurs, however, is attributable to learning rather than psychodynamic principles.

In early attempts to sketch accounts of FE in learning-based terms, Levine and colleagues (Levine, 1982; Rappaport & Levine, 1986) described a developmental trajectory guided forward by disordered defecation dynamics (rather than disordered psychodynamics) and their subsequent influence on toileting behaviors. Not surprisingly, the cardinal variable in this account is constipation. The delay increases the difficulty and discomfort that accompanies bowel movements (see section on Physical Factors Influencing Behavior), and there is a sizable literature showing that effort and discomfort can cause avoidance (Friman & Poling, 1995). Avoidance of discomfort associated with bowel movements negatively reinforces toileting resistance. In turn, successful toileting resistance leads to stool withholding, which has the same effects on bowel movements as constipation itself; thus it is possible that the resistance rather than the constipation is the more important consideration. Research on this question, however, has suggested that constipation usually precedes toileting refusal, and thus it is more likely to be the primary influence. Other research has shown that children who resist toilet training often have histories of painful bowel movements and/or constipation (Luxem, Christophersen, Purvis, & Baer, 1997; Taubman, 1997). In sum, fecal toileting and resistance of it are both behaviors that are subject to learning processes. To date, the limited research on the role of learning in fecal incontinence suggests that children exhibiting an early predisposition toward constipation are at risk for becoming encopretic through these processes.

The account offered by Levine (1982; Rappaport & Levine, 1986) includes other types of experiences that contribute to the learning-based dimensions of FE. These include an array of events that are potentially aversive but that are also often a part of the toileting training process. For example, children sitting on an adult toilet with unsupported feet can experience discomfort in their legs. Children may experience aversive levels of vulnerability if they are required to have a bowel movement away from home. To avoid such experiences, children may forestall the urge to defecate and in so doing retard the natural progression of the peristaltic process, leading to situational constipation. There are several other possible experiences, such as inconsistent schedules, family strife, inconvenient bathrooms, and isolation, and all of these can have learning-based influences on toileting and thus on the possibility of FE.

Parental Issues Because parents (or primary child caregivers) are responsible for toilet training, they are inextricably involved in their children's failure to attain continence. This failure can be attributable to a broad range of variables, from parental abuse and neglect to inability to effectively manage protracted constipation and extreme child resistance. To date, these variables have been the subject of conceptually and clinically derived descriptive accounts much more than they have been the object of focused research (e.g., Levine, 1982; Rappaport & Levine, 1986; Schaefer, 1979). Some extremely critical attributions about parental involvement in FE can be found in psychodynamic accounts. For example, the mothers are said to lack warmth and be dominating, nagging, preoccupied with children's intestinal functions, overprotective, anxious, or vague. Fathers are said to be weak and ineffectual, bossy, and tending to inhibit any show of masculine assertiveness in sons (see Hoag, Norriss, Himeno, & Jacobs, 1971, for a review). No scientific evidence is provided to support these attributions, and their functional role has never been established empirically. In fact, such interpretations of parental involvement have been shown to be the result of ideologically driven clinical descriptions or a failure to take selection biases into account when generalizing from case examples (e.g., Friman, 2002).

Nonetheless, parents can play an important role in the development and progression of FE as well as its sequelae. For example, incontinence has been described as a leading cause of child abuse (Helfer & Kempe, 1976). More frequently, it can lead to parental responses that, although not abusive, are indeed punitive. A common diagnostic question in the assessment of FE is whether the target child ever attempts to obscure evidence of accidents (e.g., hides underwear), and it is often answered in the affirmative (Friman & Jones, 1998; Levine, 1982). Such behavior is the result of punishing experiences that were initiated by parents, although not always intentionally. For example, parents faced with their children's unexpected fecal accidents may unintentionally express disappointment or frustration, which in turn can have punitive effects on children who want nothing more than to please their parents. Clearly, however, the punitive response to fecal accidents is sometimes intentional. For descriptions of how such responses may come about, refer to select early accounts of FE (e.g., Levine, 1982; Rappaport & Levine, 1986; Schaefer, 1979).

A parent variable that has some empirical support involves the extent to which parents bring their children under effective instructional control. One of the prerequisite skills for successful toilet training is the child's ability to follow multiple one-step commands. The skill is needed because toilet training is a complex process, and training episodes, especially in the early stages, require multiple parent-issued, child-followed instructions. Children may be developmentally capable of following such instructions but reluctant to do so due to general oppositionality or aversion to toileting or both. To contend with such problems, parents must be able to bring about child compliance (i.e., train) with toileting-based instructions. Related research shows that parents of children at risk for FE due to toileting refusal have significantly more difficulty setting limits and establishing instructional control than parents of children who are not at risk (Taubman, 1997). In sum, despite the extraordinarily intimate role parents (and caregivers) play in child attainment of continence, the relevant literature is surprisingly nonempirical. A small number of studies have identified a few parent-mediated functional variables (e.g., Taubman, 1997), but there is virtually no empirical support for the powerful role assigned to parents by the psychodynamic literature.

Life Events   The alimentary system is exquisitely sensitive to life events, and because fecal elimination is the terminal response of the system, it is also highly responsive to these events. However, beyond psychosocial issues that affect the quality of toilet training (e.g., poverty, size of family), life events are much more likely to contribute to secondary than primary FE. As just one example, a study on classification of incontinence (Fritz & Anders, 1979) showed a large increase in the onset of secondary FE in children who had recently experienced a stressful life event (e.g., hospitalization, parental separation). Rather than catalogue and discuss the influence of the myriad stressful life events that can precipitate fecal continence, this chapter addresses only sexual abuse, the life event that appears to figure most prominently in the general understanding of FE in nonmedical communities.

In these communities, as well as in a substantial portion of the descriptive literature, there is a seemingly intractable assumption that FE is a robust indicator of a history of sex abuse. As just one example, in a paper for clinicians on identifying sex abuse, Krugman (1986) recommended that physicians routinely consider sodomy as a contributor to cases of chronic fecal soiling. For a brief review of the relevant literature, readers should consult Mellon, Whiteside, and Friedrich (2006), who also gathered some empirical data. The data were drawn from a large population-based study whose purpose was to validate a sex abuse inventory. They showed that children with a known history of being sexually abused did exhibit significantly higher rates of fecal soiling, but these rates were no higher than rates from a group of children referred for psychiatric problems. Additionally, classifying a child as having been abused on the basis of occasional soiling was as likely to be correct as incorrect. The authors concluded that using the single behavioral symptom of occasional soiling was not useful in identifying a history of sex abuse in children.

Genetic Influences   In contrast to the substantial literature on the genetics of NE (see related section), there is only a very limited and dated literature on the genetics of FE. For example, Bellman (1966) reported that 15% of the fathers of the children in her study had a history of FE. As another example, Abraham and Lloyd-Still (1984) reported that 55% of their chronically constipated patients had a positive family history of constipation. Despite the design limitations and age of these studies, the results suggesting positive family history in the development of FE would, at a minimum, seem to supply an inducement to study genetic influences further.

Peer Influences   Conducting bowel movements at times and places that allow peer detection can significantly heighten the aversive properties of the experience and potentially lead to fecal retention, thus placing affected children at risk for future fecal accidents. Furthermore, aversive peer influences can contribute to the overall detrimental effect FE has on social and emotional development. Despite the logic of considering peer influences as potential risk factors (e.g., Levine, 1982; Rappaport & Levine, 1986; Shaefer, 1979), there is no directly supportive research. In fact, search terms including the terms "peer" and "encopresis" yielded no references in a variety of search engines, including PsychINFO.

Physical Factors That Affect Behavior   The large intestine or colon is the distal end of the alimentary tract that is sequentially composed of the esophagus, stomach, biliary tract, and the intestines (small and large). The colon is a tubular organ shaped like an inverted U that connects to the small intestine via the ileum, from which it receives nonnutritive (fecal) waste in liquid form. It is best understood in terms of six components: the ascending, transverse, descending, and sigmoid colons and the rectum and anus. The colon has three major functions: storage of, fluid absorption from, and evacuation of waste. Extended storage and planned evacuation of fecal waste into an appropriate location are the defining features of fecal continence. Evacuation is achieved through a motor function called peristalsis, involving a wavelike motion of the walls of the colon. Retrograde peristalsis in the ascending colon keeps liquid fecal waste in contact with the walls of the colon that absorb moisture, resulting in gradual solidification of the waste, which begins to move forward as it takes on mass. Movement occurs over an extended period and is potentiated by external events. Examples of these events are gross motor activity, resulting in the orthcolonic reflex, and eating, resulting in the gastrocolonic reflex.

Most of the time the rectum contains little or no fecal matter, but when colonic movement leads to contraction of the sigmoid colon, feces are propelled into the rectum, and its distension stimulates sensory receptors in the rectal mucosa and in the muscles of the pelvic floor. Two muscle-based switching systems, the internal and external sphincters, regulate fecal progression from that point. The internal sphincter is involuntary and opens only through the stimulation generated by the process described earlier. As fecal mass distends the rectum, the external sphincter can be manipulated using three muscle groups (thoracic diaphragm, abdominal musculature, levator ani) to start or stop defecation (these muscle groups are also used to start or stop urination; described more fully in the NE section). Thus fecal continence requires appropriate responses to stimulation generated by a waste-receiving organ system. The task may be easier than achieving nocturnal urinary continence because the child is awake for fecal continence training and awareness plays a crucial role. In very general terms, the purpose of fecal toilet training is to acquaint the child with the proprioceptive feedback from the colon and to coordinate the relaxing of the external anal sphincter with the appropriate positioning over a potty chair or a toilet (for additional information on bowel function, see Christophersen & Friman, 2004; Friman, in press; Friman, Hofstadter, & Jones, 2006; Friman & Jones, 1998; Weinstock & Clouse, 1987; Whitehead & Schuster, 1985).

Drugs That Affect Behavior   There are a number of medications prescribed for children that can influence elimination. As an example, most prescription-level medications for pain relief, and especially those that involve opiates or their derivatives, can cause constipation. As another example, most antibiotics can cause temporary diarrhea. Antidepressant medications, especially those involving selective serotonin reuptake inhibition, can cause either diarrhea or constipation. However, all of these medications are accompanied upon receipt with a thorough and minutely detailed description of side effects, and those that involve the gastrointestinal tract will almost certainly be familiar to the prescribing physician. Rather than go into further detail here, the most useful advice is to incorporate caution about medications and their influence on fecal elimination into questions to be asked of the supervising physician.

Cultural and Diversity Issues   As indicated, there is much less epidemiological research on FE than there is on NE. Presently, there is virtually nothing to be found in the peer-reviewed literature on cultural issues beyond the occasional suggestion that FE is more likely to be found in families with lower incomes. Yet even this suggestion has been dismissed as inaccurate and based on biases in population sampling (Fritz & Armbrust, 1982). At least some early research on prevalence indicates that FE is much more frequent in boys than girls, with the ratios ranging from 3:1 to 6:1 (e.g., Fritz & Armbrust, 1982; Wright et al., 1979). Some of the relevant research was conducted in foreign countries (e.g., Stockholm; Bellman, 1966), but the samples were primarily Caucasian from industrialized cultures and thus not substantially different from the populations studied in this country.

Medical Treatment

The successful treatment of FE always includes medical components. In fact, the medical approach, which includes some behavioral aspects (e.g., scheduled toilet sits), has been standardized sufficiently to be included as a component in comparative trials yielding empirically supported multicomponent treatment protocols (more on this in the Behavioral Treatment section). At this point in the development of treatment for FE, distinguishing between medical and behavioral treatments is a mostly rhetorical maneuver that has little direct relevance to state-of-the-art treatment. Nonetheless, the subsections that follow describe the primary components of what has been called medical treatment.

Bowel Evacuation   The primary goal of FE treatment is the establishment of regular bowel movements in the toilet, and the first step is to cleanse the bowel completely of resident fecal matter (Christophersen & Friman, 2004; Field & Friman, 2006; Friman, 2003, in press; Friman & Jones, 1998; Levine, 1982). A variety of methods are used, the most common of which involve enemas and/or laxatives. Although any properly trained professional can assist with the recommendations for these (e.g., with suggestions about timing, interactional style, behavioral management), the evacuation procedure must be prescribed and overseen by the child's physician. Typically, evacuation procedures are conducted in the child's home, but severe resistance can necessitate medical assistance, in which case they must be completed in a medical setting. The ultimate goal, however, is complete parent management of evacuation procedures because they are to be used whenever the child's eliminational pattern suggests excessive fecal retention.

Successful treatment for FE will almost always require medications that soften fecal matter and ease its migration through the colon and/or aid its expulsion from the rectum. The discovery of the therapeutic benefits of facilitating medication represents the advent of the medical approach to FE and the departure from the historically psychodynamic approach (Davidson, 1958; Davidson, Kugler, & Bauer, 1963; Levine, 1982). The decision to use medication as well as the type of medication are the consulting physician's to make, but, as with bowel evacuation, any trained professional can inform the decision and educate the parent about its use. Generally, it is best to avoid interfering with the sensitive biochemistry of the alimentary system (the colonic portion of it in particular); thus, inert or only mildly noninert substances are preferred. Formerly, the most frequently used substance was mineral oil, used either alone or in combination with other ingredients such as magnesium. As indicated, prescription of the substance is the physician's prerogative, but ensuring compliance with the prescription is typically a psychological task. Children will often resist ingesting substances with odd tastes and textures. Therefore, to gain their cooperation it is often necessary to mix the substances with a preferred liquid (e.g., orange juice) and follow ingestion with praise and appreciation. A recent development makes this task even easier while also improving outcomes for children with FE. Polyethylene glycol (trade name Miralax) is an odorless, tasteless, powdered laxative that can be mixed with food or liquid with limited possibility of child detection. The laxative has been reported to produce excellent results in treatment of childhood constipation and FE and is increasingly becoming the preferred medical treatment option (e.g., Biggs & Derry, 2006).

Dietary Changes   Diet often plays a causal role in FE, and dietary changes are often part of treatment. Increased dietary fiber increases colonic motility and the moisture in colonic contents and facilitates easier and more regular bowel movements. Dietary changes can also be enhanced with over-the-counter preparations with dense fiber content (e.g., Metamucil, Perdiem). In addition to recommendations about increases in fiber, some investigators have included recommendations about increased fluid intake. The reason for this is to ensure that a child with FE is sufficiently hydrated to maintain soft stools.

Scheduling Toilet Sits   Regular elimination in the toilet is the goal of treatment, and regular toilet sits are an important step toward this goal. The time should not be during school hours because unpleasant social responses to bowel movements in the school setting can cause regressive responses to treatment (e.g., stool retention; see Levine, 1982). Choosing among the times that remain (morning, afternoon, or evening) is guided by the child's typical habits and child-parent time constraints. Establishing a time shortly after food intake can increase chances of success through the influence of the gastrocolonic reflex. In the early stages of treatment, or in difficult cases, two scheduled attempts a day (e.g., after breakfast and dinner) are often necessary. The time the child is required to sit on the toilet should be limited to 10 or fewer minutes to avoid unnecessarily increasing the aversive properties of the toileting experience. The child's feet should be supported by a flat surface (e.g., floor or a small stool) to increase comfort, maintain circulation in the extremities, and facilitate the abdominal push necessary to expel fecal matter from the body. The time should also be unhurried and free from distraction or observation by anyone other than the managing parent. Allowing children to listen to music, read, or talk with the parent may improve the child's attitude toward toileting requirements. Generally, toileting should be a relaxed, pleasant, and ultimately private affair.

BEHAVIORAL TREATMENT

Functional Encopresis with Constipation   A broad range of components loosely grouped under the term *behavioral treatments* have been combined with medical treatments as well as medical plus biofeedback treatments. The primary component includes two types of consequential events. The first involves requiring that children participate in their own cleanup, including wiping and caring for soiled clothing. Although this component has not been independently evaluated, it is routine in most treatment programs, and there is no apparent logical basis to exclude it. The second consequential event involves rewards for efforts or success. These have been included in multiple evaluations involving successful treatment of single subjects (e.g., Houts & Peterson, 1986; O'Brien, Ross, & Christophersen, 1986) and groups of subjects (see McGrath, Mellon, & Murphy, 2000). Additional behavioral components include stimulus control procedures, enhanced scheduling, enhanced health education, relaxation techniques, and various types of monitoring. Behavioral components have been included in almost all empirically supported approaches to treatment of FE.

Over the past 20 years, several descriptive and controlled experimental studies have supplemented variations on the medical treatments (described earlier) with behavioral approaches, which has led to several comprehensive biobehavioral treatment packages for FE (e.g., Christophersen & Friman, 2004; Field & Friman, 2006; Friman, 2003, in press; Friman & Jones, 1998; McGrath et al., 2000). The research suggests that effective treatment for FE depends on core treatment components (i.e., medical treatment), and the probability of success mounts with the inclusion of other components, especially those composing the behavioral approach.

The literature on this comprehensive approach includes multiple single-subject evaluations (e.g., O'Brien et al., 1986) and group trials (e.g., Lowery, Srour, Whitehead, & Schuster, 1985). For example, in a study of 58 children with FE, 60% were completely continent after 5 months, and those who did not achieve full continence averaged a 90% decrease in accidents (Lowery et al., 1985). A more recent study reported on a comparison of three treatment conditions: (1) medical care (including enemas for disimpaction and laxatives to promote frequent bowel movements); (2) enhanced toilet training, a comprehensive approach very similar those cited earlier (Lowery et al., 1985; O'Brien et al., 1986); and (3) biofeedback (directed at relaxing the external anal sphincter during attempted defecation), along with toilet training, laxatives, and enemas. At 3 months after treatment, the enhanced toilet training group significantly benefited more children than the other two treatments, with fewer treatment sessions and lower costs (Cox, Sutphen, Borowitz, Kovatchev, & Ling, 1998).

The multiple successes of the single-subject and group evaluations of the comprehensive approach to treatment have led to evaluation of group treatment. In the initial evaluation, 18 encopretic children between the ages of 4 and 11 years and their parents were seen in groups of 3 to 5 families for 6 sessions. Noteworthy is that all of these children had previously failed a medical regimen. The sessions in this trial focused on a regimen very similar to those cited earlier (Cox et al., 1998; Lowery et al., 1985; O'Brien et al., 1986). Soiling accidents decreased by 84% across the groups, and these results were maintained or improved at 6-month follow-up (Stark et al., 1990). Additionally, the results were subsequently replicated in a much larger group (Stark et al., 1997). The successes of the comprehensive approach to treatment in small N and large N studies (focused on treating individuals) and large N studies treating groups have led to treatment being supplied entirely by an interactive Internet-based program that has been shown to be highly effective (Ritterbrand et al., 2003).

Functional Encopresis without Constipation   Treatment of nonretentive FE has been the focus of far less research than treatment of the retentive type; therefore, it would be premature to argue that any known approach is empirically supported.

From the little available literature, it appears that treatment of afflicted children should be preceded by a comprehensive psychological evaluation. Virtually all investigators who have described this subsample of children report emotional and behavioral problems and treatment resistance (e.g., Landman & Rappaport, 1985), and it is possible that some of these children's soiling is related to modifiable aspects of their social ecology. Some investigators have employed versions of the approach outlined earlier and included supportive verbal therapy (Landman & Rappaport, 1985), or they have specifically taught parents how to manage their children's misbehavior (Stark et al., 1990). Thus it appears that effective treatment of this subsample would involve only some components of the comprehensive approach to treatment (e.g., facilitating medication may not be needed), combined with some form of treatment for psychological and behavioral problems.

Case Description

Case Introduction, Presenting Complaints, History, and Assessment

Patrick, age 5, was seen in a university-based behavioral pediatric outpatient clinic. The primary presenting complaint involved large, infrequent bowel movements that occurred mostly in his clothing. A physical examination ruled out organic etiology, and a toileting history revealed that, although Patrick had achieved diurnal urinary continence, he had never been fecally continent. He wore a pullup at night and regular clothes during the day. When he had the urge for a bowel movement he asked for a diaper, which was then given to him by his parents. A development screening was negative for delays. A psychological screening for emotional and behavioral problems revealed mild to moderate opposition to instruction in the daily routine and major opposition to any attempt to have him sit on the toilet. The parents typically addressed opposition with a combination of placation, reasoning, threats, periodic privilege withdrawal, and occasional spankings. There were major disagreements between the parents about how to interpret the accidents. Patrick's mother believed there was something physically wrong with him, whereas his father believed he was lazy and stubborn.

A KUB revealed fecal impaction extending from the rectum to the proximal portion of the transverse colon and corresponding fecal distension. An interview with the parents revealed that Patrick had exhibited constipation since early infancy. A home-style method was used to assess Patrick's fecal transit time. He was fed a substantial amount of corn, and the time it took for corn residue to emerge in his diaper was used as the estimate. The process took 30 hours, which is at the far upper end of normal (Christophersen & Friman, 2004; Friman, 2003). The parents also described him as a picky eater who eschewed vegetables, fruits, and brown bread. The majority of his caloric intake was obtained through dairy products. His nondairy preferred foods included various forms of pasta, white bread, sugared cereals, puddings, and toaster breakfast items.

(continued)

Case Conceptualization

Patrick's fecal incontinence met criteria for primary FE with overflow incontinence and constipation. Its etiology was mostly biologic given his early constipation and his current high fecal transit time. But its course was exacerbated by diet, inconsistency between the parents, toileting resistance, and perpetuated use of the diaper.

Course of Treatment and Assessment of Progress

The initial step in treatment was full compliance with the "go no further" maxim described earlier. As indicated in the case description, Patrick was seen by a physician, who ruled out physiopathologic causes. At that time, a treatment partnership with the physician was sought and obtained. This was deemed critical because the presence of impaction would require a medical intervention (e.g., laxatives and enemas) to resolve. Additionally, management of Patrick's chronic constipation would require not only dietary changes but prescription-level stool softeners. Treatment began with a biobehavioral interpretation of Patrick's FE delivered to both parents. It was followed by requiring daily parental recording of bowel movements, their size and consistency, and location. Recording also included dietary intake. An instructional control protocol involving time in and time out procedures (cf. Friman & Finney, 2003) focused on direct instructions and a bedtime protocol (Friman, 2005) were also implemented. No disciplinary responses were directed toward toileting. Once Patrick regularly followed one-step parental commands and complied with bedtime procedures, direct treatment for his FE was begun. It included (a) increases in fiber-rich foods such as fruits and vegetables and reductions in highly processed foods and dairy products; (b) an increase in fluid intake (i.e., 6–8 oz glasses of fluid other than milk a day); (c) physician-supervised bowel evacuation; (d) two 10-minute toilet sits a day, once after breakfast and once during the midafternoon; (e) a daily dose of a stool softener prescribed by the physician (Miralax); (f) support for Patrick's feet while he sat on the toilet; (g) refusal to supply the diaper when he requested it; and (h) a primary reward system involving small rewards for each successful bowel movement in the toilet and praise for periodic pants checks with accident-free findings.

Progress was determined by the parental recordings and periodic interviews with Patrick. Results were graphed and placed prominently on a bulletin board at home. The graph included one mark for successful bowel movements in the toilet and one for each accident-free day. Patrick averaged 2.4 accidents a day during the 3-week baseline (a period that corresponded with the instructional control training) and .2 accidents a day during the first 4 weeks of treatment. Over the Thanksgiving holiday, Patrick relapsed, most likely because the arrival of houseguests and the disruption of the daily routine interrupted his diet and treatment program. Bowel evacuation procedures were used immediately after the holiday and the full program resumed. After 6 additional weeks of treatment, Patrick was almost accident-free and remained so through long-term follow-up.

Managed Care Considerations

The one major managed care consideration is actually a general third-party payer consideration. Specifically, since the *DSM-IV* distinction between FE with and without overflow incontinence and constipation was established, third-party payers have begun to designate FE with constipation as a medical disorder and decline to reimburse psychological services. Thus payment for treatment under the *DSM-IV* diagnostic category (786.6) increasingly involves an out-of-pocket expense for parents. Fortunately, the primary components of treatment can usually be prescribed in a small number of visits, and effective follow-up can be conducted by telephone, email, and snail mail.

Follow-Up

A 1-year follow-up telephone call revealed that Patrick rarely had accidents, and when he did, they involved either staining from incomplete cleanup or accidents due to his failure to disrupt an activity and use the bathroom. After the full year of follow-up, Patrick's Miralax medication was faded systematically, and after 20 weeks, it was discontinued altogether. However, the requirement that Patrick continue with increased fiber in his diet was maintained.

RECOMMENDATIONS FOR CLINICIANS AND STUDENTS

Beyond following empirically supported treatment protocols for treatment of FE (e.g., this paper; Field & Friman, 2006; Friman et al., 2006), there are at least seven critical recommendations for clinicians and students (each at least partially addressed earlier). The first is to include a physician as a partner in the initial evaluation and subsequent treatment. The child's primary care physician is appropriate and should be the person to determine whether referral to a gastroenterologist is needed (and it typically is not in routine cases such as this one). Although there is a small possibility of losing the case to a medical provider system, this risk is outweighed by multiple advantages. In addition to having access to medical expertise and prescriptive medications as needed, there is a good chance that physicians will consider referring new patients to a provider who has the clinical acumen to include medical professionals when faced with behavioral problems with a medical expression. The second recommendation is to become fully informed about the physiology of defecation as well as the differential diagnoses that involve fecal incontinence. The third is to do everything possible to eliminate punishment for fecal accidents. Additionally, siblings who ridicule the afflicted child should be disciplined for that practice. The fourth is to administer treatment for instructional control problems before the full treatment protocol is implemented. Although following this recommendation will take extra time, success with this treatment can obviate the detrimental effect oppositional behavior can have on FE treatment. The fifth recommendation is to not underestimate the role of diet in the expression and treatment of FE. The sixth is to be prepared for resurgence of accidents following disruptions in the family or child schedules. These are almost always resolved by full bowel evacuation if needed and a full reimplementation of treatment. The seventh recommendation is to participate as actively as possible in the afflicted child's successes (e.g., ask parents to allow the child to telephone or email success messages).

NOCTURNAL ENURESIS

DESCRIPTION AND DIAGNOSIS

Criteria for including children in enuretic study groups have varied widely in the past 3 decades. The current criteria for NE from *DSM-IV* (American Psychiatric Association, 1994) are (a) repeated urination into bed or clothing; (b) at least two occurrences per week for at least 3 months or a sufficient number of occurrences to cause clinically significant distress; (c) chronological age of 5 or, for children with developmental delays, a mental age of at least 5; (d) occurrences not due exclusively to the direct effects of a substance (e.g., diuretics) or a general medical condition (e.g., diabetes).

There are three subtypes of enuresis: nocturnal only, diurnal only, and mixed nocturnal and diurnal. There are two courses, primary and secondary. The primary course includes children who have never established continence, and the secondary course involves children who, after establishing continence, resume having accidents.

Research from several countries suggests that NE is most prevalent in the United States (Gross & Dornbusch, 1983). The National Health Examination Survey reported as many as 25% of boys and 15% of girls were enuretic at age 6, with as many as 8% of boys and 4% of girls still enuretic at age 12 (Gross & Dornbusch, 1983; see also Foxman, Valdez, & Brook, 1986). Prevalence studies from outside the United States, although more conservative, indicate at least 7% of all 8-year-old children wet their beds, with a 2:1 or 3:1 ratio of boys over girls, depending on the study (Verhulst et al., 1985; see reviews by De Jong, 1973; Mellon & Houts, 1995). Estimates of the percentage of children with NE whose condition is primary range from 80% (Mellon & Houts, 1995) to 90% (Scharf & Jennings, 1988).

ASSESSMENT

The initial stage of an NE assessment should include the "go no further" maxim described in the FE section. That is, once a toileting history has been obtained and preliminary information about NE has been shared with the parents and child, the psychologist should go no further with direct treatment until a medical examination has been conducted. There are numerous pathophysiological variables that can cause NE, and, although these are rare, they are real and must be ruled out medically before a primary treatment plan is implemented (Christophersen & Friman, 2004; Cohen, 1975; Friman, 1986, 1995, in press; Friman & Jones, 1998, 2005; Gross & Dornbusch, 1983; Mellon & Houts, 1995). This emphasis on initial medical examination should not be construed as undermining the role of the psychologist. Effective management involves direct and indirect components, and the medical examination merely precedes the direct components. There are, however, important indirect components that can be pursued immediately. For example, the parents and child will most likely have contended unsuccessfully with NE for some time, and thus it is likely to seem beyond their control. Additionally, because a residue of characterological and psychopathological interpretations of NE still remain in Western culture, it is possible that the parents and the child will have misinterpreted the problem. Thus the assessment should include some therapeutically active properties, such as optimism about outcome, deconstruction of antiquated notions about NE that sometimes lead to blaming or shaming the child (or a parent), and proscriptions about punishment.

The assessment should include questions derived from the earlier subsections on defining characteristics (e.g., primary versus secondary) as well as possible etiological factors (e.g., family history of NE, disease history, mental health history). Some screening for mental health problems should be included (e.g., behavior checklists, related inquiry). Mental health problems do not appear to have a direct forward-causal relationship with NE (i.e., they are much more likely to be caused than they are to cause NE). However, if the child presents with mental health problems, these should be addressed in the ultimate treatment plan.

In addition to addressing medical and psychological complications, the assessment should also address three other very important topics. First, all sources of punishment for wetting should be identified and proscribed. Warning parents away from punishment can do this directly, and showing them that the incontinence is beyond their child's immediate control can do it indirectly. Second, the motivation, abilities, and resources of the parents should be determined. If parents are minimally motivated and/or have limited abilities or resources (e.g., single working parent, handicapped parent), the number of treatment components they will be able to implement may be limited. Third, the motivation of the child should be assessed. Optimal treatment plans involve multiple components and require compliance from the child for completion of most steps. An unmotivated or noncompliant child would be difficult to treat with any method known to cure NE. Fortunately, NE itself usually contributes to the afflicted child's motivation. As the quantity of pleasant experiences missed (e.g., sleepovers, camp) and unpleasant experiences encountered (e.g., wetness, social detection, embarrassment) accumulate, motivation naturally increases.

CONCEPTUALIZATION

Developmental Issues The research on NE suggests that afflicted children exhibit detectable maturational delays (Scharf & Jennings, 1988). For example, children with decreased developmental scores at the ages of 1 and 3 years are significantly more likely to develop NE than children with higher scores (Fergusson, Horwood, & Sannon, 1986). There is also an inverse relationship between birth weight and NE at any age. Enuretic children tend to lag slightly behind their nonenuretic peers in Tanner sexual maturation scores, bone growth, and height (Gross & Dornbusch, 1983). The increased prevalence of NE in boys also suggests maturation lag because boys generally have a slower rate of development than girls throughout childhood and adolescence (Fergusson et al., 1986; Gross & Dornbusch, 1983; Verhulst et al., 1985). Finally, enuretic children exhibit a 15% annual spontaneous remission rate, which is consistent with the notion that they are lagging behind in the acquisition of continence, a developmental milestone for all children (Forsythe & Redmond, 1974). Despite the apparent maturational lag in many (perhaps most) enuretic children, their scores on standardized intellectual tests are usually in the average range (Gross & Dornbusch, 1983). Thus the maturational lag appears more anatomical and/or physiological than intellectual, and its cardinal expression is delayed bladder control (Barbour, Borland, Boyd, Miller, & Oppel, 1963; Gross & Dornbusch, 1983; Muellner, 1960, 1961).

Learning and Modeling   There is no direct evidence that learning plays a significant role in the development of NE (although it does in treatment). Almost all enuretic events occur while children sleep; thus, the probability of volitional urination is limited. It is possible (although not yet demonstrated by research) that incontinent episodes occur when enuretic children, already accustomed to soiled beds, merely eliminate in bed rather than get up and use the bathroom. Another possibility proposed by Gross and Dornbusch (1983) is that children in homes with limited social and material resources may be at greater risk for NE because they may have limited access to adult guidance pertaining to continence and/or to safe and convenient opportunities to eliminate after bedtime. To the extent that these conditions are present, there is a possibility of learning-based influences on incontinence, although the only supportive evidence for this position is oblique. Essentially it consists of evidence that NE is more frequent in lower socioeconomic groups and in families where there is significant social and family stress during children's preschool years (for reviews, see Cohen, 1975; Gross & Dornbusch, 1983). Another source of indirect evidence suggesting a learning basis for NE is a longitudinal study of kibbutz children in Israel (Kaffman & Elizur, 1977). Children identified in the study as being at high risk for NE based on family history were more likely to attain full continence if their toilet training was conducted earlier (i.e., at 12–15 months rather than after 20). Additionally, the higher prevalence of NE in the United States versus Great Britain has been attributed to the generally earlier and more goal-directed toilet training in the British culture (Gross & Dornbusch, 1983). Last, there is a small amount of new evidence that prolonged diaper wearing can perpetuate incontinence and inhibit toilet training (e.g., Tarbox, Williams, & Friman, 2004). In sum, there is a plausible possibility that learning processes play a role in the development of NE, but it has not yet been demonstrated by direct experimental research. The proportion of cases in which learning plays a primary role seems likely to be small.

Parental Issues   There is a substantial, although somewhat dated, literature suggesting that parents are responsible not only for their children's NE through psychodynamic processes, but also for any emotional disturbance that develops in association with it (Friman, 2002). These suggestions have never been supported by empirical research and seem to be offered more as an attempt to illuminate psychodynamic theory than as an attempt to describe the clinical phenomenology of NE (e.g., Varga, 1986). Nonetheless, that enuretic children can be treated harshly by parents and caregivers is well documented (e.g., Warzak, 1993), and, as indicated in the FE section, incontinence is a leading cause of child abuse (Friman, 1986; Helfer & Kempe, 1976). Thus, as with FE, a fundamental component of the assessment and treatment of NE is the extent of its punishment history and a proscription against punishment from the point of the assessment forward.

The clinical observation that parental attitudes toward NE can be harsh led to various attempts to assess those attitudes and the role intolerance might play in the psychological development of the enuretic child and the treatment of the condition (e.g., Butler, Redfern, & Forsythe, 1993). As an example of the relevant research, mothers in one study attributed the cause of NE to stable and uncontrollable factors that contributed to their feelings of helplessness (Butler, Brewin, & Forsythe, 1986). Maternal attitudes in that study became substantially more negative as the NE in their children persisted. This study, along with others focused on parent issues, indicates that parent attitudes toward NE are important for at least three reasons. First, enuretic children are incapable of direct control of their own condition. If parents view the condition critically, then the children can be the recipients of direct and indirect punitive parental interactions focused on a behavior that the children cannot control. Experiencing punishment for a behavior over which one has no control is a defining feature of learned helplessness, which, in turn, is a significant contributor to Major Depression (Seligman, 1975). Second, parents are the primary administrators of treatment, and negative attitudes about NE can adversely affect the parents' approach to treatment (Butler, Redfern, & Forsythe, 1993; Morgan & Young, 1975). Third, physician attitude toward NE is likely to be tolerant and optimistic, and differences of opinion between parent and physician can interfere with successful management (Shelov, McIntire, Jones, & Hegarty, 1981) and lead to treatment failures (Houts, Peterson, & Whelan, 1986).

Life Events   As indicated in the section on Description and Diagnosis, NE is subdivided into primary and secondary types, with the secondary type occurring after a period of continence has been established. Approximately 25% of cases involve the secondary type, and these are often attributed to adverse life events that cause some regression or loss of continence skills (Fritz & Armburst, 1982; Gross & Dornbusch, 1983). One well-documented life event that can cause NE is the onset of a psychotropic medication regimen (see section on Drugs That Affect Behavior). Other life events that have been said to cause secondary NE include any cause of significant distress for children, such as hospitalization, parental divorce, moving to a new home, and the birth of a sibling. In one study, such events occurred in the month before the onset of secondary NE in 81% of cases (Fritz & Anders, 1979). Despite these suggestive data and the frequent attempts to link psychosocial variables to the precipitation of NE in the literature, the majority opinion is that the etiology of NE is primarily biologic (e.g., Christophersen & Friman, 2004; Fergusson et al., 1986; Friman, 1986, 1995, in press; Friman & Jones, 1998, 2005).

Genetic Influences   The research on the genetics of NE shows that the probability of NE increases as a function of closeness or number of blood relations with a positive history (Bakwin, 1971, 1973; Hallgren, 1957; Kaffman & Elizur, 1977). These findings suggest a genetic linkage that some theorists argue against, suggesting instead that families convey tolerant attitudes toward bed-wetting, not enuretic "genes" (Kanner, 1972). But even in settings where family custom plays a minimal role in child development (such as the Israeli kibbutzim), a high correlation between family history and NE in children exists (Kaffman & Elizur, 1977). More recent and much more narrowly focused research has actually implicated several chromosomes as well as modes of transmission. The chromosomes are 13q, 12q, 8, and 22 (Arnell et al., 1997; Eiberg, Berendt, & Mohr, 1995; Von Gontard, Eiberg, Hollman, Rittig, & Lehmkuhl, 1997).

Peer Influences   There is no evidence that peers influence the development of NE, but there is indirect evidence that they can influence its social and emotional costs for affected children. There is a large literature showing that children can be highly critical of developmental and behavioral differences in their peers, especially if those differences are viewed as maladaptive and potentially under the control of the child who exhibits them (e.g., Friman, McPherson, Warzak, & Evans, 1993; Sigelman & Begley, 1987). Epidemiological research shows that by the age of 4, most children have achieved full continence (Berk & Friman, 1990); thus urinary accidents in older children that are detected by peers are likely to be viewed negatively, and ostracism is a real possibility. Most reviews of the vast NE literature describe the potential peer problems that can result from NE, yet none of these includes references to directly supportive empirical research (e.g., Christophersen & Friman, 2004; Friman, 1986, 1995, in press; Friman & Jones, 1998, 2005; Warzak, 1993). The typical assertion is that, to avoid peer detection, enuretic children may avoid developmentally important socializing events such as camp, sleepovers, and overnight trips with nonfamily members. Although obviously logical and supported by frequent case descriptions, these peer-related social responses to NE await direct experimental support.

Physical Factors That Affect Behavior

PHYSIOLOGY OF MICTURATION   The bladder is the primary organ in a complex set of physiological systems that govern urination. A comprehensive review of these systems is far beyond the scope of this chapter (for more thorough discussions, see Muellner, 1951, 1960, 1961; Vincent, 1974). An elementary description, however, is necessary to underscore the logic behind treatment approaches for NE.

The bladder is an elastic hollow organ resembling an upside-down balloon with a long narrow neck; it has two primarily mechanical functions: storage and release of urine (Vincent, 1974). Extended storage and volitional release are the defining properties of urinary continence. The body of the bladder is composed of smooth muscle, and its nerve supply is autonomic. It cannot be directly controlled by volitional maneuvers; that is, one cannot "will" the bladder to contract or relax. Yet continence requires personal control over bladder contraction and relaxation.

Fortunately, there are components of the urogenital system (other than the bladder itself) that can be volitionally controlled to establish continence. These involve three large muscle groups: the thoracic diaphragm, the lower abdominal musculature, and the pubococcygeus (anterior end of the levator ani; Muellner, 1960, 1961). Deliberate urination at all levels of bladder filling involves a coordination of these three groups, resulting in intra-abdominal pressure directed to the bladder neck. This coordinated action lowers the bladder neck, resulting in reflexive contractions of the bladder body, opening of the internal and external sphincters, and bladder emptying.

Urine retention generally involves a reversal of this process. That is, except during imminent or actual urination, pelvic floor muscles remain in a state of tonus, or involuntary partial contraction, which maintains the bladder neck in an elevated position and the sphincter muscles closed (Vincent, 1974). Even after initiation of urination has begun, contraction of the pelvic floor muscles can abruptly raise the bladder neck and terminate urination, but this requires some training and concentrated effort. Optimal bladder training requires detection of bladder filling and either urination in an appropriate location or retentive contraction of pelvic floor muscles (Christophersen & Friman, 2004; Friman, 1986, 1995, in press; Friman & Jones, 1998, 2005; Mellon, Scott, Haynes, Schmidt, & Houts, 1997).

Voluntary components of the bladder system can be used to initiate the involuntary components to achieve urination or continence. Establishing nocturnal continence involves a sequence of continence skills, including awareness of urgency, initiating urination, inhibiting actual and impending urination while awake, and inhibiting actual and impending urination while asleep. Mastery of continence skills requires abundant practice, especially for enuretic children.

FUNCTIONAL BLADDER CAPACITY   Functional bladder capacity (FBC) refers to voiding capacity as distinguished from true bladder capacity (TBC), which refers to bladder structure (Troup & Hodgson, 1971). Functional bladder capacity is established in various ways, examples of which include the higher volume in either of the first two voidings after ingestion of a specified water load (e.g., 30 ml/kg body weight; Starfield, 1967; Zaleski, Gerrard, & Shokeir, 1973), the average of all voidings in 24 hours (Hauri, 1982), or the average of all voidings in 1 week (Zaleski et al., 1973). The research suggests that the FBC of enuretic children is generally lower than that of their nonenuretic siblings (Starfield, 1967) and peers (Muellner, 1961; Starfield, 1967; Troup & Hodgson, 1971; Zaleski et al., 1973), but their TBC is about the same (Troup & Hodgson, 1971). Overall, the research on FBC suggests that many enuretic children urinate more frequently with less volume than their nonenuretic peers and siblings. Their urinary pattern has been compared to that found in infants and very young children (Muellner, 1960, 1961).

ANTIDIURETIC HORMONE   The presence of antidiuretic hormone (ADH) or arginine vasopression causes the kidneys to increase the concentration of urine (by increasing reabsorption of free water in the renal-collecting duct). Theoretically, serum ADH levels increase at night and thereby protect sleep from urinary urgency and facilitate nocturnal continence. An influential line of research has shown that a subset of enuretic children do not exhibit the normal diurnal rhythm of ADH secretion and perhaps wet their beds as a result of increased urine production while sleeping (Norgaard, Pedersen, & Djurhuus, 1985; Rittig, Knudsen, Norgaard, Pedersen, & Djurhuus, 1989). Earlier (and subsequent) related research showed that desmopressin (desamino-D-arginine vasopressin [DDAVP]), an intranasally administered vasopressin analogue, reduced nocturnal enuretic episodes in children (e.g., Dimson, 1977; and see DDAVP under Treatment). Whether the effectiveness of DDAVP is due to restoration of insufficient nocturnal ADH or is merely the result of decreased urine volume (due to increased concentration) and thus not a primary causal variable is still unknown (Houts, 1991; Key, Bloom, & Sanvordenker, 1992). In fact, support for decreased nocturnal ADH as a primary causal variable is still quite limited, for several reasons. The sample sizes in the related studies were small (Norgaard et al., 1985; Rittig et al., 1989). Subsequent studies found a much smaller proportion of children who exhibited deficient ADH (e.g., Steffens, Netzer, Isenberg, Alloussi, & Ziegler, 1993). Fewer than one-quarter of treated bed-wetting children achieve short-term dryness (Moffatt, Harlos, Kirshen, & Burd, 1993). Not all children with known urine concentrating problems wet the bed (e.g., only 50% of children with sickle cell anemia are enuretic). Lower ADH is not linked in any empirical way to why children do not awaken to full bladders, and not all children with this characteristic are bed wetters. As indicated earlier, nocturnal NE is multiply determined, and abnormality in nocturnal ADH secretion is but one of several possible causal contributors.

Drugs That Affect Behavior   Substances with bioactive properties have the potential to affect urinary elimination and thus play a potential role in the development and progress of NE, especially of the secondary type. For example, most psychotropic drugs can affect urination, and there are multiple case studies reporting secondary NE induced by medications such as risperidone (Kantrowitz, Srihari, & Tek, 2006) and paroxetine (Ginsburg, 2004), as well as lithium, valproic acid, clozapine, and theophylline (Fritz & Rockney, 2004). There are also substances that can be obtained without a prescription that can increase urinary frequency and thus contribute to NE.

The most common of these is caffeine; conventional treatment advice, whether medical or behavioral, usually includes a recommendation against allowing children to ingest caffeinated beverages near bedtime. From a different perspective, medications that influence sleep patterns can increase or decrease the probability of enuretic events depending on the type of influence they exert. Some literature indicates that depth of sleep and capacity for arousal from it play a role in NE (e.g., Gellis, 1994; Willie, 1994; Wolfish, 1999). Thus medications that have soporific properties could increase the possibility of enuretic events. Conversely, medications that lighten sleep or decrease arousal latency could decrease the possibility of enuretic events. For example, imipramine, a tricyclic antidepressant, has been used to treat NE for decades (more on this later), and its modest successes, when they occur, have been attributed to its reductive effects on depth of sleep. Because some common prescription and over-the-counter drugs can influence urination and potentially the development and/or progression of NE, when incontinence is discussed with the physician, all drugs currently being used with afflicted children should also be discussed.

Cultural and Diversity Issues   The major diversity issue in studies of NE involves sex. Enuretic boys outnumber enuretic girls by as much as 3 to 1, as indicated in the section on Description and Diagnosis. Based on the abundance of evidence indicating this disparity, one group of epidemiological researchers has recommended changing the diagnostic criteria for boys from age 5 to age 8 because the proportion of enuretic girls at age 5 is about the same as the proportion of boys at age 8 (Friman, 1986; Verhulst et al., 1985). Cross-cultural research indicates that although NE is more prevalent in the United States than in Europe (Fritz & Armbrust, 1982) and other countries such as Thailand (Hansakunachai, Ruangdaraganon, Udomsubpayakul, & Kotchabnakdi, 2005) and China (Liu, Sun, Uchiyama, Li, & Okawa, 2000), it may be more prevalent in some developing countries, such as Nigeria (Peltzer & Taiwo, 1993). Nocturnal enuresis has also been shown to have increased prevalence in populations that have lower socioeconomic status or that exhibit significant psychosocial deviancy, such as children in institutionalized settings (Fritz & Armbrust, 1982).

Medical Treatment

The primary medical treatment for NE is drug treatment, and the literature indicates that physicians prescribe it for NE more frequently than for any other treatment (Blackwell & Currah, 1973; Cohen, 1975; Fergusson et al., 1986; Rauber & Maroncelli, 1984; Vogel, Young, & Primack, 1996). Because of the necessity of physician involvement in NE, the widespread use of drug therapy by physicians, and the dominating influence of the biobehavioral model of NE, it is likely that medication will be part of treatment (e.g., Christophersen & Friman, 2004; Friman, 1986, 1995, in press; Friman & Jones, 1998, 2005; Houts, 1991; Mellon & McGrath, 2000). The two most commonly prescribed medications for NE are imipramine and DDAVP.

Imipramine   Historically, tricyclic antidepressants were the drugs of choice for treatment of NE, and imipramine was the most frequently prescribed drug treatment (Blackwell & Currah, 1973; Foxman et al., 1986; Rauber & Maroncelli, 1984; Stephenson, 1979). The mechanism by which imipramine reduces bed-wetting is still mostly unknown (Stephenson, 1979). In doses between 25 and 75 mg given at bedtime, imipramine has produced initial reductions in wetting in substantial numbers of enuretic children, often within the first week of treatment (Blackwell & Currah, 1973). Reviews of both short- and long-term studies show that NE usually recurs when tricyclic therapeutic agents are withdrawn (Ambrosini, 1984). The permanent cure produced with imipramine is reported to be 25% (ranging from 5% to 40%; Blackwell & Currah, 1973; Houts, Berman, & Abramson, 1994). There are some concerns with use of imipramine for NE, ranging from a potential detrimental effect on behavioral treatment (Houts, Peterson, & Liebert, 1984) to a large number of unpleasant and sometimes unhealthful side effects (e.g., Cohen, 1975; Friman, 1986; Herson, Schmitt, & Rumack, 1979).

Desmopressin As described earlier, Norgaard and colleagues reported on a small number of enuretic children who had abnormal circadian patterns of ADH (Norgaard et al., 1985; Rittig et al., 1989). As a result of these reports, DDAVP has rapidly become a popular treatment for NE, and it appears to have displaced the tricyclics as the most prescribed treatment. Desmopressin concentrates urine, thereby decreasing urine volume and intravesical pressure, which makes the physiological dynamics that precede urination less probable and nocturnal continence more probable. Desmopressin also has far fewer side effects than imipramine (Dimson, 1986; Ferrie, MacFarlane, & Glen, 1984; Norgaard et al., 1985; Pedersen, Hejl, & Kjoller, 1985). Recommended dosages are 10 to 20 μg taken at bedtime.

Research on DDAVP has yielded mixed results, with success in some studies (Dimson, 1986; Pederson et al., 1985; Post, Richman, & Blackett, 1983) but not in others (Ferrie et al., 1984; Scharf & Jennings, 1988). A recent review indicated that fewer than 25% of children become dry on the drug (a much larger percentage show some improvement), and, similar to tricyclics, its effects appear to last only as long as the drug is taken and are less likely to occur in younger children or children who have frequent accidents (Moffatt et al., 1993; see also Houts et al., 1994; Pederson et al., 1985; Post et al., 1983). Additionally, DDAVP is also very expensive. Nonetheless, its treatment effects, when they occur, are as immediate as imipramine but with fewer side effects. Thus DDAVP may be preferable to imipramine as an adjunct to treatment, and a review of the relevant literature suggested including it with alarm-based treatment has the potential to boost the already high success obtained by the urine alarm (discussed later) to 100% (Mellon & McGrath, 2000).

BEHAVIORAL TREATMENT

Urine Alarms The best known and most widely used behavioral treatment for NE is the urine alarm, and, if not the first, certainly the foremost early user of it was Herbert Mowrer (Mowrer & Mowrer, 1938). Since the mid-1970s, psychological research on medically uncomplicated NE in children has been dominated by either the development of alternative behavioral procedures based on operant conditioning or improving urine alarm treatments (Houts, 2000; Mellon & McGrath, 2000). Controlled evaluations of the urine alarm indicate that this relatively simple device is 65% to 75% effective, with a duration of treatment around 5 to 12 weeks and a 6-month relapse rate of 15% to 30% (Butler, 2004). Most of this research has been conducted using the bed device and, more rarely, the pajama device.

BED DEVICES The urine alarm features a moisture-sensitive switching system that, when closed by contact with urine seeped into pajamas or bedding, completes a small voltage electrical circuit and activates a stimulus theoretically strong enough to cause waking (e.g., buzzer, bell, light, or vibrator). The device is placed on the bed or sewn into the pajamas. The bed device typically involves two aluminum foil pads, one of which is perforated, with a cloth pad between them. The bed pads are placed under the sheets of the target enuretic child's bed, with the perforated pad on top. A urinary accident results in urine seeping through perforations in the top pad, collecting in the cloth pad, and causing contact with the bottom sufficient to complete an electrical circuit and activate a sound-based alarm mechanism. In principle, the awakened child turns off the alarm and completes a series of responsibility training steps associated with the child's accidents (Christophersen & Friman, 2004; Friman, 1986, 1995, in press; Friman & Jones, 1998, 2005), such as completing urination in the bathroom, changing pajamas and sheets, and returning to bed. In practice, the alarm often alerts parents first, who then waken the child and guide him or her through the training steps.

PAJAMA DEVICES   Pajama devices are similar in function yet simpler in design. The alarm itself is either placed into a pocket sewn into the child's pajamas or pinned to the pajamas. Two wire leads extending from the alarm are attached (e.g., by small alligator clamps) on or near the pajama bottoms. When the child wets during the night, absorption of urine by the pajamas completes an electrical circuit between the two wire leads and activates the alarm. A range of stimuli are available for use with the pajama devices: buzzing, ringing, vibrating, and lighting. In principle, as with the bed devices, the alarm is supposed to waken the child. In practice, the sound-based alarms sometimes alert parents first, who proceed to assist the child through the steps mentioned earlier. The light- and vibration-based alarms have yet to be subjected to controlled evaluation, and thus questions pertaining to whether they awaken parent or child, their effectiveness, and how they compare with sound-based alarms remain unanswered.

Mechanism of Action   The mechanism of action in alarm treatment was initially described as classical conditioning, with the alarm as the unconditioned stimulus, bladder distention as the conditioned stimulus, and waking as the conditioned response (Mowrer & Mowrer, 1938). More recent literature emphasizes a negative reinforcement or avoidance paradigm (Friman, 1995, in press; Friman & Jones, 1998, 2005), in which the child increases sensory awareness to urinary need and exercises anatomical responses (e.g., contraction of the pelvic floor muscles) that effectively avoid setting off the alarm (Mellon et al., 1997). Cures are obtained slowly, however, and during the first few weeks of alarm use the child often awakens only after voiding completely. The aversive properties of the alarm, however, inexorably strengthen those skills necessary to avoid it.

EVIDENCE OF EFFECTIVENESS

Reports of controlled comparative trials show that the alarm-based treatment is superior to drug treatment and other nondrug methods such as retention control training. In fact, numerous reviews of the literature show that its success rate is higher and its relapse rate lower than any other method (Christophersen & Friman, 2004; Friman, 1986, 1995, in press; Friman & Jones, 1998, 2005; Houts et al., 1994; Mellon & McGrath, 2000). One problem with interpreting the review literature on alarm treatment is that it is usually augmented by other components to improve effectiveness, resulting in treatment packages such as dry bed training (Azrin, Sneed, & Foxx, 1974) and full-spectrum home training (Houts & Liebert, 1985).

Augmenting the Alarm

RETENTION CONTROL TRAINING   Retention control training (RCT) expands functional bladder capacity by increasing children's capacity to forestall and thus increase the volume of their urinations. Training requires that children drink extra fluids (e.g., 16 oz of water or juice), notify parents of the urge to urinate, and delay urination as long as possible. Parents should establish a regular time for RCT each day and conclude the training at least a few hours before bedtime. Progress can be assessed by monitoring the amount of time the children are able to delay urination and/or the volume of urine they are able to produce in a single urination (Christophersen & Friman, 2004; Friman, 1986, 1995, in press; Friman & Jones, 1998, 2005). Either or both can be incorporated into a game context, wherein children earn rewards for progress.

OVERLEARNING   An adjunct related to RCT is overlearning. Like the RCT procedure, this method requires that children drink extra fluids—but just prior to bedtime. Overlearning is an adjunctive strategy only, and is used to enhance the maintenance of treatment effects established by alarm-based means. Thus, it should not be initiated until a dryness criterion has been reached (e.g., 7 dry nights; Houts & Liebert, 1985).

KEGEL AND STREAM INTERRUPTION EXERCISES   Kegel exercises involve purposeful manipulation of the muscles necessary to prematurely terminate urination. Originally developed for stress incontinence in women, a version of these exercises called stream interruption is often used in NE treatment packages (e.g., Christophersen & Friman, 2004; Friman, 1986, 1995, in press; Friman & Jones, 1998, 2005). For children, stream interruption requires initiating and terminating urine flow at least once a day during a urinary episode. "Dry practice" or actual Kegel exercises can be practiced far more frequently once the child has learned to detect and manipulate the requisite musculature while conducting stream interruption. Dry contraction of pelvic musculature consists of the child holding a contraction for 5 to 10 seconds, followed by a 5-second rest, at least 10 times on three separate occasions per day (Schneider, King, & Surwitt, 1994).

PAIRED ASSOCIATIONS   Paired associations involve pairing stream interruption with the urine alarm in a reward-based program (Christophersen & Friman, 2004; Friman, 1986, 1995, in press; Friman & Jones, 1998, 2005). In one version, the parent stands outside the bathroom door with the alarm and activates it two or three times while the child urinates, whereupon the child practices stream interruption. The parent can also use the alarm to cue Kegel (dry practice) exercises. Alternatively, the parent can make an audiotape of the alarm that, when played intermittently, would allow the child to practice alone with stream interruption and/or Kegel exercises. To establish and maintain motivation, the parent should use praise and a reward system, described in the next section.

REWARD SYSTEMS   Contingent rewards alone are unlikely to cure NE, but they may be critical in sustaining a child's motivation to participate in treatment, especially when the system reinforces success in small steps. An example involves a dot-to-dot drawing and a grab bag (Christophersen & Friman, 2004; Friman, 1986, 1995, in press; Friman & Jones, 1998, 2005), wherein the child identifies an affordable and desirable prize and the parent draws (or traces) a picture of it using a dot-to-dot format, with every third or fourth dot larger than the others. The child is allowed to connect two dots for each dry night; each time the line reaches a larger dot, the child earns access to a grab bag with small rewards (e.g., small toys, edibles, money, privileges, special time with parents). When all dots are connected, the child earns a prize. This system may also be used to motivate participation in other components of a package program (e.g., paired associations).

Waking Schedule This treatment component involves waking the children prior to accidents and guiding them to the bathroom for urination. Results obtained are attributed to a change in arousal, increased access to the reinforcing properties of dry nights, and increased awareness of urinary urge in lighter stages of sleep. Several schedules are possible, a minimally effortful example of which involves waking the children just before the parents go to bed and systematically waking them a half-hour earlier on nights following several successive dry nights, until the children awaken to urinate without assistance (Christophersen & Friman, 2004; Friman, 1986, 1995, in press; Friman & Jones, 1998, 2005; Houts & Liebert, 1985).

Self-Monitoring Self-monitoring provides data that can be used to evaluate progress. One simple method for monitoring NE merely requires the child to record on a calendar whether the previous night was wet or dry. A more complex and more sensitive method involves placing tracing paper over the stain resulting from an accident and tracing the outline of the stain. Next, the tracing paper is placed over a grid, and the number of squares inside the area is recorded (Friman, 1986, 1995, in press; Ruckstuhl & Friman, 2003). Beyond progress monitoring, charting these data and setting goals may have the additional therapeutic benefit of reactivity: The direction of change is determined by the valence of the behaviors that are monitored (e.g., behaviors viewed negatively are reduced).

Responsibility Training All of the skill-based components mentioned thus far (e.g., RCT, paired association) are designed to promote a mature voiding repertoire in the child. To be consistent with this goal, the child should be treated in a way that promotes independence and responsibility. For example, a child should not be left in diapers at night. Rather, the enuretic child should be assigned reasonable household responsibilities associated with his or her accidents. In younger children this may merely mean bringing their sheets to the laundry basket. Older children, however, should be expected to actually launder sheets and clothing. These responsibilities should not be presented as a punishment but as a correlate of increased responsibility and a demonstration of the parents' confidence in and respect for their maturing child (Christophersen & Friman, 2004; Friman, 1995, in press; Friman & Jones, 1998, 2005; Houts & Liebert, 1985).

Case Description

Case Introduction, Presenting Complaints, History, and Assessment

Tom, a 7-year-old boy in second grade, was seen in an outpatient behavioral pediatric clinic for assessment and treatment of NE. Beyond the presenting complaint, his medical, psychiatric, educational, and developmental histories were unremarkable. Tom had no siblings. His father was a businessman and his mother did not work (although she was a community volunteer). Both parents had graduate degrees. The history revealed that Tom had been diurnally continent since age 3 but had never had an accident-free night. He still wore a pullup at night, although he had recently begun requesting to go to bed without one. A physical examination by his primary care physician ruled out any health-related reason for the nocturnal accidents. A family history revealed that his father had been nocturnally enuretic. A developmental screening was negative for delays, as was a psychological screening for behavior and emotional problems. There was evidence of mounting social costs. Immediately prior to the clinic visit, Tom had an accident while sleeping overnight at a friend's home. Although the friend and his mother addressed the accident in a tolerant fashion, Tom told his mother that he did not want to spend the night away from home again. Assessment of parental attitudes indicated high tolerance for Tom's accidents by both, and there was no evidence of characterological or moral interpretation. Perhaps because of his own history, the father was particularly sympathetic to Tom. Both parents and Tom were eager to pursue treatment.

Case Conceptualization

Tom's urinary accidents met *DSM-IV* criteria for primary NE. Its etiology was evidently biologic, given the absence of a dry night during his lifetime and the father's positive history. The case was not complicated by extraneous factors such as psychological problems, parental misinterpretation, or low child or parent motivation.

Course of Treatment and Assessment of Progress

As indicated earlier, the primary treatment component for NE is the urine alarm, but there are several additional components that can augment the alarm. The number of components to include is best determined collaboratively by the provider, parents, and child. In Tom's case, the alarm selected was a pajama device. The additional components were (a) eliminating use of the pullup; (b) a waking schedule in which one of the parents awakened Tom fully and took him to the bathroom when they went to bed; (c) responsibility training requiring Tom to bring soiled sheets to the laundry room and to remake his own bed after an accident; (d) Kegel exercises during at least one urination a day; (e) 3 weeks of overlearning in which Tom drank extra fluids before bed; (f) RCT on the weekends; (g) a self-monitoring system in which Tom recorded accident-free nights on calendar; (h) a dot-to-dot reward system, in which dots were connected for every dry night and whenever Tom increased the volume of urine produced during RCT; and (i) DDAVP administered to Tom whenever he spent the night away from home.

Progress was evaluated by inspecting Tom's self-monitoring calendar and dot-to-dot drawing and periodic interviews with Tom and his parents. During a 2-week baseline period during which Tom had his physical examination and he and his parents had their clinic visits with the provider of his treatment program, Tom had an accident every night. For the first 3 weeks of treatment, he continued to have accidents every night, but both he and his parents noted that the size of the stain appeared to be shrinking. On the 22nd day of treatment, Tom had the first dry night of his life. His parents let him call his therapist and his grandparents to announce the result. During the next 3 weeks his dry nights averaged 2 a week, moving to 5 a week over the subsequent 6 weeks.

(continued)

Managed Care Considerations

There are no significant managed care considerations. Therapy for NE is generally covered by third-party payers, and the number of visits required to implement and follow a case as routine as this one is usually small.

Follow-Up

At 3 months, Tom was having only one accident a month, and at 1 year he was accident-free. He has remained accident-free for 2 years.

RECOMMENDATIONS FOR CLINICIANS AND STUDENTS

Beyond following empirically supported treatment protocols for treatment of NE (e.g., this paper; Christophersen & Friman, 2004; Friman, in press), there are at least eight critical recommendations for clinicians and students; they are consistent with the recommendations made for FE. The first is to request a medical examination prior to beginning treatment. The child's primary care physician is appropriate; referral to a urologist is unnecessary for uncomplicated cases of primary NE. The second is to become fully familiar with the physiology of urination as well as the differential diagnoses that involve urinary incontinence. The third recommendation is to do everything possible to eliminate all sources of punishment for urinary accidents. Additionally, siblings who ridicule the afflicted child should be disciplined for that practice. The fourth is to compose the treatment in accord with child and parent motivation to implement various components and their acceptance of them. For example, some children or parents may be reluctant to use the urine alarm. The fifth recommendation is to avoid limiting fluids before bedtime. There is no evidence that doing so influences the probability of wet nights unless the child drinks to excess. The sixth is to completely eliminate the use of absorbent undergarments (e.g., pullups). The child's exposure to the sensations associated with accidents contributes to the learning process. Steps should be taken to protect the child's bed from accidents (e.g., rubber sheets). The seventh recommendation is to suggest a small amount of medication (i.e., DDAVP or imipramine). The eighth is to participate as actively as possible in the afflicted child's successes (e.g., ask parents to allow the child to telephone or email success messages).

SUMMARY

This chapter has reviewed the two most commonly occurring elimination disorders affecting children: functional encopresis and nocturnal enuresis. To maximize the likelihood of successful intervention for elimination disorders, readers were advised to first obtain medical evaluation before attempting to treat these conditions (i.e., the "go no further with treatment" maxim). Emphasizing the importance of collaboration between the therapist, the family, and the child's physician is also likely to enhance treatment outcome.

Although psychodynamic views concerning elimination disorders continue to influence contemporary thinking, this perspective has gradually given way to a body of empirically based, peer-reviewed research on interventions that combine learning- (e.g., dry bed training) and contingency-based (e.g., token programs) approaches with medical treatment (e.g., stool softeners). Fostering a greater appreciation and understanding of the physiology of elimination appears to have greatly improved outcomes for children with elimination disorders. Following treatment guidelines spelled out in this chapter is an important step toward improving one's clinical practice with these common but extremely challenging behavioral problems.

REFERENCES

Abraham, F. P., & Lloyd-Still, J. D. (1984). Chronic constipation in childhood: A longitudinal study of 186 patients. *Journal of Pediatric Gastroenterology and Nutrition, 3,* 460–467.

Ambrosini, P. J. (1984). A pharmacological paradigm for urinary continence and NE. *Journal of Clinical Psychopharmacology, 4,* 247–253.

American Psychiatric Association. (1994). *Diagnostic and statistical manual of mental disorders* (4th ed.). Washington, DC: Author.

Arnell, H., Hjalmas, K., Jagervall, M., Lackgren, G., Stenberg, A., Bengtsson, B., et al. (1997). The genetics of primary nocturnal enuresis: Inheritance and suggestion of a second major gene on chromosome 12q. *Journal of Medical Genetics, 34,* 360–365.

Aruffo, R. N., Ibarra, S., & Strupp, K. R. (2000). Encopresis and anal masturbation. *Journal of the American Psychoanalytic Association, 48,* 1327–1354.

Azrin, N. H., Sneed, T. J., & Foxx, R. M. (1974). Dry-bed training: Rapid elimination of childhood enuresis. *Behavior Research and Therapy, 12,* 147–156.

Bakwin, H. (1971). Enuresis in twins. *American Journal of Diseases in Children, 121,* 222–225.

Bakwin, H. (1973). The genetics of enuresis. In I. Kolvin, R. C. MacKeith, & S. R. Meadow (Eds.), *Bladder control and enuresis* (pp. 73–78). Philadelphia: Lippincott.

Barbour, R. F., Borland, E. M., Boyd, M. M., Miller, A., & Oppel, T. E. (1963). Enuresis as a disorder of development. *British Medical Journal, 2,* 787–790.

Barr, R. G., Levine, M. D., Wilkinson, R. H., & Mulvihill, D. (1979). Chronic and occult stool retention: A clinical tool for its evaluation in school aged children. *Clinical Pediatrics, 18,* 674–686.

Bellman, M. (1966). Studies on encopresis. *Acta Paediatrica Scandinavica, 170*(Suppl.), 1–137.

Berk, L. B., & Friman, P. C. (1990). Epidemiological aspects of toilet training. *Clinical Pediatrics, 29,* 278–282.

Biggs, W. S., & Dery, W. H. (2006). Evaluation and treatment of constipation in infants and children. *American Family Physician, 73,* 469–484.

Blackwell, B., & Currah, J. (1973). The psychopharmacology of nocturnal enuresis. In I. Kolvin, R. C. MacKeith, & S. R. Meadow (Eds.), *Bladder control and enuresis* (pp. 231–257). Philadelphia: Lippincott.

Blum, N. J., Taubman, B., & Nemeth, N. (2004). During toilet training constipation occurs before stool toileting refusal. *Pediatrics, 113,* e520–e522.

Blum, N. J., Taubman, B., & Osborne, M. (1997). Behavioral characteristics of children with stool toileting refusal. *Pediatrics, 99,* 50–53.

Butler, R. J. (2004). Childhood nocturnal enuresis: Developing a conceptual framework. *Clinical Psychology Review, 24,* 909–931.

Butler, R. J., Brewin, C. R., & Forsythe, I. (1993). Maternal attributions and tolerance for nocturnal enuresis. *Behavior Research and Therapy, 24,* 307–312.

Butler, R. J., Redfern, E. J., & Forsythe, I. (1993). The Maternal Tolerance Scale and nocturnal enuresis. *Behavior Research and Therapy, 31,* 433–436.

Christophersen, E. R., & Friman, P. C. (2004). Elimination disorders. In R. Brown (Ed.), *Handbook of pediatric psychology in school settings* (pp. 467–488). Mahwah, NJ: Erlbaum.

Cohen, M. W. (1975). Enuresis. *Pediatric Clinics of North America, 22*, 545–560.

Cox, D., Morris, J. B., Borowitz, S., & Sutphen, J. L. (2002). Psychological differences between children with and without chronic encopresis. *Journal of Pediatric Psychology, 27*, 585–591.

Cox, D. J., Sutphen, J., Borowitz, S., Kovatchev, B., & Ling, W. (1998). Contribution of behavior therapy and biofeedback to laxative therapy in the treatment of pediatric encopresis. *Annals of Behavioral Medicine, 20*(2), 70–76.

Davidson, M. (1958). Constipation and fecal incontinence. *Pediatric Clinics of North America, 5*, 749–757.

Davidson, M., Kugler, M. M., & Bauer, C. H. (1963). Diagnosis and management in children with severe and protracted constipation and obstipation. *Journal of Pediatrics, 62*, 261–275.

De Jong, G. A. (1973). Epidemiology of enuresis: A survey of the literature. In I. Kolvin, R. C. MacKeith, & S. R. Meadow (Eds.), *Bladder control and enuresis* (pp. 39–46). London: Heinemann.

Dimson, S. B. (1977). Desmopressin as a treatment for enuresis. *Lancet, 1*, 1260

Dimson, S. B. (1986). DDAVP and urine osmolality in refractory enuresis. *Archives of Diseases in Children, 61*, 1104–1107.

Eiberg, H., Berendt, I., & Mohr, J. (1995). Assignment of dominant inherited nocturnal enuresis (ENUR1) to chromosome 13q. *National Genetics, 10*, 334–336.

Fergusson, D. M., Horwood, L. J., & Sannon, F. T. (1986). Factors related to the age of attainment of nocturnal bladder control: An 8-year longitudinal study. *Pediatrics, 78*, 884–890.

Ferrie, B. G., MacFarlane, J., & Glen, E. S. (1984). DDAVP in young enuretic patients: A double-blind trial. *British Journal of Urology, 56*, 376–378.

Field, C. E., & Friman, P. C. (2006). Encopresis. In J. E. Fisher & W. T. Odonohue (Eds.), *Practitioner's guide to evidence-based psychotherapy* (pp. 277–283). New York: Springer.

Forsythe, W., & Redmond, A. (1974). Enuresis and spontaneous cure rate study of 1129 enuretics. *Archives of Diseases in Children, 49*, 259–269.

Foxman B., Valdez, R. B., & Brook, R. H. (1986). Childhood enuresis: Prevalence, perceived impact, and prescribed treatments. *Pediatrics, 77*, 482–487.

Freud, S. (2000). Three essays on the theory of sexuality (rev. ed.). New York: Basic Books. (Original work published 1905)

Friman, P. C. (1986). A preventive context for enuresis. *Pediatric Clinics of North America, 33*, 871–886.

Friman, P. C. (1995). Nocturnal enuresis in the child. In R. Ferber & M. H. Kryger (Eds.), *Principles and practice of sleep medicine in the child* (pp. 107–114). Philadelphia: Saunders.

Friman, P. C. (2002, May). *The psychopathological interpretation of common child behavior problems: A critique and related opportunity for behavior analysis.* Invited address at the 28th annual convention of the Association for Behavior Analysis, Toronto, Canada. (Video available from ABA International)

Friman, P. C. (2003). A biobehavioral bowel and toilet training treatment for functional encopresis. In W. O'Donohue, S. Hayes, & J. Fisher (Eds.), *Empirically supported techniques of cognitive behavior therapy* (pp. 51–58). Hoboken, NJ: Wiley.

Friman, P. C. (2005). *Good night, we love you, we will miss you, now go to bed and go to sleep: Managing sleep problems in young children.* Boys Town, NE: Girls and Boys Town Press.

Friman, P. C. (in press). Evidence based therapies for enuresis and encopresis. In G. Steele, D. Elkin, & M. C. Roberts (Eds.), *Handbook of evidence-based therapies for children and adolescents.* New York: Springer.

Friman, P. C., & Finney, J. W. (2003). Teaching parents to use time out (and time in). In W. Odonohue, S. Hayes, & J. Fisher (Eds.), *Empirically supported techniques of cognitive behavior therapy* (pp. 429–435). Hoboken, NJ: Wiley.

Friman, P. C., Hofstadter, K. L., & Jones, K. M. (2006). A biobehavioral approach to the treatment of functional encopresis in children. *Journal of Early and Intensive Behavioral Interventions, 3*, 263–272.

Friman, P. C., & Jones, K. M. (1998). Elimination disorders in children. In S. Watson & F. Gresham (Eds.), *Handbook of child behavior therapy* (pp. 239–260). New York: Plenum Press.

Friman, P. C., & Jones, K. M. (2005). Behavioral treatment for nocturnal enuresis. *Journal of Early and Intensive Behavioral Intervention, 2*, 259–267.

Friman, P. C., Mathews, J. R., Finney, J. W., & Christophersen, E. R. (1988). Do children with encopresis have clinically significant behavior problems? *Pediatrics, 82*, 407–409.

Friman, P. C., McPherson, K. M., Warzak, W. J., & Evans, J. (1993). Influence of thumb sucking on peer social acceptance in first grade children. *Pediatrics, 91*, 784–786.

Friman, P. C., & Poling, A. (1995). Life does not have to be so hard: Basic findings and applied implications from research on response effort/force. *Journal of Applied Behavior Analysis, 28*, 583–590.

Fritz, G. K., & Anders, T. F. (1979). Enuresis: The clinical application of an etiologically based system. *Child Psychiatry and Human Development, 10*, 103–111.

Fritz, G. K., & Armbrust, J. (1982). Enuresis and encopresis. *Pediatric Clinics of North America, 5*, 283–296.

Fritz, G. K., & Rockney, R. (2004). Practice parameters for the assessment and treatment of children and adolescents with enuresis. *Journal of the American Academy of Child and Adolescent Psychiatry, 43*, 1540–1550.

Gabel, S., Hegedus, A. M., Wald, A., Chandra, R., & Chaponis, D. (1986). Prevalence of behavior problems and mental health utilization among encopretic children. *Journal of Developmental and Behavioral Pediatrics, 7*, 293–297.

Gellis, S. S. (1994). Are enuretics truly hard to arouse? *Pediatric Notes, 18*, 113.

Ginsburg, D. L. (2004). Paroxetine induced enuresis. *Primary Psychiatry, 11*, 24.

Gross, R. T., & Dornbusch, S. M. (1983). Enuresis. In M. D. Levine, W. B. Carey, A. C. Crocker, & R. T. Gross (Eds.), *Developmental-behavioral pediatrics* (pp. 575–586). Philadelphia: Saunders.

Hallgren, B. (1957). Enuresis: A clinical and genetic study. *ACTA Psychiatrica et Neurologica Scandinavica, 32*(Suppl. 114), 73–90. Philadelphia: Saunders.

Hansakunachai, T., Ruangdaraganon, N., Udomsubpayakul, S. T., & Kotchabnakdi, N. (2005). Epidemiology of enuresis among school-age children in Thailand. *Journal of Developmental and Behavioral Pediatrics, 26*, 356–360.

Hatch, T. F. (1988). Encopresis and constipation in children. *Pediatric Clinics of North America, 35*, 257–281.

Hauri, P. (1982). *The sleep disorders: Current concepts.* Kalamazoo, MI: Upjohn.

Helfer, R., & Kempe, C. H. (1976). *Child abuse and neglect.* Cambridge, MA: Ballinger.

Herson, V. C., Schmitt, B. D., & Rumack, B. H. (1979). Magical thinking and imipramine poisoning in two school-aged children. *Journal of the American Medical Association, 241*, 1926–1927.

Hoag, J. M., Norriss, N. G., Himeno, E. T., & Jacobs, J. (1971). The encopretic child and his family. *Journal of the American Academy of Clinical Psychiatry, 10*, 242–257.

Houts, A. C. (1991). Nocturnal enuresis as a biobehavioral problem. *Behavior Therapy, 22*, 133–151.

Houts, A. C. (2000). Commentary: Treatments for enuresis: Criteria, mechanisms, and health care policy. *Journal of Pediatric Psychology, 25*, 219–224.

Houts, A. C., Berman, J. S., & Abramson, H. (1994). Effectiveness of psychological and pharmacological treatments for nocturnal enuresis. *Journal of Consulting and Clinical Psychology, 62*, 737–745.

Houts, A. C., & Liebert, R. M. (1985). *Bedwetting: A guide for parents.* Springfield, IL: Thomas.

Houts, A. C., & Peterson, J. K. (1986). Treatment of a retentive encopretic child using contingency management and diet modification with stimulus control. *Journal of Pediatric Psychology, 11*, 375–383.

Houts, A. C., Peterson, J. K., & Liebert, R. M. (1984). The effects of prior imipramine treatment on the results of conditioning therapy with N.E. *Journal of Pediatric Psychology, 9*, 505–508.

Houts, A. C., Peterson, J. K., & Whelan, J. P. (1986). Prevention of relapse in full spectrum training for primary enuresis. *Behavior Therapy, 17*, 462–469.

Kaffman, M., & Elizur, E. (1977). Infants who become enuretics: A longitudinal study of 161 kibbutz children. *Monographs of the Society for Research on Child Development, 42*, 2–12.

Kanner, L. (1972). *Child psychiatry.* Springfield, IL: Charles C Thomas.

Kantrowitz, J. T., Srihari, V. H., & Tek, C. (2006). Three cases of risperidone-induced enuresis. *Schizophrenia Research, 84*, 174–175.

Key, D. W., Bloom, D. A., & Sanvordenker, J. (1992). Low-dose DDAVP in nocturnal enuresis. *Clinical Pediatrics, 32*, 299–301.

Krugman, R. (1986). Recognition of sexual abuse in children. *Pediatrics in Review, 8*, 25–30.

Landman, G. B., & Rappaport, L. (1985). Pediatric management of severe treatment-resistant encopresis. *Development and Behavioral Pediatrics, 6*, 349–351.

Levine, M. D. (1975). Children with encopresis: A descriptive analysis. *Pediatrics, 56*, 407–409.

Levine, M. D. (1981). The schoolchild with encopresis. *Pediatrics in Review, 2*, 285–291.

Levine, M. D. (1982). Encopresis: Its potentiation, evaluation, and alleviation. *Pediatric Clinics of North America, 29*, 315–330.

Levine, M. D., & Bakow, H. (1976). Children with encopresis: A study of treatment outcome. *Pediatrics, 58*, 845–852.

Levine, M. D., Mazonson, P., & Bakow, H. (1980). Behavioral symptom substitution in children cured of encopresis. *American Journal of Diseases in Childhood, 134*, 663–667.

Liu, X., Sun, Z., Uchiyama, M., Li, Y., & Okawa, M. (2000). Attaining nocturnal urinary control, nocturnal enuresis, and behavioral problems in Chinese children aged 6 through 16 years. *Journal of the American Academy of Clinical Psychiatry, 39*, 1557–1564.

Loening-Baucke, V. (1996). Encopresis and soiling. *Pediatric Clinics of North America, 43*, 279–298.

Loening-Baucke, V. A., Cruikshank, B., & Savage, C. (1987). Defecation dynamics and behavior profiles in encopretic children. *Pediatrics, 80*, 672–679.

Lowery, S., Srour, J., Whitehead, W. E., & Schuster, M. M. (1985). Habit training as treatment of encopresis secondary to chronic constipation. *Journal of Pediatric Gastroenterology and Nutrition, 4*, 397–401.

Luxem, M. C., Christophersen, E. R., Purvis, P. C., & Baer, D. M. (1997). Behavioral-medical treatment of pediatric toileting refusal. *Journal of Development and Behavioral Pediatrics, 18*, 34–41.

McGrath, M. L., Mellon, M. W., & Murphy, L. (2000). Empirically supported treatments in pediatric psychology: Constipation and encopresis. *Journal of Pediatric Psychology, 25*, 225–254.

McGuire, T., Rothenberg, M., B., & Tyler, D. C. (1983). Profound shock following intervention for chronic untreated stool retention. *Clinical Pediatrics, 23*, 459–461.

Mellon, M. W., & Houts, A. C. (1995). Elimination disorders. In R. T. Ammerman & M. Hersen (Eds.), *Handbook of child behavior therapy in the psychiatric setting* (pp. 341–366). New York: Wiley.

Mellon, M. W., & McGrath, M. L. (2000). Empirically supported treatments in pediatric psychology: Nocturnal enuresis. *Journal of Pediatric Psychology, 25,* 193–214.

Mellon, M. W., Scott, M. A., Haynes, K. B., Schmidt, D. F., & Houts, A. C. (1997, April). *EMG recording of pelvic floor conditioning in nocturnal enuresis during urine alarm treatment: A preliminary study.* Paper presentation at the 6th Florida Conference on Child Health Psychology, University of Florida, Gainesville.

Mellon, M. W., Whiteside, S. P., & Friedrich, W. N. (2006). The relevance of fecal soiling as an indicator of child sexual abuse: A preliminary analysis. *Developmental and Behavioral Pediatrics, 27,* 25–32.

Moffatt, M. E. K., Harlos, S., Kirshen, A. J., & Burd, L. (1993). Desmopressin acetate and nocturnal enuresis: How much do we know? *Pediatrics, 92,* 420–425.

Morgan, R. T. T., & Young, G. C. (1975). Parental attitudes and the conditioning of childhood enuresis. *Behavior Research and Therapy, 13,* 197–199.

Mowrer, O. H., & Mowrer, W. M. (1938). Enuresis: A method for its study and treatment. *American Journal of Orthopsychiatry, 8,* 436–459.

Muellner, S. R. (1951). The physiology of micturition. *Journal of Urology, 65,* 805–813.

Muellner, R. S. (1960). Development of urinary control in children. *Journal of the American Medical Association, 172,* 1256–1261.

Muellner, R. S. (1961). Obstacles to the successful treatment of primary enuresis. *Journal of the American Medical Association, 178,* 147–148.

Norgaard, J. P., Pedersen, E. B., & Djurhuus, J. C. (1985). Diurnal antidiuretic hormone levels in enuretics. *Journal of Urology, 134,* 1029–1031.

O'Brien, S., Ross, L., & Christophersen, E. R. (1986). Primary encopresis: Evaluation and treatment. *Journal of Applied Behavior Analysis, 19,* 137–145.

Partin, J. C., Hamill, S. K., Fischel, J. E., & Partin, J. S. (1992). Painful defecation and fecal soiling in children. *Pediatrics, 89,* 1007–1009.

Pedersen, P. S., Hejl, M., & Kjoller, S. S. (1985). Desamino-D-arginine vasopressin in childhood nocturnal enuresis. *Journal of Urology, 133,* 65–66.

Peltzer, K., & Taiwo, O. (1993). Enuresis in a population of Nigerian children. *Journal of Psychology in Africa, 1,* 136–150.

Post, E. M., Richman, R. A., & Blackett, P. R. (1983). Desmopressin response of enuretic children. *American Journal of Diseases in Children, 137,* 962–963.

Rappaport, L. A., & Levine, M. D. (1986). The prevention of constipation and encopresis: A developmental model and approach. *Pediatric Clinics of North America, 33,* 859–871.

Rauber A., & Maroncelli, R. (1984). Prescribing practices and knowledge of tricyclic antidepressants among physicians caring for children. *Pediatrics, 73,* 107–109.

Ritterband, L. M., Cox, D. J., Walker, L. S., Kovatchev, B., McKnight, L., Patel, K., et al. (2003). An Internet intervention as adjunctive therapy for pediatric encopresis. *Journal of Consulting and Clinical Psychology, 71,* 910–917.

Rittig, S., Knudsen, U. B., Norgaard, J. P., Pedersen, E. B., & Djurhuus, J. C. (1989). Abnormal diurnal rhythm of plasma vasopressin and urinary output in patients with enuresis. *American Journal of Physiology, 252,* F664–F671.

Ruckstuhl, L. E., & Friman, P. C. (2003, May). *Evaluating the effectiveness of the vibrating urine alarm: A study of effectiveness and social validity.* Paper presented at the 29th annual convention of the Association for Behavior Analysis, San Francisco, CA.

Schaefer, C. E. (1979). *Childhood encopresis and enuresis.* New York: Von Nostrand.

Scharf, M. B., & Jennings, S. W. (1988). Childhood enuresis: Relationship to sleep, etiology, evaluation, and treatment. *Annals of Behavioral Medicine, 10,* 113–120.

Schneider, M. S., King, L. R., & Surwitt, R. S. (1994). Kegel exercises and childhood incontinence: A new role for an old treatment. *Journal of Pediatrics, 124,* 91–92.

Seligman, M. E. (1975). *Helplessness: On depression, development, and death.* San Francisco: Freeman.

Shelov, S. P., McIntire, M. S., Jones, D. J., & Hegarty, M. C. (1981). Enuresis: A contrast of attitudes of parents and physicians. *Pediatrics, 67,* 707–710.

Sigelman, C. K., & Begley, N. L. (1987). The early development of reactions to peers with controllable and uncontrollable problems. *Journal of Pediatric Psychology, 12,* 99–114.

Sperling, M. (1994). *The major neuroses and behavior disorders in children.* Lanham, MD: Aronson.

Starfield, B. (1967). Functional bladder capacity in enuretic and nonenuretic children. *Journal of Pediatrics, 70,* 777–782.

Stark, L. J., Opipari, L. C., Donaldson, D. L., Danovsky, M. R., Rasile, D. A., & DelSanto, A. F. (1997). Evaluation of a standard protocol for retentive encopresis: A replication. *Journal of Pediatric Psychology, 22,* 619–633.

Stark, L. J., Spirito, A., Lewis, A. V., & Hart, K. J. (1990). Encopresis: Behavioral parameters associated with children who fail medical management. *Child Psychiatry and Human Development, 20,* 169–179.

Steffens, J., Netzer, M., Isenberg, E., Alloussi, S., & Ziegler, M. (1993). Vasopressin deficiency in primary nocturnal enuresis: Results of a controlled prospective study. *European Urology, 24,* 366–370.

Stephenson, J. D. (1979). Physiological and pharmacological basis for the chemotherapy of enuresis. *Psychological Medicine, 9,* 249–263.

Tarbox, R., Williams, L., & Friman, P. C. (2004). Extended diaper wearing: Effects on continence in and out of the diaper. *Journal of Applied Behavior Analysis, 37,* 97–101.

Taubman, B. (1997). Toilet training and toileting refusal for stool only: A prospective study. *Pediatrics, 99,* 54–58.

Troup, C. W., & Hodgson, N. B. (1971). Nocturnal functional bladder capacity in enuretic children. *Journal of Urology, 105,* 129–132.

Varga, A. Y. (1986). The role of the parent child relationship in the stabilization of a child's neurotic reaction (using the example of children with enuresis). *Psikhologiya, 14,* 32–38.

Verhulst, F. C., van der lee, J. H., Akkeruis, G. W., Sanders-Woudstra, J. A., Timmer, F. C., & Donkhorst, I. D. (1985). The prevalence of nocturnal enuresis: Do DSM III criteria need to be changed? *Journal of Child Psychology and Psychiatry, 26,* 989–993.

Vincent, S. A. (1974). Mechanical, electrical and other aspects of enuresis. In J. H. Johnston & W. Goodwin (Eds.), *Reviews in pediatric urology* (pp. 280–313). New York: Elsevier.

Vogel, W., Young, M., & Primack, W. (1996). A survey of physician use of treatment methods for functional enuresis. *Journal of Developmental Behavioral Pediatrics, 17,* 90–3.

Von Gontard, A., Eiberg, H., Hollman, E., Rittig, S., & Lehmkuhl, G. (1997). Clinical enuresis phenotypes in familial nocturnal enuresis. *Scandinavian Journal of Urology (Nephrology Supplement), 118,* 11–16.

Warzak, W. J. (1993). Psychosocial implications of nocturnal enuresis. *Clinical Pediatrics, 31,* 38–40.

Weinstock, L. B., & Clouse, R. E. (1987). A focused overview of gastrointestinal physiology. *Annals of Behavioral Medicine, 9,* 3–6.

Whitehead, W. E., & Schuster, M. M. (1985). *Gastrointestinal disorders: Behavioral and physiological basis for treatment.* New York: Academic Press.

Willie, N. (1994). Nocturnal enuresis: Sleep disturbances and behavioral patterns. *Acta Paediatrica, 83,* 772–774.

Wolfish, N. (1999). Sleep arousal function in enuretic males. *Urology and Nephrology, 202,* 24–26.

Wright, L., Schaefer, A. B., & Solomons, G. (1979). *Encyclopedia of pediatric psychology.* Baltimore: University Park Press.

Young, M. H., Brennen, L. C., Baker, R. D., & Baker, S. S. (1995). Functional encopresis: Symptom reduction and behavioral improvement. *Developmental and Behavioral Pediatrics, 16,* 226–232.

Zaleski, A., Gerrard, J. W., & Shokeir, H. K. (1973). Nocturnal enuresis: The importance of a small bladder capacity. In I. Kolvin, R. C. MacKeith, & S. R. Meadow (Eds.), *Bladder control and enuresis* (pp. 95–101). Philadelphia: Lippincott.

CHAPTER 22

Sleep Disorders

EMERSON M. WICKWIRE JR., MALCOLM M. S. ROLAND,
T. DAVID ELKIN, AND JULIE A. SCHUMACHER

Sleep is a phenomenon that accounts for approximately one-third of our lives, yet little is known about the exact purpose of sleep or the specific mechanisms through which sleep exerts its powerful influences. Certainly, sleep is a complex set of neurobiological processes that cross a wide range of functions at the cellular, systemic, and behavioral levels. Disturbances in sleep can cause dramatic changes in behavioral and cognitive functioning in humans, yet as a society we are ignorant of even the basic aspects of sleep. For this reason, sleep has become an important area of clinical research and practice.

Like many aspects of human behavior, sleep changes over the developmental cycle. The purpose of this chapter is to discuss sleep and sleep disturbances in children and adolescents. We describe the four most prevalent sleep problems likely to be seen in clinical practice, outline appropriate interventions, and detail a case example for each. We also explore the relationship between sleep and medical status and psychological and psychosocial functioning. Each pediatric sleep disorder is presented within a developmental perspective, so the practitioner will be able to apply these principles to individual cases.

PHYSIOLOGY OF SLEEP

An in-depth discussion of the intricate neurophysiologic functions of sleep is beyond the scope of this chapter. However, a basic understanding of the physiology of sleep is needed to appreciate more fully the sleep process and its centrality to our health and functioning. Although the exact purpose of sleep has not yet been identified, an extensive literature expanding over half a century conclusively demonstrates that humans who experience nonnormal sleep will also experience nonnormal waking and impaired daytime functioning.

At the most basic level, sleep can be divided into two categories: rapid eye movement (REM) sleep and nonrapid eye movement (NREM) sleep. These two categories of sleep are distinguished by the amount of information from the peripheral environment that reaches the cerebral cortex. This property is commonly referred to as *depth* of sleep.

To a parent standing over his or her sleeping child, NREM and REM sleep are indistinguishable. However, NREM and REM are more different than they are alike, varying at the neuroanatomic and neurochemical levels. The longest episodes of REM sleep occur in the second half of the night. During REM and NREM sleep, the brain receives varying levels of blood flow, and the stages are further differentiated by specific thalamic functioning, blood glucose utilization, and the predominant neuronal systems active in the brain. Most readers know that dreaming takes place during REM sleep. In addition, during REM sleep peripheral muscle tone is suppressed, which, as we will see, has important implications for sleep-related breathing disorders, as well as other sleep-related phenomena.

Nonrapid eye movement sleep is further divided into four stages. Stage I sleep is the lightest stage, and Stage II sleep represents a slightly deeper level of sleep. Stages III and IV represent progressively deeper stages of sleep known as *slow-wave* sleep for their characteristic slow brainwave oscillations (0.5 to 2.5 cycles per second) measured by the scalp electroencephalogram. Slow-wave sleep occurs within the first third of the night after sleep onset, and during this time it can be difficult to arouse a sleeping child. This is likely due to the fact that slow-wave sleep is associated with "thalamic gating," the process through which the thalamus restricts sensory input to the brain. This restriction may explain the unresponsiveness to environmental stimuli observed during sleep. As we will discuss, these sleep stages are most commonly identified and differentiated during an all-night sleep study, or polysomnogram (PSG). The physiological activity revealed during a PSG is typically referred to as sleep "architecture."

Although they are too brief to be remembered, short arousals during sleep are normal for humans. Adults progress through the stages of wake, NREM sleep, and REM sleep once every 60 to 90 minutes. This ultradian cycle is slightly longer in children. During this cycle, there is extensive reorganization of neuronal networks and neurotransmitters at many levels of brain function.

The brainstem plays an important role in sleep, and it is widely known that high levels of cortical activity take place during sleep (e.g., Mahowald & Schenck, 1992). More specifically, during REM sleep there is extensive reorganization of the central nervous system. Two pontine nuclei fire throughout REM sleep, and the end of REM sleep corresponds with activity within serotonergic and noradrenergic neurons. This explains why REM sleep is suppressed by many antidepressants and can be promoted by cholinergic agonists (e.g., Mindell, Owens, & Carskadon, 1999).

It is important to note that sleep is a function of distinct neuronal groups rather than a whole-brain activity. During the sleep cycle, if the transition between states is interrupted or incomplete, "mixed" or dissociative states result (Mahowald & Schenck, 1992). As we discuss later, this means that certain parts of the brain can be asleep while others are awake. Such mixed or dissociative states are characteristic of disorders of arousal that occur directly from NREM slow-wave sleep. These NREM parasomnias are discussed later in the chapter. Narcolepsy and REM sleep behavior disorder are examples of other mixed or dissociative states.

Our propensity to sleep is controlled by two basic drives. First, based on our recent waking activity, humans experience a homeostatic "sleep pressure." This sleep pressure controls the length and depth of our sleep and is related to sleep debt, as evidenced by the fact that sleep deprivation leads to increased levels of "catch-up" REM, or REM rebound. Second, our sleep is controlled by a circadian clock, a "hypothalamic pacemaker" that develops by 6 months of age and drives us to sleep during the night and wake during the day. The circadian clock is guided by the presence or absence of light; from an evolutionary perspective, it developed so we would be alert during the daytime and restful at night. For most people, the diurnal-nocturnal circadian cycle is slightly longer than 24 hours in duration, and there is variability between individuals. Our body temperature, hormone and gastric acid secretion, pulmonary function, including heart rate and blood pressure, and the responsiveness and reactivity of the immune system all fluctuate with our circadian rhythms (Mistlberger & Rusak, 2005).

For the purposes of this chapter, it is important to understand that numerous physiological phenomena can negatively affect sleep, leading to poor daytime performance (e.g., Bruni et al., 2006; Chervin et al., 2002; Gaultney, Terrell, & Gingras, 2005; Richman, Stevenson, & Graham, 1975). Electroencephalograph arousals, even if too brief to be remembered, can significantly disrupt sleep and cause it to be nonrestorative. Oxygen desaturation resulting from sleep-disordered breathing can lead to impaired organ function, excessive daytime sleepiness, and numerous psychological sequelae). These events and other causes can lead to difficulty initiating or maintaining sleep, resulting in decreased total sleep time and impaired functioning (e.g., Blunden & Beebe, 2006).

CHANGING NEEDS: SLEEP ACROSS THE LIFE SPAN

Having reviewed the basic physiological processes involved in sleep, we now consider changes in sleep behavior over the life span. At different developmental stages, our sleep needs vary considerably.

For fetuses and infants less than 6 months of age, there are only two types of sleep. Active and quiet sleep are immature precursors of REM and NREM sleep, respectively. During the fetal stage of development, the fetus sleeps roughly 16 to 20 hours per day, consisting of 8 hours of fragmented sleep at night and four naps during the day. Of these sleeping hours, 60% to 80% are spent in active sleep. Human fetuses cycle through wake, active sleep, and quiet sleep in a way analogous to the adult sleep cycle (Groome, Bentz, & Singh, 1995), and there is considerable evidence that fetuses respond to environmental stimuli. In addition, there is some suggestion that parent behavior can set fetuses' circadian clocks (e.g., Acebo et al., 2005; Wulff, Dedek, & Siegmund, 2001). Notably, fetuses are more active during sleep than they will be after they are born, which explains why pregnant mothers can feel such frequent kicking.

Although it may not seem this way to parents, Nathaniel Kleitman (1939) demonstrated as far back as the 1930s that newborn sleep is not random. Full-term newborns spend approximately 16 hours per day asleep. However, they are unable to sleep a continuous 10 to 12 hours, and sleep is equally divided between 5 to 7 episodes of 1 to 4 hours each (Mindell et al., 1999). This time is equally distributed between active and quiet sleep. The active-quiet cycle, analogous to the REM-NREM cycle, takes place every 60 minutes, considerably shorter than the 90 minutes it takes in most adults. Between 3 and 6 months of age, slow-wave sleep begins to develop. Brief periods of dense, high frequency EEG activity, called sleep spindles, also appear during this time and mark the development of cortical superstructures. By 6 months, even though circadian nocturnal-diurnal rhythms have not yet fully developed, most sleep takes place during the night. Further, active sleep turns into REM sleep and moves to the last third of the sleep architecture (Sadeh, 2000).

For neonates less than 1 year of age, PSG evidence suggests not only significant motor activity but also that sleep is entered through active sleep or REM (e.g., Anders, 1982). Irregular breathing is common during this time, and periods of apnea less than 20 seconds in duration are often present and are considered normal. Prior to the 40th week of life, homeostatic factors and parent modeling are the strongest determinants of sleep. At that time, however, regular sleep and wake times begin to emerge. Also during the first year, sleep stages become differentiated and the slow-wave activity characteristic of deep sleep develops. Slow-wave sleep will peak in early childhood, decrease by 40% during adolescence, and continue to decline gradually throughout adulthood (Carskadon, 1982). Adults spend approximately 2 hours per night in slow-wave sleep, and by older adulthood, humans spend only 15% to 20% of their total sleep time in slow-wave sleep.

By 1 year, sleep has consolidated considerably and takes place during the night. Most children this age sleep approximately 11 hours per night and take two additional daytime naps for a total of 13 to 15 hours a day (e.g., Mindell et al., 1999). By age 3, this amount has decreased to 10.5 hours with one 1.5-hour nap (e.g., Sadeh, 2000), and by age 4 or 5, most children do all their sleeping at night and have abandoned the daytime nap altogether. Between ages 5 and 12, sleep fluctuates with life demands, including social activities, season of the year, and school vacation schedule. Total sleep consolidates to approximately 10 hours. Children tend to be awake and active during the day due to clock-dependent alerting, and sleep pressure (i.e., the homeostatic sleep drive) leads to restful sleep during the night. Although up to two brief awakenings per night are not uncommon and 20% to 41% experience some sleep difficulty (Sadeh, 2000), a majority of children will experience the best sleep of their lives from the ages of 7 to 12. These preteens are typically very well-rested and tend to have difficulty falling asleep during the day, even if prompted.

Sleep needs remain vital to healthy development during puberty and adolescence. At the onset of puberty, levels of the sleep-related hormone melatonin decrease, resulting in the first major sleep-related changes since early childhood (Mindell et al., 1999). In addition, other hormone levels increase, the heart rate accelerates, and brain development continues as the cerebral cortex initiates a new stage of developmental rewiring. During sleep, numerous hormones are secreted, including testosterone, follicle stimulating hormone, luteinizing hormone, and human growth hormone. Importantly, then, teens who do not get enough sleep might be harmed due to inadequate levels of the hormones necessary for growth. At the same time, although sleep remains essential for healthy development, teenagers experience radical shifts in social demands. Early school starts, increased demands from friends to hang out, and increased levels of commitment needed to remain active in extracurricular activities such as sports, band, and theater, all lead to teenagers experiencing chronic sleep debt (e.g., Hansen, Jenssen, Schiff, Zee, & Dubocovich, 2005).

Between the ages of 15 and 17, adolescents report relatively longer sleep onset latencies and more awakenings during the night, as well as increased daytime sleepiness. It has been repeatedly documented that high school students get less sleep than they need. Although adolescents need between 9.25 and 9.5 hours of sleep per day (Howard & Wong, 2001), during the school week they often sleep as little as 5 to 6 hours per night. This shortcoming has been associated with increased automobile accidents, drug use, violence and aggression, and chronic sleep disorders.

PARENT ISSUES ESPECIALLY RELEVANT TO PEDIATRIC SLEEP DISORDERS

For quite some time now, parents have been using any and all methods to get their children to sleep. With the publication of *Solve Your Child's Sleep Problems*, Dr. Richard Ferber (1985) systematized this arduous process for millions of new parents. His technique of getting children to self-soothe has been so closely associated with his name that babies are now spoken of as being "Ferberized." Hence, it could be argued that Dr. Ferber brought parents into a more active role in the treatment of pediatric sleep disorders. An updated version of Ferber's seminal work was published in 2006.

Parenting a child's sleep behavior is much like parenting a child in general. When the child is young, the parents have a great deal of control. The process of parenting involves teaching the child self-control and gradually transferring autonomy. As with most issues related to parenting, this is a longitudinal process and is fraught with difficulties.

Parents of newborn children often find themselves at odds over how to encourage sleep in their child. One parent may want to begin a strictly regimented program of feeding and sleeping; the other may want to be more flexible. New parents need to be educated about the sleep requirements and patterns of newborns, and then encouraged to commit to a plan for sharing duties that is agreeable to both. This is true not only for helping their child sleep, but also for rearing their child in general. Several studies have supported the efficacy of training both expectant (e.g., Wolfson, Lacks, & Futterman, 1992) and new (e.g., Hall, Saunders, Clauson, Carty, & Janssen, 2006; Kerr, Jowett, & Smith, 1996) parents in helping improve their children's sleep. In both studies, children of trained parents slept better than children of parents in the control groups.

Parents of newborns are also sleep-deprived and thus may demonstrate less cognitive stamina and flexibility. Parents of newborns tend to lose about 2 hours of sleep per night until the newborn is about 5 months, then about 1 hour per night until the child is about 2 years old. In rare instances, this lack of sleep can have dire consequences; for example, parental sleepiness has been associated with shaken baby syndrome (e.g., Carbaugh, 2004). Thus, the adoption of a plan to which both parents can agree and adhere will be invaluable. This plan can vary widely from family to family; for instance, some parents would never consider sharing their bed with the child, whereas others would consider it cruel not to permit it. Regardless, parents of newborns need to decide how they will approach sleep as a family and then make provisions accordingly.

This united front approach will serve parents well as children get older. During the toddler and early grade school years, most children will resist sleep schedules and bedtimes. This is a natural (though unpleasant) attempt to establish autonomy and resist boundaries. Parents should not be surprised when a frequently disobedient child begins to use noncompliance to extend the bedtime ritual.

From the elementary years to the adolescent years, children tend to sleep well and only occasionally resist sleep. However, as noted earlier, adolescents tend to have more social demands on their time and interests and therefore tend not to sleep as much as they need. Parents should remember that during this stage, adolescents are attempting to distinguish themselves as individuals and do so with a perplexing combination of modeling adult behavior and rebelling against adult restrictions. They see adults sleeping less, so they assume this is how adults behave and they attempt to model it, even though they still need more sleep. This can be an especially trying time for parents, and they will benefit from normative education from an informed therapist.

CLASSIFICATION OF SLEEP DISORDERS

Patients with sleep disorders may present with almost any complaint, but most present with at least one of the following: the inability to sleep, nonrestful sleep, excessive daytime sleepiness, or unusual behaviors during sleep. Even though it is important for the clinician to inquire about each of these, unfortunately these symptoms are not pathognomonic for specific disorders. Most of the sleep disorders presented in this chapter could induce any of these complaints.

Clinicians who studied the disorders of sleep in the early days of the specialty developed a broad classification scheme for sleep disorders, which remains today and divides sleep disorders into two broad disease constructs. Like sleep disorders among adults, pediatric sleep disorders are divided into dysomnias and parasomnias (American Sleep Disorders Association, 2005). Dysomnias typically involve problems initiating or maintaining sleep or with the quality of sleep. Parasomnias, on the other hand, arise during sleep and present as unusual or inappropriate behaviors, such as walking or talking during sleep or enuresis.

Current sleep specialty nosology includes approximately 50 disorders, most of which can occur in children, albeit not as frequently as in adults (American Sleep Disorders Association, 2005). In this chapter, we discuss the four disorders most commonly seen in pediatric clinical practice: obstructive sleep apnea, parasomnias (i.e., sleep walking and sleep terrors), behavioral insomnias (i.e., sleep onset association disorder and limit-setting disorder), and circadian rhythm disorders (i.e., delayed sleep phase syndrome).

Many psychologists will be unfamiliar with the *International Classification of Sleep Disorders* or *ICSD* (American Sleep Disorders Association, 1997). It is noteworthy that the *Diagnostic and Statistical Manual of Mental Disorders* of the American Psychiatric Association (*DSM-IV*; 2000) utilizes slightly different terminology in describing sleep disorders. Ultimately, however, the categorization of pediatric sleep disorders among children is the same in both the *ICSD* and *DSM-IV*.

MEASURING SLEEP

When considering a physiologic process that integrates the central and peripheral nervous, respiratory, and cardiovascular systems, the task of measuring sleep may seem insurmountable. Although it is true that the physiologic components of sleep are essential to understanding and treating sleep disorders of medical origin, the most important component of any assessment is the clinical interview. A thorough clinical interview should assess the child's medical and social history, household and sleeping environment, daytime functioning, presleep routine and in-sleep behaviors, and family medical history. Typical interview questions should include the following:

- Describe bedroom: Furniture? Appliances? Electronics? Natural light? Sound?
- Describe how child falls asleep.
- Who is with child at bedtime? What do they do?
- Is cosleeping allowed?
- Are there any abnormal behaviors at bedtime? Head banging? Body rocking?
- Are nighttime arousals present? If yes, when? How often? How long do they last? How aware is child? What are the triggers (Fatigue? Food?)? Description? How much movement, if any? Injury? How do they end? Memory for event?
- Describe child's breathing during sleep.
- Other sleep problems? Seizures? Sleep apnea? Periodic limb movement disorder? Enuresis? Encopresis?
- Daily functioning? Daytime sleepiness? Performance at school?
- Family history for snoring? Sleep apnea? Arousals? Seizures? Psychiatric? Psychosocial stressors? Narcolepsy? Restless leg syndrome?

An inexpensive and effective tool for assessing sleep is the sleep diary. Sleep diaries used with adult sleep disorder patients (e.g., Morin, 1993) can be easily modified for use by parents to report their child's sleep patterns (see Table 22.1). Typically, 2 weeks of baseline sleep behavior and ecology are obtained via these daily diaries, which also serve to reinforce parent monitoring, an essential component of many behavioral interventions.

In addition to sleep diaries and a detailed history, parents' observations of their child's sleep (or video or audio recordings) can provide valuable information without

Table 22.1
Child Sleep Diary (To Be Completed by Parent or Guardian)
Child Initials: _____ Date Started: _____

DAY/DATE	SUN	MON	TUES	WEDS	THURS	FRI	SAT
Time that child woke up							
Time that child got out of bed							
Difficulty to awaken? (1 = none to 5 = severe)							
Number of naps taken yesterday							
Total nap time							
Time that child went to bed							
Difficulty to put asleep? (1 = none to 5 = severe)							
Number of awakenings during night							
Time of arousal #1 and duration?							
Time of arousal #2 and duration?							
Time of arousal #3 and duration?							
Notes:							

the inconvenience and expense of an all-night sleep study at a sleep center. Among adults, for example, it is not uncommon for spouses to bring to the clinic audio recordings of their bed partner to demonstrate snoring. Similarly, parents have on occasion provided video footage of their child's sleepwalking or breathing pauses. There are also several validated questionnaires that clinicians can use to assess pediatric sleep disorders, such as the Brief Infant Sleep Questionnaire (Sadeh, 2004), Children's Sleep Habits Questionnaire (J. A. Owens, Spirito, & McGuinn, 2000), and Pediatric Sleep Questionnaire (Chervin, Hedger, Dillon, & Pituch, 2000).

For some disorders (e.g., sleep-related breathing problems) an overnight sleep study, or PSG, is usually required. The PSG is a test that records a number of parameters during sleep: brain activity (via electroencephalogram); electrical activity of muscles (via surface electromyography); eye movements (via electrooculogram); respiratory rate; air flow, including snoring; heart rate; blood oxygen saturation; leg movement; and chest and abdominal movement. Most sleep labs also use video recording, which allows treatment providers to observe movements or other unusual behaviors during sleep.

Another physiologic measure of sleep is the Multiple Sleep Latency Test, a daytime test usually administered in a sleep center or medical setting. Using an electroencephalogram to determine the exact onset of sleep, a patient is given 4 to 5 opportunities to take a nap throughout the day. The room is dark and quiet, and each nap is separated by about 2 hours. The time from lights out to the onset of sleep is measured for each nap, and an average sleep latency serves as an objective measure of daytime sleepiness. Other, less frequently used measures of sleep behavior include the Maintenance of Wakefulness Test and actigraphy, which tracks ambulatory movement via a wristwatch-type device.

OBSTRUCTIVE SLEEP APNEA

Obstructive sleep apnea (OSA) is a disorder of breathing during sleep. It typically manifests in children as loud snoring, labored breathing, sleeping in unusual positions that facilitate breathing (e.g., with head hanging off the bed), and daytime sleepiness or irritability. Signs of labored breathing include noisy breathing, paradoxical movement of the chest and abdomen during breathing, and the use of accessory muscles of respiration. Breathing pauses or apneas during sleep, prominent in adult sleep apnea, are not as conspicuous in younger children. Nonetheless, children may have significant difficulty breathing during sleep as a result of upper airway resistance. Snoring and OSA can be understood as ends on the same continuum, and snoring alone has been identified as a cause of significant impairment in children and adults (e.g., Guilleminault, 2004; Lopes & Guilleminault, 2006). The final factor that accounts for symptoms of daytime sleepiness is sleep fragmentation, which results when the brain arouses to restore muscle tone to the narrowed (snoring) or completely obstructed (apnea) airway.

Nighttime breathing disturbances may occur concurrent with such sleep disorders as enuresis and parasomnias. These comorbidities likely reflect the effects of fragmented sleep resulting from the disordered breathing. In addition, younger children may present with uncharacteristic and somewhat subtle symptoms of OSA, including daytime behavioral disturbances (e.g., irritability, inattentiveness, and temper tantrums). In older children and adolescents, problems related to sleep-disordered breathing are sometimes confused with symptoms of Attention-Deficit/Hyperactivity

Disorder (ADHD), depression, drug use, and poor academic achievement (e.g., Archbold, 2006; Chervin, Dillon, Hedger, Archbold, & Ruzicka, 2003; Guilleminault, 2004; Nixon & Brouillette, 2005). As clinicians, it is important to realize that due to the paralysis accompanying REM sleep, these breathing disturbances are usually more evident during REM. Because REM sleep typically takes place later in the night, most parents and caregivers are themselves asleep and less likely to observe their child's sleep-disordered breathing.

Diagnosis and Assessment

In the past decade, there have been several unsuccessful efforts to diagnose OSA based on home audio recording of sleep. The gold standard for assessing physiologic aspects of sleep is PSG, and children with suspected sleep-disordered breathing should be referred to a sleep center for evaluation (e.g., Carskadon, 1982).

Conceptualization

Genetic Influences   Both familial and genetic influences have been linked to obstructive sleep apnea (e.g., Ovchinsky, Rao, Lotwin, & Goldstein, 2002).

Peer Influences   Although not directly related to the disease, peers can play an important role in OSA. Daytime sequelae of OSA such as falling asleep in class are likely to draw negative attention from peers and exacerbate the unpleasant experience for the child already struggling with OSA. In addition, some children are prescribed continuous positive airway pressure (CPAP) for OSA. This treatment is administered via a mask that covers the nose or lower face and is connected via a hose to a shoebox-size machine. The machine creates a pneumatic splint to hold the airway open. Children prescribed CPAP may be uncomfortable lugging their machine to sleepovers and social events. Peer support and acceptance can significantly reduce this burden.

Physical Factors Affecting Behavior   The cause of OSA is resistance to airflow through an abnormally narrow or collapsible upper airway (i.e., the airway immediately behind the oral cavity and the tongue). Children can have either problem: the narrow or the collapsible airway. Young, normal weight, and otherwise healthy children are likely to have large palatine or adenoid tonsils as the cause of their sleep-related breathing (e.g., Guilleminault, Lee, & Chan, 2005).

Drugs Affecting Behavior   In general, all sedating medications have the potential to worsen sleep-disordered breathing. This impairment results from a combination of decreased muscle tone in the throat and an increased arousal threshold, which makes the corrective response to upper airway obstruction less likely to occur. Alcohol and benzodiazepines are the most common culprits and should be avoided in patients with sleep-disordered breathing.

Cultural and Diversity Issues   Higher rates of OSA have been reported in children of lower socioeconomic status, among African Americans, and among overweight children (e.g., Spilsbury et al., 2006; Stores, Montgomery, & Wiggs, 2006).

Behavioral Treatment

Typically, behavioral treatments serve a complementary role in treating OSA by increasing adherence to medical interventions such as CPAP, the most frequently prescribed treatment for OSA among adults (Sadeh, 2005). Adherence to the CPAP procedure can be poor, as this can be a particularly invasive treatment. However, it is efficacious if used properly, and behavioral interventions designed to increase adherence can aid in this process (e.g., Kirk & O'Donnell, 2006; Koontz, Slifer, Cataldo, & Marcus, 2003). A recent development has been the design of colorful pediatric CPAP machines, labeled with animated characters, to increase the acceptability of CPAP to children.

Medical Treatment

In most cases, treatment of OSA in children involves referral to an ear, nose, and throat doctor for an evaluation of the appropriateness of an adenotonsillectomy. In patients who are not candidates for surgery or who have had surgery and are still symptomatic, consideration should be given to CPAP treatment and in some cases to oral appliances designed to broaden the airway. In relatively milder cases, weight loss and positional treatment may be considered (e.g., Rosen, 2004).

Case Description: Sleep-Disordered Breathing

Case Introduction

A 7-year-old boy, Timothy, was referred to a clinical psychologist by his parents because of poor school performance.

Presenting Complaints

Early in the year, Timothy's parents began to hear from his teacher that Timothy was inattentive and irritable in the classroom. His school performance had also been below average. His parents reported that although Timothy had been a happy child, he had become more temperamental and disobedient recently. Timothy's father admits to "dreading" going home after work on afternoons when Timothy is particularly difficult.

History

Timothy was born at full term following an uncomplicated pregnancy. His parents described him as healthy, aside from having tubes placed in his ears at age 4. They also noted that Timothy has "continuous" allergies and a runny nose throughout the year. He has been treated for strep throat on at least two occasions. When he is asleep, his parents can hear his loud breathing from outside his bedroom, and they note that sometimes he sleeps on his back with his head hanging off the bed. Timothy consistently breathes through his mouth at night, and he often drools. He also experiences nighttime enuresis. Almost without fail, his mother is amazed at how disheveled his bed is in the morning. Despite

(continued)

these indications of compromised sleep, Timothy's parents describe him as very active, and they deny that he has ever seemed sleepy during the day.

Prior to kindergarten, Timothy slept from 7:30 PM until 7:00 AM and took one 2- to 3-hour nap during the afternoon. While in kindergarten, he took naps at school, but his mother notes that he began to show signs of irritability in the afternoons following kindergarten, about 1 year ago.

By all accounts, Timothy's parents are happily married. His father is a lawyer and spends one afternoon a week and every weekend with his family. Timothy's mother works part time, but her hours do not overlap with Timothy's time at home. She stated that she loves her afternoons with Timothy, although these afternoons have become much more difficult in the past few months due to her son's behavior.

Assessment

Timothy appeared to be a typical 7-year-old boy. During the interview he walked around the office, touched objects, and was inattentive regarding the conversation, except when specifically directed by his parents. He seemed to be more resistant to being redirected than would otherwise be expected and had a temper tantrum when asked to sit in a chair for a brief conversation with the therapist. Despite this behavior, the therapist was able to observe very narrow nostrils that retracted visibly on inspiration, mild darkening under Timothy's red, watery eyes, and greatly enlarged tonsils. Based on these observations, the therapist concluded that Timothy's likely behavior had a medical cause.

Case Conceptualization

Timothy's case provides an excellent example of how a prevalent medical condition affecting sleep could present as a behavioral problem. The description of loud breathing during sleep, mouth breathing, drooling, and bedwetting, in addition to the behavioral complaints, are classic features of sleep-disordered breathing in children. Timothy's repetitive upper-respiratory infections are also suggestive of sleep-disordered breathing. The evolution of his symptoms is also significant. Timothy's 14 to 15 hours of sleep in previous years partially but not completely compensated for the poor quality of his sleep. During the transitions to kindergarten and first grade, his underlying sleep disturbance was unmasked.

Course of Treatment and Assessment of Progress

At the therapist's suggestion, Timothy's parents made an appointment with their pediatrician. The pediatrician confirmed the presence of enlarged tonsils and adenoids and referred them to an otolaryngologist, who requested a polysomnogram to confirm the diagnosis of OSA. Following receipt of the study, which showed tachypnea (i.e., snoring and increased arousals due to respiratory effort), the surgeon proceeded with an adenotonsillectomy.

Complicating Factors (Including Medical Management)

Fortunately, many cases of pediatric sleep-disordered breathing respond well to surgery to remove adenoids and tonsils. However, depending on the degree of allergic rhinitis and the ventilation of the home environment, humidified air, nasal saline, and antihistamines may be necessary for continued relief of nasal obstruction.

Follow-Up

Timothy and his parents were seen 1 and 3 months after the surgery. At each visit, Timothy appeared increasingly healthy and energetic. Gone were his darkened, red, watery eyes, and his parents reported that his runny nose had mysteriously disappeared. His mother had returned to enjoying their afternoons together, and his parents reported that Timothy's frequent tantrums had abruptly ended.

RECOMMENDATIONS FOR CLINICIANS AND STUDENTS

As noted, this case illustrates the connection between behavior and clinical medicine (e.g., Goll & Shapiro, 2006). Assessment of depression, poor school performance, and other psychosocial problems should be informed by the medical conditions that may contribute to the presenting complaints. Much of the data needed to evaluate the physical factors involved in obstructed breathing during sleep can be obtained without specific medical training or special equipment or may require only close observation of facial features. Collapsed nostrils, watery eyes, a small jaw, and small midfacial structures are all be suggestive of a narrow airway. Mental health professionals should be aware of these factors and refer to physicians when appropriate.

PARASOMNIAS

Parasomnias include numerous disorders that occur during sleep. Most common in younger children, parasomnias typically occur early in the nighttime cycle, 60 to 90 minutes after sleep onset. Importantly, this timing coincides with the transition out of slow-wave sleep at the end of the first ultradian cycle. Parasomnias take place during mixed states, when certain parts of the brain may be awake while others are asleep (Mahowald & Shenck, 1992). Parasomnias can last from a few seconds to over 90 minutes and are characterized by misperception of or unresponsiveness to the environment; involuntary, seemingly automatic behavior; and a high arousal threshold. Variable levels of autonomic arousal and retrograde amnesia may also be present, meaning that there can be considerable variability in behaviors observed during sleep, and the child typically will not recall the episodes at all. Parasomnias most likely to be encountered in clinical practice are somnambulism (sleepwalking), confusion arousals, sleep terrors, and rhythmic movement disorders (Laberge, Tremblay, Vitaro, & Montplaisir, 2000; Sheldon, 2004).

SLEEPWALKING

Somnambulism, or sleepwalking, is characterized by a partial arousal directly from slow-wave sleep (Gaudreau, Joncas, Zadra, & Montplaisir, 2000; Guilleminault &

Oldani, 2001). Although the symptoms are similar among patients of all ages, sleepwalking is most common among younger children, with most patients reporting onset and elimination between ages 3 and 10. Approximately 40% of parents report that their children have sleepwalked at least once, and 6% to 17% of children sleep-walk each year (Klackenberg, 1982). In a recent study, Laberge et al. (2000) reported a prevalence rate for sleepwalking of 13.8% among children ages 3 to 13. If sleepwalking quietly, a child will often go unnoticed by parents. However, inappropriate behavior (such as urinating on the bathroom floor) is not uncommon.

CONFUSION AROUSALS

Although the child may appear awake to his or her parents, a child experiencing a confusion arousal will typically be nonresponsive to parental communication or gestures, often not recognizing parents or appearing not to understand their language. The child may cry, moan, call out, or thrash in the crib or bed, and his or her expression will be one of confusion, frustration, or anger. It is thus understandable that confusion arousals are particularly distressing to parents, who cannot understand why their child is unresponsive. Confusion arousals typically last from 5 to 15 minutes, with a range of a few seconds to over an hour. Laberge et al. (2000) reported that 17.3% of children under the age of 12 experience confusion arousals.

SLEEP TERRORS

The most extreme and infrequent childhood parasomnia, sleep terrors typically last several minutes (DiMario & Emery, 1987). The child sits up in bed with eyes wide and a look of terror on his or her face. The sleep terror is often accompanied by a full-throated scream, and the child may even run from the room as if from an unseen threat. Like all parasomnias, sleep terrors can be precipitated by sleep deprivation and an irregular sleep-wake cycle, and have been reported to correlate with anxiety (Laberge, et al., 2000).

It is important to distinguish sleep terrors from nightmares. Although no consistent operational definition for nightmares exists in the literature, nightmares are differentiated from sleep terrors in that nightmares are well-remembered by the child. Nightmares are more likely than sleep terrors to take place in the extended periods of REM during the second half of sleep, and unlike sleep terrors, nightmares are common among children. Although not conceptualized as a sign of psychological impairment, there is some evidence connecting nightmares with emotional distress. Krakow et al. (2001) and others (e.g., Kohen, Calwell, Heimel, & Olness, 1984; Kohen, Mahowald, & Rosen, 1992) have reported successful treatment of nightmares using relaxation and imagery strategies.

RHYTHMIC MOVEMENT DISORDERS

Rhythmic disorders include such behaviors as body rocking and head banging. Like confusion arousals and sleep terrors, rhythmic movement disorders can be very distressing to parents disturbed by a child who is somewhat violently, repetitively banging his or her head against the crib or bedroom wall. However, in most cases, the risk of injury is low.

DIAGNOSIS AND ASSESSMENT

The most important factor in diagnosing parasomnias is a detailed clinical interview and sleep history. A polysomnogram is rarely indicated but can be used to rule out other sleep disorders, such as sleep-related breathing problems, gastroesophageal reflux disease, and seizures that may mimic or trigger arousal.

CONCEPTUALIZATION

Developmental Issues   As the time spent in REM decreases with age, the amount of slow-wave sleep also decreases dramatically. This decrease is especially marked as children enter adolescence, which explains why children tend to grow out of most childhood parasomnias (e.g., DiMario & Emery, 1987). In addition, multiple parasomnias can be present in the same child (e.g., Laberge et al., 2000). For example, some children experience both sleepwalking and confusion arousals, but at different ages. Similarly, children who sleepwalk can develop sleep terrors at a later age (Klackenberg, 1982).

Life Events   Sleepwalking has been associated with sleep deprivation and increased homeostatic sleep pressure. In addition, although sleepwalking is generally not conceptualized as a disorder reflecting underlying psychological issues, it has been associated with affective disorders, anxiety, and environmental stress.

Genetic Influences   A genetic predisposition for parasomnias has been established, with a positive family history (first-degree relative) present in 60% of children with parasomnias versus 30% of children in the general population (Kales et al., 1980). In addition, genetic factors have been implicated in sleepwalking (Kales et al., 1980).

Physical Factors Affecting Behavior   Parasomnias take place during mixed or dissociative states that arise during the transition between sleep stages. This is why parasomnias are typically short-lived: Although different neuronal systems can concurrently be in different stages of sleep, this phenomenon is unstable, and all neuronal systems soon stabilize in one state or the other. It is believed that parasomnias are related to the stability of slow-wave sleep (e.g., Gaudreau et al., 2000), which requires an electroencephalogram for assessment of the sleep architecture.

Homeostatic sleep factors also play an important role in parasomnias. As sleep pressure increases due to elevated waking activity or sleep deprivation, the frequency and severity of parasomnia episodes will also increase. This phenomenon is also observed in sleep-deprived children. Of course, these factors become even more relevant in children with a genetic predisposition for parasomnias.

Finally, sleep terrors and other parasomnias certainly exist in isolation from other medical conditions. However, sleep-disordered breathing is a common precipitant for parasomnias and, as discussed, has its own implications for a child's behavior and requires medical attention. It is important to note that any condition that fragments a child's sleep will make episodes of parasomnias more frequent. Routine pediatric infections, gastroesophageal reflux, and environments that are not conducive to sleep can aggravate a child's propensity for parasomnias.

Drugs Affecting Behavior   Caffeine will increase the likelihood of parasomnias, as will any drug that disrupts sleep.

BEHAVIORAL TREATMENT

Because parasomnias are generally benign and self-limited, behavioral treatment incorporates three components: educating children and their parents to demystify what parasomnias are, reassuring parents and their children as to the nonpathological nature of the disorder, and ensuring the safety of the child by controlling the environment. Importantly, parents should be warned not to try to intervene during some parasomnia episodes, such as a confusion arousal or sleep terror, because the child is not alert or responsive and may thus injure himself or herself or the intervening parent.

Depending on clinical presentation, it may also be necessary to secure the sleeping and household environment to protect a child experiencing parasomnia episodes. At the very least, parents can restrict access to certain kinds of sleeping arrangements (e.g., top bunk of a bunk bed) and remove all obstructions from the bedroom and nearby areas. Parents may also wish to lock doors and windows to prevent the child from leaving the home. If clinically indicated, parents should also be encouraged to consider installing a security system, hanging a bell or other triggering device on the child's door, putting a gate across the stairs, or other similar modifications.

There is a lack of rigorous evaluation of the effectiveness of behavioral treatments for parasomnias in children and adolescents. Nonetheless, several additional approaches can be found in the literature and have been used with clinical success. First, the frequency of many parasomnias (e.g., sleepwalking and sleep terrors) can be reduced simply by extending the child's sleep period and regularizing the sleep schedule (Kuhn & Weidinger, 2000). Several authors have proposed scheduled awakenings to address the problematic transitions between sleep stages that are believed to be an important mechanism underlying parasomnias. In this procedure, parents should awaken their child 15 minutes prior to the time of their usual arousals, as determined by sleep diaries. Although there are no consistent clinical guidelines, children should at least acknowledge that they are awake (Durand & Mindell, 1999; Frank & Spirito, 1997). Other authors have suggested that the child should be kept awake for at least 5 minutes (e.g., Tobin, 1993). For older children, teaching relaxation and imagery may be effective strategies for reducing parasomnias (Kohen et al., 1984; Kohen et al., 1992; Krakow et al., 2001). More extensive psychotherapy is generally unwarranted unless the child or family is experiencing significant distress related to the arousals. It is unlikely, however, that this level of distress would be exclusive to the sleep domain.

MEDICAL TREATMENT

In general, pharmacological treatment should be avoided for most parasomnias in children (Weissbluth, 1984). The reason for this is simple: There is a low risk of harm from these arousals. However, some have recommended prescription of clonazepam in severe cases, or if the child poses significant risk of harm to self or others (e.g., Mahowald, 1994).

Case Description: Parasomnias

Case Introduction
A 4-year-old girl presents for evaluation of "horrible nightmares."

Presenting Complaints
Jenna is a healthy girl whose parents are concerned about "terrifying" episodes occurring during sleep. One to 2 hours after putting their daughter to bed, Jenna's parents can hear her crying in her bedroom. This crying quickly escalates to loud screaming. Her parents then enter Jenna's bedroom and find her in a state of panic. As Jenna lashes out at her parents and continues to cry, their attempts to console her only seem to exacerbate the problem. These episodes last between 15 and 45 minutes. Jenna's parents are highly distressed, and it is apparent that their sleep is suffering.

History
Jenna's medical history was unremarkable. With the exception of nasal congestion, which had worsened recently, nothing in her history suggested broader social or psychological problems. Although Jenna's parents had observed her snoring on several occasions, they reported that Jenna was only sleepy or irritable on days when her sinuses were particularly irritated. Jenna was completely unaware of the episodes and had no recollection of the "nightmares" or of being frightened.

Assessment
Jenna's parents reported that she had met developmental milestones within normal age limits. Her emotional functioning and social interactions with the therapist were age-appropriate. She was social, appeared happy, and excepting her nocturnal arousals, presented no evidence of abnormal behavior. Her mother did note that Jenna had not been congested and had not had any awakenings the night prior to her presentation at the clinic.

Case Conceptualization
This is a classic case of sleep terrors, an NREM parasomnia that arises directly out of slow-wave sleep. Key features of Jenna's history that point to the diagnosis are the time of night in which the arousals occur, the dramatic nature of the events, and her complete lack of recall of the episodes. Sleep terrors are often particularly frightening for parents, whose sleep is usually more negatively impacted than that of their child. Like somnambulism, sleep terrors occur during slow-wave sleep, which is most common during the first third of the night. As an NREM disorder, sleep terrors lack the vivid imagery of nightmares. During these episodes, the patient remains unconscious and in deep sleep, even though body and sympathetic nervous system are highly aroused. Although quite frightening, sleep terrors are usually benign.

(continued)

Course of Treatment and Assessment of Progress

As with all parasomnias, treatment of Jenna's sleep terrors involved educating, reassuring, and supporting her parents. Her parents and the therapist met several times to review Jenna's condition and also to address their own anxiety. After this brief therapy, Jenna's parents had essentially resumed normal sleep and understood that their daughter would likely grow out of her sleep terrors.

Follow-Up

Jenna's sleep terrors became less frequent when her nasal congestion was addressed. She continued to experience symptoms of sleep terrors between her initial evaluation and a 6-month follow-up. However, her parents reported that as a result of counseling from the therapist, their anxiety regarding the episodes had been greatly reduced, and their sleep had improved as a result. The normal course for parasomnias is that as the brain continues to develop, children will outgrow their propensity for these mixed-state arousals.

RECOMMENDATIONS TO CLINICIANS AND STUDENTS

Should any repetitive movements, stereotyped behaviors, or convulsive activity be observed, medical evaluation should be sought immediately. Such events may be symptoms of epileptic seizures, which are common during sleep in predisposed individuals.

BEHAVIORAL INSOMNIAS OF CHILDHOOD

Difficulties initiating and maintaining sleep are dysomnias experienced by individuals of all ages. Importantly, however, the causes and clinical presentations associated with these sleep disturbances are typically very different for adults and children. The most common dysomnias in children are sleep onset association disorder and limit-setting sleep disorder. Although dysomnias commonly seen in adults (e.g., psychophysiological insomnia) also occur in children and adolescents, they are much less frequently seen in clinical practice than these two disorders.

SLEEP ONSET ASSOCIATION DISORDER

Sleep onset association disorder is diagnosed when the onset of sleep has been conditioned to the presence of a particular stimulus or set of stimuli, and sleep cannot be easily initiated in the absence of these stimuli. Typically observed in infants and very young children, common examples of this disorder might involve an infant who always falls asleep while nursing and experiences significant difficulty falling asleep without the presence of the breast or bottle, or a toddler who always falls asleep with his or her parent in a lighted room and experiences significant difficulty falling asleep in a darkened room without the parent present. In both cases, the difficulty is not usually limited to bedtime, as awakenings during the night will be prolonged by the child's inability to return to sleep without a feeding or without a parent's return to the room.

LIMIT-SETTING SLEEP DISORDER

Limit-setting sleep disorder is diagnosed when caregivers do not enforce an appropriate and consistent bedtime, which results in delayed sleep onset. Rather than initiating sleep at an appropriate time, a child with limit-setting sleep disorder may stall (e.g., make requests for a drink of water, another bedtime story, or an additional hour of television) or may simply refuse to comply at bedtime, perhaps throwing a tantrum. In turn, parents typically give in to these stall tactics or refusals on a variable schedule, which increases the frequency of the child's stalling or refusal behavior.

DIAGNOSIS AND ASSESSMENT

In part because children presenting with behavioral insomnias can be very young, diagnosis of both of these disorders typically relies exclusively on parental self-reports about the nature and duration of the child's sleep disturbance. Assessment must determine the role that environmental factors and parent behavior may play in maintaining the sleep disturbance, as well as rule out psychological or medical disorders that may underlie the child's behavior. In many cases, these assessments may be conducted using either a loosely structured or semi-structured clinical interview. In other cases, the clinician may request parental monitoring of bedtime and sleep behavior via a sleep diary, a thorough psychological evaluation of the child, or a medical evaluation to rule out the presence of other disorders (e.g., Sadeh, 2000, 2004)

To diagnose sleep onset association disorder, the complaints must have persisted for at least 3 weeks, and there must be evidence that insomnia is temporally associated with the absence of specific conditions or stimuli (e.g., the breast, bottle, or parent; American Sleep Disorders Association, 2005. Importantly, sleep must be normal in onset, duration, and quality as long as the conditions or stimuli needed for sleep are present. Although not necessary for diagnosis, polysomnographic monitoring of a child with sleep onset association disorder should reveal normal sleep in the presence of the conditioned stimuli and increased sleep onset latency and increases in the duration or frequency of awakenings in the absence of the conditioned stimuli. Final diagnostic considerations involve ruling out an underlying psychological or medical disorder or another sleep disorder that causes sleep initiation difficulties, such as limit-setting sleep disorder.

A diagnosis of limit-setting sleep disorder is appropriate when a child's difficulty initiating sleep is related to stalling or refusing to go to bed at an appropriate time, but the child's sleep is of normal quality and duration once he or she does go to sleep (Sadeh, 2000). Although not necessary for diagnosis, polysomnographic monitoring of a child with limit-setting sleep disorder will show no irregularities. As with sleep onset association disorder, the final diagnostic considerations require ruling out underlying psychological or medical causes, as well as other sleep disorders that may better account for the problem initiating sleep.

CONCEPTUALIZATION

Developmental Issues   As noted previously, sleep onset association disorder is most typically observed in infants and very young children. Although considered a disorder, it is intimately tied to a developmentally normal process. From an evolutionary perspective, the transition from wakefulness to sleep makes any organism vulnerable to threat. Therefore, it is important for organisms to identify environmental cues that signal it is safe to initiate sleep. Limit-setting sleep disorder can also be diagnosed in infants and very young children, but more commonly impacts older children.

Learning and Modeling   Learning plays a critical role in the development of both sleep onset association disorder and limit-setting disorder (Owens, France, & Wiggs, 2003; Sadeh 2000, 2005). In sleep onset association disorder, a child is conditioned (via classical conditioning processes) to associate a stimulus or set of conditions with the onset of sleep, which the parent either cannot maintain (e.g., entering the child's bedroom several times per night to soothe or feed the child) or does not wish to maintain (e.g., allowing the child to fall asleep with the lights on or a pacifier in his or her mouth). In limit-setting sleep disorder, the principles of operant conditioning are more relevant. Parents typically respond to children's attempts to stall or refuse bedtime with a variable reinforcement schedule. That is, sometimes the child's bedtime resistance is reinforced, such as when the parent feels too tired or overwhelmed to endure a potential escalation in a child's tantrums or other behaviors that accompany limit setting; at other times the appropriate bedtime is enforced. This inconsistent reinforcement schedule predictably leads to an escalation of bedtime refusal or stall tactics as the child learns that if he or she simply persists in these tactics, the parents may give in.

Parental Issues   Parents often play paramount causal and maintaining roles in both sleep onset association disorder and limit-setting sleep disorder. Parents of infants and young children may feel very distressed separating from their child at bedtime or when confronted with protests from their child. Parents may engage in behaviors designed to soothe or quiet their child, such as remaining in the child's bedroom until the child is able to fall asleep, or giving the child an extra feeding at bedtime, which can contribute to either disorder. Unfortunately, these parental issues can worsen over time. Children's sleep problems often disrupt parents' sleep, which over time can lead to sleepiness, irritability, and depression or other psychological sequelae which further reduce a parent's ability to tolerate the distress associated with children's sleep problems. In such situations, a "negative reinforcement trap" can develop. In this cycle, frustrated parents are negatively reinforced for giving in, the child is positively reinforced for protesting, and the pattern continues.

Life Events   Particularly arousing days or exciting activity around bedtime is likely to exacerbate behavioral insomnias of childhood. In addition, children who are sleep-deprived are likely to be grumpy and more difficult than well-rested children. Parents should view the hours before bedtime as a wind-down period. Maintaining regular sleep and wake times is essential.

Genetic Influences   The primary causes of behavioral insomnias of childhood are believed to be maladaptive bedtime conditioning.

Drugs Affecting Behavior   Certain medications or drugs may influence a child's ability to feel sleepy at bedtime. For example, children taking stimulant medications for ADHD late in the day or who consume caffeinated beverages in the late afternoon may not feel sleepy at bedtime (Cortese, Konofal, Yateman, Mouren, & Lecendreux, 2006). If the source of the problem is not identified quickly, children and parents may fall into a behavioral pattern of bedtime refusals or stalling tactics, late awakening, and daytime sleepiness or napping that does not resolve when the medication or drug is withdrawn. Hence drugs and medications could in some cases contribute to the onset of limit-setting sleep disorder. Similarly, a parent who consistently gives his or her child a sleep aid to help induce sleep, whether a drug such as an antihistamine or a home remedy such as warm milk, may contribute to the development of sleep onset association disorder, in which the child can no longer fall asleep without the sleep aid.

Cultural and Diversity Issues   Beliefs about normal and appropriate sleep behavior for children and adolescents vary across cultures and even across families. For example, in some cultures and families cosleeping with infants and young children is viewed as normative, whereas in other cultures and families infants are transitioned to independent sleeping immediately or shortly after birth. Similarly, views on appropriate bedtimes and awakening times are also widely varied. Whereas a family with children who begin school early in the morning may view a child's refusal to go to bed prior to midnight and inability to awaken refreshed before dawn as a problem and seek treatment, a family in which children are homeschooled and parents have a later start to their work day may perceive a child's bedtime refusals as nonproblematic. In assessing and treating behavioral insomnias, it is important for clinicians to be aware of the cultural or family context in which the disturbance occurs and identify treatment goals and strategies that are adaptive for that context.

BEHAVIORAL TREATMENT

Behavioral treatment of limit-setting disorder involves using extinction and limit-setting techniques, scheduling bedtime changes, and educating parents (e.g., Owens et al., 2003; Sadeh, 2005). Parents need to be willing to change their sleep schedule expectations for their child and establish clear boundaries by ignoring protesting behaviors, within limits. As the case example shows, these types of interventions work well with behavioral insomnias of childhood. Most researchers recommend a combination of behavioral interventions, as the flexibility afforded by combining these interventions yields good results (Sadeh, 2005). Notably, a thorough functional analysis is imperative to plan interventions effectively.

MEDICAL TREATMENT

In general, medications should be avoided for pediatric behavioral insomnias, as behavioral interventions have been demonstrated to be effective treatments for both limit-setting disorder and sleep onset association disorder. Parents with difficulty complying will sometimes request medication for their child. However, this should be resisted until the therapist has exhausted all behavioral options. (For a review of medications for childhood insomnias, see Pelayo, Chen, Monzon, & Guilleminault, 2004.)

Case Study: Limit-Setting Disorder

Case Introduction

Kimberly is a 9-year-old girl who presented for evaluation of "sleeping all the time."

Presenting Complaint

Kimberly's mother stated that Kimberly sleeps "too much." Upon returning from school, Kimberly will fall asleep watching television and will sleep until 11:00 PM. During that time, her mother tries unsuccessfully to awaken Kimberly, although she acknowledged that she is busy with her other two children and may not try hard enough. Her mother leaves a frozen dinner or other food for Kimberly to "heat up in the microwave," which Kimberly does after awakening and will usually stay up until 3:00 AM watching TV. At 6:00 AM the next morning, she is extremely difficult to awaken for school. Kimberly does admit to occasional daytime sleepiness, but denies falling asleep at school. She reports, and her mother confirms, no history of poor school performance.

History

A generally healthy third-grader, Kimberly was born at full term after an uncomplicated pregnancy. She lives with her mother, who is unmarried, and her two half-sisters, ages 4 and 14. Kimberly is estranged from her father, and her mother admits that she has difficulty paying all her bills because her children's fathers are not supportive.

For several years, Kimberly's mother has observed soft snoring on occasion that may be associated with airway obstruction or breathing pauses. When queried, she admits to having found her daughter sleeping on her back with her head hanging over the edge of the bed. In addition, Kimberly reports waking frequently in the middle of the night with pain in her stomach, stating that her "stomach and throat burn." This stomach pain is occasionally accompanied by nausea and vomiting.

Assessment

During the interview, Kimberly appeared shy and hesitant to make eye contact with the therapist. She was otherwise appropriate and the remainder of the interview was unremarkable.

Case Conceptualization

Kimberly's case exemplifies many of the maladaptive sleep patterns that children adopt and that parents, either actively or passively, reinforce. Kimberly's sleep-wake schedule is completely unstructured, and it is likely that a more thorough review of her daily routine would reveal pervasive failures of limit setting. She may be getting an adequate amount of sleep, but it is clearly not of the consolidated quality that is most beneficial to her development.

Course of Treatment and Assessment of Progress

As is typically the case with behavioral insomnias of childhood, treatment centered on improving Kimberly's mother's parenting skills, and specifically, improving instruction-giving and limit-setting practices. Specific recommendations included that Kimberly should adopt and maintain a consistent sleep-wake schedule and that she should not be allowed to nap during the afternoon.

To address the soft snoring and complaint of stomach pain during sleep, Kimberly's therapist referred her to a sleep medicine specialist. A polysomnogram was performed, which revealed essentially normal breathing during sleep. However, Kimberly experienced several awakenings during the night, which coincided with her complaints of "chest burning." In addition, in light of her habitual late-night eating, Kimberly's psychologist referred her to a gastroenterologist, who agreed with the diagnosis of gastroesophageal reflux disease (GERD) and instructed Kimberly and her mother that Kimberly should avoid eating within 3 hours of bedtime. Kimberly was also prescribed acid-reducing medications.

Complicating Factors (Including Medical Management)

After Kimberly was diagnosed with limit-setting disorder and GERD, her attendance at follow-up sessions declined. Her mother rescheduled each appointment multiple times. In addition, her mother had apparently misinterpreted the recommendations made by the treatment team and began seeking concessions such as rescheduling classes (i.e., for later in the day) and excuses for previously missed school work. The psychologist also received a request from the mother for another prescription of the "acid medication."

Follow-UP

Kimberly was seen following evaluation by the gastroenterologist and was having less symptomatic heartburn. Her mother was provided additional strategies for establishing clearer boundaries and had succeeded in limiting afternoon naps. In addition, Kimberly's nighttime meal had been moved to a more typical dinner time near 7 PM. Even though Kimberly continued to watch television late at night, her daytime functioning had improved dramatically, as evidenced by what Kimberly described as a new "excitement" about school.

CIRCADIAN RHYTHM DISORDERS

Circadian rhythm disorders are a collection of sleep disorders characterized by a misalignment of the major sleep and wake periods relative to societal or parental norms. Examples include the teenager who stays awake late on weekends to socialize or work and has no trouble falling asleep at her late weekend bedtime, sleeping 8 hours without difficulty and feeling fully alert after these 8 hours. During the week, however, she has difficulty waking, feels sleepy during the day, and cannot fall asleep at an appropriate bedtime. The essential features of the circadian rhythm disorders are the inability to generate sufficient quantity and quality of sleep for normal daytime functioning due to asynchronous timing between sleep and environmental demands.

Delayed sleep phase syndrome (DSPS) is the most common sleep disorder among adolescents and is characterized by sleep onset and wake times that are considerably delayed relative to societal expectations. When there is a schedule change such as the school year beginning, the patient is unable to adjust to the new sleep-wake time demands (Anstead, 2000). The patient may complain of sleep-onset insomnia, severe difficulty waking in the morning, or excessive daytime sleepiness (Mindell et al., 1999). Patients with DSPS also frequently present with academic or behavioral problems or mood disturbance.

Although it can be seen in individuals of any age, including prepubertal adolescents, DSPS is most common during the teenage years, with a prevalence rate of approximately 7% among adolescents (Mindell et al., 1999).

As with OSA, adolescents experiencing DSPS are likely to experience sleepiness-related difficulty in conforming to obligations and to experience problems in school, at work, and with friends and family. They are also at considerable risk for accidents, especially falling asleep while driving, and may report hopelessness over ever sleeping normally again.

Diagnosis and Assessment

Diagnosis of each of the circadian rhythm sleep disorders is based primarily on a thorough and detailed review of the patient's sleep habits and presenting complaints. As with all sleep disorders, sleep diaries are the preferred method for establishing sleep patterns.

At the outset, it is important to rule out possible medical or psychological causes for the presenting complaints. For example, sleep-onset insomnia, excessive daytime sleepiness, poor academic performance, behavioral problems, or depressed mood may be due to another sleep disorder, such as OSA, or may be due to an underlying psychological problem, such as Major Depressive Disorder. In general, polysomnography is not necessary to diagnose a circadian disorder, although it may be necessary to rule out another sleep disorder such as periodic limb movement disorder or a sleep-related breathing disorder. Additionally, because many teens with DSPS will attempt to self-medicate by using alcohol or other drugs, it is always necessary to assess for mood disturbance and substance abuse.

Conceptualization

Both intrinsic and extrinsic factors can influence circadian rhythm disorders. Intrinsic factors include the biologically determined length of an individual's circadian cycle, which can be significantly shorter or longer than the approximately 25-hour typical cycle. Extrinsic factors include forces that can impact the patient's bedtime and/or wake time, such as social events (staying out late with friends), watching television late at night, using the Internet, or working (e.g., Johnson, Cohen, Kasen, First, & Brook, 2004; Owens et al., 1999).

Developmental Issues   Irregular sleep schedules in infants up to the age of 6 months are normal. At approximately 6 months, infants should begin to concentrate the majority of their sleep in the nighttime or the major sleep period of their caretakers. As noted, DSPS typically begins in adolescence, concurrent with shifts in societal demands. At this time, teens also begin to stay up late and to set their own bedtime, to sleep late in the morning, and to take late afternoon naps, especially on weekends, holidays, and vacations. All of these behaviors can exacerbate problems associated with a circadian delay.

Learning and Modeling   Perhaps the social changes of adolescence represent the strongest environmental influences on DSPS. As adolescents seek to establish their autonomy, they will find no shortage of friends with whom to stay up late talking on the phone.

Parental Issues   Irregular family sleep-wake schedules and a chaotic home environment can contribute to DSPS.

Genetic Influences   DSPS has been associated with positive family history for the disorder and has been linked to polymorphisms in the *hPeriod* gene (Archer et al., 2003).

Peer Influences   Like children with OSA, DSPS patients may be regarded as "lazy" or unmotivated. Adolescents who regularly use a light box may experience similar social distress to children and teens who use CPAP.

Drugs Affecting Behavior   As indicated, many teens will try to self-medicate or alleviate their sleep difficulty by experimenting with alcohol or other drugs (Bootzin & Stephens, 2005).

BEHAVIORAL TREATMENT

The goal of therapy is to resynchronize the circadian clock with the desired 24-hour, light-dark cycle and to facilitate improved school attendance and functioning within the family. Teens must be encouraged to establish and maintain a regular sleep-wake schedule, with as little weekday-weekend variation as possible. This can be done by implementing positive bedtime rituals and an adaptive, relaxing presleep routine. Teens should be instructed not to eat heavy meals in the evening and to limit daytime napping. In addition, healthy sleep hygiene should be encouraged, with no afternoon or evening caffeine and no television or video games in the bedroom. Importantly, adolescents with DSPS should minimize physical activity and exposure to light in the evening and maximize them in the morning. The use of light-boxes, which deliver bright light at a set time to mimic the sun and thus help shift the circadian clock, has been a successful adjunctive treatment for DSPS (Chesson et al., 1999).

Clinicians commonly instruct patients suffering from DSPS to shift their sleep and wake times by 15 minutes a day until the desired bedtime is achieved. More dramatically, chronotherapy (Czeisler et al., 1981) involves the successive delay of sleep times by 3 hours daily over a 5- to 6-day period until the desired sleep time is achieved, followed by rigid adherence to a set sleep-wake schedule.

Medical Treatment

Although stimulant and hypnotic medications are sometimes prescribed in teens presenting with the symptoms of DSPS, more recent research suggests that an evening dose of melatonin may aid the sleep process and circadian shift (Mundey, Benloucif, Harsanyi, Dubocovich, & Zee, 2005).

Case Description

Case Introduction

John is a 17-year-old boy referred for evaluation of difficulty waking in the morning and sleeping at school. He is accompanied at intake by his mother.

Presenting Complaints

John is "almost impossible" to wake up in the morning. His mother starts to wake him up at 6:45 AM so that he can be at school by 7:45 AM. However, he resists for at least 15 minutes, and he is so sleepy and slow in the course of getting ready that he often skips breakfast and is late to school multiple times per week. John's parents have received weekly notes from school regarding John's tardiness and sleepiness at school. His parents have been called in and are scheduled to meet with John's teachers and the high school principal to discuss John's performance.

History

John was born at 32 weeks of gestation and was in the pediatric ICU for 2 weeks for treatment of jaundice and other problems related to premature birth. Although he was smaller than average for his first few years of life, he quickly caught up with his peers. At the time of presentation, John was of above-average height and weight, had an athletic build, and, with the exception of routine upper respiratory tract infections, was a model of adolescent health.

Assessment

During the interview, John was awake, alert, and cooperative and on gross assessment, quite intelligent. John admitted to sleeping through his first 2 classes at school but explained that he then "catches a second wind" and is able to stay awake for the remainder of the day. This pattern was reflected in his grades; during the past year, he had struggled with calculus and history, which were his first two classes each morning. In the evening, after returning home from basketball practice, John eats with his family and completes his schoolwork. He reported that his bedtime is around 10:00 PM, but admitted that he usually stays up until approximately 1:00 AM talking on the phone and watching television. John explained that he "just wasn't sleepy" at his scheduled bedtime and that he would lie awake in his bed for 30 or more minutes before he would turn on his light in frustration. On the weekends, he sleeps in until 11:00 AM and wakes feeling much more refreshed than on school days. There was no evidence of other sleep complications, such as snoring, sleepwalking, or restless sleep. Further, although there were some disputes between John's account and his mother's, they appeared to have an otherwise healthy relationship. Information obtained during the interview was believed accurate.

Case Conceptualization

Although sleeping late and resisting getting up in the morning are fairly routine occurrences among teenagers, delayed-sleep phase disorder is a very real circadian abnormality and places children at odds with societal expectations. Purists may argue that there is no disorder at all, and there is some credence to their position; if adolescents are allowed to get adequate amounts of sleep on their own schedules, most individuals with delayed-sleep phase function normally.

Course of Treatment and Assessment of Progress

A strict schedule was adopted to retrain John's biological clock. He was instructed to use eye masks and ear plugs if necessary to remove all stimuli from his sleep environment (e.g., light, noise) and to schedule a 9:30 PM bedtime. This regimen was to be rigorously adhered to 7 days a week. To further aid the resetting of his circadian clock, John was also instructed to sit in front of a light box for 30 minutes beginning at 6:30 AM.

Complicating Factors (Including Medical Management)

Compliance with such strict schedules is difficult under the best of circumstances, and working with teenagers presents numerous additional challenges. Changing the weekend schedule would likely meet with significant resistance. Light boxes are effective, but in an age group that will soon be going to college and sharing rooms, long-term compliance might be unlikely. Long-term treatment will depend on the preferences of individual patients, with some rearranging class schedules and/or choosing career paths that fit their innate circadian patterns. Fortunately for most adolescents with DSPS, their circadian rhythms will readjust as they enter adulthood.

Follow-Up

With the help of his parents, particularly his mother, John was able to comply with strict sleep restriction and reported improvement even without complying with a light box. He admitted to "feeling like death" for the first few weekends, but reported a gradual shift in becoming sleepy at progressively earlier times. Within 4 weeks of treatment, John was consistently falling asleep by 10:30 PM. At his 3-month follow-up, he was sleeping from roughly 10:00 PM to 6:30 AM, staying awake during his first two class periods, and earning improved marks in calculus and history.

(continued)

SUMMARY

Sleep disorders among children are prevalent and can contribute to substantial distress among children and their families. There is considerable overlap between symptoms of various sleep disorders, and it can often be difficult to discern whether a child's presenting complaint represents a psychological disorder (e.g., ADHD) or a sleep disorder (e.g., OSA). Due to the similarities in symptomatology and presenting complaints, it is imperative for clinicians to be familiar with sleep and its disorders and to screen for sleep disturbance as part of routine clinical practice. The most important component of assessment for all childhood sleep disorders is a detailed clinical interview; in most cases an all-night sleep study is not warranted. Fortunately, the most common sleep disorders among children typically respond well to treatment, which always involves educative and supportive components for both child and parents. Occasionally, medical intervention is necessary (e.g., adenotonsillectomy), medication is rarely warranted, and cognitive-behavioral approaches have been found to be effective in this population.

REFERENCES

Acebo, C., Sadeh, A., Seifer, R., Tzischinsky, O., Hafer, A., & Carskadon, M. A. (2005). Sleep/wake patterns derived from activity monitoring and maternal report for healthy 1- to 5-year-old children. *Sleep, 28*(12), 1568–1577.

American Psychiatric Association (2000). *Diagnostic and statistical manual of mental disorders* (4th ed., text rev.). Washington, DC: Washington, DC: Author.

American Sleep Disorders Association, Diagnostic Classification Steering Committee (2005). *International classification of sleep disorders: Diagnostic and coding manual*. Westchester, IL: American Academy of Sleep Medicine.

Anders, T. F. (1982). Neurophysiological studies of sleep in infants and children. *Journal of Child Psychology and Psychiatry, 23,* 75.

Anstead, M. (2000). Pediatric sleep disorders: New developments and evolving understanding. *Current Opinions in Pulmonary Medicine, 6,* 501–506.

Archbold, K. H. (2006). Sleep disorders and attention-deficit hyperactivity disorder in children: A missing differential diagnosis. *Journal of the American Psychiatric Nurses Association, 12*(4), 216–224.

Archer, S. N., Robilliard, D. L., Skene, D. J., Smits, M., Williams, A., Arnedt, J., et al. (2003). A length polymorphism in the circadian clock gene Per3 is linked to delayed sleep phase syndrome and extreme diurnal preference. *Sleep, 26,* 413–415.

Blunden, S. L., & Beebe, D. W. (2006). The contribution of intermittent hypoxia, sleep debt, and sleep disruption to daytime performance in children: Consideration of respiratory and non-respiratory sleep disorders. *Sleep Medicine Reviews, 10,* 109–118.

Bootzin, R. R., & Stephens, S. J. (2005). Adolescents, substance abuse, and the treatment of insomnia and daytime sleepiness. *Clinical Psychology Review, 25,* 629–644.

Bruni, O., Ferini-Strambi, L., Russo, P. M., Antignani, M., Innocenzi, M., Ottaviano, P., et al. (2006). Sleep disturbances and teacher ratings of school achievement and temperament in children. *Sleep Medicine, 7*(1), 43–48.

Carbaugh, S. (2004). Understanding shaken baby syndrome. *Advances in Neonatal Care, 4,* 105–117.

Carskadon, M. A. (1982). The second decade. In C. Guilleminault (Ed.), *Sleeping and waking disorders: Indications and techniques*. Menlo Park, CA: Addison Wesley.

Chervin, R. D., Archbold, K. H., Dillon, J. E., Pituch, K. J., Dahl, R. E., & Guilleminault, C. (2002). Associations between symptoms of inattention, hyperactivity, restless legs, and periodic limb movements. *Sleep, 25*(2), 213–218.

Chervin, R. D., Dillon, J. E., Hedger, K., Archbold, R. N., & Ruzicka, D. L. (2003). Conduct problems and symptoms of sleep disorders in children. *Journal of the Academy of Child and Adolescent Psychiatry, 42*(2), 201–208.

Chervin, R. D., Hedger, K., Dillon, J. E., & Pituch, K. J. (2000). Pediatric Sleep Questionnaire (PSG): Validity and reliability of scales for sleep-disordered breathing, snoring, sleepiness, and behavioral problems. *Sleep Medicine, 1*(1), 21–32.

Chesson, A. L. J., Littner, M., Davila, D., Anderson, W. M., Damberger, M., Hartse, K., et al. (1999). Practice parameters for the use of light therapy in the treatment of sleep disorders (Standards of Practice Committee, American Academy of Sleep Medicine). *Sleep, 22,* 641–660.

Cortese, S., Konofal, E., Yateman, N., Mouren, M. C., & Lecendreux, M. (2006). Sleep and alertness in children with attention-deficit/hyperactivity disorder: A systematic review of the literature. *Sleep, 29*(4), 504–511.

Czeisler, C. A., Rochardson, G. S., Coleman, R. M., Zimmerman, J. C., Moore-Ede, M. C., Dement, W. C., et al.(1981). Chronotherapy: Resetting the circadian clocks of patients with delayed sleep phase insomnia. *Sleep, 4*(1), 1–21.

DiMario, F. J., & Emery, E. S. (1987). The natural history of night terrors. *Clinical Pediatrics, 26,* 505.

Durand, V. M., & Mindell, J.A.(1999). Behavioral interventions for childhood sleep. terrors. *Behavior Therapy, 30,* 705–715.

Ferber, R. (1985) *Solve your child's sleep problems.* New York: Simon & Schuster.

Ferber, R. (2006). *Solve your child's sleep problems* (rev. and expanded ed.). New York: Simon & Schuster.

Frank, C., & Spirito, A. (1997). The use of scheduled awakenings to eliminate childhood sleepwalking. *Journal of Pediatric Psychology, 22,* 345–353.

Gaudreau, H., Joncas, S., Zadra, A., & Montplaisir, J. (2000). Dynamics of slow-wave activity during the NREM sleep of sleepwalkers and control subjects. *Sleep, 23,* (6), 755–760.

Gaultney, J. F., Terrell, D. F., & Gingras, J. L. (2005). Parent-reported periodic limb movement, sleep disordered breathing, bedtime resistance behaviors, and ADHD. *Behavioral Sleep Medicine, 3*(1), 32–43.

Goll, J. C., & Shapiro, C. M. (2006). Sleep disorders presenting as common pediatric problems. *Canadian Medical Association Journal, 174*(5), 617–619.

Groome, L. J., Bentz, L. S., & Singh, K. P. (1995). Behavioral state organization in normal term fetuses: The relationship between periods of undefined state and other characteristics of state control. *Sleep, 18*(2), 77–81.

Guilleminault, C. (2004). Does benign snoring ever exist in children? *Chest, 126*(5), 1396–1397.

Guilleminault, C., Lee, J. H., & Chan, A. (2005). Pediatric obstructive sleep apnea syndrome. *Archives of Pediatric and Adolescent Medicine, 159,* 775–785.

Guilleminault, C., & Oldani, A. (2001). Sleep and wakefulness in somnambulism: A spectral analysis study. *Journal of Psychosomatic Research, 51,* 411–416.

Hall, W. A., Saunders, R. A., Clauson, M., Carty, E. M., & Janssen, P. A. (2006). Effects of an intervention aimed at reducing night waking and signaling in 6- to 12-month-old infants. *Behavioral Sleep Medicine, 4*(4), 242–261.

Hansen, M., Janssen, I., Schiff, A., Zee, P. C., & Dubocovich, M. L. (2005). The impact of daily school schedule on adolescent sleep. *Pediatrics, 115*(6), 1555–1561.

Howard, B. J., & Wong, J. (2001). Sleep disorders. *Pediatrics in Review, 22,* 327–342.

Johnson, J. G., Cohen, P., Kasen, S., First, M. B., & Brook, J. S. (2004). Association between television viewing and sleep problems during adolescence and early adulthood. *Archives of Pediatric and Adolescent Medicine, 158,* 562–568.

Kales, A., Soldatos, C. R., Bixler, E. O., Ladda, R. L., Charney, D. S., Weber, G., & Schweitzer, P. K. (1980). Hereditary factors in sleepwalking and night terrors. *British Journal of Psychiatry, 137,* 111–118.

Kerr, S. M., Jowett, S. A., & Smith, L. N. (1996). Preventing sleep problems in infants: A randomized controlled trial. *Journal of Advanced Nursing, 24*(5), 938–942.

Kirk, V. G., & O'Donnell, A. R. (2006). Continuous positive airway pressure for children: A discussion on how to maximize compliance. *Sleep Medicine Reviews, 10,* 119–127.

Klackenberg, G. (1982). Somnambulism in childhood: Prevalence, course, and behavioral correlates. A prospective longitudinal study (6–16 years). *Acta Paediatrica Scandinavica, 71,* 495–499.

Kleitman, N. (1939). *Sleep and wakefulness.* Chicago: University of Chicago Press.

Kohen, D. P., Calwell, S. O., Heimel, A., & Olness, K. N. (1984). The use of relaxation-mental imagery (self-hypnosis) in the management of 505 pediatric behavioral encounters. *Journal of Developmental and Behavioral Pediatrics, 5,* 21–25.

Kohen, D. P., Mahowald, M. W., & Rosen, G. (1992). Sleep terrors disorders in children: The role of self-hypnosis in management. *American Journal of Clinical Hypnosis, 4,* 233–244.

Koontz, K. L., Slifer, K. J., Cataldo, M. D., & Marcus, C. L. (2003). Improving pediatric compliance with positive airway pressure therapy: The impact of behavioral intervention. *Sleep, 26*(8), 1010–1015.

Krakow, B., Sandoval, D., Schrader, R., Kuehne, B., McBride, L., Yau, C., et al. (2001). Treatment of chronic nightmares in adjudicated adolescent girls in a residential facility. *Journal of Adolescent Health, 29*(2), 94–100.

Kuhn, B. R. & Weidinger, D. (2000) Interventions for infant and toddler sleep disturbance: A review. *Child and Family Behavior Therapy 22*(2), 33–50.

Laberge, L., Tremblay, R. E., Vitaro, F., & Montplaisir, J. (2000). Development of parasomnias from childhood to early adolescence. *Pediatrics, 106,* 67–74.

Lopes, M. C., & Guilleminault, C. (2006). Chronic snoring and sleep in children: A demonstration of sleep disruption. *Pediatrics, 118*(3), e741–e746.

Mahowald, M. W., & Schenck, C. H. (1992). Dissociated states of wakefulness and sleep. *Neurology, 42,* 44–52.

Mahowald, M. W., & Schenck, C. H. (1994). REM sleep behavior disorder. In M. H., Kryger, T. Rothand, & W. C. Dement (Eds.). *Principles and practice of sleep medicine* (2nd ed., 574–578). Philadelphia: Saunders.

Mindell, J. A., Owens, J. A., & Carskadon, M. A. (1999). Developmental features of sleep. *Child and Adolescent Psychiatric Clinics of North America, 8*(4), 695–725.

Mistlberger, R. E., & Rusak, B. B. (2005). Circadian rhythms in mammals: Formal properties and environmental influences. In M. H. Kryger, T. Roth, & W. C. Dement (Eds.), *Principles and practice of sleep medicine* (4th ed.). Philadelphia: Saunders.

Mistlberger R. E., & Rusak, B. (2005). Circadian rhythms in mammals: Formal properties and environmental influences. In M. H. Kryger, T. Roth, W. C. Dement (Eds.), *Principles and practise of sleep medicine* (4th ed.) Philadelphia: Saunders.

Mundey, K., Benloucif, S., Harsanyi, K., Dubocovich, M. L., & Zee, P. C. (2005). Phase-dependent treatment of delayed sleep phase syndrome with melatonin. *Sleep, 28*(10), 1214–1216.

Nixon, G. M., & Brouillette, R. T. (2005). Paediatric obstructive sleep apnoea. *Thorax, 60,* 511–516.

Ovchinsky, A., Rao, M., Lotwin, I., & Goldstein, N. A. (2002). The familial aggregation of pediatric obstructive sleep apnea syndrome. *Archives of Otolaryngology—Head and Neck Surgery, 128*(7), 815–818.

Owens, J. A., Maxim, R., McGuinn, M., Nobile, C., Msall, M., & Alario, A. (1999). Television-viewing habits and sleep disturbance in children. *Pediatrics,* e27.

Owens, J. A., Spirito, A., & McGuinn, M. (2000). The Children's Sleep Habits Questionnaire (CSHQ): Psychometric properties of a survey instrument for school-aged children. *Sleep, 23*(8), 1043–1051.

Owens, J. L., France, K. G., & Wiggs, L. (2003). Behavioral and cognitive-behavioral interventions for infants and children: A review. *Sleep Medicine Reviews, 3*(4), 281–302.

Pelayo, R., Chen, W., Monzon, S., & Guilleminault, C. (2004). Pediatric sleep pharmacology: You want to give my kid sleeping pills? *Pediatric Clinics of North America, 51,* 117–134.

Richman, N., Stevenson, J. E., & Graham, P. J. (1975). Behavior problems in 3-year-old children: An epidemiological study in a London borough. *Journal of Child Psychology and Psychiatry, 12,* 5.

Rosen, C. L. (2004). Obstructive sleep apnea syndrome in children: Controversies in diagnosis and treatment. *Pediatric Clinics of North America, 51,* 153–167.

Sadeh, A. (2000). Clinical assessment of pediatric sleep disorders. In K. L. Lichstein & M. L. Perlis (Eds.) *Treating sleep disorders: Principles and practice of behavioral sleep medicine,* pp 344–364. Hoboken, NJ: Wiley.

Sadeh, A. (2004). A brief screening questionnaire for infant sleep problems: Validation and findings for an Internet sample. *Pediatrics, 113*(6), 570–577.

Sadeh, A. (2005). Cognitive-behavioral treatment for childhood sleep disorders. *Clinical Psychology Review, 25,* 612–628.

Sheldon, S. H. (2004). Parasomnias in childhood. *Pediatric Clinics of North America, 51,* 69–88.

Spilsbury, J. C., Storfer-Isser, A., Kirchner, L., Nelson, L., Rosen, C. L., Drotar, D., & Redline, S. (2006). Neighborhood disadvantage as a risk factor for pediatric sleep apnea. *Journal of Pediatrics, 149,* 342–347.

Stores, G., Montgomery, P., & Wiggs, L. (2006). The psychosocial problems of children with narcolepsy and those with excessive daytime sleepiness of uncertain origin. *Pediatrics, 118,* 1116–1123.

Tobin, J. (1993). Treatment of night terrors with anticipatory awakening. *Journal of Pediatrics, 122,* 426–427.

Weissbluth, M. (1984). Is drug treatment of night terrors warranted? *American Journal of Diseases of Children, 138,* 1086.

Wolfson, A., Lacks, P., & Futterman, A. (1992). Effects of parent training on infant sleeping patterns, parents' stress, and perceived parental competence. *Journal of Consulting and Clinical Psychology, 60*(1), 41–418.

Wulff, K., Dedek, A., & Siegmund, R. (2001). Circadian and ultradian time patterns in human behavior: Pt. 2. Social synchronization during the development of the infant's diurnal activity-rest pattern. *Biological Rhythm Research, 32*(5), 529–546.

Author Index

Subject Index